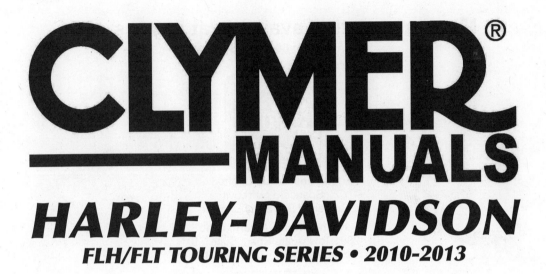

CLYMER
MANUALS

HARLEY-DAVIDSON
FLH/FLT TOURING SERIES • 2010-2013

WHAT'S IN YOUR TOOLBOX?

More information available at haynes.com
Phone: 805-498-6703

Haynes Group Limited
Sparkford Nr Yeovil
Somerset BA22 7JJ England

Haynes North America, Inc
2801 Townsgate Road, Suite 340
Thousand Oaks, CA 91361 USA

ISBN-10: 1-62092-217-7
ISBN-13: 978-1-62092-217-0
Library of Congress: 2015953373

Author: *Ed Scott*
Technical Photography: *Ed Scott with technical assistance from Jordan Engineering, Oceanside, CA*
Technical Illustrations: *Errol McCarthy*
Cover: *Photographed by Mark Clifford (www.markclifford.com), Los Angeles, CA*
2013 Road Glide Custom courtesy of Ventura Harley-Davidson, Ventura, CA

M253, 6X2, 15-672

ABCDEFGHIJKL

Common spark plug conditions

NORMAL

Symptoms: Brown to grayish-tan color and slight electrode wear. Correct heat range for engine and operating conditions.

Recommendation: When new spark plugs are installed, replace with plugs of the same heat range.

WORN

Symptoms: Rounded electrodes with a small amount of ·deposits on the firing end. Normal color. Causes hard starting in damp or cold weather and poor fuel economy.

Recommendation: Plugs have been left in the engine too long. Replace with new plugs of the same heat range. Follow the recommended maintenance schedule.

CARBON DEPOSITS

Symptoms: Dry sooty deposits indicate a rich mixture or weak ignition. Causes misfiring, hard starting and hesitation.

Recommendation: Make sure the plug has the correct heat range. Check for a clogged air filter or problem in the fuel system or engine management system. Also check for ignition system problems.

ASH DEPOSITS

Symptoms: Light brown deposits encrusted on the side or center electrodes or both. Derived from oil and/or fuel additives. Excessive amounts may mask the spark, causing misfiring and hesitation during acceleration.

Recommendation: If excessive deposits accumulate over a short time or low mileage, install new valve guide seals to prevent seepage of oil into the combustion chambers. Also try changing gasoline brands.

OIL DEPOSITS

Symptoms: Oily coating caused by poor oil control. Oil is leaking past worn valve guides or piston rings into the combustion chamber. Causes hard starting, misfiring and hesitation.

Recommendation: Correct the mechanical condition with necessary repairs and install new plugs.

GAP BRIDGING

Symptoms: Combustion deposits lodge between the electrodes. Heavy deposits accumulate and bridge the electrode gap. The plug ceases to fire, resulting in a dead cylinder.

Recommendation: Locate the faulty plug and remove the deposits from between the electrodes.

TOO HOT

Symptoms: Blistered, white insulator, eroded electrode and absence of deposits. Results in shortened plug life.

Recommendation: Check for the correct plug heat range, over-advanced ignition timing, lean fuel mixture, intake manifold vacuum leaks, sticking valves and insufficient engine cooling.

PREIGNITION

Symptoms: Melted electrodes. Insulators are white, but may be dirty due to misfiring or flying debris in the combustion chamber. Can lead to engine damage.

Recommendation: Check for the correct plug heat range, over-advanced ignition timing, lean fuel mixture, insufficient engine cooling and lack of lubrication.

HIGH SPEED GLAZING

Symptoms: Insulator has yellowish, glazed appearance. Indicates that combustion chamber temperatures have risen suddenly during hard acceleration. Normal deposits melt to form a conductive coating. Causes misfiring at high speeds.

Recommendation: Install new plugs. Consider using a colder plug if driving habits warrant.

DETONATION

Symptoms: Insulators may be cracked or chipped.· Improper gap setting techniques can also result in a fractured insulator tip. Can lead to piston damage.

Recommendation: Make sure the fuel anti-knock values meet engine requirements. Use care when setting the gaps on new plugs. Avoid lugging the engine.

MECHANICAL DAMAGE

Symptoms: May be caused by a foreign object in the combustion chamber or the piston striking an incorrect reach (too long) plug. Causes a dead cylinder and could result in piston damage.

Recommendation: Repair the mechanical damage. Remove the foreign object from the engine and/or install the correct reach plug.

CONTENTS

QUICK REFERENCE DATA

TIRE INFLATION PRESSURE (COLD)*

	kPa	psi
Front wheel	248	36
Rear wheel	275	40

* Tire pressure for OE equipment tires. Aftermarket tires may require different inflation pressure.
  These specifications apply to all different size wheel/tire combinations for all models.

FUEL, ENGINE AND DRIVE FLUID CAPACITIES

Item	Capacity
Fuel tank, total	6.0 gal (18.9 L)
Fuel tank, reserve	1.0 gal (3.8 L)
Engine oil with filter[1]	4 qt. (3.79 L)
Transmission[2]	1 qt. (0.95 L)
Primary chaincase	1.40 qt. (1.32 L)

1. When refilling, initially add 3.0 qt. (2.84L) and add additional as need to bring level within specification.
2. When refilling, initially add 28 oz. (0.83 L) and add additional as need to bring level within specification.

FRONT FORK OIL CAPACITY AND OIL LEVEL SPECIFICATIONS

Model	Capacity–each fork leg oz. (cc)	Oil level height* in. (mm)
All models except FLHR, FLHRC, FLHRSE	10.7 (316)	4.92 (125)
FLHR, FLHRC, FLHRSE models	11.0 (325)	5.92 (134)

*Measured from the top of the fork tube with fork spring removed and the fork leg fully compressed.

MAINTENANCE SPECIFICATIONS

Item	Specification
Brake pad minimum thickness (front and rear)	0.016 in. (0.41 mm)
All models except VRSCF	2008-200
Clutch cable free play	1/16-1/8 in. (1.6-3.2 mm)
Drive belt deflection	
All models except FLX, FLTRX	1/4-7/16 in. (6.4-11.1 mm)
FLX, FLTRX models	3/8-9/16 in. (9.5-14.3 mm)
Engine compression	
All models except CVO	
ARC connected	
96 cu. in	125 psi (862 kPa)
103 and 110 cu. in.	110 psi (758 kPa)
ARC disconnected	175 psi (1207 kPa)
CVO models	
ARC connected	130-170 psi (896-1172 kPa)
ARC disconnected	200-220 psi (1379-1517 kPa)
Idle speed	950-1050 rpm
Ignition timing	Non-adjustable
Rear axle alignment	1/32 in. (0.8 mm)

(continued)

MAINTENANCE SPECIFICATIONS (continued)

Item	Specification
Spark plugs	
Gap	0.038-043 in. (0.97-1.09 mm)
Type	HD No. 6R12*

* Harley-Davidson recommends that no other type of spark plug be substituted.

MAINTENANCE AND TUNE-UP TORQUE SPECIFICATIONS

	ft.-lb.	in.-lb.	N•m
Air filter			
All models except CVO			
Cover screw	–	36-60	4.1-6.8
Bracket screw	–	108-132	12.2-14.9
CVO models			
FLTRXSE			
Air filter element clamp screw	–	45-55	5.1-6.2
Back plate mounting screw	–	55-60	6.2-6.8
Breather bolts	22-24	–	29.8-32.5
Intake tube screw	–	55-60	6.2-6.8
Outer mounting ring screw	–	15-20	1.7-2.3
All models except FLTRXSE			
Insert screw	–	27-32	3.1-3.6
Cover screw	–	36-60	4.1-6.8
Air filter element screw		55-60	6.2-6.8
Clutch adjusting screw locknut	–	120	13.6
Clutch cover screws	–	84-108	9.5-12.2
Engine oil drain plug	14-21	–	19-28.5
Primary chaincase oil drain plug	14-21	–	19-28.5
Jiffy stand leg stop bolt	12-15	–	16.3-20.3
Rear axle nut	95-105	–	128.8-142.4
Sparkplug	12-18	–	16.3-24.4
Transmission oil drain plug	14-21	–	19-28.5
Transmission oil filler cap/dipstick	–	25-75	2.8-8.5
Voltage regulator flange nut	–	70-100	7.9-11.3

CHAPTER ONE

GENERAL INFORMATION

This detailed and comprehensive manual covers 2010-2013 Harley-Davidson FLT and FLR Touring models, including all Twin Cam 96, 103 and 110 cubic inch engines. The text provides complete information on maintenance, tune-up, repair and overhaul. Hundreds of photos and drawings guide the reader through every job. Each procedure is in step-by-step format and designed for the reader who may be working on the motorcycle for the first time.

MANUAL ORGANIZATION

A shop manual is a tool and, as in all Clymer manuals, the chapters are thumb-tabbed for easy reference. Main headings are listed in the table of contents and the index. Frequently-used specifications and capacities from the tables at the end of each individual chapter are listed in the *Quick Reference Data* section at the front of the manual. Specifications and capacities are provided in U.S. standard and metric units of measure.

During some of the procedures there will be references to headings in other chapters or sections of the manual. When a specific heading is called out in a step it will be *italicized* as it appears in the manual. If a sub-heading is indicated as being "in this section" it is located within the same main heading. For example, the sub-heading *Handling Gasoline Safely* is located within the main heading *SAFETY*.

This chapter provides general information on shop safety, tools and their usage, service fundamentals and shop supplies. **Tables 1-10** at the end of the chapter provide general motorcycle, mechanical and shop information.

Chapter Two provides methods for quick and accurate diagnosis of problems. Troubleshooting procedures present typical symptoms and logical methods to pinpoint and repair the problem.

Chapter Three explains all routine maintenance necessary to keep the motorcycle running well. Chapter Three also includes recommended tune-up procedures, eliminating the need to constantly consult the chapters on the various assemblies.

Subsequent chapters describe specific systems such as engine, exhaust system, clutch and primary drive system, transmission, fuel system, suspension and brakes. Each disassembly, repair and assembly procedure is discussed step-by-step.

WARNINGS, CAUTIONS AND NOTES

The terms WARNING, CAUTION and NOTE each have specific meanings in this manual.

A WARNING emphasizes areas where injury or even death could result from negligence. Mechanical damage may also occur. WARNINGS are to be taken seriously.

A CAUTION emphasizes areas where equipment damage could result. Disregarding a CAUTION could cause permanent mechanical damage, though injury is unlikely.

A NOTE provides additional information to make a step or procedure easier or clearer. Disregarding a NOTE could cause inconvenience, but would not cause equipment damage or injury.

SAFETY

Follow these guidelines and practice common sense to safely service the motorcycle.

1. Do not operate the motorcycle in an enclosed area. The exhaust gases contain carbon monoxide, an odorless, colorless and tasteless poisonous gas. Carbon monoxide levels build quickly in small enclosed areas and can cause unconsciousness and death in a short time. Make sure to properly ventilate the work area or operate the motorcycle outside.

2. Never use gasoline or any extremely flammable liquid to clean parts. Refer to *Cleaning Parts* and *Handling Gasoline Safely* in this section.

3. Never smoke or use a torch in the vicinity of flammable liquids, such as gasoline or cleaning solvent.

4. If welding or brazing on the motorcycle, remove the fuel tank to a safe distance at least 50 ft. (15 m) away.

5. Use the correct type and size of tools to avoid damaging fasteners.

6. Keep tools clean and in good condition. Replace or repair worn or damaged equipment.

7. When loosening a tight fastener, be guided by what would happen if the tool slips.

8. When replacing fasteners, make sure the new fasteners are the same size and strength as the original ones.

9. Keep the work area clean and organized.

10. Wear eye protection anytime the safety of the eyes is in question. This includes procedures that involve drilling, grinding, hammering, compressed air and chemicals.

11. Wear the correct clothing for the job. Tie up or cover long hair so it does not get caught in moving equipment.

12. Do not carry sharp tools in clothing pockets.

13. Always have an approved fire extinguisher available. Make sure it is rated for gasoline (Class B) and electrical (Class C) fires.

14. Do not use compressed air to clean clothes, the motorcycle or the work area. Debris may be blown into the eyes or skin. Never direct a compressed air hose at anyone. Do not allow children to use or play with any compressed air equipment.

15. When using compressed air to dry rotating parts, hold the part so it does not rotate. Do not allow the force of the air to spin the part. The air jet is capable of rotating parts at extreme speed. The part may disintegrate or become damaged, causing serious injury.

16. Do not inhale the dust created by brake pad and clutch wear. These particles may contain asbestos. In addition, some types of insulating materials and gaskets may contain asbestos. Inhaling asbestos particles is hazardous to health.

17. Never work on the motorcycle while someone is working under it.

18. When placing the motorcycle on a stand, make sure it is secure before walking away.

Handling Gasoline Safely

Gasoline is a volatile flammable liquid and is one of the most dangerous items in the shop. Because gasoline is used so often, many people forget it is hazardous. Only use gasoline as fuel for internal combustion gas engines. Keep in mind when working on the machine that gasoline is always present in the fuel tank, fuel line and throttle body. To

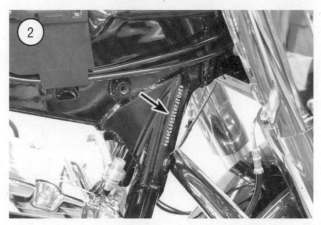

avoid a disastrous accident when working around the fuel system, carefully observe the following precautions:

1. Never use gasoline to clean parts. Refer to *Cleaning Parts* in this section.

2. When working on the fuel system, work outside or in a well-ventilated area.

3. Do not add fuel to the fuel tank or service the fuel system while the motorcycle is near open flames, sparks or where someone is smoking. Gasoline vapor is heavier than air; it collects in low areas and is more easily ignited than liquid gasoline.

4. Allow the engine to cool completely before working on any fuel system component.

5. Do not store gasoline in glass containers. If the glass breaks, a serious explosion or fire may occur.

6. Immediately wipe up spilled gasoline with rags. Store the rags in a metal container with a lid until they can be properly disposed of, or place them outside in a safe place for the fuel to evaporate.

7. Do not pour water onto a gasoline fire. Water spreads the fire and makes it more difficult to put out. Use a class B, BC or ABC fire extinguisher to extinguish the fire.

8. Always turn off the engine before refueling. Do not spill fuel onto the engine or exhaust system. Do not overfill the fuel tank. Leave air space at the top of the tank to allow room for the fuel to expand due to temperature fluctuations.

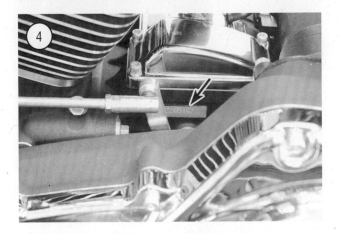

Cleaning Parts

Cleaning parts is one of the more tedious and difficult service jobs performed in the home garage. Many types of chemical cleaners and solvents are available for shop use. Most are poisonous and extremely flammable. To prevent chemical exposure, vapor buildup, fire and serious injury, observe each product warning label and note the following:

1. Read and observe the entire product label before using any chemical. Always know what type of chemical is being used and whether it is poisonous and/or flammable.

2. Do not use more than one type of cleaning solvent at a time. If mixing chemicals is required, measure the proper amounts according to the manufacturer.

3. Work in a well-ventilated area.

4. Wear chemical-resistant gloves.

5. Wear safety glasses.

6. Wear a vapor respirator if the instructions call for it.

7. Wash hands and arms thoroughly after cleaning parts.

8. Keep chemical products away from children and pets.

9. Thoroughly clean all oil, grease and cleaner residue from any part that must be heated.

10. Use a nylon brush when cleaning parts. Metal brushes may cause a spark.

11. When using a parts washer, only use the solvent recommended by the manufacturer. Make sure the parts washer is equipped with a metal lid that will lower in case of fire.

Warning Labels

Most manufacturers attach information and warning labels to the motorcycle. These labels contain instructions that are important to personal safety when operating, servicing, transporting and storing the motorcycle. Refer to the owner's manual for the description and location of labels. Order replacement labels from the manufacturer if they are missing or damaged.

SERIAL NUMBERS

Serial numbers are stamped in various locations on the frame, engine and transmission. Record these numbers in the *Quick Reference Data* section in the front of the book. Have these numbers available when ordering parts.

The VIN number label (**Figure 1**) is located on the left side frame down tube.

The frame serial number label (**Figure 2**) is stamped on the right side frame down tube.

The engine serial number is stamped on the raised pad (**Figure 3**) on the left side of the crankcase

The transmission serial number is stamped on the raised pad (**Figure 4**) on the left side of the transmission case next to the shift lever.

FASTENERS

WARNING
Do not use replacement fasteners with a lower strength classification than the originals.

Make sure replacement fasteners meet all the same requirements as the originals; failure to do so may cause equipment failure and/or damage.

Threaded Fasteners

CAUTION
To ensure that the fastener threads are not mismatched or cross-threaded, start all fasteners by hand. If a fastener is hard to start or turn, determine the cause before tightening with a wrench.

Pay particular attention when working with unidentified fasteners; mismatched thread types can damage threads. Both Standard and metric fasteners (**Figure 5**) are used on the engine and chassis.

Threaded fasteners secure most of the components on the motorcycle. Most fasteners are tightened by turning them clockwise (right-hand threads). If the normal rotation of the component being tightened would loosen the fastener, it may have left-hand threads. If a left-hand threaded fastener is used, it is noted in the text.

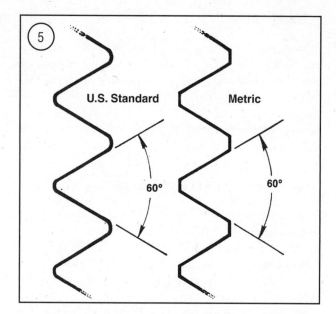

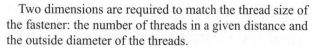

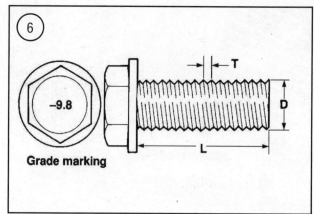

Two dimensions are required to match the thread size of the fastener: the number of threads in a given distance and the outside diameter of the threads.

The length (L, **Figure 6**), diameter (D) and pitch (T), or distance between thread crests, classify metric screws and bolts. A typical bolt may be identified by the numbers, 8–1.25 × 130. This indicates the bolt has a diameter of 8 mm, the distance between thread crests is 1.25 mm and the length is 130 mm. Always measure bolt length as shown in L, **Figure 6** to avoid purchasing replacements of the wrong length.

The numbers on the top of the fastener (**Figure 6**) indicate the strength of metric screws and bolts. The higher the number, the stronger the fastener is. Typically, unnumbered fasteners are the weakest.

Many screws, bolts and studs are combined with nuts to secure particular components. To indicate the size of a nut, manufacturers specify the internal diameter and the thread pitch.

The measurement across two flats on a nut or bolt indicates the wrench size.

Torque Specifications

The materials used in the manufacturing of the motorcycle may be subjected to uneven stresses if the fasteners of the various subassemblies are not installed and tightened correctly. Fasteners that are improperly installed or work loose can cause extensive damage. It is essential to use an accurate torque wrench as described in this chapter.

Specifications for torque are provided in Newton-meters (N•m), foot-pounds (ft.-lb.) and inch-pounds (in.-lb.). Refer to **Table 5** for general torque recommendations. To determine the torque requirement, first determine the size of the fastener as described in *Threaded Fasteners* (this section). Torque specifications for specific components are listed at the end of the appropriate chapters. Torque wrenches are covered in *Basic Tools* (this chapter).

Self-Locking Fasteners

Several types of bolts, screws and nuts incorporate a system that creates interference between the two fasteners. Interference is achieved in various ways. The most common types are the nylon insert nut and a dry adhesive coating on the threads of a bolt.

Self-locking fasteners offer greater holding strength than standard fasteners, which improves their resistance to vibration. Self-locking fasteners cannot be reused. The materials used to form the lock become distorted after the initial installation and removal. Discard and replace self-locking fasteners after removing them. Do not replace self-locking fasteners with standard fasteners.

Some fasteners are equipped with a threadlocking compound pre-applied to the fastener threads (**Figure 7**). When installing these fasteners, do not apply additional separate threadlocking compound. When it is necessary to reuse one of these fasteners, remove the threadlocking compound residue from the threads. Then apply the specified threadlocking compound.

Washers

The two basic types of washers are flat washers and lockwashers. Flat washers are simple discs with a hole to fit a screw or bolt. Lockwashers are used to prevent a fastener from working loose. Washers can be used as spacers and

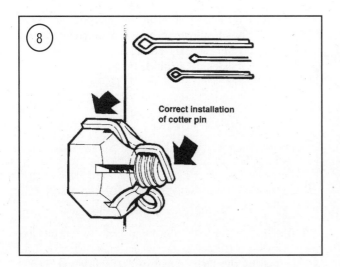

Correct installation of cotter pin

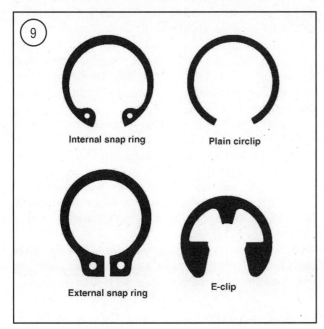

Internal snap ring

Plain circlip

External snap ring

E-clip

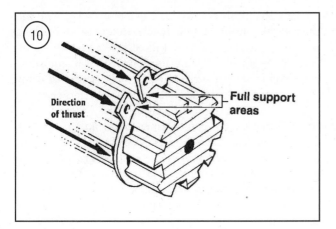

Direction of thrust

Full support areas

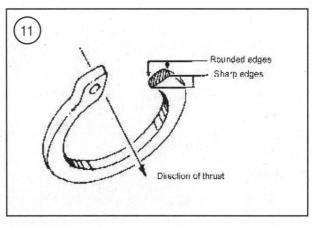

Rounded edges
Sharp edges

Direction of thrust

Cotter Pins

A cotter pin is a split metal pin inserted into a hole or slot to prevent a fastener from loosening. In certain applications, such as the rear axle on an ATV or motorcycle, the fastener must be secured in this way. For these applications, a cotter pin and castellated (slotted) nut is used.

To use a cotter pin, first make sure the diameter is correct for the hole in the fastener. After correctly tightening the fastener and aligning the holes, insert the cotter pin through the hole and bend the ends over the fastener (**Figure 8**). Unless instructed to do so, never loosen a tightened fastener to align the holes. If the holes do not align, tighten the fastener just enough to achieve alignment.

Cotter pins are available in various diameters and lengths. Measure the length from the bottom of the head to the tip of the shortest pin.

Snap Rings and E-clips

Snap rings (**Figure 9**) are circular-shaped metal retaining clips. They are required to secure parts and gears in place on parts such as shafts, pins or rods. External type snap rings are used to retain items on shafts. Internal type snap rings secure parts within housing bores. In some applications, in addition to securing the component(s), snap rings of varying thickness also determine endplay. These are usually called selective snap rings.

The two basic types of snap rings are machined and stamped snap rings. Machined snap rings (**Figure 10**) can be installed in either direction, because both faces have sharp edges. Stamped snap rings (**Figure 11**) are manufactured with a sharp and a round edge. When installing a stamped snap ring in a thrust application, install the sharp edge facing away from the part producing the thrust.

E-clips are used when it is not practical to use a snap ring. Remove E-clips with a flat blade screwdriver by prying between the shaft and E-clip. To install an E-clip, center it over the shaft groove and push or tap it into place.

Observe the following when installing snap rings:

1. Remove and install snap rings with snap ring pliers. Refer to *Basic Tools* (this chapter).

seals, or can help distribute fastener load and prevent the fastener from damaging the component.

As with fasteners, when replacing washers make sure the replacement washers are of the same design and quality.

2. In some applications, it may be necessary to replace snap rings after removing them.

3. Compress or expand snap rings just enough to install them. If overly expanded, they lose their retaining ability.

4. After installing a snap ring, make sure it seats completely.

5. Wear eye protection when removing and installing snap rings.

SHOP SUPPLIES

Lubricants and Fluids

Periodic lubrication helps ensure a long service life for any type of equipment. Using the correct type of lubricant is as important as performing the lubrication service, although in an emergency the wrong type is better than not using one. The following section describes the types of lubricants most often required. Make sure to follow the manufacturer's recommendations for lubricant types.

Engine oils

Engine oil for four-stroke motorcycle engine use is classified by three standards: the American Petroleum Institute (API) service classification, the Society of Automotive Engineers (SAE) viscosity rating and the Japanese Automobile Standards Organization (JASO) T 903 Standard classification. Always use a oil with a classification recommended by the manufacturer. Using oil with a different classification can cause engine damage.

The API service classification and the SAE viscosity index are not indications of oil quality. The API service classification indicates that the oil meets specific lubrication standards. The first letter in the classification S indicates that the oil is for gasoline engines. The second letter indicates the standard the oil satisfies. Do not use automotive oil with an SJ or higher classification. They are designed for automotive applications and contain friction modifiers that reduce frictional losses. Oils with this classification can cause engine wear in a motorcycle.

The JASO information is for oil manufactured specifically for motorcycle use.

Viscosity is an indication of the oil's thickness. Thin oils have a lower number while thick oils have a higher number. Engine oils fall into the 5- to 50-weight range for single-grade oils. The number or sequence of numbers and letter (10W-40 for example) is the viscosity rating.

Most manufacturers recommend multi-grade oil. These oils perform efficiently across a wide range of operating conditions. Multi-grade oils are identified by a W after the first number, which indicates the low-temperature viscosity.

Greases

Grease is lubricating oil with thickening agents added to it. The National Lubricating Grease Institute (NLGI) grades grease. Grades range from No. 000 to No. 6, with No. 6 being the thickest. Typical multipurpose grease is NLGI No. 2. For specific applications, manufacturers may recommend a water-resistant grease or one with an additive such as molybdenum disulfide (MoS_2).

Brake fluid

> *WARNING*
> *Use of the incorrect brake fluid may cause component damage and brake failure. Make sure the correct brake fluid is being used at all times.*

Brake fluid is the hydraulic fluid used to transmit hydraulic pressure (force) to the wheel brakes. Brake fluid is classified by the Department of Transportation (DOT) to meet particular specifications. The DOT classification, DOT 4 for example, appears on the brake fluid container.

When adding brake fluid, use only the brake fluid type recommended by the manufacturer. All models covered in this manual require DOT 4 brake fluid for the brake system, and, on Screamin' Eagle models, for the hydraulic clutch system as well.

Do not intermix different types of brake fluid. Silicone-based (DOT 5) brake fluid is not compatible with any other types or for use in systems not designed for it and may cause brake failure if so used.

Brake fluid will damage any plastic, painted or plated surface it contacts. Use extreme care when working with brake fluid and remove any spills immediately with soap and water.

Hydraulic brake systems require clean and moisture-free brake fluid. Never reuse brake fluid. Keep containers and reservoirs properly sealed.

Cleaners, Degreasers and Solvents

Many chemicals are available to remove oil, grease and other residue from the motorcycle. Before using cleaning solvents, consider how they will be used and disposed of, particularly if they are not water-soluble. Local ordinances may require special procedures for the disposal of many types of cleaning chemicals. Refer to *Safety* (this chapter).

Use brake parts cleaner to clean brake system components. Brake system parts cleaner leaves no residue. Use electrical contact cleaner to clean electrical connections and components without leaving any residue. Carburetor cleaner is a powerful solvent used to remove fuel deposits and varnish from fuel system components. Do *not* use this cleaner on any of the fuel injection components, as it may damage them.

Generally, degreasers are strong cleaners used to remove heavy accumulations of grease from engine and frame components.

Most solvents are designed to be used with a parts washing cabinet for individual component cleaning. For safety, use only nonflammable or high flashpoint solvents.

Gasket Sealant

Sealant is used in combination with a gasket or seal. In other applications, such as between crankcase halves, only a sealant is used. Follow the manufacturer's recommendation when using a sealant. Use extreme care when choosing a sealant different from the type originally recommended. Choose a sealant based on its resistance to heat, various fluids and its sealing capabilities.

A common sealant is room temperature vulcanization sealant, or RTV. This sealant cures at room temperature over a specific time period. This allows the repositioning of components without damaging gaskets.

Moisture in the air causes the RTV sealant to cure. Always install the tube cap as soon as possible after applying RTV sealant. RTV sealant has a limited shelf life and will not cure properly if the shelf life has expired. Keep partial tubes sealed and discard them if they have passed the expiration date.

Removing RTV sealant

Silicone sealant is used on some engine gasket surfaces. When cleaning parts after disassembly, a single-sided razor blade or gasket scraper is required to remove silicone residue that cannot be pulled off by hand from the gasket surface. To avoid damaging gasket surfaces, use Permatex Silicone Stripper (part No. 80647) to help soften the residue before scraping.

Applying RTV sealant

Clean all old gasket residue from the mating surfaces. Remove all gasket material from blind threaded holes to avoid inaccurate bolt torque. Spray the mating surfaces with aerosol parts cleaner and then wipe with a lint-free cloth. The area must be clean for the sealant to adhere.

Apply RTV sealant in a continuous bead 0.08-0.12 in. (2-3 mm) thick. Circle all the fastener holes with sealant unless otherwise specified. Do not allow any sealant to enter these holes. Assemble the components and tighten the fasteners to the specified torque within the time frame recommended by the sealant manufacturer.

Gasket Remover

Aerosol gasket remover can help remove stubborn gaskets. This product can speed up the removal process and prevent damage to the mating surface that may be caused by using a scraping tool. Most of these types of products are very caustic. Follow the gasket remover manufacturer's instructions for use.

Threadlocking Compound

CAUTION
Threadlock is anaerobic and will damage plastic parts. Use caution when using these products near plastic components.

Threadlock is a fluid applied to the threads of fasteners. After tightening the fastener, the fluid dries and becomes a solid filler between the threads. This makes it difficult for the fastener to work loose from vibration or heat expansion and contraction. Some types of threadlock also provide a seal against fluid leaks.

Before applying threadlock, remove any residue from both thread areas and clean them with aerosol parts cleaner. Use the threadlock sparingly. Excess fluid can run into adjoining parts.

Harley-Davidson recommends the use of Loctite Threadlocker No. 222 (purple), Loctite Threadlocker 243 (blue), Loctite 246 Medium Strength/High Temperature Threadlocker (blue) and Loctite RC/620 (green) High Temperature Retaining Compound. Use these products, or equivalent threadlock, where called for in this manual.

TOOLS

Most of the procedures in this manual can be carried out with simple hand tools and test equipment familiar to the home mechanic. Always use the correct tools for the job at hand. Keep tools organized and clean. Store them in a tool chest with related tools organized together.

Quality tools are essential. The best are constructed of high-strength alloy steel. These tools are light, easy to use and resistant to wear. Their working surface is devoid of sharp edges and carefully polished. They have an easy-to-clean finish and are comfortable to use. Quality tools are a good investment.

If purchasing tools to perform the procedures covered in this manual, consider the tool's potential frequency of use and purchase accordingly. If a tool kit is just now being started, consider purchasing a basic tool set from a quality tool supplier. These sets are available in many tool combinations and offer substantial savings when compared to individually purchased tools. As work experience grows and tasks become more complicated, specialized tools can be added.

Some of the procedures in this manual specify special tools. In many cases the tool is illustrated in use. Those with a large tool kit may be able to use a suitable substitute or fabricate a suitable replacement. However, in some cases, the specialized equipment or expertise may make it impractical for the home mechanic to attempt the procedure. When necessary, such operations come with the recommendation to have a dealership or specialist perform the task. It may be less expensive to have a professional perform these jobs, especially when considering the cost of equipment.

Refer to **Table 10** at the end of this chapter for a list of tools, their manufacturer and part number. The tools

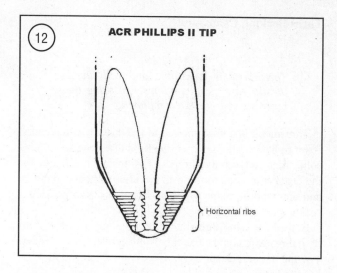

throughout this manual are either Harley-Davidson (H-D), Motion Pro (MP) or JIMS tools. Motion Pro and JIMS tools are available from dealerships and many aftermarket tool suppliers. The publisher cannot guarantee tool availability now or in the future, or that the part numbering system will remain the same. Contact the tool manufacturer for additional information.

Screwdrivers

Screwdrivers of various lengths and types are mandatory for the simplest tool kit. The two basic types are the slotted tip (flat blade) and the Phillips tip. These are available in sets that often include an assortment of tip sizes and shaft lengths.

As with all tools, use a screwdriver designed for the job. Make sure the size of the tip conforms to the size and shape of the fastener. Use them only for driving screws. Never use a screwdriver for prying or chiseling metal. Repair or replace worn or damaged screwdrivers. A worn tip may damage the fastener, making it difficult to remove.

Phillips-head screws are often damaged by incorrectly fitting screwdrivers. Quality Phillips screwdrivers are manufactured with their crosshead tip machined to Phillips Screw Company specifications. Poor quality or damaged Phillips screwdrivers can back out (camout) and round over the screw head. In addition, weak or soft screw materials can make removal difficult.

An effective screwdriver to use on Phillips screws is the ACR Phillips II screwdriver. ACR stands for the horizontal anti-camout ribs found on the driving faces or flutes of the screwdriver's tip (**Figure 12**).

Designed to be used with ACR Phillips II screws, they also work well on common Phillips screws.

Another way to prevent camout and to increase the grip of a Phillips screwdriver is to apply valve grinding compound or Permatex Screw & Socket Gripper onto the screwdriver tip. After loosening/tightening the screw, clean the screw recess to prevent engine oil contamination.

Wrenches

Box-end, open-end and combination wrenches (**Figure 13**) are available in a variety of types and sizes.

The number stamped on the wrench refers to the distance between the work areas that grip the nut or bolt. This size must match the size of the fastener head.

The box-end wrench is an excellent tool because it grips the fastener on all sides. This reduces the chance of the tool slipping. The box-end wrench is designed with either a 6 or 12-point opening. For stubborn or damaged fasteners, the 6-point provides superior holding because it contacts the fastener across a wider area at all six edges. For general use, the 12-point works well. It allows the wrench to be removed and reinstalled without moving the handle over such a wide arc.

An open-end wrench is fast and works best in areas with limited overhead access. It contacts the fastener at only two points and is subject to slipping if under heavy force, or if the tool or fastener is worn. A box-end wrench is preferred in most instances, especially when breaking loose and applying the final tightening force to a fastener.

The combination wrench has a box-end on one end and an open-end on the other. This combination makes it a convenient tool.

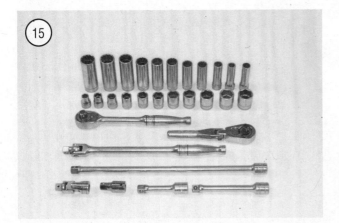

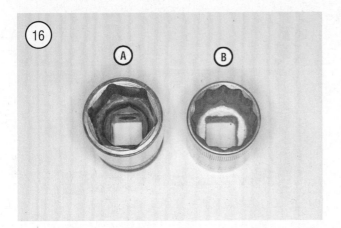

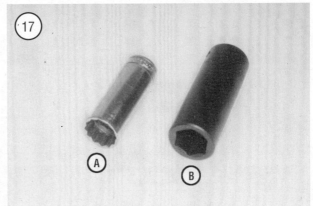

Adjustable Wrenches

An adjustable wrench or Crescent wrench (**Figure 14**) can fit nearly any nut or bolt head that has clear access around its entire perimeter. An adjustable wrench is best used as a backup wrench to keep a large nut or bolt from turning while the other end is being loosened or tightened with a box-end or socket wrench.

Adjustable wrenches contact the fastener at only two points, which makes them more subject to slipping off the fastener. Because one jaw is adjustable and may become loose, this tendency is increased. Make certain the solid jaw is the one transmitting the force.

Socket Wrenches, Ratchets and Handles

WARNING
Do not use hand sockets with air or impact tools because they may shatter and cause injury. Always wear eye protection when using impact or air tools.

Sockets that attach to a ratchet handle (**Figure 15**) are available with 6-point (A, **Figure 16**) or 12-point openings (B). As with wrenches, a 6-point socket provides superior-holding ability, while a 12-point socket needs to be moved only half as far to reposition it on the fastener. Sockets are also available in different drive sizes. The drive size in-

dicates the size of the square hole that accepts the ratchet handle. The number stamped on the socket is the size of the work area and must match the fastener head.

Sockets are designated for either hand or impact use. Impact sockets are made of thicker material for more durability. Compare the size and wall thickness of a 19-mm hand socket (A, **Figure 17**) and the 19-mm impact socket (B). Use impact sockets when using an impact driver or air tools. Use hand sockets with hand-driven attachments.

Various handles are available for sockets. Use the speed handle for fast operation. Flexible ratchet heads in varying lengths allow the socket to be turned with varying force and at odd angles. Extension bars allow the socket setup to reach difficult areas. The ratchet is the most versatile. It allows the user to install or remove the nut without removing the socket.

Sockets combined with any number of drivers make them undoubtedly the fastest, safest and most convenient tool for fastener removal and installation.

Impact Drivers

WARNING
Do not use hand sockets with air or impact tools because they may shatter and cause injury. Always wear eye protection when using impact or air tools.

An impact driver provides extra force for removing fasteners by converting the impact of a hammer into a turning motion. This makes it possible to remove stubborn fasteners without damaging them. Impact drivers and interchangeable bits (**Figure 18**) are available from most tool suppliers. When using a socket with an impact driver, make sure the socket is designed for impact use. Refer to *Socket Wrenches, Ratchets and Handles* in this section.

Allen Wrenches

Use Allen or setscrew wrenches (**Figure 19**) on fasteners with hexagonal recesses in the fastener head. These wrench-

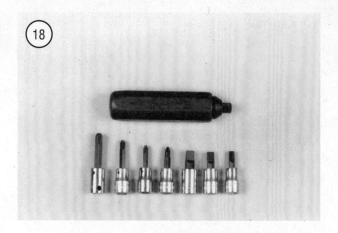

es are available in L-shaped bar, socket and T-handle types. Allen bolts are sometimes called socket bolts.

Torque Wrenches

Use a torque wrench with a socket, torque adapter or similar extension to tighten a fastener to a measured torque. Torque wrenches come in several drive sizes (1/4, 3/8, 1/2 and 3/4) and use various methods to display the torque value. The drive size indicates the size of the square drive that accepts the socket, adapter or extension. Common methods of displaying the torque value are the deflecting beam, the dial indicator and the audible click type of torque wrench (**Figure 20**).

When choosing a torque wrench, consider the torque range, drive size and accuracy needed. The torque specifications in this manual provide an indication of the range required.

A torque wrench is a precision tool that must be properly cared for to remain accurate. Store torque wrenches in cases or separate padded drawers within a toolbox. Follow the manufacturer's instructions for their care and calibration.

Torque Adapters

Torque adapters or extensions extend or reduce the reach of a torque wrench. The torque adapter is used to tighten a fastener that cannot be reached because of the size of the torque wrench head, drive and socket. If a torque adapter changes the effective lever length (**Figure 21**), the torque reading on the wrench will not equal the actual torque applied to the fastener. It is necessary to recalibrate the torque setting on the wrench to compensate for the change of lever length. When using a torque adapter at a right angle to the drive head, calibration is not required, because the effective length has not changed.

To recalculate a torque reading when using a torque adapter, use the following formula and refer to **Figure 21**.

$$TW = \frac{TA \times L}{L + A}$$

TW is the torque setting or dial reading on the wrench.

TA is the torque specification and the actual amount of torque that is applied to the fastener.

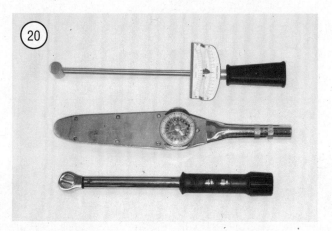

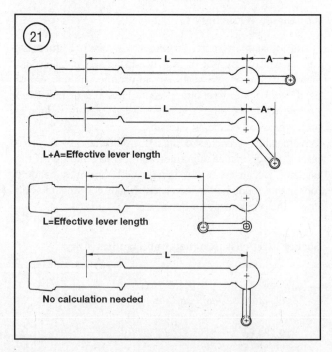

A is the amount that the adapter increases (or in some cases reduces) the effective lever length as measured along the centerline of the torque wrench.

L is the lever length of the wrench as measured from the center of the drive to the center of the grip.

The effective length is the sum of L and A.

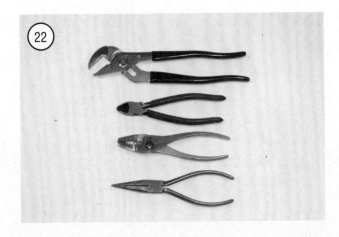

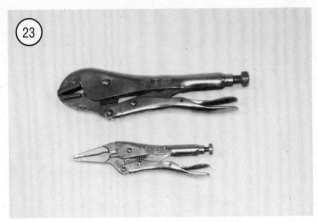

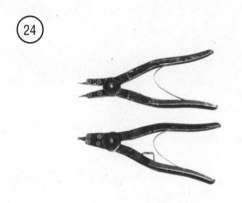

Example:
TA = 20 ft.-lb.
A = 3 in.
L = 14 in.
$$TW = \frac{20 \times 14}{14 + 3} = \frac{280}{17} = 16.5 \text{ ft.-lb.}$$

In this example, the torque wrench would be set to the recalculated torque value (TW = 16.5 ft.-lb.). When using a beam-type wrench, tighten the fastener until the pointer aligns with 16.5 ft.-lb. In this example, although the torque wrench is pre set to 16.5 ft.-lb., the actual torque applied to the fastener is 20 ft.-lb.

Pliers

Pliers come in a wide range of types and sizes. Pliers are useful for holding, cutting, bending and crimping. Do not use them to turn fasteners. **Figure 22** shows several types of useful pliers. Each design has a specialized function. Slip-joint pliers are general-purpose pliers used for gripping and bending. Diagonal cutting pliers are needed to cut wire and can be used to remove cotter pins. Use needlenose pliers to hold or bend small objects. Locking pliers (**Figure 23**), sometimes called Vise-Grips, are used to hold objects very tightly. They have many uses ranging from holding two parts together, to gripping the end of a broken stud. Use caution when using locking pliers, as the sharp jaws will damage the objects they hold.

Snap Ring Pliers

> *WARNING*
> *Snap rings can slip and fly off when removing and installing them or the plier tips may break. Always wear eye protection when using snap ring pliers.*

Snap ring pliers are specialized pliers with tips that fit into the ends of snap rings to remove and install them.

Snap ring pliers (**Figure 24**) are available with a fixed action (either internal or external) or convertible (one tool works on both internal and external snap rings). They may have fixed tips or interchangeable ones of various sizes and angles. For general use, select convertible-type pliers with interchangeable tips.

Hammers

Various types of hammers are available to fit a number of applications. Use a ball-peen hammer to strike another tool, such as a punch or chisel. Use soft-faced hammers when a metal object must be struck without damaging it. Never use a metal-faced hammer on engine or suspension components because damage will occur.

Always wear eye protection when using hammers. Make sure the hammer face is in good condition and the handle is not cracked. Select the correct hammer for the job and make sure to strike the object squarely. Do not use the handle or the side of the hammer to strike an object.

MEASURING TOOLS

The ability to accurately measure components is essential to perform many of the procedures described in this manual. Equipment is manufactured to close tolerances and obtaining consistently accurate measurements is essential to determine which components require replacement or further service.

Each type of measuring instrument (**Figure 25**) is designed to measure a dimension with a certain degree of accuracy and within a certain range. When selecting the measuring tool, make sure it is applicable to the task.

As with all tools, measuring tools provide the best results if cared for properly. Improper use can damage the tool and cause inaccurate results. If any measurement is questionable, verify the measurement using another tool. A standard gauge is usually provided with micrometers to check accuracy and calibrate the tool if necessary.

Precision of measurements can vary according to the experience of the person performing the procedure. Accurate results are only possible if the mechanic possesses a feel for using the tool. Heavy-handed use of measuring tools produces less accurate results. Hold the tool gently by the fingertips to easily feel the point at which the tool contacts the object. A feel for the equipment produces more accurate measurements and reduces the risk of damaging the tool or component. Refer to the following sections for specific measuring tools.

Feeler Gauge

Feeler or thickness gauges (**Figure 26**) are required to measure the distance between two surfaces.

A feeler gauge set consists of an assortment of steel strips of graduated thickness. Each blade is marked with its thickness. Blades can be of various lengths and angles for different procedures.

A common use for a feeler gauge is to measure valve clearance. Use wire (round) type gauges to measure spark plug gap.

Calipers

Calipers (**Figure 27**) are excellent tools for obtaining inside, outside and depth measurements. Although not as precise as a micrometer, they allow reasonable precision, typically to within 0.05 mm (0.001 in.). Most calipers have a range up to 150 mm (6 in.).

Calipers are available in dial, vernier or digital versions. Dial calipers have a dial readout that provides convenient reading. Vernier calipers have marked scales that must be compared to determine the measurement. The digital caliper uses a liquid-crystal display (LCD) to show the measurement.

Properly maintain the measuring surfaces of the caliper. There must not be any dirt or burrs between the tool and the object being measured. Never force the caliper to close around an object. Close the caliper around the highest point so it can be removed with a slight drag. Some calipers require calibration. Always refer to the manufacturer's instructions when using a new or unfamiliar caliper.

To read a vernier caliper refer to **Figure 28**. The fixed scale is marked in 1-mm increments. Ten individual lines on the fixed scale equal 1 cm. The movable scale is marked in 0.05 mm (hundredth) increments. To obtain a reading, establish the first number by the location of the 0 line on the movable scale in relation to the first line to the left on the fixed scale.

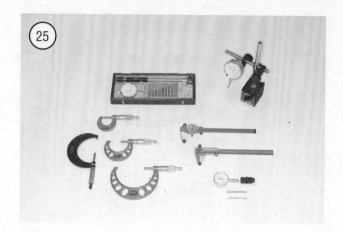

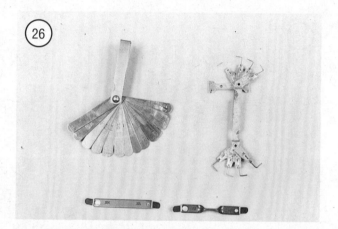

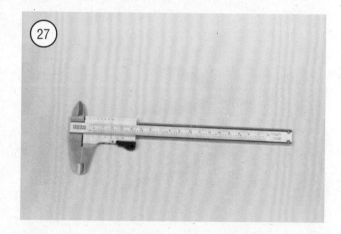

In this example, the number is 10 mm. To determine the next number, note which of the lines on the movable scale align with a mark on the fixed scale. A number of lines will seem close, but only one will align exactly. In this case, 0.50 mm is the reading to add to the first number. Adding 10 mm and 0.50 mm equals a measurement of 10.50 mm.

Micrometers

A micrometer is an instrument designed for linear measurement using the decimal divisions of the inch or meter. While there are many types and styles of micrometers (**Figure 29**), most of the procedures in this manual call

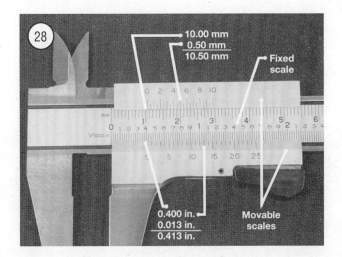

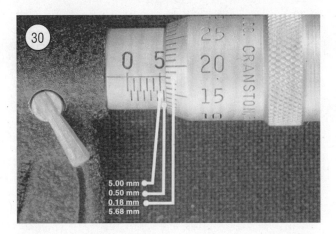

for an outside micrometer. Use the outside micrometer to measure the outside diameter of cylindrical forms and the thickness of materials.

A micrometer's size indicates the minimum and maximum size of a part that it can measure. The usual sizes are 0-25 mm (0-1 in.), 25-50 mm (1-2 in.), 50-75 mm (2-3 in.) and 75-100 mm (3-4 in.).

Micrometers that cover a wider range of measurements are available. These use a large frame with interchangeable anvils of various lengths. This type of micrometer offers a cost savings, but its overall size may make it less convenient.

Adjustment

Before using a micrometer, check its adjustment as follows:
1. Clean the anvil and spindle faces.
2A. To check a 0-1 in. or 0-25 mm micrometer:
   a. Turn the thimble until the spindle contacts the anvil. If the micrometer has a ratchet stop, use it to ensure that the proper amount of pressure is applied.
   b. If the adjustment is correct, the 0 mark on the thimble will align exactly with the 0 mark on the sleeve line. If the marks do not align, the micrometer is out of adjustment.
   c. Follow the manufacturer's instructions to adjust the micrometer.
2B. To check a micrometer larger than 1 in. or 25 mm use the standard gauge supplied by the manufacturer. A standard gauge is a steel block, disc or rod that is machined to an exact size.
   a. Place the standard gauge between the spindle and anvil and measure its outside diameter or length. If the micrometer has a ratchet stop, use it to ensure that the proper amount of pressure is applied.
   b. If the adjustment is correct, the 0 mark on the thimble will align exactly with the 0 mark on the sleeve line. If the marks do not align, the micrometer is out of adjustment.
   c. Follow the manufacturer's instructions to adjust the micrometer.

Care

Micrometers are precision instruments. They must be used and maintained with great care. Note the following:
1. Store micrometers in protective cases or in separate padded drawers of a toolbox.
2. When in storage, make sure the spindle and anvil faces do not contact each other or an other object. If they do, temperature changes and corrosion may damage the contact faces.
3. Do not clean a micrometer with compressed air. Dirt forced into the tool will cause wear.
4. Lubricate micrometers with WD-40 to prevent corrosion.

Reading

When reading a micrometer, numbers are taken from different scales and added together. The following sections describe how to read the measurements of various types of outside micrometers.

For accurate results, properly maintain the measuring surfaces of the micrometer. There cannot be any dirt or burrs between the tool and the measured object. Never force the micrometer to close around an object. Close the micrometer around the highest point so it can be removed with a slight drag.

The standard metric micrometer (**Figure 30**) is accurate to one one-hundredth of a millimeter (0.01 mm). The sleeve line is graduated in millimeter and half millimeter increments. The marks on the upper half of the sleeve line equal 1.00 mm. Each fifth mark above the sleeve line is identified with a number. The number sequence depends on the size of the micrometer. A 0-25 mm micrometer, for example, will have sleeve marks numbered 0 through 25 in 5 mm increments. This numbering sequence continues with larger micrometers. On all metric micrometers, each mark on the lower half of the sleeve equals 0.50 mm.

The tapered end of the thimble has 50 lines marked around it. Each mark equals 0.01 mm. One complete turn of the thimble aligns its 0 mark with the first line on the lower half of the sleeve line or 0.50 mm.

When reading a metric micrometer, add the number of millimeters and half-millimeters on the sleeve line to the number of one one-hundredth millimeters on the thimble. Perform the following steps while referring to **Figure 30**.

1. Read the upper half of the sleeve line and count the number of lines visible. Each upper line equals 1 mm.

2. See if the half-millimeter line is visible on the lower sleeve line. If so, add 0.50 mm to the reading in Step 1.

3. Read the thimble mark that aligns with the sleeve line. Each thimble mark equals 0.01 mm.

4. If a thimble mark does not align exactly with the sleeve line, estimate the amount between the lines. For accurate readings in two-thousandths of a millimeter (0.002 mm), use a metric vernier micrometer.

5. Add the readings from these steps together to get the final measurement.

Telescoping and Small Bore Gauges

Use telescoping gauges (**Figure 31**) and small bore gauges (**Figure 32**) to measure bores. Neither gauge has a scale for direct readings. Use an outside micrometer to determine the reading.

To use a telescoping gauge, select the correct size gauge for the bore. Compress the movable post and carefully insert the gauge into the bore. Carefully move the gauge in the bore to make sure it is centered. Tighten the knurled end of the gauge to hold the movable post in position. Remove the gauge and measure the length of the posts. Telescoping gauges are typically used to measure cylinder bores.

To use a small bore gauge, select the correct size gauge for the bore. Carefully insert the gauge into the bore. Tighten the knurled end of the gauge to carefully expand the gauge fingers to the limit within the bore. Do not overtighten the gauge because there is no built-in release. Excessive tightening can damage the bore surface and damage the tool. Remove the gauge and measure the outside dimension (**Figure 33**). Small bore gauges are typically used to measure valve guides.

Dial Indicator

A dial indicator (**Figure 34**) is a gauge with a dial face and needle used to measure variations in dimensions and

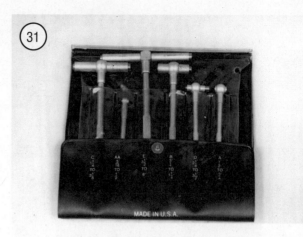

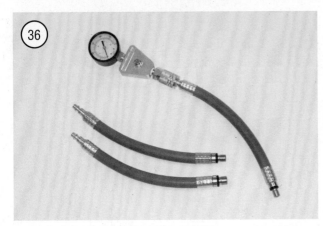

taper and out-of-round. When using a bore gauge, follow the manufacturer's instructions.

Compression Gauge

A compression gauge (**Figure 36**) measures combustion chamber (cylinder) pressure, usually in psi or kg/cm^2. The gauge adapter is either inserted or screwed into the spark plug hole to obtain the reading. Disable the engine so it will not start and hold the throttle in the wide-open position when performing a compression test. An engine that does not have adequate compression cannot be properly tuned. Refer to Chapter Three for compression test procedures.

Multimeter

A digital multimeter (**Figure 37**) is an essential tool for electrical system diagnosis. The voltage function indicates the voltage applied or available to various electrical components. The ohmmeter function tests circuits for continuity, or lack of continuity and measures the resistance of a circuit.

Some manufacturers' specifications for electrical components are based on results using a specific test meter. Results may vary if a meter not recommended by the manufacturer is used. Such requirements are noted when applicable.

If an analog ohmmeter is used, it must be calibrated. Refer to the meter manufacturer's instructions.

ELECTRICAL SYSTEM FUNDAMENTALS

Refer to *Electrical Testing* and *Electrical Troubleshooting* in Chapter Two for typical test procedures and equipment. Refer to Chapter Eleven for specific system test procedures.

Refer to the following for electrical basics necessary to perform simple diagnostic tests.

Voltage

Voltage is the electrical potential or pressure in an electrical circuit and is expressed in volts. The more pressure (voltage) in a circuit, the more work can be performed.

Direct current (DC) voltage means the electricity flows in one direction. All circuits powered by a battery are DC circuits.

Alternating current (AC) means the electricity flows in one direction momentarily and then switches to the opposite direction. Alternator output is an example of AC voltage. This voltage must be changed or rectified to direct current to operate in a battery powered system.

movements. Measuring brake rotor runout is a typical use for a dial indicator.

Dial indicators are available in various ranges and graduations. They can come with any of three basic types of mounting bases: magnetic, clamp, or screw-in stud.

Cylinder Bore Gauge

A cylinder bore gauge is similar to a dial indicator. The gauge set shown in **Figure 35** consists of a dial indicator, handle and different length adapters (anvils) to fit various bore sizes. The bore gauge is used to measure bore size,

Resistance

Resistance is the opposition to the flow of electricity within a circuit or component and is measured in ohms. Resistance causes a reduction in available current and voltage.

Measure resistance in an inactive circuit with an ohmmeter. An ohmmeter, although useful, is not always a good indicator of a circuit's actual ability under operating conditions. This is because of the low voltage (6-9 volts) the meter uses to test the circuit. The voltage in an ignition coil secondary winding can be several thousand volts. Such high voltage can cause the coil to malfunction, even though it tests acceptable during a resistance test.

Resistance generally increases with temperature. Perform all testing with the component or circuit at room temperature. Resistance tests performed at high temperatures may indicate high resistance readings and cause unnecessary replacement of a component.

Amperage

Amperage is the unit of measurement for the amount of current within a circuit. Current is the actual flow of electricity. The higher the current, the more work can be performed up to a given point. If the current flow exceeds the circuit or component capacity, it will damage the system.

SERVICE METHODS

Most of the procedures in this manual are straightforward and can be performed by anyone reasonably competent with tools. However, consider personal capabilities carefully before attempting any operation involving major disassembly.

1. *Front*, in this manual, refers to the front of the motorcycle. The front of any component is the end closest to the front of the motorcycle. The left and right sides refer to the position of the parts as viewed by the rider sitting on the seat facing forward.
2. Whenever servicing an engine or suspension component, secure the motorcycle in a safe manner.
3. Tag all similar parts for location and mark all mating parts for position. Record the number and thickness of any shims when removing them. Identify parts by placing them in sealed and labeled plastic sandwich bags.
4. Tag disconnected wires and connectors with masking tape and a marking pen. Do not rely on memory alone.
5. Protect finished surfaces from physical damage or corrosion. Keep gasoline and other chemicals off painted surfaces.
6. Use penetrating oil on frozen or tight bolts. Avoid using heat where possible. Heat can warp, melt or affect the temper of parts. Heat also damages the finish of paint and plastics.
7. When a part is a press fit or requires a special tool to remove, the information or type of tool is identified in the text. Otherwise, if a part is difficult to remove or install, determine the cause before proceeding.

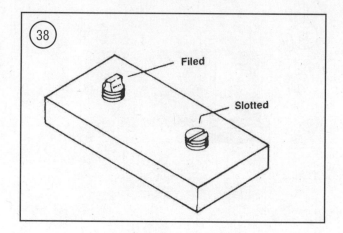

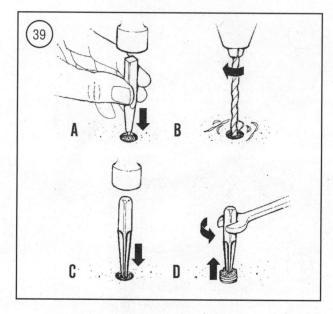

8. To prevent objects or debris from falling into the engine, cover all openings.
9. Read each procedure thoroughly and compare the illustrations to the actual components before starting the procedure. Perform the procedure in sequence.
10. Recommendations are occasionally made to refer service to a dealership or specialist. In these cases, the work can be performed more economically by the specialist than by the home mechanic.
11. The term replace means to discard a defective part and replace it with a new part. Overhaul means to remove, disassemble, inspect, measure, repair and/or replace parts as required to recondition an assembly.
12. Some operations require using a hydraulic press. If a press is not available, have these operations performed by a shop equipped with the necessary equipment. Do not use makeshift equipment that may damage the motorcycle.
13. Repairs are much faster and easier if the motorcycle is clean before starting work. Degrease the motorcycle with a commercial degreaser; follow the directions on the container for the best results. Clean all parts with cleaning solvent when removing them.

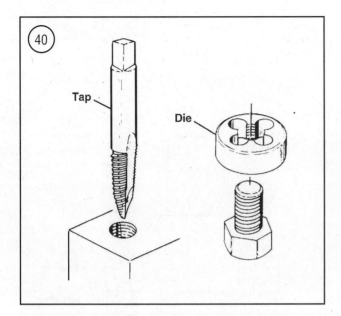

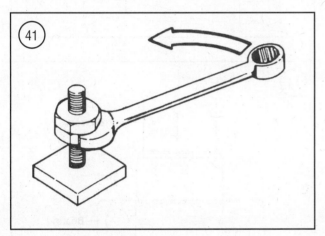

CAUTION
Do not direct high-pressure water at steering bearings, fuel hoses, transmission vent hose, wheel bearings, suspension and electrical components. Water may force grease out of the bearings and possibly damage the seals.

14. If special tools are required, have them available before starting the procedure. When special tools are required, they are described at the beginning of the procedure.

15. Make diagrams of similar-appearing parts. For instance, crankcase bolts are often not the same lengths. Do not rely on memory alone. Carefully laid out parts can become disturbed, making it difficult to reassemble the components correctly.

16. Make sure all shims and washers are reinstalled in the same location and position.

17. Whenever rotating parts contact a stationary part, look for a shim or washer.

18. Use new gaskets if there is any doubt about the condition of old ones.

19. If using self-locking fasteners, replace them with new ones. Do not install standard fasteners in place of self-locking ones.

20. Use grease to hold small parts in place if they tend to fall out during assembly. Do not apply grease to electrical or brake components.

Removing Frozen Fasteners

If a fastener cannot be removed, several methods may be used to loosen it. First, apply penetrating oil such as Liquid Wrench or WD-40. Apply it liberally and let it penetrate for 10-15 minutes. Rap the fastener several times with a small hammer. Do not hit it hard enough to cause damage. Reapply the penetrating oil if necessary.

For frozen screws, apply penetrating oil as described, and then insert a screwdriver in the slot and rap the top of the screwdriver with a hammer. This loosens the rust so the screw can be removed in the normal way. If the screw head is too damaged to use this method, grip the head with locking pliers and twist the screw out.

Avoid applying heat unless specifically instructed. Heat may melt, warp or remove the temper from parts.

Removing Broken Fasteners

If the head breaks off a screw or bolt, several methods are available for removing the remaining portion. If a large portion of the remainder projects out, try gripping it with locking pliers. If the projecting portion is too small, file it to fit a wrench or cut a slot in it to fit a screwdriver (**Figure 38**).

If the head breaks off flush, use a screw extractor. To do this, center punch the exact center of the remaining portion of the screw or bolt (A, **Figure 39**). Drill a small hole in the screw (B, **Figure 39**) and tap the extractor into the hole (C). Back the screw out with a wrench on the extractor (D, **Figure 39**).

Repairing Damaged Threads

Occasionally, threads are stripped through carelessness or impact damage. Often the threads can be repaired by running a tap (for internal threads on nuts) or die (for external threads on bolts) through the threads (**Figure 40**). To clean or repair spark plug threads, use a spark plug tap.

If an internal thread is damaged, it may be necessary to install a Helicoil or some other type of thread insert. Follow the insert manufacturer's instructions when installing it.

If it is necessary to drill and tap a hole, refer to **Table 8** or **Table 9** for the applicable tap and drill sizes.

Stud Removal/Installation

A stud removal tool is available from most tool suppliers. This tool makes the removal and installation of studs easier. If one is not available, thread two nuts onto the stud and tighten them against each other. Remove the stud by turning the lower nut (**Figure 41**). Remove and install studs as follows:

1. Measure the height of the stud above the surface.

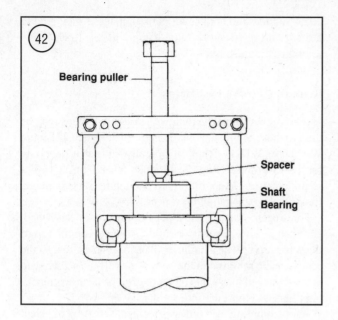

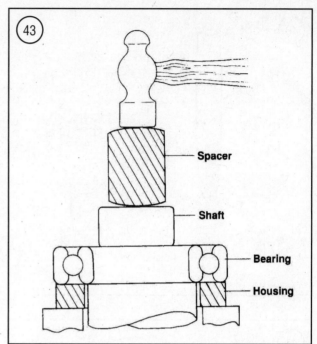

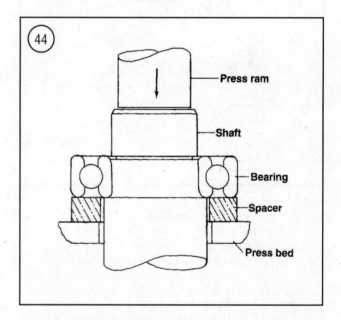

2. Thread the stud removal tool onto the stud and tighten it, or thread two nuts onto the stud.

3. Remove the stud by turning the stud remover or the lower nut.

4. Remove any threadlock residue from the threaded hole. Clean the threads with a aerosol parts cleaner.

5. Install the stud removal tool onto the new stud or thread two nuts onto the stud.

6. Apply threadlock to the threads of the stud.

7. Install the stud and tighten with the stud removal tool or the top nut.

8. Install the stud to the height noted or tighten to its torque specification.

9. Remove the stud removal tool or the two nuts.

Removing Hoses

Do not exert excessive force on the hose or fitting when removing stubborn hoses. Remove the hose clamp and carefully insert a small screwdriver or pick tool between the fitting and hose. Apply a spray lubricant under the hose and carefully twist the hose off the fitting. Clean the fitting of any corrosion or rubber hose material with a wire brush. Clean the inside of the hose thoroughly. Do *not* use any lubricant when installing the new or old hose. The lubricant may allow the hose to come off the fitting, even with the clamp secure.

Bearings

Bearings are used in the engine and transmission assembly to reduce power loss, heat and noise resulting from friction. Because bearings are precision parts, they must be maintained with proper lubrication and maintenance. If a bearing is damaged, replace it immediately. When installing a new bearing, take care to prevent damaging it. Bearing replacement procedures are included in the indi-

vidual chapters where applicable; however, use the following sections as a guideline.

NOTE
Unless otherwise specified, install bearings with the manufacturer's mark or number facing outward.

Removal

While bearings are normally removed only when damaged, there may be times when it is necessary to remove a bearing that is in good condition. However, improper bear-

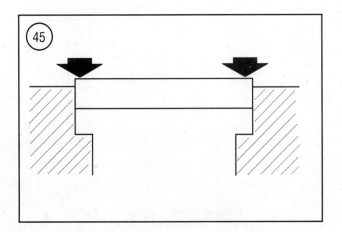

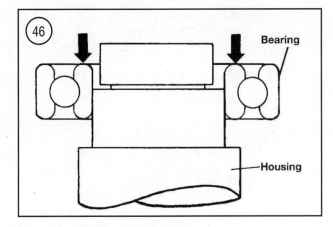

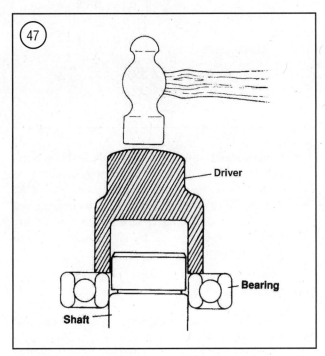

screw. In addition, place the puller arms next to the inner bearing race as shown in **Figure 42**.

2. When using a hammer to remove a bearing from a shaft, do not strike the hammer directly against the shaft. Instead, use a brass or aluminum rod between the hammer and shaft and make sure to support both bearing races with wooden blocks as shown in **Figure 43**.

3. The ideal method of bearing removal is with a hydraulic press. Note the following when using a press:

   a. Always support the inner and outer bearing races with a suitable size wooden or aluminum spacer (**Figure 44**). If only the outer race is supported, pressure applied against the balls and/or the inner race will damage them.

   b. Always make sure the press arm (**Figure 44**) aligns with the center of the shaft. If the arm is not centered, it may damage the bearing and/or shaft.

   c. The moment the shaft is free of the bearing, it drops to the floor. Secure or hold the shaft to prevent it from falling.

Installation

1. When installing a bearing into a housing, apply pressure to the outer bearing race (**Figure 45**). When installing a bearing on a shaft, apply pressure to the inner bearing race (**Figure 46**).

2. When installing a bearing, some type of driver is required. Never strike the bearing directly with a hammer or it will damage the bearing. When installing a bearing, use a piece of pipe or a driver with a diameter that matches the bearing inner race. **Figure 47** shows the correct way to use a driver and hammer to install a bearing.

3. This procedure describes how to install a bearing in a case half or over a shaft. However, when installing a bearing over a shaft and into the housing at the same time, a tight fit is required for both outer and inner bearing races. In this situation, install a spacer underneath the driver tool so that pressure is applied evenly across both races as shown in **Figure 48**. If the outer race is not supported as shown, the balls will push against the outer bearing race and damage it.

Interference fit

1. Follow this procedure when installing a bearing over a shaft. When a tight fit is required, the bearing inside diameter is smaller than the shaft. In this case, driving the bearing on the shaft using normal methods may cause bearing damage. Instead, heat the bearing before installation. Note the following:

   a. Secure the shaft so it is ready for bearing installation.

   b. Clean all residue from the bearing surface of the shaft. Remove burrs with a file or sandpaper.

   c. Fill a suitable pot or beaker with clean mineral oil. Place a thermometer rated above 120° C (248° F) in

ing removal will damage the bearing and possibly the shaft or case. Note the following when removing bearings:

1. When using a puller to remove a bearing from a shaft, take care that the shaft is not damaged. Always place a piece of metal between the end of the shaft and the puller

the oil. Support the thermometer so it does not rest on the bottom or side of the pot.

d. Remove the bearing from its wrapper and secure it with a piece of heavy wire bent to hold it in the pot. Hang the bearing in the pot so it does not touch the bottom or sides of the pot.

e. Turn the heat on and monitor the thermometer. When the oil temperature rises to approximately 120° C (248° F), remove the bearing from the pot and quickly install it. If necessary, place a socket on the inner bearing race and tap the bearing into place. As the bearing chills, it will tighten on the shaft, so installation must be done quickly. Make sure the bearing is installed completely.

2. Follow this step when installing a bearing in a housing. Bearings are generally installed in a housing with a slight interference fit. Driving the bearing into the housing using normal methods may damage the housing or cause bearing damage. Instead, heat the housing before the bearing is installed. Note the following:

CAUTION
Before heating the housing in this procedure, wash the housing thoroughly with detergent and water. Rinse and rewash the cases as required to remove all traces of oil and other chemical deposits.

a. Heat the housing to approximately 100° C (212° F) in an oven or on a hot plate. An easy way to check that it is the proper temperature is to place tiny drops of water on the housing; if they sizzle and evaporate immediately, the temperature is correct. Heat only one housing at a time.

CAUTION
Do not heat the housing with a propane or acetylene torch. Never bring a flame into contact with the bearing or housing. The direct heat will destroy the case hardening of the bearing and will likely warp the housing.

b. Remove the housing from the oven or hot plate and hold onto the housing with welding gloves. It is hot!

NOTE
Remove and install the bearings with a suitable size socket and extension.

c. Hold the housing with the bearing side down and tap the bearing out. Repeat for all bearings in the housing.

d. Before heating the bearing housing, place the new bearing in a freezer if possible. Chilling a bearing slightly reduces its outside diameter while the heated bearing housing assembly is slightly larger due to heat expansion. This makes bearing installation easier.

NOTE
Always install bearings with the manufacturer's mark or number facing outward.

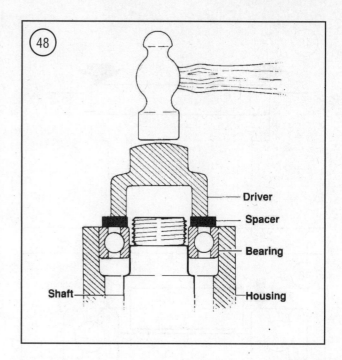

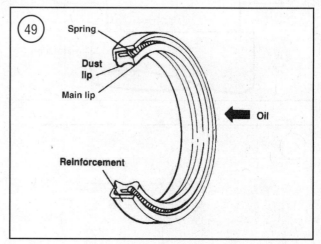

e. While the housing is still hot, install the new bearing(s) into the housing. Install the bearings by hand, if possible. If necessary, lightly tap the bearing(s) into the housing with a driver placed on the outer bearing race (**Figure 45**). Do not install new bearings by driving on the inner-bearing race. Install the bearing(s) until it seats completely.

Seal Replacement

Seals (**Figure 49**) contain oil, water, grease or combustion gases in a housing or shaft. Improperly removing a seal can damage the housing or shaft. Improperly installing the seal can damage the seal. Note the following:

1. Prying is generally the easiest and most effective method of removing a seal from the housing. However, always place a rag underneath the pry tool to prevent damage to the housing. Note the seal's installed depth or if it is installed flush.

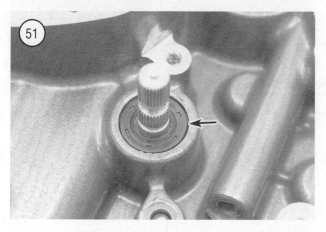

2. On small seals, screw a sheet metal screw (A, **Figure 50**) into the seal (B), being careful not to damage the bearing beneath it. Pull straight up on the screw and remove the seal.

3. Pack waterproof grease in the seal lips before the new seal is installed.

4. In most cases, install seals with the manufacturer's numbers or marks facing out.

5. Install seals with a socket or driver placed on the outside (**Figure 51**) of the seal. Drive the seal squarely into the housing until it is seated to the correct depth or flush as noted during removal. Never install a seal by hitting against the top of it with a hammer.

STORAGE

Several months of non-use can cause a general deterioration of the motorcycle. This is especially true in areas of extreme temperature variations. This deterioration can be minimized with careful preparation for storage. A properly stored motorcycle is much easier to return to service.

Storage Area Selection

When selecting a storage area, consider the following:
1. The storage area must be dry. A heated area is best, but not necessary. It should be insulated to minimize extreme temperature variations.

2. If the building has large window areas, mask them to keep sunlight off the motorcycle.
3. Avoid buildings in industrial areas where corrosive emissions may be present. Avoid areas close to saltwater.
4. Consider the area's risk of fire, theft or vandalism. Check with an insurer regarding motorcycle coverage while in storage.

Preparing the Motorcycle for Storage

The amount of preparation a motorcycle should undergo before storage depends on the expected length of non-use, storage area conditions and personal preference. Consider the following list the minimum requirement:
1. Wash the motorcycle thoroughly. Make sure all dirt, mud and road debris are removed.
2. Fill the fuel tank with a mixture of fuel and fuel stabilizer. Mix the fuel and stabilizer in the ratio recommended by the stabilizer manufacturer. Run the engine for a few minutes so the stabilized fuel can enter the fuel system. If the motorcycle will be stored for a long period, consider draining the fuel system.
3. Start the engine and allow it to reach operating temperature. Drain the engine oil regardless of the riding time since the last service. Fill the engine with the recommended type of oil.
4. Fill the fuel tank completely. There is no need to try to empty the fuel delivery or return lines since they are not vented to the atmosphere.
5. Remove the spark plugs and pour a teaspoon of engine oil into the cylinders. Place a rag over the openings and slowly turn the engine over to distribute the oil. Reinstall the spark plugs.
6. Remove the battery. Store the battery in a cool and dry location. Charge the battery once a month.
7. Cover the exhaust and intake openings.
8. Apply a protective substance to the plastic and rubber components. Make sure to follow the manufacturer's instructions for each type of product being used.
9. Place the motorcycle on blocks with the wheels off the ground.
10. Cover the motorcycle with old bed sheets or something similar that can breathe. Do not cover it with any plastic material that will trap moisture.

Returning the Motorcycle to Service

The amount of service required when returning a motorcycle to service after storage depends on the length of non-use and storage conditions. In addition to performing the reverse of the above procedure, make sure the brakes, clutch, throttle and engine run/stop switch work properly before operating the motorcycle. Refer to Chapter Three and evaluate the service intervals to determine which areas require service.

Table 1 MODEL DESIGNATIONS

FLHTC Electra Glide Classic (2010-on)
FLHTK Electra Glide Ultra Limited (2010-on)
FLHR Road King (2010-on)
FLHRC Road King Classic (2010-on)
FLTRX Road Glide Custom (2010-on)
FLTRU Road Glide Ultra (2011-on)
FLHX Street Glide (2010-on)
FLHTCUSE5 CVO Ultra Classic Electra Glide (2010)
FLHTCUSE6 CVO Ultra Classic Electra Glide (2011)
FLHTCUSE7 CVO Ultra Classic Electra Glide (2012)
FLHTCUSE8 CVO Ultra Classic Electra Glide (2013)
FLTRUSE CVO Road Glide Ultra (2011)
FLHRSE5 CVO Road Glide Custom (2013)
FLHXSE CVO Street Glide (2010)
FLHXSE2 CVO Street Glide (2011)
FLTRXSE Road Glide Custom (2012)
FLTRXSE2 Road Glide Custom (2013)

*The I designation indicates models equipped with fuel injection.

Table 2 GENERAL MOTORCYCLE DIMENSIONS

Item/model	in.	mm
Wheel base	63.5	1613
Overall length		
FLHTC	98.3	2497
FLHTCU, FLHTK, FLTRU	98.6	2504
FLHR, FLTRX, FLHX, FLHRSE	95.0	2413
FLHRC	94.2	2393
FLHTCUSE		
2010	98.2	2494.28
2011-2013	98.8	2510
FLHXSE	96.23	2444.24
FLTRUSE	98.8	2510
FLTRXSE	96.2	2443
Overall width		
FLHTC, FLHTCU, FLHTK, FLHX	38.0	965
FLTRU	36.2	319
FLHR, FLHRSE	37.4	950
FLHRC	37.5	953
FLTRX, FLTRXSE	35.8	909
FLHTCUSE, FLTRUSE	38.0	965
FLHXSE	38.38	972.31
Road clearance		
FLHTC, FLHTCU, FLHTK, FLTRU,		
FLHR, FLHRC, FLTRX	5.1	130
FLHX	4.7	119
FLHTCUSE, FLHRSE, FLTRXSE	5.1	130
FLHXSE	5.09	129.29
Overall height		
FLHTC, FLHTCU, FLHTK	61.0	1549
FLTRU	55.0	1397
FLHR, FLHRC	55.1	1400
FLTRX, FLTRXSE	50.0	1270
FLHX	52.2	1326
FLHTCUE	57.0	1447.80
FLHXSE	52.80	1341.12
FLHRSE	55.1	1400
FLTRUSE	55.4	14070
Saddle height		
FLHTC, FLHTCU, FLHTK, FLTRU	27.3	693
FLHR, FLHRSE	26.5	673
FLHRC	26.7	678
FLHRX, FLHX	26.1	663

(continued)

Table 2 GENERAL MOTORCYCLE DIMENSIONS (continued)

Item/model	in.	mm
Saddle height (continued)		
FLHTCUSE		
2010	27.4	695.96
2011-2013	27.8	706.20
FLHXSE	26.48	672.59
FLTRUSE	27.5	699
FLHRXSE	26.6	676

Table 3 MOTORCYCLE WEIGHT

Model	Dry weight lb. (kg)*	Gross vehicle weight lb. (kg)	Gross axle weight front lb. (kg)	Gross axle weight rear lb.(kg)
FLHTC	864 (391.9)	1360 (616.9)	500 (226.8)	927 (420.5)
FLHTCU	889 (403.3)	1360 (616.9)	500 (226.8)	927 (420.5)
FLHTK	901 (408.7)	1360 (616.9)	500 (226.8)	927 (420.5)
FLTRU	888 (402.8)	1360 (616.9)	500 (226.8)	927 (420.5)
FLHR	812 (368.3)	1360 (616.9)	500 (226.8)	927 (420.5)
FLHRC	810 (367.4)	1360 (616.9)	500 (226.8)	927 (420.5)
FLTRX	817 (370.6)	1360 (616.9)	500 (226.8)	927 (420.5)
FLHX	822 (372.9)	1360 (616.9)	500 (226.8)	927 (420.5)
FLHTCUSE	887 (402.34)	1360 (616.9)	500 (226.8)	927 (420.5)
FLHXSE	806.44 (365.8)	1360 (616.9)	500 (226.8)	927 (420.5)
FLHRSE	849 (385.1)	1360 (616.9)	500 (226.8)	927 (420.5)
FLTRUSE	905 (410.5)	1360 (616.9)	500 (226.8)	927 (420.5)
FLTRXSE	855 (387.8)	1360 (616.9)	500 (226.8)	927 (420.5)

*The total weight of the motorcycle as delivered with all oil/fluids and approximately 90% fuel.

Table 4 DECIMAL AND METRIC EQUIVALENTS

Fractions	Decimal in.	Metric mm	Fractions	Decimal in.	Metric mm
1/64	0.015625	0.39688	33/64	0.515625	13.09687
1/32	0.03125	0.79375	17/32	0.53125	13.49375
3/64	0.046875	1.19062	35/64	0.546875	13.89062
1/16	0.0625	1.58750	9/16	0.5625	14.28750
5/64	0.078125	1.98437	37/64	0.578125	14.68437
3/32	0.09375	2.38125	19/32	0.59375	15.08125
7/64	0.109375	2.77812	39/64	0.609375	15.47812
1/8	0.125	3.1750	5/8	0.625	15.87500
9/64	0.140625	3.57187	41/64	0.640625	16.27187
5/32	0.15625	3.96875	21/32	0.65625	16.66875
11/64	0.171875	4.36562	43/64	0.671875	17.06562
3/16	0.1875	4.76250	11/16	0.6875	17.46250
13/64	0.203125	5.15937	45/64	0.703125	17.85937
7/32	0.21875	5.55625	23/32	0.71875	18.25625
15/64	0.234375	5.95312	47/64	0.734375	18.65312
1/4	0.250	6.35000	3/4	0.750	19.05000
17/64	0.265625	6.74687	49/64	0.765625	19.44687
9/32	0.28125	7.14375	25/32	0.78125	19.84375
19/64	0.296875	7.54062	51/64	0.796875	20.24062
5/16	0.3125	7.93750	13/16	0.8125	20.63750
21/64	0.328125	8.33437	53/64	0.828125	21.03437
11/32	0.34375	8.73125	27/32	0.84375	21.43125
23/64	0.359375	9.12812	55/64	0.859375	22.82812
3/8	0.375	9.52500	7/8	0.875	22.22500
25/64	0.390625	9.92187	57/64	0.890625	22.62187
13/32	0.40625	10.31875	29/32	0.90625	23.01875
27/64	0.421875	10.71562	59/64	0.921875	23.41562
7/16	0.4375	11.11250	15/16	0.9375	23.81250
29/64	0.453125	11.50937	61/64	0.953125	24.20937
15/32	0.46875	11.90625	31/32	0.96875	24.60625
31/64	0.484375	12.30312	63/64	0.984375	25.00312
1/2	0.500	12.70000	1	1.00	25.40000

Table 5 TORQUE RECOMMENDATIONS

Type2	1/4	5/16	3/8	7/16	1/2	9/16	5/8	3/4	7/8	1
SAE 2	6	12	20	32	47	69	96	155	206	310
SAE 5	10	19	33	54	78	114	154	257	382	587
SAE 7	13	25	44	71	110	154	215	360	570	840
SAE 8	14	29	47	78	119	169	230	380	600	700

1. Convert ft.-lb. specification to N•m by multiplying by 1.3558.
2. Fastener strength of SAE bolts can be determined by the bolt head grade markings. Unmarked bolt heads and cap screws are usually mild steel. More grade markings indicate higher fastener quality.

Table 6 CONVERSION FORMULAS

Multiply:	By:	To get the equivalent of:
Fluid volume		
U.S. quarts	0.9463	Liters
U.S. gallons	3.785	Liters
U.S. ounces	29.573529	Milliliters
Liters	0.2641721	U.S. gallons
Liters	1.0566882	U.S. quarts
Liters	33.814023	U.S. ounces
Milliliters	0.033814	U.S. ounces
Milliliters	1.0	Cubic centimeters
Milliliters	0.001	Liters
Torque		
Foot-pounds	1.3558	Newton-meters
Foot-pounds	0.138255	Meters-kilograms
Inch-pounds	0.11299	Newton-meters
Newton-meters	0.7375622	Foot-pounds
Newton-meters	8.8507	Inch-pounds
Meters-kilograms	7.2330139	Foot-pounds
Volume		
Cubic inches	16.387064	Cubic centimeters
Cubic centimeters	0.0610237	Cubic inches
Temperature		
Fahrenheit	(°F − 32) 0.556	Centigrade
Centigrade	(°C 1.8) + 32	Fahrenheit
Weight		
Ounces	28.3495	Grams
Pounds	0.4535924	Kilograms
Grams	0.035274	Ounces
Kilograms	2.2046224	Pounds
Pressure		
Pounds per square inch	0.070307	Kilograms per square centimeter
Kilograms per square centimeter	14.223343	Pounds per square inch
Kilopascals	0.1450	Pounds per square inch
Pounds per square inch	6.895	Kilopascals
Speed		
Miles per hour	1.609344	Kilometers per hour
Kilometers per hour	0.6213712	Miles per hour

Table 7 TECHNICAL ABBREVIATIONS

A	Ampere
ABS	Anti-lock brake system
AC	Alternating current
ACR	Automatic compression release
A.h	Ampere hour
BAS	Bank angle sensor
C	Celsius
cc	Cubic centimeter
CDI	Capacitor discharge ignition
CKP sensor	Crank position sensor
cid	cubic inch displacement
cm	Centimeter
cu. in.	Cubic inch and cubic inches
cyl.	Cylinder

(continued)

Table 7 TECHNICAL ABBREVIATIONS (continued)

DC	Direct current
ECM	Electronic control module
ECU	Electronic control unit
ET sensor	Engine temperature sensor
F	Fahrenheit
fl. oz.	Fluid ounces
ft.	Foot
ft.-lb.	Foot pounds
gal.	Gallon and gallons
H/A	High altitude
HFSM	Hands-free security module
hp	Horsepower
Hz	Hertz
IAC	Idle air control
IAT sensor	Intake air temperature sensor
ICM	Ignition control module
ID	Inside diameter
in.	Inch and inches
in.-lb.	Inch-pounds
in. Hg	Inches of mercury
k	One-thousand ohms (2k = 2000 ohms)
kg	Kilogram
kg/cm^2	Kilogram per square centimeter
kgm	Kilogram meter
km	Kilometer
km/h	Kilometer per hour
kPa	Kilopascals
kW	Kilowatt
L	Liter and liters
L/m	Liters per minute
lb.	Pound and pounds
m	Meter
MAP sensor	Manifold absolute pressure sensor
mL	Milliliter
mm	Millimeter
N•m	Newton meter
O$_2$ sensor	Oxygen sensor
OD	Outside diameter
oz.	Ounce and ounces
psi	Pounds per square inch
pt.	Pint and pints
qt.	Quart and quarts
rpm	Revolution per minute
TCA	Throttle control actuator
TDC	Top dead center
TGS	Throttle grip sensor
TMAP sensor	Temperature and manifold absolute pressure sensor
TP sensor	Throttle position sensor
TSM	Turn signal module
TSSM	Turn signal and security module
V	Volt
VSS	Vehicle speed sensor
W	Watt

Table 8 U.S. TAP AND DRILL SIZES

Tap thread	Drill size	Tap thread	Drill size
#0-80	3/64	1/4-28	No. 3
#1-64	No. 53	5/16-18	F
#1-72	No. 53	5/16-24	I
#2-56	No. 51	3/8-16	5/16
#2-64	No. 50	3/8-24	Q
#3-48	5/64	7/16-14	U
#3-56	No. 46	7/16-20	W
#4-40	No. 43	1/2-13	27/64
#4-48	No. 42	1/2-20	29/64
		(continued)	

Table 8 U.S. TAP AND DRILL SIZES (continued)

Tap thread	Drill size	Tap thread	Drill size
#5-40	No. 39	9/16-12	31/64
#5-44	No. 37	9/16-18	33/64
#6-32	No. 36	5/8-11	17/32
#6-40	No. 33	5/18-18	37/64
#8-32	No. 29	3/4-10	21/32
#8-36	No. 29	3/4-16	11/16
#10-24	No. 25	7/8-9	49/64
#10-32	No. 21	7/8-14	13/16
#12-24	No. 17	1-8	7/8
#12-28	No. 15	1-14	15/16

Table 9 METRIC TAP AND DRILL SIZES

Metric size	Drill equivalent	Decimal fraction	Nearest fraction
3 0.50	No. 39	0.0995	3/32
3 0.60	3/32	0.0937	3/32
4 0.70	No. 30	0.1285	1/8
4 0.75	1/8	0.125	1/8
5 0.80	No. 19	0.166	11/64
5 0.90	No. 20	0.161	5/32
6 1.00	No. 9	0.196	13/64
7 1.00	16/64	0.234	15/64
8 1.00	J	0.277	9/32
8 1.25	17/64	0.265	17/64
9 1.00	5/16	0.3125	5/16
9 1.25	5/16	0.3125	5/16
10 1.25	11/32	0.3437	11/32
10 1.50	R	0.339	11/32
11 1.50	3/8	0.375	3/8
12 1.50	13/32	0.406	13/32
12 1.75	13/32	0.406	13/32

Table 10 SPECIAL TOOLS

Use the following special tools, or equivalent tools, whenever special tools are called for in this manual.

Tool Description	Part No.	Manufacturer
All-purpose claw puller	HD-95635-46	
ACR solenoid socket	HD-48498-A	H-D
Belt tension gauge	08-0350	Motion Pro
	923	JIMS
	HD-355381-A	H-D
Bearing race puller and installation tool	HD-3490-B	H-D
Camshaft assembly tool	990	JIMS
Camshaft assembly tool	HD-47956	H-D
Large guide	HD-47956-1	H-D
Small guide	HD-47956-2	H-D
Camshaft bearing puller	1280	JIMS
Camshaft bearing remover/installer	HD-43644	H-D
Camshaft remover and installer	1277	JIMS
	HD-43644	H-D
Camshaft chain tensioner tool	1283	JIMS
	HD-42313	H-D
Camshaft/crankshaft sprocket lock tool	994	JIMS
	HD-47941	H-D
Camshaft inner bearing installer	787	JIMS
Camshaft inner bearing remover tool	993	JIMS
Camshaft needle inner bearing remover/installer	HD-42325	H-D
Center stand jack	904	JIMS
Connecting rod clamping tool	1284	JIMS
Connecting rod holding tool	1284	JIMS

(continued)

Table 10 SPECIAL TOOLS (continued)

Tool Description	Part No.	Manufacturer
Crankcase bearing snap ring remover and installer	1710	JIMS
Crankcase disassembly/removing tool	995	JIMS
Crankshaft bearing remover and installer	1146	JIMS
Crankshaft bearing remover/installer base	HD-42720-5	H-D
Crankshaft bearing remover/installer pilot/driver		
Right side	HD-44065-1	H-D
Left side	B-45655	H-D
Crankshaft bearing remover/installer support tube		
Right side	HD-44065-4	H-D
Left side	HD-42720-5	H-D
Crankshaft bushing tool	1281	JIMS
	HD-42315	H-D
Crankshaft seal installation tool	39361-69	JIMS
Crankshaft guide	1288	JIMS
Crankshaft hard cap	1048	JIMS
Crankshaft support fixture	HD-44358	H-D
Crankcase stud installer	08-0148	Motion Pro
Cylinder chamfering cone	2078	JIMS
Cylinder stud steel ball	HD-8860	H-D
Cylinder torque plates	951	JIMS
All models CVO	HD-42324-A	H-D
CVO models	HD-48627	H-D
Cylinder head support stand	HD-39782-A	H-D
Cylinder head holding fixture	HD-39786	H-D
Drive sprocket lock	2260	JIMS
Driver handle and remover	HD-34740	H-D
Electrical Terminal Tools		
Deutsch connector service kit	HD-41475	H-D
Deutsch terminal crimp tool	HD-39965-A	H-D
Electrical crimper tool (Deutsch)	HD-42879	H-D
Flat blade L-hook (Deutsch)	HD-41475-100	H-D
Molex electrical connector terminal remover	HD-48114	H-D
Molex electrical crimp tool	HD-48119	H-D
Packard terminal crimp tool (Metri-pack)	HD-38125-6	H-D
Packard terminal crimper (Metri-pack)	HD-38125-7	H-D
Packard crimping tool (Metri-pack)	HD-38125-8	H-D
Packard Micro 64 terminal crimper	HD-45929	H-D
Packard Micro 64 terminal remover	HD-45928	H-D
Pin terminal tool	HD-39621-28	H-D
Socket terminal tool (AMP)	HD-39621-27	H-D
Terminal pick	GA500A	Snap-on
	1764	JIMS
Terminal tool pick	114008	Deutch
Engine stand		
Base stand	1138	JIMS
Engine stand	1140	JIMS
Engine/transmission stand	HD-42310	H-D
Exhaust oxygen O_2 sensor socket	HD-50017	H-D
	969	JIMS
Final drive sprocket shaft bearing cone installer	HD-007225-55C	H-D
Final drive sprocket shaft bearing installation tool	97225-55	JIMS
Final drive sprocket locker	HD-46282	HD
	2260	JIMS
Final drive sprocket shaft seal installer	39461-69	JIMS
Flywheel sprocket support	HD-44358	HD
Fork oil level gauge	08-0121	Motion Pro
Fork seal driver/installer	2046	JIMS
Fork stem bearing remover		
	HD-48262	HD
	1414	JIMS
Fuel pressure gauge	HD-41182	H-D
Fuel pressure gauge adapter	HD-44061	H-D

(continued)

Table 10 SPECIAL TOOLS (continued)

Use the following special tools, or equivalent tools, whenever special tools are called for in this manual.

Tool Description	Part No.	Manufacturer
Fuel pump retainer remover/installer tool	HD-48646	H-D
	954	JIMS
Heavy-duty retaining ring pliers	J-5586-A	H-D
High performance sealant, gray	HD-99650-02	H-D
Hose clamp pincer tool/pliers	1171	JIMS
	HD-97087-65B	H-D
Hub bearing removal set	08-0410	Motion Pro
	12-0024	Motion Pro
Hydraulic brake bleeder	Mityvac	
Hydraulic tensioner compression tool	HD-44063	H-D
Hydraulic tensioner retainer	HD-44408	H-D
Ignition switch alignment tool	943	JIMS
	HD-45962	H-D
Ignition switch remover	HD-45961	H-D
Intake manifold wrench	35-3975	K&L
	HD-47250	H-D
Motor sprocket shaft seal installer tool	39361-69	JIMS
Oil line remover and replacement tool	HD-44455	H-D
Passing lamp flare nut socket	FRX181	Snap-On
Piston ring compressor	HD-96333-51F	H-D
Primary drive locking tool	2315	JIMS
	HD-47977	H-D
Pushrod tool	08-0225	Motion Pro
Radio support bracket bolt remover (ball and socket)	FABL6E	Snap-On
Rear wheel alignment tool	928	JIMS
	08-0368	Motion Pro
Rim protectors	HD-01289	H-D
Rocker arm shaft reamer	94804-57	JIMS
Shift fork shaft remover	985	JIMS
Small pick	TT600-3	Snap-On
Spark tester	08-0122	Motion Pro
Sprocket shaft bearing tool	HD-97225-55C	H-D
Sprocket shaft bearing installation tool	97225-55	JIMS
Sprocket shaft bearing race tool set	94547-80A	JIMS
Sprocket shaft oil seal installer	39361-69	JIMS
Snap ring remover and installer Timkin bearing outer race	1710	JIMS
Snap ring pliers	J-5586-A	H-D
Socket-hand drive	HD-43643	H-D
Spark tester	08-01222	Motion Pro
Sprocket shaft bearing cone installer	97225-55C	JIMS
Sprocket shaft seal installer	39361-69	JIMS
Steering head bearing race remover	1414	JIMS
Steering head bearing race installer	1725	JIMS
Swing arm bearing installer	HD-45327	H-D
Threaded cylinders	HD-95952-1	H-D
Timken bearing race installer	2246	JIMS
Transmission bearing and race installer tool handle	33416-80	JIMS
Transmission sprocket locker tool	2260	JIMS
Transmission cradle	HD-42310-50	H-D
Transmission main drive gear tool set	35316-80	JIMS
Transmission main bearing remover set	1720	JIMS
Transmission side door remover	984	JIMS
Transmission shaft installer	2189	JIMS
Transmission mainshaft bearing race puller and installer	34902-84	JIMS
	HD-34902-C	H-D
Transmission main drive gear installer	981	JIMS
Transmission main drive gear remover and installer	HD-35316-B	H-D
Transmission main drive gear bearing installer	987	JIMS

(continued)

Table 10 SPECIAL TOOLS (continued)

Tool Description	Part No.	Manufacturer
Transmission main drive gear large oil seal installer	HD-47856	H-D
	972	JIMS
Transmission sprocket tool	HD-41184	H-D
Transmission main drive gear/bearing remover and installer	HD-35316-C	H-D
Transmission main drive gear wrench	989	JIMS
Transmission main drive gear seal installer	972	JIMS
	HD-47933	H-D
Transmission main drive gear bearing and seal installer tool	986	JIMS
Transmission main drive gear wedge attachment	HD-95637-46B	H-D
Transmission shaft installer	21989	JIMS
Vacuum hose identifier kit	74600	Lisle
Valve guide cleaning brush	HD-34751	H-D
Valve guide driver		
All models except CVO	B-45524-1	H-D
CVO models	HD-34740	H-D
Valve guide installer sleeve		
All models except CVO	B-45524-2A	H-D
CVO models	HD-46583	H-D
Valve guide intake seat adapter	HD-39782-3	H-D
Valve guide exhaust seat adapters	HD-39782-4	H-D
Valve guide hone		
All models except CVO	B-45525	H-D
CVO models	HD-34723	H-D
Valve guide reamer		
All models except CVO	B-45523	H-D
CVO models	HD-39932	H-D
Valve guide reamer T-handle	HD-39847	H-D
Valve guide reamer and honing lubricant	HD-39964	H-D
Valve guide seal installer	HD-48644	H-D
Valve seat cutter set, Neway	HD-35758-C	H-D
Valve spring compressor	HD-34736-B	H-D
Valve spring tester	HD-96796-47	H-D
Wheel alignment tool	08-0368	Motion Pro
Wheel bearing race remover and installer	33461	JIMS
	08-0410	Motion Pro
Wheel (rear) compensating bearing remover/installer	HD-48921	H-D

1

NOTES

TROUBLESHOOTING

This chapter describes troubleshooting procedures. Each procedure provides typical symptoms and logical methods for isolating the cause(s). Gather as much information as possible to aid in diagnosis. Never assume anything and do not overlook the obvious. Follow a systematic approach to eliminate each possibility and avoid unnecessary parts replacement.

In most cases, complicated test equipment is not required for basic troubleshooting.

However, some procedures require specialized test equipment. In such cases, eliminate all possible causes by performing any basic test(s) first, if possible. Be realistic and do not start procedures that are beyond the experience and equipment available. Many service departments will not take work that involves the re-assembly of damaged or abused equipment; if they do, expect the cost to be high. If the motorcycle does require the attention of a professional, describe symptoms and conditions accurately and fully. The more information a technician has available, the easier it will be to diagnose the problem.

Refer to **Tables 1-3** at the end of this chapter for trouble-shooting specifications and diagnostic trouble codes.

ENGINE STARTING

NOTE
Do not open the throttle when starting either a cold or warm engine. The ignition control module (ICM) or electronic control module (ECM) takes throttle position into consideration during the starting procedure.

Engine Fails to Start (Spark Test)

1. Shift the transmission into neutral and confirm that the engine run/stop switch (**Figure 1**) is in the RUN position.

WARNING
To prevent fuel from being injected into the cylinders when the engine is turned over, remove the fuel pump fuse or disconnect the fuel pump electrical connector.

2. Disconnect the fuel pump (Chapter Eight).
3. Disconnect the spark plug wire and remove the spark plug as described in Chapter Three.

NOTE
*A spark tester (Motion Pro part No. 08-0122) is a useful tool for testing spark output. The tester (**Figure 2**) is inserted into the spark plug cap and its base is grounded against the cylinder head. The tester's air gap is adjustable, and it allows the visual inspection of the spark while testing the intensity of the spark.*

4. Cover the spark plug hole with a clean shop cloth to lessen the chance of gasoline vapors being emitted from the hole.
5. Insert the spark plug (**Figure 3**), or spark tester (**Figure 4**), into a plug cap and ground the base against the cylinder head. Position the spark plug or tester so the electrode is visible.
6. Pull the clutch lever in (even with the transmission in neutral).

WARNING
Do not hold the spark plug, tester, plug wire or connector. A serious electrical shock may result.

WARNING
Position the spark plug, or tester, away from the spark plug hole in the cylinder so that the spark or tester cannot ignite the gasoline vapors in the cylinder. If the engine is flooded, do not perform this test. The firing of the spark plug can ignite fuel that is ejected through the spark plug hole.

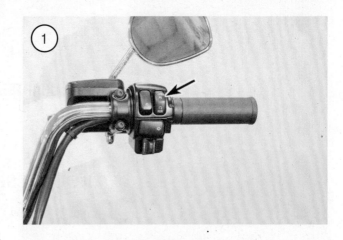

7. Turn the engine over with the starter. A crisp blue spark should be evident across the spark plug electrode or spark tester terminals. Repeat for the remaining cylinder.

8. If the spark is good, check for one or more of the following possible malfunctions:
   a. Faulty fuel system component.
   b. Low engine compression or engine damage.
   c. Flooded engine.
   d. Incorrect ignition timing.

9. If the spark is weak or if there is no spark, refer to *Engine is Difficult to Start* in this chapter.

10. Install the spark plugs as described in Chapter Three.

11. Connect the fuel pump electrical connector (Chapter Eight).

Engine Is Difficult to Start

1. After attempting to start the engine, remove one of the spark plugs (Chapter Three) and check for the presence of fuel on the plug tip. Note the following:
   a. If there is no fuel visible on the plug, remove the other spark plug. If there is no fuel on this plug, perform Step 2.
   b. If there is fuel present on the plug tip, go to Step 4.
   c. If there is an excessive amount of fuel on the plug, check for a clogged air filter, or for incorrect throttle operation (throttle plate stuck open).

2. Perform the *Fuel Pressure Test* in Chapter Eight. Note the following:
   a. If the fuel pump pressure is correct, go to Step 3B.
   b. If the fuel pump pressure is incorrect, replace the fuel pump and retest the fuel system.

3. Inspect the fuel injectors as described in Chapter Eight.

4. Check for a clogged fuel line and/or contaminated fuel system.

5. Perform the spark test as described in this section. Note the following:
   a. If the spark is weak or if there is no spark, go to Step 6.
   b. If the spark is good, go to Step 7.

6. If the spark is weak or if there is no spark, check the following:
   a. Fouled spark plug(s).
   b. Damaged spark plug(s).

   c. Loose or damaged ignition coil wire(s).
   d. Damaged electronic control module (ECM).
   e. Damaged crankshaft position sensor.
   f. Damaged ignition coil.
   g. Damaged engine run/stop switch.
   h. Damaged ignition switch.
   i. Damaged clutch interlock switch.
   j. Dirty or loose-fitting terminals.

7. If the engine turns over but does not start, the engine compression is probably low. Check for the following possible malfunctions:
   a. Leaking cylinder head gasket(s).
   b. Bent or stuck valve(s).
   c. Incorrect valve timing.
   d. Worn cylinders and/or pistons rings.

8. If the spark is good, try starting the engine by following normal starting procedures. If the engine starts but then stops, check the following conditions:
   a. Leaking or damaged rubber intake boot.
   b. Contaminated fuel.
   c. Incorrect ignition timing due to a damaged ignition coil.

Engine Does Not Crank

If the engine will not turn over, check for one or more of the following possible malfunctions:

1. Blown Main fuse (Chapter Nine).

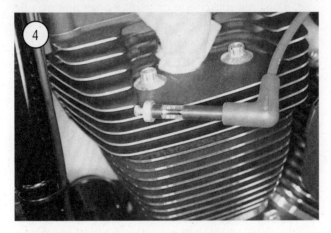

2. Discharged battery (Chapter Nine).
3. Defective starter and/or starter relay (Chapter Nine).
4. Seized piston (Chapter Five).
5. Seized crankshaft bearings (Chapter Five).
6. Broken connecting rod (Chapter Five).
7. Locked-up transmission or clutch assembly (Chapter Six or Seven).

ENGINE PERFORMANCE

If the engine runs, but performance is unsatisfactory, refer to the following procedure(s) that best describes the symptom(s).

NOTE
*The ignition timing is not adjustable. If incorrect ignition timing is suspected as being the cause of a malfunction, a defective ignition system component is indicated. Refer to **Ignition System** (this chapter).*

Engine Will Not Idle

1. Clogged air filter element.
2. Poor fuel flow.
3. Fouled or improperly gapped spark plug(s).
4. Leaking head gasket(s) or vacuum leak.
5. Leaking or damaged rubber intake boot(s).

6. Incorrect ignition timing: damaged, electronic control module (ECM), or crankshaft position sensor.
7. Obstructed or defective fuel injector(s).
8. Low engine compression.

Poor Overall Performance

1. Support the motorcycle with the rear wheel off the ground, and then spin the rear wheel by hand. If the wheel spins freely, perform the next step. If the wheel does not spin freely, check for the following conditions:
   a. Dragging rear brake.
   b. Damaged rear axle/bearing holder assembly.
   c. Damaged drive belt.
   d. Damaged drive or driven sprockets.
2. Check the clutch operation. If the clutch slips, refer to *Clutch* (this chapter).
3. If the previous steps did not locate the problem, test ride the motorcycle and accelerate lightly. If the engine speed increased according to throttle position, perform the next step. If the engine speed did not increase, check for one or more of the following problems:
   a. Clogged air filter.
   b. Restricted fuel flow.
   c. Clogged or damaged muffler(s).
4. Check for one or more of the following problems:
   a. Low engine compression.
   b. Worn spark plug(s).
   c. Fouled spark plug(s).
   d. Incorrect spark plug heat range.
   e. Clogged or defective fuel injector(s).
   f. Incorrect oil level (too high or too low).
   g. Contaminated oil.
   h. Worn or damaged valve train assembly.
   i. Engine overheating. Refer to *Engine Overheating* (this section).
   j. Incorrect ignition timing: damaged, electronic control module (ECM) or crankshaft position sensor.
5. If the engine knocks when it is accelerated or when running at high speed, check for one or more of the following possible malfunctions:
   a. Incorrect type of fuel.
   b. Lean fuel mixture.
   c. Advanced ignition timing: damaged ignition control module (ICM), or electronic control module (ECM),
   d. Excessive carbon buildup in combustion chamber.
   e. Worn pistons and/or cylinder bores.

Poor Idle or Low Speed Performance

1. Check for damaged rubber intake boots, a loose carburetor or throttle body, or loose air filter housing hose clamps.
2. Check the fuel flow and the fuel injectors as described in Chapter Eight.
3. Perform the spark test (this section). Note the following:

a. If the spark is good, test the fuel system as described in this chapter.

b. If the spark is weak, test the ignition system as described in this chapter.

Poor High Speed Performance

1. Check the fuel flow and the fuel injectors as described in Chapter Eight.

2. Incorrect valve timing and worn or damaged valve springs can cause poor high-speed performance. If the camshafts were timed just prior to experiencing this type of problem, the cam timing may be incorrect. If the cam timing was not set or changed, and all of the other inspection procedures in this section failed to locate the problem, remove the cylinder heads and inspect the camshafts and valve assembly.

Engine Overheating

1. Improper spark plug heat range.
2. Oil not circulating properly.
3. Valves leaking.
4. Heavy engine carbon deposits in combustion chamber(s).
5. Dragging brake(s).
6. Clutch slipping.

Engine Backfires

1. Incorrect ignition timing (due to loose or defective ignition system component).
2. Incorrect throttle body adjustment.

Engine Misfires During Acceleration

1. Incorrect ignition timing (due to loose or defective ignition system component).
2. Incorrect throttle body adjustment.

ENGINE NOISES

1. A knocking or pinging during acceleration is typically caused by using a lower octane fuel than recommended or poor quality fuel. Incorrect carburetor jetting (carbureted models) and an incorrect (hot) spark plug heat range can cause pinging. Refer to *Spark Plug Heat Range* in Chapter Three. Check also for excessive carbon buildup in the combustion chamber or a defective ignition module.

2. If a slapping or rattling noises at low speed or during acceleration is heard, consider excessive piston-to-cylinder wall clearance as a possible cause. Also check also for a bent connecting rod, a worn piston pin and/or a worn piston pin hole in the piston.

3. A knocking or rapping while decelerating is usually caused by excessive rod bearing clearance.

4. A persistent knocking and vibration is usually caused by worn main bearings and/or excessive crankshaft runout.

Connecting rod and piston (stuck/broken rings) problems can also exhibit this condition. However, rule out the following first:

a. Loose engine mounts.
b. Cracked frame.
c. Leaking cylinder head gasket(s).
d. Exhaust pipe leaks at cylinder head(s).

5. A rapid on-off squeal indicates a compression leak around the cylinder head gasket or spark plug.

6. If the valve train is noisy, check for the following:

a. Bent pushrod(s).
b. Defective lifter(s).
c. Valve sticking in guide.
d. Worn cam gears and/or cam.
e. Damaged rocker arm or shaft. Rocker arm may be binding on shaft.

ELECTRICAL TESTING

This section describes general electrical test procedures and equipment use. Subsequent sections cover the starting, charging and ignition systems.

After determining which system requires testing, start with the first inspection in the list and perform the indicated test(s). Each test presumes that the component tested in the prior step is working properly. The test can yield invalid results if they are performed out of sequence. If a test indicates that a component is working properly, reconnect the electrical connections and proceed to the next step. Systematically work through the procedure until the problem is found. Repair or replace faulty parts as described in the appropriate section of this manual.

If necessary, refer to the wiring diagrams located in Chapter Sixteen for component and connector identification. Trace the current paths from the power source through the circuit components to ground. Check any circuits that share the same fuse, ground or switch. If the other circuits work properly and the shared wiring is good, the cause must be in the wiring used only by the suspect circuit. If all related circuits are faulty at the same time, the probable cause is a poor ground connection or a blown fuse(s).

Electrical connections are often the weak link in the electrical system. Dirty, loose-fitting electrical connectors cause numerous electrical-related problems, especially on high-mileage motorcycles. When troubleshooting an electrical problem, carefully inspect the connectors and wiring harness.

As with all troubleshooting, analyze typical symptoms in a systematic manner. Never assume anything, and do not overlook the obvious, like a blown fuse or an electrical connector that has separated.

Electrical Component Replacement

Most dealerships and parts suppliers will not accept the return of any electrical part. Consider any test results carefully before replacing a component that tests only slightly

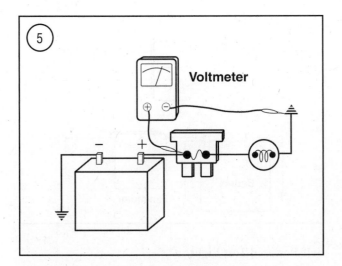

out of specification, especially for resistance. A number of variables can affect test results dramatically. These include: the testing meter's internal circuitry, ambient temperature and conditions under which the machine has been operated. All instructions and specifications have been checked for accuracy; however, successful test results depend to a great degree upon individual accuracy. If the exact cause of any electrical system malfunction cannot be determined, have a dealership retest that specific system to verify the test results before purchasing a non-returnable part.

Preliminary Checks and Precautions

Prior to starting any electrical troubleshooting procedure perform the following:

1. Check the Main Fuse as described in Chapter Nine. If the Main fuse is blown, replace it.
2. Check the individual fuses mounted in the fuse box as described in Chapter Nine. Remove the suspected fuse and replace if blown.
3. Inspect the battery as described in Chapter Nine. Make sure it is fully charged, and that the battery leads are clean and securely attached to the battery terminals.
4. Disconnect each electrical connector in the suspect circuit and check that there are no bent terminals on either side of the connector.
5. Make sure all electrical terminals are clean and free of corrosion. Clean, if necessary, and pack the connectors with dielectric grease.
6. Make sure the terminals are pushed all the way into the connector. If not, carefully push them in with a narrow blade screwdriver.
7. Check the wires where they enter the individual connectors.
8. Push the connectors together and make sure they are fully engaged and locked together.
9. Never pull on the electrical wires when disconnecting an electrical connector.

Test Light or Voltmeter

Use a test light to check for voltage in a circuit by attaching one lead to ground and the other lead to various points along the circuit. Where battery voltage is present the light bulb will light.

Use a voltmeter in the same manner as the test light to determine if battery voltage is present in any given circuit. When using a voltmeter, attach the positive lead to the component or wire to be checked and the negative lead to a good ground (**Figure 5**).

Voltage Test

Make all voltage tests with the electrical connectors still connected, unless otherwise specified. Insert the test leads into the backside of the connector and make sure the test lead touches the electrical wire or metal terminal within the connector housing. Touching the wire insulation will yield a false reading.

Always check both sides of the connector as one side may be loose or corroded thus preventing electrical flow through the connector. This type of test can be performed with a test light or a voltmeter. A voltmeter gives the best results.

NOTE
When using a test light, either lead can be attached to ground.

1. Attach the voltmeter negative test lead to a good ground. Make sure the part used for ground is not insulated with a rubber gasket or rubber grommet.
2. Attach the voltmeter positive test lead to the point (electrical connector, etc.) to be checked.
3. Turn the ignition switch to IGN. When using a test light, the test light will come on if voltage is present. When using a voltmeter, note the voltage reading. The reading should be within 1 volt of battery voltage. If the voltage is significantly less than battery voltage, there is a problem in the circuit.

Voltage Drop Test

Since resistance causes voltage to drop, a voltmeter can be used to determine resistance in an active circuit. This is called a voltage drop test. A voltage drop test measures the difference between the voltage at the beginning of the circuit and the available voltage at the end of the circuit while the circuit is operating. If the circuit has no resistance, there is no voltage drop so the voltmeter indicates 0 volts. The greater the resistance in the circuit will result in a greater the voltage drop reading. A voltage drop of 1 or more volts indicates that a circuit has excessive resistance.

Remember a 0 reading on a voltage drop test is good. Battery voltage, on the other hand, indicates an open circuit. A voltage drop test is an excellent way to check the condition of solenoids, relays, battery cables and other high-current electrical components.

1. Connect the voltmeter positive test lead to the end of the wire or device closest to the battery.

2. Connect the voltmeter negative test lead to the ground side of the wire or device (**Figure 6**).

3. Turn the components on in the circuit.

4. The voltmeter should indicate 0 volts. If there is a drop of 1 volt or more, there is a problem within the circuit. A voltage drop reading of 12 volts indicates an open in the circuit.

Ammeter

An ammeter measures the flow of current (amps) in a circuit (**Figure 7**). When connected in series in the circuit, the ammeter determines whether current is flowing in the circuit, and whether the current flow is excessive because of a short in the circuit. This current flow is usually referred to as current draw. Comparing actual current draw in the circuit or component to the manufacturer's specified current draw rating provides useful diagnostic information.

Ohmmeter

> *CAUTION*
> *Never connect an ohmmeter to a circuit that has power applied to it. Always disconnect the negative battery cable before using the ohmmeter.*

An ohmmeter reads resistance in ohms to current flow in a circuit or component. Ohmmeters may be an analog type (needle scale) or a digital type (LCD or LED readout). Both types of ohmmeters have a switch that allows the selection of different ranges of resistance for accurate readings. The analog ohmmeter also has a set-adjust control which is used to zero or calibrate the meter needle for accurate adjustments. Digital ohmmeters do not require calibration.

Use an ohmmeter by connecting its test leads to the terminals or leads of the circuit or component being tested. When using an analog meter, calibrate it by crossing the test leads and turning the set-adjust knob until the meter needle reads zero. When the leads are uncrossed, the needle should move to the other end of the scale, indicating infinite resistance.

During a continuity test, a reading of infinite indicates that there is an open in the circuit or component. A reading of zero indicates continuity, which means there is no measurable resistance in the circuit or component being tested. If the meter needle falls between the two ends of the scale, this indicates the actual resistance to current flow that is present. To determine the resistance, multiply the meter reading by the ohmmeter scale. For example, a meter reading of 5 multiplied by the R × 1000 scale is 5000 ohms of resistance.

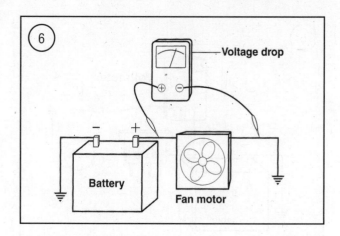

Self-Powered Test Light

> *CAUTION*
> *Never use a self-powered test light on circuits that contain solid-state devices. The solid-state device may be damaged.*

A self-powered test light can be constructed of a 12-volt light bulb, a pair of test leads and a 12-volt battery. When the test leads are touched together, the light bulb illuminates.

Use a self-powered test light as follows:

1. Touch the test leads together to make sure the light bulb goes on. If not, correct the problem prior to using it in a test procedure.

2. Disconnect the motorcycle's battery or remove the fuse(s) that protects the circuit to be tested. Refer to Chapter Nine.

3. Select two points within the circuit that should have continuity.

4. Attach one lead of the self-powered test light to each point.

5. If there is continuity, the self-powered test light bulb will come on.

6. If there is no continuity, the self-powered test light bulb will not come on. This indicates an open, or a break, in the circuit.

Continuity Test

A continuity test is used to determine the integrity of a circuit, wire or component. A circuit has continuity if it forms a complete circuit; if there are no opens, or breaks, in either the electrical wires or components within the circuit. A circuit with an open or break in it has no continuity.

This type of test can be performed with a self-powered test light or an ohmmeter. An ohmmeter gives the best results. When using an analog ohmmeter, calibrate the meter by touching the leads together and turning the set-adjust knob until the meter needle reads zero.

1. Disconnect the battery negative cable.

2. Attach one test lead (test light or ohmmeter) to one end of the part of the circuit to be tested.

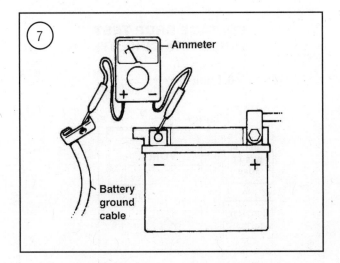

3. Attach the other test lead to the other end of the part or the circuit to be tested.

4. The self-powered test light comes on if there is continuity. An ohmmeter reads 0 or very low resistance if there is continuity. A reading of infinite resistance indicates no continuity; the circuit has an open, or a break, in it.

Jumper Wire

A jumper wire is a simple way to bypass a potential problem and isolate it to a particular point in a circuit. If a faulty circuit works properly with a jumper wire installed, an open exists between the two jumper points in the circuit.

To troubleshoot with a jumper wire, first use the wire to determine if the problem is on the ground side or the load side of a device. Test the ground by connecting the wire between the device and a good ground. If the device comes on, the problem is the connection between the device and ground. If the device does not come on with the jumper installed, the device's connection to ground is good so the problem is between the device and the power source.

To isolate the problem, connect the jumper between the battery and the device. If it comes on, the problem is between these two points. Next, connect the jumper between the battery and the fuse side of the switch. If the device comes on, the switch is good. By moving the jumper from one point to another, the problem can be isolated to a particular place in the circuit.

Note the following when using a jumper wire:

1. A jumper wire is a temporary test measures only. Do not leave a jumper wire installed as a permanent solution. This creates a severe fire hazard that could easily lead to complete loss of the motorcycle.

2. Never use a jumper wire across any load (a component that is connected and turned on). This would result in a direct short and will blow the fuse(s).

3. Install an inline fuse/fuse holder (available at most automotive supply stores or electronic supply stores) to the jumper wire.

4. Make sure the jumper wire gauge (thickness) is the same as that used in the circuit being tested. Smaller gauge wire will rapidly overhead and could melt.

5. Install insulated boots over alligator clips. This prevents accidental grounding, sparks or possible shock when working in cramped quarters.

Testing For a Short With an Ohmmeter

1. Disconnect the battery negative cable.

2. Remove the blown fuse from the fuse panel.

3. Connect one test lead of the ohmmeter (or self-powered test light) to the load side (battery side) of the fuse terminal in the fuse panel.

4. Connect the other test lead to a good ground. Make sure the part used for a ground is not insulated with a rubber gasket or rubber grommet.

5. With the ohmmeter attached to the fuse terminal and ground, wiggle the wiring harness of the suspect circuit at 6 in. (15.2 cm) increments. Start next to the fuse panel and work away from the fuse panel.

6. Watch the ohmmeter as you progress along the harness. If the ohmmeter moves when the harness is wiggled, there is a short-to-ground at that point in the harness.

Testing For a Short With a Test Light

1. Remove the blown fuse from the fuse panel.

2. Connect the test light (or voltmeter) across the fuse terminals in the fuse panel. Turn the ignition switch to IGN and check for battery voltage.

3. With the test light attached to the fuse terminals, wiggle the wiring harness of the suspect circuit at 6 in. (15.2 cm) intervals. Start next to the fuse panel and work away from the panel.

4. Watch the test light as you progress along the harness. If the test light blinks or if the needle on the voltmeter moves when the harness is wiggled, there is a short-to-ground at that point in the harness.

Wiggle Test

The wiggle test locates intermittent problems within a circuit.

1. Connect a digital volt/ohmmeter between two points within a suspected circuit.

2. Start the engine, let it idle and note the voltage.

3. Shake the harness while observing the meter. If a large change in voltage occurs, an intermittent short or open exists between the two tested points.

4. To narrow the search, move one probe closer to the other point and repeat the test until the intermittent has been isolated to a place in the circuit.

STARTING SYSTEM

The starting system consists of the battery, starter, starter relay, solenoid, starter switch, starter mechanism and related wiring.

When the ignition switch is turned to IGN and the starter switch is pushed in, current is transmitted from the battery to the starter relay. When the relay is activated, it allows electricity to flow from the battery to the starter.

Before troubleshooting the starting system, perform the following:

1. Make sure the battery is fully charged.
2. Replace damaged or undersize cables.
3. Make sure all electrical connections are clean and tight.
4. Inspect the wiring harness for worn or frayed insulation or loose harness sockets.
5. Verify fuel tank is filled with an adequate supply of fresh gasoline.

Voltage Drop Test

Before performing the steps listed in *Starter Troubleshooting* (this section), perform this voltage drop test. These steps will help find weak or damaged electrical components that may be causing the starting system problem.

1. Connect the positive voltmeter lead to the positive battery terminal, and then connect the negative voltmeter lead to the solenoid (**Figure 8**). The voltmeter lead must not touch the starter-to-solenoid terminal.
2. Shift the transmission into neutral. Pull the clutch lever in (even with the transmission in neutral).
3. Turn the ignition switch to IGN and push the starter switch while reading the voltmeter scale. Note the following:
   a. The circuit is operating correctly if the voltmeter reading is 2 volts or less. A voltmeter reading of 12 volts indicates an open circuit.
   b. A voltage drop of more than 2 volts shows a problem in the solenoid circuit.
   c. If the voltage drop reading is correct, continue with the test procedure.

NOTE
This procedure checks the voltage drop across the starter ground circuit. To check any other ground in the starting circuit, repeat this test but leave the negative voltmeter lead connected to the battery and connect the positive voltmeter lead to the ground that is being tested.

4. To check the starter ground circuit, connect the negative voltmeter lead to the negative battery terminal, and then connect the positive voltmeter lead to the starter housing (**Figure 9**).
5. Turn the ignition switch to IGN and push the starter switch while reading the voltmeter scale. The voltage drop must not exceed 0.2 volts. If it does, check the ground connections between the meter leads.

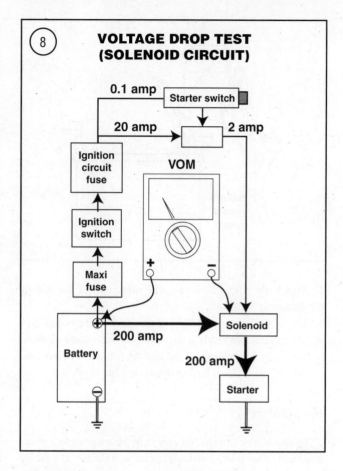

(8) **VOLTAGE DROP TEST (SOLENOID CIRCUIT)**

6. If the problem is not located, refer to *Starter Troubleshooting* in this section.

Starter Troubleshooting

The basic starter-related troubles are:
1. Starter does not spin.
2. Starter spins but does not engage.
3. The starter will not disengage after the starter switch is released.
4. Loud grinding noise when starter turns.
5. Starter stalls or spins to slowly.

CAUTION
Never operate the starter for more than 30 seconds at as time. Allow the starter to cool before reusing it. Failure to allow the starter to cool after continuous starting attempts can damage the starter.

Starter does not spin

1. Turn the ignition switch to IGN and push the starter switch while listening for a click at the starter relay in the electrical panel. Turn the ignition switch off and note the following:
   a. If the starter relay clicks, test the starter relay as described in this section. If the starter relay test readings are correct, continue with Step 2.

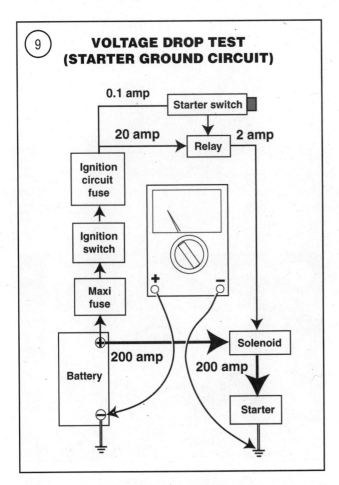

VOLTAGE DROP TEST (STARTER GROUND CIRCUIT)

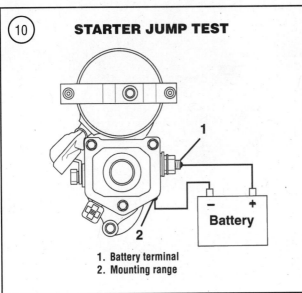

STARTER JUMP TEST

1. Battery terminal
2. Mounting range

tests and starter current draw tests described in this section.

3. Perform a voltage drop test between the battery and solenoid terminals as described in *Voltage Drop Test* (this section). The normal voltage drop is less than 2 volts. Note the following:

    a. If the voltage drop is less than 2 volts, perform Step 4.

    b. If the voltage drop is more than 2 volts, check the solenoid and battery wires and connections for dirty or loose fitting terminals; clean and repair as required.

4. Remove the starter as described in Chapter Eleven. Momentarily connect a fully charged 12-volt battery to the starter. Refer to **Figure 10**. If the starter is operational, it will turn when connected to the battery. Disconnect the battery and note the following:

    a. If the starter turns, perform the solenoid pull-in and hold-in tests as described in *Solenoid Tests* (this section).

    b. If the starter does not turn, disassemble the starter as described in Chapter Nine, and check for opens, shorts and grounds.

5. If there is no click when performing Step 1, measure voltage between the starter switch and the starter relay. The voltmeter must read battery voltage. Note the following:

    a. If battery voltage is noted, continue with Step 7.

    b. If there is no voltage, go to Step 8.

6. Check the starter relay ground at the starter relay. Note the following:

    a. If the starter relay is properly grounded, test the starter relay as described in this section.

    b. If the starter relay is not grounded, check the ground connection. Repair the ground connection, and then retest the relay.

7. Check for voltage at the starter switch. Note the following:

    a. If there is voltage at the starter switch, test the starter relay as described in this section.

    b. If there is no voltage at the starter switch, check continuity across the switch. If there is voltage leading to the starter switch, but no voltage leaving the switch, replace the switch and retest. If there is no voltage leading to the starter switch, check the switch wiring for dirty or loose-fitting terminals or damaged wiring. Clean and/or repair the terminals or wiring as required.

Starter spins but does not engage

If the starter spins but the pinion gear does not engage the ring gear, perform the following:

1. Remove the outer primary cover as described in Chapter Six.

2. Inspect the starter pinion gear (**Figure 11**). If the teeth are chipped or worn, inspect the clutch ring gear (**Figure 12**) for the same problems.

    a. If the pinion gear and ring gear are damaged, service the parts as described in Chapter Six or Chapter Eleven.

    b. If the solenoid clicks, go to Step 3.

    c. If there was no click, go to Step 6.

2. Check the wiring connectors between the starter relay and solenoid. Note the following:

    a. Repair any dirty, loose fitting or damaged connectors or wiring.

    b. If the wiring is in good condition, remove the starter as described in Chapter Nine. Perform the solenoid

b. If the pinion gear and ring gear are not damaged, continue with Step 3.

3. Remove and disassemble the starter as described in Chapter Nine. Then, check the overrunning clutch assembly (**Figure 13**) for:

    a. Roller damage (**Figure 14**).

    b. Compression spring damage (A, **Figure 15**).

    c. Excessively worn or damaged pinion teeth.

    d. Pinion does not run in overrunning direction.

    e. Damaged clutch shaft splines (B, **Figure 15**).

4. Replace worn or damaged parts as required.

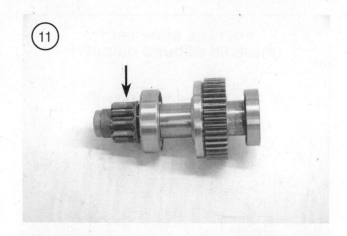

Starter will not disengage after the starter switch is released

1. A sticking solenoid, caused by a worn solenoid compression spring (A, **Figure 15**), can cause this problem. Replace the solenoid if damaged.

2. Check the starter switch and starter relay for internal damage. Test the starter switch as described in *Switches* (Chapter Nine). Test the starter relay as described in this chapter.

Loud grinding noises when the starter turns

Incorrect pinion gear and clutch ring gear engagement (B, **Figure 11**) can cause this problem. Remove and inspect the starter as described in Chapter Nine.

Starter stalls or spins too slowly

1. Perform a voltage drop test between the battery and solenoid terminals as described in *Voltage Drop Test* (this section). The normal voltage drop is less than 2 volts. Note the following:

    a. If the voltage drop is less than 2 volts, continue with Step 2.

    b. If the voltage drop exceeds 2 volts, check the solenoid and battery wires and connections for dirty or loose-fitting terminals. Clean and/or repair the terminals or wiring as required.

2. Perform a voltage drop test between the solenoid terminals and the starter as described in *Voltage Drop Test* (this section). The normal voltage drop is less than 2 volts. Note the following:

    a. If the voltage drop is less than 2 volts, continue with Step 3.

    b. If the voltage drop exceeds 2 volts, check the solenoid and starter wires and connections for dirty or loose-fitting terminals. Clean and/or repair the terminals or wiring as required.

3. Perform a voltage drop test between the battery ground wire and the starter as described in *Voltage Drop Test* (this section). The normal voltage drop is less than 2 volts. Note the following:

    a. If the voltage drop is less than 2 volts, continue with Step 4.

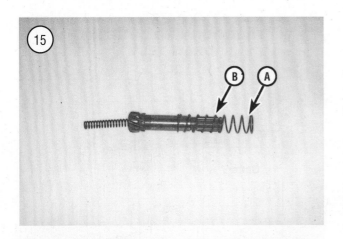

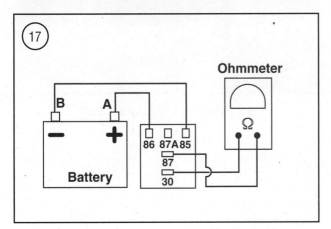

5. Remove the outer primary cover as described in Chapter Six. Check the clutch ring gear (**Figure 12**). If the teeth are chipped or worn, service this part as described in Chapter Six. Disassemble the starter and check the starter pinion gear (**Figure 11**). If the teeth are chipped or worn, service this part as described in Chapter Nine.

6. Remove and disassemble the starter as described in Chapter Nine. Check the disassembled starter for opens, shorts and grounds.

Starter Relay
Testing

Check starter relay operation with an ohmmeter, jumper wires and a fully charged 12-volt battery.

1. Carefully remove the starter relay from the fuse block assembly (**Figure 16**) as described in Chpater Nine.

> *CAUTION*
> *The battery negative lead must be connected to starter relay terminal No. 85 to avoid internal diode damage.*

2. Connect an ohmmeter and 12-volt battery between the relay terminals shown in **Figure 17**. This setup will energize the relay for testing.

3. Check for continuity through the relay contacts using an ohmmeter while the relay coil is energized. The correct reading is 0 ohm. If resistance is excessive or if there is no continuity, replace the relay.

4. If the starter relay passes this test, reconnect and install the starter relay as described in Chapter Nine.

Starter Current Draw Tests

The battery must be fully charged for these tests. Refer to *Battery* in Chapter Eleven. An inductive ammeter is required.

Loaded Current draw test (starter installed)

1. Shift the transmission into neutral.

2. Disconnect the spark plug caps from both spark plugs, and ground the plug caps with two extra spark plugs. Do *not* remove the spark plugs from the cylinder heads.

3. Connect an inductive ammeter (A, **Figure 18**) between the starter terminal and positive battery terminal (B). Connect a jumper cable from the negative battery terminal to ground.

4. Turn the ignition switch to IGN and press the starter switch for approximately 10 seconds. Typical current draw of between 160-200 amps.

> *NOTE*
> *The current draw is high when the starter switch is first pressed, and then it will drop and stabilize at a lower reading. Refer to the lower stabilized reading during this test.*

b. If the voltage drop exceeds 2 volts, check the battery ground wire connections for dirty or loose-fitting terminals. Clean and/or repair the terminals or wiring as required.

4. Perform the *Loaded Current Draw Test* (this section). Note the following:

a. If the loaded current draw is excessive, check for a damaged starter or starter drive assembly. Remove the starter as described in Chapter Eleven and perform the *Free-Running Current Draw Test* (this section).

b. If the current draw reading is correct, continue with Step 5.

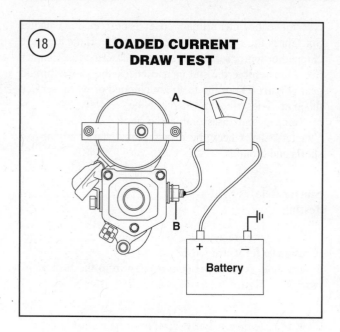

LOADED CURRENT DRAW TEST

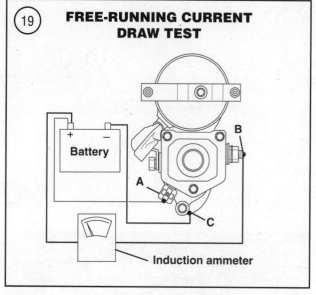

FREE-RUNNING CURRENT DRAW TEST

Induction ammeter

5. If the current draw exceeds 250 amps, check for a defective starter or starter drive mechanism. Remove and service these components as described in Chapter Eleven.
6. Disconnect the ammeter and jumper cables.

Free-running current draw test (starter removed)

A jumper wire (14 gauge minimum) and 3 jumper cables (6-gauge minimum) are required for this test.
1. Remove the starter as described in Chapter Eleven.

NOTE
The solenoid must be installed on the starter during the following tests.

2. Mount the starter in a vise with soft jaws.
3. Connect the 14-gauge jumper wire between the positive battery terminal and the solenoid relay terminal (A, **Figure 19**).
4. Connect a jumper cable between the positive battery terminal and the ammeter (**Figure 19**).
5. Connect the second jumper cable between the ammeter and the starter battery terminal (B, **Figure 19**) on the starter solenoid.
6. Connect the third jumper cable between the battery ground terminal and the starter mounting flange (C, **Figure 19**).
7. Read the ammeter; the correct ammeter reading is 90 amps. A damaged pinion gear assembly will cause an excessively high current draw reading. If the current draw reading is low, check for an undercharged battery or an open field winding or armature in the starter.

Solenoid Testing (Bench Test)

The battery must be fully charged for this test. Refer to *Battery* in Chapter Nine.

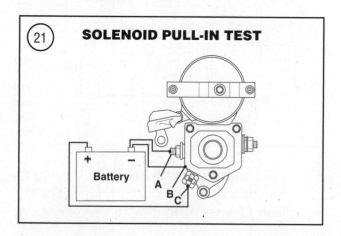

SOLENOID PULL-IN TEST

Three jumper wires are also required.
1. Remove the starter (A, **Figure 20**, typical) as described in Chapter Nine.

NOTE
*The solenoid (B, **Figure 20**) must be installed on the starter during the following tests. Do not remove it.*

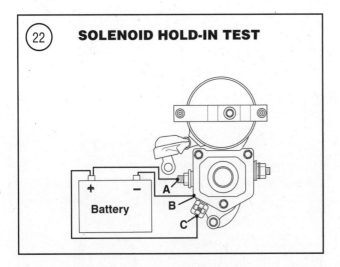

SOLENOID HOLD-IN TEST (22)

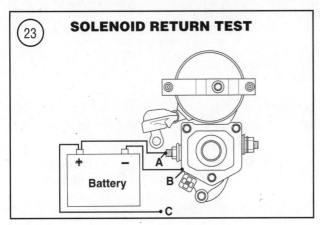

SOLENOID RETURN TEST (23)

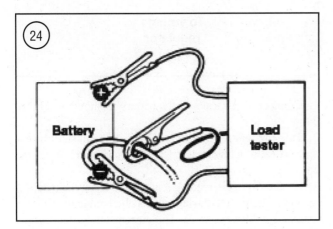

(24)

2. Disconnect the field wire terminal (C, **Figure 20**) from the solenoid before performing the following tests. Insulate the end of the wire terminal so that it cannot short out on any of the test connectors.

CAUTION
Battery voltage is being applied directly to the solenoid and starter in the following tests. Do not leave the jumper cables connected to the solenoid for more than 3-5 seconds; otherwise, the solenoid will be damaged.

NOTE
Thoroughly read the following procedure to familiarize and understand the procedures and test connections. Perform the tests in the order listed and without interruption.

3. Perform the solenoid pull-in test as follows:
   a. Connect one jumper wire from the negative battery terminal to the solenoid housing ground (A, **Figure 21**).
   b. Connect one jumper wire from the negative battery terminal to the solenoid motor terminal (B, **Figure 21**).
   c. Touch a jumper wire from the positive battery terminal to the starter relay terminal (C, **Figure 21**). The pinion shaft (D, **Figure 20**) must extend from the housing.
   d. Leave the jumper wires connected and continue with Step 4.
4. To perform the solenoid hold-in test, perform the following:
   a. With the pinion shaft retracted, disconnect the solenoid motor terminal jumper wire (**Figure 22**) from the negative battery terminal and connect it to the positive battery terminal. The pinion shaft will remain extended from the housing. If the pinion shaft returns to its normal position, replace the solenoid.
   b. Leave the jumper wires connected and continue with Step 5.
5. To perform the solenoid return test, perform the following:
   a. Disconnect the jumper wire from the starter relay terminal (**Figure 23**). The pinion shaft must return to its original position.
   b. Disconnect all of the jumper wires from the solenoid and battery.
6. Replace the solenoid as described in Chapter Nine if the starter shaft failed to operate properly during these tests.

CHARGING SYSTEM

The charging system consists of the battery, alternator and a voltage regulator/rectifier. Alternating current generated by the alternator is rectified to direct current. The voltage regulator maintains the voltage to the battery and additional electrical loads, like the lights and ignition system, at a constant voltage regardless of variations in engine speed and load.

Milliamp Draw Test

1. Turn the ignition switch off. Make sure all accessories are in the off position.
2. Disconnect the Main-Fuse as described in Chapter Nine.

CAUTION
Before connecting the ammeter into the circuit, set the meter to its highest amperage scale. This prevents a large current flow from

damaging the meter or blowing the meter's fuse.

NOTE
Even with the ignition in the off position, an initial current draw of up to 200mA will occur directly after connecting the ammeter. .

3. Connect an ammeter between both red wires of the Main-Fuse socket terminals. Note the meter reading after the initial one minute interval as follows:

    a. Add the current draw (0.5mA) to the approximate values of the TSM/TSSM/HFSM/ECM. If this total is less than the ammeter reading, then the current draw is within limits.

    b. If there is a higher reading, this indicates an excessive draw and all accessories must be checked for excessive current drain.

4. Dirt and/or electrolyte on top of the battery or a crack in the battery case can create a path for battery current to flow. If excessive current draw is noted, remove and clean the battery (Chapter Nine), and then repeat the test.

5. If the current draw is still excessive, consider the following probable causes:

    a. Faulty voltage regulator.

    b. Damaged battery.

    c. Short circuit in the system.

    d. Loose, dirty or faulty electrical connectors in the charging circuit.

6. To find the short circuit that is causing excessive current draw, refer to the wiring diagrams located in Chapter Sixteen. Then, continue to measure the current draw while disconnecting different connectors in the electrical system one by one. If the current draw returns to an acceptable level, the problem circuit is indicated. Test the circuit further to find the fault.

7. Disconnect the ammeter.

8. Connect the Main-Fuse as described in Chapter Nine.

Total Current Draw Test

This test, requiring a load tester, measures the total current load of the electrical system and any additional accessories while the engine is running. Perform this test if the battery keeps being discharged, yet the charging system output is within specifications.

If aftermarket accessories have been installed on the motorcycle, the increased current demand may exceed the charging system's capacity and result in a discharged battery.

NOTE
When using a load tester, refer to the manufacturer's instructions. To prevent tester damage caused by overheating, do not leave the load switch on for more than 20 seconds at a time.

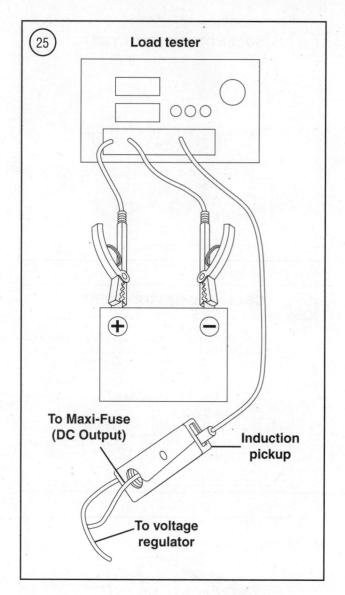

1. Connect a load tester to the battery as shown in **Figure 24**.

2. Turn the ignition switch to IGN, but do not start the engine. Then, turn on *all* electrical accessories and switch the headlight beam to HIGH.

3. Read the ampere reading (current draw) on the load tester and compare it to the test results obtained in the *Current Output Test* (this section). The current output test results must exceed the current draw by 3.5 amps for the battery to remain sufficiently charged.

4. If aftermarket accessories have been added to the motorcycle, disconnect them and repeat the test. If the current draw is now within specification, the problem is with the additional accessories.

5. If no accessories have been added to the motorcycle, a short circuit may be causing the battery to discharge.

Current Output Test

This test requires a load tester.

1. The battery must be fully charged for this test. Refer to *Battery* in Chapter Eleven.

> *NOTE*
> *When using the load tester, read and follow the manufacturer's instructions. To prevent tester damage caused by overheating, do not leave the load switch on for more than 20 seconds at a time.*

2. Connect the load tester negative and positive leads to the battery terminals. Then, place the induction pickup of the load tester around the positive voltage regulator wire (**Figure 25**).
3. Start the engine and bring the speed up to 3000 rpm while reading the load tester scale. With the engine running at 3,000 rpm, operate the load tester switch until the voltage scale reads 13.0 volts. The correct current output reading is 45-60 amps.
4. Turn the engine off and disconnect the load tester.
5. Perform the *Stator Tests* described in this section. If the results of the stator tests are acceptable, a defective voltage regulator/rectifier or a wiring short circuit is indicated. Make sure to eliminate the possibility of a poor connection or damaged wiring before replacing the voltage regulator/rectifier.

Stator Tests

Grounded stator

1. Turn the ignition switch off. Partially remove the voltage regulator (Chapter Nine) and disconnect the round connector (**Figure 26**) from the left side of the regulator.
2. Insert one of the ohmmeter probes into any of the three connector sockets and connect the other probe to ground. The correct reading is infinity. Any other reading indicates a grounded stator. Repeat this test for the other two stator sockets. Again, the correct ohmmeter reading is infinity.
3. If resistance is not as specified, replace the stator assembly as described in Chapter Nine.
4. Reconnect the round connector (**Figure 26**) and install the voltage regulator (Chapter Nine).

Open stator

1. Turn the ignition switch off, partially remove the voltage regulator (Chapter Nine), and disconnect the round connector (**Figure 26**) from the left side of the regulator.
2. Insert the ohmmeter probes between all three sockets (1-2, 2-3, 1-3). The correct reading should be less than 1 ohm (typically 0.1-0.3 ohm). If resistance is not as specified, replace the stator assembly as described in Chapter Nine.
3. Reconnect the round connector (**Figure 26**) and install the voltage regulator (Chapter Nine).

AC output

1. Turn the ignition switch off, and then disconnect the round connector (**Figure 26**) from the regulator/rectifier.
2. Connect an AC voltmeter across any two terminals.
3. Start the engine and slowly increase engine speed until the engine is running at 2000 rpm. The AC output should be 32-46 VAC .
4. If the AC voltage output reading is below the specified range, replace the stator assembly as described in Chapter Nine.
5. Reconnect the round regulator/rectifier connector (**Figure 26**).

Voltage Regulator Ground Test

The voltage regulator base must be grounded to the frame for proper operation.
1. Connect one ohmmeter lead to a good engine or frame ground and the other ohmmeter lead to the regulator base. Read the ohmmeter scale. The correct reading is 0 ohm. Note the following:
   a. If there is low resistance (0 ohm), the voltage regulator is properly grounded.
   b. If there is high resistance, remove the voltage regulator and clean its frame mounting points.
2. Remove the voltage regulator and check the connectors on the backside of the voltage regulator. They must be tight and free of corrosion.

IGNITION SYSTEM

Precautions

Before testing the ignition system, observe the following precautions to prevent damage to protect the system:
1. Never disconnect any of the electrical connectors while the engine is running.
2. Apply dielectric grease to all electrical connectors prior to reconnecting them. This will help seal out moisture.
3. Make sure all electrical connectors are free of corrosion and are securely fastened to each other.

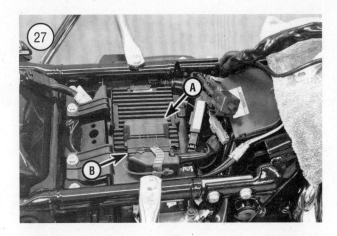

4. The electronic control module (ECM) must be mounted securely to the top caddy (A, **Figure 27**) and the electrical connector (B) must be securely fastened.

Troubleshooting Preparation

1. Refer to the wiring diagrams located in Chapter Sixteen for the specific model.
2. Check the wiring harness for visible signs of damage.
3. Make sure all connectors are fastened securely to each other and locked in place.
4. Check all electrical components for a good ground to the engine.
5. Check all wiring for short circuits or open circuits.
6. To check a blown fuse, perform the following:
   a. Remove the left side saddlebag and the left side frame cover (Chapter Fourteen).
   b. Pull out on the bottom catch (A, **Figure 28**), hinge up the cover and remove the cover (B).

NOTE
*Fuse description and location is printed on the fuse block cover (**Figure 29**).*

   c. Locate the blown fuse (**Figure 30**) and install a new fuse with the same *amperage*.

Ignition Coil Testing

   Use an ohmmeter to check the ignition coil secondary and primary resistance. Test the coil twice: first when it is cold (room temperature) and then at normal operating temperature. If the engine will not start, heat the coil with a hair dryer, and test it with the ohmmeter.
1. Remove the ignition coil as described in Chapter Nine.
2. Disconnect the primary wire connector and the secondary wires from the ignition coil.
3. Measure the primary coil resistance between terminals (**Figure 31**) as follows:
   a. Front coil: Terminal A and D.
   b. Rear coil: Terminal A and C.

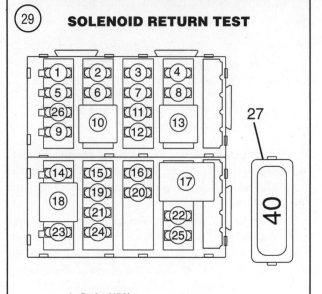

SOLENOID RETURN TEST

1. Brake (15A)
2. Accessory (15A)
3. P&A (15A)
4. Radio power (15A)
5. Radio memory (15A)
6. Battery (15A)
7. ECM power (15A)
8. Power outlet (15A) (optional)
9. Fuel pump (15A)
10. System relay
11. Power lock (optional)
12. GPS optional (2A)
13. Start relay
14. P&A ignition (2 A max.)
15. Instruments (15A)
16. Ignition (15A)
17. Lighting relay
18. Brake relay
19. Headlamp (15A)
20. Lights (15A)
21. Heated handgrips (5A)   (optional)
22. Spare (15A)
23. ABS (30A) (optional)
24. Amplifier (30A)
25. Spare (30A)
26. Spare (30A)
27. Main fuse (40A)

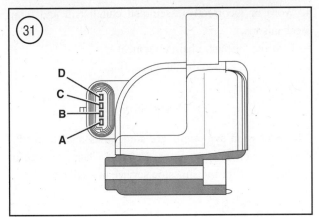

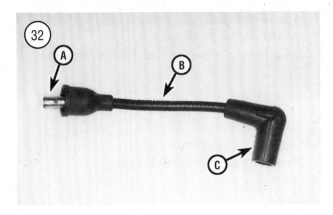

4. Set the ohmmeter on its highest scale. Measure the resistance between the secondary terminals. Specified resistance is 5500-7500 ohms

5. Compare the primary coil resistance reading of 0.5 to 0.7 ohms. Replace the ignition coil if the reading is not within specification.

6. If the resistance values are less than specified, there is most likely a short in the coil windings. Replace the coil.

7. If the resistance values are more than specified, this may indicate corrosion or oxidation of the coil's terminals. Thoroughly clean the terminals, and spray with an aerosol electrical contact cleaner. Repeat the test and if the resistance value is still high, replace the coil.

8. If the coil resistance does not meet (or come close to) either of these specifications, the coil must be replaced. If the coil exhibits visible damage, replace it as described in Chapter Nine.

9. Install the ignition coil as described in Chapter Nine.

Spark Plug Cable Resistance Test and Inspection

1. Remove the ignition coil as described in Chapter Eleven.

2. Disconnect the cables from the spark plug and ignition coil.

3. Measure the resistance of each spark plug cable (**Figure 32**) from end to end.

4. Compare the reading to the following: front cable 4188-11,172 ohms; rear cable 8688-23,178 ohms. Replace the spark plug cable if the reading is not within specification.

5. Inspect the spark plug cables for:
    a. Corroded or damaged connector ends (A, **Figure 32**).
    b. Breaks in the cable insulation (B, **Figure 32**) that could allow arcing.
    c. Split or damaged plug caps (C, **Figure 32**) that could allow arcing to the cylinder heads.

6. Connect the cables onto the spark plugs and ignition coil.

7. Install ignition coil as described in Chapter Nine.

ELECTRONIC FUEL INJECTION

Start troubleshooting the fuel system at the fuel tank and work throughout the fuel system reserving the fuel injecting system to the final point. Check for an empty fuel tank, a plugged filter, fuel pump failure, sour fuel or a clogged air filter element. Refer to *Starting the Engine* and *Engine Performance* in this chapter.

The fuel injection system is controlled by the electronic control module (ECM) component of the engine management system.

ENGINE LUBRICATION

An improperly operating engine lubrication system will quickly lead to engine damage. Check the engine oil level weekly as described in Chapter Three. Oil pump service is covered in Chapter Five.

Low Oil Warning Light

The low oil warning light, mounted on the indicator light panel, should come on when the ignition switch is turned to IGN before the engine is started. After the engine is started, the oil light should turn off when the engine speed is above idle.

If the low oil warning light does not come on when the ignition switch is turned to IGN and the engine is not running, the LED indicator lamp assembly may be damaged and must be replaced as described in Chapter Nine. If the

LED is working, check the oil pressure switch, or sender (**Figure 33**) as described in Chapter Nine.

If the oil light remains on when the engine speed is above idle, turn the engine off and check the oil level (Chapter Three). If oil level is correct, check for a clogged or damaged oil pump (Chapter Five).

Oil Consumption High or Engine Smokes Excessively

1. Worn valve guides.
2. Worn valve guide seals.
3. Worn or damaged piston rings.
4. Oil pan overfilled.
5. Oil filter restricted.
6. Leaking cylinder head surfaces.

Oil Fails to Return to Oil Pan

1. Oil pump damaged or operating incorrectly.
2. Oil pan empty.
3. Oil filter restricted.
4. Damaged oil feed pump.

Engine Oil Leaks

1. Clogged air filter breather hose.
2. Loose engine parts.
3. Damaged gasket sealing surfaces.
4. Oil pan overfilled.
5. Restricted oil filter.
6. Plugged air filter-to-breather system hose.

CLUTCH

All clutch troubles, other than adjustments (except cvo models), require partial clutch disassembly to identify and cure the problem. Refer to Chapter Six for clutch service procedures.

Clutch Chatter or Noise

This problem is usually caused by worn or warped friction and plain plates.

Clutch Slip

1. Incorrect clutch adjustment.
2. Worn friction plates.
3. Weak or damaged diaphragm spring.
4. Damaged pressure plate.

Clutch Drag

1. Incorrect clutch cable adjustment.
2. Warped clutch plain plates.
3. Worn or damaged clutch shell or clutch hub.

4. Worn or incorrectly assembled clutch ball and ramp mechanism.
5. Incorrect primary chain alignment.
6. Weak or damaged diaphragm spring.

TRANSMISSION

Transmission symptoms are sometimes hard to distinguish from clutch symptoms. Refer to Chapter Seven or Chapter Eight for transmission service procedures.

Gears Will Not Stay Engaged

1. Worn or damaged shifter parts.
2. Incorrect shifter rod adjustment.
3. Severely worn or damaged gears and/or shift forks.

Difficult Shifting

1. Worn or damaged shift forks.
2. Worn or damaged shifter clutch dogs.
3. Weak or damaged shifter return spring.
4. Clutch drag.

Excessive Gear Noise

1. Worn or damaged bearings.
2. Worn or damaged gears.
3. Excessive gear backlash.

LIGHTING SYSTEM

If bulbs burn out frequently, check for excessive vibration, loose connections that permit sudden current surges, or the installation of the wrong type of bulb.

Most light and ignition problems are caused by loose or corroded ground connections. Check these prior to replacing a bulb or electrical component.

EXCESSIVE VIBRATION

Excessive vibration is usually caused by loose engine mounting hardware. A bent axle shaft or loose suspension component will cause high-speed vibration problems. Vibration can also be caused by the following conditions:

1. Cracked or broken frame.
2. Severely worn primary chain.
3. Tight primary chain links.
4. Loose, worn or damaged engine stabilizer link(s).
5. Loose or damaged rubber mounts.
6. Improperly balanced wheel(s).
7. Defective or damaged wheel(s).
8. Defective or damaged tire(s).
9. Internal engine wear or damage.
10. Loose or worn steering head bearings.
11. Loose swing arm pivot shaft nut.

FRONT SUSPENSION AND STEERING

Poor handling may be caused by improper tire inflation pressure, a damaged or bent frame or front steering components, worn wheel bearings or dragging brakes. Possible causes for suspension and steering malfunctions are listed below.

Irregular or Wobbly Steering

1. Loose wheel axle nut(s).
2. Loose or worn steering head bearings.
3. Excessive wheel bearing play.
4. Damaged cast wheel.
5. Laced wheel out of alignment.
6. Unbalanced wheel assembly.
7. Incorrect wheel alignment.
8. Incorrect vehicle alignment.
9. Bent or damaged steering stem or frame at steering neck.
10. Tire incorrectly seated on rim.
11. Excessive front end loading from non-standard equipment.

Stiff Steering

1. Low front tire air pressure.
2. Bent or damaged steering stem or frame.
3. Loose or worn steering head bearings.

Stiff or Heavy Fork Operation

1. Incorrect fork springs.
2. Incorrect fork oil viscosity.
3. Excessive amount of fork oil.
4. Bent fork tubes.
5. Incorrect fork air pressure.

Poor Fork Operation

1. Worn or damaged fork tubes.
2. Fork oil capacity low due to leaking fork seals.
3. Bent or damaged fork tubes.
4. Contaminated fork oil.
5. Incorrect fork springs.
6. Excessive front end loading from non-standard equipment.

Poor Rear Shock Absorber Operation

1. Weak or worn springs.
2. Damper unit leaking.
3. Shock shaft worn or bent.
4. Rear shocks adjusted incorrectly.
5. Excessive rear end loading from non-standard equipment.
6. Incorrect loading.
7. Incorrect rear shock air pressure.

BRAKE PROBLEMS

Perform the maintenance specified in Chapter Three to minimize brake system problems. Brake system service is covered in Chapter Thirteen. When refilling the front and rear master cylinders, use only DOT 4 brake fluid.

Insufficient Braking Power

Worn brake pads or disc, air in the hydraulic system, glazed or contaminated pads, low brake fluid level, or a leaking brake line or hose can cause this problem. Visually check for leaks. Check for worn brake pads. Check also for a leaking or damaged primary cup seal in the master cylinder. Bleed the brakes. Rebuild a leaking master cylinder or brake caliper. Brake drag will result in excessive heat and brake fade. Refer to *Brake Drag* in this section.

Spongy Brake Feel

This problem is generally caused by air in the hydraulic system. Bleed the brakes as described in Chapter Thirteen.

Brake Drag

Check for insufficient brake pedal and/or hand lever free play. Also check for worn, loose or missing parts in the brake calipers. Check the brake disc(s) for excessive runout.

Brakes Squeal or Chatter

Check brake pad thickness and disc condition. Check that the caliper anti-rattle springs are properly installed and in good condition. Clean off any dirt on the pads. Loose components can also cause this. Check for:

1. Warped brake disc.

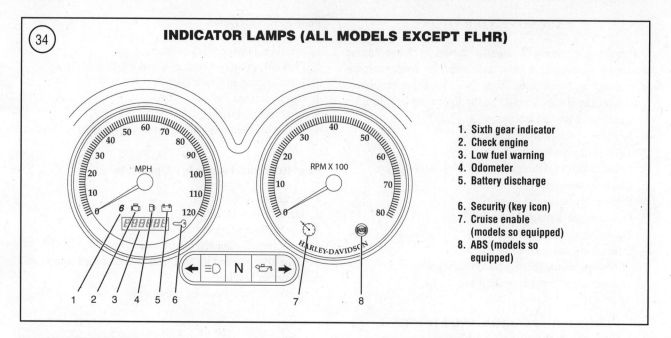

INDICATOR LAMPS (ALL MODELS EXCEPT FLHR)

1. Sixth gear indicator
2. Check engine
3. Low fuel warning
4. Odometer
5. Battery discharge

6. Security (key icon)
7. Cruise enable (models so equipped)
8. ABS (models so equipped)

2. Loose brake disc.
3. Loose caliper mounting bolts.
4. Loose front axle nut.
5. Worn wheel bearings.
6. Damaged hub.

ELECTRONIC DIAGNOSTIC SYSTEM

All models are equipped with an electronic diagnostic system that monitors the operating condition of the starting system, charging system, instruments, TSM/TSSM/HFSM, and engine management components. A serial data bus connects these components. If a malfunction occurs, a diagnostic trouble code (DTC) may be generated.

The DTC identifies an anomaly detected in a monitored component. The trouble code is stored in the memory of the ECM, the TSM/TSSM/HFSM and the speedometer.

A current DTC identifies a problem that affects present motorcycle operation. A historic DTC identifies a problem that has been resolved either through servicing or a changed condition. Historic DTC's are retained to provide information should an intermittent problem exist. A historic DTC is retained in memory until fifty start/run cycles have occurred at which time the DTC is erased or by the Harley-Davidson Digital Technician II (part No. HD-48650).

Not all malfunctions generate a DTC. Refer to **Table 1** and **Table 2**.

Startup Check

The diagnostic system indicates a normal condition or an operating problem each time the ignition key is turned to ON (ignition).

Refer to **Figure 34** or **Figure 35**.
1. During normal startup, the following occurs after the key is turned on:

a. The *check engine* symbol illuminates for four seconds, then goes out.
b. The *security* symbol illuminates for four seconds, then goes out.
2. Note the following indications of potential problems during startup:
a. If the check engine symbol or security symbol does not illuminate, the speedometer may be faulty.
b. If the check engine symbol or security symbol illuminates after 20 seconds, a serial data bus problem may exist. Check for DTCs.
c. If the check engine symbol or security symbol stays on, the speedometer may be faulty or a DTC exists.

Diagnostic Trouble Code (DTC) Retrieval

A diagnostic trouble code consists of a letter prefix followed by four numerals.

NOTE
*The message **BusEr** is a trouble code which may appear during diagnostic troubleshooting. **BusEr** indicates a problem in the serial bus data circuit.*

NOTE
Make sure engine stop switch is in the run position.

1. Press in and hold the odometer reset button on the speedometer.
2. Turn the ignition switch ON, and release the reset button. The following should occur:
a. The speedometer backlighting comes on.
b. The speedometer needle (and tachometer, models so equipped) rotates to its full deflection position.

INDICATOR LAMPS (FLHR MODELS)

1. Pursuit (law enforcement)
2. Sixth gear indicator
3. Cruse enable (models so equipped)
4. Check engine
5. Low fuel warning
6. Odometer /trip odometer/ clock window
7. Battery discharge
8. ABS (models so equipped)
9. Security (key icon)

NOTE
The security symbol may come on even though the motorcycle is not equipped with a security system.

c. The indicator lamps controlled by the serial bus (battery, security, coolant temperature, low fuel, and check engine symbols) should illuminate.

3. The message *diag* appears in the odometer window on the speedometer.

4. Press and release the odometer reset button. The letters *PSSPtb* appears in the odometer window. The letter *P* will flash indicating that information concerning the ECM is obtainable.

DTCs are stored in several devices each represented by a letter or letters. A flashing letter identifier indicates that a particular device has been selected. For example, a flashing *P* indicates the ECM has been selected. Proceeding further will provide information about the ECM.

The letters *PSSPtb* identify the following components:

    a. The letter P identifies the ECM.
    b. The letter S identifies the TSM/TSSM/HFSM.
    c. The letters SP identify the speedometer.
    d. The letter t identifies the tachometer (on models so equipped).
    e. The letter b identifies the ABS system (on models so equipped).

5. To toggle through the *PSSPtb* letter identifiers, push and quickly release the odometer reset button. The selected letter identifier will flash.

6. To obtain a DTC, select a particular device (its identifier letter[s] flashes), then push and hold the reset button for a least 5 seconds. Release the button. The code or *none* will appear in the odometer window. Record the DTC and the device (ECM, speedometer or TSM/TSSM/HFSM) where the DTC is stored.

NOTE
Press and release the reset button only long enough to display the next code. Holding in the reset button for more than 5 seconds will erase the codes.

7. Press and release the reset button as needed to read additional trouble codes until *end* appears.

8. If *none* appears, pushing and releasing the reset button causes the speedometer to display the part number of the selected device. For instance, the display may read *Pn 34246-08A or 34246-08B* for the ECM.

9. Push and release the reset button to return to the *PSSPtb* display.

10. Turn off the ignition switch to exit the diagnostic mode.

DATA LINK CONNECTOR

The data link connector provides access to the data bus and provides a testing terminal when troubleshooting. The data link connector (**Figure 36**) is located on the fuse panel beneath the left side frame side cover.

Diagnostic Tools

The Harley-Davidson Digital Technician II (part No. HD-48650), is needed to obtain or erase historic DTCs and to reprogram a new ECM or new TSM/TSSM/HFSM. At the time of publication, these tools were not available to the general public.

Table 1 DIAGNOSTIC TROUBLE CODES

DTC	Problem
B0562	Battery voltage low
B0563, P0563	Battery voltage high
B1004	Fuel level sensor low
B1005	Fuel level sensor high/open
B1006	Accessory line over voltage
B1006	Ignition line over voltage
B1008	Odometer reset switch closed
B1121	Right turn signal output fault FHSM
B1122	Left turn signal output fault FHSM
B1121	Right turn signal output fault TSM/TSSM
B1122	Left turn signal output fault FHSM
B1123	Right turn signal short to ground FHSM
B1124	Left turn signal short to ground FHSM
B1125	Right turn signal short to voltage FHSM
B1126	Left turn signal short to voltage FHSM
B1131	Alarm output low
B1132	Alarm output high
B1134	Starter relay output high
B1143	Security antenna short to ground
B1144	Security antenna short to voltage
B1145	Security antenna open
B1154	Clutch switch short to ground
B1155	Neutral switch short to ground
C1017	ABS pump motor power circuit open fault
C1018	ABS pump motor ground high resistance fault
C1021	ABS front wheel sensor speed sensors zero
C1023	ABS rear wheel sensor speed sensors zero
C1025	ABS wheel sensor signal intermittent
C1026	ABS wheel sensor signal frequency out of range
C1032	ABS front wheel speed sensor circuit open or shorted
C1034	ABS rear wheel speed sensor circuit open or shorted
C1042	ABS brake pump motor open
C1043	ABS brake pump motor stalled
C1094	ABS front brake switch always on
C1095	ABS front brake switch open
C1151	ABS front wheel release too long
C1153	ABS rear wheel release too long
C1212	ABS front or rear brake not applied during deceleration
C1214	ABS rear brake switch always on
C1216	ABS rear brake switch open
C1014	ABS ECU internal fault
C1055-1066	ABS ECU internal fault
C1118	ABS ECU internal fault
C1121	ABS ECU internal fault
P0031	O_2 sensor heater open/low
P0032	O_2 sensor heater shorted/high
P0107	MAP sensor error open/low
P0108	MAP sensor error high
P0112	IAT sensor voltage low
P0113	IAT sensor voltage open/high
P0117	ET sensor voltage low
P0118	ET sensor voltage open/high
P0120	TPS1 sensor range error
P0122	TPS1 sensor range open/low
P0123	TPS1 sensor range high
P0131	O_2 sensor (front) low or engine running lean
P0132	O_2 sensor (front) running rich
P0134	O_2 sensor (front) heater open/not responding/high
P0151	O_2 sensor (rear) low or engine running lean
P0152	O_2 sensor (rear) running rich
P0154	O_2 sensor (rear) open/not responding/high
P0220	TPS2 sensor range error
P0222	TPS2 sensor low/open
P0223	TPS2 sensor high
P0261	Fuel injector (front) open/low
P0262	Fuel injector (front) high

(continued)

Table 1 DIAGNOSTIC TROUBLE CODES (continued)

DTC	Problem
P0263	Fuel injector (rear) open/low
P0264	Fuel injector (rear) high
P0373	CKP sensor intermittent
P0374	CKP sensor synch error
P0501	Vehicle speed sensor (VSS) sensor low
P0502	Vehicle speed sensor (VSS) sensor high
P0572	Brake switch input error
P0577	Cruise control input high
P0641	Throttle control actuator 5V VREF-1 out of range
P0651	Throttle control actuator 5V VREF-2 out of range
P1001	Starter system relay coil open/low
P1002	Starter system relay coil high/shorted
P1003	Starter system relay contacts open
P1004	Starter system relay contacts closed
P1009	Incorrect password
P1010	Missing password
P1351	Ignition coil open
P1354	Ignition coil low
P1352	Ignition coil high
P1353	No combustion front cylinder
P1354	Ignition coil shorted
P1356	No combustion rear cylinder
P1357	Intermittent combustion front cylinder
P1358	Intermittent combustion rear cylinder
P1475	Exhaust actuator position failure (HDI)
P1477	Exhaust actuator open/low (HDI)
P1478	Exhaust actuator high (HDI)
P1501	Jiffy stand sensor (JSS) low
P1502	Jiffy stand sensor (JSS) high
P1510	Throttle control management
P1511	Throttle control management
P1512	Throttle control management
P1600	TCA module processor internal fault
P1655	ARC solenoid malfunction
P1656	ARC short to voltage in control circuit
P2100	Throttle actuator motor circuit open
P2101	Throttle actuator motor circuit range/performance (actuator error)
P2102	Throttle actuator motor control shorted low
P2103	Throttle actuator motor control shorted high
P2105	Throttle control system forced engine shut down
P2107	Throttle control system module—internal fault
P2119	TCA system throttle body range performance
P2122	Throttle twist grip sensor TGS 1 low/open
P2123	Throttle twist grip sensor TGS 1 high
P2127	Throttle twist grip sensor TGS 2 low/open
P2128	Throttle twist grip sensor TGS 2 high
P2135	TPS correlation error
P2138	TPS correlation error
P2170	Throttle twist grip validation error
P2176	TCA system throttle body range closed position not learned
U1016	Serial data error/missing message or loss of ECM serial data
U1040	Loss of ABS serial data at speedometer
U1064	Loss of TSM/TSSM/HFSM serial data
U1097	Loss of speedometer serial data
U1255	Serial data error/missing message

Table 2 DTC CODE PRIORITY ORDER

DTC Number	Priority	DTC Number	Priority
B0563	138	C1065	101
B1004	145	C1066	102
B1005	146	C1094	121
B1006	143	C1095	122
B1007	142	C1118	103

(continued)

Table 2 DTC CODE PRIORITY ORDER (continued)

DTC Number	Priority	DTC Number	Priority
B1008	144	C1121	104
B1121	129	C1151	126
B1121	130	C1153	127
B1123	131	C1158	106
B1124	132	C1206	119
B1125	133	C1208	120
B1126	134	C1212	125
B1121	139	C1214	123
B1132	140	C1216	124
B1134	128	P0031	82
B1135	23	P0032	82
B1136	24	P0107	19
B1141	141	P0108	20
B1142	135	P0112	58
B1144	136	P0113	59
B1145	137	P0117	56
B1151	25	P0118	57
B1152	26	P0120	38
B1153	27	P0120	38
B1154	28	P0122	40
B1155	29	P0123	41
C0562	111	P0131	84
C0563	112	P0132	86
C1014	105	P0134	88
C1017	110	P0151	85
B1018	109	P0152	87
C1021	115	P0154	89
C1023	116	P0220	39
C1025	117	P0222	42
C1027	118	P0223	43
C1032	113	P0261	66
C1034	114	P0262	68
C1042	107	P0263	67
C1043	108	P0264	69
C1055	96	P0373	18
C1056	97	P0374	21
C1057	98	P0444	77
C1061	99	P0445	78
C1062	100	P0501	72
P0502	73	P2127	35
P0505	76	P2128	36
P0562	70	P2135	44
P0563	71	P2138	37
P0572	55	P2176	50
P0577	93	U1016	7
P0603	2	U1040	8
P0605	1	U1064	6
P0641	16	U1097	5
P0651	17	U1255	9
P0661	48	U1300	3
P0662	49	U1301	4
P1001	12	U1302	147
P1002	11		
P1003	10		
P1004	13		
P1009	14		
P1010	15		
P1270	31		
P1351	60		
P1352	62		
P1353	75		
P1354	61		
P1355	63		
P1356	74		
P1357	64		
P1358	65		

(continued)

Table 2 DTC CODE PRIORITY ORDER (continued)

DTC Number	Priority	DTC Number	Priority
P1475	79		
P1477	80		
P1478	81		
P1501	53		
P1502	54		
P1510	90		
P1511	91		
P1512	92		
P1514	51		
P1600	30		
P1655	94		
P1656	95		
P1200	46		
P1201	47		
P2102	48		
P2103	49		
P2105	52		
P2107	32		
P2119	45		
P2122	33		
P2123	34		

Table 3 DEVICE PART NUMBER

Item	Part Number
ECM	HD-34236-08B
TSM module	HD-68920-07
TSSM module	HD-68924-07
HFSM remote control fob	HD-68926-07
Siren alarm (HDI)	HD-68958-07C
Siren antenna module (HDI)	HD-68956-07

NOTES

CHAPTER THREE

LUBRICATION, MAINTENANCE AND TUNE-UP

This chapter describes lubrication, maintenance and tune-up procedures.

During the inspection procedures in this chapter, compare the measurements taken to the maintenance and tune-up specifications in the tables at the end of this chapter. Replace any part that is damaged, worn or out of specification. During assembly, tighten fasteners as specified.

Refer to **Tables 1-7** located at the end of this chapter for specifications.

MAINTENANCE INTERVALS

Refer to **Table 1** for the maintenance intervals. Adherence to these recommendations helps ensure a long service life from the motorcycle. If the motorcycle is operated in high humidity, extreme temperatures, continuous stop and go traffic, areas of blowing dirt or other extreme elements, consider performing service more frequently.

PRE-RIDE INSPECTION

1. Check wheel and tire condition. Check tire pressure. Refer to *Tires and Wheels* in this chapter.
2. Check engine for oil leaks. If necessary, add oil as described in this chapter.
3. Check brake fluid level and condition. If necessary, add fluid as described in this chapter.
4. On CVO models, check clutch fluid level and condition. If necessary, add fluid as described in this chapter.
5. Check the operation of the front and rear brakes.
6A. On all models except CVO, check clutch operation. If necessary, adjust the clutch as described in this chapter.

6B. On CVO models, check clutch operation. If necessary, bleed the clutch hydraulic system as described in Chapter Six.
7. Check the throttle operation. The throttle should move smoothly and return quickly when released.
8. Inspect the front and rear suspension. They should have a solid feel with no looseness.
9. Check the exhaust system for leaks or damage.
10. Inspect the fuel system for leaks.
11. Check drive belt deflection as described in this chapter.
12. With the ignition switch turned to IGN, check the following.
   a. Pull the front brake lever and check that the brake light comes on.
   b. Push the rear brake pedal down and check that the brake light comes on soon after the pedal has been depressed.
   c. Make sure the headlight and taillight are on.
   d. Press the dimmer switch and make sure the headlight elements are working in both the high and low positions.
   e. Push the right and left turn signal switches and make sure all four turn signal lights are working.
   f. Check that all accessory lights work properly, if so equipped.
   g. Check the horn switch operation.
   h. If the horn or any light fails to work properly, refer to Chapter Nine.

TIRES AND WHEELS

Tire Pressure

Check the tire pressure often to maintain tire performance and prevent unnecessary tire wear.

Refer to **Table 2** for original equipment tire pressure.

Tire Inspection

Inspect the tires periodically for excessive wear, deep cuts and imbedded objects such as stones or nails. If a nail or other object is found in a tire, mark its location with a light crayon prior to removing the object.

Measure the depth (**Figure 1**) with a tread depth gauge or a small ruler. As a guideline, replace tires when the tread wear indicator bars appear on the tread surface and when the tread depth is 1/32 in. (0. 8 mm.) or less. Locate the arrows on the sidewall indicating the location of the tread wear indicators. Refer to Chapter Ten for tire changing and repair information.

Spoke Tension

Check laced wheels for loose or damaged spokes. Refer to Chapter Ten for wheel service.

Wheel Inspection

Check the wheel for cracks and other damage. Refer to Chapter Twelve for wheel service.

CVO LUBRICATION

Engine, Transmission and Primary Chaincase Oil Recommendations

All new CVO models use Screamin' Eagle SYN3 synthetic motorcycle lubricant. If additional oil must be added to correct oil level, and the SYN3 oil is not available, *temporarily* add the correct viscosity of HD-360 motor oil. Although both types of lubricant are compatible, the intermixed lubricant should be changed as soon as possible. If SYN3 is not going to be used permanently, completely drain the engine, transmission or primary chaincase oil and use in another type of oil recommended in **Table 4**.

ENGINE OIL AND FILTER

Engine Oil Level Check

Check the engine oil level with the dipstick/oil filler cap located on the transmission case. Be sure to observe the correct portion of the marks on the dipstick (**Figure 2**).

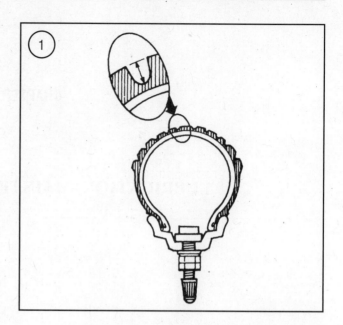

NOTE
The oil level cannot be accurately measured when the engine is cold. Do not add oil to bring the oil level on a cold engine to the FULL HOT mark on the dipstick.

1. Start and run the engine for approximately 10 minutes or until the engine has reached normal operating temperature. Turn the engine off and allow the oil to settle.

CAUTION
Holding the motorcycle straight upright will result in an incorrect level reading.

2. Place the motorcycle on a level surface and rest it on the jiffy stand.
3. Wipe the area around the oil filler cap with a clean rag. Unscrew the oil filler/dipstick (A, **Figure 3**) from the top of the transmission upper housing. Wipe off the dipstick with a clean rag and reinsert the oil filler cap/dipstick. Tighten it completely into the fill spout.
4. Unscrew and withdraw the oil filler cap/dipstick again and check the oil level on the dipstick. The oil level is correct if it registers midway (2, **Figure 2**) between FULL and ADD marks on the dipstick. If necessary, add only enough oil, listed in Table 3, to bring the level midway (2, **Figure 2**) on the dipstick.
5. Inspect the O-ring (**Figure 4**) for crack or other damage; replace if necessary.
6. Reinsert the oil filler cap/dipstick, and tighten completely into the fill spout.

Engine Oil and Filter Change

Refer to **Table 1** for the recommended oil and filter change interval, which assumes that the motorcycle is operated in moderate climates. If the motorcycle is operated

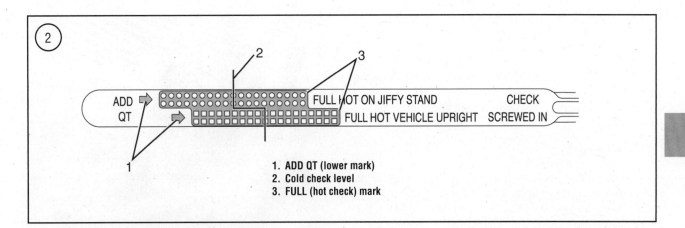

1. ADD QT (lower mark)
2. Cold check level
3. FULL (hot check) mark

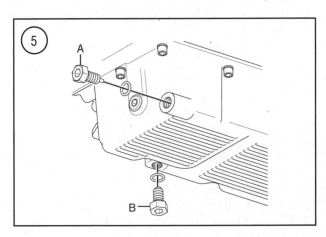

under dusty conditions, the oil becomes contaminated more quickly and should be changed more frequently.

Use a motorcycle oil with a classification recommended by the manufacturer and one specifically designated for motorcycle applications. Always try to use the same brand of oil at each change. Refer to **Table 4** for correct oil viscosity to use under anticipated ambient temperatures. Using oil additives is not recommended as they may cause clutch damage.

WARNING
Contact with oil may cause skin cancer. Wash oil from hands with soap and water as soon as possible after handling engine oil.

CAUTION
Do not use automotive oils in motorcycle engines. These oils typically contain friction modifiers that reduce frictional losses on engine components. Specifically designed for automotive engines, these oils can cause damage to motorcycle engine and clutch assemblies.

NOTE
Never dispose of motor oil in the trash, on the ground or down a storm drain. Many service stations and oil retailers will accept used oil for recycling. Do not combine other fluids with motor oil to be recycled.

1. Ride the motorcycle until engine is at normal operating temperature.
2. Turn off the engine and allow the oil to settle in oil pan. Support the motorcycle on level ground on a swing arm stand.
3. Wipe the area around the oil filler cap with a clean rag. Unscrew the oil filler cap/dipstick (A, **Figure 3**) from of the transmission case.

NOTE
*The oil pan is equipped with two drain plugs. Remove only the engine oil drain plug (A, **Figure 5**) located at the front left side of the*

*oil pan. Do not remove the transmission drain plug (B, **Figure 5**) at the base of the oil pan.*

4. Place a drain pan underneath the oil pan and remove the engine oil drain plug (A, **Figure 5**) and O-ring from the front left side of the oil pan.

5. Allow the engine oil to drain completely.

> *NOTE*
> *On models equipped with an oil cooler, the oil filter (A, **Figure 6**) is very difficult to reach due to the oil cooler adapter and related oil hoses (B). It is recommended that the oil filter wrench (part No. HD-42311 or HD-44067A) and hand tools be used to remove the oil filter. These tools also assist in reducing damage to the crankshaft position sensor (C, **Figure 6**) during filter removal.*

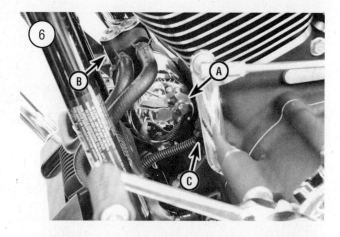

6. To replace the oil filter (A, **Figure 7**), perform the following:

  a. Temporarily install the drain bolt and O-ring finger-tight. Then, move the drain pan underneath the oil filter. Place a shop cloth (B, **Figure 7**) over the voltage regulator, and under the oil filter to catch residual oil drips after the oil filter (A) is removed.

  b. Install a socket-type oil filter wrench squarely over the oil filter (A, **Figure 7**) and turn it *counterclockwise* to loosen it. Place another shop cloth on the filter as it is hot and quickly remove the oil filter as oil will begin to run out.

  c. Position the oil filter so the open end faces up.

  d. Place the oil filter over the drain pan, turn it over and pour out the remaining oil. Place the filter in a plastic bag, seal it and dispose of it properly.

  e. Remove the shop cloth and dispose of it properly. Wipe all spilled oil from the surrounding area.

  f. Coat the new oil filter gasket with clean engine oil.

> *CAUTION*
> *Tighten the oil filter by hand. Do not over-tighten.*

  g. Screw the oil filter onto its mount and tighten it by hand until the filter gasket just touches the sealing surface. Then, tighten the filter by hand an additional 1/2 to 3/4 turn.

7. Install a *new* O-ring (**Figure 8**) onto the engine oil drain plug.

8. Lubricate the O-ring with clean engine oil before installing it. Install the engine oil drain plug and new O-ring and tighten the drain plug to 14-21 ft.-lb. (19-28.5 N•m).

9. While the engine is drained of oil, inspect the pipe plug at the front right side crankcase for leaks. If leaks have occurred, remove the pipe plug and clean the threads thoroughly in solvent and dry. Apply Loctite Pipe Sealant, or an equivalent, to the threads, and then reinstall the pipe plug and tighten it securely.

10. Add the correct type (**Table 4**) and quantity (**Table 3**) of oil into the oil pan.

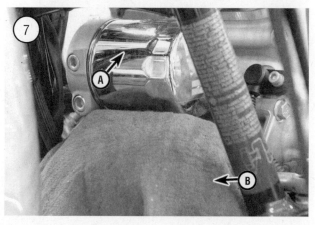

11. Thread the oil filler cap/dipstick into the fill spout and tighten completely.

> *NOTE*
> *After oil has been added, the oil level will register above the FULL HOT dipstick mark (3, **Figure 2**) until the engine runs and the filter fills with oil. To obtain a correct reading after installing a new oil filter and adding oil, follow the procedure described here.*

12. After changing the engine oil and filter, check the oil level as follows:

  a. Start and run the engine for 1 minute, and then shut it off.

  b. Check the oil level on the dipstick as described in this section.

  c. If the oil level is correct, it will register in the dipstick's safe operating level range. If so, *do not* top off or add oil to bring it to the FULL HOT level on the dipstick. (3, **Figure 2**)

  d. Ride the motorcycle until engine is at normal operating temperature.

  e. Place the motorcycle on a level surface and park it on its jiffy stand and allow the engine to idle for 1-2 minutes. Turn off the engine and recheck the oil level; adjust if necessary.

13. Check the oil filter and drain plug for leaks.

14. Dispose of the used oil properly.

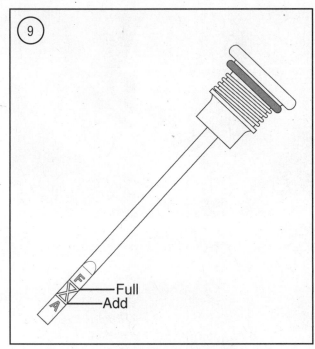

Full
Add

TRANSMISSION OIL

Transmission Oil Level Check

Table 1 lists the recommended transmission oil inspection intervals. When checking the transmission oil level, do not allow any dirt or debris to enter the transmission case opening.

> *WARNING*
> *Contact with oil may cause skin cancer. Wash oil from hands with soap and water as soon as possible after handling transmission oil.*

1. Ride the motorcycle for approximately 10 minutes and shift through all gears until the transmission oil has reached normal operating temperature. Turn off the engine and allow the oil to settle. Park the motorcycle on a level surface on the jiffystand.

2. Clean the area around the transmission filler cap/dipstick (B, **Figure 3**) on top of the transmission case and unscrew it.

3. Wipe the dipstick and reinsert it back into the clutch release cover housing, or into the transmission case; do not screw the cap/dipstick into place. Rest it on the opening and then withdraw it. The oil level is correct when it registers between the two dipstick marks (**Figure 9**).

> *CAUTION*
> *Do not add engine oil. Add only the recommended type of transmission oil listed in* **Table 5**.

4. If the oil level is low, add the recommended type of transmission oil, or equivalent, listed in **Table 5**. Do not overfill.

5. Inspect the filler cap O-ring. Replace if worn or damaged.

6. Install the transmission oil filler cap/dipstick and tighten it to 25-75 in.-lb. (2.8-8.5 N•m).

7. Wipe any spilled oil off the clutch release cover housing or transmission case.

Transmission Oil Change

Table 1 lists the recommended transmission oil change intervals.

1. Ride the motorcycle for approximately 10 minutes and shift through all gears until the transmission oil has reached normal operating temperature. Turn off the engine and allow the oil to settle in the tank. Park the motorcycle on a level surface and have an assistant support it in an upright position.

2. Clean the area around the transmission filler cap/dipstick (B, **Figure 3**) on top of the transmission case and unscrew it.

> *NOTE*
> *The oil pan is equipped with two drain plugs. Make sure to remove the transmission oil drain plug on the base of the oil pan (B, **Figure 5**) not the engine oil drain plug (A) at the front left side.*

3. Place a drain pan underneath the transmission/oil tank pan and remove the transmission oil drain plug (B, **Figure 5**) and O-ring on the base of the oil pan.

> *WARNING*
> *If any oil spills onto the ground, wipe it up immediately before it contacts the rear tire.*

4. Check the drain plug O-ring (**Figure 8**) for damage and replace if necessary.

5. The drain plug is magnetic. Check the plug for metal debris that may indicate transmission damage, and wipe the plug off. Replace the plug if damaged.

6. Install the transmission drain plug (B, **Figure 5**) and tighten to 14-21 ft.-lb. (19-28.5 N•m).

CAUTION
Add only the recommended type of transmission oil listed in **Table 5**; *do not add engine oil. Make sure to add the oil to the correct oil filler hole.*

7. Refill the transmission through the oil filler cap/dipstick hole with the recommended quantity (**Table 3**) and type (**Table 5**) of transmission oil.
8. Install the transmission oil filler cap/dipstick and tighten it to 25-75 in.-lb. (2.8-8.5 N•m).
9. Wipe any spilled oil off the clutch release cover housing or transmission case.
10. Dispose of the used oil properly.
11. Ride the motorcycle until the transmission oil reaches normal operating temperature. Shut off the engine.
12. Check the transmission drain plug for leaks.
13. Check the transmission oil level as described in this section. Readjust the level if necessary.

PRIMARY CHAINCASE OIL

Primary Chaincase Oil Level Check

The primary chaincase oil lubricates the clutch, primary chain and sprockets. **Table 1** lists the intervals for checking the chaincase oil level. When checking the primary chaincase oil level, do not allow any dirt or debris to enter the housing.
1. Ride the motorcycle for approximately 10 minutes and shift through all gears until the primary chaincase oil has reached normal operating temperature. Turn off the engine and allow the oil to settle in the case. Park the motorcycle on a level surface and have an assistant support it in an upright position. Do not support it on the jiffy stand.

CAUTION
Do not check the oil level with the motorcycle supported on its jiffy stand or the reading will be incorrect.

2. Remove the Torx screws (T27) securing the clutch cover (**Figure 10**) and gasket, or seal ring. Then, remove the cover.
3. The oil level is correct when it is even with the bottom of the clutch opening (**Figure 11**) or at the bottom of the clutch diaphragm spring.

CAUTION
Do not add engine oil. Add only the recommended type of primary chaincase lubricant listed in **Table 5**.

4. If necessary, add the recommended type of lubricant, or its equivalent, through the opening to correct the level.
5. Refer to *Oil Change* in this section to correctly install the seal ring (**Figure 12**), clutch cover and screws.

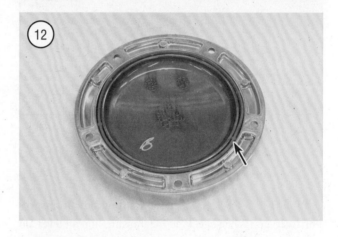

Primary Chaincase Oil Change

Table 1 lists the recommended primary chaincase lubricant replacement intervals.
1. Ride the motorcycle for approximately 10 minutes and shift through all gears until the primary chaincase oil has reached normal operating temperature. Turn off the engine and allow the oil to settle in the case. Park the motorcycle on a level surface.
2. Place a drain pan under the chaincase and remove the drain plug (**Figure 13**).
3. Allow the oil to drain for at least 10 minutes.

4. The drain plug is magnetic. Check the plug for metal debris that may indicate drive component or clutch damage, and then wipe the plug off. Replace the plug if damaged.

5. Reinstall the drain plug and tighten to 14-21 ft.-lb. (19-28.5 N•m).

6. Remove the Torx screws (T27) securing the clutch cover (**Figure 10**) and gasket, or seal ring (**Figure 12**). Then, remove the cover.

CAUTION
*Add only the recommended type of primary chaincase lubricant listed in **Table 5**. Do not add engine oil.*

7. Position a funnel (**Figure 14**) into the clutch opening, and refill the primary chaincase with the recommended quantity (**Table 3**) and type (**Table 5**) of primary chaincase oil. Do not overfill. The oil level must be even with the bottom of the clutch opening (**Figure 11**) or at the bottom of the clutch diaphragm spring.

NOTE
All lubricant must be removed from the seal ring and its mounting groove prior to installation. If any lubricant remains, there will be temporary lubricant seepage around the clutch cover.

8. Remove the seal ring (**Figure 12**) from the clutch cover. Wipe all lubricant from the seal ring and inspect it for cuts or deterioration; replace if necessary. Wipe all lubricant from the seal ring groove and install the seal ring onto the cover. Push the nibs into the ring groove walls.

9. Install the clutch cover and seal ring (**Figure 12**) onto the primary chaincase cover.

10. Install the clutch cover screws and tighten them to 84-108 in.-lb. (9.5-12.2 N•m).

11. Ride the motorcycle until the primary chaincase oil reaches normal operating temperature. Then, shut the engine off.

12. Check the primary chaincase drain plug and clutch cover for leaks.

FRONT FORK OIL

The front fork must be removed and partially disassembled in order to change the oil. Refer to Chapter Eleven.

CONTROL CABLES LUBRICATION

Lubricate the control cables at the intervals in Table 1 or sooner if they become stiff. At this time, inspect each cable for fraying and cable sheath damage. Replace any faulty cable(s). Lubricate the cables with a cable lubricant.

CAUTION
If the original equipment cables have been replaced with nylon-lined cables, do not lubricate them as described in this procedure. Oil and most cable lubricants will cause the cable liner to expand, pushing the liner against the cable sheath and binding the cable. Nylon-lined cables are normally used dry. Follow the manufacturer's instructions when servicing nylon-lined and other aftermarket cables.

CAUTION
Do not use chain lube to lubricate control cables.

NOTE
The major cause of cable damage is improper lubrication. Maintaining the cables as described in this section will ensure long service life.

1. On all models except CVO, disconnect the clutch cable ends as described in *Clutch Cable Replacement* (Chapter Six).

2. Attach a cable lubricator (**Figure 15**) to the cable following its manufacturer's instructions.

NOTE
Place a shop cloth at the opposite end of the cable to catch all excess lubricant.

3. Insert the lubricant nozzle tube into the lubricator, press the button on the can and hold it down until the lubricant begins to flow out of the other end of the cable. If the lubricant squirts out from around the lubricator, it is not clamped to the cable properly. Loosen and reposition the cable lubricator.

NOTE
If the lubricant does not flow out of the other end of the cable, check the cable for fraying, bending or other damage. Replace damaged cables.

4. Remove the lubricator and wipe off both ends of the cable.
5. Reconnect the clutch cable ends as described in *Clutch Cable Replacement* (Chapter Six).
6. Adjust the cables as described in this section.

Drive Belt
Deflection and Alignment

Inspect drive belt deflection and rear axle alignment at the intervals specified in **Table 1**. If the drive belt is severely worn, or if it is wearing incorrectly, refer to Chapter Twelve for inspection and replacement procedures.

The drive belt deflection can be inspected with the rear wheel off the ground or with the motorcycle resting on the jiffy stand without rider or luggage. A belt tension gauge (JIMS part No. 923 or Motion Pro 08-0350), or the equivalent, is needed to check drive belt defection.

NOTE
Check drive belt deflection and axle alignment when the belt is at room temperature, not after a ride.

1. Remove the left side saddlebag as described in Chapter Fourteen.
2. Support the motorcycle with the rear wheel off the ground, or position it on the Jiffy stand.
3. Shift the transmission into neutral.
4. If the rear wheel is off the ground, turn the rear wheel and check the drive belt for its tightest point. If positioned on the Jiffy stand, move the motorcycle forward for the tightest point. When this point is located, move the wheel so that the belt's tight spot is on the lower belt run, midway between the front and rear sprockets.
5. Slide the O-ring on the gauge toward the 0 lb. (0 kg) mark on the gauge.
6. Position the gauge on the lower belt strand half way between the transmission drive sprocket and rear wheel driven sprocket.
7. Push up on the gauge until the O-ring slides to the 10 lb. (4.5 kg) mark while measuring the belt deflection at the same point (**Figure 16**).
8. Rotate the rear wheel and measure the deflection at different locations on the belt.

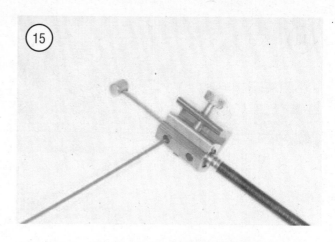

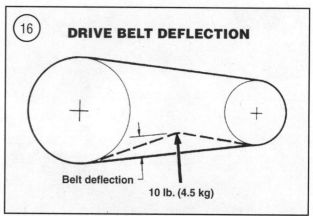

DRIVE BELT DEFLECTION

Belt deflection

10 lb. (4.5 kg)

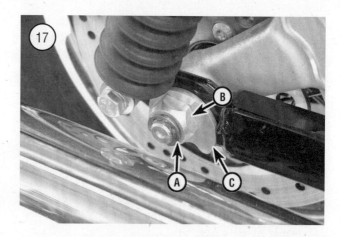

9. Compare the belt deflection measurement with the correct specification in **Table 6**. If the belt deflection measurement is correct, install the left side saddlebag. If the deflection measurement is incorrect, continue the procedure to adjust the belt tension.
10. Remove the right side muffler as described in Chapter Four.
11. Remove the e-clip (A, **Figure 17**) and loosen the rear axle nut (B).
12. Support the motorcycle with the rear wheel off the ground, if it is not already in this position.
13. Rotate the rear axle adjuster cam (C, **Figure 17**) in either direction to adjust belt deflection while maintaining

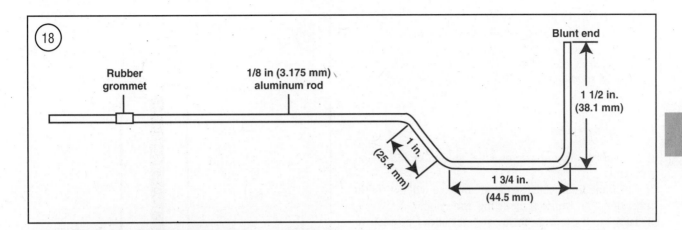

rear wheel alignment. Recheck drive belt deflection as described in this section.

14. After the drive belt deflection measurement is correct, check axle alignment as follows:

  a. Make the alignment tool as shown in **Figure 18** or use a wheel alignment tool (Motion Pro part No. 08-0368), or an equivalent.

  b. Support the motorcycle with the rear wheel off the ground.

  c. Insert the alignment tool into the swing arm index holes. Then, hold it parallel to the rear axle and slide the grommet on the tool until it aligns with the axle center point.

  d. Without repositioning the grommet, remove the tool and check the opposite side of the swing arm, comparing this position with the opposite side. Axle alignment is correct if the two measurements are identical or within 1/32 in. (0.8 mm) of each other.

  e. If the axle alignment is incorrect, adjust the axle while maintaining the correct drive belt deflection measurement.

15. Verify that the axle adjuster cam (C, **Figure 17**) contacts the swing arm boss (**Figure 19**) on each side.

16. When the drive belt deflection and axle alignment adjustments are correct, secure the axle on the left side and tighten the axle nut (B, **Figure 17**) to 95-105 ft.-lb. (128.8-142.4 N•m). Position the e-clip with the flat side facing out

and install it (A, **Figure 17**) around the axle. Make sure it is correctly seated.

17. Install the right side muffler as described in Chapter Four.

18. Lower the rear wheel to the ground.

BRAKE SYSTEM

Front Brake Lever Pivot Pin Lubrication

Inspect the front brake lever pivot pin for lubrication at the intervals specified in **Table 1**. If the pin is dry, lubricate it with light weight oil. To service the pivot pin, refer to *Front Master Cylinder* in Chapter Fifteen.

Brake Pad Inspection

1. Without removing either brake caliper, inspect the brake pads for damage.

2. If the pad material appears marginal; remove the brake pads as described in Chapter Fifteen.

3. Measure the thickness of each brake pad lining (**Figure 20**) with a ruler. Replace the brake pads if worn to the minimum specification in **Table 6**. Replace the brake pads as described in Chapter Fifteen. Always replace both brake pads as a set.

Brake Fluid Level

> *WARNING*
> *Use only DOT 4 brake fluid. Do not intermix different types of brake fluids, as they are not compatible. DOT 5 is silicone-based and the mistaken use of silicone brake fluid in these models can cause brake failure.*

> *WARNING*
> *If the brake fluid level is low enough to allow air in the hydraulic system, bleed the brakes as described in Chapter Thirteen.*

Front master cylinder

1. Support the motorcycle on level ground with a swing arm stand.
2. Block the front wheel so the motorcycle will not roll in either direction while on the swing arm stand.
3. Turn the handlebars to the straight ahead position to level the front master cylinder.
4. Observe the brake fluid level on the sight glass (**Figure 21**) on the front of the master cylinder body. The brake fluid must be visible at the sight glass.
5. If the fluid level is not visible, remove the master cylinder top cover (**Figure 22**), and diaphragm, and observe the fluid level. The fluid level should be flush with the MAX line at the front of the master cylinder body (**Figure 23**).
6. Add fresh DOT 4 brake fluid to bring the level sufficiently so the brake fluid is visible in the sight glass. Install the diaphragm, top cover and screws. Tighten the screws securely. Re-check the fluid level in the sight glass, add additional brake fluid if necessary.

Rear master cylinder

1. Support the motorcycle on level ground.
2. Observe the brake fluid level on the sight glass (**Figure 24**) on the outboard surface of the master cylinder body. The brake fluid must be visible at the sight glass.
3. If the fluid level is not visible, remove the master cylinder top cover (**Figure 25**), and diaphragm, and observe the fluid level. The fluid level should be flush with the MAX line at the rear of the master cylinder body.
4. Add fresh DOT 4 brake fluid to bring the level sufficiently so the brake fluid is visible in the sight glass. Install the diaphragm, top cover and screws. Tighten the screws securely. Re-check the fluid level in the sight glass, add additional brake fluid if necessary.

Front and Rear Brake Disc Inspection

Inspect the front (**Figure 26**) and rear brake discs for scoring, cracks or other damage. Measure the brake disc thickness, and if necessary, service the brake discs as described in Chapter Thirteen.

Brake Lines and Seals

Check the brake lines between each master cylinder and each brake caliper and at the control module on ABS models. If there are any leaks, tighten the connections and bleed the brakes as described in Chapter Thirteen.

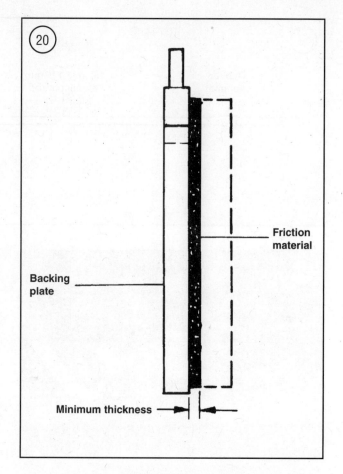

Friction material

Backing plate

Minimum thickness

Brake Fluid Change

To change brake fluid, follow the brake bleeding procedure in Chapter Thirteen.

CLUTCH SYSTEM

Clutch Lever Pivot Pin Lubrication

Inspect the clutch lever pivot pin at the intervals specified in **Table 1**. Lubricate the pin with light weight oil or silicone brake grease on CVO models. To service the pivot pin, refer to Chapter Six.

Clutch Adjustment
(All Models Except CVO)

> *CAUTION*
> *Because the clutch cable adjuster clearance increases with engine temperature, adjust the clutch when the engine is cold. If the clutch is adjusted when the engine is hot, insufficient pushrod clearance can cause the clutch to slip.*

1. Remove the Torx screws (T27) securing the clutch cover (**Figure 27**) and gasket, or seal ring. Then, remove the cover.
2. Slide the rubber boot (A, **Figure 28**) away from the clutch cable in-line adjuster.
3. Loosen the adjuster locknut (B, **Figure 28**) and turn the adjuster (C) to provide maximum cable slack.
4. Check that the clutch cable seats squarely in its perch (**Figure 29**) at the handlebar.
5. At the clutch mechanism, loosen the clutch adjusting screw locknut (A, **Figure 30**) and turn the adjusting screw (B) *clockwise* until it is lightly seated.
6. Apply the clutch lever three times to verify the clutch balls are seated in the ramp release mechanism located behind the transmission side cover.
7. Back out the adjusting screw (A, **Figure 31**) *counterclockwise* 1/2 to 1 turn. Then, hold the adjusting screw (A, **Figure 31**) and tighten the locknut (B) to 72-120 in.-lb. (8.1-13.6 N•m).

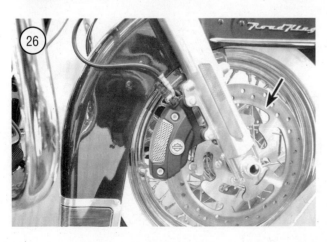

8. Once again, apply the clutch lever to its maximum limit three times to set the clutch balls and ramp release mechanism.

9. Check the free play as follows:

a. At the clutch cable in-line adjuster, turn the adjuster away from the locknut until slack is eliminated at the clutch lever.

b. Pull the clutch cable sheath away from the clutch lever, and turn the clutch cable adjuster to obtain the clearance gap (**Figure 32**) of 1/16-1/8 in. (1.6-3.2 mm).

c. When the adjustment is correct, secure the adjuster and tighten the locknut. Slide the rubber boot back over the cable adjuster.

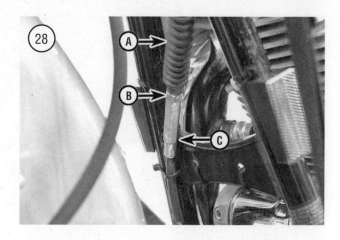

NOTE
All lubricant must be removed from the seal ring and its groove prior to installation. If any lubricant remains, there will be a temporary lubricant leak around the clutch cover.

10. Remove the seal ring (**Figure 33**) from the clutch cover. Wipe all lubricant from the seal ring and inspect it for cuts or deterioration; replace if necessary. Wipe all lubricant from the seal ring groove and install the seal ring onto the cover. Push the nibs into the ring groove walls.

11. Install the clutch cover and seal ring (**Figure 27**) onto the primary chaincase cover.

12. Install the clutch cover screws and tighten them to 84-108 in.-lb. (9.2-12.2 N•m).

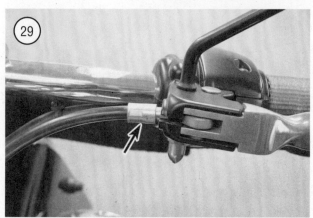

**Clutch Fluid Level
(CVO Models)**

WARNING
Use only DOT 4 brake fluid in the clutch system. Do not intermix DOT4 with DOT 5 brake fluids, as they are not compatible. DOT 5 is silicone-based and the mistaken use of silicone brake fluid in these models can cause clutch failure.

CAUTION
Be careful when handling brake fluid. Do not spill it on painted or plastic surfaces, as it damages them. Wash the area immediately with soap and water, and thoroughly rinse it.

NOTE
If the clutch fluid level is low enough to allow air in the hydraulic system, bleed the clutch as described in Chapter Six.

1. Turn the handlebars to the straight ahead position to level the clutch master cylinder.

2. Clean any dirt from the master cylinder cover prior to removing it.

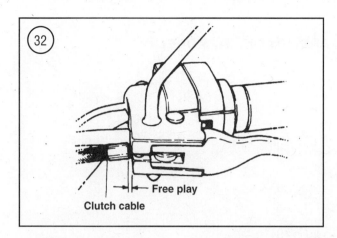

Free play

Clutch cable

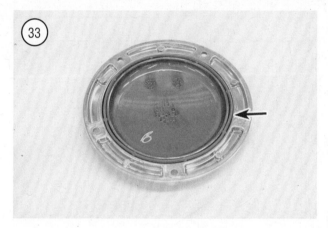

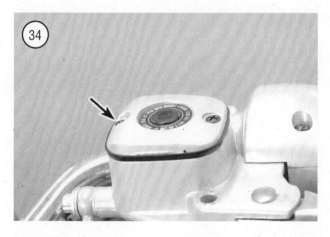

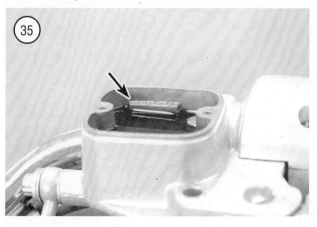

3. Remove the screws, cover, and diaphragm from the master cylinder (**Figure 34**).

4. The clutch fluid level should be flush with the top ledge (**Figure 35**) cast into the front of the clutch master cylinder body.

5. Add enough fresh DOT 4 brake fluid to correct the level. Reinstall the diaphragm and top cover. Tighten the screws securely.

Clutch Hoses and Seals
(CVO Models)

Check the clutch hose between the master cylinder and the release cylinder. If there is any leak, tighten the connections and bleed the clutch as described in Chapter Six. If this does not stop the leak or if a line is obviously damaged, cracked, or chafed, replace the hose and/or the master cylinder or release cylinder(s). Then, bleed the clutch as described in Chapter Six.

Clutch Fluid Change
(CVOModels)

A small amount of dirt and moisture enters the clutch fluid each time the reservoir cap is removed. The same thing happens if a leak occurs or when any part of the hydraulic system is loosened or disconnected. Dirt can clog the system and cause unnecessary wear. Water in the fluid vaporizes at high temperatures, impairing the hydraulic action and reducing clutch performance.

To change the clutch fluid, drain the fluid from the clutch system as described in Chapter Six. Add new fluid to the master cylinder, and bleed the clutch at the release cylinder until the fluid leaving the release cylinder is clean and free of contaminants and air bubbles. Refer to the clutch bleeding procedure in Chapter Six.

FUEL LINE INSPECTION

WARNING
A damaged or deteriorated fuel line can cause a fire or explosion if fuel spills onto a hot engine or exhaust pipe.

Inspect the fuel lines from the fuel tank to the fuel injection module, and the cross over hose at the front of the fuel tank. Replace leaking or damaged fuel lines. Make sure the hose clamps are in place and holding securely. Check the hose fittings for looseness.

WARNING
A damaged or deteriorated fuel line can cause a fire or explosion if fuel spills onto a hot engine or exhaust pipe.

AIR FILTER (ALL 96 CU. IN. AND 103 CU. IN. MODELS)

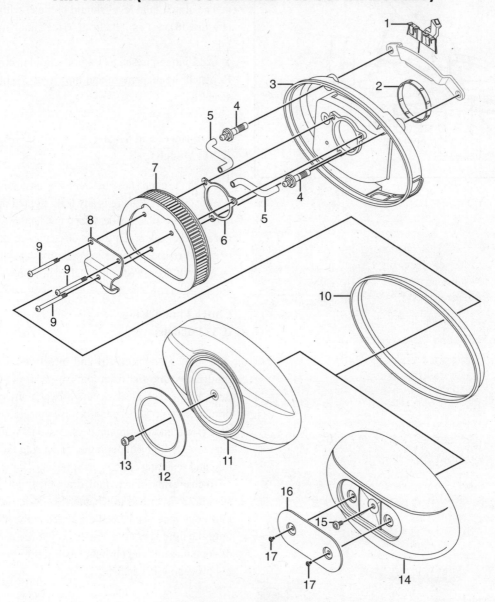

1. Clip (ARC connector cable)
2. Gasket
3. Backplate
4. Breather hollow bolt
5. Breather hose
6. Gasket
7. Air filter element
8. Mounting bracket
9. Torx screw
10. Rubber seal ring
11. Cover (All non-CVO except 2013 FLHTCUSE)
12. Insert
13. Allen screw
14. Cover (2013 FLHTCUSE)
15. Allen screw
16. Trim plate
17. Screw

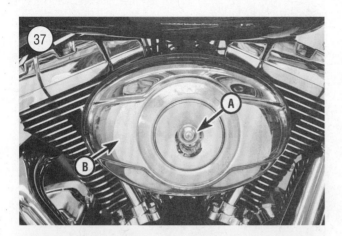

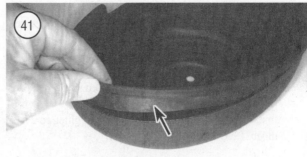

AIR FILTER

Remove and clean the air filter at the interval in **Table 1**. Replace the element whenever it is damaged or starts to deteriorate.

Removal/Installation
(All 96 cu. in. and 103 cu.in. Models)

Refer to **Figure 36**.

1A. On all models except 2013 FLHTCUSE (103 cu. in.), remove the air filter cover Allen screw (A, **Figure 37**), and remove the cover (B).

1B. On 2013 FLHTCUSE (103 cu. in.) models, remove the trim plate screw and trim plate screws and trim plate. Remove the air filter cover Allen screw, and remove the cover.

2. Remove the Torx screws (**Figure 38**) and bracket from the air filter element.

3. Gently pull the air filter element away from the backplate and disconnect the two breather hoses (A, **Figure 39**) from the breather hollow bolts on the backplate. Remove the air filter element (B, **Figure 39**).

4. Remove the gasket (A, **Figure 40**) from the inboard side of the element. Discard the gasket.

5. Clean the air filter as described in the following procedure.

6. Inspect the breather hoses (B, **Figure 40**) for tears or deterioration. Replace if necessary.

7. Inspect the seal ring (**Figure 41**) on the air filter cover for hardness or deterioration. Replace if necessary.

8. Install a *new* gasket (**Figure 42**) on the inboard side of the element.

9. Position the filter element with the flat side facing down.

10. Insert the breather hoses (**Figure 43**) about 1/4 inch (6.4 mm) onto the breather hollow bolts located on the backside of the element.

11. Move the element into position and install the mounting bracket (**Figure 38**). Install the Torx screws through the mounting bracket and element. Align the screw holes and tighten the Torx screws (T27) to 40-60 in.-lb. (4.5-6.8 N•m).

12. Apply a drop of Loctite 243 (blue), or an equivalent, threadlock to the cover screw prior to installation.

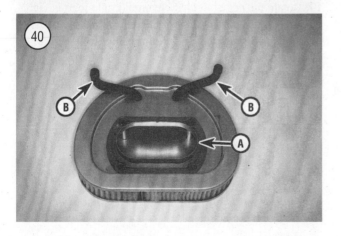

13A. On all models except 2013 FLHTCUSE (103 cu. in.) install the air filter cover (B, **Figure 37**) and Allen screw (A). Tighten the screw to 36-60 in.-lb. (4.0-6.8 N•m).

13B. On 2013 FLHTCUSE (103 cu. in.) models, perform the following:

  a. Install the cover and tighten the Allen screw to 36-60 in.-lb. (4.1-6.8 N•m).

  b. Install the trim plate and screws, and tighten to 27-32 in.-lb. (3.1-3.6 N•m).

Removal/Installation
(All 110 cu.in. Models except FLTRXSE)

Refer to **Figure 44**.

1. Remove the trim plate screw and trim plate screws and trim plate. Remove the air filter cover Allen screw, and remove the cover.

2. Remove the screws from the air filter element.

3. Gently pull the air filter element away from the backplate and remove it.

4. Clean the air filter as described in this section.

5. On models so equipped, inspect the seal ring on the air filter cover for hardness or deterioration. Replace if necessary.

6. Check the tightness of the standoff bolts. If loose, tighten the bolts to 55-60 in.-lb. (6.3-6.7 N•m).

7. Install the element onto the backplate and align the screw holes.

8. Install filter screws through the element (B). Tighten the screws to 55-60 in.-lb. (6.2-6.8 N•m).

9. Apply a drop of Loctite 243 (blue), or an equivalent, threadlock to the cover screw prior to installation.

10. Install the air filter cover and Allen screw (A). Tighten the Allen screw to 36-60 in.-lb. (4.0-6.8 N•m).

11. If removed, install the trim plate and screws. Tighten the screws to 27-32 in.-lb. (3.1-3.6 N•m).

Removal/Installation (FLTRXSE Models)

Refer to **Figure 45**.

1. Loosen the clamp screw, and remove the air filter from the intake tube.

2. Remove the four mounting screws and remove the outer mounting ring from the backside of the air filter element.

3. If necessary, remove the clamp from the rubber snout on the air filter element.

4. Remove the air filter element from the cover. Watch for foam pad within the cover.

5. Remove the clamp from the rubber snout on the air filter.

6. Clean the air filter as described in the following procedure.

7. Verify the foam pad is in place in the cover.

8. Install the air filter element onto the cover.

9. Located the cover so the Screamin' Eagle logo is facing outward and is straight.

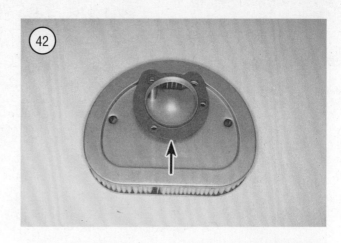

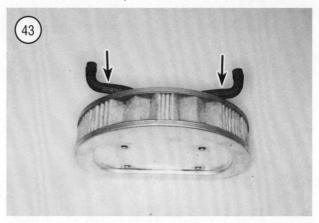

10. Install the outer mounting ring onto the backside of the air filter element. Install the screws and tighten to 15-20 in.-lb. (1.7-2.3 N•m).

11. Install the clamp onto the rubber snout on the air filter element and approximately centered in the notch with the screw slot facing down.

12. Install the air filter element assembly onto the intake tube. Press the assembly on up to the locating line (approximately 5/8 in. (16 mm).

NOTE
Hold the clamping screw in the approximate center of the notch

13. Rotate the cover so the Screamin' Eagle logo is facing out and aligned correctly. Verify that the assembly does not touch any other parts. Tighten the clamp to 45-55 in.-lb. (5.1-6.2 N•m).

Air Filter Element Cleaning
(All Models Except FLTRXSE)

WARNING
Do not clean the air filter in any type of solvent. Never clean the air filter element in gasoline or any type of low flash-point solvent. The residual solvent or vapors left by these

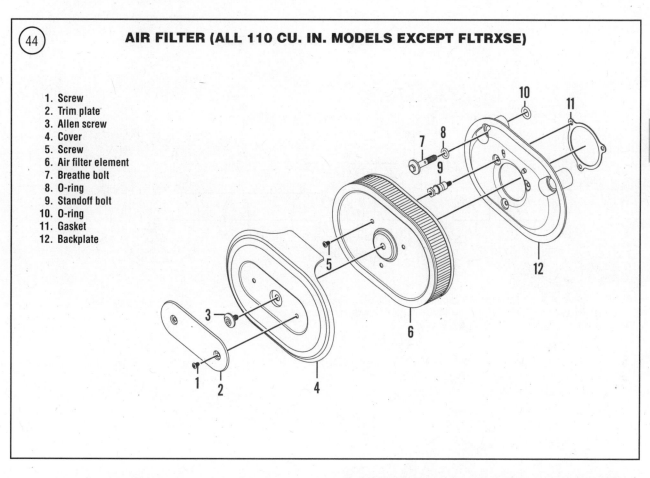

AIR FILTER (ALL 110 CU. IN. MODELS EXCEPT FLTRXSE)

1. Screw
2. Trim plate
3. Allen screw
4. Cover
5. Screw
6. Air filter element
7. Breathe bolt
8. O-ring
9. Standoff bolt
10. O-ring
11. Gasket
12. Backplate

chemicals may cause a fire or explosion after the filter is reinstalled.

CAUTION
Do not tap or strike the air filter element on a hard surface to dislodge dirt. Do not use high air pressure to dry the filter. Doing so will damage the element.

1. Remove the air filter element as described in this section.
2. Place the air filter in a pan filled with lukewarm water and mild detergent. Move the air filter element back and forth to help dislodge trapped dirt. Thoroughly rinse in clean water to remove all detergent residue.
3. Remove the air filter and hold it up to a strong light. Check the filter pores for dirt and oil. Repeat the cleaning process until there is no longer dirt and oil in the filter pores. If the air filter cannot be cleaned, or if the filter is saturated with oil or other chemicals, replace it.

CAUTION
Do not blow compressed air through the outer surface of the air filter element. Doing so can force dirt trapped on the outer filter surface deeper into the air filter element, restricting airflow and damaging the air filter element.

4. Gently apply compressed air from the inside of the air filter element to remove loosened dirt and dust trapped in the filter.
5. Inspect the air filter element. Replace if torn or damaged. Do not ride the motorcycle with a damaged filter element as it may allow dirt to enter the engine.
6. Clean the breather hoses in the same solution used for the filter. Make sure both hoses are clean and clear. Clean out with a pipe cleaner if necessary.
7. Wipe the inside of the cover and backplate with a clean, damp shop rag.

CAUTION
Air will not pass through a wet or damp filter. Make sure the filter is thoroughly dry before installing it.

8. Allow the filter to dry completely, and reinstall it as described in this section.

Air Filter Element Cleaning (FLTRXSE Models)

1. Remove the air filter element as described in this section.
2. Replace the air filter if damaged.

WARNING
Do not clean the air filter in solvent. Never clean the air filter element in gasoline or low

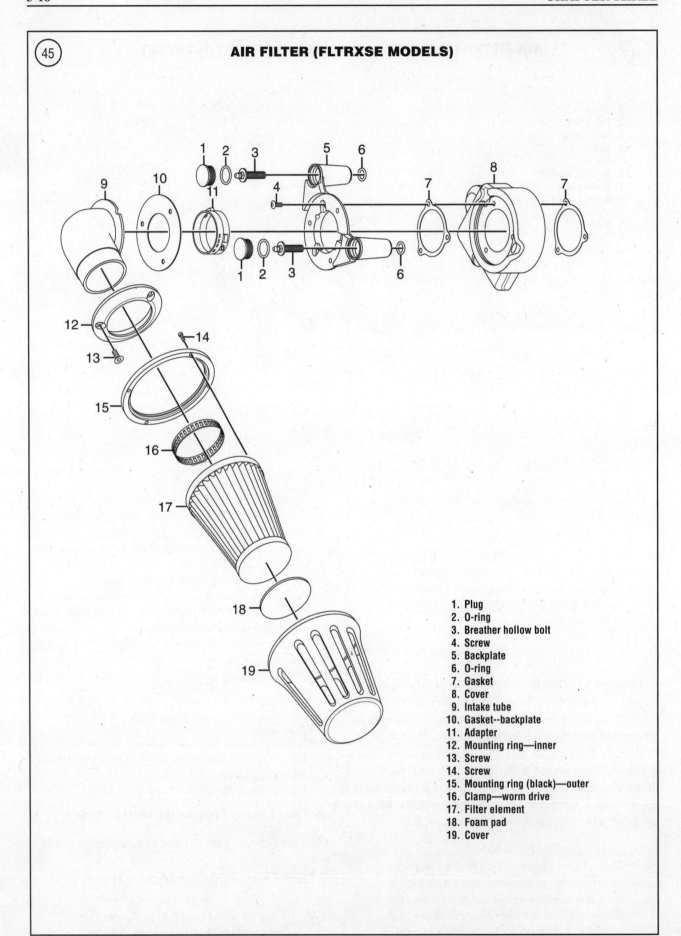

(45) **AIR FILTER (FLTRXSE MODELS)**

1. Plug
2. O-ring
3. Breather hollow bolt
4. Screw
5. Backplate
6. O-ring
7. Gasket
8. Cover
9. Intake tube
10. Gasket--backplate
11. Adapter
12. Mounting ring—inner
13. Screw
14. Screw
15. Mounting ring (black)—outer
16. Clamp—worm drive
17. Filter element
18. Foam pad
19. Cover

*flash point solvent. The residual solvent or
vapors may cause a fire or explosion after the
filter is reinstalled.*

3. Tap the air filter to dislodge dirt and debris. Brush the
filter clean with a soft, bristle brush.

4. Liberally spray the cotton filter media with K&N Air
Filter Cleaner. Let it soak for 10 minutes. If an aerosol
cleaner is not available, roll the cotton filter media through
a shallow pan of air filter cleaner. Immediately remove the
filter from the cleaner, and let it soak for 10 minutes.

5. Completely rinse the filter with low-pressure tap water.

6. Shake off excess water, and air dry the filter. DO NOT
use compressed air or heat to accelerate drying.

7. Only after the media is *completely* dry, perform Step 8.

8A. Spray aerosol air filter oil along each pleat – once
only. Hold the nozzle approximately 3 in. (76 mm) from
the filter media.

8B. If an aerosol oil is not available, use a squeeze bottle
to place oil along each pleat. Only add the oil once.

9. Set the filter aside it can absorb the oil. After 20 minutes, inspect the filter completely. Apply additional oil to
any remaining while spots, and set the filter aside so it can
absorb the oil.

10. Install the air filter element as described in this section.

SUSPENSION AND FASTENERS

Steering Play

Check the steering play as described in Chapter Eleven at the
intervals specified in **Table 1**. Adjust the bearings as necessary.

Rear Swing Arm Pivot Bolt

Check the rear swing arm pivot bolt tightness as described
in Chapter twelve at the intervals specified in **Table 1**.

REAR SHOCK ABSORBERS

Check the rear shock absorbers for oil leaks or damaged
bushings. Check the shock absorber mounting bolts and
nuts for tightness. Refer to *Shock Absorbers* in Chapter
Twelve for procedures.

ENGINE MOUNTS AND STABILIZER

Check the stabilizers and the engine and frame mounts for
loose or damaged parts. Refer to Chapter Five for procedures.

EXHAUST SYSTEM

Check all fittings, including the crossover pipe connections, for exhaust leaks at the intervals specified in **Table
1**. Tighten all bolts and nuts to the specifications listed in
Chapter Four. Replace gaskets as necessary.

FASTENERS

CAUTION
*To accurately check cylinder head mounting
bolts for tightness, refer to **Cylinder Head
Installation** in Chapter Four. Tightening
these bolts incorrectly can cause an oil leak
or cylinder head damage.*

Check the tightness of all fasteners at the intervals specified in **Table 1**, especially those on:

1. Engine mounting hardware.
2. Engine and primary covers.
3. Handlebar and front fork.
4. Gearshift levers.
5. Sprocket bolts and nuts.
6. Brake pedal and lever.
7. Exhaust system.
8. Lighting equipment.
9. Fairing and saddlebag components.

ELECTRICAL EQUIPMENT AND SWITCHES

Check all electrical equipment and switches for proper
operation at the intervals specified in **Table 1**. Refer to
Chapter Nine.

COMPRESSION TEST

A compression test is one of the most effective ways to
check the condition of the engine. If possible, check the
compression at each tune-up, record it, and then compare
the readings at subsequent tune-ups. This will help identify
any developing problems.

1. Prior to starting the compression test, make sure the following is correct:
   a. The cylinder head bolts (**Figure 46**) are tightened to
      the specified torque as described in Chapter Four.
   b. The battery is fully charged to ensure proper engine
      cranking speed.

2. Ride the motorcycle until engine is at normal operating
temperature.

3. Place the motorcycle on a level surface and park it on
the jiffy stand. Turn off the engine.

4. Remove the air filter assembly as described in Chapter
Eight.

5. Remove the spark plugs (**Figure 47**) as described in this
chapter. Reinstall the caps onto the spark plugs and place
the spark plugs against the cylinder heads to ground them.

6. Disconnect the throttle control actuator (TCA) 6-pin
electrical connector (No. 211) from the induction module
(**Figure 48**).

CAUTION
*To avoid damage to the induction module
and/or the throttle plate, do not use any me-
tallic object to hold the throttle plate open.*

7. Carefully open throttle plate. Then, *very carefully* insert a wood or plastic dowel into the throttle plate area of the induction module to hold the throttle plate in the wide open position. Use a dowel about 12 in. (305 mm) long and by 0.75 in. (19 mm) in diameter.

8. Connect the compression tester (**Figure 49**) to the front cylinder following its manufacturer's instructions.

9. Crank the engine over continuously through 5-7 full revolutions until there is no further rise in pressure.

10. Record the reading and remove the tester. The standard compression pressure is as follows:

    a. 96 cu. in. engine: 125 psi (862 kPa).

    b. 103 cu. in. and 110 cu. in. engine: 110 psi (758 kPa).

11. On 103 cu. in. and 110 cu. in. engines, disconnect the system relay (**Figure 50**) from the fuse panel (Chapter Nine).

12. Repeat the test procedure for the front cylinder with the system relay removed. The standard compression pressure this time as listed in **Table 6**.

13. Connect the system relay on the left side electrical caddy (Chapter Nine).

14. Repeat the test procedure for the rear cylinder with the system relay connected and again with it disconnected. Record the readings.

15. Carefully open the throttle plate. Then, *very carefully*, withdraw the wood or plastic dowel from the throttle plate area of the induction module.

NOTE

The removal of the system relay may set a diagnostic trouble code. Clear the diagnostic trouble code(s) as described in Chapter Fifteen, if necessary.

16. Connect the throttle control actuator (TCA) 6-pin electrical connector (No. 211) onto the induction module (**Figure 48**).

17. Reinstall the spark plugs and reconnect their caps as described in this chapter.

18. Install the filter element and air filter assembly as described in Chapter Eight.

Results

Table 6 lists the standard engine compression reading. When interpreting the results, also note any difference between the cylinder readings. The pressure must not vary between the cylinders by more than 10 percent. If a low reading is obtained or greater differences are indicated, consider worn or broken rings and/or leaky or sticky valves. Do not rule out a blown head gasket also.

If a low reading (10 percent or more) is obtained, pour about a teaspoon of engine oil into the spark plug hole. Then, perform another compression test and record the reading. If the compression increases significantly, the valves are good but the rings are defective on that cylinder. If compression does not increase, the valves require servicing.

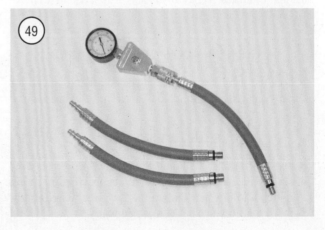

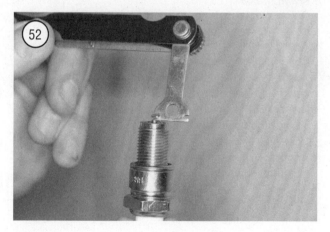

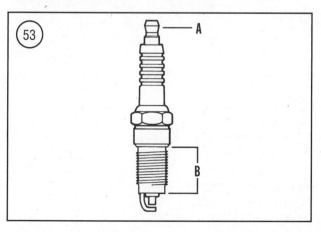

SPARK PLUGS

Removal

CAUTION
Whenever the spark plug is removed, dirt around it can fall into the plug hole.

1. Blow away any loose dirt or debris that may have accumulated around the base of the spark plug and could fall into the cylinder head.
2. Grasp the spark plug cable (**Figure 47**), and twist from side to side to break the seal loose. Then, pull the cap off the spark plug. If the cap is stuck to the plug, twist it slightly to break it loose.

NOTE
Use a spark plug socket equipped with a rubber insert that holds the spark plug. This type of socket is necessary for both removal and installation.

3. Install the spark plug socket onto the spark plug. Make sure it is correctly seated and install an open-end wrench or ratchet handle and remove the spark plug. Mark which cylinder it was removed from on the spark plug.
4. Repeat for the remaining spark plug.
5. Thoroughly inspect each plug. Look for broken center porcelain, excessively eroded electrodes and excessive carbon or oil fouling.
6. Inspect the spark plug caps and secondary wires for damage, or hardness. If any portion is damaged, the cap and secondary wire must be replaced as an assembly. The front and rear cylinder plug wire assemblies are different.

Service and Installation

Carefully gap the spark plugs to ensure a reliable, consistent spark. Use a spark plug gapping tool and a wire feeler gauge.
1. Insert a wire feeler gauge (**Figure 51**) between the center and side electrode of the plug. The correct gap is listed in **Table 6**. If the gap is correct, a slight drag will be felt as the wire gauge is pulled through. If there is no drag, or the gauge will not pass through, bend the side electrode with a gapping tool (**Figure 52**) to adjust the gap to the proper one listed in **Table 6**.
2. Install the terminal nut (A, **Figure 53**).
3. Apply a *light coat* of antiseize lubricant on the threads of the spark plug before installing it. Do *not* use engine oil on the plug threads.

CAUTION
The aluminum cylinder head is easily damaged by cross-threading the spark plug.

4. Slowly screw the spark plug into the cylinder head by hand until it seats. Very little effort is required. If force is necessary, the plug is cross-threaded; unscrew it and try again.
5. Hand-tighten the spark plug until it seats against the cylinder head, and then tighten to 12-18 ft.-lb. (16.3-24.4 N•m).

6. Install the spark plug cap and lead to the correct spark plug. Rotate the cap slightly in both directions and make sure it is attached to the spark plug.

7. Repeat the procedure for the other spark plug.

Spark Plug Heat Range

> *NOTE*
> *The manufacturer only recommends using HD-6R12 spark plugs. This specific resistor spark plug reduces radio interference created by the ignition system and also maintains optimal performance.*

Spark plugs are available in heat ranges hotter or colder than the plugs originally installed by the manufacturer.

Select a plug with a heat range designed for the loads and conditions under which the motorcycle will be operated. A plug with an incorrect heat range can foul, overheat and cause piston damage.

In general, use a hot plug for low speeds and low temperatures. Use a cold plug for high speeds, high engine loads and high temperatures. The plug should operate hot enough to burn off unwanted deposits, but not so hot that it is damaged or causes preignition. To determine if plug heat range is correct, remove each spark plug and examine the insulator.

Do not change the spark plug heat range to compensate for adverse engine or carburetion conditions.

When replacing plugs, make sure the reach (B, **Figure 53**) of the plug is correct. A longer than standard plug could interfere with the piston, causing engine damage.

Refer to **Table 6** for recommended spark plugs.

Spark Plug Reading

Reading the spark plugs can provide a significant amount of information regarding engine performance. Reading plugs that have been in use will give an indication of spark plug operation, air/fuel mixture composition and engine conditions (such as oil consumption or pistons). Before checking the spark plugs, operate the motorcycle under a medium load for approximately 6 miles (10 km). Avoid prolonged idling before shutting off the engine. Remove the spark plugs as described in this chapter. Examine each plug and compare it to those in **Figure 54** while referring to the following sections to determine the operating conditions.

On carbureted models, if the plugs are being read to determine if carburetor jetting is correct, start with *new* plugs and operate the motorcycle at the load that corresponds to the jetting information desired. For example, if the main jet is in question, operate the motorcycle at full throttle and shut the engine off and coast to a stop.

Normal condition

If the plug has a light tan- or gray-colored deposit and no abnormal gap wear or erosion, good engine, air/fuel

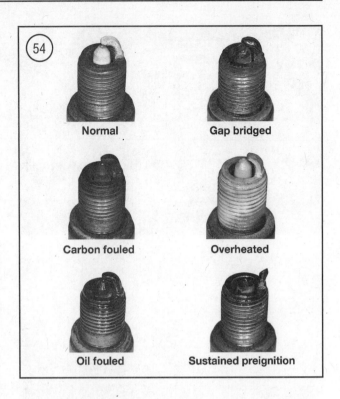

Normal	Gap bridged
Carbon fouled	Overheated
Oil fouled	Sustained preignition

mixture and ignition conditions are indicated. The plug in use is of the proper heat range and may be serviced and returned to use.

Carbon fouled

Soft, dry, sooty deposits covering the entire firing end of the plug are evidence of incomplete combustion. Even though the firing end of the plug is dry, the plug's insulation decreases when in this condition. An electrical path is formed that bypasses the electrodes, resulting in a misfire condition. Carbon fouling can be caused by one or more of the following:

1. Cold spark plug heat range.
2. Clogged air filter.
5. Improperly operating ignition component.
4. Ignition component failure.
5. Low engine compression.
6. Prolonged idling.

Oil fouled

The tip of an oil-fouled plug has a black insulator tip, a damp oily film over the firing end and a carbon layer over the entire nose. The electrodes are not worn. Oil-fouled spark plugs may be cleaned in an emergency, but it is better to replace them. It is important to correct the cause of fouling before the engine is returned to service. Common causes for this condition are:

1. Low idle speed or prolonged idling.
2. Ignition component failure.
3. Cold spark plug heat range.
4. Engine still being broken in.
5. Valve guides worn.
6. Piston rings worn or broken.

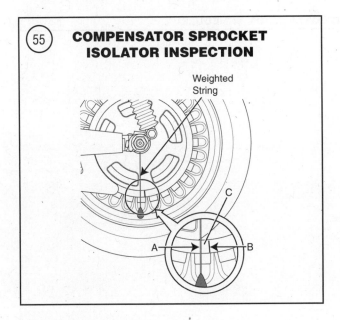

55 COMPENSATOR SPROCKET ISOLATOR INSPECTION

Weighted String

Gap bridging

Plugs with this condition exhibit gaps shorted out by combustion deposits between the electrodes. If this condition is encountered, check for excessive carbon or oil in the combustion chamber. Be sure to locate and correct the cause of this condition.

Overheating

Badly worn electrodes and premature gap wear are signs of overheating, along with a gray or white blistered porcelain insulator surface. The most common cause for this condition is using a spark plug of the wrong heat range (too hot). If spark plug is the correct heat range and is overheated, consider the following causes:
1. Improperly operating ignition component.
2. Engine lubrication system malfunction.
3. Cooling system malfunction (clogged cooling fins).
4. Engine air leak.
5. Improper spark plug installation (over-tightening).
6. No spark plug gasket.

Worn out

Corrosive gases formed by combustion and high voltage sparks have eroded the electrodes. A spark plug in this condition requires more voltage to fire under hard acceleration. Replace with a new spark plug.

Preignition

If the electrodes are melted, preignition is almost certainly the cause. Check for intake air leaks at the intake manifold, carburetor, or throttle body, and for advanced ignition timing. It is also possible that a plug of the wrong heat range (too hot) is being used. Find the cause of the preignition before returning the engine to service.

IGNITION TIMING

The ignition system is controlled by the electronic control module (ECM). There are no means of adjusting ignition timing. The manufacturer does not provide any procedure for checking the ignition timing. If an ignition related problem is suspected, inspect the ignition components as described in Chapter Nine.

Incorrect ignition timing can cause a loss of engine performance. It may also cause overheating.

IDLE SPEED ADJUSTMENT

Idle speed adjustment must be performed by a dealership with the Harley-Davidson digital technician tool.

COMPENSATOR SPROCKET ISOLATOR INSPECTION

1. Support the motorcycle with the rear wheel off the ground. Refer to *Motorcycle Stands* in Chapter Twelve.
2. Remove the left side saddlebag (Chapter Fourteen).
3. Hang a weighted string on the on the left side axle spacer as close as possible to, but not touching, the rear sprocket.
4. Apply a piece of masking tape to the face of the sprocket in the area of the weighted string where the following marks will be made.

NOTE
In the following step, do not allow the rear wheel to rotate as that would allow a false measurement.

5. Rotate the rear sprocket in either direction until it stops. Secure the rear sprocket in this place. Allow the weighted string to stop any of its movement.
6. Using a fine line permanent marking pen, carefully mark the masking tape on the sprocket edge in line with the weighted spring (A, **Figure 55**).
7. Rotate the rear sprocket in the opposite direction until it stops. Secure the rear sprocket in this place. Allow the weighted string to stop any of its movement.
8. Make the second mark the masking tape along the sprocket edge in line with the weighted spring (B, **Figure 55**).
9. Measure the distance between the two marks (C, **Figure 55**). If the measurement exceed 0.400 in. (10.2 mm); replace the rear sprocket rubber isolator (Chapter Twelve).
10. Remove the piece of masking tape from the face of the sprocket.
11. Remove the weighted string from the left side axle spacer.
12. Install the left side saddlebag (Chapter Fourteen).

Table 1 MAINTENANCE AND LUBRICATION SCHEDULE[1]

Pre-ride check
  Check tire condition and inflation pressure.
  Check wheel rim condition.
  Check light and horn operation.
  Check engine oil level; add oil if necessary.
  Check brake fluid level and condition; add fluid if necessary.
  Check clutch fluid level and condition (CVO models); add fluid if necessary.
  Check the operation of the front and rear brakes lever.
  Check throttle operation.
  Check clutch lever operation.
  Check fuel level in fuel tank; top off if necessary.
  Check fuel system for leaks.
First Service[2]
  Change engine oil and filter.
  Check the oil lines, brake lines, and clutch lines (CVO models) for leaks.
  Inspect air filter element.
  Check tire condition and inflation pressure.
  Check the wheel spokes; tighten as necessary.
  Change the primary chaincase lubricant.
  Change transmission lubricant.
  Check clutch operation; adjust if necessary.
  Check drive belt tension; adjust if necessary.
  Check drive belt and sprockets condition.
  Check front and rear brake pads and discs for wear.
  Check brake fluid level and condition; add fluid if necessary.
  Check clutch fluid level and condition; add fluid if necessary (CVO models).
  Check battery condition; clean cable connections if necessary.
  Inspect spark plugs.
  Lubricate front brake and clutch lever pivot pin.
  Lubricate clutch cable if necessary (non-CVO models).
  Check the clutch cable operation. Adjust and lubricate the cable as necessary (non-CVO models).
  Check the clutch release system (CVO models).
  Check fuel system for leaks
  Check electrical switches and equipment for proper operation
  Check the jiffy stand. Lubricate as necessary.
  Adjust the steering head bearings.
  Lubricate the hinges and latches on the fuel door, tour-pak and saddlebags.
  Check the exhaust system for leaks, cracks or loose fasteners.
  Check all fasteners for tightness[2].
  Road test the motorcycle
Every 5000 miles (8000 km)
  Change engine oil and filter.
  Check the oil lines, brake lines, and clutch lines for leaks (CVO models).
  Inspect air filter element.
  Check tire condition and inflation pressure.
  Check the wheel spokes; tighten as necessary.
  Check clutch operation; adjust if necessary.
  Check drive belt tension; adjust as necessary.
  Check the condition of the drive belt and sprockets.
  Check the clutch cable operation. Adjust and lubricate the cable as necessary.
  Check the clutch release system (CVO models).
  Check fuel system for leaks
  Check brake fluid level and condition; add fluid if necessary.
  Check clutch fluid level and condition; add fluid if necessary (CVO models).
  Inspect spark plugs.
  Check electrical switches and equipment for proper operation
  Check engine idle speed; adjust if necessary
  Lubricate the hinges and latches on the fuel door, tour-pak and saddlebags.
  Check the exhaust system for leaks, cracks or loose fasteners.
  Road test the motorcycle
Every 10,000 miles (16,000 km)
  Change engine oil and filter.
  Check the oil lines, brake lines, and clutch lines (CVO models) for leaks.
  Inspect air filter element.
  Check tire condition and inflation pressure.
  Change the primary chaincase lubricant.
  Check clutch operation; adjust if necessary.

(continued)

Table 1 MAINTENANCE AND LUBRICATION SCHEDULE[1] (continued)

Every 10,000 miles (16,000 km) (continued)
  Check drive belt tension; adjust if necessary.
  Check drive belt and sprockets condition.
  Check the clutch cable operation. Adjust and lubricate the cable as necessary (non-CVO models).
  Check the clutch release system (CVO models).
  Check fuel system for leaks
  Check electrical switches and equipment for proper operation.
  Check the jiffy stand. Lubricate as necessary.
  Check front and rear brake pads and discs for wear.
  Check brake fluid level and condition; add fluid if necessary.
  Check clutch fluid level and condition; add fluid if necessary (CVO models).
  Check the spark plugs, replace as necessary.
  Lubricate and adjust the steering head bearings.
  Inspect the windshield bushings.
  Check all fasteners for tightness[2].
  Check the exhaust system for leaks, cracks or loose fasteners.
  Road test the motorcycle
Every 15,000 miles (32,000 km)
  Perform the Every 5,000 miles (8,000 km) service.
Every 20,000 miles (32,000 km)
  Perform the 5,000 miles (8,000 km) service plus the following:
  Replace the spark plugs.
  Change the primary chaincase lubricant.
  Change the transmission lubricant.
  Check the jiffy stand. Lubricate as necessary.
  Clean and repack the swing arm bearings.
  Lubricate and adjust the steering head bearings.
  Inspect the windshield bushings.
  Check all fasteners for tightness[3].
  Check the exhaust system for leaks, cracks or loose fasteners.
  Road test the motorcycle
Every 25,000 miles (40,000 km)
  Perform the 5,000 miles (8,000 km) service plus the following:
  Replace the fuel tank filter screen.
Every 30,000 miles
  Disassemble, inspect, and lubricate the steering head bearings.
Every 50,000 miles (80,000 km)
  Change front fork oil.
Every year
  Check battery condition; clean cable connections if necessary.
  Check the exhaust system for leaks, cracks or loose fasteners.
Every 2 years
  Replace the hydraulic fluid in the brake system. On CVO models, also replace the fluid in the clutch system.

1. Consider this maintenance schedule a guide to general maintenance and lubrication intervals. If the motorcycle is ridden harder than normal or if it is exposed to mud, water or high humidity; perform most of these maintenance items more frequently than indicated.
2. Except cylinder head bolts. Cylinder head bolts must be tightened following the procedure listed in Chapter Four. Improper tightening of the cylinder head bolts may cause cylinder gasket damage and/or cylinder head leakage.

Table 2 TIRE INFLATION PRESSURE (COLD)*

	kPa	psi
Front wheel	248	36
Rear wheel	275	40

* Tire pressure for OE equipment tires. Aftermarket tires may require different inflation pressure.
  These specifications apply to all different size wheel/tire combinations for all models.

Table 3 FUEL, ENGINE AND DRIVE FLUID CAPACITIES

Item	Capacity
Fuel tank, total	6.0 gal (18.9 L)
Fuel tank, reserve	1.0 gal (3.8 L)
Engine oil with filter[1]	4 qt. (3.79 L)

(continued)

Table 3 FUEL, ENGINE AND DRIVE FLUID CAPACITIES (continued)

Item	Capacity
Transmission[2]	32 oz. (0.95 L)
Primary chaincase	38 oz. (1.12 L)

1. When refilling, initially add 3.0 qt. (2.84L) and add additional as need to bring level within specification.
2. When refilling, initially add 28 oz. (0.83 L) and add additional as need to bring level within specification.

Table 4 RECOMMENDED ENGINE OIL

Type	Viscosity	H-D Rating	Ambient operating temperature
H-D Multi-grade	SAE 10W40	HD 360	Below 40° F (4° C)
H-D Multi-grade	SAE 20W50	HD 360	Above 40° F (4° C)
H-D Regular Heavy	SAE 50	HD 360	Above 60° F (16° C)
H-D Extra Heavy	SAE 60	HD 360	Above 80° F (16° C)
Screamin' Eagle models SYN3 Synthetic Motorcycle Lubricant	SAE 20W50	HD360	Above 40° F (4° C)

Table 5 RECOMMENDED LUBRICANTS AND FLUIDS

Brake fluid	DOT4 hydraulic fluid
Clutch fluid (CVO models)	DOT4 hydraulic fluid
Front fork oil	H-D Type E fork oil
Fuel	91 pump octane or higher
Transmission oil	
All models except CVO	H-D Formula+ Transmission and Primary Chaincase lubricant
CVO models	Screamin' Eagle SYN3 Synthetic Motorcycle lubricant
Primary chaincase oil	
All models except CVO	H-D Formula+ Transmission and Primary Chaincase lubricant
CVO models	Screamin' Eagle SYN3 Synthetic Motorcycle lubricant

Table 6 MAINTENANCE SPECIFICATIONS

Item	Specification
Brake pad minimum thickness (front and rear)	0.016 in. (0.41 mm)
Clutch cable free play	1/16-1/8 in. (1.6-3.2 mm)
Drive belt deflection	
All models except FLX, FLTRX	1/4-7/16 in. (6.4-11.1 mm)
FLX, FLTRX models	3/8-9/16 in. (9.5-14.3 mm)
Engine compression	
All models except CVO	
ARC connected	
96 cu. in.	125 psi (862 kPa)
103 & 110 cu. in.	110 psi (758 kPa)
ARC disconnected	175 psi (1207 kPa)
CVO models	
ARC connected	130-170 psi (896-1172 kPa)
ARC disconnected	200-220 psi (1379-1517 kPa)
Idle speed	950-1050 rpm
Ignition timing	Non-adjustable
Rear axle alignment	1/32 in. (0.8 mm)
Spark plugs	
Gap	0.038-043 in. (0.97-1.09 mm)
Type	HD No. 6R12*

*Harley-Davidson recommends that no other type of sparkplug be substituted.

Table 7 MAINTENANCE AND TUNE-UP TORQUE SPECIFICATIONS

	ft.-lb.	in.-lb.	N•m
Air filter			
All models except CVO			
Cover screw	–	36-60	4.1-6.8
Bracket screw	–	108-132	12.2-14.9
CVO models			
FLTRXSE			
Air filter element clamp screw	–	45-55	5.1-6.2
Back plate mounting screw	–	55-60	6.2-6.8
Breather bolts	22-24	–	29.8-32.5
Intake tube screw	–	55-60	6.2-6.8
All models except FLTRXSE			
Insert screw	–	27-32	3.1-3.6
Cover screw	–	36-60	4.1-6.8
Air filter element screw		55-60	6.2-6.8
Clutch adjusting screw locknut	–	120	13.6
Clutch cover screws	–	84-108	9.5-12.2
Engine oil drain plug	14-21	–	19-28.5
Primary chaincase oil drain plug	14-21	–	19-28.5
Jiffy stand leg stop bolt	12-15	–	16.3-20.3
Rear axle nut	95-105	–	128.8-142.4
Sparkplug	12-18	–	16.3-24.4
Transmission oil drain plug	14-21	–	19-28.5
Transmission oil filler			
cap/dipstick	–	25-75	2.8-8.5
Voltage regulator flange nut	–	70-100	7.9-11.3

3

NOTES

CHAPTER FOUR

ENGINE TOP END AND EXHAUST SYSTEM

The engine is an air-cooled four-stroke, overhead-valve V-twin. Viewed from the engine's right side, engine rotation is clockwise.

Both cylinders fire once in 720° of crankshaft rotation. The rear cylinder fires 315° after the front cylinder. The front cylinder fires again in another 405°. Note that one cylinder is always on its exhaust stroke when the other fires on its compression stroke.

Refer to **Tables 1-5** at the end of the chapter for specifications.

ENGINE SERVICE PRECAUTIONS

Before working on the engine, note the following:

1. Review *Service Methods* and *Measuring Tools* in Chapter One.
2. The text frequently mentions the left and right side of the engine. This refers to the engine as it is mounted in the frame, not how it may sit on the workbench.
3. Always replace worn or damaged fasteners with those of the same size, type and torque requirements. Clearly identify each bolt before replacing it. Lubricate bolt threads with engine oil, unless otherwise noted, before tightening them. If a torque specification is not listed in **Table 5**, refer to the general torque recommendations table in Chapter One.
4. Use the correct tools as noted. Refer to Chapter One for a list of tools and their part numbers.
5. Store parts in boxes, plastic bags and containers. Use masking tape and a permanent, waterproof marking pen to label parts.
6. Use a set of assorted size and color vacuum hose identifiers (Lisle part No. 74600) to identify hoses and fittings during engine removal and disassembly.
7. Use a vise with protective jaws to hold parts.
8. Use a press and/or the specific tools listed when force is required to remove and install parts. Do not try to pry, hammer or otherwise force them on or off.
9. Replace all gaskets, O-rings and oil seals during reassembly. Lubricate new O-rings with the lubricant that is being sealed. Apply a small amount of grease to the inner lips of each new seal to prevent damage when the engine is first started. Thoroughly clean all gasket, O-ring or seal mating surfaces before installation.
10. Record the location, position and thickness of all shims as they are removed.
11. Always disarm the optional security system (TSSM/HFSM) before disconnecting the battery or pulling the Main Fuse so the siren will not sound.

SERVICING ENGINE IN FRAME

The following components can be accessed while the engine is mounted in the frame:

1. Rocker arm cover and rocker arms.
2. Cylinder heads.
3. Cylinders and pistons.
4. Camshafts.
5. Gearshift mechanism.
6. Clutch and primary drive assembly.
7. Transmission.
8. Carburetor or fuel-injection induction module.
9. Starter and gears.

10. Alternator and electrical systems.

ROCKER ARMS, PUSHRODS AND VALVE LIFTERS

Refer to **Figures 1-3.**

The rocker arm, pushrod and valve lifter procedures are shown performed on the rear cylinder. The same procedures also apply to the front cylinder. Any differences are noted.

The rear cylinder head is closer to the frame backbone than the front cylinder. In some cases, it may be possible to completely remove some of the rocker arm mounting bolts on the front cylinder that cannot be removed on the rear cylinder.

Removal

1. If the engine is mounted in the frame, perform the following:
   a. Securely support the motorcycle on a level surface. Refer to *Motorcycle Stands* in Chapter Ten.
   b. Thoroughly clean the engine of all dirt and debris.
   c. Remove the seat and right footboard as described in Chapter Fourteen.
   d. Disconnect the negative battery cable (Chapter Nine).
   e. Drain the engine oil and remove the spark plugs as described in Chapter Three.
   f. Remove the fuel tank as described in Chapter Eight.
   g. Remove the air filter and backplate as described in Eight
   h. Remove the exhaust system as described in this chapter.
   i. Remove the fuel induction module (Chapter Eight).
2. Following the sequence shown in **Figure 4**, evenly loosen the rocker arm cover bolts. Remove each bolt and its captive washer. Note and record the location of the short and long bolts during removal.
3. Remove the rocker arm cover and gasket. Discard the gasket.
4. If not already performed, remove both spark plugs as described in Chapter Three to make it easier to rotate the engine by hand.
5A. Use the pushrod tool (Motion Pro part No. 08-0255) and compress the upper and lower pushrod covers. Insert a screwdriver (**Figure 5**) and pry the spring cap retainer free and remove it.
5B. If special tool is not available, using a screwdriver, pry the spring cap retainer (**Figure 6**) from between the cylinder head and spring cap. Compress the upper (A, **Figure 7**) and lower (B) push rod covers.

CAUTION
The piston must be at top dead center (TDC) on the compression stroke to avoid damage to the pushrods and rocker arms.

6A. *With the primary chain cover in place*, position the piston for the cylinder being worked on at top dead center (TDC) on the compression stroke as follows:
   a. Support the motorcycle on a stand with the rear wheel off the ground. Refer to *Motorcycle Stands* in Chapter Twelve.
   b. Shift the transmission into fifth or sixth gear.
   c. Rotate the rear wheel in the direction of normal rotation.
   d. Stop rotating the rear wheel when the intake and exhaust valves are closed.
   e. Look into the spark plug hole with a flashlight and verify that the piston is at TDC.
   f. Wiggle both rocker arms. There should be free play that indicates that both valves are closed and that the piston is at top dead center (TDC) on the compression stroke. Also, the push rods are in the unloaded position.
6B. *With the primary chain cover removed,* position the piston for the cylinder being worked on at top dead center (TDC) on the compression stroke as follows:
   a. Shift the transmission into neurtral.
   b. Place a socket or wrench on the compensating sprocket shaft nut.
   c. Rotate the compensating sprocket shaft *counterclockwise* until the intake and exhaust valves are closed.
   d. Look into the spark plug hole with a flashlight and verify that the piston is at TDC.
   e. Wiggle both rocker arms. There should be free play that indicates that both valves are closed and that the piston is at top dead center (TDC) on the compression stroke. Also, the push rods are in the unloaded position.
7. Using a crossing pattern, completely loosen the four bolts (A, **Figure 8**) securing the rocker arm support plate. The bolts cannot be removed at this time.
8. Completely loosen the bolts securing the breather assembly (B, **Figure 8**).
9. Remove the two *right side* rocker arm support bolts (A, **Figure 9**) and the *right side* breather assembly bolt (B).

NOTE
The two left side rocker arm support bolts and left side breather assembly bolt cannot be removed until the rocker arm support plate is removed from the cylinder head.

10. Lift the right side of the rocker arm support plate (A, **Figure 10**) sufficiently to clear the push rods (B).
11. Carefully slide the rocker arm support plate out through the right side and remove it from the cylinder head.
12. Remove the two *left side* rocker arm support bolts (A, **Figure 11**) and the *left side* breather assembly bolt (B). Remove the breather assembly from the rocker arm support plate.
13. Remove the O-ring seal (A, **Figure 12**) from the rocker arm housing.

①

ROCKER ARM ASSEMBLY (2010 MODELS)

1. Bolt
2. Rocker arm cover
3. Gasket
4. Bolt
5. Breather cover
6. Gasket
7. Valve
8. Breather baffle
9. Filter element
10. Gasket
11. Bushing
12. Rocker arm
    Intake (front cylinder)
    Exhaust (rear cylinder)
13. Rocker arm shaft
14. Washer
15. Rocker arm support
16. Rocker arm
    Intake (rear cylinder)
    Exhaust (front cylinder)
17. O-ring seal
18. Rocker arm housing
19. Gasket

4

② **ROCKER ARM ASSEMBLY (2011-ON MODELS)**

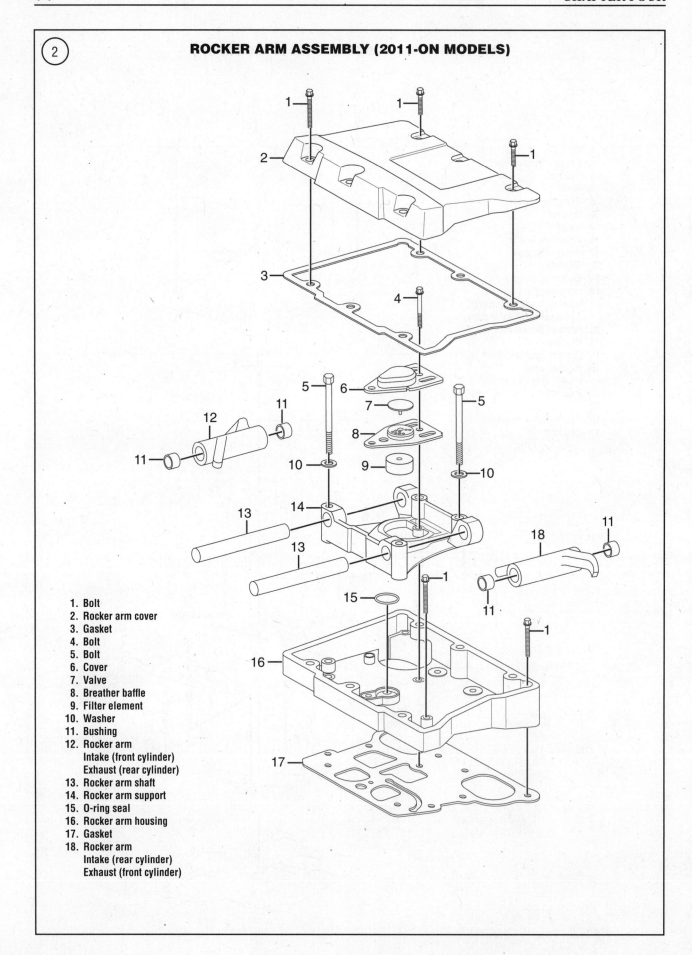

1. Bolt
2. Rocker arm cover
3. Gasket
4. Bolt
5. Bolt
6. Cover
7. Valve
8. Breather baffle
9. Filter element
10. Washer
11. Bushing
12. Rocker arm
    Intake (front cylinder)
    Exhaust (rear cylinder)
13. Rocker arm shaft
14. Rocker arm support
15. O-ring seal
16. Rocker arm housing
17. Gasket
18. Rocker arm
    Intake (rear cylinder)
    Exhaust (front cylinder)

4

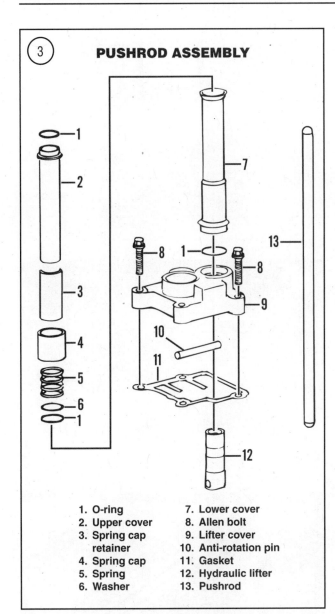

③ **PUSHROD ASSEMBLY**

1. O-ring
2. Upper cover
3. Spring cap retainer
4. Spring cap
5. Spring
6. Washer
7. Lower cover
8. Allen bolt
9. Lifter cover
10. Anti-rotation pin
11. Gasket
12. Hydraulic lifter
13. Pushrod

④ **ROCKER ARM COVER TORQUE SEQUENCE**

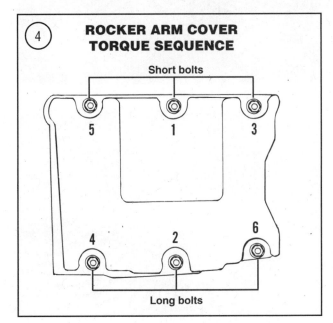

Short bolts

Long bolts

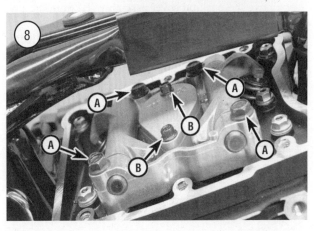

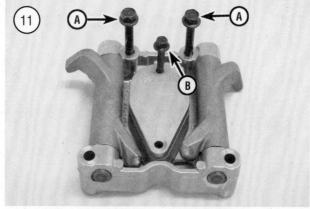

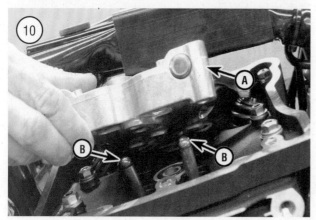

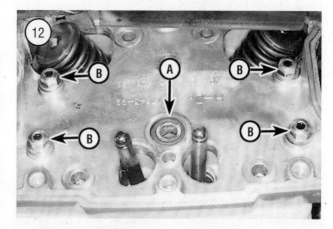

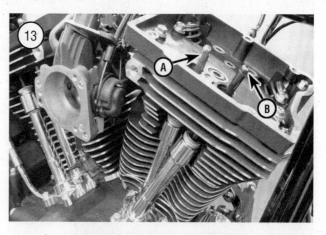

CAUTION
When removing the pushrods, do not mix the parts from each set. When reinstalling the original pushrods, install them so each end faces in its original operating position. The pushrods develop a set wear pattern and installing them upside down may cause rapid wear to the pushrod, lifter and rocker arm.

14. Lift the silver (A, **Figure 13**) intake and black (B) exhaust pushrods from the cylinder head. Mark the top and bottom of each pushrod, and mark its operating location in the cylinder head.

15. Remove the pushrod covers.
   a. Slide the upper cover (A, **Figure 14**) down, and remove the pushrod cover assembly (B) from the cylinder head and the lifter cover.
   b. Label the cover assembly so it can be reinstalled in its original location.
   c. Repeat the process to remove the remaining pushrod cover(s) on the opposite cylinder.

NOTE
*To clear the cylinder's lower cooling fins, loosen the lifter cover's two inner Allen bolts with a short 90° Allen wrench (**Figure 15**).*

16. Remove the lifter cover mounting bolts (**Figure 16**) and captive washers. Then, remove the cover.

17. Remove and discard the lifter cover gasket.

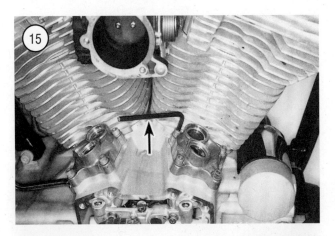

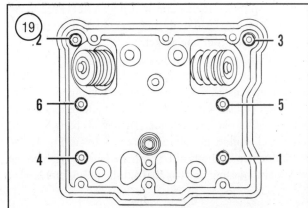

4

CAUTION
Do not mix the valve lifters when removing them. Mark them so they can be installed in their original positions.

18. Remove the anti-rotation pin (A, **Figure 17**), and then remove both valve lifters (B). Store the lifters upright in a container filled with clean engine oil until installation or inspection.

19. Cover the crankcase openings with duct tape (**Figure 18**) to prevent the entry of debris.

20. Loosen the six rocker arm housing bolts in 1/8-turn increments in the sequence shown in **Figure 19**. Remove the rocker arm housing bolts and their captive washers. Note that the two bolts on the left side of the engine are longer than the other four interior bolts (B, **Figure 12**). Mark the bolts for proper reinstallation.

21. Tap the rocker arm housing with a rubber mallet, and then lift it off the cylinder head.

22. Remove and discard the rocker arm housing gasket.

23. Disassemble and inspect the rocker arm assembly, pushrod covers or breather as described in this section.

Installation

NOTE
Figure 20 *and* ***Figure 21*** *are shown with the engine removed to clearly illustrate the steps.*

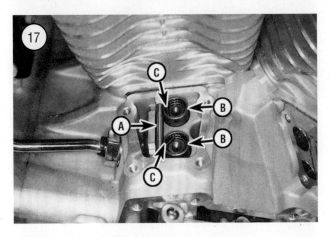

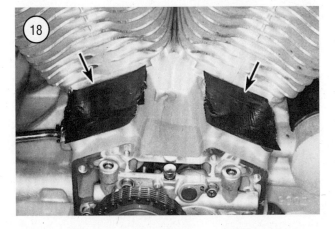

1. Position a *new* rocker arm housing gasket (**Figure 20**) onto the cylinder head so the breather channel (**Figure 21**) is covered and install the gasket.

2. Install the rocker arm housing onto the cylinder head.

3. Apply Loctite Threadlocker 243 (blue) to the bolt threads, and install the six rocker arm housing bolts along with their captive washer. Install the two long rocker arm housing bolts into the left side. Tighten all bolts by hand until snug. Following the sequences shown in **Figure 19**, evenly tighten the bolts in 1/8-turn increments. Tighten the rocker arm housing bolts to 10-14 ft.-lb. (13.6-19.0 N•m).

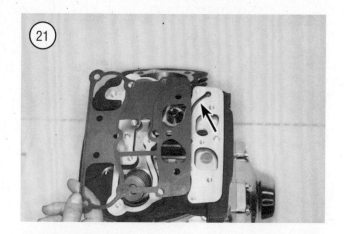

> *CAUTION*
> *The valve springs must not contact any part of the rocker arm housing.*

4. Install a *new* O-ring seal (A, **Figure 12**) onto the rocker arm housing. Apply a light coat of clean engine oil to the O-ring.

5. Check for clearance between each valve spring and the rocker arm housing. If necessary, loosen the housing bolts, and adjust the position of the rocker arm housing. Retighten the bolts as described in this section.

6. Install the breather assembly onto the rocker arm support plate, if removed.

7. Apply Loctite Threadlocker 243 (blue) to the bolt threads and install the two left side bolts (A, **Figure 11**) and left side breather assembly bolt (B) onto the rocker arm housing.

8. Remove the duct tape from the crankcase openings.

9. Install each valve lifter into the correct crankcase bore. The oil hole of each lifter (**Figure 22**) must face the inboard side of its bore and the lifter flats must face the front and rear of the engine. This is necessary for installation of the anti-rotation pin in the next step.

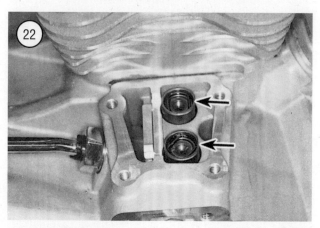

> *CAUTION*
> *Failure to install the anti-rotational pin will allow the lifter to rotate off the camshaft lobe and cause severe internal engine damage.*

10. Completely seat the anti-rotation pin (**Figure 23**) within the crankcase slot. Make sure the pin (A, **Figure 17**) rests against the flats (C) of both hydraulic lifters (B).

11. If the engine's position has been disturbed since the rocker arm components were removed, rotate the engine until both lifters for the cylinder being serviced sit on the lowest point (base circle) of the cam. The lifter's top surface should be flush with the top surface of the crankcase as shown in **Figure 24**.

12. Install a *new* lifter cover gasket (**Figure 25**) onto the crankcase.

> *NOTE*
> *To clear the cylinder's lower cooling fins, tighten the lifter cover two inner Allen bolts with a short 90° Allen wrench.*

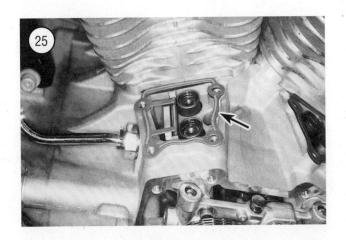

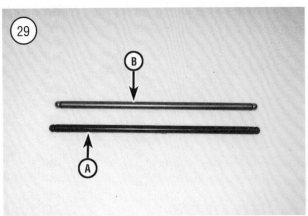

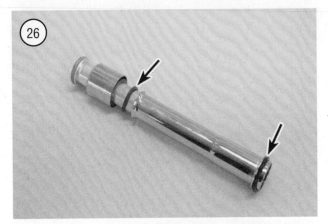

13. Install the lifter cover and the mounting bolts (**Figure 16**). Tighten the lift cover bolts to 90-120 in.-lb. (10.2-13.6 N•m).

14. Install a *new* O-ring (**Figure 26**) onto each end of the pushrod covers. Apply a light coat of clean engine oil to each O-ring.

15. If the pushrod cover assembly was disassembled, reassemble it as described in this section.

CAUTION
*The pushrod covers and the pushrods must be installed in the correct locations on the cylinder head and lifter cover as indicated in **Table 4**.*

16. Install the pushrod covers by performing the following:
   a. Compress the pushrod cover assembly, and fit the lower cover into the correct lifter cover bore (**Figure 27**).
   b. Slide the upper cover (**Figure 28**) up into the cylinder head bore. Do not install the spring cap retainer at this time.
   c. Repeat this process to install the remaining pushrod cover.

17. Install the pushrods as follows:

CAUTION
*Two different length pushrods are used in the Twin Cam engines. The black exhaust pushrods (A, **Figure 29**) are longer than the silver intake pushrods (B).*

   a. When installing the existing pushrods, install each pushrod in its original position and with the correct orientation. Refer to A, **Figure 13** for an intake pushrod, and B, **Figure 13** for an exhaust pushrod.

NOTE
Because new pushrods are symmetrical, they can be installed with either end facing up.

   b. Make sure the pushrod is centered in its respective lifter.

18A. On 2010 models, disassembled, install the breather assembly by performing the following:

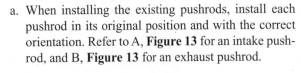

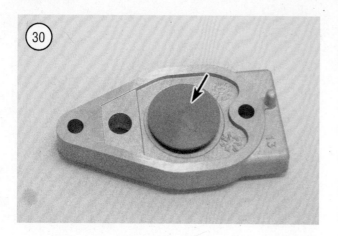

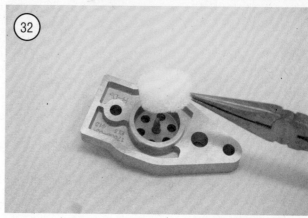

a. If removed, install a new valve (**Figure 30**) onto the breather baffle. Lubricate the valve stem with denatured alcohol or glass cleaner, insert the valve stem through the center hole in the top of the breather baffle and pull the stem (**Figure 31**) through from the other side to seat the valve.

b. Align the hole in a new filter (**Figure 32**) with the valve stem, and press the filter into the bore (**Figure 33**) on the bottom of the baffle.

c. Install a *new* breather baffle gasket (**Figure 34**).

d. Hold the filter element in place and install the breather baffle (**Figure 35**).

e. Install a *new* cover gasket (**Figure 36**).

f. Install the cover (A, **Figure 37**) and *left side* cover bolt (B).

18B. On 2011-on models, if disassembled, install the breather assembly by perform the following:

a. If removed, install a new valve (**Figure 30**) onto the breather baffle. Lubricate the valve stem with denatured alcohol or glass cleaner, insert the valve stem through the center hole in the top if the breather baffle and pull the stem (**Figure 31**) through from the outer side if the seat the valve.

b. Align the hole in the new filter (**Figure 32**) with the valve stem, and press the filter into the bore (**Figure 33**) on the bottom of the baffle.

c. Install the cover (A, **Figure 37**, typical) and *left side* bolt (B).

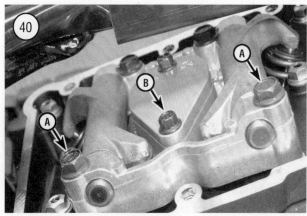

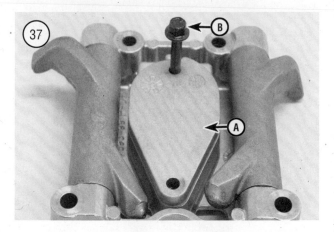

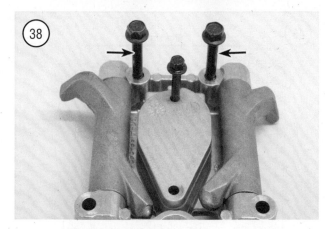

19. Install the two *left side* bolts (**Figure 38**).

20. From the right side, slide the rocker arm support plate (A, **Figure 39**) onto the rocker arm housing, and past the pushrods (B). Do not forget to install the breather assembly left side bolt (B, **Figure 37**). This bolt cannot be installed after the rocker arm support plate is in place on the cylinder head.

21. Lift the left side of the rocker arm support plate, and install the two right side bolts (A, **Figure 40**) and the right side breather assembly bolt (B). Do not tighten the bolts at this time.

CAUTION
To avoid damaging a pushrod, the rocker arms or the valves, follow a crossing pattern and tighten the rocker arm support plate bolts evenly in 1/4-turn increments. When tightening the mounting bolts, spin each pushrod by hand to ensure the rocker arm support plate is being tightened evenly. If one or both pushrods cannot be rotated, loosen the mounting bolts and determine the cause.

22. Install the rocker arm support plate bolts and finger-tighten them. Using a crossing pattern, tighten the rocker arm support plate bolts evenly to 18-22 ft.-lb. (24.4-29.8 N•m).

23. Lift each lower pushrod cover and confirm that each pushrod rotates freely.

24. Make sure the pushrod cover O-rings are correctly seated in the cylinder head and lifter cover.

25A. Use the pushrod tool (Motion Pro part No. 08-0255) to compress the upper and lower pushrod covers (**Figure 41**) and install the spring cap retainer. Repeat the process to install the remaining pushrod cover.

25B. If the pushrod tool is not available, compress the spring cap with a thin open end wrench (A, **Figure 42**), or an equivalent, and install the spring cap retainer (B). Make sure the spring cap retainer is positioned correctly on both the upper cover and the spring cap (**Figure 43**). Repeat the process to install the remaining pushrod cover.

26. Tighten the breather assembly bolts evenly to 90-120 in.-lb. (10.2-13.6 N•m).

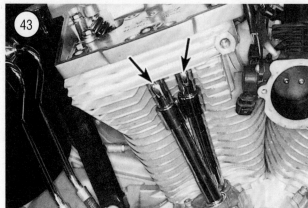

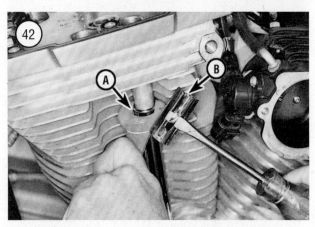

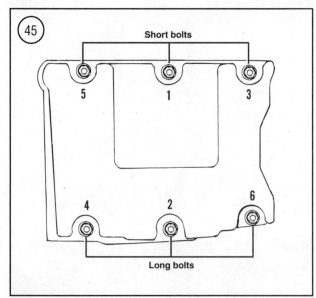

27. Install a *new* rocker arm cover gasket (**Figure 44**), and rocker arm cover.

NOTE
*There are two different length bolts (**Figure 45**) securing the rocker arm cover.*

28. Apply Loctite Threadlocker 243 (blue) to the bolt threads, and then install each rocker arm cover bolt with its captive washer. Using the sequence shown in **Figure 45**, tighten the bolts in 1/8-turn increments to 15-18 ft.-lbs. (20.3-24.4 N•m).

29. Install both spark plugs as described in Chapter Three.

30. If the engine is mounted in the frame, perform the following:

    a. Install the induction module (Chapter Eight).

    b. Install the exhaust system as described in this chapter.

    c. Install the air filter and backplate as described in Chapter Eight.

    d. Install the fuel tank as described in Chapter Eight.

    e. Refill the engine oil and install the spark plugs as described in Chapter Three.

    f. Connect the negative battery cable (Chapter Nine).

    g. Install the seat and right footboard as described in Chapter Fourteen.

Rocker Arm Disassembly/Assembly

1. Before removing the rocker arms (**Figure 46** and **47**), measure the rocker arm end clearance as follows:

    a. Insert a feeler gauge between the rocker arm and the inside of the rocker arm support plate (**Figure 48**).

    b. Record the measurement.

    c. Repeat for each end of both rocker arms.

ROCKER ARM ASSEMBLY (2010 MODELS)

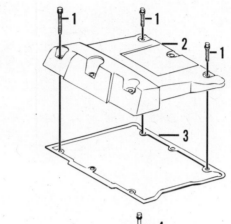

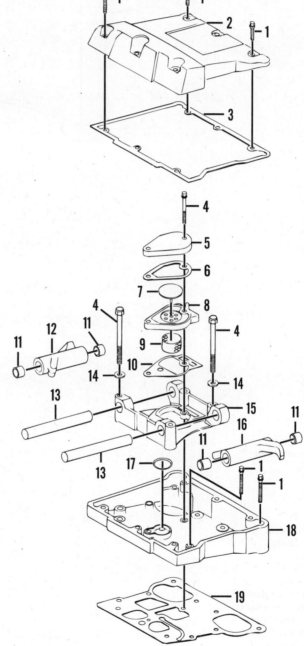

1. Bolt
2. Rocker arm cover
3. Gasket
4. Bolt
5. Breather cover
6. Gasket
7. Valve
8. Breather baffle
9. Filter element
10. Gasket
11. Bushing
12. Rocker arm
    Intake (front cylinder)
    Exhaust (rear cylinder)
13. Rocker arm shaft
14. Washer
15. Rocker arm support
16. Rocker arm
    Intake (rear cylinder)
    Exhaust (front cylinder)
17. O-ring seal
18. Rocker arm housing
19. Gasket

4

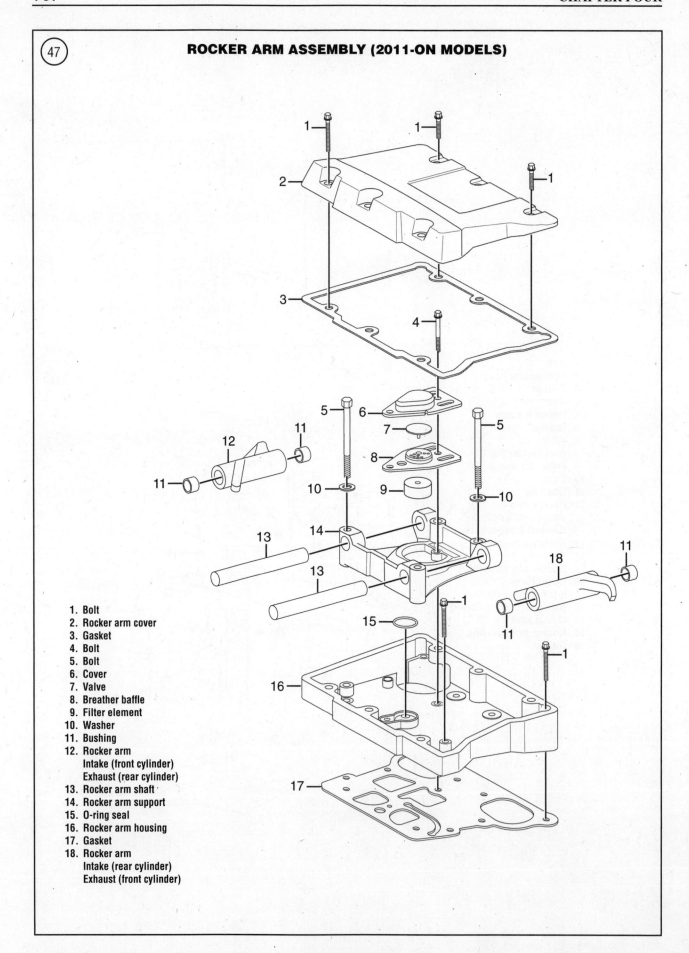

ROCKER ARM ASSEMBLY (2011-ON MODELS)

47

1. Bolt
2. Rocker arm cover
3. Gasket
4. Bolt
5. Bolt
6. Cover
7. Valve
8. Breather baffle
9. Filter element
10. Washer
11. Bushing
12. Rocker arm
    Intake (front cylinder)
    Exhaust (rear cylinder)
13. Rocker arm shaft
14. Rocker arm support
15. O-ring seal
16. Rocker arm housing
17. Gasket
18. Rocker arm
    Intake (rear cylinder)
    Exhaust (front cylinder)

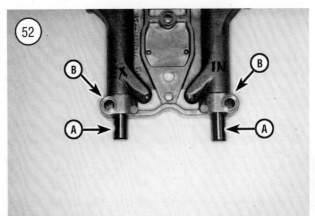

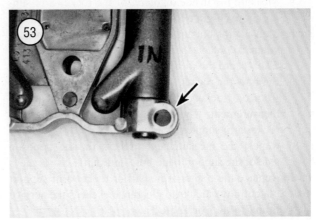

4

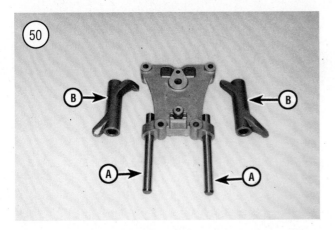

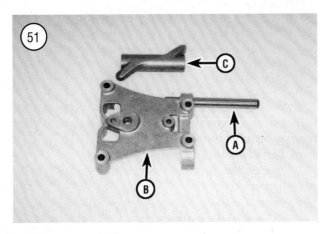

d. Replace the rocker arm and/or the rocker arm support if end clearance exceeds the service limit (**Table 2** or **Table 3**).

2. Prior to disassembling the rocker arms, mark each one with an IN for intake or an EX for exhaust (**Figure 49**) to ensure they are installed in their original positions.

3. Use a hammer and drift, and tap the left side of each rocker shaft so the notched ends come out first. Remove the rocker arm shafts (A, **Figure 50**), and then remove the rocker arms (B).

4. Clean all parts in solvent, blow compressed air through all oil passages, and inspect the components as described in this section.

5. Install the rocker arm shaft (A, **Figure 51**) part way into the rocker arm support plate (B) in its original position.

6. Install a rocker arm (C, **Figure 51**) into its original position and push the shaft part way through the rocker arm.

7. Align the notch (A, **Figure 52**) in the rocker arm shaft with the corresponding mounting bolt hole (B) in the rocker arm support and install the shaft all the way. Check for correct alignment (**Figure 53**).

8. Repeat the proccess to install the remaining rocker arm and shaft.

Rocker Arm Component Inspection

During inspection, compare any measurements to the specifications in **Table 2** or **Table 3**. Replace any part that is worn, damaged or out of specification.

1. Inspect the rocker arm pads (A, **Figure 54**) and ball sockets (B) for pitting and excessive wear.

2. Examine the rocker arm shaft for scoring, ridge wear or other damage. If these conditions are present, replace the rocker arm shaft.

3. Check the rocker arm bushing (**Figure 55**) for wear or scoring.

4. Perform the following to determine the shaft-to-rocker arm support clearance.

    a. Measure the inside diameter of the rocker arm support bore (**Figure 56**). Record the measurement.

    b. Measure the outside diameter of the rocker arm shaft where it contacts the rocker arm support bore (**Figure 57**). Record the measurement.

    c. Subtract the rocker arm shaft diameter measurement from the rocker arm support bore inside diameter measurement. The difference equals the shaft-to-rocker arm support clearance.

    d. Repeat the measurement process for the opposite side of the support plate bore and shaft.

    e. Replace the rocker arm shaft or rocker arm support plate if any calculated clearance exceeds the service limit (**Table 2** or **Table 3**).

5. Perform the following to determine the shaft-to-rocker arm bushing clearance:

    a. Measure the rocker arm bushing inside diameter (**Figure 58**). Record the measurement.

    b. Measure the diameter of the rocker arm shaft diameter where it contacts the rocker arm bushing (**Figure 57**). Record the measurement.

    c. Subtract the rocker arm shaft diameter from the inside diameter of the bushing.

    d. Repeat the measurement process for the opposite side of the rocker arm and shaft.

    e. Replace the shaft or bushing if any clearance exceeds the specified service limit (**Table 2** or **Table 3**).

6. Inspect the rocker arm support plate bores (**Figure 58**) for wear or elongation.

7. Inspect the gasket surface of the rocker arm cover for damage or warp.

8. Inspect the rocker arm support plate (**Figure 59**) for damage or warp.

9. Inspect both gasket surfaces of the rocker arm housing for damage or warp.

Rocker Arm Bushing Replacement

Each rocker arm is equipped with two bushings (**Figure 55**). Replacement bushings must be reamed after installation. Use the rocker arm bushing reamer (JIMS part No. 94804-57). If the correct size reamer is unavailable, have the bushings replaced by a dealership.

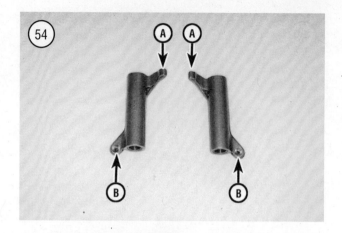

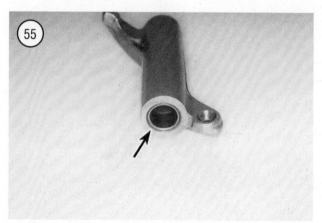

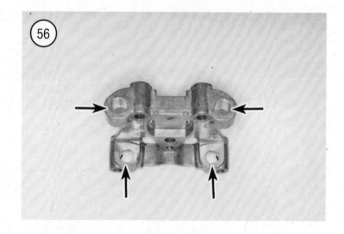

NOTE
Since the new bushings must be reamed, just remove one bushing at a time. The opposite bushing is then used as a guide to ream the first bushing.

1. Press one bushing (**Figure 55**) out of the rocker arm. Do not remove the second bushing. If the bushing is difficult to remove, perform the following:

    a. Thread a 9/16 × 18 tap into the bushing.

    b. Support the rocker arm in a press so the tap is at the bottom.

    c. Insert a mandrel through the top of the rocker arm and seat it on top of the tap.

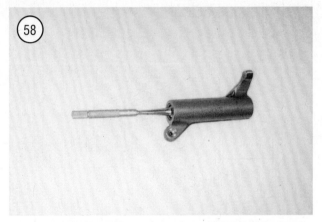

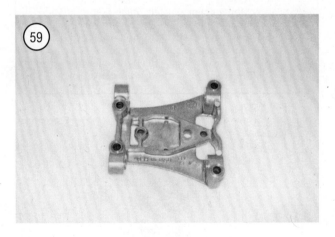

d. Press on the mandrel to force the bushing and tap out of the rocker arm.

e. Remove the tap from the bushing and discard the bushing.

2. Position the new bushing with the split portion facing toward the top of the rocker arm.

3. Press the new bushing into the rocker arm until the bushing's outer surface is flush with the end of rocker arm bore.

4. Ream the new bushing with the bushing reamer as follows:

a. Mount the rocker arm in a vise with soft jaws so the new bushing is at the bottom.

CAUTION
Only turn the reamer clockwise. Do not rotate the reamer counterclockwise or the reamer and bushing will be damaged.

b. Mount a tap handle on top of the reamer and insert the reamer into the bushing. Turn the reamer *clockwise* until it passes through the new bushing and remove it from the bottom side.

5. Remove the rocker arm from the vise and repeat the procedure to replace the opposite bushing.

6. Ream the second bushing. The first bushing now serves as a guide.

7. After installing and reaming both bushings, clean the rocker arm assembly in solvent. Then, clean it with hot, soapy water and rinse it with clear water. Dry it with compressed air.

8. Calculate the shaft-to-rocker arm bushing clearance at each end of the rocker arm as described in *Rocker Arm Component Inspection*. Each clearance must be within specification.

Valve Lifter Inspection

Figure 60 shows a valve lifter in relation to the pushrod and valve lifter cover. The valve lifters and covers are installed on the right side of the engine. During engine operation, the lifters are pumped full with engine oil, thus taking up all play in the valve train. When the engine is turned off, the lifters leak down after a period of time as some of the oil drains out. When the engine is started, the lifters click until they completely refill with oil. The lifters are working properly when they stop clicking after the engine is run for a few minutes. If the clicking persists, a problem may exist with the lifter(s).

CAUTION
Place the lifters on a clean, lint-free cloth during inspection.

1. Check the pushrod socket (**Figure 61**) in the top of the lifter for wear or damage.

2. Check the lifter roller (A, **Figure 62**) for pitting, scoring, galling or excessive wear. If the roller is excessively worn, check the mating cam lobe for the same condition.

3. Clean the lifter roller. Measure the radial play of the roller pin and the roller end clearance. Replace the lifter if either measurement clearance exceeds the wear limit.

4. Determine the lifter-to-bore clearance as follows:

a. Use an inside micrometer or a bore gauge to measure the inside diameter of the lifter bore in the crankcase.

b. Use outside micrometers to measure the lifter outside diameter (B, **Figure 62**).

c. Calculate the lifter-to-bore clearance by subtracting the lifter outside diameter from the lifter bore inside diameter.

d. Replace the lifter and/or crankcase if the lifter-to-bore clearance exceeds the service limit.

5. If a lifter does not show visual damage, it may be contaminated with dirt or have internal damage. If so, replace it. The lifters are not serviceable and must be replaced as a unit.

6. After inspecting the lifters, store them upright in a container filled with clean engine oil until installation.

7. If most of the oil has drained out of the lifter, refill it with a pump-type oil can through the oil hole in the side of the lifter.

8. Clean all gasket material from the mating surfaces of the crankcase and the lifter cover.

9. Inspect the lifter cover (**Figure 63**) for cracks or damage.

Pushrod Inspection

1. Clean the pushrods in solvent and dry them with compressed air.

2. Check the pushrods for cracks and worn or damaged ball heads (**Figure 64**).

3. Roll the pushrods on a surface plate or on a piece of glass, and check for bending.

4. Replace any damaged pushrods.

Pushrod Cover Disassembly/Inspection/Assembly

Refer to **Figure 60**.

1. Remove and discard the O-rings from their seats on the upper and lower pushrod covers.

2. Pull the lower pushrod cover (**Figure 65**) from the upper cover.

3. Slide the O-ring (A, **Figure 66**), washer (B), spring (C) and spring cap (D) from the upper pushrod cover. Discard the O-ring.

4. Clean all parts in solvent, and blow them dry with compressed air. Make sure the O-ring seats and contact surfaces of the covers are clean.

5. Check the pushrod cover assembly (**Figure 67**) as follows:
   a. Check the spring for sagging or cracking.
   b. Check the washer for deformation or damage.
   c. Check the pushrod covers for cracking or damage.

6. Replace all worn or damaged parts.

7. Assembly is the reverse of disassembly. Install new O-rings. Lubricate each O-ring with clean engine oil.

Breather Disassembly/Inspection

Refer to **Figure 46 and Figure 47**.

1. Remove the breather fasteners, and lift the breather assembly from the rocker arm support plate.

2. Remove the breather cover and gasket. Discard the gasket.

3. Remove the filter element from the breather baffle, and then remove the valve. Discard both.

4. Clean all parts in solvent. Blow them dry with compressed air.

5. Inspect the breather by performing the following:

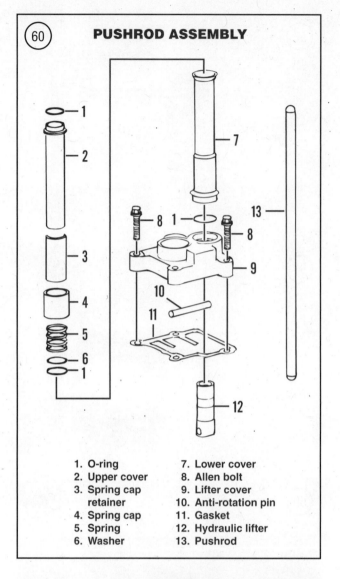

PUSHROD ASSEMBLY

60

1. O-ring	7. Lower cover
2. Upper cover	8. Allen bolt
3. Spring cap retainer	9. Lifter cover
4. Spring cap	10. Anti-rotation pin
5. Spring	11. Gasket
6. Washer	12. Hydraulic lifter
	13. Pushrod

61

a. Place a straightedge diagonally across the breather cover so the straightedge crosses opposite corners of the cover.

b. Check breather cover warp by inserting a feeler gauge at several places between the straightedge and the cover.

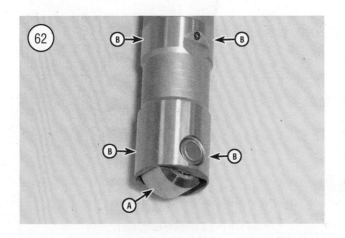

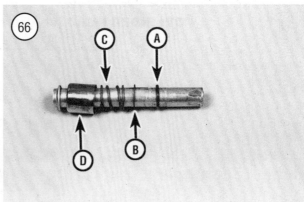

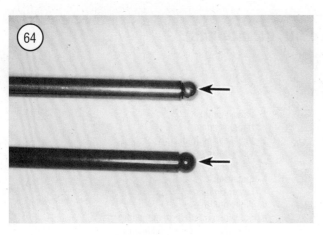

c. Repeat the process and check for warp across the opposite diagonal.

d. Replace the breather cover if any measurement exceeds the specified service limit.

e. Repeat the measurement procedure, and check the breather baffle for warp.

6. Reassemble the breather assembly as described in *Installation* (this section).

CYLINDER HEAD

The cylinder head procedures shown here are performed on the rear cylinder (**Figures 68** and **Figure 69**). The same procedures apply to the front cylinder. Any differences are noted.

NOTE
The following procedures are shown with the engine removed to clearly illustrate the steps.

Removal

1. Remove the rocker arm support plate, rocker arm housing, pushrods and pushrod covers as described in this chapter.

2. Disconnect the breather hose from the fitting on the cylinder head.

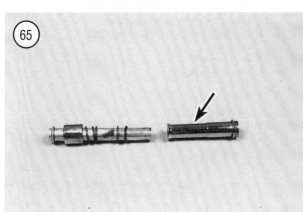

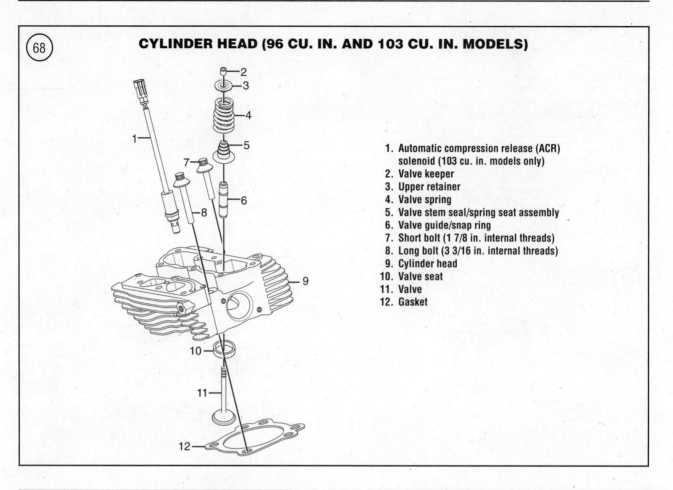

(68)

CYLINDER HEAD (96 CU. IN. AND 103 CU. IN. MODELS)

1. Automatic compression release (ACR) solenoid (103 cu. in. models only)
2. Valve keeper
3. Upper retainer
4. Valve spring
5. Valve stem seal/spring seat assembly
6. Valve guide/snap ring
7. Short bolt (1 7/8 in. internal threads)
8. Long bolt (3 3/16 in. internal threads)
9. Cylinder head
10. Valve seat
11. Valve
12. Gasket

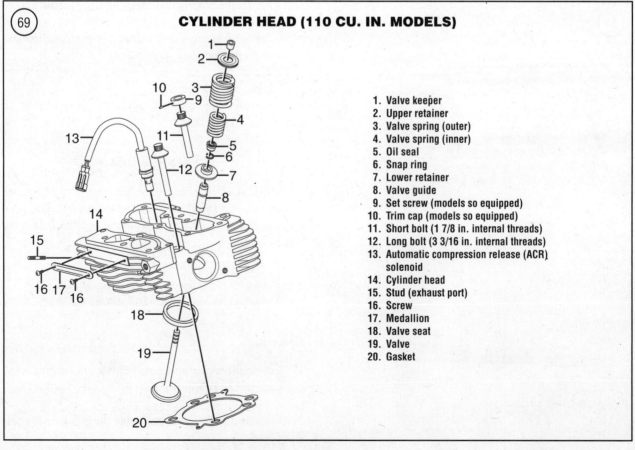

(69)

CYLINDER HEAD (110 CU. IN. MODELS)

1. Valve keeper
2. Upper retainer
3. Valve spring (outer)
4. Valve spring (inner)
5. Oil seal
6. Snap ring
7. Lower retainer
8. Valve guide
9. Set screw (models so equipped)
10. Trim cap (models so equipped)
11. Short bolt (1 7/8 in. internal threads)
12. Long bolt (3 3/16 in. internal threads)
13. Automatic compression release (ACR) solenoid
14. Cylinder head
15. Stud (exhaust port)
16. Screw
17. Medallion
18. Valve seat
19. Valve
20. Gasket

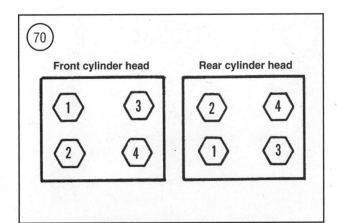

Front cylinder head   Rear cylinder head

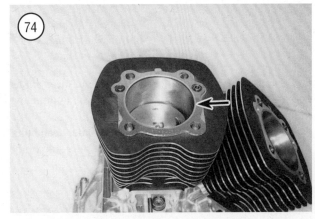

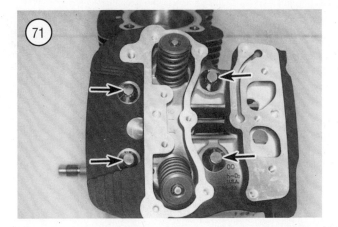

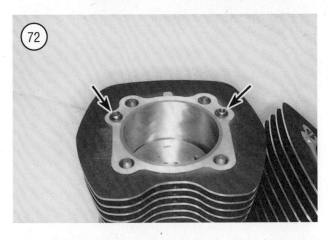

3. On CVO models, loosen the set screw, and then remove each cylinder head bolt cover from the bolt head. *Do not* remove the set screws.

4. Following the sequence shown in **Figure 70**, loosen the cylinder head bolts (**Figure 71**) in 1/4-turn increments until they are loose. Remove the four bolts. Note and mark the position of the short and long bolts.

5. Tap the cylinder head with a rubber mallet to free it, and lift it off the cylinder.

6. Remove the cylinder head gasket.

7. Remove the cylinder head dowels (**Figure 72**) and O-rings. Discard each O-ring.

8. Repeat the procedure to remove the opposite cylinder head.

Installation

1. If removed, install the piston and cylinder as described in this chapter.

2. Lubricate the cylinder head bolts as follows:
   a. Clean the cylinder head bolts in solvent and dry with compressed air.
   b. Apply clean engine oil to the cylinder head bolt threads and to the flat shoulder surface on each bolt (**Figure 73**). Wipe excess oil from the bolts, leaving only an oil film on these surfaces.

3. Install the dowels (**Figure 72**) into the top of the cylinder.

4. Install a *new* O-ring (**Figure 72**) over each dowel. Apply a light coat of clean engine oil to the O-rings.

> *CAUTION*
> *Because the O-rings center the head gasket on the cylinder, install them before installing the head gasket.*

5. Install a *new* cylinder head gasket (**Figure 74**) onto the cylinder.

> *CAUTION*
> *Do not use sealer on the cylinder head gasket. For an aftermarket head gasket, follow the gasket manufacturer's instructions for installation.*

NOTE
*The cylinder heads are **not** identical. Refer to the **FRONT** or **REAR** (**Figure 75**) identifier cast into top surface of the cylinder head.*

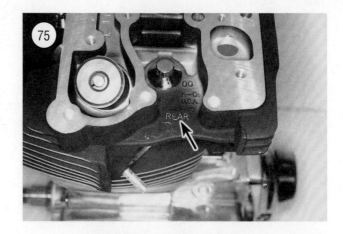

6. Lower the cylinder head (**Figure 76**) onto the cylinder and the dowels. Position the head carefully to avoid moving the head gasket out of alignment.

7. Install and lightly finger-tighten the cylinder head bolts. Make sure the short bolts are on the spark plug side of the head.

CAUTION
Failure to follow the proper torque sequence may distort the cylinder head, allowing the gasket to leak.

8. Following the torque sequence shown in **Figure 72**, tighten the cylinder head bolts as follows:
   a. Starting with bolt No. 1, evenly finger-tighten the cylinder head bolts in order.
   b. Tighten each bolt in order to 10-12 ft.-lb. (13.6-16.3 N•m).
   c. Tighten each bolt in order to 15-17 ft.-lb. (20.3-23.0 N•m).
   d. Make a vertical mark (A, **Figure 77**) with a permanent marker on each bolt head. Make another mark (B, **Figure 77**) on the cylinder head at a 90° angle or 1/4-turn from the mark on the bolt head.
   e. Following the torque sequence, tighten each bolt an additional 90° or 1/4-turn using the marks as a guide (**Figure 78**).

9. On Screamin' Eagle models, install the cylinder head bolt caps. Tighten the set screws to 60-84 in.-lb. (6.8-9.5 N•m). Make sure each set screw sits in a notch between the bolt points.

10. Connect the breather hose to its fitting.

11. Install the rocker arm assemblies, pushrods and pushrod covers as described in this chapter.

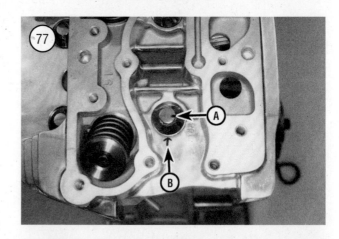

Leak Test

Before removing the valves or cleaning the cylinder head, perform the cylinder head leak test.

1. Position the cylinder head so the exhaust port faces up. Pour solvent or kerosene into each exhaust port opening (**Figure 79**).

2. After at least ten seconds, turn the head over slightly and check each exhaust valve area on the combustion chamber side. If the valves and seats are in good condition, no fluid will be found and the valve seat area will be dry. If any area is wet, the valve seat is not sealing correctly. The valve seat or face may be damaged or the valve may be bent or damaged. Remove the valve, and inspect the valve and seat as decribed in this section.

3. Pour solvent into the intake port and repeat the procedure to check the intake valve for leaks.

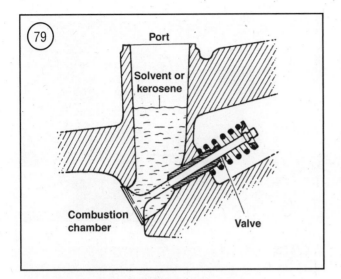

Port

Solvent or kerosene

Combustion chamber

Valve

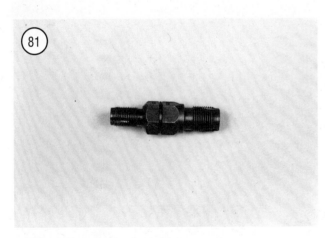

Inspection

During inspection, compare any measurements taken to the specifications listed in **Table 2** or **Table 3**. Replace any part that is worn, damaged or out of specification.

1. Perform the *Leak Test* (this section).
2. Thoroughly clean the outside of the cylinder head. Use a stiff brush, soap and water to remove all debris from the cooling fins (**Figure 80**). If necessary, use a piece of wood and scrape away any lodged dirt. Clogged cooling fins can cause overheating and lead to engine damage.

CAUTION
Cleaning the combustion chamber with the valves removed can damage the valve seat surfaces. A damaged or even slightly scratched valve seat will cause poor valve seating.

3. *Without removing the valves*, use a wire brush to remove all carbon deposits from the combustion chamber. Use a fine wire brush and dip it in solvent or make a scraper from hardwood. Be careful not to damage the cylinder head, valves or spark plug threads.

NOTE
If there is severe thread damage, restore the threads by installing a thread insert. If necessary, have this done by a machine shop.

4. Examine the spark plug threads in the cylinder head for damage. If there is minor damage or if the threads are dirty or clogged with carbon, use a spark plug thread tap (**Figure 81**) and kerosene or cutting fluid to clean the threads.
5. After all carbon is removed from the combustion chambers and valve ports, and the spark plug thread hole has been repaired, clean the entire head in solvent. Dry it with compressed air.
6. Examine the crown on the piston (**Figure 82**). The crown should show no signs of wear or damage. If the crown appears pecked or spongy-looking, also check the spark plug, valves and combustion chamber for aluminum deposits. If these deposits are found, the cylinder has overheated. Check for a lean fuel mixture or other conditions that could cause preignition.
7. Check for cracks in the combustion chamber, the intake port (**Figure 83**) and the exhaust port (**Figure 84**). Replace a cracked head if welding cannot repair it.
8. Inspect the exhaust pipe mounting studs (**Figure 85**) for damage. Repair the threads with a die if they are damaged.

CAUTION
If the cylinder head is bead-blasted, clean the head thoroughly with solvent, and then with hot soapy water. Residual grit seats in small crevices and other areas, and can be hard to get out. Also, run a tap through each exposed thread to remove grit from the threads. Any

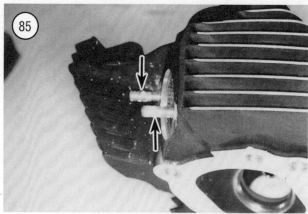

grit left in the engine will cause premature wear.

9. Thoroughly clean the cylinder head.

10. Measure the head for warp by placing a straightedge across the gasket surface at several points and attempting to insert a feeler gauge between the straightedge and the cylinder head at each location (**Figure 86**). Distortion or nicks in the cylinder head surface could cause an air leak and overheating. If warp exceeds the specified service limit, replace the cylinder head.

11. Repeat the procedure to check the rocker arm housing mating surfaces (**Figure 87**) for warp.

12. Make sure the breather channel (**Figure 88**) is clear at each end.

13. Check the valves and valve guides as described in *Valves and Valve Components* (this chapter).

VALVES AND VALVE COMPONENTS

The following procedures describe how to check the valve components for wear and how to determine what type of valve service is required.

Refer to **Figures 89** and **Figure 90**.

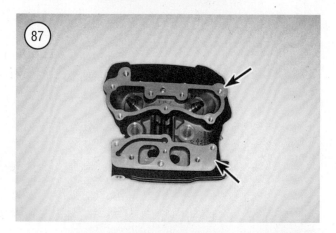

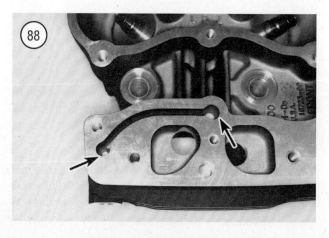

89

CYLINDER HEAD (96 CU. IN. AND 103 CU. IN. MODELS)

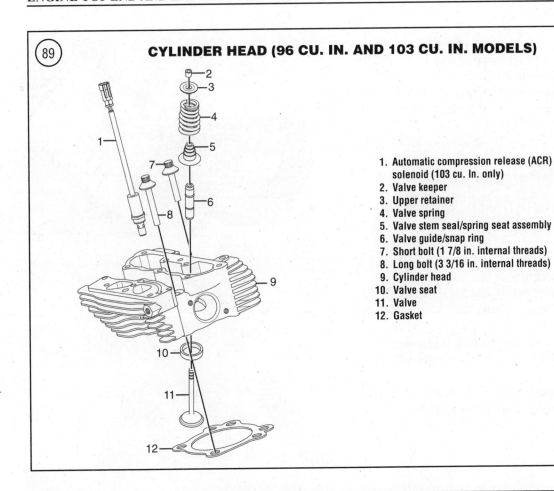

1. Automatic compression release (ACR) solenoid (103 cu. In. only)
2. Valve keeper
3. Upper retainer
4. Valve spring
5. Valve stem seal/spring seat assembly
6. Valve guide/snap ring
7. Short bolt (1 7/8 in. internal threads)
8. Long bolt (3 3/16 in. internal threads)
9. Cylinder head
10. Valve seat
11. Valve
12. Gasket

4

90

CYLINDER HEAD (110 CU. IN. MODELS)

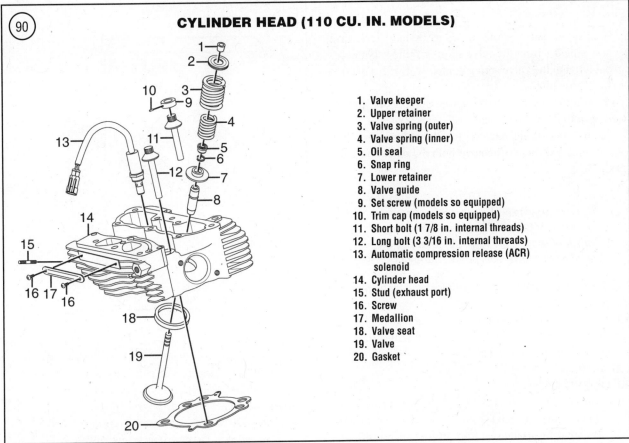

1. Valve keeper
2. Upper retainer
3. Valve spring (outer)
4. Valve spring (inner)
5. Oil seal
6. Snap ring
7. Lower retainer
8. Valve guide
9. Set screw (models so equipped)
10. Trim cap (models so equipped)
11. Short bolt (1 7/8 in. internal threads)
12. Long bolt (3 3/16 in. internal threads)
13. Automatic compression release (ACR) solenoid
14. Cylinder head
15. Stud (exhaust port)
16. Screw
17. Medallion
18. Valve seat
19. Valve
20. Gasket

Tools

The following tools, or their equivalents, are needed for valve removal and installation:
1. Valve spring compressor (H-D part No. HD-34736-B).
2. Valve guide cleaning brush (H-D part No. HD-34751-A).
3. Valve guide seal installer (H-D part No. HD-48644); CVO models only.
4. Cylinder head holding fixture (H-D part No. HD-39786-A).
5. ACR solenoid socket (H-D part No. HD-48498).

Valve Removal

1. Remove the cylinder head as described in this chapter.
2. If using the cylinder head holding fixture, install the 12-mm end of the tool into the spark plug hole. Secure the fixture in a vise.
3. On models so equipped, use the ACR solenoid socket to remove the ACR solenoid from the cylinder head.(Chapter Nine).
4. Install the valve spring compressor (**Figure 91**) squarely over the valve spring upper retainer (**Figure 92**) and against the valve head.

> *CAUTION*
> *To avoid loss of spring tension, compress the spring just enough to remove the valve keepers.*

5. Tighten the valve spring compressor until the valve keepers separate from the valve stem. Lift the valve keepers out through the valve spring compressor with a magnet or needlenose pliers.
6. Gradually loosen the valve spring compressor and remove it from the cylinder head.
7. Remove the spring retainer and the valve spring. On 110 cu. in. CVO models, remove both the outer and inner springs.

> *CAUTION*
> *Remove any burrs from the valve stem keeper groove (**Figure 93**) before removing the valve; otherwise the valve guide will be damaged as the valve stem passes through it.*

8. Remove the valve from the cylinder head while rotating it slightly.
9A. On all models except CVO, use needlenose pliers to carefully twist and remove the valve stem seal/spring seat assembly from the valve guide. Discard the valve stem seal/spring seat assembly.
9B. On CVO models:
    a. Use needlenose pliers to carefully twist and remove the valve stem seal from the valve guide. Discard the seal.
    b. Remove the spring seat from the cylinder head.

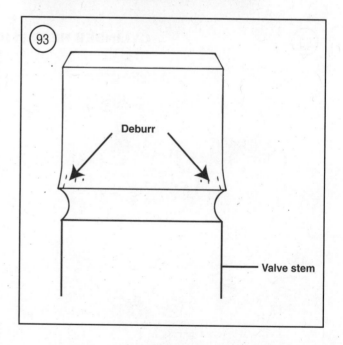

Deburr

Valve stem

> *CAUTION*
> *Keep the components of each valve assembly together. Identify the components as either intake or exhaust. If both cylinders are disassembled, also label the components front or rear. Do not mix components from the valve assemblies. Excessive wear may result.*

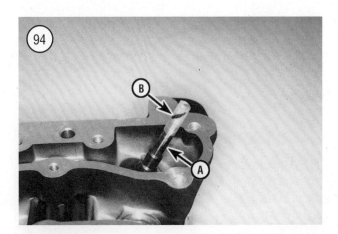

10. Repeat the procedure to remove the remaining valve.

Valve Installation

1. Run the valve cleaning brush through the valve guide to make sure it is clean.

2. Coat a valve stem with Torco MPZ, molybdenum disulfide paste or an equivalent lubricant. Install the valve part way into the guide. Slowly turn the valve as it enters the oil seal and continue turning it until the valve is installed all the way.

3. Work the valve back and forth in the valve guide to ensure the lubricant is distributed evenly within the valve guide.

4. Withdraw the valve and apply an additional coat of lubricant.

5. On all models except CVO 110cu.in. models, perform the following:

   a. Reinstall the valve into the valve guide, and push the valve (A, **Figure 94**) all the way into the cylinder head until it bottoms.

   CAUTION
   The valve seal will be torn as it passes the valve stem keeper groove if the plastic capsule is not installed. The capsule is included in the top end gasket set.

   b. Hold the valve in place and install the plastic capsule (B, **Figure 98**) onto the end of the valve stem. Apply a light coat of clean engine oil to the outer surface of the capsule.

   c. Hold the valve in place, and slowly slide the valve seal/spring seat assembly (**Figure 95**) onto the valve stem. Push the assembly down until it bottoms on the machined surface of the cylinder head (**Figure 96**).

   d. Remove the plastic capsule from the valve stem, but keep it. The capsule will be used on the remaining valves.

6. On CVO110 cu.in models, perform the following:

   a. Install the spring seat over the valve guide and into the cylinder head.

   b. Reinstall the valve into the valve guide, but do not push the valve past the top of the valve guide.

   c. Use isopropyl alcohol, or its equivalent, to thoroughly clean all grease from the outside surface of the valve guide.

   CAUTION
   Do not apply the retaining compound to the top or inside of the valve guide.

   d. Carefully apply Loctite RC620 (green) to the valve seal seating surface on the outside of the valve guide.

   e. Push the valve (A, **Figure 94**) all the way into the cylinder head until it bottoms.

   CAUTION
   The valve seal will be torn as it passes the valve stem keeper groove if the plastic capsule is not installed. The capsule is included in the top end gasket set.

   f. Hold the valve in place and install the plastic capsule (B, **Figure 94**) onto the end of the valve stem. Apply a light coat of clean engine oil to the outer surface of the capsule.

   g. Slide a new valve seal (**Figure 97**) over the capsule and down the valve stem until the seal contacts the valve guide.

h. Remove the plastic capsule from the valve stem, but keep it. The capsule will be used on the remaining valves.

i. Slide the valve guide seal installer (**Figure 98**) over the seal. Use a small hammer to gently tap the seal installer until the valve seal lightly bottoms on the valve guide.

7A On all CVO 110cu.in, position the valve spring (**Figure 99**) with the tapered end going on last and install the valve spring.

7B. On CVO 110cu.in., perform the following:

a. Install the inner valve spring (**Figure 100**) and make sure it is properly seated on the lower spring retainer.

b. Install the outer valve spring (**Figure 101**) and make sure it is properly seated on the lower spring retainer. The larger diameter flange must separate the inner and outer springs.

c. Install the spring retainer (**Figure 102**).

CAUTION
To avoid loss of spring tension, compress the springs just enough to install the valve keepers.

8. Compress the valve spring with a valve spring compressor (**Figure 91**) and install the valve keepers (**Figure 103**).

9. Make sure both keepers are seated around the valve stem prior to releasing the compressor.

10. Slowly release tension from the compressor and remove it. After removing the compressor, inspect the valve keepers to make sure they are properly seated (**Figure 104**). Tap the end of the valve stem with a *soft-faced* hammer to ensure the keepers are properly seated.

11. Repeat the procedure to install the remaining valves.

12. On models so equippedd the ACR solenoid as follows:

a. Make sure the copper washer is in place on the ACR solenoid.

b. Apply three dots of Loctite 246 Threadlocker Medium Strength/High Temperature to the lower 1/3 of the solenoid threads. Evenly space the dots of threadlock around the circumference of the threads (**Figure 105**).

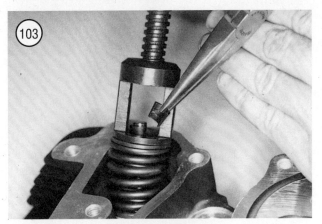

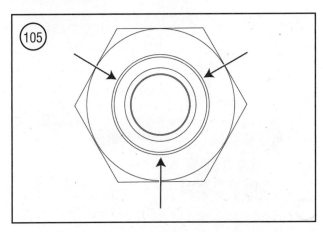

4

c. Install the ACR solenoid into the cylinder head. Using the solenoid socket, tighten the ACR solenoid to 11-15 ft.-lb. (14.9-20.3 N•m).

13. Install the cylinder head as described in this chapter.

Valve Inspection

During inspection, compare any measurements taken to the specifications listed in **Table 2** or **Table 3**. Replace any part that is worn, damaged or out of specification.

1. Clean valves in solvent. Do not gouge or damage the valve seating surface.

2. Inspect the valve face. Minor roughness and pitting (**Figure 106**) can be removed by lapping the valve as described in this section. Excessive unevenness of the valve contact surface indicates the valve is not serviceable.

3. Inspect the valve stem for wear and roughness. Then, measure the valve stem outside diameter (**Figure 107**) with a micrometer.

4. Remove all carbon and varnish from the valve guides with a stiff spiral wire brush before measuring wear.

5. Measure the valve guide inside diameter with a small bore gauge (**Figure 108**) at the top, center and bottom positions. Then, measure the small bore gauge with a micrometer.

6. Determine the valve stem-to-valve guide clearance by subtracting the valve stem outside diameter from the valve guide inside diameter.

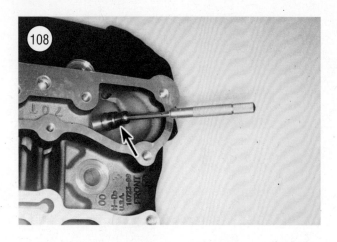

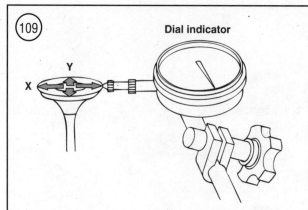

Dial indicator

7. If a small bore gauge is not available, insert each valve into its guide. Attach a dial indicator to the valve stem next to the head (**Figure 109**). Hold the valve slightly off its seat and rock it sideways in both directions 90° to each other. If the valve rocks more than slightly, the guide is probably worn. Take the cylinder head to a dealership or machine shop and have the valve guides measured.

8. Check the valve spring as follows:
   a. Inspect the valve spring(s) (**Figure 110**) for visible damage.
   b. Use a square (**Figure 111**) to visually check the spring for distortion or tilt.
   c. Measure the valve spring free length with a caliper (**Figure 112**).
   d. Repeat the measurements for each valve spring.
   e. Replace the defective spring(s).

9. Check the valve spring retainer and seat for cracks or other damage.

10. Check the valve keepers fit on the valve stem end (**Figure 113**). They should index tightly into the valve stem groove.

11. Inspect the valve seats (**Figure 114**) in the cylinder head. If they are worn or burned, they can be reconditioned as described in this section. Seats and valves in near-perfect condition can be reconditioned by lapping as described in this section.

Valve Guide Replacement

Tools

The following special tools, or their equivalent, are required to replace the valve guides.

1. Cylinder head stand (H-D part No. HD-39782-B).
2. Intake seat adapter (H-D part No. HD-39782-3).
3. Exhaust seat adapter (H-D part No. HD-39782-4).
4. Valve guide driver (all models except CVO: H-D part No. HD-B-45524-1); CVO models: H-D part No. HD-46583).
5. Valve guide installer sleeve (all models except CVO: H-D part No. 45524-2A); CVO models H-D part No. HD-48628).

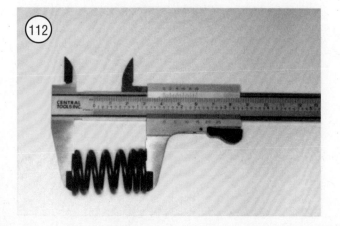

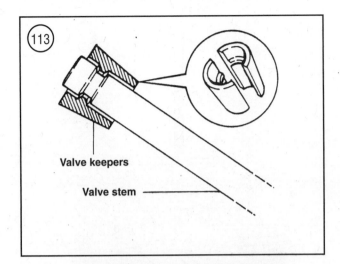

Valve keepers

Valve stem

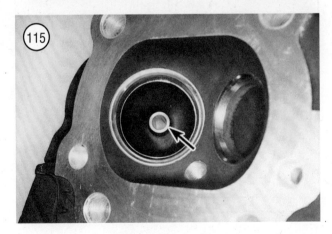

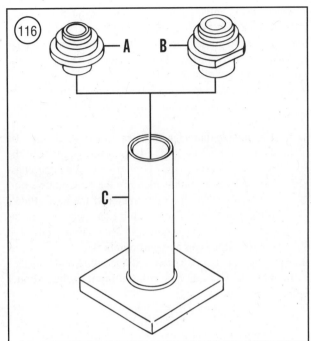

6. Valve guide brush (all models except CVO: H-D part No. HD-34751).

7. Valve guide reamer (all models except CVO: H-D part No. 45523); CVO models H-D part No. HD-39932).

8. Valve guide reamer T-handle (H-D part No. 39847).

9. Valve guide reamer honing lubricant (H-D part No. 39964).

10. Valve guide hone (all models except CVO: H-D part No. B-45525); CVO models: H-D part No. 34723-A).

11. Hydraulic press.

Procedure

CAUTION
The valve guides must be removed and installed using the proper tools to avoid damage to the cylinder head. Use the correct size valve guide removal tool to remove the valve guides or the tool may expand the end of the guide. An expanded guide will widen and damage the guide bore in the cylinder head as it passes through it.

1. Remove the old valve guide (**Figure 115**) as follows:
   a. When removing a valve guide that uses a retaining ring, remove the retaining ring from the top of the cylinder head.
   b. Install the intake (A, **Figure 116**) or exhaust (B) valve seat adapter into the tube at the top of the cylinder head support stand (C).
   c. Set the support stand onto a hydraulic press table.
   d. Install the cylinder head (A, **Figure 117**) onto the support stand (B) *centering* the cylinder head valve seat on the seat adapter.
   e. Insert the valve guide driver (C, **Figure 117**) into the valve guide bore until the driver stops on the valve guide shoulder.
   f. Center the valve guide driver under the press ram. Make sure the driver is perpendicular to the press table.
   g. Support the cylinder head, and then slowly apply ram pressure and drive the valve guide out through the combustion chamber. Discard the old valve guide.
   h. Remove the cylinder head and tools from the press bed.
   i. Repeat the process to remove for the remaining valve guides.
2. Clean the valve guide bores in the cylinder head.

3. Because the valve guide bores in the cylinder head may have been enlarged during removal of the old guides, measure each valve guide bore. Purchase the new valve guides to match their respective bore diameters. Determine the bore diameter as follows:

a. Measure the valve guide bore diameter in the cylinder head with a small bore gauge. Record the bore diameter.

b. The outside diameter of the *new* valve guide must be 0.0020-0.0033 in. (0.051-0.084 mm) larger than the valve guide bore in the cylinder head. When purchasing new valve guides, measure the new guide's outside diameter with a micrometer. If the new guide's outside diameter is not within this specification, install oversize valve guide(s). Refer to a dealership for available sizes and part numbers.

4. Apply a thin coat of Vaseline to the entire outer surface of the new valve guide before installing it in the cylinder head.

> *CAUTION*
> *When installing oversize valve guides, make sure to match each guide to its respective bore in the cylinder head.*

5. Install the *new* valve guide as follows:

a. Install the intake (A, **Figure 116**) or exhaust (B) seat adapter into the tube at the top of the cylinder head support stand (C).

b. Install the support stand onto the hydraulic press table.

c. Install the cylinder head (A, **Figure 118**) onto the support stand (B) *centering* the cylinder head valve seat on the seat adapter.

d. Install the valve guide over its bore in the cylinder head. On guides that use retaining rings, make sure the valve guide retaining ring groove faces out away from the cylinder head.

e. Install the valve guide installer sleeve (C, **Figure 118**) over the valve guide, and insert the tapered end of the valve guide driver (D) into the installer sleeve.

f. Center the valve guide driver under the press ram. Make sure the driver is perpendicular to the press table.

g. Support the cylinder head. Slowly apply ram pressure, and then start to drive the valve guide into the cylinder head receptacle. Stop and back off the press ram to allow the valve guide to center itself.

h. Verify that the support stand (B, **Figure 118**) and valve guide driver (D) are square with the press table.

i. Apply ram pressure and continue to drive the valve guide part way into the cylinder head receptacle. Once again, stop and back off the press ram to allow the valve guide to center itself.

j. Apply ram pressure again and drive the valve guide into the bore until the installer sleeve (C, **Figure 118**) contacts the machined surface of the cylinder head. Remove the valve guide driver and installer sleeve.

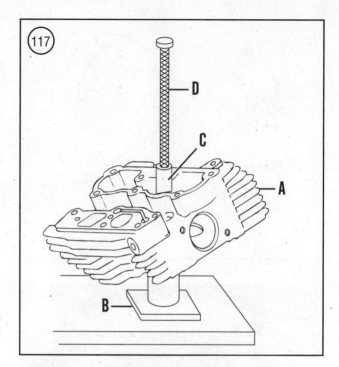

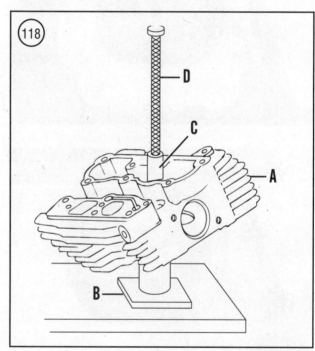

k. Install a *new* retaining ring into the groove of a valve guide that uses a retaining ring. Make sure the retaining ring is completely seated in the valve guide groove.

l. Remove the cylinder head and tools from the press bed.

m. Repeat the process to install the remaining valve guides.

6. Replacement valve guides are sold with a smaller inside diameter than the valve stem. Ream the guide to within 0.0005-0.0001 in (0.013-0.0025 mm) of its finished size as follows:

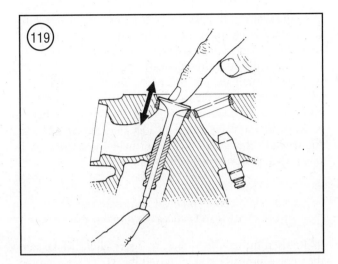

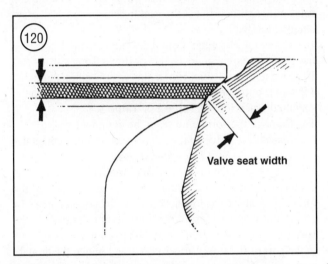

Valve seat width

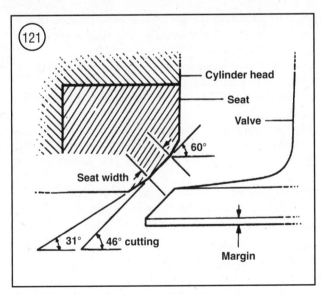

a. Install the valve guide reamer onto the T-handle.
b. Apply a liberal amount of reamer lubricant to the ream bit and to the valve guide bore.
c. Start the reamer straight into the valve guide bore at the top of the cylinder head.

CAUTION
Only apply pressure to the end of the drive socket. If pressure is applied to the T-handle, the bore will be uneven, rough cut and tapered.

d. Apply thumb pressure to the end of the drive socket portion of the T-handle while rotating the T-handle *clockwise*. Only *light* pressure is required. Apply additional lubricant to the reamer and into the valve guide while rotating the reamer.
e. Continue to rotate the reamer until the entire bit has traveled through the valve guide and the shank of the reamer rotates freely.

CAUTION
Never back the reamer out through the valve guide as the guide will be damaged.

f. Remove the T-handle from the reamer. Remove the reamer from the combustion chamber side of the cylinder head.
g. Apply low-pressure compressed air to remove the small shavings from the valve guide bore. Clean the valve guide bore with a valve guide brush.
7. Hone the valve guide as follows:
    a. Install the valve guide hone into a high-speed electric drill.
    b. Lubricate the valve guide bore and hone stones with reamer lubricant–*do not use motor oil*.
    c. Carefully insert the hone stones into the valve guide bore.
    d. Start the drill and move the hone back and forth in the valve guide bore for 10 to 12 complete strokes to obtain a 60° degree crosshatch pattern.
8. Repeat the reaming and honing process for each valve guide.
9. Soak the cylinder head in a container filled with hot, soapy water. Then, clean the valve guides with a valve guide brush or an equivalent bristle brush. *Do not use a steel brush.* Do not use cleaning solvent, kerosene or gasoline as these chemicals will not remove all of the abrasive particles produced during the honing operation. Repeat this step until all of the valve guides are thoroughly cleaned. Then, rinse the cylinder head and valve guides in clear water and dry them with compressed air.
10. After cleaning and drying the valve guides, apply clean engine oil to the guides to prevent rust.
11. Resurface the valve seats as described in *Valve Seat Reconditioning* (this section).

Valve Seat Inspection

1. Remove all carbon residue from each valve seat. Then, clean the cylinder head as described in *Valve Inspection* (this section).
2. Check the valve seats in their original locations with machinist's dye as follows:

a. Thoroughly clean the valve face and valve seat with contact cleaner.

b. Spread a thin layer of machinist's dye evenly on the valve face.

c. Insert the valve into its guide.

d. Support the valve by hand (**Figure 119**) and tap the valve up and down in the cylinder head. Do not rotate the valve or the reading will be false.

e. Remove the valve and examine the impression left by the machinist's dye. The impressions on the valve and the seat should be even around their circumferences and the width (**Figure 120**) should be within the specification in **Table 2** or **Table 3**. If the width is beyond the specification or if the impression is uneven, recondition the valve seats.

3. Closely examine the valve seat in the cylinder head (**Figure 114**). It should be smooth and even with a polished seating surface.

4. If the valve seat is in good condition, install the valve as described in this section.

5. If the valve seat is not correct, recondition the valve seat as described in this section.

Valve Seat Reconditioning

Valve seat reconditioning requires experience and a number of tools. In most cases, it is more practical to have these procedures performed by a machinist.

A valve seat cutter set H-D part No. HD-35758-C), or an equivalent, is required.

Refer to **Figure 121** for valve seat angles.

1. Clean the valve guides as described in *Valve Inspection* (this section).

2. Measure the valve stem protrusion by performing the following:

a. Insert the valve stem into the valve guide from the combustion chamber side of the cylinder head.

b. Use a caliper to measure the distance from the top of the valve stem to the cylinder head's machined surface.

c. If the measured valve stem protrusion exceeds the service limit (**Table 2** or **Table 3**), replace the valve seat or cylinder head as necessary.

3. Carefully rotate and insert the solid pilot into the valve guide. Make sure the pilot is correctly seated.

CAUTION
Valve seat cutting accuracy depends on a correctly sized and installed pilot.

4. Using the proper 46° cutter (intake or exhaust), descale and clean the valve seat with one or two turns.

CAUTION
*Measure the valve seat contact area in the cylinder head (**Figure 121**) after each cut to make sure its size and area are correct. Overgrinding will lower the valves into the cylinder head and off the valve seat far enough that the seat will have to be replaced.*

5. If the seat is still pitted or burned, turn the cutter until the surface is clean. Work slowly and carefully to avoid removing too much material from the valve seat.

6. Remove the pilot from the valve guide.

7. Apply a small amount of valve lapping compound to the valve face and install the valve. Rotate the valve against the valve seat using a valve lapping tool. Remove the valve.

8. Measure the valve seat with a caliper (**Figure 121** and **Figure 121**). Record the measurement to use as a reference point when performing the following steps.

CAUTION
The 31° cutter removes material quickly. Work carefully and check the progress often.

9. Reinsert the solid pilot into the valve guide. Make sure the pilot is properly seated. Install the 31° cutter onto the solid pilot and lightly cut the seat to remove 1/4 of the existing valve seat.

10. Install the 60° cutter onto the solid pilot and lightly cut the seat to remove the lower 1/4 of the existing valve seat.

11. Measure the valve seat width with a caliper. Fit the 46° cutter onto the solid pilot, and cut the valve seat to the specified seat width in **Table 2** or **Table 3**.

12. Remove the solid pilot from the cylinder head.

13. Inspect the valve seat-to-valve face impression as described in *Valve Seat Inspection* (this section).

14. If the contact area is too high or too wide on the valve, cut the seat with the 31° cutter. This will remove part of the top valve seat area to lower or narrow the contact area.

15. If the contact area is too low or too narrow on the valve, cut the seat with the 60° degree cutter. This will remove part of the lower area to raise and widen the contact area.

16. After obtaining the desired valve seat position and angle, use the 46° cutter and *lightly* clean off any burrs caused by the previous cuts.

17. When the contact area is correct, lap the valve as described in this section.

18. Repeat this procedure to recondition the remaining valve seats.

19. Thoroughly clean the cylinder head and all valve components in solvent. Then, wash them with detergent and hot water, and rinse them in cold water. Dry them with compressed air.

20. After cleaning and drying the cylinder head and valve components, apply a light coat of engine oil to all non-aluminum surfaces to prevent rust formation.

Valve Lapping

If valve wear or distortion is not excessive, restore the valve's sealing ability by lapping the valve to the seat.

1. Smear a light coat of fine-grade valve lapping compound on the seating surface of the valve.

2. Insert the valve into the head.

3. Wet the suction cup of the lapping tool, and stick it onto the head of the valve. Lap the valve to the seat by spinning

the tool between both hands while lifting and moving the valve around the seat 1/4-turn at a time.

4. Wipe off the valve and seat frequently to check progress. Lap the valve just enough to achieve a precise seating ring around the valve head.

5. Closely examine the valve seat in the cylinder head. The seat must be smooth and even with a polished seating ring.

6. Thoroughly clean the valves and cylinder head in solvent to remove all lapping compound residue. Compound left on the valves or the cylinder head will cause rapid engine wear.

7. After installing the valves into the cylinder head, test each valve for proper seating by performing the *Leak Test* as described in this section. If solvent leaks past any valve, disassemble the leaking valve and repeat the lapping procedure or recondition the valve seat as described in this section.

Valve Seat Replacement

Valve seat replacement requires considerable experience and equipment. Refer this work to a dealership or machine shop.

CYLINDER

Refer to **Figure 122**.

Removal

1. Remove the cylinder head as described in this chapter.
2. Remove all debris from the cylinder base.
3. Remove the dowels (**Figure 123**) from the top of the cylinder if they are still in place.
4. Turn the crankshaft until the piston is at bottom dead center (BDC).

CAUTION
The front and rear cylinders are identical (same part number). Mark each cylinder so it can be reinstalled in its original position.

5. Pull the cylinder straight up and off the piston and cylinder studs. If necessary, tap around the perimeter of the cylinder with a rubber or plastic mallet.
6. Place clean shop rags (A, **Figure 124**) into the crankcase opening to prevent objects from falling undetected into the crankcase.
7. Remove the O-rings (B, **Figure 124**) from the locating dowels in the crankcase.
8. Remove and discard the O-ring (A, **Figure 125**) from the base of the cylinder.
9. Install a hose (**Figure 126**) over each stud to protect the piston.

CAUTION
After removing the cylinder, be careful when working around the cylinder studs to avoid bending or damaging them. The slightest bend could cause the stud to fail.

10. Repeat the procedure to remove the other cylinder.

Installation

CAUTION
When a cylinder has been bored oversize, the inner lead-in angle (B, Figure 125) at the base of the bore skirt has been eliminated. This lead-in angle is necessary for the piston rings to safely enter the cylinder bore. If necessary, use a cylinder chamfering cone (JIMS part No. 2078) or a hand grinder with a fine stone to make a new lead-in angle. The finished surface must be smooth so it will not catch and damage the piston rings during installation.

1. If removed, install the pistons and rings as described in this chapter.
2. Remove gasket residue and clean the cylinder as described in *Inspection* (this section).
3. Remove the rubber hose (A, **Figure 127**) from each stud.
4. Install a *new* O-ring (**Figure 125**) onto the base of the cylinder. Apply a light coat of clean engine oil to the O-ring.
5. If removed, install the locating dowels (**Figure 128**) into the crankcase.
6. Install a *new* O-ring (B, **Figure 124**) onto each dowel. Apply a light coat of clean engine oil to each O-ring.
7. Turn the crankshaft until the piston is at top dead center (TDC).
8. Lubricate the cylinder bore, piston and piston rings liberally with clean engine oil.
9. Position the top compression ring gap so it is facing the intake port. Then, stagger the remaining piston ring end gaps as shown in **Figure 129**.
10. Compress the piston rings with a ring compressor (B, **Figure 127**).

NOTE
Install the cylinder in its original position as noted during removal.

11. Position the cylinder so the indents in the cooling fins face the right side (front facing forward). Carefully align the cylinder with the studs, and slowly slide the cylinder down (**Figure 130**) the studs until it sits over the top of the piston. Continue sliding the cylinder down past the rings. Remove the ring compressor (A, **Figure 131**) once the piston rings enter the cylinder bore. Remove the shop rag (B, **Figure 131**) from the crankcase opening.
12. Continue to slide the cylinder down until it bottoms out on the crankcase.

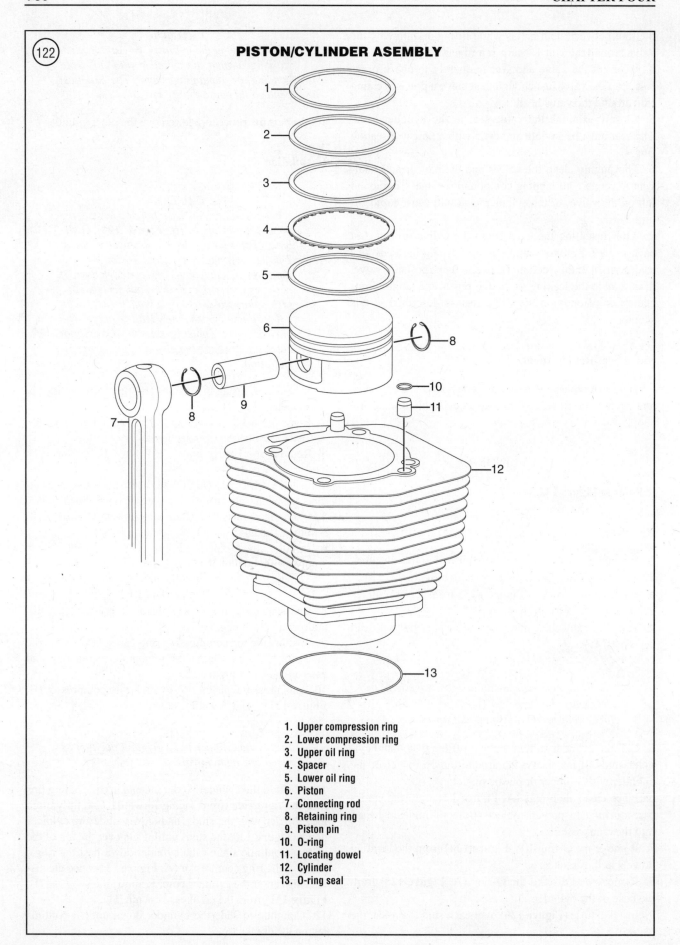

PISTON/CYLINDER ASEMBLY

1. Upper compression ring
2. Lower compression ring
3. Upper oil ring
4. Spacer
5. Lower oil ring
6. Piston
7. Connecting rod
8. Retaining ring
9. Piston pin
10. O-ring
11. Locating dowel
12. Cylinder
13. O-ring seal

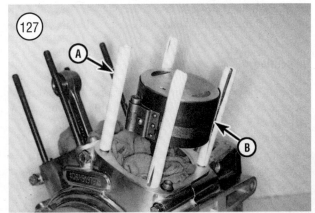

4

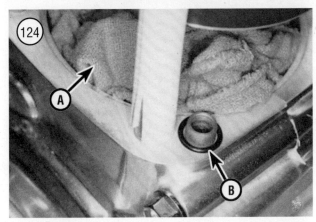

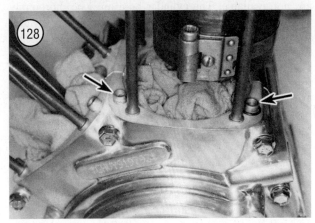

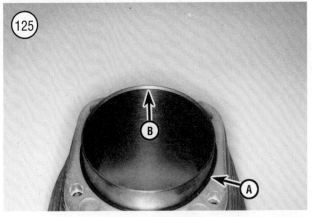

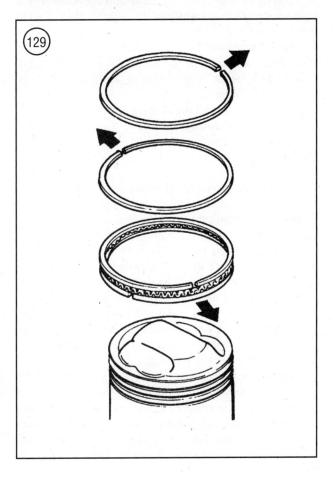

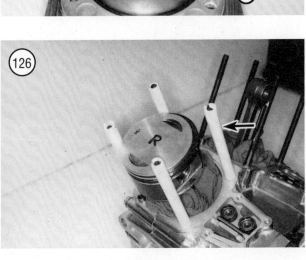

13. Repeat the process to install the other cylinder.

14. Install the cylinder heads as described in this chapter.

Inspection

During inspection, compare all measurements taken to the specifications listed in **Table 2** or **Table 3**. Replace any part that is worn, damaged or out of specification.

To obtain an accurate cylinder bore measurement, the cylinder must be tightened between cylinder torque plates (JIMS part No. 1287). Measurements made without the torque plates will be inaccurate and may vary by as much as 0.001 in. (0.025 mm). Refer this procedure to a shop equipped and experienced with this procedure if the tools are not available. The cylinder bore must be thoroughly clean and at room temperature to obtain accurate measurements. Do not measure the cylinder immediately after it has been honed as it will still be warm. Measurements can vary by as much as 0.002 in. (0.051 mm) if the cylinder block is not at room temperature.

1. Thoroughly clean the outside of the cylinder. Use a stiff brush, soap and water to clean all debris from the cooling fins (**Figure 132**). If necessary, use a piece of wood to scrape away any dirt lodged between the fins. Clogged cooling fins can cause overheating and lead to possible engine damage.

2. Carefully remove all gasket residue from the top and bottom cylinder gasket surfaces.

3. Thoroughly clean the cylinder with solvent, and dry it with compressed air. Lightly oil the cylinder block bore to prevent rust.

4. Check the top and bottom cylinder gasket surfaces for warp with a straightedge and feeler gauge (**Figure 133**). If warp exceeds the service limit in **Table 2** or **Table 3**, replace the cylinder.

5. Check the cylinder bore (**Figure 134**) for scuff marks, scratches or other damage.

6. Install the cylinder torque plates onto the cylinder (**Figure 135**) following the tool manufacturer's instructions.

7. Measure the cylinder bore inside diameter with a bore gauge or inside micrometer at the positions indicated in **Figure 136**. Perform the first measurement 0.500 in. (12.7 mm) below the top of the cylinder (**Figure 137**). Do not measure areas where the rings do not travel.

8. Measure the bore in two axes aligned with the piston pin and at 90° to the pin. If the taper or out-of-round measurements exceed the service limits, bore both cylinders to the next oversize and install oversize pistons and rings. Confirm the accuracy of all measurements and consult with a parts supplier on the availability of replacement parts before having the cylinder serviced.

9. Remove the torque plates.

10. If the cylinders were serviced, wash each cylinder in hot, soapy water to remove the fine grit material left from the boring or honing process. Run a clean white cloth through the cylinder bore. If the cloth shows traces of grit or oil, the bore is not clean. Wash the cylinder until the

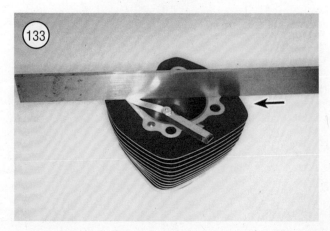

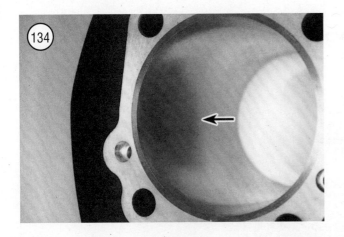

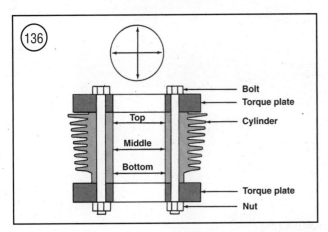

cloth passes through cleanly. When the bore is clean, dry it with compressed air, and then lubricate it with clean engine oil to prevent rust.

> *CAUTION*
> *Only hot, soapy water will completely clean the cylinder bore. Solvent and kerosene cannot wash fine grit out of the cylinder crevices. Abrasive grit left in the cylinder will cause premature engine wear.*

Cylinder Studs and Cylinder Head Bolts Inspection and Cleaning

The cylinder studs and cylinder head bolts must be in good condition and properly cleaned before the cylinder and cylinder heads are installed. Damaged or dirty studs may distort the cylinder head and cause gasket leaks.

> *CAUTION*
> *The cylinder studs, cylinder head bolts and washers consist of hardened material. Do not use a substitute.*

1. Inspect the cylinder head bolts. Replace any that are damaged.
2. Examine the cylinder studs for bending, looseness or damage. Replace studs as described in *Cylinder Stud Replacement* in Chapter Five.
3. Cover both crankcase openings with shop rags to prevent debris from falling into the engine.
4. Remove all carbon residue from the cylinder studs and cylinder head bolts as follows:
   a. Apply solvent to the cylinder stud and mating cylinder head bolt threads, and thread the bolt onto the stud.
   b. Turn the cylinder head bolt back and forth to loosen and remove the carbon residue from the threads. Remove the bolt from the stud. Wipe off the residue with a shop rag moistened in cleaning solvent.
   c. Repeat the process until both thread sets are free of carbon residue.
   d. Spray the cylinder stud and cylinder head bolt with an aerosol parts cleaner and allow them to dry.
   e. Set the clean bolt aside and install it on the same stud when installing the cylinder head.
5. Repeat the carbon removal procedure for each cylinder stud and cylinder head bolt set.

PISTONS AND PISTON RINGS

Refer to **Figure 138**.

Piston Removal

1. Remove the cylinder as described in this chapter.
2. Cover the crankcase with clean shop rags.

PISTON/CYLINDER ASEMBLY

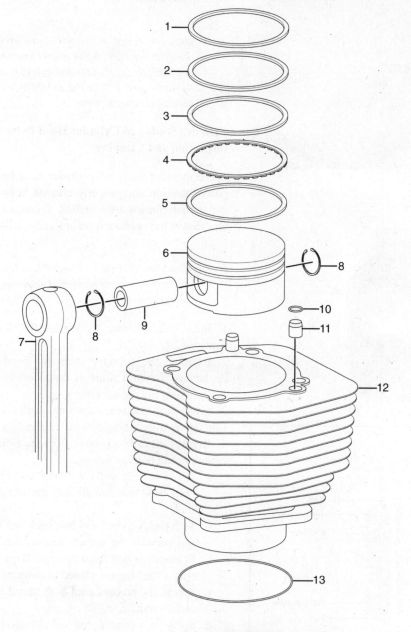

1. Upper compression ring
2. Lower compression ring
3. Upper oil ring
4. Spacer
5. Lower oil ring
6. Piston
7. Connecting rod
8. Retaining ring
9. Piston pin
10. O-ring
11. Locating dowel
12. Cylinder
13. O-ring seal

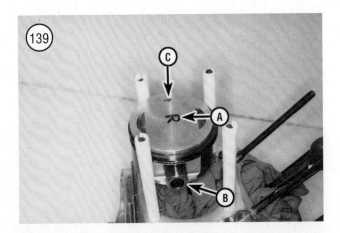

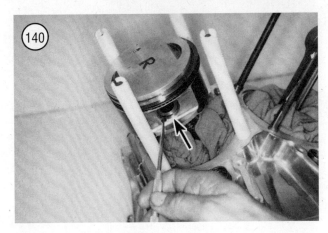

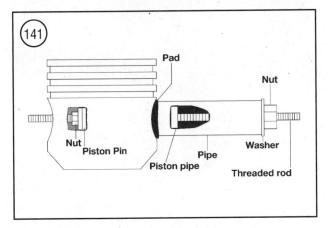

3. Lightly mark the pistons with a F for front or a R (A, **Figure 139**) for rear so they can be reinstalled onto their original connecting rods.

WARNING
The piston pin retaining rings may spring out of the piston during removal. Wear safety glasses when removing them.

4. Use an awl, and pry the piston pin retaining rings (**Figure 140**) out of the piston. Place a thumb over the hole for the piston pin to help keep the retaining rings from flying out during removal.

5. Support the piston and push out the piston pin (B, **Figure 139**). If the piston pin is difficult to remove, use a piston pin removal tool (**Figure 141**).

6. Remove the piston from the connecting rod. Keep the connecting rod propped upright so it does not hit the crankcase.

7. Fit a long piece of hose or some foam pipe insulation over each connecting rod stud so it will not be damaged.

8. If necessary, remove the piston rings as described in this section.

9. Inspect the pistons, piston pins and piston rings as described in this section.

Piston Installation

1. Cover the crankcase openings to avoid dropping a retaining ring into the engine.

2. If removed, install the piston rings as described in this section.

3. Install a *new* piston pin retaining ring into one groove in the piston. Make sure the ring seats in the groove completely.

4. Coat the connecting rod bushing and piston pin with clean engine oil.

5. Slide the piston pin (**Figure 142**) into the piston until its end is flush with the piston pin boss.

6. Place the piston over the connecting rod with the arrow mark (C, **Figure 139**) on the piston facing toward the front of the engine. Seat a used piston onto its original connecting rod. Refer to the marks made on the pistons during removal.

7. Push the piston pin (B, **Figure 139**) through the connecting rod bushing and into the other side of the piston. Push the piston pin in until it bottoms against the retaining ring.

8. Install the other *new* piston pin retaining ring (**Figure 143**) into the piston groove. Make sure it seats properly in the piston groove (**Figure 144**).

9. Repeat the process to install for the remaining piston.

10. Install the cylinders as described in this chapter.

Piston Inspection

During inspection, compare all measurements taken to the specifications listed in **Table 2** or **Table 3**. Replace any part that is worn, damaged or out of specification.

1. If necessary, remove the piston rings as described in this section.

> *CAUTION*
> *Be very careful not to gouge or otherwise damage the piston when removing carbon. Never use a wire brush to clean the piston ring grooves. Do not attempt to remove carbon from the sides of the piston above the top ring or from the cylinder bore near the top. Removal of carbon from these two areas may cause increased oil consumption.*

2. Carefully clean the carbon from the piston crown (**Figure 145**) with a soft scraper. Large carbon accumulations reduce piston cooling and cause detonation and piston damage. Make sure the piston remains properly identified.

3. After cleaning the piston, examine the crown. The crown should show no signs of wear or damage. If the crown appears pecked or spongy-looking, check the spark plug, valves and combustion chamber for aluminum deposits. If aluminum deposits are found, the engine is overheating.

4. Remove all carbon buildup and oil residue from the ring grooves with a broken piston ring. Do not gouge or remove any aluminum from the ring grooves as this will increase side clearance. Replace the piston if necessary.

5. Examine each ring groove for burrs, dented edges or other damage. Pay particular attention to the top compression ring groove as it usually wears more than the others. The oil rings and grooves generally wear less than compression rings and their grooves. If the oil ring groove is worn or if the oil ring assembly is tight and difficult to remove, the piston skirt may have collapsed due to excessive heat and is permanently deformed. Replace the piston.

6. Check the oil control holes (**Figure 147**) in the piston for carbon or oil sludge buildup. Clean the holes with wire and blow them out with compressed air.

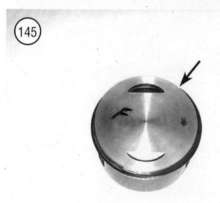

> *CAUTION*
> *The pistons have a special coating on the skirt (**Figure 147**). Do not scrape or use any type of abrasive on this surface as it will be damaged.*

> *NOTE*
> *If the piston skirt is worn or scuffed unevenly from side-to-side, the connecting rod may be bent or twisted.*

7. Check the piston skirt (**Figure 147**) for cracks or other damage. If a piston shows signs of partial seizure such as aluminum build-up on the piston skirt, replace the piston to reduce the possibility of engine noise and further piston seizure.

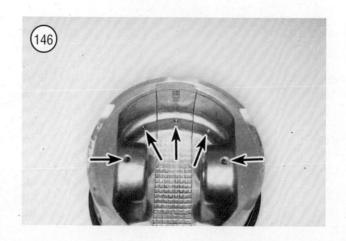

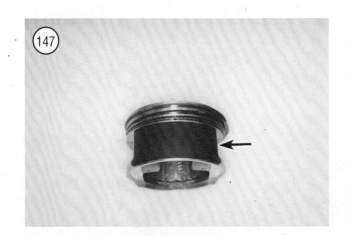

4

8. Check the circlip groove (**Figure 148**) on each side for wear, cracks or other damage. If the grooves are questionable, check the circlip fit by installing a new circlip into each groove, and then attempt to move the circlip from side-to-side. If the circlip has any side play, the groove is worn and the piston must be replaced.

9. Measure piston-to-cylinder clearance as described in *Piston Clearance* (this section).

10. If the piston needs to be replaced, select a new piston as described in *Piston Clearance* (this section). If the piston and cylinder are not damaged and are dimensionally correct, they can be reused. The manufacturer recommends that *new* piston rings be installed every time the piston is removed.

Piston Pin Inspection and Clearance

1. Clean the piston pin in solvent and dry it thoroughly.

2. Inspect the piston pin for chrome flaking or cracks. Replace it if necessary.

3. Oil the piston pin and install it in the connecting rod. Slowly rotate the piston pin and check for radial play (**Figure 149**).

4. Oil the piston pin and install it in the piston (**Figure 150**). Check the piston pin for excessive play.

5. To measure piston pin-to-piston clearance, perform the following:

    a. Measure the piston pin outside diameter with a micrometer (**Figure 151**).

    b. Measure the inside diameter of the piston pin bore (**Figure 152**) with a small bore gauge. Measure the small bore gauge with a micrometer.

    c. Subtract the piston pin outside diameter from the piston pin bore inside diameter to obtain the piston pin clearance.

6. If the piston pin clearance exceeds the service limit (**Table 2** or **Table 3**), replace the piston and/or the piston pin.

Piston Clearance

On all models except CVO, the piston has a small oval-shaped opening (**Figure 153**) on the piston skirt coating.

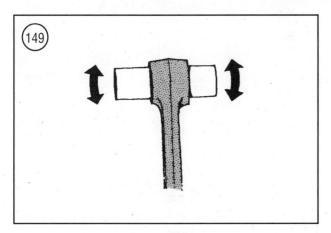

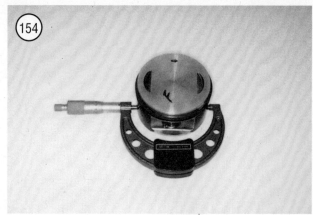

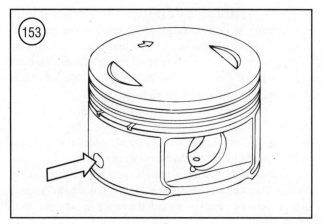

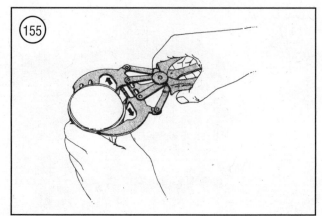

This opening is used to locate the micrometer for an accurate outer diameter measurement. This small oval-shaped opening is too small for the standard flat anvil micrometer to obtain an accurate measurement. Use a 3-4 inch blade or ball anvil style micrometer, or a 4-5 inch micrometer with spherical ball adapters to achieve a correct measurement (**Figure 154**).

1. Make sure the piston skirt (**Figure 147**) and cylinder bore (**Figure 134**) are clean and dry.

2. Measure the cylinder bore inside diameter (**Figure 137**) as described in *Cylinder Inspection* in this chapter.

3A. On all models except CVO models, measure the piston diameter with a micrometer as follows:

    a. Use the previously described special micrometer and correctly position it on the bare aluminum spot on each side of the piston as shown in **Figure 154**.

    b. Measure the piston at this location only (**Figure 153**).

3B. On CVO models, measure the piston diameter with a micrometer as follows:

    a. Set the piston on a flat surface.

    b. Mark the center of each side of the skirt at a point 0.394 in. (10 mm) up from the skirt bottom.

    c. Fit a micrometer onto these marks, and measure the piston diameter.

4. Subtract the piston diameter from the largest bore inside diameter; the difference is piston-to-cylinder clearance. If the clearance exceeds the service limit in **Table 2** or **Table 3**, replace the pistons and have the cylinders bored

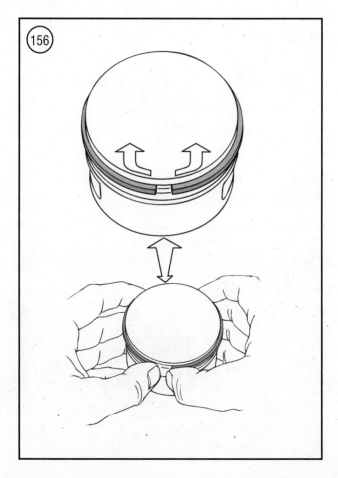

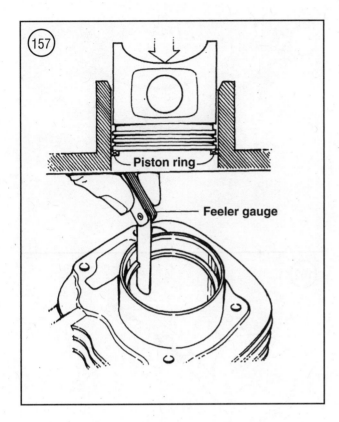

Piston ring

Feeler gauge

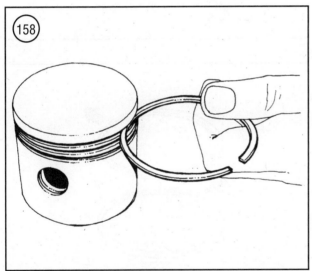

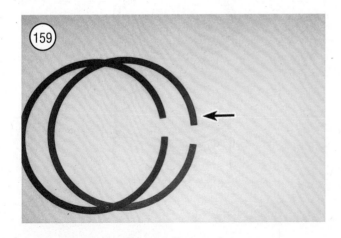

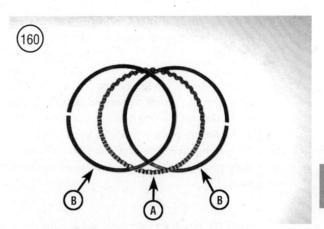

oversize, and then honed. Purchase the new pistons first. Measure their diameter and add the specified clearance to determine the proper cylinder bore diameter.

Piston Ring Removal/Inspection

During inspection, compare any measurements taken to the specifications listed in **Table 2** or **Table 3**. Replace any part that is worn, damaged or out of specification.

1. Remove the piston rings by using a ring expander tool (**Figure 155**) or by spreading them by hand (**Figure 156**)

2. Clean the piston ring grooves as described in *Piston Inspection* (this section).

3. Inspect the ring grooves for burrs, nicks, or broken or cracked lands. Replace the piston if necessary.

4. Insert one piston ring into the top of its cylinder, and tap it down approximately 1/2 in. (12.7 mm), using the piston to square it in the bore. Measure the ring end gap (**Figure 157**) with a feeler gauge and compare it with the specification in **Table 2** or **Table 3**. Replace the piston rings as a set if any one ring end gap measurement is excessive. Repeat this process for each ring.

5. Roll each compression ring around its piston groove as shown in **Figure 158**. The ring should move smoothly with no binding. If a ring binds in its groove, check the groove for damage. Replace the piston if necessary.

Piston Ring Installation

Each piston is equipped with three piston rings: two compression rings and one oil ring assembly. The top compression ring is not marked. The lower compression ring (**Figure 159**) is marked with a dot.

The manufacturer recommends that *new* piston rings be installed every time the piston is removed. Always lightly hone the cylinder before installing new piston rings.

1. Wash the piston in hot, soapy water. Rinse it with clear water, and dry it with compressed air. Make sure the oil control holes in the lower ring groove are clear.

2. Install the oil ring assembly as follows:

   a. The oil ring assembly consists of three rings: a ribbed spacer ring (A, **Figure 160**) and two steel rings (B).

b. Install the spacer ring into the lower ring groove. Butt the spacer ring ends together. Do not overlap the ring ends.

c. Insert one end of the first steel ring into the lower groove so it is below the spacer ring. Then, spiral the other end over the piston crown and into the lower groove. To prevent the ring end from scratching the side of the piston, place a piece of shim stock or a thin, flat feeler gauge between the ring and piston.

d. Repeat the process to install the other steel ring above the spacer ring.

CAUTION
*To install the compression rings, use a ring expander as shown in **Figure 155**. Do not expand the rings any more than necessary to install them.*

3. Install the *new* lower compression ring with the dot (**Figure 161**) facing up.

4. Install the *new* top compression ring with either side facing up.

5. Check the ring side clearance with a feeler gauge as shown in **Figure 162**. Check the side clearance in several spots around the piston. If the clearance is larger than the service limit in **Table 2** or **Table 3**, replace the piston.

6. Stagger the ring gaps around the piston as shown in **Figure 163**.

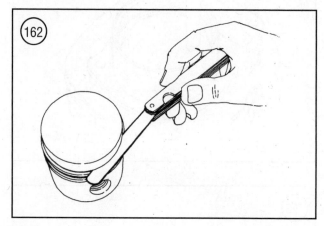

PUSHRODS

Removal/Installation

Remove and install the pushrods as described in *Rocker Arms Pushrods and Valve Lifters* (this chapter).

EXHAUST SYSTEM

Removal

Refer to **Figure 164** or **Figure 165**.

NOTE
If the system joints are corroded or rusty, spray all connections with PB Blaster, WD-40, or an equivalent. Allow the penetrating oil to soak in sufficiently to free the rusted joints.

1. Support the motorcycle on a stand or floor jack. See *Motorcycle Stands* in Chapter Ten.

2. Remove the seat as described in Chapter Fourteen.

3. Remove both saddlebags and right side frame side cover (Chapter Fourteen).

4. Remove both footboards as described in Chapter Fourteen.

5. Remove the engine guard and lower fairing assemblies (Chapter Fourteen), on models so equipped.

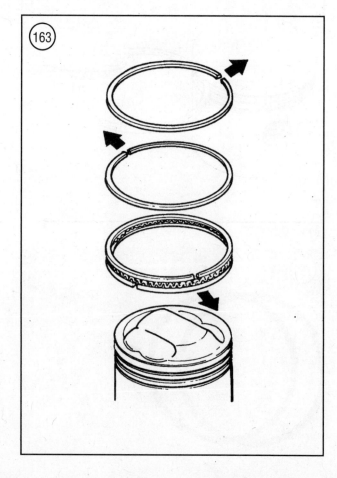

EXHAUST SYSTEM (ALL MODELS EXCEPT FLHX AND FLTRX SERIES)

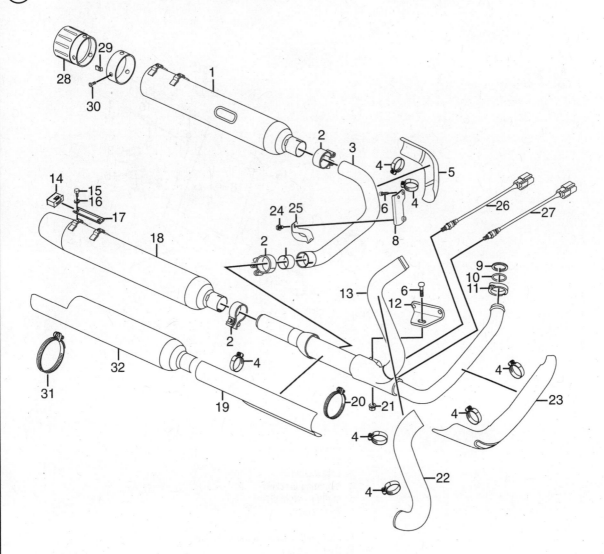

1. Muffler—left side
2. Torca clamp
3. Crossover pipe
4. Clamp—worm drive
5. Heat shield
6. Screw
7. Screw
8. Transmission
9. Gasket
10. Retaining ring
11. Clamp
12. Exhaust bracket
13. Exhaust pipe assembly
14. Rubber mount
15. Bolt
16. Lockwasher
17. Mounting bracket
18. Muffler—right side
19. Heat shield
20. Clamp—worm drive
21. Flange locknut
22. Heat shield
23. Heat shield
24. Bolt
25. Hanger—crossover pipe
26. Rear oxygen sensor
27. Front oxygen sensor
28. End cap
29. Nut clip
30. Retention ring
31. Clamp—worm drive
32. Heat shield

EXHAUST SYSTEM (FLHX AND FLTRX SERIES MODELS)

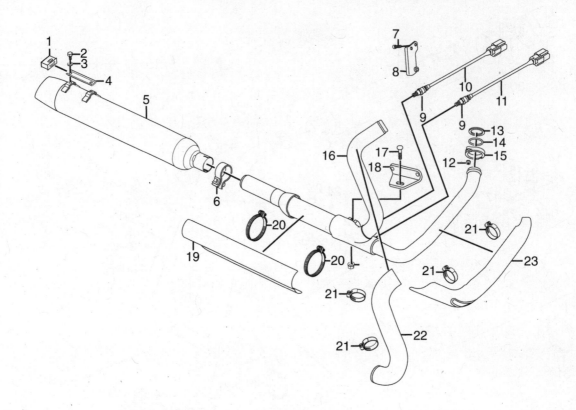

1. Rubber mount
2. Bolt
3. Lockwasher
4. Mounting bracket
5. Muffler—right side
6. Torca clamp
7. Screw
8. Mounting bracket (at transmission)
9. Oxygen sensor
10. Oxygen sensor cable—rear cylinder
11. Oxygen sensor cable—front cylinder
12. Nut
13. Gasket
14. Retaining ring
15. Flange
16. Exhaust pipe assembly
17. Screw
18. Bracket
19. Heat shield
20. Clamp—worm drive
21. Clamp—worm drive
22. Heat shield
23. Heat shield

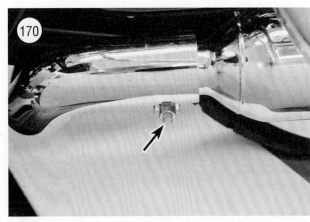

6. On HDI models, disconnect the cable from the valve actuator as described in this chapter.

7. Disconnect the O$_2$ sensor (**Figure 166**) as described in *Oxygen (O$_2$) Sensor Removal/Installation* in Chapter Eight.

8. Identify the heat shields prior to removal as this will aid during installation. They are very similar but all have slight differences. Use the numbers assigned to these parts shown in **Figure 164** or **Figure 165** to aid in identification.

9. Loosen the clamps (A, **Figure 167**) and remove all heat shields (B).

10. Protect the finish, and secure the muffler(s) to the saddlebag mounting bracket with a Bungee cord or rope.

11A. On FLHX and FLTR models, perform the following:

   a. Remove the bolts and lockwashers (**Figure 168**) securing the muffler to the saddlebag support

   b. Twist and pull straight back, and remove the muffler from the exhaust pipe assembly.

11B. On all models except FLHX and FLTR, perform the following:

   a. Loosen the clamp (**Figure 169**) between the rear cylinder exhaust pipe and the crossover pipe.

   b. Loosen the clamp (**Figure 170**) on the crossover pipe to the left side muffler.

   c. Remove the bolts and lockwashers (**Figure 168**) securing the left side muffler to the saddlebag support.

   d. Twist and pull straight back, and remove the left side muffler from the crossover pipe assembly.

   e. Remove the bolts and lockwashers securing the right side muffler to the saddlebag support.

   f. Twist and pull straight back, and remove the right side muffler from the exhaust pipe assembly.

   g. Remove the bolt on the clamp securing the crossover pipe to the mounting bracket. Remove the crossover pipe from the frame.

12. At the front cylinder head, loosen and remove the two flange nuts (A, **Figure 171**) securing the exhaust pipe to the front cylinder head. Slide the exhaust flange (B, **Figure 171**) off the cylinder head studs.

13. At the rear cylinder head, loosen and remove the two flange nuts (A, **Figure 172**) securing the exhaust pipe to

the rear cylinder head. Slide the exhaust flange (B, **Figure 172**) off the cylinder head studs.

14. Remove the flange nut and carriage bolt securing the exhaust pipe assembly to the exhaust bracket.

15. Carefully pull and twist the exhaust pipe assembly off the both cylinder heads and remove from the frame.

16. Remove the snap ring and gasket (**Figure 173**) from each cylinder head exhaust port. Discard the gaskets.

17. Inspect the exhaust system as described in this chapter.

Installation

> *NOTE*
> *To eliminate exhaust leaks. Do not tighten any of the mounting bolts and nuts or the clamp until all of the exhaust components are in place.*

1. Prior to installing the new exhaust port gaskets, scrape the exhaust port surfaces of all carbon residue. Then, wipe clean the ports with a rag.

2. Install a new exhaust gasket (**Figure 174**) into each exhaust port. Make sure the tapered side of the gasket faces out, and secure it in place with the snap ring.

3. Carefully install the exhaust pipe assembly onto the frame and both cylinder head studs.

4. Install the flange nut and carriage bolt securing the exhaust pipe assembly to the exhaust bracket. Finger-tighten the flange nut.

5. Slide the exhaust flanges onto the cylinder head studs.

6. At the front cylinder head, install the two flange nuts (A, **Figure 171**) securing the exhaust pipe to the front cylinder head. Finger-tighten the nuts

7. At the rear cylinder head, install the two flange nuts (A, **Figure 172**) securing the exhaust pipe to the rear cylinder head. Finger-tighten the nuts.

8A. On FLHX and FLTR models, perform the following:
   a. Carefully slide and push straight forward, and install the muffler onto the exhaust pipe assembly.
   b. Install the bolts and lockwashers (**Figure 168**) securing the muffler to the saddlebag support. Finger-tighten the bolts.

8B. On all models except FLHX and FLTR, perform the following:
   a. Install the crossover pipe into the frame and secure it with the bolt on the frame clamp Finger-tighten the bolt.
   b. Carefully twist and push straight forward, and install the right side muffler onto the exhaust pipe assembly.
   c. Install the bolts and lockwashers (**Figure 168**) securing the right side muffler to the saddlebag support. Finger-tighten the bolts.
   d. Carefully slide and push straight forward, and install the left side muffler onto the cross over assembly.
   e. Install the bolts and lockwashers (**Figure 168**) securing the left side muffler to the saddlebag support. Finger-tighten the bolts.

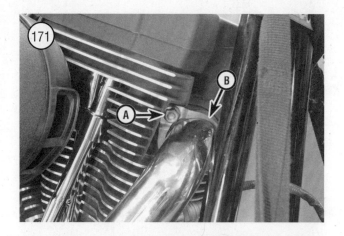

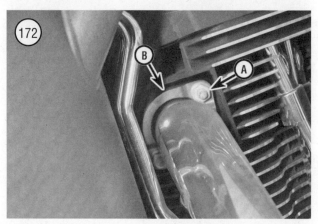

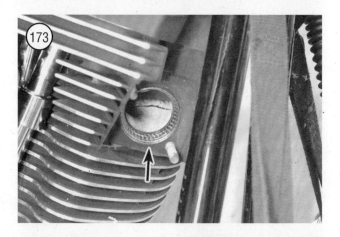

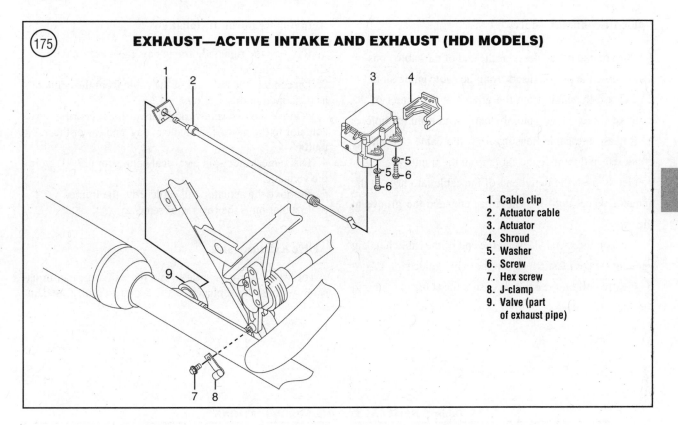

(175)

EXHAUST—ACTIVE INTAKE AND EXHAUST (HDI MODELS)

1. Cable clip
2. Actuator cable
3. Actuator
4. Shroud
5. Washer
6. Screw
7. Hex screw
8. J-clamp
9. Valve (part
   of exhaust pipe)

f. Move the clamp (**Figure 170**) into position on the crossover pipe and to the left side muffler, models so equipped. Finger-tighten the clamp

g. Finger-tighten the clamp (**Figure 169**) securing he rear exhaust pipe and the crossover pipe.

9. Check the entire exhaust system to make sure none of the exhaust components are touching the frame. If necessary, make slight adjustments to avoid any contact with the frame. Verify that no components bind while tightening the fasteners to avoid any unwanted noise or vibration.

10. Check the exhaust system alignment and then tighten the mounting bolts and nuts to the following:

a. Front cylinder head flange nuts. Tighten the upper nut to 9-18 in.lb. (1-2 N•m), and then tighten the lower nut to 110-120 in.-lb. (11.3-13.6 N•m). Re-tighten the upper nut to 120 in.-lb. (13.6 N•m).

b. Rear cylinder head flange nuts. Tighten the upper nut to 9-18 in.lb. (1-2 N•m), and then tighten the lower nut to 110-120 in.-lb. (11.3-13.6 N•m). Re-tighten the upper nut to 120 in.-lb. (13.6 N•m).

c. Tighten the exhaust pipe mounting flange locknut 20-25 ft.-lb. (27.1-33.9 N•m).

d. Tighten the crossover pipe clamp to 25-30 ft.-lb. (33.9-40.7 N•m).

e. Tighten the cross over clamp carriage bolt and nut to 14-18 ft.-lb. (19.0.1-24.4 N•m).

11. Refer to the marks made during removal identifying the heat shields. Use the numbers assigned to these parts shown in **Figure 164** or **Figure 165** to aid in identification.

12. Position the worm drive clamp screws on the outboard side in the most accessible position. Install the heat shields

(B, **Figure 167**) and tighten the clamp screws (A) to 20-40 in.-lb. (2.3-4.5 N•m).

13. Connect the O$_2$ sensor (**Figure 166**) as described in *Oxygen (O$_2$) Sensor Removal/Installation* in Chapter Eight.

14. On HDI models, connect the cable from the valve actuator as described in this chapter.

15. Install the engine guard and lower fairing assemblies (Chapter Fourteen), on models so equipped.

16. Install both footboards as described in Chapter Fourteen.

17. Install the right side frame side cover and both saddlebags (Chapter Fourteen).

18. Install the seat as described in Chapter Fourteen.

Exhaust System Inspection (All Models)

Exhaust system insepection (All Models)

Replace any rusted or damaged exhaust system components.

1. Inspect all pipes for rust or corrosion. Remove all rust from exhaust pipes and muffler mating surfaces.

2. Replace damaged exhaust pipe flanges.

3. Replace worn or damaged heat shield clamps as required.

4. Check the mounting bracket bolts and nuts for tightness. The Torca clamps are not reusable.

ACTIVE EXHAUST

Refer to **Figure 175**.

Cable Disconnect/Connect

1. Push on the metal sleeve at the end of the cable housing and release the plastic insert from the cable guide slot.

2. Release the cable from the groove at the center of the actuator wheel. Gently pull the barrel end from the hole.

3. Release the cable housing from the cable clip on the crankcase and remove the cable from the frame.

4. Gently push the barrel end of the cable into hole in the actuator wheel until the cable has engaged the groove at the center.

5. Push on the metal sleeve at the end of the cable housing and engage the plastic insert in the cable guide slot.

6. Gently pull on the cable to ensure the cable is secure in the cable housing.

Actuator Removal/ Installation

1. Remove the right side frame cover as described in Chapter Fourteen.
2. Disconnect the rear end of the cable from the actuator as described in this section.
3. Remove the two screws and flat washers securing the actuator to the base of the battery tray, and lower the actuator.
4. Disconnect the 5-pin electrical connector (179B) from the actuator.
5. Remove the actuator and cable from the frame.
6. Installation is the reverse of removal.

Active Exhaust valve

The valve is not repairable and the exhaust pipe, or assembly, must be replaced if the valve is faulty or damaged.

Table 1 GENERAL ENGINE SPECIFICATIONS

Item	Specifications
Engine type	4-stroke, 45°, OHV V-twin, Twin Cam 96, 103 and 110
Bore and stroke	
96 models	3.750 4.375 in. (95.25 111.13 mm)
103 models	3.875 4.375 in. (98.435 111.13 mm)
110 models	4.00 4.38 in. (101.60 111.13 mm)
Displacement	
96 models	96 cubic inch (1584 cc)
103 models	103 cubic inch (1690 cc)
110 models	110 cubic inch (1800 cc)
Compression ratio	
96 models	9.2 to 1
103 models	9.6 to 1
110 models	9.15 to 1

Table 2 ENGINE TOP END SPECIFICATIONS (ALL MODELS EXCEPT CVO)

Item	New in. (mm)	Service limit in. (mm)
Breather cover warp	–	0.005 (0.13)
Cylinder head		
Flatness limit	–	0.006 (0.15)
Valve guide fit in head	0.0022-0.0033 (0.051-0.084)	0.002 (0.51)
Valve seat fit in head	0.0030-0.0045 (0.076-0.114)	0.002 (0.0051)
Rocker arm		
Bushing fit in rocker arm	0.0020-0.004 (0.051-0.102)	–
End clearance	0.0030-0.013 (0.08-0.033)	0.025 (0.635)
Shaft-to-rocker arm bushing clearance (loose)		
	0.0005-0.0020 (0.013-0.051)	0.0035 (0.089)
Shaft-to-rocker arm support clearance		
	0.0007-0.0022 (0.018-0.056)	0.0035 (0.089)
Valves		
Valve stem-to-guide clearance		
Intake	0.001-0.003 (0.025-0.076)	0.0038 (0.097)
Exhaust	0.001-0.003 (0.025-0.076)	0.0038 (0.097)

(continued)

Table 2 ENGINE TOP END SPECIFICATIONS (ALL MODELS EXCEPT CVO) (continued)

Item	New in. (mm)	Service limit in. (mm)
Valves (continued)		
Seat width	0.040-0.062 (.102-1.58)	–
Valve stem protrusion from		
cylinder head boss	2.012-2.023 (51.11-51.61)	2.069 (52.55)
Valve springs		
Free length	2.325 (59.1)	–
Spring rate		
Closed	135 lbs. @ 1.850 in (61.279 kg @ 47.0 mm)	–
Open	312 lbs. @ 1.30 in. (141.5 kg @ 33.0 mm)	
Piston-to-cylinder clearance		
96 cu. in.	0.0014-0.0025 (0.036-0.064)	0.003 (0.076)
103 cu. in.	0.0007-0.0012 (0.018-0.030)	0.003 (0.076)
Piston pin-to-connecting		
rod clearance	0.0007-0.0012 (0.018-0.030)	0.002 (0.051)
Piston pin-to-piston		
clearance (fit in piston)	0.0002-0.0005 (0.005-0.013)	0.0008 (0.020)
Piston rings		
96 cu. in.		
Ring end gap		
Top ring	0.010-0.020 (0.254-0.508)	0.034 (0.0864)
Second ring	0.014-0.024 (0.356-0.610)	0.032 (0.813)
Oil control ring end gap	0.010-0.050 (0.254-1.270)	0.030 (0.762)
Ring side clearance		
Top ring	0.0012-0.0037 (0.030-0.094)	0.0032 (0.081)
Second ring	0.0012-0.0037 (0.030-0.094)	0.0032 (0.081)
Oil control ring	0.0031-0.0091 (0.079-0.231)	0.004 (0.102)
103 cu. in.		
Ring end gap		
Top ring	0.012-0.022 (0.305-0.559)	0.030 (0.762)
Second ring	0.015-0.025 (0.381-0.635)	0.034 (0.864)
Oil control ring end gap	0.010-0.050 (0.254-1.270)	0.050 (1.27)
Ring side clearance		
Top ring	0.0012-0.0037 (0.030-0.094)	0.0032 (0.081)
Second ring	0.0012-0.0037 (0.030-0.094)	0.0032 (0.081)
Oil control ring	0.0031-0.0091 (0.079-0.231)	0.004 (0.102)
Cylinder		
Taper	–	0.002 (0.051)
Out of round	–	0.002 (0.051)
Warp		
At top (cylinder head)	–	0.006 (0.152)
At base (crankcase)	–	0.004 (0.102)
Cylinder bore 96 cu. in.		
Standard	3.7500-3.7505 (95.250-95.263)	3.752 (95.301)
Oversize 0.005 in	3.7550-3.755 (95.377-95.390)	3.757 (95.428)
Oversize 0.010 in.	3.7600-3.7605 (95.505-95-517)	3.762 (95.55)
Cylinder bore 103 cu. in.		
Standard	3.8750- 3.8755 (98.425 98.438)	3.877 (98.48)
Oversize 0.005 in	N.A.	3.882 (98.60)
Oversize 0.010 in.	3.8850-3.8855 (98.679)	3.887 (98.73)
Hydraulic lifters		
Lifter-to-bore clearance		
(loose)	0.0009-0.0026 (0.002-0.066)	N.A.

N.A. Specification not available from the manufacturer.

Table 3 ENGINE TOP END SPECIFICATIONS (CVO MODELS)

Item	New in. (mm)	Service limit in. (mm)
Breather cover warp	–	0.005 (0.13)
Cylinder head		
Flatness limit	–	0.006 (0.15)
Valve guide fit in head	0.0020-0.0033 (0.051-0.084)	0.002 (0.51)
	(continued)	

Table 3 ENGINE TOP END SPECIFICATIONS (CVO MODELS) (continued)

Item	New in. (mm)	Service limit in. (mm)
Cylinder head (continued)		
Valve seat fit in head		
Intake	0.0040-0.0055 (0.102-0.140)	0.002 (0.0051)
Exhaust	0.0040-0.0055 (0.102-0.140)	0.004 (0.102)
Rocker arm		0.002 (0.0051)
Bushing fit in rocker arm	0.0020-0.004 (0.051-0.102)	–
End clearance	0.0030-0.013 (0.08-0.033)	0.025 (0.635)
Shaft-to-rocker arm bushing clearance (loose)		
	0.0005-0.0020 (0.013-0.051)	0.0035 (0.089)
Shaft-to-rocker arm support clearance		
	0.0007-0.0022 (0.018-0.056)	0.0035 (0.089)
Valves		
Valve stem-to-guide clearance		
Intake	0.011-0.0029 (0.028-0.074)	0.0038 (0.097)
Exhaust	0.011-0.0029 (0.028-0.074)	0.0038 (0.097)
Seat width	0.034-0.062 (0.86-1.58)	–
Valve stem protrusion from cylinder head boss	1.990-2.024 (50.55-51.41)	–
Valve springs		
Free length	N.A.	–
Spring rate		
Closed	175 lbs @ 1.800 in (79 kg @ 45.7 mm)	–
Open	432 lbs @ 1.250 in.	
	(196 kg @ (31.8 mm)	
Piston-to-cylinder clearance		
103 cu. in.	0.0006-0.0012 (0.015-0.030)	0.002 (0.051)
110 cu. in.	0.0018-0.0027 (0.046-0.069)	0.003 (0.076)
Piston pin-to-connecting rod clearance		
	0.0006-0.0012 (0.015-0.030)	0.002 (0.051)
Piston pin-to-piston clearance (fit in piston)		
103 cu. n.	0.0002-0.0005 (0.005-0.013)	0.0008 (0.020)
110 cu. in.	0.0005-0.0009 (0.013-0.023)	0.0009 (0.023)
Piston rings		
103 cu.in.		
Ring end gap		
Top ring	0.012-0.022 (0.305-0.559)	0.034 (0.0864)
Second ring	0.015-0.025 (0.381-0.635)	0.032 (0.813)
Oil control ring end gap	0.010-0.050 (0.254-1.270)	0.030 (0.762)
Ring side clearance		
Top ring	0.0012-0.0037 (0.030-0.094)	0.0032 (0.081)
Second ring	0.0012-0.0037 (0.030-0.094)	0.0032 (0.081)
Oil control ring	0.0031-0.0091 (0.079-0.231)	0.004 (0.102)
110 cu. in.		
Ring end gap		
Top ring	0.016-0.024 (0.406-0.610)	0.034 (0.0864)
Second ring	0.014-0.022 (0.356-0.559)	0.032 (0.813)
Oil control ring end gap	0.010-0.030 (0.254-0.762)	0.030 (0.762)
Ring side clearance		
Top ring	0.00098-0.0024 (0.025-0.061)	0.0032 (0.081)
Second ring	0.00098-0.0024 (0.025-0.061)	0.0032 (0.081)
Oil control ring	0.002-0.004 (0.051-0.102)	0.004 (0.102)
Cylinder		
Taper	–	0.002 (0.051)
Out of round	–	0.002 (0.051)
Warp		
At top (cylinder head)	–	0.006 (0.152)
At base (crankcase)	–	0.004 (0.102)
Cylinder bore 103 cu. in.		
Standard	3.875 (98.42)	4.002 (101.65)
Oversize 0.005 in	4.007 (101.78)	4.007 (101.78)
Oversize 0.010 in.	4.012 (101.90)	4.012 (101.90)
Cylinder bore 110 cu. in.		
Standard	4.000 (101.6)	4.002 (101.65)
Oversize 0.005 in	4.007 (101.78)	4.007 (101.78)
Oversize 0.010 in.	4.012 (101.90)	4.012 (101.90)

(continued)

Table 3 ENGINE TOP END SPECIFICATIONS (CVO MODELS) (continued)

Item	New in. (mm)	Service limit in. (mm)
Hydraulic lifters Lifter-to-bore clearance (loose)	0.0009-0.0026 (0.002-0.066)	N.A.
N.A. Specification not available from the manufacturer.		

Table 4 PUSHROD AND LIFTER LOCATIONS

Cylinder	Lifter bore	Cylinder head/rocker housing
Front		
Intake	Inside	Rear
Exhaust	Outside	Front
Rear		
Intake	Inside	Front
Exhaust	Outside	Rear

Table 5 ENGINE TOP END AND EXHAUST TORQUE SPECIFICATIONS

Item	ft.-lb.	in.-lb.	N•m
Automatic compression release (ARC) solenoid	11-15	–	14.9-20.3
Breather assembly bolt	–	120-156	13.6-17.6
Cylinder head bolts			
Initial	–	120-144	13.6-16.3
Final	15-17	–	20.3-23.0
Cylinder head bracket bolts	30-35	–	41-48
Cylinder stud	10-20	–	13.6-27.1
Cylinder head bolt-cover set screw (CVO models)	–	60-84	6.8-9.5
Exhaust system fasteners			
Bracket tab and stud mounting nut	12-15	–	16.3-20.3
Crossover pipe			
Hanger bolt	14-18	–	19.0-24.4
Clamp	25-30	–	33.9-40.7
Cylinder head flange nuts			
Upper nut			
Preliminary	–	9-18	1-2
Final	–	110-120	12.4-13.6
Lower nut	–	110-120	12.4-13.6
Bracket flange locknut	20-25	–	27.1-33.9
Transmission bracket bolt	–	84-132	9.5-14.9
Saddlebag mounting bracket bolt	–	96-144	10.8-16.3
Oxygen sensor	14	–	19.0
Torca clamp	38-43	–	51.5-58.3
Torca clamp support bracket nut	12-15	–	16.3-20.3
Lifter cover bolts	–	90-120	10.2-13.6
Rocker arm			
Cover bolt	15-18	–	20.3-24.4
Housing bolt	–	120-168	13.6-19.0
Support place bolt	18-22	–	24.4-29.8
Spark plug	12-18	–	16.3-24.4

4

NOTES

CHAPTER FIVE

ENGINE LOWER END

This chapter provides service and overhaul procedures for the lower end, including engine removal and installation.

Specifications are located at the end of the chapter in **Tables 1-3**.

ENGINE REMOVAL/INSTALLATION

Removal

Refer to **Figure 1**.

1. Thoroughly clean all dirt and debris from the engine.
2. Support the motorcycle on a stand or floor jack. See *Motorcycle Stands* in Chapter Ten. Note the following:
   a. The motorcycle has almost a 50/50 weight distribution at the center of the engine location on the frame. Position the jack so the motorcycle will be stable when lifted off the ground. The following procedure is shown with JIMS Center Jack (part No. 904).
   b. Use additional wooden blocks to ensure that the motorcycle remains stable during service.
   c. Tie down the motorcycle.
3. Remove the seat as described in Chapter Fourteen.
4. Remove both saddlebags, frame side covers, the windshield, and both footboards (Chapter Fourteen).
5. Remove the lower fairing assemblies, models so equipped.
6. Remove the engine guards, models so equipped.
7. Remove the fuel tank as described in Chapter Eight.
8. Remove the air filter and backplate (Chapter Eight).
9. Remove the fuel induction module (Chapter Eight).
10. Remove the exhaust system (Chapter Four).
11. Remove the rear brake pedal (Chapter Thirteen).
12. Drain the engine oil and the primary chaincase oil (Chapter Three).
13. Disconnect the following electrical connectors:
   a. Battery negative cable.
   b. Crank position sensor (CKP) mounting bolt (A, **Figure 2**) and remove the sensor (B).
   c. Alternator stator and voltage regulator.
   d. Oil pressure switch (**Figure 3**).
   e. Vehicle speed sensor (VSS) (located under the starter).
   f. Neutral switch (**Figure 4**).
   g. Engine temperature sensor (ETC) (**Figure 5**).
14. Disconnect the connector from the TSM/TSSM/HFSM (A, **Figure 6**).
15. Disconnect the HFSM antenna connector (**Figure 7**), and disconnect the siren connector from the optional security siren or from its receptacle on the left side of the fuse panel.
16. Remove the following as described in Chapter Nine.
   a. Alternator rotor, stator and the voltage regulator.
   b. Starter motor.
   c. Horn assembly.
17. Disconnect the spark plug wires and secure them out of the way to the frame backbone.
18. Cover and protect the cylinder head rocker covers with foam padding or bubble wrap.
19. Remove the primary chain case assembly, including the inner housing, as described in Chapter Six.
20A. On all models except CVO, disconnect the clutch cable from the clutch release mechanism as described in *Clutch Cable Replacement* in Chapter Six. Release the

① **ENGINE MOUNTS AND STABILIZER**

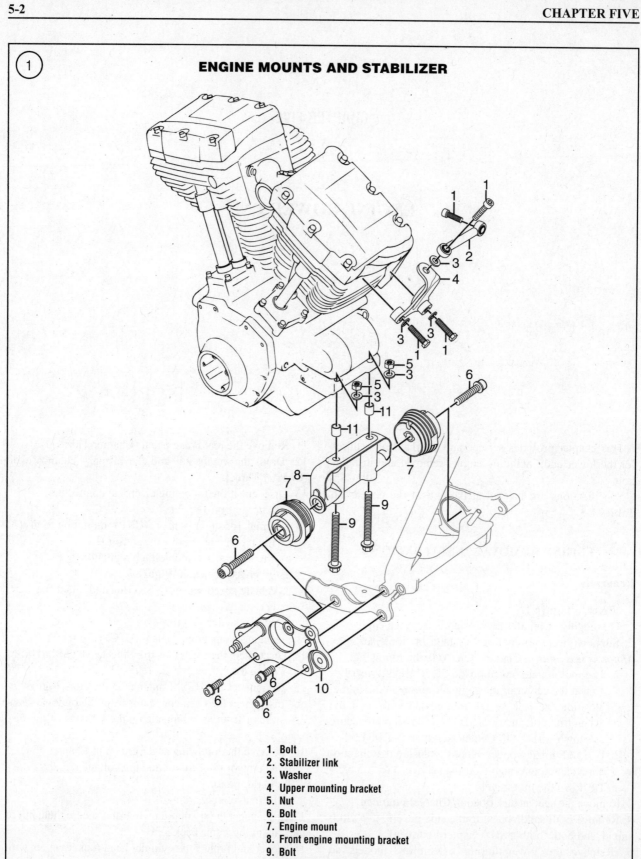

1. Bolt
2. Stabilizer link
3. Washer
4. Upper mounting bracket
5. Nut
6. Bolt
7. Engine mount
8. Front engine mounting bracket
9. Bolt
10. Front engine mount end cap
11. Dowel pin

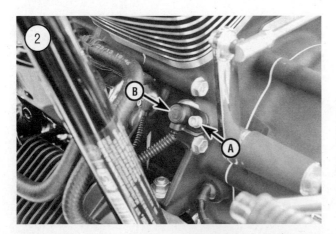

5

cable from any cable ties or holders that secure the cable to the engine or frame.

20B. On CVO models, disconnect the clutch hydraulic hose from the clutch release cover as described in *Clutch Hydraulic Hose Replacement* in Chapter Six. Release the hose from any cable ties or holders that secure the hose to the engine or frame.

21. Remove the oil cooler and hoses as described in this chapter.

22. Wrap protective tape around the frame front down tubes and lower tubes to prevent surface damage during the following steps.

23. Support the engine with a floor jack or JIMS center jack. Apply enough jack pressure to support the engine before removing the engine mounting bolts.

24. Secure the transmission to the frame with a ratchet strap to stabilize the transmission.

25. Remove the short (1/2 in.) upper bolts (**Figure 8**) and the long (9/16 in.) lower bolts (**Figure 9**) along with their washers securing the then engine to the transmission.

26. Remove the Allen bolt (**Figure 10**) securing the stabilizer link to the frame on the left side.

27. Remove the Allen bolt (A, **Figure 11**) securing the stabilizer link to the upper mounting bracket (B) on the right side. Remove the stabilizer link (C, **Figure 11**).

28. Remove the bolts and washers (**Figure 12**) securing the upper mounting bracket to the front cylinder head, and remove the mounting bracket.

29. Remove the front engine mount as follows:

    a. Loosen, *but do not remove* the two long Allen bolts securing each engine mount to the front engine mounting bracket.

    b. Remove the two hex head bolts, washers and nuts securing the front engine mounting bracket to the engine.

    c. On the right side, remove the three short Allen bolts securing the engine cap to the frame. Remove the end cap from the frame and the right side engine mount.

    d. Remove front engine mounting bracket and both engine mounts as an assembly from the frame receptacle on the left side. Watch for the two hollow dowel pins that fall out or may stay with the mounting bracket.

30. Check the engine to make sure all electrical wiring, hoses and other related components have been disconnected from the engine. Make sure nothing will interfere with engine removal.

> *CAUTION*
> *Due to the weight of the engine assembly, at least two people are required to safely remove the engine from the frame.*

31. Move the engine forward enough the clear the transmission case dowels, and remove the engine from the right side of the frame.

32. If available, mount the engine in the twin cam 88B engine base stand (JIMS part No.1138) and engine stand (JIMS part No.1142) or an equivalent stand (**Figure 13**).

33. Clean the front engine mount bolts and washers in solvent. Dry them thoroughly.

34. Replace leaking or damaged fuel lines.

Installation

> *CAUTION*
> *Due to the weight of the engine assembly, a minimum of two people are required to safely install the engine into the frame.*

1. Make sure all electrical wires, hoses and other related components are out of the way and will not interfere with engine installation.

2. Correctly position a floor jack, or JIMS center jack, and piece of wood under the frame to support the engine when it is set into the frame.

3. Cover and protect the cylinder head rocker covers with foam padding or bubble wrap.

4. Secure the transmission to the frame ratchet strap, if removed.

5. Remove the engine from the engine stand and base stand, if used.

6. If removed, install the two lower locating dowels (**Figure 14**) into the transmission case.

7. Thoroughly clean the gasket mating surface of the transmission case and crankcase.

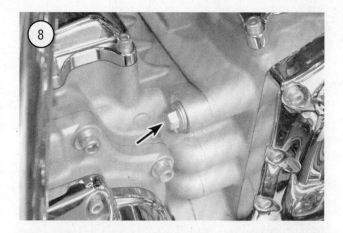

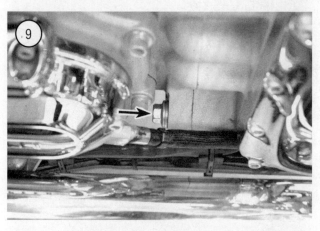

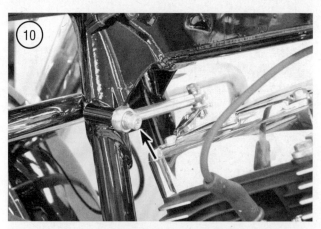

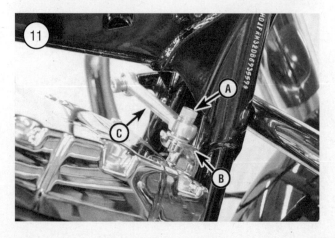

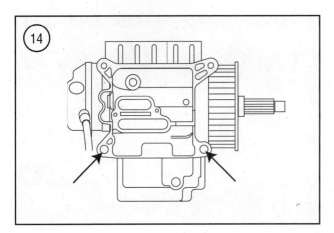

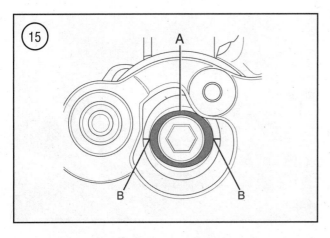

8. Apply a light coat of gasket sealer to the transmission side of the new gasket.

9. Position the gasket with the alignment pins facing the transmission and install it onto the transmission case. Press the gasket into place until the alignment pin shave seated into the transmission case receptacles.

10. Correctly position the floor jack or enter jack to accept the engine as it is moved into position.

11. Install the engine from the right side of the frame, and place it on the piece of wood and floor jack. Apply enough jack pressure to support the engine before installing the engine mounting bolts.

12. Correctly position the engine. Make sure the engine engages the dowels in the transmission case, and align the engine through-bolt holes with those in the frame.

13. Install the short (1/2 in.) upper bolts (**Figure 8**) and the long (9/16 in.) lower bolts (**Figure 9**) along with their washers securing the then engine to the transmission.

14. Tighten the engine-to-transmission bolts as follows:
   a. Initially tighten the bolts using a crisscross pattern to 15 ft.-lb. (20.3 N•m).
   b. Tighten the bolts to the final torque using a crisscross pattern to 34-39 ft.-lb. (46.1-52.9 N•m).

15. Install the two hollow dowel pins into the receptacles in the front mounting bracket.

16. Install the engine front mounting bracket and both engine mounts as an assembly from the right side. Index it into the frame receptacle on the left side.

17. On the right side, thread the three short Allen bolts securing the end cap to the frame. Do not tighten the bolts at this time.

18. Install the two hex head bolts through the mounting bracket, two hollow dowel pins and through the holes in the crankcase. Hold the mounting bracket in place.

19. Apply threadlocking compound (Loctite Threadlock 243 blue, or equivalent) to the nut threads. Install the nuts and washers onto the two hex head bolts. Tighten the nuts finger-tight at this time.

20. Verify that the rubber snubber (A, **Figure 15**) of each engine front mount is centered fore and aft with (B) and are approximately equal.

21. Tighten the two hex head bolts to Verify that the rubber snubbers (A, **Figure 15**) are still centered; adjust if necessary.

22. On the right side, tighten the engine cap short Allen bolts to 42-48 ft.-lb. (56.9-65.0 N•m).

23. Install the upper mounting bracket onto the front cylinder head. Install the bolts and washers (**Figure 12**) and tighten to 30-35 ft.-lb. (41-48 N•m).

24. Install the stabilizer link (C, **Figure 11**) onto the frame upper mounting bracket (B). Install the Allen bolt and tighten to 18-22 ft.-lb. (24.4-29.8 N•m).

25. Move the stabilizer link into position and install the Allen bolt (**Figure 10**) securing the stabilizer link to the frame on the left side. Tighten both Allen bolts to18-22 ft.-lb. (24.4-29.8 N•m).

26. Remove the floor jack or JIMS center jack from under the crankcase.

27. Remove the protective padding from the cylinder head rocker covers and frame.

28A. On all models except CVO, connect the clutch cable to the clutch release cover as described in *Clutch Cable Replacement* in Chapter Six. Route the cable as noted during removal, and secure it to the same locations on the engine and frame.

28B. On CVO models, connect the clutch hydraulic hose to the clutch release cover as described in *Clutch Hydraulic Hose Replacement* in Chapter Six. Route the hose as noted during removal, and secure it to the same locations on the engine and frame.

29. Install the primary chain case assembly, including the inner housing, as described in Chapter Six.

30. Connect the spark plug wires.

31. Install the following as described in Chapter Nine.

a. Alternator rotor, stator and the voltage regulator.

b. Starter motor.

c. Horn assembly.

32. Connect the HFSM antenna connector (**Figure 7**), and connect the siren connector onto the optional security siren or onto its receptacle on the left side of the fuse panel.

33. Connect the connector onto the TSM/TSSM/HFSM (A, **Figure 6**).

34. Connect the following electrical connectors:

    a. Battery negative cable.

    b. Install the crank position sensor and (A, **Figure 2**). Tighten the bolt securely.

    c. Alternator stator and voltage regulator.

    d. Oil pressure switch (**Figure 3**).

    e. Vehicle speed sensor (VSS) (located under the starter).

    f. Neutral switch (**Figure 4**).

    g. Engine temperature sensor (ETC) (**Figure 5**).

35. Refill the engine oil and the primary chaincase oil (Chapter Three).

36. Install the rear brake pedal (Chapter Thirteen).

37. Install the exhaust system (Chapter Eight).

38. Install the fuel induction module (Chapter Eight).

39. Install the air filter backplate and air filter (Chapter Eight).

40. Install the fuel tank (Chapter Eight).

41. Install the engine guards, models so equipped.

42. Install the lower fairing assemblies, models so equipped.

43. Install both frame side covers, both saddlebags, the windshield, and both footboards (Chapter Fourteen).

44. Connect the battery negative cable (Chapter Nine).

45. Install the seat as described in Chapter Fourteen.

46. Start the engine and check for leaks

Cleaning and Inspection

1. Remove any corrosion from the engine mount bolts with a wire wheel.

2. Clean and dry the engine mount bolts.

3. Clean and inspect the engine mounting bolt threads and the threads in the frame for damage.

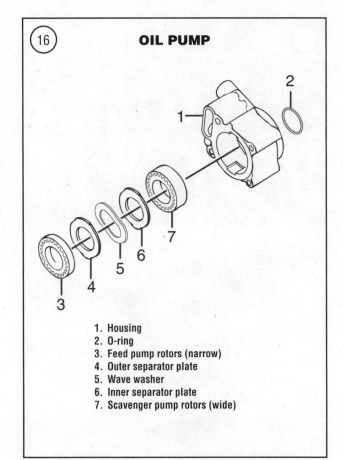

OIL PUMP

1. Housing
2. O-ring
3. Feed pump rotors (narrow)
4. Outer separator plate
5. Wave washer
6. Inner separator plate
7. Scavenger pump rotors (wide)

4. Replace damaged fasteners.

5. Inspect the jiffy stand bracket for cracks and fractures.

6. Check the wire harness routing in the frame. Check the harness cover and wires for chafing or other damage. Replace harness cable guides and clips as required.

7. Clean the electrical connectors with contact cleaner.

8. On CVO models, check the clutch hydraulic line for kinks or damage. Check the fasteners for damage.

OIL PUMP

The oil pump is located on the right side of the crankcase under the camshaft support plate. The oil pump consists of two sections: a feed pump (narrow rotors) which supplies oil under pressure to the engine components and a scavenger pump (wide rotors) which returns the oil from the engine to the oil pan in the base of the transmission case. The oil travels directly from the engine to the transmission case via oil flow channels within both components.

Disassembly/Removal

The oil pump can be removed with the engine in the frame. Refer to **Figure 16**.

1. Drain the engine oil as described in Chapter Three.

2. Remove the camshaft support plate assembly as described in this chapter.

3. Remove the feed pump outer (**Figure 17**) and inner (**Figure 18**) rotors.

4. Remove the outer separator plate (A, **Figure 19**), wave washer (**Figure 20**) and the inner separator plate (A, **Figure 21**).

5. Remove the scavenger pump outer (**Figure 22**) and inner (**Figure 23**) rotors.

6. Carefully pull the oil pump body (**Figure 24**) straight off the crankshaft.

7. Remove the O-ring (A, **Figure 25**) from the backside of the oil pump housing.

Assembly/Installation

NOTE
*Position both inner and outer rotor sets with the punch marks (**Figure 26**, typical) facing out. If the rotor set is not marked, position the rotors in either orientation.*

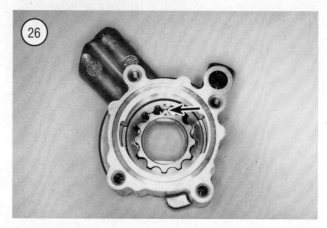

1. Install a *new* O-ring (A, **Figure 25**) onto the backside of the oil pump. Apply clean engine oil to the O-ring.
2. Carefully push the oil pump body (**Figure 24**) straight onto the crankshaft. Align the O-ring and fitting to the crankcase fitting (B, **Figure 25**). Push it on until it bottoms. Make sure the O-ring seats correctly in the crankcase fitting.
3. Align the flat on the scavenger inner rotor with the flat on the crankshaft, and install the inner rotor (**Figure 23**).
4. Install the scavenger outer rotor (**Figure 22**) into the oil pump. Push it on until it is meshed with the inner rotor and the oil pump housing.
5. Align the tangs on the inner separator plate with the oil pump grooves (B, **Figure 21**), and install the inner separator plate (A).
6. Install the wave washer (**Figure 20**).
7. Align the tangs on the outer separator plate with the oil pump grooves (B, **Figure 19**), and install the outer separator plate (A).
8. Align the flat on the feed pump inner rotor with the flat on the crankshaft and install the inner rotor (**Figure 18**).
9. Install the feed pump outer rotor (**Figure 17**) into the oil pump housing. Push in on the outer rotor until it is meshed with the inner rotor and the oil pump housing.
10. Install the camshaft support plate assembly as described in this chapter.
11. Refill the engine oil as described in Chapter Three.

Inspection

1. Clean all parts thoroughly in solvent and place them on a clean, lint-free cloth (**Figure 27**).
2. Inspect both sets of inner and outer rotors (**Figure 28**) for scratches and abrasion.

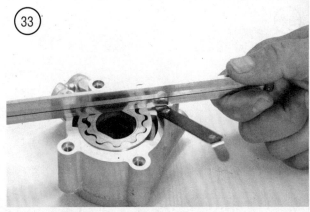

5

3. Inspect the oil pump housing (**Figure 29**) for scratches caused by the rotors.

4. Inspect the interior passageways of the oil pump housing. Make sure all oil sludge and debris are removed. Blow low-pressure compressed air through all passages in the pump housing.

5. Install an inner rotor into its outer rotor. Use a flat feeler gauge to measure the clearance (**Figure 30**) between the tips of the inner and outer rotors. Replace the rotors as a set if the clearance exceeds the service limit (**Table 1**). Also measure the other set of rotors.

6. Measure the thickness of the inner (**Figure 31**) and outer (**Figure 32**) rotors. Compare the two measurements. If the difference exceeds 0.001 in. (0.025 mm), replace the rotors as a complete set. Also measure the other set of rotors.

7. Perform the following to check the feed rotor height:

   a. Assemble the oil pump (**Figure 16**).

   b. Set the pump on the bench with the feed rotors facing up.

   c. Place a straightedge across the feed rotors. Use a feeler gauge to measure the distance from the pump housing to the bottom of the straightedge (**Figure 33**).

   d. If this measurement is less than the service limit (**Table 1**), replace the wave washer.

   e. Assemble the pump with the new wave washer, and measure the feed rotor height. If it is still out of specification, replace the pump.

OIL COOLER, COVER AND ADAPTER (103 AND 110 CU. IN. ENGINES)

The oil cooler and mount are located at the front of the engine and can be removed with the engine in the frame.

NOTE
The original equipment (OE) hose clamps at the oil cooler will be cut and destroyed when they are removed. The same new OE clamps may be installed or a quality screw-type hose clamp can be used. The OE hose clamps must be installed using JIMS hose clamp pliers (part No. 1171), or H-D (part No. HD-97087-65B).

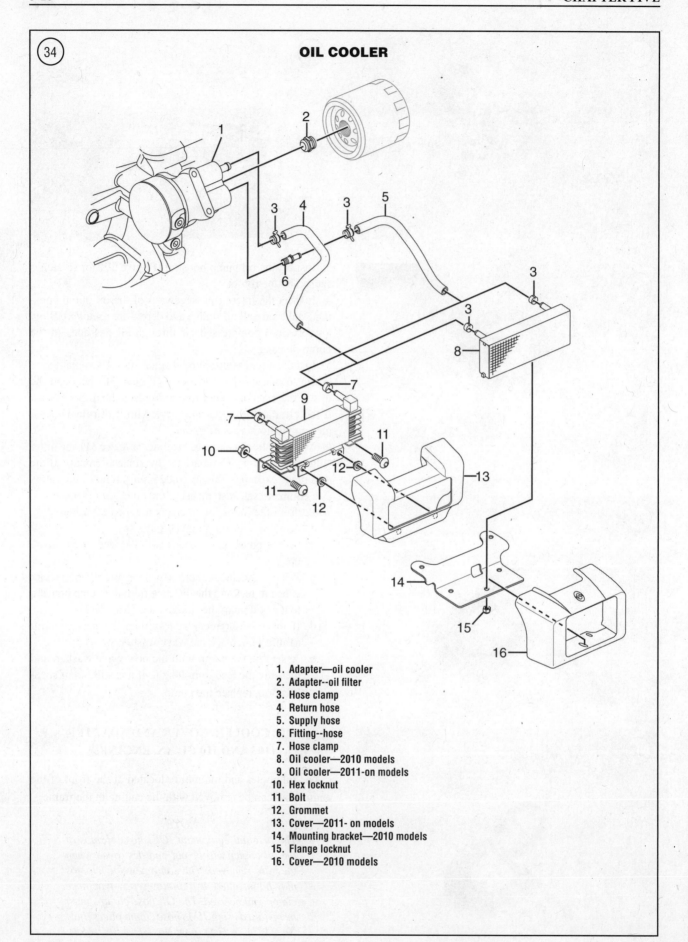

OIL COOLER

1. Adapter—oil cooler
2. Adapter--oil filter
3. Hose clamp
4. Return hose
5. Supply hose
6. Fitting--hose
7. Hose clamp
8. Oil cooler—2010 models
9. Oil cooler—2011-on models
10. Hex locknut
11. Bolt
12. Grommet
13. Cover—2011- on models
14. Mounting bracket—2010 models
15. Flange locknut
16. Cover—2010 models

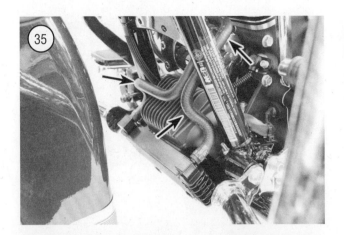

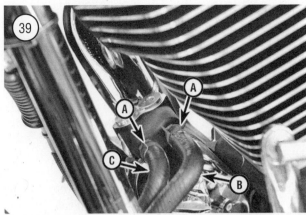

5

The hose clamps at the oil cooler adapter are reusable.

Oil Cooler and Cover
Removal/Installation

Refer to **Figure 34**.
1. Place the motorcycle on level ground.
2. If the motorcycle has recently been ridden, allow the engine to cool to room temperature as the oil cooler will be hot.
3. Remove the left side lower fairing assemblies, models so equipped (Chapter Fourteen).
4. Place a drain pan under the oil cooler assembly.
5. Label the hoses to their respective fittings on the oil cooler and adapter. Always use OE hoses as they are formed to the correct location (**Figure 35**).
6A. On 2010 models, remove the locknuts securing the oil cooler and cover to the mounting bracket.
6B. On 2011-on models, pull out on the bottom of the cover (**Figure 36**) and disengage the pins, then pull up and remove the cover.

NOTE
If the oil hoses are going to be replaced, cut the hose clamps at the oil cooler while the oil cooler is still installed in the frame as it provides a good holding fixture.

7. Use the previously described hose clamp pliers, or side cutting pliers, and cut the hose clamp (A, **Figure 37**) on the supply hose (B, **Figure 37**) and the hose clamp (A, **Figure 38**) on the return hose (B, **Figure 38**) at the oil cooler.
8. At the oil cooler adapter, release and slide the reusable clamps (A, **Figure 39**) down onto both oil hoses.
9. Place several shop cloths under the oil cooler adapter to catch any oil.
10. Disconnect the return hose (B, **Figure 39**) and supply hose (C) from the oil cooler adapter.
11. On 2011-on models, remove the screw (A, **Figure 40**) on each side securing the oil cooler (B) to the frame.
12. Disconnect both hoses from the fitting on the oil cooler adapter and remove the oil cooler and hoses from the

frame. Plug the ends of the hoses and adapter fittings to prevent the entry of debris.

13. Drain residual oil from the oil cooler and hoses.

14. Remove the shop cloths from under the oil cooler adapter and dispose of properly. Clean all spilled oil from the crankcase and voltage regulator area.

15. On 2010 models, if replacement of the oil cooler mounting bracket is necessary, after first remove the voltage regulator (Chapter Nine).

16. Install by reversing these removal steps. Note the following:

    a. Install new hose clamps securing the oil hoses to the oil cooler fittings. Use hose clamp pliers to crimp the new hose clamps in place if using the OE style clamps.

    b. Install the reusable clamps (A, **Figure 39**) onto both oil hoses prior to installing the assembly into the frame area. Position the clamps facing UP.

    c. On 2010 models, tighten the locknuts securing the oil cooler to the mounting bracket to 70-100 in.-lb. (7.9-11.3 N•m).

    d. Check the oil level and add additional to the correct the level (Chapter Three).

    e. Start the engine and check for oil leaks.

Oil Cooler Adapter
Removal/Inspection/Installation

Refer to **Figure 41**.

1. Remove the oil filter as described in Chapter Three.

2. Remove the hoses from the oil cooler adapter as described in this section.

3. Unscrew and remove the oil filter adapter from the crankcase.

4. Remove the oil cooler adapter and gasket from the crankcase.

5. Inspect the gasket, and replace if damaged or there is evidence of oil leaks.

6. Thoroughly clean the oil cooler adapter in solvent and dry with compressed air, especially through the oil hose fitting ports.

7. Clean off all gasket residue from the gasket surface on the oil cooler adapter and crankcase.

8. Install a *new* gasket onto the oil cooler adapter, if necessary.

9. Align the positioning bosses on the oil cooler adapter to those on the crankcase mounting surface, and install the oil cooler adapter and gasket onto the crankcase. Make sure it is positioned correctly; readjust if necessary.

10. Apply Loctite Threadlocker 246 (red) to the threads of the oil filter adapter prior to installation.

11. Make sure the oil cooler adapter is positioned correctly and hold it in place.

> *CAUTION*
> *The threaded area of the oil filter adapter is small and easily damaged.*

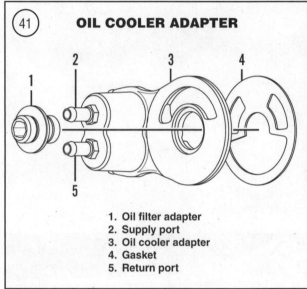

OIL COOLER ADAPTER

1. Oil filter adapter
2. Supply port
3. Oil cooler adapter
4. Gasket
5. Return port

12. Position the oil filter adapter with the Allen bolt receptacle facing out and carefully install the adapter into the crankcase. Tighten the oil filter adapter to 18-22 ft.-lb. (24.4-27.3 N•m).

13. Attach the hoses to the oil cooler adapter as described in this section.

14. Install a *new* oil filter as described in Chapter Three.

15. Check engine oil level and add additional oil to the correct level as described in Chapter Three.

16. Start the engine and check for oil leaks.

CAMSHAFT SUPPORT PLATE

A camshaft locking tool (JIMS part No. 994 or H-D part No. HD-47941), or an equivalent, is needed.

Refer to **Figure 42**.

Removal

1. Remove the exhaust system as described in Chapter Four.

2. Drain the engine oil as described in Chapter Three.

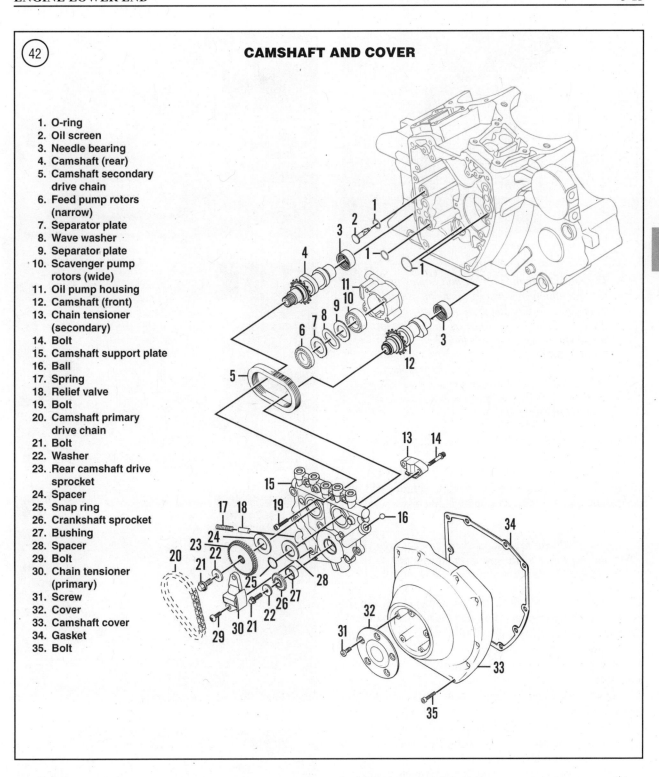

CAMSHAFT AND COVER

1. O-ring
2. Oil screen
3. Needle bearing
4. Camshaft (rear)
5. Camshaft secondary drive chain
6. Feed pump rotors (narrow)
7. Separator plate
8. Wave washer
9. Separator plate
10. Scavenger pump rotors (wide)
11. Oil pump housing
12. Camshaft (front)
13. Chain tensioner (secondary)
14. Bolt
15. Camshaft support plate
16. Ball
17. Spring
18. Relief valve
19. Bolt
20. Camshaft primary drive chain
21. Bolt
22. Washer
23. Rear camshaft drive sprocket
24. Spacer
25. Snap ring
26. Crankshaft sprocket
27. Bushing
28. Spacer
29. Bolt
30. Chain tensioner (primary)
31. Screw
32. Cover
33. Camshaft cover
34. Gasket
35. Bolt

3. Remove the rocker arm support plate, pushrods, pushrod covers and valve lifters as described in *Rocker Arms, Pushrods, and Valve Lifters* (Chapter Four).

4. Using a crossing pattern, evenly loosen, and then remove the camshaft cover bolts and their captive washers. Remove the cover (**Figure 43**, typical) and its gasket. Discard the gasket.

5. To ensure the camshaft primary drive chain is reinstalled with its original direction of travel, mark one of the link plates with a permanent marking pen or a scribe.

6. Insert a wire into the hole (A, **Figure 44**) in the primary chain tensioner to keep the tensioner parts assembled.

7. Remove the primary chain tensioner bolts (B, **Figure 44**), and remove the tensioner (C).

8. Install the camshaft locking tool (A, **Figure 45**, typical) so it engages the teeth of the rear camshaft sprocket and the crankshaft sprocket.

9. Loosen the crankshaft sprocket bolt (B, **Figure 45**, typical).

CAUTION
*The rear camshaft sprocket bolt comes from the manufactuer secured with threadlock. Attempt to loosen the bolt with an impact driver or air impact wrench. If this is not successful, evenly heat the bolt head with a propane torch, or high temperature heat gun. Use caution, as excessive heat may damage the tensioner assembly. Do **not** use excessive force to remove the bolt. If necessary, have a dealership remove the bolt.*

10. Loosen the rear camshaft sprocket bolt (C, **Figure 45**, typical).

11. Remove the sprocket locking tool (A, **Figure 45**).

12. Remove camshaft sprocket bolt (C, **Figure 45**) and crankshaft sprocket bolt (B) along with their washers.

NOTE
If it is difficult to loosen either sprocket from its respective shaft, use a small pry bar to gently loosen the sprocket from its shaft.

13. Remove the rear camshaft drive sprocket (A, **Figure 46**), the crankshaft sprocket (B), and the primary camshaft drive chain (C) as an assembly. Pull the assembly straight off the shafts.

14. Remove the sprocket spacer (**Figure 47**) from the rear camshaft.

15. Remove the camshaft support plate bolts in the following sequence:

   a. Evenly loosen the four center camshaft support plate bolts in the sequence shown in **Figure 48**, and then remove the bolts.

   b. Evenly loosen the remaining six perimeter camshaft support plate bolts in the order shown in **Figure 49**, and then remove the bolts.

16. Withdraw the camshaft support plate assembly from the crankcase. If necessary, carefully pry the plate loose from the crankcase in the areas where the dowels are located (**Figure 50**).

17. Remove the lower O-ring from (A, **Figure 51**) from the lower crankcase flange.

18. Remove the upper O-ring from (B, **Figure 51**) and the oil screen (**Figure 52**) from behind the O-ring.

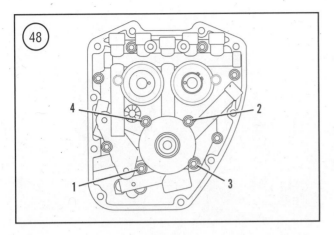

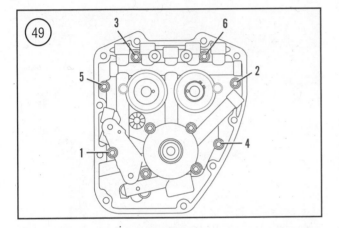

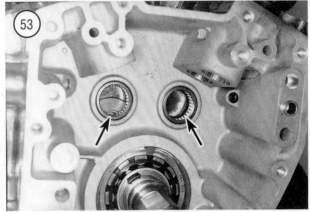

19. Remove the dowels (C, **Figure 51**).

20. If necessary, disassemble and remove the camshafts as described in this section.

Installation

1. If performed, assemble and install the camshafts as described in this section.

2. If removed, press on the oil pump assembly until it bottoms.

3. Install a new O-ring (A, **Figure 51**) into the lower crankcase flange. Apply a light coat of clean engine oil to the O-ring.

4. Install the oil screen (**Figure 52**) and a new O-ring (B, **Figure 51**). Apply a light coat of clean engine oil to the O-ring.

5. Lubricate the camshaft needle bearings (**Figure 53**) in the crankcase and the camshaft journals with clean engine oil.

6. Make sure the timing marks (**Figure 54**) on the camshafts align with each other. If the marks are not aligned, reposition the camshafts before installing the assembly into the crankcase.

7. If removed, install the two locating dowels (C, **Figure 51**) onto the crankcase.

CAUTION
Do not force the camshaft support plate as-
sembly into the crankcase. During installa-
tion the camshaft ends may not be correctly
aligned with the needle bearings. If force is
applied, the needle bearing(s) will be dam-
aged.

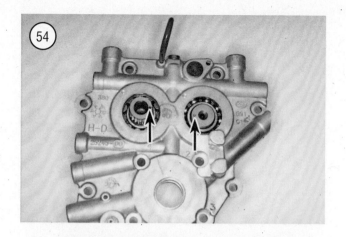

8. Slowly install the camshaft support plate assembly (A, **Figure 55**) into the crankcase. Guide the camshaft ends into the crankcase needle bearings (**Figure 53**). If necessary, slightly rotate and/or wiggle the end of the rear cylinder camshaft (B, **Figure 55**) to assist in the alignment.

CAUTION
When properly aligned, the camshaft sup-
port plate assembly fits snugly against the
crankcase mating surface. If they do not meet
correctly, do not attempt to pull the parts to-
gether with the mounting bolts. Remove the
camshaft support plate assembly and deter-
mine the cause of the interference.

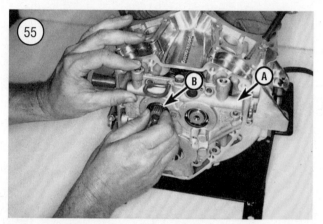

9. Push the camshaft support plate assembly into the crankcase until it engages the dowels and bottoms against the crankcase mating surface.

10. Make sure the timing marks (**Figure 56**) on each camshaft are still aligned. If they are not aligned (**Figure 57**), correct the problem at this time.

11. Tighten the six perimeter camshaft support plate bolts in the following sequence:
   a. Install and finger-tighten the six Allen bolts.
   b. Using the sequence shown in **Figure 49**, tighten the six bolts to 90-120 in.-lb. (10.2-13.6 N•m).

12. Tighten the four center camshaft support plate bolts in the following sequence:
   a. Loosely install the four bolts around the oil pump housing. Evenly tighten the bolts until they just contact the support plate, and then back them out 1/4 turn.
   b. Rotate the engine until the oil pump finds its neutral center with no load on it.
   c. Tighten bolts 1 and 2 until they are snug against the support plate.
   d. Tighten bolts 3 and 4 until each is snug against the support plate.
   e. Using the sequence shown in **Figure 48**, tighten the bolts to 40-45 in.-lb. (4.5-5.1 N•m). Then, tighten them again, using the same sequence, to 90-120 in.-lb. (10.2-13.6 N•m).

13. Check the outer edge of the support plate to make sure it is evenly seated against the crankcase mating surface.

14A. If new parts have been installed, perform the alignment procedure described in *Rear Camshaft Sprocket and Crankshaft Drive Sprocket Alignment* (this section) now.

14B. If the original parts are being re-installed, continue with installation procedure.

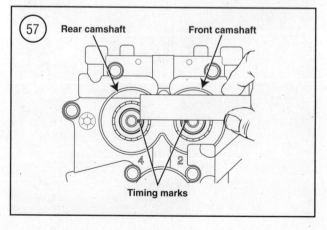

Rear camshaft   Front camshaft

Timing marks

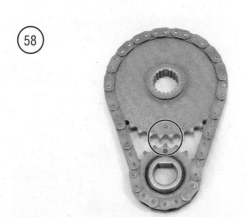

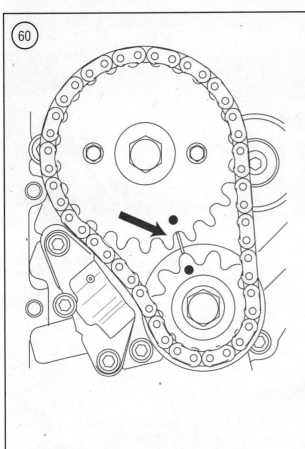

15. Install the sprocket spacer (**Figure 47**) onto the rear camshaft with the manufacturer's marks facing the crankcase.

CAUTION
Refer to the mark made before removal and position the camshaft primary drive chain so it will travel in the original direction. If it is installed incorrectly, the drive chain will wear prematurely.

16. Assemble the rear camshaft sprocket, the crankshaft drive sprocket and the primary drive chain as an assembly. Align the index mark on both sprockets so they face each other as shown in **Figure 58**.

17. Install the rear camshaft drive sprocket (A, **Figure 46**), the crankshaft sprocket (B), and the primary camshaft drive chain (C) as an assembly. Align the camshaft sprocket key with the keyway on the rear camshaft, align the flat on the crankshaft sprocket with the flat on the crankshaft (A, **Figure 59**), and seat each sprocket on its shaft. Check the alignment (**Figure 60**) of the index mark on both sprockets. They must still face each other as shown in **Figure 60** Remove the chain/sprocket assembly and realign the sprocket index marks as necessary to achieve the correct alignment.

18. Install *new* crankshaft and rear-camshaft sprocket bolts as follows:

   a. Apply clean engine oil beneath the flange of the sprocket bolts.

NOTE
If new sprocket bolts are unavailable, oil the flange of the bolts and apply a small amount of Loctite Threadlocker 262 (red) to the threads of each sprocket bolt.

   b. Install the correct flat washer onto each sprocket bolt. The washers are not interchangeable.

   c. Install the rear camshaft sprocket bolt and crankshaft sprocket bolt. Finger-tighten the bolts snugly at this time.

19. Install the camshaft/crankshaft sprocket lock tool (A, **Figure 45**) between the camshaft and crankshaft sprockets.

20. Tighten both sprocket bolts as follows:

   a. Tighten both bolts to 15 ft.-lb. (20.3 N•m).

   b. Loosen both bolts one complete revolution (360°).

   c. Tighten the rear camshaft sprocket bolt (C, **Figure 45**) to 34 ft.-lb. (46.1 N•m).

   d. Tighten the crankshaft sprocket bolt to (B, **Figure 45**) 24 ft.-lb. (32.5 N•m).

21. Remove the sprocket lock tool (A, **Figure 45**).

22. Install the primary chain tensioner (C, **Figure 44**). Tighten the cam chain tensioner mounting bolts (B, **Figure 44**) to 100-120 in.-lbs. (11.3-13.6 N•m). Remove the wire (A, **Figure 44**) from the tensioner.

23. Install a *new* camshaft cover gasket onto the crankcase.

24. Install the camshaft cover (**Figure 61**) onto the crankcase, and then install the cover bolts. Following the se-

quence shown in **Figure 62**, tighten the camshaft cover bolts to 125-155 in.-lb. (14.1-17.5 N•m).

25. Install the valve lifters, pushrod covers, pushrods, and the rocker arm support plate as described in *Rocker Arms, Pushrods, and Valve Lifters* (Chapter Four).

26. Refill the engine oil as described in Chapter Three.

27. Install the exhaust system as described in Chapter Four.

Rear Camshaft Sprocket and Crankshaft Drive Sprocket Alignment

This procedure is required if the camshaft support plate, one or both camshafts, the rear camshaft sprocket, the crankshaft drive sprocket and/or the crankshaft assembly have been replaced.

If alignment between the rear camshaft sprocket and the crankshaft drive sprocket is incorrect, the primary drive chain and both sprockets will bind and cause premature wear.

1. Install the sprocket spacer (**Figure 63**) onto the rear camshaft with the manufacturer's marks facing toward the crankcase.

2. Apply clean engine oil to the camshaft splines and to the rear camshaft sprocket splines.

3. Install the rear camshaft sprocket onto the camshaft. Install the *used* rear camshaft sprocket bolt (A, **Figure 64**) and flat washer. Finger-tighten the bolt at this time.

> *NOTE*
> *Use a washer with a smaller outside diameter than the original washer installed on the crankshaft sprocket bolt. This creates room for a straightedge to be placed against the flat surface of the crankshaft sprocket face.*

4. Install the crankshaft sprocket onto the crankshaft. Install the *used* crankshaft sprocket bolt and a washer (B, **Figure 64**) with a smaller outside diameter than the original washer (see previous note). Finger-tighten the bolt at this time.

5. Install the camshaft/crankshaft sprocket lock (A, **Figure 45**) between the camshaft and crankshaft sprockets.

6. Tighten both crankshaft and rear camshaft sprocket bolts as follows:

   a. Tighten both bolts to 15 ft.-lb. (20.3 N•m).
   b. Loosen both bolts one complete revolution (360°).
   c. Tighten the rear camshaft sprocket bolt (C, **Figure 45**) to 34 ft.-lb. (46.1 N•m).
   d. Tighten the crankshaft sprocket bolt to (B, **Figure 45**) 24 ft.-lb. (32.5 N•m).
   e. Remove the sprocket lock tool (A, **Figure 45**).

7. If the engine was not removed from the engine, install the compensating sprocket (Chapter Six) to pull the crankshaft to the left side.

8. Press the crankshaft and rear camshaft into the crankcase to eliminate any end play.

9. Place a straightedge (C, **Figure 64**) against the face of both sprockets.

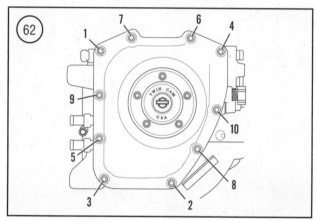

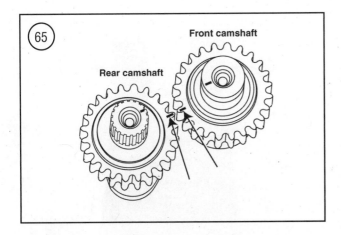

Front camshaft

Rear camshaft

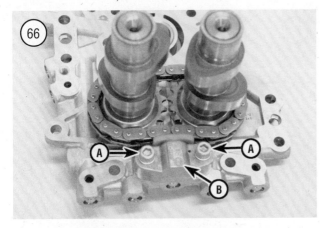

10. Try to insert a 0.010 in. (0.254mm) feeler gauge (D, **Figure 64**) between the straightedge and the each sprocket face.

11A. If the 0.010 in. (0.254 mm) feeler gauge cannot be inserted at either location, the sprockets are correctly aligned. Remove both sprockets and complete installation of the components as described in *Camshaft Support Plate Installation* (this section).

11B. If a different thickness feeler gauge can be inserted, indicating a height difference other than 0.010 in. (0.254 mm), the rear camshaft spacer must be changed. Continue to insert feeler gauges of different thicknesses until the off-set dimension is determined. Record this dimension. It will be used to choose a new spacer.

12. Remove the rear camshaft sprocket bolt, washer and sprocket.

13. Remove the existing sprocket spacer (**Figure 63**) from the rear camshaft. Compare the part number stamped on the spacer with the part numbers in **Table 2** to determine its thickness.

14A. If the crankshaft sprocket sits more than 0.010 in. (0.254 mm) above the rear camshaft sprocket, install the next *thicker* size spacer behind the camshaft sprocket.

14B. If the rear camshaft sprocket sits more than 0.010 in. (0.254 mm) above the crankshaft sprocket, install the next *thinner* size spacer behind the rear camshaft sprocket.

15. Install a new spacer and repeat the measurement process until the sprockets are correctly aligned.

16. After the correct spacer thickness is established, remove the sprockets from the rear camshaft and crankshaft, and complete installation of the components as described in *Camshaft Support Plate Installation* (this section).

Camshaft Removal

1. Remove the camshaft support plate as described in this section.

2. Remove the tensioner bolts (A, **Figure 66**) and remove the secondary chain tensioner (B).

3. Remove the snap ring (A, **Figure 67**) and spacer (B) from the front cylinder camshaft. Mark the spacer so it will not be confused with the rear camshaft spacer. They are not interchangeable.

4. Pull the camshaft and secondary chain assembly from the camshaft support plate.

5. Use a permanent marker to mark a link (**Figure 68**, typical) on the outboard side of the secondary cam chain so the chain can be installed with the same orientation.

6. Remove each camshaft from between the runs of the secondary chain.

Camshaft Installation

The camshaft assembly tool (JIMS part No. 990 or H-D part No. HD-47956), or an equivalent, is needed for this procedure.

NOTE
On some models, the index marks are lines as shown in Figure 65. On others, these marks are dots.

1. Position the camshafts so the index marks (**Figure 65**) on the sprockets align with each other.

2. Position the secondary chain with the marked link plate facing up (**Figure 68**, typical), and install the secondary chain onto both camshafts.

3. Rotate the camshafts in either direction several times, and check the alignment of the index marks. If necessary, adjust one of the camshafts to attain correct alignment (**Figure 65**).

4. Set the inboard end of each camshaft into the camshaft assembly tool base (A, **Figure 69**). Make sure the timing marks (B, **Figure 69**) still align.

5. Place the small guide (A, **Figure 70**) onto the rear camshaft and the large guide (B) over the front camshaft.

6. Apply engine oil to the camshaft bores in the camshaft support plate, and lower the support plate (A, **Figure 71**) over the guides (B) and onto the camshafts.

7. Remove the guides (B, **Figure 109**) and base (A, **Figure 69**) from the assembly.

8. Use a straightedge (**Figure 72**) to confirm that the camshaft index marks are still correctly aligned. If necessary, remove the camshafts and realign the index marks.

9. Install the front camshaft spacer (B, **Figure 67**) onto the front camshaft, and install a *new* snap ring (A) so its sharp edge faces out. Make sure the snap ring is completely seated in the camshaft groove.

10. Rotate the camshafts several complete revolutions and check for binding.

11. Install the secondary chain tensioner (B, **Figure 66**). Tighten the camshaft chain tensioner mounting bolts (A, **Figure 66**) to 100-120 in.-lb. (11.3-13.6 N•m).

Camshaft and Sprocket Inspection

The manufacturer does not provide camshaft specifications. Visually inspect the camshafts to determine if they require replacement.

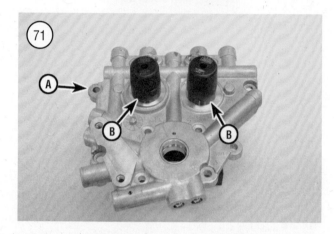

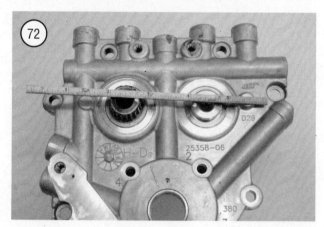

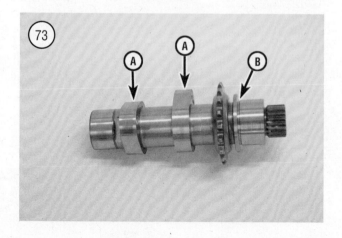

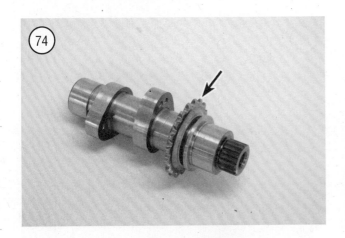

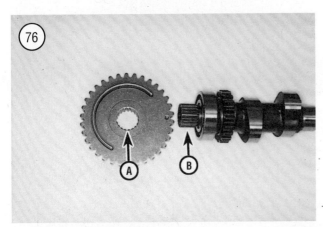

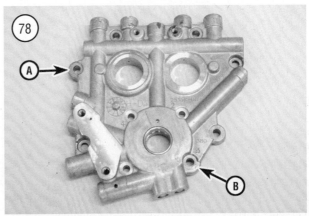

5

1. Check the camshaft lobes (A, **Figure 73**) for wear. The lobes should not be scored and the edges should be square.

2. Inspect the camshaft secondary drive chain sprocket for broken or chipped teeth. Refer to **Figure 74**. Also check the teeth for cracking or rounding. If the sprocket is damaged or severely worn, replace the camshaft.

3. If the camshaft secondary drive chain sprockets are worn, check the camshaft secondary drive chain. (**Figure 75**).

4. Inspect the external splines (A, **Figure 76**) on the rear cylinder's camshaft and the internal splines (B) on the rear camshaft primary drive chain sprocket. Check for worn or damaged splines and replace either or both parts as necessary. The sprocket must fit tightly on the camshaft.

5. Inspect the crankshaft and rear camshaft primary drive chain sprockets for broken or chipped teeth. Also check the teeth for cracking or rounding. Replace a damaged or severely worn sprocket. Inspect the primary drive chain for damage if the rear camshaft primary drive chain sprocket is worn or damaged.

6. Check the snap ring groove (B, **Figure 73**) on the front camshaft for wear or damage.

7. Inspect the crankshaft bushing (**Figure 77**) for wear or damage.

Camshaft Support Plate Inspection

1. Check the six perimeter (A, **Figure 78**) and the four center (B) mounting bolt holes on the camshaft support plate for cracks or fractures. Replace the support plate as necessary.

2. Check the crankcase mating surface (**Figure 79**) for warping and/or surface damage, and replace as necessary.

Needle Bearing Replacement

A camshaft inner bearing remover (JIMS part No. 993), and installer (JIMS part No. 787), or camshaft inner bearing remover/installer (part No. HD-42325), or equivalent tools, are needed for this procedure.

NOTE
*The camshaft needle bearings (**Figure 53**) can be removed with the engine mounted in the frame after the camshaft support plate is removed.*

NOTE
Replace both needle bearings as a set even if only one requires replacement.

1. Remove the camshaft support plate assembly from the engine as described in this section.
2. Install the puller portion of the tool set (A, **Figure 80**) part way into the needle bearing. Install a small hose clamp onto the end that is closest to the needle bearing (B, **Figure 80**) and tighten it. This closes the end of the tool so it can pass through the needle bearing. Push the puller all the way through the needle bearing and remove the hose clamp.
3. Assemble the remainder of the tool components onto the puller following the manufacturer's instructions.
4. Place a 5/8 in. wrench on the flats of the puller (A, **Figure 81**).
5. Place a 1-1/8 in. wrench, or an adjustable wrench, on the large nut (B, **Figure 81**).

CAUTION
Do not turn the 5/8 in. wrench as this will damage the tool and the crankcase receptacle.

6. Hold the 5/8 in. wrench (A, **Figure 81**) to keep the puller from rotating. Turn the 1-1/8 in. wrench (B, **Figure 81**) *clockwise* on the large nut (C). Tighten the large nut and pull the needle bearing out of the crankcase bore.
7. Disassemble the tool, and remove the needle bearing from it.
8. Repeat the process to remove the other needle bearing.
9. Apply a light coat of clean engine oil, or press lube, to the outer surface of the *new* needle bearing(s) and to the crankcase needle bearing bore(s) (**Figure 82**, typical).
10. Apply a light coat of clean engine oil to the threads of the screw portion and to the installer plate.
11. Insert the screw portion of the tool part way into the installer plate.
12. Push the installer onto the screw until it locks into place.
13. Position the *new* bearing (A, **Figure 83**) on the installer (B) with the manufacturer's marks facing out on the installer.
14. Postition the installer plate on the crankcase, aligning the tool to the bearing bore.
15. Install the thumb screws (A, **Figure 84**) through the installer plate and into the crankcase threaded holes. Tighten the thumb screws securely.
16. Slowly tighten the installer screw (B, **Figure 84**) until the bearing starts to enter the crankcase bore. Continue to tighten it until the installer contacts the crankcase surface. This correctly positions the needle bearing within the crankcase.

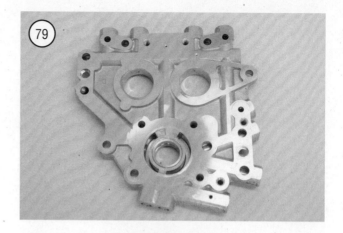

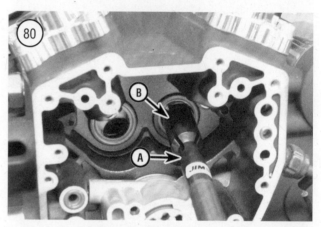

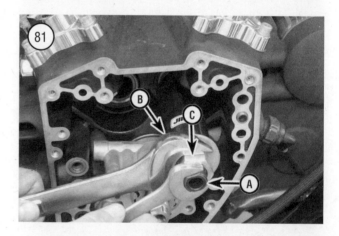

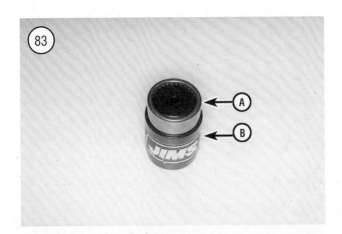

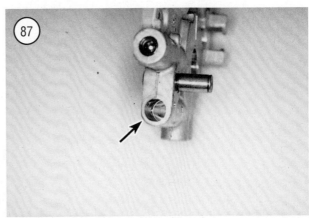

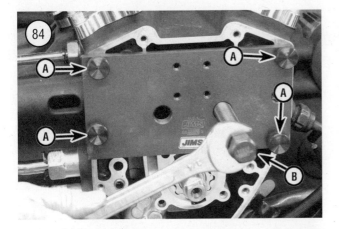

17. Remove the tools.

18. Repeat the process to install the remaining needle bearing.

**Oil Pressure Relief Valve
Removal/Inspection/Installation**

*NOTE
This procedure is shown with the camshaft assembly removed to clearly illustrate the steps.*

1. Remove the camshaft support plate assembly from the engine as described in this section.

2A. If the camshafts are still in place, secure the camshaft support plate in a vise with soft jaws.

2B. If the camshafts have been removed, place the camshaft support plate on a piece of soft wood.

3. Before disassembling the valve, measure the seated depth of the valve body in the bore by performing the following:

    a. Insert a stiff wire down through the valve spring until it reaches bottom inside the valve body.

    b. Mark the wire where it aligns with the outside edge of the bore.

    c. Remove the wire and measure the distance from the end of the wire to the mark. It should approximately equal the valve seated depth (**Table 1**).

    d. If the measurement is out of specification, the spring is fatigued. Replace the spring.

4. Use a 1/8 in. punch to drive the roll pin (**Figure 85**) from the camshaft support plate. Discard the roll pin.

5. Remove the valve body (A, **Figure 86**) and spring (B) from the relief-valve port of the camshaft support plate.

6. Inspect the spring for signs of stretching, cracks or wear. Replace it if worn.

7. Inspect the valve body and the relief-valve port (**Figure 87**) for burrs, scoring or metal chips. If found, replace the valve body and the support plate.

8. Determine the running clearance by performing the following:

    a. Measure the outside diameter of the valve body (**Figure 88**).

    b. Measure the inside diameter of the relief-valve port in the camshaft support plate.

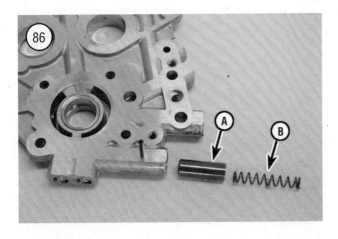

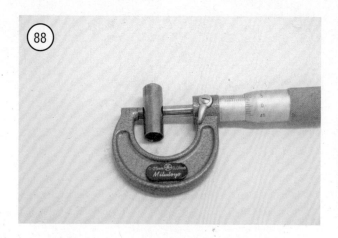

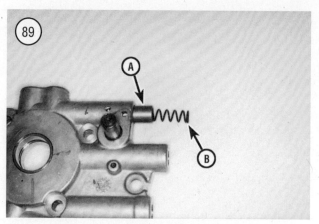

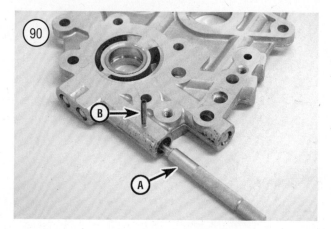

c. Subtract the valve body outside diameter from the relief-valve port inside diameter. This is the running clearance.

d. If running clearance exceeds specification (**Table 1**), replace the valve body. Measure the outside diameter of the new valve body and recalculate the running clearance. If the running clearance still exceeds specification, replace the valve body and camshaft support plate.

9. Apply a light coat of clean engine oil to the bypass port and to the valve body.

10. Install the valve body (A, **Figure 89**) so its closed end goes into the bypass port first.

11. Install the spring (B, **Figure 89**) into the valve body.

12. Push the valve body and spring into the bypass port. Hold them in place (A, **Figure 90**) and install a *new* roll pin (B). Tap the roll pin in until it sits flush with the support plate (**Figure 85**).

Chain Tensioner Inspection

1. Visually inspect the tensioner shoe (A, **Figure 91**). Replace the tensioners if the contact surface of the shoe is less than 0.060 in. (1.52 mm) thick.

2. If tensioner was disassembled, assemble it by performing the following:

    a. Insert the piston (A, **Figure 92**) and spring (B) into the tensioner housing.

    b. Align the shoe (C, **Figure 92**) with the cutouts in the housing, and press the shoe into the housing (D).

    c. Insert a wire (B, **Figure 91**) through the hole in the tensioner housing to hold the assembly together.

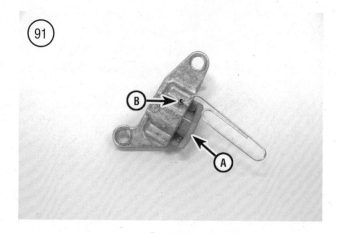

CRANKCASE AND CRANKSHAFT

Crankcase Disassembly

An engine stand (JIMS part No, 1140), base stand (JIMS part No.1138) and crankshaft disassembly/removing tool (JIMS part No. 995) are used in some of the following procedures.

Refer to **Figure 93** and **Figure 94**.

1. Remove the engine as described in this chapter.

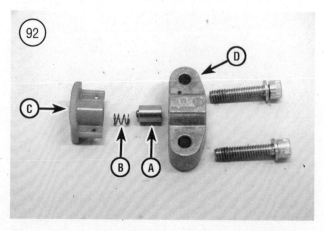

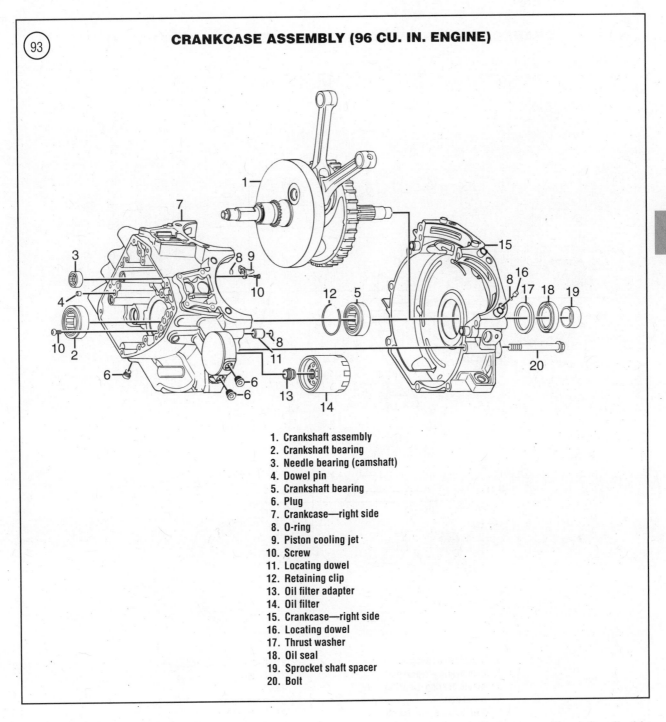

CRANKCASE ASSEMBLY (96 CU. IN. ENGINE)

93

1. Crankshaft assembly
2. Crankshaft bearing
3. Needle bearing (camshaft)
4. Dowel pin
5. Crankshaft bearing
6. Plug
7. Crankcase—right side
8. O-ring
9. Piston cooling jet
10. Screw
11. Locating dowel
12. Retaining clip
13. Oil filter adapter
14. Oil filter
15. Crankcase—right side
16. Locating dowel
17. Thrust washer
18. Oil seal
19. Sprocket shaft spacer
20. Bolt

CAUTION
Do not lift the crankcase assembly by the cylinder studs. Bent or damaged cylinder studs may cause an oil leak.

2. Remove the following components:
   a. Rocker arms, pushrods and valve lifters as described in Chapter Four.
   b. Cylinder heads, pistons and cylinders as described in Chapter Four.
   c. Camshaft support plate and oil pump as described in this chapter.

d. Alternator rotor and stator assembly as described in Chapter Eleven.

NOTE
Leave the bolts for the left side off so the case halves can be separated in the following steps.

3. Attach the crankcase assembly to an engine stand (**Figure 95**) following the manufacturer's instructions.
4. Secure the engine stand to the workbench.
5. Following the sequence shown in **Figure 96**, loosen the bolts (**Figure 97**) from the left side of the crankcase in two to three stages. Then, remove the bolts.

94 CRANKCASE ASSEMBLY (103 CU. IN. AND 110 CU. IN. ENGINE)

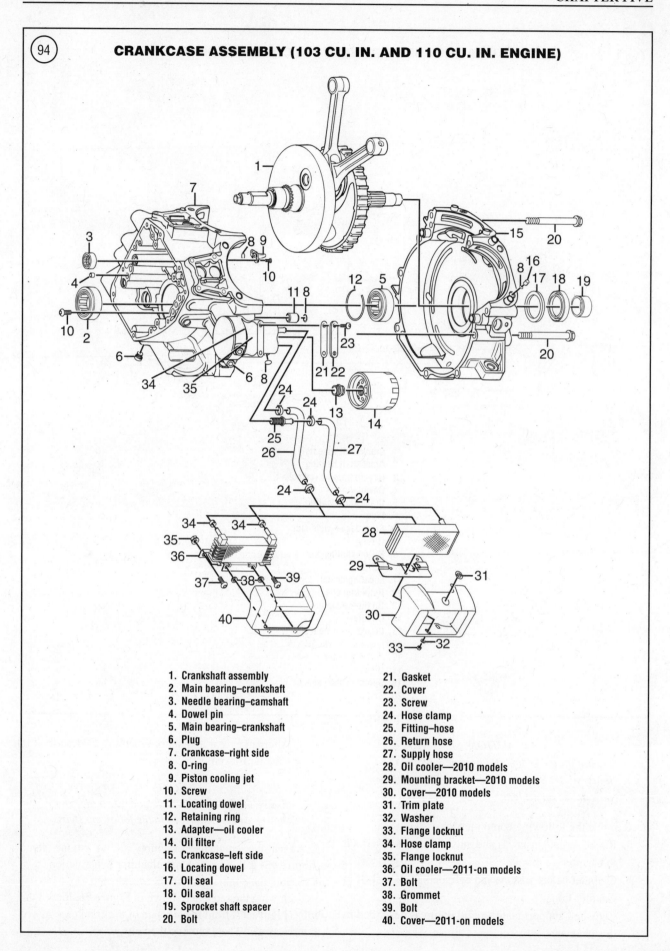

1. Crankshaft assembly
2. Main bearing–crankshaft
3. Needle bearing–camshaft
4. Dowel pin
5. Main bearing–crankshaft
6. Plug
7. Crankcase–right side
8. O-ring
9. Piston cooling jet
10. Screw
11. Locating dowel
12. Retaining ring
13. Adapter—oil cooler
14. Oil filter
15. Crankcase–left side
16. Locating dowel
17. Oil seal
18. Oil seal
19. Sprocket shaft spacer
20. Bolt

21. Gasket
22. Cover
23. Screw
24. Hose clamp
25. Fitting–hose
26. Return hose
27. Supply hose
28. Oil cooler—2010 models
29. Mounting bracket—2010 models
30. Cover—2010 models
31. Trim plate
32. Washer
33. Flange locknut
34. Hose clamp
35. Flange locknut
36. Oil cooler—2011-on models
37. Bolt
38. Grommet
39. Bolt
40. Cover—2011-on models

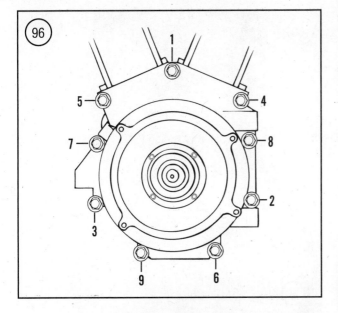

6. Place the crankcase assembly on wooden blocks with the camshaft cover side facing up. Use wooden blocks thick enough so the crankshaft clears the workbench surface (**Figure 98**).

7. Tap around the perimeter of the crankcase with a plastic mallet and remove the right crankcase half (**Figure 99**).

8. If the crankcase halves will not separate easily, perform the following:

a. Install the separation tool(s) (A, **Figure 100**) onto the left side of the crankcase following the manufacturer's instructions.

b. Make sure the right side engine stand bolts (A, **Figure 101**) are *not* installed onto the crankcase half.

c. Apply clean engine oil, or press lube, to the end of the center screw and install it into the tool.

CAUTION
Do not use a hand impact driver or air impact wrench on the center screw. These will damage the crankcase halves and the tool(s).

d. Slowly turn the center screw (B, **Figure 100**) with a wrench 1/2 turn at a time. After each turn, tap on the

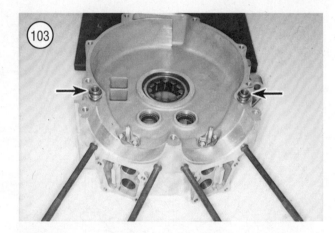

end of the center screw with a brass mallet to relieve the stress on the center screw and the tool.

e. Repeat the process until the center screw turns freely and the crankcase halves begin to separate (B, **Figure 101**).

f. Remove the crankcase from the engine stand.

g. Remove the right side crankcase half (**Figure 102**).

h. Remove the separation tool from the left side crankcase half unless the crankshaft is going to be removed.

9. Remove the locating dowels (**Figure 103**) and O-rings from the right side crankcase half.

> *CAUTION*
> *Do not drive the crankshaft out of the crankcase half with a hammer.*

10A. If a hydraulic press is available, press the crankshaft out of the right crankcase half as follows:

a. Support the right crankcase half in a press on wooden blocks with the outer surface facing up.

b. Center the press ram onto the end of the crankshaft, and then press the crankshaft out of the right crankcase half. Have an assistant support the crankshaft as it is being pressed out.

c. Remove the crankshaft.

d. Remove the right crankcase half from the press bed and move it to workbench for further service.

10B. If a hydraulic press is not available, perform the following:

a. Install the crankshaft disassembly/removing tool (A, **Figure 104**) onto the left side of the crankcase following the manufacturer's instructions.

b. Apply clean engine oil, or press lube, to the end of the center screw and install it into the tool.

> *CAUTION*
> *Do not use a hand impact driver or air impact wrench on the center screw, as these will damage the crankcase and the tool(s).*

c. Secure the right side of the crankshaft with a wrench (B, **Figure 104**) to prevent it from rotating.

d. Slowly turn the center screw with a wrench (C, **Figure 104**) 1/2 turn at a time. After each turn, tap

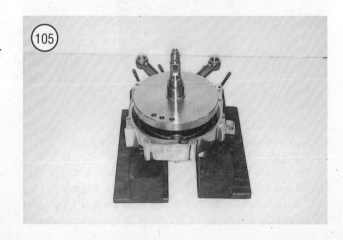

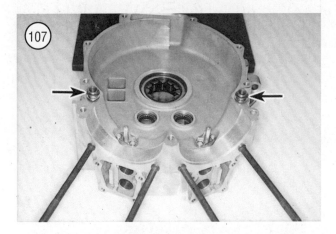

on the end of the center screw with a brass mallet to relieve the stress on the center screw and the tool.

e. Repeat the process until the center screw pushes the crankshaft out of the left side crankcase half.

f. Remove the tool from the left side crankcase half.

11. To remove the crankshaft outer roller bearing and oil seal assembly from the left crankcase half, perform the following:

a. Place the left crankcase half on the workbench with the outer surface facing up.

b. Carefully pry the sprocket shaft spacer out of the oil seal.

c. Carefully pry the oil seal out of the crankcase using a wide-blade screwdriver. Support the screwdriver with a rag to prevent damage to the crankcase.

d. Lift the outer roller bearing from the crankcase.

Crankcase Assembly

A crankshaft guide (JIMS part No. 1288), or an equivalent tool, is required to assemble the crankcase halves.

1. Perform Steps 1-9 of *Crankcase Cleaning and Inspection* (this section).

2. Support the left crankcase half on wooden blocks (**Figure 105**) so the inboard side faces up. Make sure the blocks are thick enough so the left side of the crankshaft will clear the workbench surface.

3. Install the locating dowels (**Figure 106**) and *new* O-rings in both locations in the right crankcase half. Apply clean engine oil to the O-rings (**Figure 107**).

4. Fit the crankshaft guide (**Figure 108**) onto the crankshaft sprocket shaft (left side), and install the crankshaft into the left crankcase half . Make sure each connecting rod sits in the correct cylinder cutout.

5. Thoroughly clean and dry the crankcase gasket surface of each crankcase half.

6. Apply a thin coat of a non-hardening gasket sealant to the crankcase mating surfaces. Use High Performance Sealant, Gray (H-D part No. HD-99650-02), or an equivalent.

7. Align the crankcase halves and carefully lower the right crankcase half over the crankshaft and onto left crankcase half (**Figure 109**). Press it down until it is seated correctly on the locating dowels. If necessary, carefully tap around the perimeter of the right crankcase half until it is completed seated on the left half (**Figure 110**).

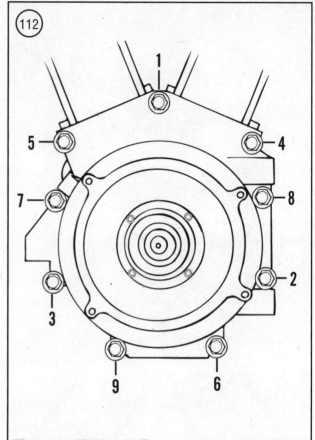

CAUTION
When properly aligned, the crankcase halves will fit snugly against each other around the entire perimeter. If they do not meet correctly, do not attempt to pull the case halves together with the mounting bolts. Separate the crankcase assembly and investigate the cause of the interference.

8. Pull the crankshaft guide from the crankshaft.

9. If available, place the crankcase assembly in an engine stand (A, **Figure 111**). Secure the engine stand to the workbench.

10. Install the crankcase bolts into the left crankcase half (B, **Figure 111**) and tighten them as follows:

    a. Alternately finger-tighten the bolts.

    b. Following the torque sequence shown in **Figure 112**, tighten the bolts to 10 ft.-lb. (13.6 N•m).

    c. Following the same sequence, tighten the crankcase bolts to 15-19 ft.-lb. (20.3-25.8 N•m).

11. Apply clean engine oil to the outer surface of the sprocket shaft spacer (**Figure 113**) and install it onto the crankshaft and into the new oil seal.

12. Install the following components:

    a. Alternator rotor and stator assembly as described in Chapter Eleven.

    b. Camshaft support plate and oil pump as described in this chapter.

    c. Cylinder heads, pistons and cylinders as described in Chapter Four.

    d. Rocker arms, pushrods and valve lifters as described in Chapter Four.

Crankcase Cleaning and Inspection

1. Clean both crankcase halves in solvent and dry with compressed air.

2. Apply a light coat of oil to the races to prevent rust.

3. Inspect the right (**Figure 114**) and left (**Figure 115**) crankcase halves for cracks or other damage.

4. Inspect the case studs (**Figure 116**) for bending, cracks or other damage. Check the exposed stud threads for dam-

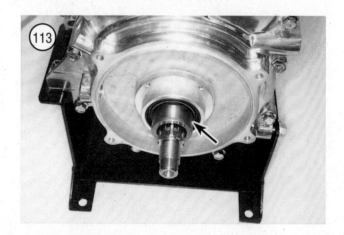

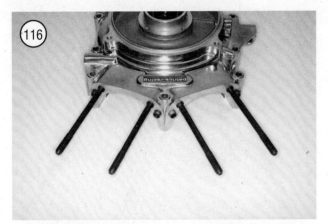

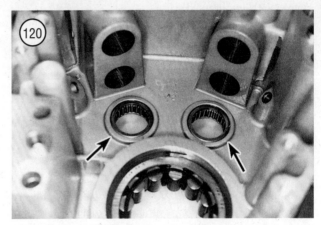

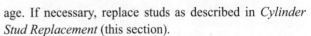

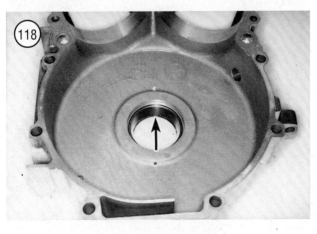

age. If necessary, replace studs as described in *Cylinder Stud Replacement* (this section).

5. Inspect the left side main bearing races. Refer to **Figure 117** for the outer bearing race and **Figure 118** for the inner bearing race. Also, check the roller bearings for wear or damage. The bearings must turn smoothly with no roughness. If any of these parts are worn, replace the bearing assembly as described in *Left Side Main Bearing Assembly Replacement* (this chapter).

6. Inspect the right side main roller bearing (**Figure 119**) for wear or damage. The bearing must turn smoothly with no roughness. If damaged, replace the bearing assembly as described in *Right Side Main Bearing Replacement* (this chapter).

7. Inspect the camshaft needle bearings (**Figure 120**) in the right crankcase half for damage. To replace one or both of these bearings, refer to *Camshaft Support Plate* (this chapter).

8. Inspect the valve lifter bore receptacles (**Figure 121**) for wear or damage. Refer to *Valve Lifter Inspection* (Chapter Four).

NOTE
If the original piston cooling jets are being reinstalled, apply Loctite No. 222 (purple), or an equivalent threadlock, to the screw threads prior to installation.

9. Make sure the piston cooling jets (**Figure 122**) are clear. If necessary, remove the Torx mounting screws (T20), and then remove the cooling jets and O-rings. Clean the oil jets with compressed air. Install *new* O-rings and tighten the mounting screws securely.

Crankshaft and Connecting Rods Cleaning and Inspection

If any portion of the crankshaft and/or connecting rods are worn or damaged, they must be replaced as one assembly. If necessary, have the crankshaft overhauled by a dealership.

1. Clean the crankshaft assembly in solvent and dry thoroughly with compressed air.

2. Hold the shank portion of each connecting rod where it attaches to the crankshaft (**Figure 123**). Pull up and down on each connecting rod. Any slight amount of up and down movement indicates excessive lower bearing wear. If there is movement, the crankshaft must be overhauled.

3. Measure connecting rod side play with a feeler gauge (**Figure 124**). Compare the results with the service limit in **Table 2**.

4. Inspect the pinion shaft (**Figure 125**) on the right side and the sprocket shaft (**Figure 126**) on the left side for excessive wear or damage.

5. Support the crankshaft on a truing stand (A, **Figure 127**) and check the runout with a dial indicator (B) at the machined surfaces of the crankshaft near each end. If the runout exceeds the service limit in Table 2, have the crankshaft trued or overhauled.

6. Inspect the crankshaft position sensor timing teeth (**Figure 128**) on the left side flywheel for damaged or missing teeth.

Cylinder Stud Replacement

Replace bent or otherwise damaged cylinder studs (A, **Figure 129**) to prevent cylinder block and cylinder head leaks.

1. If the engine lower end is assembled, block off the lower crankcase opening with clean shop cloths.

2A. If the stud has broken off flush with the top surface of the crankcase, remove it as described in Chapter One.

2B. If the whole stud is still in place, perform the following:

   a. Thread a 3/8-16 nut onto the top of the stud.

   b. Thread an additional nut onto the stud and tighten it against the first nut so that they are locked.

   c. Turn the bottom nut *counterclockwise* and unscrew the stud.

3. Clean the stud threads in the crankcase with a spiral brush, and then clean with an aerosol parts cleaner. If necessary, clean the threads with an appropriate size tap.

NOTE
New studs may have a patch of threadlock already applied to the lower stud threads. If

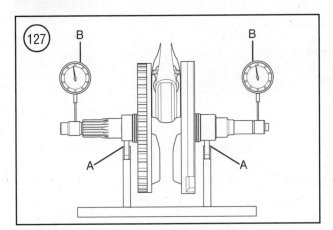

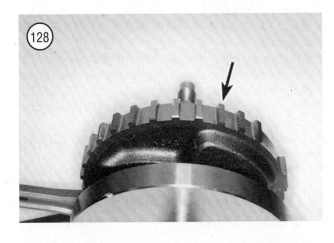

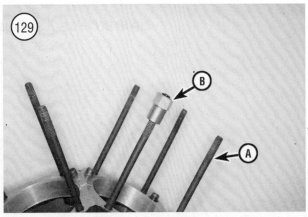

5

so, do not apply any additional threadlock to these studs.

4. If the new stud does not have the patch of threadlock already applied, apply ThreeBond TB1360, or an equivalent, to the lower stud threads.

NOTE
The cylinder studs have a shoulder on one end and this end must be installed next to the crankcase surface.

5A. Install a stud installation tool (Motion Pro part No. 08-0148) on the stud (B, **Figure 129**).

5B. To protect the end of the stud, place a 0.313 in. (7.95 mm) diameter steel ball (H-D part No. 8860) onto the cylinder head hollow stud. Then thread the bolt onto the end of the new stud without the collar.

6. Position the stud with the shoulder end going in first and hand-thread the new stud into the crankcase.

CAUTION
Do not use a breaker bar, ratchet or similar tool to install the studs. These tools may bend the stud and cause the engine to leak oil.

7. Hold an air impact wrench directly in-line with the stud. *Slowly* tighten the new stud with an air impact wrench until the stud shoulder contacts the top surface of the crankcase.

8. Use a torque wrench and hand-tighten the stud to 10-20 ft.-lb. (13.6-27.1 N•m).

9. Remove the cylinder head bolt and steel ball from the cylinder stud.

10. Repeat the procedure to install any additional studs.

CRANKCASE BEARING REPLACEMENT

Right Side Main Bearing Replacement

Refer to **Figures 130** and **Figure 131**.

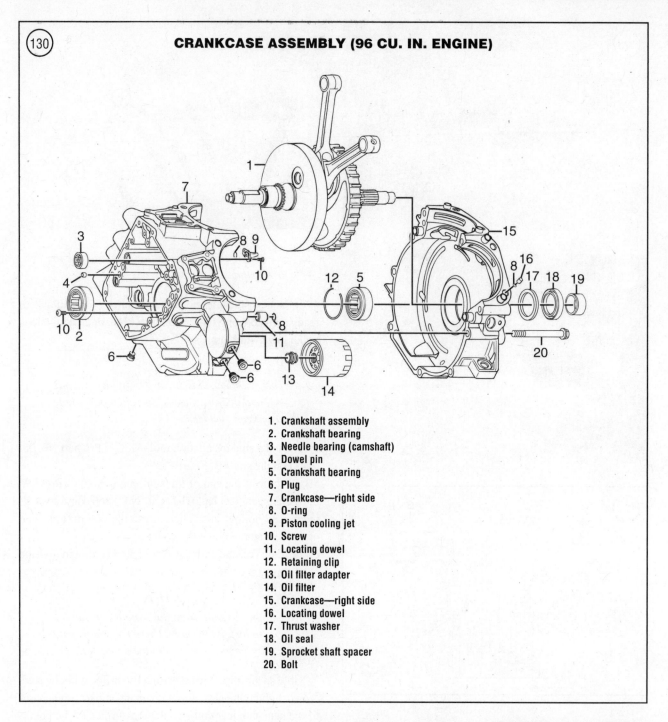

CRANKCASE ASSEMBLY (96 CU. IN. ENGINE)

1. Crankshaft assembly
2. Crankshaft bearing
3. Needle bearing (camshaft)
4. Dowel pin
5. Crankshaft bearing
6. Plug
7. Crankcase—right side
8. O-ring
9. Piston cooling jet
10. Screw
11. Locating dowel
12. Retaining clip
13. Oil filter adapter
14. Oil filter
15. Crankcase—right side
16. Locating dowel
17. Thrust washer
18. Oil seal
19. Sprocket shaft spacer
20. Bolt

Tools

The following tools, or their equivalents, are required to remove and install the right side main bearing:
1. Hydraulic press.
2. Crankshaft bearing support tube (H-D part No. 42720-5) marked with either *A* or *B*.
3. Pilot/driver (H-D part No. B-45655).

Removal

1. On 2011-on models, remove the two screws securing the main bearing to the crankcase.

2. Place the support tube on the press bed with the *A* side facing up.
3. Position the right crankcase half with the outboard side facing up and position the bearing directly over the support tube on the press bed.
4. Install the pilot/driver shaft (A, **Figure 132**) through the bearing and into the support tube.
5. Center the press driver (B, **Figure 132**) over the pilot/driver shaft.
6. Hold the crankcase half parallel to the press bed and have an assistant slowly apply ram pressure on the pilot shaft until the bearing is free from the crankcase half.
7. Remove the crankcase half and tools from the press bed.

131 **CRANKCASE ASSEMBLY (103 CU. IN. AND 110 CU. IN. ENGINE)**

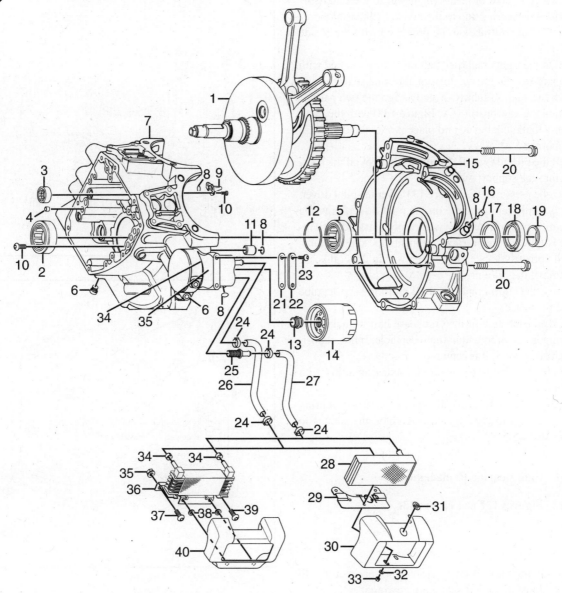

5

1. Crankshaft assembly	21. Gasket
2. Main bearing--crankshaft	22. Cover
3. Needle bearing--camshaft	23. Screw
4. Dowel pin	24. Hose clamp
5. Main bearing--crankshaft	25. Fitting--hose
6. Plug	26. Return hose
7. Crankcase--right side	27. Supply hose
8. O-ring	28. Oil cooler—2010 models
9. Piston cooling jet	29. Mounting bracket—2010 models
10. Screw	30. Cover—2010 models
11. Locating dowel	31. Trim plate
12. Retaining ring	32. Washer
13. Adapter—oil cooler	33. Flange locknut
14. Oil filter	34. Hose clamp
15. Crankcase--left side	35. Flange locknut
16. Locating dowel	36. Oil cooler—2011-on models
17. Oil seal	37. Bolt
18. Oil seal	38. Grommet
19. Sprocket shaft spacer	39. Bolt
20. Bolt	40. Cover—2011-on models

Installation

1. Apply a light coat of clean engine oil to the outer surface of the *new* bearing and to the crankcase bearing bore.
2. Place the support tube on the press bed with the *B* side facing up.
3. Position the right crankcase half onto the press bed with the outboard side facing up. Position the crankshaft bearing bore over the support tube. Correctly align the two parts.
4. Position the *new* bearing (A, **Figure 133**) with the manufacturer's marks facing up and place it over the crankcase bearing bore.
5. Install the pilot/driver (B, **Figure 133**) through the bearing and into the support tube.
6. Center the press ram (C, **Figure 133**) over the pilot driver.
7. Slowly apply ram pressure on the pilot driver, pressing the bearing into the crankcase half. Apply pressure until resistance is felt and the bearing bottoms in the support tube. This will correctly locate the bearing within the crankcase half. Remove the pilot driver.
8. Remove the right crankcase half and the support tube from the press bed.
9. Check on each side of the crankcase half to make sure the bearing is centered within the receptacle. If not, reposition the bearing until it is centered correctly.
10. Spin the bearing to make sure it rotates smoothly with no binding.
11. On 2011-on models, install two new screws securing the main bearing to the crankcase. Tighten the screws to 40-70 in.-lb. (4.5-7.9 N•m).

Left Side Main Bearing Replacement

Refer to **Figures 130** and **Figure 131**.

Tools

The following tools, or their equivalents, are required to remove and install the left side main bearing:
1. Hydraulic press.
2. Crankshaft bearing support tube (H-D part No. HD-42720-5) marked with either *A* or *B*.
3. Pilot/driver (H-D part No. B-45655).

Removal

1. Place the left crankcase half on the workbench with the inner surface facing up.
2. If still in place, remove the crankshaft spacer from the bearing bore.
3. Carefully pull the thrust washer from the outboard side of the crankcase past the oil seal.
4. Place the support tube on the workbench with the *A* side facing up.
5. Position the crankcase half with the outer surface facing up and place the bearing bore over the support tube.

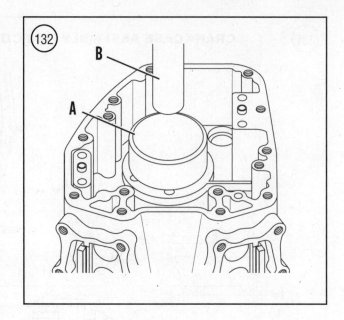

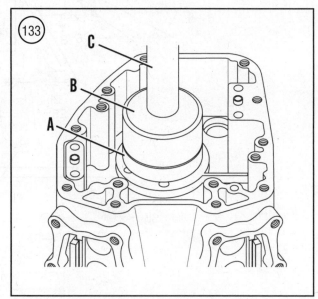

6. Use a suitable size drift and tap the oil seal out of the bearing bore. Discard the oil seal.
7. Turn the crankcase half over with the inner surface facing up.

CAUTION
Do not damage the crankcase retaining ring groove with the screwdriver. The groove must remain sharp to correctly seat the retaining ring.

8. The roller bearing (A, **Figure 134**) is secured in the crankcase half with a retaining ring (B) fit into a groove on the inner surface of the bearing bore. Remove the retaining ring as follows:
   a. Use a flat-bladed screwdriver (C, **Figure 134**) and place it under the retaining ring. Carefully lift the edge of the retaining ring up and out of the crankcase groove.

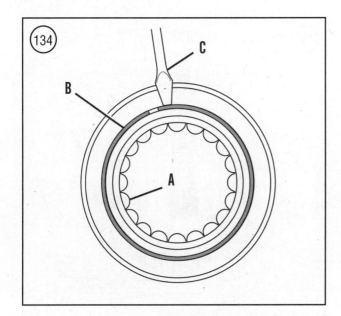

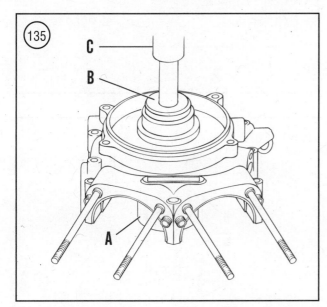

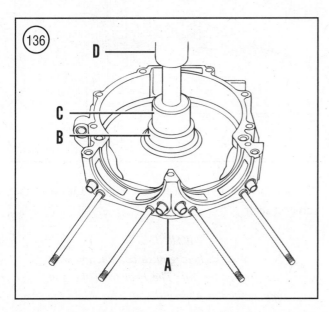

b. Slide the tip of the screwdriver around the edge of the bearing and continue to lift the retaining ring out of the crankcase groove.

c. Remove the retaining ring.

9. Position the support tube (A, **Figure 135**) on the press bed with the *A* side facing up.

10. Position the left crankcase half onto the press bed with the outboard side facing up. Position the crankshaft's bearing bore over the support tube. Correctly align the two parts.

11. Slide the pilot/driver (B, **Figure 135**) through the crankcase bearing and into the support.

12. Center the press ram (C, **Figure 135**) directly over the pilot/driver (B) and slowly press the bearing out of the crankcase half.

13. Remove the crankcase half and tools from the press bed.

14. Clean the crankcase half in solvent and dry it with compressed air.

Installation

1. Apply clean engine oil, or press lube, to the bearing receptacle in the crankcase half and to the outer race of the *new* bearing.

2. Position the support tube (A, **Figure 136**) on the press bed with the *A* side facing up.

3. Position the crankcase half with the inboard side facing up and position the crankshaft bearing bore over the support tube. Correctly align the two parts.

4. Correctly position the *new* bearing (B, **Figure 136**) over the crankcase bearing bore with the manufacturer's marks facing down.

5. Slide the pilot/driver (C, **Figure 136**) through the new bearing and crankcase half and into the support tube.

6. Center the press ram (D, **Figure 136**) directly over the pilot/driver (C) and slowly press the bearing into the crankcase half until it *lightly* bottoms in the crankshaft bearing bore.

7. Remove the crankcase half and tools from the press.

8. Make sure the bearing has been pressed in past the retaining ring groove. If the groove is not visible above the bearing, repeat the installation process until the groove is visible.

9. Position the crankcase half on the workbench with the inboard side facing up.

> *CAUTION*
> *Do not damage the crankcase retaining ring groove with the screwdriver. The groove must remain sharp to correctly seat the retaining ring. If the retaining ring will not correctly seat in the crankcase groove, the bearing is not correctly seated in the crankcase bore. Repeat the installation process until the retaining ring groove is accessible.*

10. Install a *new* bearing retaining ring as follows:

a. Work the retaining ring into the crankcase groove, being careful not to damage the crankcase groove.

b. Use a flat-bladed screwdriver and push the retaining ring into the groove. Continue to push the retaining ring into the crankcase until it fully engages the groove. Make sure it is correctly seated in the groove.

Crankshaft Left Side Main Bearing Inner Race Replacement

Refer to **Figures 130** and **Figure 131**.

Removal

1. Support the crankshaft in a support fixture (H-D part No. HD-44358), or an equivalent (A, **Figure 137**), with the bearing side facing up.

2. Place a hardened plug (B, **Figure 137**) between the bearing puller and the end of the crankshaft.

3. Install the bearing splitter (C, **Figure 137**) under the bearing inner race.

4. Attach a bearing puller (D, **Figure 137**) to the splitter. Apply graphite lubricant to the bearing puller center screw before installing it.

> *WARNING*
> ***Never** use the heat gun in conjunction with the penetrating oil. The heat from the gun may ignite the oil resulting in a fire.*

5A. Use a high temperature heat gun and apply heat uniformly to the bearing inner race for approximately 30 seconds.

5B. If a heat gun is not available, apply penetrating oil to the inner race and crankshaft and allow the oil to penetrate for 30 minutes.

6. Make sure the bearing puller is square to the crankshaft so the bearing inner race is not out of alignment with the crankshaft shoulder.

7. Slowly tighten the bearing puller center screw (E, **Figure 137**) and withdraw the bearing inner race (F) from the crankshaft shoulder.

8. Remove the bearing puller, splitter and bearing inner race from the crankshaft.

9. Remove the thrust washer from the crankshaft. Discard the thrust washer, it cannot be re-used.

10. Clean the sprocket shaft with contact cleaner. Check the sprocket shaft for cracks or other damage. If it is damaged, refer service to a dealership.

Installation

The sprocket shaft bearing cone installer (H-D part No. HD-97225-55C) is required to install the sprocket shaft bearing inner race.

1. Support the crankshaft in a support fixture (H-D part No. HD-44358), or an equivalent (A, **Figure 138**), with the bearing side facing up.

2. Thread the tool pilot shaft (B, **Figure 138**) onto the crankshaft until it contacts the crankshaft.

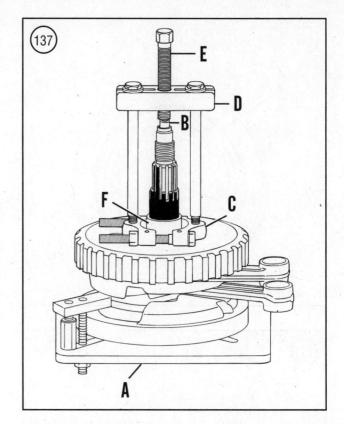

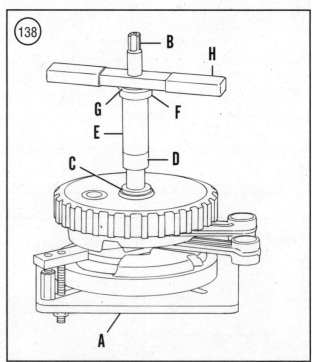

3. Slide the *new* thrust washer (C, **Figure 138**) over the sprocket shaft.

> *WARNING*
> ***Never** use the heat gun in conjunction with the penetrating oil. The heat from the gun may ignite the oil resulting in a fire.*

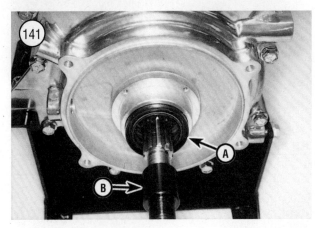

4A. Place the *new* bearing race on the workbench. Use a heat gun and uniformly heat the bearing race for approximately 60 seconds. Wear heavy duty gloves and install the new inner race (D, **Figure 138**) onto the crankshaft.

4B. If a heat gun is not available, apply penetrating oil to the inner surface of the bearing race and to the crankshaft shoulder. Install the new inner race (D, **Figure 138**) onto the crankshaft.

5. Apply graphite lubricant to the threads of the pilot shaft and flat washer.

6. Slide the tool sleeve (E, **Figure 138**) onto the crankshaft until it contacts the bearing inner race.

7. Slide the tool installer bearing (F, **Figure 138**) and flat washer (G) over the pilot shaft until it contacts the top of the sleeve.

8. Thread the tool handle (H, **Figure 138**) onto the pilot shaft (B).

9. Slowly tighten the handle *clockwise* until the bearing inner race bottoms on the crankshaft shoulder.

10. Unscrew and remove all parts of the tool.

Crankcase Left Side Oil Seal Replacement

Refer to **Figure 130** and **Figure 131**

Tools

The following tools, or their equivalent, are required to install the oil seal.

1. Sprocket shaft seal installer tool (JIMS part No. 39361-69).

2. Sprocket shaft bearing cone installer (H-D part No. HD-97225-55C).

Removal/Installation

1. Remove the sprocket shaft spacer (**Figure 139**) from the crankshaft and the oil seal.

2. Carefully pry the old oil seal (**Figure 140**) out of the bearing bore and discard it.

3. Position the *new* oil seal so the side with the manufacturer's marks faces out.

4. Install the oil seal (A, **Figure 141**) onto the crankshaft and center it within the bearing bore.

5. Apply clean engine oil or press lube to the installer tool threads, both washers and the radial bearing.

6. Install the main tool body (B, **Figure 141**) onto the crankshaft and screw it on until it stops.

7. Install the rest of the shaft seal installer tool following the manufacturer's instructions.

8. Hold the handle (A, **Figure 142**) of the main tool body and slowly tighten the large nut (B) with a wrench. Tighten the large nut slowly and make sure the oil seal (**Figure 143**) is entering straight into the bearing bore.

9. Tighten the large nut until the shaft seal installer tool contacts the crankcase surface (**Figure 144**).

10. Remove the tools.

11. Apply clean engine oil to the outer surface of the sprocket shaft spacer (**Figure 139**), and install it onto the crankshaft and into the oil seal.

ENGINE BREAK-IN

Following cylinder service (boring, honing, new rings) and major lower end work, the engine must be broken in just as though it were new. The service and performance life of the engine depends on a careful and sensible break-in.

1. For the first 50 mi. (80 km), maintain engine speed below 2500 rpm in any gear. However, do not lug the engine. Do not exceed 50 mph during this period.

2. From 50-500 mi. (80-805 km), vary the engine speed. Avoid prolonged steady running at one engine speed. During this period, increase engine speed to 3000 rpm. Do not exceed 55 mph during this period.

3. After the first 500 mi. (805 km), the engine break-in is complete.

Table 1 ENGINE LOWER END SPECIFICATIONS

Item	New In. (mm)	Service limit In. (mm)
Camshaft support plate		
Camshaft chain tensioner shoe	–	Less than 0.060 (1.52)
Camshaft bore in plate	–	1.1023 (27.998)
Connecting rod		
Connecting rod-to-crankpin clearance	0.0004-0.0017 (0.018-0.030)	0.002 (0.051)
Piston pin clearance in connecting rod		
All models except CVO	0.0007-0.00012 (0.018-0.030)	0.002 (0.051)
CVO models	0.0006-0.00012 (0.015-0.030)	0.002 (0.051)
Connecting rod side play	–	0.020 (0.508)
Oil pump pressure (at 230º F (110º C)	30-38 psi (207-262 kN/m²) @ 2000 rpm	–
Oil pump rotor thickness differential between		
rotors	–	0.001 (0.025)
Crankshaft		
Runout		
Shaft measured in case	–	0.012 (0.305)
Measured in truing stand	–	0.005 (0.127)
End play	–	0.013 (0.330)
Oil pressure relief valve		
Valve seated depth	2.25 in. (57.15 mm)	–
Running clearance	0.003 in. (0.076 mm)	–

Table 2 REAR CAMSHAFT SPROCKET SPACERS

Part No.	in.	mm
25729-06	0.100	2.54
25731-06	0.110	2.79
25734-06	0.120	3.05
25736-06	0.130	3.30
25737-06	0.140	3.56
25738-06	0.150	3.81

Table 3 ENGINE LOWER END TORQUE SPECIFICATIONS

Item	ft.-lb.	in.-lb.	N•m
Breather cover bolts	–	120-156	13.6-17.6
Camshaft cover bolts	–	125-155	14.1-17.5
Camshaft support plate			
Perimeter six bolts	–	90-120	10.2-13.6
Center four bolts (adjacent to oil pump)			
Initial	–	40-45	4.5-5.1
Final	–	90-120	10.2-13.6
Sprocket bolts			
Preliminary	15	–	20.3
Rear camshaft sprocket bolt	34	–	46.1
Crankshaft sprocket bolt	24	–	32.5
Cam chain tensioner bolt	–	90-120	10.2-13.6
Crank position sensor bolt	–	100-120	11.3-13.6
Crankshaft drive sprocket bolt	See text		
Crankcase bolts			
Initial	10	–	13.6
Final	15-19	–	20.3-25.8
Crankshaft right side main bearing screws	–	40-70	4.5-7.9
Cylinder stud	10-20	–	13.6-27.1
Initial	10	–	13.6
Final	15-19	–	20.3-25.8
Cylinder stud	10-20	–	13.6-27.1
Engine-to-transmission bolt			
Preliminary	15	–	20.3
Final	34-39	–	46.1-52.9
Upper mounting bracket to cylinder head hex bolts	30-35	–	41-48
Stabilizer link-to-frame weldment Allen bolt	18-22	–	24.4-29.8
Stabilizer link-to-upper mounting bracket Allen bolt	18-22	–	24.4-29.8
End cap Allen bolts	42-48	–	56.9-65.0
Oil cooler			
Adapter inspection cover	–	90-120	10.2-13.6
Mounting screws	20-22	–	27.1-29.8
Mounting bracket locknuts (2010 models)	–	70-100	7.9-11.3
Oil cooler adapter	18-22	–	24.4-29.8
Piston oil jet screw	–	25-35	2.8-4.0

5

NOTES

CHAPTER SIX

CLUTCH AND PRIMARY DRIVE

PRIMARY CHAINCASE COVER

Removal

Refer to **Figure 1**.

> *WARNING*
> *Disconnect the negative battery cable or pull the main fuse before working on the clutch or any primary drive component to avoid accidentally activating the starter.*

> *NOTE*
> *Always disarm the optional TSM/TSSM/ HFSM security system before disconnecting the battery or pulling the main fuse so the alarm will not sound.*

1. Disconnect the negative battery cable (Chapter Nine).
2. Remove the left side footboard (Chapter Fourteen).
3. Remove the clamp bolt (A, **Figure 2**) and remove the heel shift lever (B).
4. Drain the primary chaincase oil (Chapter Three).

> *NOTE*
> *Two different length bolts secure the primary chaincase cover. Note and mark the location of the short (S) and long (L) bolts (**Figure 3**). They must be reinstalled in the correct location.*

5. Evenly loosen the primary chaincase cover bolts (**Figure 3**).

6. Pull the cover bolts along with their washers, and remove the chaincase cover and cover gasket. Watch for the dowel pins (A, **Figure 4**) behind the cover.

Installation

1. If removed, install the dowel pins A, **Figure 4** into the primary chaincase housing.

> *CAUTION*
> *The manufacturer specifies that a new gasket must be installed every time the primary chaincase cover is removed.*

> *NOTE*
> *The gasket is very thin and it may shift before the installation of the cover bolts.*

2. Apply a couple of small dabs of gasket sealer to the backside of the new gasket to help hold it in place on the dowel pins.
3. Install the new gasket over the dowel pins (A, **Figure 4**), and seat it against the gasket surface (B) of the chaincase housing.
4. Slide the primary cover over the dowels, and seat it against the gasket.
5. Insert the short (S) and long (L) bolts, with their washers, into the locations noted during removal (**Figure 3**). Following the torque sequence shown in **Figure 3**, tighten the primary chaincase cover bolts to144-156 in.-lb. (16.3-17.6 N•m). Make sure the gasket seats flush around the cover.

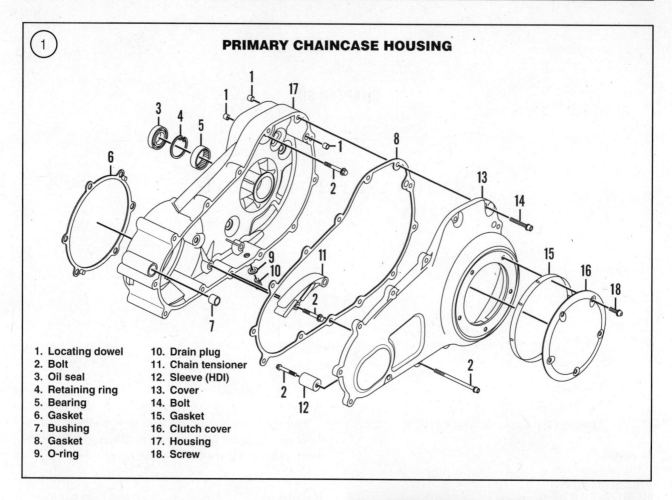

PRIMARY CHAINCASE HOUSING

1. Locating dowel
2. Bolt
3. Oil seal
4. Retaining ring
5. Bearing
6. Gasket
7. Bushing
8. Gasket
9. O-ring
10. Drain plug
11. Chain tensioner
12. Sleeve (HDI)
13. Cover
14. Bolt
15. Gasket
16. Clutch cover
17. Housing
18. Screw

6. Install the heel shift lever (B, **Figure 2**) and clamp bolt (A). Tighten the bolt securely.

7. Install the left footboard (Chapter Fourteen).

8. Fill the primary chaincase with the type and quantity of the specified oil as described in Chapter Three.

9. Connect the negative battery cable or install the main fuse (Chapter Nine).

Inspection

1. Remove all gasket residue from the chaincase cover (**Figure 5**) and chaincase housing gasket surfaces (B, **Figure 4**).

2. Clean the primary cover in solvent. Dry it with compressed air.

3. Inspect the primary chaincase cover for cracks or damage.

PRIMARY CHAINCASE HOUSING

The primary chaincase housing mounts to both the engine and transmission. It houses the primary drive assembly, alternator rotor, and the mainshaft oil seal and bearing assembly.

Refer to **Figure 6**.

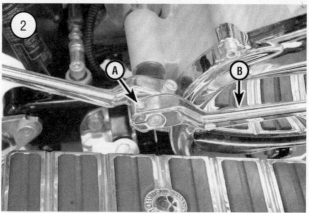

Removal

NOTE
Always disarm the optional TSSM/HFSM security system before disconnecting the battery or pulling the Main-Fuse so the alarm will not sound.

1. Disconnect the negative battery cable as described in Chapter Nine.

2. Remove the primary chaincase cover and the primary drive assembly as described in this chapter.

3. Remove the starter as described in Chapter Eleven.

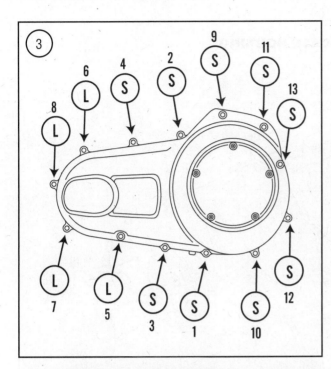

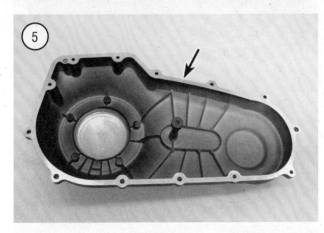

4. Remove the five primary chaincase housing bolts (**Figure 7**). Discard the bolts as they cannot be reused.

5. Tap the housing loose.

6. Remove the housing from the crankcase, transmission and gearshift shaft.

7. Remove the gasket (**Figure 8**) from the engine crankcase flange and discard it.

8. If still in place, remove the gasket locating pins from the crankcase flange or old gasket.

9. If still in place, remove the two locating dowels from the transmission case.

Installation

1. Confirm that the swing arm pivot shaft is properly tightened. Refer to Chapter Twelve.

2. Thoroughly clean the *outer surface* of the five primary chaincase housing bolt holes.

3. Thoroughly clean the mating surfaces of the housing, transmission and crankcase.

4. Install the locating dowels (A, **Figure 9**) into the transmission case or the inboard side of the primary housing.

5. Ensure the two gasket locating pins (**Figure 10**) are in place on a new crankshaft gasket. Apply engine oil to the rubber portion of the gasket.

6. Install the *new* gasket (**Figure 8**) onto the engine crankcase flange so the gasket locating pins engages the crankcase flange holes.

7. To prevent the transmission mainshaft splines from damaging the oil seal in the housing, wrap the mainshaft splines with 1-2 layers of smooth tape (no duct tape) (A, **Figure 11**). Apply clean primary crankcase oil to the tape and to the lips of the oil seal (B, **Figure 11**).

8. If removed, install the drive belt before installing the housing.

9. Align the housing dowels (A, **Figure 9**) with their mating holes transmission case, install the housing and press it securely against the crankcase and transmission case. Remove the tape (A, **Figure 11**) from the mainshaft splines.

10. Install the five *new* primary chaincase bolts fingertight. Do *not* apply lubricant to the captive rubber seal on the bolts.

11. Following the torque sequence shown in **Figure 12**, tighten the primary chaincase housing bolts evenly in two-to-three stages 26-28 ft.-lb. (35.3-38.0 N•m) .

12. Install the starter as described in Chapter Nine.

13. Install the primary drive assembly and the primary chaincase cover as described in this chapter.

14. Connect the negative battery cable or install the Main-Fuse as described in Chapter Nine.

Inspection

1. Remove all gasket material from the housing gasket surfaces on the outboard (B, **Figure 9**) and inboard (**Figure 13**) sides of the primary chaincase housing.

2. Clean the inner housing in solvent. Dry it thoroughly.

3. Check the housing for cracks or other damage.

4. Turn the mainshaft bearing (**Figure 14**) by hand. If necessary, replace the bearing as follows:

PRIMARY CHAINCASE HOUSING

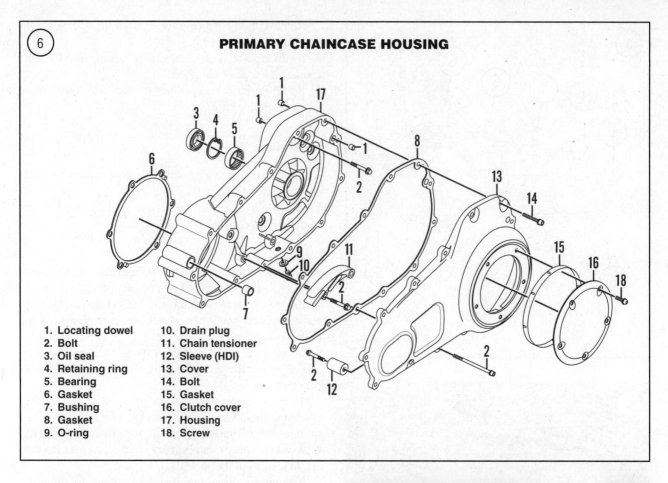

1. Locating dowel
2. Bolt
3. Oil seal
4. Retaining ring
5. Bearing
6. Gasket
7. Bushing
8. Gasket
9. O-ring
10. Drain plug
11. Chain tensioner
12. Sleeve (HDI)
13. Cover
14. Bolt
15. Gasket
16. Clutch cover
17. Housing
18. Screw

a. Remove the oil seal (**Figure 15**) as described in this section.

b. Remove the bearing snap ring (A, **Figure 16**) that sits beneath the oil seal. Discard the snap ring.

c. Support the housing in a press with the clutch side facing up (**Figure 13**) and press the bearing from the housing.

d. Apply engine oil to the *new* bearing and the bearing bore in the primary chaincase housing.

e. Support the housing in the press so the transmission side faces up.

f. Position the bearing so the side with the manufacturer's marks face up. Then, press in the bearing until it bottoms in the bearing bore. Use a driver or socket that matches the outside diameter of the bearing.

g. Install a *new* snap ring (A, **Figure 16**) so it is completely seated within the groove in the housing. Position the snap ring so it does not block the oil hole (B, **Figure 16**).

h. Install a *new* oil seal as described in this section.

5. If necessary, replace the mainshaft bearing inner race (**Figure 17**) as described in *Transmission Side Door Assembly* (Chapter Seven).

6. Inspect the oil seal (**Figure 15**) for excessive wear, tearing or other damage. To replace the oil seal, perform the following:

a. Use a flat-bladed screwdriver to pry the oil seal from the transmission side (inboard) of the housing.

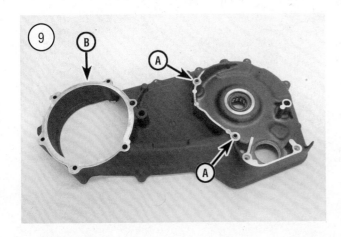

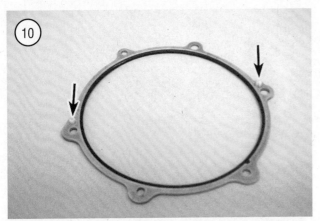

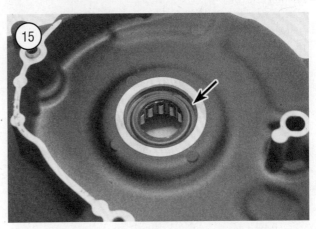

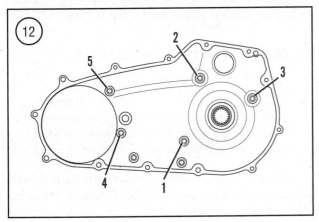

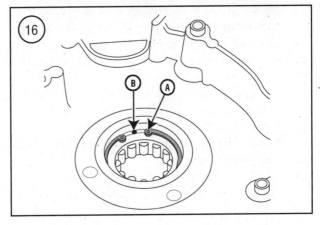

b. Clean the oil seal bore.

c. Pack the lip of the new oil seal with a waterproof bearing grease.

d. Position the oil seal so the side marked *OIL SIDE* faces the bearing. Using a driver (**Figure 18**) or a socket that presses against the outside edge of the seal, press the *new* oil seal into the housing until its outer surface sits flush with the edge of the bearing bore.

CLUTCH ASSEMBLY

This section describes removal, inspection and installation of the clutch plates. If the clutch requires additional service, refer to *Clutch Shell, Hub and Sprocket* in this chapter.

Refer to **Figures 19-21**.

Removal

NOTE
Always disarm the optional TSSM/HFSM security system before disconnecting the battery or pulling the Main-Fuse so the alarm will not sound.

1. Disconnect the negative battery cable as described in Chapter Eleven.

2. Remove the primary chaincase cover (**Figure 22**) as described in this chapter.

3A. On all models except CVO, perform the following:

a. At the clutch, loosen the clutch adjusting screw locknut (A, **Figure 23**) and turn the adjusting screw (B) *counterclockwise* to allow slack against the diaphragm spring.

b. Remove the snap ring (C, **Figure 23**), and then remove the release plate/adjusting screw assembly (**Figure 24**).

3B. On 2012 CVO models, perform the following:

a. Remove the large snap ring (A, **Figure 25**) securing the release bearing plate.

b. Pull the release bearing plate (B, **Figure 25**) and the pushrod (C) from the pressure plate as an assembly.

c. Remove the small snap ring (D, **Figure 25**). If necessary, pull the push rod from the release bearing.

3C. On all models except 2013 CVO models, perform the following:

a. Using a crisscross pattern, evenly loosen the diaphragm spring retainer bolts (A, **Figure 26**). Remove the bolts and the retainer (B, **Figure 26**).

b. Remove the diaphragm spring (**Figure 27**) and pressure plate (**Figure 28**).

3D. On 2013 CVO models, perform the following:

a. Using a crisscross pattern, evenly loosen the three bolts securing the stopper plate to the clutch hub.

NOTE
The small spring seats will fall out when the three bolts and springs are removed.

b. Remove the three bolts, springs and spring seats securing the stopper plate. Watch for the spring seats.

c. Remove the stopper plate and pressure plate.

d. Remove the two narrow friction plates and the narrow plain plate from the backside of the pressure plate.

4. Remove each friction disc and plain plate (**Figure 29**) from the clutch shell, keeping them in the order of removal.

5. Remove the damper spring (**Figure 30**) and damper spring seat (**Figure 31**) from the clutch shell.

6. Inspect the parts as described in this section.

Installation (All Models Except 2013 CVO)

NOTE
*The original equipment clutch set (**Figure 29**) has nine friction discs, eight plain plates, one damper spring and one damper spring seat. Make sure each part is installed.*

1. Soak the clutch friction disc and clutch plates in new primary drive oil for approximately 5 minutes before installing them.

CLUTCH (ALL MODELS EXCEPT CVO)

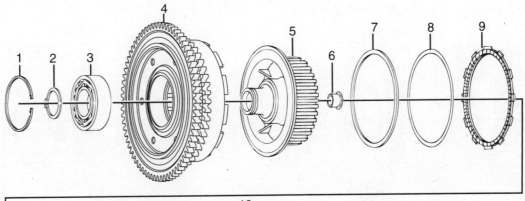

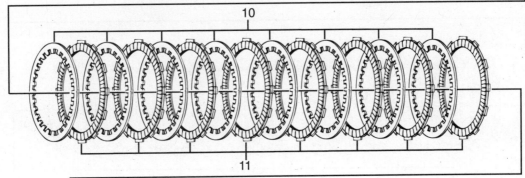

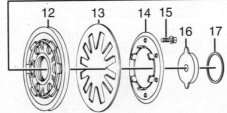

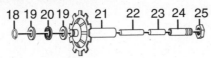

1. Snap ring
2. Snap ring
3. Bearing
4. Clutch shell and sprocket
5. Clutch hub
6. Clutch nut
7. Damper spring seat
8. Damper spring
9. Friction disc B
10. Plain plates
11. Friction disc A
12. Pressure plate
13. Diaphragm spring

14. Diaphragm spring retainer
15. Bolt
16. Release plate
17. Snap ring
18. Snap ring
19. Thrust washer
20. Radial bearing
21. Oil slinger
22. Pushrod—right side
23. Pushrod—left side
24. Adjust screw
25. Locknut

6

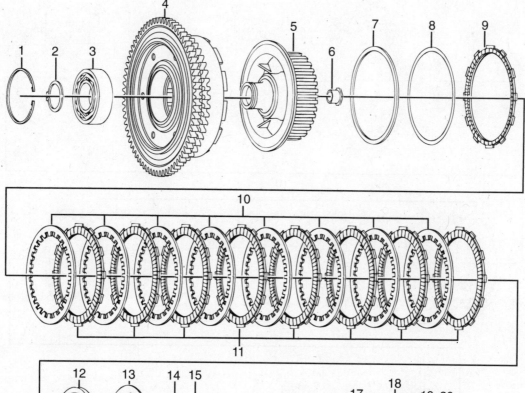

CLUTCH (2012 CVO MODELS)

1. Snap ring
2. Snap ring
3. Bearing
4. Clutch shell and sprocket
5. Clutch hub
6. Clutch nut
7. Damper spring seat
8. Damper spring
9. Friction disc B
10. Plain plates
11. Friction disc A
12. Pressure plate
13. Diaphragm spring
14. Diaphragm spring retainer
15. Bolt
16. Pushrod
17. Bearing
18. Release bearing plate
19. Snap ring–small
20. Snap ring–large

CLUTCH (2013 CVO MODELS)

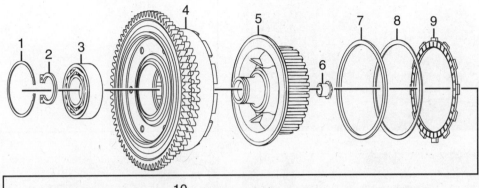

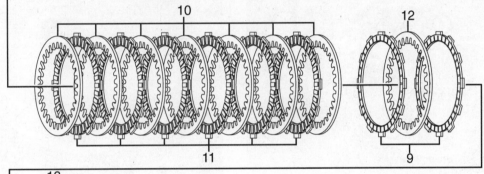

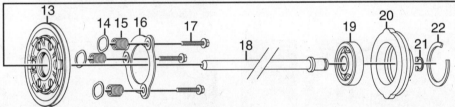

1. Snap ring
2. Snap ring
3. Bearing
4. Clutch shell and sprocket
5. Clutch hub
6. Clutch nut
7. Damper spring seat
8. Damper spring
9. Friction disc B–narrow
10. Plain plates–wide
11. Friction disc A–wide
12. Plain plate–narrow
13. Pressure plate
14. Spring seat
15. Spring
16. Stopper plate
17. Bolt
18. Pushrod
19. Bearing
20. Release bearing plate
21. Snap ring–small
22. Snap ring–large

6

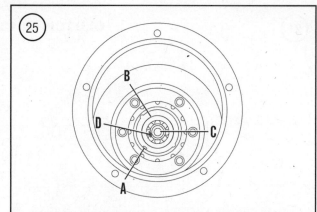

NOTE
*The clutch uses two different types of friction discs (**Figure 32**). The wider friction disc A (A, **Figure 32**) is the normal width disc. The narrower friction disc B (B, **Figure 32**) is installed first, as it works in conjunction with the damper spring and damper spring seat.*

2. Install friction disc B (**Figure 33**) so its tangs engage the slots in clutch shell. Push the disc all the way in until it bottoms within the clutch hub.

3. Install the damper spring seat (**Figure 31**) onto the clutch hub and push it in until it seats within friction disc B.

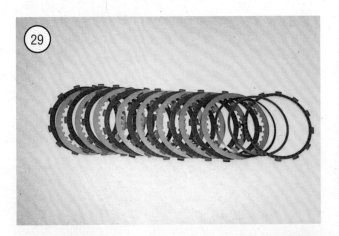

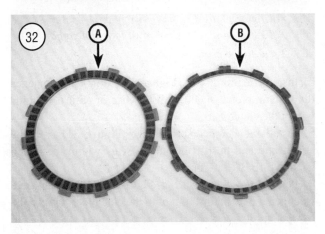

4. Position the damper spring (**Figure 30**) with the concave side facing out and install it onto the clutch hub against the damper spring seat.

5. Install a plain plate (**Figure 34**) so its inner teeth engage the clutch hub, and then install a friction disc A (**Figure 35**). Continue to alternately install the clutch plates and friction discs A. The last part installed is a friction disc A (**Figure 35**).

6. Install the pressure plate (**Figure 28**) onto the clutch hub.

7. Position the diaphragm spring (**Figure 27**) with its concave side facing in, and seat it onto the pressure plate.

8. Install the diaphragm spring retainer (B, **Figure 26**) so its tabs sit between the fingers of the diaphragm spring, and then install the retainer bolts (A).

9. Using a crossing pattern, evenly tighten the diaphragm-spring-retainer bolts to 70-100 in-lb. (7.9-11.3 N•m).

10A. On all models except CVO, install the release plate/adjuster assembly (**Figure 24**) so the ears of the release plate engage the cutouts (**Figure 36**) in the pressure plate. Make sure the side of the release plate marked OUT faces out. Install the snap ring (C, **Figure 23**).

10B. On CVO models, refer to **Figure 20** and perform the following:

    a. Press a new bearing into the release plate.

    b. Install the pushrod into the bearing, and install a new small snap ring into the pushrod groove.

    c. Slide the pushrod/release plate assembly into the mainshaft bore so the ears of the release plate engage the cutouts in the pressure plate.

    d. Install a new large snap ring.

11. Install the primary chaincase cover as described in this chapter.

12A. On all models except CVO, adjust the clutch as described in Chapter Three.

12B. On CVO models, inspect the clutch pushrod and release plate as described in this chapter.

NOTE
All lubricant must be removed from the seal ring and its groove prior to installation. If any lubricant remains there will be temporary lubricant seepage around the inspection cover.

13. Remove the seal ring from the clutch cover. Wipe all lubricant from the seal ring and inspect it for cuts or deterioration, replace if necessary. Wipe all lubricant from the seal ring groove and install the seal ring onto the cover. Push the nibs into the ring groove walls.

14. Install the clutch cover and seal ring (**Figure 37**) onto the primary chaincase cover.

15. Install the clutch cover screws (**Figure 38**). Then, using a crossing pattern, evenly tighten the clutch cover screws to 84-108 in.-lb. (9.5-12.2 N•m).

16. Connect the negative battery cable as described in Chapter Nine.

Installation
(2013 CVO Models)

1. Soak the clutch friction disc and clutch plates in new primary drive oil for approximately 5 minutes before installing them.

NOTE
*The clutch uses two different types of friction discs. The wider friction disc A (A, **Figure 32**) is the normal width disc. The narrow friction disc B (B, **Figure 32**) is installed first, as it works in conjunction with the damper spring and damper spring seat adjacent to*

the clutch hub. There are two narrow friction discs B along with a narrow plain plate adjacent to the pressure plate.

2. Install friction disc B (**Figure 33**) so its tangs engages the slots in clutch shell. Push the disc in until it bottoms within the clutch hub.

3. Install the damper spring seat (**Figure 31**) onto the clutch hub and push it in until it seats within the clutch friction disc B.

4. Position the damper spring (**Figure 30**) with the concave side facing out and install it onto the clutch hub against the damper spring seat.

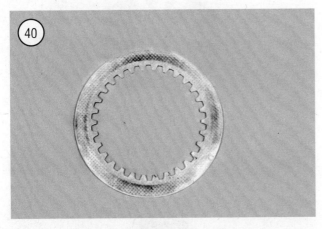

12. Install the pushrod (18, **Figure 21**) into the bearing, and install a new small snap ring (21) into the pushrod groove. Make sure the snap ring is seated correctly.

13. Slide the pushrod/release plate assembly into the mainshaft bore so the ears of the release plate engage the cutouts in the pressure plate.

14. Install a new large snap ring (22, **Figure 21**).

15. Install the primary chaincase cover as described in this chapter.

16. Check the clutch pushrod and release plate movement as described in this chapter.

17. Install the primary chaincase cover as described in this chapter.

18. Connect the negative battery cable or install the main fuse (Chapter Nine).

Inspection

Compare any measurements taken to the specifications listed in **Table 1** when inspecting clutch components. Replace any parts that are worn, damaged or out of specification.

1. Clean all parts in solvent. Thoroughly dry them with compressed air.

2. Inspect the friction discs as follows:

NOTE
*If any friction disc need replacing, replace **all nine** friction discs as a set. Never replace only one or two discs.*

a. Inspect the friction material (**Figure 32**) for excessive or uneven wear, cracks and other damage.

NOTE
If the friction disc tangs are damaged, inspect the clutch shell fingers carefully as described in this chapter.

b. Check the disc tangs for surface damage. The sides of the disc tangs must be smooth where they contact the clutch shell slots; otherwise, the discs cannot engage and disengage correctly.

c. Measure the thickness (**Figure 39**) of each friction disc with a caliper at several places around the disc.

3. Inspect the plain plates (**Figure 40**) as follows:

a. Inspect the plain plates for cracks, damage or color change. Overheated clutch plates have a bluish discoloration.

b. Check the plain plates for oil glaze buildup. Remove any glaze by lightly sanding both sides of each plate with 400 grit sandpaper placed on a surface plate or piece of glass.

c. Place each plain plate on a flat surface, and check for warp (**Figure 41**) with a feeler gauge.

5. Install a plain plate (**Figure 34**) so its inner teeth engage the clutch hub, and then install a friction disc A (**Figure 35**).

6. Continue to alternately install the wide pain plates and wide friction discs A until all of the wide parts are installed. The last part installed is a *wide plain plate*.

7. Insert the three bolts into the outside surface of the stopper plate. Turn it over with the bolts sticking up. Install the three springs and three spring seats onto these three bolts.

8. Install one narrow friction disc B, one narrow plain plate and one narrow friction disc B onto the pressure plate.

9. Secure the friction and plain plates onto the pressure plate and install the assembly onto the stopper plate and three bolts.

10. Align the bolts and threaded bosses and, install the pressure plate assembly onto the clutch hub. Assuring correct alignment, push the assembly in until it bottoms. Evenly tighten the bolts finger tight, then using a crisscross pattern, tighten them to 70-100 in.-lb. (7.9-11.3 N•m).

11 Press a new bearing (19, **Figure 21**) into the release plate (20).

NOTE
If the clutch plate teeth are damaged, inspect the clutch hub splines carefully as described in this chapter.

d. The clutch plate inner teeth mesh with the clutch hub splines. Check the clutch plate teeth for any roughness or damage. The teeth contact surfaces must be smooth; otherwise, the plates cannot engage and disengage correctly.

4. Inspect the diaphragm spring (**Figure 42**) for cracks or damage.

5. Inspect the diaphragm spring retainer (**Figure 43**) for cracks or damage. Check also for bent or damaged fingers.

6. Inspect outer surface of the pressure plate (**Figure 44**) for wear caused by contact with the diaphragm spring. Check also for cracks or other damage.

7. On all models except CVO models, perform the following:

a. Inspect the release plate, left pushrod and locknut for wear or damage.

b. Inspect the pressure-plate snap ring groove for damage.

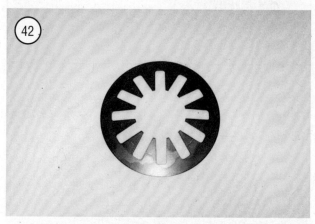

CLUTCH PUSHROD AND RELEASE PLATE INSPECTION (CVO MODELS)

1. Remove the clutch cover (**Figure 38**) from the primary chaincase cover.

2. Mount a dial indicator to one of the clutch cover bolt holes or to a suitable stationary stand.

3. Position the dial indicator anvil against the end of the clutch pushrod (C, **Figure 25**).

4. Fully apply the clutch lever, and note the pushrod movement.

5. The pushrod must move a minimum of 0.065 in. (1.65 mm) to guarantee complete clutch disengagement.

NOTE
Correct the clutch fluid level and bleed the clutch system if pushrod movement is greater than 0.065 in. (1.65 mm).

6. If the push rod movement is less than specified, the clutch fluid level is low and the clutch system must be bled as described in this chapter.

NOTE
All lubricant must be removed from the seal ring and its groove prior to installation. If any lubricant remains there will be temporary lubricant seepage around the inspection cover.

7. Remove the seal ring from the clutch cover. Wipe all lubricant from the seal ring and inspect it for cuts or deterioration; replace if necessary. Wipe all lubricant from the seal ring groove and install the seal ring onto the cover. Push the nibs into the ring groove walls.

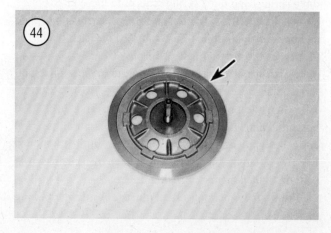

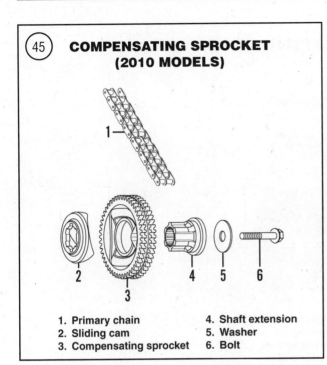

45 COMPENSATING SPROCKET (2010 MODELS)

1. Primary chain
2. Sliding cam
3. Compensating sprocket
4. Shaft extension
5. Washer
6. Bolt

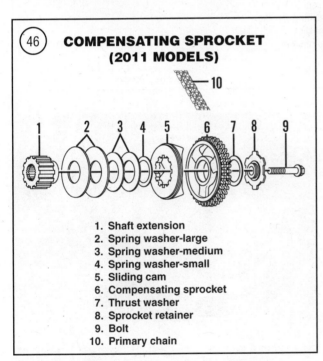

46 COMPENSATING SPROCKET (2011 MODELS)

1. Shaft extension
2. Spring washer-large
3. Spring washer-medium
4. Spring washer-small
5. Sliding cam
6. Compensating sprocket
7. Thrust washer
8. Sprocket retainer
9. Bolt
10. Primary chain

8. Install the clutch cover (**Figure 38**) and seal ring (**Figure 37**) onto the primary chain case cover.

   g. Install the clutch cover screws. Then, using a crossing pattern, evenly tighten the Torx screws (T27) to 84-108 in.-lb. (9.5-12.2 N•m).

PRIMARY DRIVE ASSEMBLY

The primary drive assembly consists of the clutch shell, compensating sprocket and primary chain. These must be removed and installed as an assembly.

The primary drive locking tool (JIMS part No. 2312 or H-D part No. HD-47977) is needed to remove and install the primary drive assembly.

Removal

Refer to **Figures 45-47**.

NOTE
Always disarm the optional TSSM/HFSM security system before disconnecting the battery or pulling the Maxi-Fuse so the alarm will not sound.

1. Disconnect the negative battery cable as described in Chapter Nine.
2. Remove the primary chaincase cover as described in this chapter.
3A. On all models except CVO perform the following:
   a. Loosen the clutch adjusting screw locknut (A, **Figure 48**) and turn the adjusting screw (B) *counterclockwise* to allow slack against the diaphragm spring.
   b. Remove the snap ring (C, **Figure 48**).
   c. Make sure the locknut (A, **Figure 49**) is still on the adjusting screw (B), and remove the release plate.
3B. On 2010-2012 CVO models, perform the following:
   a. Loosen the large snap ring (A, **Figure 50**) securing the release bearing plate.
   b. Pull the release bearing plate (B, **Figure 50**) and the pushrod (C) from the pressure plate as an assembly.
3C. On 2013 CVO models, perform the following:
   a. Loosen the large snap ring (A, **Figure 51**) securing the release bearing plate.
   b. Pull the release bearing plate (B, **Figure 51**) with release bearing (D) and the pushrod (C) from the pressure plate as an assembly.

CAUTION
Failure to secure the tensioner in the compressed position will result in damage to the last 2-3 threads of the primary chain tensioner bolts during removal.

4. Secure the tensioner assembly in the compressed position with a cable strap. Insert the cable strap under the tensioner and over the top of the tensioner shoe, leaving the tail of the cable strap (A, **Figure 52**) in place. It serves as a reminder to remove the cable strap during installation.
5. Remove the primary chain tensioner bolts (B, **Figure 52**), and remove the tensioner assembly.
6. Install the primary drive locking tool (A, **Figure 53**) between the teeth of the primary chain sprocket on the clutch hub and compensating sprocket to prevent the clutch from rotating.

CAUTION
*The clutch nut has **left-hand threads**. Turn the clutch nut clockwise to loosen it.*

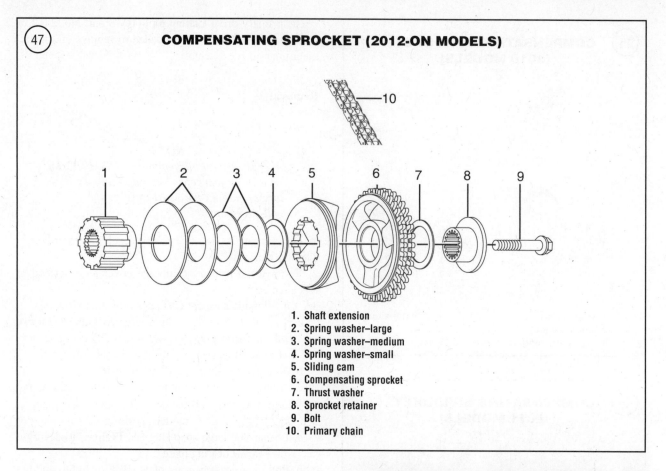

COMPENSATING SPROCKET (2012-ON MODELS)

1. Shaft extension
2. Spring washer–large
3. Spring washer–medium
4. Spring washer–small
5. Sliding cam
6. Compensating sprocket
7. Thrust washer
8. Sprocket retainer
9. Bolt
10. Primary chain

7. Loosen the clutch nut (B, **Figure 53**) *clockwise* with an impact wrench, and remove the clutch nut.

8. Reposition the primary drive locking tool (A, **Figure 54**) to prevent the compensating sprocket from rotating.

9. Loosen the compensating sprocket bolt (B, **Figure 54**) with an impact wrench.

10. Remove the compensating sprocket bolt (**Figure 55**), washer and shaft extension (**Figure 56**).

11. Use a permanent marker pen or scribe to mark an outboard link on the primary chain. The primary chain should be reinstalled so it rotates in its original direction to prolong chain life. Refer to these marks during installation.

12A. On 2010 models, perform the following:

   a. Remove the compensating sprocket (**Figure 57**), primary chain and clutch shell assembly (**Figure 58**) all at the same time.

   b. Remove the sliding cam (A, **Figure 59**) located behind the compensating sprocket (B).

12B. On 2011-on models, perform the following:

   a. Remove the compensating sprocket bolt, sprocket retainer and the thrust washer.

   b. Remove the compensating sprocket (**Figure 57**), primary chain and clutch shell assembly (**Figure 58**) all at the same time.

   c. Remove the sliding cam (A, **Figure 59**) located behind the compensating sprocket (B).

   d. Remove the small spring washer, two medium spring washers and two large spring washers from the engine sprocket shaft.

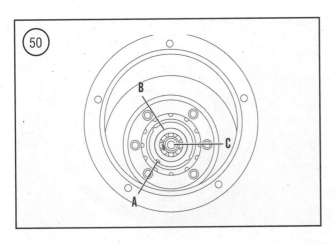

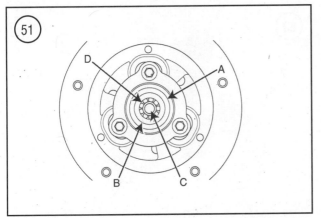

6

e. Remove the shaft extension from the engine sprocket shaft.

13 Inspect the various components as described in this chapter.

Installation

1. Remove all threadlock residue from the threads of the crankshaft, mainshaft, compensating sprocket bolt and the clutch nut.

2. Remove all gasket material from the primary housing gasket surfaces.

NOTE
If reinstalling the old primary chain tensioner, compress the tensioner.

3. Assemble the tensioner (**Figure 60**) if necessary. Then, compress the tensioner as follows:
   a. Position the spring rod end on the roll pin.
   b. Slide the wedge (A, **Figure 61**) toward the roll pin until all travel is removed.
   c. Push tensioner shoe (B, **Figure 61**) down until it contacts the wedge and hold it in this position. Keep tension on shoe to keep wedge in place.
   d. Install a cable strap around the shoe and tensioner so the end of the strap is located outboard of the tensioner assembly (**Figure 62**). The end of the strap must hang below the primary chain cover to insure it is visible after the tensioner is installed so it will be cut and removed.

NOTE
*The chain tensioner is sold as an assembly, but may become disassembled during shipment as shown in **Figure 60**.*

4. If installing a new chain tensioner, assemble the tensioner, if necessary, and then compress it as follows:
   a. Compress the spring rod into the wedge, and seat the end of the spring rod onto the roll pin.
   b. Slide the wedge (A, **Figure 63**) to the very end of the spring rod (B).
   c. Lower the wedge so its rear-most tooth engages the rear-most tooth on the tensioner serrations. Hold the wedge in this position.
   d. Push the tensioner shoe (C, **Figure 63**) down against the wedge. Hold it in this position.
   e. Use a cable strap to secure the tensioner (**Figure 64**) in this compressed position. The cable strap end must sit on the outboard side of the tensioner so it can be cut and removed after tensioner installation.

5. Apply a light coat of primary chaincase oil to the inside bore of the compensating sprocket and to the splines of the shaft extension.

6A. On 2010 models, perform the following:
   a. Lubricate the ramps of the sliding cam (A, **Figure 59**) and fit the sliding cam on back of the compensating sprocket (B).

b. Slide the washer onto the compensating sprocket bolt.
   c. Refer to the marks made on the primary chain during removal to ensure it will rotate in the original direction. Fit the primary chain onto compensating sprocket and onto the primary chain sprocket on the clutch shell.
   d. Install the compensating sprocket (**Figure 57**), primary chain and clutch assembly (**Figure 58**) at the same time. Rotate the compensating sprocket and clutch hub slightly to ease installation.
   e. Install the shaft extension (**Figure 56**) into the compensating sprocket.

6B. On 2011-on models, perform the following:
   a. Position the bearing journal side of the shaft extension going on last and install the shaft extension into the engine sprocket shaft.
   b. Position the two large spring washers so the concave side of the washers face each other (**Figure 65**) and install them onto the shaft extension.
   c. Position the medium spring washers so the concave side of each washer face each other (**Figure 65**) and install them next to the two large washers on the shaft extension.
   d. Install the small spring washer so its concave side faces out.
   e. Install the sliding cam onto the shaft extension.

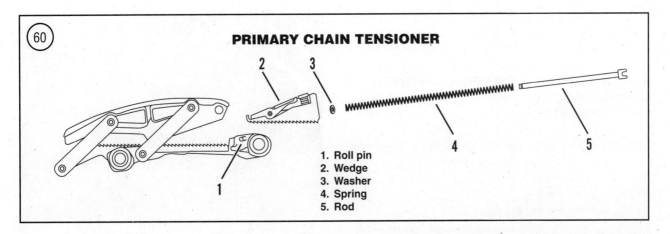

PRIMARY CHAIN TENSIONER

1. Roll pin
2. Wedge
3. Washer
4. Spring
5. Rod

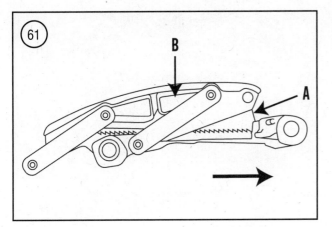

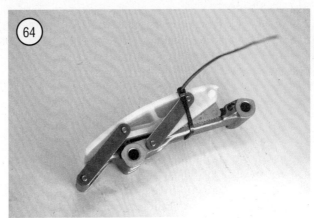

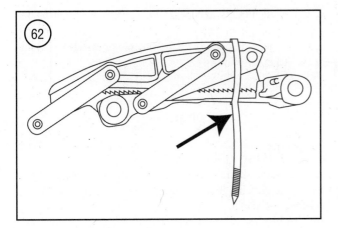

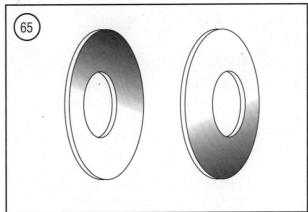

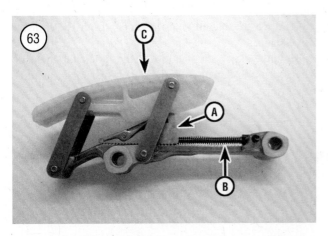

f. Install the compensating sprocket (**Figure 57**), primary chain and clutch assembly (**Figure 58**) at the same time. Rotate the compensating sprocket and clutch hub slightly to ease installation.

g. Install the thrust washer, sprocket retainer and the sprocket bolt.

CAUTION
If the primary chain tensioner is not installed, the primary chain could be pinched against the primary chain housing when the compensating sprocket bolt is tightened.

6

7. Insert the primary chain tensioner under the primary chain, and seat it against its mounting boss. Install the tensioner mounting bolts (B, **Figure 52**) and finger-tighten them.

8. Apply two drops of Loctite Threadlocker 262 (red) to the threads of the *new* compensating sprocket bolt. Install the bolt (**Figure 55**) and washer. Then, finger-tighten the bolt.

9. Position the primary drive locking tool (A, **Figure 66**) to keep the compensating sprocket from rotating.

10. Tighten the compensating sprocket bolt (B, **Figure 66**) to 100 ft.-lb. (135.6 N•m).

11. Loosen the bolt one full turn (360°).

12. Re-tighten the compensating sprocket bolt to 140 ft.-lb. (189.8 N•m).

13. Position the primary drive locking tool (A, **Figure 67**) to keep the clutch from rotating.

14. Apply two drops of Loctite Threadlocker 262 (red) to the clutch nut.

NOTE
*The clutch nut has **left-hand threads**. Turn the nut counterclockwise to tighten it.*

15. Install the clutch nut (B, **Figure 67**), and tighten it *counterclockwise* to 70-80 ft.-lb. (94.9-108.5 N•m).

16. Remove the primary drive locking tool.

17. Tighten the primary chain tensioner bolts (B, **Figure 52**) to 21-24 ft.-lb. (28.5-32.5 N•m).

NOTE
The tensioner will not completely release and adjust the primary chain until the motorcycle has been ridden a short distance.

18. Cut and remove the cable strap (A, **Figure 52**). Make sure no portion of the strap remains in the primary chaincase.

19A. On CVO models, refer to **Figure 50** or **Figure 51** and perform the following::
  a. Press a new bearing into the release plate.
  b. Install the pushrod into the bearing, and install a *new* small snap ring into the pushrod groove.
  c. Slide the pushrod/release plate assembly into the mainshaft bore so the ears of the release plate engage the cutouts in the pressure plate.
  d. Install a *new* large snap ring.

19B. On all models except CVO, install the release plate/adjuster assembly so the ears (**Figure 24**) of the release plate engage the cutouts (**Figure 36**) in the pressure plate. Make sure the side of the release plate marked OUT faces out. Install a *new* snap ring (C, **Figure 23**) and make sure it is seated correctly.

20. If removed, install the clutch plates, friction discs, pressure plate and diaphragm spring as described in *Clutch Assembly* (this chapter).

21. Install the primary chaincase cover as described in this chapter.

22. On all models except CVO, adjust the clutch as described in Chapter Three.

23. Connect the negative battery cable or install the Maxi-Fuse (Chapter Nine).

CLUTCH SHELL, HUB AND SPROCKET

Inspection

The clutch shell is a subassembly consisting of the clutch shell, the clutch hub, the bearing and two snap rings. Refer to **Figures 68-70**.

1. Remove the primary drive assembly as described in this chapter.

2. Remove the clutch shell assembly from the primary drive chain.

3. Hold the clutch shell and rotate the clutch hub by hand. The bearing is damaged if the clutch hub binds or turns roughly.

4. Check the primary chain sprocket (A, **Figure 71**) and the starter gear (B) on the clutch shell for cracks, deep scoring, excessive tooth wear or heat discoloration.

5. If the sprocket or the gear are worn or damaged, replace the clutch shell. If the primary chain sprocket is worn, also check the primary chain and the compensating sprocket as described in this chapter.

6. Inspect the clutch hub for the following:

68 **CLUTCH (ALL MODELS EXCEPT CVO)**

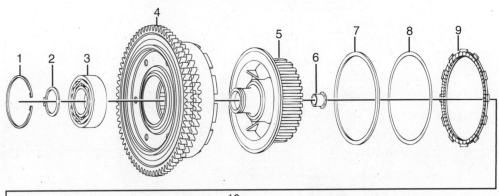

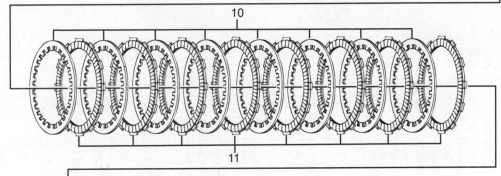

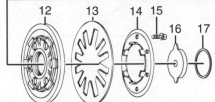

6

1. Snap ring
2. Snap ring
3. Bearing
4. Clutch shell and sprocket
5. Clutch hub
6. Clutch nut
7. Damper spring seat
8. Damper spring
9. Friction disc B
10. Plain plates
11. Friction disc A
12. Pressure plate
13. Diaphragm spring
14. Diaphragm spring retainer
15. Bolt
16. Release plate
17. Snap ring
18. Snap ring
19. Thrust washer
20. Radial bearing
21. Oil slinger
22. Pushrod—right side
23. Pushrod—left side
24. Adjust screw
25. Locknut

CLUTCH (2012 CVO MODELS)

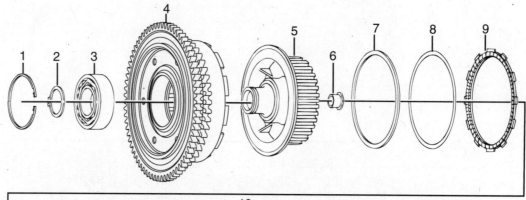

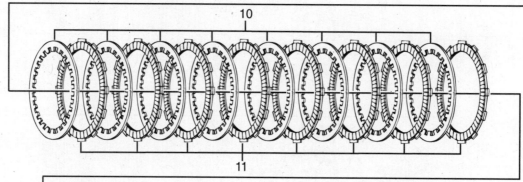

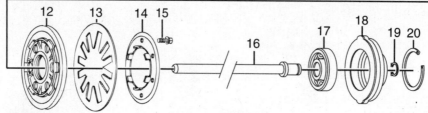

1. Snap ring
2. Snap ring
3. Bearing
4. Clutch shell and sprocket
5. Clutch hub
6. Clutch nut
7. Damper spring seat
8. Damper spring
9. Friction disc B
10. Plain plates
11. Friction disc A
12. Pressure plate
13. Diaphragm spring
14. Diaphragm spring retainer
15. Bolt
16. Pushrod
17. Bearing
18. Release bearing plate
19. Snap ring–small
20. Snap ring–large

CLUTCH (2013 CVO MODELS)

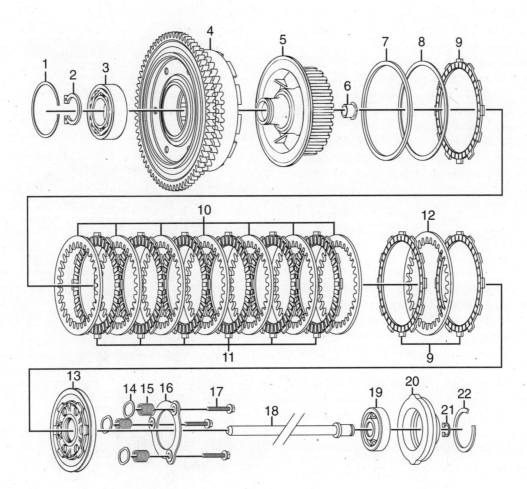

1. Snap ring
2. Snap ring
3. Bearing
4. Clutch shell and sprocket
5. Clutch hub
6. Clutch nut
7. Damper spring seat
8. Damper spring
9. Friction disc B—narrow
10. Plain plate—wide
11. Friction disc A—wide
12. Plain plate--narrow
13. Pressure plate
14. Spring seat
15. Spring
16. Stopper plate
17. Bolt
18. Pushrod
19. Bearing
20. Release bearing plate
21. Snap ring—small
22. Snap ring—large

a. The clutch plate teeth must slide in the clutch hub splines. Inspect the splines (A, **Figure 72**) for rough spots, grooves or other damage. Repair minor damage with a file or oil stone. If the damage is severe, replace the clutch hub.

b. Inspect the bolt towers (B, **Figure 72**) for thread damage or cracks at the base of the tower. Repair any thread damage with the correct size metric tap. If a tower is cracked or damaged, replace the clutch hub.

c. The friction disc tangs must slide in the clutch shell slots (C, **Figure 72**). Inspect the slots for cracks or galling. Repair minor damage with a file. If the damage is severe, replace the clutch housing.

7. Inspect the clutch hub inner splines (**Figure 73**). Check for galling, severe wear or other damage. Repair minor damage with a fine cut file. If damage is severe, replace the clutch hub.

8. If the clutch hub, the clutch shell or bearing are damaged, replace them as described in this section.

Disassembly/Assembly

Do not separate the clutch shell and hub unless the bearing or either part must be replaced. The bearing will be damaged when the shell and hub are separated. Removal and installation of the bearing requires the use of a hydraulic press.

1. Remove the friction discs and plain plates as described in *Clutch Assembly* (this chapter).

2. Remove the primary drive assembly as described in this chapter.

3. Remove the clutch shell assembly from the primary drive chain.

4. Place the clutch hub on the bench with the starter gear side facing up.

5. Remove the small snap ring (**Figure 74**) from the clutch hub groove.

6. Support the clutch shell on the press bed with the starter gear side *facing up*.

7. Place a suitable size arbor or socket on the clutch hub surface (**Figure 75**), and press the clutch hub from the bearing.

8. Remove the clutch shell from the press bed.

9. Remove the large snap ring (**Figure 76**) from the clutch shell groove.

> *CAUTION*
> *Press the bearing out from the primary chain sprocket side of the clutch shell. The bearing bore has a shoulder on the starter ring gear side.*

10. Support the clutch shell in the press with the primary chain sprocket side *facing up*.

11. Place a suitable size arbor or socket on the bearing inner race (**Figure 77**), and press the bearing out of the clutch shell.

12. Thoroughly clean the clutch hub and shell in solvent. Dry them with compressed air.

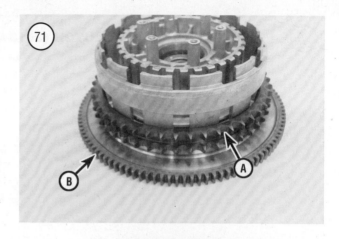

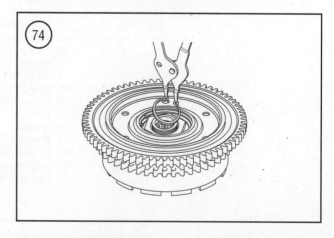

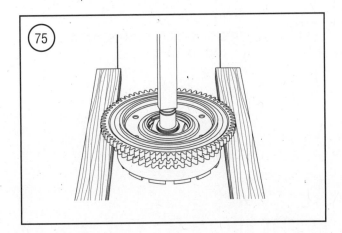

75

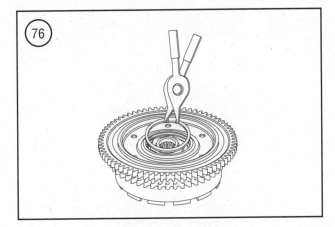

76

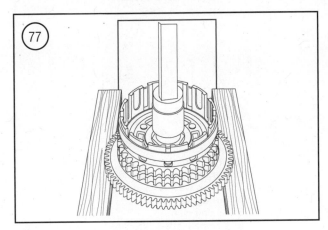

77

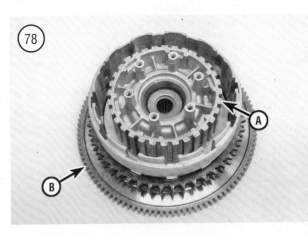

78

13. Inspect the bearing bore in the clutch shell for damage or burrs. Clean off any burrs that would interfere with new bearing installation.

14. Support the clutch shell in the press with the starter gear side *facing up*.

15. Apply chaincase lubricant to the bearing bore in the clutch shell and to the outer surface of the bearing.

16. Align the bearing with the clutch shell bore.

17. Place a suitable size arbor on the bearing outer race, and slowly press the bearing into the clutch shell until it bottoms on the lower shoulder. Press only on the outer bearing race. Applying force to the bearing's inner race will damage the bearing. Refer to *Bearings* (Chapter One) for additional information.

18. Position the *new* large snap ring with its flat side against the bearing (**Figure 76**), and install the large snap ring into the clutch shell groove. Make sure the snap ring completely seats in the clutch shell groove.

19. Press the clutch hub into the clutch shell as follows:

CAUTION
Failure to support the inner bearing race properly will cause bearing and clutch shell damage.

a. Place the clutch shell in a press so the starter gear side *faces down*. Support the inner bearing race with a sleeve that matches the bearing inner race.

b. Align the clutch hub with the bearing, and slowly press the clutch hub into the bearing until the clutch hub shoulder seats against the bearing inner race.

c. Turn the assembly over, and install a *new* small snap ring (**Figure 74**) into the clutch hub. Make sure the snap ring is completely seated in the clutch hub groove.

20. After completing assembly, hold the clutch hub (A, **Figure 78**) and rotate the clutch shell (B) by hand. The shell must turn smoothly with no roughness or binding. If the clutch shell binds or turns roughly, the bearing was installed incorrectly. Repeat the assembly procedure until this problem is corrected.

PRIMARY CHAIN AND TENSIONER INSPECTION (ALL MODELS)

1. Remove the primary chain as described in this chapter.

2. Remove the compensating sprocket and the clutch shell from the primary chain.

3. Clean the primary chain in solvent and dry thoroughly.

4. Inspect the primary chain (**Figure 79**) for excessive wear, cracks or other damage. If the chain is worn or damaged, check both sprockets for wear and damage.

NOTE
If the primary chain is near the end of its adjustment level or if no more adjustment is available, and the tensioner shoe is not worn or damaged; the primary chain is excessively worn. Specifications for chain wear are not available.

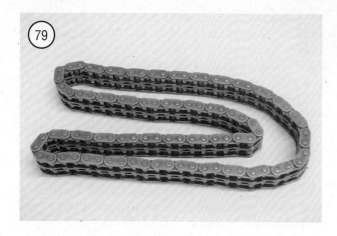

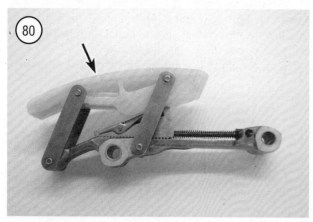

NOTE
The tensioner assembly cannot be serviced.
It must be replaced if any portion is worn or
damaged.

5. Inspect the chain tensioner shoe assembly (**Figure 80**) for cracks, severe wear or other damage. Replace the chain tensioner assembly if necessary.

COMPENSATING
SPROCKET INSPECTION

Refer to **Figures 81-83**.
1. Remove the compensating sprocket assembly as described in this chapter.
2. Clean all parts in solvent. Dry them with compressed air.
3. Check the shaft extension splines for wear or galling.
4. Inspect the bolt threads for damage.
5. Inspect the surfaces of the medium and large dished washers (**Figure 84**) for wear or distortion. Replace as a pair if damaged.

CLUTCH CABLE
(ALLMODELS EXCEPT CVO)

Replacement

Refer to **Figure 85**.

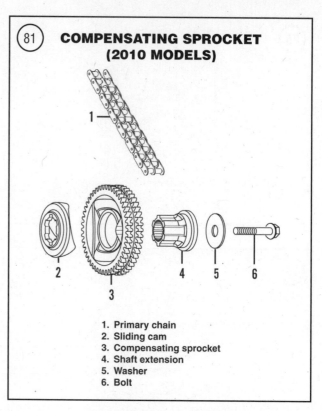

**COMPENSATING SPROCKET
(2010 MODELS)**

1. Primary chain
2. Sliding cam
3. Compensating sprocket
4. Shaft extension
5. Washer
6. Bolt

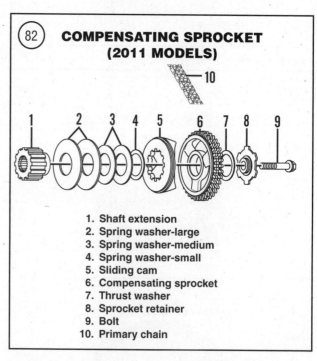

**COMPENSATING SPROCKET
(2011 MODELS)**

1. Shaft extension
2. Spring washer-large
3. Spring washer-medium
4. Spring washer-small
5. Sliding cam
6. Compensating sprocket
7. Thrust washer
8. Sprocket retainer
9. Bolt
10. Primary chain

1. Before removing the clutch cable, make a drawing of the cable's path from the handlebar, down the left frame-down tube, under the engine mounting spacer and on to the clutch release cover. The new cable must be routed along the same path.
2. Perform the following at the clutch cable adjuster:
  a. Release the clutch cable from the clamp (A, **Figure 86**) and slide the boot (B) away from the adjuster.

83

COMPENSATING SPROCKET (2012-ON MODELS)

10

1 2 3 4 5 6 7 8 9

1. Shaft extension
2. Spring washer–large
3. Spring washer–medium
4. Spring washer–small
5. Sliding cam
6. Compensating sprocket
7. Thrust washer
8. Sprocket retainer
9. Bolt
10. Primary chain

6

84

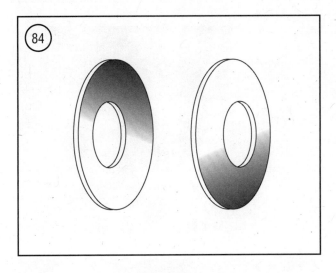

b. Loosen the locknut (C, **Figure 86**), and turn the adjuster (D) to provide maximum slack.

3. Disconnect the clutch cable (**Figure 87**) from the clutch release mechanism and remove it from the release cover as described in *Clutch Release Cover Disassembly* (this chapter).

4. Remove the snap ring from the bottom of the clutch lever pivot pin.

5. Remove the pivot pin (A, **Figure 88**), and slide the clutch lever (B) from the lever bracket.

6. Remove the anchor pin (**Figure 89**), and disconnect the clutch cable from the lever.

7. Check the clutch lever components (**Figure 90**) for worn or damaged parts.

8. Make sure the anti-rattle spring screw (**Figure 91**) on the bottom of the clutch lever is tight.

9. On fork mounted front fairing models, withdraw the clutch cable from the inner fairing rubber grommet (**Figure 92**)

10. Following the path noted prior to removal, route the new clutch cable from the handlebar to the clutch release cover.

11. Fit the clutch cable end into its lever. Secure it with the anchor pin (**Figure 89**).

12. Slide the clutch lever (B, **Figure 88**) into the bracket, and install the pivot pin (A).

13. Secure the pivot pin with the snap ring.

14. Reconnect the clutch cable (**Figure 87**) to the clutch release mechanism as described in *Clutch Release Cover Assembly* (this chapter).

15. Adjust the clutch as described in Chapter Three.

CLUTCH LEVER ASSEMBLY (ALL MODELS EXCEPT CVO)

Removal

1. If necessary, disconnect the clutch cable from the lever assembly as described in *Clutch Cable Replacement* (this chapter).

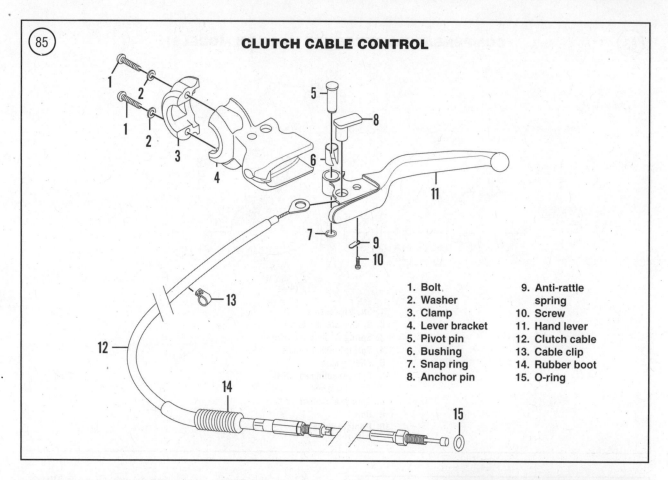

CLUTCH CABLE CONTROL

1. Bolt
2. Washer
3. Clamp
4. Lever bracket
5. Pivot pin
6. Bushing
7. Snap ring
8. Anchor pin
9. Anti-rattle spring
10. Screw
11. Hand lever
12. Clutch cable
13. Cable clip
14. Rubber boot
15. O-ring

2. Remove the handlebar switch housing screws (C, **Figure 88**) from the left handlebar switch assembly.

3. Separate the halves of the handlebar switch, and slide the assembly from the handlebar. Note how the ribs on the outside of the handlebar assembly engage the groove (**Figure 93**) in the handlebar grip.

4. Remove the clutch lever assembly clamp bolts (A, **Figure 94**). Then, remove the clutch lever assembly and its clamp (B, **Figure 94**) from the handlebar.

5. If necessary, remove the handlebar grip (C, **Figure 94**) from the handlebar.

Installation

1. If removed, install a new handlebar grip (C, **Figure 94**) by performing the following:

    a. Clean all adhesive from the handlebar.

    b. Pour adhesive into the new grip and roll the grip to evenly spread the adhesive on the grip's inner surface.

    c. Roll the new grip onto the handlebar. Clean away any excess adhesive.

2. Fit the left handlebar switch onto the handlebar so the switch ribs engage the groove (**Figure 93**) in the handlebar grip.

3. Install and finger-tighten the handlebar switch housing screws (C, **Figure 88**).

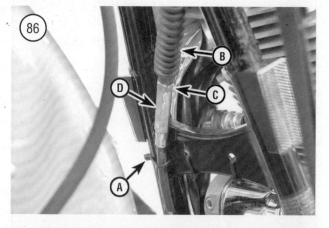

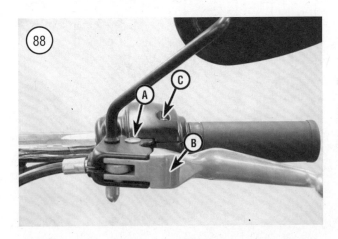

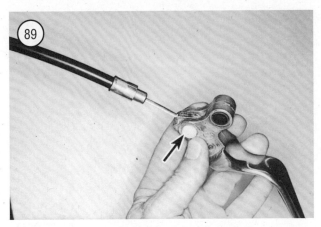

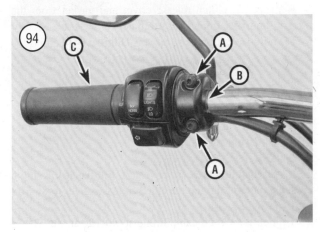

6

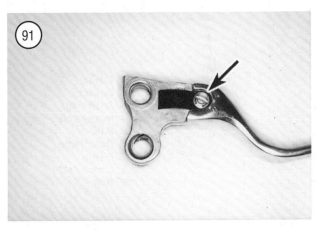

4. Position the clutch lever assembly onto the handlebar so the notch (A, **Figure 95**; typical) in the clutch lever assembly engages the tab (B) in the lower handlebar switch housing.

5. Fit the clamp (B, **Figure 94**) into position and install the clutch lever assembly clamp bolts (A).

6. Tighten the upper clutch control clamp bolt first, and then the lower bolt. Tighten each bolt 72-80 in.-lb. (8.1-12.0 N•m).

7. Starting with the bottom screw, tighten the handlebar switch housing screws (C, **Figure 88**) securely.

8. If removed, install the clutch cable as described in *Clutch Cable Replacement* (this chapter).

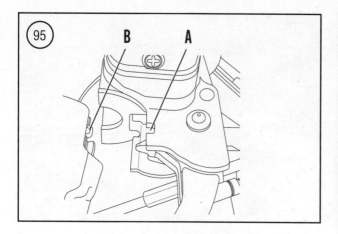

CLUTCH RELEASE COVER
(ALL MODELS EXCEPT CVO)

Removal

1. Remove the exhaust system as described in Chapter Four.
2. Drain the transmission oil as described in Chapter Three.

NOTE
If the cover is difficult to remove, apply the clutch lever after the mounting bolts have been removed. This usually breaks the cover loose.

3. Remove the mounting bolts (A, **Figure 96**) securing the clutch release cover.
4. Remove the clutch release cover and gasket from the transmission side door. Discard the cover gasket.
5. Do not lose the locating dowels (**Figure 97**) behind the cover.

Installation

1. If removed, install the locating dowels (**Figure 97**) into the transmission side door.
2. Install a *new* gasket.
3. Install the clutch release cover (A, **Figure 96**). Using a crossing pattern, tighten the clutch release cover to 84-108 in.-lb. (9.5-12.2 N•m).
4. Tighten the clutch cable fitting to 90-120 in.-lb. (10.2-13.6 N•m).
5. Refill the transmission with oil as described in Chapter Three.
6. Install the exhaust system as described in a Chapter Four.
7. Adjust the clutch as described in Chapter Three.

Disassembly

Refer to **Figure 98**.
1. Remove the clutch release cover as described in this section.
2. Perform the following at the clutch cable adjuster:
   a. Release the clutch cable from the clamp (A, **Figure 86**), and slide the boot (B) away from the adjuster.

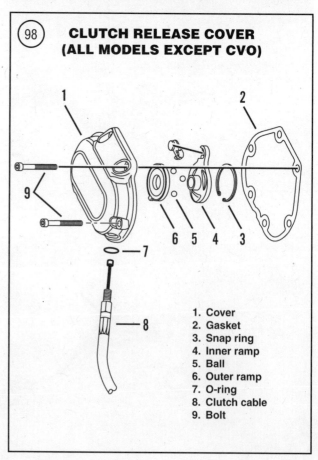

CLUTCH RELEASE COVER
(ALL MODELS EXCEPT CVO)

1. Cover
2. Gasket
3. Snap ring
4. Inner ramp
5. Ball
6. Outer ramp
7. O-ring
8. Clutch cable
9. Bolt

b. Loosen the locknut (C, **Figure 86**), and turn the adjuster (D) to provide maximum slack.

NOTE
*Before removing the snap ring, note that the snap ring opening (A, **Figure 99**) is centered on the cover slot. The snap ring must be reinstalled with the opening in the same position.*

3. Remove the snap ring (B, **Figure 99**) from the groove in the side cover.
4. Disconnect the ramp coupling (A, **Figure 100**) from the inner ramp (B).
5. Disconnect the cable end (**Figure 101**) from the ramp coupling, and remove the coupling.
6. Lift the inner ramp (**Figure 102**) from the release cover.
7. Remove the three balls (**Figure 103**) from the outer ramp.
8. Remove the outer ramp (A, **Figure 104**).
9. If necessary, loosen the clutch cable fitting (**Figure 105**), and remove the cable from the clutch release cover.

Assembly

1. If removed, insert the cable and thread the clutch cable fitting (**Figure 105**) into the clutch release cover. Do not tighten the cable fitting at this time.
2. Install the outer ramp (A, **Figure 104**) into the cover and engage the ramp's tab (B) with the cover slot. The ball sockets in the outer ramp must face up.

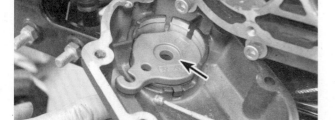

3. Seat a ball (**Figure 103**) into each socket in the outer ramp. Center each ball in its socket.

4. Align the inner ramp socket with the balls, and install the inner ramp (**Figure 102**) into the cover.

5. Connect the cable end (**Figure 101**) to the ramp coupling. Then, connect the ramp coupling (A, **Figure 100**) to the inner ramp (B).

6. Install the snap ring (B, **Figure 99**) into the clutch release cover groove. Position the snap ring so its opening (A, **Figure 99**) is centered on the slot in the cover. Make sure the snap ring is completely seated in the groove.

7. Tighten the cable fitting (**Figure 105**) securely.

Inspection

1. Clean the side cover and all components thoroughly in solvent, and dry them with compressed air.

2. Check the release mechanism balls (A, **Figure 106**), inner ramp sockets (B) and outer ramp sockets (C) for cracks, deep scoring or excessive wear.

3. Check the clutch release cover for cracks or damage. Check the clutch cable threads and the coupling snap ring groove for damage. Check the ramp bore in the release cover for excessive wear, or grooves that could catch and bind the ramps causing improper clutch adjustment.

4. Replace the clutch cable O-ring.

5. Replace all worn or damaged parts.

CLUTCH SERVICE (CVO MODELS)

The hydraulic release system transmits hydraulic pressure from the master cylinder to the clutch release mechanism in the clutch release cover. As the clutch components wear, the clutch release piston moves out. As this occurs, the fluid level in the master cylinder reservoir goes down. Occasionally adding fluid compensates for this drop.

Proper operation of the hydraulic clutch system depends on a supply of clean brake fluid (DOT 4). Always work in a clean environment when servicing this system. Even tiny particles of debris that enter the system can damage components and cause poor clutch performance.

Brake fluid is hygroscopic (easily absorbs moisture), and moisture in the system reduces clutch performance. Purchase brake fluid in small containers and properly discard any small quantities that remain. Small quantities of fluid quickly absorb moisture in the container. Use only fluid clearly marked DOT 4. Other types of brake fluid are not compatible with DOT 4. If possible, always use the same brand of brake fluid. Fluids from different manufacturers may not be compatible with one another. Do not reuse drained fluid. Properly discard all old brake fluid. Do not mix it with other fluids for recycling.

Perform clutch service procedures carefully. Do not use any sharp tools inside the master cylinder or release mechanism piston. Damage to these components could cause a loss in the system's ability to maintain hydraulic pressure. If there is any doubt about the ability to correctly and safe-

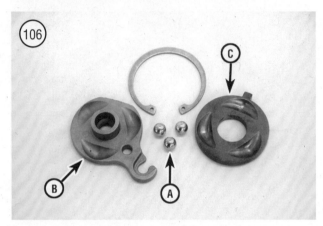

ly service the clutch system, have a professional technician perform the task.

Consider the following when servicing the hydraulic clutch system:

1. The hydraulic components rarely require disassembly. Make sure it is necessary. Not all models are equipped with a piston assembly repair kit as shown in 13, Figure 107.

2. Keep the reservoir cover in place to prevent the entry of moisture and debris.

3. Clean parts with an aerosol brake parts cleaner or isopropyl alcohol. Never use petroleum-based solvents on internal clutch system components. They will cause seals to swell and distort.

4. Do not allow brake fluid to contact plastic, painted or plated parts. It quickly damages these surfaces.

5. Dispose of used brake fluid properly.

6. If the hydraulic system, not including the reservoir cover, has been opened, bleed the system to remove air from the system. Refer to *Clutch System Bleeding* in this chapter.

CLUTCH MASTER CYLINDER (CVO MODELS)

Read *Clutch Service* in this chapter before servicing the clutch master cylinder.

Refer to **Figure 107** and **Figure 108**.

(107)

CLUTCH MASTER CYLINDER (CVO MODELS)
(2010 FLHTCUSE BUILT PRIOR TO FEBRUARY 2010)

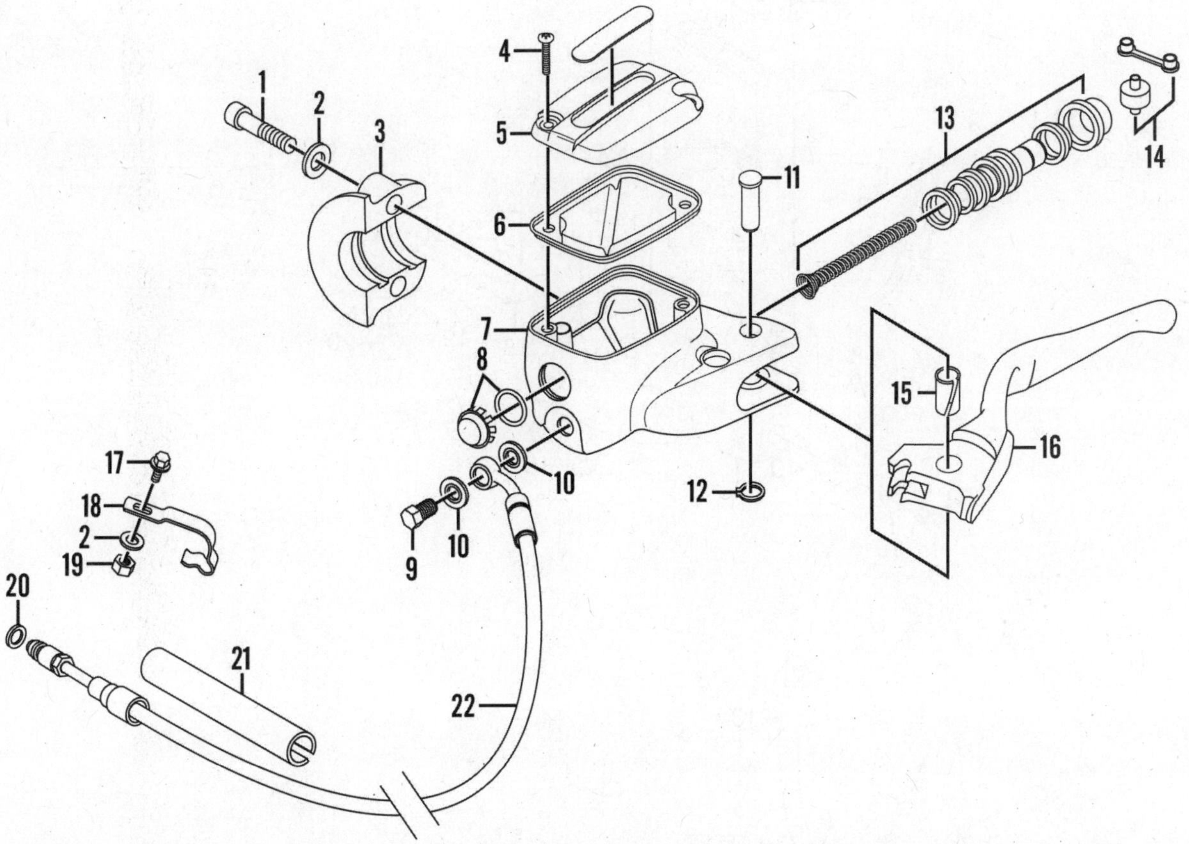

1. Bolt
2. Washer
3. Clamp
4. Screw
5. Top cover
6. Diaphragm
7. Body
8. Sight glass and gasket
9. Banjo bolt
10. Sealing washer
11. Pivot pin
12. Snap ring
13. Piston assembly
14. Bushing and roller
15. Bushing
16. Clutch lever
17. Bolt
18. Cable retainer
19. Nut
20. O-ring
21. Tubing
22. Hose

6

(108)

CLUTCH MASTER CYLINDER (CVO MODELS)
(ALL MODELS EXCEPT 2010 FLHTCUSE* BUILT PRIOR TO FEBRUARY 2010)

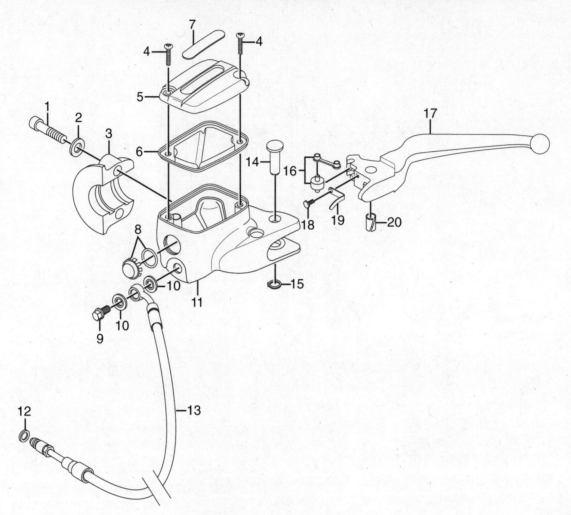

1. Bolt
2. Washer
3. Clamp
4. Screw
5. Top cover
6. Diaphragm
7. Plate
8. Sight glass and gasket
9. Banjo bolt
10. Sealing washer
11. Body
12. O-ring
13. Clutch hose
14. Pivot pin
15. Snap ring
16. Bushing and roller
17. Clutch lever
18. Spring
19. Screw
20. Bushing

*The 2010 FLHFTCUSE models, built after mid February
2010-on are equipped with this clutch master cylinder.
There are no piston assembly repair kits available for
these models.

Removal/Installation

1. Use a swing arm stand to support the motorcycle on level ground.

2. Block the front wheel so the motorcycle cannot roll in either direction while on the swing arm stand.

3. If the master cylinder will be serviced, perform the following:

    a. Cover the fuel tank, front fairing and front fender with a heavy cloth or plastic tarp to protect them from accidental brake fluid spills.

CAUTION
Wash brake fluid off any surface immediately, as it damages the finish. Use soapy water and rinse completely.

    b. Drain the clutch system as described in this chapter.

    c. Remove the banjo bolt and washers securing the clutch hose to the master cylinder. Seal the clutch hose in a plastic bag so brake fluid cannot drip onto the motorcycle. Tie the loose end of the hose to the handlebar.

    d. Plug the bolt opening in the master cylinder to prevent dripping when removing the master cylinder in the following steps.

4. Remove the clutch master cylinder clamp bolts, washers and the clamp, and lower the clutch master cylinder from the handlebar.

5A. If necessary, service the master cylinder as described in this section.

5B. If the master cylinder will not be serviced, suspend it from the motorcycle. Use a bungee cord so the clutch hose is not strained, and keep the master cylinder upright.

6. Clean the handlebar, master cylinder and clamp mating surfaces.

7. Mount the master cylinder onto the handlebar and position it to rider's preference.

8. Install the master cylinder clamp, clamp bolts and washers.

NOTE
When the master cylinder clamp is correctly installed, the upper edge of the clamp touches the master cylinder mating surface, leaving a gap at the bottom.

9. Tighten the upper master cylinder clamp bolt first, and then tighten the lower bolt. Tighten each bolt to 60-80 in.-lb. (6.8-9.0 N•m).

10. If removed, install a *new* sealing washer on each side of the clutch hose and secure the clutch hose to the master cylinder with the banjo bolt. Tighten the banjo bolt to 12.5-14.5 ft.-lb. (16.9-19.7 N•m).

11. Bleed the clutch system as described in this chapter.

12. Test ride the motorcycle to ensure the clutch is operating correctly.

Disassembly

NOTE
On the 2010 FLHTCUSE, 2011 FLHXSE and 2012 FLTRXSE models, the master cylinder internal components cannot be serviced individually. If the piston assembly is leaking brake fluid, the master cylinder body/piston assembly must be replaced as a unit. This does not include the clutch lever components.

1. Remove the master cylinder as described in this section.

2. If still in place, remove the master cylinder cover and diaphragm. Pour out and discard the remaining brake fluid.

3. Remove the snap ring from the clutch lever pivot pin.

4. Apply light hand pressure to the clutch lever to remove some of the spring pressure on the pivot pin.

5. Withdraw the pivot pin from the body, and then remove the clutch lever. Watch for the bushing and roller in the lever.

NOTE
Step 6 and Step 7 apply to models with a removable piston assembly.

6. Remove the rubber boot from the groove in the body at the end of the piston.

NOTE
If brake fluid is leaking from the piston bore, the piston cups are worn or damaged. Replace the piston assembly with the repair kit.

7. Remove the piston assembly and spring from the master cylinder bore. Do not remove the primary and secondary cups from the piston as they cannot be replaced separately

Assembly

NOTE
Steps 1-5 relate only those models that have the removable piston assembly.

1. If installing a new piston repair kit assembly as described in *Inspection* in this section.

2. Lubricate the piston (A, **Figure 109**), primary cup (B), secondary cup (C), rubber boot (D) and cylinder bore with DOT 4 brake fluid.

3. Install the narrow end of the spring (E, **Figure 109**) into the piston.

CAUTION
Do not allow the piston cups to tear or turn inside out when installing the piston into the master cylinder bore. Both cups are larger than the bore. To ease installation, lubricate the cups and piston with DOT 4 brake fluid.

4. Insert the spring and piston assembly into the master cylinder bore. Press the end of the piston until the entire assembly sits in the bore.

CAUTION
The rubber boot must completely seat in the master cylinder groove. Slowly push and release the piston a few times to make sure it moves smoothly and that the rubber boot does not pop out.

5. Hold the piston in place, and carefully install the rubber boot into the groove in the master cylinder bore. Make sure the entire perimeter of the boot is correctly seated in the groove.

6. Lubricate the pivot pin and bushing with silicone brake grease.

7. If removed, install the bushing and roller kit into the end of the clutch lever. Position the bushing so it sits flush with both sides of the clutch lever.

8. Install the clutch lever onto the body, and install the pivot pin part way in from the top.

9. Apply slight hand pressure to the clutch lever to compress the spring, and push the piston in all the way.

10 Install a *new* snap ring onto the pivot pin. Make sure it is correctly seated in the groove.

11. Check that the clutch lever moves freely. If there is any binding or roughness, remove the pivot pin and clutch lever, and inspect the parts.

12. Temporarily install the diaphragm and cover. Install and finger-tighten the cover screws. Do not fully tighten the screws, as brake fluid will be added later.

13. Install the master cylinder as described in this chapter.

Inspection

NOTE
Steps 1-5 relate only those models that have the removable piston assembly.

The manufacturer does not supply specifications for the clutch master cylinder. Replace visibly worn or damaged parts as described in this section.

1. Clean and dry the master cylinder assembly as follows:
   a. Handle the brake components carefully when servicing them.

CAUTION
Do not get any oil or grease onto any of the master cylinder components. These chemicals cause the rubber parts in the brake system to swell, permanently damaging them.

   b. Use only DOT 4 brake fluid or isopropyl alcohol to wash rubber parts (rubber boot and piston assembly) in the clutch system. Never allow any petroleum-based cleaner to contact the rubber parts. These

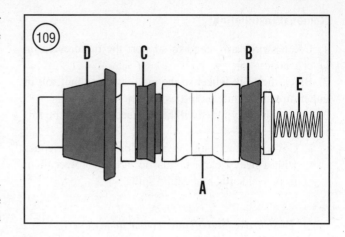

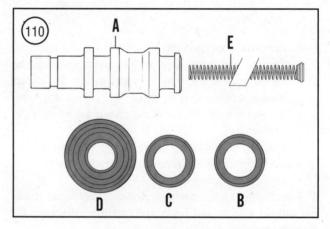

chemicals cause the rubber to swell, requiring their replacement.
   c. Clean the master cylinder piston rubber boot groove carefully. Use a small pick or brush to clean the groove. If a hard varnish residue has built up in the groove, soak the master cylinder in solvent to help soften the residue. Then, wash in soapy water and rinse completely.
   d. Blow the master cylinder dry with compressed air to remove any solvent residue.
   e. Place cleaned parts on a clean, lint-free cloth until assembly.

CAUTION
Do not remove the primary and secondary cups from the piston assembly for cleaning or inspection purposes.

2A. Check the piston assembly for the following defects:
   a. Scratched or corroded piston (A, **Figure 110**).
   b. Worn, cracked, damaged or swollen primary (B, **Figure 110**) and secondary (C) cups.
   c. Worn or damaged rubber boot (D, **Figure 110**).
   d. Broken, distorted or collapsed piston return spring (E, **Figure 110**).

2B. If any of these parts are worn or damaged, replace the piston assembly.

3. To assemble a *new* piston assembly, perform the following:

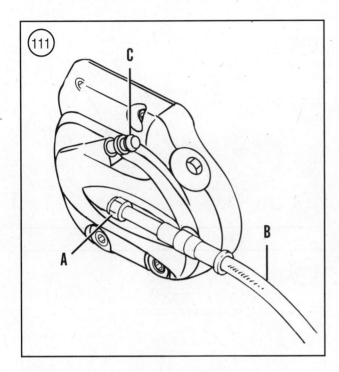

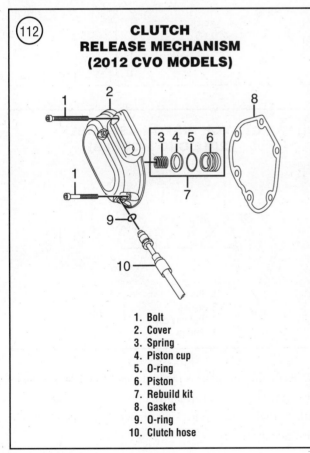

**CLUTCH
RELEASE MECHANISM
(2012 CVO MODELS)**

1. Bolt
2. Cover
3. Spring
4. Piston cup
5. O-ring
6. Piston
7. Rebuild kit
8. Gasket
9. O-ring
10. Clutch hose

a. Install the *new* primary and secondary cups onto the piston. Use the original piston assembly as a reference when installing the new cups onto the piston.

b. Before installing the new piston cups, lubricate them with DOT 4 brake fluid.

c. Clean the new piston (A, **Figure 110**) in brake fluid.

d. Install the primary cup (B, **Figure 110**) onto the spring end of the piston, and then the secondary (C) cup.

4. Inspect the master cylinder bore. Replace the master cylinder if the bore is corroded, cracked or damaged in any way. Do not hone the master cylinder bore to remove scratches or other damage.

5. Make sure the fluid passageway in the reservoir is clear. Clean it out with compressed air if necessary.

6. Check the banjo bolt threads for damage.

7. Inspect the diaphragm and cover for deterioration and other damage.

8. Check the clutch lever assembly for the following defects:

a. Damaged clutch lever.

b. Excessively worn or damaged pivot pin.

c. Worn or damaged bushing.

CLUTCH RELEASE COVER
(2012 CVO MODELS)

Refer to **Figure 111** and **Figure 112**.

Removal

NOTE
*On the 2013 CVO models, the clutch release cover is part of the **Clutch Secondary Actuator (2013 CVO Models)** in this chapter.*

1. Use a swing arm stand to support the motorcycle on level ground.

2. Block the front wheel so the motorcycle cannot roll in either direction while on the swing arm stand.

3. Remove the exhaust system as described in Chapter Four.

4. Drain the transmission oil as described in Chapter Three.

CAUTION
Wash brake fluid off any surface immediately, as it damages the finish. Use soapy water and rinse completely.

5. Cover the frame under the transmission case with a heavy cloth or plastic tarp to protect it from accidental brake fluid spills.

6. Slightly loosen the clutch release cover bolts, and apply the clutch lever. This helps break the cover loose from the transmission side door.

7. Drain the hydraulic fluid from the clutch system as described in this chapter.

8. Carefully loosen the flare nut (A, **Figure 111**, typical) securing the clutch hose (B) to the cover. Do not scratch the chrome cover.

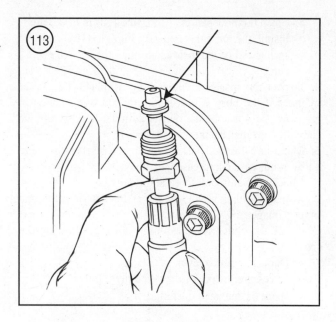

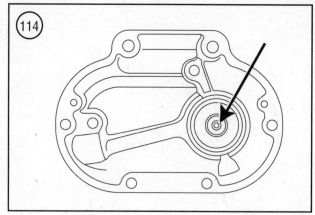

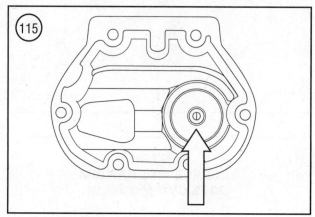

9. Disconnect the clutch hose (B, **Figure 112**, typical) from the cover, and place the end into a plastic bag. Remove the O-ring (**Figure 113**, typical) from the end of the clutch hose, or if necessary, remove the O-ring from the threaded outlet within the cover.

NOTE
Note that two different length cover bolts are used. Two short bolts are used at the top of the cover; long bolts are used at the four remaining locations.

10. Remove the clutch release cover bolts, and then remove the cover. Watch for the dowels (**Figure 97**, typical) behind the cover.
11. Remove and discard the cover gasket.

Installation

1. If removed, install the locating dowels (**Figure 97**, typical).
2. Install a *new* gasket over the locating dowels.
3. Install the clutch release cover.
4. Install the two short bolts at the top of the clutch release cover and the long bolts at the four remaining locations. Using a crossing pattern, tighten the clutch release cover bolts to 10-12 ft.-lb. (13.6-16.3 N•m).
5. Install a *new* O-ring (**Figure 113**) onto the end of the clutch hose.
6. Connect the clutch hose (B, **Figure 112**) to the cover. Manually thread the flare nut into the cover until it bottoms. Tighten the clutch hose flare nut to 72-120 in.-lb. (8.1-13.6 N•m). Do not cross thread the flare nut or scratch the cover.
7. Refill the transmission oil as described in Chapter Three.
8. Install the exhaust system as described in Chapter Four.

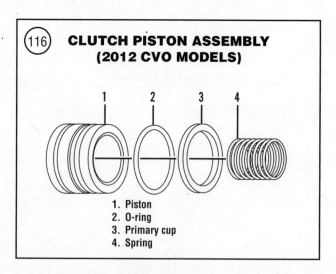

CLUTCH PISTON ASSEMBLY (2012 CVO MODELS)

1. Piston
2. O-ring
3. Primary cup
4. Spring

9. Refill the clutch master cylinder and bleed the system as described under in this chapter.
10. Start the engine, check for proper clutch operation, and test ride the motorcycle.

CLUTCH SECONDARY ACTUATOR (2012 CVO MODELS)

1. Remove the clutch release cover as described in this chapter.

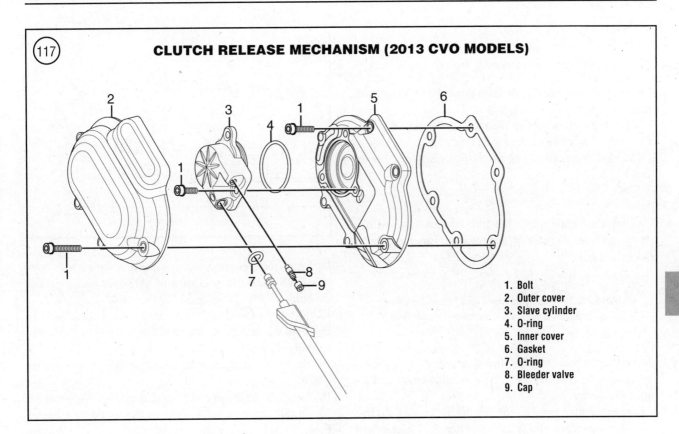

CLUTCH RELEASE MECHANISM (2013 CVO MODELS)

1. Bolt
2. Outer cover
3. Slave cylinder
4. O-ring
5. Inner cover
6. Gasket
7. O-ring
8. Bleeder valve
9. Cap

2. If removed, install the bleed valve and tighten to 12-15 in.-lb. (1.4-1.7 N•m).

3. To remove the piston (**Figure 114**), perform the following:

   a. Place a piece of soft wood on the work bench.

   b. Position the release cover with the piston side facing toward the work bench.

   c. Apply compressed air through the clutch hose port in the cover, and force the piston part way out of the cover receptacle.

4. Withdraw the piston assembly and spring (**Figure 115**) from the cover receptacle.

5. If the primary cup was removed from the piston, install the cup so its raised leading-edge lip faces the spring end of the piston.

6. Apply DOT 4 brake fluid to the *new* primary cup, O-ring and piston (**Figure 174**). Also apply DOT 4 brake fluid to the cylinder in the cover.

7. Install the spring into the piston, and install the assembly into the cover cylinder. Guide the primary cup into the receptacle to prevent the lips from turning over.

8. Push the piston and spring in until they bottom. Press the piston into the bore and check that the spring pushes it back out part way. The piston must move freely within the bore.

9. Install the clutch release cover as described in this chapter.

Inspection

Replacement parts are not available for the piston assembly (**Figure 116**). If any part is worn or damaged, replace the piston and spring as an assembly.

1. Clean the cylinder bore and piston in DOT 4 brake fluid or isopropyl alcohol. Dry them with compressed air.

2. Inspect the spring for fractures or sagging.

3. Check the O-ring and primary cup for hardness or deterioration.

4. Check the piston and cylinder bore for scratches, scoring or other damage.

5. Check the piston O-ring and primary cup grooves for damage.

6. Inspect the threaded flare nut hole in the cover. If it is worn or damaged, clean it out with a thread tap or replace the cover.

7. Inspect the threaded bleed valve hole in the cover. If it is worn or damaged, clean it out with a thread tap or replace the cover.

8. Inspect the bleed valve. Apply compressed air to the opening and make sure it is clear. Clean it out, if necessary with brake fluid. Install the bleed valve and tighten to 12-15 in.-lb. (1.4-1.7 N•m).

CLUTCH SECONDARY ACTUATOR (2013 MODELS)

Removal/Installation

Refer to **Figure 117**.

NOTE
The clutch secondary actuator is not service-able and must be replaced if faulty.

1. Support the motorcycle on level ground on a swing arm stand.

2. Block the front wheel so the motorcycle cannot roll in either direction while on the swing arm stand.

3. Remove the exhaust system as described in Chapter Four.

4. Drain the transmission oil as described in Chapter Three.

5. Cover the frame under the transmission case with a heavy cloth or plastic tarp to protect it from accidental brake fluid spills.

CAUTION
Wash brake fluid off any surface immediately, as it damages the finish. Use soapy water and rinse completely.

6. Remove the transmission filler plug and level dipstick.

7. Remove the bolts securing the outer side cover and remove the cover.

8. Loosen the fitting and disconnect the hydraulic fluid line from the secondary clutch actuator. Residual brake fluid will drain out after the fluid line is removed. Place the end into a reclosable plastic bag.

NOTE
The O-ring may remain within the secondary clutch actuator receptacle. Use a non-metal-lic pick, withdraw and discard the O-ring.

9. If necessary, remove the bolts securing the secondary clutch actuator to the inner side cover. Remove and discard the large O-ring.

10. Remove the bolts securing the inner side cover to the transmission side door.

11. Remove the secondary clutch actuator and inner side cover and gasket from the transmission side door. Watch for two small locating dowels on the side door. Discard the gasket.

12. Clean the inner side cover with denatured alcohol only.

13. Ensure the two small locating dowels are installed on the transmission side door.

14. Install a new gasket on the locating dowels.

15. If the secondary clutch actuator was removed from the inner side cover, perform the following:

a. Apply transmission oil to the large O-ring prior to installation.

b. Install a new large O-ring into the groove within the inner side cover.

c. Install the secondary clutch actuator onto the inner side cover. Install and tighten the bolts to 100-120 in.-lb. (11.2-13.6 N•m).

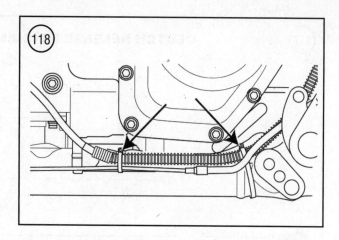

16. Install the secondary clutch actuator and inner side cover assembly onto the transmission side door Install tighten the bolts to 100-120 in.-lb. (11.2-13.6 N•m).

17. Install a new O-ring and connect the hydraulic fluid line onto the secondary clutch actuator. Tighten the fitting securely.

18. Refill the transmission oil as described in Chapter Three.

19. Install the transmission filler plug and level dipstick.

20. Install the exhaust system as described in Chapter Four.

CLUTCH HYDRAULIC HOSE REPLACEMENT (CVO MODELS)

1. Use a swing arm stand to support the motorcycle on level ground.

2. Block the front wheel so the motorcycle cannot roll in either direction while on the swing arm stand.

3. Before removing the hose, make a drawing of its path from the handlebar to the clutch release cover. The new hose must be routed along the same path.

4. Remove the front exhaust pipe as described in Chapter Four.

5. Cover the frame under the transmission case with a heavy cloth or plastic tarp to protect it from accidental brake fluid spills.

CAUTION
Wash brake fluid off any surface immediately, as it damages the finish. Use soapy water and rinse completely.

6. Drain the fluid from the clutch system as described in this chapter.

7. Carefully loosen the flare nut (A, **Figure 112**, typical) securing the clutch hose to the clutch release cover. Do not scratch the chrome cover.

8. Disconnect the clutch hose (B, **Figure 112**, typical) from the cover, and place the loose end in a container.

9. Continue to apply the clutch lever and drain the brake fluid out of the clutch hose.

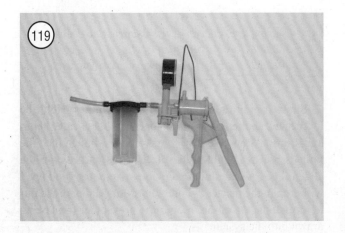

10. Remove the O-ring (**Figure 113**) from the end of the clutch hose, or if necessary, remove the O-ring within the cover threaded outlet.

11. Remove the banjo bolt and washers securing the clutch hose to the master cylinder. Separate the hose from the master cylinder.

12. Seal both ends of the hose in a small plastic bag and tape them closed so brake fluid does not drip onto the motorcycle.

13. Release the hose from any clamps (**Figure 118**) securing it to the frame. Note the location of each hose clamp.

14. Carefully pull the clutch hydraulic hose and fitting out through the inner fairing, on models so equipped. Clean any clutch fluid from the inner fairing immediately.

15. Plug the bolt opening in the master cylinder and clutch release cover to prevent any leaks and the entry of foreign matter.

16. Install the *new* clutch hydraulic hose through the frame and along the same path noted during removal. Secure it with the hose clamps (**Figure 118**) noted during removal.

17. Secure the clutch hose to the master cylinder with the banjo bolt and two *new* washers, one on each side of the clutch hose. Tighten the banjo bolt to 12.5-14.5 ft.-lb (16.9-19.7 N•m).

18. Install a *new* O-ring (**Figure 113**) onto the end of the clutch hose.

19. Connect the clutch hose (B, **Figure 112**, typical) to the cover. Thread the flare nut all the way into the cover by and until it bottoms. Do not cross threat the flare nut or scratch the cover. Tighten the flare nut to the following:

    a. 2006-2012 models: 72-120 in.-lb. (8.1-13.6 N•m).

    b. 2013 models: 96-144 in.-lb. (10.9-16.3 N•m).

20. Bleed the clutch as described in *Clutch System Bleeding* (this chapter).

21. Test ride the motorcycle to ensure the clutch is operating correctly.

CLUTCH SYSTEM FLUSHING (CVO MODELS)

CAUTION
Never reuse old brake fluid. Properly discard all brake fluid flushed from the system.

When flushing the clutch system, use DOT 4 brake fluid as a flushing fluid. Flushing consists of pulling *new* brake fluid through the clutch system until the new fluid appears at the release cover bleed valve without the presence of any air bubbles. To flush the clutch system, follow one of the bleeding procedures described in this chapter.

CLUTCH SYSTEM DRAINING (CVO MODELS)

To drain the system, follow one of the bleeding procedures, but do not add fluid to the reservoir. Bleed the system until all fluid has been removed from the reservoir and hydraulic lines.

CLUTCH SYSTEM BLEEDING (CVO MODELS)

Bleeding Process

This procedure uses a hydraulic brake bleeding kit (**Figure 119**) that is commonly available from automotive or motorcycle supply stores.

1. Remove the dust cap from the bleed valve on the clutch release cover.

2. Place a clean shop cloth over the exhaust pipe and frame to protect it from accidental brake fluid spills.

3. Assemble the vacuum bleeder tool according to its manufacturer's instructions. Secure it to the bleed valve.

4. Clean all dirt and foreign matter from the top of the master cylinder.

5. Turn the handlebars to level the clutch master cylinder. Then, remove the screws, reservoir cover and diaphragm.

6. Fill the reservoir almost to the top with DOT 4 brake fluid and reinstall the diaphragm and cover. Leave the cover in place during this procedure to prevent the entry of dirt.

NOTE
Carefully monitor the fluid level in the reservoir. It will drop quite rapidly. Stop often and check the brake fluid level. Keep the level 3/8 in. (10 mm) from the top of the reservoir so air will not be drawn into the system. If this occurs, the procedure must be repeated.

7. Operate the pump several times to create a vacuum in the line, and open the bleed valve approximately a half turn. Fluid will be quickly drawn from the system and into the pump's reservoir. Maintain vacuum with the pump while the bleed valve is still open. Tighten the bleed valve well before the fluid in the master cylinder runs empty. To prevent air from being drawn through the master cylinder, frequently add fluid to maintain its level at or near the top of the reservoir.

8. Continue the bleeding process until the fluid drawn from the bleed valve is bubble-free. If bubbles are withdrawn with the fluid, more air is still trapped in the line.

Repeat the bleeding procedure, making sure to refill the master cylinder often to prevent air from being drawn into the system.

9. When the system is free of bubbles, tighten the bleed valve to the following:
   a. 2010-2012 models: 12-15 in.-lb. (1.4-1.7 N•m).
   b. 2013 models: 32-41 in.-lb. (3.5-5.6 N•m).

NOTE
Dispose of the used fluid responsibly. Do not reuse the old fluid.

10. If necessary, add fluid to correct the level in the master cylinder reservoir. When topping off the clutch master cylinder, turn the handlebar until the reservoir is level; add fluid to the full level mark in the reservoir.

11. Reinstall the reservoir diaphragm and cover. Install the reservoir cover screws, and tighten them to 6-8 in.-lb. (0.7-0.9 N•m).

12. Test the feel of the clutch lever. It must be firm and offer the same resistance each time it's operated. If it feels spongy, it is likely that there is still air in the system and it must be bleed again. After bleeding the system, check for leaks and tighten all fittings and connections as necessary.

WARNING
Do not ride the motorcycle until the clutch lever is operating correctly with full hydraulic advantage.

13. Test ride the motorcycle slowly at first to make sure that the clutch is operating properly.

Without a Brake Bleeder

NOTE
Before bleeding the clutch, check that all hoses and lines are tight.

1. Remove the dust cap from the bleed valve on the clutch release cover.

2. Place a clean shop cloth over the exhaust pipe and frame to protect it from accidental brake fluid spills.

3. Connect a length of clear tubing to the bleed valve on the release cover. Place the other end of the tube into a clean container. Fill the container with enough fresh DOT 4 brake fluid to keep the end of the tube submerged. The tube must be long enough so that a loop can be made higher than the bleeder valve to prevent air from being drawn into the release cylinder during bleeding.

4. Clean all dirt and foreign matter from the top of the clutch master cylinder.

5. Remove the screws securing the master cylinder cover, and then remove the cover and the diaphragm.

6. Fill the reservoir almost to the top with DOT 4 brake fluid. Then, reinstall the diaphragm and cover. Leave the cover in place during this procedure to prevent the entry of dirt.

NOTE
During this procedure, it is important to check the fluid level in the master cylinder reservoir often. If the reservoir runs dry, more air will enter the system.

7. Slowly apply the clutch lever several times. Hold the lever in the applied position and open the bleed valve about a half turn. Allow the lever to travel to its limit. When the limit is reached, tighten the bleed valve and release the clutch lever. As the fluid enters the system, the fluid level will drop in the master cylinder reservoir. Maintain the fluid level at the top of the reservoir to prevent air from being drawn into the system.

8. Continue the bleeding process until the fluid emerging from the hose is completely free of air bubbles. If the fluid is being replaced, continue until the fluid emerging from the hose is clean.

NOTE
If bleeding is difficult, allowing the fluid to stabilize for a few hours. Repeat the bleeding procedure when the tiny bubbles in the system settle out.

9. Hold the lever in this applied position and tighten the bleed valve to the following:
   a. 2012 models: 12-15 in.-lb. (1.4-1.7 N•m).
   b. 2013 models: 32-41 in.-lb. (3.5-5.6 N•m).

Remove the Bleed Tube and Install the Bleed Valve Dust Cap.

NOTE
Dispose of the used fluid responsibly. Do not reuse the old fluid.

10. If necessary, add fluid to correct the level in the master cylinder reservoir. When topping off the front master cylinder, turn the handlebar until the reservoir is level; add fluid to the full level mark in the reservoir.

11. Reinstall the reservoir diaphragm and cover. Install the reservoir cover screws, and tighten them to 6-8 in.-lb. (0.7-0.9 N•m).

12. Test the feel of the clutch lever. It must be firm and offer the same resistance each time it's operated. If it feels spongy, it is likely that there is still air in the system and it must bleed it again. After bleeding the system, check for leaks and tighten all fittings and connections as necessary.

WARNING
Do not ride the motorcycle until the clutch is operating correctly with full hydraulic advantage.

13. Test ride the motorcycle slowly at first to make sure that the clutch is operating properly.

Table 1 CLUTCH SPECIFICATIONS AND SPROCKET SIZES

Item	Specification
Clutch type	Wet-multi-plate disc
Clutch lever free play	1/16-1/8 in. (1.6-3.2 mm)
Clutch screw adjustment	Loosen 1/2 turn after lightly seated
Clutch friction plate thickness service limit	0.143 in. (3.63 mm)
Clutch plain plate warp service limit	0.006 in. (0.15 mm)
Compensation sprocket	34 teeth
Clutch sprocket	46 teeth
Rear wheel sprocket	68 teeth
Transmission sprocket	32 teeth
Clutch pushrod and release plate movement (CVO models)	
2010 models	0.065 in. (1.65 mm)
2011-on models	0.080 in. (2.03 mm)

Table 2 CLUTCH AND PRIMARY CHAINCASE TORQUE SPECIFICATIONS

Item	ft.-lb.	in.-lb.	N•m
Clutch cable fitting	–	90-120	10.2-13.6
Clutch hose flare nut—			
CVO models			
2012 models	–	72-120	8.1-13.6
2013 models	–	96-144	10.9-16.3
Clutch inspection cover			
Torx bolts (T27)	–	84-108	9.5-12.2
Clutch lever clamp bolt	–	72-108	8.1-12.0
Clutch nut	70-80	–	94.9-108.5
Clutch master cylinder (CVO models)			
Banjo bolt	12.5-14.5	–	16.9-19.7
Reservoir cover screw	–	6-8	0.7-0.9
Clutch release cover bolts			
Non-CVO models	–	84-108	9.5-12.2
2010-2012 CVO models	10-12	–	13.3-16.3
2013 CVO models	–	100-120	11.2-13.6
Clutch secondary actuator (2013 CVO models)			
Mounting bolts	–	100-120	11.2-13.6
Side door-to-transmission side door	–	100-120	11.2-13.6
Bleed valve—CVO models			
2012 models	–	12-15	1.4-1.7
2013 models	–	32-41	3.5-5.6
Compensating sprocket bolt	see text		
Diaphragm spring retainer bolts	–	70-100	7.9-11.3
Pressure plate-to-clutch hub (2013 CVO models)	–	70-100	11.3
Primary chain tensioner bolt	21-24	–	28.5-32.5
Primary chaincase			
Cover bolts	–	144-156	16.3-17.6
Housing bolt	26-28	–	35.3-38.0
Stopper plate bolts (2013 CVO models)	–	70-100	7/9-11.3
Transmission sprocket nut	see text		

NOTES

CHAPTER SEVEN

TRANSMISSION AND GEARSHIFT MECHANISM

This chapter covers procedures for the transmission, shift linkage and oil pan. All 2007-2009 models are equipped with a six-speed transmission, which is separate from the engine. The transmission shaft assemblies and the shift assemblies can be serviced with the transmission case mounted in the frame.

Refer to **Tables 1-4** at the end of this chapter for specifications.

SHIFT ASSEMBLY

The shift assembly (**Figure 1 And Figure 2**) consists of the external shift linkage, internal shift cam and shift arm components.

If a shift problem is encountered, refer to the troubleshooting procedures in Chapter Two and eliminate all clutch and shift mechanism possibilities *before* considering transmission repairs. On all models except CVO, improper clutch adjustment (Chapter Three) is often a cause of poor shifting.

Shift Linkage Adjustment

The shift linkage assembly connects the transmission shift rod lever to the foot-operated shift levers. The shift linkage does not require adjustment unless the shift linkage is replaced or the transmission gears do not engage properly.

> *NOTE*
> *Always disarm the optional TSSM/HFSM security system prior to disconnecting the*

battery or pulling the Main-Fuse so the siren will not sound.

1. Remove the Main-Fuse as described under *Fuses* in Chapter Nine.
2. Loosen the two shift linkage rod locknuts (A, **Figure 3** and **Figure 4**).
3. Remove the acorn nut (B, **Figure 3**) and washers securing the shift linkage rod to the inner shift lever. Do not remove the rod from the shift lever.
4. Turn the shift linkage rod (C, **Figure 3**) as necessary to change the linkage adjustment.
5. Securely tighten the shift linkage rod to the shift rod lever.
6. Tighten the shift linkage rod locknuts to 80-120 in.-lb. (9.0-13.6 N•m).
7. Recheck the shifting. Readjust if necessary.
8. If proper shifting cannot be obtained by performing this adjustment, check the shift linkage for any interference problems. Then, check the shift linkage assembly for worn or damaged parts.
9. Once linkage is properly adjusted, reinstall the Main-Fuse as described in Chapter Nine.

EXTERNAL SHIFT MECHANISM

Removal/Installation

Refer to **Figure 1,** and **Figure 2**

> *NOTE*
> *Always disarm the optional TSSM/HFSM security system prior to disconnecting the*

① **SHIFTER ASSEMBLY* (2010 MODELS)**

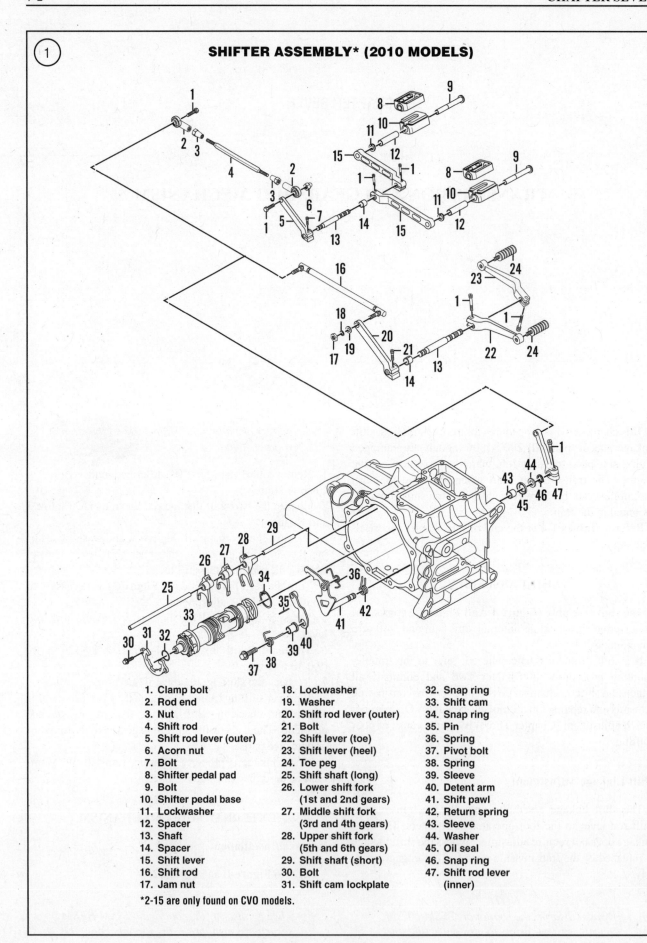

1. Clamp bolt	18. Lockwasher	32. Snap ring
2. Rod end	19. Washer	33. Shift cam
3. Nut	20. Shift rod lever (outer)	34. Snap ring
4. Shift rod	21. Bolt	35. Pin
5. Shift rod lever (outer)	22. Shift lever (toe)	36. Spring
6. Acorn nut	23. Shift lever (heel)	37. Pivot bolt
7. Bolt	24. Toe peg	38. Spring
8. Shifter pedal pad	25. Shift shaft (long)	39. Sleeve
9. Bolt	26. Lower shift fork	40. Detent arm
10. Shifter pedal base	(1st and 2nd gears)	41. Shift pawl
11. Lockwasher	27. Middle shift fork	42. Return spring
12. Spacer	(3rd and 4th gears)	43. Sleeve
13. Shaft	28. Upper shift fork	44. Washer
14. Spacer	(5th and 6th gears)	45. Oil seal
15. Shift lever	29. Shift shaft (short)	46. Snap ring
16. Shift rod	30. Bolt	47. Shift rod lever
17. Jam nut	31. Shift cam lockplate	(inner)

*2-15 are only found on CVO models.

(2) **SHIFTER ASSEMBLY* (2011-ON MODELS)**

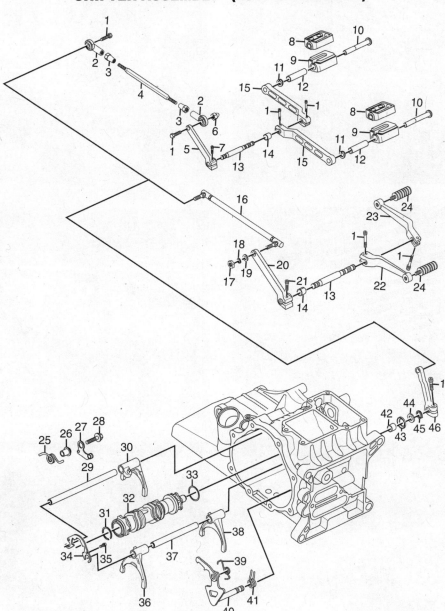

7

1. **Clamp bolt**	18. **Lockwasher**	34. **Shift cam lockplate**
2. **Rod end**	19. **Washer**	35. **Bolt**
3. **Nut**	20. **Shift rod lever–outer**	36. **Lower shift fork**
4. **Shift rod**	21. **Bolt**	**(1st and 2nd gears)**
5. **Shift rod lever–outer**	22. **Shift lever–toe**	37. **Shift shaft (short)**
6. **Acorn nut**	23. **Shift lever–heel**	38. **Middle shift fork**
7. **Bolt**	24. **Toe peg**	**(3rd and 4th gears)**
8. **Shifter pedal pad**	25. **Return spring**	39. **Spring**
9. **Bolt**	26. **Sleeve**	40. **Shift pawl**
10. **Shifter pedal base**	27. **Detent arm**	41. **Return spring**
11. **Lockwasher**	28. **Bolt**	42. **Sleeve**
12. **Spacer**	29. **Shift shaft–long**	43. **Oil seal**
13. **Shaft**	30. **Upper shift fork**	44. **Washer**
14. **Spacer**	**(5th and 6th gears)**	45. **Snap ring**
15. **Shift lever**	31. **Snap ring**	46. **Shift rod lever–inner**
16. **Shift rod**	32. **Shift cam**	*** Items 2-15 are used only**
17. **Jam nut**	33. **Snap ring**	**on CVO models.**

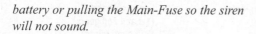

battery or pulling the Main-Fuse so the siren will not sound.

1. Remove the Main-Fuse as described in *Fuses* (Chapter Nine).

2. Remove the front left footboard as described in Chapter Fourteen.

3. Make an alignment mark on the heel shift lever and the end of the shift lever shaft.

4. Remove the clamp bolt (A, **Figure 5**) and remove the heel shift lever (B).

5. Make an alignment mark on the toe shift lever and the end of the shift lever shaft.

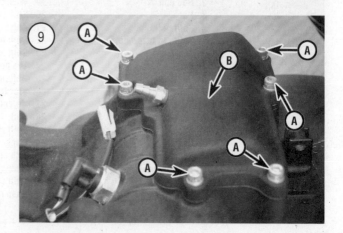

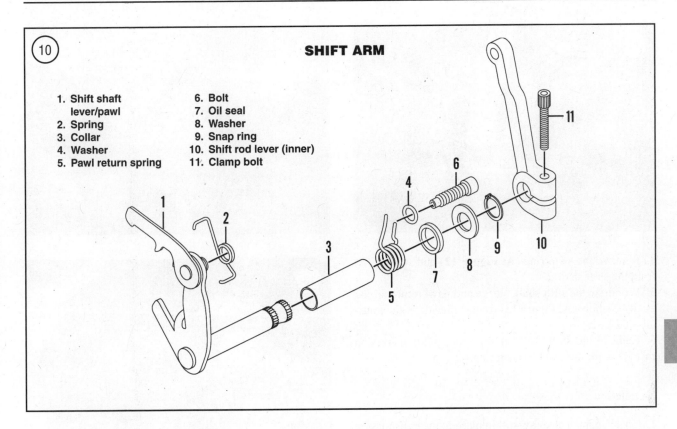

SHIFT ARM

1. Shift shaft lever/pawl
2. Spring
3. Collar
4. Washer
5. Pawl return spring
6. Bolt
7. Oil seal
8. Washer
9. Snap ring
10. Shift rod lever (inner)
11. Clamp bolt

6. Remove the clamp bolt (C, **Figure 5**) and remove the toe shift lever (D).

7. Remove the spacer (**Figure 6**) from the shift lever shaft.

8. On CVO models, remove the jiffy stand as described in Chapter Seventeen.

9. Remove the primary chaincase assembly as described in Chapter Six.

10. Remove the nut, washer and lockwasher securing the shift rod to the outer shift lever.

11. Remove the clamp bolt (A, **Figure 7**) securing the inner shift rod lever (B) to the transmission case.

12. Remove the outer shift rod lever (A, **Figure 7**), shift rod (B), inner shift lever and shift lever shaft as an assembly.

13. Install by reversing the removal steps. Tighten the shift rod lever clamp bolts to 18-22 ft.-lb. (24.4-29.8 N•m).

TRANSMISSION COVER

The transmission cover assembly can be serviced with the transmission installed in the frame.

Removal/Installation

NOTE
Always disarm the optional TSSM/HFSM security system prior to disconnecting the battery or pulling the Main-Fuse so the siren will not sound.

1. Remove the Main-Fuse as described in *Fuses* (Chapter Eleven).

2. Remove the right side exhaust system as described in Chapter Four.

3. Remove the clamp, and disconnect the vent hose from the transmission cover fitting.

4. Remove the bolts (A, **Figure 9**) securing the transmission cover to the transmission case. Remove the cover (B, **Figure 9**) and the gasket.

5. Remove the gasket residue from the transmission cover and transmission case mating surfaces.

6. Install a *new* gasket onto the transmission case. ·

7. Install the transmission cover, the bolts and the washers. Using a crossing pattern, tighten the transmission cover bolts to 90-120 in.-ib. (10.2-13.6. N•m)

8. Reconnect the vent hose (**Figure 8**) to the fitting and install a *new* hose clamp.

9. Reinstall the Main-Fuse as described in *Fuses* (Chapter Nine).

10. Install the right side exhaust system as described in Chapter Four.

SHIFT ARM ASSEMBLY

Removal

Refer to **Figure 10**.

1. Remove the transmission side door assembly as described in this chapter.

2. Make an alignment mark on the shift shaft (A, **Figure 11**) that relates to the split part (B) of the shift rod lever.

3. Remove the clamp bolt (C, **Figure 11**), and then remove the shift rod lever (D) from the shift shaft.

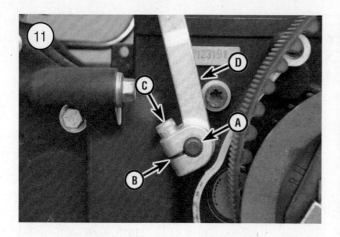

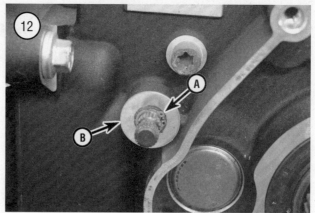

4. Remove the snap ring (A, **Figure 12**) and washer (B) from the shift shaft.

5. Withdraw the shift shaft, sleeve and pawl return spring as an assembly (A, **Figure 13**) from the inside of the transmission case.

6. Remove the shift shaft oil seal from the transmission case. Discard the seal and snap ring.

Installation

1. Check that the sleeve is still in place in the transmission case.

2. Make sure the arms of the shift shaft spring straddle (A, **Figure 14**) the tab on the shift shaft body.

3. If removed, install the shift pawl return spring.

4. Install the shift shaft assembly (A, **Figure 13**) into the transmission case so the arms of the shift shaft spring straddle the centering pin (B, **Figure 13**) in the case.

5. Carefully install a new oil seal over the shift shaft and into the transmission case. Make sure the shift shaft splines do not damage the seal.

6. Install the washer (B, **Figure 12**) and a *new* snap ring (A) onto the shaft. Make sure the snap ring is correctly seated in the shaft.

7. Refer to the indexing marks made during removal and install the inner shift rod lever onto the end of the shift shaft. Push the lever on until its clamp bolt hole aligns with the shift shaft groove.

8. Install the shift rod lever clamp bolt (C, **Figure 11**) and tighten the bolt to 18-22 ft.-lb. (24.4-29.8 N•m).

9. Install the transmission side door assembly as described in this chapter.

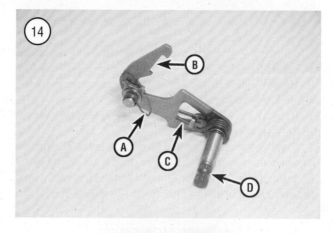

Inspection

Replace any part that is worn or damaged.

1. Check the shift shaft spring (A, **Figure 14**) and pawl return spring (C) for fatigue or damage.

2. Check the shift pawl (B, **Figure 14**) for wear. Replace the shift shaft assembly if the pawl is damaged.

3. Check the shift shaft for wear or damage. Make sure the end splines (D, **Figure 14**) are in good condition.

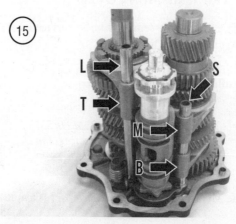

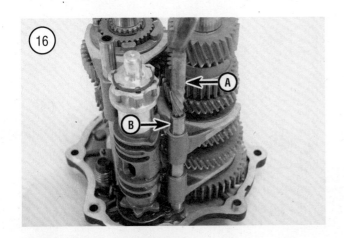

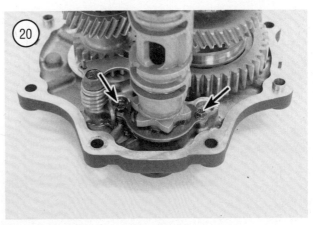

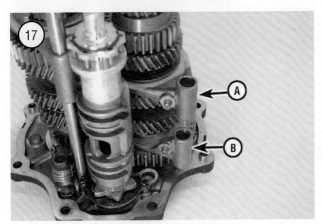

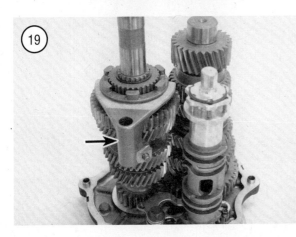

4. Check the inner shift rod lever (D, **Figure 11**) for wear or damage. Make sure the internal splines are in good condition.

SHIFT FORKS AND SHIFT CAM

The 6-speed shift fork shaft remover (JIMS part No. 985), a twist-type screw extractor, or an equivalent tool, is needed for this procedure.

Refer to **Figure 1**.

Removal

1. Remove the transmission side door assembly as described in this chapter.
2. If still installed, remove the clutch push rod from the mainshaft tunnel.

NOTE
*Use a waterproof felt-tip pen or scribe and mark the installed position of each shift fork (T, M, B, **Figure 15**) as it sits in the transmission. Each shift fork is unique and must be reinstalled in the groove of a particular dog ring. Also mark the top of the long (L, **Figure 15**) or short (S) shift fork shafts so they can be reinstalled with the original orientation.*

3. Carefully install the shift fork shaft remover (A, **Figure 16**) and remove the short shift fork shaft (B).
4. Remove the middle (3rd/4th gear) shift fork (A, **Figure 17**) and the bottom (1st/2nd gear) shift fork (B).
5. Carefully install the shift fork shaft remover (A, **Figure 18**), and remove the long shift fork shaft (B).
6. Remove the top (5th/6th gear) shift fork (**Figure 19**).
7. Remove the shift drum lock plate bolts (**Figure 20**), and remove the shift cam lock plate (**Figure 21**). Discard the bolts.
8. Use a flat-bladed screwdriver to gently push the detent arm (A, **Figure 22**) away from the shift cam.
9. Pull straight up and withdraw the shift cam (B, **Figure 22**) and bearing from the bore in transmission door.

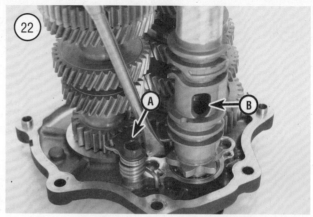

10. If necessary, remove the detent arm assembly (A, **Figure 23**) by performing the following:

   a. Before removal, note how the lower arm of the detent spring engages the boss (B, **Figure 23**) in the side door. The assembly must be reinstalled so this arm engages the correct boss.

   b. Remove the detent arm pivot bolt (C, **Figure 23**) and remove the detent arm (D). Note how the upper arm of the detent spring passes through the hole in the detent arm.

   c. Remove the sleeve and the detent spring. Discard the pivot bolt.

11. Inspect all parts as described in this section.

Installation

NOTE
Refer to the marks made during removal and install each shift fork in the correct location.

1. Coat all bearing and sliding surfaces with transmission oil.

2. If removed, install the detent arm assembly (A, **Figure 23**) by performing the following:

   a. Assemble the detent arm with a *new* pivot bolt (C, **Figure 23**). Make sure the detent spring's upper arm engages the hole in the detent arm.

   b. Lower the assembly into the side door so the spring's lower arm engages the boss (B, **Figure 23**) noted during removal.

   c. Install the detent arm pivot bolt (C, **Figure 23**), and then tighten the bolt to 120-150 in.-lb. (13.6-17.0 N•m).

3. Move the detent arm out of the way, and hold it in this position.

4. Lower the shift cam (A, **Figure 24**) so it's bearing engages the bore (B) in transmission side door. Carefully push straight down on the shift cam (B, **Figure 22**) until the bearing bottoms. Once the shift cam is correctly installed, release the detent arm onto the shift cam.

5. Install the shift cam lock plate (**Figure 21**) and install *new* lock plate bolts. Tighten the shift cam lock plate bolts (**Figure 20**) to 57-63 in.-lb. (6.4-7.1 N•m).

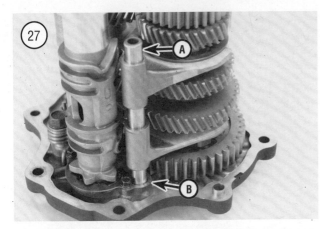

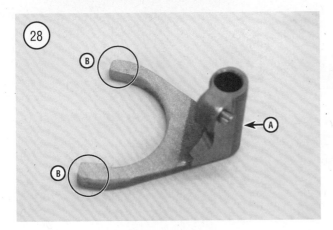

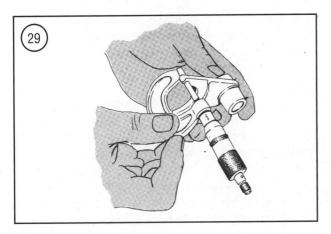

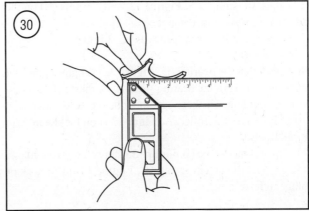

6. Install the top (5th/6th gear) shift fork (**Figure 19**) into the slot of the dog ring atop mainshaft 5th gear.

7. Move the shift fork into alignment with the shift-fork-shaft receptacle in the side door. Position the long shift fork shaft with the marked end facing up, and install it (**Figure 25**) through the shift fork and into the shaft receptacle in the side door (**Figure 26**). Tap the shaft in until it bottoms in the receptacle.

8. Install the bottom (1st/2nd gear) shift fork (B, **Figure 17**) into slot of the dog ring between countershaft 1st and 2nd gear.

9. Install the middle (3rd/4th gear) shift fork (A, **Figure 17**) into slot of the dog ring between countershaft 3rd and 4th gear.

10. Move the shift forks so the receptacles align with the shift-fork-shaft boss in the side door. Position the short shift fork shaft with the marked end facing up, and install it (A, **Figure 27**) through both shift forks and into the shaft receptacle (B) in the side door. Tap the shaft in until it bottoms in the receptacle.

11. The clutch pushrod will be installed in the mainshaft channel once the transmission side door assembly is installed in the transmission case.

Inspection

Replace any part that is worn, damaged or out of specification.

1. Inspect each shift fork (A, **Figure 28**) for excessive wear or damage. Replace worn or damaged shift forks as required.

2. Measure the thickness (**Figure 29**) of each shift fork finger (B, **Figure 28**) where it contacts the dog ring groove. Replace the shift fork if any finger is worn to the service limit (**Table 3**).

3. Inspect the shift forks for any arc-shaped wear or burn marks.

4. Place each shift fork and shaft along the side of a square (**Figure 30**) and check for bending.

5. Roll each shift fork shaft on a flat surface and check for bending.

6. Install each shift fork onto its shift shaft and slide it back and forth (**Figure 31**). Each shift fork must slide smoothly with no binding or tight spots.

7

7. Check the ramps (A, **Figure 32**) and the pins (B) on the shift cam for wear or damage.

8. Inspect the shift cam grooves (C, **Figure 32**) for wear or roughness.

9. Check that the bearing (D, **Figure 32**) is tight on the end of shift cam. Turn the bearing by hand. It must rotate freely with no binding. The bearing cannot be replaced separately.

10. Make sure the roller (A, **Figure 33**) on the detent arm turns freely.

11. Inspect the sleeve (B, **Figure 33**) for wear or roughness.

12. Inspect the detent spring (C, **Figure 33**) for cracks or other signs of fatigue.

TRANSMISSION SIDE DOOR ASSEMBLY

Refer to **Figure 34**.

The transmission side door assembly includes the side door, mainshaft, countershaft, shift forks and shift cam. The transmission side door assembly can be serviced with the transmission case installed in the frame.

Tools

The following tools are used during side door assembly removal/installation or disassembly/assembly:

1. The mainshaft bearing race puller and installation tool (JIMS part No. 34902-84 or H-D part No. HD-34902-C).

2. The transmission main drive gear installer (JIMS part No. 981).

3. The transmission side door puller tool (JIMS part No. 984).

4. The transmission mainshaft pulley locknut socket (JIMS part No. 989).

Removal

1. Remove the exhaust system as described in Chapter Four.

2. Drain the transmission oil and the primary chaincase oil as described in Chapter Three.

3. Remove the transmission filler plug/dipstick (**Figure 35**). If left in place it will interfere with the removal of the transmission side door assembly.

4. Remove the primary chaincase housing and the clutch release cover as described in Chapter Six.

5. On all models except CVO, remove the oil slinger (**Figure 36**) from the mainshaft.

6. Withdraw the clutch pushrod (**Figure 37**).

7. Remove the bearing inner race (A, **Figure 38**) from the mainshaft as follows:

    a. Attach the mainshaft bearing race puller and installation tool (A, **Figure 39**) against the inner bearing race (B) following the tool manufacturer's instructions.

    b. Tighten the puller center bolt and withdraw the inner race (B, **Figure 39**) from the mainshaft (C).

    c. Remove the tool and the inner race.

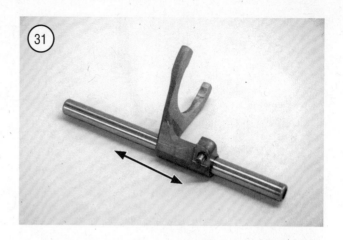

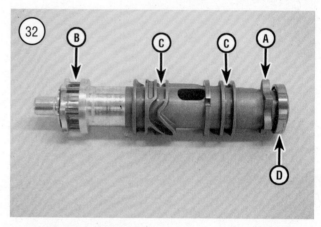

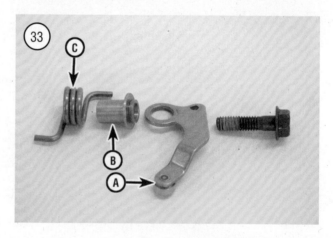

    d. Tape the clutch splines (B, **Figure 38**) on the mainshaft so they will not damage the needle bearings in the main drive gear.

8. Remove the transmission cover as described in this chapter.

9. Lift the shift pawl (**Figure 40**) from the shift cam pins, and set it onto the transmission cover gasket surface.

10. If the transmission shaft assemblies will be removed from the side door, perform the following:

    a. Turn the transmission by hand and shift the transmission into 6th gear to keep the shafts from turning.

    b. Loosen, but do not remove, the countershaft (A, **Figure 41**) and mainshaft (B) locknuts.

TRANSMISSION CASE BEARINGS AND COVERS

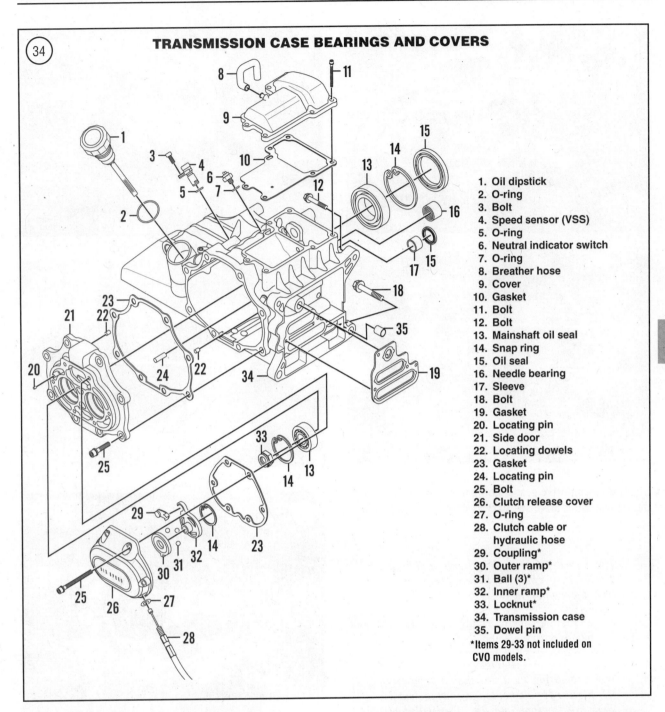

1. Oil dipstick
2. O-ring
3. Bolt
4. Speed sensor (VSS)
5. O-ring
6. Neutral indicator switch
7. O-ring
8. Breather hose
9. Cover
10. Gasket
11. Bolt
12. Bolt
13. Mainshaft oil seal
14. Snap ring
15. Oil seal
16. Needle bearing
17. Sleeve
18. Bolt
19. Gasket
20. Locating pin
21. Side door
22. Locating dowels
23. Gasket
24. Locating pin
25. Bolt
26. Clutch release cover
27. O-ring
28. Clutch cable or
    hydraulic hose
29. Coupling*
30. Outer ramp*
31. Ball (3)*
32. Inner ramp*
33. Locknut*
34. Transmission case
35. Dowel pin

*Items 29-33 not included on
CVO models.

7

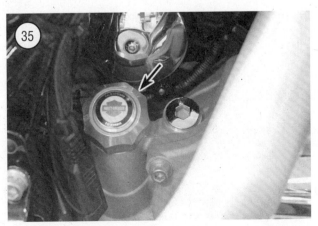

11. If the main drive gear is going to be removed, remove the transmission drive sprocket as described in this chapter.

NOTE
*There are two different length side door bolts. The two longer bolts (C, **Figure 41**) are located in the bottom two holes of the side door.*

12. Using a crossing pattern, evenly loosen the side door bolts, and then remove the bolts.

CAUTION
*When removing the transmission side door (D, **Figure 41**), do not tap against the mainshaft from the opposite side. This will damage the side door bearings.*

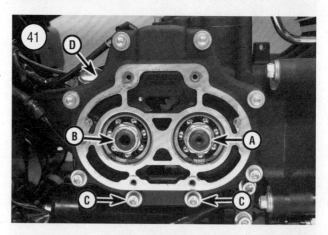

13A. Install the transmission side door puller (**Figure 42**) onto the side door following the tool manufacturer's instructions. Tighten the outside screws one-half turn at a time, alternating from side-to-side until the side door releases from the transmission case. Remove the tool.
13B. If the remover tool is not available, use a soft-face mallet, and carefully tap against the transmission side door to loosen its seal against the transmission case. If necessary, insert a large, flat-bladed screwdriver into the pry points (**Figure 43**) and work the door loose (**Figure 44**).
14. Slowly withdraw the transmission side door assembly and the transmission shafts (**Figure 45**) from the trans-

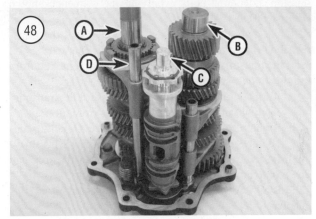

mission case, and then remove it. Do not lose the locating dowels behind the side door.

15. Remove and discard the transmission side door gasket.

16. If necessary, service the side door and transmission assembly as described in *Transmission Shafts* (this chapter).

Installation

1. If the main drive gear was removed, install it as described in this chapter.

2. Remove all gasket residue from mating surfaces of the side door and transmission case.

3. If removed install the dowels, and then install a *new* side-door gasket onto the transmission case.

4. Wrap the clutch splines (B, **Figure 38**) on the mainshaft with tape to protect the main drive gear needle bearings and oil seal during installation.

5. Apply clean transmission oil to the following:

    a. The main drive gear small oil seal (A, **Figure 46**), the outer needle bearing (B) and the inner needle bearing (A, **Figure 47**).

    b. The countershaft needle bearings (B, **Figure 47**).

    c. The journals on the mainshaft (A, **Figure 48**), countershaft (B), and the shift cam (C).

    d. The end of the long shift fork shaft (D, **Figure 48**).

6. Slowly and carefully slide the side door assembly into the transmission case (**Figure 45**) so the mainshaft passes through the main drive gear needle bearings (A, **Figure 47**),

and the countershaft seats in its needle bearing (B). Also, make sure the shift cam seats in its transmission case receptacle (A, **Figure 49**) and that the long shift fork shaft sits in its receptacle (B). Check all of these items if the side door does not seat directly against the transmission case.

NOTE
There are two different length side door bolts. The two longer bolts (C, Figure 41) are located in the bottom two holes of the side door.

7. Install the two longer side door bolts and captive washers and finger-tighten the bolts. Install the remaining six shorter bolts and finger-tighten the bolts. Tighten the transmission side door bolts evenly in the sequence shown (**Figure 50**) to 13-18 ft.-lb. (17.6-24.4 N•m).

8. If the main drive gear was removed, install the transmission drive sprocket as described in this chapter.

9. If the transmission shaft assemblies were removed from the side door, perform the following:
   a. Turn the transmission by hand and shift the transmission into 6th gear to keep the gears from turning.
   b. Tighten the countershaft (A, **Figure 41**) and mainshaft (B) locknuts to 55-65 ft.-lb. (74.6-88.1 N•m).

10. Move the shift pawl forward and lower the free end down onto engagement with the shift cam pins.

11. Install the transmission cover as described in this chapter.

12. Install the mainshaft bearing inner race (A, **Figure 38**) onto the mainshaft by performing the following:
   a. Assemble the mainshaft bearing race puller and installation tool according to the tool manufacturer's instructions.
   b. Apply clean oil to the mainshaft shaft bearing surface, shaft threads and to the inner surface of the inner race.
   c. Position the bearing inner race with the chamfered end goes on first. Slide the bearing inner race onto the mainshaft until it stops prior to being pressed on.
   d. Thread the extension shaft (A, **Figure 51**) onto the mainshaft.
   e. Place the pusher tube (B, **Figure 51**) over the extension shaft, add the two flat washers (C). Thread on the nut (D, **Figure 51**) and hand tighten securely against the flat washers.

CAUTION
Install the inner bearing race to the dimension listed. This aligns the race with the bearing outer race installed in the primary chaincase. Installing the wrong race or installing it incorrectly will damage the bearing and race assembly.

   f. Secure the extension shaft (A, **Figure 51**) and tighten the nut (D) to press the bearing inner race onto the mainshaft. Install the race so that it's inside edge is 0.100-0.125 in. (2.540-3.180 mm) away from the main drive gear.

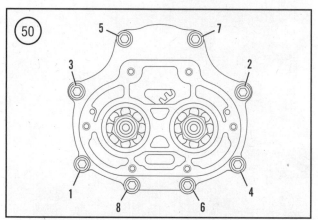

   g. Remove the tools.

13. Install the clutch pushrod (**Figure 37**) into the mainshaft.

14. On all models except CVO, install the oil slinger assembly (**Figure 36**) into the mainshaft.

15. Install the primary chaincase housing, primary drive and clutch release cover as described in Chapter Six.

16. Install the drain plugs, and add oil to the transmission and to the primary chaincase described in Chapter Three.

17. Install the transmission filler plug/dipstick (**Figure 35**).

18. Install the exhaust system as described in Chapter Four.

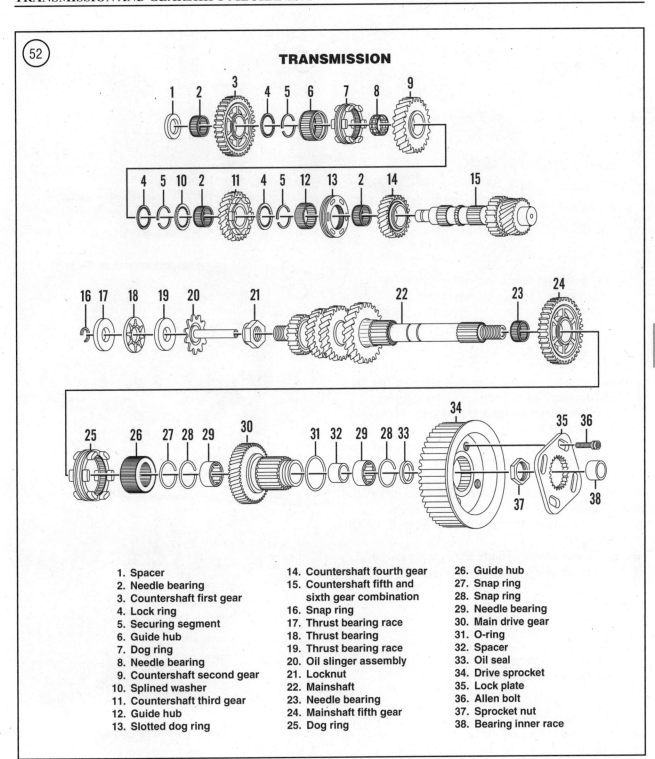

52   TRANSMISSION

1. Spacer
2. Needle bearing
3. Countershaft first gear
4. Lock ring
5. Securing segment
6. Guide hub
7. Dog ring
8. Needle bearing
9. Countershaft second gear
10. Splined washer
11. Countershaft third gear
12. Guide hub
13. Slotted dog ring

14. Countershaft fourth gear
15. Countershaft fifth and
    sixth gear combination
16. Snap ring
17. Thrust bearing race
18. Thrust bearing
19. Thrust bearing race
20. Oil slinger assembly
21. Locknut
22. Mainshaft
23. Needle bearing
24. Mainshaft fifth gear
25. Dog ring

26. Guide hub
27. Snap ring
28. Snap ring
29. Needle bearing
30. Main drive gear
31. O-ring
32. Spacer
33. Oil seal
34. Drive sprocket
35. Lock plate
36. Allen bolt
37. Sprocket nut
38. Bearing inner race

19. Test-ride the motorcycle slowly and check for proper transmission operation.

TRANSMISSION SHAFTS

The snap rings are very difficult to loosen and remove even with high quality snap ring pliers. It is recommended that heavy-duty retaining ring pliers (H-D part No. J-5586), or an equivalent, be used.

Store all of the transmission gears, snap rings, washers and split bearings in their order of removal.

Refer to **Figure 52**.

Mainshaft Disassembly

First, second, third and forth gears are an integral part of the mainshaft assembly and cannot be replaced separately. If any one of these is damaged, the mainshaft must be replaced.

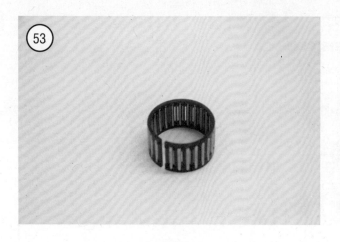

NOTE
The mainshaft needle bearings are split bearings (Figure 53) and must be partially opened during removal. Doing so weakens the plastic cage securing the needles. Discard all removed needle bearings and always install new bearings during assembly.

1. Remove the transmission side door assembly, the shift forks and the shift cam as described in this chapter.
2. If still in place, remove the dowels (**Figure 54**) from the inboard side of the side door.
3. Remove the locknut (A, **Figure 55**) from the right end of the mainshaft. If the countershaft will also be serviced, remove the locknut (B, **Figure 55**) from the countershaft.
4. Remove the snap ring (**Figure 56**) from the left end of the mainshaft.
5. Slide the dog ring (A, **Figure 57**) and its guide hub (B) from the mainshaft.
6. Remove fifth gear (A, **Figure 58**) from the mainshaft.
7. Remove fifth gear needle bearing (**Figure 59**).
8. Place the transmission assembly on the hydraulic press with the side door (A, **Figure 60**) facing up. Make sure the side door lies flat on the press bed.

CAUTION
Do not apply pressure on the bearing inner race as the bearing and/or side door will be damaged.

9. Place an appropriate size mandrel or socket (B, **Figure 60**) onto the end of the mainshaft.
10. Secure the lower end of the mainshaft assembly, and slowly press the assembly out of the side door bearing. Carefully guide the mainshaft gears past the countershaft gears.
11. If the countershaft also requires service, remove it as described in *Countershaft Disassembly* (this section).

NOTE
Replace the side door bearing whenever the shaft(s) is removed.

12. Replace the side door bearing as described in this chatper.
13. Inspect all parts (**Figure 61**) as described in this section.

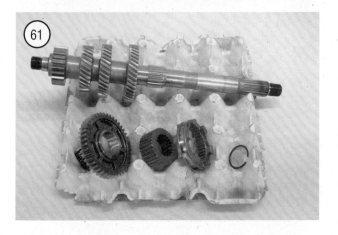

Mainshaft Assembly

CAUTION
*Install a new snap ring to ensure proper gear alignment and engagement. Never reinstall a snap ring that has been removed since it has become distorted and weakened and may fail. Make sure the **new** snap ring is correctly seated in its respective shaft groove.*

1. If the countershaft was serviced, install it into the side door as described in *Countershaft Assembly* (this section).
2. Apply a light coat of clean transmission oil to the side door bearing inner race and to the mainshaft bearing surface.
3. Place the mainshaft on the press plate supported by fourth gear.
4. Place the side door and countershaft assembly next to the mainshaft, and align both transmission shaft assemblies.
5. Position the countershaft so it clears the press bed. Have an assistant secure both shaft assemblies in this position.

CAUTION
*The countershaft dog ring (A, **Figure 62**) must be fully engaged with countershaft third gear (B). Failure to do so will push the shafts out of alignment and cause damage to the bearings and gears on both shafts. Do **not** press the side door onto the mainshaft while this dog ring engages countershaft fourth gear.*

6. Have the assistant lift the countershaft dog ring (A, **Figure 62**) up so it is fully engaged with countershaft third gear (B) during the mainshaft assembly procedure.
7. Place an appropriate size mandrel or socket (**Figure 63**) onto the side door bearing inner race. The outer diameter of the mandrel or socket must only rest on the inner race of the side door bearing.
8. Slowly press the side door bearing onto the mainshaft until the bearing inner race contacts mainshaft first gear. The gear must contact the bearing inner race to ensure correct alignment between both shaft assemblies.
9. Release ram pressure, and remove the side door assembly from the press bed.

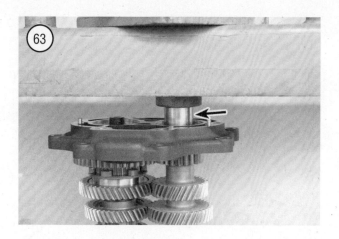

10 Slowly rotate both shaft assemblies within the side door (**Figure 64**) to ensure the gears are aligned correctly. Do not spin too hard as the locknuts are not in place.

11. Install a *new* needle bearing (**Figure 59**) onto the mainshaft. Make sure it is seated correctly on the shaft.

12. Position mainshaft fifth gear (A, **Figure 58**) with the dog ring slot side (B) going on last and install the fifth gear.

13. Position the guide hub (**Figure 65**) with the counter bored end going on first (facing fifth gear with the flat side facing out), and then install the guide hub.

14. Install the dog ring (A, **Figure 57**) onto fifth gear and make sure it is correctly seated.

15. Install a *new* snap ring (A, **Figure 56**). Make sure it is seated correctly in the mainshaft groove.

16. Refer to **Figure 66** to ensure the correct placement of the gears. Also check that the gears mesh properly with an adjoining gear where applicable. This is the last opportunity to check the shaft assemblies before they are installed into the transmission case.

CAUTION
The transmission shaft assembly must be installed in the transmission case prior to tightening the locknuts to achieve for correct alignment. The side door bearings can be damaged if the locknuts are tightened while the assembly is on the bench.

17. If removed, install the dowels (**Figure 54**) into the inboard side of the transmission door.

18. Use the dog rings to lock the two shafts together, and temporarily install the side door and transmission assembly into the transmission case.

19. Thread a *new* locknut on the mainshaft (A, **Figure 55**) and the countershaft (B).

20. Tighten each locknut (**Figure 67**) 55-65 ft.-lb. (74.6-88.1 N•m).

21. Remove the side door assembly, and install the shift forks and the shift cam as described in this chapter.

22. Install the transmission side door assembly as described in this chapter.

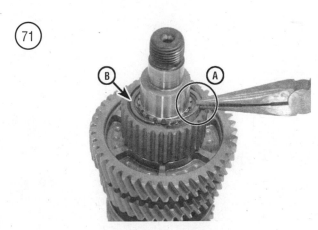

Countershaft Disassembly

Fifth and sixth gear are an integral part of the countershaft assembly and cannot be replaced separately. If either of these gears is damaged, the countershaft must be replaced.

> *NOTE*
> *The countershaft needle bearings are split bearings (**Figure 53**) and must be partially opened during removal. Doing so weakens the plastic cage securing the needles. Discard all removed needle bearings and always install new bearings during assembly.*

1. Remove the transmission side door assembly, shift forks and shift cam as described in this chapter.
2. Press the mainshaft from the side door as described in *Mainshaft Disassembly* (this section).
3. Remove the locknut (B, **Figure 55**) from the right side of the countershaft.
4. Place the transmission assembly in the hydraulic press with the side door (A, **Figure 68**) facing up. Make sure the side door lies flat on the press bed.

> *CAUTION*
> *Do not apply pressure to the bearing inner race as the bearing and/or side door will be damaged.*

5. Place an appropriate size mandrel or socket (B, **Figure 68**) onto the end of the countershaft.
6. Secure the lower end of the countershaft assembly, and slowly press the countershaft out of the side door bearing.
7. Remove the side door and countershaft assembly from the press bed.
8. Remove the spacer (A, **Figure 69**) and first gear (B) from the side door end of the countershaft.
9. Remove the needle bearing (A, **Figure 70**), the lock ring (B), and the dog ring (C).
10. Remove both securing segments (A, **Figure 71**) from the guide hub counter bore (B).
11. Remove the guide hub (A, **Figure 72**).
12. Remove second gear (A, **Figure 73**) and its needle bearing (**Figure 74**) from the shaft.

13. Remove the lock ring (**Figure 75**), both securing segments (**Figure 76**) and the splined washer (**Figure 77**) from the shaft.

14. Remove third gear (A, **Figure 78**) and its needle bearing (**Figure 79**) from the countershaft.

15. Remove the lock ring (**Figure 80**).

16. Remove both securing segments (**Figure 81**) and the slotted dog ring (**Figure 82**) from the shaft.

17. Remove the guide hub (A, **Figure 83**) and fourth gear (B).

18. Remove fourth gear needle bearing (**Figure 84**).

19. Replace the side door bearings as described in this chapter.

20. Inspect all parts (**Figure 85**) as described in this section.

Countershaft Assembly

1. Apply a light coat of clean transmission oil to all sliding surfaces and needle bearings.

2. Install a *new* needle bearing (**Figure 84**). Make sure it is seated correctly on the shaft.

3. Position countershaft fourth gear with the shift dogs (C, **Figure 83**) facing up, and then install countershaft fourth gear (B).

4. Install the guide hub (A, **Figure 83**) and the slotted dog ring (**Figure 82**).

5. Install both securing segments (**Figure 81**) so their straight sides face the guide hub. Each segment must be completely seated in the shaft groove.

NOTE
When installing lock rings next to securing segments, make sure the shouldered side of the lock ring faces and surrounds the securing segments. The parts are properly installed when the securing segments are nested within the lock ring.

6. Position the lock ring (**Figure 80**) so its shouldered side faces and surrounds the securing segments. Install the lock ring.

7. Install a *new* needle bearing (**Figure 79**). Make sure it is seated correctly on the shaft.

8. Position countershaft third gear with the shouldered side (B, **Figure 78**) faces out, and install the third gear (A).

9. Install the spline washer (**Figure 77**).

10. Seat both securing segments (**Figure 76**) in the shaft groove so their straight sides face the splined washer.

11. Position the lock ring (**Figure 75**) so it's shouldered side faces and surrounds the securing segments. Install the lock ring.

12. Install a *new* needle bearing (**Figure 74**). Make sure it is seated correctly on the shaft.

13. Position second gear so its engagement slots (B, **Figure 73**) face out, and then install second gear (A).

14. Position the guide hub with the recessed side (B, **Figure 72**) facing out. Install the guide hub (A, **Figure 72**).

15. Seat both securing segments (**Figure 71**) in the guide hub so their straight sides face the hub.

16. Install the dog ring (**Figure 86**) onto the guide hub.

17. Position the lock ring (B, **Figure 70**) so it's shouldered side faces and surrounds the securing segments. Install the lock ring.

18. Install a *new* needle bearing (A, **Figure 70**). Make sure it is seated correctly on the shaft.

19. Position countershaft first gear so its engagement slots face the dog ring, and then install countershaft first gear (B, **Figure 69**).

20. Install the spacer (A, **Figure 69**).

21. Refer to **Figure 87** to ensure all gears are in the correct location.

Transmission Inspection

Maintain the alignment of the transmission components when cleaning and inspecting the individual parts in the following section. To prevent mixing parts, work on only one shaft at a time.

Refer to **Table 2** when inspecting the service clearance and end play of the indicated gears and shafts. Replace parts that are worn, damaged or out of specification.

1. Clean and dry the shaft assemblies.

2. Inspect the mainshaft (**Figure 88**) and countershaft (**Figure 89**) for:

   a. Worn or damaged splines (A, **Figure 88**).

   b. Excessively worn or damaged bearing surfaces (A, **Figure 89**).

   c. Cracked or rounded-off securing segment grooves (B, **Figure 89**).

   d. Worn or damaged threads (B, **Figure 88**).

3. Check each gear for excessive wear, burrs, pitting, or chipped or missing teeth (A, **Figure 90**).

4. Check the gear bearing surface (B, **Figure 90**) for wear, cracks or other damage.

5. To check gears for wear, install them on their correct shaft and in the original operating position. If necessary, use the old snap rings to secure them in place. Then, spin the gear by hand. The gear should turn smoothly. A rough turning gear indicates heat damage–check for a dark bluish coloring or galling on the operating surfaces. Rocking indicates excessive wear, either to the gear or shaft or both.

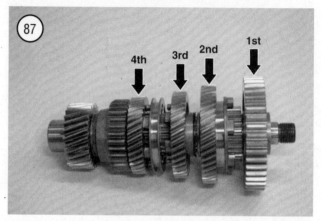

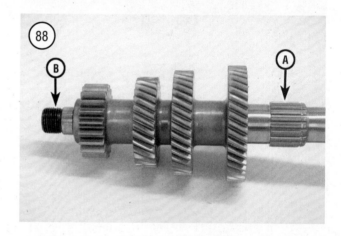

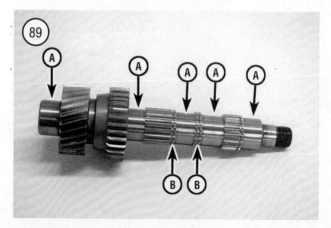

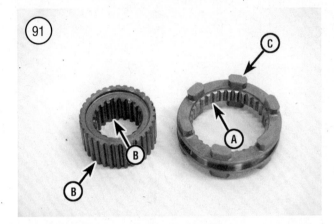

6. Check for excessive wear or damage on the inner splines of the dog rings (A, **Figure 91**) and on the inner and outer splines of the guide hubs (B).

7. To check the dog rings and guide hubs, install them onto their correct shaft and in their original operating position. They should slide back and fourth without any binding or excessive play.

8. Check the shift fork groove on each dog ring (A, **Figure 92**) for wear or damage.

NOTE
*If there is excessive or uneven wear to the gear engagement dogs, check the shift forks carefully for bending and other damage. Refer to **Shift Assembly** in this chapter.*

9. Check the dogs on the gears (**Figure 93**) and dog rings (C, **Figure 91**) for excessive wear, rounding, cracks or other damage. When wear is noticeable, make sure it is consistent on each gear dog. If one dog is worn more than the others, the others will be overstressed during operation and will eventually crack and fail.

10. Check each engagement slot in the gears (C, **Figure 90**) and slotted dog ring (B, **Figure 92**) for cracks, rounding and other damage.

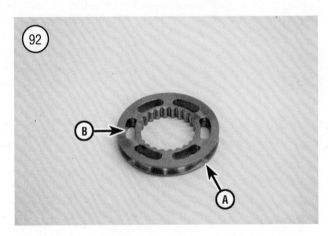

NOTE
Replace defective gears along with their mating gears, though they may not show as much wear or damage.

11. Check engaging gears by installing the two gears on their respective shaft and in their original operating position. Mesh the gears together. Twist one gear against the other, and then check the dog engagement. Then, reverse the thrust load to check in the other operating position. Make sure the engagement in both directions is positive and without any slippage. Check that there is equal engagement across all of the engagement dogs.

12. Check the split bearings (**Figure 94**) for excessive wear or damage. Replace all of the split bearings during re-assembly.

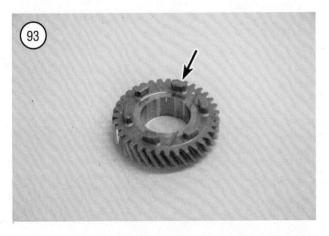

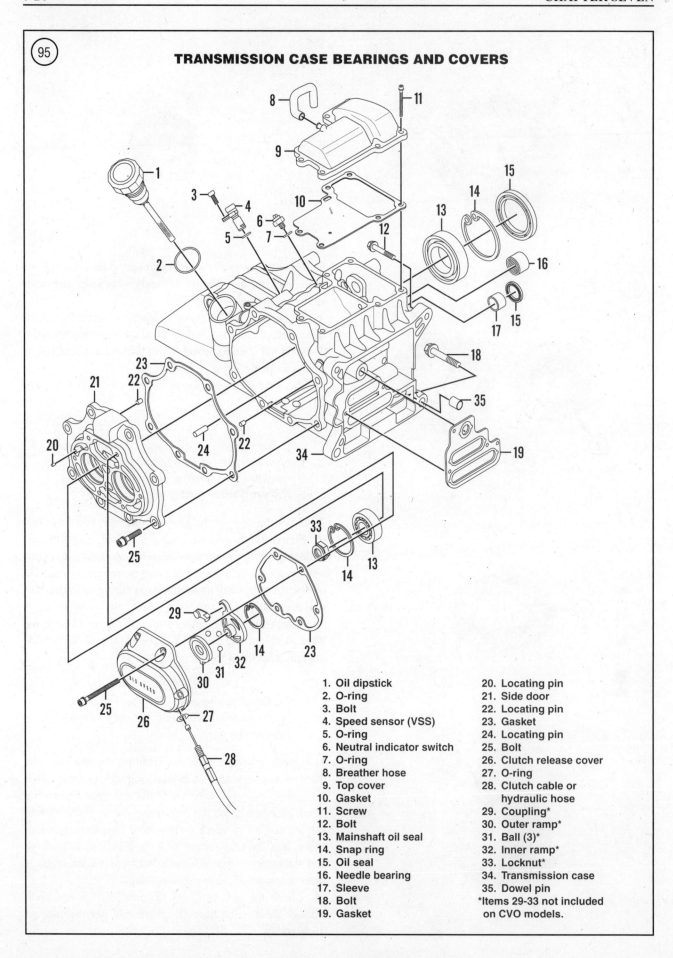

TRANSMISSION CASE BEARINGS AND COVERS

95

1. Oil dipstick
2. O-ring
3. Bolt
4. Speed sensor (VSS)
5. O-ring
6. Neutral indicator switch
7. O-ring
8. Breather hose
9. Top cover
10. Gasket
11. Screw
12. Bolt
13. Mainshaft oil seal
14. Snap ring
15. Oil seal
16. Needle bearing
17. Sleeve
18. Bolt
19. Gasket
20. Locating pin
21. Side door
22. Locating pin
23. Gasket
24. Locating pin
25. Bolt
26. Clutch release cover
27. O-ring
28. Clutch cable or
    hydraulic hose
29. Coupling*
30. Outer ramp*
31. Ball (3)*
32. Inner ramp*
33. Locknut*
34. Transmission case
35. Dowel pin
*Items 29-33 not included
on CVO models.

13. Replace all of the snap rings during re-assembly. In addition, check the washers for burn marks, scoring or cracks. Replace the washers as necessary.

14. Check the spacers for wear or damage.

15. Check the securing segments for cracks, wear or other damage.

SIDE DOOR BEARINGS

Replacement

The side door bearings (**Figure 95**) are pressed into place and secured with a snap ring. They can be removed and installed using the transmission side door bearing remover and installer (JIMS part No. 911). If the tool set is not available, a press is required.

Replace the side door bearings whenever the transmission shafts have been removed.

1. Clean the side door and bearings in solvent, and dry them with compressed air.

2. Remove each snap ring (**Figure 96**) from the outer surface of the side door.

3A. If the tool set is used, follow the tool manufacturer's instructions and remove the bearings.

3B. If a press is used, perform the following:

    a. Support the side door on the press bed with its inner surface facing up.

    b. Use a driver or socket that matches the diameter of the bearing inner races, and press the bearing out of the side-door bore (**Figure 97**).

    c. Repeat the process to remove the opposite bearing.

4. Clean the side door again in solvent and dry thoroughly.

5. Inspect the bearing bores in the side cover for cracks or other damage. Replace the side door if damaged.

> *NOTE*
> *Both side door bearings have the same part number.*

6A. If the tool set is used, follow the tool manufacturer's instructions and install the bearings.

6B. If a press is used, perform the following:

    a. Support the side door in a press with its outer surface acing up.

    b. Center the bearing in the bore so the side with the manufacturer's marks faces up.

    c. Using a driver that presses against the bearing outer race, press the bearing (**Figure 98**) into the bore until it bottoms.

    d. Repeat the process to install the opposite bearing.

7. Install *new* snap rings so the side with the sharp edge faces the bearing outer race. Make sure the snap rings (**Figure 99**) are correctly seated in the side door groove.

MAIN DRIVE GEAR

The main drive gear assembly (**Figure 100**) is pressed into the transmission case. Whenever the main drive gear

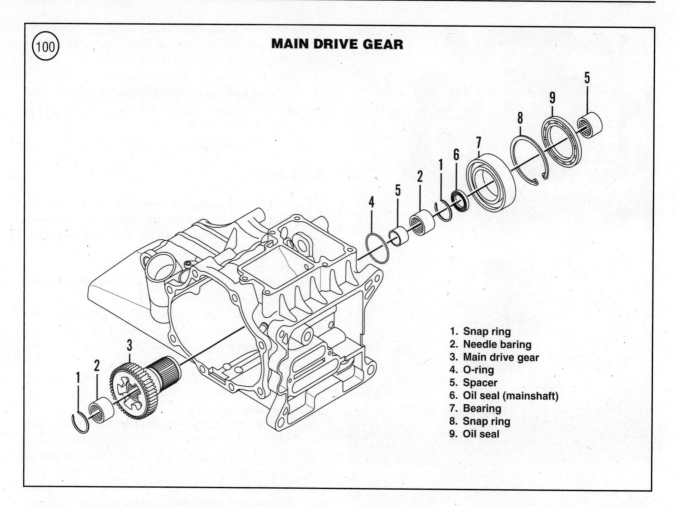

MAIN DRIVE GEAR

1. Snap ring
2. Needle baring
3. Main drive gear
4. O-ring
5. Spacer
6. Oil seal (mainshaft)
7. Bearing
8. Snap ring
9. Oil seal

is removed, the main drive bearing is damaged and must be replaced at the same time.

Tools

If the transmission case is installed in the frame, the following tools are used to remove and install the main drive gear and the main drive bearing:

1. The main drive gear/bearing remover and installer (JIMS part No. 987 or H-D part No. HD-35316-C).
2. The transmission main drive gear large seal installer (JIMS part No. 972 or H-D part No. HD-47856) is required to install the large oil seal.
3. The transmission main drive gear installer (JIMS part No. 981).

If the transmission case has been removed, use a press to remove and install the main drive gear and main drive bearing.

Removal

1. Remove the transmission side door assembly and the transmission drive sprocket as described in this chapter.
2. Remove large oil seal (A, **Figure 101**) from the main drive gear.

3. Remove the snap ring from the main drive bearing behind the large seal.

NOTE
If the main drive gear will not release from the bearing due to corrosion, remove the tools and heat the bearing with a heat gun.

4. Assemble the tool set onto the main drive gear following the tool manufacturer's instructions. Tighten the puller nut slowly to pull the main drive gear from the main drive bearing in the transmission case.
5. Remove the main drive bearing from the transmission case as described in this section.

NOTE
The main drive bearing inner race may remain on the main drive gear. If the main drive gear will be reinstalled, the inner race must be removed.

6. Remove the bearing inner race from the main drive gear by performing the following:
   a. Install the transmission main drive gear wedge attachment (H-D part No HD-95637-46B) or a bearing puller (A, **Figure 102**) beneath the inner race.
   b. Support the tool in a hydraulic press (B, **Figure 102**), and press the main drive gear (C) from the inner race.

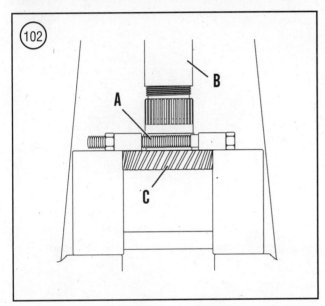

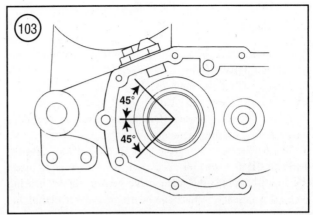

c. Be prepared to catch the main drive gear as it is released from the bearing.

Installation

1. Install a new main drive bearing as described in this section.

2. Install a *new* snap ring so its flat side faces the bearing.

3. Position the snap ring with the open end facing the rear of the transmission and within a 45° angle to horizontal (**Figure 103**). Make sure it is fully seated in the snap ring groove.

4. Lubricate a new O-ring with engine oil, and install it into the groove on the main drive gear.

5. Apply transmission oil to the main drive bearing inner race and to the outer surface of the main drive gear. Also apply oil to the nut and threaded shaft of the installer tool.

6. Insert the main drive gear into the main drive gear bearing as far as it will go. Hold it in place and assemble the tool onto the main drive gear and transmission case following the tool manufacturer's instructions.

7. Slowly tighten the puller nut to pull the main drive gear into the bearing in the transmission case. Continue until the gear bottoms in the bearing inner race.

8. Disassemble and remove the installation tool.

9A. If the transmission main drive gear seal installer (Jims part No.987 or H-D part No. HD-47856) is available; install the large oil seal per the tool manufacturer's instructions.

9B. If the seal installer is not available, perform the following:

    a. Lubricate the lips of a *new* main-drive-gear large oil seal with clean transmission oil.

    b. Position the seal in the bearing bore so its closed side faces out.

    c. Using a mandrel that matches the diameter of the seal, drive the seal into the bore until the seal is flush with the outer edge of the transmission case (A, **Figure 101**).

10. Install the transmission side door assembly and the transmission drive sprocket as described in this chapter.

NOTE
If a new small oil seal was not installed into the main drive gear during needle bearing installation or if the small oil seal is damaged, it can be replaced now. The transmission main drive gear bearing and seal installer tool (JIMS part No. 972 or H-D part No. HD-47933) is needed for this procedure.

11. If necessary, install the small oil seal by performing the following:

    a. Install the protector sleeve over the mainshaft.

    b. Lubricate the sleeve and the small oil seal with clean transmission oil.

    c. Fit the oil seal over the protector sleeve so the seal's closed side faces out.

    d. Slide the seal driver onto the protector, and manually press the seal into the main drive gear. The seal is properly seated when the tool bottoms against the main drive gear.

Inspection

CAUTION
Do no allow solvent to enter the inside of the main drive gear. The solvent will wash contaminants behind the needles in the bearings.

If this occurs, the needle bearing must be replaced.

1. Clean the main drive gear in solvent, and dry with compressed air, if available.

2. Check each gear tooth (A, **Figure 104**) for excessive wear, burrs, galling and pitting. Check for missing teeth.

3. Check the gear splines (B, **Figure 104**) for excessive wear, galling or other damage.

4. Inspect the two main drive gear needle bearings (**Figure 105** and **Figure 106**) for excessive wear or damage. Insert the mainshaft into the main drive gear to check bearing wear. If necessary, replace the bearings as described in this section.

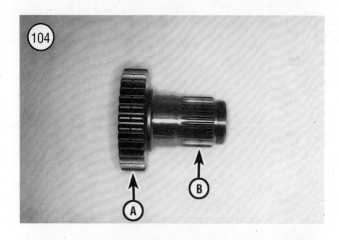

Needle Bearing Replacement

Both main drive gear needle bearings must be installed to the correct depth within the main drive gear. The correct depth is obtained with a main drive gear bearing and seal installer tool (JIMS part No. 986 or H-D part No HD-47933). This tool (**Figure 107**) is also used to install the small oil seal.

If the seal installer is not available, measure the depth of both bearings before removing them.

Replace both main drive gear needle bearings as a set.

> ### CAUTION
> *Never reuse a main drive gear needle bearing, as it is distorted during removal.*

1. Remove O-ring (**Figure 108**) from the main drive gear. Discard the O-ring.

2. Remove the small oil seal (**Figure 109**) from the clutch side of the main drive gear.

3. Remove the retaining ring from each end of the main drive gear bore. Discard the rings.

4. If the seal installer is not available, measure and record the depth of both bearings.

5. Use a blind bearing puller to remove the needle bearings and spacer.

6. Clean the main drive gear and its bearing bore in solvent. Dry it thoroughly.

7. Apply transmission oil to the bearing bore in the main drive gear and to the outer surface of both bearings.

> ### NOTE
> *Install each needle bearing with the manufacturer's marks facing out.*

8. Set the main drive gear (A, **Figure 110**) in the press so its clutch side faces up. Center the main drive gear bore under the press ram.

9. Set a *new* needle bearing into the clutch side of the drive gear bore. Insert the 0.400-in. (10.16 mm) step of the seal installer (B, **Figure 110**) into the bearing.

10. Press the bearing into the bore until the tool lightly contacts the main drive gear.

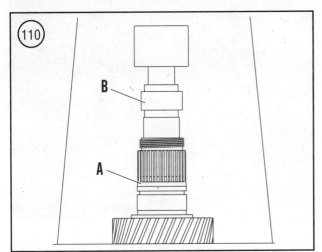

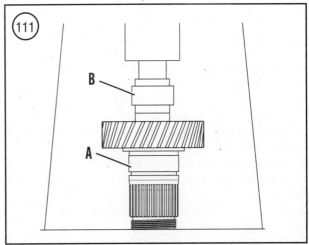

16. Insert the tool's 0.188-in. (4.78 mm) step into the needle bearing, and press the bearing into the bore until the tool (B, **Figure 111**) lightly contacts the main drive gear.

17. Install a *new* retaining ring into the main drive gear. Make sure the ring is completely seated in its groove.

18. Install a *new* small oil seal (B, **Figure 101**) into the clutch side of the main drive gear.

19. Install a *new* O-ring into the main drive gear.

20. Install the main drive gear as described in this section.

Main Drive Bearing Replacement

The main drive bearing (**Figure 100**) is pressed into the transmission case. Whenever the main drive gear is removed, the main drive bearing is damaged and must be replaced at the same time.

CAUTION
Failure to use the correct tools can cause premature bearing failure.

The transmission main drive gear/bearing remover and installer (Jims part No.35316-80, or H-D part No. HD-35316-C) and the transmission main drive gear bearing installer (JIMS part No. 987) are used to remove and install the main drive bearing if the transmission case is installed in the frame.

If the transmission has been removed, a press can be used to remove the main drive bearing.

1. Remove the main drive gear from the transmission case as described in this section.

2. Assemble the tool set onto the main drive bearing following the tool manufacturer's instructions. Tighten the bolt and nut slowly to pull the main drive gear bearing from the transmission case.

3. Clean the bearing bore and dry with compressed air. Check the bore for nicks or burrs and check the snap ring groove for damage.

11. Raise the press ram. Install a *new* retaining ring so the ring's flat side faces the bearing.

12. Insert a new small oil seal into the drive gear bore. The side with the manufacturer's marks must face out.

13. Insert the 0.090-in. (2.29 mm) end of the seal installer into the oil seal, and press the seal into the bore until the tool lightly contact the main drive gear.

14. Turn the main drive gear (A, **Figure 111**) over so it transmission side faces up, install the spacer, and center the bore under the press ram.

15. Start a *new* needle bearing into the bore.

NOTE
Install the bearing into the transmission case
with the manufacturer's marks facing out.

4. Apply transmission oil to the bearing bore in the transmission case and to the outer surface of the bearing. Also apply oil to the nut and threaded shaft of the installer tool.

5. Install the bearing onto the installation tool and assemble the installation tool following the tool manufacturer's instructions.

6. Slowly tighten the puller nut to pull the bearing into the transmission case. Continue until the bearing bottoms in the case.

7. Disassemble and remove the installation tool.

TRANSMISSION DRIVE SPROCKET

Removal/Installation

The transmission drive sprocket locker tool (JIMS part No. 2260 or H-D part No. HD-46282) and the mainshaft pulley locknut socket (JIMS part No. 989 or H-D part No. HD-47910 and part No. HD-94660-2) are used to remove the transmission drive sprocket.

NOTE
It is not necessary to remove the mainshaft
bearing inner race when removing the transmission drive sprocket.

1. Remove the primary chaincase assembly as described in Chapter Six.

2. If necessary, remove the belt guard and debris deflector.

3. Perform the following to create sufficient slack in the drive belt.

    a. Remove the E-clip (A, **Figure 112**) and loosen the rear axle nut (B).

    b. Support the motorcycle with the rear wheel off the ground.

    c. Turn each axle adjuster (C, **Figure 112** and **Figure 113**) in equal amounts.

    d. Push the rear wheel forward to provide sufficient slack in the drive belt.

4. Remove the two Allen bolts (A, **Figure 114**) and the lock plate (B).

5. Install a sprocket locker tool (A, **Figure 115**) onto the transmission drive sprocket, following the tool manufacturer's instructions.

6. Install the tool inner collar (B, **Figure 115**) onto the mainshaft.

7. Install the pulley nut socket (**Figure 116**), and then loosen the pulley nut.

8. Remove the tools and the sprocket nut (C, **Figure 115**) from the mainshaft.

9. Carefully slide the transmission drive sprocket (**Figure 117**) from the mainshaft so the bearing inner race (D, **Figure 115**) is not damaged.

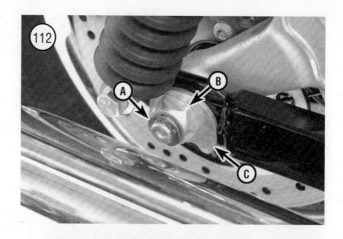

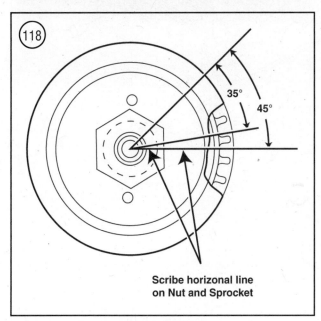

**Scribe horizonal line
on Nut and Sprocket**

10. Fit the drive belt onto the pulley, and slide the transmission drive pulley onto the mainshaft.

11. Finger-tighten the pulley nut onto the main drive gear.

   a. If installing a new sprocket nut, apply a very light coat of clean engine oil onto the inboard side of the new nut. Do not allow any oil to contact the patch of threadlock on the pulley nut threads.

   b. If reinstalling the old nut, apply Loctite High Strength Threadlocker 271 (red) to the nut threads. Also apply a very light coat of clean engine oil onto the inboard face of the locknut and to the surface of the sprocket where the nut makes contact.

12. Install the tool inner collar (B, **Figure 115**) and the drive sprocket nut (**Figure 116**).

13. Tighten the drive sprocket mounting nut to 35 ft.-lb. (47.5 N•m).

14. On all models, perform the following:

CAUTION
*Once the nut has been re-tightened to 35 ft.-lb. (47.5 N•m), the final tightening of the nut must not exceed 45°, which is 1/8th of a turn. If further tightening is needed, watch the scribe lines so total nut movement does not exceed 45° (**Figure 118**).*

   a. Loosen the nut, and then retighten it to 35 ft.-lb. (47.5 N•m).

   b. Scribe a horizontal line onto the sprocket nut and onto the sprocket as shown in **Figure 118**).

CAUTION
Do not tighten the nut more than an additional 45° to align the lockplate bolt holes. The nut will be damaged.

   c. Tighten the nut an additional 35-40° until the lockplate holes align with the holes on the drive sprocket.

15. Remove the tools.

16. Install the lockplate (B, **Figure 114**) over the nut, aligning two of the opposite holes with the threaded holes in the sprocket nut. Remove and refit the lockplate until two opposite holes align. If hole alignment cannot be achieved; tighten the nut additionally as needed. However, the total movement of the nut must not exceed maximum of 45°.

NOTE
New lockplate bolts have threadlock pre-applied to the threads and can be reused up to three times. They must be replaced after the fourth use.

NOTE
Apply Loctite High Strength Threadlocker 271 (red) if reusing the old bolts. Do not apply threadlock when using new bolts.

17. Install and tighten the lockplate bolts (A, **Figure 114**) to 90-120 in.-lb. (10.2-13.6 N•m).

18. Adjust the belt deflection as described in Chapter Three.

TRANSMISSION CASE

Only remove the transmission case (**Figure 119**) if it requires replacement, when performing extensive frame re-

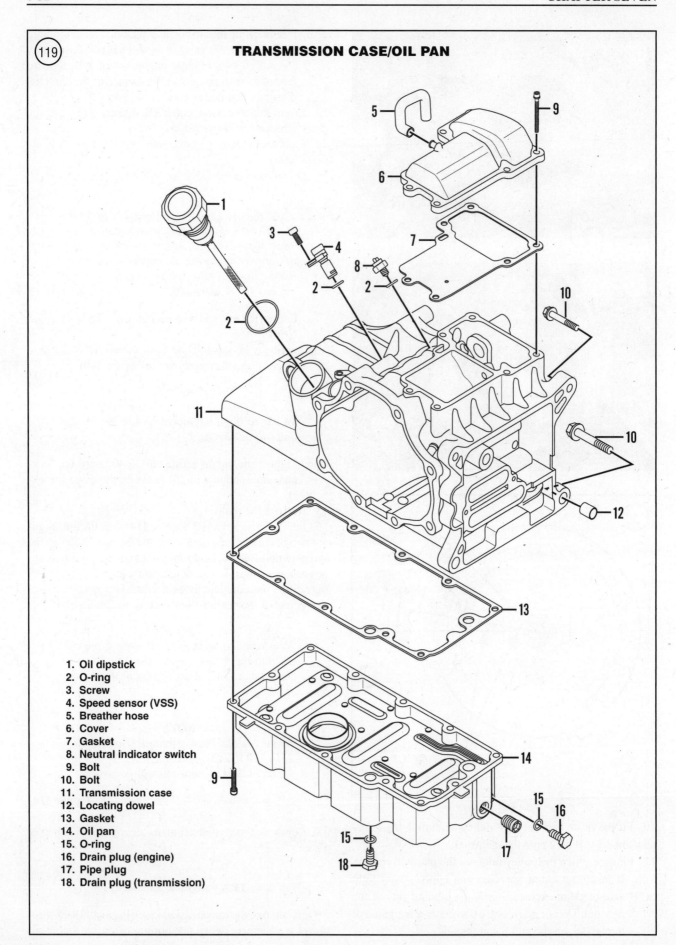

119

TRANSMISSION CASE/OIL PAN

1. Oil dipstick
2. O-ring
3. Screw
4. Speed sensor (VSS)
5. Breather hose
6. Cover
7. Gasket
8. Neutral indicator switch
9. Bolt
10. Bolt
11. Transmission case
12. Locating dowel
13. Gasket
14. Oil pan
15. O-ring
16. Drain plug (engine)
17. Pipe plug
18. Drain plug (transmission)

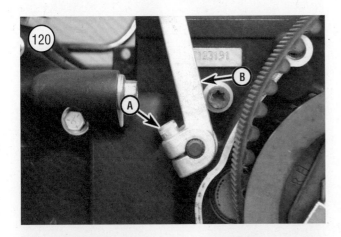

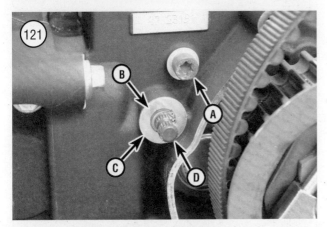

pair or if replacing the frame. All internal components can be removed with the case in the frame.

Removal/Installation

NOTE
Always disarm the TSSM/HFSM security system before disconnecting the battery or pulling the Main-Fuse so the alarm will not sound.

1. Remove the Main-Fuse as described in Chapter Nine.
2. Drain the transmission oil and primary chaincase lubricant as described in Chapter Three.

3. Remove the exhaust system as described in Chapter Four.
4. Remove the starter as described in Chapter Nine.
5. Remove the neutral switch as described in Chapter Nine.
6. Disconnect the electrical connector from the vehicle speed sensor (VSS), located on top of the transmission case under the starter.
7. Disconnect the ground post from the top of the transmission case.
8. Remove the main power cable from the clip on the T-stud at the front of the battery tray, Move it toward the left side of the motorcycle.
9. Remove the primary chaincase cover as described in Chapter Six.
10. Remove the clutch assembly as described in Chapter Six.
11. Remove the clutch release cover and the clutch release mechanism (Chapter Six).
12. Remove the primary chaincase housing as described in Chapter Six.
13. Remove the transmission drive sprocket as described in this chapter.
14. Remove the side door and transmission shaft assemblies as described in this chapter, if necessary.
15. Remove the external shift linkage from the transmission as described in this chapter.
16. Make an alignment mark on the shift rod lever and the end of the shift shaft.
17. Remove the clamping bolt (A, **Figure 120**) securing the shift rod lever (B).
18. Use a Torx driver (T50) and back out the centering screw (A, **Figure 121**) until it clears the centering slot in the shift pawl assembly.
19. Remove the snap ring (B, **Figure 121**) and flat washer (C) from the shift shaft (D).
20. Remove the rear wheel as described in Chapter Ten.
21. Remove the engine oil dipstick (**Figure 122**).
22. Support the swing arm. Then, remove the swing arm pivot bolt as described in Chapter Twelve.
23. Place a jack under the crankcase to support the engine after the transmission case is removed.
24. Remove the short (1/2 in.) upper (**Figure 123**) and the long (9/16 in.) lower (**Figure 124**) bolts and washers on each side securing the engine to the transmission.
25. Move the transmission case to the rear to clear the two lower locating dowels, and rest it on the frame cross member.
26. Move the transmission toward the left side and remove the transmission case from the frame.
27. Install the transmission case by reversing the removal steps, while noting the following:
   a. Make sure the two locating dowels (**Figure 125**) are in place on the engine or transmission case.
   b. Install the shorter (1/2 in.) transmission mounting bolts at the lower locations and the longer (9/16 in.) bolts at the upper locations.

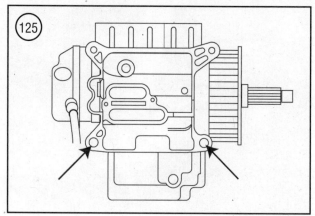

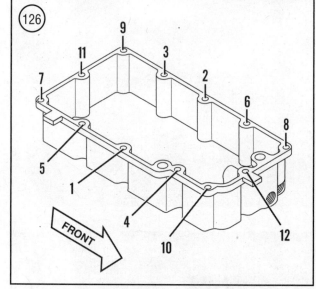

c. On all models, use a crossing pattern to tighten the transmission-to-engine mounting bolts. Tighten the bolts evenly, in two steps, to the specification listed in **Table 4**.

d. Tighten the oil pan bolts in the sequence shown in **Figure 126** to 84-132 in.-lb. (9.5-14.9 N•m).

e. Install the ground post on top of the transmission.

OIL PAN

The oil pan (**Figure 119**) mounts onto the bottom of the transmission case. It can be removed with the transmission mounted in the frame.

Removal

1. Drain the engine oil as described in Chapter Three.

2. Drain the transmission oil as described in Chapter Three.

CAUTION
The dipstick will be damaged if left in place during oil pan removal.

3. Remove the engine oil dipstick (**Figure 122**).

4. Remove the left side muffler, crossover pipe and crossover pipe clamp bracket from the transmission as described in Chapter Four.

NOTE
Access hidden bolts through the holes in the frame cross member.

5. Use 3/16 inch ball hex socket driver, and remove the twelve bolts securing the oil pan to the transmission case.

6. Lower and slide the oil pan toward the rear and remove it from the transmission case and the frame.

7. Remove the gasket.

Installation

1. Thoroughly clean the gasket surface of the oil pan.

2. Coat the oil pan gasket surface with a thin coat of Hylomar gasket sealer, or an equivalent. Allow the sealer to dry until tacky.

3. Install a *new* oil pan gasket on the oil pan.

4. Install the baffle and both baffle springs into the oil pan.

5. Install the oil pan onto the bottom of the transmission case.

6. Hold the oil pan in place, install the twelve bolts and tighten them just 2 full turns.

7. Check that the oil pan is still positioned correctly. Tighten the oil pan bolts in the sequence shown in **Figure 126** to 84-132 in.-lb. (9.5-14.9 N•m).

8. Install the left side muffler, crossover pipe and crossover pipe clamp bracket from the transmission as described in Chapter Four.

9. If necessary, replace the engine oil filter as described in Chapter Three.

10 Refill the engine with *new* engine oil as described in Chapter Three and install the dipstick.

11. Refill the transmission with *new* oil as described in Chapter Three.

12. Start the engine and check for leaks.

Inspection

1. Clean the oil pan in solvent and dry thoroughly.

2. Remove all old gasket residue from the oil pan and transmission case mating surfaces.

3. Inspect the oil pan for cracks or damage. Replace if necessary.

Table 1 TRANSMISSION GENERAL SPECIFICATIONS

Transmission type	6-speed, constant mesh
Gear ratios	
First	3.34
Second	2.31
Third	1.72
Fourth	1.39
Fifth	1.18
Sixth	1.00
Transmission fluid capacity	32 U.S. oz. (946.4 ml)

Table 2 TRANSMISSION SERVICE SPECIFICATIONS

Item	In.	mm
Countershaft		
Runout	0.000-0.003	0.00-0.08
Endplay	0.001-0.003	0.025-0.08
First gear		
Clearance (radial)	0.0004-0.0020	0.010-0.052
End play (axial)	0.001-0.023	0.03-0.08
Second gear		
Clearance (radial)	0.0004-0.0020	0.010-0.052
End play (axial)	0.001-0.40	0.03-1.02
Third gear		
Clearance (radial)	0.0004-0.0020	0.010-0.052
End play (axial)	0.001-0.028	0.03-1.07
Fourth gear		
Clearance (radial)	0.0004-0.0020	0.010-0.052
End play (axial)	0.001-0.028	0.03-0.71
Mainshaft		
Runout	0.00-0.003	0.00-0.08
Endplay	None	
Fifth gear		
Clearance (radial)	0.0004-0.0020	0.010-0.052
End play (axial)	0.002-0.026	0.05-0.66
Main drive gear (sixth)		
Bearing fit in transmission case	0.0003-0.0017	0.0076-0.043
Fit in bearing (press-fit)	0.001-0.003	0.025-0.076
End play	None	
Shift dog service limit		
First	0.013-0.121	0.33-3.07
Second	0.016-0.138	0.41-3.51
Third	0.010-0.125	0.25-3.17
Fourth	0.018-0.129	0.46-3.28
Fifth	0.007-0.117	0.18-2.97
Sixth	0.022-0.131	0.56-3.33
Shift forks		
Shift fork-to-shift cam groove end play	0.004-0.012	0.102-0.305
Shift fork-to-dog ring groove end play	0.004-0.016	0.102-0.4060
Finger thickness service limit		
1st/2nd gear shift fork	0.258	6.55
3rd/4th gear shift fork	0.198	5.03
5th/6th gear shift fork	0.258	6.55

7

Table 3 TRANSMISSION SIDE DOOR BEARING SPECIFICATIONS

Item	In. (mm
Fit in side door	0.001-0.0014 (0.0025-0.0356)
Fit on countershaft	
Tight fit	0.0004 (0.010)
Loose fit	0.0012 (0.030)
Fit on mainshaft	
Tight fit	0.0004 (0.010)
Loose fit	0.0012 (0.030)

Table 4 TRANSMISSION TORQUE SPECIFICATIONS

Item	ft.-lb.	in.-lb.	N•m
Detent arm pivot bolt	–	120-150	13.6-17.0
Oil pan bolts	–	84-132	9.5-14.9
Shift cam detent arm pivot bolt			
Shift cam lock plate bolt	–	57-63	6.4-7.1
Shift rod locknuts	–	80-120	9.0-13.6
Shift rod lever clamp bolt	18-22	–	24.4-29.8
Swing arm pivot shaft nut	90-110	–	122-149.1
Top cover bolts	–	90-120	10.2-13.6
Transmission-to-engine bolt			
Initial torque	15	–	20.3
Final torque	34-39	–	46.1-52.9
Transmission drain plug	14-21	–	19.0-28.5
Transmission drive sprocket			
lockplate screws	–	84-108	9.5-12.2
Transmission drive sprocket nut	35	–	47.5
Transmission mainshaft/			
countershaft locknuts			
at side door	55-65	–	74.6-88.2
Transmission side door bolt	13-18	–	17/6-24.4
Mounting nut	see text		
Lock plate bolts	–	90-120	10.2-13.6

CHAPTER EIGHT

AIR/FUEL AND EMISSION CONTROL SYSTEMS

This chapter covers the fuel injection system. Refer to Chapter Nine for the emission control systems on all California models. Air filter maintenance is covered in Chapter Three. Refer to *Safety* in Chapter One.

Specifications are located in **Table 1** and **Table 2** at the end of the chapter.

WARNING
Gasoline is carcinogenic and flammable. Handle gasoline carefully. Wear nitrile gloves to avoid skin contact. If gasoline does contact skin, immediately and thoroughly wash the area with soap and warm water.

AIR FILTER AND BACKPLATE
(ALL 96 CU. IN. AND 103 CU.IN. MODELS)

Refer to **Figure 1**.

Removal

1. Support the motorcycle on level ground on a swing arm stand.
2. Remove the air filter cover screw (A, **Figure 2**) and remove the cover (B).
3. Remove the Torx (**Figure 3**) and the bracket from the air filter element.
4. Gently pull the air filter element away from the backplate. And disconnect the two breather hoses (A, **Figure 4**) from its fitting on the breather bolt. Remove the air filter element (B, **Figure 4**) and its gasket. Discard the gasket.

5. Use a deep socket to remove the breather bolts (A, **Figure 5**).
6. Pull the backplate (B, **Figure 5**) away from the cylinder heads, and remove backplate and its gasket (A, **Figure 6**). Remove the O-rings (B, **Figure 5**) from the breather bolt bosses in the backplate. Discard the O-rings.
7. Remove and discard the backplate and air filter gaskets (**Figure 7**). New gasket must be installed.

Installation

1. Apply a small amount of gasket sealer to a new backplate gasket, and fit it onto the back of the backplate (**Figure 7**).
2. Install new O-rings (B, **Figure 6**) into the inboard side of the breather bolt bosses in the backplate.
3. Position the backplate (B, **Figure 5**) against the fuel injection module. Reposition the gasket as necessary to align its bolts holes with those of the induction module.
4. Install the breather bolts (A, **Figure 5**), and secure backplate to the cylinder heads. Tighten the breather bolts to 22-24 ft.-lb. (29.8-32.5 N•m).
5. Install the breather hoses (A, **Figure 4**) onto the breather bolt fittings.
6. Apply a small amount of gasket sealer to a new air filter gasket. Fit the gasket onto air filter element.
7. Position the element with the flat side facing down, and insert the breather hoses (A, **Figure 4**) to the backside of the element

NOTE
If an aftermarket air filter element is being installed, position it onto the backplate following the manufacturer's instructions.

① **AIR FILTER (ALL NON-CVO MODELS EXCEPT 2013 FLHTCUSE MODELS)**

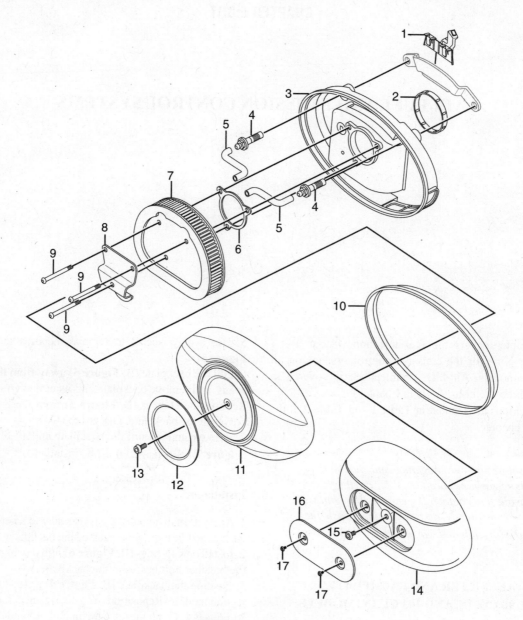

1. Clip (ARC connector cable)
2. Gasket
3. Backplate
4. Breather hollow bolt
5. Breather hose
6. Gasket
7. Air filter element
8. Mounting bracket
9. Torx screw
10. Rubber seal ring
11. Cover (All non-CVO except 2013 FLHTCUSE)
12. Insert
13. Allen screw
14. Cover (2013 FLHTCUSE)
15. Allen screw
16. Trim plate
17. Screw

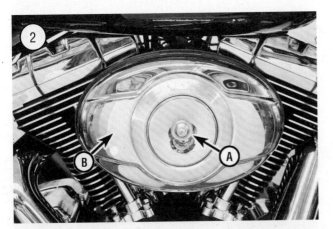

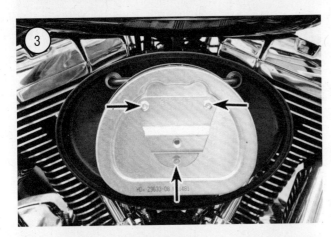

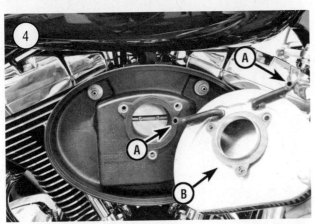

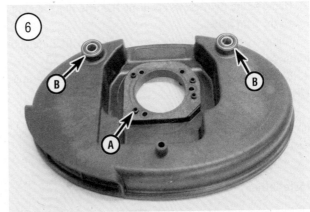

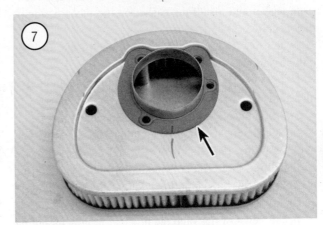

8

8. Set the element into position in the backplate. Install the mounting bracket and bracket Torx screws (**Figure 3**). Tighten the Torx screws to 108-132 in.-lb. (12.2-14.9 N•m).

9. Inspect the air filter cover seal ring (**Figure 8**) for hardness or deterioration; replace as necessary.

10. Apply threadlocking compound (Loctite Threadlock 243 blue, or equivalent) to the screw threads prior to installation.

11. Install the air filter cover (B, **Figure 2**) and the screw (A). Tighten the cover screw to 36-60 in.-lb. (4.1-6.8 N•m).

Inspection

1. Inspect the backplate (**Figure 9**) for damage.

2. Make sure the breather hollow bolts and breather hoses (**Figure 10**) are clear. Clean out if necessary.

AIR FILTER AND BACKPLATE (ALL 110 CU. IN. MODELS EXCEPT FLTRXSE)

Refer to **Figure 11**.

Removal

1. Support the motorcycle on level ground with a swing arm stand.

2. Remove the two screws securing the trim plate, and remove the trim plate.

3. Remove the three screws securing the air filter element to the back plate. Remove the air filter.

4. Remove the two breather mounting bolts and O-rings. Discard the O-rings.

5. Remove the backplate three standoff mounting bolts.

6. Remove the backplate and gasket from the fuel injection induction module. Discard the gasket.

Installation

1. Apply a small amount of gasket sealer to the new backplate gasket and install the gasket on the inboard side of the backplate.

2. Install new O-ring to the inboard side of the breather bolt bosses on the backplate.

3. Install the backplate against the fuel injection induction manifold. Reposition the inboard gasket if necessary to align the bolt holes with those in the induction model.

4. Install the breather hollow mounting bolts and tighten to 22-24 ft.-lb. (29.8-32.5 N•m).

5. Install the three standoff mounting bolts securing the backplate to the induction module and tighten to 96-144 in.-lb. (10.8-16.3 N•m).

6. Install new O-rings onto the breather hollow mounting bolts. Install the bolts and tighten to 22-24 ft.-lb. (29.8-32.5 N•m).

7. Install the three air filter cover Torx screws.

8. Install the trim plate and the two mounting screws. Tighten the screws securely.

AIR FILTER AND BACKPLATE (110 CU. IN. FLTRXSE MODELS)

Refer to **Figure 12**.

Removal

1. Support the motorcycle on level ground with a swing arm stand.

2. Remove the screws securing the intake tube and air filter assembly to the backplate. Remove as an assembly.

3. Remove the two plugs from the backplate.

4. Remove the two breather hollow mounting bolts located under the plugs.

5. Remove the adapter from the backplate.

6. Remove the three screws securing the backing plate and cover to the induction module.

7. Remove from induction module.

8. Remove and discard the gasket from each side of the cover.

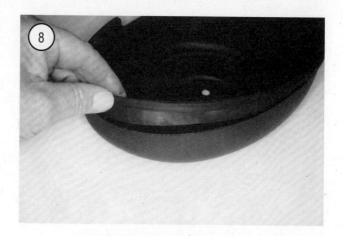

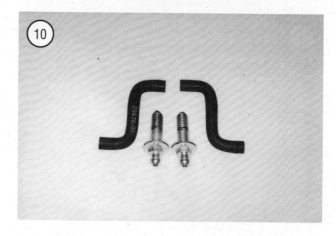

Installation

1. Apply a couple dabs of gasket sealer to the new cover gaskets and install on each side of the cover.

2. Install new O-rings into the inboard side of the breather bolt boss in the backing plate.

3. Install the cover onto the backplate and install this assembly against the fuel injection induction manifold. Reposition the inboard gasket if necessary to align the bolt holes with those in the induction model.

4. Install the three screws securing the backplate to the induction module and tighten to 55-60 in.-lb. (6.2-6.8 N•m).

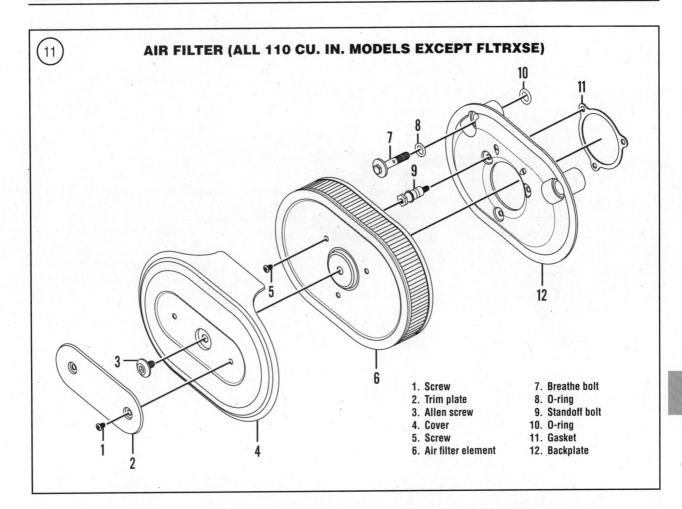

AIR FILTER (ALL 110 CU. IN. MODELS EXCEPT FLTRXSE)

1. Screw
2. Trim plate
3. Allen screw
4. Cover
5. Screw
6. Air filter element
7. Breathe bolt
8. O-ring
9. Standoff bolt
10. O-ring
11. Gasket
12. Backplate

5. Install the breather hollow mounting bolts and tighten to 22-24 ft.-lb. (29.8-32.5 N•m).

6. Install new O-rings onto the plugs and install the plugs over the breather hollow bolts. Press in until they bottom.

7. Install the adapter onto the backing plate.

8. Install a new gasket onto the backside of the intake tube

9. Install the intake tube and air filter assembly onto the backing plate.

10. Align the gasket bolt holes and install the three screws securing the intake tube and air filter assembly to the backing plate. Tighten the screws to 55-60 in.-lb. (6.2-6.8 N•m)

DEPRESSURIZING THE FUEL SYSTEM

WARNING
The fuel system is under pressure at all times, even when the engine is not operating. The system must be depressurized prior to loosening fittings or disconnecting any fuel lines within the fuel injection system. Gasoline will spurt out unless the system is depressurized.

1. Remove the left side saddlebag and left side frame cover as described in Chapter Fourteen.

NOTE
*The location of some fuses varies during model years. Check the diagram on the cover of the fuse/relay panel (**Figure 13**) to determine the precise location of the fuel pump fuse on a particular model.*

2. Lift the cover from the fuse/relay panel, and pull the fuel pump fuse from the panel.

3. Start the engine. Let it idle until it runs out of gasoline.

4. After the engine has stopped, operate the starter for three seconds to eliminate any residual gasoline in the fuel lines.

5. After all service procedures have been completed, install the fuel pump fuse.

6. Install the left side cover and left side saddlebag as described in Chapter Fourteen.

FUEL TANK

WARNING
Some fuel may spill from the fuel tank hose during this procedure. Because gasoline is extremely flammable and explosive, perform this procedure away from all open flames, including appliance pilot lights and sparks.

⑫   **AIR FILTER (FLTRXSE 110 CU. IN. MODELS)**

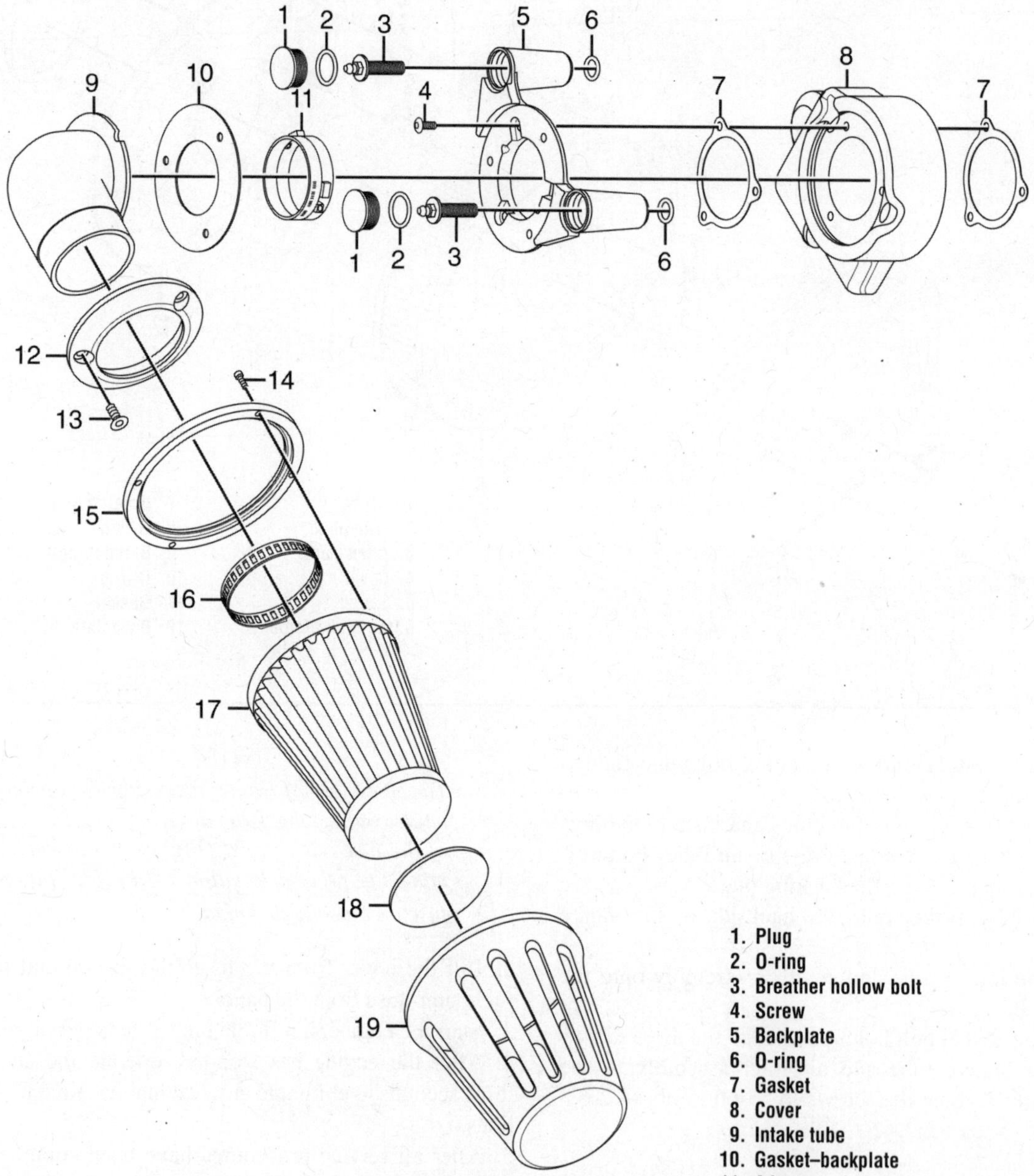

1. Plug
2. O-ring
3. Breather hollow bolt
4. Screw
5. Backplate
6. O-ring
7. Gasket
8. Cover
9. Intake tube
10. Gasket–backplate
11. Adapter
12. Mounting ring–inner
13. Screw
14. Screw
15. Mounting ring (black)–outer
16. Clamp–worm drive
17. Filter element
18. Foam pad
19. Cover

Do not smoke or allow anyone to smoke in the work area, as an explosion and fire may occur. Always work in a well-ventilated area. Wipe up any spills immediately.

WARNING
Make sure to route the fuel tank vapor hoses so that they cannot contact any hot engine or exhaust component. These hoses contain flammable vapors. If a hose melts from contacting a hot part, leaking vapors may ignite, causing a fire.

Draining

1. Depressurize the fuel system as described in this chapter.
2. Disconnect the negative battery cable as described in Chapter Nine.
3. Remove the fuel filler cap.
4. Insert a siphon tool and withdraw the gasoline from the tank.
5. Store the gasoline in a safe container designed or fuel storage.
6. Install the fuel filler cap and tighten securely.
7. Connect the negative battery cable as described in Chapter Nine.

Removal/Installation

Refer to the **Figures 14-16**.

NOTE
Always disarm the TSM/TSSM/HFSM security system prior to disconnecting the battery or pulling the main fuse so the siren will not sound.

1. Depressurize the fuel system as described in this chapter.
2. Disconnect the negative battery cable as described in Chapter Nine.
3. Remove the seat as described in Chapter Fourteen.

4. Partially remove the fuel tank console (A, **Figure 17**) as described in this chapter.
5. Disconnect the fuel pump electrical connector (B, **Figure 17**) and vapor vent hose (C) from the fuel tank.
6. Drain the fuel tank as described in this section.
7. On models with a fuel level gauge; on the lower left side of the fuel tank, gently pull the convoluted tubing down. Carefully pull down and disconnect the electrical connector (**Figure 18**) for the fuel level gauge.

WARNING
A small amount of fuel will dribble from the fuel tank when the fuel line is disconnected from the tank. Place several shop cloths under the fuel line fitting to catch any spilled fuel before disconnecting them. Discard the shop cloths in a suitable safe manner.

CAUTION
Do not twist the plastic fuel line fitting as it may cause a small crack leading to fuel leaks.

8. On the left side, lift the chrome sleeve (A, **Figure 19**) on the quick connect fitting, and disconnect the fuel line (B) from the fuel tank fitting.
9. On models so equipped, remove the lower fairing cap on each side to gain access to the front mounting bolts as described in Chapter Fourteen.
10. At the front of the fuel tank, remove the trip cover from the mounting bolt on each side.
11. Remove the mounting bolt (**Figure 20**) on each side securing the fuel tank to the frame.
12. At the rear of the fuel tank, remove the mounting bolt(s) (**Figure 21**) from the frame mount. On some models, this bolt was previously removed during fuel tank console removal.
13. Lift off and remove the fuel tank.
14. Drain any remaining fuel into the gas can and store correctly.

CAUTION
Store the fuel tank in a safe place away from open flames or where it could be damaged.

15. Inspect the fuel tank (this section).
16. Installation is the reverse of these steps while noting the following:
   a. Tighten the front mounting bolts to 15-20 ft.-lb. (20-27 N•m). Install the trim covers over the bolts.
   b. Tighten the rear mounting bolt to 15-20 ft.-lb. (20-27 N•m).
   c. Refill the tank and check for leaks.

Inspection

1. Inspect the quick-disconnect fitting for leaks. Replace as necessary.

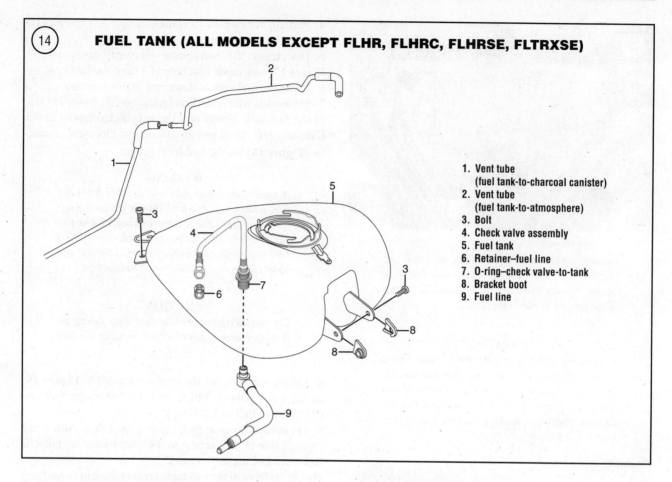

(14)   **FUEL TANK (ALL MODELS EXCEPT FLHR, FLHRC, FLHRSE, FLTRXSE)**

1. Vent tube
   (fuel tank-to-charcoal canister)
2. Vent tube
   (fuel tank-to-atmosphere)
3. Bolt
4. Check valve assembly
5. Fuel tank
6. Retainer–fuel line
7. O-ring–check valve-to-tank
8. Bracket boot
9. Fuel line

2. Inspect the front mounting tabs (**Figure 22**) and rear mounting tab (**Figure 23**) for cracks or fractures.

3. Inspect the console front mounting tab (**Figure 24**) for thread damage. Repair threads if necessary.

4. Inspect the engagement slots (**Figure 25**) in the fuel tank collar for cracks or damage.

5. Remove the fuel filler cap and inspect the interior of the fuel tank for rust or contamination. If there is a rust buildup inside the tank, clean and flush the tank.

6. Inspect the fuel tank for leaks.

FUEL SUPPLY CHECK VALVE

Removal/Installation

The check valve is mounted in the quick-connect fitting. The valve keeps fuel from draining from the tank when the external line is disconnected.

Refer to **Figure 26**.

1. Remove the fuel tank as described in this chapter.

2. Remove the fuel pump/level sender assembly (this chapter).

3. Place several towels or blanket on the work bench to protect the fuel tank finish.

4. Turn the fuel tank upside down on the towels or blanket.

5. Install a 7/8 in. deep socket over the quick-connect fitting and onto its hex head.

6. Remove the fitting, and then carefully remove the check valve and fuel line from the fuel tank.

7. Remove and discard the O-ring from the fitting.

8. Lubricate a *new* O-ring with a light coat of clean engine oil, and install the O-ring onto the fitting.

9. Insert the fuel line into the fuel tank opening. Manually thread the quick-connect fitting into the tank until it is snug. Tighten the quick-connect fitting to 18 ft.-lb. (24.4 N•m).

10. Install fuel pump/level sender assembly as described in this chapter.

11. Install the fuel tank as described in this chapter.

FUEL PUMP AND FUEL FILTER

Refer to **Figure 27**.

Fuel Tank Top Plate

Removal

1. Depressurize the fuel system as described in this chapter.

2. Remove the seat as described in Chapter Fourteen.

3. Partially remove the fuel tank console as described in this chapter.

4. Drain the fuel tank as described in this chapter. Do not remove the fuel tank as it must be secured while using the special tools to loosen the cam ring in the next step.

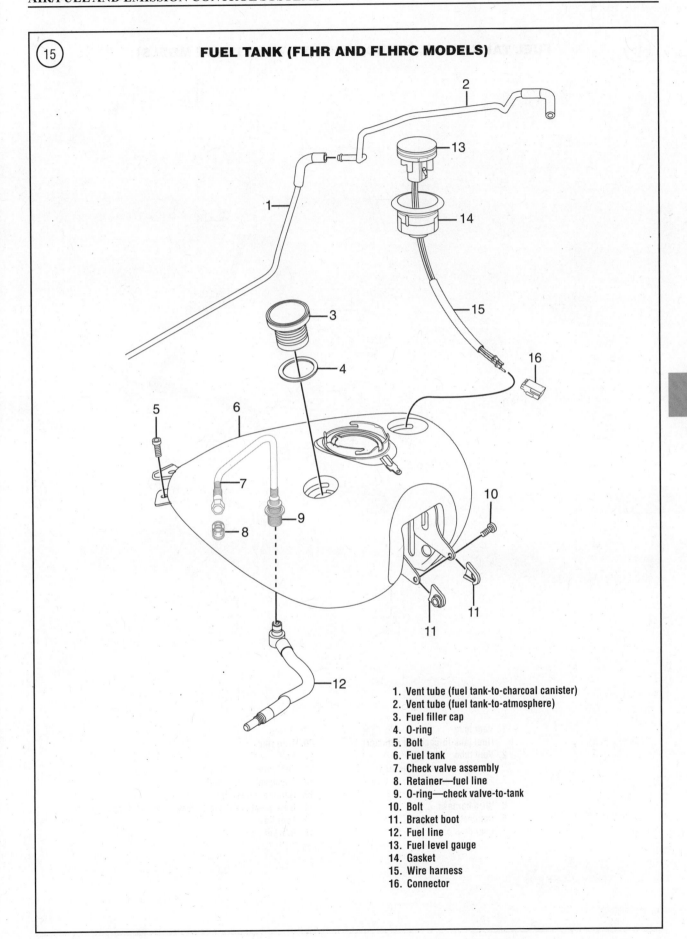

FUEL TANK (FLHR AND FLHRC MODELS)

15

8

1. Vent tube (fuel tank-to-charcoal canister)
2. Vent tube (fuel tank-to-atmosphere)
3. Fuel filler cap
4. O-ring
5. Bolt
6. Fuel tank
7. Check valve assembly
8. Retainer—fuel line
9. O-ring—check valve-to-tank
10. Bolt
11. Bracket boot
12. Fuel line
13. Fuel level gauge
14. Gasket
15. Wire harness
16. Connector

⑯ **FUEL TANK (FLHR, FLHRC, FLHRSE AND FLTRXSE MOELS)**

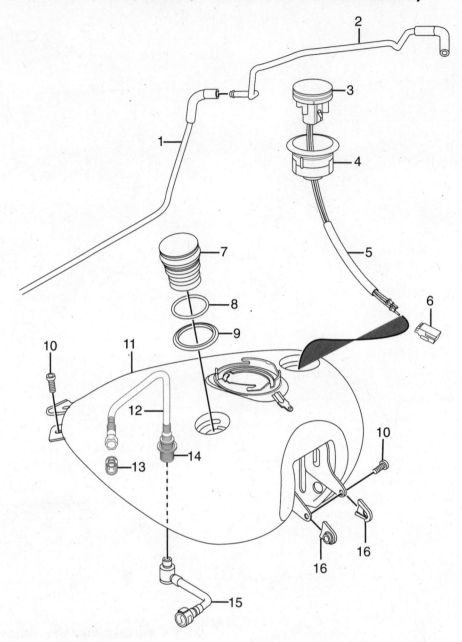

1. Vent tube	8. O-ring
(fuel tank-to-charcoal canister)	9. Trim ring
2. Vent tube	10. Bolt
(fuel tank-to-atmosphere)	11. Fuel tank
3. Fuel level gauge	12. Check valve assembly
4. Gasket	13. Retainer—fuel line
5. Wire harness	14. O-ring—check valve-to-tank
6. Connector	15. Fuel line
7. Fuel filler cap	16. Bracket boot

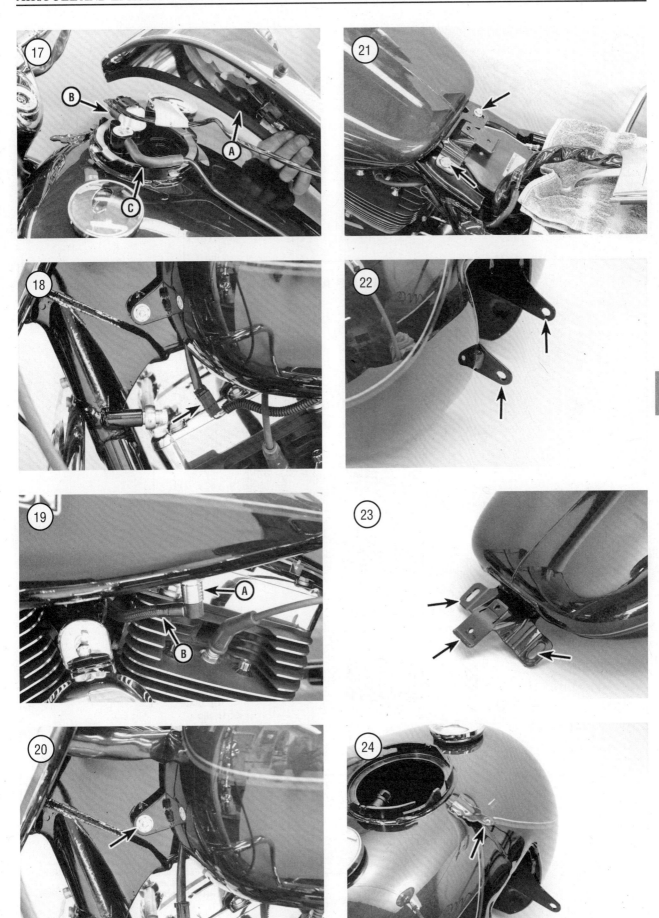

(25)

(26)

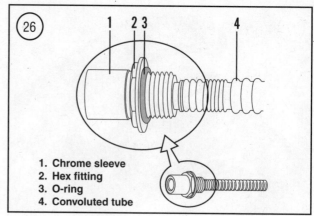

1. Chrome sleeve
2. Hex fitting
3. O-ring
4. Convoluted tube

(27)

FUEL PUMP AND FILTER

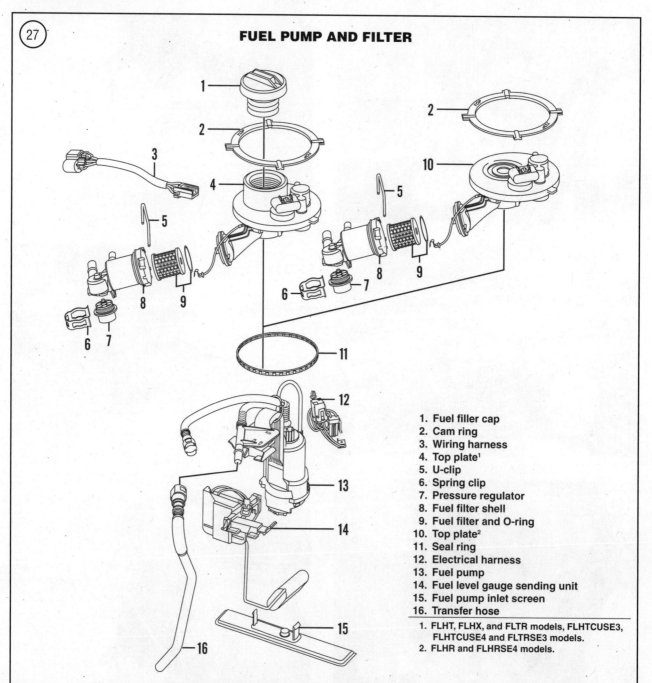

1. Fuel filler cap
2. Cam ring
3. Wiring harness
4. Top plate[1]
5. U-clip
6. Spring clip
7. Pressure regulator
8. Fuel filter shell
9. Fuel filter and O-ring
10. Top plate[2]
11. Seal ring
12. Electrical harness
13. Fuel pump
14. Fuel level gauge sending unit
15. Fuel pump inlet screen
16. Transfer hose

1. FLHT, FLHX, and FLTR models, FLHTCUSE3, FLHTCUSE4 and FLTRSE3 models.
2. FLHR and FLHRSE4 models.

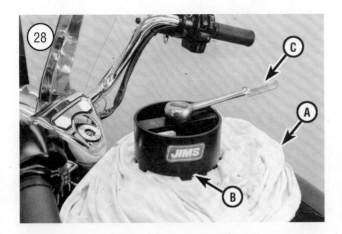

NOTE
Do not try to loosen the cam ring without the correct tool. The tabs on the cam ring are fragile and will break off if pried on or tapped on. Using an incorrect tool may also damage the fuel tank finish.

5. Wrap the neck of an old T-shirt (A, **Figure 28**) around the neck of the fuel tank collar to protect the fuel tank finish.

6. Install the cam ring tool (JIMS part No. 954 or H-D part no HD-48646) onto the top plate cam ring. Align the tool notches with the four projected tabs (B, **Figure 28**) on the cam ring.

7. Use a 1/2 inch drive ratchet (C, **Figure 28**) and press down on the ratchet and special tool to prevent the tool from slipping. Slowly rotate the cam ring *counterclockwise* until it is free from the engagement slots in the fuel tank collar. The tool has to rotate only about 20° to release the cam ring.

8. Carefully remove the special tools and the T-shirt from the fuel tank collar.

9. Completely remove the cam ring (**Figure 29**) from the fuel tank. Discard the cam ring.

10. Use needle nose pliers and release the electrical connector from the console electrical terminal on the top plate (**Figure 30**).

11. Press on the retainer tab and release the fitting (**Figure 31**) on the smaller diameter fuel line and disconnect it from the fuel filter.

12. Press on the retainer tab and release the fitting (**Figure 32**) on the larger diameter fuel line and disconnect it from the fuel filter.

13. Disconnect the ground spade terminal (A, **Figure 33**) from the top plate and remove the top plate assembly (B) from the fuel tank.

14. Place the wiring harness from the console electrical connector outside of the fuel tank (**Figure 34**) to keep it from falling back into the tank.

15. Remove the seal ring (C, **Figure 33**) and inspect it for cuts, tears or deterioration; replace as necessary.

8

Installation

1. If removed, install the séal ring (C, **Figure 33**) into the top plate groove. Ensure that the seal ring nubs contact the groove walls.

2. Position the top plate assembly with the fuel line fittings facing toward the rear.

3. Partially install the top plate assembly (B, **Figure 33**) into the fuel tank.

4. Connect the ground spade terminal (A, **Figure 33**) onto the top plate.

5. Align the fuel line fitting latch with the raised barb on the fuel filter tube. Push the larger diameter fuel line (**Figure 32**) on the fuel filter until an audible click is heard. Pull on the fuel line to ensure it is locked in place.

6. Repeat Step 5 for the smaller fuel line (**Figure 31**). Pull on the fuel line to ensure it is locked in place.

7. Carefully install the top plate into the fuel tank along with the wiring harness from the console electrical connector.

8. Connect the electrical connector onto the console electrical terminal on the top plate (**Figure 30**).

9. Install a new cam ring (**Figure 35**) with the TOP stamp facing up.

10. Wrap the neck of an old T-shirt (A, **Figure 36**) around the neck of the fuel tank collar to protect the fuel tank finish.

11. Install the cam ring tool (JIMS part No. 954 or H-D part no HD-48646) onto the top plate cam ring. Align the tool notches with the four projected tabs (B, **Figure 36**) on the cam ring.

12. Use the palm of your hand and press down on the special tool. Slowly rotate the special tool *clockwise* until each of the four index tabs begin the engage the slots in the fuel tank collar.

13. Install the 1/2 inch drive ratchet (C, **Figure 36**) onto the special tool and rotate it until the cam ring is fully seated in the fuel tank collar. The tool has to rotate only about 20º to lock the cam ring into place.

14. Carefully remove the special tools and the T-shirt from the fuel tank.

15. Install the fuel tank console as described in this chapter.

16. Refill the fuel tank and check for leaks. Start the engine and repeat the inspection.

17. Install the seat as described in Chapter Fourteen.

Fuel Filter

Removal/Installation

1. Remove the top plate as described in this section.

2. Insert a small, flat-bladed screwdriver through the small window and depress the tang on the ground wire. Pull the wire terminal from the slot (A, **Figure 37**).

3. Carefully raise the locking arm and pull the U-clip (B, **Figure 37**) from the holes in the fuel filter shell.

4. Remove fuel filter shell from top plate.

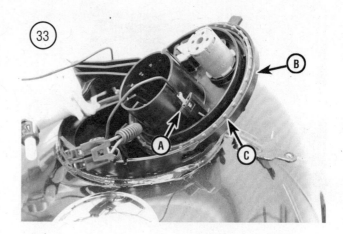

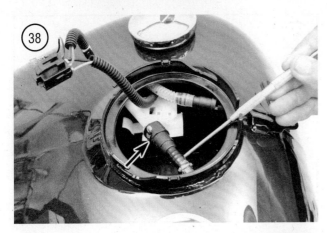

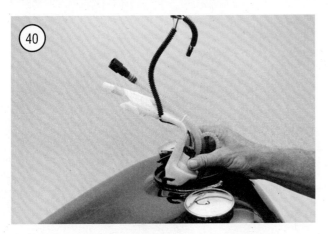

5. Withdraw the fuel filter from the filter shell and remove the O-ring from the shell.

6. Install a *new* fuel filter into the shell.

7. Install a *new* O-ring into the counter bore at the top of the fuel filter. Make sure it is correctly seated.

8. Position the fuel filter shell so the slot in the shell engages the top cap index pin, and install the fuel filter shell.

9. Push the U-clip through the holes on the locking arm of the fuel filter shell until the ends exit the holes on the opposite side. Retract the U-clip until contact is made with the step in the locking arm of the filter shell.

NOTE
If the terminal does not lock in place, use a small Xacto knife blade to slightly bend the tang away from the terminal body.

10. Route the ground wire around the index pin side of the end cap and install the terminal into the slot in the fuel filter shell. Gently pull on the wire to make sure the terminal is locked in place.

11. Install the top plate as described in this section.

Fuel Pump

Removal

1. Remove the top plate as described in this section.

2. Remove the fuel level sender as described in this section.

3. Pull up on the transfer tube bracket and release the two tabs at the bottom of the slots at the top of the fuel pump bracket.

4. Depress the collar (**Figure 38**) on each side of the transfer hose and disconnect the hose from the fuel pump bracket.

5. Reach down in the fuel tank (**Figure 39**), and pull up on the rear finger. Slide the fuel pump bracket forward and free the four ears on the bracket from the catches at top of the fuel tank tunnel.

6. On the left side of the fuel tank, rotate the fuel pump 90° *clockwise* so the transfer hose is facing toward the rear (**Figure 40**). Carefully withdraw the fuel pump and filter from the fuel tank.

7. To remove the fuel filter, depress the fingers on the fuel filter and release it from the base of the fuel pump.

Installation

1. If removed, install the fuel filter onto the base of the fuel pump. Press it on until it clicks into place.

2. Position the fuel pump with the transfer hose pointing toward the rear (**Figure 40**) and insert the fuel pump into the fuel tank (**Figure 39**).

3. Rotate the fuel pump 90° *counterclockwise* and check that the fuel pump inlet screen is laying flat on the bottom of the fuel tank. Ensure that the screen ends are not folded under.

4. Check that the wiring harness is still captured in the folded clip at the front of the fuel pump bracket.

5. Reach down into the fuel tank, and make sure the finger on the fuel pump bracket is pointing toward the rear. Push the fuel pump toward the rear and engage the four ears on the bracket onto the catches at top of fuel tank tunnel.

6. Connect the transfer hose (**Figure 38**) onto the fuel pump bracket. Install the two tabs on the bottom of the transfer hose into the slots on the fuel pump bracket. Check that the transfer hose is captured in the weldclip on the right side of the tunnel (**Figure 41**) and the free end contacts the bottom of the fuel tank.

7. Install the fuel level sender as described in this section.

8. Install the top plate as described in this section.

Fuel Pump and Fuel Level Sender
Electrical Harness Replacement

> *WARNING*
> *Use only OEM Teflon-coated wiring if the harness requires replacement. Standard wiring insulation materials will deteriorate when exposed to gasoline.*

1. Remove the fuel pump as described in this section.

2. Carefully cut the cable strap (A, **Figure 42**) and separate the harness (B) from the fuel pump bracket.

3. Release the electrical connector from the fuel pump molded clip (A, **Figure 43**), and disconnect the electrical connector from the fuel pump. Remove the harness.

4. Connect the electrical connector onto the fuel pump. Make sure the connector snaps into place.

5. Route the harness toward the rear and then toward the front under the arm of the fuel pump bracket.

6. Install a *new* cable strap (B, **Figure 43**) at the elbow, securing the fuel pump hose (C) and the transfer hose (D) at the top of the arm and the harness at the bottom of the bracket.

7. Route the harness through the fuel pump molded clip (A, **Figure 43**).

8. Install the fuel pump as described in this section.

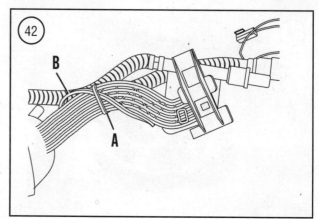

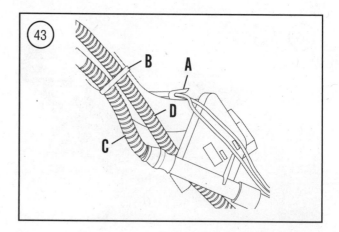

Fuel Pressure Regulator
Removal/Installation

1. Remove the fuel pump as described in this section.

2. Insert a small screwdriver through the small window (A, **Figure 44**) and depress the tang on the ground wire. Pull the terminal from the slot on the fuel filter shell.

3. Free one side of the spring clip first (B, **Figure 44**), and then the other. Then remove the spring clip from the fuel pressure regulator.

4. Remove the fuel pressure regulator assembly (C, **Figure 44**) from the filter shell.

5. Remove the regulator seat, large O-ring, screen and small O-ring from the regulator body.

6. Inspect all O-rings, regulator seat and screen for hardness and deterioration. Replace the fuel pressure regulator

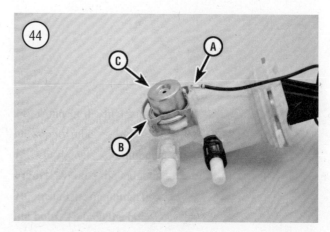

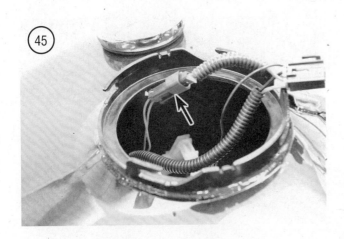

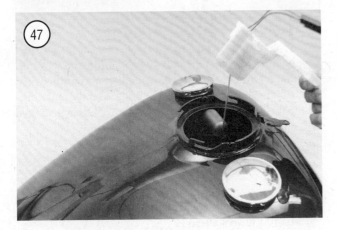

if any parts require replacement as they are not available separately.

7. Install the small O-ring onto the top of the pressure port bore.

8. Position the screen so the sleeve faces the small O-ring, and install the screen.

9. Install the regulator seat and evenly press the screen correctly into place. Remove the regulator seat.

10. Install the large O-ring at the top of the screen.

11. Install the regulator seat and make sure it seats correctly.

12. Install the fuel pressure regulator onto the fuel filter shell.

13. Install the spring clip so the indented sides engage the top of the center rib of the fuel pressure regulator. The rounded side must engage the bottom tabs of the fuel filter shell.

NOTE
If the terminal does not lock in place, use a small Xacto knife blade to slightly bend the tang away from the terminal body.

14. Route the ground wire around the index pin side of the end cap and install the terminal into the slot in the fuel filter shell. Gently pull on the wire to make sure the terminal is locked in place.

15. Install the top plate as described in this section.

Fuel Level Sender
Removal/Installation

1. Remove the top plate as described in this section.

2. Disconnect the 2-pin electrical connector from the harness (**Figure 45**).

3. Look down into the fuel tank at the left side of the top tunnel. Note the orientation of the front and rear fingers on top of the fuel level sensor (**Figure 46**).

4. Reach into the fuel tank and pull up on the front finger while sliding the fuel level sensor toward the rear. Move the senor back until the four ears on the bracket are free from the fuel tank tunnel mounts.

5. Carefully withdraw the fuel level sensor from the left side of the fuel tank (**Figure 47**).

6. Position the fuel level sensor with the front finger facing toward the front of the fuel tank.

7. Install the fuel level sensor into the left side of the fuel tank.

8. Move the fuel level sensor toward the rear and engage the four ears of the bracket onto the fuel tank tunnel mounts. Push it forward until it locks into place.

9. Connect the 2-pin electrical connector onto the harness.

10. Install the top plate as described in this section.

FUEL PRESSURE TEST

WARNING
This procedure is performed adjacent to a hot exhaust system while handling gasoline-related test equipment. Have an approved fire extinguisher rated for gasoline fires (Class B) available.

1. The following tools, or their equivalents, are required for this test:
   a. Fuel pressure gauge (H-D part No. HD-41182).
   b. Two fuel pressure gauge adapters (H-D part No. HD-44061).

2. Depressurize the fuel system as described in this chapter.

8

3. Lift the chrome sleeve (A, **Figure 48**) on the quick-connect fitting, and disconnect the fuel line (B) from the fuel tank fitting.

4. Install the pressure gauge adapters as follows:

    a. Pull in the knurled sleeve on the female end of the first fuel pressure gauge adapter.

    b. Insert male end of second adapter into the first adapter, and push down on knurled sleeve until locked. Gently tug on the adapters to make sure they are locked in place and will not come loose.

    c. Pull in the knurled sleeve on the second fuel pressure gauge adapter. Insert the male end of fuel supply line (A, **Figure 49**) into the second adapter, and then pull down on the knurled sleeve until locked place. Gently tug on the fuel supply fitting to make sure it is locked in place and will not come loose.

    d. Pull up on the fuel tank quick-connect chrome sleeve (B, **Figure 49**), insert the male end of the first fuel pressure gauge adapter. Pull down on the chrome sleeve until locked. Gently tug on the adapter to make sure it is locked in place and will not come loose.

5. Make sure the fuel valve and the air bleed petcock on the fuel pressure gauge are in the *closed* position.

6. Remove the protective cap from the Schrader valve on the fuel pressure gauge adapter closest to the fuel tank. Connect the fuel pressure gauge (C, **Figure 49**) to this Schrader valve.

7. Gently tug on the fuel pressure gauge to make sure it is locked in place and will not come loose.

8. Install the fuel pump fuse.

WARNING
The exhaust system warms up rapidly, protect yourself accordingly.

9. Start the engine to pressurize the fuel system. Allow the engine to idle.

10. Slowly open the fuel valve (D, **Figure 49**) and allow fuel to flow to the pressure gauge.

11. Position the clear air bleed tube into a suitable container and open and close the air bleed petcock to purge the air from the fuel gauge and hose. Repeat this several times until only bubble-free fuel flows from the bleed tube into the container. Close the petcock.

12. Increase engine above idle, and then decrease engine speed several times. Note the gauge readings. The fuel pressure should remain constant as specified in **Table 2** at all engine speeds. Repeat several times.

13. Turn the engine off.

14. Open the bleed valve petcock to relieve all fuel pressure and purge fuel from the pressure gauge.

15. Place a shop cloth beneath the Schrader valve to catch any remaining fuel, and disconnect the fuel pressure gauge from the Schrader valve. Dispose of the shop cloth in a suitable manner.

16. Install the protective cap onto the Schrader valve, and tighten it securely.

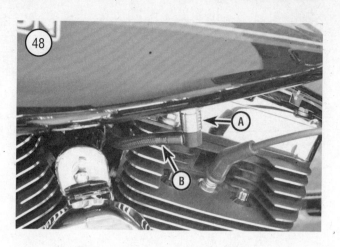

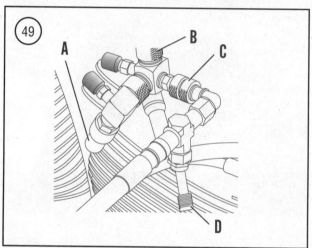

17. Disconnect the fuel pressure adapters from the fuel supply line and from the quick-connect fitting on the tank.

18. Pull up the chrome sleeve of quick-connect fitting, and insert fuel supply line onto tank fitting. Gently pull down on the fuel supply line to make sure it is locked in place and will not come loose.

FUEL TANK CONSOLE

Removal/Installation

Refer to **Figures 50-53**.

NOTE
Always disarm the TSSM/HFSM security system prior to disconnecting the battery or pulling the Main-Fuse so the siren will not sound.

1. Disconnect the negative battery cable as described in Chapter Nine.

2. Remove the seat as described in Chapter Fourteen.

3. Make a drawing or take a photo of the wiring harness, fuel vapor tube and overflow hose routing under the rear of the console prior to removal. These items must be reinstalled in the correct location to avoid damage.

4. On and 2013 FLHRSE models, perform the following:

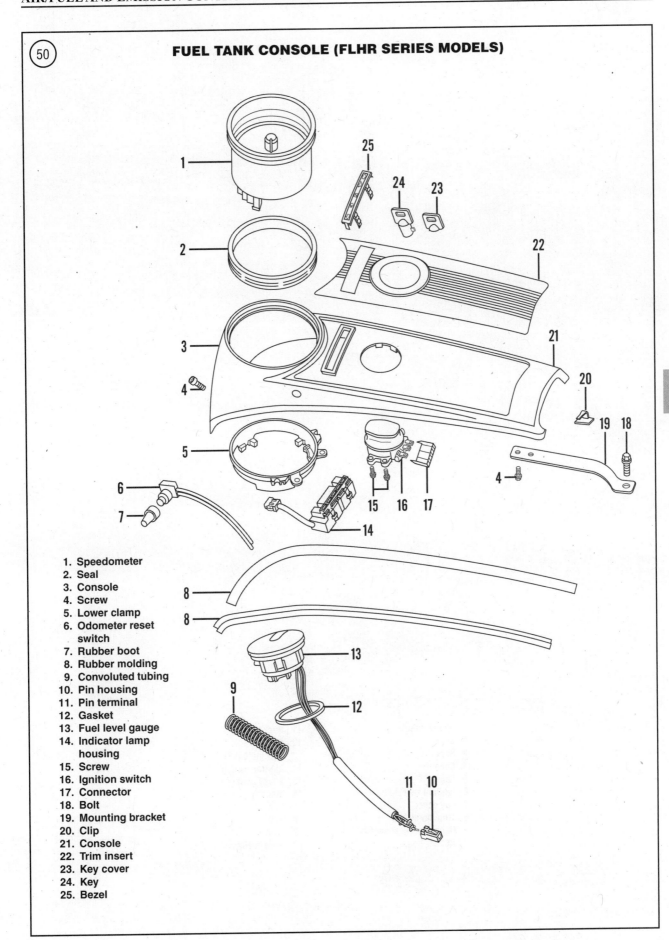

(50) **FUEL TANK CONSOLE (FLHR SERIES MODELS)**

8

1. Speedometer
2. Seal
3. Console
4. Screw
5. Lower clamp
6. Odometer reset switch
7. Rubber boot
8. Rubber molding
9. Convoluted tubing
10. Pin housing
11. Pin terminal
12. Gasket
13. Fuel level gauge
14. Indicator lamp housing
15. Screw
16. Ignition switch
17. Connector
18. Bolt
19. Mounting bracket
20. Clip
21. Console
22. Trim insert
23. Key cover
24. Key
25. Bezel

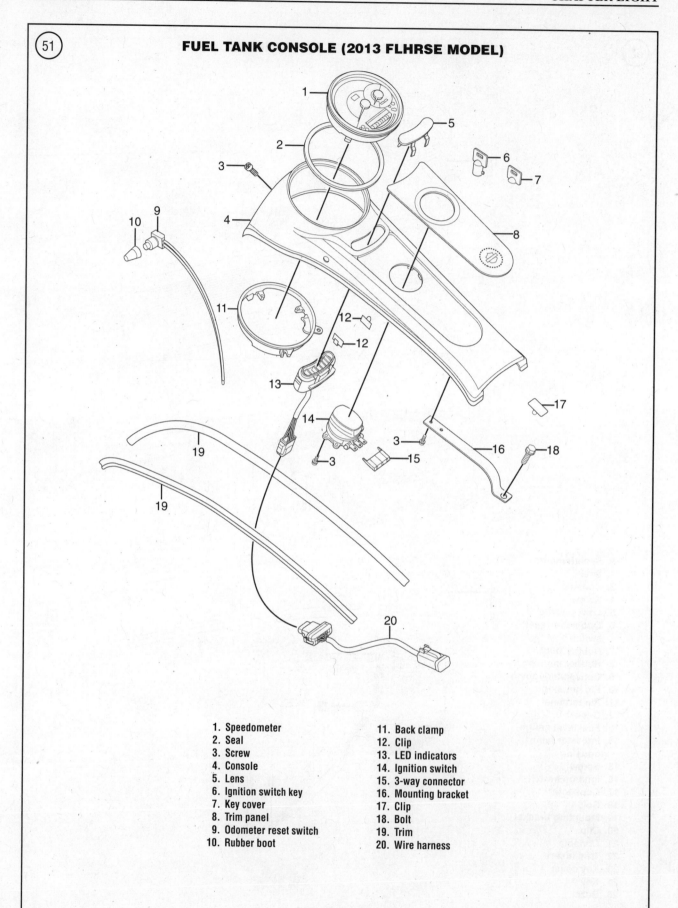

FUEL TANK CONSOLE (2013 FLHRSE MODEL)

51

1. Speedometer
2. Seal
3. Screw
4. Console
5. Lens
6. Ignition switch key
7. Key cover
8. Trim panel
9. Odometer reset switch
10. Rubber boot
11. Back clamp
12. Clip
13. LED indicators
14. Ignition switch
15. 3-way connector
16. Mounting bracket
17. Clip
18. Bolt
19. Trim
20. Wire harness

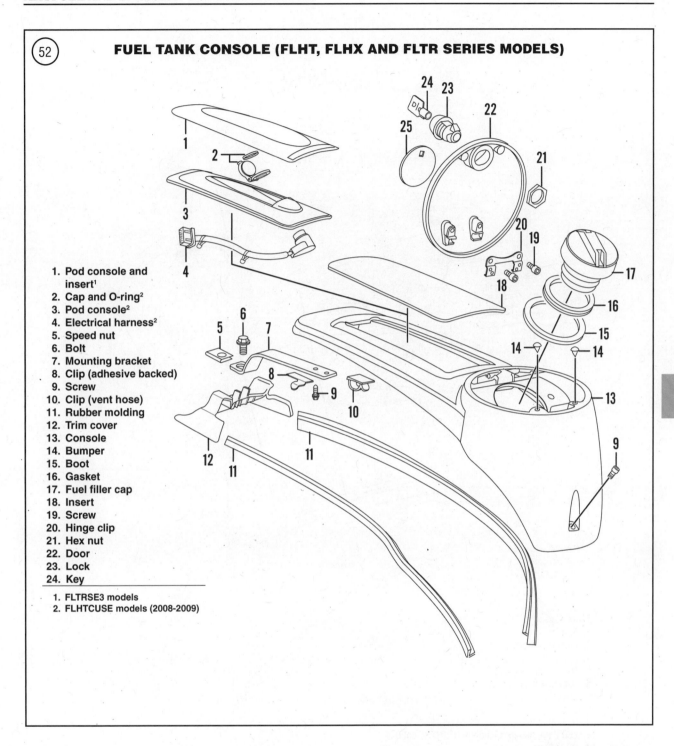

FUEL TANK CONSOLE (FLHT, FLHX AND FLTR SERIES MODELS)

52

1. Pod console and insert[1]
2. Cap and O-ring[2]
3. Pod console[2]
4. Electrical harness[2]
5. Speed nut
6. Bolt
7. Mounting bracket
8. Clip (adhesive backed)
9. Screw
10. Clip (vent hose)
11. Rubber molding
12. Trim cover
13. Console
14. Bumper
15. Boot
16. Gasket
17. Fuel filler cap
18. Insert
19. Screw
20. Hinge clip
21. Hex nut
22. Door
23. Lock
24. Key

1. FLTRSE3 models
2. FLHTCUSE models (2008-2009)

8

a. Carefully cut the cable strap securing the fuel level sender wires to the main harness on the left side frame rail.

b. Remove the front screw (**Figure 54**) and the rear bolt (**Figure 55**) securing the console to the frame and fuel tank.

c. Lift the console partially up off the fuel tank and disconnect the fuel level sensor electrical connector (**Figure 56**).

d. Turn the console over and lay it upside down in shop cloths on the rear fender.

e. Disconnect the electrical connector from the ignition switch (A, **Figure 57**) and indicator lamp housing (B).

5. On FLHT, FLTR and FLHX models, perform the following:

a. Remove the screw (A, **Figure 58**) securing the rear of the console to the fuel tank.

b. Remove the screw securing the front of the console to the fuel tank.

c. Unscrew the fuel filler cap.

⑤³ **FUEL TANK CONSOLE (FLHTSE AND FLTRXSE MODELS)**

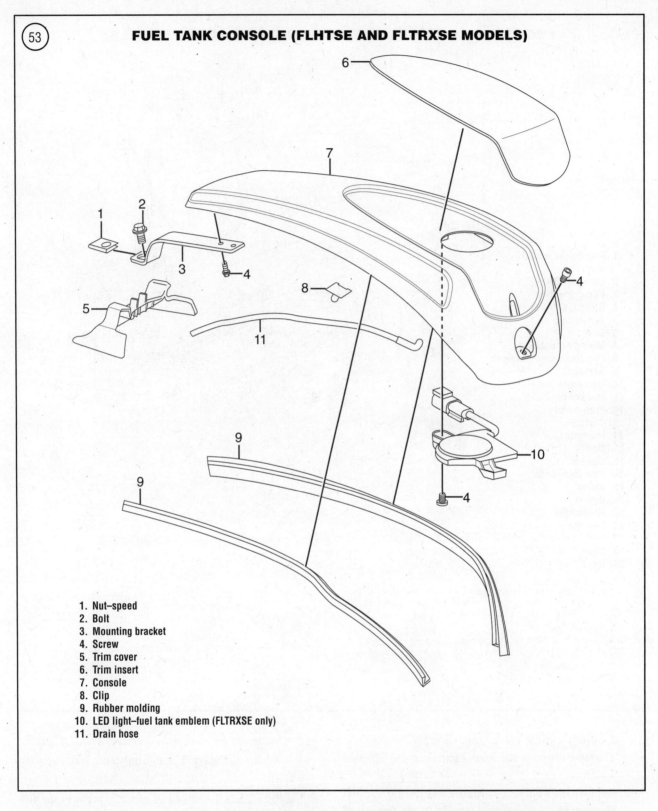

1. Nut–speed
2. Bolt
3. Mounting bracket
4. Screw
5. Trim cover
6. Trim insert
7. Console
8. Clip
9. Rubber molding
10. LED light–fuel tank emblem (FLTRXSE only)
11. Drain hose

d. Lift the console part way off the fuel tank and disconnect the electrical connector from the ignition switch, on models so equipped.

6. On 2013 FLHXSE and FLTRXSE models, perform the following:

a. Remove the front screw and the rear bolt securing the console to the frame and fuel tank.

b. Lift the console partially up off the fuel tank and disconnect the light electrical connector.

c. Remove the console from the fuel tank.

7. On all models except FLHR, FLHRC and 2013 FLHXSE and FLTRXSE, carefully remove the console and lay it upside down in shop cloths on the work bench.

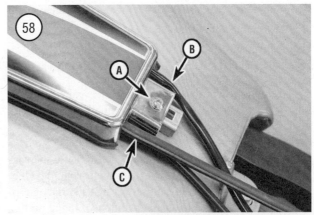

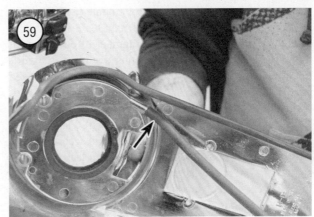

8

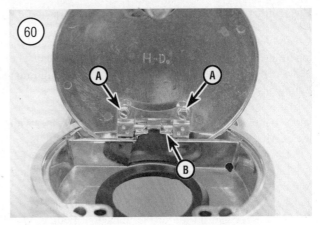

8. On FLHT, FLTR and FLHX models, disconnect the overflow hose (**Figure 58**) from the lower fitting. Reinstall the fuel filler cap.

9. On FLHT, FLTR and FLHX models, check the tightness of the clip mounting screws (A, **Figure 60**) and the hinge pin (B).

10. Install by reversing the removal steps, while noting the following:

    a. Make sure the trim pieces or the rubber boot is in place prior to installation.

    b. Correctly and carefully route the electrical cables (B, **Figure 58**) and hoses (C) between the console and

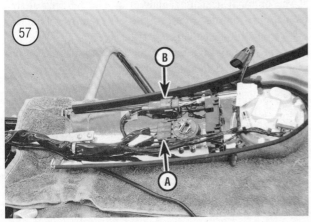

fuel tank so they will not get pinched or damaged, on models so equipped.

ELECTRONIC FUEL INJECTION (EFI)

This section describes the components and the operation of the electronic, sequential-port fuel injection (EFI) system. Fuel injection eliminates an inefficient cold start enrichment device, yet it provides accurate idle-speed control. It also improves torque characteristics while increasing fuel economy and reducing exhaust emissions. The fuel injection system constantly adjusts the air/fuel ratio and ignition timing to match the load conditions. Engine performance can be modified by simply changing the operating parameters of the electronic control module (ECM).

Complete service of the system requires a H-D digital technician, a breakout box and a number of other special tools. However, basic troubleshooting diagnosis is no different on a fuel-injected motorcycle than on a carbureted one. If the check engine light comes on or if there is a drivability problem, troubleshoot the system as described in *Electronic Diagnostic System* (Chapter Two). Make sure all related electrical connections are clean and secure. A high or erratic idle speed may indicate a vacuum leak. If the basic tests fail to reveal the cause of a problem, refer service to a dealership. Incorrectly-performed diagnostic procedures can result in damage to the fuel injection system.

Electronic Control Module (ECM) and Sensors

The electronic control module, or ECM, is located on top of the electrical caddy (**Figure 61**), under the seat. The ECM determines the optimum fuel injection and ignition timing based on input from six or seven sensors.

Make sure the ECM is securely mounted on the rubber isolators to prevent damage from vibration. Do not tamper with the ECM; it is sealed to prevent moisture contamination.

The engine-mounted sensors are shown in **Figure 62**. Additional sensors and their locations (**Figure 63**) and functions are as follows:

1. The temperature and manifold absolute pressure sensor (TMAP) is located on top of the induction module. One portion of the TMAP measures temperature of the air entering the induction manifold and the remaining portion measures air pressure within the induction module.

2. The throttle grip sensor (TGS) is mounted on the right side of the handlebar. It is a Hall-effect sensor that operates the TCA in the induction module.

3. The throttle control actuator (TCA) is mounted on the induction module. The TCA receives inputs from the TGS, throttle position sensors and the ECM. The TCA controls the throttle plates within the induction module.

4. The crankshaft position (CKP) sensor, located on the forward position of the left crankcase, is an inductive type sensor. The ECM determines the engine speed by how fast the machined teeth on the flywheel pass by the sensor.

5. The engine temperature (ET) sensor, is located on the front cylinder head. The ECM adjusts the injector opening time based on input from this sensor.

6. The bank angle sensor (BAS), located within the turn signal module (TSM) or the turn signal security module (TSSM), interrupts the ignition and shuts off the engine if the motorcycle's lean angle is greater than 45° from vertical for more than one second.

7. Vehicle speed sensor (VSS) is located on top of the crankcase behind the transmission cover. The VSS monitors gear tooth movement on the top gear and sends data to the ECM.

8. Oxygen (O_2) sensors are screwed into the front and rear exhaust header. The O_2 sensors monitor the oxygen content of the exhaust system, and adjust the air/fuel mixture to maintain the desired 14.7:1 air/fuel mixture.

9. Active intake solenoid (HDI models only) is located in the air filter backplate. The solenoid opens a valve in the backplate to allow additional air to enter the engine and change the air/fuel mixture at speeds greater than 43 mph (70 kph) when the throttle opening is greater than 50%.

10. Active exhaust system (HDI models only) is attached to the base of the battery case and operates a valve in the rear cylinder's exhaust pipe. The valve's position automatically adjusts, enhancing engine performance.

Heat Management System (2007-2009 Models)

The optional heat management system reduces engine temperature for rider comfort. The system turns off the rear cylinder fuel injector whenever the following four conditions are present; high engine temperature, engine is running at idle speed, motorcycle is not moving and when the clutch lever is pulled in or the transmission is in neutral.

Idle speed is maintained even though the rear cylinder is no longer firing, but it acts like an air pump to help cool the engine. This cooling continues until one of the previously mentioned conditions is no longer evident at which time the fuel injector is activated and the rear cylinder fires normally.

During the cooling mode, the idle cadence is different and there is a unique exhaust odor. Both of these are normal and they not to be construed as an idle problem.

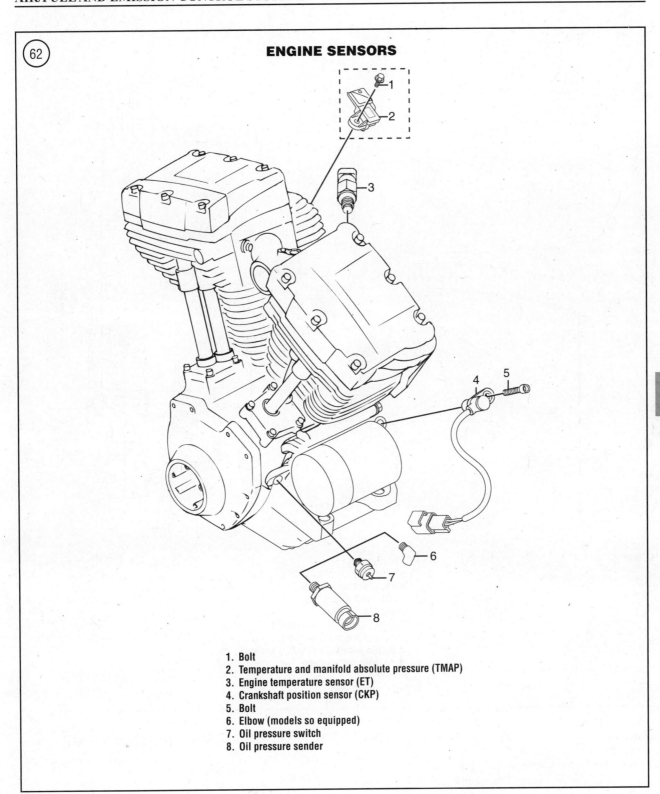

ENGINE SENSORS

62

1. Bolt
2. Temperature and manifold absolute pressure (TMAP)
3. Engine temperature sensor (ET)
4. Crankshaft position sensor (CKP)
5. Bolt
6. Elbow (models so equipped)
7. Oil pressure switch
8. Oil pressure sender

Fuel Supply System

Fuel pump and filters

The fuel pump and filter assembly is located inside the fuel tank. This assembly is part of the removable top plate that is attached to the top of the fuel tank. The top plate allows for easy removal and installation of the attached components without having to work within the fuel tank cavity. To provide maximum filtration prior to the fuel reaching the fuel injectors there is an inlet screen on the fuel pump and then a secondary fuel filter canister located downstream from the fuel pump.

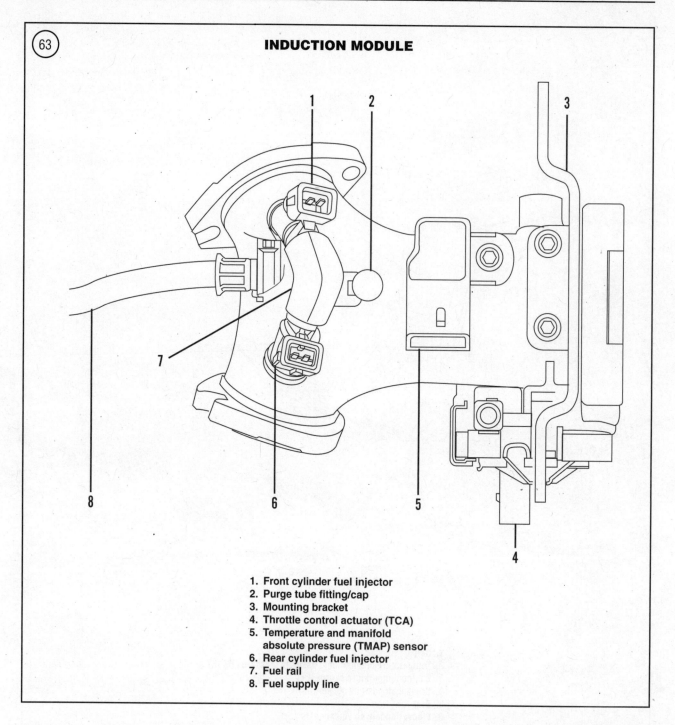

INDUCTION MODULE

1. Front cylinder fuel injector
2. Purge tube fitting/cap
3. Mounting bracket
4. Throttle control actuator (TCA)
5. Temperature and manifold absolute pressure (TMAP) sensor
6. Rear cylinder fuel injector
7. Fuel rail
8. Fuel supply line

Fuel lines

One fuel line is equipped with a quick-connect fitting at the base of the fuel tank. The supply fuel line is pressurized at 58 psi (400 kPa) and is controlled by the pressure regulator.

A check valve is located on both the supply and return lines where they attach to the fuel tank.

Fuel injectors

The solenoid-actuated constant-stroke pintle-type fuel injectors consist of a solenoid plunger, needle valve and housing. The fuel injector's opening is fixed and fuel pressure is constant. The fuel injectors are part of the fuel rail assembly.

The ECM controls the time the injectors open and close.

Fuel pump and filters

The fuel pump and filter assembly is an integral unit that is located within the fuel tank.

This assembly can easily be removed from the top of the fuel tank and serviced on the workbench.

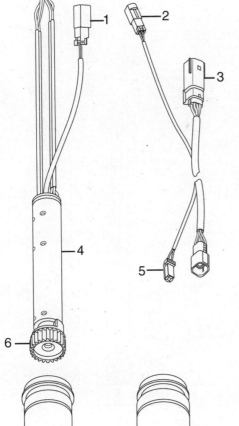

⑥④

**THROTTLE TWIST GRIP SENSOR
(ALL MODELS EXCEPT CVO)**

1. Connector
2. Connector
3. Jumper harness
4. Throttle grip sensor
5. Connector
6. Seal cap
7. Throttle grip—non-heated
8. Throttle grip—heated
9. End cap

Induction module

The induction module consists of two fuel injectors, throttle position sensor (TPS), intake air temperature (IAT) sensor, manifold absolute pressure (MAP) sensor, idle air control (IAC) sensor, fuel rail, fuel supply tube and purge tube fitting (California models).

THROTTLE CONTROL ACTUATOR (TCA)

The Throttle Control Actuator (TCA) is an internal component of the induction module. If the TCA is defective, the induction module must be replaced as described in this chapter.

THROTTLE OR TWIST GRIP SENSOR

Refer to **Figure 64** or **Figure 65**.

NOTE
Some models are also equipped with the heated right and left side hand grips. The heated hand grip procedures are located in Chapter Nine.

NOTE
Always disarm the TSM/TSSM security system prior to disconnecting the battery negative cable or pulling the main fuse so the siren will not sound.

Removal

1. Disconnect the negative battery cable as described in Chapter Nine.
2. Remove the left side frame cover and saddlebag as described in Chapter Fourteen.
3. On models with heated handgrips, pry the end cap from the handgrip and pull the connector out through the end of the handgrip. It is not necessary to disconnect the heated handgrip power or interconnect connectors.
4. Remove the front brake master cylinder as described in Chapter Thirteen.
5. Remove the right side switch assembly as described in Chapter Nine.
6. Tug slightly on the throttle grip to release the index pins in the throttle grip from the seal cap receptacle of the twist grip sensor. Remove the throttle grip from the handlebar.
7. Remove two wiring harness clips from the holes in the handlebar, on models so equipped.
8A. On Road King models, perform the following:
   a. Remove the headlight and nacelle as described in Chapter Nine.
   b. Disconnect the 6-pin twist grip sensor jumper wire connector (245) (**Figure 66**).

c. Withdraw the jumper wire and connector through the opening in the headlight case.

d. Remove the jumper wire from the t-stud on the fork stem lockplate on the right side.

8B. On fork-mounted fairing models, perform the following:

a. Remove the upper front fairing and windshield as described in Chapter Fourteen.

b. Disconnect the 6-pin twist grip sensor jumper wire connector.

c. Withdraw the jumper wire and connector through the opening in the fairing.

d. Remove the jumper wire from the t-stud on the inboard top right side support brace.

8C. On frame-mounted fairing models, perform the following:

a. Remove the front upper fairing and windshield (**Figure 67**) as described in Chapter Fourteen.

b. Disconnect black 6-pin twist grip sensor jumper wire connector (**Figure 68**).

c. Withdraw the jumper wire and connector through the opening in the headlight case.

CAUTION
Do not pull too hard on the twist grip sensor or the external latch on the pin housing will break. If broken, the twist grip sensor will not reconnect positively and the twist grip sensor must be replaced.

9. Gently withdraw the twist grip sensor part way out of the handlebar sufficiently to gain access to the sensor connector. Straighten the conduit on the connector end of the jumper harness. Feed it though the slot at the front of the handlebar while pulling. If the harness sticks inside the handlebar, carefully pull on the connector end and retract the conduit slightly. Gently work the conduit back and forth until the connector is past the handlebar opening.

CAUTION
Do not pry the connector, or twist it with the screwdriver; the external latch on the pin housing will break. If broken, the twist grip sensor harness will not reconnect positively and the twist grip sensor jumper harness must be replaced.

10. Carefully insert a small, flat-bladed screwdriver (A, **Figure 69**) between the pin and socket housing. When the bottom edge of the latch is disengaged, pull the pin housing from the socket housing (B, **Figure 69**).

11. On models with heated handgrips, disconnect the interconnect harness from the sensor harness.

12. Remove the twist grip sensor (**Figure 70**) from the handlebar.

Installation

1. If necessary, purchase a new seal cap O-ring.

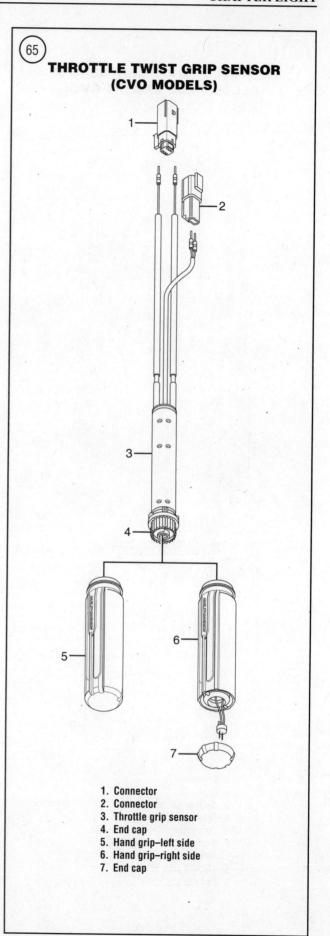

(65)

**THROTTLE TWIST GRIP SENSOR
(CVO MODELS)**

1. Connector
2. Connector
3. Throttle grip sensor
4. End cap
5. Hand grip–left side
6. Hand grip–right side
7. End cap

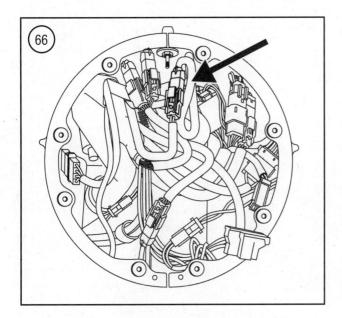

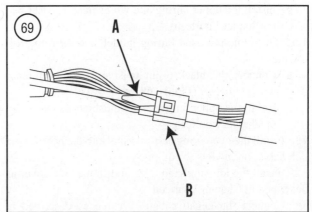

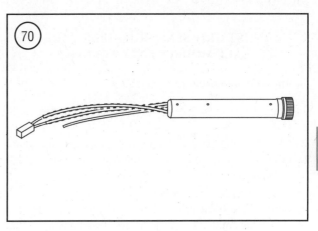

8

2. On models with heated handgrips, connect the interconnect harness onto the sensor harness.

3. Make sure the seal cap is in place in the end of the twist grip sensor, and verify that the seal cap is engaged on the index pins at the end of the sensor.

4. Install the new seal cap, engaging the legs into the slots in the end of the twist grip sensor. Install one leg first, and depress the second leg with a small, flat-bladed screwdriver

(A, **Figure 71**). Push down on the seal cap (B, **Figure 71**) until it bottoms.

5. Connect the jumper harness to the twist grip sensor.

6. Slowly pull on the jumper harness Molex connector and draw the twist grip sensor into the handlebar.

7. Carefully twist the twist grip sensor and align the grips' index tabs (A, **Figure 72**) with the slots (B) in the handlebar. Ensure that the small index tab is aligned with the small slot in the handlebar.

8. Slowly pull the twist grip sensor into the handlebar until it bottoms. The twist grip sensor is now secure to the handlebar and will not slide out.

9. Install the throttle grip onto the handlebar and onto the twist grip sensor, engaging the index pins.

10. Install the right side switch assembly as described in Chapter Nine.

11. Install the front brake master cylinder as described in Chapter Thirteen.

12A. On Road King models, perform the following:

  a. Connect the black 6-pin twist grip sensor jumper wire connector (**Figure 66**) onto the t-stud on the fork stem lock plate.

  b. Install the headlight and nacelle as described in Chapter Nine.

12B. On fork-mounted fairing models, perform the following:

  a. Connect the black 6-pin twist grip sensor jumper wire connector onto the t-stud on inboard top right side fairing support brace.

b. Install the upper fairing and windshield as described in Chapter Fourteen.

12C. On frame-mounted fairing models, perform the following:

a. Connect the black 6-pin twist grip sensor jumper wire connector (**Figure 68**).

b. Install the upper fairing and windshield as described in Chapter Fourteen.

13. Install the two wiring harness clips into the holes in the handlebar, on models so equipped.

14. Install the left side saddlebag and frame side cover as described in Chapter Fourteen.

15. Connect the negative battery cable as described in Chapter Nine.

TWIST GRIP SENSOR JUMPER WIRE (ALL MODELS EXCEPT CVO)

Removal/Installation

1. Remove the twist grip sensor as described in this chapter.

2. Use a length of fish wire long enough to span the entire length between the openings of the handlebar with an additional 24 inches (610 mm) left over.

3. Securely attach the fish wire to the jumper wire conduit inboard of the twist grip connector (**Figure 73**). Tie the wire onto the conduit to prevent it from bunching up within the handlebar when being pulled.

4. Secure the loose end of the fish wire to the frame to prevent it from working its way completely through the handlebar.

5. At the handlebar center opening, gently pull the jumper wire harness though the center slot in the handlebar. If the harness binds within the handlebar, gently pull on the fish wire at the other end of the handlebar to free it. Try again and pull the jumper wire harness out of the center opening slot of the handlebar with the fish wire.

6. Untie the fish wire from the old jumper wire.

7. Securely attach the fish wire to the *new* jumper wire conduit inboard of the twist grip connector. Tie the fish wire onto the conduit to prevent it from bunching up within the handlebar when being pulled.

8. Guide the electrical connector and conduit through the slot in the handlebar. Keep the harness straight and feed it into the handlebar slot while pulling on the fish wire.

9. At the twist grip end of the handlebar, gently pull the jumper wire harness though the center slot in the handlebar. If the harness binds within the handlebar, gently pull on the fish wire at the other end of the handlebar to free it. Try again and pull the jumper wire harness toward the twist grip end of the handlebar with the fish wire.

10. Only pull the fish wire and jumper harness sufficiently to gain access to the twist grip electrical connector. Disconnect the fish wire from the harness and the frame.

11. Install the twist grip sensor as described in this chapter.

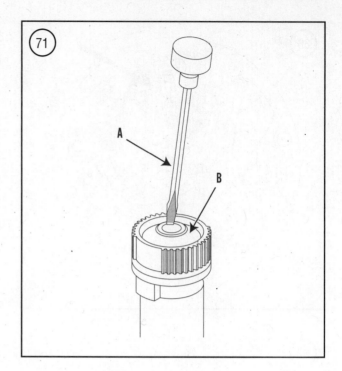

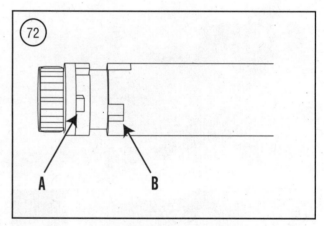

INDUCTION MODULE

Tools

The induction module is secured with Allen bolts that are difficult to reach and remove. Use the intake manifold wrench (K&L part No. 35-3975 or H-D part No. HD-47250). If this tool is not available, make a special tool as follows:

1. Cut a 9/16 in. (14 mm) long section (A, **Figure 74**) from a 1/4-in. Allen wrench.

2. Use the shortened wrench (B, **Figure 74**) when leverage is needed to break loose or tighten an Allen bolt.

3. Use the stub (A, **Figure 74**) and a 1/4-in. wrench (C, **Figure 74**) to remove or thread in an Allen bolt.

Removal

Refer to **Figure 75** and **Figure 76**.

1. Remove the fuel tank as described in this chapter.

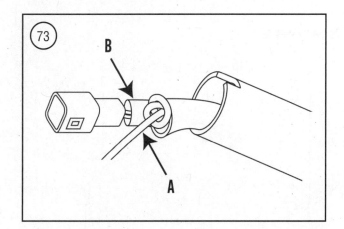

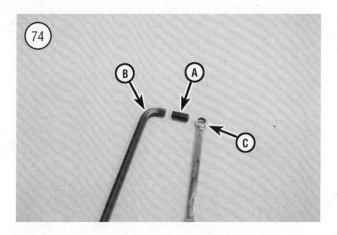

2. Remove the air filter and backplate as described in this chapter.

3. Remove the horn as described in Chapter Nine.

4. On models so equipped, remove the ARC electrical connector (A, **Figure 77**) and retainer from the mounting bracket (B).

5. Remove the mounting bolts and remove the mounting bracket (B, **Figure 77**).

6. On models so equipped, disconnect the purge hose (A, **Figure 78**) from the induction module.

7. Disconnect the fuel supply line from the induction module supply tube.

8. Disconnect the electrical connector (B, **Figure 78**) from the TMAP sensor.

9. Disconnect the electrical connector from the front fuel injector (84) (A, **Figure 79**) and rear fuel injector (85) (B).

10. Disconnect the electrical connector from TCA (211) (A, **Figure 80**). Carefully cut the cable strap and release the connector and harness (B, **Figure 80**) from the front right side of the induction module.

11. Pull back on the boot, and disconnect the connector from the engine temperature (ET) sensor (A, **Figure 81**).

12. On the left side of the motorcycle, loosen the lower Allen bolts (B, **Figure 81**) securing the induction module to the front and rear cylinders. Leave the bolts loosely in place in the cylinder heads.

13. On the right side of the motorcycle, use the Allen wrench stub and 1/4 in. wench and remove the upper Allen bolts (**Figure 82**).

NOTE
Each flange rotates on the induction module port.

14. Slide the induction module flanges off the lower Allen bolts, and partially remove the induction module from the right side. Be careful not to damage the fuel line.

15. Remove the mounting flanges (A, **Figure 83**), and discard the seals (B). Mark each flange to it can be reinstalled on the correct port.

16. Inspect the induction module as described in this section.

Installation

1. Refer to the marks made during removal and install the flanges (**Figure 84**) onto the correct sides of the induction module. Make sure the seal counter bore of each flange faces outward away from the induction module.

2. Install a new seal (B, **Figure 83**) into the flange so the beveled side faced into the flange.

3. On the right side, carefully position the induction module (A, **Figure 85**) between the cylinder head intake ports. Slide the flanges into place on the lower Allen bolts (B, **Figure 85**).

4. Align the mounting flanges with the cylinder head ports. Install and finger-tighten the two upper Allen bolts (**Figure 82**).

5. To ensure the correct alignment it the induction module to the cylinder heads, perform the following:

   a. Fit the air filter backplate (A, **Figure 86**) into place against the cylinder heads. Install and finger-tighten the breather bolts (B, **Figure 86**).

   b. Install the air filter bracket screws (C, **Figure 86**) to secure the backplate to the induction module, and finger-tighten the screws.

6. Working on the right side of the motorcycle, tighten the two upper Allen bolts (**Figure 82**) until snug. Do not tighten to the final torque specification at this time. Use same tool set-up used to loosen the Allen bolts.

7. Remove the air filter backplate.

8. Working on the left side of the motorcycle, tighten the two lower Allen bolts (**Figure 81**) to 96-144 in.-lb. (10.8-16.3 N•m).

9. Working on the right side of the motorcycle, tighten the two upper Allen bolts (**Figure 82**) to 96-144 in.-lb. (10.8-16.3 N•m).

10. Connect the connector onto the engine temperature (ET) sensor (A, **Figure 81**), and push the boot back onto the sensor.

11. Connect the electrical connector (211) onto TCA (**Figure 80**). Move the harness (B, **Figure 80**) back into place on the front right side of the induction module.

8

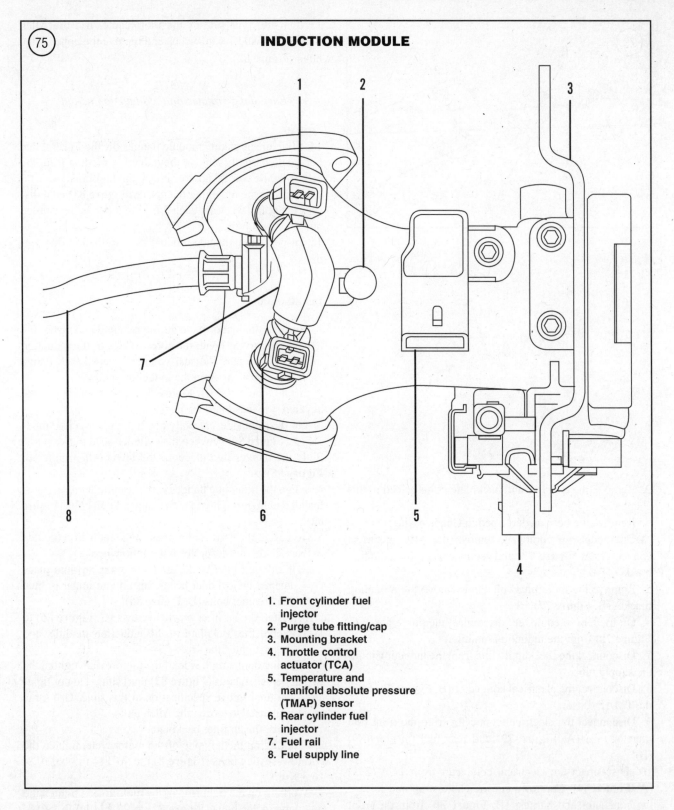

75

INDUCTION MODULE

1. Front cylinder fuel injector
2. Purge tube fitting/cap
3. Mounting bracket
4. Throttle control actuator (TCA)
5. Temperature and manifold absolute pressure (TMAP) sensor
6. Rear cylinder fuel injector
7. Fuel rail
8. Fuel supply line

Secure with a new cable strap, and remove any excess material.

12. Connect the electrical connector (A, **Figure 79**) onto the front fuel injector (84) and onto the rear fuel injector (B) (85).

13. Connect the electrical connector (B, **Figure 78**) onto the TMAP sensor (80).

14. Connect the fuel supply line from the induction module supply tube.

15. On models so equipped, connect the purge hose (A, **Figure 78**) onto the induction module.

16. Install the mounting bracket (B, **Figure 77**) and mounting bolts. Tighten the bolts securely.

76

FUEL INDUCTION MODULE AND SENSORS

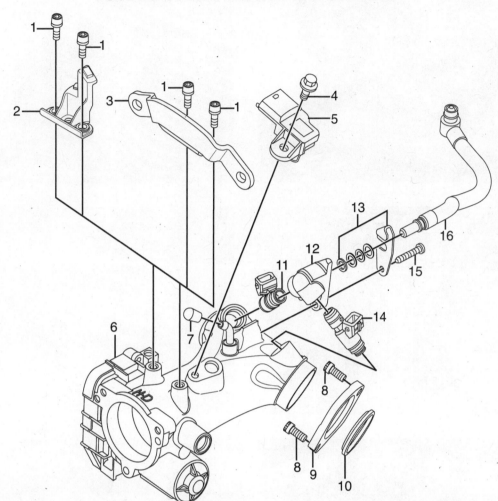

8

1. Bolt
2. Mounting bracket–CVO models
3. Mounting bracket–all models except CVO
4. Bolt
5. Temperature and manifold absolute pressure (TMAP)
6. Induction module
7. Purge tube cap
8. Bolt
9. Mounting flange
10. Seal
11. Fuel injector–rear cylinder
12. Fuel rail
13. Throttle cable bracket assembly
14. Fuel injector–front cylinder
15. Screw
16. Fuel hose

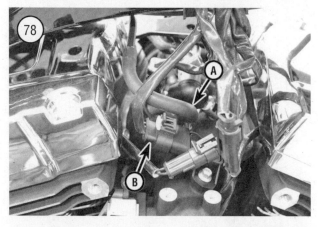

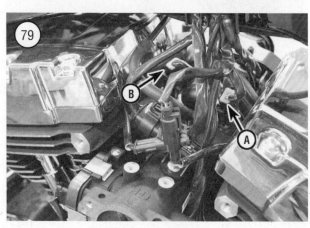

17. On models so equipped, install the ARC electrical connector (A, **Figure 77**) and retainer onto the mounting bracket (B).

18. Install the horn as described in Chapter Nine.

19. Install the backplate and the air filter as described in this chapter.

20. Install the fuel tank as described in this chapter.

Inspection

1. Check the induction module for wear, deterioration or other damage.

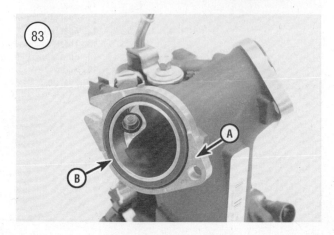

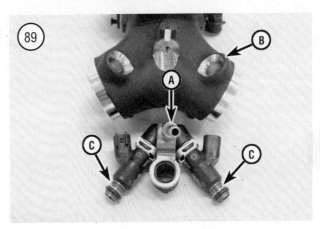

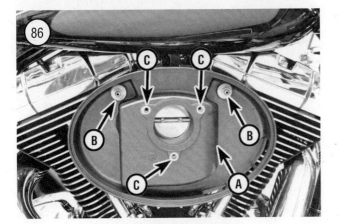

2. Inspect each flange (A, **Figure 87**) and its seal (B) on the induction module for cracks or distortion.

FUEL INJECTORS

Removal

1. Remove the induction module as described in this chapter.

2. Remove the fuel supply tube bolt (A, **Figure 88**) and washer.

3. Gently rock the fuel injector and fuel rail assembly (B, **Figure 88**) back and forth while pulling up, and remove the assembly (A, **Figure 89**) from the induction module (B). Do not lose the bottom O-ring (C, **Figure 89**) on each fuel injector.

4. Rotate the fuel injector 90° so the closed end (A, **Figure 90**) of the spring clip is accessible. Note that the arms of the spring clip straddle the tab (B, **Figure 90**) on the injector.

5. Remove the spring clip (A, **Figure 91**), and pull the fuel injector (B) from the fuel rail. Gently rock the injector back and forth, if necessary.

6. Remove and discard the top (A, **Figure 92**) and bottom (B) O-rings.

7. Repeat the process to remove the remaining fuel injector.

8. Remove the Torx screw (A, **Figure 93**) securing the fuel supply tube clamp bracket (B) and fuel rail.

9. Rotate the bracket (A, **Figure 94**) 90° *clockwise* and remove it from the fuel supply tube.

10. Withdraw the fuel supply tube (B, **Figure 94**) from the fuel rail. Remove a washer, an O-ring, a washer and an O-ring from the end of the fuel supply tube. These items may remain within the fuel rail. These items must be removed to ensure correct fuel tube installation to avoid fuel leaks.

Installation

1. Apply a light coat of clean engine oil to all *new* O-rings.

2. Insert the fuel supply tube into the fuel rail bore. Push it in until it bottoms. Rotate the fuel supply tube *clockwise* until the fuel tank quick-connect fitting is point upward. Now rotate the fuel supply tube and additional 90° so the fitting is pointing toward the TCA sensor on the induction module.

3. Engage the fuel supply tube clamp bracket into the slot in the fuel supply hose fitting.

4. Rotate the bracket (A, **Figure 94**) 90° *counterclockwise* until the flange of the bracket bottoms on the fuel rail.

5. Align the screw hole in the clamp bracket with the induction module, and then install the Torx screw (A, **Figure 93**). Tighten the screw to 66-82 in.-lb. (7.5-9.3 N•m).

6. Install the O-ring (A, **Figure 92**) with the thicker base and smaller ID onto the fuel rail end of the fuel injector. Install the remaining O-ring (B, **Figure 92**) onto the induction module and of the fuel injector.

7. Push the electrical connector side of each fuel injector (B, **Figure 91**) into the fuel rail until it bottoms.

8. Position the concave side of the spring clip (A, **Figure 91**) toward the fuel rail, and press the spring clip into the slot in the fuel injector. When properly installed, the spring clip engages the lip on each side of the fuel injector and the fingers on the back of the clip straddle the tab (B, **Figure 90**) on the fuel injector.

9. Rotate the fuel injectors so the closed side of the spring clip faces the fuel rail (C, **Figure 90**).

10. Position the fuel rail assembly onto the induction module so each injector (**Figure 95**) is started into its port.

11. Carefully install the fuel injectors into the induction module ports until the fuel rail tab (**Figure 96**) engages the slot at the top of the induction module.

12. Install the induction module assembly as described in this chapter.

Inspection

1. Inspect the fuel injectors for damage. Check for corrosion on the electrical connector pins; clean if necessary.

2. Inspect the fuel rail and fuel supply tube for damage.

3. Inspect the injector ports (**Figure 97**) in the induction module.

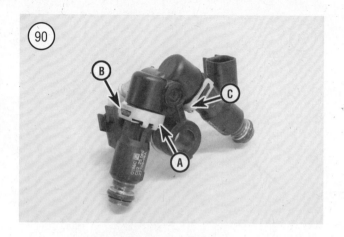

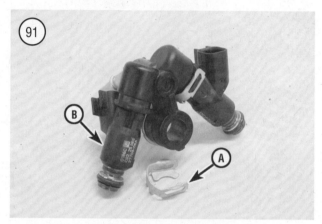

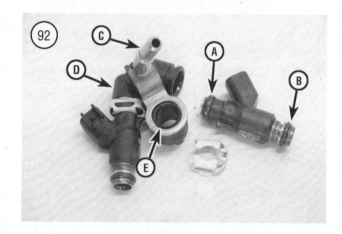

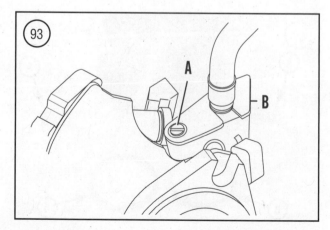

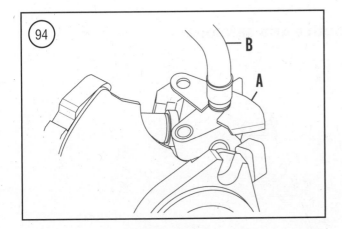

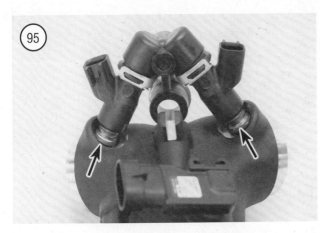

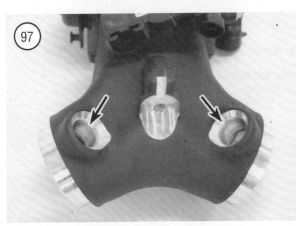

4. Replace any worn or damaged part.

INDUCTION MODULE SENSORS

NOTE
Always disarm the TSM/TSSM security system prior to disconnecting the battery negative cable or pulling the main fuse so the siren will not sound.

Refer to **Figure 98**.

Temperature Manifold Absolute Pressure Sensor (TMAP)

Removal/Installation

1. Remove the fuel tank as described in this chapter.
2. Remove the air filter and backplate as described in this chapter.
3. Remove the horn as described in Chapter Nine.
4. On models so equipped, remove the ARC electrical connector (A, **Figure 99**) and retainer from the mounting bracket (B).
5. Remove the mounting bolts and remove the mounting bracket (B, **Figure 99**).
6. Disconnect the electrical connector (A, **Figure 100**) from the TMAP sensor (80). Remove the mounting hex bolt (B, **Figure 100**). Rotate the TMAP sensor slightly, pull straight up, and release the pressure port from the hole in the top of the induction module.
7. Inspect the O-ring for tears or deterioration; replace if necessary.
8. Position the electrical connector facing toward the rear cylinder head. Align the bolt hole with the induction module bolt hole and carefully install the pressure port of the sensor into the hole in the induction module. Push the sensor in until it bottoms.
9. Install a new hex bolt and tighten to 84-108 in.-lb. (9.5-12.2 N•m).
10 Connect the electrical connector (A, **Figure 100**) onto the TMAP sensor (80).
11. Install the mounting bracket (B, **Figure 100**) and mounting bolts. Tighten the bolts securely.
12. On models so equipped, install the ARC electrical connector (A, **Figure 99**) and retainer onto the mounting bracket (B).
13. Install the horn as described in Chapter Nine.
14. Install the backplate and the air filter as described in this chapter.
15. Install the fuel tank as described in this chapter.

Engine Temperature (ET) Sensor
Removal/Installation

Refer to *Sensors* in Chapter Nine.

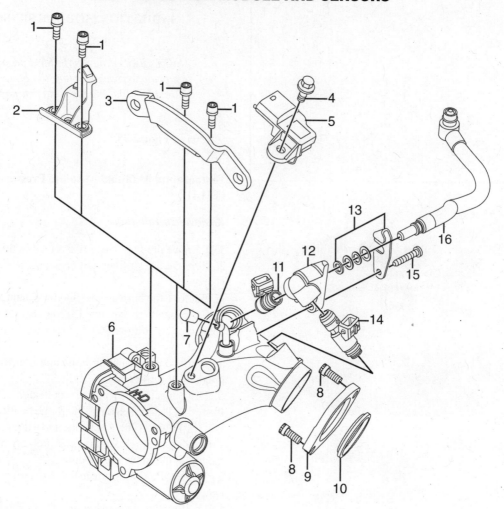

98

FUEL INDUCTION MODULE AND SENSORS

1. Bolt
2. Mounting bracket–CVO models
3. Mounting bracket–all models except CVO
4. Bolt
5. Temperature and manifold absolute pressure (TMAP)
6. Induction module
7. Purge tube cap
8. Bolt
9. Mounting flange
10. Seal
11. Fuel injector—rear cylinder
12. Fuel rail
13. Throttle cable bracket assembly
14. Fuel injector—front cylinder
15. Screw
16. Fuel hose

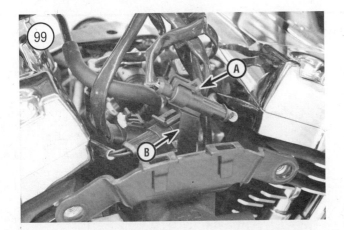

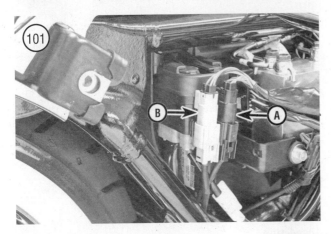

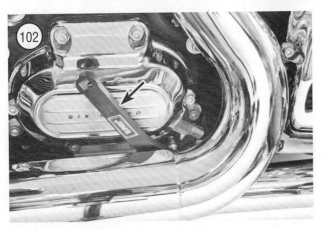

Oxygen (O₂) Sensor
Removal/Installation

The oxygen sensors are located on the inboard side of the front and rear exhaust pipes. An oxygen sensor socket (JIMS part No. 969 or H-D part No. HD-48262), or an equivalent must be used to remove and install the sensors after the exhaust system is removed. To remove the oxygen sensor with the exhaust system installed use JIMS O2 sensor wrench (part No. 784).

1. Disconnect the negative battery cable as described in Chapter Nine.

2. Removed the seat as described in Chapter Fourteen.

3. Remove the right side saddlebag and right side frame cover as described in Chapter Fourteen.

4. Follow the O_2 sensor wiring harness along the right side of the frame and exhaust system to the connectors located to the left of the ABS hydraulic unit. Note this routing as the wiring harness must be reinstalled in the same location.

5. Disconnect the front O_2 sensor (A, **Figure 101**) or rear O_2 sensor (B) from the harness connectors.

6. Release any cable ties securing the harness to the frame and rear brake hose.

7A. To remove the sensor with the exhaust system in place, perform the following:

    a. Allow the exhaust system to cool down to shop temperature.

    b. Thoroughly clean the entire area from road dirt and debris.

    c. Protect the finish on the exhaust system and the clutch release cover with duct tape, or an equivalent.

    d. Carefully withdraw the 2-pin electrical connector and wiring harness down and out of the frame. Lay the harness out straight on the shop floor in a straight line from where the sensor is attached to the exhaust system.

    e. Correctly install the wrench on the sensor (**Figure 102**) and use a 3/8 in. drive, loosen the sensor. Reposition the wrench on the sensor and completely loosen it.

    f. Remove the wrench and completely unscrew the O_2 sensor from the exhaust pipe by hand while turning the wiring harness at the same to avoid kinking the fragile wiring harness.

7B. To remove the sensor with the exhaust system removed, perform the following:

    a. Allow the exhaust system to cool down to shop temperature.

    b. Thoroughly clean the entire area from road dirt and debris.

    c. Install the O_2 sensor socket onto the O_2 sensor (**Figure 102**) without damage to the electrical wires.

NOTE
Do not install an oxygen sensor that has been dropped or damaged by other components. It may be damaged, and will not function correctly.

8

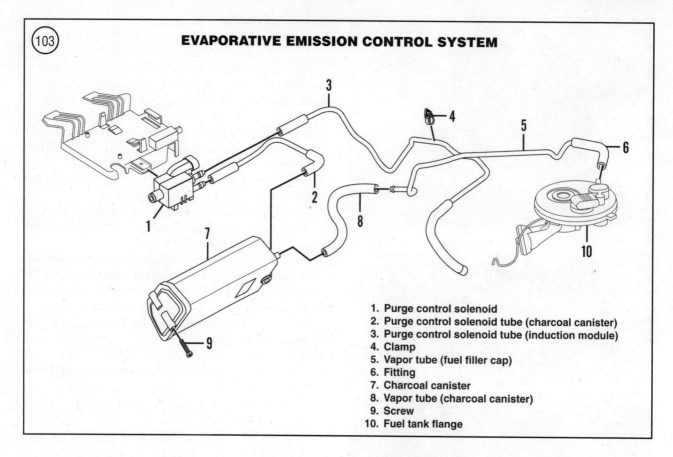

EVAPORATIVE EMISSION CONTROL SYSTEM

1. Purge control solenoid
2. Purge control solenoid tube (charcoal canister)
3. Purge control solenoid tube (induction module)
4. Clamp
5. Vapor tube (fuel filler cap)
6. Fitting
7. Charcoal canister
8. Vapor tube (charcoal canister)
9. Screw
10. Fuel tank flange

NOTE
The threads of new O_2 sensor assemblies are coated with anti-seize lubricant and new seal rings. It is not necessary to add additional anti-seize lubricant

CAUTION
Do not allow and anti-seize lubricant to get onto the O_2 sensor tip of the as it will not function correctly.

8. Apply a light coat of Loctite Anti-Seize to the threads prior to installation.
9. Carefully thread the O_2 sensor onto the exhaust pipe by hand. Do not cross thread it.
10. Install the socket, or wrench, on the O_2 sensor and tighten to14 ft.-lb. (19 N•m).
11. Rote the wiring harness through the frame along the same patch as noted during removal.
12. Secure the harness to the frame and rear brake hose with new cable ties in the exact same location as noted during removal.
13. Connect the front O_2 sensor (A, **Figure 101**) or rear (B).
14. Install the right side frame cover and saddlebag cover as described in Chapter Fourteen.
15. Install the seat.
16. Connect the negative battery cable as described in Chapter Nine.

EVAPORATIVE EMISSION CONTROL SYSTEM

The evaporative emission control system prevents gasoline vapors from escaping into the atmosphere on models sold in different areas.

When the engine is not running, the system directs the fuel vapor from the fuel tank through the vapor valve and into the charcoal canister. When the engine is running, these vapors are drawn through a purge hose, routed into the induction module, and then burned in the combustion chambers.

Refer to **Figure 103**.

Charcoal Canister
Inspection

Before removing the hoses from any part, mark the hose and fitting with a piece of masking tape to identify them. Hoses must be reconnected to the correct fittings during assembly.

1. Check all emission control lines and hoses to make sure they are correctly routed and connected.

WARNING
Make sure the fuel tank vapor hoses are routed so they cannot contact hot engine or exhaust components. These hoses contain flammable vapor. If a hose melts from contact with a hot part, leaking vapor may ignite causing severe motorcycle damage and rider injury.

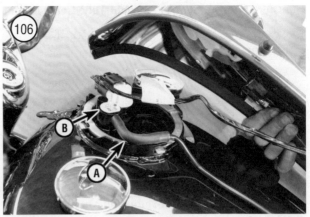

8. Remove the nut and disconnect three ground ring terminals from left ground stud.

9. Remove the nut and disconnect two ground ring terminals from right ground stud.

10. Remove the mounting screws and remove the canister from the frame cross member.

11. Installation is the reverse of removal.

    a. Securely connect each hose to the fitting noted during removal.

    b. Tighten the canister mounting screws to 10-15 in.-lb. (1.1-1.7 N•m).

    c. Secure the main harness to the frame with new cable ties.

Purge Solenoid Replacement

1. Remove the seat as described in Chapter Fourteen.

2. Partially remove the top caddy to gain access to the purge solenoid.

3. Disconnect the electrical connector (A, **Figure 105**) from the purge solenoid.

4. Disconnect the solenoid-to-induction module purge tube (B, **Figure 105**).

5. Disconnect the canister-to-solenoid purge tube (C, **Figure 105**).

6. Remove the purge solenoid from the frame.

7. Installation is the reverse of removal. Ensure that the tubes are not kinked or pinched.

Vapor Vent Tube Replacement

1. Remove the seat as described in Chapter Fourteen.

2. Partially remove the fuel tank console as described in this chapter.

3. Have an assistant secure the console, and disconnect the fuel vapor vent tube (A, **Figure 106**) from the fuel tank top plate (B).

4. Disconnect the vent tube (8, **Figure 103**) from the fitting on the canister (7).

5. Remove the vent tube from the frame.

6. Installation is the reverse of removal. Ensure that the vent tube is not kinked or pinched.

2. Make sure the lines or hoses are not kinked. Also inspect the hoses and lines routed near engine hot spots for excessive wear or burning.

3. Check the physical condition of all lines and hoses in the system. Check for cuts, tears or loose connections. These lines and hoses are subjected to various temperatures and operating conditions, and they eventually become brittle and crack. Replace damaged lines and hoses.

4. Check all components in the emission control system for damage, such as broken fittings.

Charcoal Canister Replacement

1. Support the motorcycle on a work stand with the rear wheel off the ground. See *Motorcycle Stands* in Chapter Twelve.

2. Remove the seat, both saddlebags and both frame side covers as described in Chapter Fourteen.

3. Remove the battery as described in Chapter Nine.

4. On the left side, carefully remove the cable straps securing the main harness to the frame adjacent to the left side caddy.

5. Remove the two bolts (A, **Figure 104**) securing the left side caddy (B) to the frame.

6. Disconnect the fuel vapor vent tube (8, **Figure 103**) from the canister fitting marked *tank*.

7. Disconnect the purge tube (2, **Figure 103**) from the canister fitting marked *purge*.

Canister-to-Purge Control Solenoid Tube Replacement

1. Remove the seat as described in Chapter Fourteen.
2. Partially remove the top caddy to gain access to the purge solenoid.
3. Disconnect the canister-to-solenoid purge tube.
4. Disconnect the canister-to-solenoid purge tube from the lower fitting on the canister.
5. Remove the purge tube from the frame.
6. Installation is the reverse of removal. Ensure that the purge tube is not kinked or pinched.

Purge Control Solenoid-to-Induction Module Tube Replacement

1. Remove the seat as described in Chapter Fourteen.
2. Remove the fuel tank as described in this chapter.
3. Partially remove the top caddy to gain access to the purge solenoid.
4. Disconnect the solenoid-to-induction module purge tube.

5. Remove the cable clip securing the purge tube to the frame backbone.
6. Disconnect the purge tube (**Figure 107**) from the induction module.
7. Remove the purge tube from the frame.
8. Installation is the reverse of removal. Ensure that the purge tube is not kinked or pinched.

Table 1 FUEL SYSTEM SPECIFICATIONS

Item	Specification
Idle speed	950-1050 rpm
Fuel pressure	55-62 psi (380-425 kPa)
Fuel tank capacity	6.0 gal (18.9 L)
Fuel tank reserve*	1.0 gal (3.79 L)
Recommended fuel	91 pump octane or higher
*Low fuel warning light on.	

Table 2 FUEL SYSTEM TORQUE SPECIFICATIONS

Item	ft.-lb.	in.-lb.	N•m
Air filter			
All models except CVO			
Cover screw	–	36-60	4.1-6.8
Bracket Torx screw	–	108-132	12.2-14.9
CVO models			
FLTRXSE			
Air filter element clamp screw	–	45-55	5.1-6.2
Back plate mounting screw	–	55-60	6.2-6.8
Breather bolts	22-24	–	29.8-32.5
Intake tube screw	–	55-60	6.2-6.8
All models except FLTRXSE			
Insert screw	–	27-32	3.1-3.6
Cover screw	–	36-60	4.1-6.8
Air filter element screw		55-60	6.2-6.8
Charcoal canister screw	–	10-15	1.1-1.7
Engine temperature sensor	–	120-180	13.6-20.3
Fuel supply tube Torx screw	–	66-82	7.5-9.3
Fuel tank check valve	18	–	24.4
Fuel tank front and			
rear mounting bolt	15-20	–	20.3-27.1
Fuel tank quick connect fitting	22-26	–	29.8-35.3
Temperature manifold absolute			
pressure sensor (TMAP)			
hex bolt	–	84-108	9.5-12.2
Induction module mounting			
flange bolts	–	96-144	10.8-16.3
Oxygen sensor	14	–	19

CHAPTER NINE

ELECTRICAL SYSTEM

This chapter contains service and test procedures for electrical system components. Refer to Chapter Three for spark plugs service.

Specifications are located in **Tables 1-7** at the end of the chapter. Wiring diagrams are located in Chapter Sixteen of this manual.

ELECTRICAL COMPONENT REPLACEMENT

Most dealerships and parts suppliers will not accept the return of any electrical part. If the exact cause of an electrical system malfunction cannot be determined, have a dealership retest the specific system to verify test results. If a new electrical component is installed and the system still does not work, the unit, in all likelihood, cannot be returned for a refund.

Consider any test results carefully before replacing a component that tests only slight out of specification, especially when testing for resistance. A number of variables affect test results dramatically. These include the test meter's internal circuitry, ambient air temperature, and the condition under which the machine has been operated. All instructions and specifications have been checked for accuracy. However, successful test results depend largely upon individual accuracy.

FUSES

All models are equipped with a series of fuses to protect the electrical system. The number of fuses varies depending on the model. Refer to **Table 3** for fuse specifications.

The fuse panel is located under the seat, behind the battery. If there is an electrical failure, first check for a blown fuse. A blown fuse has a break in the element.

Whenever a fuse blows, find the reason for the failure before replacing the fuse. Usually, the trouble is a short circuit in the wiring. This may be caused by worn-through insulation or a disconnected wire shorted to ground. Check the circuit that the fuse protects.

Spare fuses are included in the fuse block. When a spare fuse is used, replace it as soon as possible. Consider carrying additional spare fuses.

> *NOTE*
> *Always disarm the optional security system (TSSM/HFSM) before disconnecting the battery or before pulling the Main Fuse so the siren will not sound.*

Fuse Replacement

1. Remove the seat as described in Chapter Fourteen.
2. Remove the right side saddlebag and the frame right side cover (Chapter Fourteen).
3. Remove the main fuse as described in this section.
4. Pull the fuse panel out from the bottom and remove the fuse panel cover.

> *NOTE*
> *Fuse description and typical location is printed on the fuse block cover **Figure 1** and **Figure 2**. Always refer to the location print-*

9

ed on the fuse block cover for your specific model.

5. Locate the blown fuse and install a new fuse with the same amperage.

MAIN FUSE

NOTE
Always disarm the optional security system (TSM/TSSM/HFSM) before disconnecting the battery or main fuse so the siren will not sound.

The main 40-amp fuse functions as the electrical system main fuse.
1. Remove the seat as described in Chapter Fourteen.
2. Remove the right side saddlebag and the frame right side cover (Chapter Fourteen).
3. Pull the main fuse (**Figure 3**) straight out from the fuse panel and remove it.
4. Install the main fuse (**Figure 3**) straight into the fuse panel and press it in until it bottoms.
5. Install the right side saddlebag and the frame right side cover (Chapter Fourteen).
6. Install the seat as described in Chapter Fourteen.

BATTERY

NOTE
Always disarm the optional security system (TSSM/HFSM) before disconnecting the battery or before pulling the Main Fuse so the siren will not sound.

A sealed, maintenance-free battery is installed on all models. The battery electrolyte level cannot be serviced. When replacing the battery, use a sealed type; do not install a non-sealed battery as the electrolyte will leak out. Never attempt to remove the sealing caps from the top of the battery. The battery does not require periodic electrolyte inspection or refilling.

Disconnect the negative (ground) cable first, and then the positive cable, when removing the battery. This minimizes the chance of a tool shorting to ground when disconnecting the battery positive cable.

Refer to Chapter Two for charging system troubleshooting.

Negative Cable Disconnect

Some procedures in this manual require disconnecting the negative battery cable as a safety precaution.
1. Remove the seat as described in Chapter Fourteen.
2. Partially remove the top caddy as described in this chapter to gain access to the top surface of the battery.

NOTE
Always disarm the optional security system (TSM/TSSM/HFSM) before disconnecting the battery or main fuse so the siren will not sound.

3. Note how the negative cable (black) is routed from the negative terminal to the frame ground.
4. Remove the bolt (A, **Figure 4**), and disconnect the negative cable (black) from the battery. Move the cable away from the battery to avoid accidental contact with the battery negative post.
5. Connect the negative cable (black) onto the battery post, and install the bolt (B, **Figure 4**). Tighten the bolt to 60-70 in.-lb. (6.8-7.9 N•m).
6. Apply a light coat of petroleum jelly, or dielectric grease to both battery terminals to retard corrosion and decomposition of the terminals.
7. Install the partially removed the top caddy as described in this chapter.
8. Install the seat as described in Chapter Fourteen.

Cable Service

To ensure good electrical contact between the battery and the electrical cables, the cables must be clean and free of corrosion.
1. If the electrical cable terminals are badly corroded, disconnect them from the motorcycle's electrical system.
2. Thoroughly clean each connector with a wire brush and a baking soda solution. Rinse thoroughly with clean water and wipe dry with a clean cloth.
3. After cleaning, apply a thin layer of dielectric grease to the battery terminals before reattaching the cables.
4. Reconnect the electrical cables to the motorcycle's electrical system if they were disconnected.
5. After connecting the electrical cables, apply a light coat of dielectric grease to the connectors to retard corrosion.

Removal/Installation

1. Turn the ignition switch off.

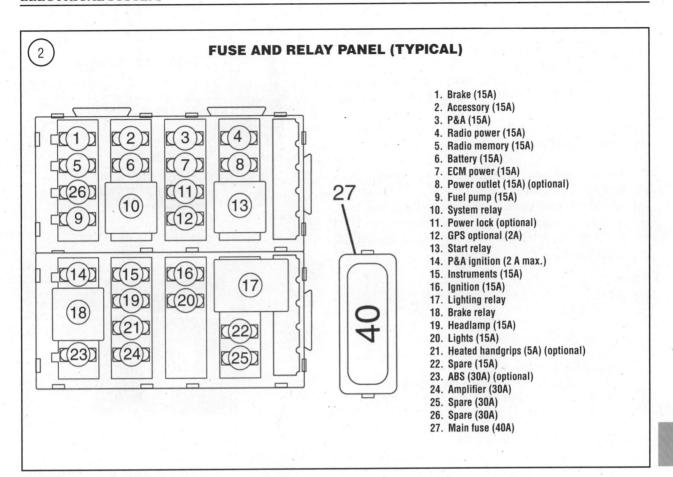

FUSE AND RELAY PANEL (TYPICAL)

1. Brake (15A)
2. Accessory (15A)
3. P&A (15A)
4. Radio power (15A)
5. Radio memory (15A)
6. Battery (15A)
7. ECM power (15A)
8. Power outlet (15A) (optional)
9. Fuel pump (15A)
10. System relay
11. Power lock (optional)
12. GPS optional (2A)
13. Start relay
14. P&A ignition (2 A max.)
15. Instruments (15A)
16. Ignition (15A)
17. Lighting relay
18. Brake relay
19. Headlamp (15A)
20. Lights (15A)
21. Heated handgrips (5A) (optional)
22. Spare (15A)
23. ABS (30A) (optional)
24. Amplifier (30A)
25. Spare (30A)
26. Spare (30A)
27. Main fuse (40A)

9

2. Remove the seat and frame left side cover as described in Chapter Fourteen.

3. Partially remove the top caddy as described in this chapter. Rotate the top caddy out of the way and onto the rear fender.

4. On models so equipped, disarm the security system.

5. Remove the bolt (A, **Figure 4**) and disconnect the negative cable (black) from the battery. Move the cable away from the battery to avoid accidental contact with the battery negative post.

6. Remove the bolt (B, **Figure 4**) and disconnect the positive cable (red) from the battery. Move the cable away from the battery to avoid accidental contact with the battery positive post.

7. Unfold the lifting strap. Grasp the lifting strap loop end and lift the battery sufficiently to a firm grip is possible under the battery.

8. Lift up and remove the battery from the battery tray and frame.

9. Release the lifting strap.

10. Inspect the battery tray for corrosion or damage. Clean or replace as necessary.

11. Run the lifting strap toward the rear, first down the center of the battery tray then up and across he frame crossmember.

12. Position the battery with the negative terminal facing toward the left side of the frame.

13. Reinstall the battery into the battery tray in the frame.

14. Connect the positive cable (red) onto the battery positive post. Install the bolt (B, **Figure 4**) and tighten to 60-70 in.-lb. (6.8-7.9 N•m).

15. Connect the negative cable (black) onto the battery negative post. Install the bolt (A, **Figure 4**) and tighten to 60-70 in.-lb. (6.8-7.9 N•m).

16. Carefully reposition the top caddy onto the battery hold-down bracket. Install the bolts but do not tighten at this time.

17. Install the top caddy as described in this chapter.

18. Apply a light coat of petroleum jelly, or dielectric grease to both battery terminals to retard corrosion and decomposition of the terminals.

19. Install the frame left side cover and seat as described in Chapter Fourteen.

Inspection

> *WARNING*
> *Electrolyte is extremely harmful to the eyes. Always wear safety glasses while working with a battery. If electrolyte gets into the eyes, call a physician immediately. Force the eyes open, and flood them with cool, clean water for approximately 15 minutes.*

The battery electrolyte level cannot be serviced in a maintenance-free battery. *Never* attempt to remove the sealing bar cap from the top of the battery. The battery does not require periodic electrolyte inspection or water refilling. Refer to the label (A, **Figure 5**) on top of the battery.

Even though the battery is sealed, protect eyes, skin and clothing. The corrosive electrolyte may have spilled out and can cause severe chemical skin burns and permanent injury. The battery case may be cracked and leaking electrolyte. If electrolyte is spilled or splashed on clothing or skin, immediately neutralize it with a baking soda and water solution, and flush with an abundance of clean water.

1. Remove the battery as described in this section. Do not clean the battery while it is mounted in the frame.

2. Set the battery on a stack of newspapers or shop cloths to protect the surface of the workbench.

3. Check the entire battery case (**Figure 6**) for cracks or other damage. If the battery case is warped, discolored or has a raised top, the battery has been overcharged and overheated.

4. Check the battery terminal bolts, spacers and nuts (B, **Figure 5**) for corrosion or damage. Clean parts thoroughly with a baking soda and water solution. Replace corroded or damaged parts.

5. If the top of the battery is corroded, clean it with a stiff bristle brush using the baking soda and water solution.

6. Check the battery cable ends for corrosion and damage. If corrosion is minor, clean the battery cable ends with a stiff wire brush. Replace severely corroded or damaged cables.

7. Perform the open circuit voltage test (this section).

8. Inspect the battery case for contamination or damage. Clean it with a baking soda and water solution.

9. Install the battery as described in this section.

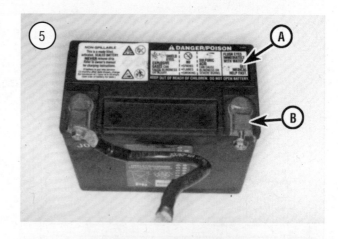

Open Circuit Voltage Test

1. Remove the battery as described in this section.

2. Connect a digital voltmeter between the battery negative and positive terminals. Note the following:

   a. If the battery voltage is 12.7 volts (at 68° F [20° C]), or greater, the battery is fully charged. At 12.6 volts, it is 75% charged.

   b. If the battery voltage is 12.0 to 12.5 volts (at 68° F [20° C]), or lower, the battery is undercharged and requires charging.

3. If the battery is undercharged, charge it as described in this section. Then, test the charging system as described in Chapter Two.

Load Test

A load test checks the battery's performance under full current load and is the best indication of battery condition.

A battery load tester is required for this procedure. When using a load tester, follow the manufacturer's instructions. **Figure 7** shows a typical load tester and battery arrangement.

1. Remove the battery from the motorcycle as described in this section.

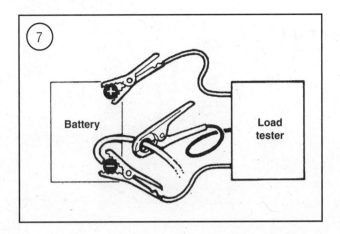

9

NOTE
Let the battery stand for at least one hour if the battery has been recently charged before performing this test.

2. The battery must be fully charged before beginning this test. If necessary, charge the battery as described in this section.

WARNING
The battery load tester must be turned off prior to connecting or disconnecting the test cables to the battery. Otherwise, a spark could cause the battery to explode.

CAUTION
To prevent battery damage during load testing, do not load test a discharged battery. Performing a load test on a discharged battery can cause permanent battery damage. Do not load test the battery for more than 20 seconds.

3. Load test the battery as follows:
   a. Connect the load tester cables to the battery following the tester manufacturer's instructions.
   b. Load the battery at 50% of the cold cranking amperage (CCA) or 135 amperes.
   c. After 15 seconds, the voltage reading with the load still applied should be 9.6 volts or higher at 70° F (21° C). Now quickly remove the load and turn the tester OFF.

4. If the voltage reading is 9.6 volts or higher, the battery output capacity is good. If the reading is below 9.6 volts, the battery is defective.

5. With the tester OFF, disconnect the cables from the battery.

6. Install the battery as described in this section.

Charging

Refer to *Battery Initialization* (this section) if the battery is new.

To recharge a maintenance-free battery, a digital voltmeter and a charger with an adjustable amperage output are required. If this equipment is not available, have the battery charged by a repair shop with the proper equipment. Excessive voltage and amperage from an unregulated charger can damage the battery and shorten service life.

The battery should only self-discharge approximately one percent of its given capacity each day. If a battery not in use, without any loads connected, loses its charge within a week after charging, the battery is defective.

If the motorcycle is not used for long periods of time, an automatic battery charger with variable voltage and amperage outputs is recommended for optimum battery service life.

WARNING
During charging, highly explosive hydrogen gas is released from the battery. Only charge the battery in a well-ventilated area away from open flames, including pilot lights on appliances. Do not allow smoking in the area. Never check the charge of the battery by arcing across the terminals; the resulting spark can ignite the hydrogen gas.

CAUTION
Always disconnect the battery cables from the battery. If the cables are left connected during the charging procedure, the charger may damage the diodes within the voltage regulator/rectifier.

1. Remove the battery from the motorcycle as described in this section.

2. Set the battery on a stack of newspapers or shop cloths to protect the surface of the workbench.

3. Make sure the battery charger is turned off prior to attaching the charger leads to the battery.

4. Connect the positive charger lead to the positive battery terminal and the negative charger lead to the negative battery terminal.

5. Set the charger at 12 volts. If the output of the charger is variable, select the low setting.

6. The charging time depends on the discharged condition of the battery. Refer to **Table 2** for the suggested charging time. Normally, a battery should be charged at 1/10th its given capacity.

CAUTION
If the battery emits an excessive amount of gas during the charging cycle, decrease the charge rate. If the battery becomes hotter than 110° F (43° C) during the charging cycle, turn the charger off and allow the battery to cool. Then continue with a reduced charging rate and continue to monitor the battery temperature.

7. Turn the charger on.

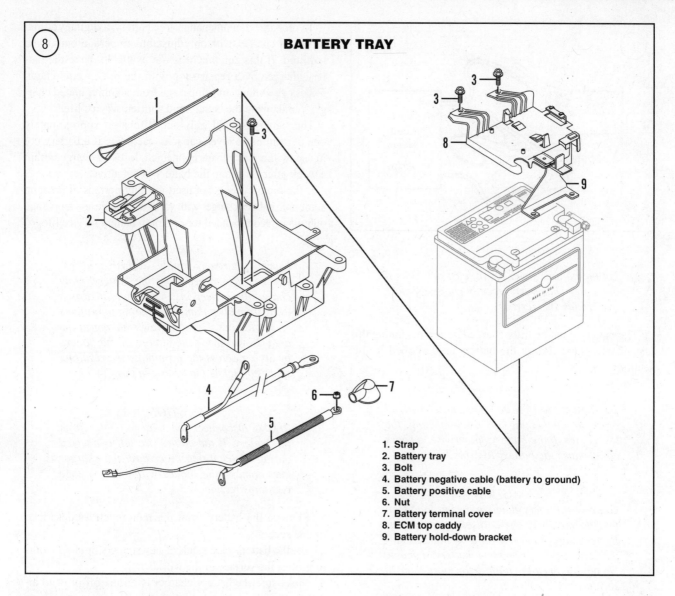

⑧ **BATTERY TRAY**

1. Strap
2. Battery tray
3. Bolt
4. Battery negative cable (battery to ground)
5. Battery positive cable
6. Nut
7. Battery terminal cover
8. ECM top caddy
9. Battery hold-down bracket

8. After the battery has been charged for the predetermined time, turn the charger off, disconnect the leads and measure the battery voltage. Refer to the following:

   a. If the battery voltage is 12.7 volts (at 68° F [20° C]), or greater, the battery is fully charged.

   b. If the battery voltage is 12.5 volts (at 68° F [20° C]), or lower, the battery is undercharged and requires additional charging time.

9. If the battery remains stable for one hour, the battery is charged.

10. Install the battery as described in this section.

Battery Initialization

A new battery must be *fully* charged to a specific gravity of 1.260-1.280 before installation. To bring the battery to a full charge, give it an initial charge. Using a new battery without an initial charge will cause permanent battery damage. The battery will never be able to hold more than an 80% charge. Charging a new battery after it has been used will not bring its charge to 100%. When purchasing a new battery, verify its charge status.

NOTE
Recycle the old battery. When a new battery is purchased, turn in the old one for recycling. Most motorcycle dealerships will accept the old battery in trade for a new one. Never place an old battery in the household trash since it is illegal, in most states, to place any acid or lead (heavy metal) in landfills.

BATTERY TRAY

Removal/Installation

Refer to **Figure 8**.

1. Remove the battery from the motorcycle as described in this chapter.

2. Remove both frame side covers as described in Chapter Fourteen.

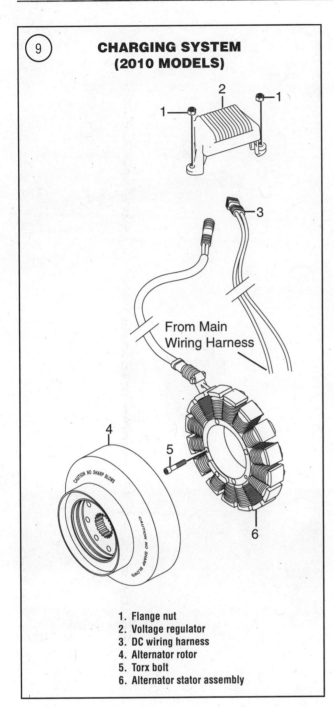

**⑨ CHARGING SYSTEM
(2010 MODELS)**

1. Flange nut
2. Voltage regulator
3. DC wiring harness
4. Alternator rotor
5. Torx bolt
6. Alternator stator assembly

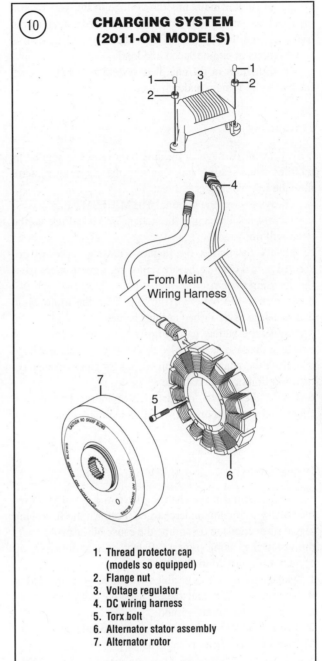

**⑩ CHARGING SYSTEM
(2011-ON MODELS)**

1. Thread protector cap
   (models so equipped)
2. Flange nut
3. Voltage regulator
4. DC wiring harness
5. Torx bolt
6. Alternator stator assembly
7. Alternator rotor

9

3. Remove both saddlebags as described in Chapter Fourteen.

4. Remove the rear wheel as described in Chapter Ten.

5. Remove the left side electrical caddy as described in this chapter.

6. Disconnect the Tour-Pak electrical connectors if routed through side of battery tray, on models so equipped.

7. Remove the ignition coil as described in this chapter.

8. Remove the ABS module, on models so equipped.

9. Pull the Turn Signal Security Module away from the battery tray, do not disconnect it.

10. Remove the four bolts securing the battery tray to the frame.

11. Carefully pull the battery tray toward the rear and remove it through the frame.

12. Inspect the battery tray for damage and/or corrosion. Thoroughly clean the tray and replace it if necessary.

13. Install by reversing the removal steps. Tighten the four battery tray mounting bolts to 72-96 in.-lb. (8.1-10.9 N•m).

CHARGING SYSTEM

Refer to **Figure 9** and **Figure 10**.

The charging system consists of the battery, alternator and a voltage regulator/rectifier. Alternating current generated by the alternator is rectified to direct current. The voltage regulator maintains the voltage to the battery and provides power for additional electrical loads, such as the lights and ignition system, at a constant voltage regardless of variations in engine speed and load.

A malfunction in the charging system generally causes the battery to remain undercharged.

Precautions

To prevent damage to the alternator and the regulator/ rectifier when testing and repairing the charging system, note the following precautions:

1. Always disarm the optional TSSM/HFSM security system before disconnecting the battery or Main Fuse so the siren will not sound.

2. Always disconnect the negative battery cable, as described in this chapter, before removing a component from the charging system.

3. To charge the battery, remove it from the motorcycle and recharge as described in this chapter.

4. Inspect the battery case (**Figure 6**). Look for bulges or cracks in the case, leaking electrolyte or corrosion build-up.

5. Check the charging system wiring for signs of chafing, deterioration or other damage.

6. Check the wiring for corroded or loose connections. Clean, tighten or reconnect wiring as required. Replace any damaged parts.

Inspection

A malfunction in the charging system generally causes the battery to remain undercharged. Perform the following visual inspections to determine the cause of the problem. If the visual inspection proves satisfactory, test the charging system as described in Chapter Two.

1. Make sure the battery cables are properly connected to the battery terminals and that the negative cable is properly connected to the frame ground.

2. Inspect the terminals for loose or corroded connections. Tighten or clean them as required.

3. Inspect the battery case. Look for bulges or cracks in the case, leaking electrolyte or corrosion buildup.

4. Carefully check all connections at the alternator to make sure they are clean and tight.

5. Check the circuit wiring for corroded or loose connections. Clean, tighten or connect wiring as required.

ALTERNATOR

WARNING
*All models have a laminated high-output rotor that is equipped with **very strong** magnets. On CVO models, a rotor puller must be used for rotor removal and installation. During installation, the magnets will quickly pull the rotor into place, avoid trapping fingers*

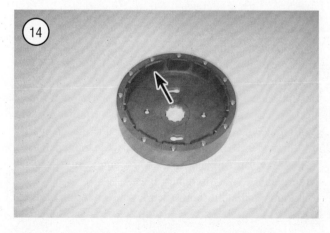

between the rotor (**Figure 11**) and the sharp
edge of the crankcase.

NOTE

*Always disarm the optional security system
(TSM/TSSM/HFSM) before disconnecting
the battery or pulling the main fuse so the siren will not sound.*

Rotor Removal/Installation
(CVO Models)

Refer to **Figure 10**.

1. Disconnect the negative battery cable as described in
this chapter.
2. Remove the primary chaincase cover and housing as described in Chapter Six.
3. Remove the primary chain, clutch assembly, chain tensioner assembly and compensating sprocket components
as an assembly (Chapter Six).
4. If still in place, remove the shaft extension and washer
from the crankshaft.
5. Assemble the rotor puller (**Figure 12**) or use a generic
bearing puller and two 5/16 in. × 3 in. coarse thread bolts.
6. Install the rotor puller over the crankshaft and against
the rotor.
7. Secure the rotor puller to the rotor with the two bolts
(A, **Figure 13**).
8. Slowly turn the center bolt (B, **Figure 13**) and withdraw
the rotor from the stator coils.
9. Remove the rotor and puller. Separate the puller from
the rotor.
10. Inspect the rotor magnets (**Figure 14**) for small bolts,
washers or other metal debris that may have been picked
up by the magnets. These small metal bits can cause severe
damage to the alternator stator assembly.
11. Check the inner splines (**Figure 15**) for wear or damage. Replace the rotor if necessary.
12. Install by reversing the removal steps. Align the rotor
splines with the crankshaft splines.

Rotor Removal/Installation
(All Models Except CVO)

Refer to **Figure 9**.

1. Disconnect the negative battery cable as described in
this chapter.
2. Remove the primary chaincase cover and housing as described in Chapter Six.
3. Remove the primary chain, clutch assembly, chain tensioner assembly and compensating sprocket components
as an assembly (Chapter Six).
4. If still in place, remove the shaft extension and washer
from the crankshaft.
5. Install a large bearing puller (**Figure 16**) or strap-type
flywheel holder (**Figure 17**) onto the rotor.
6. Pull on the bearing puller or flywheel holder and remove the rotor from the crankshaft.
7. Separate the tool from the rotor.
8. Inspect the rotor magnets for small bolts, washers or
other metal debris that may have been picked up by the
magnets. These small metal bits can cause severe damage
to the alternator stator assembly.
9. Check the inner splines for wear or damage. Replace
the rotor if necessary.
10. Install by reversing the removal steps. Align the rotor
splines with the crankshaft splines.

9

Stator Removal

NOTE
Some of the photographs in this procedure are shown with the engine removed to better illustrate the step.

1. Remove the rotor as described in this chapter.
2. On CVO models, remove the thread protector caps from the mounting studs.
3. Remove the flange nuts (A, **Figure 18**) securing the voltage regulator (B) to the frame studs.
4. Lift the voltage regulator (B, **Figure 18**) off the studs, release the wiring harness from the cable clip on the left side of the voltage regulator, and lower the regulator.
5. Disconnect the round 3-pin stator connector (A, **Figure 19**) from the base of the voltage regulator.
6. Remove the four Torx screws (**Figure 20**) securing the stator assembly to the crankcase. New Torx screws must be used on installation.
7. Insert a small awl (A, **Figure 21**), or screwdriver, into the space between the grommet and the crankcase and carefully lift the capped rib (B) on the grommet away from the crankcase opening (C). Tilt the awl slightly and squirt isopropyl alcohol or glass cleaner into the opening. Repeat this at one or two additional locations around the opening.
8. Push on the capped rib (B, **Figure 21**) from the outside of the opening. Place needlenose pliers on the cable stop, and withdraw the grommet through the crankcase bore. Rock the grommet back and forth to ease removal if necessary. Be careful not to damage the grommet ribs if the stator is going to be reused.
9. Remove the stator assembly.

Inspection

1. Inspect the stator mounting surface on the crankcase for any oil residue that may have passed by a damaged oil seal. Clean off if necessary.
2. Inspect the stator wires (A, **Figure 22**) for fraying or damage.
3. Inspect the rubber grommet (B, **Figure 22**) for deterioration or hardness.
4. Check the stator electrical connector pins for corrosion, looseness or damage.

Stator Installation

1. Thoroughly clean the grommet with isopropyl alcohol so the ribs are free of oil residue and debris.
2. Apply a light coat of glass cleaner to the wiring harness grommet to help ease it into the crankcase boss receptacle.

NOTE
Figure 23 is shown with the engine removed to better illustrate the step.

3. Insert the electrical harness and grommet into the crankcase boss receptacle and carefully pull it through until the grommet is correctly seated (**Figure 23**).

CAUTION
New Torx screws (T27) must be installed. The threadlock originally applied to the Torx screws is sufficient for one time use only. If a used Torx screw is installed it can work loose and cause engine damage.

4. Move the stator into position on the crankcase and install four *new* Torx screws (**Figure 20**). Tighten the stator screws (T27) to 55-75 in.-lb. (6.2-8.5 N•m).

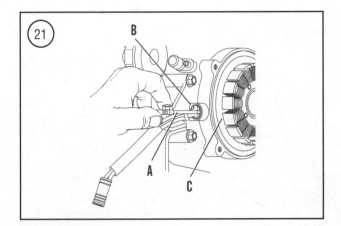

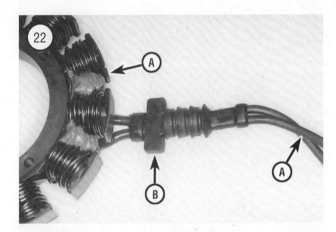

5. Insert the electrical harness under the front engine stabilizer link and then forward along the outboard side of the voltage regulator.

6. Secure the electrical harness in the cable clip under the left side of the voltage regulator. Remove all slack in the harness so it will not rub against the engine stabilizer link.

7. Connect the round 3-pin stator connector (A, **Figure 19**) onto the base of the voltage regulator. Push it on until it bottoms.

8. Move the voltage regulator (B, **Figure 18**) onto the mounting studs and install the flange nuts (A, **Figure 18**). Tighten the flange nuts to 70-100 in.-lb. (7.9-11.3 N•m).

9. Install the rotor as described in this section.

VOLTAGE REGULATOR

Removal/Installation

1. Disconnect the negative battery cable as described in this chapter.

2. On CVO models, remove the thread protector caps from the mounting studs.

3. Remove the flange nuts (A, **Figure 18**) securing the voltage regulator (B) to the frame studs.

4. Lift the voltage regulator (B, **Figure 18**) off the studs, release the wiring harness from the cable clip on the left side of the voltage regulator, and then turn it over.

5. Disconnect the round 3-pin stator connector (A, **Figure 19**) and the 2-pin square electrical connector (B) from the base of the voltage regulator.

6. Remove the voltage regulator from the frame.

7. Install by reversing the removal steps while noting the following:

   a. Install both electrical connectors onto the voltage regulator. Push them on until they click and lock into place.

   b. When installing the voltage regulator onto the lower frame member studs, move the electrical wires away from the studs. Make sure they are not pinched between frame member and the voltage regulator flange.

   c. Install the flange nuts (A, **Figure 27**) and tighten to 70-100 in.-lb. (7.9-11.3 N•m).

IGNITION SYSTEM

Operation

The ignition system consists of an ignition coil, two spark plugs, the electronic control module (ECM), crankshaft position sensor (CKP), manifold absolute pressure sensor (TMAP), intake air temperature sensor (IAT), idle air control (IAC), engine temperature sensor (ET) and vehicle speed sensor (VSS). Refer to **Figure 24** for sensor locations on the engine. The remaining sensors are located on the induction module.

The ECM is located on the top electrical caddy under the rider seat.

The ECM determines the spark advance for correct ignition timing based on signals from the IAT, ET, TP and O_2 sensors. The ignition system fires the spark plugs near top dead center for starting, and then varies the spark advance from 0° to 50°depending on engine speed, crankshaft position, and intake manifold pressure. It also regulates the low-voltage circuits between the battery and the ignition coil.

The ECM modules are not repairable and must be replaced if defective.

The crankshaft position (CKP) sensor is located in the front left side of the crankcase. The CKP sensor takes readings off the 30 teeth on the left side flywheel. There is a two-tooth wide gap in the rotor. This gap creates a reference point to determine engine speed so the ECM can regu-

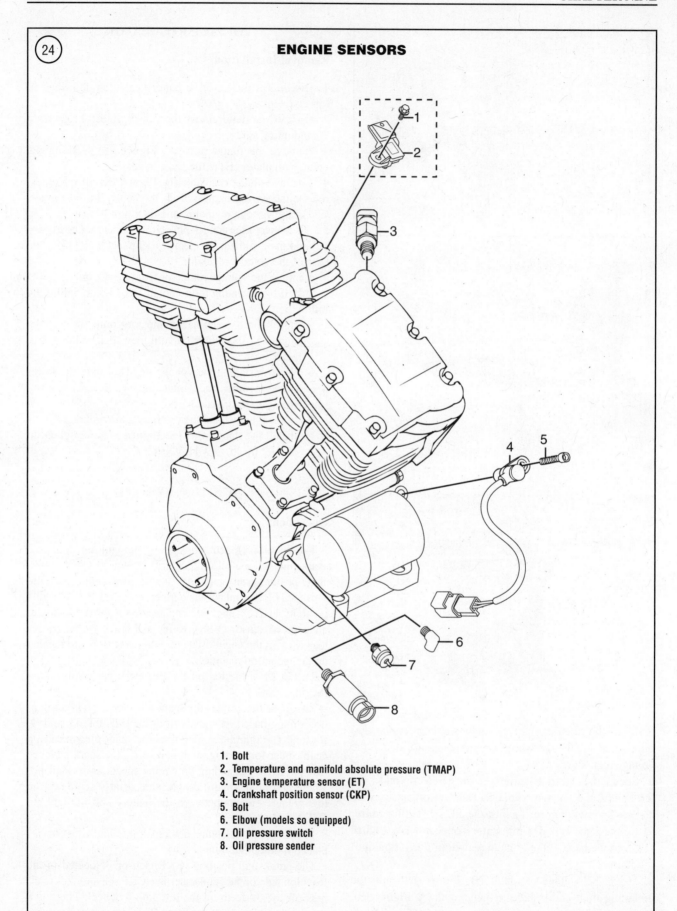

ENGINE SENSORS

(24)

1. Bolt
2. Temperature and manifold absolute pressure (TMAP)
3. Engine temperature sensor (ET)
4. Crankshaft position sensor (CKP)
5. Bolt
6. Elbow (models so equipped)
7. Oil pressure switch
8. Oil pressure sender

late ignition timing. The gap can also be used as a reference point to establish TDC.

The TMAP sensor is located on top of the intake manifold or induction module. This sensor monitors the intake manifold vacuum and sends this information to the electronic control module. The module adjusts the ignition timing advance curve for maximum performance.

The bank angle sensor is an integral part of the turn signal/turn signal security module (TSM/TSSM/HFSM). The sensor consists of a small magnetic disc that rides within a V-shaped channel. If the motorcycle is tilted at a 45° angle for more than one second, the ignition system shuts off. Once the sensor is activated, the motorcycle must be up-righted and the ignition must be turned off, and then back on so the ignition system is operational and the engine can be restarted.

The ignition systems components are shown in **Figure 25**. When servicing the ignition system, refer to the wiring diagrams located in Chapter Sixteen of this manual. Refer to Chapter Two for trouble shooting procedures.

IGNITION COIL

Removal/Installation

Refer to **Figure 25**.

> *NOTE*
> *Always disarm the optional security system (TSM/TSSM/HFSM) before disconnecting the battery or pulling the main fuse so the siren will not sound.*

1. Remove the top electrical caddy as described in this chapter.
2. Remove the battery as described in this chapter.
3. Disconnect the secondary wire (**Figure 26**) from each spark plug
4. Disconnect the front cylinder (A, **Figure 27**) and rear cylinder (B) secondary wire from the ignition coil.
5. Remove the bolts securing the ignition coil to the battery hold down bracket and battery tray.
6. Remove the battery hold down bracket from the frame.
7. Loosen the ground terminal nut, but do not remove it. Hold the ground terminal out of the way and remove the ignition coil from the frame.
8. Install the ignition coil by reversing these removal steps, note the following:
   a. Tighten the ground terminal nut to 50-90 in.-lb. (5.7-10.2 N•m).
   b. Tighten the ignition coil, hold down bracket bolts to 32-40 in.-lb. (3.6-4.5 N•m).

Performance Test

1. Disconnect the plug wire and remove one of the spark plugs as described in Chapter Three.

> *NOTE*
> *A spark tester (**Figure 28**) is a useful tool for testing the ignition system spark output. This tool (Motion Pro part No. 08-0122), or its equivalent, is inserted in the spark plug cap and its base is grounded against the cylinder head. The tool's air gap is adjustable, and it allows the visual inspection of the spark while testing the intensity of the spark.*

2. Insert a clean shop cloth into the spark plug hole in the cylinder head to lessen the chance of gasoline vapors being emitted from the hole.

> *WARNING*
> *The firing of the spark plug can ignite fuel that is ejected through the spark plug hole. Mount the spark plug, or tester, away from the spark plug hole. If the engine is flooded, do not perform this test.*

3. Insert a new spark plug (**Figure 29**), or a spark tester (**Figure 30**), into the spark plug cap and touch the base of the plug or tester against the cylinder head to ground it. Position the spark plug or tester so the electrical contacts are visible.

> *WARNING*
> *If necessary, hold onto the spark plug wire with a pair of insulated pliers. Do **not** hold the spark plug, wire or connector or a serious electrical shock may result.*

4. Turn the engine over with the starter. A fat blue spark should be evident across the spark plug electrode or spark tester. If there is strong sunlight on the plug, or tester, shade it so the spark is more visible. Repeat test for the other cylinder.
5. If a fat blue spark occurs, the ignition coil is good. If not, perform a resistance test as described in this section.

Resistance Test

> *NOTE*
> *Refer to **Electrical Component Replacement** at the beginning of this chapter.*

1. Remove the ignition coil as described in this section.
2. Disconnect the secondary wires from the ignition coil.
3. Measure the primary coil resistance between the terminals shown in **Figure 31**.
   a. Front coil: Terminal A and D.
   b. Rear coil: Terminal A and C.
4. Set the ohmmeter on its highest scale. Measure the resistance between the secondary terminals.
5. If the resistance values are less than specified in **Table 1**, there is most likely a short in the coil windings. Replace the coil (this section).

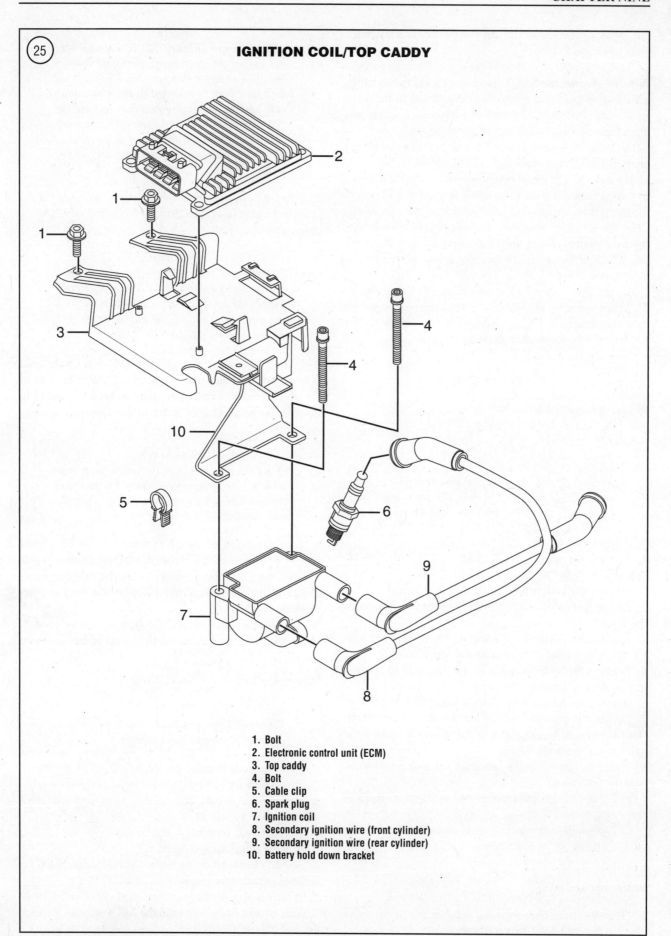

25

IGNITION COIL/TOP CADDY

1. Bolt
2. Electronic control unit (ECM)
3. Top caddy
4. Bolt
5. Cable clip
6. Spark plug
7. Ignition coil
8. Secondary ignition wire (front cylinder)
9. Secondary ignition wire (rear cylinder)
10. Battery hold down bracket

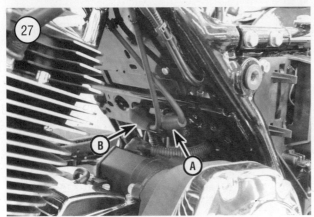

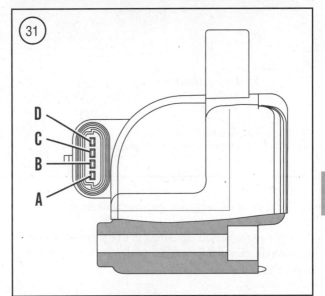

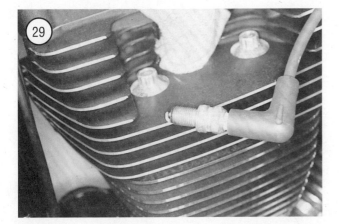

6. If the resistance values are more than specified, this may indicate corrosion or oxidation of the coil's terminals. Thoroughly clean the terminals, and spray with an aerosol electrical contact cleaner. Repeat the test and if the resistance value is still high, replace the coil (this section).

7. If the coil resistance does not meet (or come close to) either of these specifications, replace the coil. If the coil exhibits visible damage, replace it as described in this section.

8. Install the ignition coil as described in this section.

ELECTRONIC CONTROL MODULE (ECM)

Removal/Installation

NOTE
Always disarm the optional security system (TSSM/HFSM) before disconnecting the battery or before pulling the Main-Fuse so the siren will not sound.

Refer to **Figure 25**.

9

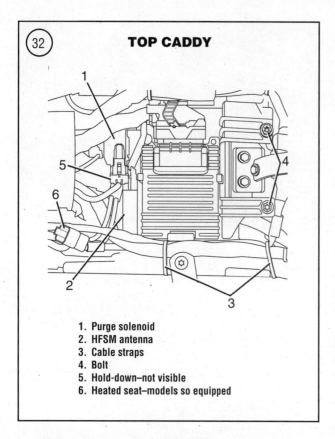

TOP CADDY

1. Purge solenoid
2. HFSM antenna
3. Cable straps
4. Bolt
5. Hold-down–not visible
6. Heated seat–models so equipped

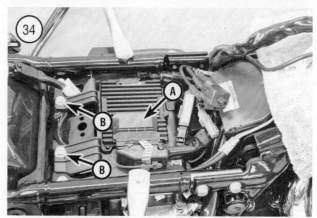

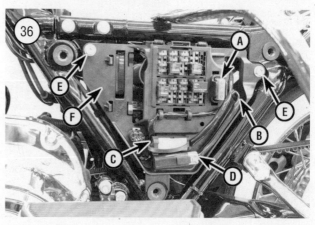

1. Disconnect the negative battery cable as described in this chapter.

2. Remove the seat as described in Chapter Fourteen.

3. Push the rear catch away, and carefully lift the ECM up and off the electrical caddy.

> *CAUTION*
> *Do not force the socket housing with the latches partially engaged. Doing so will damage the connector.*

4. Depress the button on the socket housing, and rotate the locking bar until it is seated in the rear most position. The locking bar index pin should now be engaged with the rear notch in the socket housing.

5. Gently pull the 73-pin Delphi connector from the ECM.

6. Install the ECM by reversing the removal steps. Ensure the ECM is correctly installed on the electrical caddy and that the rear catch is securely engaged.

ELECTRICAL CADDIES

Top Electrical Caddy
Removal/Installation

Refer to **Figure 32**.

1. Turn the ignition switch off.

2. Remove the seat and left side cover as described in Chapter Fourteen.

3. On models so equipped, move the purge solenoid (A, **Figure 33**) toward the side and release if from the top caddy.

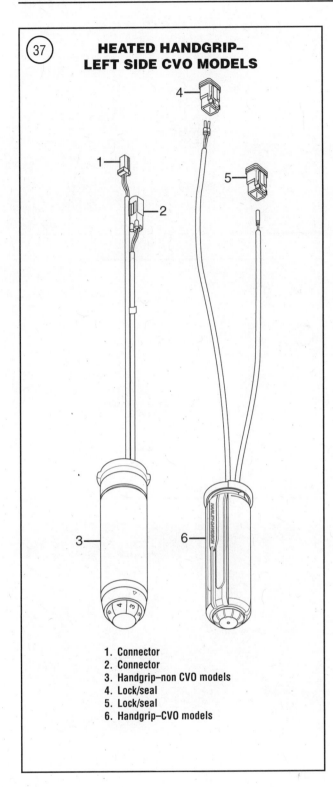

(37) HEATED HANDGRIP–
LEFT SIDE CVO MODELS

1. Connector
2. Connector
3. Handgrip–non CVO models
4. Lock/seal
5. Lock/seal
6. Handgrip–CVO models

4. On models so equipped, release the HFSM antenna (B, **Figure 33**) from the top caddy and model it out of the way.

5. Release the mounting clip on each side and lift the ECM (A, **Figure 34**) up and of the electrical caddy. Move it out of the way.

6. Remove the two mounting bolts (B, **Figure 34**) securing the top caddy.

7. Carefully remove the two cable ties securing wiring harness to the frame.

8. Carefully release the top caddy (**Figure 35**) from the battery hold-down bracket, rotate the top caddy out of the way and remove it from the frame.

9. Install by reversing these removal steps. Tighten the mounting bolts to 72-96 in.-lb. (8.1-10.9 N•m).

**Left Side Electrical Caddy
Removal/Installation**

> *NOTE*
> *Always disarm the optional security system (TSM/TSSM/HFSM) before disconnecting the battery or pulling the main fuse so the securing siren will not sound.*

1. Remove the seat as described in Chapter Fourteen

2. Remove the left side saddlebag and left side cover as described in Chapter Fourteen.

3. Remove the fuse block cover.

4. Remove the main fuse (A, **Figure 36**) as described in this chapter.

5. Disconnect the rear fender tip harness electrical connector (B, **Figure 36**) and slide the connector body off the mounting tab.

6. Carefully cut the strap securing the excess AM/FM antenna wire loop, on models so equipped.

7. Disconnect the sire and remove it from the side caddy, on models so equipped.

8. Remove the data link connector (C, **Figure 36**).

9. Remove the ABS diode pack (D, **Figure 36**), on models so equipped.

10. Remove the two mounting screws (E, **Figure 36**) securing the side caddy (F) to the frame.

11. Carefully cut the front and rear cable straps seucring the side caddy to the main wiring harness.

12. Reach around and remove the harness cover from the backside of the caddy.

13. Carefully remove the wiring harness through the square opening in the side caddy.

14. On the backside of the side caddy, squeeze the tabs at the top and bottom of the main fuse holder, and pull it away from the side caddy.

15. On the backside of the caddy, pull the tabs securing the fuse block to the daddy and remove it.

16. Remove the left side caddy from the frame.

17. Install by reversing these removal steps. Tighten the mounting screws to 72-96 in.-lb. (8.1-10.9 N•m).

HEATED LEFT SIDE HANDGRIP
(MODELS SO EQUIPPED)

Removal/Installation

Refer to **Figure 37**.

1. Remove the handlebar as described in Chapter Eleven.

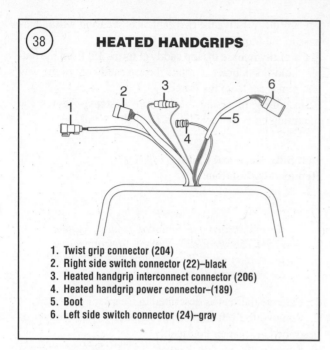

HEATED HANDGRIPS

38

1. Twist grip connector (204)
2. Right side switch connector (22)–black
3. Heated handgrip interconnect connector (206)
4. Heated handgrip power connector–(189)
5. Boot
6. Left side switch connector (24)–gray

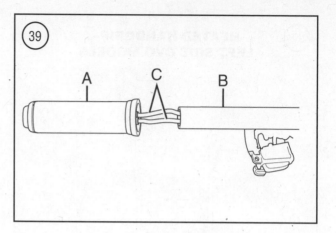

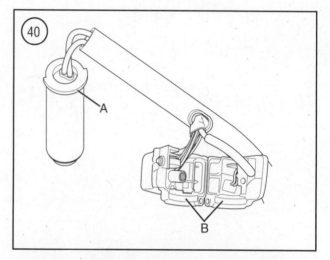

2. Disassemble the handlebar as described in Chapter Eleven to gain access to the electrical connectors (**Figure 38**).

3. Slide the handgrip (A, **Figure 39**) off the end of the handlebar (B).

NOTE
Refer to the instructions relating to the fish wire in Chapter Eleven. Make sure the end of the fish wire is still protruding from the center hole in the handlebar.

4. Grasp the handgrip interconnect and power harness (C, **Figure 39**) and gently pull the harness leads and fish wire from the handlebar.

5. Install by reversing these removal steps, note the following:

   a. Install the left side switch housing and over inboard end of handgrip.

   b. Position the rim of the handgrip (A, **Figure 40**) so it fits into the switch housing grooves (B). Install the switch housing screws and finger-tighten.

SENSORS

TMAP Sensor
Removal/Installation

NOTE
Always disarm the optional security system (TSM/TSSM/HFSM) before disconnecting the battery or pulling the main fuse so the siren will not sound.

1. Disconnect the negative battery cable as described in this chapter

2. Remove the fuel tank as described in Chapter Eight.

3. Remove the air filter and backing plate assembly as described in Chapter Eight.

4. Seal off the induction module opening to prevent the entry of debris.

5. Disconnect the electrical connector (A, **Figure 41**) from the TMAP sensor.

6. Remove the bolt (B, **Figure 41**) securing the TMAP sensor to the induction module.

7. Pull the TMAP sensor straight up and out of the induction module.

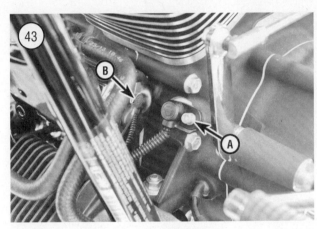

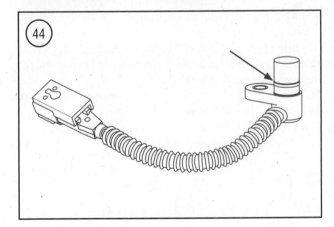

8. Install by reversing these removal steps. Tighten the bolts to 84-108 in.-lb. (9.5-12.2 N•m).

Crankshaft Position Sensor (CKP) Sensor Removal/Installation

NOTE
Always disarm the optional security system (TSSM/HFSM) before disconnecting the battery or before pulling the Main-Fuse so the siren will not sound.

1. Disconnect the negative battery cable as described in this chapter.

2. Remove the flange nuts (A, **Figure 42**) securing the voltage regulator (B) to the mounting bracket or frame.

3. Move the voltage regulator off the studs and lower it.

4. On the front, left side of the motorcycle, remove the Allen screw (A, **Figure 43**) and withdraw the CKP sensor and O-ring from the crankcase. Discard the O-ring.

5. Follow the wiring harness (B, **Figure 43**) down under the frame lower cross member, and locate the 2-pin CKP connector.

6. Disengage the small end of slot on attachment clip from T-stud on the bracket.

7. Depress the button on socket terminal side and disconnect the electrical connector.

8. Note the path of the harness and tubing out behind the lower stabilizer link and through the frame.

9. Carefully pull the wiring harness and convoluted tube out from under the voltage regulator mounting area. The harness and tube must be routed along the same path noted during removal.

10. Install by reversing the removal steps while noting the following:

    a. Apply clean engine oil to a *new* O-ring (**Figure 44**) on the CKP sensor prior to installation.

    b. Install the sensor and tighten the Allen screw to 100-120 in.-lb. (11.3-13.6 N•m).

Engine Temperature (ET) Sensor Removal/Installation

NOTE
Always disarm the optional security system (TSSM/HFSM) before disconnecting the battery or before pulling the Maxi-Fuse so the siren will not sound.

1. Disconnect the negative battery cable as described in this chapter.

2. Remove the fuel tank as described in Chapter Eight.

3. Remove the horn assembly (A, **Figure 45**) as described in this chapter.

4. On the left rear side of the front cylinder head, pull the rubber boot (B, **Figure 45**) back off the ET sensor.

5. Disconnect the electrical connector from the ET sensor.

6. Use a 3/4 in. deep socket and loosen the sensor. When the socket turns easily, remove the socket and completely unscrew the sensor by hand.

7. Install a new sensor and start it by hand. Using the socket, tighten the ET sensor to 120-180 in.-lb. (13.6-20.3 N•m).

8. Install the electrical connector and push it on until it locks into place.

9 Pull the rubber boot back over the electrical connector.

10. Install the horn assembly (A, **Figure 45**) as described in this chapter.

11. Install the fuel tank as described in Chapter Eight.

12. Connect the negative battery cable as described in this chapter.

Bank Angle (BAS) Sensor

The bank angle sensor is an integral part of the Turn Signal Security Module.

1. Remove the starter as described in this chapter.
2. Disconnect the 3-pin VSS connector (**Figure 46**) on the top of the transmission case.
3. Remove the screw securing the VSS to the top right side of the transmission housing and withdraw the sensor from the transmission case.
4. Install by reversing the removal steps while noting the following:
   a. Apply clean engine oil to a *new* O-ring on the VSS sensor prior to installation.
   b. Install the sensor and tighten the Allen screw to 84-132 in.-lb. (9.5-14.9 N•m).

STARTING SYSTEM

When servicing the starting system, refer to the wiring diagrams located in Chapter Sixteen of this manual.

CAUTION
Do not operate the starter for more than five seconds at a time. Let it cool approximately 10 seconds before operating it again.

Troubleshooting

Refer to Chapter Two.

STARTER

Refer to **Figure 47**.

Removal

1. Remove the seat as described in Chapter Fourteen.
2. Remove the exhaust system as described in Chapter Four.
3. Remove the battery and battery tray as described in this chapter.
4. Remove the engine oil dipstick from the transmission.
5. Wipe the area around the oil filler cap with a clean rag. Unscrew the oil filler cap/dipstick out of the transmission case. Cover the fill spout to keep out debris.
6. Remove the cover screw and chrome cover, on models so equipped.
7. Remove the nut from the bracket tab and remove the exhaust pipe support bracket.
8. Slide back the rubber boot, and remove the terminal nut from the battery-terminal post, and disconnect the positive battery cable ring terminals from the post.
9. Disconnect the solenoid connector (A, **Figure 48**) from the starter.

10. Remove the starter mounting bolts (B, **Figure 48**) and washers.
11. From the right side of the motorcycle, pull the starter straight out of the crankcase and remove it. Do not lose the locating dowels (A, **Figure 49**).
12. Close off the primary chaincase opening (B, **Figure 49**) with a shop cloth to prevent the entry of debris.
13. If necessary, service the starter, drive housing or solenoid housing as described in this section.

Installation

1. Remove the shop cloth from the crankcase opening (B, **Figure 49**).
2. Press the locating dowels (A, **Figure 49**) into the crankcase, if removed.
3. Install the starter, and push it in until it bottoms.
4. Apply Loctite Threadlocker 243 (blue) to the bolt threads. Install the starter mounting bolts (B, **Figure 48**) and washers.Tighten the mounting bolts to 25-27 ft.-lb. (33.9-36.6 N•m).
5. Connect the solenoid connector (A, **Figure 48**) to the starter.
6. Connect the positive battery cable onto the battery-terminal post, and install the terminal nut. Tighten the nut securely, and slide the rubber boot into position. .
7. Install the exhaust pipe support bracket and nut onto the bracket tab, and tighten the nut securely.

STARTER

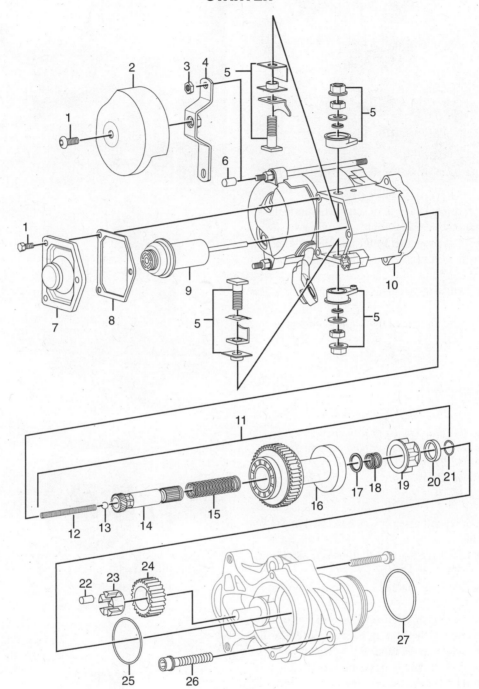

1. Screw	12. Return spring	23. Idle gear bearing
2. Cover	13. Ball	24. Idle gear
3. Nut	14. Drive shaft	25. O-ring
4. Mounting bracket	15. Drive spring	26. Bolt
5. Motor-terminal post	16. Starter clutch	27. O-ring
6. Cap--thread protector	17. Spring seat	
7. Solenoid cover	18. Spring	*All parts indicated as number
8. Rubber gasket	19. Pinion gear	11 are included in the Clutch
9. Plunger	20. Cup	Assembly rebuild kit, and none
10. Field coil/armature	21. Snap ring	of these parts are available
11. Clutch assembly*	22. Roller bearing	separately.

9

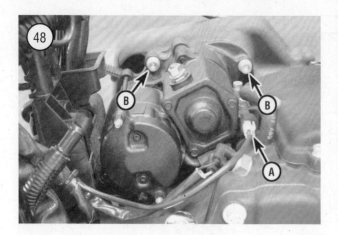

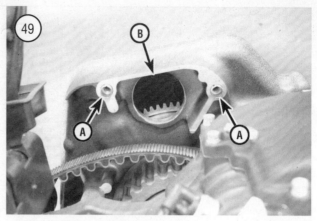

8. Install the chrome cover and screw, on models so equipped. Tighten the screw securely.

9. Uncover the fill spout and screw the oil filler cap/dipstick into of the transmission case. Tighten the dipstick securely.

10. Install the battery tray (this chapter).

11. Install the exhaust system as described in Chapter Four.

12. Install the seat as described in Chapter Fourteen.

Drive Housing

Disassembly/Inspection

> *NOTE*
> *Many of the individual parts of the starter drive housing are no longer sold separately. Items No. 12-21 in **Figure 47** are now available only as an assembly called the **Clutch Subassembly**.*

1. Remove the field coil assembly as described in *Starter Disassembly* (this section).

2. Remove the two drive housing Phillips screws (**Figure 50**).

3. Tap the drive housing, and remove it from the solenoid housing.

4. Remove the idler gear (**Figure 51**) from the bearing cage, and then remove the bearing cage (**Figure 52**). Do not lose the five rollers in the cage.

5. Push the drive shaft, and remove the starter clutch assembly (A, **Figure 53**) from the housing.

6. If necessary, disassemble the starter clutch assembly by performing the following:

    a. Compress the assembly's internal springs, and remove the snap ring from the end of the drive shaft.

    b. Remove the cup and pinion gear (**Figure 54**).

    c. Remove the short spring and spring seat.

    d. Press the splined end of the drive shaft, and remove it from the starter clutch.

    e. Remove the return spring (A, **Figure 55**) from the drive shaft (B) bore or from the solenoid plunger shaft (**Figure 56**) in the solenoid housing.

    f. Remove the steel ball from the drive shaft bore.

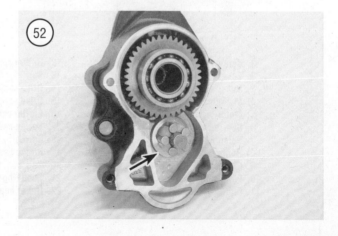

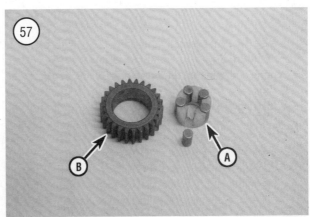

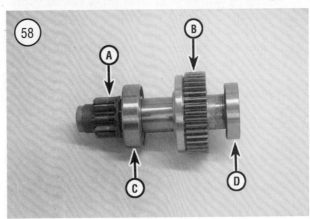

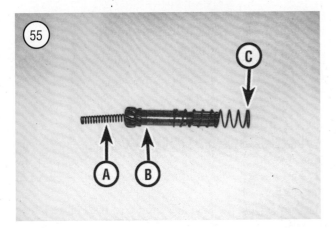

g. Remove the drive spring (C, **Figure 55**) from the drive shaft.

7. Inspect the idler gear bearing and cage assembly (A, **Figure 57**) for worn or damaged parts.

8. Inspect the springs for kinks or fatigue.

9. Check the idler gear (B, **Figure 57**), pinion gear (A, **Figure 58**) and starter clutch gear (B) for worn or damage teeth.

10. Inspect the bearings (C, **Figure 58**). They should rotate freely with no roughness.

11. Inspect the drive shaft (B, **Figure 55**) for worn or damaged splines or gear teeth.

12. Inspect the drive housing outer O-ring (B, **Figure 53**) and the O-ring in the housing bore. Replace as needed.

Assembly

1. Lubricate the starter drive shaft (B, **Figure 55**) with a high-temperature grease and install the return spring (C) into the shaft.

2. Lubricate the drive housing outer O-ring (B, **Figure 53**) and the O-ring in the housing bore with a high-temperature grease.

3. If disassembled, assemble the starter clutch assembly by performing the following:

   a. Slide the drive spring (A, **Figure 55**) onto the splined end of the drive shaft (C).

b. Slide the splined end of the drive shaft into the gear end of the starter clutch bore.

c. Select a deep socket that matches the outside diameter of the drive shaft. Insert the socket into the starter clutch bore, and stand the socket upright on the bench.

d. Press the starter clutch down so the socket presses the drive shaft into the starter clutch bore until the splined end of the shaft emerges from the starter clutch bearing.

e. Install the spring seat, short spring, pinion gear and cup onto the splined end of the drive shaft. The collar on the pinion gear and the concave side of the cup must face up away from the starter clutch.

f. Continue to compress the assembly, and install a new snap ring onto the drive shaft. Make sure the ring is completely seated in the shaft groove. Release the tension on the starter clutch and check the snap ring. It must be completely seated within the concave part of the cup.

g. Remove the socket from the starter clutch bore.

4. Lubricate the starter clutch bearing (A, **Figure 53**) with a high-temperature grease, and install the starter clutch into the drive housing (C). Make sure the clutch bearing is seated in the bearing bore.

5. Lubricate the bearing rollers and bearing cage with a high-temperature grease. Install the rollers into the cage (A, **Figure 57**), and then install the bearing cage (**Figure 52**) onto the shaft in the drive housing.

6. Lubricate the idler gear (**Figure 51**) with a high-temperature grease, and install it over the bearing cage.

7. Install the ball (**Figure 59**) into the drive shaft bore.

8. Apply a high-temperature grease to the solenoid plunger shaft, and slide the return spring (**Figure 56**) onto the shaft.

9. Fit the drive housing onto the solenoid housing so the return spring (**Figure 56**) will slide into the drive shaft bore within the starter clutch.

10. Install the two drive housing Phillips screws (**Figure 50**) and tighten securely.

11. Install the field coil assembly as described in *Starter Assembly* (this section).

Solenoid Housing Disassembly/Inspection/Assembly

Refer to **Figure 60**.

1. Remove the field coil assembly as described in *Starter Disassembly* (this section).

2. Remove the two drive housing Phillips screws (**Figure 50**).

3. Tap the drive housing, and remove it from the solenoid housing. If the return spring (**Figure 56**) remains with the solenoid plunger, do not lose the ball (**Figure 59**) in the starter clutch bore.

4. Remove the solenoid cover bolts (A, **Figure 61**), and remove the solenoid cover (B) and gasket.

5. Remove the plunger assembly from the solenoid housing.

6. Inspect the rubber cap (A, **Figure 62**) for hardness or deterioration; replace if necessary.

7. Inspect the plunger (B, **Figure 62**) and shaft (C) for wear or damage; replace if necessary.

8. Inspect the solenoid housing (A, **Figure 63**) for wear, cracks or other damage.

9. Inspect each terminal post assembly on the solenoid housing. If any part is worn or damaged, install a new solenoid repair kit. Individual terminal parts are not available.

10. Assemble the solenoid housing by reversing the disassembly steps while noting the following:

a. Lubricate the solenoid plunger with a high-temperature grease.

b. Install a new gasket.

c. Install the field coil assembly as described in *Starter Assembly* (this section).

Solenoid Contacts Removal/Installation

Refer to **Figure 60**.

NOTE
A solenoid contact repair kit is available from the manufacturer.

1. Purchase a solenoid contact repair kit prior to starting this procedure.

2. Perform *Solenoid Housing Disassembly* as described in this section.

3. Disassemble the field coil short post (B, **Figure 63**) as follows:

a. Remove the hex nut, if still in place.

b. Remove the jam nut, wave washer, round bushing and O-ring from the post.

c. On the inside, remove the post bolt, hold-in terminal contact plate and square bushing.

4. Disassemble the battery long post (C, **Figure 63**) as follows:

a. Remove the hex nut, if still in place.

b. Remove the jam nut, wave washer, round bushing and O-ring from the post.

c. On the inside, remove the post bolt, contact plate, square bushing and paper insulator washer.

5. Assemble the field coil short post (B, **Figure 63**) as follows:

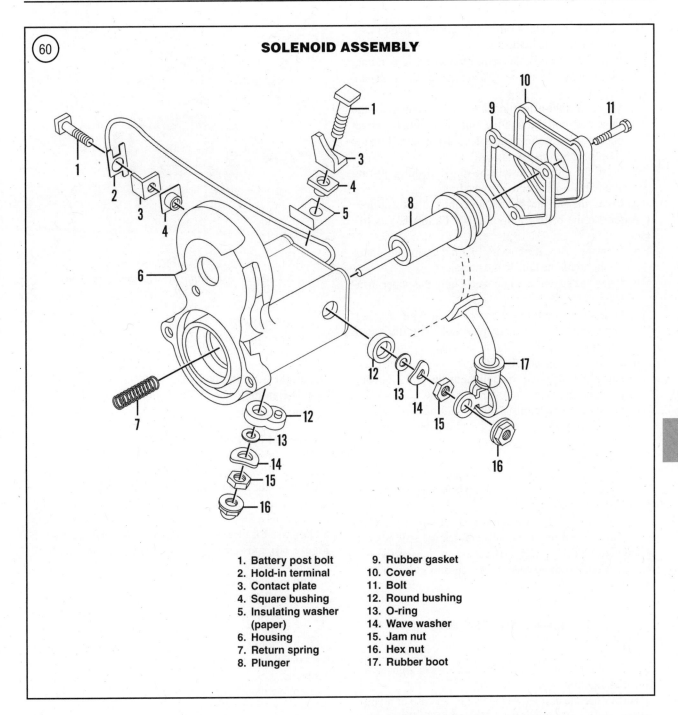

SOLENOID ASSEMBLY

1. Battery post bolt
2. Hold-in terminal
3. Contact plate
4. Square bushing
5. Insulating washer (paper)
6. Housing
7. Return spring
8. Plunger
9. Rubber gasket
10. Cover
11. Bolt
12. Round bushing
13. O-ring
14. Wave washer
15. Jam nut
16. Hex nut
17. Rubber boot

9

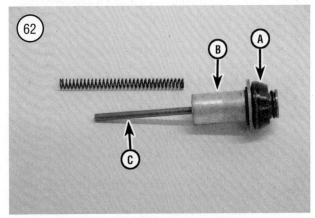

a. Working inside the housing, insert the square bushing into the hole in the housing.
b. Hold the inboard foot against the solenoid winding, and then align the contact plate hole with the square bushing.
c. Move the hold-in terminal into position and insert the short post bolt through the hold-in terminal, contact plate, square bushing and solenoid housing. Hold the short post bolt in place.
d. From the outside, install the round bushing, O-ring and wave washer onto the post bolt.
e. Install the jam nut, but do not tighten it at this time.

6. Assemble the battery long post (C, **Figure 63**) as follows:
a. Working inside the housing, align the paper insulator washer with the hole in the housing.
b. Insert the square bushing sleeve into the paper insulator.
c. Hold the inboard foot against the solenoid winding, and then align the contact plate hole with the square bushing.
d. Insert the long post bolt through the contact plate, square bushing and solenoid housing. Hold the long post bolt in place.
e. From the outside, install the round bushing, O-ring and wave washer onto the post bolt. Make sure that the round bushing index pin enters the blind hole in the solenoid housing.
f. Install the jam nut, but do not tighten it at this time.

7. Complete the *Solenoid Housing Assembly* procedure as described in this section.
8. Alternately tighten the jam nuts to 60-80 in.-lb. (7.3-9.0 N•m). Ensure that the contact plates are still correctly aligned with the plunger. If necessary, loosen the jam nut(s), reposition the contact plates and retighten the jam nuts to specification.

LIGHTING SYSTEM

The lighting system consists of a headlight, passing lights, taillight/brake light combination, turn signals and Tour-Pak lighting.

Always use the correct wattage bulb. The use of a larger wattage bulb will give a dim light and a smaller wattage bulb will burn out prematurely. Refer to **Table 4** or **Table 5** for bulb specifications.

Many of the following procedures refer to disconnecting a specific electrical connector located within the headlight or the front fairing assembly. Refer to *Electrical Connector Location and Identification* (this chapter).

HEADLIGHT

WARNING
If the headlight has just burned out or just been turned off, it will be hot. To avoid burned fingers, allow the bulb to cool prior to removal.

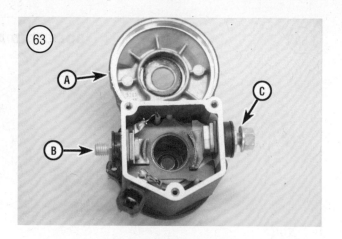

CAUTION
All models are equipped with a quartz-halogen bulb. Do not touch the bulb glass. Traces of body oil left on the bulb will drastically reduce its life. Clean all traces of oil from the bulb glass with a cloth moistened in alcohol or lacquer thinner.

**Headlight Bulb Replacement
(Single Headlight Road King and Fork Mounted Fairing Models)**

Refer to **Figure 64** and **Figure 65**.
1. Place a shop cloth or towel on the front bumper to protect the finish.
2. Remove the screw (A, **Figure 66**) at the base of the trim bezel (B), and then remove the trim bezel from the headlight lens assembly. Do not lose the two springs on the trim bezel.
3. Remove the three screws securing the retaining ring (B, **Figure 66**) and remove the ring while holding the headlight lens assembly in place.
4. Pull the lens assembly (**Figure 67**) out of the front fairing, or headlight nacelle.
5. On models so equipped, squeeze the two external tabs to release the electrical connector from the lens assembly.
6. Pull *straight out* and disconnect the electrical connector from the bulb (**Figure 68**) and remove the headlight assembly.
7. Remove the rubber cover (**Figure 69**) from the back of the headlight lens. Check the rubber boot (**Figure 70**) for tears or deterioration; replace if necessary.
8. Unhook the light bulb retaining clip (**Figure 71**) and pivot it out of the way.
9. Remove and discard the blown bulb (**Figure 72**).
10. Align the tangs on the new bulb with the notches in the headlight lens and install the bulb.
11. Securely hook the retaining clip over the bulb (**Figure 71**).
12. Install the rubber boot (**Figure 70**) and makes sure it is correctly seated against the bulb and the retainer.
13. Correctly align the electrical plug terminals with the bulb and connect it. Push it *straight on* until it bottoms on the bulb and the rubber cover (**Figure 69**).
14. Check headlight operation.

64 HEADLIGHT ASSEMBLY (FORK MOUNT FAIRING MODELS)

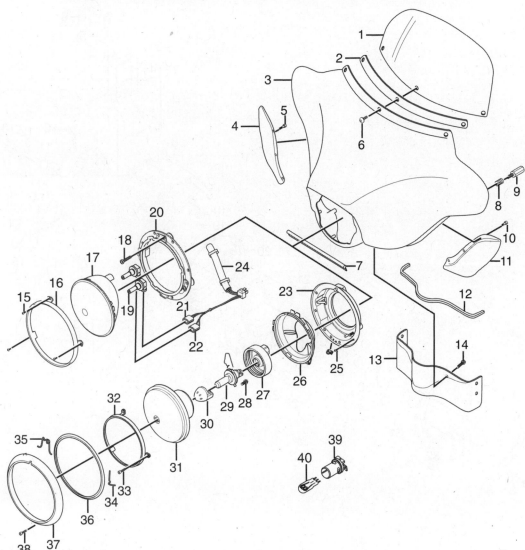

1. Windshield
2. Tape
3. Front fairing
4. Air deflector (models so equipped)
5. Screw
6. Screw
7. Seal strip
8. Insert
9. Nut extension
10. Screw
11. Air deflector (models so equipped)
12. Trim
13. Chrome mounting bracket
14. Screw
15. Screw*
16. Retaining ring*
17. Headlamp lens*
18. Bulbs—low and high beam*
19. Screw*
20. Mounting ring assembly*
21. Bulb socket—gray*

22. Bulb socket--black*
23. Headlight housing
24. Wiring harness*
25. Screw
26. Mounting ring
27. Rubber boot
28. Bolt
29. Bulb
30. Bulb cover
31. Headlight lens
32. Retaining ring
33. Screw
34. Bottom spring
35. Top spring
36. Gasket
37. Trim bezel
38. Screw
39. Socket (HDI only)
40. Position lamp socket (HDI only)
   *CVO models only

9

HEADLIGHT AND NACELLE (ROAD KING MODELS)

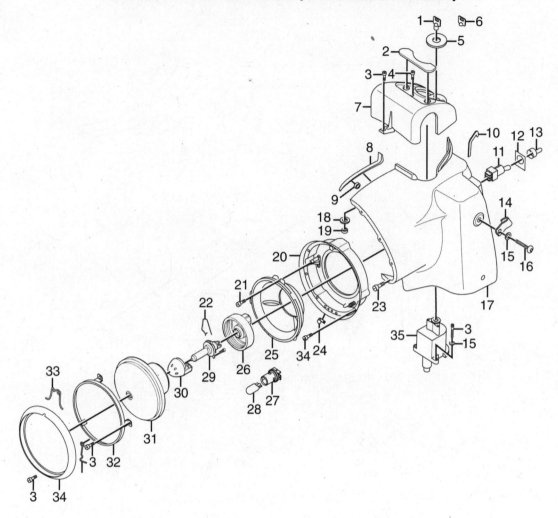

1. Key
2. Trim plate
3. Screw
4. Screw
5. Trim plate
6. Key cover
7. Handlebar cover
8. Trim
9. Speed nut
10. Trim
11. Switch
12. Label
13. Rubber boot
14. Clamp
15. Washer
16. Screw
17. Headlight nacelle (left side shown)
18. Washer

19. Nut with washer
20. Headlight housing
21. Screw
22. Retaining clip
23. Screw
24. Screw
25. Mounting ring
26. Rubber boot
27. Position lamp socket (HDI only)
28. Position lamp (HDI only)
29. Bulb
30. Bulb cover
31. Headlight lens
32. Retaining ring
33. Top spring
34. Headlight lens
35. Ignition switch

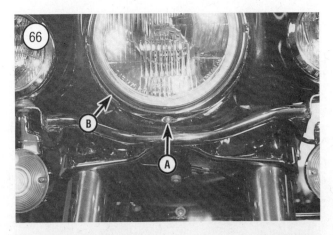

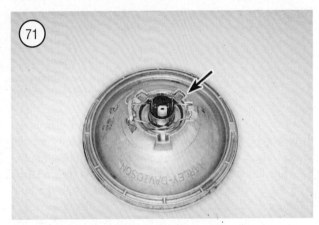

9

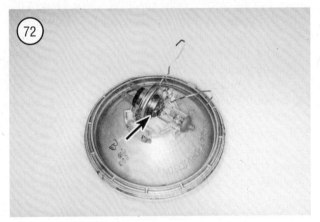

15. Insert the lens assembly (**Figure 68**) into the headlight housing and seat it correctly.

16. Install the retaining ring (B, **Figure 66**) and the three screws. Tighten the screws (A, **Figure 66**) securely.

17. Install the square portion of the top spring (**Figure 73**) into the slot in the trim bezel and snap the trim bezel into place. Install the screw and tighten securely.

18. Check headlight adjustment as described in this section.

Headlight Bulb Replacement
(Single Headlight FLHRSE Models)

Refer to **Figure 74**.

1. Place a shop cloth or towel on the front bumper to protect the finish.

2. Remove the screw at the base of the trim bezel, and then remove the trim bezel from the headlight lens assembly. Do not lose the top spring on the trim bezel.

3. Support the headlight lens and remove the three Phillips screws (A, **Figure 75**).

4. Carefully pull straight out on the bottom of the ring (B, **Figure 75**). Lift the ring up and remove it from the headlight lens while holding the headlight lens assembly in place. Lay the lens assembly on cloths covering the front fender.

5. Pinch the two latches on the low beam electrical connector (A, **Figure 76**) and remove it from the bulb socket (B).

6. Grasp the low bulb socket (B, **Figure 76**) and turn it approximately 1/8 turn *counterclockwise*. Withdraw it from the headlight shell and discard the blown low beam bulb.

7. Pinch the two latches on the high beam electrical connector (C, **Figure 76**) and remove it from the bulb socket (D).

8. Grasp the bulb socket (D, **Figure 76**) and turn it approximately 1/8 turn *counterclockwise*. Withdraw it from the headlight shell and discard the blown high beam bulb.

9. Align the tangs on the new low beam bulb (green label) with the notches in the headlight lens and install the bulb (B, **Figure 76**). Turn it approximately 1/8 turn *clockwise*.

10. Align the tangs on the new high beam bulb (yellow label) with the notches in the headlight lens and install the bulb (D, **Figure 76**). Turn it approximately 1/8 turn *clockwise*.

11. Attach the connector to each bulb assembly. Push on each of the connectors until it clicks into place.

12. Check headlight function.

13. Move the headlight lens assembly into place, install the retaining ring and the three Phillips screws (A, **Figure 75**). Tighten the screws to 23-28 in.-lb. (2.6-3.2 N•m).

14. Make sure the rubber gasket is in place in the trim bezel and is held in place with the three small springs.

15. Make sure the top spring is in place at the top center location.

16. Position the trim bezel onto the top portion of the headlight case. Fit the square shaped section of the spring into the slot at the top of the back plate.

17. Carefully press the trim bezel down until it is positioned correctly with equal amounts of gasket visible between the headlight assembly and the trim bezel.

18. Install the screw at the base of the trim ring and tighten securely.

19. Check headlight adjustment as described in this section.

Headlight Bulb Replacement (Dual Headlight Models)

Refer to **Figure 77** or **Figure 78**.

1. Remove the front fairing and windshield assembly as described in Chapter Fourteen.

2. Place the front fairing on a workbench covered with several towels to protect the finish.

3. Remove the rubber boot (**Figure 79**) from the back of the lens assembly. Check the rubber boot for tears or deterioration; replace if necessary.

4. Rotate the bulb retainer (A, **Figure 80**) *counterclockwise* and remove it from the lens assembly.

5. Remove and discard the blown bulb (B, **Figure 80**).

6. Position the new bulb with the wider tab at the top. Insert this tab under the flange, and push the bottom of bulb flange so the lower two tabs side fit snugly in the slot of the bulb housing.

7. Place the bulb retainer (B, **Figure 80**) over the bulb, and carefully rotate it *clockwise* until it is secure in the lens assembly.

8. Install the rubber boot (**Figure 79**) and make sure it is correctly seated against the bulb and the retainer.

9. Repeat the process to replace the other bulb if necessary.

10. Install the front fairing and windshield assembly as described in Chapter Fourteen.

11. Check headlight operation.

12. Check headlight adjustment as described in this section.

Headlight Lens Removal/Installation (Dual Headlight Models)

Refer to **Figure 77** or **Figure 78**.

1. Remove the front fairing and windshield assembly as described in Chapter Fourteen.

2. Place the front fairing on workbench covered with several towels to protect the finish.

3. On the inboard surface of the outer fairing, carefully depress the two upper tabs (**Figure 81**) of the lens cover with a flat-bladed screwdriver. Repeat for the two lower tabs and remove the lens cover (**Figure 82**) from the front side of the fairing.

4. Remove the plastic protective sleeve (A, **Figure 83**) from the top center hex adjuster stud.

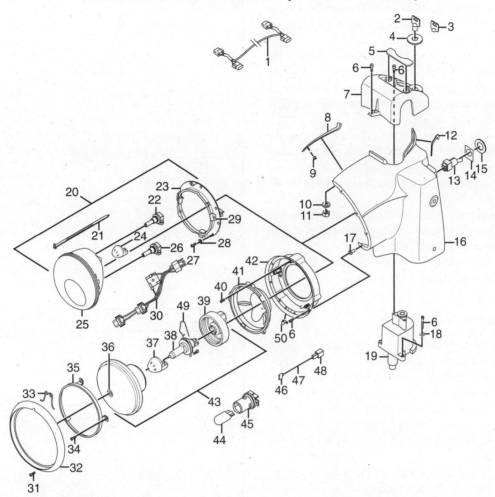

HEADLIGHT AND NACELLE (FLHRSE MODELS)

74

9

1. Harness
2. Key
3. Key cover
4. Trim plate
5. Plate
6. Screw
7. Handlebar cover
8. Trim
9. Screw
10. Washer
11. Nut with washer
12. Trim
13. Switch
14. Label
15. Rubber boot
16. Headlight nacelle (left side shown)
17. Retaining clip*
18. Washer
19. Ignition switch
20. Headlight assembly (CVO models)
21. Cable strap
22. Bulb–low beam
23. Mounting ring
24. Bulb cover
25. Headlight lens
26. Bulb–high beam
27. Screw
28. Washer
29. Screw
30. Wiring harness
31. Screw
32. Trim bezel
33. Top spring
34. Screw
35. Retaining ring
36. Headlight lens
37. Bulb cover*
38. Bulb*
39. Rubber boot*
40. Screw
41. Mounting ring
42. Headlight housing
43. Headlight assembly
44. Position lamp*
45. Position lamp socket*
46. Terminal*
47. Jumper harness*
48. Terminal*
49. Retaining clip*
50. Clamp
 * HDI models only

5. Depress the mounting clips on all three hex adjuster studs (B, **Figure 83**) and carefully remove the lens assembly (C) from the front side of the front fairing (D). Do not damage the stud holes in the front fairing during lens removal.

6. Align the lens hex adjuster studs with the holes in the front fairing, and slowly push the lens assembly into the front fairing until the mounting clips engage the inboard side of the outer fairing. Ensure that all three studs are fully engaged with the outer fairing.

7. To avoid cutting or chafing headlight wiring, install the plastic protective sleeve (A, **Figure 83**) onto the top center hex adjuster stud.

8. Clean the outer surface of the lens assembly and the inner surface of the lens cover.

9. Carefully snap the lens cover bottom two tabs into place in the inner fairing. Repeat for the upper two tabs and make sure the lens cover is securely held in place.

10. Install the front fairing and windshield assembly as described in Chapter Seventeen.

Headlight Adjustment (All Models)

1. Park the motorcycle on a level surface approximately 25 ft. (7.6 m) from the wall (**Figure 84**).

2. Check tire inflation pressure, readjust to the correct pressure if necessary as described in Chapter Three.

3. Draw a horizontal line on the wall at is same height above floor at the center of the headlight.

4. Have a helper the approximate weight of the principal rider sit on the seat.

5. Aim the headlight at the wall and turn on the headlight. Switch the headlight to the high beam.

6. Position the front wheel directly at straight ahead.

7. Check the headlight beam alignment. The broad, flat pattern of light (main beam of light) should be centered on the horizontal line (equal area of light above and below line).

8. Turn the key switch to the ignition position.

9. Now check the headlight beam lateral alignment. With the headlight beam pointed straight ahead (centered), there should be an equal area of light to the left and right of center.

10A. On dual head light models, if the beam is incorrect as described in this section, adjust the headlight as follows.

> *NOTE*
> *Figure 85 is shown with the meter assembly removed. Do not remove the meter assembly for this procedure. The hex-adjusters are located on each side of the lower inner surface of the front fairing.*

  a. Use a 4.5 mm socket on a flexible extension and adjust the hex-adjuster (**Figure 85**).
  b. Refer to **Table 5** for the correct rotation of the adjusters to achieve correct headlight aim.

10B. On all other models, if the beam is incorrect as described in this section, adjust the headlight as follows.

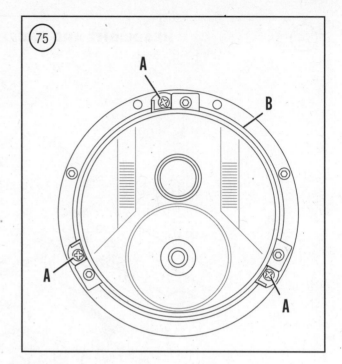

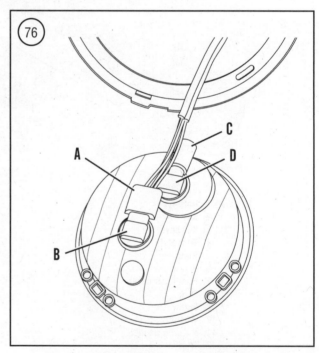

  a. Turn the top vertical adjuster (A, **Figure 86**) to adjust headlight vertically.
  b. Turn the right side horizontal adjuster (B, **Figure 86**) to adjust headlight horizontally.

PASSING LIGHTS AND FRONT TURN SIGNALS

Passing Light and Front Turn Signal Bulb Replacement (FLHR and FLHT Series Models)

Refer to **Figure 87**.

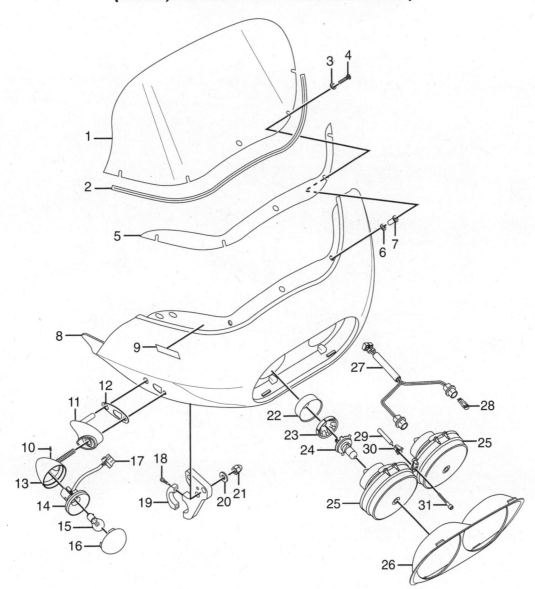

(77)

**HEADLIGHT AND FRONT RURN SIGNAL
(FLTRX, FLTRXSE AND FLTRUSE MODELS)**

1. Windshield
2. Trim
3. Washer
4. Screw
5. Decal
6. Rubber washer
7. Well nut
8. Front fairing
9. Isolator strip
10. Set screw
11. Turn signal housing
12. Mounting bracket
13. Gasket
14. Socket assembly
15. Bulb
16. Lens

17. Terminal
18. Screw
19. Clamp and fairing mount
20. Washer
21. Acorn nut
22. Rubber boot
23. Bulb retainer
24. Bulb
25. Lens assembly
26. Trim
27. Wiring harness
28. Bulb
29. Thread protector
30. Thread protector cap
31. Adjustment stud

9

(78) **HEADLIGHT AND FRONT TURN SIGNAL (2013 FLTRXSE MODELS)**

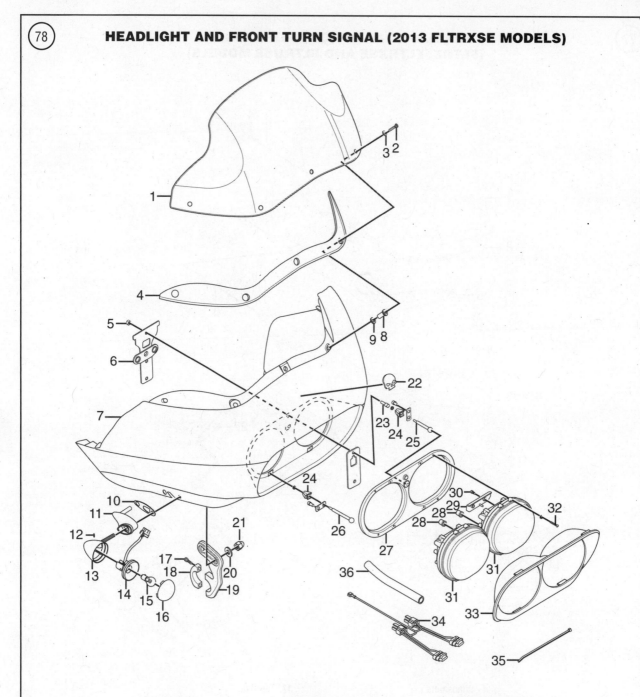

1. Windshield	13. Housing	25. Adjustment stud
2. Screw	14. Socket assembly	26. Adjustment stud
3. Washer	15. Bulb	27. Trim
4. Decal	16. Lens	28. Bushing
5. Nut	17. Screw	29. Mounting clip
6. Bracket	18. Clamp	30. Screw
7. Front fairing	19. Fairing mount	31. Headlamp
8. Well nut	20. Washer	32. Screw
9. Rubber washer	21. Acorn nut	33. Trim
10. Gasket	22. Medallion	34. Wiring harness
11. Mounting bracket	23. Tread protector cap	35. Cable strap
12. Set screw	24. Mounting clip	

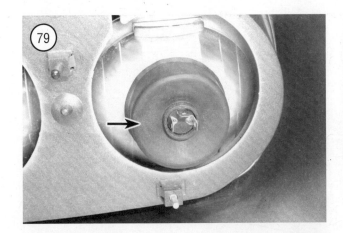

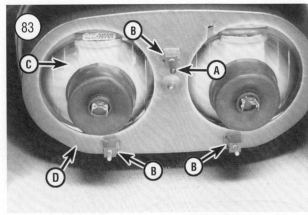

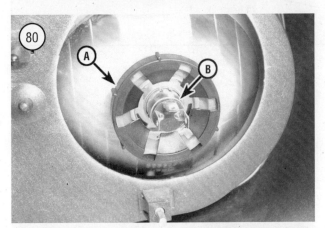

1. To remove the passing light bulb, perform the following:

    a. Remove the screw (**Figure 88**) at the base of the trim bezel and remove the trim bezel from the passing light housing.

    b. Carefully pull the bulb/lens assembly partially out of the housing.

    c. Disconnect the electrical connector (**Figure 89**) from the bulb/lens assembly. Remove the bulb/lens assembly from the housing.

    d. Remove the bulb from the lens assembly and install a new one. Push the bulb in until it bottoms.

    e. Connect the electrical connector (**Figure 89**) onto the bulb/lens assembly.

    f. Install the bulb/lens assembly from the housing and tighten the screw (**Figure 88**) securely.

2. To remove the front turn signal bulb, perform the following:

    a. Remove the screws securing the lens (**Figure 90**).

    b. Push in on the bulb (**Figure 91**), rotate it, and then remove the faulty bulb.

    c. Install the new bulb and rotate it into place.

    d. Install the lens and tighten the screw securely. Do not overtighten the screws as the lens may crack.

Passing Light and Front Turn Signal Bulb Replacement (FLHTCUSE Models)

Refer to **Figure 92**.

1. Remove the passing light bulb as follows:

    a. Loosen the clamping screw at the base of the trim bezel and remove the trim bezel from the passing light housing.

    b. Carefully pull the bulb reflector partially out of the housing.

    c. Disconnect the electrical connector from the bulb socket on the backside of the bulb reflector.

    d. Remove the bulb reflector from the housing.

    e. Remove the nesting ring from the bulb reflector.

    f. Secure the bulb reflector with one hand and rotate the bulb/socket assembly *counterclockwise* approximately 1/8 turn. Remove the bulb/socket assembly and discard it.

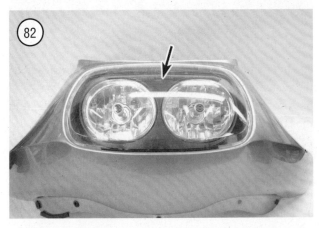

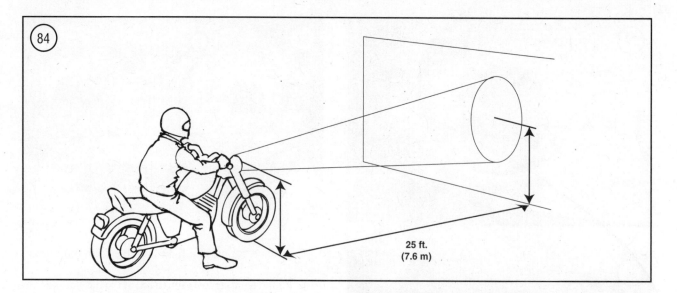

25 ft.
(7.6 m)

g. Install a *new* bulb/socket assembly into the backside of the bulb reflector.

h. Secure the bulb reflector with one hand and rotate the bulb/socket assembly *clockwise* approximately 1/8 turn to secure it.

i. Position the nesting ring with the concave side facing out and install the nesting ring into the bulb reflector. Index the nesting ring slots into the bulb reflector tabs.

j. Connect the electrical connector onto the bulb/socket assembly. Push it on until it clicks into place.

k. Carefully install the bulb reflector into the housing and hold it in place.

Install the trim bezel onto the passing light housing and rotate it so the clamping screw is located at the base of the housing. Tighten the clamping screw securely.

2. Remove the front turn signal bulb as follows:

a. Locate the notch in the lens cap.

b. Insert a coin into the notch and carefully twist the coin until the lens cap (A, **Figure 93**) comes off the housing.

c. Push in on the bulb (B, **Figure 93**), rotate it and remove it.

d. Install a new bulb.

e. Push the lens cap into the housing until is snaps into place.

**Passing Light Adjustment
(All Models)**

Refer to **Figure 94**.

1. Check the headlight aim and adjust if necessary as described in this chapter.

2. Park the motorcycle on a level surface approximately 25 ft. (7.6 m) from the wall.

3. Check tire inflation pressure. Readjust it if necessary, as described in Chapter Three.

4. Have a helper the approximate weight of the principal rider sit on the seat.

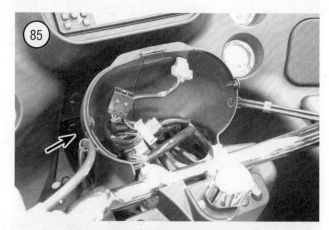

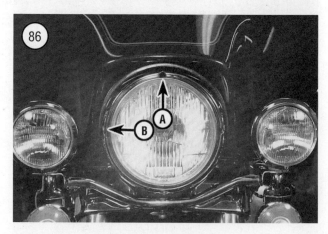

5. Draw a horizontal line on the wall the same height as the center of the headlight (**Figure 84**).

6. Aim the headlight at the wall. Switch the headlight to the HIGH beam. Point the front wheel straight ahead.

7. Check the headlight beam alignment. The broad, flat pattern of light (main beam of light) should be centered on the horizontal line with an equal area of light above and below line. Mark this location on the wall (A, **Figure 94**).

8. Turn off the headlight.

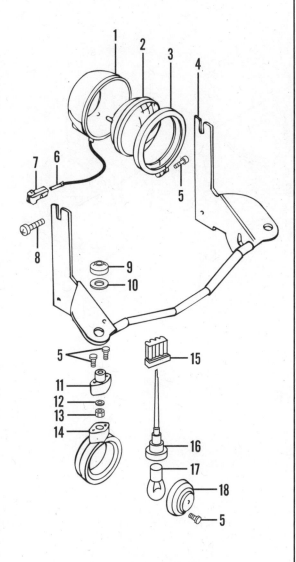

87 **PASSING LIGHTS/FRONT TURN SIGNALS (FLHR AND FLHT SERIES MODELS)**

1. Passing light housing
2. Passing light lens/bulb assembly
3. Trim bezel
4. Mounting bracket
5. Screw
6. Wiring harness
7. Terminal housing
8. Bolt
9. Swivel block
10. Dished washer
11. Clamp block
12. Washer
13. Locknut
14. Turn signal housing
15. Socket connector
16. Bulb socket
17. Turn signal bulb
18. Turn signal lens

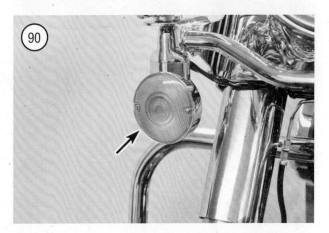

9

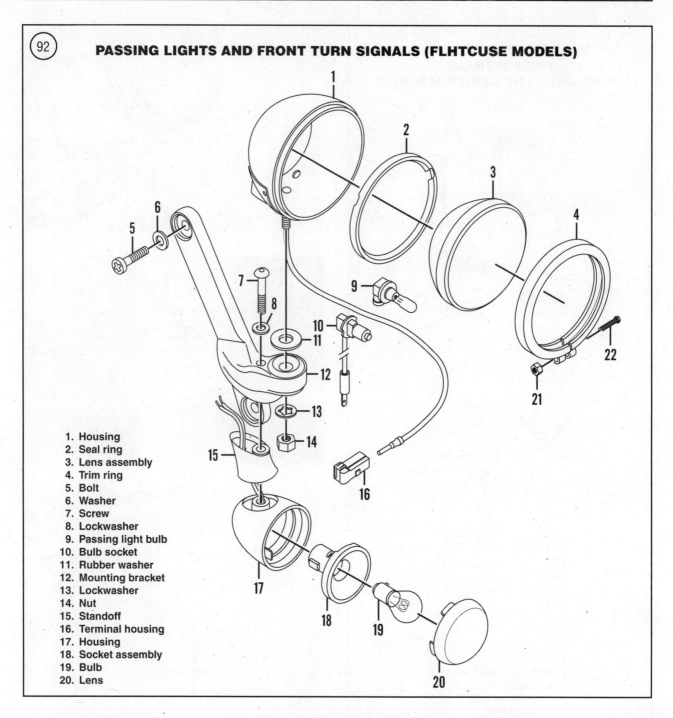

92 **PASSING LIGHTS AND FRONT TURN SIGNALS (FLHTCUSE MODELS)**

1. Housing
2. Seal ring
3. Lens assembly
4. Trim ring
5. Bolt
6. Washer
7. Screw
8. Lockwasher
9. Passing light bulb
10. Bulb socket
11. Rubber washer
12. Mounting bracket
13. Lockwasher
14. Nut
15. Standoff
16. Terminal housing
17. Housing
18. Socket assembly
19. Bulb
20. Lens

9. Measure the distance from the horizontal centerline of the headlight to the horizontal centerline of the left side passing light. Note the dimension.

10. Measure the distance from the vertical centerline of the headlight to the vertical centerline of the passing light. Note the dimension.

11. Repeat the vertical and horizontal measurement process for the right side passing light. Note both dimensions.

12. Refer to the dimensions recorded for the left and right passing light, and then mark these locations on the wall as shown in B and C, **Figure 94**.

13. Have the same helper sit on the seat and turn the headlight to HIGH beam. Verify that the headlight beam is still

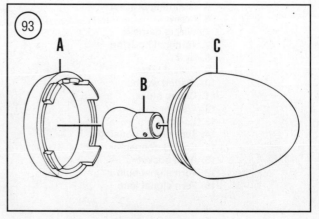

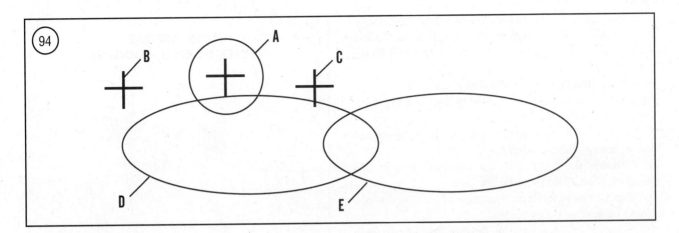

correctly aligned with the vertical and horizontal center-lines on the wall.

14. Turn the headlight to LOW beam.

15. Completely cover the headlight and the right side passing light so their beam is not visible on the wall.

16. Observe the location of the left side passing light on the wall. It should be within the area indicated in D, **Figure 94**. If the location is incorrect, adjust the passing light as described in this section.

17. Remove the cover from the right side passing light and place it over the left side passing light, so its beam is not visible on the wall.

18. Leave the headlight still covered so its beam is not visible on the wall. Make sure it is still on LOW beam.

19. Observe the location of the right side passing light on the wall. It should be within the area indicated in E, **Figure 94**. If the location is incorrect, adjust the passing light as described in this section.

20A. On all models except FLHTCUSE, adjust the passing light as follows:

   a. Turn off the headlight and passing lights.

   b. Remove the two screws securing the turn signal light assembly to the mounting bracket, and lower the turn signal light assembly.

   c. Insert a flare nut socket (Snap-On part No. FRX181), or an equivalent, into the bottom of the turn signal mounting bracket and loosen the adjust nut.

   d. Move the housing in the desired direction to correct the aim.

   e. Tighten the adjust nut to 15-18 ft.-lb. (20.30-24.4 N•m).

   f. Tighten the turn signal mounting screws to 36-60 in.-lb. (4.1-6.8 N•m).

   g. Recheck alignment and repeat if necessary.

20B. On FLHTCUSE models adjust the passing light as follows:

   a. Loosen the nut securing the passing light to the mounting bracket.

   b. Move the housing in the desired direction to correct the aim.

   c. Tighten the nut to 15-18 ft.-lb. (20.3-24.4 N•m).

TURN SIGNALS

Front Turn Signal Bulb Replacement (FLHX Models)

Refer to **Figure 95**.

1. Locate a notch in the lens and insert a coin into it. Carefully twist the coin until the lens (A, **Figure 93**) comes off the housing (C).

2. Push in on the bulb (B, **Figure 93**), rotate it and remove it from the socket.

3. Install a *new* bulb and rotate it until locked into place.

4. Push the lens into the housing until it snaps into place.

Front Turn Signal Removal/Installation (FLHT and FLHR series Models)

Refer to **Figure 87**.

1. Support the motorcycle with the front wheel off the ground as described in *Motorcycle Stands* (Chapter Ten).

2. Disconnect the negative battery cable as described in this chapter.

3A. On FLHR series models, perform the following:

   a. Remove the headlight lens assembly as described in this chapter.

   b. Locate the 6-pin Multilock connector for the front turn signal located within the headlight housing (**Figure 96**). Depress the locking button and disconnect the connector.

3B. On FLHT series models, perform the following:

   a. Remove the front fairing and windshield as described in Chapter Fourteen.

   b. Locate both 4-pin Multilock connectors for the front turn signals situated adjacent to the speakers in the inner fairing. Depress the locking button and disconnect the connectors.

4. Disconnect the appropriate terminals from within the socket housing. Refer to *Amp Multilock Connectors* (this chapter). Note the wire color location within the connector as they must be installed in the correct location.

5. Securely attach a piece of flexible fish wire to each wire terminal. Make each length of wire long enough to run from the connector, under the front fairing, through

9

the wiring conduit, and to the front turn signal assembly. Apply liquid glass cleaner, or an equivalent, to the fish wire and wiring to assist in pulling the wires through the conduit.

6. Remove the two Allen bolts and remove the turn signal from the mounting bracket. Slowly lower the assembly from the mounting bracket.

7. Carefully pull one wire at a time out from the conduit and withdraw all three wires.

8. Withdraw the wires from the mounting bracket and standoff. Then, disconnect the fish wire.

9. Strip 3/16 in. (4.8 mm) of insulation from the *new* wires. Crimp on *new* socket terminals.

10. Securely attach a piece of flexible fish wire to each new wire terminal.

11. Insert the wires into the standoff and mounting bracket.

12. Carefully pull one wire at a time into the conduit and remove the fish wire.

13A. On the right side of FLHT series models, install the wires into the following terminal sockets:

    a. Socket 1: blue.

    b. Socket 2: brown.

    c. Socket 3: black.

13B. On the left side of FLHT series models, install the wires into the following terminal sockets:

    a. Socket 1: blue.

    b. Socket 2: violet.

    c. Socket 3: black.

13C. On the right side of FLHR series models, install the wires into the following terminal sockets:

    a. Socket 1: black.

    b. Socket 2: brown.

    c. Socket 3: blue.

13D. On the left side of FLHR series models, install the wires into the following terminal sockets:

    a. Socket 1: blue.

    b. Socket 2: violet.

    c. Socket 3: black.

14. Install the turn signal assembly onto the mounting bracket. Make sure the wiring conduit is located within the slot at the back of the bracket and that it is not pinched.

15. Install the screws and lockwashers. Tighten the screws to 36-60 in.-lb. (4.1-6.8 N•m).

16. Connect the two 4-pin Multilock connectors for the front turn signals.

17. Connect the 6-pin Multilock connector for the front turn signal.

18. Connect the negative battery cable as described in this chapter.

19. Check operation of the turn signal(s) prior to installing the front fairing and windshield.

20. Install the front fairing and windshield as described in Chapter Seventeen or install the headlight as described in this chapter.

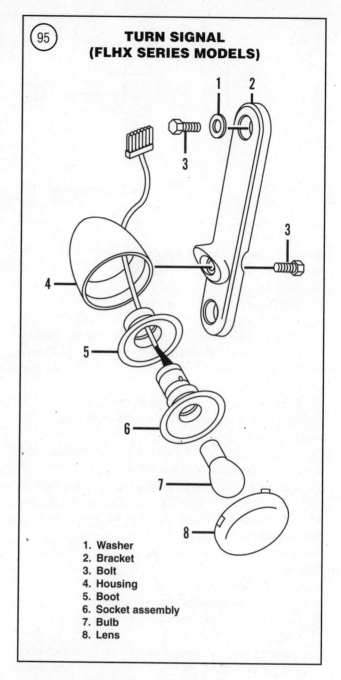

95 TURN SIGNAL (FLHX SERIES MODELS)

1. Washer
2. Bracket
3. Bolt
4. Housing
5. Boot
6. Socket assembly
7. Bulb
8. Lens

Front Turn Signal Removal/Installation (FLHR and FLHRSE Models)

Refer to **Figure 97**.

1. Support the motorcycle with the front wheel off the ground as described in *Motorcycle Stands* (Chapter Twelve).

2. Disconnect the negative battery cable as described in this chapter.

3. Remove the headlight lens and nacelle assembly as described in this chapter.

4. Locate the 6-pin Multilock connector for the front turn signal located within the headlight housing (**Figure 96**). Depress the locking button and disconnect the connector.

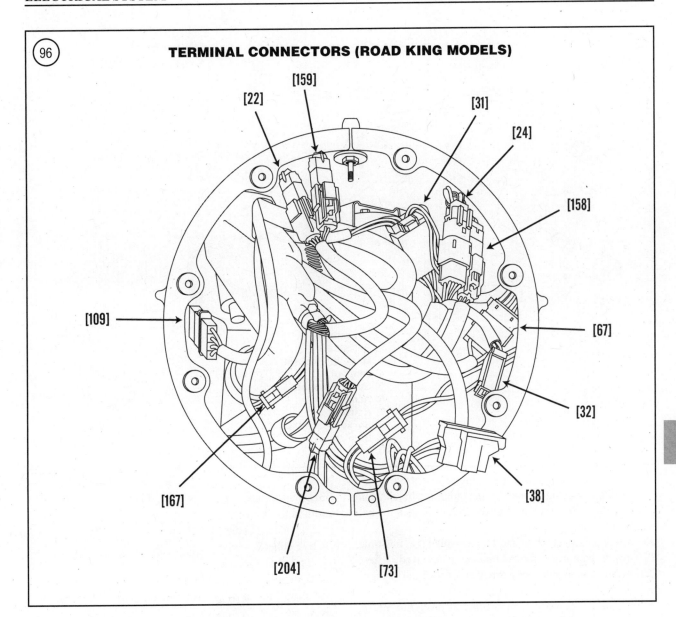

96

TERMINAL CONNECTORS (ROAD KING MODELS)

5. Disconnect the appropriate terminals from within the socket housing. Refer to *Amp Multilock Connectors* in this chapter. Note the wire color location within the connector as they must be installed in the correct location.

6. Cut the cable strap and release the wiring conduit from the lower handlebar clamp.

7. Remove the clips securing the conduit to the bottom of the handlebar.

8. Remove the acorn nut, star washer and mounting bracket from the stem of the mirror.

9. Remove the set screw from the bracket.

10. Use an Allen wrench and remove the ball stud from the housing.

11. Remove the jam nut from the ball stud.

12. Remove the ball stud from the turn signal light bracket.

13. Push the grommet at the end of the conduit into the light housing.

14. Insert a small screwdriver into the slot at the bottom of the lens and remove the lens.

15. Remove the bulb from the socket.

16. Insert the blade of a small screwdriver between the outer edge of the grommet and the inside of the housing. Gently pry and release the socket assembly.

17. Carefully pull the socket assembly, conduit and terminals out through the housing opening.

18. Remove the grommet from the housing, if necessary.

19. Insert the conduit and terminals through the interior of the housing opening.

20. Carefully pull until the socket is against the backside of the housing.

21. Install the socket tab with the slot in the housing. Carefully push on the socket until it is fully seated.

22. Install the bulb into the socket.

23. Install the lens onto the housing.

24. Install the ball stud through the mounting bracket and thread the jam nut all the way onto the ball stud.

9

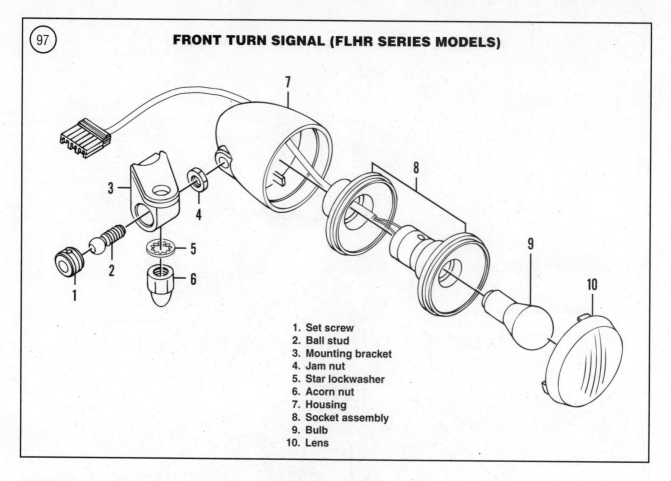

FRONT TURN SIGNAL (FLHR SERIES MODELS)

1. Set screw
2. Ball stud
3. Mounting bracket
4. Jam nut
5. Star lockwasher
6. Acorn nut
7. Housing
8. Socket assembly
9. Bulb
10. Lens

25. Hold the housing in place on the mounting bracket and thread the ball stud onto the bracket. Finger-tighten the ball stud at this time.

26. Install a *new* set screw and finger-tighten it at this time.

27. Install the mirror onto the bracket, if removed.

28. Install a *new* star lockwasher and acorn nut. Finger-tighten the acorn nut.

29. Sit on the motorcycle in an upright position with the front wheel straight ahead. Properly adjust the mirror, and then tighten the acorn nut to 60-96 in.-lb. (6.8-10.8 N•m).

30. Correctly position the housing straight ahead and tighten the set screw to 50-70 in.-lb. (5.7-7.9 N•m).

NOTE
After the set screw is tightened, do not completely remove it for any adjustment. If necessary, only loosen the set screw 1/8 turn, adjust the housing and tighten to 50-70 in.-lb. (5.7-7.9 N•m).

31. Secure the housing and tighten the jam nut securely.

32. Feed the loose ends of the electrical conduit into the top of the headlight nacelle. Stay outboard of the lower handlebar clamp.

33A. On the right side, install the wires into the following terminal sockets:
   a. Socket 1: black.
   b. Socket 2: brown.
   c. Socket 3: blue.

33B. On the left side, install the wires into the following terminal sockets:
   a. Socket 1: blue.
   b. Socket 2: violet.
   c. Socket 3: black.

34. Connect the 6-pin Multilock connector (**Figure 96**).

35. Install the clips securing the conduit to the bottom of the handlebar.

36. Install a new cable strap securing the wiring conduit onto the lower handlebar clamp.

37. Install the headlight lens and nacelle assembly as described in this chapter.

38. Connect the negative battery cable as described in this chapter.

Front Turn Signal Removal/Installation (FLHX Series Models)

Refer to **Figure 95**.

1. Support the motorcycle with the front wheel off the ground as described in *Motorcycle Stands* (Chapter Twelve).

2. Remove the Main-Fuse as described in this chapter.

3. Remove the outer front fairing and windshield as described in Chapter Seventeen.

4. Locate the 4-pin Multilock connectors for both front turn signals situated adjacent to the speakers in the inner

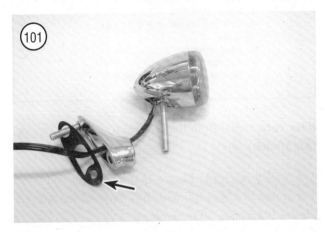

fairing. Depress the locking button and disconnect the connectors.

5. Remove the two Torx screws (T40) and washers securing the turn signal mounting bar to the upper and lower fork brackets.

6. Remove the electrical harness from the fame.

7. Position the turn signal mounting bar onto the upper and lower fork brackets.

8. Partially install the two Torx screws and washers into the mounting bar.

9. Correctly position the harness so it is routed forward through the relief at the front of the bracket, and then inboard using the relief in the upper outboard corner of the fork bracket skirt.

10. Alternately tighten the two Torx screws to 15-20 ft.-lb. (20.3-27.1 N•m).

11. Install the front fairing and windshield as described in Chapter Fourteen.

12. Reinstall the Main-Fuse as described in this chapter.

Front Turn Signal Removal/Installation (FLTR Series and FLTRSE3 Models)

Refer to **Figure 77 or Figure 78**.

1. On the inboard side of the left fairing support, remove the rear acorn nut (**Figure 98**) and washer from the turn signal light bracket. Remove the front acorn nut and washer.

2. Carefully pull the front turn signal light assembly (**Figure 99**) from the fairing.

3. Disconnect the electrical connector (**Figure 100**) and remove the assembly.

4. Install the gasket (**Figure 101**) onto the turn signal mounting bracket.

5. Install by reversing the removal steps. Tighten the acorn nut to 96-120 in.-lb. (10.8-13.6 N•m).

Front Turn Signal Removal/Installation (FLHTCUSE Models)

Refer to **Figure 92**.

1. Support the motorcycle with the front wheel off the ground as described in *Motorcycle Stands* (Chapter Twelve).

2. Disconnect the negative battery cable as described in this chapter.

3. Remove the front outer fairing and windshield as described in Chapter Seventeen.

4. Locate both 4-pin Multilock connectors for the front turn signal (**Figure 97**) in the fairing. Depress the locking button and disconnect the connectors.

NOTE
The gray/black wire within the connector is for the passing lights and does not have to be disconnected.

5. Disconnect the appropriate terminals from within the socket housing. Refer to *Amp Multilock Connectors* in this

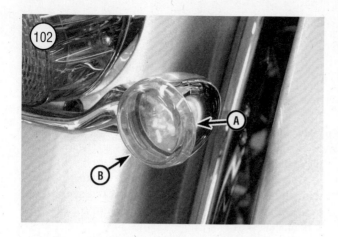

chapter. Note the wire color location within the connector as they must be installed in the correct location.

6. Securely attach a piece of flexible fish wire to each wire terminal. Make each length of wire long enough to run from the connector, under the front fairing, through the wiring conduit, and to the front turn signal assembly. Apply liquid glass cleaner, or an equivalent, to the fish wire and wiring to assist in pulling the wires through the conduit.

7. Remove the screws and lockwashers securing the turn signal assembly to the mounting bracket and slowly lower the assembly from the mounting bracket.

8. Carefully pull one wire at a time out from the conduit and withdraw all three wires.

9. Withdraw the wires from the mounting bracket and standoff.

10. Insert the new wires into the standoff and mounting bracket.

11. Carefully pull one wire at a time into the conduit, and then remove the fish wire.

12. Install the turn signal assembly onto the mounting bracket and install the screws and lockwashers. Tighten the screws to 96-120 in.-lb. (10.8-13.6 N•m).

13. Strip 3/16 in. (4.8 mm) of insulation from the new wires. Crimp on *new* socket terminals.

14A. On the right side, install the wires into the following terminal sockets:

   a. Socket 1: blue.

   b. Socket 2: brown.

   c. Socket 3: black.

14B. On the left side, install the wires into the following terminal sockets:

   a. Socket 1: blue.

   b. Socket 2: violet.

   c. Socket 3: black.

15. Connect both 4-pin Multilock connectors for the front turn signals.

16. Connect the negative battery cable as described in this chapter.

17. Check operation of the turn signal(s) prior to installing the front fairing and windshield.

18. Install the front outer fairing and windshield as described in Chapter Fourteen.

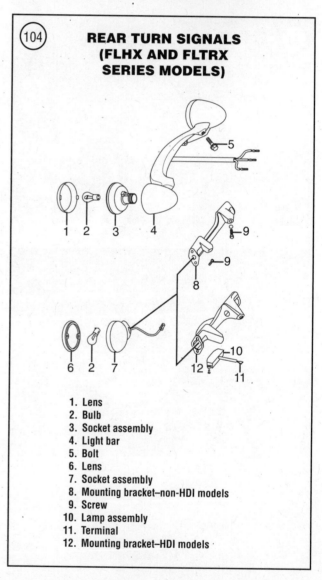

REAR TURN SIGNALS (FLHX AND FLTRX SERIES MODELS)

1. Lens
2. Bulb
3. Socket assembly
4. Light bar
5. Bolt
6. Lens
7. Socket assembly
8. Mounting bracket–non-HDI models
9. Screw
10. Lamp assembly
11. Terminal
12. Mounting bracket–HDI models

Rear Turn Signal Bulb Replacement (All Models)

1. Locate a notch (A, **Figure 102**) in the lens and insert a coin into it. Carefully twist the coin until the lens (B, **Figure 102**) comes off the housing.

105 REAR TURN SIGNALS (FLHTCUSE MODELS)

1. Lens
2. Bulb
3. Socket assembly
4. Light bar
5. License plate light assembly
6. Screw
7. Upper bracket
8. Washer
9. Lockwasher
10. Screw
11. Lower bracket (HDI)
12. Rubber bumper
13. Grommet

107 CIRCUIT BOARD CONNECTORS

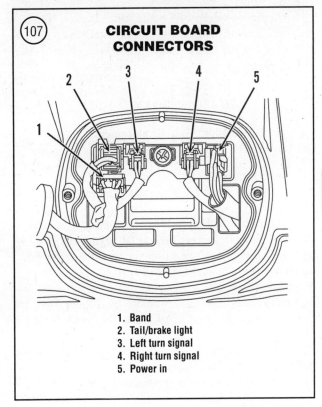

1. Band
2. Tail/brake light
3. Left turn signal
4. Right turn signal
5. Power in

9

2. Push in on the bulb, rotate it and remove it from the socket.

3. Install a *new* bulb (**Figure 103**), push it in and rotate it until locked into place.

4. Push the lens into the housing until it snaps into place.

Rear Turn Signal Bracket Removal/Installation (All Models)

Refer to **Figure 104** and **Figure 105**.

NOTE
Always disarm the optional security system (TSSM/HFSM) before disconnecting the bat-tery or before pulling the Maxi-Fuse so the siren will not sound.

1. Support the motorcycle on a swing arm stand with the rear wheel off the ground.

2. Disconnect the negative battery cable as described in this chapter.

3. Remove both saddlebags as described in Chapter Fourteen.

4. Remove the screw (A, **Figure 106**) on each side secur-ing the taillight lens (B) and remove the lens.

5. Disconnect the 4-pin taillight Multilock connector from the chrome base.

6. Use a pick or small, flat-bladed screwdriver and depress the release button on both 2-pin connectors. Disconnect the connectors (**Figure 107**) from the circuit board.

7. Carefully feed the connector and harness out through the opening on each side of the printed circuit board.

8. Reach under the rear fender and release the harness from the cable anchored on the T-stud.

9. Carefully pull the harness out of the rear fender opening and allow it to hang down below the turn signal bracket.

10. Insert a long-shank, ball-end socket (Snap-On part No. FABL5), or equivalent, through the channel in the bracket. Remove the screw on each side.

11. Remove the two flange bolts and remove the bracket assembly (C, **Figure 106**) from the rear fender.

12. Install by reversing the removal steps, while noting the following:

    a. Tighten the taillight lens screws to 20-24 in.-lb. (2.3-2.7 N•m).

    b. Apply one drop of Loctite Threadlocker No. 271 (red) to the flange bolts prior to installation.

    c. Tighten the flange bolts to 84-144 in.-lb. (9.5-16.3 N•m).

TAILLIGHT/BRAKE LIGHT

Taillight/Brake Light Bulb Replacement (FLHT, FLHR, FLTR SERIES Models)

Refer to **Figure 108**.

1. Remove the screw (A, **Figure 106**) on each side securing the lens (B).

2. Pull the lens (A, **Figure 109**) off the base.

3. Rotate the bulb/socket assembly (B, **Figure 109**) 1/4 turn *counterclockwise* and pull it from the backside of the lens.

4. Gently the bulb out of the socket assembly.

5. Install a new bulb into socket.

6. Rotate the bulb/socket assembly (B, **Figure 109**) 1/4 turn *clockwise* and push it back into the backside of the lens.

7. Inspect the gasket (C, **Figure 109**) for deterioration or damage; replace if necessary.

8. Make sure the gasket is in place on the lens.

9. Install the lens and screws. Tighten the screws to 20-24 in.-lb. (2.3-2.7 N•m). Do not overtighten as the lens may crack.

Taillight/Brake Light/Rear Turn Signal Replacement (FLTXSE, FLTRXSE AND FLHRSE MODELS)

Refer to **Figure 110**.

NOTE
The taillight, brake light and turn signal base is an integral assembly. If any portion of the base is defective, replace the complete assembly.

1. Remove the saddlebag from the side being serviced as described in Chapter Fourteen.

2. Disconnect the 2-pin electrical connector from the base.

3. Remove the three screws securing the base to the rear fender fascia.

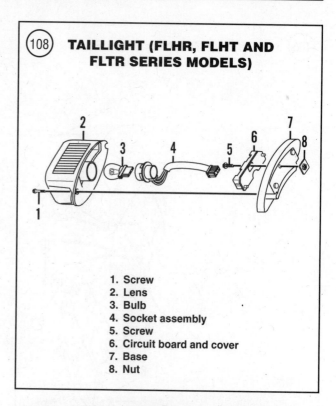

108 TAILLIGHT (FLHR, FLHT AND FLTR SERIES MODELS)

1. Screw
2. Lens
3. Bulb
4. Socket assembly
5. Screw
6. Circuit board and cover
7. Base
8. Nut

4. Pull straight back and remove the base from the rear fender fascia.

5. Install the base onto the posts on the rear fender fascia. Push it on until it bottoms.

6. Install the three screws securing the base to the rear fender fascia, and tighten securely. Do not overtighten the screws as the fascia posts may crack.

7. Connect the 4-pin electrical connector onto the base.

8. Install the saddlebag as described in Chapter Fourteen.

9. Repeat the procedure for the remaining side if necessary.

Taillight/Brake Circuit Board/Chrome Base Removal/Installation (FLHT, FLHR, FLHX and FLTR SERIES Models)

Refer to **Figure 108**.

1. Remove the screw (A, **Figure 106**) on each side securing the lens (B).

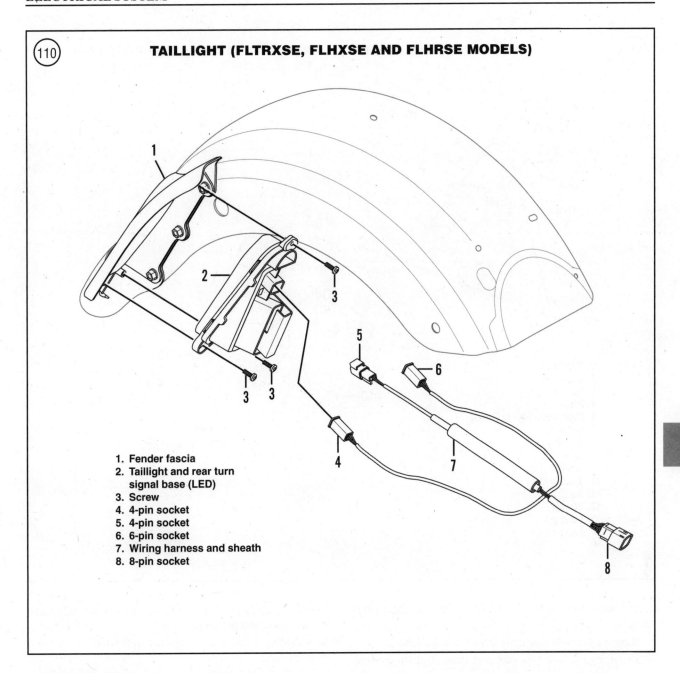

110   **TAILLIGHT (FLTRXSE, FLHXSE AND FLHRSE MODELS)**

1. Fender fascia
2. Taillight and rear turn
   signal base (LED)
3. Screw
4. 4-pin socket
5. 4-pin socket
6. 6-pin socket
7. Wiring harness and sheath
8. 8-pin socket

2. Pull the lens off the base and remove the bulb.

3. Disconnect the bulb connector.

4. Disconnect the rear fender tip light connector, on models so equipped.

5. Disconnect the rear fender light connector.

6. Use a pick or small, flat-bladed screwdriver and depress the release button on both 2-pin connectors. Disconnect the connectors (**Figure 107**) from the circuit board.

7. Remove the screw and captive washer securing the center of the printed circuit board and chrome base to the rear fender.

8. Use both thumbs and push the chrome base upward to free it from the rear fender, and remove it from the rear fender.

9. Carefully feed the wiring harness and terminal connectors out through the openings in the chrome base.

10. Remove the pin housing from the circuit board.

11. Install by reversing the removal steps. Tighten the screw and captive washer to 40-48 in.-lb. (4.5-5.4 N•m).

FENDER TIP LIGHT

Front Fender Tip Light
Removal/Installation

1. Insert the tip of a flat-bladed screwdriver into the slot at the top of the fender tip lens. Slowly rotate the screwdriver and unsnap the lens from the light base.

2. Secure the Keps nuts under the front fender to keep them from rotating.

3. Unscrew the two screws from the Keps nuts and partially remove the light base from the front fender.

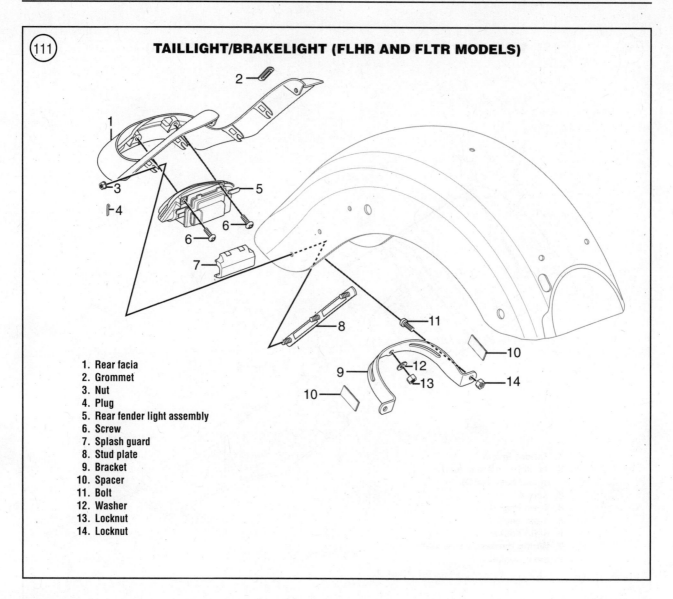

111 **TAILLIGHT/BRAKELIGHT (FLHR AND FLTR MODELS)**

1. Rear facia
2. Grommet
3. Nut
4. Plug
5. Rear fender light assembly
6. Screw
7. Splash guard
8. Stud plate
9. Bracket
10. Spacer
11. Bolt
12. Washer
13. Locknut
14. Locknut

4. Disconnect the light's 2-pin connector from the wiring harness.

5. Remove the light assembly from the front fender.

6. Install by reversing the removal steps. Tighten the two screws securely.

Rear Fender Tip Light
Removal/Installation

1. Remove the two screws securing the light assembly to the rear fender.

2. Insert the tip of a flat blade screwdriver into the slot at the top of the fender tip lens. Slowly rotate the screwdriver and unsnap the lens from the light base.

3. Remove the two screws securing the base to the rear fender, and partially remove the light base from the rear fender.

4. Disconnect the fender tip light 2-pin connector from the wiring harness.

5. Feed the socket housing through opening in the chrome base and fender.

6. Release the wiring harness from the cable clip anchored on the T-stud and the fender clip.

7. Secure the Keps nuts under the rear fender to keep them from rotating.

8. Unscrew the two screws from the Keps nuts and partially remove the light base from the front fender.

9. Withdraw the wiring harness and connector out through the large hole in the rear fender.

10. Install by reversing these removal steps. Tighten the two screws to 20-25 in.-lb. (2.3-2.8 N•m).

REAR FACIA LIGHT

Replacement (FLHX and FLTRX Models)

Refer to **Figure 111.**

1. Remove the rear facia as described in Chapter Fourteen.

2. On the left side, remove the bolt/flat washer and remove the passenger seat strap and saddlebag front mounting bracket from the frame tube chrome cover.

3. Remove the Phillips screw and the chrome cover from the frame.

4. Release the fascia light wires from the clip at the top of the radio antenna cable bracket.

5. Carefully cut the cable strap securing the rear fascia light wires and radio antenna cable to the slotted hole in the rear fender support.

6. Carefully cut the cable strap securing the rear fascia light wires and radio antenna cable to the shoulder on the upper frame tube, just in front of the air valve mounting bracket.

NOTE
The rear fascia light connector also serves as the Tour-Pak connector on FLHTC and FLHTCU models.

7. Disconnect the 3-pin rear fascia light connector from the harness at the inboard side of the upper frame tube.

8. Install by reversing the removal steps. Tighten the Phillips screws to 25-40 in.-lb. (2.8-4.5 N•m). Tighten the bolt securing the passenger seat strap and saddlebag to 60-96 in.-lb. (6.8-10.8 N•m).

LICENSE PLATE LIGHT

Bulb Replacement (FLHX And FLTRX Models)

Refer to **Figure 105**.

1. Remove the two Allen screws securing the lens assembly to the rear turn signal housing.

2. Lower the lens while being careful not to stress the wiring.

3. Remove the light bulb(s).

4, Apply a liberal amount of dielectric grease to the sockets and to the bulb contacts.

5. Install new bulb(s).

6. Carefully push the lens assembly back into the rear turn signal housing. Do not pinch the wiring.

7. Install the two Allen screws and tighten securely.

License Plate Light Assembly Removal/Installation (FLHX And FLTRX Models)

1. Remove the two Allen screws securing the lens assembly to the rear turn signal housing.

2. Lower the lens while being careful not to stress the wiring.

3. Remove the screws securing the taillight/brake light lens.

4. Pull the lens off the base and disconnect the 3-pin electrical connector (2, **Figure 107**).

5. Reach under the rear fender and release the harness from the cable anchored on the T-stud on the left side.

6. Disconnect the terminals from within the socket housing. Refer to *Amp Multilock Connectors* (this chapter). Note the wire color location within the connector as they must be installed in the correct location.

7. Carefully withdraw the wiring harness out through the hole in the rear fender.

8. Install by reversing the removal steps. Tighten the Allen screws securely.

License Plate Light and Bracket Assembly Removal/Installation (2013 FLHRSE Models)

Refer to **Figure 112**.

1. Remove the rear wheel as described in Chapter Ten.

NOTE
Always disarm the optional security system (TSM/TSSM/HFSM) before disconnecting the battery or pulling the main fuse so the siren will not sound.

2. Disconnect the negative battery cable as described in this chapter.

3. Remove the flange nut and remove the electrical connector cover.

4. Disconnect the electrical connector from the main harness.

5. Separate the electrical connector from the terminals within the connector as described in this chapter.

6. Secure the stud plate under the rear fender.

7. Remove the two screws securing the bracket assembly and stud plate to the rear fender. Remove the bracket assembly from the outer surface of the rear fender.

8. Remove the two screws securing the light assembly to the bracket and remove the light assembly.

9. Remove the gasket from the rear fender or light assembly. Discard the gasket.

10. Install by reversing these removal steps, note the following:

    a. Install the screws securing the license plate light assembly to the plate bracket and tighten to 60-80 in.-lb. (6.8-9.0 N•m).

    b. Install the light assembly screws and tighten securely.

    c. Install the electrical connector cover flange nut and tighten to 30-45 in.-lb. (3.4-5.1 N•m).

TOUR-PAK

Side Marker Light Replacement (FLHTCU and FLHTK Models)

1. Open the cover and keep it open.

2. Open the map pocket and remove the acorn nuts and washers securing the map pocket and molded liner. Remove the molded liner from the lower case.

3. Depress the external latch and remove the bulb socket.

4. Remove the bulb from the socket and install a new bulb.

5. Install the bulb socket into the receptacle and push it in until it bottoms.

6. Install the molded liner, and secure with the washers and acorn nuts. Tighten the nuts securely.

9

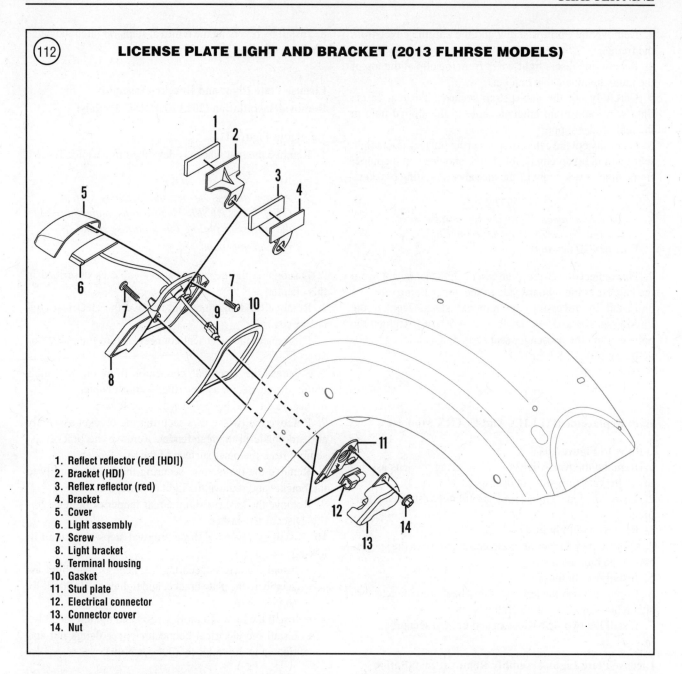

LICENSE PLATE LIGHT AND BRACKET (2013 FLHRSE MODELS)

1. Reflect reflector (red [HDI])
2. Bracket (HDI)
3. Reflex reflector (red)
4. Bracket
5. Cover
6. Light assembly
7. Screw
8. Light bracket
9. Terminal housing
10. Gasket
11. Stud plate
12. Electrical connector
13. Connector cover
14. Nut

Wrap-Around Light Housing Removal/Installation (FLHTCU and FLHTK Models)

Refer to **Figure 113**.

1. Open the cover and keep it open.

2. Open the map pocket and remove the acorn nuts and washers securing the map pocket and molded liner. Remove the molded liner from the lower case.

3. Depress the external latch and remove the bulb socket from both sides.

4. Disconnect the CB antenna cable connector on the right side.

5. Release the cable from the adhesive clip at the bottom of the Tour-Pak.

6. Remove the Keps nut, ring terminal and flat washer from the antenna loading coil stud.

7. Secure the hex head screw, and then remove the flange nut from the loading coil stud.

8. Secure the hex screw, and then remove the flange nut at the base of the Tour-Pak.

9. Remove the hex screw, with external tooth washer, and loading coil from the frame.

10. Remove the loading coil stud.

11. Remove the loading mast from the light housing.

12. On the left side, turn the knurled lock ring *counter-clockwise*, and disconnect the radio antenna cable connector. Release the cable from the rear clip on the bottom of the Tour-Pak.

13. Remove the jam nut from the radio antenna cable connector at the back of the Tour-Pak. Remove the internal tooth lockwasher, ring terminal and large flat washer from the connector.

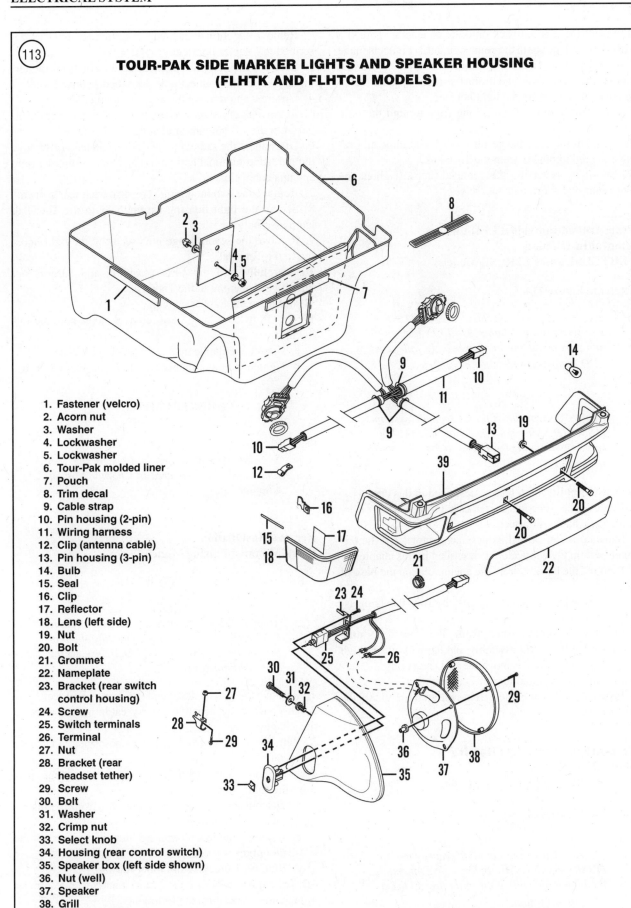

⑬

**TOUR-PAK SIDE MARKER LIGHTS AND SPEAKER HOUSING
(FLHTK AND FLHTCU MODELS)**

1. Fastener (velcro)
2. Acorn nut
3. Washer
4. Lockwasher
5. Lockwasher
6. Tour-Pak molded liner
7. Pouch
8. Trim decal
9. Cable strap
10. Pin housing (2-pin)
11. Wiring harness
12. Clip (antenna cable)
13. Pin housing (3-pin)
14. Bulb
15. Seal
16. Clip
17. Reflector
18. Lens (left side)
19. Nut
20. Bolt
21. Grommet
22. Nameplate
23. Bracket (rear switch
    control housing)
24. Screw
25. Switch terminals
26. Terminal
27. Nut
28. Bracket (rear
    headset tether)
29. Screw
30. Bolt
31. Washer
32. Crimp nut
33. Select knob
34. Housing (rear control switch)
35. Speaker box (left side shown)
36. Nut (well)
37. Speaker
38. Grill
39. Light housing

9

14. Install the jam nut back onto the connector. Thread a 1/2 in.-20 UNF nut onto the connector until contact is made with the jam nut. Turn the jam nut *counterclockwise* and remove the connector stud from the radio antenna mast. Remove the mast from the light housing.

15. Carefully remove the caulking from around the bulb housing.

16. Remove the four flange nuts and metal clips and remove the light housing from the Tour-Pak.

17. Install by reversing the removal steps. Tighten the flange nuts and acorn nuts securely.

Wrap-Around Individual LED Light Removal/Installation (FLHTCUSE and FLTRUSE Models)

Refer to **Figure 114**.

NOTE
The wrap-around lights use LED lamps. If any portion of the lamp assembly fails, the LED lamp assembly must be replaced.

NOTE
Always disarm the optional security system (TSSM/HFSM) before disconnecting the battery or pulling the main fuse so the siren will not sound.

1. Disconnect the main fuse as described in this chapter.

2. Remove the Tour-Pak lower case molded liner as described in Chapter Fourteen.

3. Separate the electrical harness connector from the terminals within the connector as described in this chapter.

4. Remove the harness from the anchor clip on the base of the lower case.

5. Secure the LED assembly against the Tour-Pak lamp assembly.

6. Unscrew nut/lockwasher from the threaded stud. Carefully pull the LED assembly and harness out through the lamp assembly and remove the LED assembly.

7. Repeat for any remaining LED assemblies.

8. Install by reversing these removal steps. Tighten the nut/lockwasher securely.

Wrap-Around LED Light Housing Removal/Installation (FLHTCUSE and FLTRUSE Models)

Refer to **Figure 114**.

NOTE
Always disarm the optional security system (TSM/TSSM/HFSM) before disconnecting the battery or pulling the main fuse so the siren will not sound.

1. Disconnect the main fuse as described in this chapter.

2. Remove the Tour-Pak lower case molded liner as described in Chapter Fourteen.

3. Separate the electrical harness connector from the terminals within the connector as described in this chapter.

4. Unscrew and remove the antenna adapter stud.

5. Remove the nut/lockwasher, flat washer and ring terminal from the CB antenna stud at the right side corner.

6. Disconnect the radio antenna cable connector. Remove the nut. Ring terminal and large flat washer from the ratio antenna connector.

7. Remove the two mounting screws at each rear corner.

8. Secure the light housing assembly onto the Tour-Pak lamp assembly.

9. Remove the seven flange nuts securing the light housing to the Tour Pak.

10. Carefully pull the LED assembly and harness out through the opening in the Tour-Pak.

11. Remove the light assembly.

12. Install by reversing these removal steps, note the following:
   a. Tighten the flange nuts to 15 in.-lb. (1.7 N•m).
   b. Tighten the mounting screws to 12 in.-lb. (1.3 N•m).

INSTRUMENTS

NOTE
Speedometers that are housed in the fuel tank console are covered in Chapter Nine or Chapter Ten.

Removal/Installation (Fork Mounted Fairing Models)

Refer to **Figure 115** and **Figure 116**.

NOTE
Always disarm the optional security system (TSSM/HFSM) before disconnecting the battery or before pulling the Main-Fuse so the siren will not sound.

1. Remove the seat as described in Chapter Fourteen.

2. Disconnect the negative battery cable as described in this chapter.

3. Remove the outer front fairing as described in Chapter Fourteen.

4A. To remove the 2 inch (51 mm) diameter gauge, perform the following:
   a. Disconnect the electrical connector from the instrument to be removed.
   b. Remove the nuts securing the instrument to the mounting bracket.
   c. Remove gauge(s) from inner fairing.

4B. To remove the 4 inch (102 mm) diameter speedometer or tachometer, perform the following:
   a. Disconnect the 12-pin Packard connector from the backside of the speedometer or tachometer.

(114) **TOUR-PAK WRAP AROUND LIGHTS FLHTCUSE AND FLTRUSE MODELS**

1. Light assembly–right side
2. Light assembly–center
3. Light assembly–left side
4. Antenna adapter
5. Trim–HDI models
6. Light housing
7. Washer
8. Screw
9. Locknut/washer
10. Plug assembly
11. Screw
12. Seal pin
13. Pin housing
14. Connector
15. Connector
16. Connector
17. Connector

9

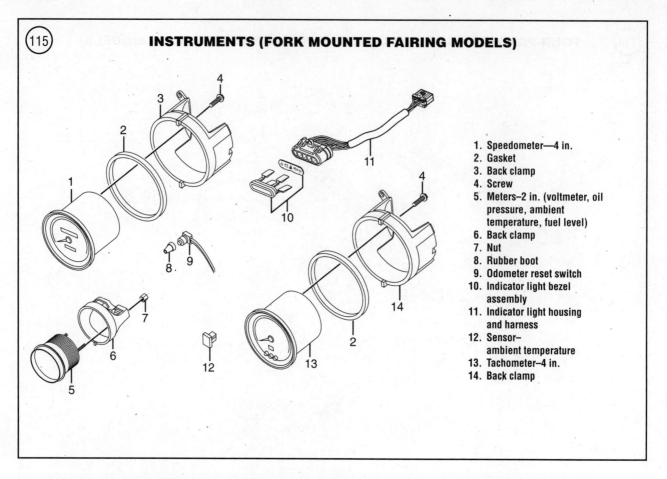

INSTRUMENTS (FORK MOUNTED FAIRING MODELS)

1. Speedometer—4 in.
2. Gasket
3. Back clamp
4. Screw
5. Meters—2 in. (voltmeter, oil pressure, ambient temperature, fuel level)
6. Back clamp
7. Nut
8. Rubber boot
9. Odometer reset switch
10. Indicator light bezel assembly
11. Indicator light housing and harness
12. Sensor— ambient temperature
13. Tachometer—4 in.
14. Back clamp

b. Remove the two Phillips screws securing the instrument to the mounting bracket.

c. Push the instrument toward the rear, out of the gasket, and remove it from the inner fairing.

5. Store the meters in a safe place.

6. If removed, install the gasket onto the speedometer and tachometer mounting brackets.

NOTE
If necessary, apply alcohol or glass cleaner to the gasket surfaces to ease installation of the meters.

7. Install by reversing the removal steps, while noting the following:

a. Install the instruments into the mounting brackets. Press firmly until the instrument is correctly seated and secure with the screws or nuts. Tighten the screws or nuts securely.

b. Connect the negative battery cable as described in this chapter.

Removal/Installation (Frame Mounted Fairing Models)

Refer to **Figure 117**.

1. Place the motorcycle on level ground on the jiffy stand.

2. Remove the seat as described in Chapter Fourteen.

NOTE
Always disarm the optional TSSM/HFSM security system before disconnecting the battery or pulling the Main-Fuse so the siren will not sound.

3. Disconnect the negative battery lead as described in this chapter.

4. Remove the Torx screw (**Figure 118**) on each side securing the instrument bezel to the housing.

5. Pull up on the top of the instrument bezel (A, **Figure 119**) and detach it from the locking tabs (B) on the housing.

6. Slightly raise the bezel and remove the anchor on the ambient temperature sensor from the inboard ear of the speedometer bracket.

7. Disconnect the following electrical connectors from the interconnect harness as follows:

a. The 12-pin Packard connector (A, **Figure 120**) from the speedometer.

b. The 12-pin Packard connector (B, **Figure 120**) from the tachometer.

c. The 10-pin Multilock connector (C, **Figure 120**) from the indicator lights.

8. Remove the bezel from the instrument housing.

9. Remove the two screws (**Figure 121**) securing the instrument(s) to the mounting bracket(s).

10. Carefully separate the instrument bezel and housing halves and remove each one from the frame. Store the panels in a safe place.

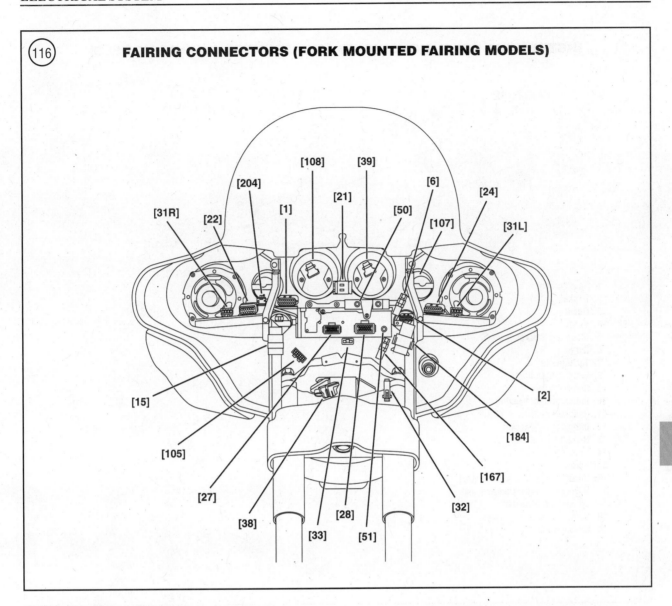

116 FAIRING CONNECTORS (FORK MOUNTED FAIRING MODELS)

[108] [39] [6] [24] [204] [21] [50] [107] [31L] [31R] [22] [1] [15] [2] [184] [105] [167] [27] [32] [38] [28] [33] [51]

9

11. Carefully push the speedometer and/or tachometer out through the gasket and the front of bezel.

12. Store the meters in a safe place.

13. If removed, install the gasket onto the speedometer and tachometer.

NOTE
If necessary, apply alcohol or glass cleaner to the gasket surfaces to ease installation of the meters.

14. Install by reversing the removal steps, while noting the following:

   a. Install the instruments into the correct side of the mounting brackets. Install the speedometer (A, **Figure 122**) on the left side and the tachometer (B) on the right side.

   b. Press firmly until the instrument is correctly seated and secure it with the screws. Tighten the bracket screws securely.

AUTOMATIC COMPRESSION RELEASE SOLENOID (ARC) (103 CU. IN AND 110 CU. IN. MODELS)

Tools

An ARC solenoid socket (H-D part No. HD-48498), or equivalent, is needed for this procedure.

Removal/Installation

1. Remove the rocker arm support plate as described in *Rocker Arms, Pushrods and Valve Lifters* (Chapter Four).

2. Use the tool to remove the ACR solenoid from the cylinder head.

3. Installation is the reverse of removal. Note the following:

   a. Apply three dots of Loctite 246 Threadlocker to the bottom third of the threads on the ACR solenoid.

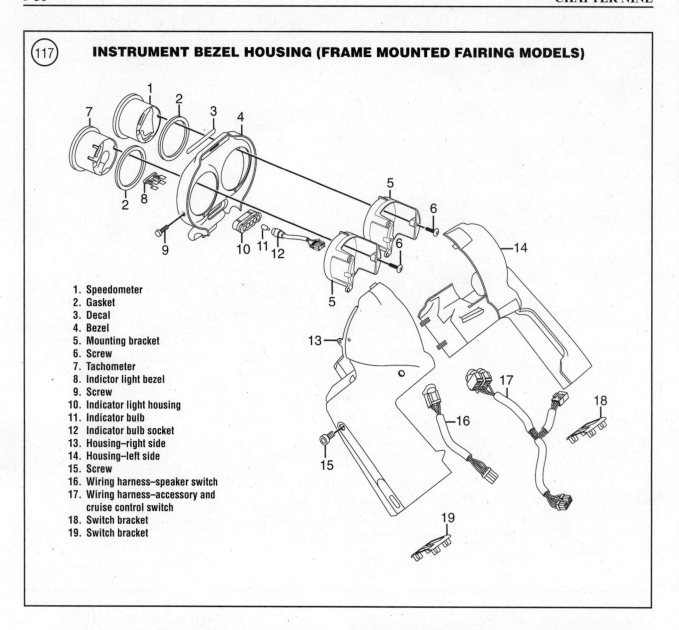

117 **INSTRUMENT BEZEL HOUSING (FRAME MOUNTED FAIRING MODELS)**

1. Speedometer
2. Gasket
3. Decal
4. Bezel
5. Mounting bracket
6. Screw
7. Tachometer
8. Indictor light bezel
9. Screw
10. Indicator light housing
11. Indicator bulb
12. Indicator bulb socket
13. Housing–right side
14. Housing–left side
15. Screw
16. Wiring harness–speaker switch
17. Wiring harness–accessory and
    cruise control switch
18. Switch bracket
19. Switch bracket

Equally space the dots around the outer circumference of the threads.

b. Tighten the ACR solenoid to 11-15 ft.-lb. (14.9-20.3 N•m).

SWITCHES

Testing

Test switches for continuity by using an ohmmeter or a self-powered test light at the switch connector while moving the switch to its various operating positions. Compare the results with the switch operating schematic included in the wiring diagrams (located in Chapter Sixteen of this manual).

For example, **Figure 123** shows the continuity diagram for a typical ignition switch. The horizontal lines on the diagram indicate which terminals should show continuity when the switch is in a given position. When the switch is

set to ignition, there should be continuity between the red/black, red and red/gray terminals. An ohmmeter connected between these three terminals should indicate little or no resistance, or a test light should light. When the switch is off, there should be no continuity between the same terminals.

Replace a switch if it does not perform properly.

When testing the switches, note the following:

1. Check the battery as described in this chapter. Charge or replace the battery if necessary.

NOTE
Always disarm the optional security system (TSSM/HFSM) before disconnecting the battery or before pulling the Main-Fuse so the siren will not sound.

2. Disconnect the negative battery cable as described in this chapter.

3. Detach all connectors located between the switch and the electrical circuit.

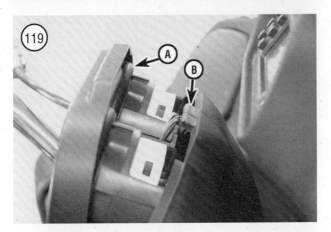

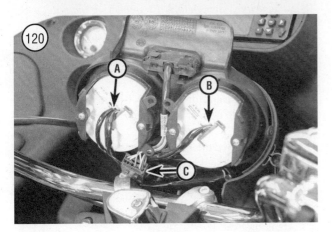

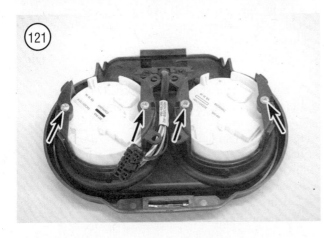

CAUTION
Do not attempt to start the engine with the battery disconnected.

4. When separating a connector, pull on the connector housings and not the wires.

5. After locating a defective circuit, check the connectors to make sure they are all clean and properly mated. Check all wires going into a connector housing to make sure each wire is positioned properly and the wire end is not loose.

6. To reconnect a connector, push the housings together until they click or snap into place.

Handlebar Switches

Left handlebar switch description

The left side handlebar switch housing (**Figure 124**) is equipped with the following switches:
1. Headlight high/low beam.
2. Horn.
3. Left side turn signal.
4. Audio controls (on/off).
5. CB control.
6. Cruise control, on/off (models so equipped).
7. Clutch interlock switch.

Right handlebar switch description

The right side handlebar switch housing (**Figure 125**) is equipped with the following switches:
1. Engine stop/run.
2. Starter.
3. Right side turn signal.
4. Front brake light.
5. Mode select up/down (models so equipped).
6. Cruise control, set/resume (models so equipped).

Handlebar switch replacement

1. Remove the screws securing the left side switch housing (**Figure 126**) to the handlebar. Then, carefully separate the switch housing (**Figure 127**) to access the defective switch.

(123)   **SWITCH**

Position \ Switch	Red/Black	Red	Red/Gray
Off		•	
Acc.		•—————————————————	————————————•
Ignition	•—————————————	•—————————————	————————————•

2. Remove the screws securing the right side switch housing (**Figure 128**) to the handlebar. Then, carefully separate the switch housing to access the defective switch.

NOTE
To service the front brake light switch, refer to ***Front Brake Light Switch Replacement*** *(this section).*

3A. On models without splices, remove the screw and bracket.
3B. On models with splices, remove the cable strap.
4. Pull the switch(es) out of the housing.
5. Cut the switch wire(s) from the defective switch(es).
6. Slip a piece of heat shrink tubing over each cut wire.
7. Solder the wire end(s) to the new switch. Then, shrink the tubing over the wire(s) by heating it.
8. Install the switch by reversing the removal steps, while noting the following:
   a. When clamping the switch housing onto the handlebar, check the wiring harness routing position to make sure it is not pinched between the housing and handlebar.
   b. Tighten the housing screws securely.

Front Brake Light Switch Replacement

The front brake light switch is mounted in the right side switch lower housing.
1. Separate the right side switch housing as described in this section.
2. If still in place, remove the spacer between the switch and the switch housing.
3. While depressing the switch plunger, slowly rotate the switch upward, rocking it slightly, and remove it from the switch housing.
4. Cut the switch wires from the defective switch.
5. Slip a piece of heat shrink tubing over each cut wire.
6. Solder the wire ends to the new switch. Then, shrink the tubing over the wires.

7. Install the switch by reversing the removal steps while noting the following.
8. When clamping the switch housing onto the handlebar, check the wiring harness routing position to make sure it is not pinched between the housing and handlebar.

Ignition/Light Key Switch
Removal/Installation (Road King Models)

NOTE
Always disarm the optional TSSM/HFSM security system before disconnecting the battery or pulling the Main-Fuse so the siren will not sound.

1. Disconnect the negative battery cable as described in this chapter.
2. Remove the seat as described in Chapter Fourteen.
3. Lay several towels or a blanket on the frame and rear fender.
4. Partially remove the fuel tank console as follows:
   a. Remove the socket screw at the front of the fuel tank console.
   b. Remove the rear hex screw and release the rear of the fuel tank console bracket from the clip nut on the fuel tank bracket.
5. Turn the fuel tank console over onto towels and disconnect the 3-pin Packard connector (A, **Figure 129**) from the ignition switch.
6. Release the wiring harness from the clip (B, **Figure 129**).
7. Remove the four screws (C, **Figure 129**) securing the ignition switch to the bottom surface of the fuel tank console.
8. Remove the ignition switch.
9. Install by reversing the removal steps, while noting the following:
   a. Install the new ignition switch with the electrical connector terminal facing toward the rear of the fuel console.

(124) **HANDLEBAR SWITCH
(LEFT SIDE)**

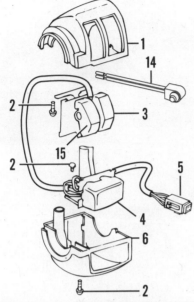

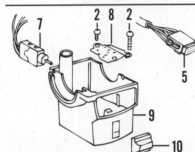

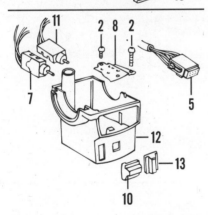

(125) **HANDLEBAR SWITCH
(RIGHT SIDE)**

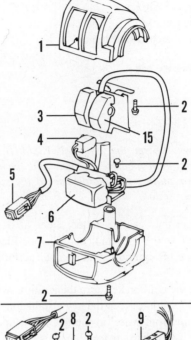

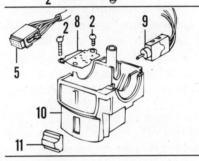

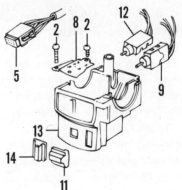

9

1. Upper housing
2. Screw
3. Headlight high/
   low switch
4. Left turn
   signal switch
5. Electrical
   connector
6. Lower housing
   (FLHR series)
7. Audio control
   switch (+/−)
8. Bracket
9. Lower housing
   (FLHT series)
10. Audio control
    knob (+/−)
11. Cruise control
    ON/OFF switch
12. Lower housing
    (FLTR series)
13. CB control knob
14. Clutch interlock
    switch
15. Horn switch

1. Upper housing
2. Screw
3. Engine starter
   switch
4. Front brake
   light switch
5. Electrical
   connector
6. Right turn
   signal switch
7. Lower housing
   (FLHR series)
8. Bracket
9. Mode select
   (up/down) switch
10. Lower housing
    (FLHT series)
11. Mode select
    (up/down) knob
12. Cruise control
    set/resume switch
13. Lower housing
    (FLTR series)
14. Cruise control
    set/resume knob
15. Engine run/stop switch

b. Tighten the four screws to 36-60 in.-lb. (4.1-6.8 N•m).

Ignition/Light Switch
Removal/Installation
(All Models Except Road King)

Refer to **Figure 130**.

Removal

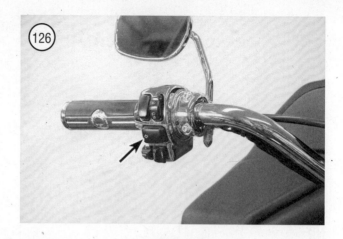

> *NOTE*
> *Always disarm the optional TSSM/HFSM security system before disconnecting the battery or pulling the Main-Fuse so the siren will not sound.*

1. Disconnect the negative battery cable as described in this chapter. Remove the handlebar (Chapter Elevem)
2. To remove the ignition switch knob, perform the following:
   a. Using the ignition key, turn the ignition switch to the unlock position. Keep the key installed in the knob.
   b. Turn the front wheel to the left fork stop. Turn the ignition switch to the fork lock position.
   c. Insert a small, flat-bladed screwdriver (A, **Figure 131**) under the left side of the switch knob and depress the release button. Keep it depressed.

> *NOTE*
> *The spring will drop out of the underside of the knob as the knob is removed.*

   d. Push the ignition key down, turn the ignition key 60° *counterclockwise* (B, **Figure 131**). Lift up and remove the switch knob.
3. To reposition switch after the switch knob has been removed, insert the ignition switch alignment tool (JIMS part No. 943 or H-D part No. HD-45962) into the switch housing until the bottom of the tool handle bottoms on the threaded post (**Figure 132**).
4. Turn the front wheel to the right fork stop.
5. Use a 7/8 in. open end wrench and loosen the ignition switch nut (**Figure 133**). Unscrew and remove the nut from the threaded post.

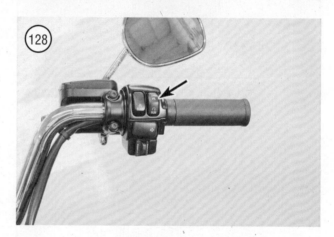

6. Remove the collar and spacer (**Figure 134**) from the threaded post.
7A. On FLHX and FLHT series models, pull on the tabs and remove the decal plate (**Figure 135**) from the slots in the fairing cap.
7B. On FLTR series models, pull on the tabs and remove the decal plate (**Figure 135**) from the slots in the instrument nacelle.
8A. On FLHX and FLHT series models, perform the following:
   a. Remove the outer fairing as described in Chapter Fourteen.

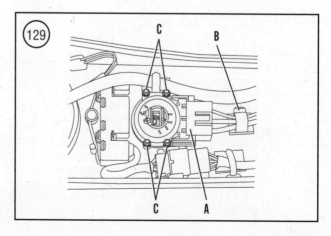

IGNITION SWITCH
(ALL MODELS EXCEPT ROAD KING AND FLHTCUSE, FLTRUSE)

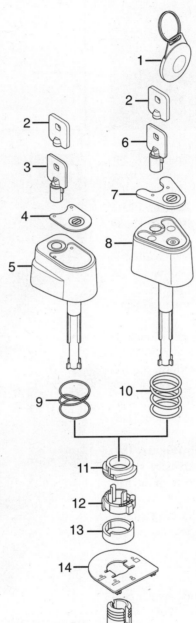

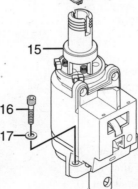

1. Remote control FOB
2. Cover
3. Key (HDI)
4. Decal (HDI)
5. Ignition switch (HDI)
6. Key
7. Decal
8. Ignition switch
9. Spring (HDI)

10. Spring
11. Nut
12. Collar
13. Spacer
14. Decal plate
15. Ignition switch
16. Allen bolt
17. Washer

9

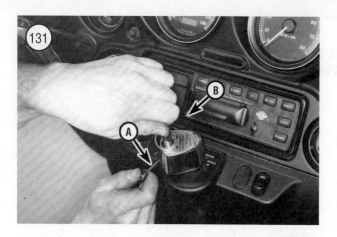

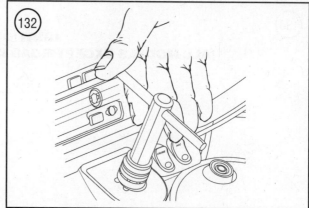

b. Insert a long shaft ball end socket (Snap-On part No. FABL6E), or an equivalent, through the oblong holes in the fairing brackets and remove the four Allen bolts. Release the radio, or storage box (on FLHT series models), from the right and left radio support brackets and move it to one side.

c. Carefully cut the straps securing the main harness to the lower right side corner of the radio, or storage box.

d. Remove the fairing cap as described in Chapter Fourteern.

8B. On FLTR series models, remove the headlight nacelle as described in this chapter.

9. On FLHX and FLHT series models, perform the following:

a. Remove the Torx screws (**Figure 136**) and washers securing the fairing cap on each side of the inner fairing.

b. Carefully disengage the fairing cap (**Figure 137**) and pull it down. Disconnect the auxiliary switch electrical connectors (A, **Figure 138**) from the harness.

c. Carefully remove the auxiliary switch wiring harness (B, **Figure 138**) from the ignition switch and remove the fairing cap from the inner fairing.

10. Disconnect the 3-pin ignition switch Packard connector at the front of the ignition as follows:

a. Carefully insert the end of the ignition switch connector remover (H-D part No. HD-45961), or an equivalent, into the slot in the ignition switch housing until it bottoms.

b. Hold onto the tool (A, **Figure 139**) and the wiring harness and pull on both parts at the same time, and release the socket housing (B) from the ignition switch.

11. Remove the handlebar upper clamp (Chapter Eleven) and move the handlebar assembly out of the way.

12A. On non-HDI models, remove the two Allen screws (A, **Figure 140**) and flat washers securing the ignition switch to the upper fork bracket. Remove the ignition switch (B, **Figure 140**).

12B. On HDI models, remove the break-away screws as follows:

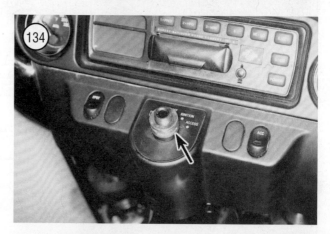

a. Make a pilot divot in the top of the screws (A, **Figure 140**) with a center punch and hammer. Make it deep enough to guide the drill bit in the next step.

b. Install a 1/8 inch left-handed drill bit into the drill and set the drill to *reverse direction*.

c. Center the drill bit in the divot. Turn the drill at low speed and spin out the break-away screw.

d. Repeat for the remaining screw.

e. Remove the ignition switch (B, **Figure 140**).

Installation

1. Insert the ignition switch into the upper fork bracket bore.

2A. On non-HDI models, install the two screws and flat washers securing the ignition switch. Tighten the screws to 36-60 in.-lb. (4.1-6.8 N•m).

2B. On HDI models, perform the following:

a. Thoroughly clean the screw threads in the fork bracket.

b. Install *new* screws and flat washers securing the ignition switch. Slowly tighten the screws until the heads snap off.

3. Install the handlebar as described in Chapter Eleven.

4. Connect the 3-pin ignition switch Packard connector onto the front of the ignition switch.

5A. On FLHT series and FLHX series models, perform the following:

a. Install a *new* strap securing the ignition switch main harness to the lower right side of the radio (or storage box).

b. Install the fairing cap as described in Chapter Seventeen.

c. Move the radio, or storage box on FLHT series models, back into position.

d. Install the four Allen screws securing the radio, or storage box on FLHT series models, onto the right and left radio support brackets. Tighten the screws to 35-45 in.-lb. (4.0-5.1 N•m).

e. Install the outer fairing as described in Chapter Fourteen.

5B. On FLTR series models, install the headlight nacelle as described in this chapter.

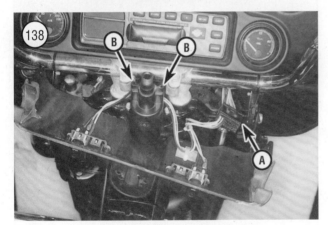

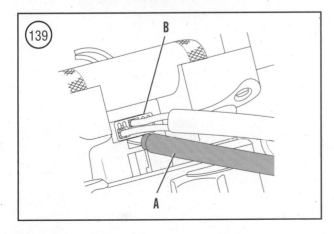

6A. On FLHT series and FLHX series models, install the decal plate tabs (**Figure 135**) into the slots in the fairing cap.

6B. On FLTR series models, install the decal plate tabs (**Figure 135**) into the slots in the instrument nacelle.

7. Position the spacer with the widest side facing forward and so the inside tabs align with the slots in the threaded post. Install the spacer (**Figure 134**) and push it down until it contacts the decal plate.

8. Position the collar so the outside tab is facing forward and the inside tabs align with the slots in the threaded post. Install the collar (**Figure 134**) and push it down until it contacts the spacer.

9. Position the nut with the flange side going on first and thread the nut onto the threaded post.

10. Turn the front wheel to the right fork stop. Use a 7/8 in. open-end crowfoot and tighten the nut to 85-115 in.-lb. (9.6-13.0 N•m).

11. Install the spring into the bore on the underside of the knob.

12. Position the knob pointing toward the FORK LOCK position and install the knob onto the threaded post.

13. Hold the knob down, insert the knob shaft into the threaded post. Hold the known down, turn the knob *clockwise* to the UNLOCK position until a click is heard. This indicates that the knob and switch are properly engaged. Release the knob and rotate it through all four positions and verify proper operation.

14. Connect the negative battery cable as described in this chapter.

POWER LOCK IGNITION SWITCH KNOB (FLTRUSE AND 2012-ON FLHTCUSE MODELS)

Removal

Refer to **Figure 141**.

> *NOTE*
> *The power lock ignition switch knob is not serviceable. If defective, it must be replaced.*

> *NOTE*
> *Always disarm the optional security system (TSM/TSSM/HFSM) before disconnecting the battery or pulling the main fuse so the siren will not sound.*

1. Disconnect the negative battery cable as described in this chapter

2. Remove the headlight assembly as described in this chapter.

3. Within the outer fairing, release the electrical harness from the anchored cable straps on the base of the radio chassis. Disconnect the power lock 2-pin electrical connector (**Figure 142**) from the harness.

4. Secure a length of mechanics wire, or heavy cord, to the power lock electrical connector harness. Tie the loose end to the front fork.

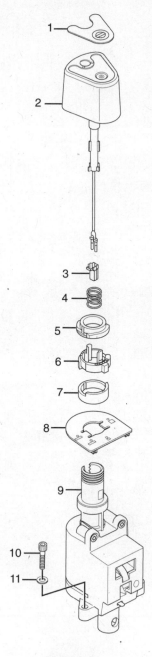

(141)

IGNITION SWITCH/POWER LOCK (FLHTCUSE, FLTRUSE MODELS)

1. Decal plate
2. Ignition switch
3. Socket
4. Spring
5. Nut
6. Collar
7. Spacer
8. Decal plate
9. Ignition switch
10. Allen bolt
11. Washer

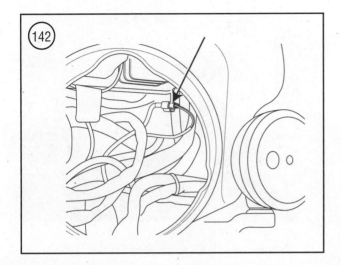

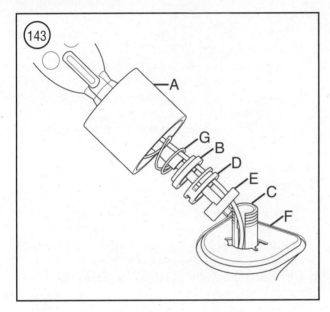

5. Release the ignition switch knob as follows:
   a. Using the ignition key, turn the ignition switch to the ACC position. Keep the key installed in the knob.
   b. Turn the key *counterclockwise* while pressing button on bottom of knob to release knob.
   c. Lift the knob (A, **Figure 143**) until the shaft clears the switch (C).
6. Remove the nut (B, **Figure 143**) and pull the collar (D) and spacer (E) off the switch (C).
7. Make sure the loose end of the mechanics wire, or heavy cord, is still attached to the front fork.
8. Carefully pull straight up and remove the knob, spring, nut, collar, spacer and switch decal plate and mechanics wire, or heavy cord, up through the notch in the fairing cap opening.
9. Untie the mechanics wire, or heavy cord, from wiring harness but leave it within the fairing cap area. This will be used to pull the wiring harness back through the fairing cap.
10. In order to remove all parts from the wiring harness, disconnect the two individual wires from the 2-pin electri-

cal. Remove these parts from the harness and keep in the order shown in **Figure 141**.

Installation

1. If removed, install all parts removed in *Removal Step 10* in the correct order shown in **Figure 141**.
2. If disconnected, connect the two individual wires onto the 2-pin electrical connector as follows:
   a. Terminal 1: green wire.
   b. Terminal 2: blue wire.
3. Install the spacer (E, **Figure 143**) and switch decal plate (F) over the wiring harness and the mechanics wire, or heavy cord.
4. Install the switch decal plate (F, **Figure 143**) back onto the tabs in the fairing cap. Make sure it is locked into place.
5. Install the spacer (E, **Figure 143**) and collar (D) onto the switch (C) and thread on the nut (B). Make sure all parts are on place and tighten the nut to 85-115 in.-lb. (9.6-13.0 N•m).
6. Install the ignition switch knob as follows:
   a. Turn the key (ital)counterclockwise(end) to the UNLOCK position.

CAUTION
Take caution to not scrape off any insulation from the wiring harness in the next step.

   b. Position the knob pointing toward ACC position; insert the shaft into the switch assembly while carefully, and slowly, pull the mechanics wire, or heavy cord, and the switch knob components back through the fairing cap and headlight housing while inserting the knob into the switch.
   c. Hold the knob down and turn the key *clockwise*. When correctly engaged an audible click will be heard indicating the knob and switch are properly engaged.
   d. Rotate the knob through all four positions to verity correct operation.
7. Within the outer fairing, secure the electrical harness onto the anchored cable straps on the base of the radio chassis. Connect the power lock 2-pin electrical connector (**Figure 142**) onto the harness.
8. Install the headlight assembly as described in this chapter.
9. Connect the negative battery cable as described in this chapter.
10. Test the power lock operation.

Oil Pressure Switch/Sender

Operation

The oil pressure switch, or sender, is located on the front right side of the crankcase.

A pressure-actuated, diaphragm-type oil pressure switch, or sender, is used. When the oil pressure is low or when oil is not circulating through a running engine, spring tension inside the switch, or sender, holds the switch contacts closed. This completes the signal light circuit and causes the oil pressure indicator lamp to light.

NOTE
The oil pressure indicator light may not come on when the ignition switch is turned off and then back on immediately. This is due to the oil pressure retained in the oil filter housing. Test the electrical part of the oil pressure switch as described in this section. If the oil pressure switch, indicator light and related wiring are in good condition, inspect the engine lubrication system as described in Chapter Two.

The oil pressure signal light should turn on when any of the following occurs:
1. The ignition switch is turned on prior to starting the engine.
2. The engine idle is below idle speed of 950-1050 rpm.
3. The engine is operating with low oil pressure.
4. Oil is not circulating through the running engine.

Testing/replacement

1A. On FLHR series models including CVO, pull on the elbow connector and disconnect the electrical connector from the switch.
1B. On FLHT, FLHX and FLTR series models, pull the external latch outward, use a rocking motion, and disconnect the 4-pin Delphi connector from the sender (**Figure 144**).
2. Turn the ignition switch on.
3A. On FLHR series models with switch, ground the switch wire to the engine.
3B. On all models except FLHR series with a switch, ground the brown/green terminal within the Delphi connector to the engine with a jumper wire.
4. The oil pressure indicator light on the instrument panel should light.
5. If the indicator lamp does not light, check for a defective indicator light and inspect all wiring between the switch or sender, and the indicator light.
6A. If the oil pressure warning light operates properly, attach the electrical connector to the pressure switch. Make sure the connection is tight and free from oil. On models with a switch, slide the rubber boot back into position.
6B. If the warning light remains on when the engine is running, shut the engine off. Check the engine lubrication system as described in Chapter Two.
7A. To replace the switch, perform the following:
   a. Use a 15/16 in. open-end crowfoot wrench and unscrew it from the engine.
   b. Apply Loctite pipe sealant with Teflon 565 to the switch threads prior to installation.
   c. Install the switch and tighten to 96-144 in.-lb. (10.8-16.3 N•m).

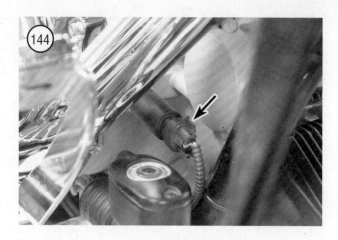

   d. Test the new switch as described in this section.
7B. To replace the oil pressure sending unit, perform the following:
   a. Use a 1-1/16 in. open-end crowfoot wrench and unscrew it from the engine.
   b. Apply Loctite pipe sealant with Teflon 565 to the sender threads prior to installation.
   c. Install the sender and tighten to 96-144 in.-lb. (10.8-16.3 N•m).
   d. Test the new sender as described in this section.

Neutral Indicator Switch
Testing/Replacement

The neutral indicator switch is located on the rear left side of the transmission case. The neutral indicator light on the instrument panel should light when the ignition is on and the transmission is in neutral.

1. Disconnect the electrical connector (**Figure 145**) from the neutral indicator switch.
2. Turn the ignition switch to IGN.
3. Ground the neutral indicator switch wire to the transmission case.
4. If the neutral indicator lamp lights, the neutral switch is defective. Replace the neutral indicator switch and retest.
5. If the neutral indicator lamp does not light, check for a defective indicator light, faulty wiring or a loose or corroded connection.

NOTE
The electrical connector can be attached to either stud on the switch.

6A. If the neutral switch operates correctly, attach the electrical connector to the neutral switch. Make sure the connection is tight and free from oil.
6B. If the neutral switch is defective, replace the neutral indicator switch as described in this section.
7. To replace the old switch, perform the following:
   a. Shift the transmission into neutral.
   b. Unscrew and remove the old switch and O-ring from the transmission cover.
   c. Apply clean transmission oil to the *new* O-ring seal.

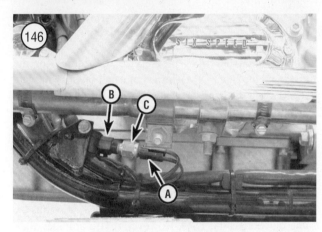

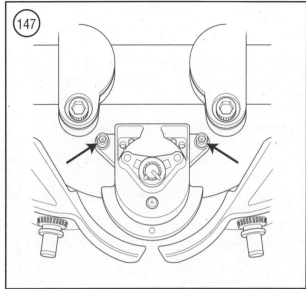

d. Install the new neutral switch and tighten to 120-180 in.-lb. (13.6-20.3 N•m).

Rear Brake Light Switch
Testing/Replacement

A hydraulic, normally-open rear brake light switch is used on all models. The rear brake light is attached to the rear brake caliper hose assembly. When the rear brake pedal is applied, hydraulic pressure closes the switch contacts, providing a ground path so the rear brake light comes on. If the rear brake light does not come on, perform the following.

NOTE
Removal of the exhaust system is not necessary, but it does provide additional work room.

1. If necessary, remove the exhaust system from the right side as described in Chapter Four.
2. Turn the ignition switch off.
3. Disconnect the electrical connector (A, **Figure 146**) from the switch.
4. Connect an ohmmeter between the switch terminals and check the following:
   a. Apply the rear brake pedal. There should be continuity.
   b. Release the rear brake pedal. There should be no continuity.

c. If the switch fails either of these tests, replace the switch as described in the section.
5. Place a drip pan under the switch, as some brake fluid will drain out when the switch is removed.
6. Secure the brake line fitting (B, **Figure 146**) with a suitable size wrench to prevent it from rotating.
7. Unscrew the switch (C, **Figure 146**) from the fitting (B).
8. Apply Loctite pipe sealant with Teflon 565 to the switch threads prior to installation.
9. Install the *new* switch and tighten it to 12-15 ft.-lb. (16.3-20.3 N•m).
10. Reconnect the switch electrical connector.
11. Bleed the rear brake as described in Chapter Thirteen.
12. Check the rear brake light with the ignition switch turned on and the rear brake applied.
13. If removed, install the right side exhaust system as described in Chapter Four.

FORK LOCK (ROAD KING MODELS)

Removal/installation

Refer to **Figure 147**.

1. Remove the instrument bezel housing as described in Chapter Fourteen.
2. Remove the two screws and flat washers securing the fork lock assembly to the upper fork bridge.
3. Remove the fork lock.
4. Install the fork lock and flat washers and tighten to 36-60 in.-lb. (4.1-6.8 N•m).
5. Install the instrument bezel housing as described in Chapter Fourteen.

HORN

Testing

1. Remove the seat as described in Chapter Fourteen.
2. Partially remove the cover and horn (**Figure 148**) to access the backside of the horn.
3. Disconnect only the yellow/black electrical connector (A, **Figure 149**) from the backside of the horn.
4. Connect a voltmeter as follows:
    a. Positive test lead to the yellow/black electrical connector.
    b. Negative test lead to ground.
5. Turn the ignition switch to IGN.
6. Depress the horn button. If battery voltage is present the horn is faulty or is not grounded properly. If there is no battery voltage, either the horn switch or the horn wiring is faulty.
7. Replace the horn or horn switch as necessary.

Replacement

NOTE
Always disarm the optional TSSM/HFSM security system before disconnecting the battery or pulling the Main-Fuse so the siren will not sound.

1. Remove the seat as described in Chapter Fourteen.
2. Disconnect the negative battery cable as described in this chapter.
3. Remove the acorn nut (**Figure 148**) and washer securing the horn assembly to the frame's rubber mount stud.
4. Disconnect the elbow electrical terminals from the horn spade terminals (A and B, **Figure 149**). Open the J-clamp (C, **Figure 149**).
5. Remove the 10-mm flange nut (D, **Figure 149**) from the backside of the horn mounting bracket. Remove the horn from the cover.
6. Install the horn onto the chrome cover inserting the stud on the backside through the mounting bracket hole.
7. Apply several drops of Loctite Threadlocker No. 222 (purple) onto the horn stud.
8. Install the 10-mm flange nut (D, **Figure 149**) onto the horn stud and tighten to 80-100 in.-lb. (9.0-11.3 N•m).
9. Connect the elbow electrical terminals onto the horn spade terminals (A and B, **Figure 149**).
10. Capture the wiring harness into the J-clamp (C, **Figure 149**) and install the horn bracket onto the rubber mount.
11. Install the flat washer and acorn nut. Tighten the acorn nut to 80-120 in.-lb. (9.0-13.6 N•m).
12. Connect the negative battery cable as described in this chapter.
13. Check that the horn operates correctly.
14. Install the seat as described in Chapter Fourteen.

TURN SIGNAL SECURITY MODULE (TSM, TSSM AND HFSM)

This section describes the service procedures for the turn signal module (TSM), turn signal and security module (TSSM), and the hands-free security module (HFSM).

The turn signal module (TSM) is an electronic microprocessor that controls the turn signals and four-way hazard flasher. The turn signal module receives its information from the speedometer and turn signal switches. The bank angle sensor (BAS) is integrated into the module and provides motorcycle movement signals to the ECM.

The turn signal and security module (TSSM) performs the same function as the TSM. However, it also provides additional security and immobilization functions. When activated, the security system alternately flashes the left and right turn signals and sounds an optional siren on models so equipped.

The hands-free security system (HFSM) performs the same function as the TSSM, but it includes a key fob for convenient arming and disarming of the security system.

Whenever the TSM/TSSM/HFSM is replaced, the new device must be reprogrammed using the Harley-Davidson digital technician tool. Take the motorcycle to a dealership or other qualified shop for reprogramming.

NOTE
The security system is activated, and the optional siren sounds, whenever the ignition circuit is tampered with, if the vehicle is moved, or whenever the battery or ground connection is broken. Always disarm the security system before servicing the motorcycle, before disconnecting the negative battery cable or before pulling the Maxi-Fuse.

Removal/Installation

NOTE
Always disarm the optional security system TSM/TSSM/HFSM before disconnecting the battery or pulling the main fuse so the siren will not sound.

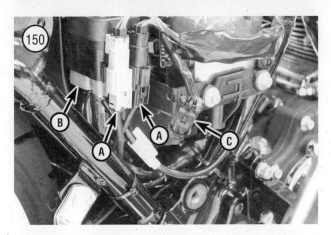

NOTE
If the vehicle is equipped with the optional **Harley-Davidson Smart Security System**, *verify that the security status icon on the speedometer face is* **not** *flashing before proceeding. If not, turn off the system.*

1. With the security fob in the immediate area of the motorcycle, turn the ignition switch ON.
2. Remove the main fuse as described in this chapter.
3. Remove the seat as described in Chapter Fourteen.
4. Remove the right side saddlebag as described in Chapter Fourteen.

NOTE
It is not necessary to disconnect or remove the oxygen sensor connectors (A, **Figure 150)** *from the upper retainer.*

5. Pull out on the bottom of the TSM/TSSM/HFSM module (B, **Figure 150**) and release it from the retainer in the battery tray.
6. On models so equipped, release the ABS wheel connector (C, **Figure 150**) from the battery tray.
7. Remove the module from the upper retainer and disconnect the TSM/TSSM module.
8. On models so equipped, disconnect the HFSM antenna jumper harness connector.

9. Installation is the reverse of removal steps. A new password must be learned if installing a new TSM/TSSM/HFSM module.
10. Test all turn signal functions and security system prior to riding the motorcycle.

Turn Signal Operation

Automatic cancellation

NOTE
The turn signal security module will not cancel the signal before the turn is actually completed.

1. When the turn signal switch is depressed, then released, the system begins a 20 count. As long as the motorcycle is moving above 7 MPH (11 KPH) the turn signals will always cancel after the 20 bulb flashes, providing the system does not receive any additional input.
2. If the motorcycle's speed drops to 7 MPH (11 KPH) or less, including stopping, the turn signals will continue to flash. The counting will continue when the motorcycle reaches 8 MPH (13 KPH) and will automatically cancel when the count total equals 20 bulb flashes.
3. The turn signals will cancel within two seconds after the turn of 45° or more is completed.

Manual cancellation

1. After the turn signal switch is depressed, and then released, the system begins a 20 count. To cancel the turn signal from flashing, depress the turn signal switch a second time.
2. If the turn direction is to be changed, depress the opposite turn signal switch. The primary signal is cancelled and the opposite turn signal will flash.

Four-way flashing

1. Turn the ignition switch to IGN. On models so equipped, disarm the security system. Press the right and left turn signal switches at the same time. All four turn signals will flash.
2. On models with the security system, the system can be armed so all four signals flash for up to two hours. Turn the ignition switch off and arm the security system. Press both the right and left turn signal switches at the same time.
3. To cancel the four-way flashing, disarm the security system, on models so equipped, and press both the right and left turn signal switches at the same time.

Bank angle sensor (BAS)

The bank angle sensor automatically shuts off the engine if the motorcycle tilts more than 45° for longer than one second. The shutoff occurs even at a very slow speed. The sensor is an integral part of the TSM/TSSM/HFSM unit.

9

To restart the motorcycle, return the motorcycle to vertical. Turn the ignition switch off, and back to IGN. Then, restart the engine.

Security System Operation

If a theft attempt is detected when the TSSM/HFSM is armed, the system immobilizes the starting and ignition systems. It also alternately flashes the right and left turn signals and sounds the siren, if so equipped. The following conditions activate the armed security system.

1. If the system detects tampering with the ignition system or detects vehicle movement, it issues the first warning: the turn signals flash three times and the optional siren chirps once. If the motorcycle is not returned to its original position within four seconds, the system issues a second warning. If the tampering continues, the system goes into full alarm: the turn signals alternately flash and the optional siren sounds for 30 seconds. If the motorcycle is not returned to its original position after a ten second pause, the system repeats full alarm. It repeats this cycle (30-seconds on/10-seconds off) for ten times or for a total of five minutes.

2. If the system detects a battery or ground disconnect, the optional siren sounds but the turn signals do not flash.

NOTE
Always disarm the optional TSSM/HFSM before disconnecting the battery or the siren will sound. If the TSSM is in auto-alarming mode, disarm the system with two clicks of the key fob, and disconnect the battery or remove the TSSM fuse before the 30-second arming period expires.

HFSM ANTENNA

Removal/Installation

1. Remove the seat as described in Chapter Fourteen.
2. Release the HFSM antenna (**Figure 151**) from the top of the top electrical caddy.
3. Disconnect the HFSM antenna jumper harness.
4. If necessary, remove the HFSM jumper harness as follows:
   a. Release the HFSM from the top of the top electrical caddy.
   b. Disconnect the HFSM antenna jumper harness.
   c. Carefully cut the cable strap retaining the jumper harness and main harness to the frame down tube.
   d. Remove the jumper harness through the opening in the right side.
5. Installation is the reverse of removal steps.

SMART SIREN (OPTIONAL)

Removal/Installation

1. Remove the seat as described in Chapter Fourteen.
2. Remove the left side saddlebag and left side cover as described in Chapter Fourteen.

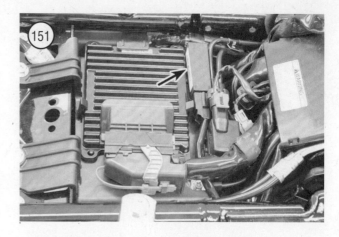

3. With the smart securing system disarmed, remove the main fuse as described in this chapter.
4. Separate the electrical connector from the smart siren.
5. Release the smart siren from the retainers on the left side fuse panel.
6. Installation is the reverse of removal steps. The siren is operating correctly if it responds with two chirps.

ADVANCED AUDIO SYSTEM (FLHTCUSE MODELS)

Removal/Installation

Refer to **Figure 152**.

NOTE
Figure 152 illustrates the major electrical connectors for the advanced audio system. Some models are equipped with various components and connectors and they are located within the inner fairing compartment. Not all connectors are shown in the illustration.

NOTE
Always disarm the optional security system TSM/TSSM/HFSM before disconnecting the battery or pulling the main fuse so the siren will not sound.

1. Remove the negative battery cable as described in this chapter.
2. Remove the outer fairing as described in Chapter Fourteen.
3. Within the inner fairing, disconnect the electrical connector for the specific component to be removed as follows:
   a. XM module 12-pin connector (185).
   b. XM antenna connector.
   c. CB transceiver 12-pin connector (184).
   d. AM/FM/WB antenna connector (51).
   e. AM/FM/WB 23-pin connector (27) and 35-pin connector (28).
   f. iPod module 8-pin connector (274).
   g. CB antenna (50).

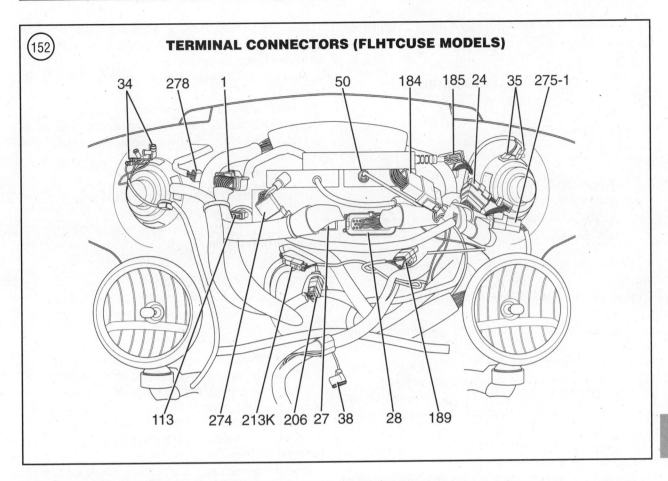

TERMINAL CONNECTORS (FLHTCUSE MODELS)

152

34 278 1 50 184 185 24 35 275-1

113 274 213K 206 27 38 28 189

9

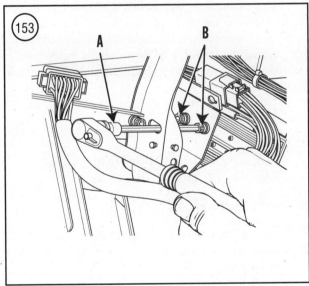

153

A B

NOTE

The AM/FM/WB radio, CB transceiver and iPod module may be all removed as an assembly. The XM Satellite Radio module and bracket is secured with the radio mounting screws and must be removed prior to removing the remaining audio system assembly.

4. Disconnect the CB, XM and iPod antenna connectors.

5. Disconnect the XM module 12-pin connector (185).

6. Disconnect the CB transceiver 12-pin connector (184).

7. Disconnect the AM/FM/WB 23-pin connector (27) and 35-pin connector (28).

8. Disconnect the iPod module 8-pin connector (274) and XM antenna connector.

NOTE
Record the location of all cable straps, prior to removal. The straps must be reinstalled in the same location.

9. Carefully remove the cable straps securing the ignition switch harness to the bottom of the radio chassis.

10. On modes so equipped, carefully remove the cable straps securing the heated handgrip power connector to the bottom of the radio chassis.

11. Use a long-shank, ball-end socket (Snap-On part No. FABL6E (A, **Figure 153**), or an equivalent tool, and remove the four screws (B) securing the radio to the right and left side support brackets (**Figure 154**).

12. Remove the XM Satellite Radio module and mounting bracket from the top of the advanced audio system.

13. Carefully pull straight forward and lifting up slightly and remove the advanced audio sound system clearing the fairing radio bezel.

14. Remove the CB module and iPod module from the radio.

15. Installation is the reverse of removal steps. Tighten all screws securely.

ADVANCED AUDIO RADIO
(FLTRXSE MODELS)

Radio Removal/Installation

NOTE
Always disarm the optional security system TSM/TSSM/HFSM before disconnecting the battery or pulling the main fuse so the siren will not sound.

1. Remove the negative battery cable as described in this chapter
2. Remove the outer fairing as described in Chapter Fourteen.
3. Disconnect the antenna connector from the backside of the radio.
4. Remove the adhesive backed cable strap mounts securing the antenna and harness to the radio top surface.
5. Use 3M General Purpose Adhesive Remover, or an equivalent, and remove adhesive residue from the radio top surface.
6. Disconnect the AM/FM/WB ratio 23-pin connector (28) and receiver 35-pin connector (27).
7. Remove the four mounting screws and pull the radio forward and remove it from the rider's side of the inner fairing.
8. Installation is the reverse of removal steps, note the following:
    a. Correctly position the cable strap mounts onto the radio top surface, and adhere them into place.
    b. Tighten the screws to 35-45 in.-lb. (4.0-5.1 N•m).

Hidden Antenna
Removal/Installation

NOTE
Always disarm the optional security system TSM/TSSM/HFSM before disconnecting the battery or pulling the main fuse so the siren will not sound.

1. Remove the negative battery cable as described in this chapter.
2. Remove the outer fairing as described in Chapter Fourteen.
3. Disconnect the antenna connector from the backside of the radio.
4. Remove the antenna module.
5. Remove the adhesive backed cable strap mounts securing the antenna and harness to the radio top surface, and the inner fairing.

6. Use 3M General Purpose Adhesive Remover, or an equivalent, and remove adhesive residue from the radio top surface and inner fairing.
7. Installation is the reverse of removal steps, note the following:
    a. Install new cable strap mounts.
    b. Correctly position the cable strap mounts onto the radio top surface and inner fairing, and adhere them into place.

ADVANCED AUDIO AMPLIFIER
(FLHTCUSE MODELS)

Removal/Installation

NOTE
The advanced audio amplifier is attached to the underside of the Tour-Pac support and bracket.

1. Remove the main fuse as described in this chapter.
2. Remove the seat as described in Chapter Fourteen.
3. Place a wide tip flat blade screwdriver under the advanced audio amplifier multi-pin connector and pull the latch down to release the connector (149).
4. Carefully remove the cable straps securing the wiring harness to the Tour-Pak support bar.
5. Remove the passenger headset socket from the clip.
6. Place a clean shop cloth or mall hand towel on the rear fender to protect the finish.
7. Secure the amplifier and remove the four nuts and washers securing the amplifier to the mounting bracket under the Tour-Pak. Lower the amplifier and slide out the right side of the frame.
8. Installation is the reverse of removal steps. Tighten the nuts securely.

AUDIO AMPLIFIER
(FLTRXSE MODELS)

Removal/Installation

1. Remove the main fuse as described in this chapter.
2. Remove the left side saddlebag liner as described in Chapter Fourteen.
3. Separate the connector from the audio amplifier.
4. Remove the top mounted screw.
5. Pull the audio amplifier up and remove it from the bracket.
6. If necessary, carefully pry the bracket from the base of the saddlebag.
7. Use general purpose adhesive remover and remove the adhesive residue from the base of the saddlebag.
8. Carefully position bracket into place and adhere into place.
9. Insert the audio amplifier into place making sure the pins and grommets are correctly engaged.

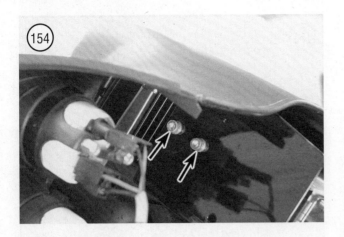

10. Install the top mounting screw and tighten to 15-20 in.-lb. (1.78-2.3 N•m).

11. Attach the connector onto the audio amplifier.

12. Install the left side saddlebag liner as described in Chapter Fourteen.

13. Install the main fuse as described in this chapter.

XM SATELLITE RADIO MODULE (FLHTCUSE MODELS)

Removal/Installation

NOTE
Always disarm the optional security system TSM/TSSM/HFSM before disconnecting the battery or pulling the main fuse so the siren will not sound.

1. Remove the negative battery cable as described in this chapter.

2. Remove the outer fairing as described in Chapter Fourteen.

3. Disconnect the XM module 12-pin connector (185).

4. Disconnect the XM module antenna.

5. Remove the nut securing the XM module to the radio.

6. Installation is the reverse of removal steps. Tighten the nut to 30-40 in.-lb. (3.4-4.5 N•m).

XM SATELLITE RADIO MODULE ANTENNA (FLHTCUSE MODELS)

Removal

NOTE
Figure 152 illustrates the major electrical connectors for the advanced audio system. Some models are equipped with various components and connectors and they must be located within the inner fairing compartment.

NOTE
Always disarm the optional security system TSM/TSSM/HFSM before disconnecting the battery or pulling the main fuse so the siren will not sound.

1. Remove the negative battery cable as described in this chapter.

2. Remove the outer fairing as described in Chapter Fourteen.

3. Disconnect the XM module antenna.

NOTE
The antenna is secured to the bracket with adhesive.

4. Gently pry the antenna from the mounting bracket above the transmitter.

Installation

1. Remove old adhesive residue from the antenna and the antenna mount.

2. Clean all old adhesive from the mount with isopropyl alcohol. Allow to dry.

3. Remove the adhesive backing from the new antenna. If reinstalling the existing antenna apply permanent mounting foam tape to the antenna.

NOTE
After installing the antenna, do not touch or move for it approximately 20 minutes.

4. Correctly position the antenna with the wire lead facing the receiver and center the antenna over the module. Press and hold the antenna for 60 seconds to ensure a good contact.

5. Bundle the antenna lead and secure to harness.

6. Install the outer fairing as described in Chapter Fourteen.

7. Connect the negative battery cable as described in this chapter.

RADIO ANTENNA CABLE

Tour-Pak Equipped Models

Removal/Installation

1. Remove the fuel tank as described in Chapter Eight.

2. Remove the seat and left side saddlebag as described in Chapter Fourteen.

3. Remove the left side frame cover as described in Chapter Fourteen.

4. Remove the' outer fairing as described in Chapter Fourteen.

5. Disconnect the radio antenna connector from the radio.

6. Carefully remove the cable straps securing the antenna cable.

7. Remove the rivet and P-clamp and release the main wiring harness to the left side of steering head.

8. Starting at the front, remove the cover from the wire trough on the frame rail.

9. Note the routing of the antenna cable through the wire trough and frame as it must be installed in the same locations.

10. Starting at the front, remove the antenna cable through the frame cable trough.

11. Carefully remove the cable straps securing the main harness to the left side upper frame tube.

12. Remove the Tour-Pak lower case molded liner as described in Chapter Fourteen.

13. Disconnect the radio antenna cable connector from antenna base as described in this section. Release the antenna cable from the two adhesive clips (A, **Figure 155**) at the bottom of the Tour-Pak.

14. On models so equipped, disconnect the Tour-Pak connector (B, **Figure 155**) and power connector.

15. Pull the grommet (C, **Figure 155**) into the Tour-Pak and remove it from the harness.

16. Pull the radio antenna and Tour-Pack light wiring harness out through hole where the grommet was located (C, **Figure 155**) in the Tour-Pak.

17. Carefully remove the cable straps securing the main harness conduit to the luggage rack rail.

18. Remove the antenna cable from the frame.

19. Install by reversing these removal steps.

Models Without Tour-Pak

Removal/Installation

1. Remove the fuel tank as described in Chapter Eight.

2. Remove the seat and left side saddlebag as described in Chapter Fourteen.

3. Remove the left side frame cover as described in Chapter Fourteen.

4. Remove the outer fairing as described in Chapter Fourteen.

5. Disconnect the radio antenna connector from the radio.

6. Remove the rivet and P-clamp and release the main wiring harness to the left side of steering head.

7. Starting at the front, remove the cover from the wire trough on the frame rail.

8. Note the routing of the antenna cable through the wire trough and frame as it must be installed in the same locations.

9. Starting at the front, remove the antenna cable through the cable trough of the frame.

10. Carefully remove the cable straps securing the antenna cable to the left side rear fender support, air valve mounting bracket and saddlebag support.

11. Remove the antenna cable from the frame.

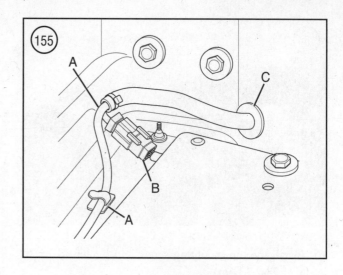

CB ANTENNA CABLE
(FLHT SERIES AND FLTRU SERIES MODELS)

Removal/Installation

1. Remove the fuel tank as described in Chapter Eight.

2. Remove the seat and left side saddlebag as described in Chapter Fourteen.

3. Remove the left side frame cover as described in Chapter Fourteen.

4. Remove the outer fairing as described in Chapter Fourteen.

5. Disconnect the CB antenna connector from the radio.

6. Starting at the front, remove the cover from the wire trough on the frame rail.

7. Carefully remove the cable straps securing the CB antenna to the upper frame tube and luggage rack rail.

8. Remove the Tour-Pak lower case molded liner as described in Chapter Fourteen.

9. Pull the grommet into the Tour-Pak and remove it from the harness.

10. Pull the radio antenna and Tour-Pack light wiring harness out through hole where the grommet was located in the Tour-Pak.

11. Disconnect the CB antenna cable connector within the Tour-Pak.

12. Release the CB antenna from the front cable clip.

13. Remove the antenna cable from the frame.

14. Install by reversing these removal steps

REAR AUDIO HARNESS
(FLHT SERIES AND FLTRU SERIES MODELS)

Removal/Installation

1. Remove the fuel tank as described in Chapter Eight.

2. Remove the seat and both saddlebags as described in Chapter Fourteen.

3. Remove both side frame covers as described in Chapter Fourteen.

4. Remove the outer fairing as described in Chapter Fourteen.

5. Within the inner fairing, disconnect the electrical connector for the specific component:

a. CB antenna cable (50).

b. CB module (184).

c. Radio (28).

d. Audio to interconnect harness (6).

6. Remove the rivet and P-clamp and release the main wiring harness to the left side of steering head.

7. Carefully pull the interconnect harness toward the rear and out of fairing cap.

8. Remove the Tour-Pak lower case molded liner as described in Chapter Fourteen.

9. Pull the grommet into the Tour-Pak and remove it from the harness.

10. Disconnect the CB antenna cable connector within the Tour-Pak.

11. Release the CB antenna from the front cable clip.

12. Pull the CB antenna cable through the Tour-Pak hole.

13. Carefully pull the rear speaker/passenger control out of the right side speaker box and disconnect. Repeat for the left side speaker/passenger control.

14. Release rear headset receptacle from bracket at bottom left side speaker box and disengage spring.

15. At the rear of the battery tray, release 12-place console connector (53) from attachment clip anchored to hole in frame weldment. Disconnect the 12-place console connector (53).

16. Carefully remove the cable straps securing the audio harness to both frame tubes.

17. Starting at the front, remove the cover from the wire trough on the frame rail.

18. Use making tape and permanent pen, draw a line on the audio harness conduit where it enters and exits the wire trough.

19. Also, mark both sides of each cable strap that secures the audio harness. Repeat for the main harness where possible.

20. Carefully remove the cable straps securing the audio harness.

21. Remove the audio harness from the motorcycle.

22. Install by reversing these removal steps. If installing a new audio harness, lay the new and oil harness side by side and transfer the marks made in Step 19 and Step 20 onto the new harness.

iPOD MODULE

Removal/Installation

1. Open right side saddlebag top.

2. Remove the two screws securing the cover strap and remove the strap.

3. Disconnect the iPod module connector from the harness.

4. Pull back the locking sleeve and disengage the lock. Separate the 8-pin audio connector (274).

5. Remove the three screws securing the iPod module and bracket to the saddlebag top. Remove the iPod module and mounting bracket.

6. If necessary, remove the screw and separate the bracket from the iPod module.

7. Install by reversing these removal steps. Tighten all screws to 15-20 in.-lb. (1.7-2.3 N•m).

ROAD TECH ZUMO 660 GPS

Removal/Installation

Refer to **Figure 156**.

> *NOTE*
> *Always disarm the optional security system TSM/TSSM/HFSM before disconnecting the battery or pulling the main fuse so the siren will not sound.*

1. Remove the main fuse as described in this chapter

2. Remove the outer fairing as described in Chapter Fourteen.

3. Working on the front side of the inner fairing, disconnect the cable strap (A, **Figure 157**) securing the GPS audio jack (B) and NIM connector (D).

4. Working on the rider's side of the inner fairing, perform the following:

   a. Remove the weather cap,

   b. Remove the four screws securing the cradle to the mount. Allow the cradle to gently hang from the harness.

5. Working on the front side of the inner fairing, secure the two locknuts and the retainer.

6. Working on the rider's side of the inner fairing, secure the mount and remove the two mounting screws. Remove the mount, the retainer, screws and locknuts.

7. Working on the front side of the inner fairing, disconnect the GPS audio jack (B, **Figure 157**) and the power connector (C).

> *NOTE*
> *Note the location of the cable straps prior to removal as they must be reinstalled in the some location.*

8. Cut the cable straps as needed and carefully pull the harness out though the inner fairing opening.

9. Install by reversing these removal steps. Tighten all screws to 20-25 in.-lb. (2.3-2.8 N•m).

NAVAGATION INTERFACE MODULE (NIM)

Refer to **Figure 157**.

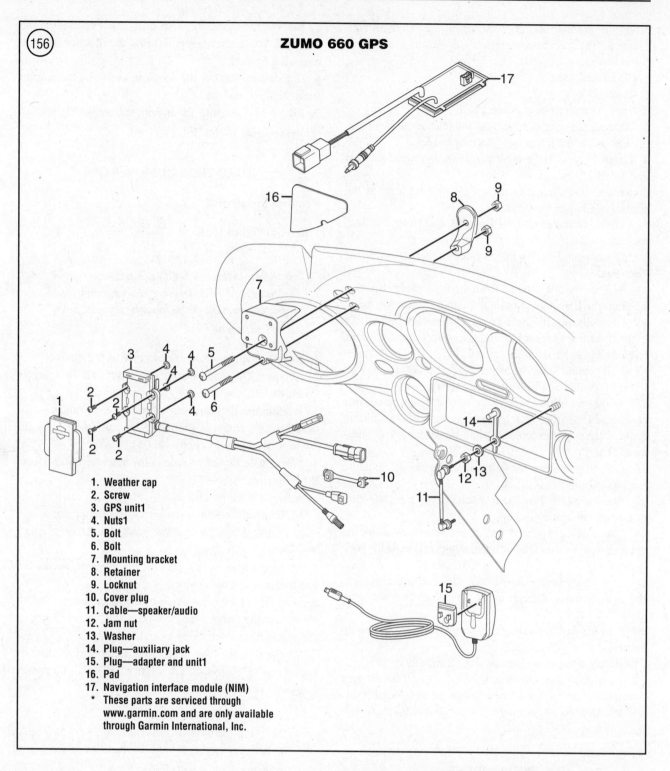

ZUMO 660 GPS

1. Weather cap
2. Screw
3. GPS unit1
4. Nuts1
5. Bolt
6. Bolt
7. Mounting bracket
8. Retainer
9. Locknut
10. Cover plug
11. Cable—speaker/audio
12. Jam nut
13. Washer
14. Plug—auxiliary jack
15. Plug—adapter and unit1
16. Pad
17. Navigation interface module (NIM)
* These parts are serviced through
  www.garmin.com and are only available
  through Garmin International, Inc.

Removal

NOTE
Always disarm the optional security system TSM/TSSM/HFSM before disconnecting the battery or pulling the main fuse so the siren will not sound.

1. Remove the main fuse as described in this chapter.
2. Remove the outer fairing as described in Chapter Fourteen.

3. Disconnect the NIM connector (D, **Figure 157**).
4. Disconnect the GPS power connector (C, **Figure 157**).
5. Carefully the NIM module from the inner fairing surface.

Installation

1. Clean all old adhesive from the module surface on the inner fairing with isopropyl alcohol. Allow to dry.
2. Remove the adhesive backing from the new NIM.

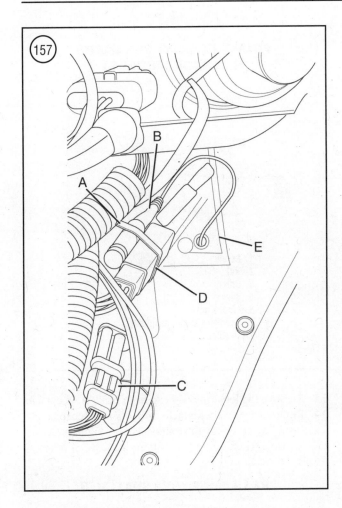

3. Position the NIM module connector wire toward the bottom and press it into place on the inner fairing surface. Hold the NIM module in position for 20 minutes for the adhesive to become secure.

4. Connect the GPS power connector (C, **Figure 157**).

5. Connect the NIM connector (D, **Figure 157**).

6. Connect the main fuse as described in this chapter.

FRONT FAIRING SPEAKERS (FORK MOUNTED FAIRING MODELS)

Removal/Installation

NOTE
Always disarm the optional TSSM/HFSM security system before disconnecting the battery or pulling the Main-Fuse so the siren will not sound.

1. Disconnect the negative battery cable as described in this chapter.

2. Remove the outer front fairing as described in Chapter Fourteen.

3. Carefully, pull straight out and disconnect the socket terminals from the speaker spade terminals.

4. Remove the three screws securing the speaker to the speaker adapter. Note the location of the screws as they are different lengths.

5. Carefully withdraw the speaker from the adapter and remove it.

6. Position the speaker with the spade terminals toward the bottom of the adapter, and install the speaker onto the adapter.

7. Thread the two top long screws securing the speaker and adapter to inner fairing.

NOTE
The lower inboard screw hole is not used.

8. Thread the lower short screw into the lower outboard hole, while positioning the washer between the adapter and support plate.

9. Tighten the single lower outboard screw to 22-28 in.-lb. (2.5-3.2 N•m).

10. Tighten the two upper screws to 35-50 in.-lb. (4.0-5.7 N•m).

11. Connect the socket terminals onto the speaker spade terminals. Push the connectors on until they bottom.

12. Install the outer front fairing as described in Chapter Fourteen.

13. Connect the negative battery cable as described in this chapter.

FRONT FAIRING SPEAKERS (FRAME MOUNTED MODELS)

Main Speakers
Removal/Installation

NOTE
Always disarm the optional security system TSM/TSSM/HFSM before disconnecting the battery or pulling the main fuse so the siren will not sound.

1. Remove the negative battery cable as described in this chapter

2. Remove the outer fairing as described in Chapter Fourteen.

3. Carefully, pull straight out and disconnect the socket terminals from the speaker spade terminals.

4. Disconnect the teeter jumper wire from the tweeter.

5. Remove the four screws securing the speaker to the adapter and remove the speaker (**Figure 158**).

6. If necessary, remove the flange nut and screws securing the adapter to the inner fairing and remove the adapter.

7. Install by reversing these removal steps, note the following:

    a. Tighten the adapter flange nut to 15-20 in.-lb. (1.7-2.3 N•m).

    b. Tighten the adapter screws to 10-15 in.-lb. (1.1-1.7 N•m).

    c. Tighten the speaker screws to 10-15 in.-lb. (1.1-1.7 N•m).

Tweeter Speakers
Removal/Installation

> *NOTE*
> *Always disarm the optional security system TSM/TSSM/HFSM before disconnecting the battery or pulling the Main Fuse so the siren will not sound.*

1. Remove the negative battery cable as described in this chapter.
2. Remove the outer fairing as described in Chapter Fourteen.
3. Carefully, pull straight out and disconnect the socket terminals from the speaker spade terminals.
4. Disconnect the teeter jumper wire from the tweeter.
5. Secure the tweeter and remove the two nuts securing the clamp to the backside of the inner fairing.
6. Remove the tweeter from the rider's side of the inner fairing.
7. Install by reversing these removal steps. Tighten the two nuts to 10-20 in.-lb. (1.1-2.3 N•m).

FRONT HEADSET RECEPTACLE
(FLHTCUSE MODELS)

Removal/Installation

> *NOTE*
> *Always disarm the optional TSSM/HFSM security system before disconnecting the battery or pulling the Main-Fuse so the siren will not sound.*

1. Remove the Main-Fuse as described in this chapter.
2. Remove the seat as described in Chapter Fourteen.
3. Remove the left saddlebag and frame side cover as described in Chapter Fourteen.
4. At the front and rear saddlebag rail, carefully cut the two cable straps securing the headset receptacle wiring conduit and audio harness to the inboard side of the left upper frame rail.
5. Release the 12-pin radio-to-headset harness connector from the attachment clip at the hole in the frame cross member at the rear of the battery. Disconnect the connector halves.
6. Place several towels or blanket over the forward part of the rear fender.
7. Remove the Allen screw securing the console at the rear to the fuel tank.
8. Remove the console and place it on the rear fender.
9. Release the fuel door on the console, and remove the fuel filler cap.
10. Bend back the clips securing the wiring harness to the front headset receptacle.
11. Turn the fuel tank console over onto the blanket. Install the fuel filler cap.
12. Raise the headset receptacle cap. Place a small punch in either notch of lock ring and rotate it *counterclockwise* until loose.

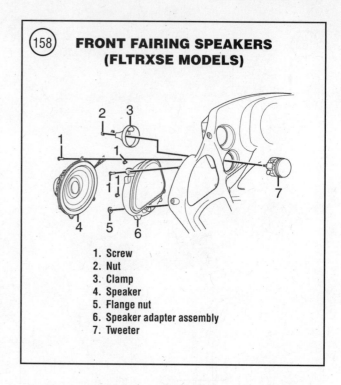

**158 FRONT FAIRING SPEAKERS
(FLTRXSE MODELS)**

1. Screw
2. Nut
3. Clamp
4. Speaker
5. Flange nut
6. Speaker adapter assembly
7. Tweeter

13. Remove the lock ring and cap from headset receptacle.
14. Remove headset receptacle from console receptacle.
15. Install by reversing the removal steps. Tighten the fuel tank console Allen screw to 25-30 in.-lb. (2.8-3.4 N•m).

REAR PASSENGER SWITCHES

Removal/Installation

> *NOTE*
> *Always disarm the optional TSSM/HFSM security system before disconnecting the battery or pulling the Main-Fuse so the siren will not sound.*

1. Disconnect the negative battery cable as described in this chapter.
2. Open the cover on the Tour-Pak and leave it open.
3. Remove the four screws securing the speaker grill and remove it from the lower case.
4. Withdraw the speaker from the lower case, and carefully pull straight out and disconnect the socket terminals from the speaker spade terminals.
5. Remove the trim ring and carefully pull on wire harness. Withdraw the 6-pin rear speaker/passenger control connector from the speaker box. Disconnect the electrical connector.
6. Withdraw the socket portion of the electrical connector back into the speaker box and pull out through speaker opening.
7. Remove the two screws and release the switch bracket from inside of speaker box.
8. Carefully pull the switch housing assembly, wiring harness, speaker terminals and socket housing from speaker box through the hole on the outboard side.

⑤⑨ SADDLEBAG SPEAKER (FLTRXSE, FLHRSE MODELS)

1. Speaker grille
2. Grommet
3. Screw
4. Speaker
5. Gasket
6. Screw
7. Basket

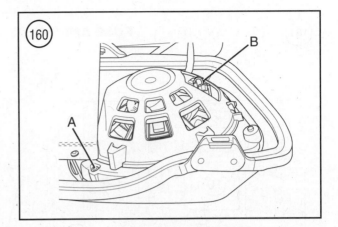

REAR SPEAKERS

Removal/Installation

NOTE
Always disarm the optional TSSM/HFSM security system before disconnecting the battery or pulling the Main-Fuse so the siren will not sound.

1. Disconnect the negative battery cable as described in this chapter.
2. Open the cover on the Tour-Pak and leave it open.
3. Remove the four screws securing the speaker grill and remove it from the lower case.
4. Withdraw the speaker from the lower case, and carefully, pull straight out and disconnect the socket terminals from the speaker spade terminals.
5. Install by reversing the removal steps. Tighten the screws securely.

SADDEBAG SPEAKERS (2013 FLTRUSE Models)

Speaker Removal/Installation

Refer to **Figure 159**.
1. Open the saddlebag cover. Remove the screws securing the check strap and remove the check strap (A, **Figure 160**).
2. Disconnect the speaker connector (B, **Figure 160**).
3. Remove the screws securing the speaker grille and remove the grille.
4. Remove the securing the speaker to the saddlebag top cover. Remove the speaker from the topside of the saddlebag top cover.
5. Press on the latch and remove the basket from the underside of the saddlebag top cover.
6. Install by reversing thesc removal steps, note the following:
   a. Check strap screw: 18-20 in.-lb. (2.0-2.3 N•m).
   b. Speaker grille and grille screws: 10-15 in.-lb. (1.1-1.7 N•m).

9. Carefully pull the keycap from the switch shaft, and remove switch from housing.

10. Note the wire colors and terminal locations in switch housing. Remove all four terminals from the housing.

11. Pull one wire at a time and withdraw all four wires from the wiring harness.

12. Repeat the procedure to remove the remaining switch.

13. Install by reversing these removal steps. Tighten the screws securely.

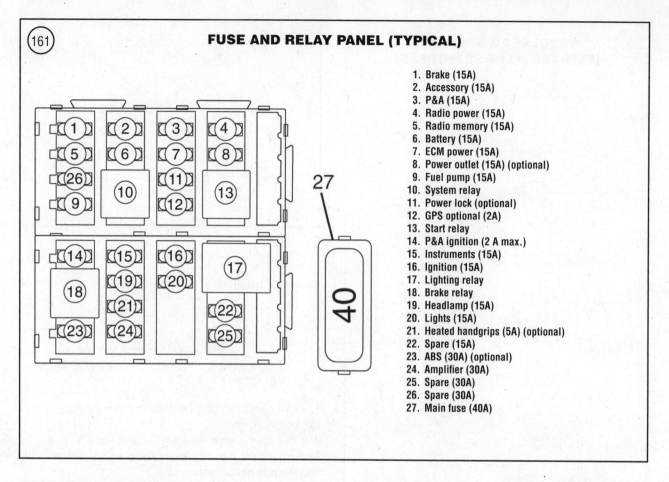

FUSE AND RELAY PANEL (TYPICAL)

161

1. Brake (15A)
2. Accessory (15A)
3. P&A (15A)
4. Radio power (15A)
5. Radio memory (15A)
6. Battery (15A)
7. ECM power (15A)
8. Power outlet (15A) (optional)
9. Fuel pump (15A)
10. System relay
11. Power lock (optional)
12. GPS optional (2A)
13. Start relay
14. P&A ignition (2 A max.)
15. Instruments (15A)
16. Ignition (15A)
17. Lighting relay
18. Brake relay
19. Headlamp (15A)
20. Lights (15A)
21. Heated handgrips (5A) (optional)
22. Spare (15A)
23. ABS (30A) (optional)
24. Amplifier (30A)
25. Spare (30A)
26. Spare (30A)
27. Main fuse (40A)

Harness Removal/Installation

Right side saddlebag

1. Open the saddlebag cover.
2. Disconnect the electrical harness from the speaker and iPod module.
3. Remove the screws securing the cover and connector to the saddlebag.
4. Remove mounting screw and hole plug on inside surface of saddlebag.
5. Withdraw harness out though hole in saddlebag.
6. Install by reversing these removal steps. Tighten cover screws to 35-45 in.-lb. (4.0-4.5 N•m).

Left side saddlebag

1. Remove the rear audio amplifier as described in this chapter.
2. Disconnect speaker connector from speaker. Remove the speaker harness from the three clamps, and remove harness from on base of saddlebag bottom.
3. Remove screws securing the cover and connector to the saddlebag.
4. Remove the speaker harness out through the amplifier mount.
5. Remove mounting screw and hole plug on inside surface of saddlebag.

6. Withdraw harness out though hole in saddlebag.
7. Insert harness in though hole in saddlebag.
8. Fully open the saddle bag cover is not pulled too tight; loosen if necessary.
9. Install the speaker harness in through the amplifier mount and secure with the three clamps.
10. Insert speaker connector under speaker web (B, **Figure 160**) and attach to speaker.
11. Install the rear audio amplifier as described in this chapter.
12. Tighten cover screws to 35-45 in.-lb. (4.0-4.5 N•m).

CB MODULE (FLHTCU MODELS)

Removal/Installation

NOTE
Always disarm the optional TSSM/HFSM security system before disconnecting the battery or pulling the Main-Fuse so the siren will not sound.

1. Disconnect the negative battery cable as described in this chapter.
2. Remove the outer front fairing as described in Chapter Fourteen.
3. Disconnect the following electrical connectors:

a. The CB antenna cable connector from the backside of the radio.

b. The 12- pin CB module connector from the backside of the radio.

4. Remove the screw(s) and release the CB module flange from the radio. Then, remove the CB module.

5. Install by reversing the removal steps. Tighten the screw(s) to 35-45 in.-lb. (4.0-5.1 N•m).

RELAYS

All relays are located within the fuse panel located under the frame left side cover. Actual number of fuses and relays (**Figure 161**) depend on the model and options.

NOTE
Always disarm the optional security system TSM/TSSM/HFSM before disconnecting the battery or pulling the main fuse so the siren will not sound.

1. Remove the negative battery cable as described in this chapter.

2. Remove the seat and left side saddlebag as described in Chapter Fourteen.

3. Remove the left side frame cover as described in Chapter Fourteen.

4. Pull the fuse panel out from the bottom and remove the fuse panel cover.

NOTE
*Relay description is located on the fuse panel block cover (**Figure 162**).*

5. Locate the faulty relay (**Figure 163**) and install a new one with the same part number.

6. Install the left side frame cover as described in Chapter Fourteen.

7. Install the seat and left side saddlebag as described in Chapter Fourteen.

8. Connect the negative battery cable as described in this chapter.

CRUISE CONTROL

System Components and Operation

The cruise control system is controlled by the Electronic Control Module (ECM).

The cruise control module receives command signals from the cruise control SET/RESUME switch on the right side handlebar switch. The cruise control receives information on operating the conditions from the speedometer output signal.

The cruise control system will set and automatically maintain any speed between 30-85 mph (48-137 km/h). To set the cruise control, turn the cruise control ON/OFF switch to the ON position. Power is then supplied to the cruise control module through the 5-amp fuse located in the fuse block under the frame left side cover.

After reaching the desired speed, momentarily push the SET/RESUME switch to the SET position. The ECM monitors the vehicle speed sensor (VSS) to establish the desired vehicle speed. The ECM then modulates the throttle control actuator to maintain vehicle speed. The cruise enabled/engaged lamp on the speedometer, or tachometer, turns from orange to greed indicating the indicated cruising speed is locked in.

The ECM monitors both the engine RPM and the VSS speed signal and the output speed signal. The ECM signals the throttle control actuator to open or close the throttle to keep the speedometer output signal constant. The engine RPM is monitored to detect engine overspeed, a condition which automatically causes disengagement.

The ECM automatically disengages cruise mode whenever the ECM receives one of the following:

1. Front or rear brake is applied.

2. Throttle is "rolled back" or closed, thereby actuating throttle roll-off (disengaged) command.

3. Motorcycle clutch is engaged; ECM senses too great increase in RPM.

4. Cruise control switch placed in the off position.

5. Handlebar-mounted engine off/run switch is placed in the OFF position.

9

6. Handlebar-mounted cruise SET/RESUME switch is pressed to SET and held in that position until vehicle speed drops below 30 mph (48 km/h) or pushed to RES until vehicle speed exceeds 90 mph (145 km/h).

Switch Replacement

ON/OFF switch replacement

NOTE
New replacement switch wires are cut to a length of 2 in. (50 mm) and the insulation partially stripped.

1A. On the FLHT series models and FLHX models, perform the following:
   a. Partially remove the inside front fairing cap as described in Chapter Fourteen.
   b. Remove the switch from the underside of the front fairing cap.
   c. Cut the wire about 1 1/2 in. from the old ON/OFF switch.
   d. Discard the old switch.
1B. On all models except the FLHT series models and FLHX models, perform the following:
   a. Disassemble the left side switch assembly (**Figure 164**) as described in Chapter Nine.
   b. Locater the switch and partially disassemble it from the switch housing. Separate the ON/OFF switch from the reminder of the switch assemblies.
   c. Cut the wire about 1 1/2 in. from the old ON/OFF switch.
   d. Discard the old switch.
2. Slide a one-inch piece of dual-wall heat shrink tubing, supplied the new switch, over each wire.
3. Securely splice the new switch onto the existing wires and solder the connection.
4. Cover each splice with duel wall head shrink tubing.
5A. On the FLHT series models and FLHX models, perform the following:
   a. Install switch onto the underside of the front fairing cap.
   b. Install the inside front fairing cap as described in Chapter Fourteen.
5B. On all models except the FLHT series models and FLHX models, assemble the left side switch assembly.

SET/RESUME switch replacement

1. Disassemble the right side switch assembly (**Figure 165**) as described in Chapter Nine.
2. Locater the switch and partially disassemble it from the switch housing. Separate the SET/RESUME switch from the reminder of the switch assemblies.
3. Cut the wire about 1 1/2 in. from the old SET/RESUME switch.
4. Discard the old switch.

5. Slide a one-inch piece of dual-wall heat shrink tubing, supplied the new switch, over each wire.
6. Securely splice the new switch onto the existing wires and solder the connection.
7. Cover each splice with duel wall head shrink tubing.
8. Assemble the right side switch assembly.

ELECTRICAL CONNECTOR LOCATION AND IDENTIFICATION

Refer to **Figures 166-170**.

The majority of the electrical connectors are located either within the headlight case and/or within the front inner fairing assembly. These illustrations will assist in locating most of the specific connectors and parts referred to in the text. The electrical connector terminal number for a specific part can be determined from the wiring diagrams located in Chapter Sixteen of this manual.

The manufacturer provides limited information on electrical connector locations for the CVO models. Some of the connector terminal locations are similar to those on non-CVO models and may be found within the standard model illustrations.

ELECTRICAL CONNECTOR SERVICE

Different types of electrical connectors are used throughout the electrical system.

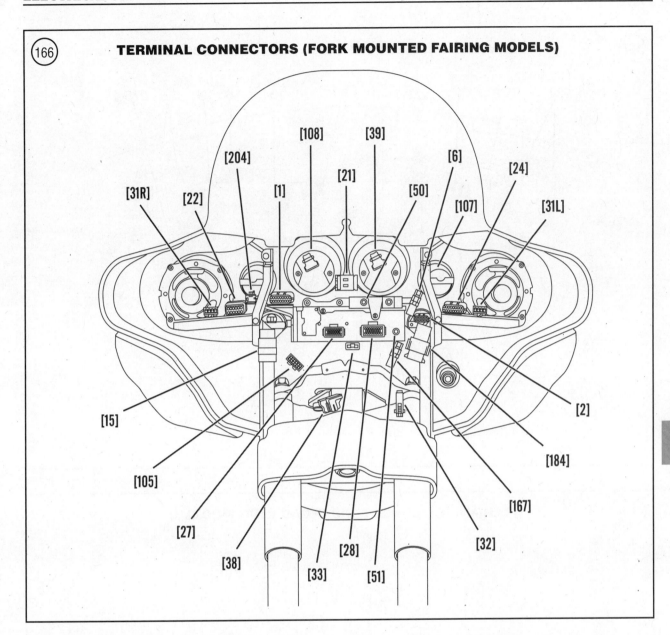

⑯ **TERMINAL CONNECTORS (FORK MOUNTED FAIRING MODELS)**

9

The following procedures describe the disassembly of the connectors so individual wires can be replaced.

NOTE
On models with an optional security system, disarm the system before disconnecting the battery cable or pulling the Maxi-Fuse so the siren will not sound.

Deutsch DT Electrical Connectors Socket Terminal Removal/Installation

Refer to **Figure 171** and **Figure 172**.

This procedure shows how to remove and install the socket terminals. This procedure is shown on a 12-pin Deutsch connector, which also applies to 2-, 3-, 4- and 6-pin Deutsch connectors.

1. Remove the Maxi-Fuse as described in this chapter.
2. Disconnect the connector housing.

3. Remove the secondary locking wedge as follows:
 a. Locate the secondary locking wedge in **Figure 171** or **Figure 172**.
 b. Insert a wide-bladed screwdriver between the socket housing and the secondary locking wedge. Turn the screwdriver 90° to force the wedge up (**Figure 173**).
 c. Remove the locking wedge.
4. Lightly press the terminal latches inside the socket housing and remove the socket terminal through the holes in the wire seal.
5. Repeat the process for each remaining socket terminal.
6. If necessary, remove the wire seal.
7. Install the wire seal into the socket housing, if it was removed.
8. Hold onto the socket housing and insert each socket terminal through the hole in the wire seal so it enters the correct chamber. Continue until the socket terminal locks

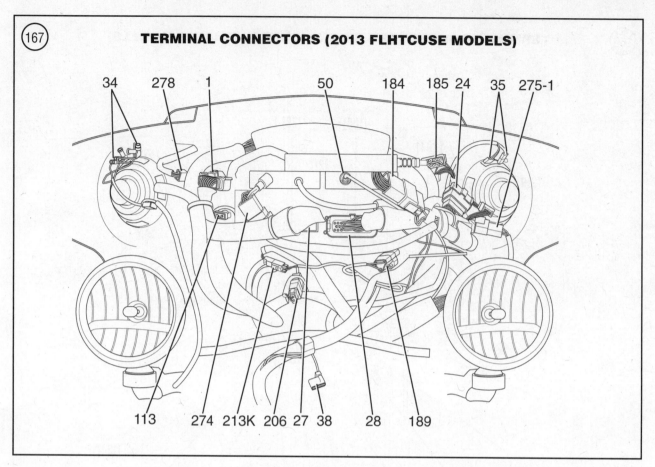

167

TERMINAL CONNECTORS (2013 FLHTCUSE MODELS)

34   278   1   50   184   185 24   35   275-1

113   274 213K 206 27 38   28   189

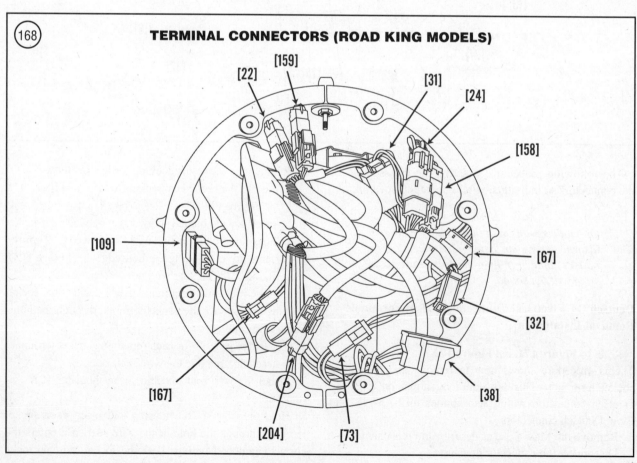

168

TERMINAL CONNECTORS (ROAD KING MODELS)

[159]

[22]   [31]   [24]

[158]

[109]   [67]

[32]

[167]   [38]

[204]   [73]

169 **TERMINAL CONNECTORS (FRAME MOUNTED FAIRING MODELS)**

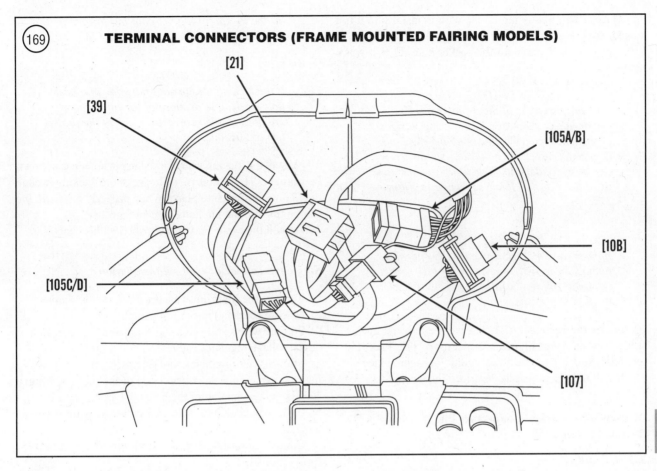

170 **TERMINAL CONNECTORS (FRAME MOUNTED FAIRING MODELS)**

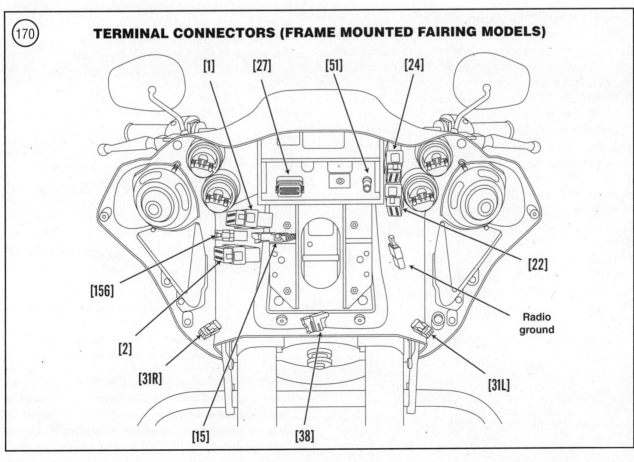

9

into place. Then, lightly tug on the wire to make sure it is locked into place.

9. Set the internal seal onto the socket housing if it was removed.

> *NOTE*
> *With the exception of the 3-pin Deutsch connector, all of the secondary locking wedges are symmetrical. When assembling the 3-pin connector, install the connector so the arrow on the secondary locking wedge points toward the external latch as shown in **Figure 174**.*

> *NOTE*
> *If the secondary locking wedge does not slide into position easily, one or more of the socket terminals are not installed correctly. Correct the problem at this time.*

10. Install the secondary locking wedge into the socket housing as shown in **Figure 171** or **Figure 172**. Press the secondary locking wedge down until it locks into place.

11. Install the Main-Fuse as described in this chapter.

Deutsch DT Electrical Connectors Pin Terminal Removal/Installation

2, 3, 4, 6 and 12- pin

Refer to **Figure 171** or **Figure 172**.

This procedure shows how to remove and install the pin terminals. This procedure is shown on a 12-pin Deutsch connector, which also applies to all Deutsch connectors (2-, 3-, 4- and 6-pin).

1. Remove the Main-Fuse as described in this chapter.
2. Disconnect the connector housing.
3. Use needlenose pliers to remove the locking wedge.
4. Lightly press the terminal latches inside the pin housing, and remove the pin terminal(s) through the holes in the wire seal.
5. Repeat the process for each remaining pin terminal.
6. If necessary, remove the wire seal.
7. Install the wire seal into the pin housing, if it was removed.
8. Hold onto the pin housing and insert the pin terminals through the holes in the wire seal so they enter the correct chamber. Continue until the pin terminal locks into place. Lightly tug on the wire to make sure it is locked into place.
9. Set the internal seal onto the socket housing if it was removed.

> *NOTE*
> *With the exception of the 3-pin Deutsch connector, all of the locking wedges are symmetrical. When assembling the three-pin connector, install the connector so the arrow*

on the locking wedge is pointing toward the external latch as shown in **Figure 174**.

> *NOTE*
> *If the locking wedge does not slide into position easily, one or more of the pin terminals are not installed correctly. Correct the problem at this time.*

10. Install the locking wedge into the pin housing as shown in **Figure 171** or **Figure 172**. Press the locking wedge down until it locks into place. When properly installed, the wedge fits into the pin housing center groove.

11. Install the Main-Fuse as described in this chapter.

Single pin connector removal/installation

1. Remove the Main-Fuse as described in this chapter.
2. Disconnect the connector housing.
3. Pull the wire seal from back of the housing, and slide it down voltage regulator cable.
4. Insert the terminal pick tool (Deutsch part No. 114008) into the cable until the tapered end of the tool (A, **Figure 175**) is in the wire end of the housing (B).
5. Push pick tool into wire end of housing until it bottoms.
6. Gently tug on housing, and pull wire (C, **Figure 175**) from terminal.
7. Remove tool from electrical cable.
8. Insert the wire into the terminal until it *clicks* and is locked into place. Slightly pull on the wire to ensure it is locked into place.
9. Install the Main-Fuse as described in this chapter.

Delphi Electrical Connectors

Micro 64 removal/installation

1. Remove the Maxi-Fuse as described in this chapter.
2. Bend back the external latches slightly and separate the connector.
3. Locate the head of the secondary lock (A, **Figure 176**).
4. Insert the tip of a narrow, flat-bladeded screwdriver between the center ear of the lock and the housing. Pry out the lock and remove it.

> *NOTE*
> *Connector terminals are numbered 1-6 in one row and 7-12 in the remaining row. The numbers 1, 6, 7 and 12 are stamped on the connector to identify the row numbers.*

5. Locate the pin hole (B, **Figure 176**) between terminals on the mating end of the connector. Refer to C, **Figure 176** for terminal number locations.
6. Push the adjacent terminal all the way into the connector housing. Insert the Packard Terminal Remover (H-D

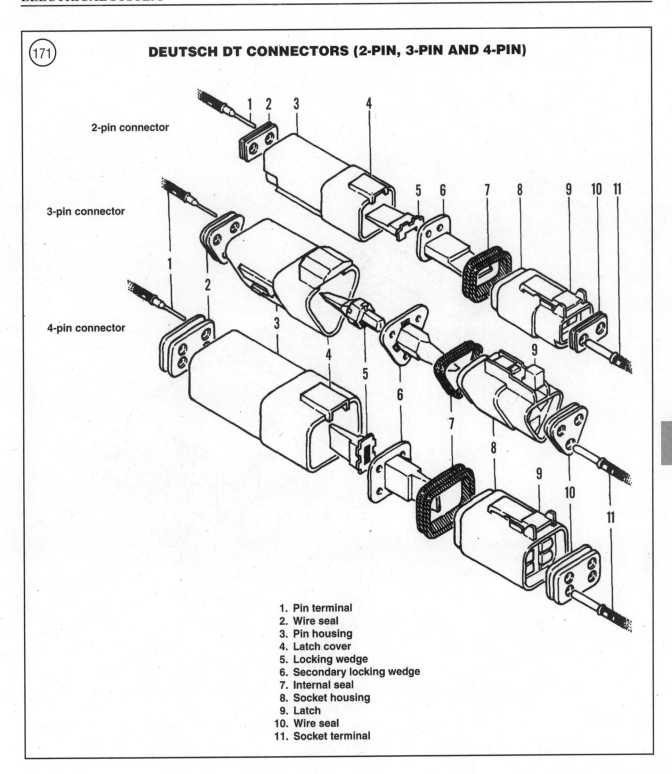

DEUTSCH DT CONNECTORS (2-PIN, 3-PIN AND 4-PIN)

2-pin connector

3-pin connector

4-pin connector

1. Pin terminal
2. Wire seal
3. Pin housing
4. Latch cover
5. Locking wedge
6. Secondary locking wedge
7. Internal seal
8. Socket housing
9. Latch
10. Wire seal
11. Socket terminal

part No. HD-45928) into the hole (A, **Figure 177**). Press on it until it bottoms.

7. With the tool in place, gently pull on the wires (B, **Figure 177**) and pull one or both terminals from wire end of connector. Remove the tool.

8. To install the terminal, insert wire and terminal into the correct location on the wire end of the connector. Push on the terminal until it bottoms. Slightly pull on the wire and wiggle it a little to ensure it is locked into place.

9. The special tool releases two terminals at the same time. Repeat the removal and installation process for the adjacent terminal even if it was not removed.

10. Position the head of the secondary lock (A, **Figure 176**) facing the mating end of the connector. Press in on the secondary lock until it is flush with the connector housing.

11. Push the connector halves together until the latches lock together.

12. Install the Main-Fuse as described in this chapter.

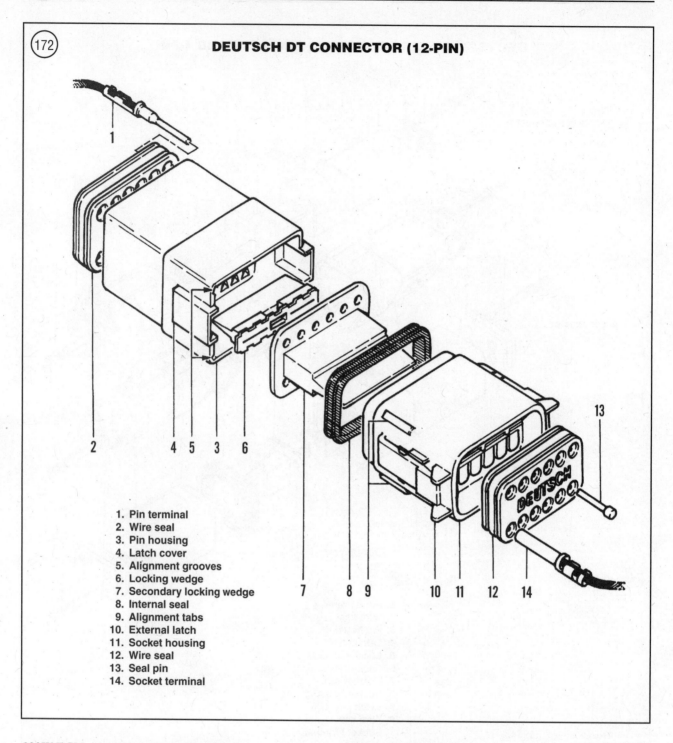

DEUTSCH DT CONNECTOR (12-PIN)

1. Pin terminal
2. Wire seal
3. Pin housing
4. Latch cover
5. Alignment grooves
6. Locking wedge
7. Secondary locking wedge
8. Internal seal
9. Alignment tabs
10. External latch
11. Socket housing
12. Wire seal
13. Seal pin
14. Socket terminal

100W ECM connector removal/installation

1. Remove the Maxi-Duse as described in this chapter.

2. Disconnect the connector housing from the ECM (this chapter).

3. Press the latch (A, **Figure 178**) on each end of the connector, and remove the secondary lock (B).

4. Clip the cable strap (C, **Figure 178**), and release the strain relief collar (D) from the conduit (E).

5. Insert a thin blade, like an X-Acto knife, into the housing seam, and pry the housing halves apart at A, **Figure**

179 until the pins release. Pivot the housing halves away from one another.

6. Push the relevant wire, and remove the socket (B, **Figure 179**) from the housing.

7. Insert the new wire into the relevant chamber of the housing, and carefully pull the wire until the socket is seated in the housing chamber.

8. Carefully close the housing halves together so no wires are pinched. Press the halves together until the pins lock (A, **Figure 178**).

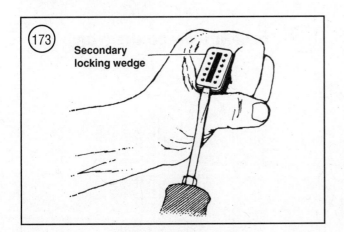

(173) Secondary locking wedge

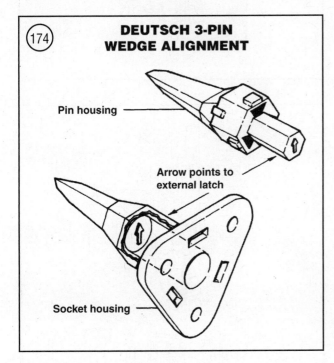

(174) **DEUTSCH 3-PIN WEDGE ALIGNMENT**

Pin housing

Arrow points to external latch

Socket housing

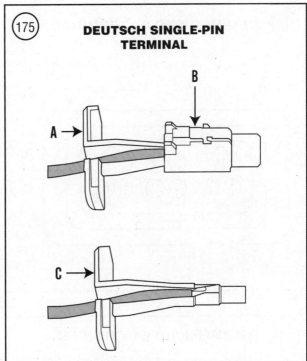

(175) **DEUTSCH SINGLE-PIN TERMINAL**

9. Install a new cable strap (C, **Figure 178**) so the strap seats in the groove of the strain relief collar (D). Make sure the collar secures the conduit (E, **Figure 178**) in place.

10. Install the secondary lock (B, **Figure 178**) over the terminals, and lock it in place.

11. Install the Main-Fuse as described in this chapter.

150 Metri-pack connector removal/installation

This procedure shows how to remove and install the electrical terminals from the Packard 150 Metri-pack connectors shown in **Figure 180**.

1. Remove the Main-Fuse as described in this chapter.

2. Bend back the external latch(es) slightly and separate the connector.

3. On push-to-seat connectors, remove the wire lock (A, **Figure 181**) from the connector housing.

4. Look into the mating end of the connector, on the external latch side, and locate the locking tang (A, **Figure 182**)

in the middle chamber. On locking ear connectors, the tang is on the side opposite the ear.

5A. On pull-to-seat connectors, insert the point of a one-inch safety pin (B, **Figure 182**) about 1/8 in. into the middle chamber. Pivot the end of the safety pin up toward the terminal body until a click is heard.

5B. On push-to-seat connectors, insert the pin (B, **Figure 181**) into the small opening in the housing until a click is heard.

6. Repeat this process several times. The click is the tang returning to the locked position as it slips from the point of the safety pin. Continue to pick at the tang until the clicking stops and the safety pin seems to slide in at a slightly greater depth indicating the tang has been depressed. Remove the safety pin.

7A. On pull-to-seat connectors, push the wire end of the lead and remove the terminal and wire (C, **Figure 182**) from the connector. If additional slack is necessary, pull back on the harness conduit, and remove the wire seal at the back of the connector.

7B. On push-to-seat connectors, pull the wire, and remove the terminal (C, **Figure 181**) from the housing.

8. To install the terminal and wire back into the connector, use a thin flat blade of an X-Acto knife to carefully bend the tang away from the terminal (D, **Figure 182** or D, **Figure 181**).

9. Carefully pull or push the lead and terminal into the connector until a click is heard indicating the terminal is seated correctly within the connector. Gently push or pull on the lead to ensure the terminal is correctly seated.

10. If necessary, install the wire seal and push the harness conduit back into position on the backside of the connector.

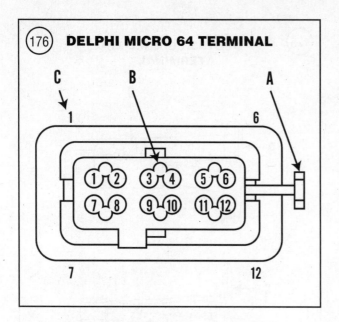

(176) **DELPHI MICRO 64 TERMINAL**

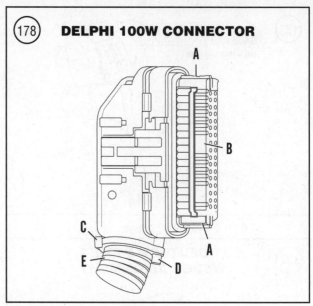

(178) **DELPHI 100W CONNECTOR**

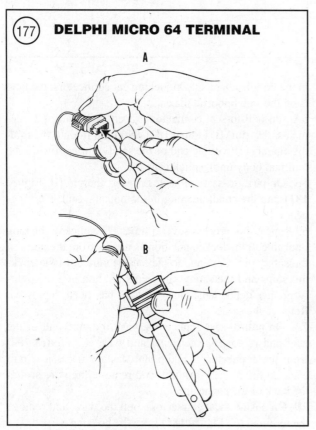

(177) **DELPHI MICRO 64 TERMINAL**

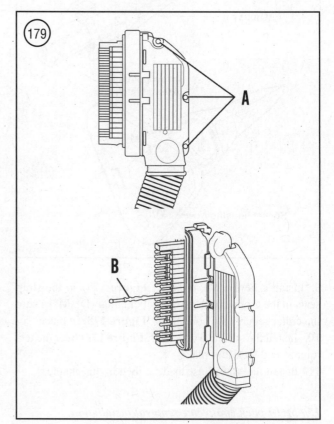

(179)

11. Push the socket halves together until the latch(es) are locked together.

12. Install the Main-Fuse as described in this chapter.

480 Metri-pack connector removal/installation

1. Use a small-bladed screwdriver to press the button on the lock (A, **Figure 183**), and separate the connector halves.

2. Slightly pry the latch up and release one side of the secondary lock (B, **Figure 183**). Repeat on the other side of the housing, and open the secondary lock (C, **Figure 183**).

3. Examine the mating end of the housing chamber(s). Note that the tang on each terminal sits against the side of the chamber with a square-shaped opening. Insert a large pin into the chamber so the pin (D, **Figure 183**) sits between the tang and the chamber wall.

4. Press the pin toward the terminal to compress the tang.

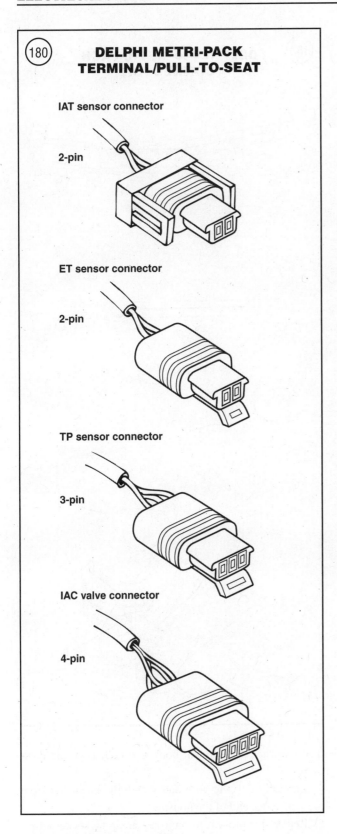

180 **DELPHI METRI-PACK TERMINAL/PULL-TO-SEAT**

IAT sensor connector

2-pin

ET sensor connector

2-pin

TP sensor connector

3-pin

IAC valve connector

4-pin

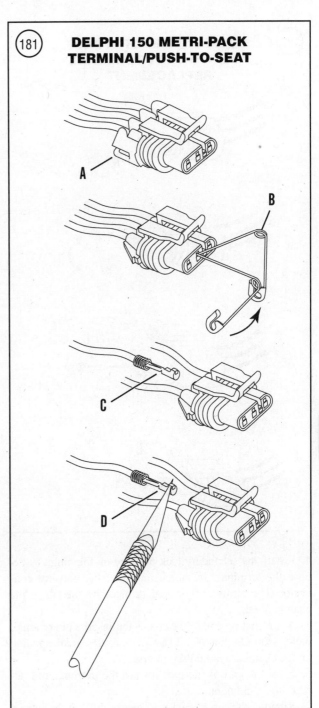

181 **DELPHI 150 METRI-PACK TERMINAL/PUSH-TO-SEAT**

9

5. Remove the pin, and pull the wire until the terminal emerges from the housing.

6. Use a thin blade, like an X-Acto knife, to bend the tang away from the terminal.

7. Insert the terminal into the chamber until it clicks into place. Make sure the tang faces the chamber side with the square-shaped opening.

630 Metri-pack connector removal/installation

1. Remove the Main-Fuse as described in this chapter.

2. Bend back the external latch slightly and separate the socket halves.

3. Bend back the latch slightly and free one side of the secondary lock. Repeat for the latch on the remaining side.

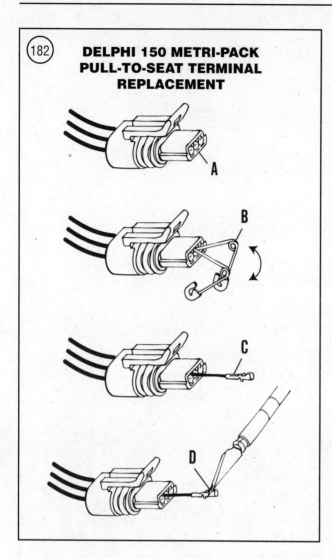

(182) DELPHI 150 METRI-PACK PULL-TO-SEAT TERMINAL REPLACEMENT

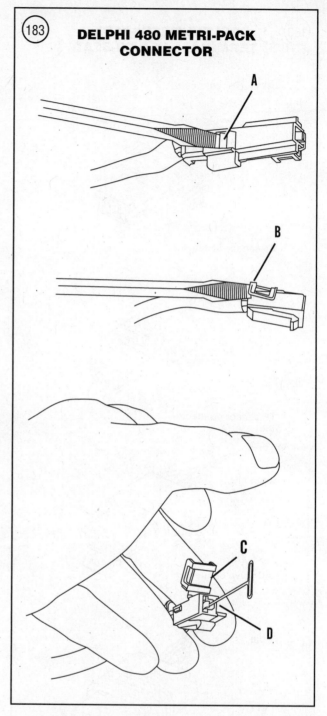

(183) DELPHI 480 METRI-PACK CONNECTOR

4. Rotate the secondary lock outward on the hinge to expose the terminals in the chambers of the housing connector. The terminal is locked in place by the rib in the chamber wall.

5. At the mating end of the connector, insert a pin or small pick (Snap-On part No. TT600-3) into the small opening on the chamber wall until it bottoms.

6. Pivot the end of the pick toward the terminal and depress the locking tang.

7. Remove the pin or pick and gently pull on the wiring and pull the terminal from the wire end of the connector. Repeat this step if the terminal is still locked in place.

8. Install the Maxi-Fuse as described in this chapter.

800 Metri-pack connectors removal/installation

1. Remove the Main-Fuse as described in this chapter.

2. Gently pull the socket housing and disengage the slots on the secondary lock (A, **Figure 184**) from the tabs (B) on the socket housing. Remove the secondary lock from the cable.

3. Carefully insert the blade of a small screwdriver (C, **Figure 184**) into the opening until it stops. Pivot the screw-

driver toward the terminal body and hold it in this position.

4. Carefully pull the wire and withdraw the socket from the wire cable end of the housing.

5. Repeat this process to remove remaining socket terminal, if necessary.

6. Use a flat-bladed screwdriver and carefully bend the tang away from terminal body.

7. Insert socket and wire lead into wire end of socket housing until it *clicks* into place. Gently pull on the wire to ensure the terminal is correctly seated.

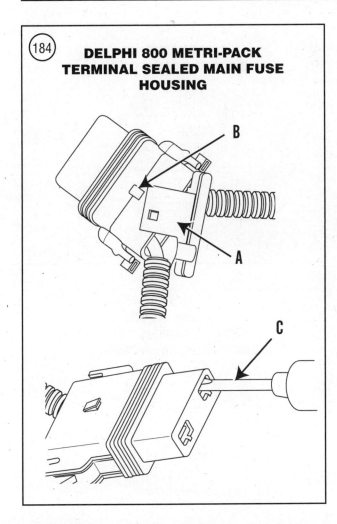

184 **DELPHI 800 METRI-PACK TERMINAL SEALED MAIN FUSE HOUSING**

5. Look into the terminal side of the connector that is opposite the secondary lock and note the location of each connector and cavity.

6. Insert a pin or a pick tool into the terminal cavity until it stops.

NOTE
Use the connector release button to determine the up and down side of the connector. The release button is on the top of the connector.

7. Press the tang in the housing to release a terminal. A click is heard when the tang is released:
   a. Press down on the tang (7, **Figure 185**) in the housing to release a pin.
   b. Lift up on the socket tang (8, **Figure 185**) to release the socket.

NOTE
Do not pull too hard on the wire. If the tang is bent downward, the terminal will be difficult to remove. If necessary, repeat the process and release the tang.

8. Gently pull on the wire to pull the wire and terminal (5, **Figure 185**) from the terminal chamber. Note the wire location number on the connector.

9. Hold the pin terminal so the catch faces (7, **Figure 185**) the tang in the chamber:
   a. On the pin side of the connector, the tangs sit on the bottom of the housing. Install a pin sit it catch faces down.
   b. On the socket side of the connector, the tangs sit at the top of the housing. Install a socket so its catch faces up.

10. Inset the terminal into the secondary lock side of the housing, and push the wire and terminal into the correct location until it snaps into place. Gently pull on the lead to ensure the terminal is correctly seated.

11. Rotate the hinged secondary lock inward until the tabs are fully engaged with the latches on both sides of the connector. Pull upward to make sure the tabs are locked in place.

12. Insert the socket housing into the pin housing and push it in until it locks into place.

13. Install the Main Fuse as described in this chapter.

8. Push rubber seal back into place on the wire end of socket terminal, if necessary.

9. Repeat this process to install remaining socket terminal, if necessary.

10. Install the secondary lock (A, **Figure 184**) onto the cable and then push it onto the wire end of the socket housing until the slots engage the tabs (B) on the sides of the socket housing.

11. Install the Main-Fuse as described in this chapter.

Amp Multilock Connectors)

3-, 6- and 10-pin connector and pin terminals removal/installation

Refer to **Figure 185**.

1. Remove the Main-Fuse as described in this chapter.

2. Slide the connector attachment clip T-stud to the large end of the opening.

3. Press the release button on the socket on the terminal side and pull the connector apart.

4. Slightly bend the latch (1, **Figure 185**) back and free one side of the secondary lock (2). Repeat for the other side of the secondary lock.

Delphi Electrical Connectors Removal/Installation

1. Remove the Main Fuse as described in this chapter.

2. Bend back the external latches (**Figure 186**) and separate the socket halves.

3. Free one side of the wire lock (A, **Figure 187**) from the ear on the wire end of the socket housing. Release the wire lock on the other side.

4. Release the wires from the channels in the wire lock, and remove them from the socket housing.

9

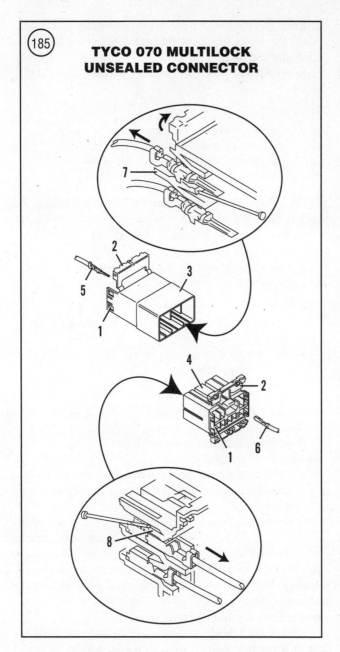

185
TYCO 070 MULTILOCK
UNSEALED CONNECTOR

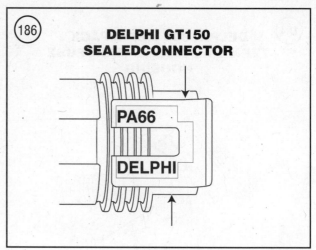

186
DELPHI GT150
SEALEDCONNECTOR

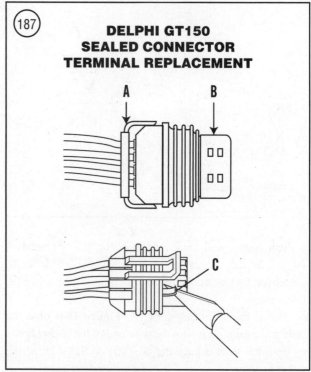

187
DELPHI GT150
SEALED CONNECTOR
TERMINAL REPLACEMENT

5. Remove the terminal lock (B, **Figure 187**) from the socket housing.

6. Use a thin blade (unsharpened end of an X-Acto knife), and gently pry the tang outward away from the terminal (C, **Figure 187**).

7. Carefully pull the wire to back the terminal out of the connector, and remove it. Do not pull the wire until the terminal is released or it will be difficult to remove it.

8. Gently push the tang on the socket housing inward toward the chamber.

9. Position the terminal so its open side faces the tang, insert the terminal into the wire end of the housing, and seat the terminal in its chamber. Gently pull the wire to ensure the terminal is correctly seated.

10. Install the terminal lock (B, **Figure 187**) onto the socket housing.

11. Install the wire lock (A, **Figure 187**) onto each side of the socket housing. Make sure they are correctly seated.

12. Push the connector halves together until the external latches engage (**Figure 186**).

13. Install the Main-Fuse as described in this chapter.

Molex MX150 Electrical Connector
Removal/Installation

1. Remove the Main-Fuse as described in this chapter.

2. Pull the secondary lock approximately 3/16 in (4.8 mm) away from the terminals until it stops by performing the following. Do not remove the secondary lock.

   a. On the socket housing, insert a flat-bladed screwdriver into the pry slot (A, **Figure 188**) and pry the secondary lock from the terminals.

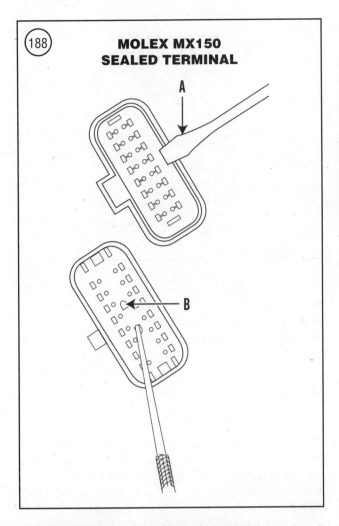

MOLEX MX150
SEALED TERMINAL

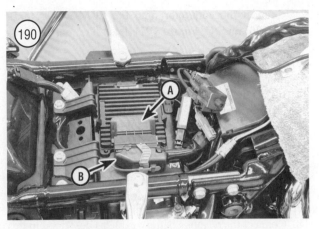

the cavity until it bottoms. Gently pull on the wire lead to ensure the terminal is correctly seated.

7. Push the secondary lock into the socket housing, and lock the terminals into the housing.

8. Install the socket housing into the terminal.

Delphi GT 280 Sealed 73-pin Terminal ECM Connector

Removal/installation

1. Turn the ignition switch off.

2. Remove the seat and left side cover as described in Chapter Fourteen.

3. On models so equipped, move the purge solenoid (A, **Figure 189**) toward the side and release if from the top caddy.

4. On models so equipped, release the HFSM antenna (B, **Figure 189**) from the top caddy and model it out of the way.

5. Release the mounting clip on each side and lift the ECM (A, **Figure 190**) up and of the electrical caddy. Move it out of the way.

NOTE
The ECM is shown removed from the top electrical caddy for clarity.

6. Remove the strap. Press on the latch (A, **Figure 191**), and rotate the lock lever (B) to the released position.

7. Disconnect the connector from the ECM. Refer to B, **Figure 190** and C, **Figure 191** .

8. Cut the cable strap and release the harness from the strain relief on the connector housing.

9. Release the latch (A, **Figure 192**) on each side and release the cover (B) from the housing (C). Remove the cover.

10. Install the cover (B, **Figure 192**) onto the housing (C) and rotate the lock lever to the locked position.

11. Install a new cable strap onto the harness in the original location.

   b. On the pin housing, use a hooked pick or needle nose pliers and loosen the secondary lock (B, **Figure 188**).

3. Insert the Molex Electrical Connector Terminal Remover (H-D part No. HD-48114) into the desired terminal pin hole. Push it in until the tool bottoms.

4. Gently pull on the wire lead and remove it from the housing cavity.

5. Insert the wire into the correct terminal chamber.

6. Orient the terminal so the tang opposite the crimp engages the slot in the terminal cavity. Push the terminal into

12. Connect the connector onto the ECM. Refer to B, **Figure 190**) and (C, **Figure 191**). Push it on until it locks into place.

13. Rotate the lock lever (B, **Figure 191**) to the locked position.

14. Install the ECM (A, **Figure 190**), straight down onto the top electrical caddy. Make sure it is locked in place.

15. On models so equipped, install the HFSM antenna (B, **Figure 189**) onto the top caddy.

16. On models so equipped, move the purge solenoid (A, **Figure 189**) back into position and secure it to the top caddy.

17. Install the seat as described in Chapter Fourteen.

18. Connect the negative battery cable as described in this chapter.

Connector terminals removal/installation

This procedure shows how to remove and install the electrical terminals in the socket housing.

1. To remove the terminals with in the connector, refer to *Micro 64 removal/installation* (this section).

2. To remove the ground terminal, perform the following:
   a. Remove the ground secondary lock (D, **Figure 192**), and the secondary lock E from the terminal housing (C).
   b. Use a thin-bladed screwdriver (**Figure 193**), and gently pry the ground terminal retainer from the terminal housing (C, **Figure 192**).
   c. Use a thin-bladed screwdriver, release the latch (**Figure 194**) and pull the ground wire, wire seal and terminal from the cover side of the housing.
   d. Connect the terminal into place from the cover side of the terminal housing (C, **Figure 192**) until the cover latch (A) engages. Gently pull on the wire to ensure the terminal is correctly seated.
   e. Correctly position the secondary lock (one short leg and one long leg), and install it (E, **Figure 192**) into the terminal housing. Push it in until it bottoms, and install the ground secondary lock (D, **Figure 192**).

Delphi 280 Metri-Pack Unsealed Connectors

Removal/installation

1. Remove the left side electrical caddy as described in this chapter.

2. Remove all fuses and relays from the fuse blocks.

3. Install all fuses and relays into the fuse blocks.

4. Install the left side electrical caddy as described in this chapter.

Connector terminals removal/installation

This procedure shows how to remove and install the electrical terminals in the fuse blocks.

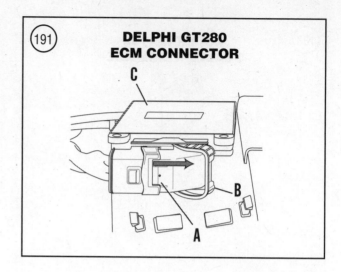

191 DELPHI GT280 ECM CONNECTOR

1. Note the exact wire color and its cavity location in the fuse block(s). The fuse block terminal cavity locations are identified by letter (1, **Figure 195**) and letter (B) coordinates. The wires must be reinstalled into the correct cavity locations.

> *NOTE*
> *Start on the outboard side of the locking wedge secondary lock.*

2. To remove the secondary locks, insert a thin-bladed screwdriver (A, **Figure 196**)under the lip of the locking wedge (B) and gently pry up the secondary lock.

3. Looking down into the chamber at top of fuse block observe the tang next to each socket terminal.

4. Use a thin blade of an X-Acto knife and carefully push the tang away from the terminal. Tug on the wire and back it out of the terminal.

5. Refer to the note in Step 1 and insert the wires into their correct cavity (**Figure 195**). If necessary, refer to the color wiring diagrams in Chapter Sixteen of this manual.

6. With the open end of the socket terminal facing the tang, push the wire lead into the correct chamber at the wire end side of the fuse block. Push it in until a "click" is heard indicating it is locked into place and is properly engaged.

7. Gently tug on the wire to ensure the terminal is correctly seated.

8. Position the locking wedges above the tangs in each chamber and slide the flat side of the secondary lock into slot (between rows), and push down until it bottoms. Repeat for all locking wedges.

Molex MX150 Connector Repair (2011-on Models)

This procedure describes the removal and installation of electrical terminals in the socket and pin housing.

1. Note the exact wire color and its cavity location number (1, **Figure 197**) are stamped on the housing side of the connector. The wires (2, **Figure 197**) must be reinstalled into the correct cavity locations (3, **Figure 197**).

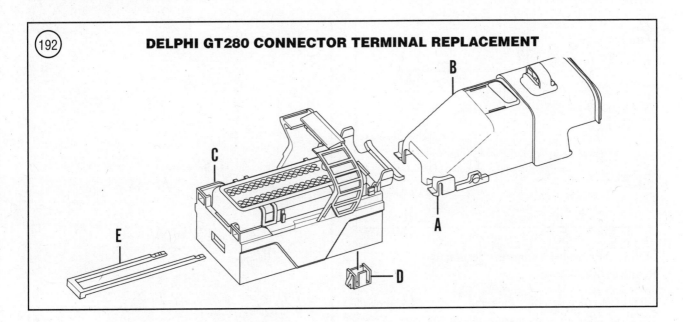

DELPHI GT280 CONNECTOR TERMINAL REPLACEMENT

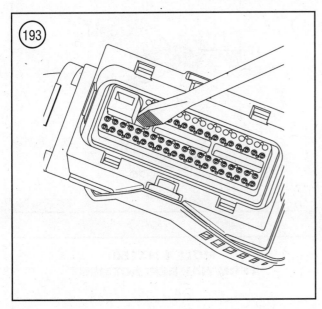

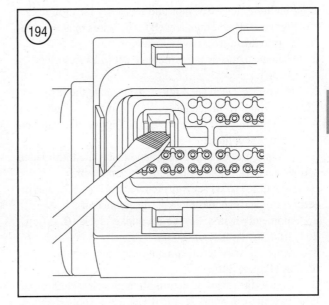

2. Disconnect the negative battery cable as described in this chapter.

3. Press on the latch while pulling the pin and socket apart and separate the connector.

4. Pull the secondary lock approximately 3/16 in. (4.8 mm) away from the terminals until it stops by performing the following. Do not remove the secondary lock.

    a. On the socket housing, insert a flat-bladed screwdriver into the pry slot (A, **Figure 198**) and pry the secondary lock from the terminals.

    b. On the pin housing, use a hooked pick (B, **Figure 198**) or needle nose pliers and loosen the secondary lock.

5. Insert the Molex Electrical Connector Terminal Remover (H-D part No. HD-48114) into the correct terminal pin hole until the tool bottoms (**Figure 199**):

    a. On the socket housing, the pin holes are inside the terminal openings.

    b. On the pin housing, the pin holes are outside the terminal openings.

6. Press the terminal remover to the bottom of the pin hole, gently pull on the wire and remove the wire terminal from its cavity.

7. Insert the wire into the correct numbered terminal connector cavity.

8. Orient the terminal so the tangs (2, **Figure 197**) are opposite the cramped engages the slot in the terminal cavity. Push the terminal into the cavity until it bottoms. Carefully pull on the wire lead to ensure the terminals correctly seated.

9. Push the secondary lock into the socket housing, and lock the terminals into the housing.

10. Install the socket housing into the terminal.

11. Disconnect the negative battery cable as described in this chapter.

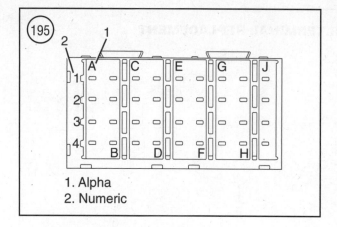

1. Alpha
2. Numeric

Molex CMC Sealed Connector Terminals Removal/Installation

This procedure describes the removal and installation of electrical terminals in the socket and pin housing.

1. Note the exact wire color and its cavity location letters (A, **Figure 200**) and numbers (B). The wires must be reinstalled into the correct cavity locations.
2. Disconnect the negative battery cable as described in this chapter.
3. Press on the catch (A, **Figure 201**), rotate the lever arm (B) down, and lift the connector (C) from the component.
4. Use a thin-bladed screwdriver (A, **Figure 202**), and insert it into the connector.
5. Maintain pressure on the cap and insert the thin-bladed screwdriver (B, **Figure 202**) into the connector.
6. Use a thin-bladed screwdriver (A, **Figure 203**), and insert it into the secondary lock in the connector.
7. Completely withdraw the secondary lock (B, **Figure 203**) from the connector.
8. Locate the wire terminal using the letter/number coordinates (**Figure 200**).
9. Identify the size of terminal, and select either the CMC extractor 0.6mm Terminal Extractor Tool (H-D part No. HD-50423), or the CMC extractor 1.5 mm Terminal Extractor Tool (H-D part No. HD-50424).
10. Insert the pins of the CMC extractor tool (A, **Figure 204**) into the access slots (B) of the terminal cavity, and extract the connector lead and terminal (C).
11. Insert the terminal and connector lead into the correct cavity access slot until it locks into place. Gently pull on the connector lead to ensure the terminal is correctly seated.
12. Slide the cap (C, **Figure 202**) over the connector lead bundle. Push it on until it locks into place.

JAE MX19 Sealed Connector Terminals Removal/Installation

This procedure describes the removal and installation of electrical terminals in the socket and pin housing.

1. Disconnect the negative battery cable as described in this chapter.

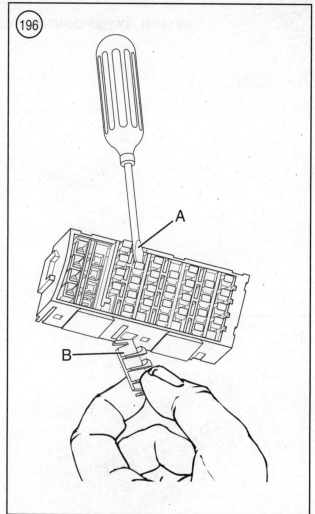

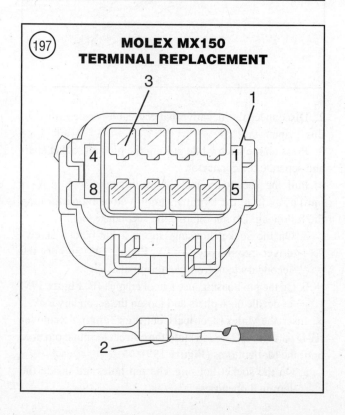

MOLEX MX150 TERMINAL REPLACEMENT

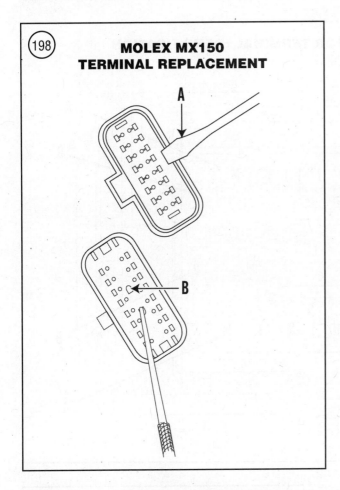

MOLEX MX150 TERMINAL REPLACEMENT

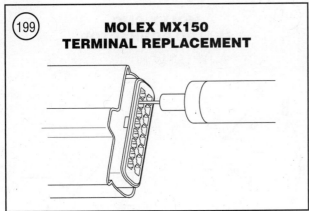

MOLEX MX150 TERMINAL REPLACEMENT

7. Attach the connector halves together and ensure they are locked together.

8. Connect the negative battery cable as described in this chapter.

TYCO Sealed Connector Terminals Removal/Installation

This procedure describes the removal and installation of electrical terminals in the housing.

Large terminal removal

1. Note the exact wire color and its cavity location numbers (**Figure 207**). The wires must be reinstalled into the correct cavity locations.

2. Disconnect the negative battery cable as described in this chapter.

3. Disconnect the electrical connector (**Figure 208**) from the ABS hydraulic unit.

4. Remove the cover from the back of the connector (**Figure 209**).

5. Insert a thin flat-bladed screwdriver all the way to the bottom behind the tab of the secondary lock.

6. Use a thin flat-bladed screwdriver and gently slide the secondary lock (**Figure 210**) out of the connector.

7. Use a terminal pick (JIMS Receptacle Extractor part No. 1764 or Snap-On part No. GA500A), and insert the smallest pins into the gaps (**Figure 211**) on each side of the socket to compress the tangs on each side of the terminal.

8. Gently pull on the wire and remove the wire and terminal.

Small terminal removal

1. Note the exact wire color and its cavity location numbers (**Figure 207**). The wires must be reinstalled into the correct cavity locations.

2. Disconnect the negative battery cable as described in this chapter.

3. Disconnect the electrical connector (**Figure 208**) from the ABS hydraulic unit.

4. Remove the cover from the back of the connector (**Figure 209**).

5. Insert a thin flat-bladed screwdriver all the way to the bottom behind the tab of the secondary lock.

6. Use a thin flat-bladed screwdriver and gently slide the secondary lock (**Figure 210**) out of the connector.

7. File a 45° angle on the front edge of the terminal extractor (H-D part No. HD-B-50085).

8. Insert the extractor (**Figure 212**) into the terminal opening outside of the terminal.

9. Tilt the extractor to lift the lift the molding latch, and release the terminal.

10. Gently pull on the connector lead and remove the terminal out of the housing.

2. Press the release button (**Figure 205**) on each side of the connector, and separate the connector.

3. File a 45° angle on the front edge of the terminal extractor (H-D part No. HD-B-50085).

4. Insert the extractor (A, **Figure 206**) into the terminal opening above the terminal, and press the plastic molding (B) up and out of the way.

5. Pull the connector lead and terminal out of the back of the housing.

6. Insert the terminal and connector lead into the housing until it clicks into place. Gently pull on the connector lead to ensure the terminal is correctly seated.

9

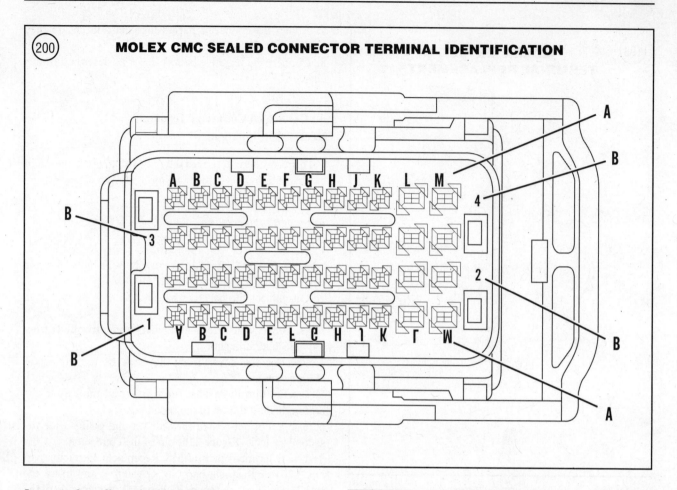

(200) **MOLEX CMC SEALED CONNECTOR TERMINAL IDENTIFICATION**

Large and small terminal installation

1. Install the wires into the correct cavity locations (**Figure 207**) as noted during removal.
2. Use a thin blade of an X-Acto knife and carefully push the tang away from the terminal.
3. Align the socket, and push it in until it "clicks" into place. Gently pull on the connector lead to ensure the terminal is correctly seated.
4. Push the secondary lock back into the connector.
5. Install the over back into place on the back of the connector (**Figure 209**).
6. Connect the electrical connector (**Figure 208**) onto the ABS hydraulic unit.
7. Connect the negative battery cable as described in this chapter.

BOSCH COMPACT 1.1 M CONNECTOR TERMINALS

Removal/Installation

This procedure describes the removal and installation of electrical terminals in the socket.

1. Remove the fuel tank as described in Chapter Eight.
2. Note the exact wire color and its cavity location numbers. The wires must be reinstalled into the correct cavity locations.

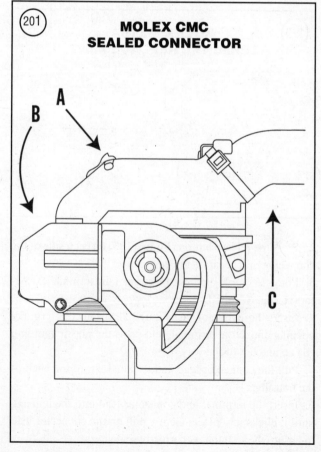

(201) **MOLEX CMC SEALED CONNECTOR**

(202)

**MOLEX CMC
SEALED CONNECTOR
TERMINAL REPLACEMENT**

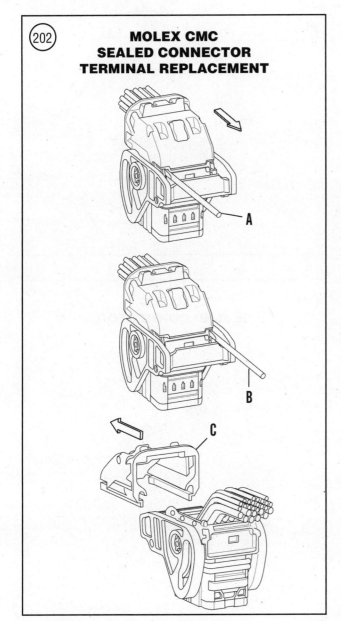

(203)

**MOLEX CMC
SEALED CONNECTOR
TERMINAL REPLACEMENT**

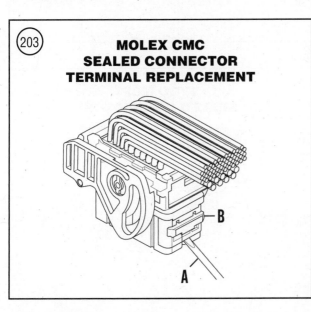

(204)

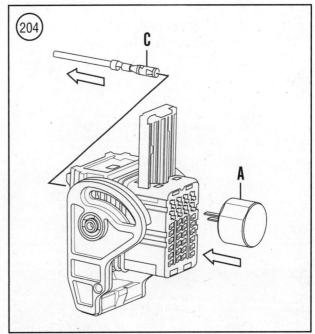

(205)

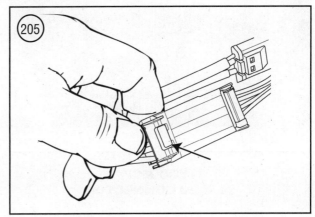

(206)

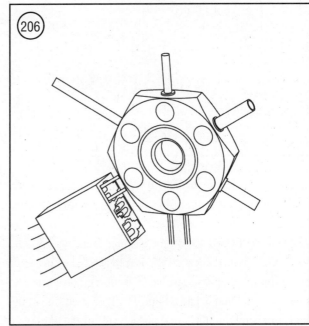

9

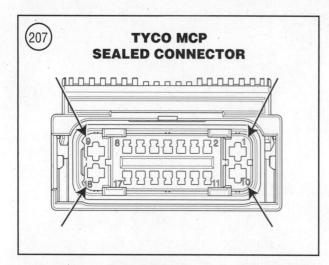

207

**TYCO MCP
SEALED CONNECTOR**

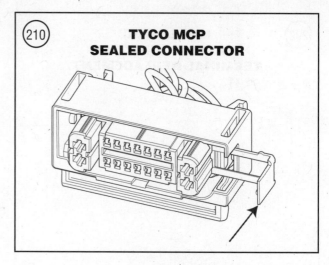

210

**TYCO MCP
SEALED CONNECTOR**

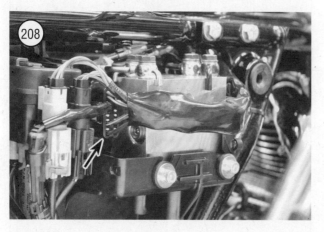

208

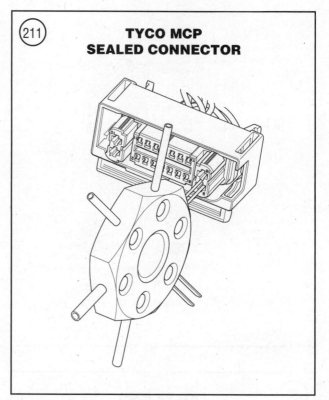

211

**TYCO MCP
SEALED CONNECTOR**

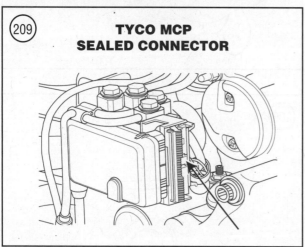

209

**TYCO MCP
SEALED CONNECTOR**

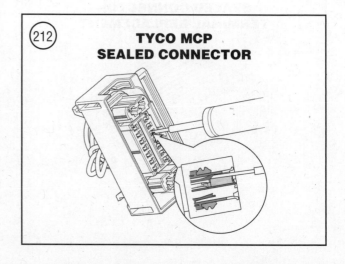

212

**TYCO MCP
SEALED CONNECTOR**

3. Snap back the secondary lock then press on the latch while pulling the socket from the TMAP sensor (**Figure 213**) on the induction module.

4. Slide the locking bar off the terminal housing.

5. Use a terminal pick (JIMS Receptacle Extractor part No. 1764 or Snap-On part No. GA500A), and insert the smallest pins into the gaps (**Figure 214**) on each side of the socket to compress the tangs on each side of the terminal.

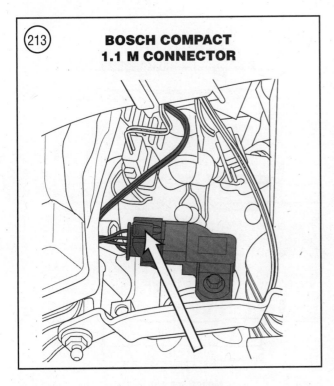

BOSCH COMPACT 1.1 M CONNECTOR

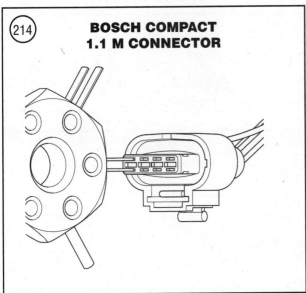

BOSCH COMPACT 1.1 M CONNECTOR

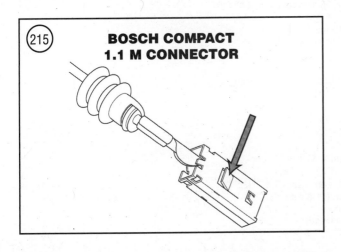

BOSCH COMPACT 1.1 M CONNECTOR

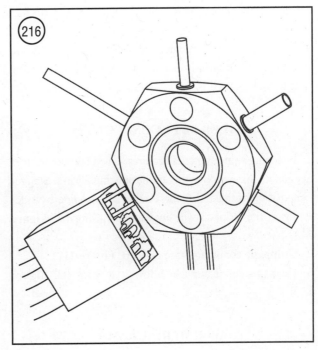

6. Gently pull on the wire and remove the wire and terminal.

7. Use a thin blade of an X-Acto knife and carefully bend the tangs (**Figure 215**) one each side of the terminal outward.

8. Align the wire and terminal to the correct socket, and push it in until it "clicks" into place. Gently pull on the connector lead to ensure the terminal is correctly seated.

9. Position the teeth on the locking face down, and slide the locking bar onto the terminal housing.

10 Install socket onto the TMAP sensor (**Figure 213**) on the induction module, and push it on until it "clicks" into place.

11. Install the fuel tank as described in Chapter Eight.

AUTOFUSE ELECTRICAL CONNECTORS

The Autofuse electrical connector terminals are located in the ignition switch and on some fuse blocks. Use a terminal pick (JIMS Receptacle Extractor part No. 1764 or Snap-On part No. GA500A) for this procedure.

1. Insert the smallest pair of the terminal picks (**Figure 216**) into the mating chamber on the end of the socket housing. Simultaneously depress the tangs on each side of the terminal housing.

2. Gently pull on the wire and remove the terminal from the socket housing.

3. Crimp *new* terminals onto the end of the wires, if necessary.

4. Use a thin blade (unsharpened end of an X-Acto knife), and gently pry the tang outward away from the terminal body.

5. Position the open side of the terminal with the rib facing down.

6. Insert the terminal into the wire side of the chamber and carefully push it until it locks in place. Pull gently on the wire to make sure it is locked in place.

SEALED BUTT CONNECTORS

Replacing some switches requires sealed butt connectors to connect the switch wiring to the existing wiring. Stagger the position of the connectors so they are not side-by-side.

1. Insert the stripped wire into the connector (A, **Figure 217**).

2. Crimp the connector/wire ends (B, **Figure 217**).

3. Heat the connector and allow it to cool (C, **Figure 217**).

WIRING DIAGRAMS

Color wiring diagrams for all models are located in Chapter Sixteen of this manual.

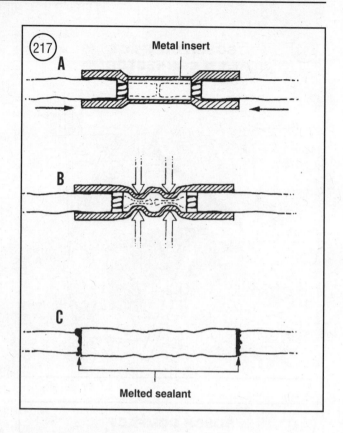

Table 1 ELECTRICAL SYSTEM SPECIFICATIONS

Item	Specification
ACR solenoid compression test	
All models except CVO	
ARC connected	110 psi (758 kPa)
ARC disconnected	175 psi (1207 kPa)
CVO models	
ARC connected	130-170 psi (896-1172 kPa)
ARC disconnected	200-220 psi (1379-1517 kPa)
Alternator	
AC voltage output	16-23 VAC per 1000 rpm
Stator coil resistance	0.1-0.2 ohms
Voltage regulator	
Voltage output @ 3600 rpm	14.3-14.7 @ 75° F (24° C)
Amps	35-50 amps @ 3000 rpm
Battery capacity	12 volts, 28 amp hour/405 CCA*
Ignition coil	
Primary resistance	0.5-0.7 ohms
Secondary resistance	5500-7500 ohms
Spark plug	
Size	12 mm
Gap	0.038-0.043 in. (0.97-1.09 mm)
Type	H-D No. 6R12
Spark plug cable resistance	
Short front cable (16.75 in./425 mm)	4,188-11,172 ohms
Long rear cable (34.75 in./883 mm)	8,688-23,178 ohms
Starter	
Minimum free speed (no load)	3000 rpm @ 11.5 volts
Maximum free current (no load)	90 amp @ 11.5 volts
Cranking current	200 amp maximum @ 68º F (20º C)
Brush length (minimum)	0.433 in. (11.0 mm)

(continued)

Table 1 ELECTRICAL SYSTEM SPECIFICATIONS (continued)

Item	Specification
Starter (continued)	
Commutator	
Runout	0.01 in. (0.41 mm)
Diameter-minimum	1.141 (28.98 mm)
Mica depth-minimum	0.008 in. (0.203 mm)
* CCA. Cold cranking amperage	

Table 2 BATTERY CHARGING RATES/TIMES (APPROXIMATE)

Voltage	% of charge	3 amp charger	6 amp charger	10 amp charger	20 amp charger
12.8	100%	–	–	–	–
12.6	75%	1.75 hours	50 minutes	30 minutes	15 minutes
12.3	50%	3.5 hours	1.75 hours	1 hour	30 minutes
12.0	25%	5 hours	2.5 hours	1.5 hours	45 minutes
11.8	0%	6 hours and 40 minutes	3 hours and 20 minutes	2 hours	1 hours

Table 3 FUSE SPECIFICATIONS (AMPERES)

Item	Specification
ABS (models so equipped)	30
Accessory	15
Amplifier (models so equipped)	30
Battery	15
Brakes	15
ECM power	15
Engine control	
Active e haust (HDI models)	15
Fuel pump	15
GPS (model so equipped)	2
Hand grips–heated (model so equipped)	5
Headlamp	15
Instruments	15
Ignition	15
Lighting	15
Main	40
P&A	2
Power outlet (model so equipped)	15
Power lock (model so equipped)	15
Radio power/siren	15
Radio memory	15

Table 4 REPLACEMENT BULBS (ALL MODELS EXCEPT CVO)

Item	Current draw amperage x Quantity
Headlamp (high beam/low beam)	
FLHTC/U, FLHR/C, FLHX, FLHTK	4.58/5.0 x 1
FLTRX, FLTRU	4.58/5.0 x 2
Position lamp (HDI)	0.32 x 1
Tail/stop	0.59/2.10 x 1
Front turn signals	
Front/running (domestic)	2.25/0.59 x 2
Front/running (HDI)	2.25 x 2
Front—FLHX (HDI)	1.75 x 2
Rear turn signals	
FLHTC/U, FLHR/C, FLHTK, FLTU	2.25 x 2
FLHX, FLTRX (domestic)	2.25/0.59 x 2
FLHX, FLTRX (HDI)	LED1
FLHX, FLTRX (Canada)	2.25 x 2

(continued)

Table 4 REPLACEMENT BULBS (ALL MODELS EXCEPT CVO)* (continued)

Item	Current draw amperage x Quantity
Tour-Pak side lamps (LED)	
FLHTCU, FLHTK, FLTRU	0.14
Tour-Pak tail/stop	2.25-0.59 x 2
Fender tip	
Front	0.30 x 1
Rear (LED)	–
License plate (HDI)	
FLHTC/U, FLHR, FLHTK, FLTRU (LED)	1
License plate (Canada) FLHX, FLTRX	0.35 x 2
Auxiliary lamps	2.1 x 2
Fog lamp (HDI)	2.1 x 2
Instrument panel lamps (LED)	
High beam, oil pressure, neutral and	
turn signal indicators	
Gauge bulbs–all models except FLHR, FLHRC	
Speedometer/tachometer (LED)	–
Oil pressure	0.24 x 1
Voltmeter	0.24 x 1
Air temperature	0.24 x 1
Fuel gauge	0.24 x 1
Gauge bulbs–FLHR, FLHRC (LED)	
Speedometer, odometer, fuel gauge, check engine	

*Illuminated with LEDs. If failure occurs, replace the unit assembly.

Table 5 HEADLIGHT AIM ADJUSTMENTS (FLTR MODELS)

Hex adjuster	Rotation	Beam movement
Left bulb	Clockwise	To the right
Right bulb	Counterclockwise	To the right
Left bulb	Clockwise	To the left
Right bulb	Counterclockwise	To the left
Left and right bulb equally	Clockwise	Upward
Left and right bulb equally	Counterclockwise	Downward

Table 6 REPLACEMENT BULBS (CVO MODELS)[1]

Item	Wattage x Quantity
Headlamp (high beam/low beam)	
FLHTCUSE	(domestic)
2010	2.7/4.3 x 1
2011-on	5.1/4.3 x 1
FLHTCUSE (HDI)	4.85/5.0 x 1
FLTRXSE, FLTRUSE	4.85/5.0 x 1
FLHRSE, FLHXSE	
Domestic	2.7/4.3 x 1
HDI	4.58/5.0 x 1
Position lamp (HDI)	0.32 x 1
Rear facia (FLHRSE, FLHXSE)[2]	LED
Tail/stop (all models except	
FLHRSE, FLHXSE)	0.59/2.10 x 1
Front turn signals (all models	
except FLHRSE, FLHXSE)	
Domestic	2.25/0.59 x 2
HDI	1.75 x 2
Front turn signals (FLHRSE, FLHXSE models)	
Domestic	2.10/0.59 x 2
HDI	1.75 x 2
Rear turn signals (all models	
except FLHRSE, FLHXSE)	
Domestic	2.25 x 2
HDI	1.75 x 2

(continued)

Table 6 REPLACEMENT BULBS (CVO MODELS)[1] (continued)

Item	Wattage × Quantity
License plate	
FLHTCUSE models (HDI)	0.37 1
FLHRSE, FLHXSE models	LED
Tour-Pak side lamps (LED)	
(all models except FLHRSE, FLHXSE)	LED
Tour-Pak wrap-around lamps (LED)	
(all models except FLHRSE, FLHXSE)	LED
Tour-Pak interior lamp (FLHTCUSE)	LED
Saddlebag interior lamp (FLHTCUSE)	LED
Auxliary lamps FLHTCUSE	
Domestic	2.1 x 2
HDI	2.7 x 2
Instrument panel lamps (LED)	
High beam, oil pressure, neutral and	
turn signal indicators	
Gauge bulbs—all models except FLHR, FLHRC	
Speedometer/tachometer (LED)	–
Oil pressure	0.24 x 1
Voltmeter	0.24 x 1
Air temperature	0.24 x 1
Fuel gauge	0.24 x 1
Gauge bulbs—FLHR, FLHRC models	
Speedometer/tachometer (LED)	–
Fuel gauge (LED)	–

1. Illuminated with LEDs. If failure occurs, replace the unit assembly.
2. The rear facia on FLHRSE, FLHXSE models contains the right and left rear turn signals and tail lamps.

Table 7 ELECTRICAL SYSTEM TORQUE SPECIFICATIONS*

Item	ft.-lb.	in.-lb.	N•m
Alternator stator screws		55-75	6.2-8.5
Automatic compression			
release solenoid	11-15	–	14.9-20.3
Auxiliary lamp bracket hardware	–	72-120	10.8-13.6
Auxiliary lamp bracket to fork			
bracket			
Screw FLHTC/U, FLHTK	15-20	–	20-27
Acorn nut FLHHR/C	–	72-80	8.1-12.2
Bank angle sensor	–	84-113	9.5-14.9
Battery terminal bolt	–	60-70	6.8-7.9
Battery tray screw	–	72-96	8.1-10.9
Brake clamp fasteners	–	72-108	8.1-12.2
CB module to radio screw	–	35-45	4.0-5.1
Crank position sensor (CKP)			
screw	–	100-120	11.3-13.6
Engine temperature sensor (ET)	–	120-180	13.6-20.3
Electrical caddy			
Top caddy screws	–	72-96	8.1-10.9
Left side caddy screw	–	72-96	8.1-10.9
Fairing cap screws	–	25-30	2.8-3.4
Fairing speaker (FLHS, FLHTC/U)			
Lower screw	–	22-28	2.5-3.2
Upper screw	–	35-50	4.0-5.7
Fork lock screw (FLHR)	–	36-60	4.1-6.8
Front fender tip lamp			
Bracket screw	–	20-25	2.3-2.8
Trim strip tee bolt	–	10-15	1.1-1.7
Front turn signal lamp mounting			
bracket			
screws (bullet style; fork			
mounted)	15-20	–	20-27
Front turn signal lamp mounting			
bracket screw			
(FLHR/C, FLHT/C/U)	–	30-60	4.1-6.8

(continued)

9

Table 7 ELECTRICAL SYSTEM TORQUE SPECIFICATIONS* (continued)

Item	ft.-lb.	in.-lb.	N•m
Fuel tank console screws	–	30-60	4.1-6.8
Ground terminal nut (ignition coil)	–	50-90	5.7-10.2
Handlebar clamp to clutch lever bracket screw	–	72-108	8.1-12.2
Handlebar switch housing screws	–	35-45	4.0-5.0
Harness ground stud flange nut	–	50-90	5.7-10.2
Headlamp adjuster mounting screw			
Dual headlamp models	–	35-45	4.0-5.1
Headlamp mounting screw			
Dual headlamp models	–	15-25	1.7-2.8
Headlamp door screw	–	9-18	1.0-2.0
Headlamp retaining screws			
Fairing equipped models	–	22-32	2.5-3.6
Headlamp retaining screws			
Non-fairing equipped models		9-18	1.0-2.0
Horn bracket acorn nut	–	80-120	9.0-13.6
Horn stud flange nut	–	80-120	9.0-13.6
Fork lock (FLHR, FLHRC) mounting screw	–	36-60	4.1-6.8
Ignition coil			
Mounting bolt	–	32-40	3.6-4.5
Ground terminal nut	–	50-90	5.7-10.2
Ignition switch			
Housing nut	–	85-115	9.6-13.0
Housing screw	–	36-60	4.1-6.8
Screws (FLHR/C)	–	20-30	2.3-3.4
Instrument bezel (FLTRU, FLTRUSE)			
Screws	–	10-15	1.1-1.7
Instrument nacelle to fork bracket screws (FLTRU, FLTRUSE)	15-20	–	20-27
Instrument console screw (FLHR/C)	–	36-60	4.1-6.8
License plate bracket screw	–	60-80	6.8-9.0
Neutral switch	–	120-180	13.6-20.3
Oil pressure			
Sender	–	96-144	10.8-16.3
Switch	–	96-144	10.8-16.3
Passenger seat strap bolt	–	60-96	6.8-10.8
Radio storage box to support bracket screw	–	35-45	4.0-5.1
Radio support bracket screw	–	35-45	4.0-5.1
Rear facia (FLHX-FLTRX) Phillips screw	–	25-40	28-45
Rear fender light harness stud plate flange nut (FLHX, FLTR)	–	60-96	6.8-10.9
Rear fender tip lamp screws	–	20-25	2.3-2.8
Rear brake light switch	12-15	–	16.3-20.3
Rear turn signal			
Lamp bracket screw	–	84-144	9.5-16.3
Lamp to lamp bracket screw	–	30-50	3.4-5.6
Speedometer bracket screw (FLHT, FLHX)	–	10-20	1.1-2.3
Starter solenoid			
Contact post jam nut	–	60-80	7.3-9.0
Ring terminal nut	–	70-90	7.9-10.2
Starter			
End cover screw	–	90-110	10.2-12.4
Mounting bolts	25-27	–	33.9-36.6
Ring terminal hex nut	–	70-90	7.9-10.2
Terminal post nut	–	70-90	7.9-10.2
Through bolts	–	39-65	4.4-7.3
TMAP senor bolt	–	84-108	9.5-12.2

(continued)

Table 7 ELECTRICAL SYSTEM TORQUE SPECIFICATIONS* (continued)

Item	ft.-lb.	in.-lb.	N•m
Tachometer bracket screw (FLHT, FLHX)	–	10-20	1.1-2.3
Tail lamp (FLHTC/U, FLHTC, FLHR/C, FLHTK, FLTRU)			
Circuit board/chrome base screw	–	40-80	4.5-5.4
Tail lamp lens screw	–	20-24	2.3-2.7
Turn signal lamp			
Acord nut or screws	–	96-120	10.8-13.6
Mounting bracket bolt	–	88-144	9.5-16.3
Lamp to auxiliary lamp stud locknut	15-18	–	20.3-24.4
Voltage regulator flange locknut	–	70-100	7.9-11.3

*Components listed in this table also relate to CVO models unless otherwise noted as relating to a specific model number(s).

Table 8 ELECTRICAL SYSTEM TORQUE SPECIFICATIONS (UNIQUE TO CVO MODELS)

Item	ft.-lb.	in.-lb.	N•m
Advanced audio (FLHTCUSE, FLTRUSE)			
Module mounting screw	–	17-21	1.9-2.4
Advanced audio			
Amplifier locknut	–	96-108	10.8-12.2
Amplifier (FLHRSE, FLTRXSE)			
Mounting screw	–	15-20	1.7-2.3
Antenna cable strap screws	–	35-45	4.0-5.1
Auxiliary lamp/turn signal bracket screw	15-20	–	20.3-27.1
CB module to radio screw (FLHXSE)	–	35-45	4.0-5.1
Garage door opener mounting bracket screw (FLHTCUSE)	–	35-45	3.9-5.1
GPS Zumo 660 (FLHTCUSE, FLTRUSE)			
Headset receptacle (FLHTCUSE)	–	25-30	2.8-3.4
Inner fairing pad screw	–	20-25	2.3-2.8
GPS unit			
Bracket screw	–	20-25	2.3-2.8
Cradle screw	–	14-20	1.6-2.3
Headlamp			
Door screw	–	9-18	1.0-2.0
Mounting screw (FLTRXSE)	–	15-25	1.7-2.8
Retaining ring screw FLHXSE, FLHRSE)	–	23-28	2.6-3.2
iPod module (FLHXSE)			
Bracket screw	–	15-20	1.7-2.3
Screw	–	15-20	1.7-2.3
Ignition switch			
Power lock nut (FLHTCUSE)	–	85-115	9.6-13.0
Ignition/light switch nut (FLTRUSE)	–	85-115	9.6-13.0
License plate light & bracket (2013 FLHRSE)			
Bracket screw	–	57-69	6.4-7.8
Electrical connector cover flange nut	–	30-45	3.4-5.1
Power lock module (FLHTCUSE, FLTRUSE)			
Bracket fastener	–	30-50	3.4-5.6
Fastener	–	20-40	2.3-4.5
Radio chassis mounting screw (FLTRSE)	–	35-45	4.0-5.1

(continued)

9

Table 8 ELECTRICAL SYSTEM TORQUE SPECIFICATIONS (UNIQUE TO CVO MODELS) (continued)

Item	ft.-lb.	in.-lb.	N•m
Road Tech Zumo 660 GPS			
Mounting screws	–	20-25	2.3-2.8
Speakers			
Main speaker screws (FLTRXSE)	–	10-15	1.1-1.7
Midrange mounting screws (FLHXSE)	–	35-50	3.9-5.6
Saddlebag (FLHRSE, FLTRXSE)			
Cover screw	–	35-45	4.0-4.5
Check strap screw	–	18-20	2.0-2.3
Mounting screw	–	10-15	1.1-1.7
Speaker grille screw	–	10-15	1.1-1.7
Adapter flange nut (FLTRXSE)	–	15-20	1.7-2.3
Adapter screws (FLTRXSE)	–	10-15	1.1-1.7
Tweeter mounting nuts	–	10-20	1.1-2.3
Tour-Pak (FLHTCUSE, FLTRUSE)			
Latch hook nut	–	25-35	2.8-3.9
Lockset retaining nut	–	30-45	3.4-5.1
Wrap around light			
Flange nut	–	15	1.7
Screw	–	12	1.3
Tweeter screws (FLHXSE, FLTRXSE)	–	10-20	1.2-2.2
XM radio (FLHTCUSE, FLTRUSE)			
Module to radio mounting screw	–	35-45	4.0-5.1
Radio nut	–	30-40	3.4-4.5

CHAPTER TEN

WHEELS, HUBS AND TIRES

This chapter includes procedures for repair of the front and rear wheels, and hubs and tire service. Refer to Chapter Three for maintenance procedures.

Specifications are in **Tables 1-4** at the end of the chapter.

MOTORCYCLE STANDS

Many procedures in this chapter require that the front or rear wheel be lifted off the ground. A motorcycle front end stand (**Figure 1**), or suitable size jack is required. Before purchasing or using a stand, check with the manufacturer to make sure the stand will work with the specific model being worked on. If any adjustments or accessories are required to the motorcycle and/or stand, perform the necessary adjustments or install the correct parts before lifting the motorcycle. When using the stand, have an assistant standing by to help. Some means to tie down one end of the motorcycle may also be required. After lifting on a stand, make sure the motorcycle is properly supported before walking away from it.

FRONT WHEEL

Removal

CAUTION
On ABS-equipped models, keep the ABS sensor and the ABS encoder wheel bearings away from any magnetic fields or they will be damaged.

1. Support the motorcycle with the front wheel off the ground. Refer to *Motorcycle Stands* in this chapter.

2. On ABS-equipped models, push in on lip at the rear of clip (A, **Figure 2**) and release it. Rotate the ABS tab (B, **Figure 2**) toward the rear until the clip is perpendicular to the bracket. Remove the clip and move the cable out of the way.

3. On models so equipped, loosen the set screw and remove the cover from the axle nut.

4. On the right side, insert a drift (**Figure 3**) or screwdriver through the front axle hole to prevent it from rotating.

5. On the left side, loosen the axle nut (**Figure 4**).

6. On the left side, remove the axle nut and washer (Figure 5).

7. On the right side, loosen the nuts (**Figure 6**) on the fork slider cap.

8. Remove the caliper mounting bolts (A, **Figure 7**), and remove both calipers as described in Chapter Thirteen. On ABS models, do not lose the clip (B, **Figure 7**) located under the mounting bolts on the left side caliper.

9. On non-ABS models, prior to removing the front axle, note the location of the short right side spacer and long left side spacer. The spacers are not interchangeable and must be reinstalled on the same side during installation.

10. Use the drift or screwdriver and withdraw the front axle (A, **Figure 8**) from the fork sliders and front wheel. Remove the tool from the axle.

CAUTION
Never pull the ABS cable taut or use the cable to support the suspension components as the cable will be damaged.

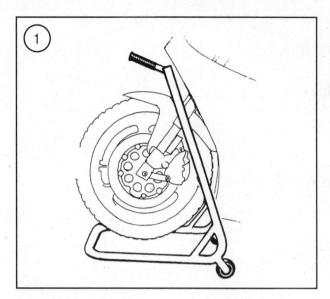

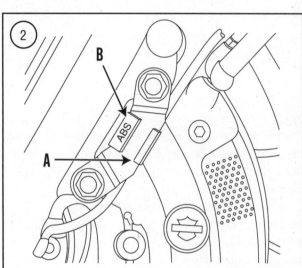

CAUTION
Do not try to remove the ABS sensor without first completely removing the front axle. The sensor is captured within a recess in the front hub assembly and the fork slider.

11A. On ABS-equipped models, perform the following:
  a. Slowly pull the wheel away from the fork sliders. Remove the ABS sensor (**Figure 9**) from the left side hub and remove the wheel.
  b. Remove the spacer (B, **Figure 8**) from the right side.
11B. On all other models, perform the following:
  a. Pull the wheel away from the fork sliders and remove it.
  b. Identify the spacers before removing them.
  c. Remove the short right side spacer and the long left side spacer from the wheel hub.
12. Inspect the front wheel assembly as described in this section.

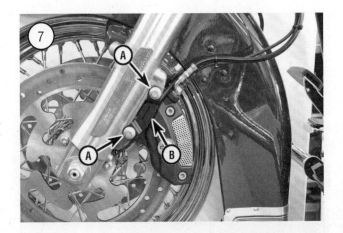

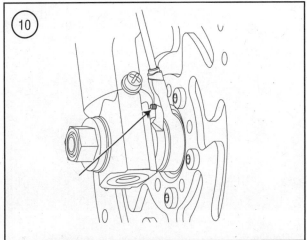

10

Installation

1. Clean the axle in solvent and dry thoroughly. Make sure the axle bearing surfaces on both fork sliders and the axle are free of burrs and nicks.

2. Apply an antiseize lubricant to the axle shaft prior to installation.

3. If the oil seals or bearings were replaced, confirm the front axle spacer alignment is correct as described in *Front Hub* (this chapter).

NOTE
Position the axle spacer(s) with the groove facing outboard away from the wheel.

4A. On ABS-equipped models, perform the following:
  a. Install the spacer on the right side of the wheel.
  b. Move the ABS sensor **Figure 9** into position adjacent to the left fork leg.
  c. Install the wheel between the fork tubes and correctly position the ABS sensor onto the hub.
  d. Install the axle from the right side.
  e. Rotate the ABS sensor *counterclockwise* until the index pin (**Figure 10**) makes contact with the left fork slider.

4B. On all other models, perform the following:
  a. Install the short right side spacer (**Figure 11**) and the long left side spacer (**Figure 12**) into the correct side of the wheel.
  b. Install the wheel between the fork tubes.
  c. Check that axle spacers are still located correctly.
  d. Install the axle from the right side.

5. On the left side, install the washer (**Figure 5**) and axle nut (**Figure 4**). Finger-tighten the axle nut. Check that the spacer(s), or ABS sensor (**Figure 9**), are installed correctly.

6. On the right side, insert a drift (**Figure 3**) or screwdriver through the front axle hole to prevent it from rotating.

7. Tighten the front axle nut to 60-65 ft.-lb. (81.3-88.1 N•m).

8. Use the drift, and pull fork leg up against the slider.

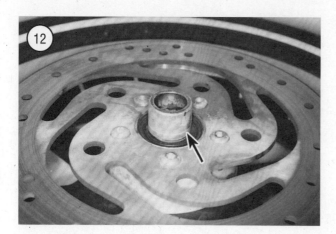

9. Tighten the nuts (B, **Figure 6**) on the fork slider cap to 132-180 in.-lb. (14.9-20.3 N•m).

10. Remove the drift from the front axle.

11. On models so equipped, install the axle nut cover. Apply a small amount of medium strength thread lock on the set screw and tighten to 60-84 in.-lb. (6.8-9.5 N•m).

12. Install both front brake calipers as described in Chapter Thirteen. On ABS models, make sure the clip (B, **Figure 7**) is located under the mounting bolts on the left side caliper.

13. Secure the wheel sensor cable as follows:
   a. Move the cable into position in the bracket.
   b. Rotate the ABS tab (B, **Figure 2**) toward the front until the clip is inline with the bracket. Press on the tab until the tab lip is engaged.
   c. Push in on lip at the rear of clip (A, **Figure 2**) and lock it in place.

14. With the front wheel off the ground, rotate it several times and apply the front brake to seat the brake pads against the discs.

15. Remove the stand and lower the front wheel onto the ground.

Inspection

Replace any worn or damaged parts as described in this section.

1. Turn each bearing inner race by hand. The bearing must turn smoothly. Some axial play (end play) is normal, but radial play (side play) as shown in **Figure 13** must be negligible. If one bearing is damaged, replace both bearings as a set. Refer to *Front and Rear Hubs* in this chapter.

2. Clean the axle and axle spacers in solvent to remove all grease and dirt. Make sure the axle contact surfaces are clean and free of dirt and old grease.

3. Check the axle runout with a set of V-blocks and dial indicator (**Figure 14**).

4. Check the spacers for wear, burrs and damage. Replace as necessary.

5. Check the brake disc bolts (**Figure 15**) for tightness. To service the brake disc, refer to Chapter Thirteen.

6. Check wheel runout as described in this chapter.

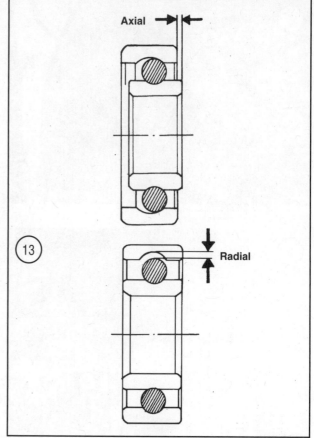

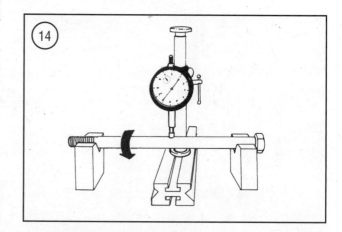

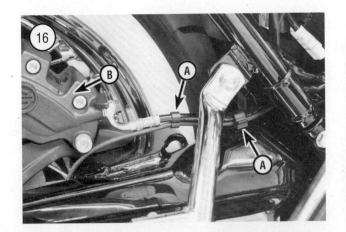

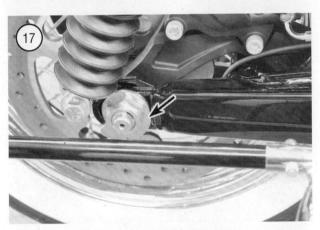

REAR WHEEL

Removal

> *CAUTION*
> *On ABS-equipped models, keep the ABS sensor and ABS encoder wheel bearings away from any magnetic field or they will be damaged.*

1. Remove both saddlebags as described in Chapter Fourteen.

2. Remove the muffler(s) as described in Chapter Four.

3. Support the motorcycle with the rear wheel off the ground on appropriate jack or stand.

4. On ABS-equipped models, remove the clip (A, **Figure 16**) securing the rear wheel sensor to the rear caliper brake hose.

5. Remove the rear brake caliper (B, **Figure 16**) from the mounting bracket as described in Chapter Thirteen, and tie it up to the frame with a bungee cord or wire.

6. Remove the large E-clip from the rear axle nut and axle. Discard the E-clip. It must not be reused.

7. Loosen and remove the axle nut (**Figure 17**) and adjuster cam (**Figure 18**).

8. Using a soft faced mallet, gently tap the rear axle (**Figure 19**) toward the left side.

> *NOTE*
> *The rear wheel is heavy and can be difficult to remove. Check the tire-to-ground clearance before removing the rear axle. If necessary, have an assistant help in the removal.*

9. From the left side, withdraw the rear axle (**Figure 20**) while holding the rear wheel.

> *CAUTION*
> *Never pull the ABS cable taut or use the cable to support the suspension components as the cable will be damaged.*

CAUTION
Do not try to remove the ABS sensor without first completely removing the rear axle. The sensor is captured within a recess in the rear hub assembly and the swing arm.

NOTE
Secure the compensator bowl to the driven sprocket to prevent it from falling off.

10A. On ABS-equipped models, perform the following:
   a. Slowly pull the wheel away from the swing arm and to the ground. Remove the ABS sensor (**Figure 21**) from the right side hub and remove the wheel.
   b. Remove the spacer from the left side.
10B. On all other models, perform he following:
   a. Slowly pull the wheel away from the swing arm and to the ground.
   b. Identify the spacers before removing them.
   c. Remove the short right side spacer (**Figure 22**) and the long left side spacer (**Figure 23**) from the wheel hub.
11. Disengage the drive belt from the driven sprocket and remove the rear wheel.
12. Remove the rear brake caliper mounting bracket from the wing arm weldment.

CAUTION
Do not set the wheel down on the brake disc surface, as it may be damaged.

13. Inspect the wheel as described in this chapter.

Installation

1. Clean the axle in solvent and dry thoroughly. Make sure the bearing surfaces on the axle are free from burrs and nicks.
2. Apply an antiseize lubricant to the axle shaft prior to installation.
3. Install the rear caliper mounting bracket onto the swing arm weldment.
4. Position the rear wheel between the swing arm sides and place the drive belt on the driven sprocket.
5A. On ABS-equipped models, install the spacer onto the left side of the wheel.
5B. On all other models, install the short right side spacer (**Figure 22**) and the long left side spacer (**Figure 23**) onto the wheel hub.
6. Install the compensating sprocket bowl onto the driven sprocket, if removed.
7. Lift the rear wheel into position and partially install the rear axle (**Figure 20**) from the left side and into the wheel hub.
8A. On ABS models, perform the following:
a. Move the ABS sensor (**Figure 21**) into position on the right side hub.

b. Continue to push the rear axle through the ABS sensor, rear caliper mounting bracket and the other side of the swing arm. Push the rear axle in until it bottoms.
8B. On all other models, continue to push the rear axle through the rear caliper mounting bracket and the other side of the swing arm. Push the rear axle in until it bottoms.
9. After the rear axle is completely installed, check that both axle spacer(s), or the spacer, and the ABS sensor are still in place.
10. On ABS equipped models, rotate the ABS sensor until the index pin (A, **Figure 24**) makes contact with the caliper bracket notch (B).

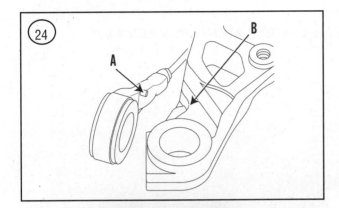

11. Install the rear caliper (B, **Figure 16**) onto the caliper bracket as described in Chapter Thirteen.

12. On ABS-equipped models, install the clips (A, **Figure 16**) securing the rear wheel sensor to the rear caliper brake hose.

13. Install the adjuster cam (**Figure 18**) and the axle nut (**Figure 17**).

14. Tighten the rear axle nut to 15-20 ft.lb. (20-27 N.m). This is an initial torque setting, not the final one.

15. Rotate the wheel several times to make sure it rotates freely. Then apply the rear brake several times to seat the pads against the disc.

16. Inspect the drive belt deflection and alignment as described in Chapter Three.

17. Adjust drive belt tension as described in Chapter Three. This procedure includes tightening the axle nut to its final torque of 95-105 ft.-lb. (128.8-142.4 N.m) and installing a new E-clip on the axle.

18. If removed, install the mufflers as described in Chapter Four.

19. Remove the jack and lower the rear wheel to the ground.

20. Install the saddlebags as described in Chapter Fourteen.

Inspection

Replace any worn or damaged parts as described in this section.

1. Turn each bearing inner race by hand. The bearing must turn smoothly. Some axial play (end play) is normal, but

radial play (side play), as shown in **Figure 13**, must be negligible. If one bearing is damaged, replace both bearings as a set. Refer to *Front and Rear Hubs* in this chapter.

2. Clean the axle and axle spacers in solvent to remove all grease and dirt. Make sure the axle contact surfaces are free of dirt and old grease.

3. Check the axle runout with a set of V-blocks and a dial indicator (**Figure 14**).

4. Check the spacers for wear, burrs and damage. Replace as necessary.

5. Check the brake disc bolts (**Figure 15**) for tightness. To service the brake disc, refer to Chapter Twelve.

6. Check the driven sprocket bolts (**Figure 25**) for tightness as decribed in this chapter.

7. Check wheel runout as described in this chapter.

FRONT AND REAR HUBS

Sealed ball bearings are installed on each side of the hub. Do not remove the bearing assemblies unless they require replacement. On models with ABS, install the encoder bearing onto the correct side of the hubs. At the front wheel, install it on the left side. At the rear wheel, install the encoder bearing on the right side.

Preliminary Inspection

Inspect each wheel bearing prior to removing it from the wheel hub.

CAUTION
Do not remove the wheel bearings for inspection purposes as they will be damaged during the removal process. Remove wheel bearings only if they are to be replaced.

1. Remove the front or rear wheel as described in this chapter.

2. If still in place, remove the axle spacers from the hub.

3. If necessary, remove the bolts securing the disc, and then remove the disc as described in Chapter Fifteen.

4. Turn each bearing by hand. The bearings must turn smoothly with no roughness.

5. Inspect the play of the inner race of each wheel bearing. Check for excessive axial play and radial play (**Figure 13**). Replace the bearing if it has an excess amount of free play.

Disassembly

This procedure applies to both the front and rear wheel and hub assemblies. Where differenced occur they are identified. Refer to **Figures 26-31** for the front wheel/hub and **Figures 32-38** for the rear wheel/hub assemblies.

1A. Remove the front wheel as described in this chapter.

1B. Remove the rear wheel as described in this chapter.

2. If still in place, remove the axle spacer(s) from each side of the hub.

10

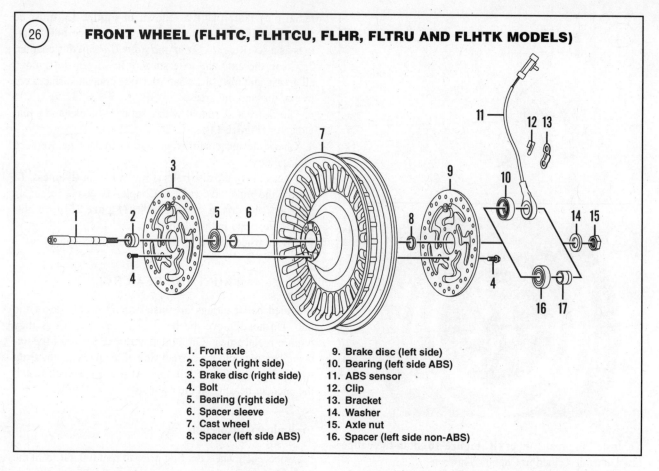

㉖ **FRONT WHEEL (FLHTC, FLHTCU, FLHR, FLTRU AND FLHTK MODELS)**

1. Front axle
2. Spacer (right side)
3. Brake disc (right side)
4. Bolt
5. Bearing (right side)
6. Spacer sleeve
7. Cast wheel
8. Spacer (left side ABS)
9. Brake disc (left side)
10. Bearing (left side ABS)
11. ABS sensor
12. Clip
13. Bracket
14. Washer
15. Axle nut
16. Spacer (left side non-ABS)

3. If necessary, remove the bolts securing the brake disc and remove the disc.

4. Before proceeding further, inspect the wheel bearings as described in this section. If they must be replaced, proceed as follows.

5A. To remove the bearings without the bearing removal set, perform the following:

   a. To remove the right- and left-hand bearings and spacer sleeve, insert a soft aluminum or brass drift into one side of the hub.

   b. Push the spacer sleeve over to one side and place the drift on the inner race of the lower bearing.

   c. Tap the bearing out of the hub with a hammer, working around the perimeter of the inner race (**Figure 39**). Remove the bearing and spacer sleeve.

   d. Repeat the process to remove the bearing on the other side.

WARNING
Be sure to wear safety glasses while using the wheel bearing remover set.

5B. To remove the bearings with a bearing removal set (Motion Pro part No. 08-0410), perform the following:

   a. Select the correct size of adapter and insert it into the bearing.

   b. Turn the wheel over and insert the remover shaft into the backside of the adapter. Tap the wedge and force

it into the slit in the adapter (**Figure 40**). This will force the adapter out against the bearing inner race.

   c. Tap on the end of the wedge bar (**Figure 41**) with a hammer and drive the bearing out of the hub. Remove the bearing and the spacer sleeve.

   d. Repeat the process to remove the bearing on the other side.

6. Clean the inside and the outside of the hub with solvent. Dry with compressed air.

Assembly

CAUTION
*The removal process will generally damage the bearings. Replace the wheel bearings in pairs along with the one located within the driven sprocket drum. **Never** reinstall the bearings after they have been removed. Always install **new** bearings.*

NOTE
On ABS models, the encoder bearing must be installed into the correct side of the wheel hub in order for the ABS system to operate correctly. The encoder bearing must be installed on the left side of the front wheel and on the right side of the rear wheel.

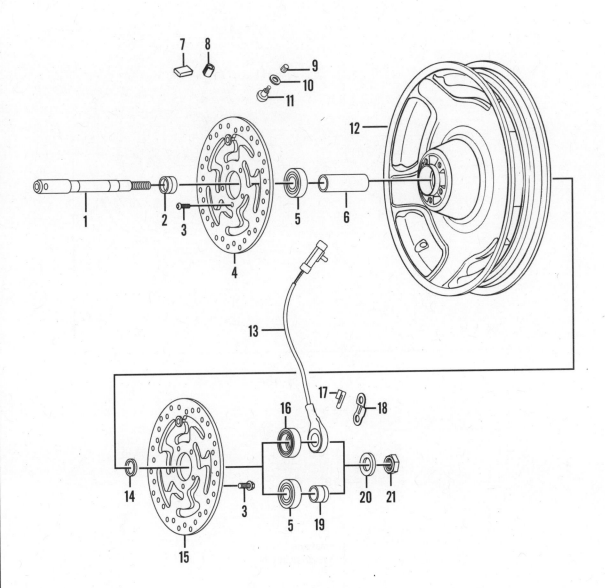

FRONT WHEEL (FLHX AND FLTRX MODELS)

27

1. Front axle
2. Spacer (right side)
3. Bolt
4. Brake disc (right side)
5. Bearing
6. Spacer sleeve
7. Balance weight (cast wheel)
8. Balance weight (laced wheel)
9. Valve stem cap
10. Seal
11. Valve stem
12. Cast wheel
13. ABS sensor
14. Spacer (left side ABS)
15. Brake disc (left side)
16. Bearing (left side ABS)
17. Clip
18. Bracket
19. Spacer (left side non-ABS)
20. Washer
21. Axle nut

10

FRONT LACED WHEEL (FLHRC MODELS)

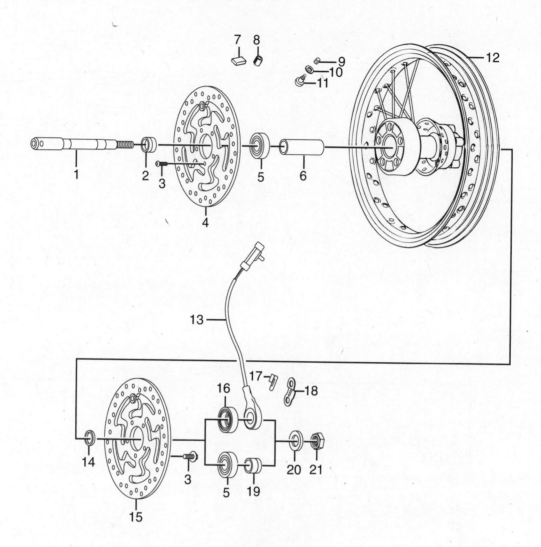

1. Front axle
2. Spacer–right side
3. Bolt
4. Brake disc–right side
5. Bearing
6. Spacer sleeve
7. Balance weight
8. Balance weight
9. Valve stem cap
10. Seal
11. Valve stem
12. Wheel
13. ABS sensor
14. Spacer–left side ABS models
15. Brake disc–left side
16. Bearing–left side ABS
17. Clip
18. Bracket
19. Spacer–left-side non-ABS
20. Washer
21. Axle nut

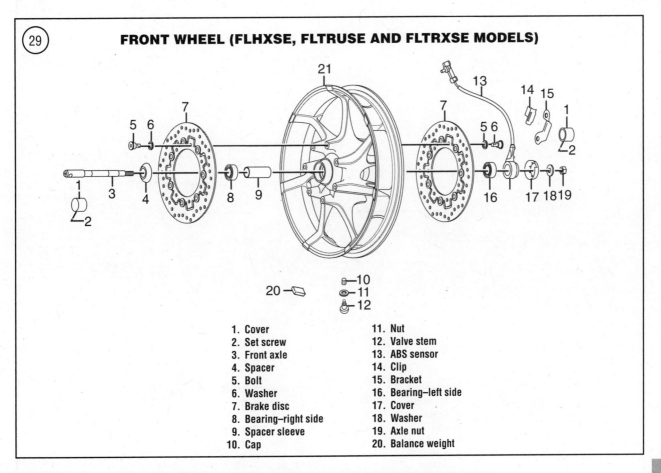

FRONT WHEEL (FLHXSE, FLTRUSE AND FLTRXSE MODELS)

1. Cover
2. Set screw
3. Front axle
4. Spacer
5. Bolt
6. Washer
7. Brake disc
8. Bearing–right side
9. Spacer sleeve
10. Cap
11. Nut
12. Valve stem
13. ABS sensor
14. Clip
15. Bracket
16. Bearing–left side
17. Cover
18. Washer
19. Axle nut
20. Balance weight

10

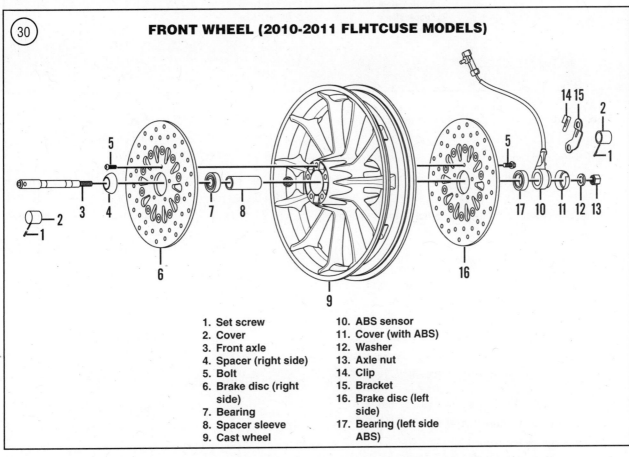

FRONT WHEEL (2010-2011 FLHTCUSE MODELS)

1. Set screw
2. Cover
3. Front axle
4. Spacer (right side)
5. Bolt
6. Brake disc (right side)
7. Bearing
8. Spacer sleeve
9. Cast wheel
10. ABS sensor
11. Cover (with ABS)
12. Washer
13. Axle nut
14. Clip
15. Bracket
16. Brake disc (left side)
17. Bearing (left side ABS)

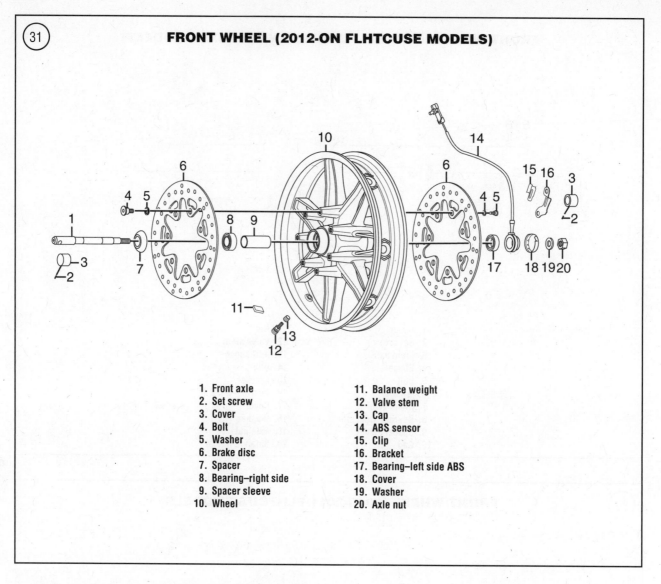

FRONT WHEEL (2012-ON FLHTCUSE MODELS)

1. Front axle
2. Set screw
3. Cover
4. Bolt
5. Washer
6. Brake disc
7. Spacer
8. Bearing—right side
9. Spacer sleeve
10. Wheel
11. Balance weight
12. Valve stem
13. Cap
14. ABS sensor
15. Clip
16. Bracket
17. Bearing—left side ABS
18. Cover
19. Washer
20. Axle nut

1. Blow any debris out of the hub prior to installing the new bearings.

2. Apply a light coat of wheel bearing grease to the bearing seating areas of the hub. This will make bearing installation easier.

3. Select a driver with an outside diameter slightly smaller than the bearing's outside diameter.

CAUTION
Install non-sealed bearings with the single sealed side facing outward. Do not tap on the inner race or the bearing might be damaged. Tap on the outer race only and make sure the bearings seat squarely into place. Be sure that the bearings are completely seated.

4. Position the right side bearing into place, and then tap the bearing into the hub bore until it bottoms. Be sure that the bearing is completely seated.

CAUTION
Do not set the wheel down on the brake disc surface, as it may be damaged.

5. Turn the wheel over (right side up) on the workbench and install the spacer collar.

6. Use the same tool set-up and drive in the left side bearing.

7. If the brake disc was removed, install it as described in Chapter Fifteen.

8A. Install the front wheel as described in this chapter.

8B. Install the rear wheel as described in this chapter.

DRIVEN SPROCKET ASSEMBLY

Preliminary Inspection

Inspect the sprocket teeth (**Figure 42**). If the teeth are visibly worn, replace the drive belt along with both the drive and driven sprockets.

REAR WHEEL (FLHTC, FLHTCU, FLHR, AND FLHTK MODELS)

32

1. E-clip
2. Axle nut
3. Adjuster cam
4. Spacer (right side)
5. Brake disc
6. Bearing
7. Cast wheel
8. Bolt
9. Balance weight (cast wheel)
10. Balance weight (laced wheel)
11. Cap
12. Valve stem
13. Spacer sleeve
14. Driven sprocket
15. Spacer (left side)
16. Rear axle
17. Washer
18. Bolt

10

(33)   **REAR WHEEL (FLHX AND FLTRX MODELS)**

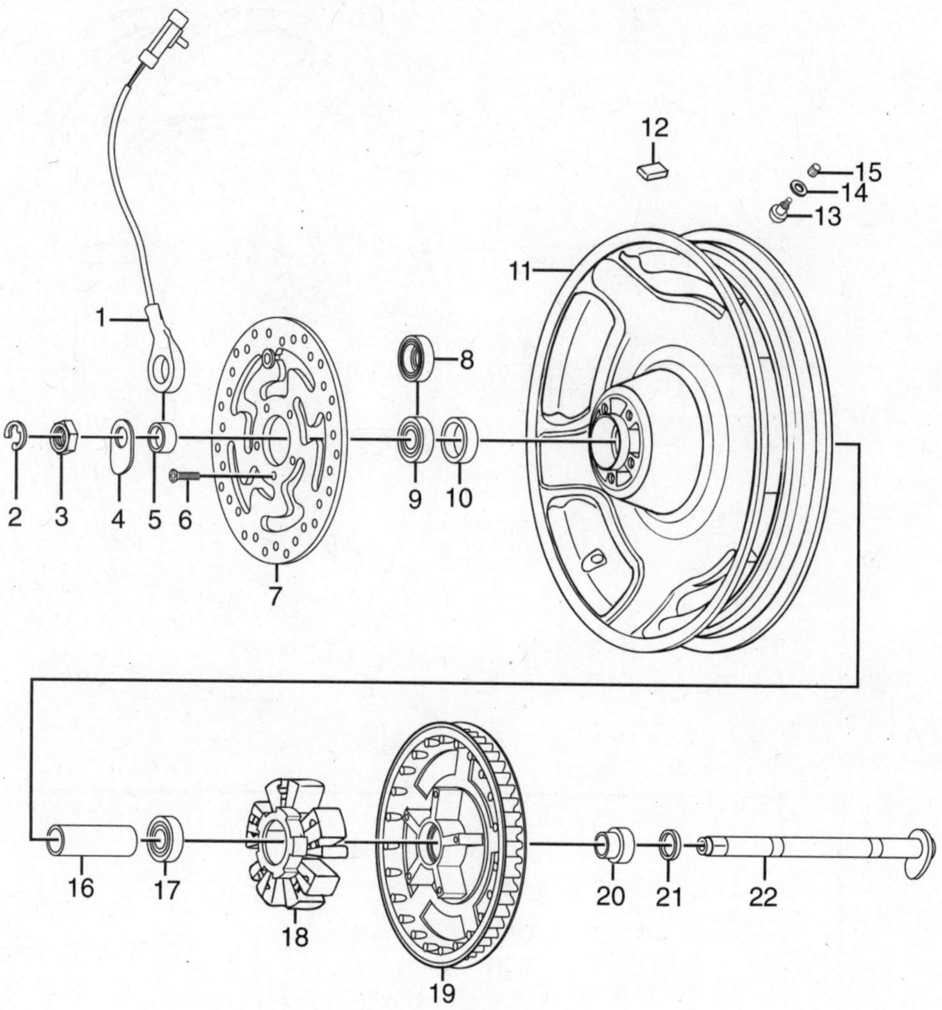

1. ABS sensor
2. E-clip
3. Axle nut
4. Adjuster cam
5. Spacer–non ABS
6. Bolt
7. Brake disc
8. Bearing–right side ABS
9. Bearing–right side non-ABS
10. Spacer
11. Wheel
12. Balance weight
13. Valve stem
14. Nut
15. Cap
16. Spacer sleeve
17. Bearing–left side
18. Rubber isolator
19. Driven sprocket
20. Spacer–left side
21. Spacer
22. Rear axle

(34)

REAR NARROW RIM LACED WHEEL
(FLHTC, FLHTCU, FLHR, FLHRC MODELS)

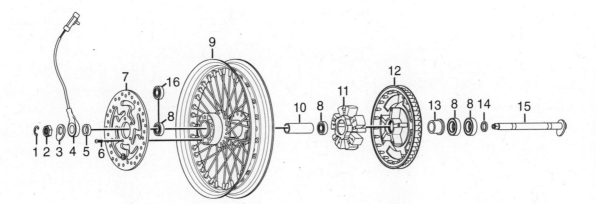

1. E-clip
2. Axle nut
3. Adjuster cam
4. ABS sensor
5. Spacer–non ABS
6. Bolt
7. Brake disc
8. Bearing–right side ABS
9. Wheel
10. Spacer sleeve
11. Rubber isolator
12. Driven sprocket
13. Spacer–left side
14. Spacer
15. Rear axle
16. Bearing–right side–non ABS

10

(35)

REAR WIDE RIM LACED WHEEL
(FLHTC, FLHTCU, FLHR, FLHRC AND FLTRU MODELS)

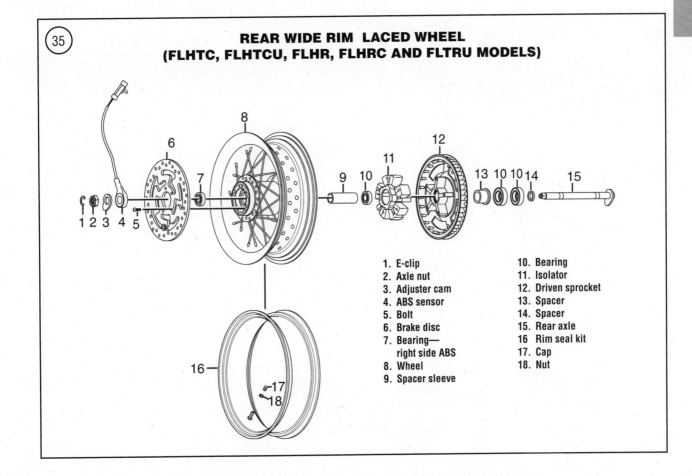

1. E-clip
2. Axle nut
3. Adjuster cam
4. ABS sensor
5. Bolt
6. Brake disc
7. Bearing—right side ABS
8. Wheel
9. Spacer sleeve
10. Bearing
11. Isolator
12. Driven sprocket
13. Spacer
14. Spacer
15. Rear axle
16. Rim seal kit
17. Cap
18. Nut

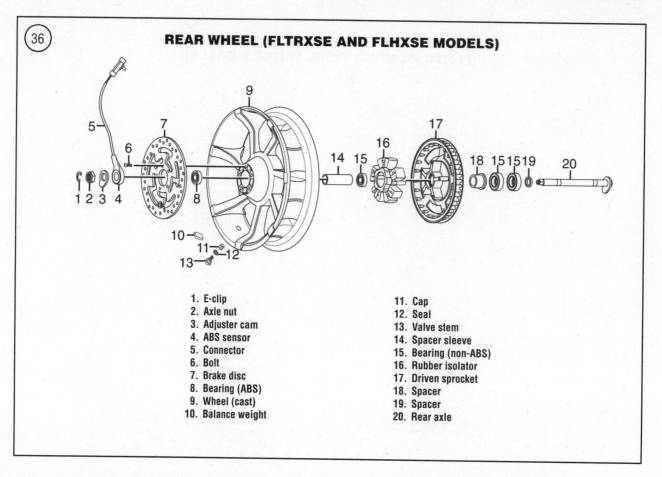

36

REAR WHEEL (FLTRXSE AND FLHXSE MODELS)

1. E-clip
2. Axle nut
3. Adjuster cam
4. ABS sensor
5. Connector
6. Bolt
7. Brake disc
8. Bearing (ABS)
9. Wheel (cast)
10. Balance weight
11. Cap
12. Seal
13. Valve stem
14. Spacer sleeve
15. Bearing (non-ABS)
16. Rubber isolator
17. Driven sprocket
18. Spacer
19. Spacer
20. Rear axle

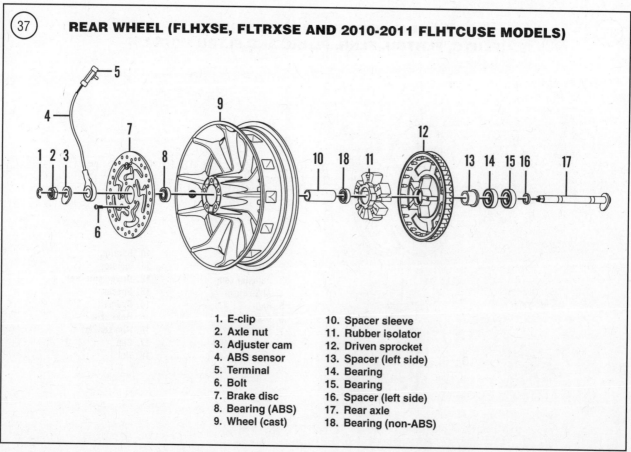

37

REAR WHEEL (FLHXSE, FLTRXSE AND 2010-2011 FLHTCUSE MODELS)

1. E-clip
2. Axle nut
3. Adjuster cam
4. ABS sensor
5. Terminal
6. Bolt
7. Brake disc
8. Bearing (ABS)
9. Wheel (cast)
10. Spacer sleeve
11. Rubber isolator
12. Driven sprocket
13. Spacer (left side)
14. Bearing
15. Bearing
16. Spacer (left side)
17. Rear axle
18. Bearing (non-ABS)

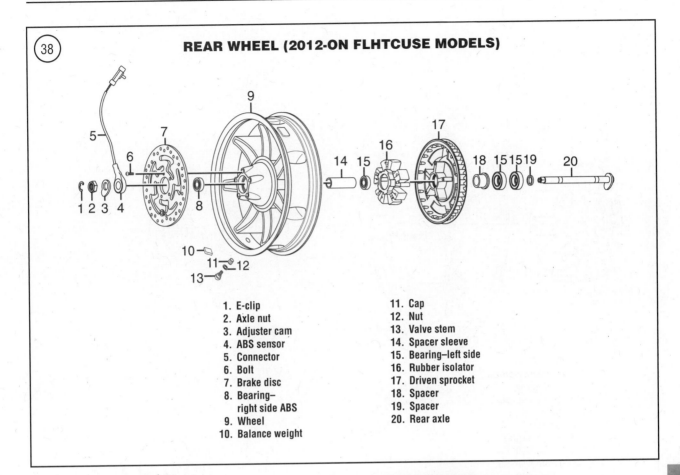

REAR WHEEL (2012-ON FLHTCUSE MODELS)

1. E-clip
2. Axle nut
3. Adjuster cam
4. ABS sensor
5. Connector
6. Bolt
7. Brake disc
8. Bearing–right side ABS
9. Wheel
10. Balance weight
11. Cap
12. Nut
13. Valve stem
14. Spacer sleeve
15. Bearing–left side
16. Rubber isolator
17. Driven sprocket
18. Spacer
19. Spacer
20. Rear axle

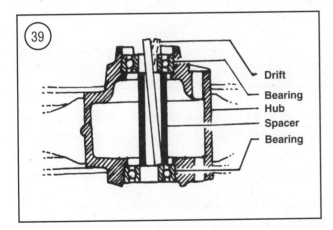

Drift
Bearing
Hub
Spacer
Bearing

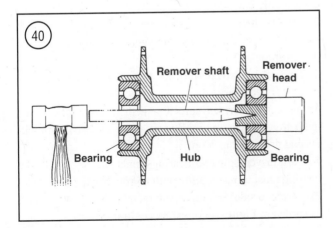

Remover shaft
Remover head
Bearing
Hub
Bearing

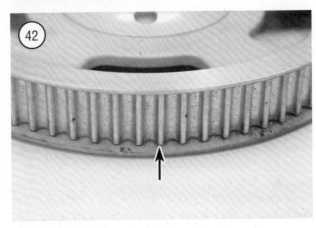

10

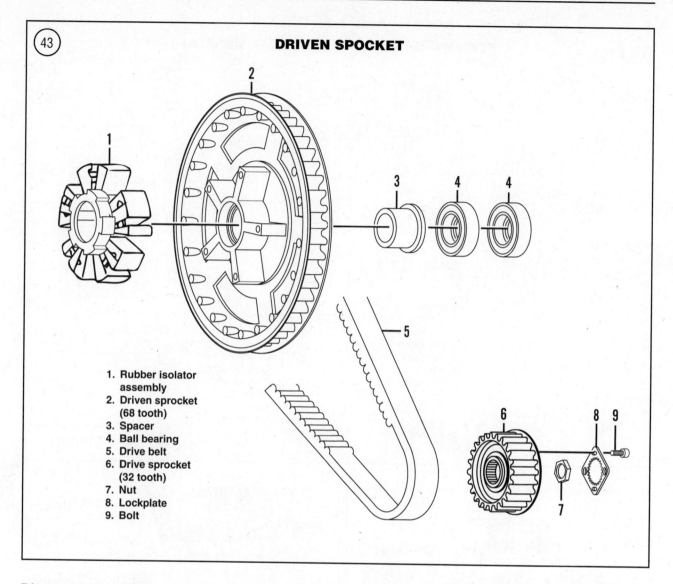

DRIVEN SPOCKET

43

1. Rubber isolator
   assembly
2. Driven sprocket
   (68 tooth)
3. Spacer
4. Ball bearing
5. Drive belt
6. Drive sprocket
   (32 tooth)
7. Nut
8. Lockplate
9. Bolt

Disassembly/Assembly

Refer to **Figure 43**.

1. Remove the rear wheel as described in this chapter.

2. Pull straight up and remove the driven sprocket from the rear hub and the compensator bowl. If the driven sprocket is difficult to remove from the hub, tap on the backside of the sprocket (from the opposite side of the wheel through the wheel spokes) with the wooden handle of a hammer.

3. Pull the rubber isolator assembly straight up and out of the compensator bowl on the rear hub.

4. Inspect the components as described in this section.

5. Lubricate the rubber isolator assembly with a 50:50 mixture of isopropyl alcohol and water. Lubricate their contact area within the compensator bowl.

6. Align the rubber isolator assembly with the raised ribs in the wheel hub, and install the assembly. Push the isolator assembly down until it bottoms and the strap engages in each rib. Make sure it is flush against the ribs side walls.

7. Align the driven sprocket bosses with the grooves of the compensator isolators and install the driven sprocket.

8. Push down evenly around the driven sprocket perimeter and press it down until it bottoms against the rear hub.

Inspection

1. Inspect the rubber isolators, or rubber isolator assembly, for signs of cracking or deterioration. Replace all isolators even if only one is damaged.

2. Inspect the raised webs in the driven sprocket. Check for cracks or wear. If any damage is visible, replace the driven sprocket.

3. Inspect the driven sprocket for cracks or damage; replace it if necessary.

4. Inspect the driven sprocket teeth (**Figure 42**). If the teeth are visibly worn, replace the drive and driven sprockets and drive belt as a set.

5. Turn driven sprocket bearings inner race by hand. The bearing must turn smoothly with no roughness. Some axial play (side to side) is normal, but radial play (up and down), as shown in **Figure 44**, must be negligible.

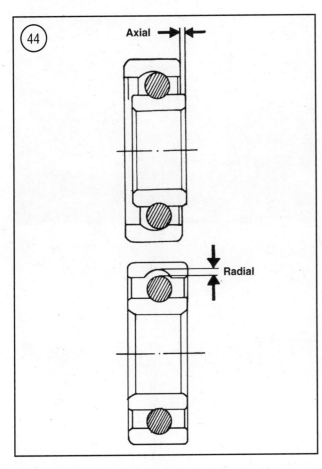

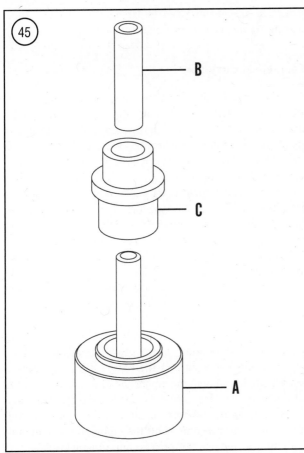

6. Carefully check the bearing outer seal for buckling or other damage that would allow dirt to enter the bearing.

Bearing Replacement

Remove and install the bearing with the rear wheel compensator bearing remover/installer (H-D part No. HD-48921) tool set (**Figure 45**), or an equivalent, and a hydraulic press.

1. Remove the driven sprocket as described in this section.

2. Remove the isolators or isolator assembly from the driven sprocket, as described in this section.

3. Position the tool base (A, **Figure 45**) on the hydraulic press bed supports with the long portion of the pin facing down.

4. Install the sleeve (B, **Figure 45**) onto the short portion of the pin (C).

5. Position the inboard side of the sprocket facing up and slide the sprocket over the sleeve (B, **Figure 45**) until it rests on the tool base (A).

6. Slide the small outer diameter of the driver (C, **Figure 45**) over the sleeve (B) until it contacts the spacer within the hub.

7. Center the driven sprocket and driver (C, **Figure 45**) directly under the press ram.

8. Slowly apply ram pressure and drive the bearings and spacer out of the hub of the driven sprocket.

9. Remove the driven sprocket and tools from the press bed. Discard the bearings.

10. Thoroughly clean the driven sprocket bearing bore and check it for nicks or gouges. Thoroughly dry the bearing bore.

11. Position the tool base (A, **Figure 45**) on the hydraulic press bed supports with the long portion of the pin facing down.

12. Install the sleeve (B, **Figure 45**) onto the short portion of the pin (C).

13. Position the outboard side of the sprocket facing up and slide the sprocket over the sleeve (B, **Figure 45**) until it rests on the tool base (A).

14. Position the *new* bearing with the sealed side facing up and center it in the bearing bore.

15. Center the driver (C, **Figure 45**) with the large outer diameter on the bearing. Make sure it contacts the outer race around the entire perimeter.

16. Center the driven sprocket and driver (C, **Figure 45**) directly under the press ram.

17. Slowly apply ram pressure and drive the bearing into the hub until the driver makes contact with the driven sprocket hub. Relieve ram pressure.

18. Repeat the procdure and install the remaining *new* bearing.

10

19. Install the isolators or isolator assembly, as described in this section.

20. Install the driven sprocket as described in this section.

DRIVE SPROCKET

The drive sprocket is covered in *Transmission Drive Sprocket* (Chapter Seven).

DRIVE BELT

CAUTION
When handling a new or used drive belt, never wrap the belt in a loop that is smaller than 5 in. (130 mm) in diameter, or bend it sharply in any direction. This will weaken or break the belt fibers and cause premature belt failure.

Removal/Installation

1. Remove the rear wheel as described in this chapter.
2. Remove the swing arm as described in Chapter Twelve.
3. Remove the compensating sprocket, clutch shell and chain tensioner as described in Chapter Six.
4. Remove the primary chaincase housing as described in Chapter Six.

NOTE
If the existing drive belt is going to be rein-stalled, it must be installed so it travels in the same direction. Before removing the belt, draw an arrow on the top surface of the belt facing forward.

5. Remove the drive belt (**Figure 46**) from the drive sprocket.
6. Installation is the reverse of removal. Adjust the drive belt deflection as described in Chapter Three.

Inspection

Do not apply any type of lubricant to the drive belt. Inspect the drive belt and teeth (**Figure 47**) for severe wear, damage or oil contamination.

Refer to **Figure 48** for various types of drive belt wear or damage. Replace the drive belt if worn or damaged.

LACED WHEEL SERVICE

The laced or wire wheel assembly consists of a rim, spokes, nipples and hub (containing the wheel bearings, spacer sleeve and seals).

Loose or improperly tightened spokes can cause hub damage. Periodically inspect the wheel assembly for loose,

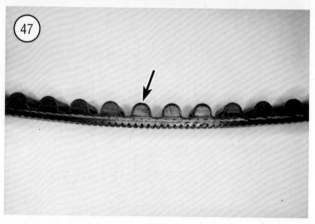

broken or missing spokes, rim damage and runout. Wheel bearing service is described in this chapter.

Component Condition

Wheels are subjected to a significant amount of punishment. Inspect the wheels regularly for lateral (side-to-side) and radial (up and down) runout, even spoke tension, and visible damage. When a wheel has a noticeable wobble, it is out of true. Loose spokes usually cause this, but it can be caused by impact damage.

Truing a wheel corrects the radial and lateral runout to bring the wheel back into specification. The condition of the individual wheel components will affect the ability to successfully true the wheel. Note the following:

1. Do not attempt to true a wheel with bent or damaged spokes. Doing so places an excessive amount of tension on the spoke and rim. The spoke may break and/or pull through the hole in the rim. Inspect spokes carefully and replace any that are damaged.
2. When truing a wheel, the nipple should turn freely on the spoke. It is common for the spoke threads to become corroded and make turning the nipple difficult. Spray a penetrating liquid onto the nipple and allow sufficient time for it to penetrate. Use a spoke wrench and work the nipple in both directions and apply additional penetrating liquid. If the spoke wrench rounds off the nipple, remove the tire from the rim and cut the spoke(s) out of the wheel.

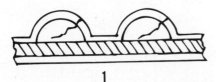

DRIVE BELT INSPECTION

1

2

3

Stone

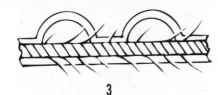

4

5

6

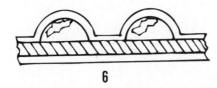

7

1. Internal tooth cracks
2. Missing teeth
3. Fuzzy edge core
4. Stone damage
5. External tooth cracks
6. Chipping
7. Hook wear

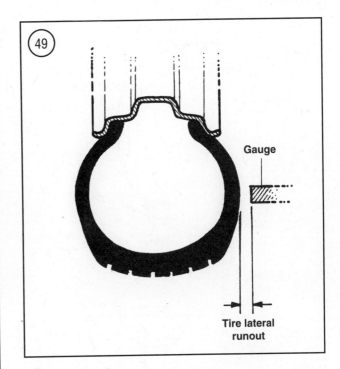

Gauge

Tire lateral runout

3. Minor rim damage can be corrected by truing; however, trying to correct excessive runout caused by impact damage will damage the hub and rim due to over-tightened spokes. Inspect the rims for cracks, flat spots or dents. Check the spoke holes for cracks or enlargement.

Wheel Truing Preliminaries

Before checking runout and truing the wheel, note the following:

1. Make sure the wheel bearings are in good condition.

2. A small amount of runout is acceptable, do not attempt to true the wheel to a perfect zero reading. Refer to **Table 2** for runout specifications.

3. Perform a quick runout check with the wheel on the motorcycle by placing a pointer against the fork or swing arm and slowly rotating the wheel (**Figure 49**).

4. Perform major wheel truing with the tire removed and the wheel mounted in a wheel truing stand.

5. Use a spoke nipple wrench of the correct size. Using the wrong type of tool or one that is the incorrect size will round off the spoke nipples, making further adjustment difficult. Quality wrenches grip the nipple on four corners to prevent damage. Tighten spokes to minimum of 55 in.-lb. (6.2 N•m).

Wheel Truing Procedure

1. Set the wheel in a truing stand.

2A. When using a dial indicator, check rim runout as follows:

    a. Measure the radial runout with a dial indicator positioned as shown in **Figure 50**. If radial runout ex-

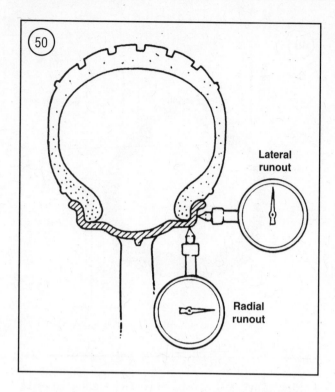

Lateral runout

Radial runout

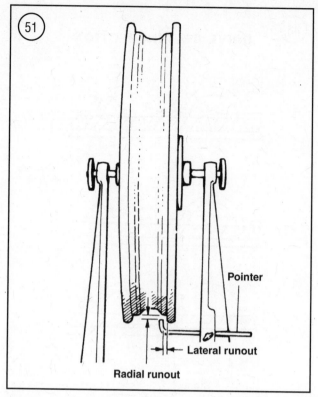

Pointer

Lateral runout

Radial runout

ceeds the service limit specified in **Table 2**, replace the rim.

b. Measure the lateral runout with a dial indicator positioned as shown in **Figure 50**. If lateral runout exceeds the service limit specified in **Table 2**, replace the rim.

2B. If a dial indicator is not available, check rim runout as follows:

a. Position a pointer facing toward the rim as shown in **Figure 51**. Spin the wheel slowly and check the lateral runout.

b. Adjust the position of the pointer and check the radial runout.

3. If lateral runout is out of specification, the rim needs to be moved relative to the centerline of the wheel. To move the rim to the left, for example, tighten the spoke(s) on the left of the rim and loosen the opposite spoke(s) on the right. Refer to **Figure 52**.

> *NOTE*
> *The number of spokes to loosen and tighten will depend on the amount of runout. As a minimum, always adjust two or three spokes in the vicinity of the rim runout. If runout affects a greater area along the rim, adjust a greater number of spokes.*

4. If radial runout is excessive, the hub is not centered within the rim. The rim needs to move relative the centerline of the hub. Draw the high point of the rim toward the centerline of the hub by tightening the spokes in the area of the high point and by loosening spokes on the low side. Tighten and loosen the spokes in equal amounts to prevent distortion. Refer to **Figure 53**.

5. Rotate the wheel and check runout. Continue adjusting the spokes until runout is within the specification listed in

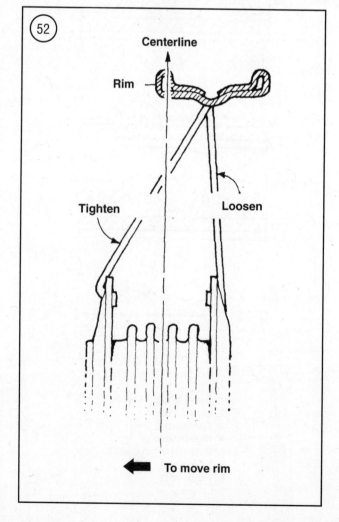

Centerline

Rim

Tighten   Loosen

To move rim

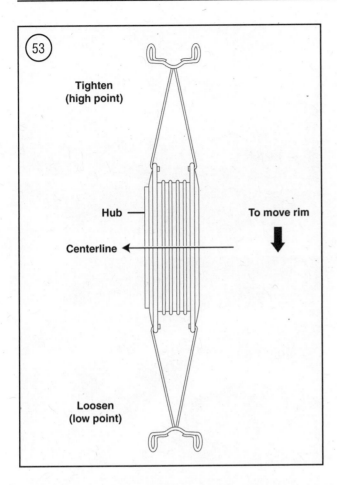

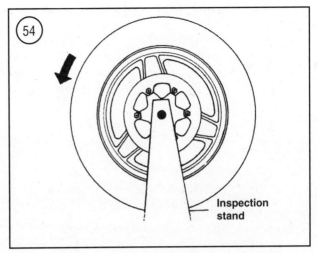

Table 2. Be patient and thorough, adjusting the position of the rim a little at a time.

6. After truing the wheel, seat each spoke in the hub by tapping it with a flat nose punch and hammer. Recheck the spoke tension and wheel runout. Readjust if necessary.

7. Check the ends of the spokes on the tube side of the rim. Grind off any spoke that protrudes from the nipple so it will not puncture the tube.

WHEEL BALANCE

An unbalanced wheel is unsafe. Depending on the degree of unbalance and the speed of the motorcycle, a rider may experience anything from a mild vibration to a violent shimmy that may result in loss of control.

Before balancing a wheel, thoroughly clean the wheel assembly. Make sure the wheel bearings are in good condition and properly lubricated. The wheel must rotate freely. Also make sure the balance mark on the tire aligns with the valve stem. If not, break the tire loose from the rim and align it before balancing the wheel. Refer to *Tire Changing* in this chapter.

NOTE
Balance the wheels with the brake disc and driven sprocket assembly attached. These components rotate with the wheel and affect the balance.

1. Remove the wheel as described in this chapter.
2. Make sure the valve stem and the valve cap are tight.
3. Mount the wheel on a stand such as the one shown in **Figure 54** so it can rotate freely.
4. Check the wheel runout as described in this chapter. Do not try to balance a wheel with excessive runout.
5. Remove any balance weights mounted on the wheel.
6. Give the wheel a spin and let it coast to a stop. Mark the tire at the highest point (12 o'clock). This is the wheel's lightest point.
7. Spin the wheel several more times. If the wheel keeps coming to rest at the same point, it is out of balance. If the wheel stops at different points each time, the wheel is balanced.

NOTE
Adhesive test weights are available from motorcycle dealerships. These are adhesive-backed weights that can be cut to the desired length and attached directly to the rim.

8. Loosely attach a balance weight (or tape a test weight) at the upper or light side (12 o'clock) of the wheel.
9. Rotate the wheel 1/4 turn (3 o'clock). Release the wheel and observe the following:
   a. If the wheel does not rotate (if it stays at the 3 o'clock position), the correct balance weight was installed. The wheel is balanced.
   b. If the wheel rotates and the weighted portion goes up, replace the weight with the next heavier size.
   c. If the wheel rotates and the weighted portion goes down, replace the weight with the next lighter size.
   d. Repeat this process until the wheel remains at rest after being rotated 1/4 turn. Then, rotate the wheel another 1/4 turn, another 1/4 turn, and another to see if the wheel is correctly balanced.
10. Remove the test weight and install the correct weight.
   a. On laced wheels, firmly crimp the balance weight (**Figure 55**) onto the spoke(s) with a pair of pliers.
   b. On alloy wheels, crimp the balance weight (**Figure 56**) onto the rim.

TIRE CHANGING (LACED WHEELS)

The laced or wire wheels can easily be damaged during tire removal. Special care must be taken with tire irons to avoid scratches and gouges to the outer rim surface. Insert rim protectors or scraps of leather between the tire iron and the rim.

Removal

> *CAUTION*
> *Support the wheel on two blocks of wood, so the brake disc does not contact the floor.*

1. Remove the wheel as described in this chapter.
2. If the tire will be reinstalled, place a balance mark on the tire opposite the valve stem location (**Figure 57**) so the tire can be reinstalled in the same position for easier balancing.
3. Remove the valve core to deflate the tire.
4. Press the entire bead on both sides of the tire away from the rim and into the center of the rim.
5. Lubricate both beads with soapy water.

> *NOTE*
> *Use rim protectors between the tire irons and the rim to protect the rim from damage. Also, use only quality tire irons without sharp edges. If necessary, file the ends of the tire irons to remove rough edges.*

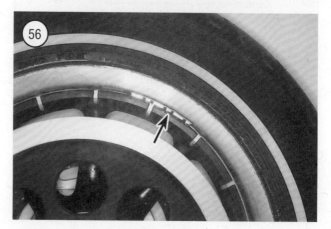

6. Insert the tire iron under the upper bead next to the valve stem (**Figure 58**). Press the lower bead into the center of the rim and pry the upper bead over the rim with the tire iron.
7. Insert a second tire iron next to the first to hold the bead over the rim (**Figure 59**). Work around the tire, prying the bead over the rim with the first tool. Be careful not to pinch the inner tube with the tire irons.
8. When the upper bead is off the rim, remove the nut from the valve stem. Remove the valve from the hole in the rim and remove the tube from the tire (**Figure 60**).
9. Stand the wheel upright. Force the second bead into the center of the rim. Insert the tire iron between the second bead and the side of the rim that the first bead was pried over. Pry the second bead off the rim (**Figure 61**), and continue working around the wheel with two tire irons until the tires is free of the rim.
10. Inspect the rim as described in this chapter.

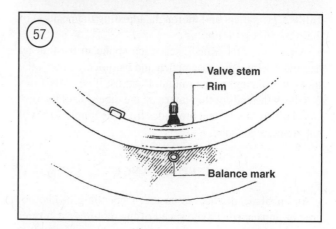

Installation

> *NOTE*
> *Before installing the tire, place it in the sun or in a hot, closed car. The heat will soften the rubber and ease installation.*

1. Install a *new* rubber rim band. Align the hole in the band with the valve hole in the rim.

2. Liberally sprinkle the inside of the tire with talcum powder to reduce chafing between the tire and tube.

3. Most tires have directional arrows on the sidewall. Install the tire so the arrow points in the direction of forward rotation.

4. If the tire was removed, lubricate the lower bead of the tire with soapy water and place the tire against the rim. Align the valve stem balance mark (**Figure 57**) with the valve stem hole in the rim.

5. Using your hand, push as much of the lower bead past the upper rim surface as possible. Work around the tire in both directions (**Figure 62**).

6. Install the valve core into the valve stem in the inner tube.

7. Put the tube into the tire and insert the valve stem through the hole in the rim. Inflate the tube just enough to round it out. Too much air will make tire installation difficult; too little air increases the chance of pinching the tube with the tire irons.

8. Lubricate the upper tire bead and rim with soapy water.

9. Press the upper bead into the rim opposite the valve stem. Pry the bead into the rim on both sides of this initial point with your hands and work around the rim to the valve stem. If the tire pulls up on one side, either uses a tire iron or a knee to hold the tire in place. The last few inches are usually the toughest and also the place where most tubes are pinched. If possible, continue to push the tire into the rim with your hands. Re-lubricate the bead if necessary. If the tire bead pulls out from under the rim, use both of your knees to hold the tire in place. If necessary, use a tire iron and rim protector for the last few inches (**Figure 63**).

CAUTION
*Make sure the valve stem is not cocked in the rim (**Figure 64**).*

10. Wiggle the valve stem to make sure the tube is not trapped under the bead. Set the valve squarely in its hole.

WARNING
*Seat the tire on the rim by inflating the tire to approximately 10% above the recommended inflation pressure listed in **Table 3**. Do not*

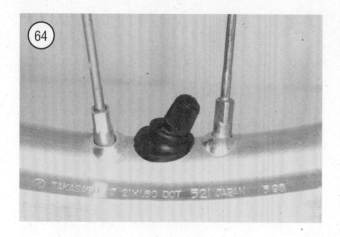

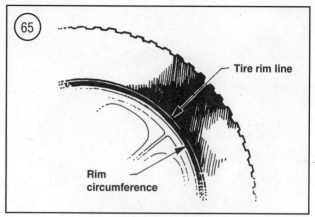

Tire rim line

Rim circumference

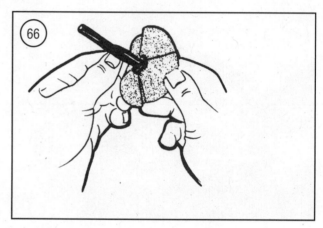

exceed 10%. Never stand directly over a tire while inflating it. The tire could burst and cause severe injury.

11. Check the bead on both sides of the tire for an even fit around the rim, and then re-lubricate both sides of the tire. Inflate the tube to seat the tire on the rim. Check to see that both beads are fully seated and the tire rim lines (**Figure 65**) are the same distance from the rim all the way around the tire. If the beads will not seat, release the air from the tire. Lubricate the rim and beads with soapy water, and re-inflate the tube.

12. Bleed the tire pressure down to the recommended pressure listed in **Table 3**. Install the valve stem nut, and tighten it against the rim. Then, install the valve stem cap.

13. Balance the wheel as described in this chapter.

Inspection

1. Remove and inspect the rubber rim band. Replace the band if it is deteriorated or broken.

2. Clean the inner and outer rim surfaces of all dirt, rust, corrosion and rubber residue.

3. Inspect the valve stem hole in the rim. Remove any dirt or corrosion from the hole.

4. Inspect the rim profiles for any cracks or other damage.

5. If the tube will be reused, reinstall the valve core, inflate the tube and check it for any leaks.

6. While the tube is inflated, clean it with water.

7. When reusing the tire, carefully check it inside and outside for damage. Replace the tire if there is any damage.

8. Make sure the spoke ends do not protrude from the nipples into the center of the rim. If necessary, grind off the end of the spokes.

TIRE CHANGING (ALLOY WHEELS)

WARNING
Do not install an inner tube inside a tubeless tire. The tube will cause an abnormal heat buildup in the tire.

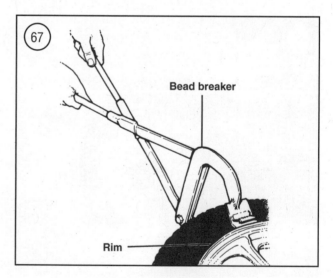

Bead breaker

Rim

Tubeless tires have the word TUBELESS molded in the tire sidewall and the rims have TUBELESS cast or stamped into them.

If the tire is punctured, remove it from the rim to inspect the inside of the tire and apply a combination plug/patch from inside the tire (**Figure 66**). A plug applied from the outside of the tire should only be used as a temporary roadside repair.

Follow the repair kit manufacturer's instructions as to applicable repairs and any speed limitations. Replace a patched or plugged tire as soon as possible.

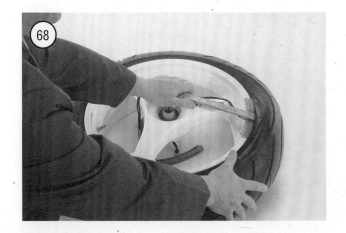

Removal

The alloy or cast wheels can easily be damaged during tire removal. Special care must be taken with tire irons to avoid scratching and gouging the outer rim surface. Protect the rim by using rim protectors or scraps of leather between the tire iron and the rim. The stock alloy wheels are designed for use with tubeless tires.

When removing a tubeless tire, be careful not to damage the tire beads, inner liner of the tire or the wheel rim flange. Use tire levers or flat-handled tire irons with rounded ends.

NOTE
While removing a tire, support the wheel on two blocks of wood, so the brake disc does not contact the floor.

1. Place a balance mark opposite the valve stem (**Figure 57**) on the tire sidewall so the tire can be reinstalled in the same position for easier balancing.
2. Remove the valve core to deflate the tire.

CAUTION
*Removal of tubeless tires from their rims can be very difficult because of the exceptionally tight bead/rim sealing surface. Breaking the bead seal may require the use of a bead breaker (**Figure 67**). Do not scratch the inside of the rim or damage the tire bead.*

3. Press the entire bead on both sides of the tire into the center of the rim.
4. Lubricate the beads with soapy water.

NOTE
Use rim protectors or insert scraps of leather between the tire irons and the rim to protect the rim from damage.

5. Insert the tire iron under the bead next to the valve stem (**Figure 68**). Force the bead on the opposite side of the tire into the center of the rim and pry the bead over the rim with the tire iron.
6. Insert a second tire iron next to the first to hold the bead over the rim (**Figure 69**). Then, work around the tire with the first tool prying the bead over the rim.
7. Set the wheel on its edge. Insert a tire tool between the second bead and the same side of the rim that the first bead was pried over (**Figure 70**). Force the bead on the opposite side from the tool into the center of the rim. Pry the second bead off the rim, and continue working around the wheel with two tire irons until the tire is free of the rim.
8. Inspect the valve stem seal. Because rubber deteriorates with age, it is advisable to replace the valve stem when replacing a tire.

Installation

1. Carefully inspect the tire for any damage, especially inside.
2. A new tire may have balancing rubbers inside. These are not patches and should not be disturbed.
3. Manufacturers place a colored spot near the bead, indicating a lighter point on the tire. Install the tires so this balance mark (either the manufacturer's or the one made during removal) sits opposite the valve stem (**Figure 57**).
4. Most tires have directional arrows on the sidewall that indicate the direction of rotation. Install the tire so the arrow points in the direction of forward rotation.
5. Lubricate both beads of the tire with soapy water.
6. Place the backside of the tire into the center of the rim. The lower bead should go into the center of the rim and the

10

upper bead outside. Work around the tire in both directions (**Figure 71**).

7. Starting at the side opposite the valve stem, press the upper bead into the rim (**Figure 72**). Pry the bead into the rim on both sides of the initial point with a tire tool, working around the rim to the valve (**Figure 73**).

8. Check the bead on both sides of the tire for an even fit around the rim.

9. Place an inflatable band around the circumference of the tire. Slowly inflate the band until the tire beads are pressed against the rim. Inflate the tire enough to seat it against the rim. Deflate and remove the band.

> *WARNING*
> *Never exceed 40 psi (279 kPa) inflation pressure as the tire could burst causing severe injury. Never stand directly over the tire while inflating it.*

10. After inflating the tire, check to see that the beads are fully seated and the tire rim lines are the same distance from the rim all the way around the tire (**Figure 65**). If the beards will not seat, deflate the tire, re-lubricate the rim and beads with soapy water, and then re-inflate the tire.

11. Inflate the tire to the required pressure. Refer to tire inflation pressure specifications listed in **Table 3**. Screw on the valve stem cap.

12. Balance the wheel assembly as described in this chapter.

TIRE REPAIRS

> *NOTE*
> *Changing or patching a tire on the road is very difficult. A can of pressurized tire inflator and sealer may inflate the tire and seal the hole, although this is only a temporary fix.*

> *WARNING*
> *Do not install an inner tube inside a tubeless tire. The tube will cause an abnormal heat buildup in the tire.*

Tubeless tires have the TUBELESS molded into the sidewall and the rims have SUITABLE FOR TUBELESS TIRES or equivalent stamped or cast on them.

If the tire is punctured, it must be removed from the rim to inspect the inside of the tire and to apply a combination plug/patch from inside the tire (**Figure 66**). Never attempt to repair a tubeless motorcycle tire using a plug or cord patch applied from outside the tire.

After repairing a tubeless tire, do not exceed 50 mph (80 km/h) for the first 24 hours.

As soon as possible, replace the patched tire with a new one.

Repair

Do not rely on a plug or cord patch applied from outside the tire. Use a combination plug/patch applied from inside the tire (**Figure 66**).

1. Remove the tire from the wheel rim as described in this chapter.

2. Inspect the rim inner flange. Smooth any scratches on the sealing surface with emery cloth. If a scratch is deeper than 0.020 in. (0.5 mm), replace the wheel.

3. Inspect the tire inside and out. Replace a tire if any of the following is found:

    a. A puncture larger than 1/8 in. (3 mm) diameter.

    b. A punctured or damaged side wall.

    c. More than 2 punctures in the tire.

4. Apply the plug/patch following the manufacturer's instructions included with the patch kit.

5. As soon as possible, replace the patched tire with a new one.

Table 1 LACED WHEEL OFFSET

Wheel type/size	Rim size	Offset in. (mm)
Steel wheel		
Front	16 3	1.551-1.571 (39.4-39.9)
Rear	16 5	1.098-1.118 (27.9-28.4)
Chrome/aluminum wheel		
Front	16 3	1.282-1.312 (32.56-33.32)
Front	17 3	1.282-1.312 (32.56-33.32)
Front	18 3.5	1.026-1.056 (26.06-26.82)
Rear	16 5	0.845-0.874 (21.47-22.23)

Table 2 WHEEL RUNOUT (MAXMUM)

Item	in.	mm
Laced and case wheel (front and rear)		
Lateral	0.30	7.6
Radial	0.30	7.6

Table 3 TIRE INFLATION PRESSURE (COLD)*

	kPa	psi
Front wheel	248	36
Rear wheel	275	40

* Tire pressure for OE equipment tires. Aftermarket tires may require different inflation pressure.
  These specifications apply to all different size wheel/tire combinations for all models.

Table 4 WHEEL TORQUE SPECIFICATIONS

	ft.-lb.	in.-lb.	N•m
Brake disc bolts			
Front wheel	16-24	–	21.7-32.5
Rear wheel	30-45	–	40.7-61.0
Front fork slider cap nuts	–	132-180	14.9-20.3
Front axle nut	60-65	–	81.3-88.1
Front axle nut cover set screw			
(models so equipped)	–	60-84	6.8-9.5
Rear axle nut	see text		
Spoke nipples–minimum	–	55	6.2

10

NOTES

CHAPTER ELEVEN

FRONT SUSPENSION AND STEERING

This chapter covers the handlebar, steering head and front fork.

Refer to **Table 1** and **Table 2** at the end of the chapter for specifications.

HANDLEBAR (ALL MODELS EXCEPT CVO)

Removal/Installation

Refer to **Figure 1**.

1. Disconnect the negative battery cable as described in Chapter Nine.

2A. On Road King models, remove the headlight nacelle as described in Chapter Nine.

2B. On fork mounted front fairing models, refer to Chapter Fourteen and perform the following:

    a. Remove the outer fairing.

    b. Partially remove the inner fairing (A, **Figure 2**) until the handlebar forward mounting bolts (B) are accessible. It is not necessary to completely remove the inner fairing.

2C. On frame mounted front fairing models, remove the instrument nacelle and housing (A, **Figure 3**) as described in Chapter Nine.

3. Support the motorcycle with the front wheel off the ground as described in *Motorcycle Stands* (Chapter Ten).

NOTE
Cover the fuel tank with a heavy cloth or plastic tarp to protect it from accidental scratches or dents when removing the handlebar.

NOTE
Before removing the handlebar, make a drawing of the clutch and throttle cable routing from the handlebar and through the frame. This information will prove helpful when reinstalling the handlebar and connecting the cables.

4. On the right side of the handlebar, perform the following:

    a. Unscrew and remove the mirror (A, **Figure 4**).

    b. Remove the screws securing the master cylinder (B, **Figure 4**). Do not disconnect the hydraulic brake line.

    c. Secure the master cylinder to the frame with a bungee cord or wire. Make sure the reservoir remains upright.

    d. Remove the screws joining the right side switch (C, **Figure 4**) halves and separate the housing. Remove the switch assembly from the handlebar.

    e. Disconnect the twist grip sensor wire as described in Chapter Nine.

5. On the left side of the handlebar, perform the following:

    a. Unscrew and remove the mirror (A, **Figure 5**).

    b. Remove the screws joining the left side switch (B, **Figure 5**) halves and separate the housing. Remove the switch assembly from the handlebar.

    c. Remove the clutch lever clamp mounting bolts (C, **Figure 5**) and washers and separate the clamp halves. Remove the lever assembly from the handlebar.

6. On FLHR and FLHRC models, perform the following:

a. Carefully remove the decorative trim plate from the handlebar clamp shroud.

b. Remove the three screws securing the handlebar cover, and then remove the cover.

7. Disconnect or remove any wiring harness clamps at the handlebar.

8. Remove the two handlebar front clamp bolts (B, **Figure 3**), and then the rear clamp bolts (C). Remove the holder(s) and the handlebar.

9. Install the handlebar by reversing the removal steps, while noting the following:

a. Check the knurled rings on the handlebar for galling and bits of aluminum. Clean the knurled section with a wire brush.

b. Check the handlebar for cracks, bends or other damage. Replace the handlebar if necessary. Do not attempt to repair it.

c. Thoroughly clean the clamp halves of all residue.

d. After installing the handlebar, reposition it while sitting on the motorcycle.

e. Tighten the handlebar clamp bolts to 16-20 ft.-lb. (21.7-27.1 N•m).

f. Adjust both mirrors.

Lower Clamp Rubber Bushing Replacement

1. Turn the front fork fully to the right and loosen the bolt securing the left side lower clamp.

2. Turn the front fork fully to the left and loosen the bolt securing the right side lower clamp.

3. Remove the handlebar assembly as described in this section.

4. On the right side, perform the following:

a. Secure the lower clamp to prevent rotation and remove the bolt.

b. Remove the flat washer and upper cup washer from the top of the upper fork bridge.

c. Remove the upper bushing from the upper fork bridge and discard it.

d. Remove the large, flat washer and cup washer from the bottom of the upper fork bridge.

e. Remove the spacer from lower bushing and discard the bushing.

5. On the left side, perform the following:

a. Secure the lower clamp to prevent rotation and remove the bolt.

b. Remove the ground cable and upper cup washer from the top of the upper fork bridge.

c. Remove the upper bushing from the upper fork bridge and discard it.

d. Remove the cup washer from the bottom of the upper fork bridge.

e. Remove the spacer from lower bushing and discard the bushing.

6. Install the *new* bushings onto the spacers until they are flush with the bottom of the spacer.

7. On the right side, perform the following:

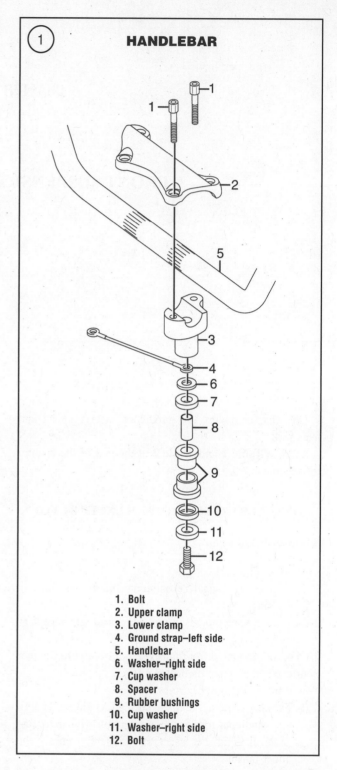

① HANDLEBAR

1. Bolt
2. Upper clamp
3. Lower clamp
4. Ground strap–left side
5. Handlebar
6. Washer–right side
7. Cup washer
8. Spacer
9. Rubber bushings
10. Cup washer
11. Washer–right side
12. Bolt

a. Insert the bushing spacer assembly into the bottom surface of the upper fork bridge. Fit the collar of the bushing over the lip of the boss.

b. Install the large flat washer onto the bolt.

c. Position the cup washer with the concave side going on last and install it onto the bolt.

d. Insert the bolt into the bushing. Index the concave side of the cup washer over the collar of the bushing. Push the bolt up until it bottoms.

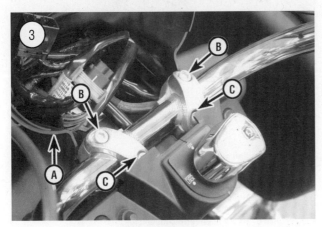

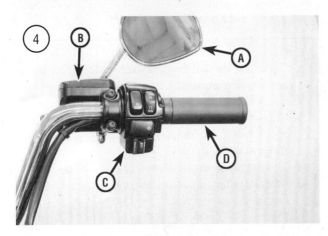

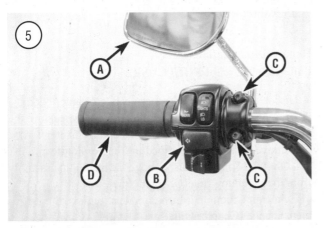

e. Install the upper bushing onto the bolt and into the bore of the upper fork bridge. Fit the collar of the bushing over the lip of the boss.

f. Position the cup washer with the concave side going on first and install the cup washer over the bolt and onto the bushing. Push the cup washer down until it bottoms.

g. Install the flat washer onto the bolt.

h. Apply medium-strength (blue) threadlock to the bolt threads.

i. Install the lower clamp onto the bolt and secure it to prevent rotation.

j. Finger-tighten the bolt.

8. On the left side, perform the following:

a. Insert the bushing spacer assembly into the bottom surface of the upper fork bridge. Fit the collar of the bushing over the lip of the boss.

b Position the cup washer with the concave side going on last and install it onto the bolt.

c. Insert the bolt into the bushing. Index the concave side of the cup washer over the collar of the bushing. Push the bolt up until it bottoms.

d. Install the upper bushing onto the bolt and into the bore of the upper fork bridge. Fit the collar of the bushing over the lip of the boss.

e. Position the cup washer with the concave side going on first and install the cup washer over the bolt and onto the bushing. Push the cup washer down until it bottoms.

f. Install the ground strap onto the bolt.

g. Apply medium-strength (blue) threadlock to the bolt threads.

h. Install the lower clamp onto the bolt and secure it to prevent rotation.

i. Finger-tighten the bolt.

9. Install the handlebar assembly as described in this section.

10. Turn the front fork fully to the right and tighten the left side bolt to 30-40 ft.-lb. (40.7-54.2 N•m).

11. Turn the front fork fully to the left and tighten the right side bolt to 30-40 ft.-lb. (40.7-54.2 N•m).

HANDLEBAR
(CVO MODELS)

The electrical cables relating to the right and left hand handlebar switches and the throttle control twist grip are routed within the handlebar tubing. Extra care must be taken during the removal and installation to avoid scraping off any wiring insulation.

The connector terminal numbers are shown in the wiring diagrams in Chapter Sixteen.

Removal/Installation
(FLHTCUSE Models)

Refer to **Figure 1**.

11

1. Disconnect the negative battery cable as described in Chapter Eleven.

2. Support the motorcycle with the front wheel off the ground as described in *Motorcycle Stands* (Chapter Ten).

CAUTION
Cover the fuel tank to protect it when removing the handlebar.

3. Remove the seat as described in Chapter Fourteen.

4. Remove the outer front fairing and fairing cap as described in Chapter Fourteen.

5. Label and identify the connectors and their wire colors to assist in reconnecting.

6. Disconnect the following electrical connectors:
   a. Right-side handlebar switch 12-pin connector.
   b. Left-side handlebar switch 16-pin and 3-pin connectors.
   c. Handgrip heater power 3-pin connector.
   d. Handgrip heater 3-pin interconnect connector.
   e. Twist grip sensor connector.

7. Remove the radio as described in Chapter Nine.

8. Remove the twist grip throttle control (Chapter Eight).

9. On the right side of the handlebar, perform the following:
   a. Unscrew and remove the mirror (A, **Figure 4**).
   b. Remove the brake master cylinder (B, **Figure 4**) clamp mounting bolts and washers, and separate the clamp. Do not disconnect the hydraulic brake hose.
   c. Secure the master cylinder to the frame with a bungee cord, or wire. Make sure the reservoir remains upright.
   d. Remove the screws joining the right side switch (C, **Figure 4**) halves and separate the housing. Remove the switch housing from the handlebar.

10. On the left side of the handlebar, perform the following:
    a. Unscrew and remove the mirror (A, **Figure 5**).
    b. Remove the screws joining the left side switch (B, **Figure 5**) halves and separate the housing. Remove the switch assembly from the handlebar.
    c. Remove the clutch master cylinder clamp mounting bolts (C, **Figure 5**) and washers and separate the clamp. Do not disconnect the hydraulic brake line.
    d. Secure the clutch master cylinder to the frame with a bungee cord or wire. Make sure the reservoir remains upright.

11. Make a drawing of the electrical cable routing within the inner fairing and where it exits the inner fairing.

12. Carefully withdraw the connectors and electrical cables out through the back side of the inner fairing.

13. Remove the two front handlebar clamp bolts, and then the rear clamp bolts. Remove the holder(s) and the handlebar. Take handlebar assembly to the work bench for further disassembly if necessary.

14. Install the handlebar by reversing the removal steps, while noting the following:

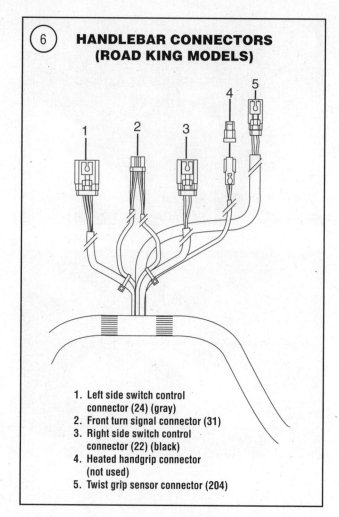

6 **HANDLEBAR CONNECTORS (ROAD KING MODELS)**

1. **Left side switch control connector (24) (gray)**
2. **Front turn signal connector (31)**
3. **Right side switch control connector (22) (black)**
4. **Heated handgrip connector (not used)**
5. **Twist grip sensor connector (204)**

   a. Check the knurled rings on the handlebar for galling and bits of aluminum. Clean the knurled section with a wire brush.
   b. Check the handlebar for cracks, bends or other damage. Replace the handlebar if necessary. Do not attempt to repair it.
   c. Thoroughly clean the clamp halves of all residue.
   d. After installing the handlebar, reposition it while sitting on the motorcycle.
   e. Tighten the handlebar clamp bolts to 16-20 ft.-lb. (21.7-27.1 N•m).
   f. Adjust both mirrors.

Removal/Installation
(All Models Except FHLTCUSE)

1. Disconnect the negative battery cable (Chapter Nine).

2. Support the motorcycle with the front wheel off the ground as described in *Motorcycle Stands* (Chapter Ten).

3. Remove the seat as described in Chapter Fourteen.

4A. On Road King models, remove the headlight assembly from the mounting ring (Chapter Nine).

4B. On frame mounted fairing models, remove the instrument nacelle (Chapter Nine).

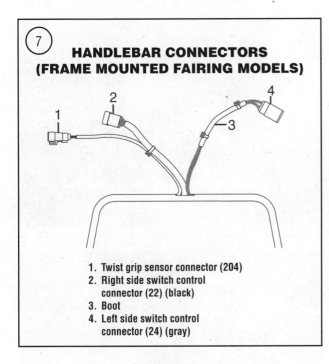

HANDLEBAR CONNECTORS (FRAME MOUNTED FAIRING MODELS)

1. Twist grip sensor connector (204)
2. Right side switch control connector (22) (black)
3. Boot
4. Left side switch control connector (24) (gray)

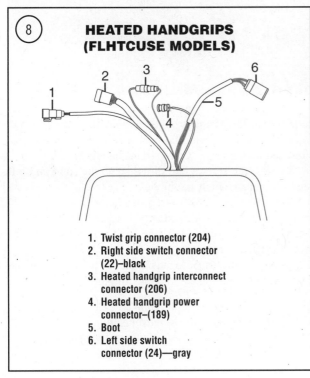

HEATED HANDGRIPS (FLHTCUSE MODELS)

1. Twist grip connector (204)
2. Right side switch connector (22)–black
3. Heated handgrip interconnect connector (206)
4. Heated handgrip power connector–(189)
5. Boot
6. Left side switch connector (24)—gray

4C. On fork mounted fairing models, remove the fairing cap (Chapter Fourteen).

5. Label and identify the connectors and their wire colors to assist in reconnecting.

6A. On Road King models, refer to **Figure 6** and appropriate wiring diagram (located in Chapter Sixteen of this manual), to help identify, located and the disconnect the following electrical connectors:

    a. Right-side switch control connector (22).

    b. Left-side switch control connector (24).

    c. Twist grips sensor connector (204).

    d. Heated hand grip connector (189) (not used on these models).

    e. Front turn signal connector (32).

6B. On frame mounted fairing models, refer to **Figure 7** and appropriate wiring diagram (located in Chapter Sixteen of this manual), to help identify, located and the disconnect the following electrical connectors:

    a. Right-side switch control connector [22] (black).

    b. Left-side switch control connector [24] (gray).

    c. Twist grips sensor connector (204).

6C. On fork mounted fairing models, refer to **Figure 8** and appropriate wiring diagram (located in Chapter Sixteen of this manual), to help identify, located and the disconnect the following electrical connectors:

    a. Right-side switch control connector [22] (black).

    b. Left-side switch control connector [24] (gray).

    c. Twist grips sensor connector (204).

    d. Heated handgrip power harness connector (189).

7. Attach a length of heavy-duty fish wire to all of the disconnected electrical connector terminals. Wrap the connectors and wire with electrical tape to assist in withdrawing the connectors and wiring from the headlight nacelle.

8. Loosen, but do not remove the handlebar cover retaining nut and large washer inside the nacelle.

9. Loosen, but do not remove the four acorn nuts and separate the headlight nacelle halves.

10. Remove the handlebar cover from the handlebar.

11. On the right side of the handlebar, perform the following:

    a. Unscrew and remove the mirror (A, **Figure 4**).

    b. Remove the brake master cylinder clamp mounting bolts and washers and separate the clamp. Do not disconnect the hydraulic brake line.

    c. Secure the master cylinder to the frame with a bungee cord or wire. Make sure the reservoir remains upright.

    d. Remove the screws joining the right side switch (C, **Figure 4**) halves and separate the housing. Remove the switch assembly from the handlebar.

    e. Slide the throttle housing assembly (D, **Figure 4**) off the handlebar.

    f. Disconnect the twist grip sensor wire as described in Chapter Nine.

12. On the left side of the handlebar, perform the following:

    a. Unscrew and remove the mirror (A, **Figure 5**).

    b. Remove the screws joining the left side switch (B, **Figure 5**) halves and separate the housing. Remove the switch assembly from the handlebar.

    c. Remove the clutch master cylinder clamp mounting bolts (C, **Figure 5**) and washers and separate the clamp. Do not disconnect the hydraulic brake line.

    d. Secure the clutch master cylinder to the frame with a bungee cord or wire. Make sure the reservoir remains upright.

11

13. Carefully withdraw the connectors, electrical cables and fish wire out through the back side of the headlight nacelle or fairing.

14. Remove the electrical tape and fish wire from the electrical cables. Leave the fish wire running through the headlight nacelle as it will be used to pull the connectors and electrical cables back through the nacelle.

15. Remove the two front handlebar clamp bolts, and then the rear clamp bolts. Remove the holder(s) and the handlebar. Take handlebar assembly to the workbench for further disassembly if necessary.

16. Install the handlebar by reversing the removal steps, while noting the following:

    a. Check the knurled rings on the handlebar for galling and bits of aluminum. Clean the knurled section with a wire brush.

    b. Check the handlebar for cracks, bends or other damage. Replace the handlebar if necessary. Do not attempt to repair it.

    c. Thoroughly clean the clamp halves of all residue.

    d. After installing the handlebar, reposition the handlebar while sitting on the motorcycle.

    e. Tighten the handlebar clamp bolts to 16-20 ft.-lb. (21.7-27.1 N•m).

    f. Adjust both mirrors.

Handlebar Disassembly (All Models)

CAUTION
The electrical cables for the handlebar switches and the throttle control twist grip are routed within the handlebar tube. Take extra care during the removal and installation to avoid scraping off any wiring insulation.

1. Remove the handlebar assembly as described in this section.

2. Note their locations, and carefully cut and remove all cable straps on the wiring.

3. Separate the heated handgrip interconnect harness connector, on models so equipped.

4. Make a drawing and write down the exact wire color and its respective chamber number within the Molex and/or Deutsch connector. The wires *must* be installed into the correct chamber location for the switch or component to operate correctly.

5. Separate the wiring terminals from the Molex and/or Deutch connectors as described under *Electrical Connector Service* in Chapter Nine.

6. Slide the boot off of the left-hand switch wiring and terminal. Save the boot as it will be reused.

7. Separate the wiring harness from the left and the right side of the handlebar.

8. Attach a 3 ft. (91.4 cm) length of fish wire to the end of each set of separated wiring harness and secure the fish wire in place. Bundle the harness together and wrap with several layers of electrical tape to prevent damage to the

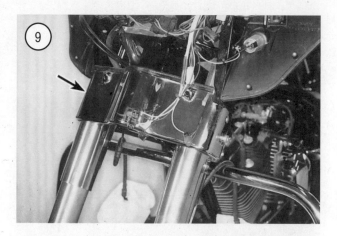

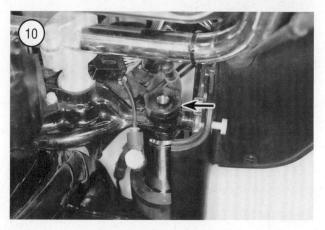

terminals as the wiring is pulled through the handlebar. Do not make the bundle too fat or it will be difficult to withdraw the wiring harness through the handle bar.

9. Remove the screws and disassemble the right and left side handlebar switch assemblies.

10. Remove the throttle twist grip assembly (D, **Figure 4**) from the right side as described in Chapter Eight.

11. Gently remove the left-side hand grip (D, **Figure 5**) from the handlebar.

12. Apply glass cleaner to the bundles of wiring to ease the removal of the wiring assemblies from the handlebar.

CAUTION
The electrical wire(s) must be replaced if any insulation is scraped off during removal and installation.

NOTE
Do not pull the loose end of the fish wire out of the handlebar as it will be used to pull the new wiring harness back through.

13. Slowly and carefully, guide the right side wiring harness assembly through the center opening in the handlebar to the outer end being careful to avoid scraping off any insulation.

14. Repeat to remove the left side wiring harness.

15. Remove the electrical tape and detach the fish wire from the wiring harness.

16. Repair or replace any defective switch or wiring sockets as described in Chapter Nine, if necessary.

Handlebar Assembly (All Models)

1. Make sure the rubber grommets are in place on the oval holes near the end of the handlebar.
2. Attach the end of the fish wire to the end of one of the sets of wiring harness and secure it in the same manner used during removal.
3. Apply liquid glass cleaner to the bundle of wiring to ease the installation of the wiring harness assemblies into the handlebar.

> *CAUTION*
> *If there is any resistance in pulling the wiring harness assembly back into the handlebar, stop and solve the problem immediately. Do not damage any portion of the assembly.*

4. Slowly pull on the fish wire and feed the wiring harness assembly into the outer end of the handlebar.
5. Continue to pull until the wiring harness is pulled into the correct location. Remove the electrical tape and detach fish wire.
6. Repeat the process to install the remaining wiring harness assembly.
7. Install the throttle twist grip assembly as described in Chapter Eight.

8. Assemble the right and left side handlebar switch assemblies and tighten the screws securely.
9. Slide the boot onto the left-hand switch wiring and terminal.
10. Refer to the drawings and notes made in *Handlebar Disassembly*. The wires *must* be installed into the correct chamber location in the Molex and/or Deutsch connector for the switch or component to operate correctly.
11. Assemble the wiring terminals into the Molex and/or Deutch connectors as described under *Electrical Connector Service* in Chapter Nine.
12. Connect the heated handgrip power connector and the interconnect harness connector.
13. Install new cable straps in the original locations.
14. Install the handlebar assembly as described in this section.

FRONT FORK

Front Fork Service

To simplify fork service and to prevent the mixing of parts, remove, service and install the fork legs individually.

Removal (No Service)

1A. On Road King models, remove the headlight assembly from the mounting ring (Chapter Nine).
1B. On frame mounted fairing models, remove the instrument nacelle (Chapter Nine).
1C. On fork mounted fairing models, remove the fairing cap (Chapter Fourteen).
2. On all models except FLTR Series, remove the passing light assembly (Chapter Nine).
3. Support the motorcycle with the front wheel off the ground as described in *Motorcycle Stands* (Chapter Ten).
4. Remove the front wheel as described in Chapter Ten.
5. Remove the front fender as described in Chapter Fourteen.
6. Remove the screws securing the chrome mounting bracket (**Figure 9**) and remove the bracket, on models so equipped.
7. If both fork legs are going to be removed, mark them with an R (right side) and L (left side) so the legs will be reinstalled on the correct side.
8. Loosen the fork cap bolt (**Figure 10**) from top of the fork tube, but do not remove it yet.
9. Loosen the lower fork bridge pinch bolt (**Figure 11**) at the lower fork bridge, but do not remove it yet.
10. Spray a little glass cleaner all around the fork tube above the fork stop.
11. Slide the fork tube up against the upper fork bracket.
12. Secure the fork leg and remove the fork cap bolt (**Figure 10**).
13. Slide the fork leg down and remove the rubber stop (**Figure 12**) from the fork tube.

11

14. Continue to slide the fork tube out of the lower fork bracket. It may be necessary to rotate the fork tube slightly while pulling it down and out. Remove the fork leg and keep it vertical.

15. Tighten the fork cap bolt (**Figure 10**) securely to avoid the loss of fork oil.

16. Take the fork leg to the workbench for service. If the fork is not going to be serviced, wrap it in a large towel or blanket to protect the surface from damage.

17. Repeat the procedure to remove the remaining fork leg.

Installation (Not Serviced)

1. Hold the fork leg vertical and remove the fork cap bolt (**Figure 10**).

2. Install the fork tube through the lower fork bracket and install the rubber fork stop (**Figure 12**).

3. Continue to push the fork tube up through the lower fork bracket until it bottoms against the upper fork bracket.

4. Install the fork cap bolt (**Figure 10**) onto top of the fork tube and tighten it securely.

5. Tighten the lower fork bridge pinch bolt (**Figure 11**) to 53-57 ft.-lb. (71.9-77.3 N•m).

6. Tighten the fork cap bolt (**Figure 10**) to 60-70 ft.-lb. (81.4-94.8 N•m).

7. Install the chrome mounting bracket, on models so equipped. Install the screws and tighten securely.

8. Install the front fender as described in Chapter Fourteen.

9. Install the front wheel as described in Chapter Ten.

10. On all models except FLTR Series, install the passing light assembly described in Chapter Nine.

11A. On Road King models, install the headlight assembly from the mounting ring as described in Chapter Nine.

11B. On frame mounted fairing models, install the instrument nacelle as described in Chapter Nine.

11C. On fork mounted fairing models, install the fairing cap as described in Chapter Fourteen.

12. Apply the front brake and pump the front forks several times to seat the forks and front wheel.

Removal (For Service)

1A. On Road King models, remove the headlight assembly from the mounting ring (Chapter Nine).

1B. On frame mounted fairing models, remove the instrument nacelle (Chapter Nine).

1C. On fork mounted fairing models, remove the fairing cap (Chapter Fourteen).

2. On all models except FLTR series, remove the passing light assembly as described in Chapter Nine.

3. Support the motorcycle with the front wheel off the ground as described in *Motorcycle Stands* (Chapter Ten).

4. Remove the front wheel (A, **Figure 13**) as described in Chapter Twelve.

5. Remove the front fender as described in Chapter Fourteen.

6. Remove the screws securing the chrome mounting bracket (**Figure 9**) and remove the bracket, on model so equipped.

7. If both fork tube legs are going to be removed, mark them with an R (right side) and L (left side) so the legs will be reinstalled on the correct side.

8. Remove the fork cap bolt (**Figure 10**) from top of the fork tube.

9. Loosen the pinch bolt (**Figure 11**) at the lower fork bridge.

10. Slide the fork leg part way down and securely retighten the pinch bolt .

11. Place a drain pan under the fork slider to catch the fork oil.

12. Remove the drain bolt (B, **Figure 13**) and washer, and then drain the fork oil. Pump the slider several times to expel most of the fork oil. Reinstall the drain bolt and washer and tighten.

13. Use an 8-mm Allen wrench and impact driver and loosen the damper rod bolt at the base of the slider. Do not remove.

14. Remove the stopper ring from the fork slider.

15. Lower the fork slider on the fork tube.

NOTE
It may be necessary to slightly heat the area on the slider around the oil seal prior to removal. Use a rag soaked in hot water; do not apply a flame directly to the fork slider.

16. There is an interference fit between the bushing in the fork slider and the bushing on the fork tube. In order to remove the fork tube from the slider, pull hard on the fork tube using quick in-and-out strokes (**Figure 14**). This will withdraw the bushing and the oil seal from the slider.

17. Remove the slider from the fork tube. If still in place, remove the oil lock piece from the damper rod if it is still in place.

18. Loosen the pinch bolt (**Figure 11**). Slide the fork tube out of the lower fork bracket and remove the rubber stop (**Figure 12**) from the fork tube. It may be necessary to rotate the fork tube slightly while pulling it down and out. Remove the fork leg and take it to the workbench for service.

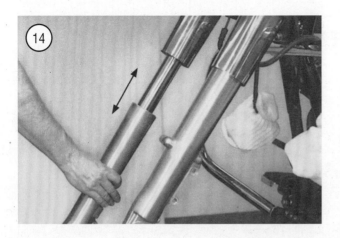

19. Repeat the procedure to remove the remaining fork leg.

20. Disassemble the fork leg as described in this section.

Installation (Serviced)

1. Assemble the fork and refill the fork oil as described in this section.

2. Install the fork tube through the lower fork bracket and install the rubber fork stop (**Figure 11**).

3. Continue to push the fork tube up through the lower fork bracket until it bottoms against the upper fork bracket.

4. Tighten the lower fork bridge pinch bolt (**Figure 10**) to 55-57 ft.-lb. (71.9-77.3 N•m).

5. Tighten the fork tube plug to 60-70 ft.-lb. (81.4-94.8 N•m).

6. Install the fork cap bolt (**Figure 9**) onto top of the fork tube and tighten to 60-70 ft.-lb. (81.4-94.8 N•m).

7. Install the front fender as described in Chapter Seventeen.

8. Install the front wheel (A, **Figure 13**) as described in Chapter Twelve.

9. Make sure the drain bolt (B, **Figure 13**) is tightened securely.

10. On all models except FLTR Series, install the passing light assembly (Chapter Nine).

11A. On Road King models, install the headlight assembly from the mounting ring (Chapter Nine).

11B. On frame mounted fairing models, install the instrument nacelle (Chapter Nine).

11C. On fork mounted faring models, install the fairing cap (Chapter Fourteen).

12. Apply the front brake and pump the front forks several times to seat the fork and the front wheel.

Fork Tube
Disassembly

Refer to **Figure 15**.

NOTE
A fork holding tool is required to disassemble and assemble this fork assembly. The fork

spring cannot be compressed sufficiently by hand to loosen and remove the fork tube plug.

1. Separate the fork tube from the slider as described in this section.

2. To protect the fork tube, place a steel washer (A, **Figure 16**) over the fork damper rod and up against the base of the fork tube.

3. Tighten the bolt (B, **Figure 16**) so it seated below the steel washer. Do not over tighten as the damper rod will be damaged. Make sure the tool is indexed properly against the steel washer.

4. Install the holding tool's upper bolt into the hole in the fork tube plug following the manufacturer's instructions. Make sure the tool (A, **Figure 17**) is indexed properly in the hole in the fork tube plug.

WARNING
Be careful when removing the fork tube plug as the spring is under pressure. Protect eyes and face accordingly.

5. Hold onto the fork tube and loosen the fork tube plug (B, **Figure 17**). Slowly loosen the tool while unscrewing the fork tube plug.

6. When the fork tube plug is completely unscrewed from the fork tube, remove the tool from the fork leg.

7. Remove the fork tube plug and fork spring and drain out any residual fork oil. Dispose of the fork oil properly.

8A. On non-fairing equipped models, turn the fork tube upside down, remove the damper rod and rebound spring.

8B. On fairing equipped models, turn the fork tube upside down, remove the damper valve, damper rod and rebound spring.

Fork Tube and Slider
Assembly

1. Coat all parts with H-D Type E, or an equivalent, fork oil before assembly.

2. Install the rebound spring (A, **Figure 18**) onto the damper rod and slide the damper rod (B) into the fork tube until it extends out the end of the fork tube.

3. Install the oil lock piece (**Figure 19**) onto the end of the damper rod.

4. Slide the fork slider bushing (A, **Figure 20**) and oil seal spacer (B) down into the fork tube. Position the oil seal (C, **Figure 20**) with the letters facing up and slide it down the fork tube.

CAUTION
To protect the oil seal lips, place a thin plastic bag on top of the fork tube. Before installing the seal in the following steps, lightly coat the bag and the seal lips with fork oil.

5. Push the fork tube (A, **Figure 21**) and damper rod into the fork slider (B). Insert a Phillips screwdriver through

11

FRONT FORK

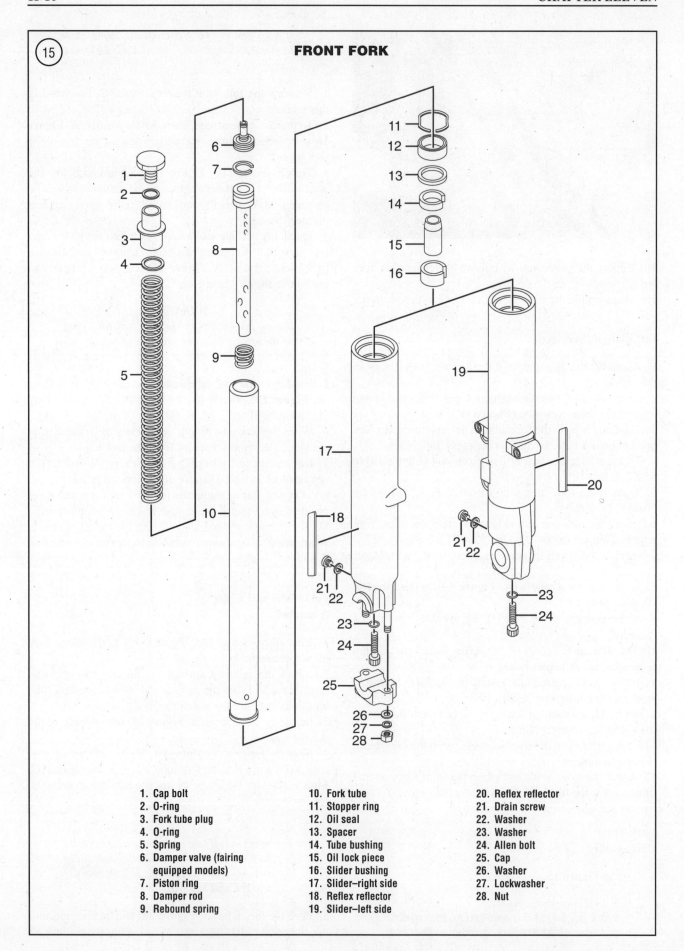

1. Cap bolt
2. O-ring
3. Fork tube plug
4. O-ring
5. Spring
6. Damper valve (fairing equipped models)
7. Piston ring
8. Damper rod
9. Rebound spring
10. Fork tube
11. Stopper ring
12. Oil seal
13. Spacer
14. Tube bushing
15. Oil lock piece
16. Slider bushing
17. Slider–right side
18. Reflex reflector
19. Slider–left side
20. Reflex reflector
21. Drain screw
22. Washer
23. Washer
24. Allen bolt
25. Cap
26. Washer
27. Lockwasher
28. Nut

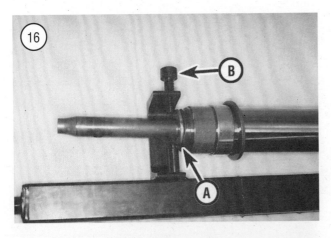

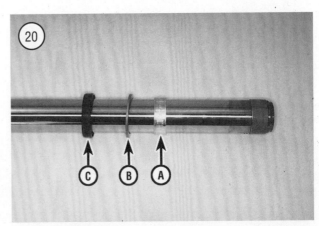

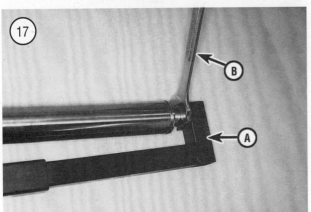

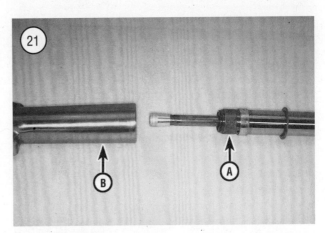

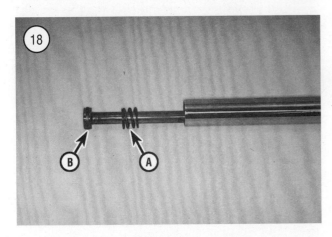

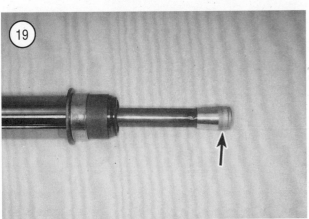

the opening in the bottom of the fork slider and guide the damper rod end into the receptacle in the base of the slider. Remove the screwdriver.

6. Slide the oil seal (**Figure 22**) down into the fork tube receptacle.

NOTE
*A fork seal driver (A, **Figure 23**) is required to install the fork tube bushing and seal into the fork tube. A number of different aftermarket fork seal drivers (JIMS part No. 2046) are available. Another method is to use a piece of pipe or metal collar with correct dimensions to slide over the fork tube and*

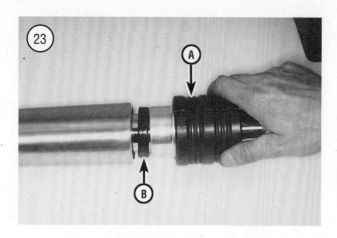

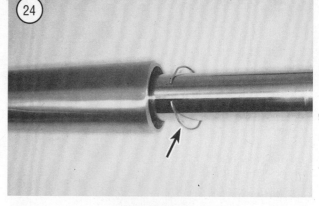

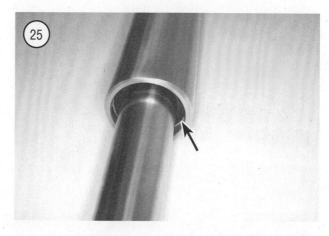

seat against the seal. When selecting or fabricating a driver tool, it must have sufficient weight to drive the bushing and oil seal into the fork tube.

7. Slide the fork seal driver down the fork tube and seat it against the oil seal (B, **Figure 23**).

8. Operate the fork seal driver, or an equivalent, and drive the fork slider bushing and new seal into the fork tube. Continue to operate the driver until the stopper ring groove in the tube is visible above the fork seal. Remove the fork seal driver tool.

9. Install the stopper ring (**Figure 24**) into the slider groove. Make sure the retaining ring seats in the groove (**Figure 25**).

10. Temporarily install the spring into the fork tube and onto the top of the damper rod.

11. Place several shop rags on the floor.

12. Hold the spring in place and turn the fork assembly upside down and place it vertically on the shop cloths.

13. Install a *new* washer on the Allen bolt.

14. Apply a medium-strength threadlock to the damper rod Allen bolt threads prior to installation. Insert the Allen bolt (**Figure 26**) through the lower end of the slider and thread it into the damper rod. Tighten the Allen bolt to 132-216 in.-lb. (14.9-24.4 N•m).

15. Hold onto the spring and invert the fork assembly. Remove the fork spring.

16. Fill the fork oil and adjust the oil level. Refer to *Fork Oil Filling and Adjustment* in this section.

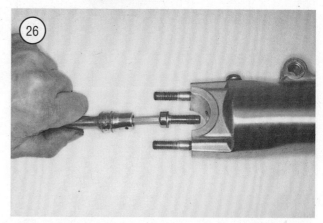

NOTE
Keep the fork assembly upright to avoid the loss of fork oil.

17A. On non-fairing equipped models, position the fork spring with the closer wound coils going in first and install the spring (**Figure 27**) into the fork tube.

17B. On fairing equipped models, perform the following:

　a. Position the fork spring with the closer wound coils going in first and install the small end of the damper valve onto the lower end of the fork spring.

　b. Install the fork spring and damper valve assembly into the fork tube and onto the top of the damper rod.

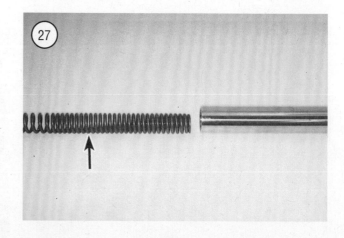

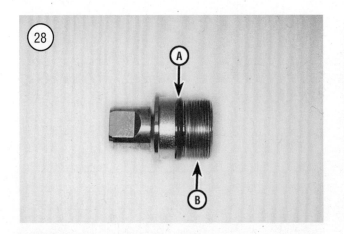

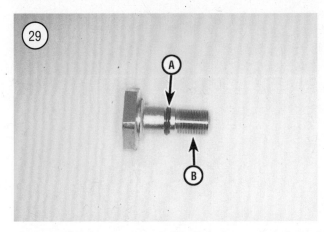

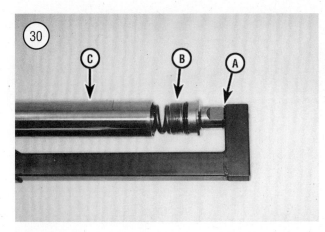

18. Install a *new* O-ring (A, **Figure 28**) onto the fork tube plug (B).

19. Install a *new* O-ring (A, **Figure 29**) onto on the fork cap bolt (B).

20. Position the fork tube plug (B, **Figure 28**) onto the top of the fork spring.

21. Install the fork holding tool's upper bolt into the hole in the fork tube plug (A, **Figure 30**) following the tool manufacturer's instructions. Make sure the tool is indexed properly in the hole in the fork tube plug.

22. Install the lower end of the fork assembly into the tool following the tool manufacturer's instructions. Make sure the tool is indexed properly in the hole in the fork tube plug.

> *CAUTION*
> *While tightening the tool, do not force the fork tube plug into the threaded portion of the fork tube. Doing so will damage the threads on either or both parts.*

23. Hold onto the fork tube plug and slowly tighten the tool while guiding the fork tube plug (B, **Figure 30**) into the top of the fork tube (C).

24. Place wrench on the fork tube plug (B, **Figure 17**) and screw the fork tube plug into the fork tube while tightening the tool. Once the fork tube plug has started to thread sufficiently into the fork tube, loosen the tool and remove it from the fork assembly.

25. Place the slider in a vise with soft jaws and tighten the fork tube plug (**Figure 31**) securely. It will be tightened to the final torque specification (**Table 2**) after the fork has been installed as decribed in this section.

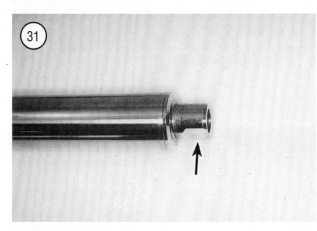

Inspection

1. Thoroughly clean all parts in solvent and dry them. Check the fork tube for signs of wear or scratches.

2. Check the fork tube for bending, nicks, rust or other damage. Place the fork tube on a set of V-blocks and check runout with a dial indicator (**Figure 32**). If these tools are not available, roll the fork tube on a large plate glass or other flat surface.

11

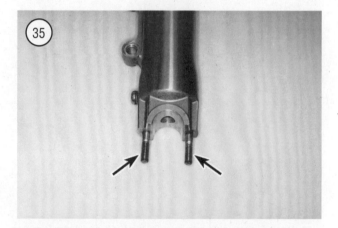

3. Check the internal threads (**Figure 33**) in the top of the fork tube for stripping, cross-threading or sealer residue. Use a tap to true up the threads and to remove sealer deposits.

4. Check the external threads on the fork tube plug (B, **Figure 28**) for stripping, cross-threading or sealer residue. Use a die to true up the threads and to remove sealer deposits.

5. Check the external threads on the fork cap bolt (B, **Figure 29**) for stripping, cross-threading or sealer residue. Use a die to true up the threads and to remove sealer deposits.

6. Check the slider for dents or other exterior damage. Check the retaining ring groove (**Figure 34**) in the top of the slider for cracks or other damage.

7. Check the threaded studs (**Figure 35**) at the base of the right side slider for damage. Repair if necessary.

8. Check the front caliper mounting bosses (**Figure 36**) for cracks or damage.

9. Check the slider and fork tube bushings for excessive wear, cracks or damage.

10. Remove the fork tube bushing as follows:
   a. Expand the bushing slit (**Figure 37**) with a screwdriver and then slide the bushing off the fork tube.
   b. Coat the new bushing with new fork oil.
   c. Install the new bushing by expanding the slit slightly with a screwdriver.
   d. Seat the new bushing into the fork tube groove.

11. Check the damper rod piston ring(s) (A, **Figure 38**) for excessive wear, cracks or other damage. If necessary, replace both rings as a set.

12. Check the damper rod (B, **Figure 38**) for straightness with a set of V-blocks and a dial indicator (**Figure 39**) or by rolling it on a piece of plate glass. Specifications for runout are not available. If the damper rod is not straight, replace it.

13. Make sure the oil passage hole in the damper rod (C, **Figure 38**) is open. If clogged, flush with solvent and dry with compressed air.

14. Check the internal threads in the bottom of the damper rod for stripping, cross-threading or sealer residue. Use a tap to true up the threads and to remove sealer deposits.

15. Check the damper rod rebound spring and the fork spring for wear or damage. Service limit specifications for

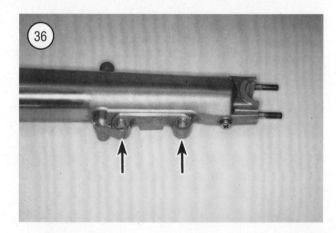

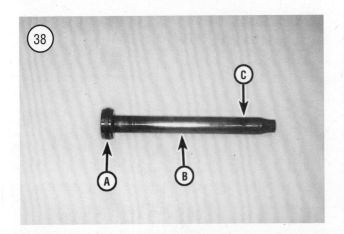

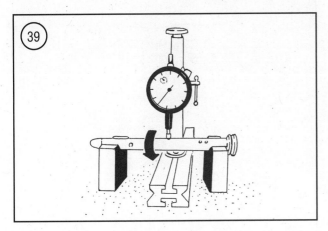

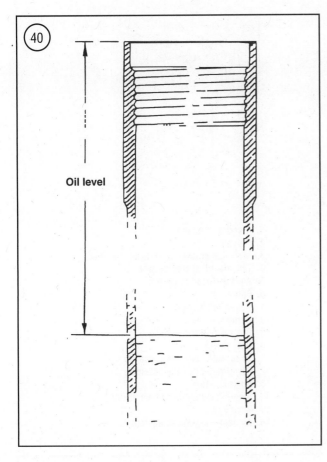

spring free length are not available from the manufacturer. If necessary, replace both springs as a set.

16. Replace the oil seal whenever it is removed. Always replace both oil seals as a set.

Fork Oil Filling and Adjustment

This section describes filling the fork with oil, setting the oil level and completing fork assembly.

1. Perform Steps 1-15 of *Fork Tube And Slider Assembly* (this section).

2. Secure the fork leg upright in a vise with soft jaws and fully compress the fork leg.

3. Fill the fork leg with approximately 11 oz. (319 ml) of H-D Type E fork oil, or an equivalent.

4. Hold the slider with one hand and slowly move the fork tube up and down. Repeat until the fork tube moves smoothly with the same amount of tension throughout the compression and rebound travel strokes. Stop when the fork tube has bottomed.

5. Set the fork assembly in a vertical position for approximately 5 minutes to allow any suspended air bubbles to surface and dissipate.

6. Set the oil level (**Figure 40**) as follows:

   a. Make sure the fork tube is bottomed against the slider and placed in a vertical position.

   b. Use a fork oil level gauge (**Figure 41**), or a caliper **Figure 42**, and set the oil level to the specification in **Table 1**.

   NOTE
   If no oil is drawn out when setting the oil level, not enough oil is in the fork tube. Add more oil and reset the level.

   c. If used, remove the fork oil level gauge.

7. Repeat the process for the remaining fork leg. Set the oil to exactly the same level in both fork legs.

8. Keep the fork leg vertical and perform Steps 17-25 of *Fork Tube And Slider Assembly* (this section).

11

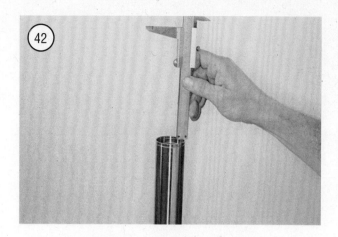

STEERING HEAD AND STEM

Removal

Refer to **Figure 43**.

1A. On Road King models, remove the headlight assembly from the mounting ring (Chapter Nine).

1B. On frame mounted fairing models, remove the instrument nacelle (Chapter Nine).

1C. On fork mounted fairing models, remove the fairing cap (Chapter Fourteen).

2. On all models except FLTR Series, remove the passing light assembly (Chapter Nine).

3. Support the motorcycle with the front wheel off the ground as described in *Motorcycle Stands* (Chapter ten).

4. Remove the front wheel as described in Chapter ten.

5. Remove the front fender as described in Chapter Seventeen.

6. Remove both front fork legs as described in this chapter.

7. Remove the handlebar as described in this chapter.

8. Remove the bolt (**Figure 44**) securing the front brake line assembly to the bottom of the lower fork bracket. Do not disconnect any brake line connections.

9. On models so equipped, remove the screw (A, **Figure 45**) and washer on each side securing the air dam (B) to the backside of the lower fork bracket and remove it.

10. On fairing equipped models, remove the interconnect harness ground socket terminal from the spade terminal on the upper fork bridge.

11. Move all electrical harnesses away from the area.

12. Pry the tabs on the locking plate away from the steering stem nut.

13. Loosen and remove the steering stem hex nut (**Figure 46**).Remove the roll pin and the mounting bracket.

14. Remove the upper fork bracket. (**Figure 47**).

NOTE
Hold or secure the steering stem as it may fall down after removing the bearing adjuster.

15. Remove the bearing adjuster (**Figure 48**) and dust shield (**Figure 49**).

16. Use a rubber mallet and tap the steering stem/lower fork bracket to free it from the upper bearing cone.

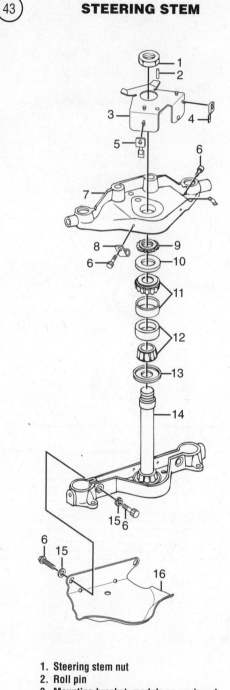

STEERING STEM

1. Steering stem nut
2. Roll pin
3. Mounting bracket–models so equipped
4. Tab–electrical connector
5. Anchor–T-stud connector
6. Bolt
7. Upper fork bracket
8. Harness guide
9. Bearing adjuster
10. Dust shield
11. Upper roller bearing assembly
12. Lower roller bearing assembly
13. Dusts shield
14. Steering stem/lower fork bracket
15. Washer
16. Air dam—models so equipped

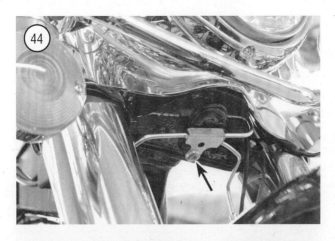

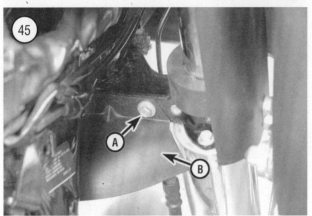

17. Slide the steering stem/lower fork bracket down and out (**Figure 50**) of the steering head.

18. Remove the upper bearing.

19. Remove the lower bearing and dust shield (**Figure 51**) from the lower fork bracket as described in this chapter, if necessary.

20. Inspect the steering stem and bearing assembly as described in this section.

Installation

1. Make sure to seat both steering head bearing races in the frame.

2. Wipe the bearing races with a clean lint-free cloth. Then lubricate each race with bearing grease.

3. Pack the upper and lower bearings with a quality bearing grease.

4. If removed, install a *new* lower dust shield on the steering stem and press it down until seated.

NOTE
Before installing the steering stem, make sure the threads on the stem are clean. Any dirt, grease or other residue on the threads affects the steering stem adjustment.

5. If removed, install the lower bearing onto the steering stem. Press the bearing into place with both thumbs until it bottoms against the dust seal.

6. Install the upper bearing (**Figure 52**) and seat it into to the upper race.

7. Insert the steering stem up (**Figure 50**) into the frame steering head through the upper bearing and hold it firmly in place.

8. Install the upper dust shield (**Figure 49**) and seat it in the upper race.

9. Install the bearing adjuster (**Figure 48**) and tighten to remove all bearing play within the steering head.

10. Install the upper fork bracket (**Figure 47**) over the steering stem.

11.Install the roll pin and the lock plate.

12. Install the steering stem hex nut (**Figure 46**). Hand-tight the nut at this time.

13. Install the front fork legs as described in this chapter.

CAUTION
Do not overtighten the steering stem nut or damage will occur to the bearings and races. Final adjustment of the fork stem will take place after the front wheel is installed.

14. Tighten the steering stem hex nut until the steering stem can be turned from side to side with no noticeable axial or lateral play. When the steering play feels correct, tighten the steering stem hex nut to 70-80 ft.-lb. (94.9-108.4 N•m).

15. Bend the tabs on the locking plate up against the flats on the steering stem nut.

16. On fairing-equipped models, install the interconnect harness ground socket connector onto the spade terminal on the upper fork bridge.

17. On models so equipped, install the air dam (B, **Figure 45**) onto the backside of the lower fork bracket. Install the screws (A, **Figure 45**) and washer on each side. Tighten the screws to 120-144 in.-lb. (13.6-16.3 N•m).

18. Move the front brake line assembly onto the bottom of the lower fork bracket. Install the bolt (**Figure 44**) and tighten securely.

19. Install the handlebar as described in this chapter.

20. Install both front fork legs as described in this chapter.

21. Install the front fender as described in Chapter Fourteen.

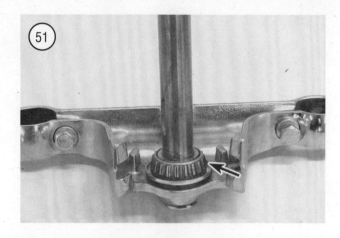

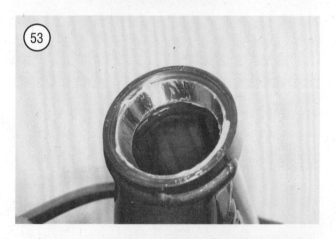

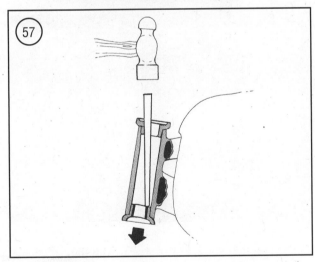

22. Install the front wheel as described in Chapter Ten.

23. On all models except FLTR Series, install the passing light assembly (Chapter Nine).

24A. On Road King models, install the headlight assembly from the mounting ring (Chapter Nine).

24B. On frame mounted fairing models, install the instrument nacelle (Chapter Nine).

24C. On fork mounted fairing models, install the fairing cap (Chapter Fourteen).

25. Adjust the steering play as described in *Steering Play Inspection and Adjustment* (this chapter).

Inspection

The bearing outer races are pressed into the steering head. Do not remove them unless they are going to be replaced as described in this chapter.

1. Wipe the bearing races with a solvent-soaked rag, and then dry with compressed air or a lint-free cloth. Check the races in the steering head (**Figure 53** and **Figure 54**) for pitting, scratches, galling or excessive wear. If any of these conditions exist, replace the races as described in this chapter. If the races are okay, wipe each race with grease.

2. Clean the bearings in solvent to remove all of the old grease. Blow the bearing dry with compressed air, making sure not to allow the air jet to spin the bearing. Do not remove the lower bearing from the fork stem unless it is to be replaced. Clean the bearing while installed on the steering stem.

3. After the bearings are dry, hold the inner race with one hand and turn the outer race with the other hand. Turn the bearing slowly, the bearing must turn smoothly with no roughness. Visually check the bearing (**Figure 55**) for pitting, scratches or visible damage. If the bearings are worn, check the dust covers for wear or damage or for improper bearing lubrication. Replace the bearing if necessary. If a bearing is going to be reused, pack it with grease and wrap it with wax paper or some other type of lint-free material until it is reinstalled. Do not store the bearings for any length of time without lubricating them to prevent rust.

4. Check the steering stem for cracks or damage. Check the threads at the top of the stem for damage. Check the steering stem nut for damage. Thread it onto the steering stem; make sure the nut threads on easily with no roughness.

5. Replace all worn or damaged parts. Replace bearing races as described in this chapter.

6. If necessary, replace the lower steering stem bearing and the dust shield as described in this chapter.

7. Check for broken welds on the frame around the steering head. If any are found, have them repaired.

STEERING HEAD BEARING RACES

The upper and lower bearing outer races are pressed into the frame. Do not remove the bearing races unless replacement is necessary. If removed, replace both the outer race along with the bearing at the same time. Never reinstall an outer race that has been removed as it is no longer true and will damage the bearing if reused.

Steering Head Bearing Replacement

1. Remove the steering stem as described in this chapter.

2. To remove a race (**Figure 56**), insert an aluminum or brass rod into the steering head and carefully tap the race out from the inside (**Figure 57**). Tap all around the race so that neither the race nor the steering head is bent.

11

3. Clean the steering head with solvent and dry thoroughly.

4A. Install the bearing races with a steering head bearing race installer (JIMS part No. 1725), or an equivalent, by following the manufacturer's instructions.

4B. If the installer tool (**Figure 58**) is not available, install the bearing races as follows:

a. Place the new bearing races in the freezer for one hour. This will slightly reduce the outer diameter.

b. Clean the race thoroughly before installing it.

c. Position the bearing with the bevel side facing out.

d. Align the *new* outer race with the frame steering head and tap it slowly and squarely in place. Make sure not to contact the bearing race surfaces. Drive the race into the steering head tube until it bottoms out on the bore shoulder. Refer to **Figure 59**.

e. Repeat the process to install the lower race into the steering head tube.

5. Apply bearing grease to the face of each race.

Fork Stem Lower Bearing Replacement

Do not remove the steering stem lower bearing and lower seal unless they are going to be replaced. The lower bearing can be difficult to remove. If the lower bearing cannot be removed as described in this procedure, take the steering stem to a dealership and have them remove it and reinstall a new part.

Never reinstall a lower bearing that has been removed as it is no longer true and will damage the rest of the bearing assembly if reused.

1A. Remove the lower bearing with fork stem bearing remover tool (JIMS part No. 1414) following the tool manufacturer's instructions.

1B. If the remover tool (**Figure 60**) is not available, remove the bearing as follows:

a. Install the steering stem nut onto the top of the steering stem to protect the threads.

b. Loosen the lower bearing from the shoulder at the base of the steering stem with a screwdriver or chisel as shown in **Figure 61**. Withdraw the lower bearing and grease seal from the steering stem.

2. Clean the steering stem with solvent and dry thoroughly.

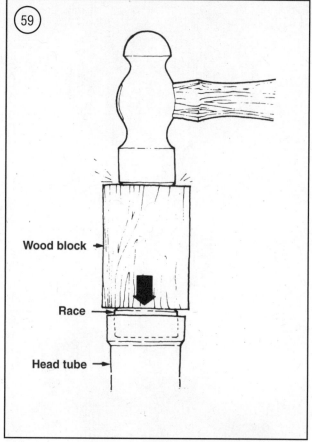

Wood block →

Race →

Head tube →

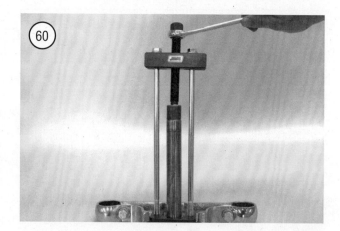

3. Position the *new* lower dust seal with the flange side facing up, and install it onto the steering stem.

4. Slide the *new* lower bearing onto the steering stem until it stops on the raised shoulder.

5. Align the lower bearing with the machined shoulder on the steering stem. Press the bearing down with both thumbs until it bottoms on the dust seal.

STEERING PLAY INSPECTION AND ADJUSTMENT

If aftermarket components have been installed, they could affect this adjustment.

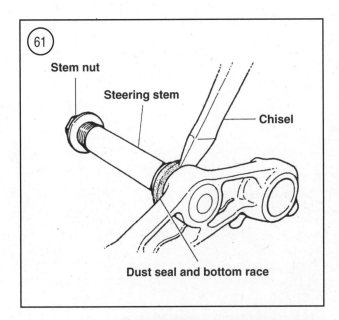

Stem nut

Steering stem

Chisel

Dust seal and bottom race

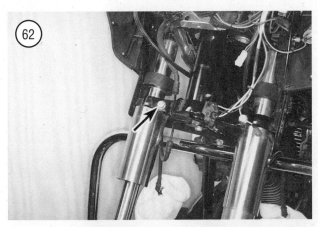

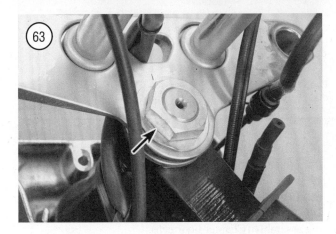

Swing Pattern

1. Use a centrally-located floor jack under the frame to support the motorcycle with both the front and rear wheels off the ground the same distance. If necessary, place a wooden block(s) under the rear wheel until the motorcycle is level.

2. Turn the front wheel full left and let it go.

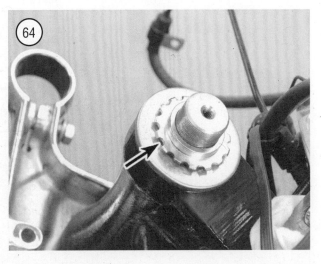

3. The front wheel should swing right, left, then right and stop. The wheel does not need to stop in the center or straight ahead position, but it must make at least a partial third swing to the right.

4. If the swing pattern is too short or too long, adjust the movement as described in this section.

Adjustment

1A. On Road King models, remove the headlight assembly from the mounting ring as described in Chapter Nine.

1B. On frame mounted fairing models, remove the instrument nacelle as described in Chapter Nine.

1C. On fork mounted fairing models, remove the front fairing assembly as described in Chapter Fourteen.

2. Working at the base of the steering stem, loosen the lower fork bridge pinch bolt (**Figure 62**) on the fork legs.

3. To prevent any binding, slide the rubber fork stop up several inches on the both fork tubes.

4. Pry the tabs on the locking plate away from the steering stem hex nut.

5. Loosen and remove the steering stem hex nut (**Figure 63**).

> *NOTE*
> *Turning the bearing adjuster (**Figure 64**) one notch will make a noticeable difference in the swing pattern.*

6. Make an adjustment tool from 1/4 inch drill rod that is 16 inches long as shown in **Figure 65**.

7. Working under the upper fork bracket, loosen the steering stem bearing adjuster with the drill rod tool.

8. To decrease the number of swings, stand on the *right side* of the motorcycle and insert the adjustment tool into the notches of the bearing adjuster. Push forward and rotate the adjuster *counterclockwise*.

9. To increase the number of swings, stand on the *left side* of the motorcycle and insert the adjustment tool into the notches of the bearing adjuster. Push forward and rotate the adjuster (**Figure 64**) *clockwise*.

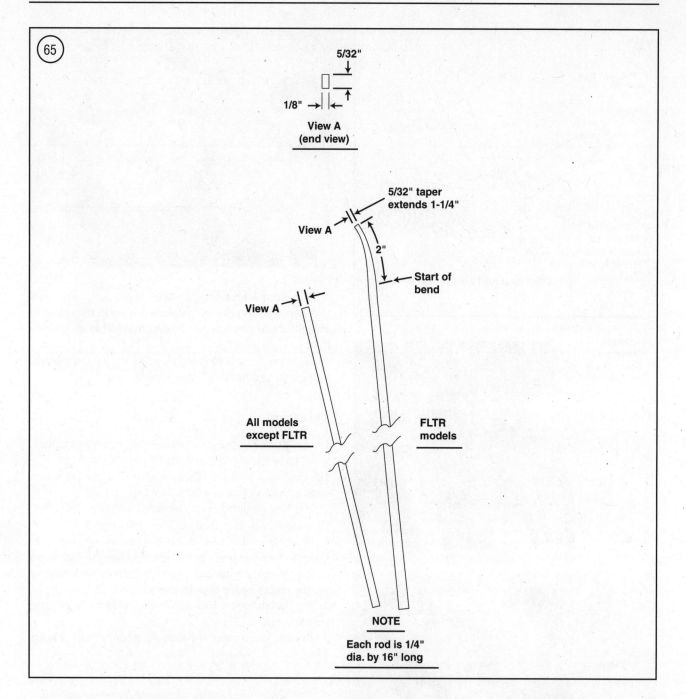

65

5/32"

1/8" →|

View A
(end view)

5/32" taper
extends 1-1/4"

View A →

2"

Start of
bend

View A →

All models
except FLTR

FLTR
models

NOTE

Each rod is 1/4"
dia. by 16" long

10. Tighten the steering stem hex nut (**Figure 63**) to 70-80 ft.-lb. (94.9-108.4 N•m).

11. Recheck the swing pattern as previously described, and if necessary, repeat the adjustment procedure.

12. Tighten the lower fork bridge pinch bolt on both fork legs to 30-35 ft.-lb. (40.7-47.5 N•m).

13. Slide the rubber fork stop back down into position.

14A. On Road King models, install the headlight assembly from the mounting ring (Chapter Nine).

14B. On frame mounted fairing models, install the instrument nacelle as (Chapter Nine).

14C. On fork mounted fairing models, install the front fairing assembly (Chapter Fourteen).

15. Lower the motorcycle to the ground.

Table 1 FRONT FORK OIL CAPACITY AND OIL LEVEL SPECIFICATIONS

Model	Capacity—each fork leg oz. (cc)	Oil level height* in. (mm)
All models except FLHR, FLHRC, FLHRSE	10.7 (316)	4.92 (125)
FLHR, FLHRC, FLHRSE models	11.0 (325)	5.92 (134)

*Measured from the top of the fork tube with fork spring removed and the fork leg fully compressed.

Table 2 FRONT SUSPENSION TORQUE SPECIFICATIONS

	ft.-lb.	in.-lb.	N•m
Front axle nut	60-65	–	81.3-88.1
Front axle set nut screw (models so equipped)	–	60-84	6.8-9.5
Front-slider axle-clamp nut	–	132-180	14.9-20.3
Front fork			
Cap bolt	60-70	–	81.4-94.8
Tube plug	60-70	–	81.4-94.9
Lower fork bridge pinch bolt	53-57	–	71.9-77.3
Damper rod Allen bolt	–	132-216	14.9-24.4
Handlebar			
Clamp bolt	16-20	–	21.7-27.1
Lower clamp rubber bushing bolt	53-57	–	71.9-77.3
Steering stem			
Hex nut	70-80	–	94.9-108.4
Air dam (models so equipped)	–	120-144	13.6-16.3

11

NOTES

CHAPTER TWELVE

REAR SUSPENSION AND FINAL DRIVE

This chapter covers repair and replacement procedures for the rear suspension components. **Tables 1-4** are located at the end of this chapter.

WARNING
All rear suspension fasteners must be replaced with the exact same type of part. Do not use a substitute design of fastener, as it may affect the performance of the rear suspension or fail, leading to loss of control of the motorcycle. Refer to the torque specifications in Table 1.

SHOCK AIR PRESSURE ADJUSTMENT (AIR PRESSURE TYPE)

WARNING
Use caution when releasing the air from the rear shock absorber air valve. Moisture combined with oil may spurt out when the air pressure is released. Protect your eyes accordingly.

CAUTION
The air chambers within the rear shock are very small and will fill rapidly. Do not use compressed air. Only use only a small hand-held or foot-operated small air pump.

1. Place the motorcycle on the jiffy stand.
2. Remove the left side saddlebag as described in Chapter Fourteen.

3. Remove the air valve cap (**Figure 1**).
4. Use a no-loss air gauge to check air pressure. Refer to the recommended air pressure listed in **Table 2** and **Table 3**.
5. Increase or decrease air pressure to achieve the desired ride and control with a small, hand-held air pump.
6. Install the air valve cap and the saddlebag.

SHOCK AIR PRESSURE LOSS INSPECTION (AIR PRESSURE TYPE)

If there is a gradual loss of air pressure in the system, inspect the hoses, fittings and air valve assembly.
1. Check that the valve stem core is tightened securely.
2. Adjust the shock absorbers to the correct air pressure and wait overnight.
3. In the morning recheck the air pressure.
4A. If air pressure is okay, the system is holding the correct amount of air.
4B. If there is a loss of 5-10 psi (35-69 kPa), check the system as described in this section.
5. Remove the saddlebag(s) as described in Chapter Fourteen.
6. Adjust the shock absorbers to the correct air pressure.
7. Inspect the air line fittings (**Figure 2**) at the shock absorbers. Spray or brush a light film of soapy water onto the compression fittings on both shock absorbers and the air inlet tee-fitting. If air bubbles appear, perform the following:
   a. Cover the rear brake assembly and wheel prior to releasing the compressed air from the rear air valve. If necessary, wipe off any oil reside that may have been ejected from the air valve.

b. Remove the air valve cap (**Figure 1**). Use a no-loss air gauge and add 3-5 psi (21-35 kPa) to purge the air lines of any oil.

c. Slowly depress the air valve to evacuate the air from both shock absorbers.

d. Use a thumb to depress the collar (A, **Figure 3**) on the fitting, and then carefully pull the air hose (B) from the fitting.

e. Inspect the end of the air hose for burrs or damage. If damaged, cut off the damaged area and reinsert the air hose into the collar. Gently pull on the hose to ensure it is secure in the fitting.

8. Pressurize the system and recheck for air leaks. If there is still an air leak, perform the following to replace the fittings:

a. Remove the air hose from the fitting, and remove the fitting from the shock absorber.

b. Install a *new* fitting. Apply pipe sealant with Teflon to the fitting's threads and install the fitting into the shock absorber. Tighten the fitting securely.

c. Install the air line(s) into the new fitting(s). Gently pull on the hose to ensure it is secure in the fitting.

9. Pressurize the system as described in *Shock Air Pressure Adjustment* (this chapter). Spray or brush a light film of soapy water onto the compression fitting(s) on both shock absorber(s) and check for air bubbles. If bubbles appear, repeat the process until the leak is repaired.

10. Inspect the air lines at the air valve assembly. Spray or brush a light film of soapy water onto the fittings at the air valve assembly fittings. If air bubbles appear, perform the following:

a. Remove the frame side cover (A, **Figure 4**).

b. Remove the hex fitting (B, **Figure 4**) securing the air valve assembly to the frame bracket.

c. Carefully remove the air valve assembly from the frame bracket.

d. Depress the collars on the outlet tee (C, **Figure 4**) and remove both air tubes from the air valve assembly. Discard the air valve assembly.

e. Install the air tubes into the *new* air valve assembly and install the air valve assembly into the frame bracket.

f. Install the air valve hex fitting (B, **Figure 4**) and tighten to 40-50 in.-lb. (4.5-5.7 N•m).

g. Pressurize the system as described in *Shock Air Pressure Adjustment* (this chapter).

SHOCK ABSORBER (AIR PRESSURE TYPE)

These models are equipped with an air-adjustable suspension. The amount of air pressure in the rear shock absorbers can be varied to suit personal comfort. The lower the air pressure, the softer the ride and the higher the air pressure, the firmer the ride. Refer to **Table 2** and **Table 3** for the recommended air pressure for the rear shock absorbers.

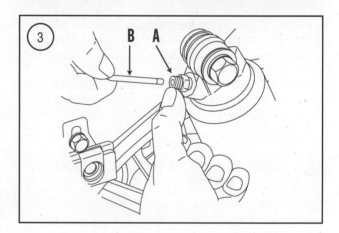

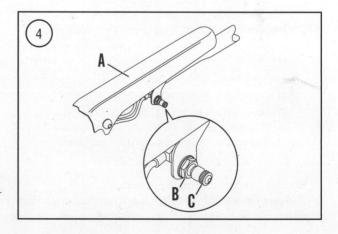

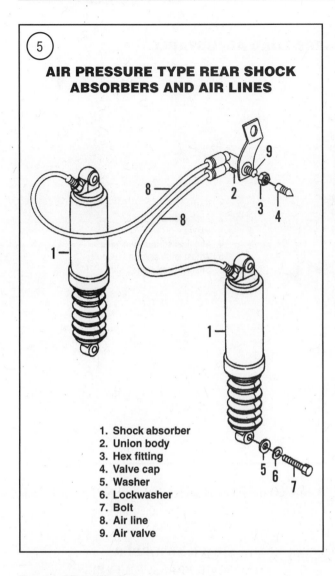

AIR PRESSURE TYPE REAR SHOCK ABSORBERS AND AIR LINES

1. Shock absorber
2. Union body
3. Hex fitting
4. Valve cap
5. Washer
6. Lockwasher
7. Bolt
8. Air line
9. Air valve

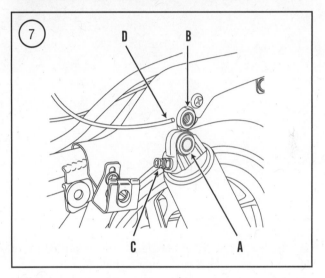

Removal/Installation

Refer to **Figure 5**.

When servicing the rear shocks, remove one shock at a time. If it is necessary to remove both shocks, support the motorcycle on a suitable floor jack, with the rear wheel off the ground.

1. Support the motorcycle with the rear wheel off the ground. Refer to *Motorcycle Stands* in Chapter Ten, if necessary.

2. Place wooden blocks under the rear wheel to place the rear wheel in a neutral position with no strain on the shock absorber mounting hardware.

3. Remove the saddlebag(s) as described in Chapter Fourteen.

WARNING
Use caution when releasing the air from the rear shock absorber air valve. Moisture combined with oil may spurt out when the air pressure is released. Protect your eyes accordingly.

4. Cover the rear brake assembly and wheel prior to releasing the compressed air from the rear air valve. If nec-

essary, wipe off any oil reside that may have been ejected from the air valve.

5. Remove the air valve cap (**Figure 1**). Use a no-loss air gauge and add 3-5 psi (21-35 kPa) to purge the air lines of any oil.

6. Slowly depress the air valve to evacuate the air from both shock absorbers.

7. Use a thumb, and depress the collar (A, **Figure 3**) on the fitting and carefully pull the air hose (B) from the fitting.

8. Loosen both the upper (A, **Figure 6**) and lower (B) mounting bolts securing the shock absorber to the frame and to the swing arm.

9. Remove the lower bolt (B, **Figure 6**), lockwasher and washer securing the shock absorber to the swing arm.

10. Remove the upper bolt (A, **Figure 6**), lockwasher and washer securing the shock absorber to the frame.

11. Remove the shock absorber (C, **Figure 6**) from the motorcycle and store it in an *upright position* to avoid the loss of oil. Any loss of oil requires replacement of the shock absorber as oil cannot be added to the unit.

12. Repeat the procedure to remove the other shock absorber, if necessary.

13. Inspect the shock absorber as described in this section.

14. Install the shock absorber (A, **Figure 7**) into position on the frame boss (B).

12

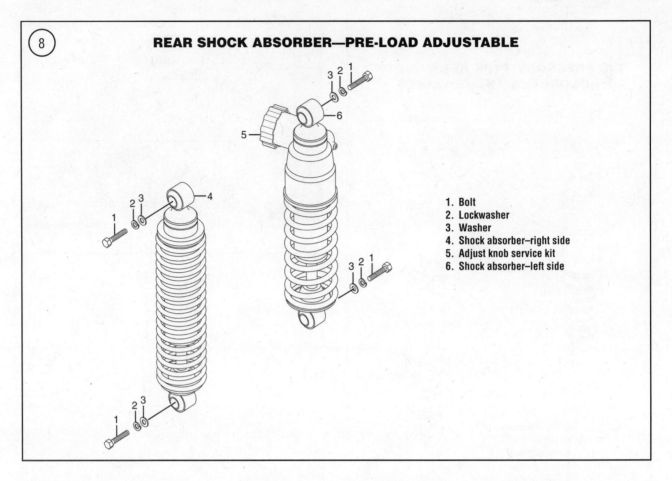

REAR SHOCK ABSORBER—PRE-LOAD ADJUSTABLE

8

1. Bolt
2. Lockwasher
3. Washer
4. Shock absorber–right side
5. Adjust knob service kit
6. Shock absorber–left side

15. Apply a few drops of Loctite 243 (blue) threadlock, or an equivalent, to the shock mounting bolt threads.

16. Install the washers, the lockwashers and bolts. Tighten the bolts to 35-40 ft.-lb. (47.5-54.2 N•m).

17. Use a thumb to depress the collar (C, **Figure 7**) on the fitting. Insert the air hose (D, **Figure 7**) into the fitting until it bottoms, and release the fitting. Gently pull on the hose to ensure it is secure in the fitting.

18. Adjust the shock absorber air pressure as described in this chapter.

19. Install the saddlebag(s) as described in Chapter Seventeen.

20. Remove the wood block under the rear tire, and lower the motorcycle.

21. Test ride the motorcycle slowly at first to make the rear suspension is working properly.

Inspection

There are no shock replacement parts available for these models. If any part, other than the mounting hardware, is damaged, replace the shock assembly.

1. Remove the shock absorber as described in this section. Keep the shock absorber in an *upright position* to avoid the loss of oil.

2. Inspect the upper shock bushing and lower shock bushing for wear and deterioration.

3. Inspect the shock absorber. If the rubber boot portion is cracked or deteriorated, replace the shock absorber.

**SHOCK ABSORBERS
(NON-AIR PRESSURE TYPE)**

These shock absorbers are the non-air pressure type and can be adjusted for preload.

Removal/Installation

Refer to **Figure 8**.

> *NOTE*
> *When servicing the shock absorbers, remove one shock at time. If it is necessary to remove both shocks at the same time, support the motorcycle on a suitable floor jack with the rear wheel off the ground.*

1. Support the motorcycle with the rear wheel off the ground. Refer to *Motorcycle Stands* in Chapter Ten.

2. Place a wooden block(s) under the rear wheel to relieve in a neutral position with no strain on the shock absorber mounting hardware.

3. Remove the saddlebags as described in Chapter Fourteen.

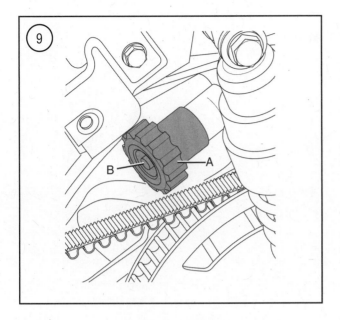

4. Remove the lower bolt, Lockwasher and washer securing the lower bolt to the swing arm.

5. Remove the upper bolt, Lockwasher and securing the upper bolt to the swing arm.

6. Remove the shock absorber from the frame and store it in an *upright position* to avoid the loss of oil. Any loss of oil requires the replacement of the shock absorber as oil cannot be added to the unit.

7. Repeat this procedure for the remaining shock absorber, if necessary.

8. Inspect the shock absorber as described in this section.

9. Apply a few drops of threadlocking compound (Loctite 243 blue or equivalent), or an equivalent, to the shock mounting bolts.

10. Install the shock absorber into position on the frame.

11. Install the Lockwasher, washers and bolt and tighten to 35-40 ft.-lb. (47.5-54.2 N•m).

12. Install the saddlebag(s) as described in Chapter Fourteen.

13. Remove the wooden block(s) from under the rear wheel, and lower the motorcycle.

14. Test ride the motorcycle slowly to make sure the rear suspension is working properly.

Knob Replacement

The knob is the only part of the shock absorber that is replaceable in kit form.

1. Remove the left side saddlebag as described in Chapter Fourteen.

2. Rotate the knob *counterclockwise* until it stops. This is the minimal amount of preload.

NOTE
The detent spring and ball will fall out when the knob is removed.

3. Hold a shop cloth under the knob (A, **Figure 9**) to catch the spring and steel ball during knob removal.

4. Remove the screw (B, **Figure 9**) and washer securing the knob. Slowly remove the knob watching for the detent spring and steel ball.

5. Remove the detent steel ball and spring from the adjuster housing, if necessary.

6. Place the spring into the bore, if removed.

7. Press the steel ball onto the end of the spring and install the knob onto the adjuster housing.

8. Hold the knob in place, install the screw and tighten securely.

9. Adjust the preload as described in this section.

10. Install the left side saddlebag as described in Chapter Fourteen.

Preload Adjustment

1. Remove the left side saddlebag as described in Chapter Fourteen.

2. Rotate the knob (A, **Figure 9**) *counterclockwise* until it stops. This is the minimal amount of preload.

3. Rotate the knob *clockwise* the recommended number of turns to increase the preload for the *total weigh* of the rider, passenger and cargo. The knob will click after each full rotation. Refer to Table 4.

REAR SWING ARM

Refer to **Figure 10**.

Bearing Play Inspection

The swing arm needle bearings wear over time and require replacement. Worn or damaged needle bearings can produce erratic and dangerous handling. Common symptoms are wheel hop, pulling to one side during acceleration and pulling to the other side during braking.

1. Remove the rear wheel (A, **Figure 11**) as described in Chapter Twelve.

2. Remove the bolt, lockwasher and washer securing both shock absorbers (B, **Figure 11**) to the swing arm. Move them up away from the swing arm.

3. Make sure both nuts on the swing arm pivot shaft are tight.

4. Have an assistant hold the motorcycle securely.

5. Grasp the back of the swing arm and try to move it from side to side. Any play between the swing arm and the frame, or swing arm and transmission may suggest worn or damaged needle bearings. If there is any play, remove the swing arm and inspect the needle bearing assemblies.

6. Install all components removed.

12

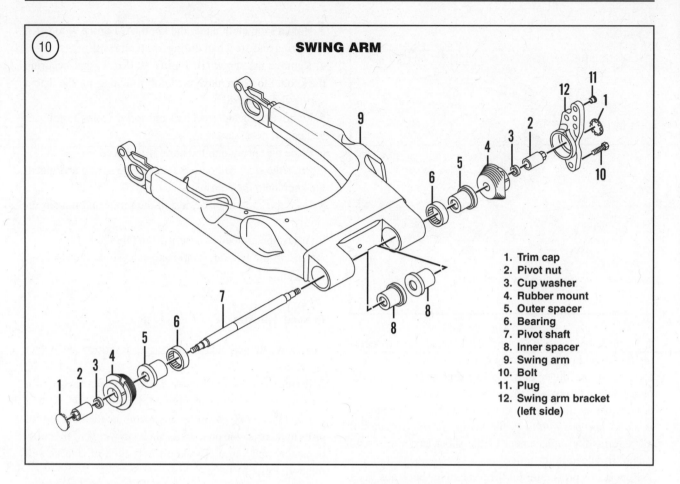

SWING ARM

1. Trim cap
2. Pivot nut
3. Cup washer
4. Rubber mount
5. Outer spacer
6. Bearing
7. Pivot shaft
8. Inner spacer
9. Swing arm
10. Bolt
11. Plug
12. Swing arm bracket (left side)

Removal

1. Remove both saddlebags as described in Chapter Fourteen.

2. Remove both passenger footboards as described in Chapter Fourteen.

3. Remove the exhaust system as described in Chapter Four.

4. Remove the bolts securing the drive belt guard and remove the guard.

5. Place wooden blocks or a floor jack under the transmission and engine assembly to support it after the swing arm pivot shaft is removed.

6. Remove the rear wheel (A, **Figure 10**) as described in Chapter Twelve.

7. Remove the rear caliper bracket from the anchor weldment on swing arm.

8. Loosen the bolt securing both shock absorbers (B, **Figure 11**) to the swing arm. Do not remove the bolt at this time.

9. Remove the trim cap (A, **Figure 12**) from the bracket.

10. Remove the bolts (B, **Figure 12**), securing the bracket on the left side. Remove the bracket (C, **Figure 12**) from the frame.

11A. On models without ABS, unhook the rear brake caliper hose from the clips on the right side of the swing arm.

11B. On models with ABS, unhook the rear brake caliper hose and the ABS rear wheel sensor from the clips on the right side of the swing arm.

12. On the left side, secure the nut (A, **Figure 13**) within the rubber mount (B) with a socket to keep it from rotating during removal.

13. On the right side, loosen and remove the nut or pivot nut securing the pivot shaft.

14. Support the swing arm on a box.

15. Use a suitable size drift and tap on the right side the pivot shaft with a drift. Drive the pivot shaft assembly part way out through the left side.

16. Remove the pivot shaft assembly (C, **Figure 13**) consisting of the pivot shaft, pivot nut, cup washer, rubber mount and outer spacer, from the frame and transmission case.

17. Remove the bolt, lockwasher and washer securing both shock absorbers (B, **Figure 11**) to the swing arm. Move them up away from the swing arm.

18. Slowly pull back and withdraw the swing arm from the transmission case and swing arm brackets.

19. Remove the outer spacer from the right side of the swing arm pivot point.

20. Remove the rubber mount from behind the right side swing arm bracket, or frame mount on 2009 models.

21. Inspect the swing arm as described in this section.

Installation

1. On the right side, position the slot (D, **Figure 13**) in the rubber mount between the twelve and one o'clock position,

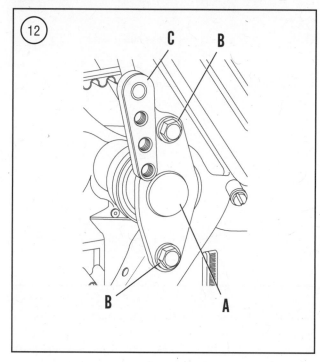

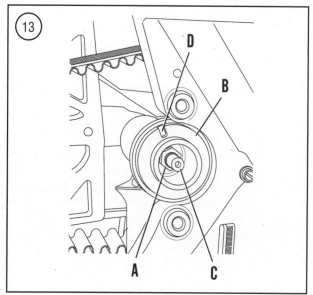

7. Install the outer spacer onto pivot shaft.

8. Position the rubber mount with the flat side going on first and install onto the pivot shaft.

9. On the left side, position the cup washer with the concave side going on first and install it onto the pivot shaft.

10. On the left side, rotate the rubber mount to position the slot in the rubber mount between the eleven and twelve o'clock position. Make sure the index tab on the inboard side of the bracket engages the slot in the rubber mount. Reposition the components, if necessary, to achieve this alignment.

11. On the left side, install the swing arm bracket. Apply a few drops of Loctite 243 (blue) threadlock, or an equivalent, to the mounting bolts. Install the swing arm bracket bolts and tighten to 55-65 ft.-lb. (74.6-88.1 N•m).

12. Apply a few drops of Loctite 243 (blue) threadlock, or an equivalent, to the threads on the locknuts, or pivot nuts.

13. Tighten the left side locknut, or pivot nut, to approximately 55-65 ft.-lb. (4.6-89.6 N•m).

14. Secure the left side locknut, or pivot nut, and tighten the right side locknut, or pivot nut to 55-65 ft.-lb. (4.6-89.6 N•m).

15. If necessary, repeat the process and tighten the left side locknut, or pivot nut, to approximately 55-65 ft.-lb. (4.6-89.6 N•m).

16. Remove the lower bolts, washers and lockwashers securing the rear shock absorbers to the swing arm.

17. Slowly raise and lower the swing arm to verify ease of movement without binding. If binding occurs, repeat the tightening procedure and correct the problem.

18. Install the chrome trim caps onto both frame brackets.

19. Move the shock absorbers into position and install the bolt, lockwasher and washer securing both shock absorbers (B, **Figure 11**) to the swing arm. Tighten the bolts to 35-40 ft.-lb. (47.5-54.2 N•m).

20A. On models without ABS, hook the rear brake caliper hose onto the clips on the right side of the swing arm.

and install it into the backside of the swing arm bracket. Make sure the index tab on the inboard side of the bracket engages the slot in the rubber mount. Reposition the components, if necessary, to achieve this alignment.

2. Install the outer spacer into the right side of the swing arm pivot point.

3. Position the drive belt on the inboard side of the swing arm and position the swing arm onto the pivot area of the transmission case and support it in this position. If necessary, use soft faced mallet and tap the swing arm into position.

4. Move the shock absorbers into position on the swing arm and loosely install the bolt, lockwasher and washer securing both shock absorbers (B, **Figure 11**) to the swing arm. Do not tighten at this time.

5. Coat the pivot shaft with Loctite antiseize, or an appropriate type of grease. Do not get any grease on the exposed threads.

6. Install the pivot shaft assembly through the left side of the frame, transmission and the swing arm.

12

20B. On models with ABS, hook the rear brake caliper hose and the ABS rear wheel sensor onto the clips on the right side of the swing arm.

21. Install the rear caliper bracket onto the anchor weldment on swing arm.

22. Install the rear wheel (A, **Figure 10**) as described in Chapter Twelve.

23. Remove the wooden blocks or floor jack from under the transmission and engine assembly.

24. Install the drive belt guard and tighten the bolts securely.

25. Install the exhaust system as described in Chapter Four.

26. Install both passenger footboards as described in Chapter Fourteren.

27. Install both saddlebags as described in Chapter Fourteen.

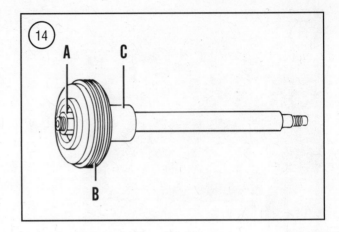

Inspection

1. Clean the exterior of the swing arm in solvent and thoroughly dry with compressed air.

2. Inspect the welded sections on the swing arm for cracks or fractures.

3. Inspect the right and left side rubber mounts on the pivot shaft. If replacement of the left side mount is necessary, hold onto the pivot shaft to keep it from rotating. Remove the locknut (A, **Figure 14**), rubber mount (B) and outer spacer (C) from the pivot shaft. Replace the rubber mounts as a pair if either one is starting to deteriorate or harden.

4. Inspect the pivot shaft for surface cracks, deep scoring, wear or heat distortion. Replace it if necessary.

5. Turn the needle bearings with a finger. The bearing should turn smoothly with no signs of roughness or damage. If necessary, replace the needle bearings as described in this section. Replace the needle bearings as a pair if either is damaged.

Needle Bearing and Inner Spacer Replacement

Remove and install the needle bearings only if the bearing must be replaced. Never install a needle bearing that has been removed. Both the needle bearings and inner spacer must be replaced as a set.

A hydraulic press and several tools are required for bearing and inner race replacement.

1. Place the swing arm on the press bed with the left side facing down (**Figure 15**). Place a wooden block on the press bed to protect the swing arm finish.

2. Place a socket with an inner diameter larger than the needle bearing under the left side pivot point.

3. Select a long socket extension with another socket attached that matches the outer diameter of the needle bearing. Insert this tool setup down through the right side of the pivot point and place it on the left side needle bearing.

4. Make sure the swing arm pivot areas are square with the press bed.

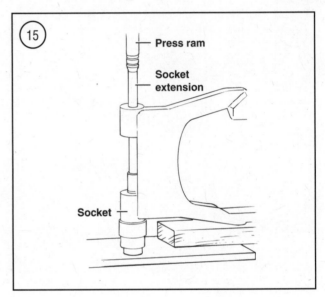

5. Hold the swing arm vertical and square. Then, slowly apply ram pressure on the long extension and drive the needle bearing and inner spacer out of the left side pivot bore and into the receiving socket.

6. Release ram pressure and remove the tools from the swing arm.

7. Turn the swing arm over, and repeat the process to remove the remaining needle bearing and inner spacer.

8. Clean the swing arm bearing bores with solvent and dry with compressed air.

9. Install the inner spacer into the *new* needle bearing (**Figure 16**) as follows:

   a. Place the bearing on a smooth, flat press plate.

   b. Position the spacer with the collar facing up and start the spacer into the needle bearing.

   c. Center the assembly under the press ram and apply pressure. Press the spacer into the bearing until it bottoms on the press plate.

   d. Repeat this process for the remaining spacer and bearing.

NOTE
There are two bearing installers in the swing arm bearing installer set (H-D part No. HD-

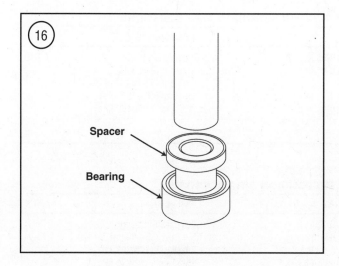

16

Spacer

Bearing

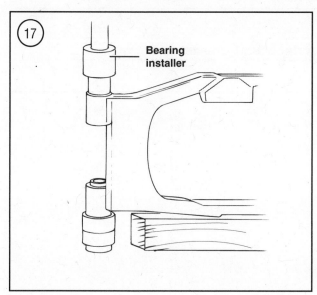

17

Bearing
installer

45327). The longer installer is used on the left side (drive side) and the shorter installer is used on the right side (brake side).

10. Place the swing arm on the press bed so the right side faces up (**Figure 17**). Place a wooden block on the press bed first to protect the swing arm finish.

11. Make sure the pivot areas are square with the press bed.

12. Position the *new* needle bearing assembly wit the spacer side facing out.

13. Place the *new* needle bearing assembly over the right side bearing bore. Place the shorter *Brake Side* installer onto the bearing assembly.

14. Make sure the pivot areas are square with the press bed.

15. Hold the swing arm so it vertical and square. Then, slowly apply ram pressure on the installer, and drive the needle bearing assembly into the right side pivot bore. Press the bearing assembly into the swing arm until the shoulder of the installer tool makes contact with the swing arm.

16. Release the pressure and remove the installer from the swing arm.

CAUTION
*The longer drive side installer shoulder **must not** make contact with the swing arm on the left side. Only press the needle bearing assembly into the pivot bore until the bearing bottoms. Do not press it in until the installer shoulder contacts the swing arm as the swing arm will be damaged.*

17. Turn the swing arm over and repeat the process to install the remaining needle bearing assembly into the left side of the swing arm. Use the longer *Drive Side* installer to install the left side bearing assembly. Press the bearing assembly into the swing arm until the bearing bottoms.

12

Table 1 REAR SUSPENSION TORQUE SPECIFICATIONS

Item	ft.-lb.	in.-lb.	N•m
Shock absorber			
Air valve hex fitting	–	40-50	4.5-5.7
Mounting bolts	35-40	–	47.5-54.2
Swing arm			
Left side swing arm bracket bolt	55-65	–	74.6-88.1
Left side pivot shaft pivot nut	55-65	–	74.6-88.1
Right side pivot shaft pivot nut	55-65	–	74.6-88.1

Table 2 FLHT, FLHR and FLTR MODELS REAR SUSPENSION AIR PRESSURE*

Load	Total weight	Pressure
Solo rider	up to 150 lb. (0-68 kg)	0 psi (0 kPa)
Solo rider	150-200 lb. (68-91 kg)	0-10 psi (0-69 kPa)
Solo rider	200-250 lb. (91-113 kg)	5-15 psi (35-103 kPa)
Passenger	up to 150 lb. (0-68 kg)	10-15 psi (69-103 kPa)
Passenger	up to 200 lb. (0-91 kg)	20-25 psi (138-172 kPa)

*Includes CVO models.

Table 3 FLHX MODELS REAR SUSPENSION AIR PRESSURE

Load	Total weight	Pressure
Solo rider	up to 160 lb. (0-73 kg)	0-5 psi (0-35 kPa)
Solo rider	over 200 lb. (over 91 kg)	5-10 psi (35-69 kPa)
Passenger	up to 150 lb. (0-68 kg)	20-30 psi (128-207 kPa)
Passenger	up to 200 lb. (over 68 kg)	25-35 psi (172-241 kPa)

Table 4 SHOCK ABSORBER PRELOAD SETTINGS (NON-AIR PRESSURE TYPE)

Preload turns from minimum	Load* LB	KG
0	Under 220	Under 100
1	220	100
2	230	104
3	240	109
4	250	113
5	260	118
6	270	122
7	280	127
8	290	132
9	300	136
10	310	141
11	320	145
12	330	150
13	340	154
14	350	159
15	360	163
16	370	168
17	380	172
18	390	177
19	400 to GVWR	181 to GVWR

1. Load includes the total weight of the rider, passenger and cargo.

CHAPTER THIRTEEN

BRAKES

This chapter covers the brake system. Specifications are located in **Table 1** and **Table 2** at the end of this chapter.

BRAKE SERVICE PREFORM

WARNING
Do not ride the motorcycle without a properly functioning brake system. After any brake system service/repair, verify proper brake operation.

WARNING
Do not intermix DOT 4 with DOT 5 brake fluids, as they are not compatible. DOT 5 is silicone-based and the mistaken use of silicone brake fluid in these models can cause brake failure.

WARNING
*When working on the brake system, do **not** inhale brake dust. It may contain asbestos. Do **not** use compressed air to blow off brake dust. Use an aerosol brake parts cleaner. Wear a face mask and wash thoroughly after completing the work.*

The brake system transmits hydraulic pressure from the master cylinders to the brake calipers. This pressure is transmitted from the caliper(s) to the brake pads, which grip both sides of the brake disc(s) and slow the motorcycle. As the pads wear, the pistons move out of the caliper bores to automatically compensate for wear. As this occurs, the fluid level in the master cylinder reservoir goes down. Compensate for this by occasionally adding fluid. Check the fluid levels at the intervals noted in Chapter Three.

Consider the following when servicing the brake system:

1. The hydraulic components rarely require disassembly. Make sure disassembly is necessary.
2. Use the correct DOT 4 brake fluid. Make sure the brake fluid is in good condition. Small quantities of brake fluid stored in the original container will absorb moisture from the air in the container. Brake system performance depends on a supply of clean brake fluid and a clean service enviroN•ment. Any debris entering the system can damage components.
3. Do not intermix brake fluid types and try to use the same brand of fluid if possible. Dispose of used or contaminated brake fluid properly.
4. Keep the reservoir covers in place to prevent the entry of moisture and debris contamination.
5. Do not allow brake fluid to contact plastic, painted or plated parts. It will damage the surface. When adding brake fluid, punch a small hole into the edge of the container's seal to help control the fluid flow. Cover all that may be contaminated by spilled fluid.
6. Clean up any spilled brake fluid with soapy water and rinse thoroughly.
7. If the hydraulic system, excluding the reservoir cover, has been opened, bleed the system to remove air from the system. Refer to *Brake Bleeding* in this chapter.
8. Clean parts with an aerosol brake parts cleaner or isopropyl alcohol. Never use petroleum-based solvents on internal brake system components. They will cause seals to swell and distort.

9. During overhaul, replace O-rings and seals. Never reuse these components.

10. The manufacturer does not provide wear limit specifications for the caliper and master cylinder assemblies. When inspecting these components, consult a dealer for advice. Brake pad and disc thickness specifications are provided.

FRONT BRAKE PADS

There is no recommended mileage interval for changing the brake pads. Pad wear depends greatly on riding habits and conditions. Frequently check the brake pads for wear. Increase the inspection interval when the wear indicator reaches the edge of the brake disc. After removal, measure the thickness of each brake pad with a caliper or ruler and compare to the dimensions in **Table 1**.

Always replace both pads in the caliper at the same time to maintain an even brake pressure on the discs. Also, replace both brake pads in *both calipers* at the same time. Do not disconnect the hydraulic brake hose from the brake caliper for brake pad replacement. Disconnect the hose only if the caliper assembly is going to be removed.

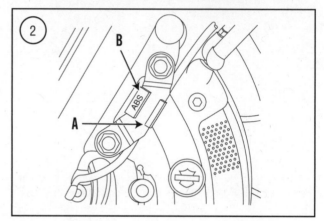

> *CAUTION*
> *Check the pads more frequently when the lining approaches the pad metal backing plate. If pad wear happens to be uneven for some reason, the backing plate may come in contact with the disc and cause damage.*

> *CAUTION*
> *On ABS equipped models, keep the ABS sensor away from all magnetic fields or it will be damaged.*

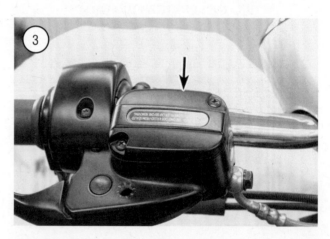

Replacement

1. Read *Brake Service Perform* in this chapter.
2. Support the motorcycle on level ground on a swing arm stand.
3. Block the front wheel so the motorcycle will not roll in either direction with the rear wheel off the ground.
4. Place a spacer between the brake lever and the throttle grip and secure it in place. This prevents the brake lever from being accidently applied forcing the piston out of the caliper. The caliper is not serviceable and would require replacement.
5A. On the left side ABS models caliper only, perform the following:

   a. Remove the clips (**Figure 1**) securing the front fender tip lamp wires (models so equipped) and wheel speed sensor wires to the left side caliper brake hose.

   b. Push in on the lip of the rear of clip (A, **Figure 2**) and release it. Rotate the ABS tab (B, **Figure 2**) toward the rear until the clip is perpendicular to the bracket. Remove the clip and move the cable out of the way.

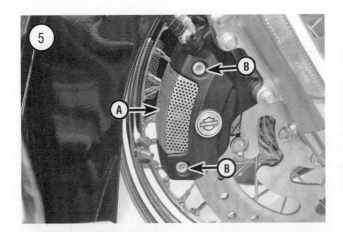

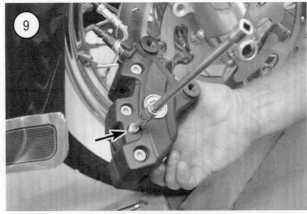

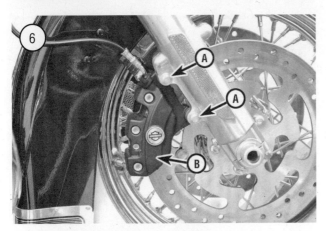

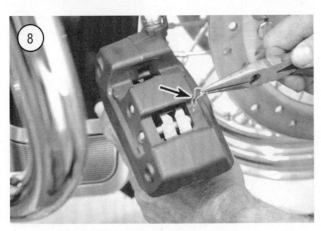

5B. On all other models so equipped, remove the clips securing the front fender tip lamp wires (models so equipped) and wheel speed sensor wires to the right side caliper brake hose

6. To prevent the master cylinder from overflowing while reposition the pistons in the brake caliper, perform the following:

   a. Clean all dirt from the top of the master cylinder.

   b. Remove the cover screws and remove the cover (**Figure 3**) and diaphragm (**Figure 4**).

   c. Use a shop syringe and remove about 50% of the reservoir to prevent overflow. Do no drain more than 50% of the brake fluid or air will enter the system. Discard the brake fluid properly.

7. Remove the cover (A, **Figure 5**) from the caliper. Do *not* try to loosen the caliper assembly bolts (B), the caliper cannot be disassembled.

8. Remove the bolts (A, **Figure 6**) securing the caliper (B) to the fork slider. On ABS equipped models, do not lose the clip located under the mounting bolts.

> *CAUTION*
> *The brake disc is thin and easily damaged. When pushing against the disc in the following step, support the disc adjacent to the caliper to prevent damage.*

9. Hold the outboard side of the caliper body and push it toward the brake disc. This pushes the outer pistons into the caliper cylinders to make room for the new brake pads. Constantly check the reservoir. Remove fluid, if necessary, before it overflows. Install the diaphragm and cover. Tighten the cover screws finger-tight.

10. Carefully side the caliper off the brake disc (**Figure 7**).

11. Remove the retaining clip (**Figure 8**) from the pad pin groove.

12. Unscrew and remove the pad pin (**Figure 9**) and discard it.

13. Remove the inboard and outboard brake pads from the caliper.

14. Remove the pad spring (**Figure 10**) if damaged or worn.

13

15. Check the brake pads for wear or damage. Measure the thickness of the brake pad friction material. Replace the brake pads if they are worn to the service limit in Table 1.

16. Carefully remove any rust or corrosion from the brake disc.

17. Thoroughly clean any corrosion or debris from the pad pins.

18. Check the friction surface of the new pads for debris or manufacturing residue. If necessary, clean them off with an aerosol brake cleaner.

NOTE
When purchasing new pads, check with the dealership to make sure the friction compound of the new pad is compatible with the disc material. Remove roughness from the backs of the new pads with a fine-cut file then thoroughly clean them off.

19. Ensure the pad spring (**Figure 10**) is in place.

20. Insert the inboard brake pad (**Figure 11**) into the caliper engaging the square corner of the pad in the caliper slot (**Figure 12**).

21. Insert the outboard brake pad (**Figure 13**) into the caliper engaging the square corner of the pad in the caliper slot (**Figure 14**).

22. Ensure that both brake pads are centered on the spring, and that the friction material is facing the brake disc.

23. Press down on the pad spring and install a new pad pin (**Figure 9**). Thread it in and tighten to 75-102 in.-lb. (8.5 -11.5 N•m).

24. Install the retaining clip (**Figure 8**) into the pad pin groove. Make sure it is seated correctly.

25. Insert the caliper onto the brake disc (**Figure 7**) being careful to not damage the leading end of the pads.

26. Install the bolts (A, **Figure 6**) securing the caliper (B) to the fork slider. On ABS equipped models, install the clip located under the mounting bolts. Tighten the bolts to 28-38 ft.-lb. (37.9 -51.5 N•m).

27. Engage the two prongs (A, **Figure 15**) on the screen beneath the caliper lower slot. Press the screen on and engage the single prong (B, **Figure 15**) is engaged, ensure engagement.

28. Make sure there is sufficient brake fluid in the master cylinder reservoir. Top it off as necessary.

29. On the left side caliper only, install the clips (**Figure 1**) securing the front fender tip lamp wires (models so equipped) and wheel speed sensor wires to the left side caliper brake hose.

30. Remove the swing arm stand.

31. Release the brake lever and pump the brake lever to reposition the brake pads against the brake disc. Roll the motorcycle back and forth. Continue to pump the brake pedal as many times as it takes to refill the cylinders in the caliper and correctly position the brake pads against the disc.

WARNING
Do not ride the motorcycle until the front brake is operating correctly with full hydrau-

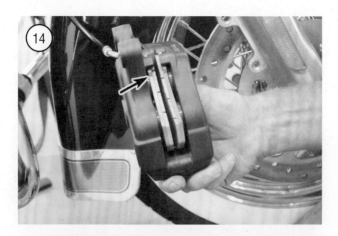

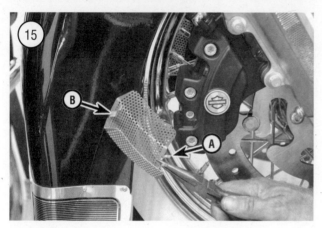

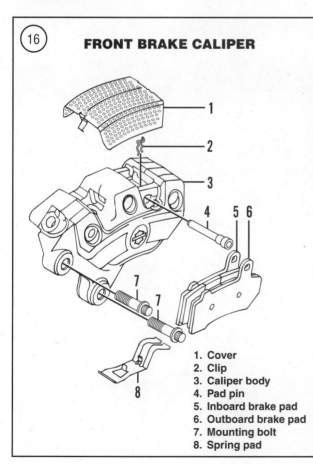

FRONT BRAKE CALIPER

1. Cover
2. Clip
3. Caliper body
4. Pad pin
5. Inboard brake pad
6. Outboard brake pad
7. Mounting bolt
8. Spring pad

lic advantage. If necessary, bleed the brakes as described in this chapter.

CAUTION
The break-in period for new brake pads is the first 100 miles (160 kilometer) of use. During the break-in period, avoid hard braking. Moderately apply the brakes for the first 100 miles (160 kilometers) of operation.

32. Refill the master cylinder reservoir, if necessary, to maintain the correct fluid level as indicated on the side of the reservoir. Install the diaphragm and the top cover. Tighten the screws to the 10-12 in.-lb. (1.1-1.4 N•m).

FRONT BRAKE CALIPER

CAUTION
On ABS equipped models, keep the ABS sensor away from all magnetic fields or it will be damaged.

Removal/Installation

Refer to **Figure 16**.
1. Read *Brake Service Perform* in this chapter.
2. Support the motorcycle on level ground on a swing arm stand.
3. Block the rear wheel so the motorcycle will not roll in either direction.
4A. On the left side caliper only, perform the following:
   a. Remove the clips (**Figure 17**) securing the front fender tip lamp wires (models so equipped) and wheel speed sensor wires to the left side caliper brake hose.
   b. Push in on the lip of the rear of clip (A, **Figure 18**) and release it. Rotate the ABS tab (B, **Figure 18**) toward the rear until the clip is perpendicular to the bracket. Remove the clip and move the cable out of the way.
4B. On all other models so equipped, remove the clips securing the front fender tip lamp wires (models so equipped)

13

and wheel speed sensor wires to the right side caliper brake hose

5. Remove the bleed valve (**Figure 19**) and copper washers securing the brake hose to the caliper assembly. Discard the copper washers.

6. Place the loose end of the brake hose in a plastic bag to prevent the entry of debris and to contain any residual brake fluid leaking out.

7. Remove the bolts (A, **Figure 20**) securing the caliper (B) to the fork slider and remove the caliper from the fork slider **Figure 21**. On ABS equipped models, do not lose the clip located under the mounting bolts. Place the caliper in a plastic bag it is going to be left off for an extended period of time to keep it clean.

8. Insert the caliper onto the brake disc (**Figure 21**) being careful to not damage the leading end of the pads.

9. Install the bolts (A, **Figure 20**) securing the caliper (B) to the fork slider. On ABS equipped models, install the clip located under the mounting bolts. Tighten the bolts to 28-38 ft.-lb. (37.9 -51.5 N•m).

10A. On ABS equipped models, perform the following:

   a. Rotate the ABS tab until the clip is perpendicular to the bracket and install the cable.

   b. Rotate the ABS tab (B, **Figure 18**) toward the front until the clip is in-line with the bracket, and apply pressure to the tab until it is engaged. Gently tug on the cable to make sure the clip is properly installed.

   c. Install the first new clip 2.5 in. (63.5 mm) above the bottom of the brake hose crimp capturing the front wheel sensor cable and brake hose.

   d. Install the second new clip 2.5 in. (63.5 mm) below the top of the brake hose crimp capturing the front wheel sensor cable and brake hose. On models so equipped, also secure the front fender tip lamp wires within this clip.

10B. On non-ABS models equipped models, position the front fender tip lamp wires onto the left-side brake caliper hose. Secure with new cable clip.

NOTE
On some models, an O-ring may have been installed on the bleed valve. On models so equipped, remove and replace the O-ring in the bleed valve. Ensure that no O-ring particles or residue remains in the bleed valve receptacle in the caliper. Thoroughly clean the caliper receptacle to ensure proper sealing and tightening of the bleed valve.

11. Install the bleed valve (**Figure 19**) and new copper washers securing the brake hose to the caliper assembly. Tighten to 17-19 ft.-lb. (23.1-25.8 N•m).

12. Bleed the brakes as described in this chapter.

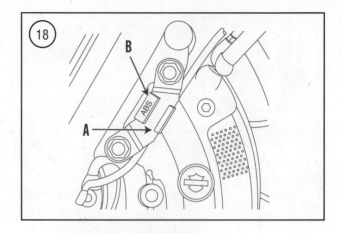

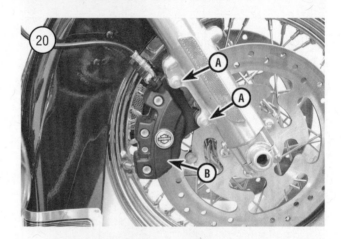

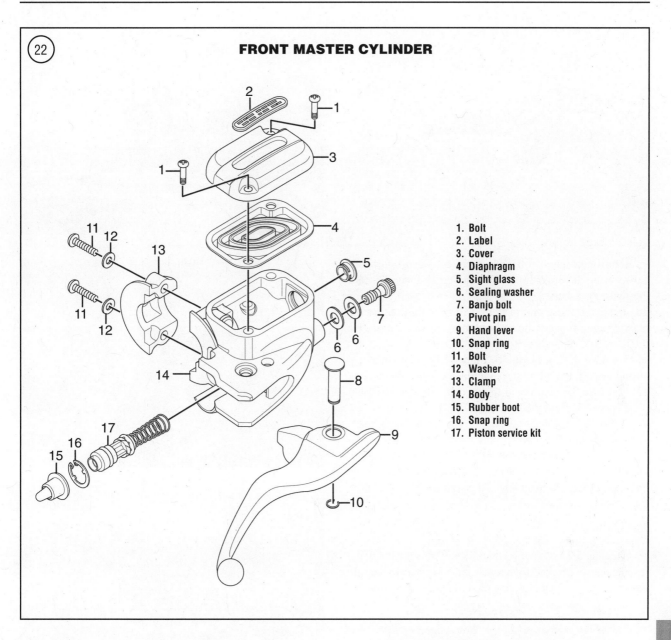

FRONT MASTER CYLINDER

1. Bolt
2. Label
3. Cover
4. Diaphragm
5. Sight glass
6. Sealing washer
7. Banjo bolt
8. Pivot pin
9. Hand lever
10. Snap ring
11. Bolt
12. Washer
13. Clamp
14. Body
15. Rubber boot
16. Snap ring
17. Piston service kit

13

Disassembly

The Brembo caliper assembly cannot be disassembled for service. The only replacement parts available are shown in **Figure 16**.

FRONT MASTER CYLINDER

Removal

Read *Brake Service* in this Chapter and refer to **Figure 22**.

1. Support the motorcycle on level ground on a swing arm stand.

2. Block the rear wheel so the motorcycle will not roll in either direction.

3. Remove the mirror (A, **Figure 23**) from the master cylinder.

4. Clean all debris off the top of the master cylinder.

Caution
*Failure to install the spacer (***Figure 24***) will result in damage to the rubber boot and plunger on the brake light switch within the right side switch assembly.*

5. Insert a 5/32 in. (4 mm) thick spacer (**Figure 24**) between the brake lever and the lever bracket. Ensure the spacer stays in place during the removal procedure.

6. Remove the screws securing the top cover (A, **Figure 25**) and remove the cover and diaphragm (**Figure 26**).

7. Use a shop syringe to draw all of the brake fluid out of the master cylinder reservoir.

8. Temporarily reinstall the diaphragm and the cover. Install the cover screws and finger-tighten them.

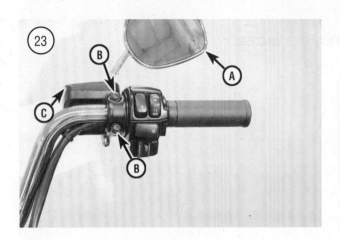

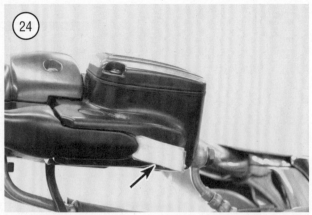

9. Remove the banjo bolt (B, **Figure 25**) and sealing washers securing the brake hose to the master cylinder. Discard the sealing washers.

10. Place the loose end of the brake hose in a reclosable plastic bag to prevent the entry of moisture and debris. Tie the loose end of the hose to the handlebar.

11. Remove the Torx bolts (B, **Figure 23**) and washers securing the clamp and master cylinder to the handlebar.

12. Remove the clamp and the master cylinder assembly (C, **Figure 23**) from the handlebar.

13. Drain any residual brake fluid from the master cylinder and dispose of it properly.

14. If the master cylinder assembly is not going to be serviced, attach the clamp to the master cylinder and reinstall the Torx bolts. Place the assembly in a plastic bag to protect it.

Installation

1. Insert the 5/32 in. (4 mm) thick spacer between the brake lever and lever bracket (**Figure 27**), if not in place. Make sure the spacer stays in place during the installation procedure.

> *CAUTION*
> *Do not damage the front brake light switch and rubber boot when installing the master cylinder.*

2. Position the front master cylinder onto the handlebar. Align the master cylinder notch (**Figure 28**) with the locating tab on the lower portion of the right side switch.

3. Position the clamp and install the Torx bolts (B, **Figure 23**) and washers. Tighten the upper, and then the lower clamp bolt to 71-80 in.-lb (8-9 N•m).

4. Apply clean DOT 4 brake fluid to *new* copper sealing washers prior to installation.

5. Install *new* sealing washers on each side of the hose fitting.

6. Install the banjo bolt (B, **Figure 25**) securing the brake hose to the master cylinder. Tighten the banjo bolt to 12.5-14.5 ft.-lb. (16.9-19.7 N•m).

7. Remove the spacer (**Figure 24**) from the brake lever.

8. Temporarily install the diaphragm (**Figure 26**) and top cover (A, **Figure 25**) onto the reservoir, if not in place. Install the screws and finger-tighten them at this time.

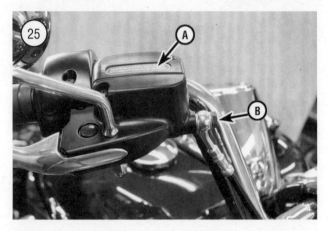

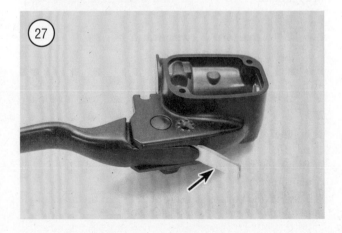

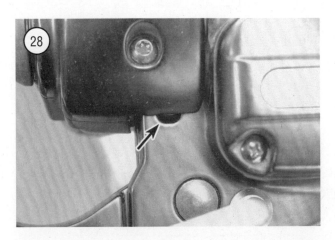

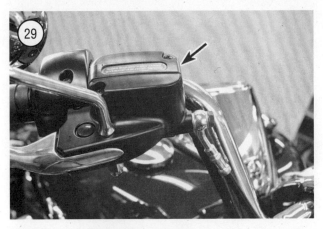

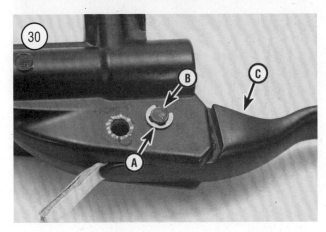

9. Install the mirror onto the master cylinder and adjust to rider preference.

10. Refill the master cylinder reservoir and bleed the front brake system as described in this chapter.

11. Install the diaphragm and cover. Install the cover screws and tighten to 10-12 in.-lb. (1.1-1.4 N•m).

Disassembly

1. Remove the master cylinder assembly as described in this section.

2. Store the master cylinder components in a divided container, such as a restaurant-size egg carton, to help maintain their correct alignment positions.

3. Remove the top cover (**Figure 29**) and the diaphragm (**Figure 26**) from the master cylinder.

4. Remove the E-clip (A, **Figure 30**) and the pivot pin (B) securing the hand lever to the master cylinder. Remove the hand lever (C, **Figure 30**).

5. Remove the pushrod (A, **Figure 31**) and rubber boot (B) from the area where the hand lever actuates the piston assembly.

6. Push down on the piston assembly and remove the snap ring (**Figure 32**).

7. Remove the piston assembly and the spring (**Figure 33**).

8. Inspect all parts as described in this section.

13

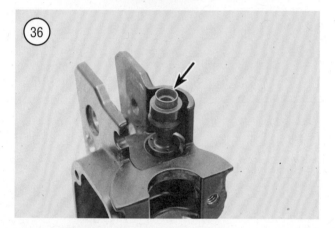

Assembly

1. Coat the inside of the cylinder bore and piston seals with DOT 4 brake fluid, prior to the assembly of parts.
2. Install a bolt into the threaded banjo bolt hole and mount the master cylinder in a vise (**Figure 34**).
3. Position the piston assembly with the spring end going in first (**Figure 35**) and install the piston assembly (**Figure 36**).

> *CAUTION*
> *When installing the piston assembly, do not allow the cup to turn inside out as it will be damaged and allow brake fluid leaks within the cylinder bore.*

4. Push down on the piston assembly (**Figure 36**) and install the snap ring (**Figure 32**). Make sure the snap ring is seated correctly in the master cylinder groove (**Figure 37**).
5. Install the rubber boot (B, **Figure 31**) and pushrod (A). Make sure the rubber boot is seated correctly in the master cylinder groove.
6. Make sure the bushing is in place in the hand lever pivot area.
7. Install the hand lever (C, **Figure 30**) into the master cylinder. Install the pivot pin (B, **Figure 30**) and secure it with the snap ring (A). Make sure the snap ring is correctly seated in the pivot pin groove.
8. Slowly apply the lever to make sure it pivots freely.
9. Install the master cylinder as described in this section.

Inspection

1. Clean all parts in denatured alcohol or clean DOT 4 brake fluid. Inspect the master cylinder bore surface (**Figure 38**) for signs of wear and damage. If it is less than perfect, replace the master cylinder assembly. The body cannot be replaced separately.
2. Make sure the fluid passage (**Figure 39**) in the bottom of the master cylinder body is clear. Clean it out if necessary.
3. Check the hand lever pivot lugs (A, **Figure 40**) in the master cylinder body for cracks or elongation.
4. Inspect the threaded mirror hole (B, **Figure 40**) in the master cylinder body. If it is worn or damaged, clean it out with a thread tap or replace the master cylinder assembly.

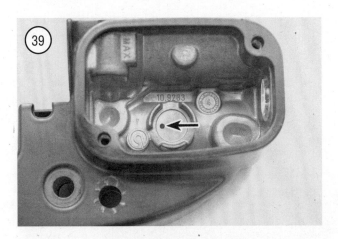

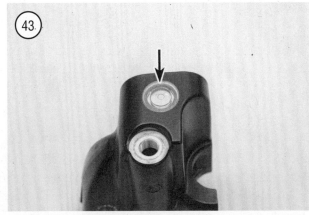

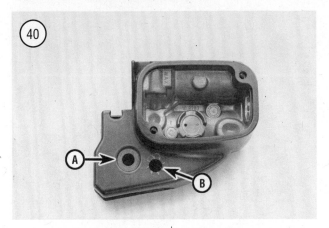

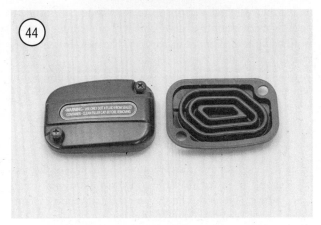

5. Inspect the hand lever pivot hole and bushing (A, **Figure 41**) and the pivot pin (B) for wear, cracks or elongation.

6. Inspect the threaded banjo bolt hole (**Figure 42**). If it is worn or damaged, clean it out with a thread tap or replace the master cylinder assembly.

7. Check the sight glass (**Figure 43**) for signs of brake fluid leaks; replace if necessary.

8. Check the top cover and diaphragm (**Figure 44**) for deterioration, damage or deterioration.

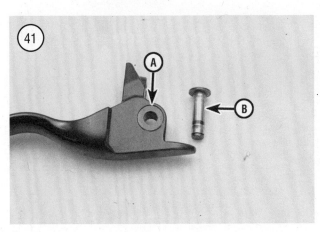

REAR BRAKE PADS

CAUTION
On ABS equipped models, keep the ABS sensor away from all magnetic fields or it will be damaged.

Replacement

1. Read *Brake Service* in this chapter.

2. Support the motorcycle on level ground on a swing arm stand.

3. Block the front wheel so the motorcycle will not roll in either direction with the rear wheel off the ground.

4. Remove the right side saddlebag as described in Chapter Fourteen.

5. Remove the right side muffler as described in Chapter Four.

13

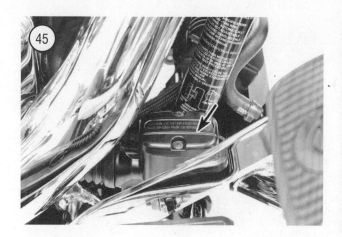

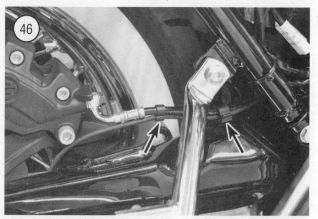

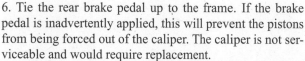

6. Tie the rear brake pedal up to the frame. If the brake pedal is inadvertently applied, this will prevent the pistons from being forced out of the caliper. The caliper is not serviceable and would require replacement.

7. To prevent the master cylinder from overflowing while reposition the pistons in the brake caliper, perform the following:

    a. Clean all dirt from the top of the master cylinder.

    b. Remove the cover screws and remove the cover (**Figure 45**) and diaphragm.

    c. Use a shop syringe and remove about 50% of the reservoir to prevent overflow. Do no drain more than 50% of the brake fluid or air will enter the system. Discard the brake fluid properly.

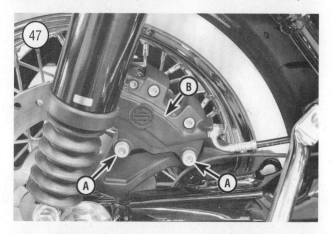

8. Place several shop cloths on the saddlebag support rail to protect the finish.

9. On ABS equipped models, remove the clips (**Figure 46**) securing the ABS cable to the rear brake hose.

10. Remove the bolts (A, **Figure 47**) securing the caliper (B) to the caliper mounting bracket.

CAUTION
The brake disc is thin and easily damaged.
When pushing against the disc in the following step, support the disc adjacent to the caliper to prevent damage.

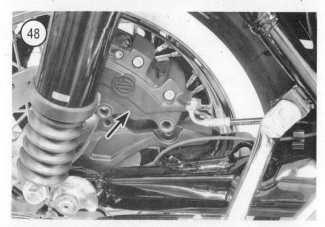

11. Hold the outboard side of the caliper body and push it toward the brake disc. This pushes the outer pistons into the caliper cylinders to make room for the new brake pads. Constantly check the reservoir. Remove fluid, if necessary, before it overflows. Install the diaphragm and cover. Tighten the cover screws finger-tight.

12. Carefully side the caliper off the brake disc (**Figure 48**).

13. Remove the retaining clip (**Figure 49**) from the pad pin groove.

14. Unscrew and remove the pad pin (**Figure 50**) and discard it.

15. Remove the inboard and outboard brake pads from the caliper.

16. Remove the pad spring (**Figure 51**) if damaged or worn.

17. Check the brake pads for wear or damage. Measure the thickness of the brake pad friction material. Replace the brake pads if they are worn to the service limit in Table 1.

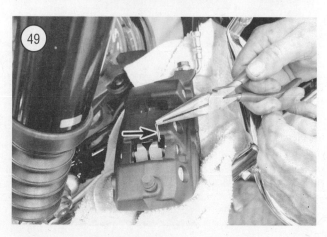

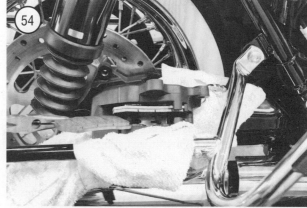

18. Carefully remove any rust or corrosion from the brake disc.

19. Thoroughly clean any corrosion or debris from the pad pins.

20. Check the friction surface of the new pads for debris or manufacturing residue. If necessary, clean them off with an aerosol brake cleaner.

NOTE
When purchasing new pads, check with the dealership to make sure the friction compound of the new pad is compatible with the disc material. Remove roughness from the backs of the new pads with a fine-cut file then thoroughly clean them off.

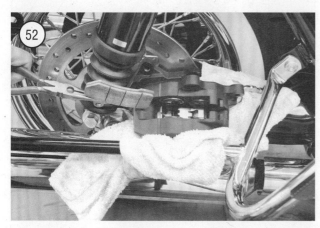

21. Ensure the pad spring (**Figure 51**) is in place. If removed, seat the new pad spring in the flat in the caliper so the clips on the spring engage the indentations in the caliper. Ensure the forked end of the spring is on the pad pin side of the caliper.

22. Insert the outboard brake pad (**Figure 52**) into the caliper engaging the square corner of the pad in the caliper slot (**Figure 53**).

23. Insert the inboard brake pad (**Figure 54**) into the caliper engaging the square corner of the pad in the caliper slot (**Figure 55**).

24. Ensure that both brake pads are centered on the spring, and that the friction material is facing the brake disc.

13

25. Press down on the pad spring and install a new pad pin (**Figure 50**). Thread it in and tighten to 75-102 in.-lb. (8.5 -11.5 N•m).

26. Install the retaining clip (**Figure 49**) into the pad pin groove. Make sure it is seated correctly.

27. Insert the caliper onto the brake disc (**Figure 48**) being careful to not damage the leading end of the pads.

28. Install the bolts (A, **Figure 47**) securing the caliper (B) to the caliper mounting bracket. On ABS equipped models, install the clips (**Figure 46**) securing the ABS cable to the rear brake hose. Tighten the bolts to 43-48 ft.-lb. (58.3 -65.1 N•m).

29. Make sure there is sufficient brake fluid in the master cylinder reservoir. Top it off as necessary.

30. Remove the swing arm stand.

31. Release the brake pedal and pump the brake pedal to reposition the new brake pads against the brake disc. Roll the motorcycle back and forth. Continue to pump the brake pedal as many times as it takes to refill the cylinders in the caliper and correctly position the brake pads against the disc.

WARNING
Do not ride the motorcycle until the rear brake is operating correctly with full hydraulic advantage. If necessary, bleed the brakes as described in this chapter.

CAUTION
The break-in period for new brake pads is the first 100 miles (160 kilometer) of use. During the break-in period, avoid hard braking. Moderately apply the brakes for the first 100 miles (160 kilometers) of operation.

32. Refill the master cylinder reservoir, if necessary, to maintain the correct fluid level as indicated on the side of the reservoir. Install the diaphragm and the top cover. Tighten the screws to the 12-15 in.-lb. (1.4-1.7 N•m).

33. Install the right side muffler as described in Chapter Four.

34. Install the right side saddlebag as described in Chapter Fourteen.

REAR BRAKE CALIPER

CAUTION
On ABS equipped models, keep the ABS sensor away from all magnetic fields or it will be damaged.

Removal/Installation

1. Read *Brake Service Preform* in this chapter.
2. Support the motorcycle on level ground on a swing arm stand.

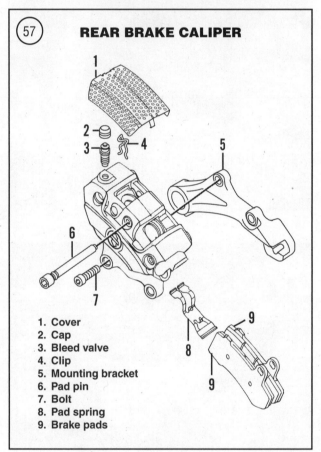

REAR BRAKE CALIPER

1. Cover
2. Cap
3. Bleed valve
4. Clip
5. Mounting bracket
6. Pad pin
7. Bolt
8. Pad spring
9. Brake pads

3. Block the front wheel so the motorcycle will not roll in either direction.

4. Remove the right side saddlebag as described in Chapter Fourteen.

5. Remove the right side muffler as described in Chapter Four.

6. Tie the rear brake pedal up to the frame. If the brake pedal is inadvertently applied, this will prevent the pistons from being forced out of the caliper. The caliper is not serviceable and would require replacement.

7. On ABS equipped models, remove the clips (**Figure 46**) securing the ABS cable to the rear brake hose.

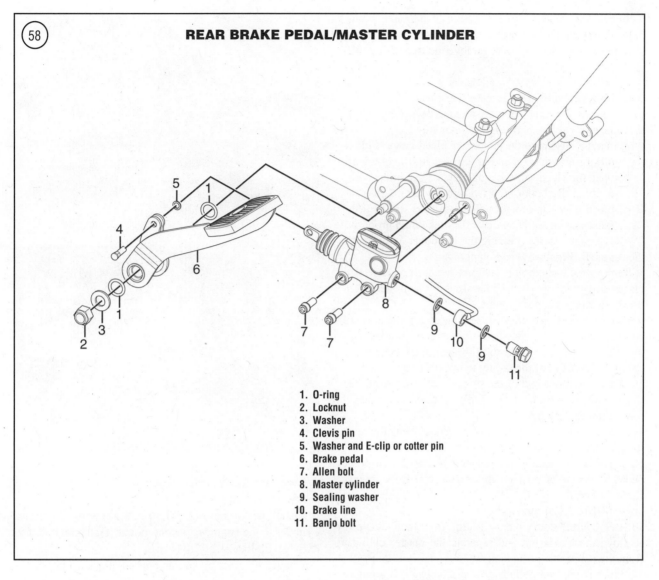

58

REAR BRAKE PEDAL/MASTER CYLINDER

1. O-ring
2. Locknut
3. Washer
4. Clevis pin
5. Washer and E-clip or cotter pin
6. Brake pedal
7. Allen bolt
8. Master cylinder
9. Sealing washer
10. Brake line
11. Banjo bolt

8. Remove the banjo bolt (A, **Figure 56**) and copper wash-ers securing the brake hose to the caliper assembly. Discard the copper washers.

9. Place the loose end of the brake hose in a plastic bag to prevent the entry of debris and to contain any residual brake fluid leaking out.

10. Remove the bolts (B, **Figure 56**) securing the caliper to the caliper mounting bracket. Place the caliper in a plastic bag it is going to be left off for an extended period of time to keep it clean.

11. Insert the caliper onto the brake disc being careful to not damage the leading end of the pads.

12. Install the bolts (B, **Figure 56**) securing the caliper (A) to the caliper mounting bracket. Tighten the bolts to 43-48 ft.-lb. (58.3 -65.1 N•m).

13. Install the banjo bolt (A, **Figure 56**) and new copper washers securing the brake hose to the caliper assembly. Tighten to 17-19 ft.-lb. (23.1-25.8 N•m).

14. Bleed the brakes as described in this chapter.

15. Install the right side muffler as described in Chapter Four.

16. Install the right side saddlebag as described in Chapter Fourteen.

Disassembly

The Brembo brake caliper cannot be disassembled for ser-vice. The only replacement parts are shown in **Figure 57.**

**REAR MASTER CYLINDER
AND BRAKE PEDAL**

Removal

Refer to **Figure 58**.

1. Read *Brake Service Preform* in this chapter.

2. Support the motorcycle on level ground on a swing arm stand.

3. Block the front wheel so the motorcycle will not roll in either direction.

13

4. Remove the exhaust system as described in Chapter Four.

5. Refer to Chapter Fourteen and perform the following:

    a. On models so equipped, remove the right side lower fairing.

    b. Remove the right side saddlebag.

    c. Remove the right side frame side cover.

    d. Remove the right side rider footboard (A, **Figure 59**).

6. At the rear caliper, perform the following:

    a. Insert a hose onto the end of the bleed valve (**Figure 60**). Insert the open end of the hose into a container.

    b. Open the bleed valve and operate the rear brake pedal to drain the brake fluid from the system. Close the bleed valve and remove the hose after draining the master cylinder. Dispose of the brake fluid properly.

7. Remove the screws securing the top cover and remove the cover (B, **Figure 59**) and diaphragm.

8. Remove the banjo bolt (C, **Figure 59**) and copper washers securing the brake hose to the front of the master cylinder. Discard the copper washers.

9. Release any clips or ties securing the rear brake line and wiring harness to the chassis. Remove only enough to allow slack in the break line to allow removal of the brake line from the front of the master cylinder fitting.

10. Place the loose end of the brake hose in a plastic bag to prevent the entry of debris and to contain any residual brake fluid leaking out.

11. Remove the two bolts (D, **Figure 59**) securing the master cylinder to the engine cap front mount.

12. Remove the locknut and washer securing the rear brake pedal to the pivot post on the engine cap front mount. Remove and discard the O-ring seal on each side of the brake pedal. Discard the locknut.

13. Remove the cotter pin, or E-clip, from the clevis pin. Remove the clevis pin and separate the master cylinder from the rear brake pedal flange.

14. Place the master cylinder in a plastic bag it is going to be left off for an extended period of time to keep it clean.

Installation

1. If the master cylinder was disconnected from the brake pedal flange, perform the following:

    a. Reposition the master cylinder onto the rear brake pedal.

    b. Support the assembly in a vise and tap the clevis pin into both parts from the outboard side of the brake pedal. Tap it in until it bottoms.

    c. Install the washer and a new cotter pin or E-clip. If a cotter pin is used, bend the ends if the pin over completely.

2. Install a new O-ring on each side of the brake pivot bore.

3. Apply a light coat of wheel bearing grease to the brake shaft pivot bore and pivot post on the engine cap front mount.

4. Install the rear master cylinder and rear brake assembly on to the pivot post.

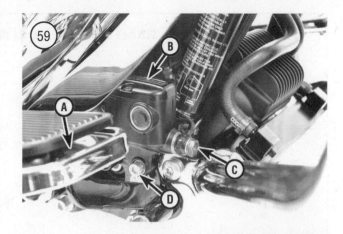

5. Install the washer and new locknut. Tighten the locknut to 15-20 ft.-lb. (20.3-27.1 N•m).

6. Install the two bolts (D, **Figure 59**) securing the master cylinder to the engine cap front mount. Tighten the bolt to 125-150 in.-lb. (14.2-17.0 N•m).

7. Connect the rear brake line onto the front of the master cylinder.

8. Install the banjo bolt (C, **Figure 59**) and new copper washers securing the brake hose to the master cylinder. Tighten to 12.5-14.5 ft.-lb. (16.9-19.7 N•m).

9. Securing the rear brake line and wiring harness to the chassis with *end* clips. Ensure the clips are secure.

10. Bleed the rear brake as described in this chapter.

11. Refer to Chapter Fourteen and perform the following:

    a. Install the right side rider footboard (A, **Figure 59**).

    b. Install the right side frame side cover.

    c. Install the right side saddlebag.

    d. On models so equipped, install the right side lower fairing.

12. Install the exhaust system as described in Chapter Four.

Rear Brake Pedal Inspection

Refer to **Figure 61** or and **Figure 62**.

1. If still in place, remove both O-rings from the pivot bore.

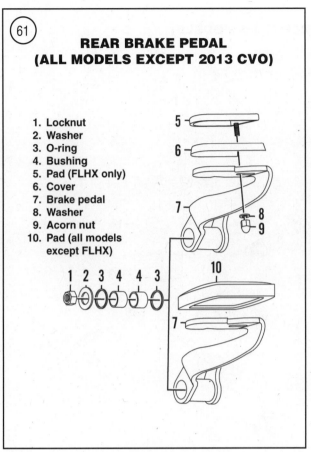

61 REAR BRAKE PEDAL
(ALL MODELS EXCEPT 2013 CVO)

1. Locknut
2. Washer
3. O-ring
4. Bushing
5. Pad (FLHX only)
6. Cover
7. Brake pedal
8. Washer
9. Acorn nut
10. Pad (all models except FLHX)

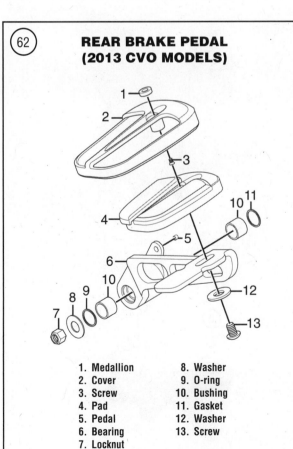

62 REAR BRAKE PEDAL
(2013 CVO MODELS)

1. Medallion	8. Washer
2. Cover	9. O-ring
3. Screw	10. Bushing
4. Pad	11. Gasket
5. Pedal	12. Washer
6. Bearing	13. Screw
7. Locknut	

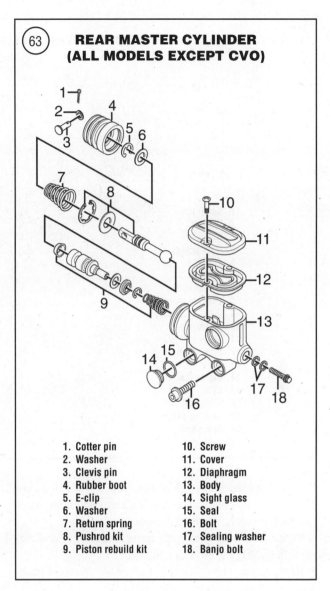

63 REAR MASTER CYLINDER
(ALL MODELS EXCEPT CVO)

1. Cotter pin	10. Screw
2. Washer	11. Cover
3. Clevis pin	12. Diaphragm
4. Rubber boot	13. Body
5. E-clip	14. Sight glass
6. Washer	15. Seal
7. Return spring	16. Bolt
8. Pushrod kit	17. Sealing washer
9. Piston rebuild kit	18. Banjo bolt

2. Inspect the pivot bushings within the pivot bore for wear or damage.

3. Carefully press out the old bushings and install new bushings, if necessary.

4. Install a new O-ring on each side of the brake pivot bore.

5. Inspect the rear brake pedal for cracks or damage; replace as necessary.

REAR MASTER CYLINDER

Disassembly

Refer to **Figure 63** or **Figure 64**.

1. Remove the master cylinder as described in this chapter.

2. Clean the exterior of the master cylinder housing with clean DOT 4 brake fluid or isopropyl alcohol. Completely dry it with compressed air.

13

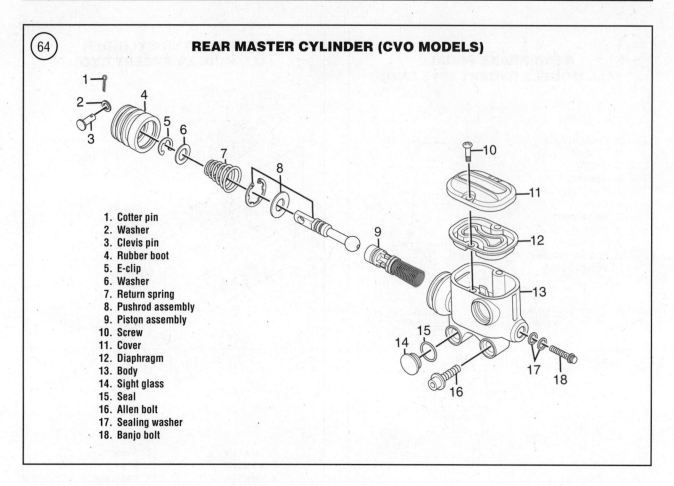

REAR MASTER CYLINDER (CVO MODELS)

1. Cotter pin
2. Washer
3. Clevis pin
4. Rubber boot
5. E-clip
6. Washer
7. Return spring
8. Pushrod assembly
9. Piston assembly
10. Screw
11. Cover
12. Diaphragm
13. Body
14. Sight glass
15. Seal
16. Allen bolt
17. Sealing washer
18. Banjo bolt

3. Store the master cylinder components in a divided container, such as a restaurant-size egg carton, to help maintain their correct alignment positions.

4. Remove the master cylinder cover (**Figure 65**) and diaphragm (A, **Figure 66**) if is still installed.

5. Remove the rubber boot (B, **Figure 66**) from the pushrod.

> *WARNING*
> *On 2013 CVO models, the return spring is very strong as it also the brake pedal return spring. Protect your hands accordingly.*

6. Compress the return spring and remove the E-clip and washer (**Figure 67**). Carefully release the pressure on the spring.

7. Stand the master cylinder on its fluid port so the reservoir clears the edge of the bench. Press the large washer to compress the piston assembly, and remove the snap ring (**Figure 68**).

8. Remove the pushrod assembly (**Figure 69**).

9. Remove the piston assembly (**Figure 70**) from the cartridge.

Assembly

1. Coat all parts with clean DOT 4 brake fluid.

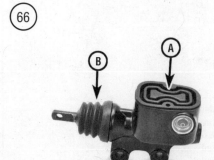

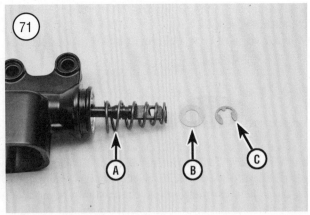

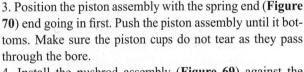

2. Soak the primary cup, O-ring and piston assembly in clean DOT 4 brake fluid for 15 minutes to make them pliable. Coat the inside of the cartridge bore with clean brake fluid prior to the assembling the parts.

CAUTION
When installing the piston assembly, do not allow the primary cup to turn inside out as it will be damaged and allow brake fluid leaks in the cartridge cylinder bore.

3. Position the piston assembly with the spring end (**Figure 70**) end going in first. Push the piston assembly until it bottoms. Make sure the piston cups do not tear as they pass through the bore.

4. Install the pushrod assembly (**Figure 69**) against the pushrod assembly.

5. Turn the reservoir on its end on a shop cloth. Carefully push the piston assembly into the cartridge with a Phillips screwdriver. Push the piston assembly in and let it move out several times to check for ease of movement.

6. Position the pushrod onto the end of the piston and push the piston into the cartridge. Hold the pushrod in place and install the snap ring (**Figure 68**). Make sure the snap ring is correctly seated in the cartridge groove.

7. Install the spring (A, **Figure 71**) onto the pushrod.

8. Compress the spring (A, **Figure 72**) and install the washer (B, **Figure 71**) and E-clip (C, **Figure 71**) onto the push-

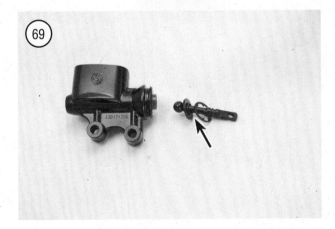

13

rod. Ensure the E-clip (B, **Figure 72**) is properly seated in the pushrod groove.

9. Install the dust boot (B, **Figure 66**) down, and seat it on the reservoir bore lip.

10. Install the diaphragm (A, **Figure 66**) and reservoir cover (A, **Figure 65**).

Inspection

1. Clean all parts in clean DOT 4 brake fluid or isopropyl alcohol and dry them with compressed air. Replace worn or damage parts as described in this section. It is recommended that a new cartridge rebuild kit assembly be installed every time the master cylinder is disassembled.

2. Check for wear or damage on the surface of the cylinder bore (**Figure 73**) in the cartridge body. Do not hone the bore to clean or repair it. If it is less than perfect, replace the cartridge and/or the master cylinder reservoir.

3. Inspect the banjo bolt thread hole (**Figure 74**) for thread damage and repair if necessary.

NOTE
The piston and spring are available only as an assembly.

4. Check the piston primary and secondary cups (A, **Figure 75**) for deterioration or damage.

5. Check the spring (B, **Figure 75**) for bent, unequally spaced coils or corrosion.

6. Inspect the boot for tears or deterioration.

7. Check the clevis/pushrod/spacer assembly and snap ring for bending, wear or damage.

8. Check the reservoir body (**Figure 76**) for corrosion or other damage.

9. Check the reservoir cap and diaphragm for damage.

BRAKE HOSE AND LINE REPLACEMENT (NON-ABS MODELS)

A combination of metal brake pipes and flexible brake hoses connect the master cylinder to the brake calipers. Banjo fittings connect brake hoses to the master cylinder and brake calipers. At each connection, the banjo bolt is sealed with combination steel/rubber sealing washers. Replace the sealing washers every time a fitting is disassembled.

Replace the brake line assembly if the flexible portion is swelling, if cracking or other damage is visible, if the metal brake pipes leak or if there are dents or cracks. When replacing a new brake line assembly, make sure the length and angle of the steel pipe portions are correct. Install *new* banjo bolt sealing washers at the same time.

Read *Brake Service* in this chapter.

Front Brake Hose Removal/Installation

Refer to **Figure 77**.

1. Support the motorcycle on level ground on a swing arm stand.

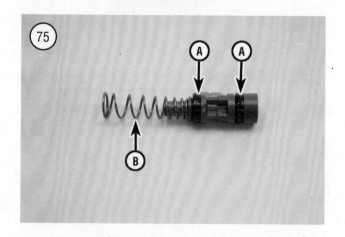

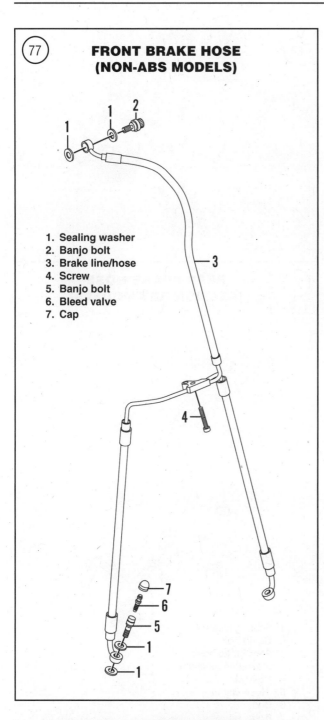

77 **FRONT BRAKE HOSE (NON-ABS MODELS)**

1. Sealing washer
2. Banjo bolt
3. Brake line/hose
4. Screw
5. Banjo bolt
6. Bleed valve
7. Cap

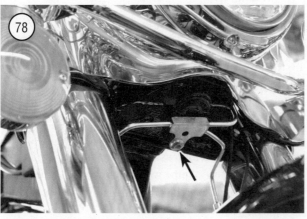

78

79

2. Block the rear wheel so the motorcycle will not roll in either direction.

3. On models so equipped, refer to Chapter Fourteen and remove all necessary front fairing panels necessary to gain access to the front brake line where it attaches to the lower steering stem.

4. Drain the front brake systems as described in *Brake Fluid Draining* (this chapter).

5. Remove the fuel tank as described in Chapter Eight.

6. Before removing the brake line assembly, note the brake line routing from the master cylinder to the calipers. In addition, note the number and position of any metal hose clamps and/or plastic ties used to hold the brake lines in place. Install the brake hose assembly along its original path. The metal clamps can be reused.

7. Cut any plastic ties securing the brake line assembly and discard them.

8. Remove the bolt (**Figure 78**) securing the brake hose mounting plate to the lower steering stem. On models so equipped, do not lose the guide plate between the hose mounting plate and the steering stem.

9. Remove the screw or nut securing the metal clamps around the brake line. Spread the clamp and remove it from the brake line.

10. Remove the banjo bolt (**Figure 79**) and washers securing the hose to each front brake caliper.

11. Remove the banjo bolt (**Figure 80**) and washers securing the hose to the front master cylinder.

12. Cover the ends of the brake hoses to prevent brake fluid from leaking onto the motorcycle.

13. Carefully remove the brake hose assembly from the frame.

14. If the existing brake hose assembly is going to be reinstalled, inspect it as follows:

    a. Check the metal pipes where they enter and exit at the flexible hoses. Check the crimped clamp for looseness or damage.

    b. Check the flexible hose portions for swelling, cracks or other damage.

    c. If any wear or damage is found, replace the brake hose assembly.

13

15. Install the brake hose, washers and banjo bolts in the reverse order of removal while noting the following:

    a. Install *new* sealing washers on each side of the hose fitting.

    b. Carefully install the clips and guides to hold the brake hose in place.

    c. Tighten the banjo bolts to the specification listed in **Table 2**.

    d. Refill the front master cylinder with clean DOT 4 brake fluid. Bleed the front brake system as described in this chapter.

Rear Brake Hose
Removal/Installation

Refer to **Figure 81**.

1. Support the motorcycle on level ground on a swing arm stand.

2. Block the front wheel so the motorcycle will not roll in either direction while the rear wheel is off ground.

3. Remove the right side frame side cover and the saddlebag as described in Chapter Seventeen.

4. Remove the right passenger footboard as described in Chapter Seventeen.

5. Remove the exhaust system as described in Chapter Four.

6. Drain the hydraulic brake fluid from the rear brake system as follows:

    a. Connect a hose to the rear caliper bleed valve. Refer to A, **Figure 82** (typical).

    b. Insert the loose end of the hose in a container to catch the brake fluid.

    c. Open the caliper bleed valve and operate the rear brake pedal to pump the fluid out of the master cylinder and brake line assembly. Continue until all of the fluid is removed.

    d. Close the bleed valve and disconnect the hose.

7. Before removing the brake line assembly, note the brake line routing from the master cylinder to the caliper. In addition, note the number and position of the metal hose clamps, plastic clips and plastic ties used to hold the brake line in place. Install the brake hose assembly along its original path. The metal clamp and plastic clips can be reused. However, new plastic ties must be installed.

8. Insert a screwdriver into the plastic clip and release the top portion. Repeat for the second clip and release the brake line from the frame.

9. Disconnect the electrical connector from the rear brake line switch.

10. Secure the fitting on the rear brake line with a wrench and unscrew the brake light switch from the fitting. Remove the bake light switch and place in a re-closable plastic bag if it is going to be reinstalled.

11. Remove the bolt securing the mounting bracket, below the brake light switch, to the frame.

12. Remove the banjo bolt (**Figure 82**) and sealing washers securing the brake hose to the caliper.

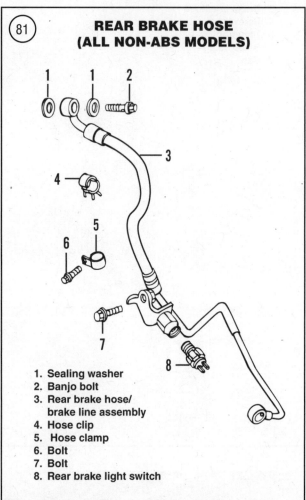

REAR BRAKE HOSE (ALL NON-ABS MODELS)

1. Sealing washer
2. Banjo bolt
3. Rear brake hose/ brake line assembly
4. Hose clip
5. Hose clamp
6. Bolt
7. Bolt
8. Rear brake light switch

13. Remove the banjo bolt (**Figure 83**) and sealing washers securing the brake hose to the master cylinder.

14. Carefully move the rear brake line assembly forward and away from the swing arm bracket.

15. If the existing brake hose assembly is going to be reinstalled, inspect it as follows:

    a. Check the metal pipe where it is attached to the flexible hose. Check the crimped clamp for looseness or damage.

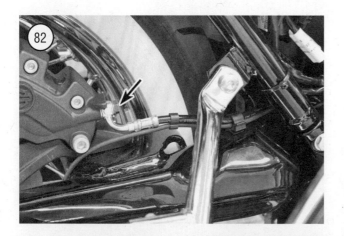

b. Check the rear flexible hose portion for swelling, cracks or other damage.

c. Check the metal pipe for any dent(s) or corrosion.

d. If any wear or damage is found, replace the brake hose.

16. If the brake light switch was removed, apply Loctite Pipe Sealant with Teflon 565 to the threads prior to installation. Secure the rear brake line fitting with a wrench and thread in the brake light switch. Tighten the switch to 12.5-14.5 ft.-lb. (16.9-19.7 N•m).

17. Install by reversing these removal step. Note the following:

a. Install new sealing washers on each side of the brake hose fittings.

b. Install the mounting bracket to the frame, indexing the locating tab into the slot in the frame. Tighten the bolt to 80-100 in.-lb. (9.0-11.3 N•m).

c. Carefully install the brake hose into the frame clips and lock the clips closed.

d. Tighten the banjo bolts to 12.5-14.5 ft.-lb. (16.9-19.7 N•m).

ABS BRAKE SYSTEM

The Anti-lock Brake System (ABS) is designed to prevent wheel lockup.

The ABS system consists of the ABS module assembly that controls the sensing and control functions of the system. The ABS module receives a signal from the ABS sensors located at each wheel, and they relay information regarding wheel rotation speed from the sensors to the ABS module.

The ABS module assembly consists of the hydraulic control unit (HCU) and the electronic control unit (ECU) they are separate components and can be replaced separately, if necessary. The hydraulic control unit (HCU) contains four solenoid valves (an apply valve and release valve for each wheel), two pumps, a pump motor and accumulators. The ABS module assembly is located on the right side in the battery caddy along with the battery. Also, there is an ABS diode pack attached to the fuse block under the left frame side cover.

The ABS module assembly interprets the signals from the wheel sensors (encoder wheel bearings located within each wheel hub) and sends this information to the various solenoid valves to prevent wheel lockup. When the master cylinder lever or pedal is applied, hydraulic pressure at the master cylinder is transmitted through the pressure modulator and then to the caliper assembly for braking action. During ABS braking there will be rapid pulsations felt in the brake lever and/or pedal. These pulsations are caused by the rapid changes in the positions of the individual solenoid valves within the module. This is normal.

Brake pressure is critical in an ABS system. The brake hoses are designed with specific characteristics. When replacing the brake hoses, or hose and metal brake line assembly, install only hoses specifically designed for use with the specific ABS system. Using a brake hose of an alternate design may the change the characteristics of the brake system.

If the ABS system malfunctions, the brakes will operate without ABS assist. If the ABS icon illuminates on the speedometer face, refer to *Electronic Diagnostic System* in Chapter Two for fault codes and troubleshooting information.

The ABS indicator icon will illuminate after start up and will go off after the motorcycle reaches a speed greater than 10 mph (16 km/h). The icon will illuminate during a bulb check and will stay on when a malfunction has occurred within the system and a DTC has been set.

After more than one brake line has been removed, the system must be checked by a dealership with the H-D digital technician to make sure the system is properly connected. This must be done for safety concerns as well as maintaining any applicable warranty.

ABS WHEEL SPEED SENSORS

CAUTION
Keep the ABS sensor and the ABS encoder wheel bearings away from magnetic fields or they will be damaged.

13

Front Wheel

Removal

1A. On frame mounted fairing models, perform the following:

    a. Turn the front wheel to the full left fork stop.

    b. Follow the speed sensor wire from the front sensor, up the fork leg and the left side of the front fairing bracket.

    c. Gently pull the front sensor wire until the 2-pin electrical connector (167A), containing one red and one black wire, is visible. Disconnect the connector.

    d. Pull the wire and connector housing down through the opening in the front fork bracket.

1B. On Road King and fork mounted fairing models, perform the following:

    a. Turn the front wheel to the full left fork stop.

    b. Follow the speed sensor wire from the front sensor and reach under the headlamp nacelle, or front fairing, on the left side of the steering head.

    c. Gently pull the front sensor wire until the 2-pin electrical connector (167A), containing one red and one black wire is visible. Disconnect the connector.

    d. Pull the wire and connector housing down through the opening in the front fork bracket.

2. Carefully cut the two cable straps and release the wheel sensor wire from the front brake hose and front fender tip lamp cables, if equipped.

3. Release the wheel sensor wire as follows:

    a. Push in on lip at the rear of clip (A, **Figure 84**) and release it.

    b. Rotate the ABS tab (B, **Figure 84**) toward the rear until the clip is perpendicular to the bracket. Remove the clip and move the cable out of the way.

CAUTION
Do not try to remove the ABS sensor without first completely removing the front axle. The sensor is captured within a recess in the front hub assembly and the fork slider.

4. Remove the front wheel (A, **Figure 85**) as described in Chapter Ten. Remove the wheel sensor (B, **Figure 85**). Remove the wheel sensor and partially reinstall the front wheel to secure the motorcycle.

Installation

1. Remove the front wheel (A, **Figure 85**) as described in Chapter Ten.

2. Move the wheel sensor (B, **Figure 85**) into position and reinstall the front wheel (Chapter Ten).

3. Rotate the ABS sensor *counterclockwise* until the index mark (**Figure 86**) makes contact with the left fork slider.

4A. On frame mounted fairing models, perform the following:

    a. Turn the front wheel to the full left fork stop.

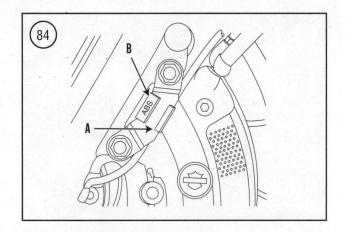

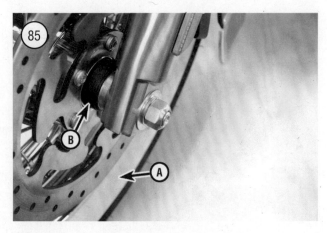

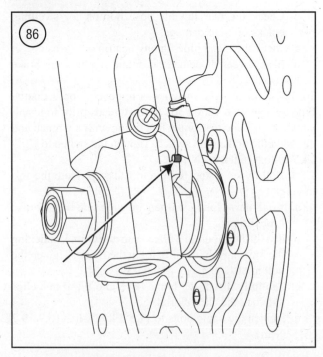

    b. Locate the harness 2-pin connector on the left side of the front fairing bracket.

    c. Feed the front wheel speed sensor wire and connector, up the fork leg and the left side of the front fairing bracket.

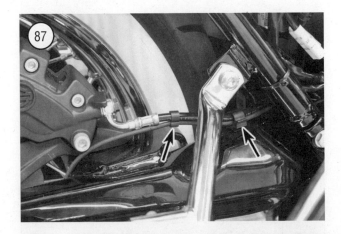

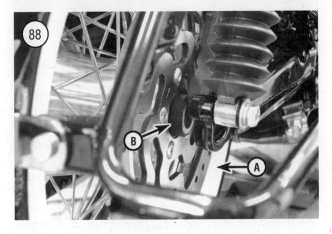

c. Push in on lip at the rear of clip (A, **Figure 84**) and lock it in place.

Rear Wheel

Removal

1. Remove the right saddlebag and frame side cover as described in Chapter Seventeen.
2. On the right side of the electrical caddy, pull the anchor on the rear wheel sensor wire through the hole in the caddy.
3. Disconnect the electrical connector.
4. Insert a small flat blade screwdriver into the gap at the side of the clip. Gently rotate the screwdriver and open cable clip on T-stud on top of swing arm.
5. Refer to Chapter Twelve and partially remove the rear axle until the wheel sensor is free. Remove the wheel sensor and push the rear axle back through the right side of the swing arm. Install the axle nut finger-tight.

Installation

1. Remove the rear axle nut and withdraw the rear axle (Chapter Twelve) sufficiently to install the wheel sensor.
2. Move the ABS sensor into position adjacent to the rear brake caliper mounting bracket and align the front axle holes. Push the rear axle from the left side until it bottoms.
3. Refer to Chapter Twelve and complete the installation of the rear axle and nut.
4. Rotate the ABS sensor until the index pin (A, **Figure 157**) makes contact with the caliper bracket notch (B).

Rear Wheel

Removal

1. Remove the right side saddlebag and frame side cover as described in Chapter Fourteen.
2. Follow the rear wheel speed sensor electrical wire cable up toward the left side of the battery tray, and disconnect the electrical connector.
3. Carefully cut, or release, the clips (**Figure 87**) securing the rear wheel speed sensor electrical cable to the rear caliper brake hose.

CAUTION
Do not try to remove the ABS sensor without first completely removing the rear axle. The sensor is captured within a recess in the rear hub assembly and the caliper mounting bracket.

4. Remove the rear wheel (A, **Figure 88**) as described in Chapter Ten. Remove the wheel sensor (B, **Figure 88**). Remove the wheel sensor and partially reinstall the rear wheel to secure the motorcycle.

d. Reconnect the speed sensor 2-pin electrical connector onto the harness connector. Push on connector until it locked into place.

4B. On Road King and fork mounted fairing models, perform the following:
  a. Turn the front wheel to the full left fork stop.
  b. Locate the harness 2-pin connector adjacent to the opening in the front fork bracket.
  c. Feed the front wheel speed sensor wire and connector up through the headlamp nacelle, or front fairing, on the left side of the steering head.
  d. Reconnect the speed sensor 2-pin electrical connector onto the harness connector. Push on connector until it locked into place.

5. Install a new cable strap 2.5 in. (63.5 mm) above the bottom of the brake hose crimp. Secure the front wheel sensor wire and front fender tip lamp electrical wires, if equipped.
6. Install a second new cable strap 2.5 in. (63.5 mm) above the top of the brake hose crimp. Secure the front wheel sensor wire and front fender tip lamp electrical wires, if equipped.
7. Secure the wheel sensor wire as follows:
  a. Move the wire into position in the bracket.
  b. Rotate the ABS tab (B, **Figure 84**) toward the front until the clip is inline with the bracket. Press on the tab until the tab lip is engaged.

13

Installation

1. Lift the rear wheel into position and partially install the rear axle from the left side and into the wheel hub.
2. Move the ABS sensor (B, **Figure 88**) into position on the right side hub.
3. Continue to push the rear axle through the ABS sensor, rear caliper mounting bracket and the other side of the swing arm. Push the rear axle in until it bottoms.
4. Rotate the ABS sensor until the index pin (A, **Figure 89**) makes contact with the caliper bracket notch (B).
5. Continue installation of rear wheel (A, **Figure 88**) as described in Chapter Ten.
6. Install the clips (**Figure 87**) securing the to the rear caliper brake hose.
7. Connect the rear wheel sensor electrical connector.
8. Install the right side frame side cover and saddlebag as described in Chapter Fourteen.

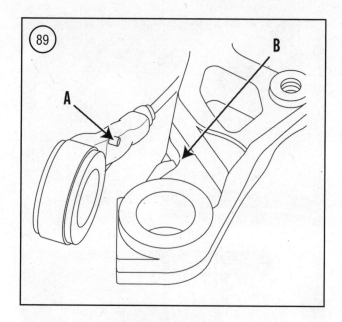

ABS BRAKE MODULE

Refer to **Figures 90** and **Figure 91**.

CAUTION
The ECU portion of the ABS module is sensitive to electrostatic discharge and can be easily damaged. Whenever handling the ABS module, or the ECU itself, ground yourself to the frame prior to touching the ABS module. Always touch the motorcycle frame or grounded surface before handling any portion of the ABS unit. This is especially true in areas with a very low air humidity index.

Removal

1. Support the motorcycle on level ground on a swing arm stand.
2. Block the front wheel so the motorcycle will not roll in either direction.
3. Remove the right frame side cover and saddlebag as described in Chapter Fourteen.
4. Remove the battery as described in Chapter Nine.
5. Drain the front and rear brake systems as described in *Brake Fluid Draining* (this chapter).

CAUTION
Ground yourself to the frame before handling the ABS module or connectors.

6. Disconnect the 18-pin electrical connector (A, **Figure 92**) from the ABS module.
7. Place several shop cloths the each brake line fitting to catch residual brake fluid when the fittings are disconnected.
8. Refer to **Figure 93** for brake line fitting locations on the ABS module. Remove the banjo bolt and copper washers (B, **Figure 92**) securing each brake line fitting to the ABS

module. Discard all copper washers unless the existing ABS unit is going to be reinstalled.
9. Remove the three screws (C, **Figure 92**) securing the ABS module to the ABS/battery caddy. Remove all three screws (only two are shown).
10. Carefully pull the ABS module up and out of the caddy and remove it.
11. If the ABS module assembly is going to be reinstalled, install the banjo bolts and old copper washers at each hose port to prevent the entry of foreign matter.

Installation

1. Inspect the rubber grommets for damage and deterioration. Replace as a set if one is damaged to ensure correct retention of the ABS module.
2. Make sure the bushing is in place on each side of the rubber grommets. Both bushings must be in place on each rubber grommet and the rubber grommet must be installed correctly in the caddy receptacles.

CAUTION
Ground yourself to the frame before handling the ABS module or connectors.

3. Position the ABS module with the brake hose ports on the right side, and carefully install the module assembly into the caddy. The caddy must sit flat and bottom in the caddy.
4. Install the three ABS module Allen screws and tighten alternately to 39-60 in.-lb. (4.4-6.8 N•m).
5. Remove the banjo bolts and *old* copper washers from the hose ports. Discard the copper washers.
6. The ABS module ports are marked to ensure correct placement of each banjo fitting (**Figure 93**) as follows:
   a. To front brake calipers: F.
   b. To rear brake caliper: R.
   c. From front master cylinder: MF.

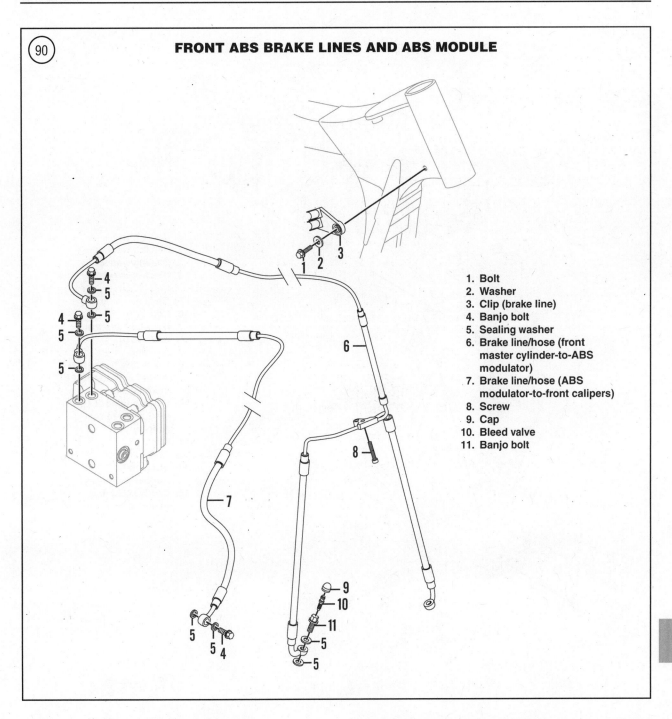

⑨⁰ **FRONT ABS BRAKE LINES AND ABS MODULE**

1. Bolt
2. Washer
3. Clip (brake line)
4. Banjo bolt
5. Sealing washer
6. Brake line/hose (front master cylinder-to-ABS modulator)
7. Brake line/hose (ABS modulator-to-front calipers)
8. Screw
9. Cap
10. Bleed valve
11. Banjo bolt

d. From rear master cylinder: MR.

7. Position the fitting of each hose to the correct port on the ABS modulator. Route the front caliper brake line fittings beneath the front master cylinder brake line.

8. Install the banjo bolt with a *new* copper washer on each side of the fitting. Alternately tighten the ABS module banjo bolts to 12.5-14.5 ft.-lb. (17.0-19.7 N•m).

9. Connect the 18-pin connector onto the ABS modulator.

10. Install the battery as described in Chapter Nine.

11. Fill both brake systems with DOT 4 brake fluid and bleed each of the systems as described in this chapter.

12. Install the right saddlebag and frame side cover as described in Chapter Fourteen.

13. The system must be checked by a dealership with the H-D digital technician to make sure the system is properly connected. This must be done for safety concerns as well as maintaining any applicable warranty.

Separation

The hydraulic control unit (HCU) can be separated from the electronic control unit (ECU) if one of the units fails. Refer to **Figure 91**.

1. Remove the ABS module as described in this section and take unit to the workbench.

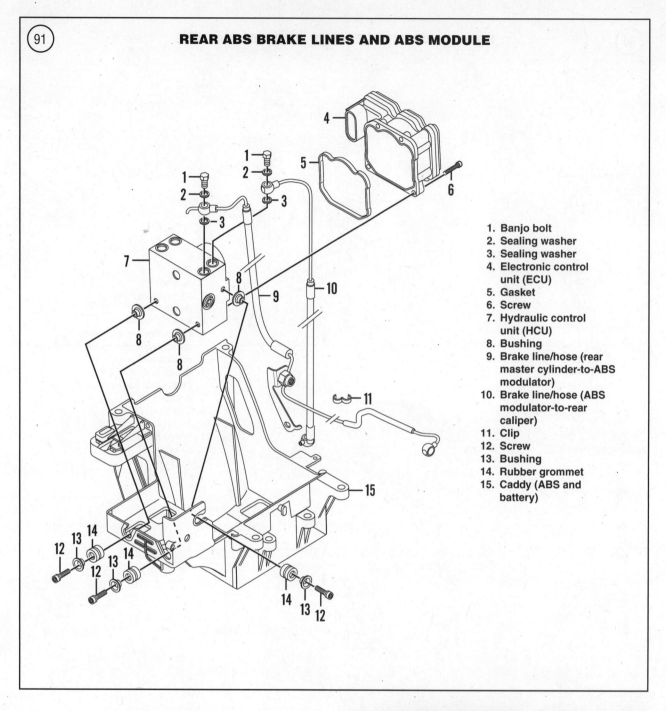

91   REAR ABS BRAKE LINES AND ABS MODULE

1. Banjo bolt
2. Sealing washer
3. Sealing washer
4. Electronic control unit (ECU)
5. Gasket
6. Screw
7. Hydraulic control unit (HCU)
8. Bushing
9. Brake line/hose (rear master cylinder-to-ABS modulator)
10. Brake line/hose (ABS modulator-to-rear caliper)
11. Clip
12. Screw
13. Bushing
14. Rubber grommet
15. Caddy (ABS and battery)

CAUTION
Ground yourself to the frame before proceeding.

2. Remove the four screws mating the ECU to the HCU and separate the two units.

3. Remove the gasket from the ECU, if necessary.

4. If removed, install the gasket into the groove in the ECU and make sure it seats correctly around the ECU.

5. Mate the HCU to the ECU and make sure they are correctly aligned.

6. Install the four mating screws and tighten to 35-45 in.-lb. (4.0-5.1 N•m).

7. Install the ABS module as described in this section.

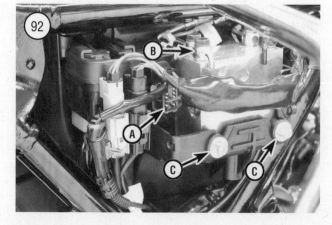

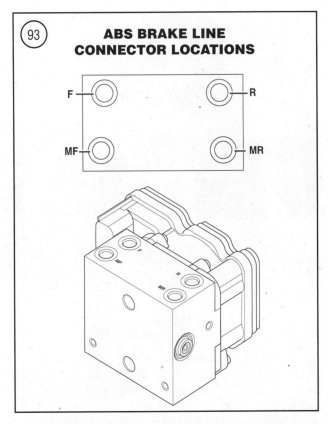

ABS BRAKE LINE CONNECTOR LOCATIONS

ABS DIODE PACK

Replacement

1. Remove the left side frame side cover as described in Chapter Fourteen.

2. Pull the ABS diode pack (**Figure 94**) out of the clip on the fuse panel.

3. Disconnect the 4-pin connector from the diode pack and remove the diode pack.

4. Connect the 4-pin connector onto the diode pack and press it on until it bottoms.

5. Install the diode pack onto the clip on the base of the fuse panel.

6. Install the left frame side cover as described in Chapter Fourteen.

BRAKE LINES (ABS MODELS)

The master cylinders are connected to the calipers by a combination of steel and flexible brake line assemblies. Banjo bolts connect brake hoses to individual components and are sealed with copper washers on each side of the fitting.

Replace the brake line assembly if the flexible portion shows swelling, cracking or other damage. Likewise, replace the brake line assembly if the metal portion leaks or if there are dents or cracks.

Refer to **Figures 90** and **Figure 91**.

CAUTION
The ECU portion of the ABS module is sensitive to electrostatic discharge and can be easily damaged. Whenever handling the ABS module, or the ECU itself, ground your self prior to touching the ABS module. Always touch the motorcycle frame or grounded surface before handling any portion of the ABS unit. This is especially true in areas with a very low air humidity index.

Front Master Cylinder-to-ABS Module

Removal

1. Support the motorcycle on level ground on a swing arm stand.

2. Block the front wheel so the motorcycle will not roll in either direction.

3. Remove the right frame side cover and saddlebag as described in Chapter Fourteen.

4. Remove the fuel tank as described in Chapter Eight.

5. Remove the top of the electrical caddy as described in Chapter Nine.

6. On models so equipped, refer to Chapter Fourteen and remove all front fairing panels necessary to gain access to the front brake line where it attaches to the lower steering stem.

7. Before removing the brake line assembly, note the brake line routing from the master cylinder to the calipers.

8. Remove the bolt **Figure 95** securing the brake hose mounting plate to the lower steering stem.

13

9. Release the brake line as follows:
   a. Cut cable strap securing front brake line to right side handlebar riser or right handlebar.
   b. Cut cable strap securing front brake lines to bracket on right side of handlebar.
   c. Cut cable strap securing front brake lines to narrow ledge at side of frame wiring trough.
   d. Remove three double sided clips and separate brake lines from frame backbone.
   e. Release brake lines from frame channel at front of wiring trough.
   f. On FLHTCU models, cut cable strap and release audio harness from upper right frame tube, if so equipped.

10. Remove the banjo bolt and washers (**Figure 96**) securing the brake hose to each front brake caliper. Discard the copper washers.

11. Remove the banjo bolt and washers (**Figure 97**) securing the brake hose to the front master cylinder. Discard the copper washers.

12. Remove the banjo bolt and washers securing the brake hose to the ABS module MF port (A, **Figure 98**). Discard the copper washers.

13. Cover the ends of the hoses to prevent brake fluid leaks.

14. Release the brake lines from the frame wire trough (**Figure 99**).

15. Pull the front section of the brake line up through the upper fork bridge. Pull the rear section up and away from the frame backbone (**Figure 100**). Remove the brake line assembly from the frame.

Installation

1. Position the brake line and hose assembly as follows:
   a. Place the assembly over the frame behind the steering head.
   b. Place the brake line along the right side of the frame wire trough with the rear banjo fitting adjacent to the ABS module.
   c. Insert the front section toward the front along the right side of the steering head.
   d. Move it up over the top fork bride and toward the rear following the right side of the handlebar to the front master cylinder.

2. Position the rear fitting onto the ABS module MF port. Install the banjo bolt and new copper washers into the MF port (A, **Figure 98**), do not tighten it at this time.

3. Position the front fitting onto the front master cylinder port. Install the banjo bolt and new copper washers (**Figure 97**), do not tighten it at this time.

4. Secure the front brake line assembly as follow:
   a. On fork mounted fairing models, install a new cable strap 2.5 in. (63.5 mm) rear of the fairing opening. Secure the brake hose and right side switch wiring to the right side handlebar riser. Secure the strap.

   b. On Road King and frame mounted fairing models, install a new cable strap and secure the brake hose and right sides switch wiring harness to the right side handlebar riser. Secure the strap.
   c. On all models, install a *new* cable strap and secure the brake hose and the bracket on the right side steering head. Secure the strap. Install a *new* cable strap and secure the brake hose from the master cylinder to the frame top channel and the brake hose to the calipers to the frame bottom channel.
   d. Press the brake line in the frame channel at front of wiring trough.

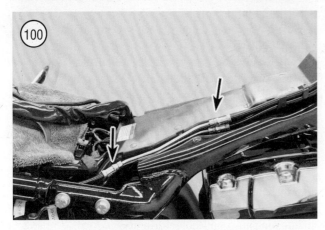

e. Press the brake line on narrow ledge at side of wire trough. At the rear ledge, install a *new* cable strap and secure the brake line to the wire trough.

f. Install the brake lines into the three double-sided clips.

g. On FLHTCU models, install a *new* cable strap and secure the audio harness to the right side upper frame tube, if equipped.

5. Install the brake hose onto the front master cylinder. Install the banjo bolt with two *new* sealing washers.

6. Tighten all banjo bolts to 12.5-14.5 ft.-lb. (17.0-19.7 N•m).

7. Refill the front brake line circuit with clean DOT 4 brake fluid. Bleed the front brake system as described in this chapter.

8. On models so equipped, refer to Chapter Fourteen and install all front fairing panels that were removed.

9. Install the top of the electrical caddy as described in Chapter Nine.

10. Install the fuel tank as described in Chapter Eight.

11. Install the right frame side cover and saddlebag as described in Chapter Fourteen.

12. Have the system checked by a dealership with the H-D digital technician to make sure the system is properly connected. This must be done for safety concerns as well as maintaining any applicable warranty.

ABS Module-to-Front Brake Calipers

Removal

1. Support the motorcycle on level ground on a swing arm stand.

2. Block the front wheel so the motorcycle will not roll in either direction.

3. Remove the right frame side cover and saddlebag as described in Chapter Fourteen.

4. Remove the fuel tank as described in Chapter Eight.

5. Remove the top of the electrical caddy as described in Chapter Nine.

6. On models so equipped, refer to Chapter Fourteen and remove all front fairing panels necessary to gain access to the front brake line where it attaches to the lower steering stem.

7. Before removing the brake line assembly, note the brake line routing from the master cylinder to the calipers.

8. On Road King series models, remove the left side of headlight nacelle as described in Chapter Nine.

9. On fork mounted fairing series models, remove the following:

    a. Remove the outer fairing front fairing and fairing cap (Chapter Fourteen).

    b. On FLHT series models, remove the front passing lights (Chapter Nine).

    c. On FLHX series models, remove the front turn signals (Chapter Nine).

10. On all models, remove the chrome skirt.

11. Cut two cable straps securing the front wheel sensor cable and front fender tip lamp electrical wires to the left caliper brake hose, if equipped.

12. Release the brake line as follows:

    a. Cut cable strap securing front brake line to right side handlebar riser or right handlebar.

    b. Cut cable strap securing front brake line to bracket on right side of steering head.

    c. Cut cable strap securing front brake lines to narrow ledge at side of frame wiring trough.

    d. Remove three double sided clips and separate brake lines from frame backbone.

    e. Release brake lines from frame channel at front of wiring trough.

    f. On FLHTCU models, cut cable strap securing the audio harness to the right upper frame tube.

13. Remove the Torx screw (T40) at base of lower fork bridge, and release brake line from bracket.

14. Remove the banjo bolt and washers (**Figure 96**) securing the brake hose to each front brake caliper. Discard the copper washers.

15. Remove the banjo bolt and washers securing the brake hose to the ABS module F port (B, **Figure 98**). Discard the copper washers.

16. Cover the ends of the hoses to prevent brake fluid leaks.

17. Release the brake lines from the frame wire trough (**Figure 99**).

13

18. Pull the front section of the brake line up through the upper fork bridge. Pull the rear section up and away from the frame backbone (**Figure 100**). Remove the brake line assembly from the frame.

Installation

1. Position the brake line and hose assembly as follows:
   a. Place the assembly over the frame behind the steering head.
   b. Place the brake line along the right side of the frame wire trough with the rear banjo fitting adjacent to the ABS module.
   c. Insert the front section toward the front along the right side of the steering head.
   d. Move it up over the top fork bridge and toward the rear following the right side of the handlebar to the front master cylinder.
2. Locate brake line bracket with the base of lower fork bridge and install the Torx screw (T40), but do not tighten it yet.
3. Position the rear fitting onto the ABS module F port (B, **Figure 93**). Install the banjo bolt and two *new* copper washers into the MF port, but do not tighten it yet.
4. Position the fittings onto both front calipers. Install the banjo bolt and two *new* copper washers into each of the calipers, but do not tighten them yet.
5. Secure the brake line assembly as follows:
   a. On all models, install a *new* cable strap and secure the front brake line to the bracket on the right side of the steering head. Secure the strap. Install a *new* cable strap and secure the brake hose from the master cylinder to the frame top channel. Install a *new* cable strap and secure the brake hose from the calipers to the frame bottom channel.
   b. Press the brake line in the frame channel at front of wiring trough.
   c. Press the brake line onto narrow ledge at side of wire trough. At the rear ledge, install a *new* cable strap and secure the brake line to the wire trough.
   d. Install the brake lines into the three double-sided clips at the following locations: one in front of the ignition coil bracket, one above wire trough through breakouts, and one in front of the fuel tank bracket threaded bolt receptacle.
   e. On FLHTCU models, install a *new* cable strap and secure the audio harness to the right side upper frame tube, if equipped.
6. From the rear of the motorcycle, verify that the front brake lines are equal distance from their specific fork sliders. Tighten the brake line bracket Torx screw (**Figure 95**) (T40) to 120-180 in.-lb. (13.6-20.3 N•m).
7. Tighten the ABS module F port banjo bolt to 12.5-14.5 ft.-lb. (17.0-19.7 N•m).
8. On all models, tighten two *new* cable straps as follows:
   a. Install cable strap 2.5 in. (63.5 mm) above the bottom of the brake hose crimp and capture the front

wheel sensor cable and front fender tip lamp electrical wires, on models so equipped.
   b. Install cable strap 2.5 in. (63.5 mm) above the top of the brake hose crimp and capture the front wheel sensor cable and front fender tip lamp electrical wires, on models so equipped.
9. Refill the front brake line circuit with clean DOT 4 brake fluid. Bleed the front brake system as described in this chapter.
10. On all models, install the chrome skirt.
11. On fork mounted fairing series models, following:
a. Install the outer fairing front fairing and fairing cap (Chapter Fourteen).
b. On FLHT series models, install the front passing lights (Chapter Nine).
c. On FLHX series models, install the front turn signals (Chapter Nine).
12. On Road King series models, install the left side of headlight nacelle (Chapter Nine).
13. Install the top of the electrical caddy as described in Chapter Nine.
14. Install the fuel tank as described in Chapter Eight.
15. Install the right frame side cover and saddlebag as described in Chapter Fourteen.
16. Have the system checked by a dealership with the H-D digital technician to make sure the system is properly connected. This must be done for safety concerns as well as maintaining any applicable warranty.

Rear Master Cylinder-to-ABS Module

Removal

1. Support the motorcycle on level ground on a swing arm stand.
2. Block the front wheel so the motorcycle will not roll in either direction while the rear wheel is off ground.
3. Remove the exhaust system as described in Chapter Four.
4. Remove the right frame side cover and saddlebag as described in Chapter Fourteen.
5. Remove the right side footboards as described in Chapter Fourteen.
6. Before removing the brake line assembly, note the brake line routing from the master cylinder to the ABS module.
7. Disconnect the electrical connector from the rear brake light switch.
8. Remove the screw securing the rear brake light switch. Push on the bracket and release the locking tab from frame weldment.
9. On the right side next to the swing arm bracket, cut the cable strap in the middle frame down tube hole securing the brake line to the main wiring harness.
10. Remove the banjo bolt and washers securing the brake hose to the ABS module MR port (C, **Figure 98**). Discard the copper washers.

11. Remove the banjo bolt and washers (**Figure 101**) securing the brake hose to rear master cylinder. Discard the copper washers.

12. Remove the rear brake master cylinder and brake pedal assembly as described in this chapter.

13. Cover the ends of the hoses to prevent brake fluid leaks.

14. Remove the brake line and hose assembly from the frame.

Installation

1. Position the brake line and hose assembly as follows:
   a. Place the assembly onto the brake pedal shaft on frame.
   b. From bottom inboard side of rear exhaust header, feed the rear section of the brake line upward at front of frame middle down tube crossing, and under the rear of the down tube at the bottom of frame cross member.
   c. Move the front section inboard of the frame weldment at bottom of the frame down tube.

2. Position the rear fitting onto the ABS module MR port (C, **Figure 98**). Install the banjo bolt and two *new* copper washers into the MF port, but do not tighten it yet.

3. Install the rear master cylinder and brake pedal assembly as described in this chapter.

4. Position the fitting onto the rear caliper. Install the banjo bolt and two *new* copper washers into the caliper, but do not tighten it yet.

5. Engage the locating tab on the rear brake light switch onto the frame weldment and install the screw. Tighten the screw securely.

6. Connect the electrical connector to the rear brake light switch.

7. Install a *new* cable strap through the middle frame down tube hole and secure the brake line to the main wiring harness.

8. Tighten the ABS module MR port banjo bolt to 12.5-14.5 ft.-lb. (17.0-19.7 N•m).

9. Refill the rear brake line circuit with clean DOT 4 brake fluid. Bleed the rear brake system as described in this chapter.

10. Install the exhaust system as described in Chapter Four.

11. Install the right side footboards as described in Chapter Seventeen.

12. Install the right frame side cover and saddlebag as described in Chapter Seventeen.

13. Have the system checked by a dealership with the H-D digital technician to make sure the system is properly connected. This must be done for safety concerns as well as maintaining any applicable warranty.

ABS Module-to-Rear Brake Caliper

Removal

1. Support the motorcycle on level ground on a swing arm stand.

2. Block the front wheel so the motorcycle will not roll in either direction while the rear wheel is off ground.

3. Remove the right frame side cover and saddlebag as described in Chapter Fourteen.

4. Remove the fuel tank as described in Chapter Eight.

5. Remove the right side electrical caddy as described in Chapter Nine.

6. Before removing the brake line assembly, note the brake line routing from the ABS module to the calipers.

7. Cut cable strap securing the rear wheel sensor to the rear brake hose.

8. Remove the banjo bolt and washers securing the brake hose to the ABS module R port (D, **Figure 98**). Discard the copper washers.

9. Remove the banjo bolt and washers securing the brake hose to the rear brake caliper. Discard the copper washers.

10. Remove the brake line from the top and bottom sections of the front edge channel of the battery tray.

11. Cover the ends of the brake hoses to prevent brake fluid leaks.

12. Remove the brake line and hose assembly from the frame.

Installation

1. Position the brake line and hose assembly as follows:
   a. Place the assembly at top of swing arm with the rear banjo fitting adjacent to the rear caliper.
   b. Turn the forward portion of the assembly up toward the ABS module near the frame cross member.

2. Place the brake hose into the two cable clips on the T-stud at the top of rear swing arm.

3. Move the rear wheel speed sensor next to the brake hose and close the rear cable clip onto both components. Snap both cable clips closed.

4. Install the brake line onto the top and bottom sections of the front edge channel of the battery tray.

5. Position the rear fitting onto the ABS module R port (D, **Figure 98**). Install the banjo bolt and two *new* copper washers into the R port, but do not tighten it yet.

13

6. Position the fitting onto the rear caliper. Install the banjo bolt and two *new* copper washers into the caliper, but do not tighten it yet.

7. Tighten the ABS module R port banjo bolt to 12.5-14.5 ft.-lb. (17.0-19.7 N•m).

8. Tighten the brake caliper banjo bolt to 17-19 ft.-lb. (23.1-25.8 N•m).

9. Install cable strap 1.2 in. (30.48 mm) in front of the rear brake hose crimp and capture the rear wheel sensor cable and brake hose.

10. Install the right side electrical caddy as described in Chapter Nine.

11. Install the fuel tank as described in Chapter Eight.

12. Install the right frame side cover and saddlebag as described in Chapter Fourteen.

13. Refill the rear brake line circuit with clean DOT 4 brake fluid. Bleed the rear brake system as described in this chapter.

14. Have the system checked by a dealership with the H-D digital technician to make sure the system is properly connected. This must be done for safety concerns as well as maintaining any applicable warranty.

BRAKE DISC

Inspection

The front and rear brake discs can be inspected while installed on the motorcycle.

Small nicks on the disc are not important, but deep scratches or other marks may reduce braking effectiveness and increase brake pad wear. If these grooves are evident and the brake pads are wearing rapidly, replace the brake disc.

Refer to **Table 1** for brake disc specifications. Each disc is also marked with the minimum (MIN) thickness. If the specification marked on the brake disc differs from the one in **Table 1**, use the specification found on the brake disc.

1. Support the motorcycle with the wheel (front or rear) off the ground.

2. Measure the thickness (**Figure 102**) of the brake disc at several locations around the disc. Replace the disc if the thickness in any area is less than the minimum allowable specification stamped on the brake disc, or less than the service limit in **Table 1**.

3. Make sure the disc mounting bolts are tight.

4. Position the dial indicator stem against the brake disc (**Figure 103**). Zero the dial gauge and slowly turn the wheel and measure the runout. If the runout is excessive:

   a. Check for loose or missing fasteners.

   b. Remove the front and/or rear wheel and check the wheel bearing condition.

5. Clean the disc of any corrosion and wipe clean with brake cleaner. Never use an oil-based solvent that may leave an oily residue on the disc.

Removal/Installation

1. Remove the front or rear wheel as described in Chapter Twelve.

2. Mark the disc with a R (right side) and L (left side) prior to removal.

3. Remove the bolts (**Figure 104**) securing the brake disc to the hub and remove the disc. Discard the bolts as they cannot be reused.

4. Check the threaded brake disc bolt holes in the wheel hub for thread damage. Clean out with a tap if necessary.

5. Clean the disc and the disc mounting surface thoroughly with brake cleaner or contact cleaner. Allow the surfaces to dry before installation.

NOTE
On FLHTCUSE models, front brake discs are symmetrical and can be installed on either side. When installing used discs, install them on the same side as noted during removal.

6. Install the disc onto the correct side of the wheel hub.

7. Install *new* Torx bolts and tighten to the following:

   a. Front wheel Torx bolt (T40): 16-24 ft.-lb. (21.7-32.5 N•m).

   b. Rear wheel Torx bolt (T45): 30-45 ft.-lb. (40.7-61.0 N•m).

8. Install the front or rear wheel as described in Chapter Twelve.

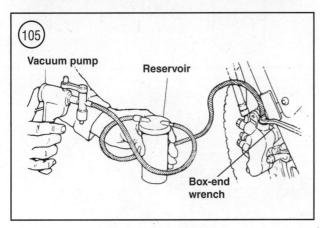

bleed valve is opened, the looser the valve becomes. This allows air to be drawn into the system from around the bleed valve threads.

7. If air is suspected of entering from around the bleed valve threads, remove the bleed valve and wrap a small amount of Teflon tape around the bleed valve threads to seal the threads. Install the bleed valve.

8. If the system is difficult to bleed, tap the banjo bolt on the master cylinder several times, it is not uncommon for air bubbles to become trapped in the hose connection where the brake fluid exits the master cylinder. When a number of bubbles appear in the master cylinder reservoir after tapping the banjo bolt, it means air was trapped in this area. Also, tap the other bolt and the line connections at the caliper and other brake units.

BRAKE BLEEDING

General Bleeding Tips

1. Clean the bleed valves and the area around the valves of all dirt and debris. Make sure the passageway in the end of the bleed valve is open and clear.

2. Use a box-end wrench to open and close the bleed valves. This prevents damage to the bleed valve hex-head. Replace bleed valves with damaged hex-heads. These are difficult to loosen and cannot be tightened fully.

3. Install the box-end wrench on the bleed valve before installing the catch hose. This allows operation of the wrench without having to disconnect the hose.

4. Use a clear catch hose to allow visual inspection of the brake fluid as it leaves the brake caliper. Air bubbles visible in the catch hose indicate there still may be air trapped in the brake system.

5. Depending on the amount of play at the bleed valve when it is loosened, it is possible to see air exiting through the catch hose even though there is no air in the brake system. A damaged catch hose can also cause air leaks. In both cases, air is being introduced into the bleed system at the bleed valve threads and catch hose connection and not from within the brake system itself. This condition can be misleading and can cause excessive brake bleeding when there is not air in the system.

6. Open the bleed valve just enough to allow fluid to pass through the screw and into the catch bottle. The farther the

Vacuum Bleeding

Vacuum bleeding can be accomplished by using either a hand-operated bleeder or an air-tool bleeder powered by compressed air. The tools (**Figure 105**) described in this section can be used by one person to drain and bleed the brake system.

Hand-operated vacuum pump

1. Connect the catch hose between the bleed valve and catch bottle. Connect the other hose between the catch bottle and vacuum pump. Refer to the tool manufacturer's instructions for additional information.

2. Secure the vacuum pump to the motorcycle with a length of wire so it is possible to check and refill the master cylinder reservoir without having to disconnect the catch hose.

3. Remove the dust cap from the brake caliper bleed valve.

4. Place a clean shop cloth over the caliper to protect it from accidental brake fluid spills.

5. Clean all dirt and debris off the top of the master cylinder.

6. Remove the screws securing the master cylinder top cover. Remove the cover and diaphragm.

7. Fill the reservoir almost to the top with clean DOT 4 brake fluid and reinstall the diaphragm and cover. Leave the cover in place during this procedure to prevent the entry of dirt.

8. Operate the vacuum pump to create a vacuum in the catch hose connected to the bleed valve. Then, open the bleed valve with the wrench to allow the brake fluid to be drawn through the master cylinder, brake hoses and lines. Close the bleed valve before the brake fluid stops flowing from the system (no more vacuum in the line) or before the master cylinder reservoir runs empty.

NOTE
Do not allow the master cylinder reservoir to empty during the bleeding operation or more air will enter the system. If this occurs, the bleeding procedure must be repeated.

13

9. Continue the bleeding process until the fluid running through the vacuum hose is a clear and solid stream without any air bubbles. Tighten the bleed valve and remove the brake bleeder assembly. Reinstall the bleed valve dust cap.

10. If necessary, add fluid to correct the level in the front master cylinder reservoir. When topping off the front master cylinder, turn the handlebar until the reservoir is level.

   a. Add fluid until the level is level should be level with the boss, or ridge within the master cylinder body, or within the viewing port.

   b. If necessary, add fluid to correct the level in the rear master cylinder reservoir. When topping off the rear master cylinder, secure the motorcycle until the reservoir is level.

   c. Add fluid until the brake fluid level should be level with the ledge or within the viewing port.

11. Reinstall the reservoir diaphragm and cover. Install the screws and tighten to 6-8 in.-lb. (0.7-0.9 N•m).

12. Test the feel of the brake lever or pedal. It should be firm and offer the same resistance each time it is operated. If it feels spongy, there is probably still air in the system. Bleed the system again. After bleeding the system, check for leaks and tighten all fittings and connections as necessary.

Compressed air vacuum pump

> *NOTE*
> *This system is highly recommended for models with ABS due to the number of brake lines and hoses.*

1. Assemble the tool, following the manufacturer's instructions.

2. Connect the box-end wrench onto the bleed screw. Connect the vacuum hose onto the bleed valve.

3. Connect a compressed air source to the vacuum tool.

> *NOTE*
> *Always close the bleed valve before releasing the lever on top of the pump.*

4. Depress the lever on top of the pump and open the bleed valve slightly. As long as the lever is depressed, a vacuum is created in the canister and brake fluid will evacuate from the brake line. Releasing the lever stops the vacuum. Because this tool will drain the master cylinder rapidly, check the master cylinder fluid level often.

5. Continue until the brake fluid running through the vacuum hose is a clear and steady stream without bubbles. Air drawn in around the bleed valve will cause bubbles to form in the vacuum hose. While this is normal, it is misleading as it always appears there is air in the system, even when the system has been bled completely. If necessary, remove the bleed valve and wrap a small amount of Teflon tape around the bleed valve threads to seal the threads. Install the bleed valve.

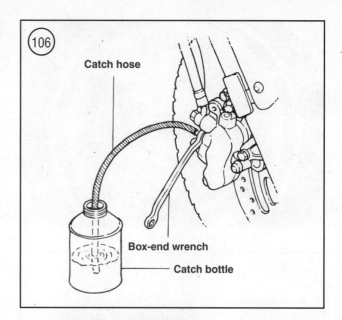

Catch hose

Box-end wrench

Catch bottle

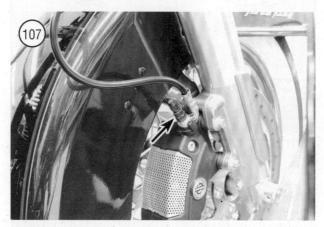

Manual Bleeding

This is a one-person procedure that requires a reservoir bottle, length of clear hose (catch hose), wrench and the specified brake fluid (**Figure 106**).

1. Connect the catch hose to the bleed valve on the caliper. Submerge the other end of the hose into a bottle partially filled with clean DOT 4 brake fluid. This prevents air from being drawn into the catch hose and back into the brake system.

2. Apply the front brake lever or rear brake pedal until it stops and hold in this position.

3. Open the bleed valve with a wrench and let the lever or pedal move to the limit of its travel. Then, close the bleed valve; make sure to close the bleed valve before releasing the brake lever or pedal. This prevents air from being drawn back into the system on the lever's or pedal's return stroke if the bleed valve was left open.

4. Release the lever or pedal slowly, and then repeat the process until the brake fluid exiting the system is clear and air-free.

Brake Fluid Draining

Before disconnecting a brake hose from the front or rear brake component, drain the brake fluid as described in this section. Doing so reduces the amount of brake fluid that can spill out when disconnecting the brake hoses and lines from the system.

Front master cylinder line

1. Support the motorcycle on level ground on a swing arm sand.
2. Block the front wheel so the motorcycle will not roll in either direction while on the swing arm stand.
3. Turn the handlebars to the straight ahead position to level the front master cylinder and remove the screws, cover and diaphragm.
4. Connect a brake bleeder to the front brake caliper bleed valve (**Figure 107**). Open the bleed valve and operate the brake bleeder until the fluid stops flowing. Tighten the bleed valve to 80-100 in.-lb. (9.0-11.3 N•m).
5. Repeat the process to drain the other caliper.
6. Disconnect the bleeder tool.

Rear master cylinder line

1. Support the motorcycle on level ground on a swing arm stand.

2. Block the front wheel so the motorcycle will not roll in either direction.
3. Remove the screws, cover and diaphragm from the reservoir.
4. Connect a brake bleeder to the rear brake caliper bleed valve (**Figure 108**). Open the bleed valve and operate the brake bleeder until the fluid stops flowing. Tighten the bleed valve.
5. Disconnect the bleeder tool.

Bleeding The System

Front brake line

1. Support the motorcycle on level ground on a swing arm stand.
2. Block the front wheel so the motorcycle will not roll in either direction while on the swing arm stand.
3. Turn the handlebars to the straight ahead position to level the front master cylinder and remove the screws, cover and diaphragm (**Figure 109**).
4. Connect a brake bleeder to the front brake caliper bleed valve (**Figure 107**). Open the bleed valve and operate the brake bleeder to bleed the brake line. Repeat until the brake fluid exiting the catch hose is clear and free of air. Tighten the bleed valve.
5. Repeat this process as necessary until the front brake lever feels firm when applying it there are not air bubbles in the catch hose.
6. Repeat the procedure to bleed the other front caliper.
7. After bleeding the system and making sure there are no air bubbles appearing in the catch hose, test the feel of the brake lever. It should be firm and should after the same resistance each time it is operated. If the brake lever feels spongy, air is still trapped in the system and the bleeding procedure must be continued.
8. Tighten the bleed valve to 80-100 in.-lb. (9.0-11.3 N•m).
9. Remove the brake bleeder.
10. If necessary, add clean DOT 4 brake fluid to correct the level in the master cylinder reservoir. Observe the brake fluid level within the master cylinder body.
11. Install diaphragm and cover. Tighten the screws to 6-8 in.-lb. (0.7-0.9 N•m).

Rear brake line

1. Support the motorcycle on level ground on a swing arm stand.
2. Block the front wheel so the motorcycle will not roll in either direction while on the swing arm stand.
3. Remove the cover (**Figure 110**) and diaphragm from the reservoir.
4. Connect a brake bleeder to the rear brake caliper bleed valve (**Figure 108**). Open the bleed valve and operate the brake bleeder to bleed the brake line. Repeat until the brake fluid exiting the catch hose is clear and free of air. Tighten the bleed valve securely.

13

5. After bleeding the bleed valves and the system so no air bubbles appear in the catch hose, test feel of the brake pedal. It should be firm and should offer the same resistance each time it is operated. If the brake pedal feels spongy, air is still trapped in the system and the bleeding procedure must be continued.

6. Tighten the bleed valve to 80-100 in.-lb. (9.0-11.3 N•m).

7. Remove the brake bleeder.

8. If necessary, add clean DOT 4 brake fluid to correct the level in the master cylinder reservoir. The correct level is flush with the top ledge cast into the Rear Step within the reservoir.

9. Install diaphragm and cover. Tighten the screws to 6-8 in.-lb. (0.7-0.9 N•m).

FLUSHING THE BRAKE SYSTEM

When flushing the brake system, use the recommended brake fluid as a flushing fluid. Flushing consists of pulling new brake fluid through the system until the new fluid appears at the caliper and without the presence of any air bubbles. To flush the brake system, follow one of the bleeding procedures described in this chapter.

Table 1 BRAKE SPECIFICATIONS

Item	Specification
Brake fluid type	DOT 4
Brake fluid height[1]	
Front master cylinder	Flush with the MAX line at front of master cylinder body
Rear master cylinder	Flush with the MAX line at rear of master cylinder body
Brake disc	
Lateral runout, maximum	0.008 in. (0.2 mm)
Minimum thickness[2]	
Front disc	0.18 in. (4.6 mm)
Rear disc	0.25 in. (6.35 mm)
Brake pads minimum thickness	
Front and rear pads	0.16 in. (0.4 mm)

1. Brake fluid should be visible in sight glass at all times.
2. The minimum thickness is stamped on the side of the brake disc.

Table 2 BRAKE TORQUE SPECIFICATIONS

Item	ft.-lb.	in.-lb.	N•m
ABS module			
Allen mounting screw	–	39-60	4.4-6.8
Banjo bolt	12.5-14.5	–	17.0-19.7
ABS brake module/control unit			
mating screw	–	35-45	4.0-5.1
ABS front brake line bracket			
Torx screw	–	120-180	13.6-20.3
(continued)			

Table 2 BRAKE TORQUE SPECIFICATIONS

Item	ft.-lb.	in.-lb.	N•m
Banjo bolt			
Front and rear master cylinder	–	12.5-14.5	16.9-19.7
Front and rear caliper	–	17-19	23.1-25.8
Banjo bleed bolt at front cylinder	17-19	–	23.1-25.8
Bleed valve	–	80-100	9.0-11.3
Brake caliper mounting bolt			
Front wheel	28-38	–	37.9-51.5
Rear wheel			
(to caliper mounting bracket)	43-48	–	58.3-65.1
Brake disc Torx bolt			
Front wheel	16-24	–	21.7-32.5
Rear wheel	30-45	–	40.7-61.0
Front brake line Torx screw	–	120-180	13.6-20.3
Master cylinder			
Reservoir top screw			
Front wheel	–	10-12	1.1-1.4
Rear wheel	–	12-15	1.4-1.7
Rear brake master			
cylinder-to-frame bolt	–	126-150	14.2-17.0
Front master cylinder			
clamp Torx bolt	–	71-80	8.0-9.0
Rear brake light switch	12.5-14.5	–	16.9-19.7
Caliper pad pin	–	75-102	8.5-11.5
Rear master cylinder			
Pivot post locknut	15-20	–	20.3-27.1
Engine strap bolt	–	125-130	14.2-17.0

13

NOTES

CHAPTER FOURTEEN

BODY AND FRAME

This chapter describes the removal and installation of the body and frame components. Handle the body panels carefully to protect the finish and note that many are fragile. Once the component is removed, attach all loose mounting hardware to avoid misplacing them. If a component is going to be left off for a period of time, wrap it with a blanket or towel and place it in a safe location.

Table 1 is located at the end of this chapter.

SEATS

Removal/Installation
Single Seat Non Tour-Pak Models

Refer to **Figure 1**.

1. Place the motorcycle on level ground on the jiffy stand.
2. Remove the left side saddlebag as described in this chapter.
3. On the left side, remove the bolt and washer securing the passenger seat strap and mounting bracket to the frame. Carefully slide the loose end of the seat strap through the seat slot. Allow the seat strap to hang free on the left side.
4. Remove the screw (**Figure 2**) securing the back of the seat to the rear fender.
5. Slightly lift up on the rear of the seat, slide it toward the rear and remove it (**Figure 3**).

6. Inspect the screw (**Figure 4**) securing the rear mounting tab and the front hook (**Figure 5**) for damage. Replace as necessary.
7. Place the seat on the frame. Firmly push down on the front of the seat and push it forward to engage the bracket into the slot of the frame backbone. Push the seat down and install the screw (**Figure 2**) securing the back of the seat to the rear fender. Tighten the screw to 48-72 in.-lb. (5.4-8.1 N•m).
8. Pull back on the seat to ensure the seat front hook is secured in place in the frame backbone.
9. Correct position the passenger seat strap onto the seat. Carefully insert the seat strap and mounting bracket through the slot in the seat.
10. Install the mounting bracket bolt and washer, and tighten to 48-72 in.-lb. (5.4-8.1 N•m).
11. Install the left side saddlebag as described in this chapter.

Removal/Installation
Rider and Pillion Seat (FLTRXSE MODELS)

Refer to **Figure 6**.

Pillion seat removal/installation

1. Place the motorcycle on level ground on the jiffy stand.

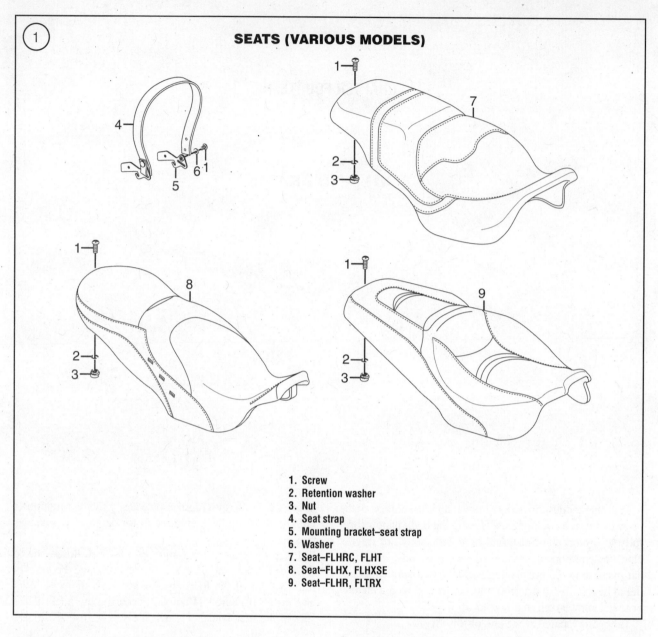

① **SEATS (VARIOUS MODELS)**

1. Screw
2. Retention washer
3. Nut
4. Seat strap
5. Mounting bracket–seat strap
6. Washer
7. Seat–FLHRC, FLHT
8. Seat–FLHX, FLHXSE
9. Seat–FLHR, FLTRX

2. Remove the thumb screw and washer.

3. Slide the pillion seat toward the rear and away from the two mounting studs on the fender. Remove the pillion seat.

4. Tuck the seat strap under the flap at the rear of the rider's seat, if necessary.

> *NOTE*
> *A decorative fender plug is attached to the base of the pillion seat. If the motorcycle is going to be ridden without the pillion installed, install the plug into the rear fender thumbscrew hole.*

5. Remove the seat strap from under the flap at the rear of the rider's seat, if necessary.

6. Place the pillion seat onto the rear fender, side it forward and engage the two mounting studs on the fender. Push forward until it bottoms.

7. Align the thumbscrews holes and install the washer and thumbscrew. Tighten the thumbscrew securely.

Rider's seat removal/installation

1. Remove the pillion seat as described in this section.

2. Remove the two thumbnuts securing the rear of the seat.

3. Lift up on the rear of the seat, to clear the threaded studs on the rear fender.

4. Pull the seat rearward and remove it.

5. Remove the seat strap, if necessary.

6. Install the seat strap onto the fenders threaded studs.

7. Side the seat forward to engage the tongue on the frame into the seat slot, while lowering the seat onto the threaded studs.

8. Install the two thumbnuts securing the rear of the seat, and seat strap and tighten securely.

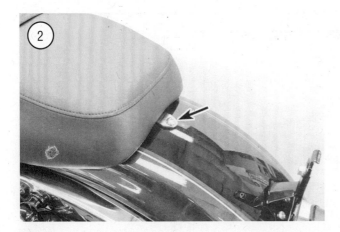

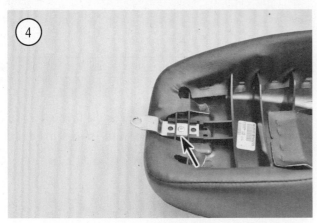

9. Install the pillion seat, if necessary as described in this section.

10. Pull up on both seats to ensure the seats are is secured in place on the rear fender.

Removal/Installation
Single Seat and Backrest Tour-Pak Models (FLHTCUE, FLTRUSE , FLHTC, FLHTCU, FLHTK and FLTRU Models)

Refer to **Figure 7** or **Figure 8**.

1. Place the motorcycle on level ground on the jiffystand.

2. Remove the left side saddlebag as described in this chapter.

3. Remove the rider's backrest, models so equipped, (this section).

4. Open the Tour-Pak lid and pivot the backrest up and out of the way.

5. On either side, remove the bolt and washer securing the passenger seat strap and mounting bracket to the frame. Allow the seat strap to hang free on either side.

6. Remove the screw securing the back of the seat to the rear fender.

7. Slightly lift up on the rear of the seat, slide it toward the rear and partially remove it and set it on the frame.

8. Toward the rear right side of the electrical caddy, disconnect the 4-pin (one orange/red wire and one black wire) heated seat connector (191) terminal from the harness.

9. Remove the seat.

10. Place the seat on the right side of the frame and plug in the heated seat connector (191) terminal into the harness. Press the connector until it locks in place. Tuck the harness down into the frame cavity making sure it will not get pinched between the seat pan and the frame rail.

11. Move the seat partially into position and hold the rear of the seat approximately 3 in. (76.2 mm) above the fender. Firmly push down on the front of the seat and push it forward to engage the bracket into the slot of the frame backbone. Push the seat down and install the screw securing the back of the seat to the rear fender. Tighten the screw to 48-72 in.-lb. (5.4-8.1 N•m).

12. Pull back on the seat to ensure the seat front hook is secured in place in the frame backbone.

13. Install the grab strap mounting bracket bolt and washer, and tighten to 48-72 in.-lb. (5.4-8.1 N•m).

14. Install the left side saddlebag as described in this chapter.

15. Install the rider's backrest, models so equipped, as described in this section.

RIDER AND PASSENGER BACKRESTS

Rider Backrest and Bracket (FLHTCUSE and FLTRUSE Models)

Removal/installation

Refer to **Figure 7**.

1. Park the motorcycle on level ground.

14

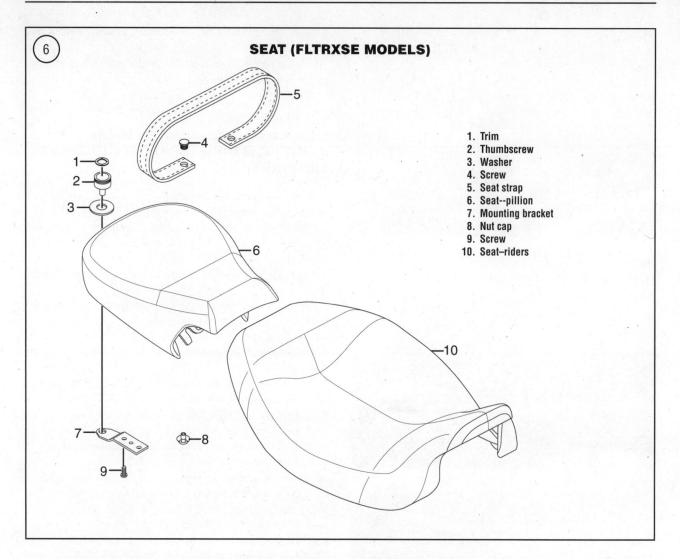

⑥ **SEAT (FLTRXSE MODELS)**

1. Trim
2. Thumbscrew
3. Washer
4. Screw
5. Seat strap
6. Seat--pillion
7. Mounting bracket
8. Nut cap
9. Screw
10. Seat–riders

2. Carefully spread the seat covering (A, **Figure 9**) at the base of the backrest.

3. Squeeze together the two spring (B, **Figure 9**) loaded backrest arms (C).

4. Carefully pull straight up and remove the back rest from the mounting pocket.

5. Carefully spread the seat covering (A, **Figure 10**) to expose the backrest mounting bracket (B).

6. Squeeze together the two spring (B, **Figure 9**) loaded backrest arms (C).

7. Carefully push straight down and install the back rest into the mounting pocket.

NOTE
Move the backrest up or down to select one of the three sets of vertical adjustment locations.

8. Release the locking arms and lock the backrest into the mounting bracket.

9. Test to ensure the backrest is secured into the mounting bracket.

Adjusting tilt

Using a 3/26 in. hex wrench, tighten the hex screw (D, **Figure 9**) to move the backrest forward, or loosen the hex screw to tilt the backrest backward.

Adjusting front to rear

1. Remove the rider backrest and seat (this section).

2. Loosen but do not remove the bolt (A, **Figure 11**) securing the flat mounting bracket to the angled mounting bracket.

3. Remove the bolt and flange locknut (B, **Figure 11**) securing the flat mounting bracket (C) to the backrest mounting bracket. Pivot the flat mounting bracket out of the way.

4. Remove the locknut (D, **Figure 11**) on each side securing the backrest mounting bracket to the rear fender threaded studs. Lift the backrest mounting bracket (E, **Figure 11**) off the threaded studs.

5. Ensure the large nylon washers are still in place on the rear fender threaded studs.

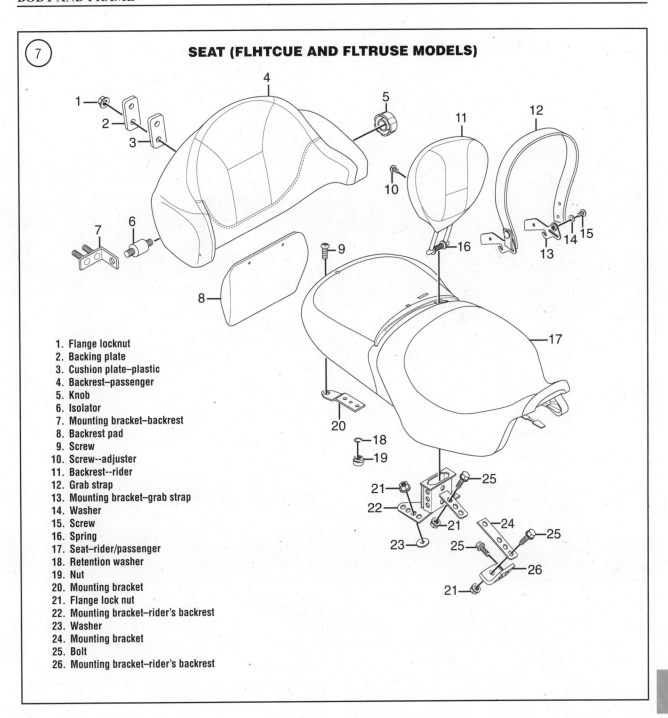

⑦ **SEAT (FLHTCUE AND FLTRUSE MODELS)**

1. Flange locknut
2. Backing plate
3. Cushion plate–plastic
4. Backrest–passenger
5. Knob
6. Isolator
7. Mounting bracket–backrest
8. Backrest pad
9. Screw
10. Screw--adjuster
11. Backrest--rider
12. Grab strap
13. Mounting bracket–grab strap
14. Washer
15. Screw
16. Spring
17. Seat–rider/passenger
18. Retention washer
19. Nut
20. Mounting bracket
21. Flange lock nut
22. Mounting bracket–rider's backrest
23. Washer
24. Mounting bracket
25. Bolt
26. Mounting bracket–rider's backrest

14

6. Reposition the backrest mounting bracket (E, **Figure 11**) onto the threaded studs in selected pair of horizontal adjustment holes (F, **Figure 11**).

7. Install the locknut (D, **Figure 11**) on each side securing the backrest mounting and tighten to 60-96 in. lb. (6.8-10.8 N•m).

8. Move the flat mounting bracket (C, **Figure 11**) onto the backrest mounting bracket and install the bolt and flange locknut (B, **Figure 11**). Tighten to 132-180 in. lb. (15-20 N•m).

9. Tighten the bolt (A, **Figure 11**) securing the flat mounting bracket to the angled mounting bracket to 60-96 in. lb. (6.8-10.8 N•m).

10. Install the rider backrest and seat as described in this section.

Passenger Backrest
(FLHXSE and FLHRSE Models)
Removal/Installation

Refer to **Figure 12**.

1. To remove the passenger backrest, perform the following:

   a. Push in on the spring-loaded locking latches, and pull the swivel latches toward the rear.

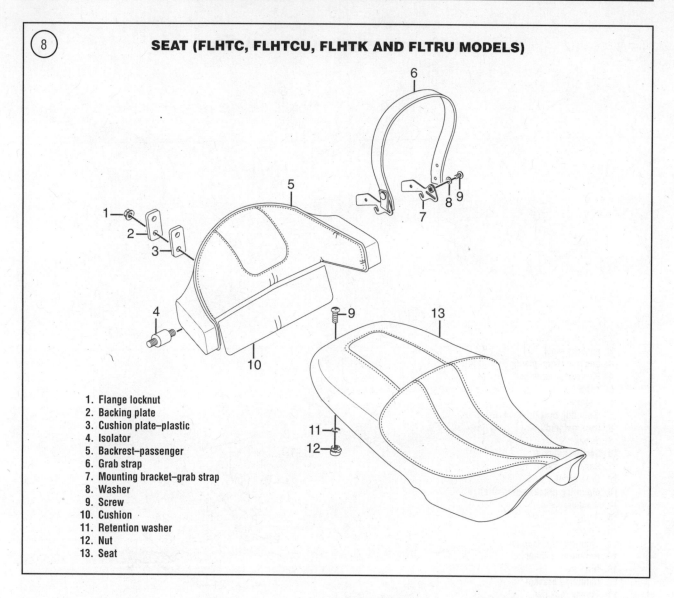

⑧ SEAT (FLHTC, FLHTCU, FLHTK AND FLTRU MODELS)

1. Flange locknut
2. Backing plate
3. Cushion plate–plastic
4. Isolator
5. Backrest–passenger
6. Grab strap
7. Mounting bracket–grab strap
8. Washer
9. Screw
10. Cushion
11. Retention washer
12. Nut
13. Seat

   b. Lift up on the backrest, and then move it toward the rear and release the backrest from the front docking point on the frame (F, **Figure 11**).

   c. Remove the passenger backrest from the frame.

2. To replace the front docking point bushing, remove the screw, washer and bushing from the frame. Repeat for the remaining side if necessary.

3. To replace the backrest brackets, perform the following:

   a. On the right side, remove the bolt and washer securing the bracket to the frame, and remove the bracket.

   b. On the left side, remove the bolt and washer securing the bracket and antenna bracket to the frame. Remove the bracket and antenna bracket.

4. Install the backrest, and antenna bracket, and tighten the screw to 16.7 ft.-lb. (22.6 N•m).

5. Install the backrest bushing assembly and tighten the screw to 120 in.-lb. (13.6 N•m).

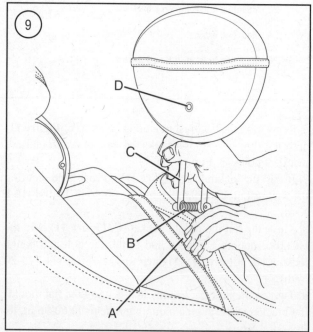

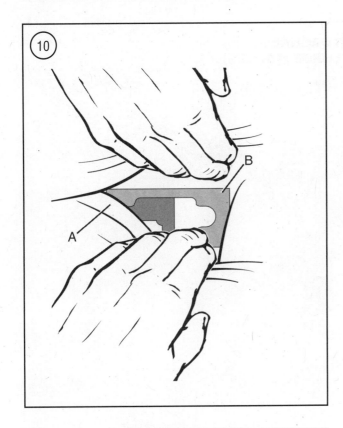

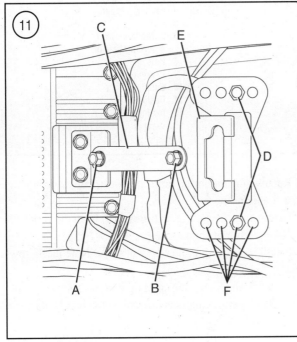

3. Remove the left frame side cover as described in this chapter.

4. Remove both saddlebags as described in this chapter.

5. Remove the Tour-Pak assembly as described in this chapter.

6. Remove the screws securing the top electrical caddy and move it out of the way as described in Chapter Nine.

7. Remove the battery and battery tray as described in Chapter Nine.

8. Note the location of the straps securing the wiring harness on each side of the rear frame. Cut the straps and move the wiring harnesses out of the way.

9. Remove both shock absorbers as described in Chapter Twelve.

10. Remove the luggage rack as follows:
   a. Remove the bolts and washers securing the seat strap and forward saddlebag bracket. Remove the seat strap and the bracket.
   b. Remove the two bolts securing the frame cover and part of the luggage rack on each side. Then, remove the cover.
   c. Remove the remaining two bolts on each side and remove the luggage rack.

11. Remove the two bolts securing the left side electrical caddy and move it out of the way as described in Chapter Nine.

12. Remove the three bolts and hardened washers on each side securing the rear frame to the main frame. Carefully pull the rear frame toward the rear and remove it. Install the bolts and washers onto the rear frame to avoid misplacing them.

13. Install the rear frame and luggage by reversing the removal steps. Note the following bolt torque specifications:
   a. Rear frame bolts and hardened washers: 40-50 ft.-lb. (54.2-67.8 N•m).
   b. Left side electrical caddy screws: 72-96 in.-lb. (8.1-10.8 N•m).
   c. Battery tray screws: 72-96 in.-lb. (8.1-10.8 N•m).
   d. Luggage rack screws: 15-20 ft.-lb. (20.3-27.1 N•m).
   e. Seat strap and forward saddlebag bracket screw: 15-20 ft.-lb. (20.3-27.1 N•m).
   f. Top electrical caddy: 72-96 in.-lb. (8.1-10.8 N•m).

FRONT FENDER

Removal/Installation
(All models Except CVO)

Refer to **Figure 14**.

1. Support the motorcycle with the front wheel off the ground as described in *Motorcycle Stands* in Chapter Ten.

NOTE
Always disarm the optional security system (TSM/TSSM/HFSM) before disconnecting the battery or pulling the main fuse so the siren will not sound.

Rear Frame/Luggage Rack
Removal/Installation
(FLTRU and FLHT Series Models)

Refer to **Figure 13**.

1. Support the motorcycle with the rear wheel off the ground.

2. Remove the rider and passenger seats as described in this chapter.

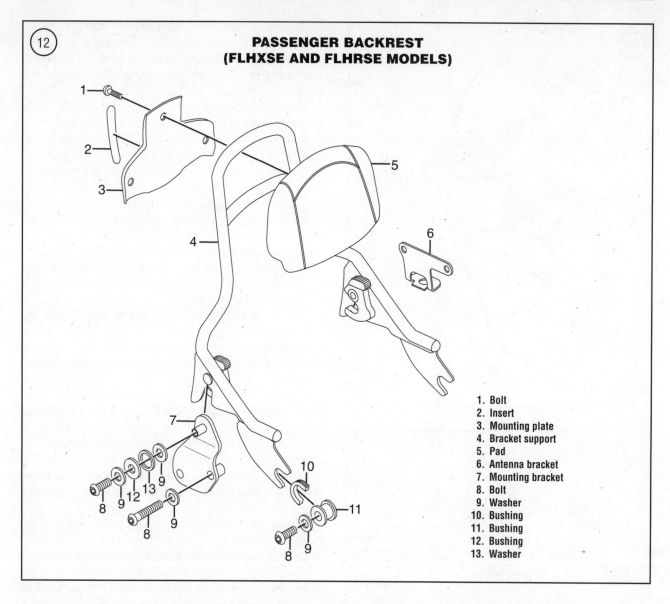

**PASSENGER BACKREST
(FLHXSE AND FLHRSE MODELS)**

1. Bolt
2. Insert
3. Mounting plate
4. Bracket support
5. Pad
6. Antenna bracket
7. Mounting bracket
8. Bolt
9. Washer
10. Bushing
11. Bushing
12. Bushing
13. Washer

2. Disconnect the battery negative cable (Chapter Nine).

3A. On fork mounted fairing models, perform the following:

    a. Remove the lower portion of the front fairing as described in this chapter.

    b. On the left side of the front fairing, locate and disconnect the 2-pin front fender tip lamp connector (32) (**Figure 15**).

    c. Carefully pull the electrical connector and harness free from the inner front fairing.

3B. On Road King models, perform the following:

    a. Remove the headlight as described in Chapter Nine.

    b. Within the headlight case, locate and disconnect the 2-pin front fender tip lamp connector (32) (**Figure 16**).

    c. Carefully pull the electrical connector and harness free from within the headlight case.

4. Remove the front wheel as described in Chapter Ten.

5. Straighten the locking tabs away from the front fender mounting bolts (**Figure 17**).

6. Remove the mounting bolts and lock plates securing the front fender to the fork sliders.

7. Remove the front fender (**Figure 18**) from the fork sliders. Be careful not scratch the paint.

8. Install by reversing the removal steps. Note the following:

    a. Install the lock plates and tighten the bolts securely.

    b. Bend the locking tabs up against the bolt heads.

**Removal/Installation
(CVO Models)**

Refer to **Figure 19**.

1. Support the motorcycle with the front wheel off the ground as described in *Motorcycle Stands* (Chapter Twelve.

2. Straighten the locking tabs away from the front fender mounting bolts (**Figure 17**).

3. Remove the mounting bolts and lock plates securing the front fender to the fork sliders.

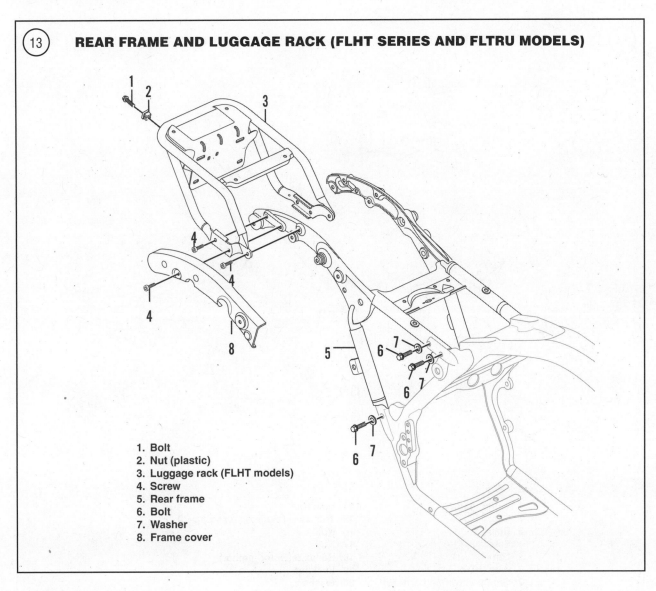

⑬ **REAR FRAME AND LUGGAGE RACK (FLHT SERIES AND FLTRU MODELS)**

1. Bolt
2. Nut (plastic)
3. Luggage rack (FLHT models)
4. Screw
5. Rear frame
6. Bolt
7. Washer
8. Frame cover

4. Remove the front fender from the fork sliders. Be careful not scratch the paint.

5. Install by reversing these removal steps while noting the following:

    a. Install the lock plates, on models so equipped, and install the front fender mounting bolts. Tighten the bolts securely.

    b. Bend the locking tabs, on models so equipped, up against the bolt heads.

REAR FENDER (ALL MODELS EXCEPT CVO)

Removal/Installation

Refer to **Figure 20** and **Figure 21**.

NOTE
Elevate the rear of the motorcycle sufficiently to allow the rear fender to roll back and over the rear wheel, as well as clear the frame rear cross member.

1. Support the motorcycle with the rear wheel slightly off the ground.

NOTE
Always disarm the optional TSSM/HFSM security system before disconnecting the battery or pulling the Main Fuse so the siren will not sound.

2. Disconnect the negative battery cable as described in Chapter Nine.

3. Remove the seat(s) as described in this chapter.

4. Remove both saddlebags as described in this chapter.

5. Remove both frame side covers as described in this chapter.

6. Remove the rear wheel as described in Chapter Ten.

7. On models so equipped, remove the rear facia as described in this chapter.

14

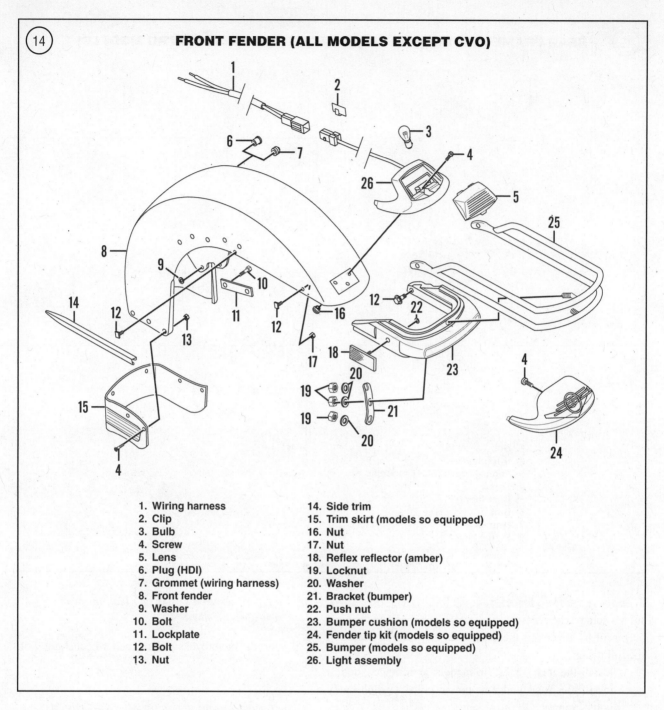

FRONT FENDER (ALL MODELS EXCEPT CVO)

1. Wiring harness
2. Clip
3. Bulb
4. Screw
5. Lens
6. Plug (HDI)
7. Grommet (wiring harness)
8. Front fender
9. Washer
10. Bolt
11. Lockplate
12. Bolt
13. Nut
14. Side trim
15. Trim skirt (models so equipped)
16. Nut
17. Nut
18. Reflex reflector (amber)
19. Locknut
20. Washer
21. Bracket (bumper)
22. Push nut
23. Bumper cushion (models so equipped)
24. Fender tip kit (models so equipped)
25. Bumper (models so equipped)
26. Light assembly

8A. On all models except FLHX and FLTR, disconnect the rear lighting connector (**Figured 22**) from the top of the rear fender. Release the connector anchor pin from the fender hole **Figure 23**

8B. On FLHX and FLTR models, remove the connector shield and disconnect the rear lighting connector (**Figure 24**) from the facia lamp assembly. Release the harness from the retainers on the left side.

9. Remove the four hex screws and lockwashers securing the license plate bracket and remove it from the luggage rack.

10. At the rear of the rear fender, remove the inboard Torx bolt (**Figure 25**) and flange nut securing the rear bumper

support rail to the saddlebag support bracket and saddlebag support rail. Repeat for the other side.

11. Working under the rear bumper, remove the flange nut with the flat washer and release the bumper bracket from the fender weld stud. Remove the rear bumper and rear bumper cushion.

12. Remove the Torx bolt (**Figure 26**; left side and **Figure 27**; right side) securing the fender to the clip nut below the frame side cover rubber grommet. Repeat for the other side.

13. Remove the rear bolt (A, **Figure 28** and A, **Figure 29**) securing the saddlebag support to the frame support. Repeat for the other side.

⑮ **TERMINAL CONNECTORS (FORK MOUNTED FARING MODELS)**

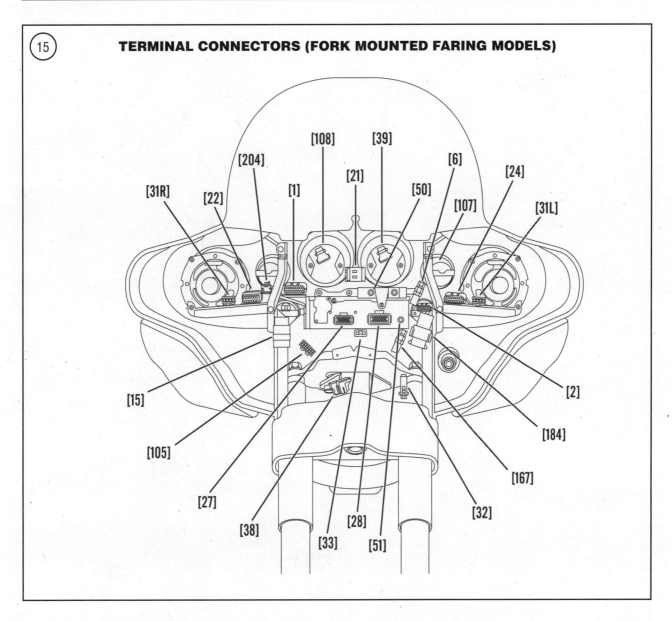

CAUTION
Hold onto the rear fender as it will drop down slightly when the following front bolt is removed.

14. Hold onto the rear fender and remove the front bolt (B, **Figure 28** and B, **Figure 29**) securing the saddlebag support to the frame support. Repeat for the other side.

15. Have an assistant spread the saddlebag supports outward. Slowly roll the rear fender back and off the rear wheel (**Figure 30**), staying away from the saddlebag supports and mufflers. Be careful not scratch the fender paint on any of the surrounding brackets.

16. Install by reversing the removal steps. Tighten all bolts and nuts as follows:
   a. Rear fender-to-battery box Torx bolt (T40) to 15-20 ft.-lb. (20.3-27.1 N•m).
   b. Saddlebag support bracket Torx bolt to 15-20 ft.-lb. (20.3-27.1 N•m).

   c. Fender side mounting Torx bolt to 15-20 ft.-lb. (20.3-27.1 N•m).
   d. Flange nut-to-weld stud to 45-85 in.-lb. (5.1-9.6 N•m).

REAR FENDER (CVO MODELS)

Removal/Installation
(FLHTCUSE and FLTRUSE Models)

Refer to **Figure 31**.

NOTE
Elevate the rear of the motorcycle sufficiently to allow the rear fender to roll back and over the rear wheel, as well as clear the frame rear cross member.

1. Support the motorcycle with the rear wheel slightly off the ground.

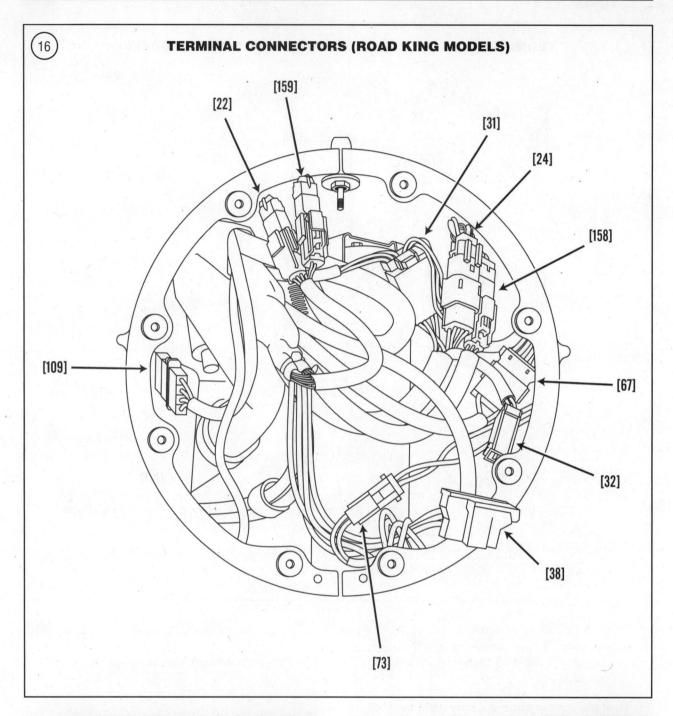

(16) TERMINAL CONNECTORS (ROAD KING MODELS)

[22] [159] [31] [24] [158] [109] [67] [32] [38] [73]

(17)

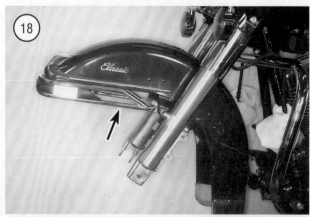

(18)

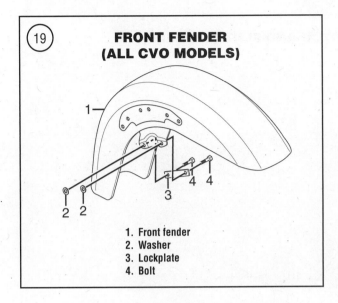

FRONT FENDER (ALL CVO MODELS)

1. Front fender
2. Washer
3. Lockplate
4. Bolt

NOTE
Always disarm the optional TSSM/HFSM security system before disconnecting the battery or pulling the Main Fuse so the siren will not sound.

2. Disconnect the negative battery cable as described in Chapter Nine.

3. Remove the seat as described in this chapter.

4. Remove both saddlebags as described in this chapter.

5. Remove both frame side covers as described in this chapter.

6. Remove the rear wheel as described in Chapter Ten.

7. Remove the passenger's seat backrest as described in this chapter.

8. Remove the saddlebag support brackets as described in this chapter.

9. Remove the bolts and lockwashers on each side securing the luggage rack to the frame. Remove the luggage rack from the frame.

10. Remove the following components only if the rear fender is going to be replaced:
   a. Remove the rear fascia as described in this chapter.
   b. Remove the rider seat backrest as described in this chapter.
   c. Remove the rear turn signal assembly as described in Chapter Nine.
   d. Remove the taillight assembly as described in Chapter Nine.

11. At the rider backrest support, remove the screws securing the support strap to the mounting bracket. Remove the support strap.

12. Disconnect the rear lighting harness connector and press the connector hold-down clip out of the rear fender.

13. Remove the locknut and washer securing the fender support bracket to the rear fender.

14. Remove the screw and clip nut securing the front of the rear fender to the frame.

15. Have an assistant support the rear fender, and remove the nuts/spacers and washers on each side.

16. Slowly roll the rear fender back and off the rear wheel (**Figure 30**), staying away from the saddlebag supports and mufflers. Be careful not scratch the fender paint on any of the surrounding brackets.

17. Install by reversing the removal steps. Note the following bolt torque specifications:
   a. Clip nut and bolt securing the front of fender-to-frame: 17-22 ft.-lb. (23.1-29.8 N•m).
   b. Passenger backrest support screws: 15-20 in.-lb. (20.3-27.1 N•m).
   c. Frame clip nut: 35-40 in.-lb. (4.0-4.5 N•m).
   d. Support bracket-to-fender locknut: 45-85 in.-lb. (5.1-9.6 N•m).

Removal/Installation (FLTRXSE, FLHXSE and FLHRSE Models)

Refer to **Figure 32**.

NOTE
Elevate the rear of the motorcycle sufficiently to allow the rear fender to roll back and over the rear wheel, as well as clear the frame rear cross member.

1. Support the motorcycle with the rear wheel slightly off the ground.

NOTE
Always disarm the optional TSSM/HFSM security system before disconnecting the battery or pulling the Main Fuse so the siren will not sound.

2. Disconnect the negative battery cable as described in Chapter Nine.

3. Remove the seat as described in this chapter.

4. Remove both saddlebags as described in this chapter.

5. Remove both frame side covers as described in this chapter.

6. Remove the rear wheel as described in Chapter Ten.

7. Remove the passenger's seat backrest as described in this chapter.

8. Remove the saddlebag support guards as described in this chapter.

9. Remove the bolts and lockwashers on each side securing the luggage rack to the frame. Remove the luggage rack from the frame.

10. Remove the following components only if the rear fender is going to be replaced:
   a. Remove the rear fascia as described in this chapter.
   b. Remove the taillight/brake light/rear turn signal assembly from each side as described in Chapter Eleven.
   c. Remove the license plate bracket as described in this chapter.

14

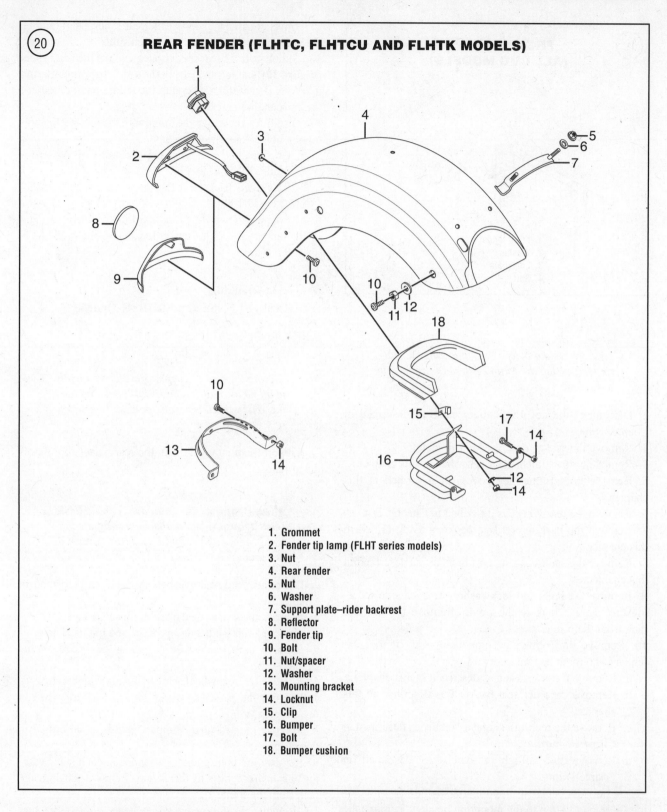

REAR FENDER (FLHTC, FLHTCU AND FLHTK MODELS)

1. Grommet
2. Fender tip lamp (FLHT series models)
3. Nut
4. Rear fender
5. Nut
6. Washer
7. Support plate–rider backrest
8. Reflector
9. Fender tip
10. Bolt
11. Nut/spacer
12. Washer
13. Mounting bracket
14. Locknut
15. Clip
16. Bumper
17. Bolt
18. Bumper cushion

11. At the rider backrest support, remove the screws securing the support strap to the mounting bracket. Remove the support strap.

12. Disconnect the air lines from both rear shock absorbers as described in Chapter Twelve.

13. Disconnect the rear lighting harness connector (**Figure 24**) and press the connector hold-down clip out of the rear fender.

14. Remove the locknut and washer securing the fender support bracket to the rear fender.

15. Remove the screw and nut slip securing the front of the rear fender to the frame.

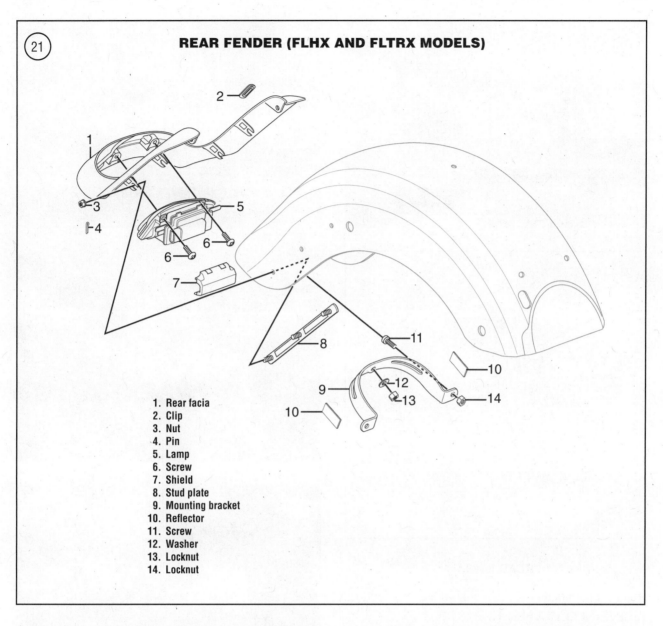

REAR FENDER (FLHX AND FLTRX MODELS)

1. Rear facia
2. Clip
3. Nut
4. Pin
5. Lamp
6. Screw
7. Shield
8. Stud plate
9. Mounting bracket
10. Reflector
11. Screw
12. Washer
13. Locknut
14. Locknut

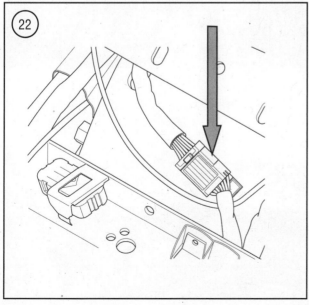

16. Have an assistant support the rear fender, and remove the nut/spacers and washers on each side.

17. Slowly roll the rear fender back and off the rear wheel (**Figure 30**), staying away from the saddlebag supports and mufflers. Be careful not scratch the fender paint on any of the surrounding brackets.

18. Install by reversing the removal steps. Note the following bolt torque specifications:

   a. Bolts securing the front of fender to frame: 15-20 ft.-lb. (20.3-27.1 N•m).

   b. Saddlebag support-to-fender and frame: 15-20 ft.-lb. (20.3-27.1 N•m).

   c. Passenger backrest support screws: 16.7 ft.-lb. (22.6 N•m).

14

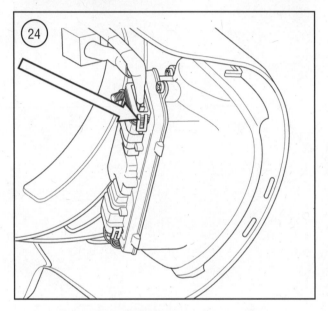

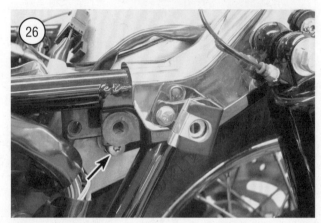

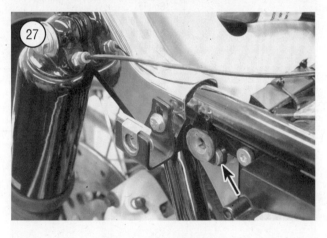

REAR FACIA

Removal/Installation
(FLHX and FLTRX Models)

Refer to **Figure 21**.

1. Support the motorcycle with the rear wheel slightly off the ground.

> *NOTE*
> *Always disarm the optional TSSM/HFSM security system before disconnecting the battery or pulling the Main Fuse so the siren will not sound.*

2. Disconnect the negative battery cable as described in Chapter Nine.

3. Remove the seat as described in this chapter.

4. Remove both saddlebags as described in this chapter.

5. Along the side of the rear fender, remove the three flange nuts from the studs on each side.

6. On the left side, loosen the set screw and unscrew the radio antenna mast from the bracket.

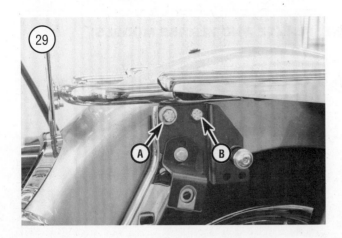

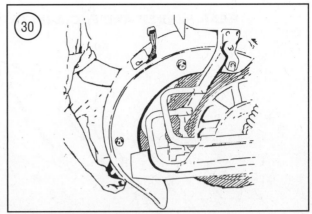

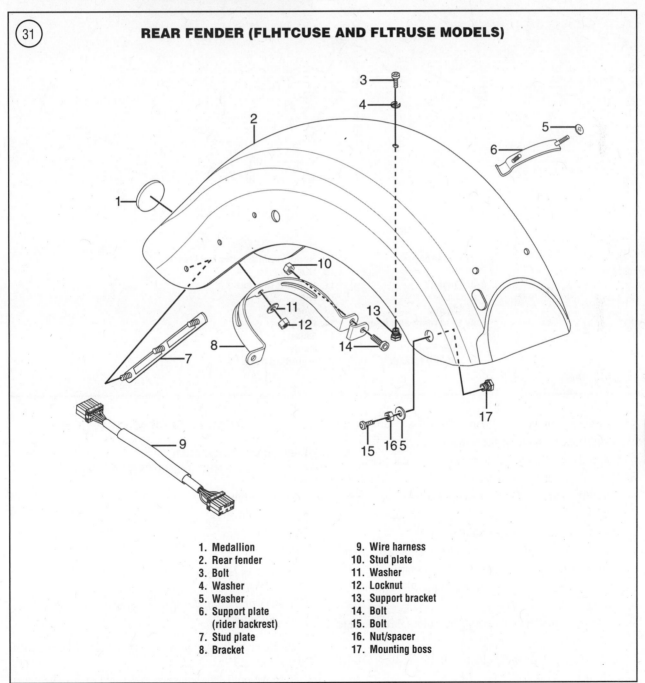

REAR FENDER (FLHTCUSE AND FLTRUSE MODELS)

1. Medallion
2. Rear fender
3. Bolt
4. Washer
5. Washer
6. Support plate
   (rider backrest)
7. Stud plate
8. Bracket
9. Wire harness
10. Stud plate
11. Washer
12. Locknut
13. Support bracket
14. Bolt
15. Bolt
16. Nut/spacer
17. Mounting boss

14

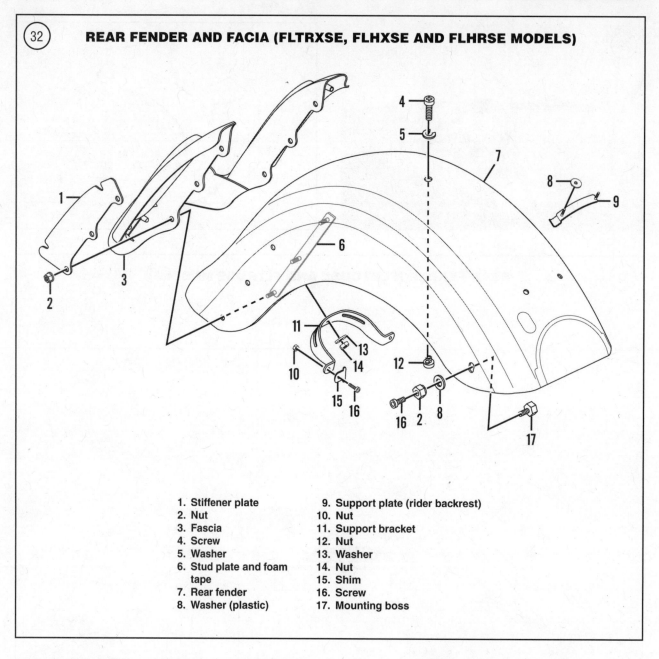

③② **REAR FENDER AND FACIA (FLTRXSE, FLHXSE AND FLHRSE MODELS)**

1. Stiffener plate
2. Nut
3. Fascia
4. Screw
5. Washer
6. Stud plate and foam tape
7. Rear fender
8. Washer (plastic)
9. Support plate (rider backrest)
10. Nut
11. Support bracket
12. Nut
13. Washer
14. Nut
15. Shim
16. Screw
17. Mounting boss

7. Carefully open the conduit on the rear fascia lamp wires at the split line and release the wires.

8. Carefully spread the top sections of the rear fascia and release if from the studs on each side.

9. Carefully pull straight down and release the fascia from the rear fender. Gently wiggle the fascia if necessary. Be careful not scratch the fender paint.

10. Remove the two Torx screws (T20), and then remove the lamp assembly from the fascia, if necessary.

11. Install by reversing the removal steps, while noting the following:

   a. Apply a small dab of Loctite 243 (blue) threadlock to the studs.

   b. Tighten the flange nuts to 30-45 in.-lb. (3.4-5.1 N•m).

REAR FENDER AND FACIA

Removal and Installation
(FLHXSE, FLHRSE and FLTRSE Models)

Refer to **Figure 32**.

1. Support the motorcycle with the rear wheel slightly off the ground.

NOTE
Always disarm the optional TSSM/HFSM security system before disconnecting the battery or pulling the Main Fuse so the siren will not sound.

2. Disconnect the negative battery cable as described in Chapter Nine.

3. Remove both saddlebags as described in this chapter.

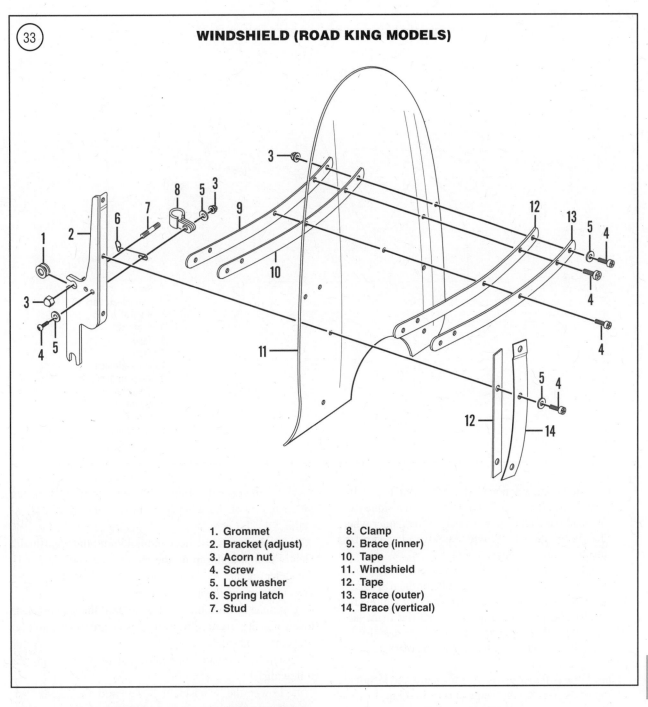

WINDSHIELD (ROAD KING MODELS)

1. Grommet
2. Bracket (adjust)
3. Acorn nut
4. Screw
5. Lock washer
6. Spring latch
7. Stud
8. Clamp
9. Brace (inner)
10. Tape
11. Windshield
12. Tape
13. Brace (outer)
14. Brace (vertical)

14

4. Remove the taillight/brake light/rear turn signal assembly from each side as described in Chapter Nine.

5. Remove the two lower flange nuts on each side securing the stiffener plate and rear fascia to the rear fender.

6. Secure the rear fascia and remove the upper flange nut on each side and remove the stiffener plates from each side.

7. Carefully pull one side of the rear fascia and remove it from the studs on that side stud plate. Then, repeat the process for the other side.

8. Carefully remove the rear fascia from the rear fender. Do not scratch the rear fender finish.

9. Remove the stud plate assembly from the inside of the rear fender, if necessary. Repeat for the other side, if necessary.

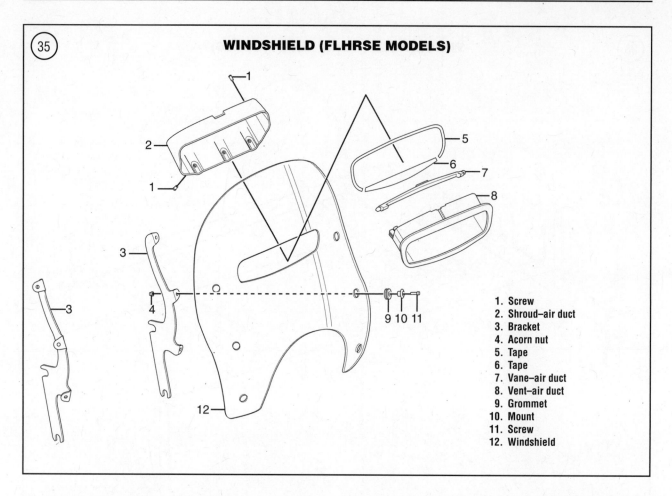

WINDSHIELD (FLHRSE MODELS)

1. Screw
2. Shroud–air duct
3. Bracket
4. Acorn nut
5. Tape
6. Tape
7. Vane–air duct
8. Vent–air duct
9. Grommet
10. Mount
11. Screw
12. Windshield

10. If the stud plate was removed, perform the following:
   a. Thoroughly scrape off all old foam tape residue from the stud plate and the underside of the fender where the stud plate was secured. Remove old foam tape residue with isopropyl alcohol.
   b. Apply two *new* sections of foam tape to the stud plate where it attaches to the under side of the rear fender.
   c. Install the stud plate onto the inner surface of the rear fender and press onto place to seat the foam tape. Repeat for the remaining stud plate, if necessary.
11. Carefully install the rear fascia onto the rear fender and the studs on each side.
12. Install the stiffener plates over the studs and install the six flange nuts. Tighten the flange nuts to 30-45 in.-lb. (3.4-5.1 N•m).
13. Install the taillight/brake light/rear turn signal assembly onto each side as described in Chapter Nine.
14. Install both saddlebags as described in this chapter.
15. Connect the negative battery cable as described in Chapter Nine.

WINDSHIELD

Road King Models
Removal/Installation

Refer to **Figure 33**.
1. Place the motorcycle on level ground on the jiffy stand.

2. Use a finger and lift up on the wire form latch spring on each side of the windshield next to the headlight nacelle.
3. Straddle the front wheel and hold onto the windshield. Gently pull straight up on the top of the windshield until the upper notches on the side brackets are free of the upper grommets on the passing light support.
4. Continue to raise the windshield until the side brackets lower notches are free from the lower grommets, and remove the windshield.
5. Install by reversing the removal steps while noting the following:
   a. Lower the windshield down until the latches are firmly seated on the grommet on each side.
   b. Push down on the wire form latch springs until they overhang the rubber grommets.
   c. To adjust, loosen the retaining screws and rotate the latch springs into the proper location.
   d. Make sure the windshield is securely in place prior to riding.FLHRCSE Models

FLHRSE Models
Removal/Installation

Refer to **Figure 35**.
1. Place the motorcycle on level ground on the jiffy stand.

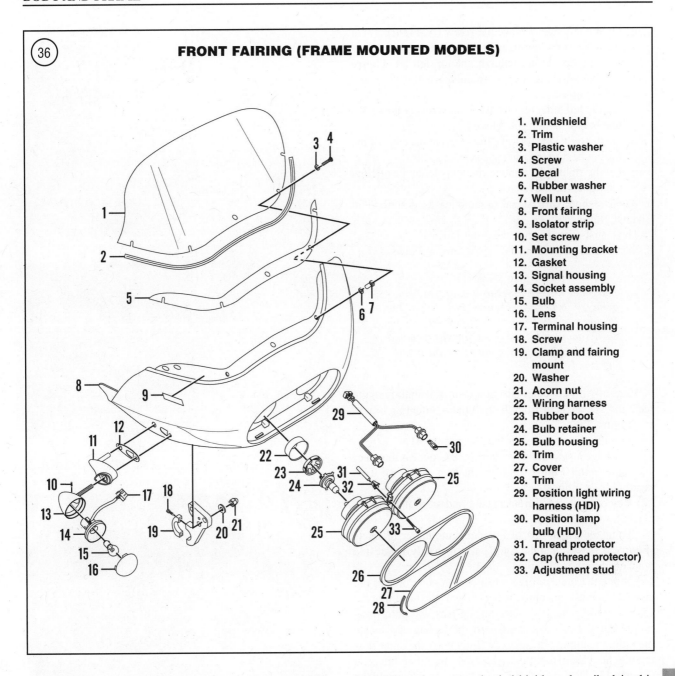

FRONT FAIRING (FRAME MOUNTED MODELS)

36

1. Windshield
2. Trim
3. Plastic washer
4. Screw
5. Decal
6. Rubber washer
7. Well nut
8. Front fairing
9. Isolator strip
10. Set screw
11. Mounting bracket
12. Gasket
13. Signal housing
14. Socket assembly
15. Bulb
16. Lens
17. Terminal housing
18. Screw
19. Clamp and fairing mount
20. Washer
21. Acorn nut
22. Wiring harness
23. Rubber boot
24. Bulb retainer
25. Bulb housing
26. Trim
27. Cover
28. Trim
29. Position light wiring harness (HDI)
30. Position lamp bulb (HDI)
31. Thread protector
32. Cap (thread protector)
33. Adjustment stud

2. Straddle the motorcycle and hold onto the windshield. Gently pull up on windshield until the bracket notches are clear of the upper and lower headlight nacelle grommets.

3. Continue to raise the windshield until the side brackets are free and remove the windshield.

4. Install by reversing these removal steps. Make sure the windshield is secure prior to riding.

FRONT FAIRING (FRAME MOUNTED MODELS)

Outer Front Fairing
Removal/Installation

Refer to **Figure 36**.

1. Place the motorcycle on level ground using the jiffy stand.

2. Remove the seat and windshield as described in this chapter.

NOTE
Always disarm the optional TSSM/HFSM security system before disconnecting the battery or pulling the Main Fuse so the siren will not sound.

3. Disconnect the negative battery cable as described in Chapter Nine.

4. Cover the front fender with towels or a blanket to protect the painted finish.

5. Remove the six Torx screws (T25) securing the outer fairing to the inner fairing in the following order:

14

   a. On the left side, remove the screw (A, **Figure 37**) at the edge of the fairing next to the left speaker.
   b. Loosen, but do not remove, the top left (B, **Figure 37**) and top right side screws outboard of the fuel and volt gauges.
   c. On the left side, remove the long screw (**Figure 38**) just below the left side glove box.
   d. On the right side, remove the screw at the edge of the fairing next to the right speaker.
   e. On the right side, remove the long screw just below the right side glove box.

6. Remove both turn signal assemblies as described in Chapter Nine.

7. Have an assistant secure the outer fairing.

8. Remove the top left and top right fairing screws.

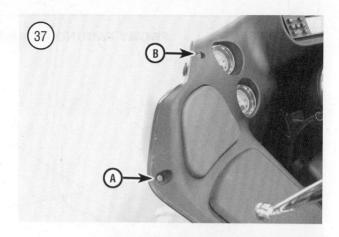

CAUTION
*The outer fairing is secured onto two radio-mounted brackets (**Figure 39**). The outer fairing mounting notches (**Figure 40**) can be easily damaged if the outer fairing is pulled on too hard during its release from the mounting brackets.*

9. Carefully lift the outer fairing up, move it slightly to the rear, and disengage it from the two radio mounting brackets (**Figure 39**).

10. Partially lower the outer fairing (**Figure 41**).

11. Working inside the outer fairing, disconnect the electrical connector (**Figure 42**) from the backside of the each headlight assembly.

12. Remove the outer front fairing and store it in a safe place.

13. Paint the outer tips of the radio mounting brackets (**Figure 43**) with a light color paint to easily locate the brackets during installation.

14. Move the outer fairing into position and connect the electrical connectors onto the backside of the headlights.

15. Carefully move the outer fairing part way into position (**Figure 41**). Look down into the fairing and locate the radio mounting brackets. Carefully hook the outer fairing notches (**Figure 40**) onto the radio mounting brackets (**Figure 43**). Do not force the outer fairing as damage to the notches will occur.

16. Align the tabs on the inner fairing to the outside of those on the outer fairing. Make sure this condition exists on both sides of the fairing (A, **Figure 44**).

17. Align the trim edge (B, **Figure 44**) between the two fairing panels.

18. Hold the fairing in position and install the top left (B, **Figure 37**) and top right side screws outboard of the fuel and volt gauges, but do not tighten them yet.

19. Install the screws (A, **Figure 37**) at the edge of the fairing next to the speakers on each side, but do not tighten them yet.

20. Install the long screw (**Figure 38**) just below the glove box on each side, but do not tighten them yet.

21. Using a crossing pattern, tighten the four short fairing screws to 6-12 in.-lb. (0.7-1.4 N•m).

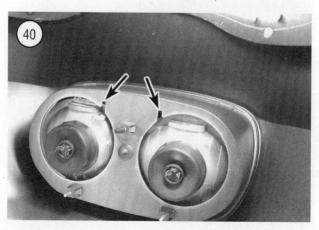

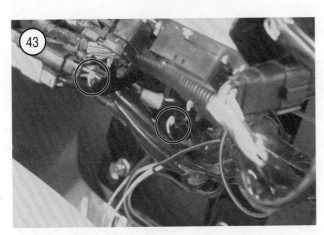

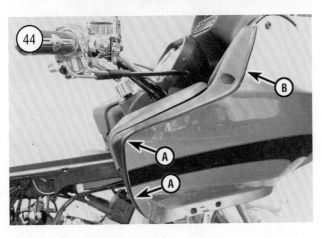

22. Tighten the two long screws to 10-15 in.-lb. (1.1-1.7 N•m), alternating from side to side. Do not overtighten as the plastic surrounding the screw hole may fracture.

23. Install the front turn signal light assembly as described in Chapter Nine.

Instrument Bezel Housing
Removal/Installation

Refer to **Figure 45**.

1. Place the motorcycle on level ground using the jiffy stand.
2. Remove the seat as described in this chapter.

> *NOTE*
> *Always disarm the optional TSSM/HFSM security system before disconnecting the battery or pulling the Main Fuser so the siren will not sound.*

3. Disconnect the negative battery cable as described in Chapter Nine.
4. Remove the instruments (A, **Figure 46**) and bezel as described in Chapter Nine.
5. Remove the ignition switch knob (A, **Figure 47**), nut, collar and washer as described in *Switches* (Chapter Nine).
6. Remove the clutch cable clip (**Figure 48**) from the hole on the left side of the instrument housing.
7. Remove the throttle cable clip (B, **Figure 46**) from the hole on the right side of the instrument housing.
8. Remove the two Torx screws (T25) and washers (B, **Figure 47**) securing the right and left side housing to the upper and lower fork bracket.
9. On the left side of the housing, unscrew the rubber boot from the odometer reset switch (C, **Figure 47**).
10. Partially remove the left side of the housing (D, **Figure 47**). Pull the odometer reset switch from the hole.
11. At the front portion of the instrument bezel housing, disconnect the 12-pin electrical connector (**Figure 49**) for the instrument switches from the interconnect harness.
12. Carefully separate the instrument bezel and housing halves and remove each one from the frame. Store the panels in a safe place.
13. Install by reversing the removal steps. Tighten the Torx screws (T25) to 15-20 ft.-lb. (20.3-27.1 N•m).

Inner Front Fairing
Removal/Installation

Refer to **Figure 50** and **Figure 51**.

1. Place the motorcycle on level ground using the jiffy stand.
2. Remove the seat as described in this chapter.

> *NOTE*
> *Always disarm the optional TSSM/HFSM security system before disconnecting the battery or pulling the Main fuse so the siren will not sound.*

14

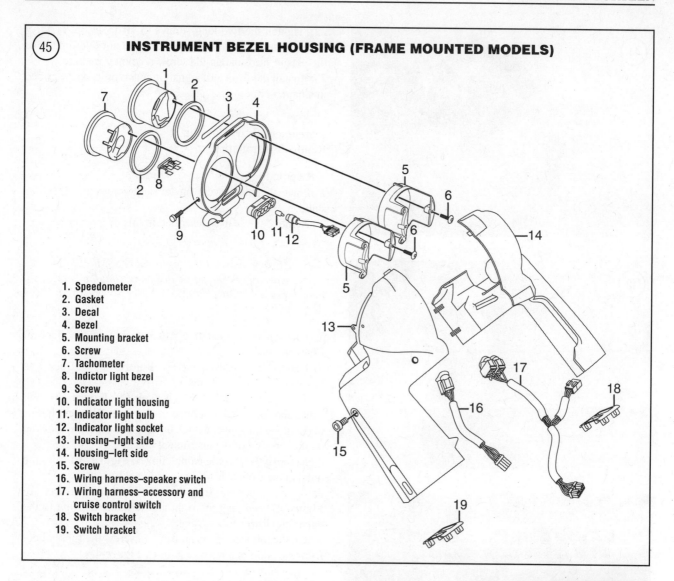

45 **INSTRUMENT BEZEL HOUSING (FRAME MOUNTED MODELS)**

1. Speedometer
2. Gasket
3. Decal
4. Bezel
5. Mounting bracket
6. Screw
7. Tachometer
8. Indictor light bezel
9. Screw
10. Indicator light housing
11. Indicator light bulb
12. Indicator light socket
13. Housing–right side
14. Housing–left side
15. Screw
16. Wiring harness–speaker switch
17. Wiring harness–accessory and cruise control switch
18. Switch bracket
19. Switch bracket

3. Disconnect the negative battery cable as described in Chapter Nine.

4. Cover the front fender with towels or a blanket to protect the painted finish.

5. Remove the instrument bezel housing as described in this section.

6. Remove the outer front fairing as described in this section.

NOTE
Due to the large number of electrical connectors to be disconnected in the following steps, be sure identify each mating half of the connectors to assist during installation.

7. Refer to **Figure 51** and to the wiring diagrams located in Chapter Sixteen. Disconnect the main harness from the interconnect harness electrical connectors as follows:
   a. The black 16-pin interconnect harness connector located on the right side below the radio.
   b. The gray 12-pin main harness to interconnect harness connector located on the right side below the radio.

46

c. The black 4-pin main power-to-interconnect harness connector located on the right side below the radio.

8. Refer to **Figure 51** and disconnect the radio cable and ground connectors as follows:
   a. The radio antenna cable connector located on the left side at the back of the radio.
   b. Radio ground, single spade and socket terminal located on the left side below the radio.

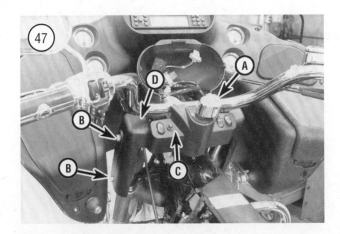

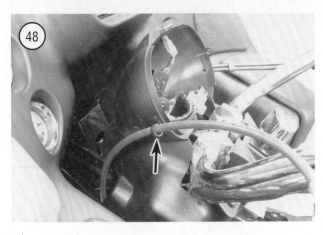

9. Disconnect the handlebar switch controls from the interconnect harness as follows:

    a. The gray 16-pin left side handlebar switch connector secured to the T-stud on the left side radio bracket.

    b. The black 12-pin right side handlebar switch connector secured to the T-stud on the right side radio bracket.

    c. The 6-pin front turn signal connector located on the right side below the radio.

    d. The radio ground single spade and socket terminal.

10. Carefully pull the main harness, handlebar switch conduit, radio ground wire and antenna cable as far forward as possible. Rest the connector of the longer harnesses on the front fender.

11. Refer to **Figure 49**, and disconnect the instrument nacelle switches and air temperature sensor from the interconnect harness as follows:

    a. The 12-pin instrument nacelle switch connector.

    b. 3-pin air temperature sensor connector.

12. Wrap the harness bundle tightly with shop cloths and secure them with tape or string. This bundle of wires must pass through the front opening (A, **Figure 52**) in the inner fairing and bracket tunnel.

13. Carefully pull the interconnect harness connectors from the instrument nacelle through the front fairing tunnel.

14. Disconnect the ignition switch as follows:

    a. Disconnect the 3-pin ignition switch connector at the front of the switch.

    b. Use the ignition switch connector remover (H-D part No. HD-45961). Gently insert the tool into the switch housing until it stops.

    c. Grasp the main harness conduit and the tool, and pull at the same time, releasing the socket from the ignition switch housing.

15. Pull the ignition switch branch of the main harness forward and out of the instrument nacelle. Pull it through the fairing bracket tunnel, toward the front of the inner fairing.

16. Separate all interconnect harness branches that may be tangled with the main wiring harness conduit. Let the interconnect harness hang down along the left side of the front fender.

17. Carefully gather and bundle all of the disconnected harnesses and electrical connectors. Wrap the harness bundle tightly with shop cloths and secure them with tape or string. This bundle of wires must pass through the front opening (A, **Figure 52**) in the inner fairing and bracket tunnel.

18. Hold onto the inner front fairing and remove the four locknuts (B, **Figure 52**) securing the inner front fairing and radio mounting bracket to the fairing mounting bracket.

19. Remove the inner front fairing and radio mounting bracket from the frame. Store it in a safe place.

20. Install by reversing the removal steps, while noting the following:

    a. Tighten the four locknuts to 96-144 in.-lb. (10.9-16.3 N•m).

    b. Correctly reconnect all electrical connectors by referring to the wiring diagrams located in Chapter Sixteen of this manual and to **Figure 51**.

FRONT FAIRING (FORK MOUNTED FAIRING MODELS)

Outer Front Fairing
Removal/Installation

Refer to **Figure 53** and **Figure 54**.

1. Place the motorcycle on level ground using the jiffy stand.

2. Remove the seat as described in this chapter.

NOTE
Always disarm the optional TSSM/HFSM security system before disconnecting the battery or pulling the Main Fuse so the siren will not sound.

3. Disconnect the negative battery cable as described in Chapter Nine.

4. Cover the front fender with towels or a blanket to protect the painted finish.

5. At the front of the outer front fairing, locate the three Torx screws (**Figure 55**) securing the windshield and the

14

49 **FAIRING TERMINAL CONNECTORS (FRAME MOUNTED FAIRING MODELS)**

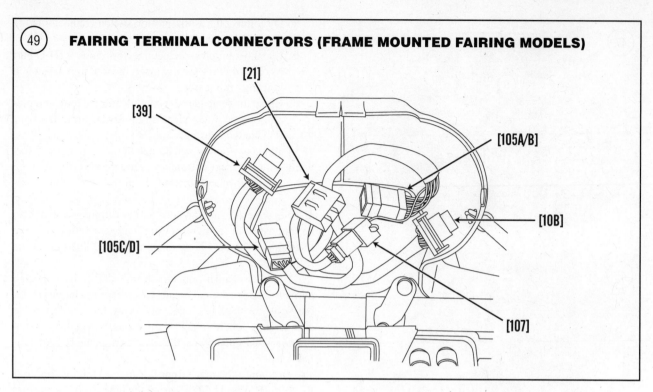

50 **INNER FRONT FAIRING (FRAME MOUNTED FAIRING MODELS)**

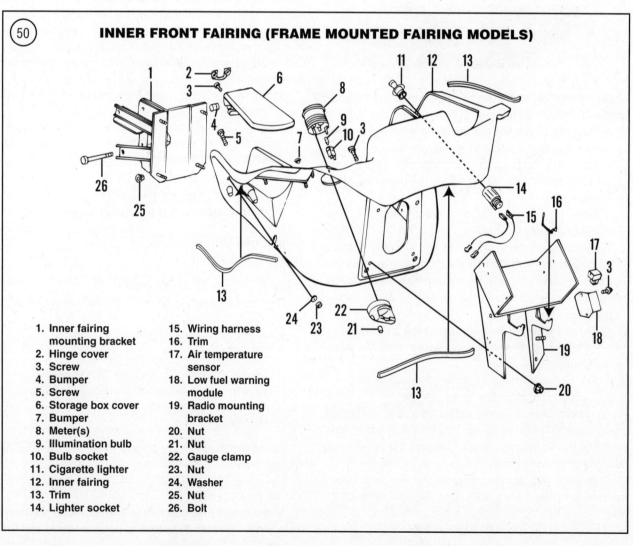

1. Inner fairing
   mounting bracket
2. Hinge cover
3. Screw
4. Bumper
5. Screw
6. Storage box cover
7. Bumper
8. Meter(s)
9. Illumination bulb
10. Bulb socket
11. Cigarette lighter
12. Inner fairing
13. Trim
14. Lighter socket
15. Wiring harness
16. Trim
17. Air temperature
    sensor
18. Low fuel warning
    module
19. Radio mounting
    bracket
20. Nut
21. Nut
22. Gauge clamp
23. Nut
24. Washer
25. Nut
26. Bolt

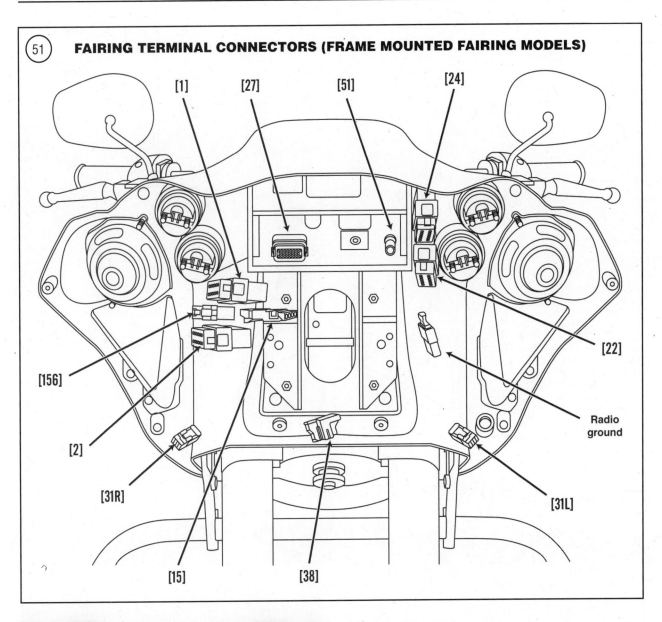

51 **FAIRING TERMINAL CONNECTORS (FRAME MOUNTED FAIRING MODELS)**

[1] [27] [51] [24]

[22]

Radio ground

[156]

[2]

[31R]

[31L]

[15] [38]

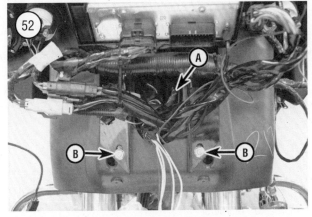

52

outer fairing to the inner fairing. Using an alternating pattern, loosen but do not remove, the screws at this time.

6. Carefully raise the windshield from between the inner and outer front fairings.

7. While working on the inner fairing side, remove the Torx screw (T25) at corner (**Figure 56**) on each side of the inner fairing.

8. Turn the front wheel all the way to the left. Working below the fairing cap, remove the screw (**Figure 57**) securing the outer front fairing to the mounting bracket.

NOTE
On FLHX models, have an assistant hold onto the front outer fairing as it will be loose after removal of the fastener.

9. Turn the front wheel all the way to the right. Working below the fairing cap, remove the other screw securing the outer front fairing to the mounting bracket.

10. Remove the three loosened Torx screws and washers.

11. Tilt the outer front front fairing forward and disconnect the headlight connector from the headlight assembly.

14

53

HEADLIGHT ASSEMBLY (FORK MOUNTED FAIRING MODELS)

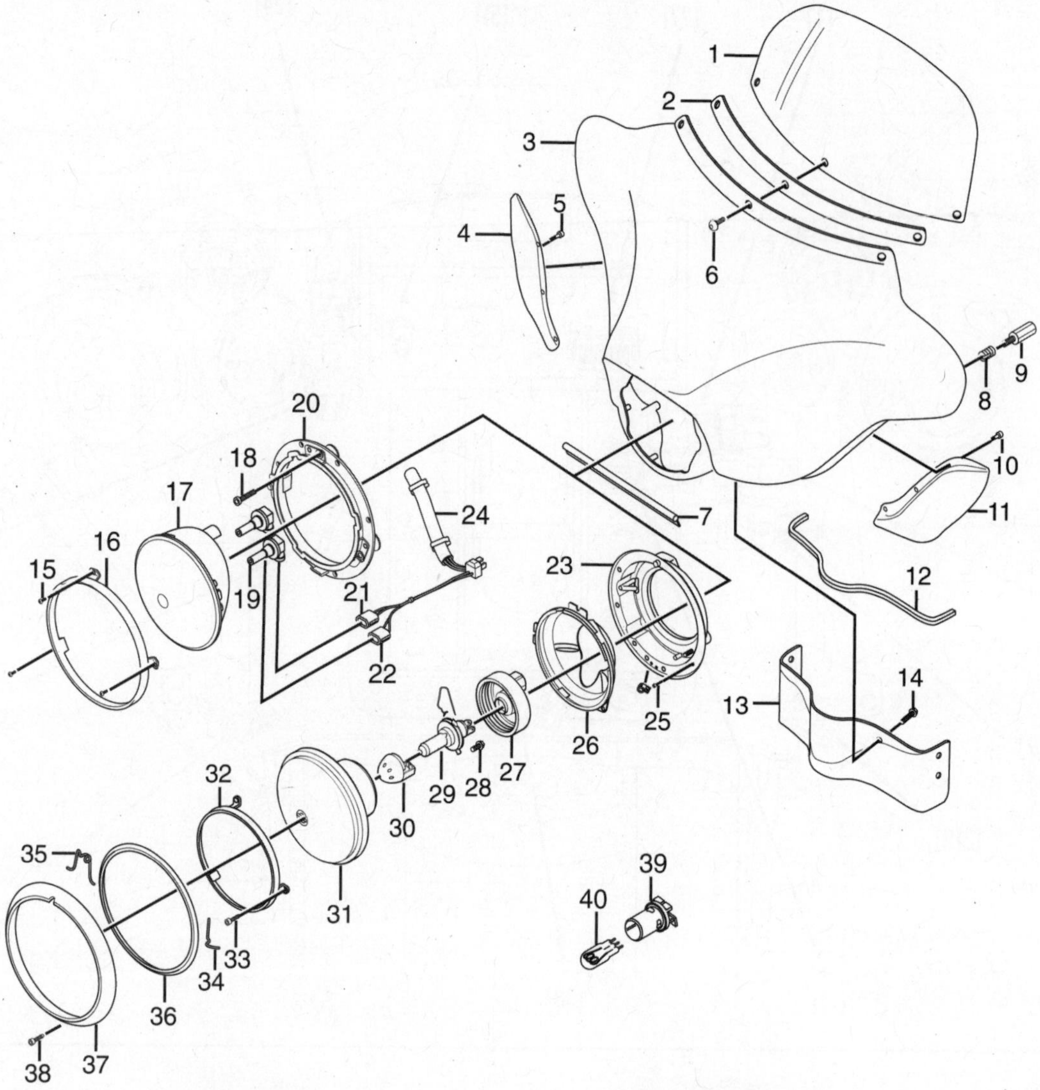

1. Windshield
2. Tape
3. Front fairing
4. Air deflector (models so equipped)
5. Screw
6. Screw
7. Seal strip
8. Insert
9. Nut extension
10. Screw
11. Air deflector (models so equipped)
12. Trim
13. Chrome mounting bracket
14. Screw
15. Screw*
16. Retaining ring*
17. Headlamp lens*
18. Bulbs–low and high beam*
19. Screw*
20. Mounting ring assembly*
21. Bulb socket–gray*
22. Bulb socket–black*
23. Headlight housing
24. Wiring harness*
25. Screw
26. Mounting ring
27. Rubber boot
28. Bolt
29. Bulb
30. Bulb cover
31. Headlight lens
32. Retaining ring
33. Screw
34. Bottom spring
35. Top spring
36. Gasket
37. Trim bezel
38. Screw
39. Socket (HDI only)
40. Position lamp socket (HDI only)

*SVO models only.

54 **FAIRING TERMINAL CONNECTORS (FORK MOUNTED FAIRING MODELS)**

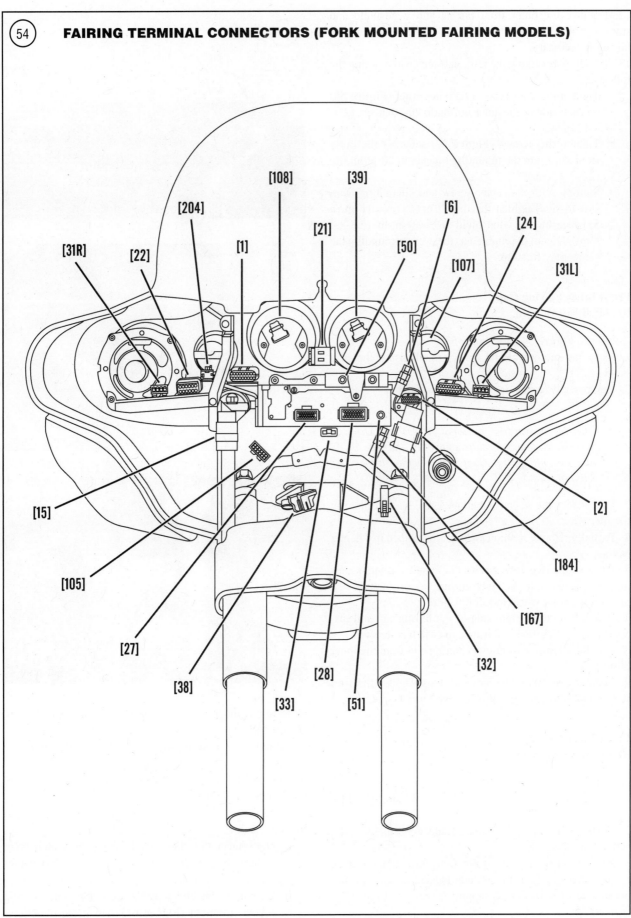

14

12. Remove the outer front fairing and windshield and store it in a safe place. Remove the windshield from the fairing if necessary.

13. Install by reversing the removal steps while noting the following:

    a. Tighten the Torx screw (T25) at corner (**Figure 56**) on each side of the inner fairing to 20-30 in.-lb. (2.3-3.4 N•m).

    b. Tighten the screws (**Figure 57**) securing the outer front fairing to the mounting bracket to 20-30 in.-lb. (2.3-3.4 N•m).

    c. Starting with the center screw and alternating from side-to-side, tighten the three Torx screws (**Figure 55**) securing the windshield to 25-30 in.-lb. (2.8-3.4 N•m). Do not overtighten as the area surrounding the screw may fracture.

Front Inner Fairing Cap
Removal/Installation

Refer to **Figure 54** and **Figure 58**.

1. Place the motorcycle on level ground using the jiffy stand.

2. Remove the seat as described in this chapter.

> *NOTE*
> *Always disarm the optional TSSM/HFSM security system before disconnecting the battery or pulling the Maxi-Fuse so the siren will not sound.*

3. Disconnect the negative battery cable as described in Chapter Nine.

4. Partially remove ignition switch as described in Chapter Nine.

5. Remove the two Torx screws (T27) and washers securing the fairing cap to the inner fairing.

6. Turn the front wheel to full left stop.

7. Reach behind the right side of the fairing cap and disconnect the black 12-pin fairing cap switch connector.

8. Carefully remove front inner fairing cap from the inner fairing.

9. Install by reversing the removal steps. Tighten the Torx screws (T27) to 25-30 in.-lb. (2.8-3.4 N•m).

Front Inner Fairing
Removal/Installation

Refer to **Figure 54** and **Figure 58**.

1. Place the motorcycle on level ground using the jiffy stand.

2. Remove the outer front fairing and windshield as described in this section.

3. Disconnect both of the 4-pin front turn signal/passing light connectors from the T-studs located at the top, outboard side of both fairing support braces (A, **Figure 59**, typical).

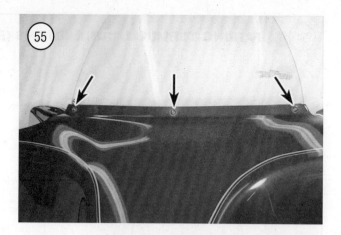

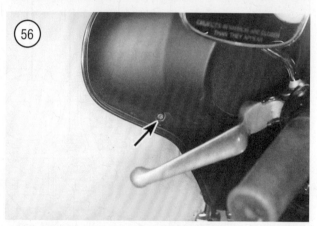

4. Remove the passing light assembly as described in Chapter Nine.

5. Remove the inner fairing cap as described in this section.

6. Remove the screws securing the chrome mounting skirt (**Figure 60**) and remove it.

7A. On all models except FLHTCUSE, perform the following:

    a. Disconnect the clutch cable from the clutch lever as described in *Clutch Cable Replacement* (Chapter Six).

    b. Withdraw the clutch cable from the inner fairing rubber grommet (**Figure 61**). Move the clutch ca-

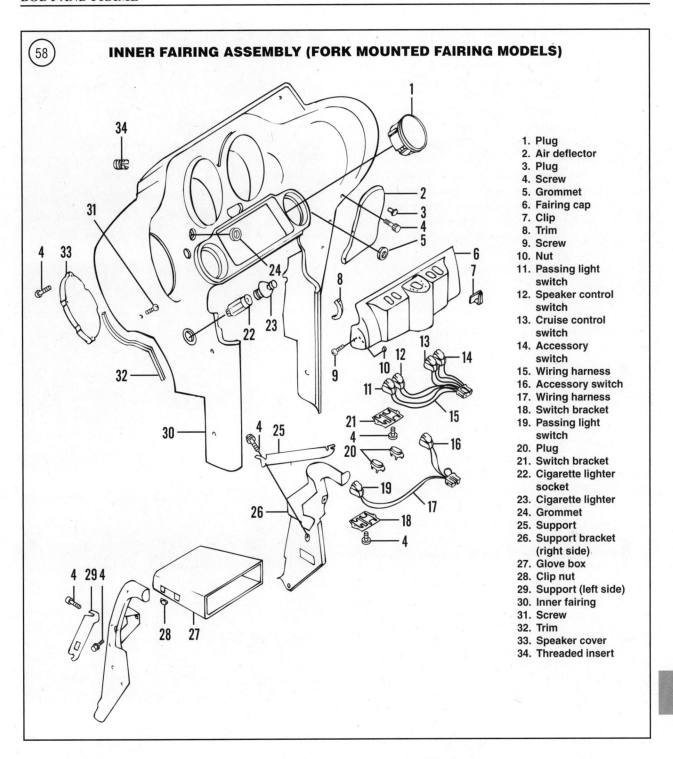

58   **INNER FAIRING ASSEMBLY (FORK MOUNTED FAIRING MODELS)**

1. Plug
2. Air deflector
3. Plug
4. Screw
5. Grommet
6. Fairing cap
7. Clip
8. Trim
9. Screw
10. Nut
11. Passing light switch
12. Speaker control switch
13. Cruise control switch
14. Accessory switch
15. Wiring harness
16. Accessory switch
17. Wiring harness
18. Switch bracket
19. Passing light switch
20. Plug
21. Switch bracket
22. Cigarette lighter socket
23. Cigarette lighter
24. Grommet
25. Support
26. Support bracket (right side)
27. Glove box
28. Clip nut
29. Support (left side)
30. Inner fairing
31. Screw
32. Trim
33. Speaker cover
34. Threaded insert

14

ble forward and out of the way. Remove the rubber grommet.

7B. On FLHTCUSE models, remove the clutch master cylinder from the handlebar as described in Chapter Six.

8. Remove the front brake master cylinder from the handlebar as described in Chapter Thirteen.

9. Separate the right side handlebar switch housing as described in Chapter Nine.

10. Disconnect the spade terminals from the cigarette lighter (B, **Figure 59**). Hold the socket to keep if from rotating and unscrew the outer shell.

11. Remove the socket from the inner fairing and reinstall the shell onto the socket.

12. Disconnect the spade terminals (C, **Figure 59**) from both speakers.

13. Remove the Torx screws (T25) securing the speaker adapter (D, **Figure 59**) to the inner fairing. Repeat for the remaining adapter.

14. On the left side of the inner fairing, unscrew the rubber boot and remove the odometer reset switch from the housing.

15. Disconnect the speedometer connector and tachometer connector from the instrument assembly.

16. Remove the Phillips screws securing the speedometer and tachometer (**Figure 62**) to the mounting brackets. Remove the speedometer and tachometer from the inner fairing. Leave the anchors on the interconnect harness installed on the outboard ears of the brackets. Push the gauges toward the rear of the motorcycle and remove both gauges from the inner fairing.

17. Disconnect the 10-pin indicator light connector.

18. Carefully cut the cable strap securing the indicator light connector between the speedometer and tachometer brackets.

19. Release the four paddles and free the indicator bulb housing from the lens assembly. Remove the lens assembly from the inner fairing.

20. Disconnect the voltmeter light connector and voltmeter connector.

21. Disconnect the fuel gauge light connector and fuel gauge connector.

22. Remove the four Allen bolts securing the inner fairing to the fairing mounting bracket.

23. Spread the bottom of the inner fairing and free it from the locating dowels in the lower fork bracket. Spread the bottom of the inner fairing bracket and release if from the same locating dowels.

24. Slightly raise the inner fairing and the support brackets further up to prevent the reengagement of the locating dowels. Raise the lower fairing and support brackets sufficiently high enough to gain access to the lower row of gauges.

25. On FLHTCU and FLHTCUSE models, disconnect the following electrical connectors:

    a. The oil pressure gauge light and oil pressure gauge connectors.

    b. The air temperature gauge light and air temperature gauge connectors.

26. Raise the inner fairing and fairing bracket together as an assembly. Pull the fairing bracket toward the front of the motorcycle and inner fairing toward the rear, and then separate them.

27. As the inner fairing is free of the radio, remove the inner fairing. Move it to the workbench and place it on towels or a blanket.

28. Reposition the fairing bracket, radio and interconnect harness onto the frame. Align the holes with the locating dowels in the lower fork bracket. Install the Allen screws and finger-tighten the screws at this time.

29. On all models, remove the hex nuts securing the voltmeter and fuel level gauges to the mounting brackets. Then, remove the voltmeter and fuel level gauge from the inner fairing, if necessary.

30. On FLHTCU and FLHTCUSE models, remove the hex nuts securing the oil pressure and air temperature gauges to the mounting brackets. Remove the oil pressure and air temperature gauges from the inner fairing, if necessary.

31. Install by reversing the removal steps while noting the following:

    a. Install the two or four gauges into the inner fairing and slide the brackets over the threaded studs. Install

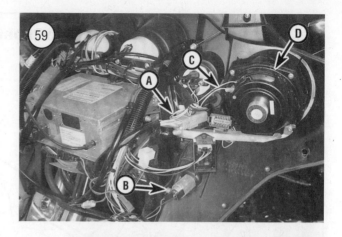

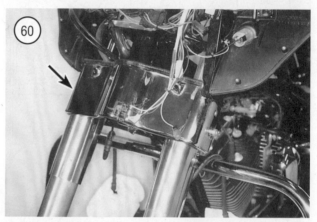

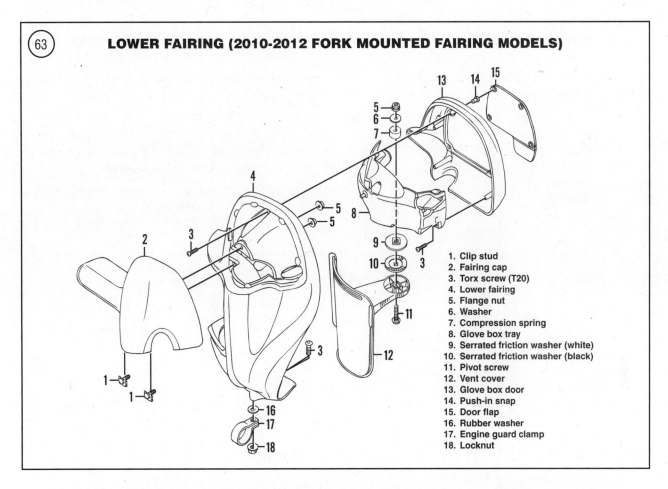

63 **LOWER FAIRING (2010-2012 FORK MOUNTED FAIRING MODELS)**

1. Clip stud
2. Fairing cap
3. Torx screw (T20)
4. Lower fairing
5. Flange nut
6. Washer
7. Compression spring
8. Glove box tray
9. Serrated friction washer (white)
10. Serrated friction washer (black)
11. Pivot screw
12. Vent cover
13. Glove box door
14. Push-in snap
15. Door flap
16. Rubber washer
17. Engine guard clamp
18. Locknut

the hex nuts and finger-tighten them. Correctly align the gauges and tighten the hex nuts to 10-20 in.-lb. (1.1-2.3 N•m).

b. Install the speedometer and tachometer into the inner fairing. Install the Phillips screws finger-tight, correctly align the gauges, and then tighten the screws to 10-20 in.-lb. (1.1-2.3 N•m).

c. Install both speaker adapters (D, **Figure 59**). Install the long Torx screws (T25) at the top and tighten to 35-50 in.-lb. (4.0-5.7 N•m). Install the short Torx screws (T25) at the bottom and tighten to 22-28 in.-lb. (2.5-3.2 N•m).

d. On all models except FLHTCUSE, adjust the clutch as described in Chapter Three.

Air Deflectors (FLHTCU and FLHTCUSE Models) Removal/Installation

Refer to **Figure 53**.

1. Remove the three knurled thumb screws securing the air deflector to the lower fairing, and remove the deflector. Repeat for the remaining side if necessary.

2. Install the air deflector and the knurled thumb screws. Tighten the thumb screws to 25-30 in.-lb. (2.8-3.4 N•m).

Lower Fairing (Fork Mounted Fairing Models)

Removal

Refer to **Figure 63** and **Figure 64**.

1. Position the front wheel in the straight ahead position to protect finish on the fender and lower fairing during removal.

2. Carefully pull out and release the door flap push-in snaps. Release all four snaps and remove the door flap.

3. Reach into the glove box and remove the two flange nuts from the clip studs.

4. Push in on end of both studs. Carefully pull straight out and remove the fairing cap from the lower fairing. Do not twist the fairing cap during removal as it will be damaged.

5. On FLHRSE models, disconnect the speaker wire from the connector on the speaker. Allow the harness to remain with the motorcycle, if necessary.

6. Secure the upper portion of the lower fairing to the engine guard with tape or twine.

7. Secure the locknut below the engine guard clamp and remove the Torx screw (T40) securing the lower fairing to the engine guard.

8. Carefully remove the lower fairing from the engine guard.

9. Remove and discard the rubber washer located between the lower fairing and the clamp.

10. Repeat the procedure for the other side, if necessary.

14

(64) **LOWER FAIRING/SPEAKER BOX (2013 FORK MOUNTED FAIRING MODELS)**

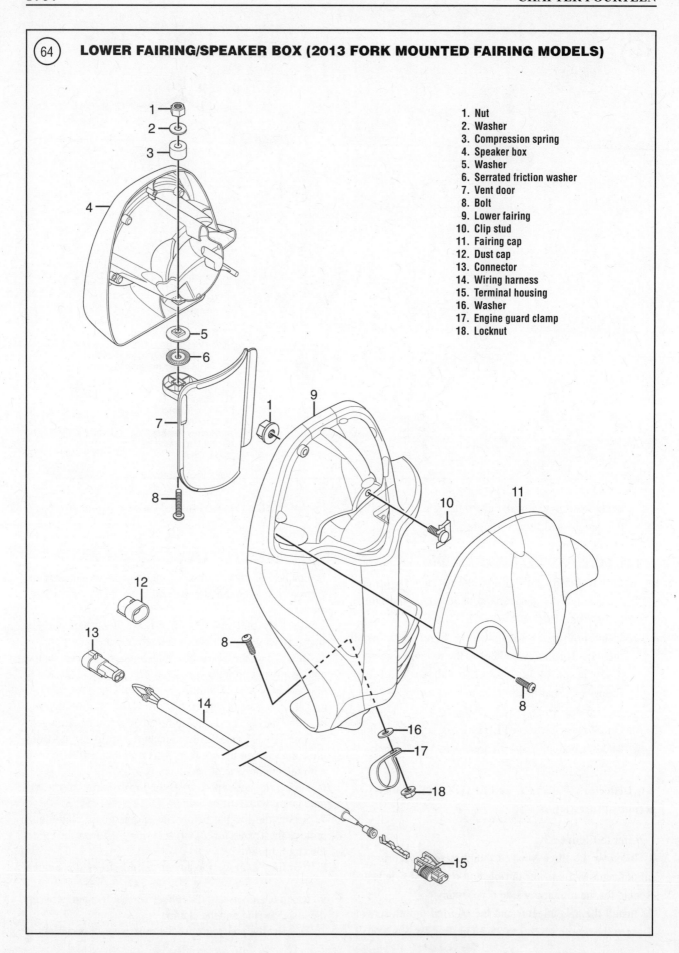

1. Nut
2. Washer
3. Compression spring
4. Speaker box
5. Washer
6. Serrated friction washer
7. Vent door
8. Bolt
9. Lower fairing
10. Clip stud
11. Fairing cap
12. Dust cap
13. Connector
14. Wiring harness
15. Terminal housing
16. Washer
17. Engine guard clamp
18. Locknut

Installation

1. Make sure the front wheel is in the straight ahead position.

2. Install the lower fairing onto the engine guard and secure it with tape or twine.

3. On FLHRSE models, connect the speaker wire onto the speaker. Push the connector until it locks into place.

4. Install the Torx screw (T40) through the lower fairing, *new* rubber washer and engine guard clamp.

5. Install the locknut onto the Torx screw and finger-tighten the nut.

6. Make sure the clip studs are in place on the fairing cap.

7. Position the fairing cap against the engine guard and against the fairing lower while aligning the clips suds with the holes in the lower fairing.

8. Secure both parts and install the flange nuts onto the clip studs.

9. Make sure the lower fairing is centered on the engine guard, and alternately tighten the flange nuts to 35-40 in.-lb. (4.0-4.5 N•m).

10. Secure the locknut on the engine guard clamp and tighten the Torx screw (T40) to 90-100 in.-lb. (10.2-11.3 N•m).

11. Repeat the procedure for the other side, if necessary.

Disassembly

1. Remove the Torx screws (T20) securing the glove box door and tray to the lower fairing. Separate the parts.

2 Remove the Torx screws (T20) securing the glove box tray to the door. Separate the parts.

3. Remove the locknut, washer and compression spring (rubber sleeve) glove box tray and two serrated washers from the pivot screw in vent door arm.

4. Remove the pivot screw from the vent door arm.

Assembly

1. Slide threaded end of pivot screw up through hole in center of vent door arm and hold it in place with tape or other means.

2. Position the *new* black serrated friction washer with the teeth facing up and install it over the pivot screw.

3. Install the serrated friction washer's square shaped boss onto the square recess in the vent door arm, and seat it correctly.

NOTE
Always use two washers of different colors. If two black or two white washers are installed there will be a chirping sound when the lower fairing is adjusted.

4. Position the *new*, white, serrated friction washer with the teeth facing down, and install it over the pivot screw. The teeth on the two washers must engage.

5. Install the glove box tray over the pivot screw and engage the square boss of the white serrated washer. Engage the glove box tray's pin with the slot at the top of the vent door.

6. Install the compression spring, flat washer and locknut onto the pivot screw.

7. Tighten the locknut against the flat washer until it is snug against it. Do not allow the flat washer to rotate, and then tighten the locknut an additional 1 1/2 turns. Move the vent door and check for ease of movement. It is recommended that the compression spring should be compressed to a height of 0.420-0.460 in (10.7-11.7 mm). Readjust if necessary.

8. Install the glove box door onto the glove box tray. Align the two holes in the glove box tray with the two bosses in the glove box door and install the two Torx screws (T20). Alternately tighten the Torx screws (T20) to 20-25 in.-lb. (2.3-2.8 N•m). Do not overtighten the screws as the screw mounting posts may crack or strip out.

9. Install the glove box tray into the top of the lower fairing and align the three holes in the lower fairing with the holes in the glove box tray, and the bosses in the glove box door. Install the two Torx screws (T20). Alternately tighten the Torx screws (T20) to 20-25 in.-lb. (2.3-2.8 N•m). Do not overtighten the screws as the screw mounting posts may crack or strip out.

10. Install the anchor on draw string of glove box flap into the hole in the glove box door. Install the glove box door flap and fasten snaps.

FRAME SIDE COVERS

Removal/Installation

1. Carefully pull out on the bottom of the side cover (A, **Figure 65**). Then, pull on each corner of the top (B, **Figure 65**) and remove the side cover from the frame grommets.

2. Install the side cover onto the frame grommets and tap into place with the palm of hand. Make sure the side cover posts are completely engaged with the frame grommets.

14

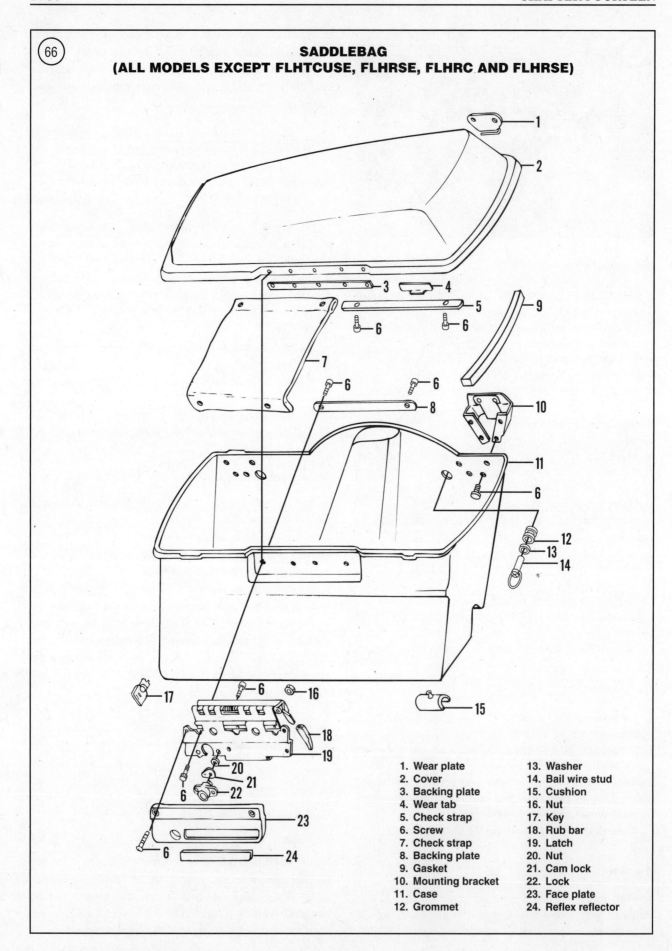

66

SADDLEBAG
(ALL MODELS EXCEPT FLHTCUSE, FLHRSE, FLHRC AND FLHRSE)

1. Wear plate
2. Cover
3. Backing plate
4. Wear tab
5. Check strap
6. Screw
7. Check strap
8. Backing plate
9. Gasket
10. Mounting bracket
11. Case
12. Grommet
13. Washer
14. Bail wire stud
15. Cushion
16. Nut
17. Key
18. Rub bar
19. Latch
20. Nut
21. Cam lock
22. Lock
23. Face plate
24. Reflex reflector

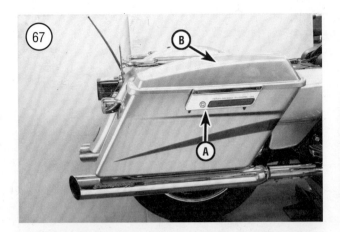

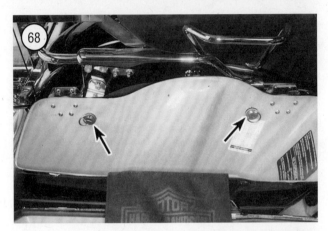

SADDLEBAGS

All Models Except FLHRC, FLHTCUSE, FLHRSE and FLTRXSE

Removal/installation

Refer to **Figure 66**.

1. Place the motorcycle on level ground using the jiffy stand.

2. Unlock the handle latch.

3. Pull out on bottom of latch (A, **Figure 67**) and open the cover (B).

4. Within the saddlebag case, grasp the latch bail wire (**Figure 68**), rotate the latch stud 1/4 turn counterclockwise and release the stud from the mounting bracket (**Figure 69**). Repeat for the other latch stud.

5. Carefully pull the saddlebag up and out of the bracket or guards.

6. Inspect the latch mounting brackets (**Figure 70** and **Figure 71**) for damage.

7. Install by reversing the removal steps. Make sure the saddlebag is locked securely into place.

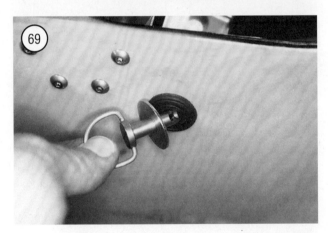

FLHRC Models

Removal/installation

Refer to **Figure 72**.

1. Place the motorcycle on level ground using the jiffy stand.

2. Raise the decorative buckle and press on the tabs on both sides of the catch. Repeat for the remaining buckle and catch. Open the cover.

3. Within the saddlebag case, grasp the latch bail wire, rotate the latch stud 1/4 turn counterclockwise and release the stud from the mounting bracket. Repeat for the remaining stud.

4. Carefully pull the saddlebag up and out of the bracket or guards.

5. Inspect the latch mounting brackets (**Figure 70** and **Figure 71**) for damage.

6. Install by reversing the removal steps. Make sure the saddlebag is locked securely into place.

14

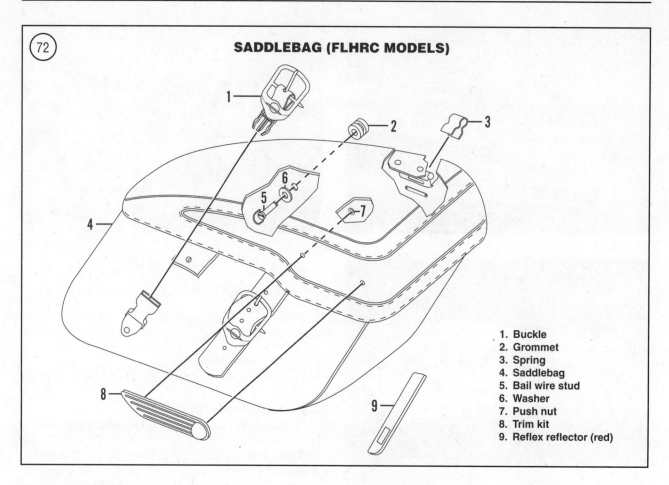

⑦②

SADDLEBAG (FLHRC MODELS)

1. Buckle
2. Grommet
3. Spring
4. Saddlebag
5. Bail wire stud
6. Washer
7. Push nut
8. Trim kit
9. Reflex reflector (red)

FLHTCUSE Models

Removal/installation

Refer to **Figure 73** and **Figure 74**.

1. Place the motorcycle on level ground using the jiffy stand.

2. Pull out on bottom of latch (A, **Figure 67**) and open the cover (B).

CAUTION
Hold onto the saddlebag while removing the second latch to avoid damage to the wiring harness.

3. Within the saddlebag case, grasp the latch bail wire (**Figure 69**), rotate the latch stud 1/4 turn counterclockwise and release the stud from the mounting bracket (**Figure 69**). Repeat for the remaining stud.

4. Tilt the top of the saddlebag away from the guard and disconnect the electrical connector for the power lock and iPod.

5. Carefully pull the saddlebag up and out of the bracket or guards.

6. Install by reversing the removal steps. Make sure the saddlebag is locked securely into place.

Latch replacement

1. Place the motorcycle on level ground using the jiffy stand.

2. Unlock the handle latch.

3. Pull out on bottom of latch (A, **Figure 67**) and open the cover (B).

4. Pull straight up and remove the felt liner.

5. Remove the two screws from the check strap and the latch cover.

6. Loosen the locknut on the cable end, and then remove the barrel and cable from the inner cam arm.

7. Remove the e-clip, spacer, spring, inner cam and outer cam.

8. Remove the two inner screws and remove the cam plate from the saddlebag.

9. Install by reversing the removal steps. Tighten the two inner screws to 25 in.-lb. (2.8 N•m).

2013 FLHRSE and FLTRXSE Models

Removal/installation

Refer to **Figure 75** and **Figure 76.**

1. Place the motorcycle on level ground on the jiffy stand.

2. Pull out on bottom of latch (A, **Figure 67**) and open the cover (B).

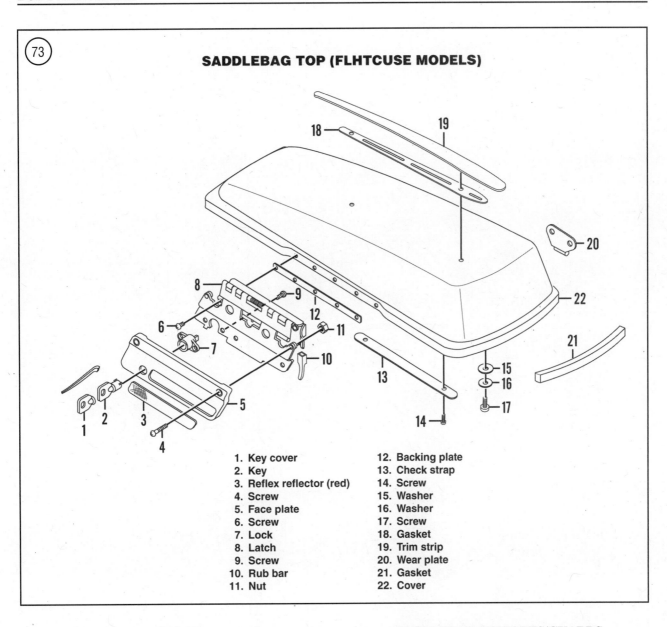

(73)

SADDLEBAG TOP (FLHTCUSE MODELS)

1. Key cover
2. Key
3. Reflex reflector (red)
4. Screw
5. Face plate
6. Screw
7. Lock
8. Latch
9. Screw
10. Rub bar
11. Nut
12. Backing plate
13. Check strap
14. Screw
15. Washer
16. Washer
17. Screw
18. Gasket
19. Trim strip
20. Wear plate
21. Gasket
22. Cover

CAUTION

Hold onto the saddlebag while removing the second latch to avoid the wiring harness.

3. Within the saddlebag case, grasp the latch bail wire (**Figure 68**), rotate the latch 1/4 turn *counterclockwise* and release the stud from the mounting bracket (**Figure 69**).

4. Close the cover and tilt the top of the saddlebag way from the guard and disconnect the speaker electrical connector. Refer to **Figure 77** or **Figure 78**.

5. Carefully full the saddlebag up and out of the bracket or guards on lower support rail.

6. Install by reversing these removal steps. Make sure the saddlebag is locked securely into place.

SADDLEBAG SUPPORTS/GUARDS

The following procedures explain the complete removal and installation of the entire assembly. Follow the procedure only as far as necessary to reach the damaged part.

All Models Except CVO
Removal/Installation

Refer to **Figure 79**.

Saddlebag lower support rail

1. Place the motorcycle on level ground using the jiffy stand.
2. Remove the saddlebag as described in this chapter.
3. Remove the bolts (**Figure 80**), lockwashers and nuts securing the rail to the frame bracket and rear fender.

14

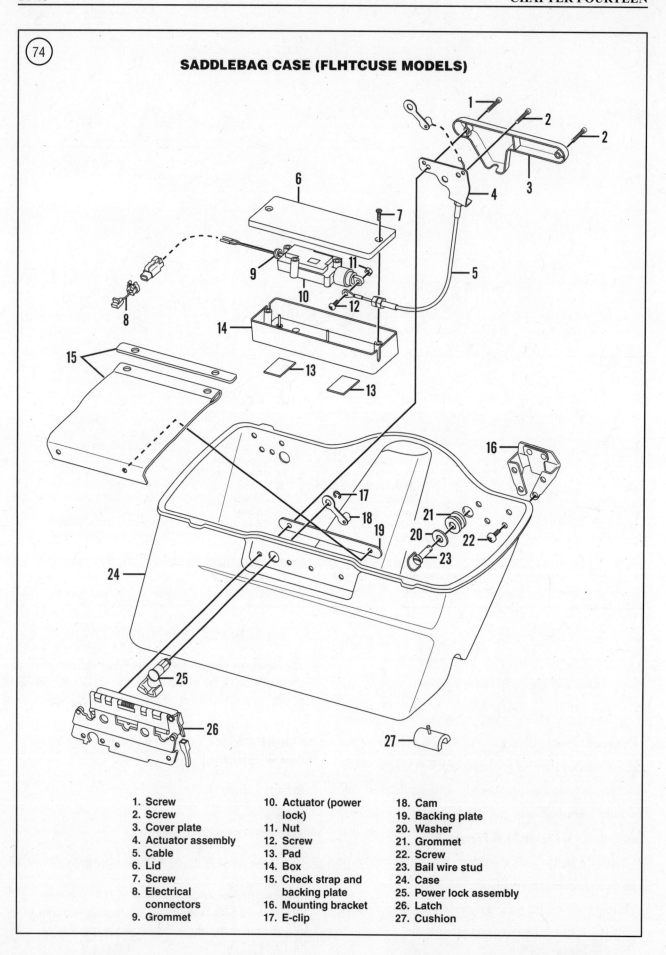

74

SADDLEBAG CASE (FLHTCUSE MODELS)

1. Screw
2. Screw
3. Cover plate
4. Actuator assembly
5. Cable
6. Lid
7. Screw
8. Electrical connectors
9. Grommet
10. Actuator (power lock)
11. Nut
12. Screw
13. Pad
14. Box
15. Check strap and backing plate
16. Mounting bracket
17. E-clip
18. Cam
19. Backing plate
20. Washer
21. Grommet
22. Screw
23. Bail wire stud
24. Case
25. Power lock assembly
26. Latch
27. Cushion

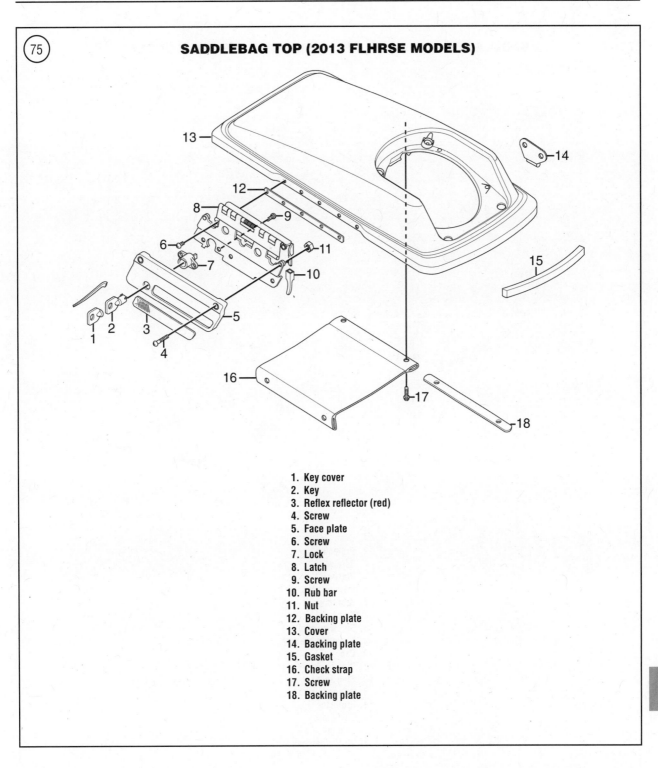

SADDLEBAG TOP (2013 FLHRSE MODELS)

75

1. Key cover
2. Key
3. Reflex reflector (red)
4. Screw
5. Face plate
6. Screw
7. Lock
8. Latch
9. Screw
10. Rub bar
11. Nut
12. Backing plate
13. Cover
14. Backing plate
15. Gasket
16. Check strap
17. Screw
18. Backing plate

4. Remove the bolts (**Figure 81**) securing the muffler to the support rail.

5. Support the rear of the muffler to the frame with a Bungee cord or rope.

6. Remove the Torx bolt (**Figure 82**) securing the support rail to the frame weldment and remove the support rail.

7. Remove the bolt and washer (A, **Figure 83**, typical) securing the support bracket (B), if necessary. Remove the bracket and spring plate assembly.

8. Install by reversing the removal steps. Tighten all bolts and nuts as follows:

   a. Saddlebag support rail-to-support bracket bolts: 15-20 ft.-lb. (20.3-27.1 N•m).

   b. Support rail to rear fender and frame bolt and nut: 15-20 ft.-lb. (20.3-27.1 N•m).

   c. Support rail to muffler bolts: 96-144 in.-lb. (10.8-16.3 N•m).

   d. Support bracket assembly bolt: 15-20 ft.-lb. (20.3-27.1 N•m).

14

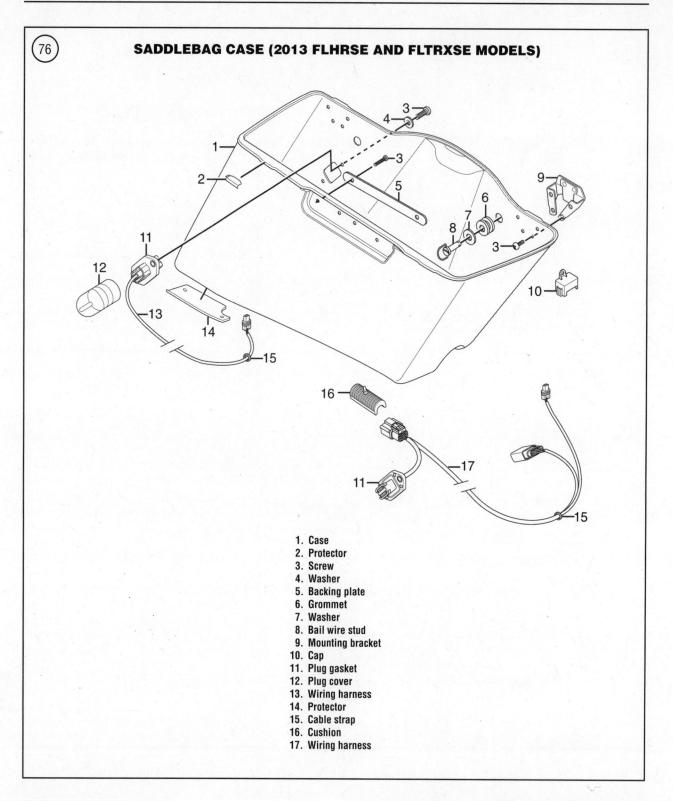

(76) **SADDLEBAG CASE (2013 FLHRSE AND FLTRXSE MODELS)**

1. Case
2. Protector
3. Screw
4. Washer
5. Backing plate
6. Grommet
7. Washer
8. Bail wire stud
9. Mounting bracket
10. Cap
11. Plug gasket
12. Plug cover
13. Wiring harness
14. Protector
15. Cable strap
16. Cushion
17. Wiring harness

Saddlebag support guards

1. Place the motorcycle on level ground using the jiffy stand.

2. Remove the saddlebag as described in this chapter.

3. Remove the front lower bolt (**Figure 84**) and locknut securing the guard to the frame.

4. Remove the bolts (A, **Figure 85**, typical) and lockwashers securing the saddlebag support rail to the muffler.

5. Remove one of the bolts (B, **Figure 85**) securing the rear support bracket to the frame bracket and rear fender. Loosen the other bolt at this time, but leave it in place.

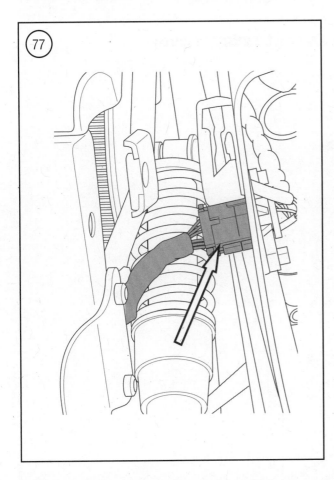

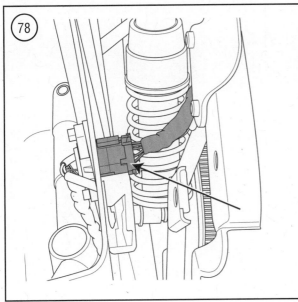

9. Support the rear of the muffler to the frame with a Bungee cord or rope.

10. Remove the bolt and washer (A, **Figure 83**, typical) securing the support bracket (B), if necessary. Remove the bracket and spring plate assembly.

11. Disassemble the assembly as necessary.

12. Install by reversing the removal steps. Tighten all bolts and nuts as follows:

    a. Saddlebag mounting bracket screws: 60-96 in.-lb. (6.8-10.8 N•m).

    b. Saddlebag support bracket bolts: 15-20 ft.-lb. (20.3-27.1 N•m).

    c. Saddlebag support rail-to-support bracket bolts: 15-20 ft.-lb. (20.3-27.1 N•m).

    d. Front guard-to-frame bolts, or bolts and nuts: 15-20 ft.-lb. (20.3-27.1 N•m).

    e. Support rail-to-guard screws: 70-100 in.-lb. (7.9-11.3 N•m).

    f. Front guard-to-saddlebag guard screws: 70-120 in.-lb. (7.9-13.6 N•m).

    g. Saddlebag guard-to-clamp screws: 30-50 in.-lb. (3.4-5.7 N•m).

CVO Models
Removal/Installation

Refer to **Figures 88** and **Figure 89**.

1. Remove both frame side covers as described in this chapter.

2. Remove both saddlebags as described in this chapter.

3A. On FLHTCUSE and FLTRUSE models, perform the following:

    a. Remove the two bolts, washers and spacers securing the filler panel to the support bracket, or support rail.

    b. Remove the two screws and lockwashers securing the support rail to the muffler. Remove the muffler mounting bracket and rubber mount from the support rail.

    c. Remove the bolt securing the support rail to the frame.

    d. Remove the bolt and locknut securing the guard to the frame.

    e. Remove the support rail and guard assembly.

3B. On FLHRSE, FLHXSE and FLTRXSE models, perform the following:

    a. Remove the front bolt and locknut securing the support rail to the frame.

    b. Remove the bolts and locknuts securing the support rail to the mounting bracket.

    c. Remove the support rail.

4. Install by reversing the removal steps. Tighten all bolts and nuts as follows:

    a. Tighten the bolts and nuts securing the support rail to the support bracket to 15-20 ft.-lb. (20.3-27.1 N•m).

    b. Tighten the bolts securing the guard to the frame to 15-20 ft.-lb. (20.3-27.1 N•m).

6. Hold onto the saddlebag support and remove the front upper bolt (**Figure 86**) securing the front guard to the frame.

7. Remove the remaining bolt securing the rear support bracket to the frame bracket.

8. Remove the saddlebag guard assembly (**Figure 87**) from the frame.

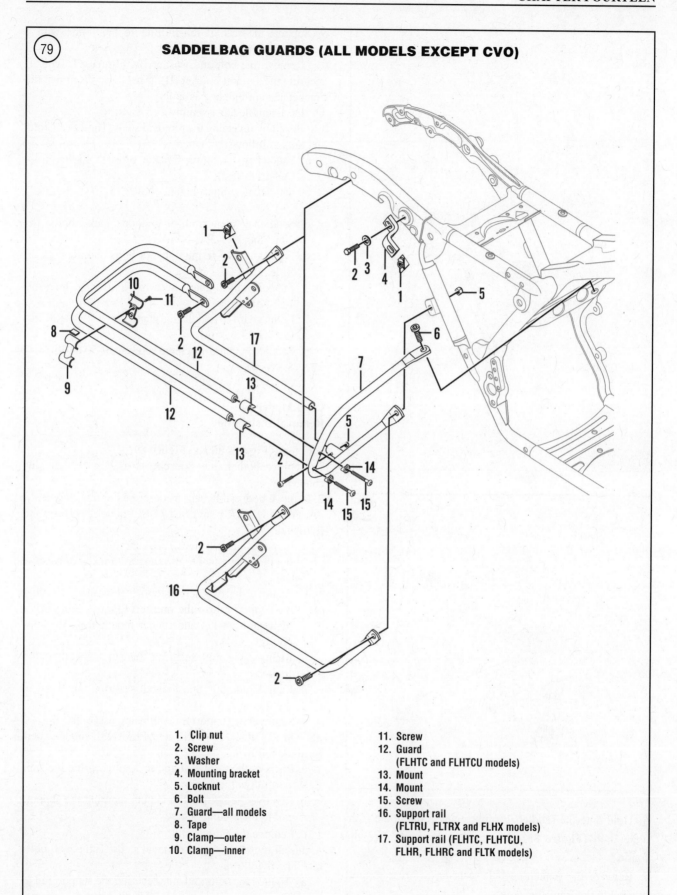

79

SADDELBAG GUARDS (ALL MODELS EXCEPT CVO)

1. Clip nut
2. Screw
3. Washer
4. Mounting bracket
5. Locknut
6. Bolt
7. Guard—all models
8. Tape
9. Clamp—outer
10. Clamp—inner
11. Screw
12. Guard
    (FLHTC and FLHTCU models)
13. Mount
14. Mount
15. Screw
16. Support rail
    (FLTRU, FLTRX and FLHX models)
17. Support rail (FLHTC, FLHTCU,
    FLHR, FLHRC and FLTK models)

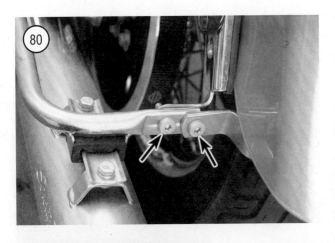

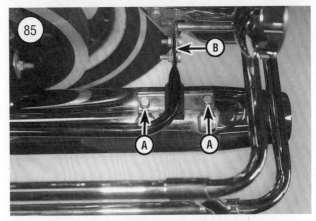

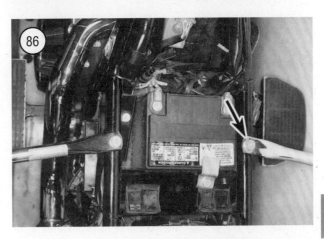

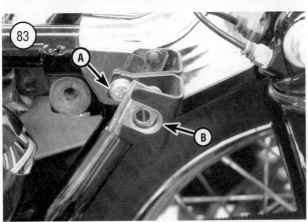

14

c. Tighten the screw and nut securing the support rail to the guard to 70-100 in.-lb. (7.9-11.3 N•m).

d. Tighten the remaining bolts securely.

Support Bracket (All Models)
Removal/Installation

1. Remove the radio antenna (A, **Figure 90**) as described in Chapter Nine, on models so equipped.

2. Remove the saddlebag guards (B, **Figure 90**) attached to the support bracket, as described in this chapter on models so equipped.

3. Remove the bolts and washers securing the support bracket and upper bracket (C, **Figure 90**) to the frame.

4. Remove the support bracket from the frame and rear fender.

5. Install by reversing the removal steps, while noting the following:

a. Tighten the upper bracket bolt to 60-96 in.-lb. (6.8-10.8 N•m).

b. Tighten the support bracket bolts to 15-20 ft.-lb. (20.3-27.1 N•m).

ENGINE GUARD

Removal/Installation

Refer to **Figure 91**.

1. Support the motorcycle with the front wheel off the ground as described in *Motorcycle Stands* (Chapter Ten).

2. Cover the backside of the front fender with a towel or blanket to protect the finish.

3. On FLHTCU and FLHTCUSE models, remove the lower fairing assembly from each side as described in this chapter.

4. Remove the lower Torx bolt (T40) and locknut from the frame weldment on each side.

5. Remove the bolt, washer, mounting strap and washer securing the engine guard to the frame.

6. Carefully pull the engine guard forward and remove from the frame.

7. Install by reversing the removal steps. Tighten all mounting bolts and nuts to 15-20 ft.-lb. (20.3-27.1 N•m).

JIFFY STAND

Removal

Refer to **Figure 92**.

1. Support the motorcycle with the front wheel off the ground as described in *Motorcycle Stands* (Chapter Ten).

2. The motorcycle must be raised sufficiently to allow room for full movement of the jiffy stand.

3. Move left side rider footboard up away from the jiffy stand.

4. Move the jiffy stand down to the full forward position.

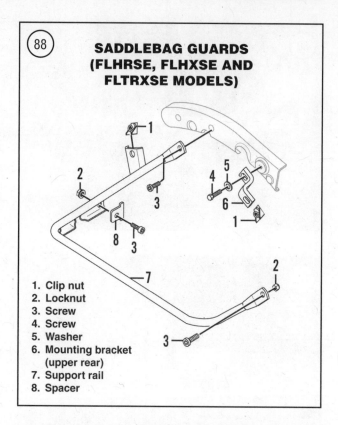

88

SADDLEBAG GUARDS (FLHRSE, FLHXSE AND FLTRXSE MODELS)

1. Clip nut
2. Locknut
3. Screw
4. Screw
5. Washer
6. Mounting bracket (upper rear)
7. Support rail
8. Spacer

5. Remove the return spring (A, **Figure 93**) from the jiffy stand leg and the hole in the frame weldment.

6. Remove the four bolts (B, **Figure 93**) and lockwashers securing the bracket and front footboard to the frame.

7. Inspect the jiffy stand leg and bracket as described in this section.

Installation

1. Install the bracket and the four bolts and lockwashers.

2. Align the rear of the bracket to the footboard and tighten the front bolts to 36-42 ft.-lb. (48.8-56.9 N•m).

3. Tighten the rear bracket bolts to 36-42 ft.-lb. (48.8-56.9 N•m).

4. Hook the return spring onto *front* of the frame weldment. If installed on the rear, the spring will rub on the leg when it is moved.

5. Hook the return spring onto the hole in the leg. Make sure return spring is secure on both the frame and leg.

6. Hold the leg in the normal down position.

7. Secure the leg in this position and check the tightness of the top hex bolt. Tighten the hex bolt to 15-20 ft.-lb. (20.3-27.1 N•m), if necessary.

8. Extend and retract the leg several times to ensure proper operation. The jiffy stand must move freely from the fully extended to the fully retracted positions.

9. If removed, install the bumper onto the leg.

10. Remove the motorcycle from the stand.

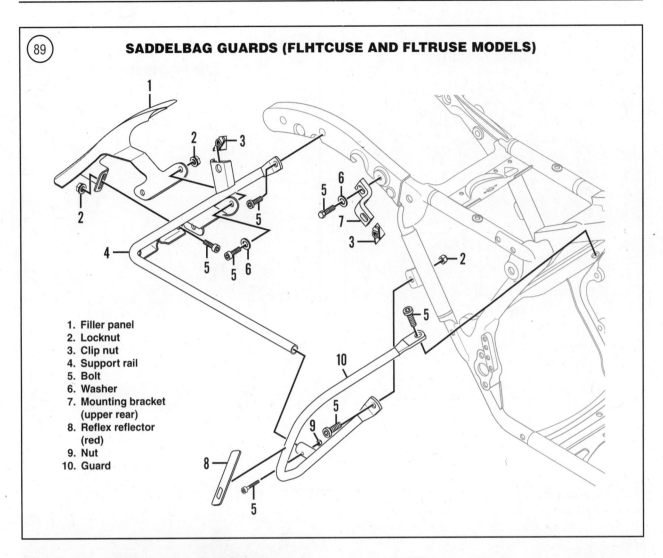

SADDELBAG GUARDS (FLHTCUSE AND FLTRUSE MODELS)

1. Filler panel
2. Locknut
3. Clip nut
4. Support rail
5. Bolt
6. Washer
7. Mounting bracket (upper rear)
8. Reflex reflector (red)
9. Nut
10. Guard

Inspection

1. Thoroughly clean all old grease and road debris from the pivot point in the bracket and the pivot post of the leg.

2. Inspect the leg for cracks or other damage. Replace if necessary.

3. Inspect the threaded end of the leg for damage. Clean out with a thread tap if necessary.

4. Inspect the bracket mounting holes for damage and elongation. Replace as necessary.

Interlock Sensor
(HDI Models)
Replacement

1. At the jiffy stand bracket, locate the wiring harness to the base of the voltage regulator.

2. Remove the anchor on the interlock sensor connector from the hole in the front cross member.

3. Carefully cut the strap securing the wiring harness to the frame.

4. Disconnect the 3-pin interlock sensor connector.

5. Move the jiffy stand to the full forward (down) position.

6. Remove the Allen bolt, and then remove the sensor from the bracket.

7. Apply a small dab of Loctite Threadlocker 243 (Blue) to the Allen bolt prior to installation. Install the bolt and tighten to 96-120 in.-lb. (10.8-13.6 N•m).

8. Route the cable over the top of the frame weldment, behind the front down tube and toward the voltage regulator.

14

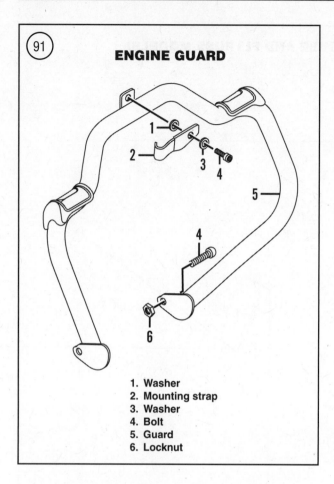

ENGINE GUARD

1. Washer
2. Mounting strap
3. Washer
4. Bolt
5. Guard
6. Locknut

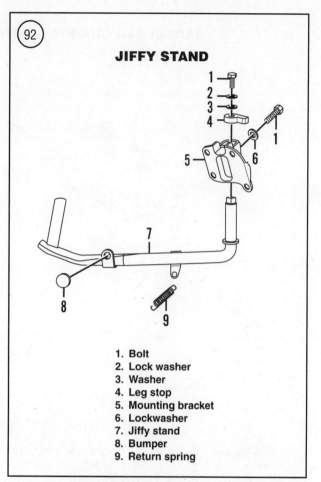

JIFFY STAND

1. Bolt
2. Lock washer
3. Washer
4. Leg stop
5. Mounting bracket
6. Lockwasher
7. Jiffy stand
8. Bumper
9. Return spring

9. Connect the 3-pin sensor connector, and then push the anchor into the hole in the front frame cross member.
10. Install a new cable strap and secure the wiring harness.

TOUR-PAK

FLHTC, FLHTCU AND FLHTK MODELS
Removal/Installation

Refer to **Figure 94**.
1. Place the motorcycle on level ground using the jiffy stand.
2. Remove the seat as described in this chapter.

> *NOTE*
> *Always disarm the optional TSSM/HFSM security system before disconnecting the battery or pulling the Main Fuse so the siren will not sound.*

3. Disconnect the negative battery cable as described in Chapter Nine.
4. Remove both saddlebags as described in this chapter.
5. Open the cover and remove the bottom liner. Leave the cover open for the remainder of this procedure.
6. On FLHTCU models, perform the following:
   a. Open the map pocket and remove the acorn nuts and flat washers securing the molded inner liner to the

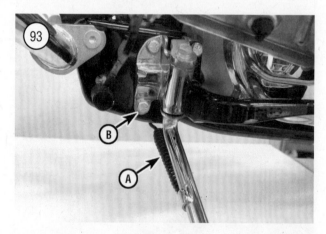

lower case. Remove the map pocket and molded liner.
   b. Depress the latch and rotate the housing and release the bulb socket from the left side of the lower case.

7. Rotate the knurled locking ring *counterclockwise* and disconnect the radio antenna cable pin and socket connector. Release the cable from the two clips on the base of the lower case.

8. Disconnect the 3-pin Tour-Pak connector. Pull the grommet into the lower case and remove it from the wire harness.

9. Feed the harness down and through the opening in the bottom of the lower case.

10. On FLHTCU models, perform the following:

    a. Release the headrest receptacle from the bottom of the left side speaker box.

    b. Remove the trim ring and carefully pull the wire harness out of the left side speaker box. Disconnect the 6-pin speaker and controller connector.

    c. On the right side, disconnect the CB antenna cable connector, and then release the cable from the two clips on the bottom of the lower case.

    d. Pull the grommet surrounding the CB antenna cable into the lower case and remove it from the cable.

    e. Feed the CB antenna down and through the opening in the bottom of the lower case.

    f. Remove the trim ring and carefully pull the wire harness out of the right and left side speaker housing. Disconnect the left and right 6-pin speaker and controller connectors.

11. Secure the locknut below each mounting bolt, and then remove the four bolts, washers and nuts securing the Tour-Pak lower case to the luggage rack. Remove the nuts and spacers from the luggage rack.

NOTE
Have an assistant hold onto the Tour-Pak during removal of the last bolt and nut. The Tour-Pak is top heavy on the left side with the cover open.

12. Secure the remaining mounting bolt underneath the lower case. Remove nut and flat washer from the inside of the lower case. Remove the bolt and spacer from the luggage rack.

13. Remove the Tour-Pak from the luggage rack.

14 On FLHTCU models, to remove the speaker box, perform the following:

    a. Remove the trim ring and carefully pull the wire harness out of the right and left side speaker housing. Disconnect the 6-pin speaker and controller connectors.

    b. Open map pocket, remove the acorn nuts and washers, and then remove the map pocket.

    c. Remove the three bolts and washers securing the speaker housing. Pull straight out and remove the speaker housing from the lower case.

15. Install by reversing these removal steps. Tighten the Tour-Pak mounting bolts and nuts to 90-108 in.-lb. (10.2-12.2 N•m).

CVO Series Models
Removal/Installation

Refer to **Figures 95** and **Figure 96**.

1. Place the motorcycle on level ground using the jiffy stand.

2. Remove the seat as described in this chapter.

NOTE
Always disarm the optional TSSM/HFSM security system before disconnecting the bat-
tery or pulling the Main Fuse so the siren will not sound.

3. Disconnect the negative battery cable as described in Chapter Nine.

4. Remove both saddlebags as described in this chapter.

5. Open the cover and remove the bottom liner. Leave the cover open for the remainder of this procedure.

6. Unscrew the AM/FM/WB antenna cable connector from the antenna mount on the left rear corner. Disconnect the antenna cable from the clip on the bottom left side of the bottom case.

7. Disconnect the power lock connector at the left rear side of the bottom case, on models so equipped.

8. Unplug the interior lighting harness connectors.

9. Remove the split grommet from the exit hole in the left front side of the bottom case. Carefully feed the AM/FM/WB antenna cable down and out through this exit hole.

10. Unplug the CB antenna cable connector at the bottom right side of the bottom case. Disengage the cable from the clips on the bottom right side of the bottom case.

11. Remove the split grommet from the exit hole in the right front side of the bottom case. Carefully feed the CB antenna cable down and out through this exit hole.

12. Carefully feed the speaker wiring harness out of the hole in the right and left speaker box. Disconnect the left and right 6-pin speaker and controller connectors.

13. Disconnect the 24-pin amplifier connector from the under the right side of the Tour-Pak.

14. Hold onto the passenger headset DIN connector and carefully pull it partially out from under the Tour-Pak. Carefully pull down on the wiring and release it from the cable clip.

15. Place a towel or small blanket on top of the rear fender to protect it during amplifier removal.

16. Note the location of which five mounting bolts are used to secure the lower case to the luggage rack as the location varies with different years.

17. Secure the locknut below each mounting bolt, and then remove the four bolts, washers and nuts securing the Tour-Pak lower case to the luggage rack. Remove the nuts and spacers from the luggage rack.

18. Slide the amplifier out the right side and lower it onto the rear fender.

NOTE
Have an assistant hold onto the Tour-Pak during removal of the last bolt and nut. The Tour-Pak is top heavy on the left side with the cover open.

19. Secure the remaining mounting bolt underneath the lower case. Remove nut, flat washer and antenna ground strap from the top of the lower case. Remove the bolt and spacer from the luggage rack.

20. Remove the Tour-Pak from the luggage rack.

21. To remove the speaker box, perform the following:

    a. Remove the trim ring and carefully pull the wire harness out of the right and left side speaker housing.

14

94

TOUR-PAK (FLHTC, FLHTCU AND FLHTK MODELS)

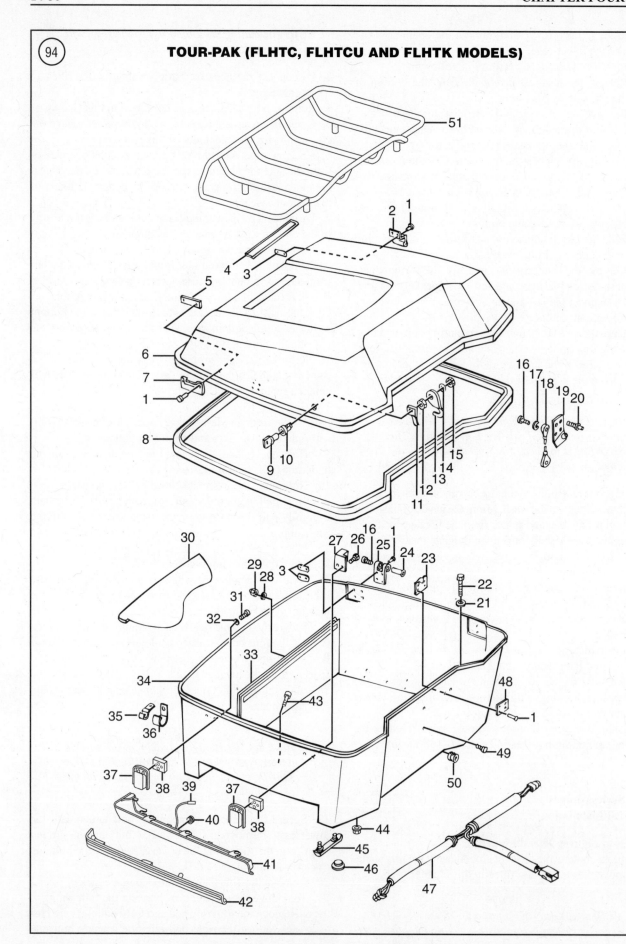

1. Rivet
2. Hinge
3. Backing plate
4. Nameplate
5. Backing plate
6. Cover
7. Upper catch
8. Gasket
9. Key
10. Lock
11. Lock guide
12. Nut
13. Cam hook
14. Lockwasher
15. Nut
16. Screw
17. Spring washer
18. Cable brace
19. Bracket
20. Nylon rivet
21. Washer
22. Screw
23. Bracket
24. Hinge pin
25. Hinge
26. Screw

27. Lower catch
28. Washer
29. Nut
30. Rubber mat
31. Screw
32. Washer
33. Pouch
34. Lower case
35. Antenna cable clip
36. Clamp
37. Catch body
38. Spacer
39. Electrical connector
40. Grommet
41. Light–right side (left side not shown)
42. Trim–right side (left side not shown)
43. Screw
44. Flange nut
45. Bumper
46. Grommet
47. Wiring harness
48. Backing plate
49. Screw
50. Grommet
51. Rack

TOUR-PAK COVER (FLHTCUSE AND FLHTRUSE MODELS)

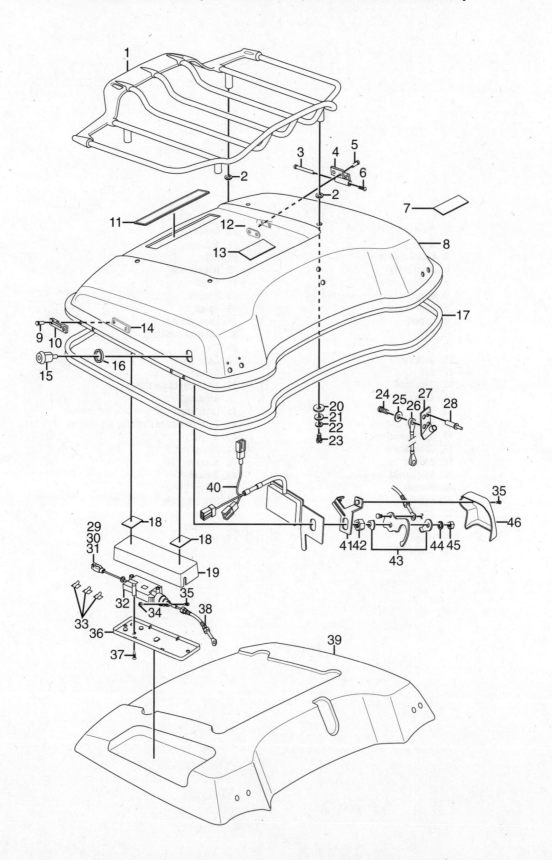

1. Rack
2. Spacer
3. Hinge pin
4. Hinge cover
5. Screw
6. Screw
7. Pad
8. Lid
9. Rivet
10. Hasp
11. Trim plate
12. Backing plate
13. Label
14. Backing plate
15. Lock
16. Grommet
17. Gasket
18. Pad
19. Cover
20. Pad
21. Lockwasher
22. Washer
23. Screw
24. Screw
25. Washer
26. Tether
27. Bracket
28. Rivet
29. Socket housing
30. Secondary lock
31. Terminal socket
32. Grommet
33. Actuator
34. Locknut
35. Screw
36. Base
37. Screw
38. Cable assembly
39. Lid liner
40. Light assembly
41. Bracket
42. Nut
43. Power lock kit
44. Lockwasher
45. Nut
46. Cover

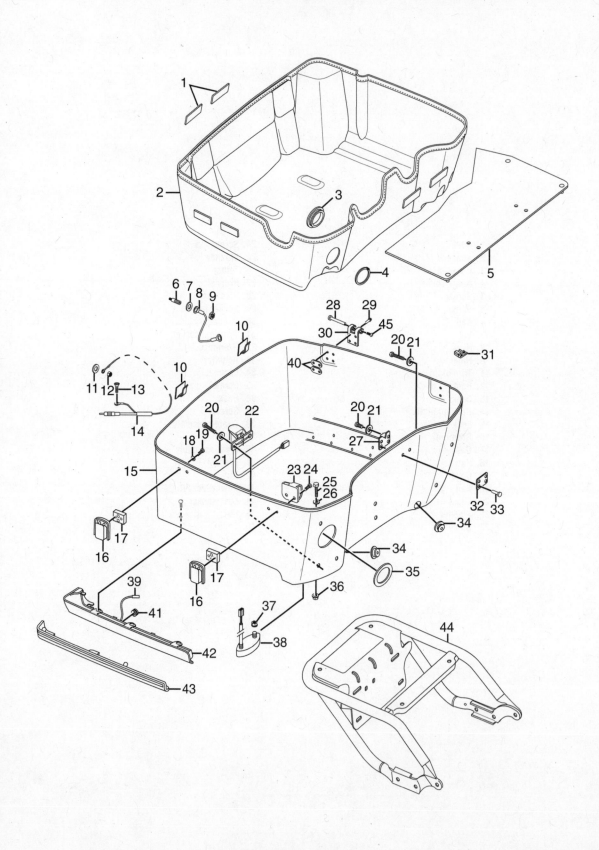

96

TOUR-PAK BOTTOM (FLHTCUSE AND FLHTRUSE MODELS)

1. Velcro–liner kit
2. Molded liner
3. Port assembly
4. Retaining ring--port
5. Reinforcing plate
6. Plug assembly
7. Washer
8. Cable
9. Nut
10. Clip
11. Washer
12. Nut/lock washer
13. Screw
14. Cable extension–CB antenna
15. Case
16. Latch body
17. Bracket
18. Washer
19. Screw
20. Screw
21. Washer
22. Power outlet
23. Lower catch
24. Screw
25. Bolt
26. Washer
27. Bracket-cable mounting
28. Hinge pin
29. Rivet
30. Hinge
31. Clip
32. Backing plate
33. Rivet
34. Velcro–liner kit
35. Mesh gasket
36. Locknut
37. Nut
38. Light assembly
39. Connector
40. Backing plate
41. Grommet
42. Light--side marker
43. Trim—HDI models
44. Luggage rack

14

97 **FOOTBOARDS (ALL MODELS EXCEPT CVO)**

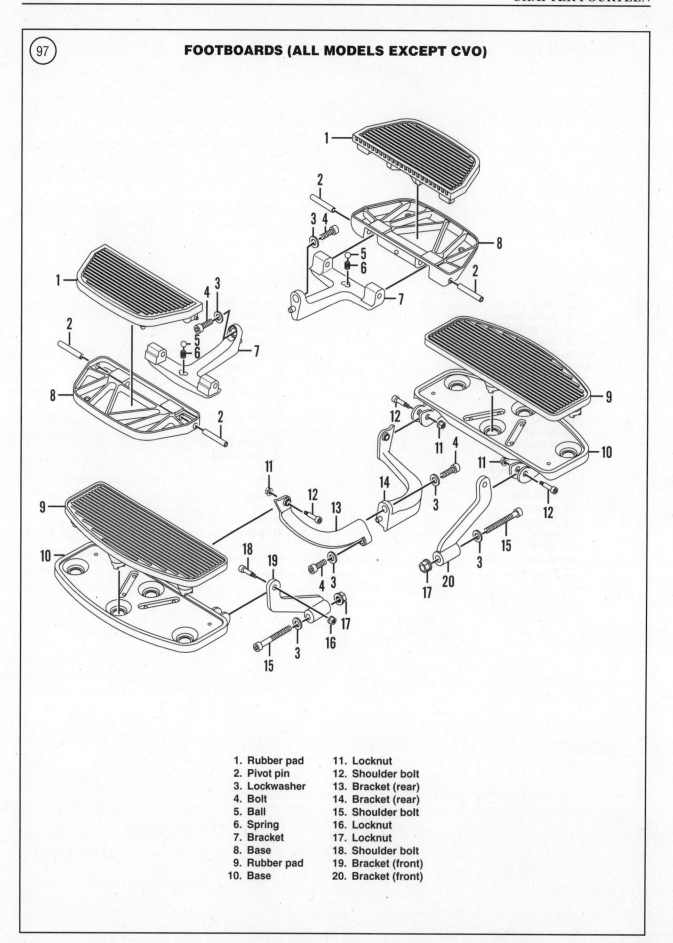

1. Rubber pad	11. Locknut
2. Pivot pin	12. Shoulder bolt
3. Lockwasher	13. Bracket (rear)
4. Bolt	14. Bracket (rear)
5. Ball	15. Shoulder bolt
6. Spring	16. Locknut
7. Bracket	17. Locknut
8. Base	18. Shoulder bolt
9. Rubber pad	19. Bracket (front)
10. Base	20. Bracket (front)

Disconnect the 6-pin speaker and controller connectors.

b. Open map pocket, remove the acorn nuts and washers, and then remove the map pocket.

c. Remove the three bolts and washers securing the speaker housing. Pull straight out and remove the speaker housing from the lower case.

d. Install speaker box by reversing the removal steps. Tighten the three mounting bolts to 25-35 in.-lb. (2.8-4.0 N•m)..

22. Install Tour-Pak by reversing the removal steps. Tighten the bolts and nuts to 96-108 in.-lb. (10.8-12.2 N•m).

FOOTBOARDS AND HIGHWAY FOOT PEGS

Refer to **Figure 97** and **Figure 98**.

Rider Footboard

Removal/installation

1. Support the motorcycle with the front wheel off the ground as described in *Motorcycle Stands* (Chapter Twelve).

2. To remove the footboard only and leave the mounting brackets in place, perform the following:

a. Remove the shoulder bolts (A, **Figure 99**) and washers, and then remove the footboard (B).

b. Clean all oxidation and road debris from the shoulder bolts.

c. Install the shoulder bolts and nuts and tighten to 60-80 in.-lb. (6.8-9.0 N•m).

3A. On the right side, perform the following:

a. Working on the inner side of the frame side rail, loosen and remove the Allen bolt, lockwasher and washer securing the front mounting bracket to the frame.

b. Working on the inner side of the frame side rail, loosen and remove the lower hex bolt and lockwasher securing the rear mounting bracket to the frame.

3B. On the left side, working on the inner side of the frame side rail, loosen and remove the Allen bolt(s), lockwasher(s) and washer(s) securing the front (A, **Figure 100**) and rear mounting brackets (B) to the frame.

4. Remove the footboard assembly from the frame.

5. If necessary, remove the rubber pad (**Figure 101**) from the footboard and install a new one. Push the locating pins all the way through the footboard to secure the rubber pad in place.

6. Inspect the pivot bolts (**Figure 102**) and nuts for looseness. Replace if necessary.

7. Inspect the footboard and the mounting brackets for damage and fractures. Replace as necessary.

8A. On all models except CVO, install the footboard onto the frame and tighten the Allen and hex bolts 36-42 ft.-lb. (48.8-56.9 N•m).

8B. On all CVO models, install the footboard onto the frame and tighten the Allen bolts to 36-42 ft.-lb. (48.8-56.9 N•m).

Disassembly/assembly

1. Remove the footboard as described in this section.

2. From underside of footboard, use a large, flat-bladed screwdriver to push in on the pad's rubber anchors. Then, remove the pad from the footboard.

3. Remove the nut and pivot bolt, and then remove the mounting bracket from the base of the footboard. Repeat for the remaining bracket.

4. Install the bracket to the footboard. Install the pivot bolt so the nut will be located on the inboard side.

5. Apply a small amount of soapy water to the rubber anchors and place on footboard. Use pliers and pull the rubber anchors through the footboard receptacles until they bottom.

6. Install the nut and pivot bolt. On CVO models, tighten the fasteners to 60-80 in.-lb. (6.8-9.0 N•m).

Passenger Footboard

Removal/installation

1. Support the motorcycle with the front wheel off the ground as described in *Motorcycle Stands* (Chapter Ten).

2. Remove the Allen bolt (A, **Figure 103**) and lockwasher securing the passenger footbaord (B) to the frame and remove it.

3. Repeat for the other side if necessary.

4. If necessary, remove the rubber pad (**Figure 104**) from the footboard and install a new one. Push the locating pins all the way through the footboard to secure the rubber pad in place.

5. Inspect the pivot pins (**Figure 105**) for looseness. Replace if necessary.

6. Install the footboard onto the frame and tighten the Allen bolt 36-42 ft.-lb. (48.8-56.9 N•m).

Disassembly/assembly

1. Remove the footboard as described in this section.

2. From underside of footboard, use a small, flat-bladed screwdriver to push in on the pad's rubber anchors and remove the pad from the footboard.

3. Turn the footboard upside down on shop cloths.

4. Tap the pivot pins toward the center of the footboard with a small drift punch and hammer.

5. Remove the footboard from the bracket and remove the small steel ball and spring from the bracket.

6. Inspect the pivot pins, steel ball and spring for wear or damage.

7. Turn the bracket upside down on shop cloths.

8. Install the spring into the bracket receptacle and place the steel ball on top of it.

9. Lower the footboard onto the bracket and make sure the steel ball remains in place.

10. Align the holes and install the pivot pins. Tap the pins into place until centered in the bracket lugs.

14

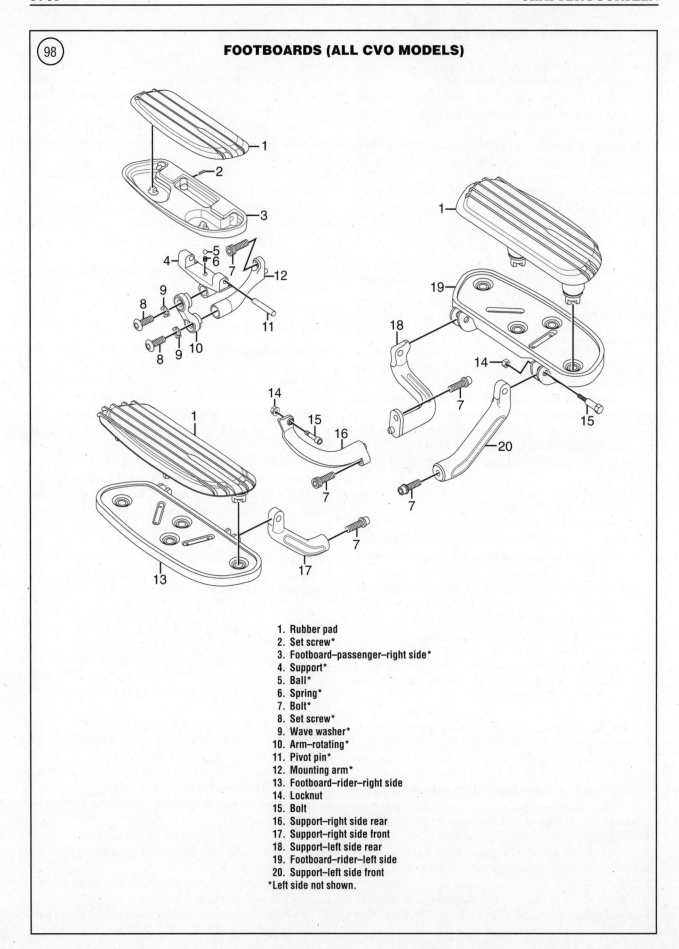

FOOTBOARDS (ALL CVO MODELS)

1. Rubber pad
2. Set screw*
3. Footboard–passenger–right side*
4. Support*
5. Ball*
6. Spring*
7. Bolt*
8. Set screw*
9. Wave washer*
10. Arm–rotating*
11. Pivot pin*
12. Mounting arm*
13. Footboard–rider–right side
14. Locknut
15. Bolt
16. Support–right side rear
17. Support–right side front
18. Support–left side rear
19. Footboard–rider–left side
20. Support–left side front
*Left side not shown.

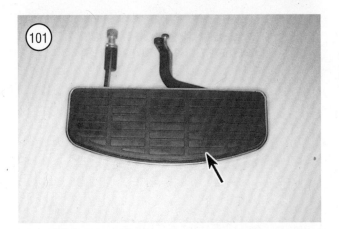

14

11. Apply a small amount of soapy water to the rubber anchors and place on footboard. Use pliers and pull the rubber anchors through the footboard receptacles until they bottom.

Passenger Footrest

Refer to **Figures 106-108**.

Removal/installation

1. Support the motorcycle with the front wheel off the ground as described in *Motorcycle Stands* (Chapter Ten).

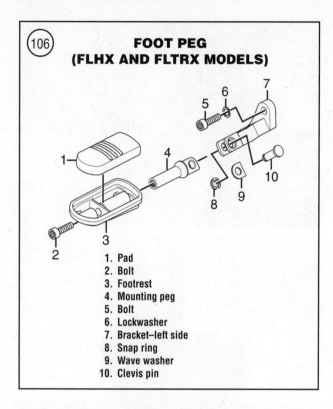

106 FOOT PEG
(FLHX AND FLTRX MODELS)

1. Pad
2. Bolt
3. Footrest
4. Mounting peg
5. Bolt
6. Lockwasher
7. Bracket–left side
8. Snap ring
9. Wave washer
10. Clevis pin

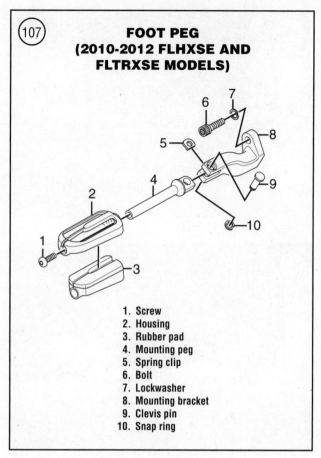

107 FOOT PEG
(2010-2012 FLHXSE AND
FLTRXSE MODELS)

1. Screw
2. Housing
3. Rubber pad
4. Mounting peg
5. Spring clip
6. Bolt
7. Lockwasher
8. Mounting bracket
9. Clevis pin
10. Snap ring

2. Remove the Allen bolt and lock washer securing the footrest to the frame. Then, remove the footrest.

3. Repeat for the other side if necessary.

4. Inspect the footrest for wear or damage.

5. Install the footrest onto the frame.

6. Tighten the Allen bolt 36-42 ft.-lb. (48.8-56.9 N•m).

Disassembly/assembly

1. Remove the footrest as described in this section.

2. Remove the Allen bolt and slide the footrest assembly off the mounting peg.

3. Remove the snap ring from the pivot pin and remove the pivot pin.

4. Remove the pivot pin and wave washer, and remove mounting peg from mounting bracket.

5. From underside of footrest, use a small, flat-bladed screwdriver to push in on the pad's rubber anchor. Then, remove the pad from the footrest.

6. Inspect the footrest for wear or damage.

7. Apply a small amount of soapy water to the rubber anchor and place on footrest. Use pliers and pull the rubber anchor through the footrest receptacle until it bottoms.

8. Correctly position the convex side of the wave washer facing up toward the pivot pin. Hold it in this position.

9. Position the mounting peg with the flat surface facing down and install it onto the mounting bracket. Do not dislodge the spring washer.

10. Install the pivot down from the top and install a *new* snap ring. Make sure it seats correctly in the pivot pin groove.

11. Install the footrest assembly onto the mounting peg.

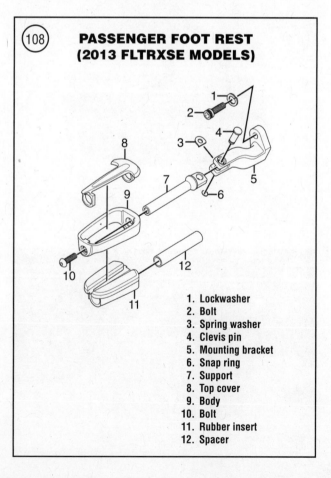

108 PASSENGER FOOT REST
(2013 FLTRXSE MODELS)

1. Lockwasher
2. Bolt
3. Spring washer
4. Clevis pin
5. Mounting bracket
6. Snap ring
7. Support
8. Top cover
9. Body
10. Bolt
11. Rubber insert
12. Spacer

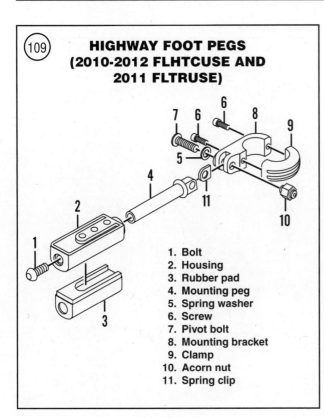

**HIGHWAY FOOT PEGS
(2010-2012 FLHTCUSE AND
2011 FLTRUSE)**

1. Bolt
2. Housing
3. Rubber pad
4. Mounting peg
5. Spring washer
6. Screw
7. Pivot bolt
8. Mounting bracket
9. Clamp
10. Acorn nut
11. Spring clip

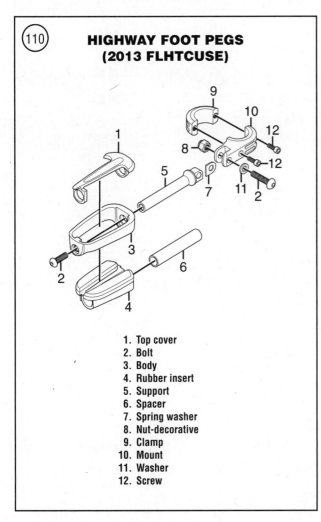

**HIGHWAY FOOT PEGS
(2013 FLHTCUSE)**

1. Top cover
2. Bolt
3. Body
4. Rubber insert
5. Support
6. Spacer
7. Spring washer
8. Nut-decorative
9. Clamp
10. Mount
11. Washer
12. Screw

12. Apply a small dab of Loctite Threadlocker 243 (Blue) to the Allen bolt prior to installation. Install the Allen bolt and tighten to 15-20 ft.-lb. (20.3-27.1 N•m).

Highway Foot Pegs

Refer to **Figure 109** And **Figure 110**.

Removal/installation

1. Place the motorcycle on level ground using the jiffy stand.
2. Place a strip of masking tape above and below the foot peg bracket on the engine guard, if the foot peg location is satisfactory.
3. Remove the two screws securing the clamp bracket and separate it from the mounting bracket.
4. Remove the foot peg assembly from the engine guard.
5A. Install the foot peg in the same location as marked, unless a different location is required.
5B. Use a grease pencil and mark a line on the engine guard down 6.5 in. (165 mm) from the top of the upper rail as a beginning point, if a new location is desired.
6. Correctly position the mounting bracket so it will not contact the lower fairings.
7. Position the mounting bracket onto the engine guard with the pivot screw and mounting screws facing forward.
8. Match the flair on the clamp bracket with the bevel on the mounting bracket. Install the bracket and clamp on the engine guard at the new, or desired, location at a 25° angle toward the rear and secure it in this position.
9. Install and tighten both clamp screws to 14 ft.-lb. (19.0 N•m).

Disassembly/assembly

1. Place the motorcycle on level ground using the jiffy stand.
2. Remove the end screw and slide the rubber pad and housing off the mounting peg.
3. Remove the pivot bolt, washer and acorn nut.
4. Remove the mounting peg and spring washer from the mounting bracket.
5. Apply a small dab of Loctite 243 (blue) threadlock to the pivot screw.
6. Correctly position the square edge of the spring clip facing the mounting bracket slot, and insert it in the mounting bracket. Hold it in this position.
7. Position the mounting peg with the flat surface facing down and install it onto the mounting bracket. Do not dislodge the spring washer.
8. Install the pivot bolt, washer and acorn nut. Tighten the acorn nut to 14-19 ft.-lb. (19.0-25.8 N•m).
9. Install the housing and rubber pad onto the mounting peg. Push it on until it bottoms.
10. Apply a small dab of Loctite 243 (blue) threadlock to the end screw.
11. Install the end screw and tighten to 19 ft.-lb. (25.8 N•m).

14

Table 1 BODY AND FRAME TORQUE SPECIFICATIONS

Item	ft.-lb.	in.-lb.	N•m
Air deflector thumb screws (FLHTCU and FLHTCUSE models)	–	25-35	2.8-4.0
Backrest			
Locknut	–	132-180	15-20
Flat mounting bracket bolt	–	60-96	6.8-10.8
Battery tray screws	–	72-96	8.1-10.8
Engine guard mounting bolts and nuts	15-20	–	20.4-27.1
Footboards (rider)			
Footboard shoulder bolts and nuts	–	60-80	6.8-9.0
Footboard complete disassembly all bolts	36-42	–	48.8-56.9
Rider footboards complete disassembly (CVO models) Allen and hex bolts	36-42	–	48.8-56.9
Footboard-to-mounting bracket pivot bolt and nut	–	60-80	6.8-9.0
Foot pegs (highway)			
Allen mounting bolts	14	–	19
Disassembly/assembly			
Pivot bolt and acorn nut	14-19	–	19.0-25.8
End screw	19	–	25.8
Footrest–passenger Allen bolt	36-42	–	48.8-56.9
Front fairing (frame mounted models)			
Outer fairing			
Four short screws	–	6-12	0.7-1.4
Two long screws	–	10-15	1.1-1.7
Instrument bezel housing			
Torx screws	15-20	–	20.3-27.1
Inner fairing-to-radio bracket locknuts	–	96-144	10.9-16.3
Front fairing (fork mounted models)			
Outer fairing			
Torx screws (T25)	–	20-30	2.3-3.4
Fairing-to-mounting bracket	–	20-30	2.3-3.4
Windshield Torx screws	–	25-30	2.8-3.4
Inner fairing cap-to-inner fairing			
Torx screws	–	25-30	2.8-3.4
Inner fairing			
Gauge-to-bracket hex nuts	–	10-20	1.1-2.3
Speedometer & tachometer mounting screws	–	10-20	1.1-2.3
Speaker adapter			
Long Torx screw (T25)	–	35-50	4.0-5.7
Short Torx screw (T25)	–	22-28	2.5-3.2
Jiffy stand			
Bracket-to-foot board bolt	36-42	–	48.8-56.9
Jiffy stand-to-bracket top hex bolt	15-20	–	20.3-27.1
Interlock Allen bolt	–	96-120	10.8-13.6
License plate bracket (FLTRUSE models)			
Connector cover flange nut	–	30-45	3.4-5.1
Light bracket screw	–	57-69	7.8
Lower fairing (fork mounted fairing models)			
Engine guard clamp Torx screw (T40)	–	90-100	10.2-11.3
Glove box door Torx screw (T20)	–	20-25	2.3-2.8

(continued)

Table 1 BODY AND FRAME TORQUE SPECIFICATIONS (continued)

Item	ft.-lb.	in.-lb.	N•m
Lower fairing (fork mounted fairing models) (continued)			
Lower fairing-to-engine guard flange nut	–	35-40	4.0-4.5
Passenger backrest (FLHRSE & FLTRUSE models)			
Backrest and antenna bracket mounting bolt	16.7	–	22.6
Backrest bushing assembly bolt	–	120	13.5
Fender mounting bracket bolt	15-20	–	20.3-27.1
Rear docking bolt	15-20	–	20.3-27.1
Rear frame/luggage rack			
Battery tray screws	–	72-96	8.1-10.8
Electrical caddy (left side) and top caddy screws	–	72-96	8.1-10.8
Luggage rack screw	15-20	–	20.3-27.1
Mounting bolts	40-50	–	54.2-67.8
Seat strap and forward luggage bracket screw	15-20	–	20.3-27.1
Rear fender (all models except CVO)			
Flange nut-to-battery Torx bolt	15-20	–	20.3-27
Saddlebag support bracket Torx bolt	15-20	–	20.3-27
Side mounting Torx bolt	15-20	–	20.3-27.1
Flange nut-to-weld stud	–	45-85	5.1-9.6
Rear fender (all CVO models except FLTRXSE)			
Back rest support screws	15-20	–	20.3-271
Fender-to-frame clip nut and bolt	17-22	–	23.1-29.8
Frame clip nut	–	35-40	4.0-4.5
Support bracket-to-fender locknut	–	45-85	5.1-9.6
Rear fender (FLTRXSE models)			
Fender-to-frame bolt	15-20	–	20.3-27.1
Passenger back rest support screws	16.7	–	22.6
Saddlebag support-to-fender and frame	15-20	–	20.3-27.1
Rear fender facia			
FLHX models flange nut	–	30-45	3.4-5.1
FLHRSE models flange nut	–	30-45	3.4-5.1
FLTRSE models flange nut	–	30-45	3.4-5.1
Saddlebag (FLHTCUSE models)			
Latch mount inner screws	–	25	2.8
Saddlebag guards/support (all models except CVO)			
Lower support rail			
Support rail-to-support bracket bolts	15-20	–	20.3-27.1
Support rail-to-rear fender and frame bolt and nut	15-20	–	20.3-27.1
Support rail-to-muffler bolt	–	96-144	10.8-16.3
Support rail bracket bolt	15-20	–	20.3-27.1
Support guards			
Saddlebag mounting bracket screw	–	60-96	6.8-10.8
Support bracket bolts	15-20	–	20.3-27.1
Support rail-to-support bracket bolt	15-20	–	20.3-27.1
Front guard-to-frame bolt and nut	15-20	–	20.3-27.1
Support guard-to-support rail screw	–	70-100	7.9-11.3

(continued)

14

Table 1 BODY AND FRAME TORQUE SPECIFICATIONS (continued)

Item	ft.-lb.	in.-lb.	N•m
Saddlebag guards/support (all models except CVO) (continued)			
Support guards (continued)			
Front guard-to-saddlebag guard screw	–	70-100	7.9-11.3
Guard clamp screw	–	30-50	3.4-5.7
Saddlebag guards/support (CVO models)			
Support rail-to-support bracket bolt	15-20	–	20.3-27.1
Support rail-to-guard	–	70-100	7.9-11.3
Seat-to-rear fender screw	–	48-72	5.4-8.1
Support bracket (all models)			
Upper bracket bolt	–	60-96	6.8-10.8
Bracket bolts	15-20	–	20.3-27.1
Tour-Pak			
FLHTC, FLHTCU models bolts and nuts	–	90-108	10.2-12.2
CVO models			
Mounting bolts and nuts	–	96-108	10.8-12.2
Speaker box mounting bolts	–	25-35	2.8-4.0
Windshield screws (Road King models)	–	6-13	0.7-1.5

INDEX

2010 FLHX, FLHT, FLHTC, FLHTCU, FLTRX AND FLHTK MODELS

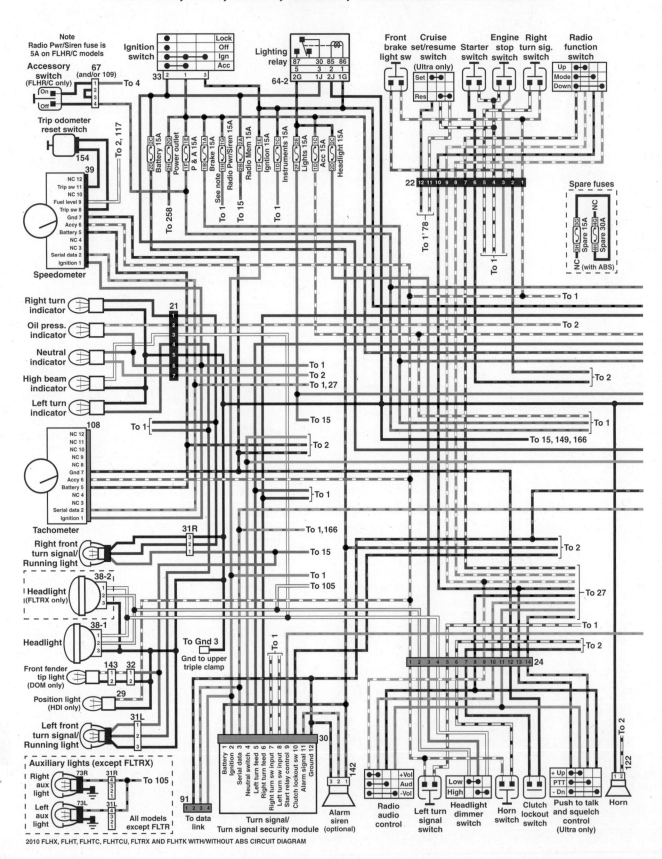

2010 FLHX, FLHT, FLHTC, FLHTCU, FLTRX AND FLHTK WITH/WITHOUT ABS CIRCUIT DIAGRAM

Active exhaust connector (HDI only)
179
5 4 3 2 1

Crank position sensor
79 2 1

Oil press. sender
80
139 A B
To 2

TMAP sensor
4 3 2 1
224
204

Twist grip sensor
Left Right
1 2 3 4 5 6
Tubing Tubing
4 5 6 1 2 3

Engine temp. sensor
A B
90

Jiffy stand sensor (HDI)
3 2 1
133

Vehicle speed sensor
3 2 1
65

Rear brake light sw
121 1 2
(To ABS)

Fuel pump/ Sender assembly
Inside fuel tank
A B C D
141
13 1 2 3 4
To 2

Neutral switch
131 B A

Brake relay
87 30 85 86
5 3 2 1
3A 2B 2A 3B

To Tour-Pak
3 2 1 12

Diagram Key
Connectors
Ground (Gnd)
Frame ground
Connection
No connection (NC)
Twisted pair
LED

Accessory connector
4
1
2
3
To 2, 67

Fender tip/ Lic. plate light
1 2 3
45

To 166, 201
To 201
To 166

FLHTCU, FLHTK, FLHR & FLHC
19

Right rear turn signal
1 2 3 4
Running light (DOM)
93

Tail/ brake light
Brake light
Running light (HDI)

Left rear turn signal
18

7
1
2
3
4
5
6
7
8

94
1
2
3
4
5
6

NC 1B 1A
P & A Ign (MAX) 2A
3B 3A
Exh. control 15A

4A 4B
ABS 30A
2E 2F
ECM Pwr 15A
4B 4A
Fuel pump 15A

Gnd 1 (left)

203FB
Front ACR
2 1
FLHTCU & FLHTK models only
203RB
Rear ACR
2 1

85
Rear fuel injector
B A

84
Front fuel injector
B A

Gnd 2 (right)
To 15

95
Purge solenoid
A B

211
1
2
3
4
5
6
Throttle control actuator

To 1
To 1
To 1

83
A Pwr
B Ion sense
C Coil rear
D Coil front
Ignition coil

Spark plugs

160
B+ 1

Main fuse 40A
B A

128 1
Starter

138
4 3 2 1

ECM
ACR ground 19
Purge solenoid 20
Exhaust actuator 21
Cruise/Set/Coast 22
Rear fuel injector 23
TMAP sensor input 24
Brake switch 25
System relay enable 26
Front fuel injector 27
Twist grip input 28
Twist grip Lo 29
HO2 Heater ground 31
Ion sense 33
Cruise resume/Accel 34
Cruise enable 35
TPS 1 37
TPS 2 39
Exhaust feedback 38
Vehicle speed input 40
CKP sensor (-) 43
HO2 return 48
IAT 49
5V sensor power 1 50
ET 51
System relay power 52
Rear ignition coil 53
Front ignition coil 54
TGS 1 59
5V sensor ground 1 61
5V sensor ground 2 62
CKP sensor (+) 63
Vehicle speed ground 64
Front HO2 sensor 66
5V sensor power 2 68
Serial data 69
12V battery 71
Engine stop switch 72
Ground 73

To Front HO2 sensor

78

137
4 3 2 1
To Rear HO2 sensor

DC 2 1 77
Voltage regulator
AC 47

Stator

System relay
4D 3C 3D 4C
1 2 3 5
86 85 30 87

Starter relay
4H 3G 3H 4G
1 2 3 5
86 85 30 87

Battery
- +

16

2010 FLHX, FLHT, FLHTC, FLHTCU, FLTRX AND FLHTK WITH/WITHOUT ABS CIRCUIT DIAGRAM

2010 FLHX, FLHT, FLHTC, FLHTCU, FLTRX AND FLHTK MODELS

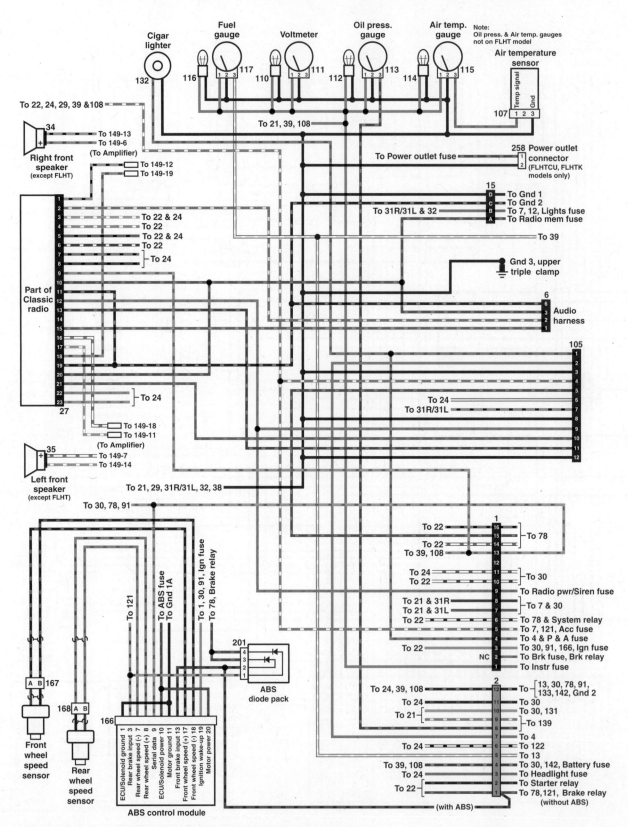

2010 FLHX, FLHT, FLHTC, FLHTCU, FLTRX AND FLHTK GAUGES, RADIO, FRONT SPEAKERS AND ABS CIRCUIT DIAGRAM

2010 FLHR, FLHRC AND FLHX MODELS

Left & right handlebar control switches on FLHR, FLHRC AND FLHX models only

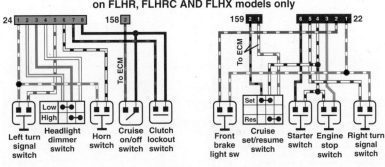

Fairing switches

Hands-free security module

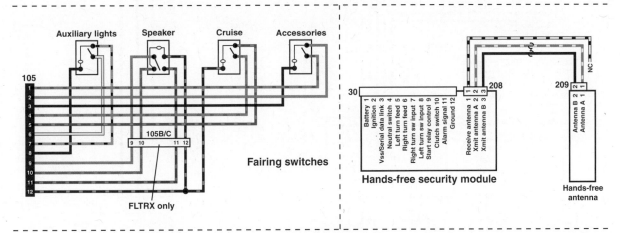

Heated hand grips
(except FLTRX)

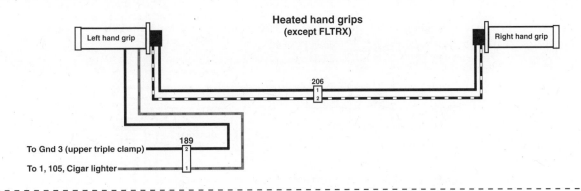

Tour-Pak lights

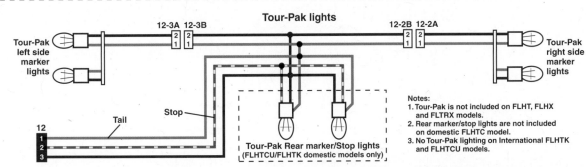

Notes:
1. Tour-Pak is not included on FLHT, FLHX and FLTRX models.
2. Rear marker/stop lights are not included on domestic FLHTC model.
3. No Tour-Pak lighting on International FLHTK and FLHTCU models.

2010 FLHR, FLHRC AND FLHX LEFT/RIGHT HANDLE BAR SWITCHES, FAIRING SWITCHES, HANDS FREE SECURITY MODULE, HEATED HAND GRIPS AND TOUR-PAK LIGHTS CIRCUIT DIAGRAMS

16

2010 FLHR AND FLHRC MODELS

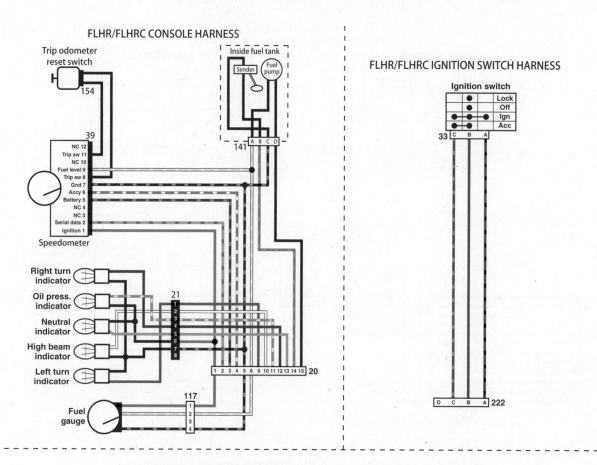

FLHR/FLHRC CONSOLE HARNESS

FLHR/FLHRC IGNITION SWITCH HARNESS

FLHR, FLHRC AND FLHX AUXILIARY LIGHT AND TURN SIGNAL HARNESS

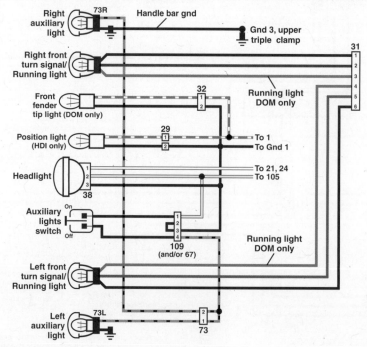

2010 FLHR, FLHRC CONSOLE, IGNITION SWITCH AND AUXILIARY LIGHTS WITHOUT/WITH ABS CIRCUIT DIAGRAMS

2010 DOMESTIC, CANADA AND INTERNATIONAL MODELS

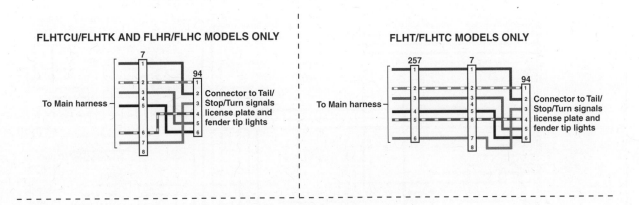

FLHTCU/FLHTK AND FLHR/FLHC MODELS ONLY

To Main harness

Connector to Tail/Stop/Turn signals license plate and fender tip lights

FLHT/FLHTC MODELS ONLY

To Main harness

Connector to Tail/Stop/Turn signals license plate and fender tip lights

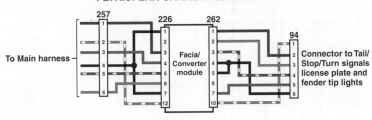

FLTRX/FLHX CANADA MODELS ONY

To Main harness

Facia/Converter module

Connector to Tail/Stop/Turn signals license plate and fender tip lights

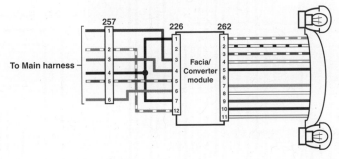

FLTRX/FLHX HDI MODELS ONLY

To Main harness

Facia/Converter module

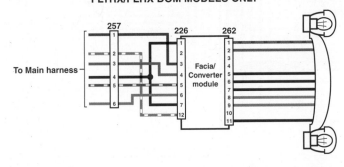

FLTRX/FLHX DOM MODELS ONLY

To Main harness

Facia/Converter module

2010 FLHX, FLHT, FLHTC, FLHTCU, FLTRX AND FLHTK MODELS

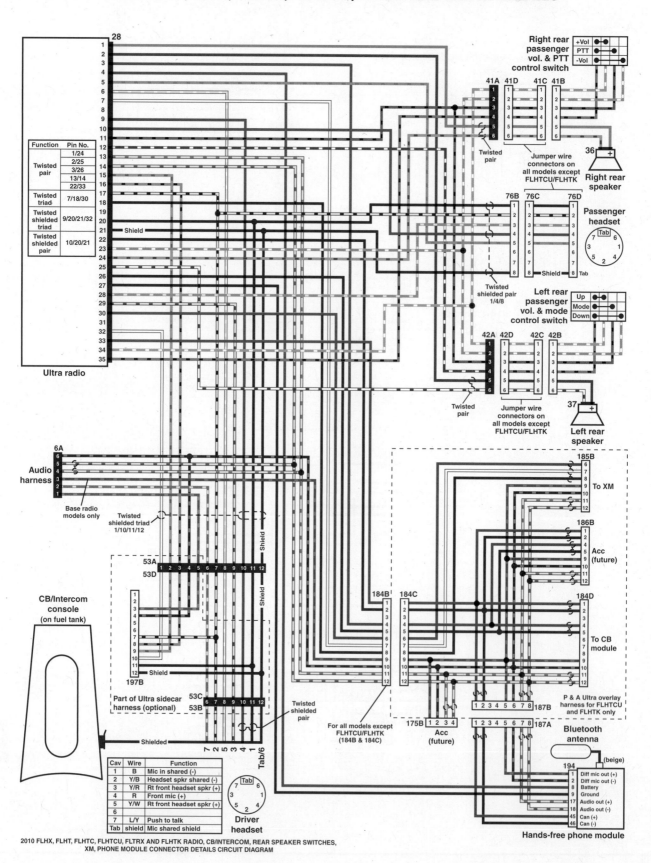

2010 FLHX, FLHT, FLHTC, FLHTCU, FLTRX AND FLHTK RADIO, CB/INTERCOM, REAR SPEAKER SWITCHES, XM, PHONE MODULE CONNECTOR DETAILS CIRCUIT DIAGRAM

2010 FLHX, FLHT, FLHTC, FLHTCU AND FLTR MODELS

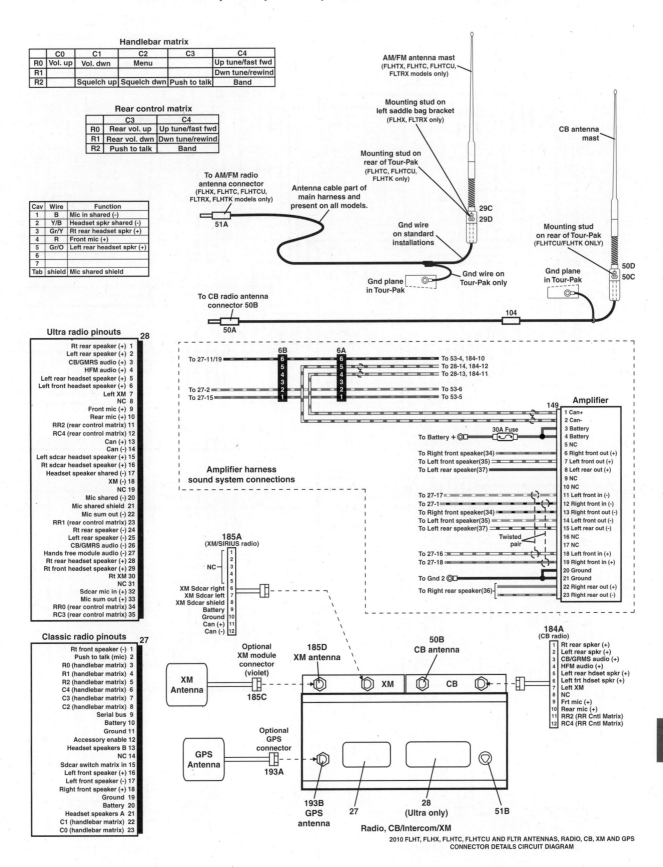

Handlebar matrix

	C0	C1	C2	C3	C4
R0	Vol. up	Vol. dwn	Menu		Up tune/fast fwd
R1					Dwn tune/rewind
R2		Squelch up	Squelch dwn	Push to talk	Band

Rear control matrix

	C3	C4
R0	Rear vol. up	Up tune/fast fwd
R1	Rear vol. dwn	Dwn tune/rewind
R2	Push to talk	Band

Cav	Wire	Function
1	B	Mic in shared (-)
2	Y/B	Headset spkr shared (-)
3	Gr/Y	Rt rear headset spkr (+)
4	R	Front mic (+)
5	Gr/O	Left rear headset spkr (+)
6		
7		
Tab	shield	Mic shared shield

To AM/FM radio antenna connector (FLHX, FLHTC, FLHTCU, FLTRX, FLHTK models only)

51A

Antenna cable part of main harness and present on all models.

AM/FM antenna mast (FLHTX, FLHTC, FLHTCU, FLTRX models only)

Mounting stud on left saddle bag bracket (FLHX, FLTRX only)

Mounting stud on rear of Tour-Pak (FLHTC, FLHTCU, FLHTK only)

CB antenna mast

29C
29D

Gnd wire on standard installations

Mounting stud on rear of Tour-Pak (FLHTCU/FLHTK ONLY)

Gnd plane in Tour-Pak

Gnd wire on Tour-Pak only

50D
50C

Gnd plane in Tour-Pak

To CB radio antenna connector 50B

50A

104

Ultra radio pinouts   28

Rt rear speaker (+)	1
Left rear speaker (+)	2
CB/GMRS audio (+)	3
HFM audio (+)	4
Left rear headset speaker (+)	5
Left front headset speaker (+)	6
Left XM	7
NC	8
Front mic (+)	9
Rear mic (+)	10
RR2 (rear control matrix)	11
RC4 (rear control matrix)	12
Can (+)	13
Can (-)	14
Left sdcar headset speaker (+)	15
Rt sdcar headset speaker (+)	16
Headset speaker shared (-)	17
XM (-)	18
NC	19
Mic shared (-)	20
Mic shared shield	21
Mic sum out (-)	22
RR1 (rear control matrix)	23
Rt rear speaker (-)	24
Left rear speaker (-)	25
CB/GMRS audio (-)	26
Hands free module audio (-)	27
Rt rear headset speaker (+)	28
Rt front headset speaker (+)	29
Rt XM	30
NC	31
Sdcar mic in (+)	32
Mic sum out (+)	33
RR0 (rear control matrix)	34
RC3 (rear control matrix)	35

Classic radio pinouts   27

Rt front speaker (-)	1
Push to talk (mic)	2
R0 (handlebar matrix)	3
R1 (handlebar matrix)	4
R2 (handlebar matrix)	5
C4 (handlebar matrix)	6
C3 (handlebar matrix)	7
C2 (handlebar matrix)	8
Serial bus	9
Battery	10
Ground	11
Accessory enable	12
Headset speakers B	13
NC	14
Sdcar switch matrix in	15
Left front speaker (+)	16
Left front speaker (-)	17
Right front speaker (+)	18
Ground	19
Battery	20
Headset speakers A	21
C1 (handlebar matrix)	22
C0 (handlebar matrix)	23

6B   6A

To 27-11/19

To 27-2
To 27-15

To 53-4, 184-10
To 28-14, 184-12
To 28-13, 184-11
To 53-6
To 53-5

149   **Amplifier**

1	Can+
2	Can-
3	Battery
4	Battery
5	NC
6	Right front out (+)
7	Left front out (+)
8	Left rear out (+)
9	NC
10	NC
11	Left front in (-)
12	Right front in (-)
13	Right front out (-)
14	Left front out (-)
15	Left rear out (-)
16	NC
17	NC
18	Left front in (+)
19	Right front in (+)
20	Ground
21	Ground
22	Right rear out (+)
23	Right rear out (-)

To Battery +   30A Fuse

To Right front speaker(34)
To Left front speaker(35)
To Left rear speaker(37)

Amplifier harness sound system connections

To 27-17
To 27-1
To Right front speaker(34)
To Left front speaker(35)
To Left rear speaker(37)

Twisted pair

To 27-16
To 27-18

To Gnd 2

To Right rear speaker(36)

185A (XM/SIRIUS radio)

NC	1
	2
	3
	4
	5
XM Sdcar right	6
XM Sdcar left	7
XM Sdcar shield	8
Battery	9
Ground	10
Can (+)	11
Can (-)	12

Optional XM module connector (violet)

185C

XM Antenna

185D XM antenna

50B CB antenna

184A (CB radio)

1	Rt rear spker (+)
2	Left rear spkr (+)
3	CB/GRMS audio (+)
4	HFM audio (+)
5	Left rear hdset spkr (+)
6	Left frt hdset spkr (+)
7	Left XM
8	NC
9	Frt mic (+)
10	Rear mic (+)
11	RR2 (RR Cntl Matrix)
12	RC4 (RR Cntl Matrix)

XM   CB

Optional GPS connector

GPS Antenna

193A

193B GPS antenna

27

28 (Ultra only)

51B

Radio, CB/Intercom/XM

2010 FLHT, FLHX, FLHTC, FLHTCU AND FLTR ANTENNAS, RADIO, CB, XM AND GPS CONNECTOR DETAILS CIRCUIT DIAGRAM

16

2011 ALL TOURING MODELS

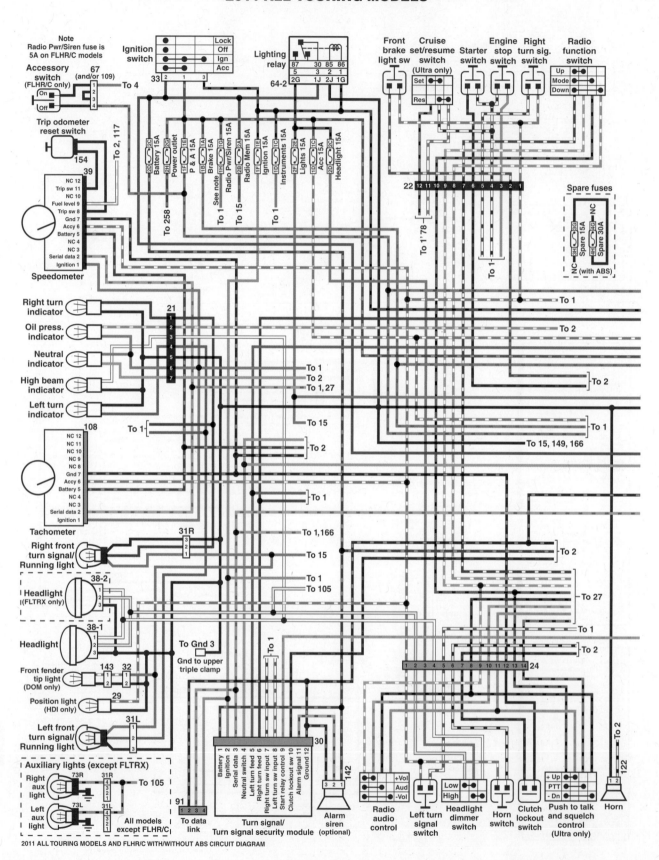

2011 ALL TOURING MODELS AND FLHR/C WITH/WITHOUT ABS CIRCUIT DIAGRAM

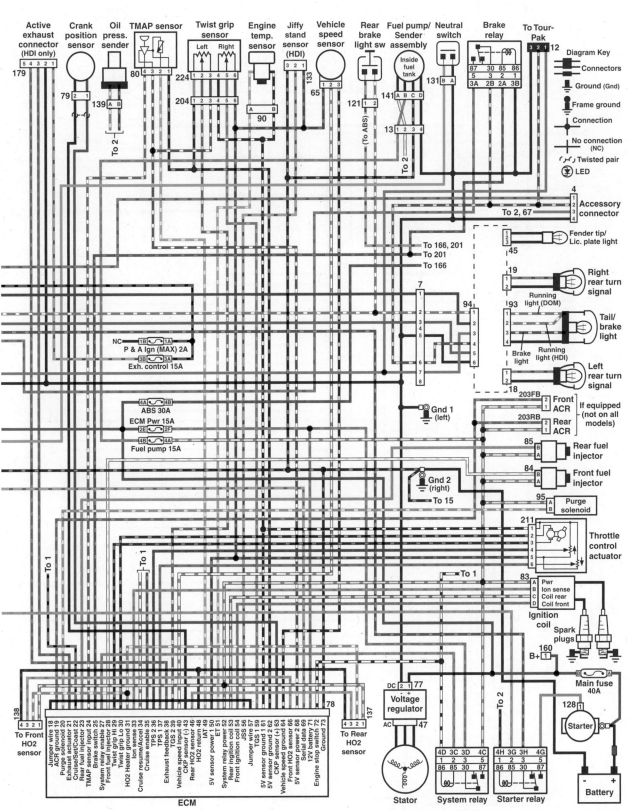

Active exhaust connector (HDI only)
Crank position sensor
Oil press. sender
TMAP sensor
Twist grip sensor
Engine temp. sensor
Jiffy stand sensor (HDI)
Vehicle speed sensor
Rear brake light sw
Fuel pump/ Sender assembly
Neutral switch
Brake relay
To Tour-Pak

Diagram Key
Connectors
Ground (Gnd)
Frame ground
Connection
No connection (NC)
Twisted pair
LED

Accessory connector
Fender tip/ Lic. plate light
Right rear turn signal
Running light (DOM)
Tail/ brake light
Brake light
Running light (HDI)
Left rear turn signal

Front ACR
Rear ACR
If equipped (not on all models)
Rear fuel injector
Front fuel injector
Purge solenoid
Throttle control actuator
Pwr
Ion sense
Coil rear
Coil front
Ignition coil
Spark plugs
Main fuse 40A
Starter

NC
P & A Ign (MAX) 2A
Exh. control 15A
ABS 30A
ECM Pwr 15A
Fuel pump 15A
Gnd 1 (left)
Gnd 2 (right)
To 15

Voltage regulator
Stator
System relay
Starter relay
Battery

To Front HO2 sensor
ECM
To Rear HO2 sensor

2011 ALL TOURING MODELS AND FLHR/C WITH/WITHOUT ABS CIRCUIT DIAGRAM

16

WIRING DIAGRAMS

2011 FLHX, FLHT, FLHTC, FLHTCU, FLTRX AND FLHTK MODELS

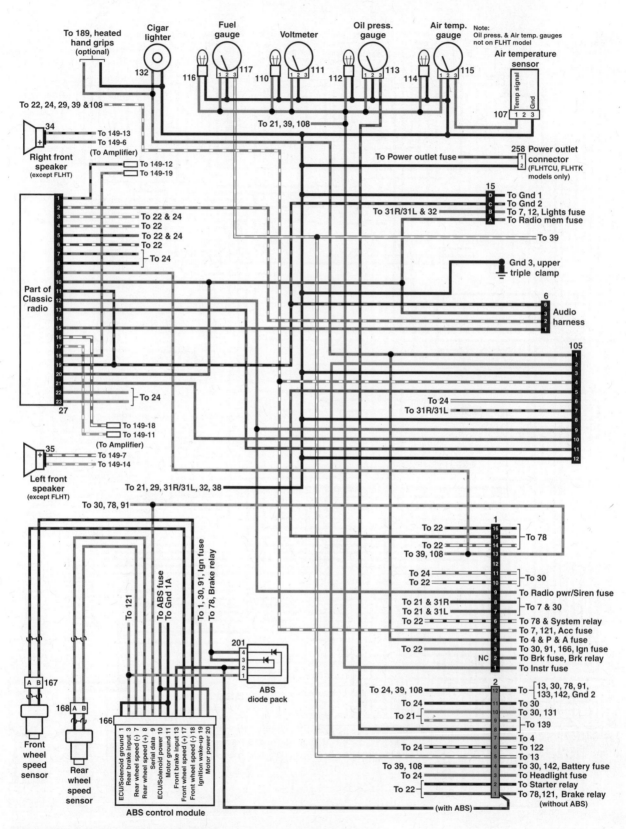

2011 FLHX, FLHT, FLHTC, FLHTCU, FLTRX AND FLHTK GAUGES, RADIO, FRONT SPEAKERS AND ABS CIRCUIT DIAGRAM

2011 FLHR AND FLHRC MODELS

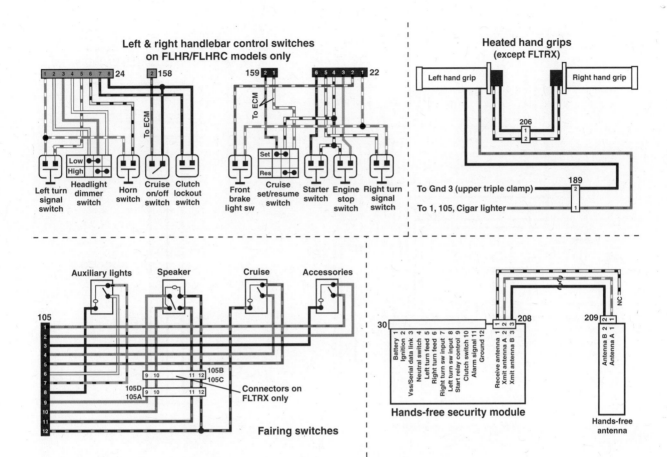

Left & right handlebar control switches on FLHR/FLHRC models only

Left turn signal switch | Headlight dimmer switch | Horn switch | Cruise on/off switch | Clutch lockout switch

Front brake light sw | Cruise set/resume switch | Starter switch | Engine stop switch | Right turn signal switch

Heated hand grips (except FLTRX)

Left hand grip | Right hand grip

To Gnd 3 (upper triple clamp)

To 1, 105, Cigar lighter

Auxiliary lights | Speaker | Cruise | Accessories

Connectors on FLTRX only

Fairing switches

Battery 1 / Ignition 2 / Vss/Serial data link 3 / Neutral switch 4 / Left turn feed 5 / Right turn feed 6 / Right turn sw input 7 / Left turn sw input 8 / Start relay control 9 / Clutch switch 10 / Alarm signal 11 / Ground 12

Receive antenna 1 / Xmit antenna A 2 / Xmit antenna B 3

Hands-free security module

Antenna B 2 / Antenna A 1

Hands-free antenna

SECURITY CIRCUIT WITH ANTI-THEFT TRACKING MODULE

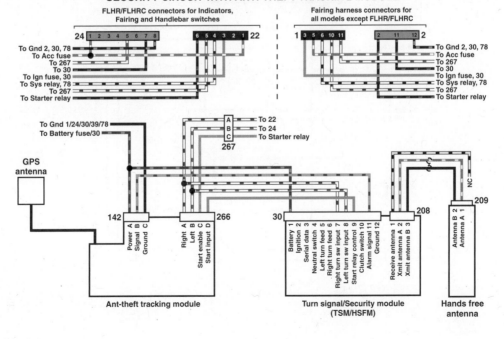

FLHR/FLHRC connectors for Indicators, Fairing and Handlebar switches

Fairing harness connectors for all models except FLHR/FLHRC

To Gnd 2, 30, 78
To Acc fuse
To 267
To 30
To Ign fuse, 30
To Sys relay, 78
To 267
To Starter relay

To Gnd 2, 30, 78
To Acc fuse
To 267
To 30
To Ign fuse, 30
To Sys relay, 78
To 267
To Starter relay

To Gnd 1/24/30/39/78
To Battery fuse/30

A — To 22
B — To 24
C — To Starter relay
267

GPS antenna

142 — Power A / Signal B / Ground C

266 — Right A / Left B / Start enable C / Start input D

Ant-theft tracking module

30 — Battery 1 / Ignition 2 / Serial data 3 / Neutral switch 4 / Left turn feed 5 / Right turn feed 6 / Right turn sw input 7 / Left turn sw input 8 / Start relay control 9 / Clutch switch 10 / Alarm signal 11 / Ground 12

208 — Receive antenna 1 / Xmit antenna A 2 / Xmit antenna B 3

Turn signal/Security module (TSM/HSFM)

209 — Antenna B 2 / Antenna A 1

Hands free antenna

16

2011 FLHR AND FLHRC MODELS

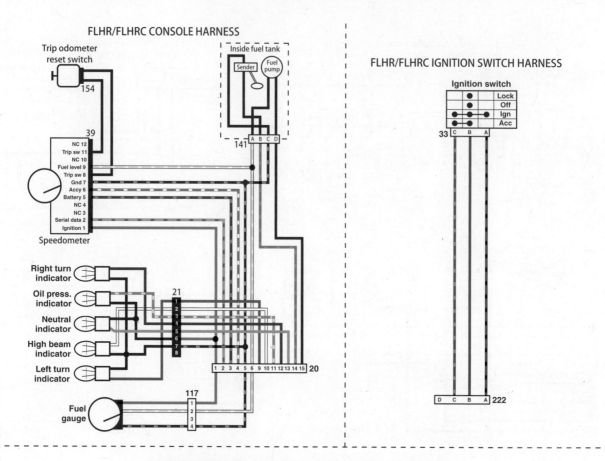

FLHR/FLHRC CONSOLE HARNESS

FLHR/FLHRC IGNITION SWITCH HARNESS

FLHR/FLHRC AUXILIARY LIGHT AND TURN SIGNAL HARNESS

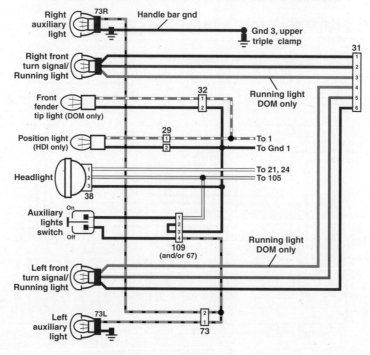

2011 FLHR, FLHRC CONSOLE, IGNITION SWITCH AND AUXILIARY LIGHTS WITHOUT/WITH ABS CIRCUIT DIAGRAMS

2011 DOMESTIC, CANADA AND INTERNATIONAL MODELS

FLHTCU/FLHTK AND FLHR/FLHC MODELS ONLY

FLHTC MODELS ONLY

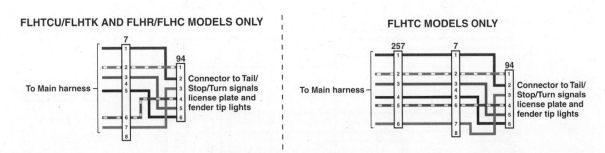

FLTRX/FLHX CANADA MODELS ONY

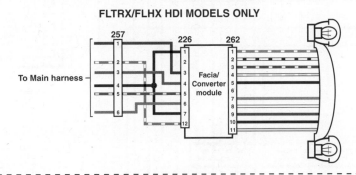

FLTRX/FLHX HDI MODELS ONLY

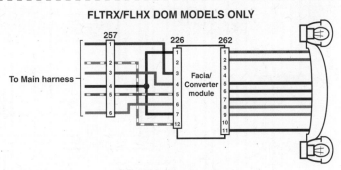

FLTRX/FLHX DOM MODELS ONLY

Tour-Pak lights

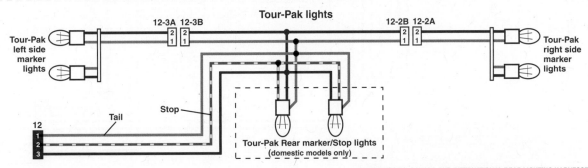

2011 DOMESTIC, CANADA AND INTERNATIONAL REAR LIGHTING HARNESSES
AND TOUR-PAK CIRCUIT DIAGRAMS

16

2011 ALL TOURING MODELS

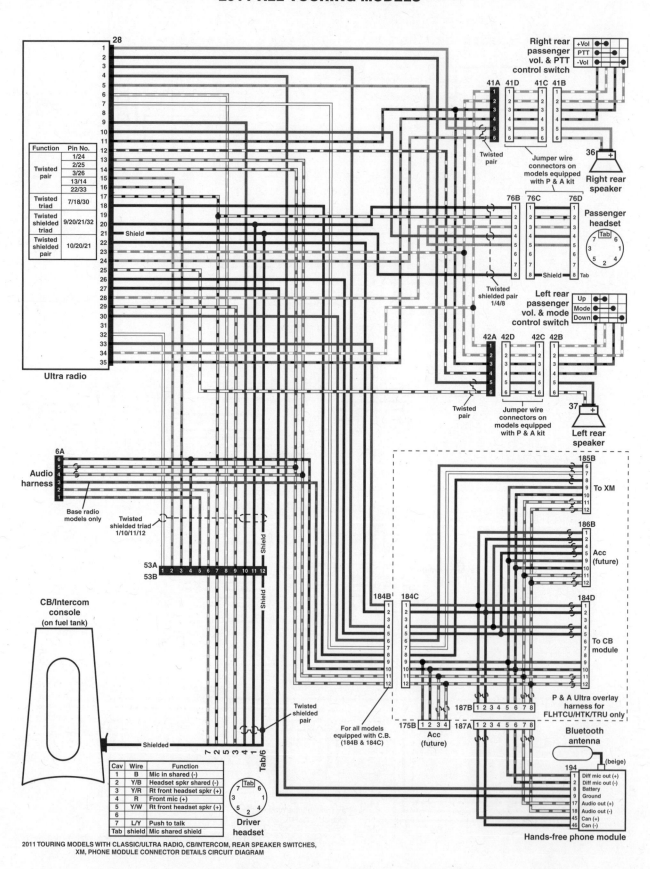

2011 TOURING MODELS WITH CLASSIC/ULTRA RADIO, CB/INTERCOM, REAR SPEAKER SWITCHES,
XM, PHONE MODULE CONNECTOR DETAILS CIRCUIT DIAGRAM

2011 ALL TOURING MODELS

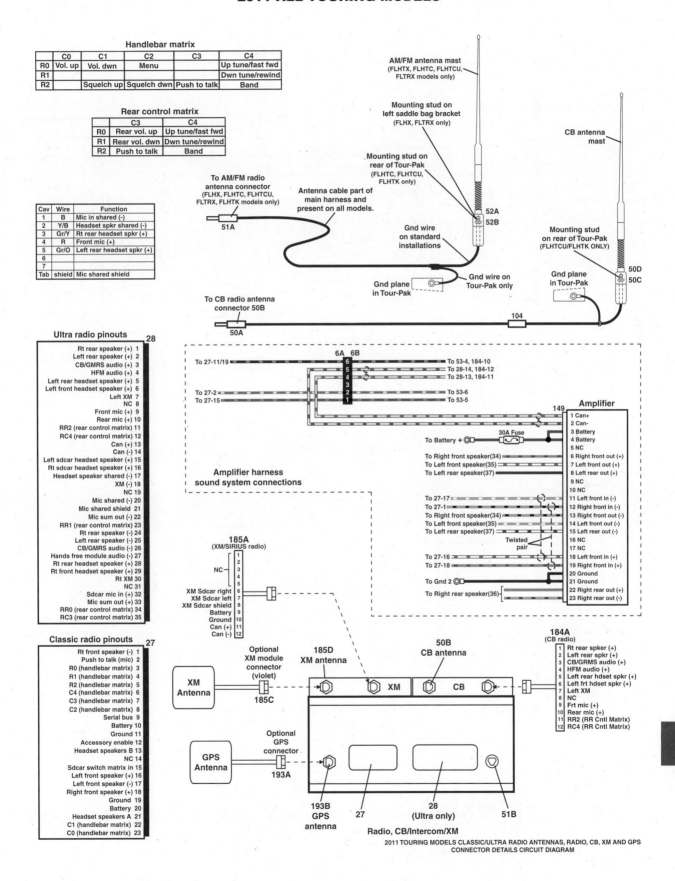

2011 TOURING MODELS CLASSIC/ULTRA RADIO ANTENNAS, RADIO, CB, XM AND GPS
CONNECTOR DETAILS CIRCUIT DIAGRAM

2011 ULTRA MODELS

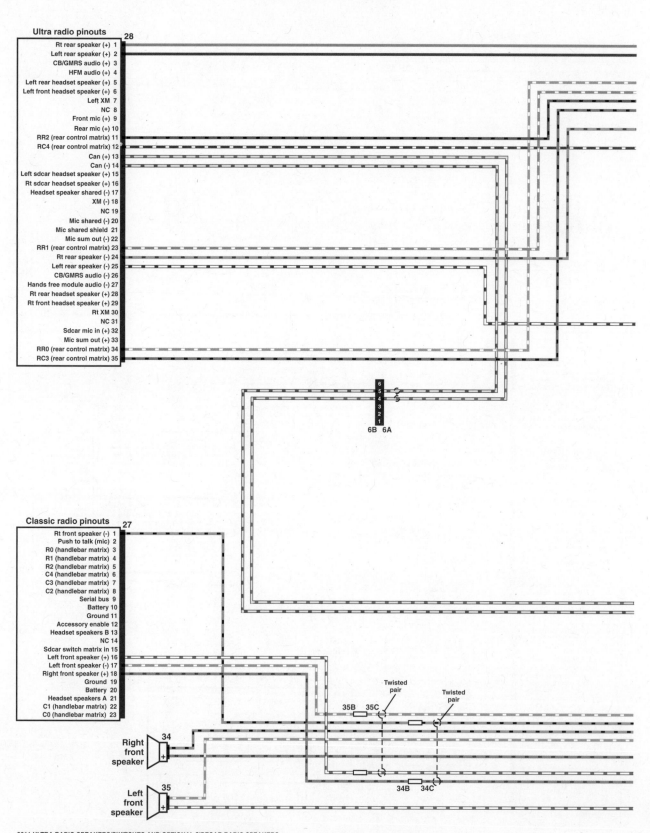

Ultra radio pinouts | 28

Rt rear speaker (+)	1
Left rear speaker (+)	2
CB/GMRS audio (+)	3
HFM audio (+)	4
Left rear headset speaker (+)	5
Left front headset speaker (+)	6
Left XM	7
NC	8
Front mic (+)	9
Rear mic (+)	10
RR2 (rear control matrix)	11
RC4 (rear control matrix)	12
Can (+)	13
Can (-)	14
Left sdcar headset speaker (+)	15
Rt sdcar headset speaker (+)	16
Headset speaker shared (-)	17
XM (-)	18
NC	19
Mic shared (-)	20
Mic shared shield	21
Mic sum out (-)	22
RR1 (rear control matrix)	23
Rt rear speaker (-)	24
Left rear speaker (-)	25
CB/GMRS audio (-)	26
Hands free module audio (-)	27
Rt rear headset speaker (+)	28
Rt front headset speaker (+)	29
Rt XM	30
NC	31
Sdcar mic in (+)	32
Mic sum out (+)	33
RR0 (rear control matrix)	34
RC3 (rear control matrix)	35

6B 6A

Classic radio pinouts | 27

Rt front speaker (-)	1
Push to talk (mic)	2
R0 (handlebar matrix)	3
R1 (handlebar matrix)	4
R2 (handlebar matrix)	5
C4 (handlebar matrix)	6
C3 (handlebar matrix)	7
C2 (handlebar matrix)	8
Serial bus	9
Battery	10
Ground	11
Accessory enable	12
Headset speakers B	13
NC	14
Sdcar switch matrix in	15
Left front speaker (+)	16
Left front speaker (-)	17
Right front speaker (+)	18
Ground	19
Battery	20
Headset speakers A	21
C1 (handlebar matrix)	22
C0 (handlebar matrix)	23

Right front speaker 34

Left front speaker 35

Twisted pair

35B 35C

Twisted pair

34B 34C

2011 ULTRA RADIO SPEAKERS/SWITCHES AND OPTIONAL SIDECAR RADIO SPEAKERS
AND CONTROL CONNECTOR DETAILS CIRCUIT DIAGRAM

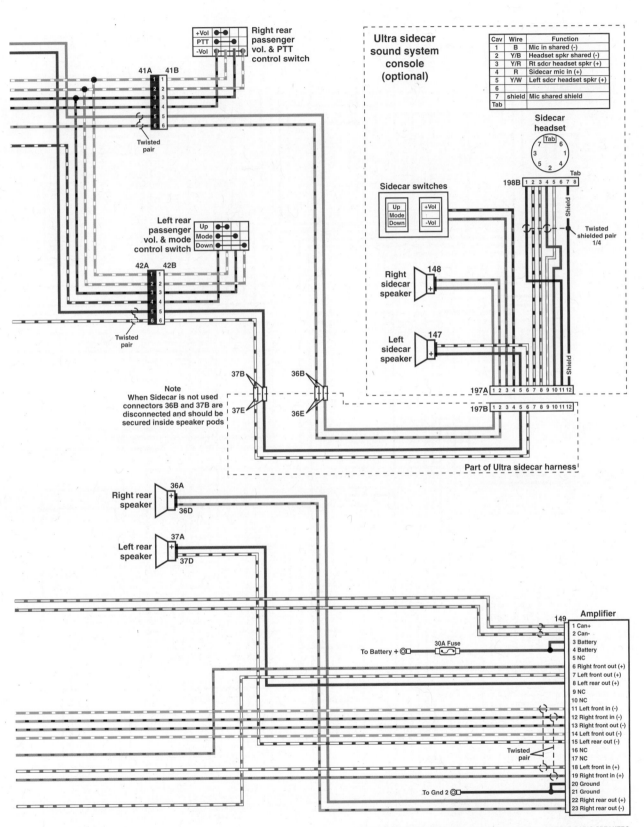

Cav	Wire	Function
1	B	Mic in shared (-)
2	Y/B	Headset spkr shared (-)
3	Y/R	Rt sdcr headset spkr (+)
4	R	Sidecar mic in (+)
5	Y/W	Left sdcr headset spkr (+)
6		
7	shield	Mic shared shield
Tab		

Ultra sidecar sound system console (optional)

Right rear passenger vol. & PTT control switch

+Vol
PTT
-Vol

41A 41B

Twisted pair

Left rear passenger vol. & mode control switch

Up
Mode
Down

42A 42B

Twisted pair

Sidecar switches

Up
Mode
Down

+Vol
-Vol

Right sidecar speaker 148

Left sidecar speaker 147

Sidecar headset

Tab

198B

Twisted shielded pair 1/4

Shield

197A

Shield

37B 36B

Note
When Sidecar is not used connectors 36B and 37B are disconnected and should be secured inside speaker pods

37E 36E

197B

Part of Ultra sidecar harness

Right rear speaker 36A
36D

Left rear speaker 37A
37D

Amplifier 149

1	Can+
2	Can-
3	Battery
4	Battery
5	NC
6	Right front out (+)
7	Left front out (+)
8	Left rear out (+)
9	NC
10	NC
11	Left front in (-)
12	Right front in (-)
13	Right front out (-)
14	Left front out (-)
15	Left rear out (-)
16	NC
17	NC
18	Left front in (+)
19	Right front in (+)
20	Ground
21	Ground
22	Right rear out (+)
23	Right rear out (-)

To Battery +   30A Fuse

Twisted pair

To Gnd 2

2011 ULTRA RADIO SPEAKERS/SWITCHES AND OPTIONAL SIDECAR RADIO SPEAKERS
AND CONTROL CONNECTOR DETAILS CIRCUIT DIAGRAM

16

2012 ALL TOURING MODELS

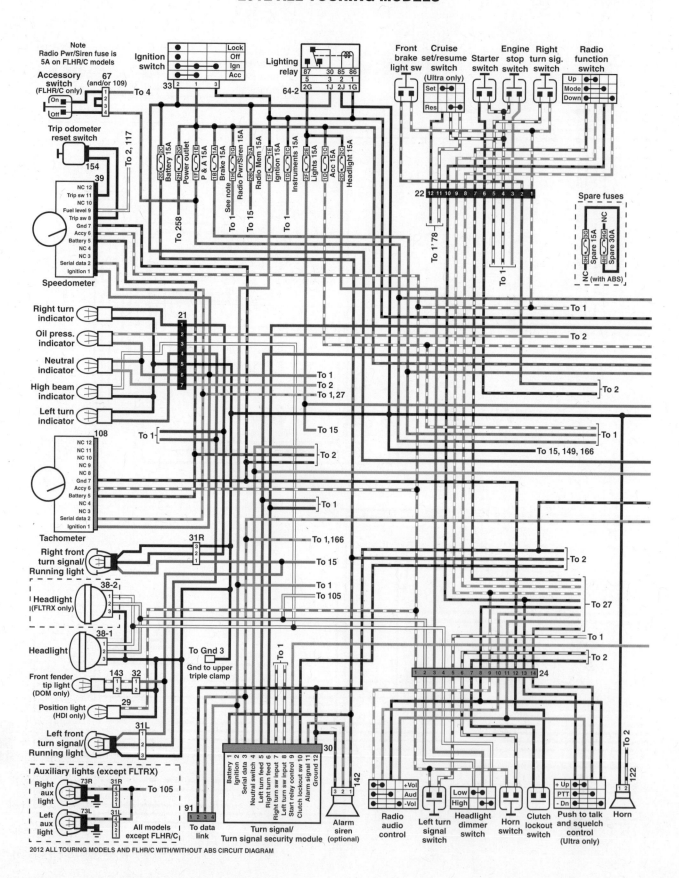

2012 ALL TOURING MODELS AND FLHR/C WITH/WITHOUT ABS CIRCUIT DIAGRAM

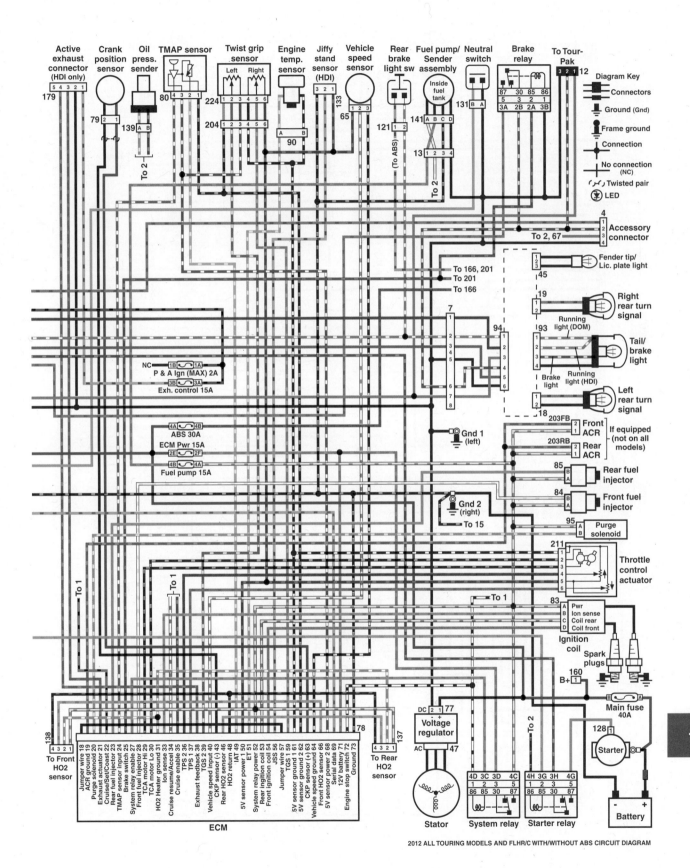

2012 ALL TOURING MODELS AND FLHR/C WITH/WITHOUT ABS CIRCUIT DIAGRAM

2012 FLHX, FLHT, FLHTC, FLHTCU, FLTRX AND FLHTK MODELS

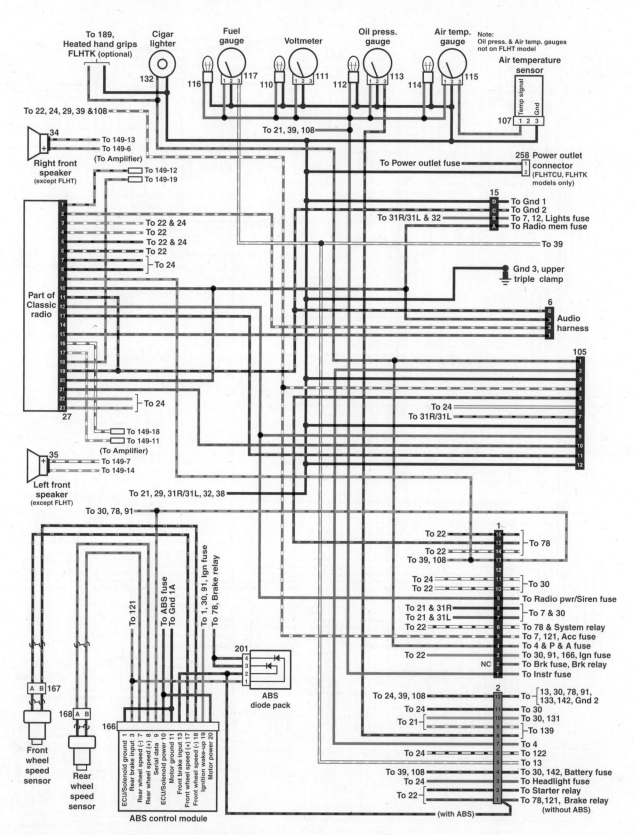

2012 FLHX, FLHT, FLHTC, FLHTCU, FLTRX AND FLHTK GAUGES, RADIO, FRONT SPEAKERS AND ABS CIRCUIT DIAGRAM

2012 ALL TOURING MODELS

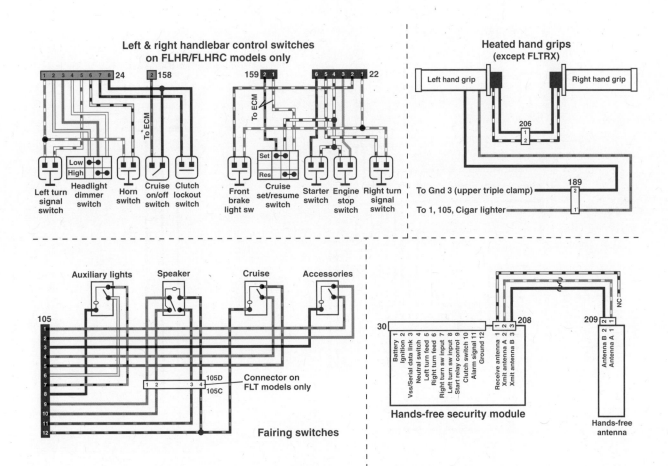

Left & right handlebar control switches on FLHR/FLHRC models only

Heated hand grips (except FLTRX)

Auxiliary lights · Speaker · Cruise · Accessories

Fairing switches

Hands-free security module

Hands-free antenna

SECURITY CIRCUIT WITH ANTI-THEFT TRACKING MODULE

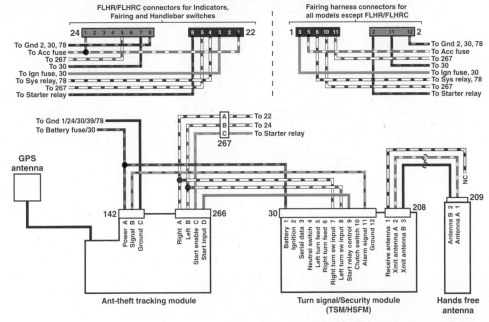

Ant-theft tracking module

Turn signal/Security module (TSM/HSFM)

Hands free antenna

GPS antenna

2012 TOURING MODELS LEFT/RIGHT HANDLE BAR SWITCHES, HEATED HAND GRIPS, FAIRING SWITCHES, HANDS FREE SECURITY MODULE AND SECURITY CIRCUIT WITH ANTI-THEFT TRACKING MODULE CIRCUIT DIAGRAMS

16

2012 FLHR AND FLHRC MODELS

FLHR/FLHRC CONSOLE HARNESS

FLHR/FLHRC IGNITION SWITCH HARNESS

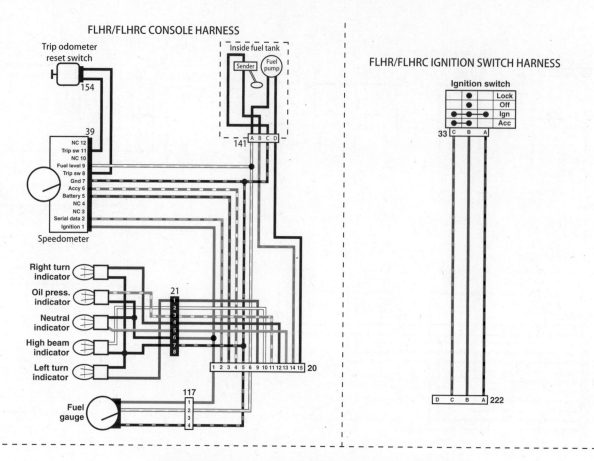

FLHR/FLHRC AUXILIARY LIGHT AND TURN SIGNAL HARNESS

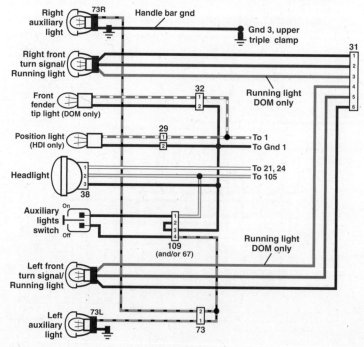

2012 FLHR, FLHRC CONSOLE, IGNITION SWITCH AND AUXILIARY LIGHTS WITHOUT/WITH ABS CIRCUIT DIAGRAMS

2012 DOMESTIC, CANADA AND INTERNATIONAL MODELS

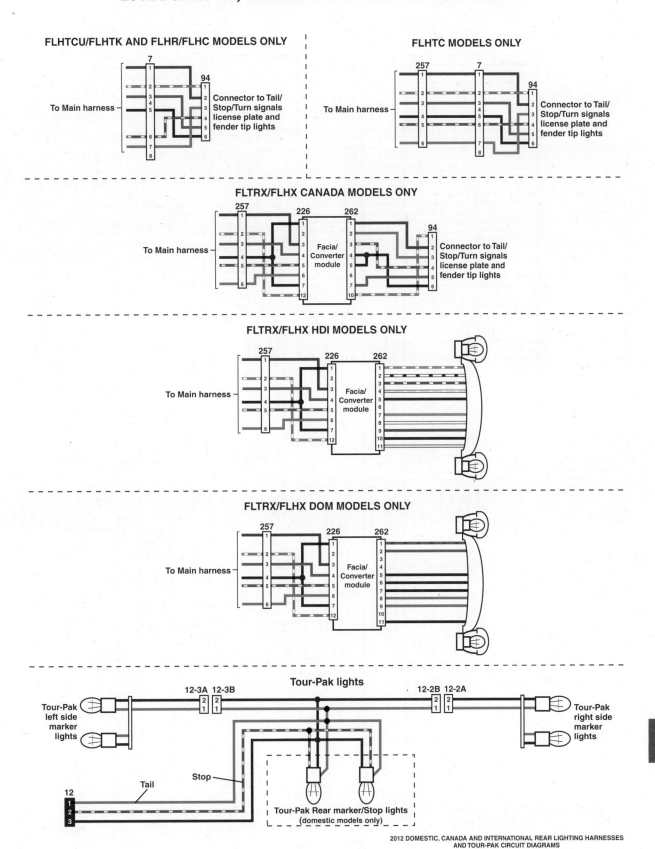

FLHTCU/FLHTK AND FLHR/FLHC MODELS ONLY

To Main harness

Connector to Tail/Stop/Turn signals license plate and fender tip lights

FLHTC MODELS ONLY

To Main harness

Connector to Tail/Stop/Turn signals license plate and fender tip lights

FLTRX/FLHX CANADA MODELS ONY

To Main harness

Facia/Converter module

Connector to Tail/Stop/Turn signals license plate and fender tip lights

FLTRX/FLHX HDI MODELS ONLY

To Main harness

Facia/Converter module

FLTRX/FLHX DOM MODELS ONLY

To Main harness

Facia/Converter module

Tour-Pak lights

Tour-Pak left side marker lights

12-3A 12-3B

12-2B 12-2A

Tour-Pak right side marker lights

Tail

Stop

Tour-Pak Rear marker/Stop lights (domestic models only)

2012 DOMESTIC, CANADA AND INTERNATIONAL REAR LIGHTING HARNESSES AND TOUR-PAK CIRCUIT DIAGRAMS

16

2012 ALL TOURING MODELS

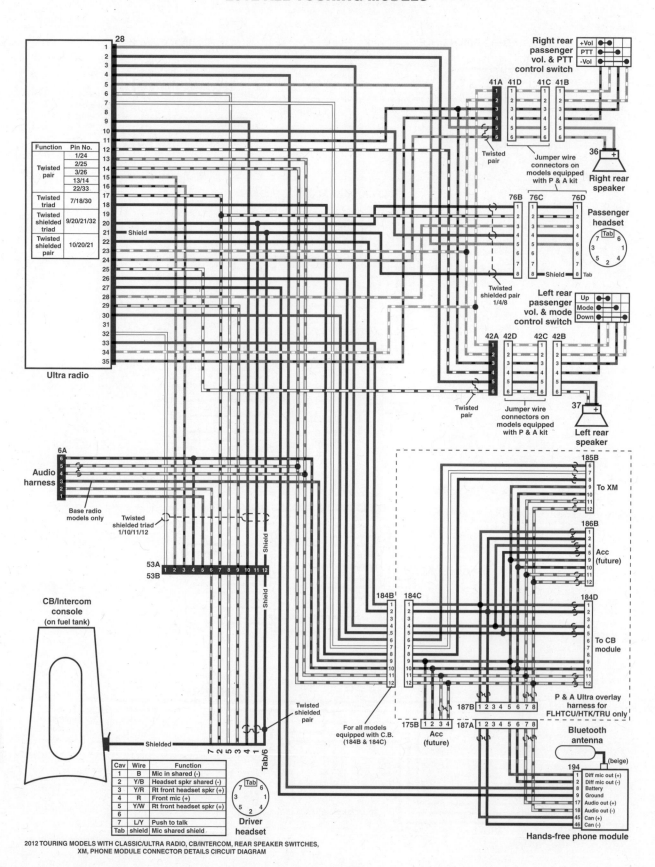

Function	Pin No.
Twisted pair	1/24
	2/25
	3/26
	13/14
	22/33
Twisted triad	7/18/30
Twisted shielded triad	9/20/21/32
Twisted shielded pair	10/20/21

Ultra radio

Right rear passenger vol. & PTT control switch

+Vol
PTT
-Vol

Twisted pair

Jumper wire connectors on models equipped with P & A kit

Right rear speaker

Passenger headset

Twisted shielded pair 1/4/8

Left rear passenger vol. & mode control switch

Up
Mode
Down

Twisted pair

Jumper wire connectors on models equipped with P & A kit

Left rear speaker

Audio harness

Base radio models only

Twisted shielded triad 1/10/11/12

CB/Intercom console (on fuel tank)

Shielded

Twisted shielded pair

Driver headset

Cav	Wire	Function
1	B	Mic in shared (-)
2	Y/B	Headset spkr shared (-)
3	Y/R	Rt front headset spkr (+)
4	R	Front mic (+)
5	Y/W	Rt front headset spkr (+)
6		
7	L/Y	Push to talk
Tab	shield	Mic shared shield

For all models equipped with C.B. (184B & 184C)

Acc (future)

P & A Ultra overlay harness for FLHTCU/HTK/TRU only

Bluetooth antenna

(beige)

To XM

Acc (future)

To CB module

194		
1	Diff mic out (+)
2	Diff mic out (-)
8	Battery
9	Ground
17	Audio out (+)
18	Audio out (-)
45	Can (+)
46	Can (-)

Hands-free phone module

2012 TOURING MODELS WITH CLASSIC/ULTRA RADIO, CB/INTERCOM, REAR SPEAKER SWITCHES, XM, PHONE MODULE CONNECTOR DETAILS CIRCUIT DIAGRAM

2012 ALL TOURING MODELS

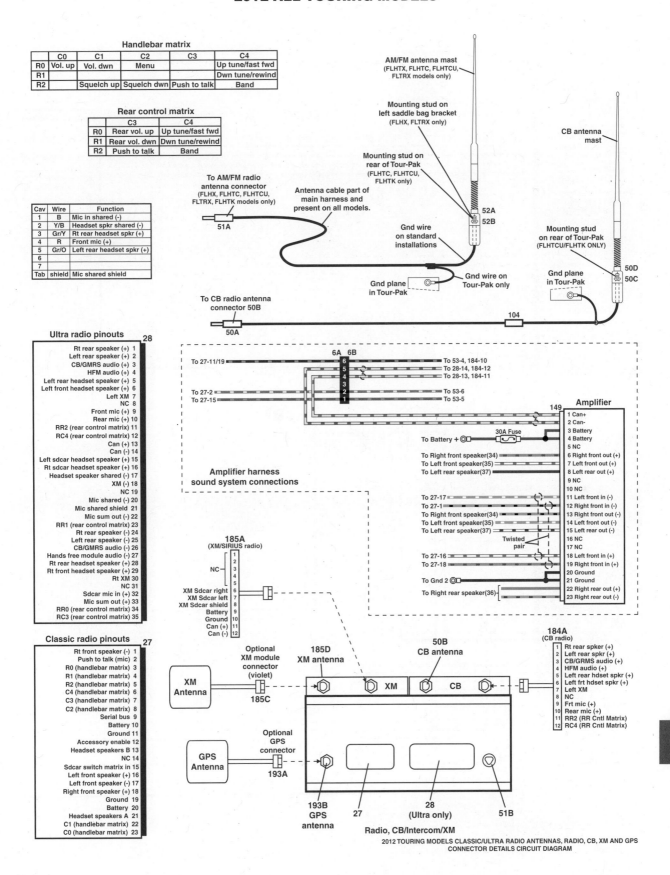

Handlebar matrix

	C0	C1	C2	C3	C4
R0	Vol. up	Vol. dwn	Menu		Up tune/fast fwd
R1					Dwn tune/rewind
R2		Squelch up	Squelch dwn	Push to talk	Band

Rear control matrix

	C3	C4
R0	Rear vol. up	Up tune/fast fwd
R1	Rear vol. dwn	Dwn tune/rewind
R2	Push to talk	Band

Cav	Wire	Function
1	B	Mic in shared (-)
2	Y/B	Headset spkr shared (-)
3	Gr/Y	Rt rear headset spkr (+)
4	R	Front mic (+)
5	Gr/O	Left rear headset spkr (+)
6		
7		
Tab	shield	Mic shared shield

Ultra radio pinouts 28

Rt rear speaker (+)	1
Left rear speaker (+)	2
CB/GMRS audio (+)	3
HFM audio (+)	4
Left rear headset speaker (+)	5
Left front headset speaker (+)	6
Left XM	7
NC	8
Front mic (+)	9
Rear mic (+)	10
RR2 (rear control matrix)	11
RC4 (rear control matrix)	12
Can (+)	13
Can (-)	14
Left sdcar headset speaker (+)	15
Rt sdcar headset speaker (+)	16
Headset speaker shared (-)	17
XM (-)	18
NC	19
Mic shared (-)	20
Mic shared shield	21
Mic sum out (-)	22
RR1 (rear control matrix)	23
Rt rear speaker (-)	24
Left rear speaker (-)	25
CB/GMRS audio (-)	26
Hands free module audio (-)	27
Rt rear headset speaker (+)	28
Rt front headset speaker (+)	29
Rt XM	30
NC	31
Sdcar mic in (+)	32
Mic sum out (+)	33
RR0 (rear control matrix)	34
RC3 (rear control matrix)	35

Classic radio pinouts 27

Rt front speaker (-)	1
Push to talk (mic)	2
R0 (handlebar matrix)	3
R1 (handlebar matrix)	4
R2 (handlebar matrix)	5
C4 (handlebar matrix)	6
C3 (handlebar matrix)	7
C2 (handlebar matrix)	8
Serial bus	9
Battery	10
Ground	11
Accessory enable	12
Headset speakers B	13
NC	14
Sdcar switch matrix in	15
Left front speaker (+)	16
Left front speaker (-)	17
Right front speaker (+)	18
Ground	19
Battery	20
Headset speakers A	21
C1 (handlebar matrix)	22
C0 (handlebar matrix)	23

AM/FM antenna mast
(FLHTX, FLHTC, FLHTCU,
FLTRX models only)

CB antenna
mast

Mounting stud on
left saddle bag bracket
(FLHX, FLTRX only)

Mounting stud on
rear of Tour-Pak
(FLHTC, FLHTCU,
FLHTK only)

To AM/FM radio
antenna connector
(FLHX, FLHTC, FLHTCU,
FLTRX, FLHTK models only)

Antenna cable part of
main harness and
present on all models.

Gnd wire
on standard
installations

Mounting stud
on rear of Tour-Pak
(FLHTCU/FLHTK ONLY)

51A

52A
52B

50D
50C

Gnd plane
in Tour-Pak

Gnd wire on
Tour-Pak only

Gnd plane
in Tour-Pak

To CB radio antenna
connector 50B

Gnd plane
in Tour-Pak

50A

104

6A 6B

To 27-11/19

6
5
4
3
2
1

To 53-4, 184-10
To 28-14, 184-12
To 28-13, 184-11

To 27-2
To 27-15

To 53-6
To 53-5

**Amplifier harness
sound system connections**

149

Amplifier

1	Can+
2	Can-
3	Battery
4	Battery
5	NC
6	Right front out (+)
7	Left front out (+)
8	Left rear out (+)
9	NC
10	NC
11	Left front in (-)
12	Right front in (-)
13	Right front out (-)
14	Left front out (-)
15	Left rear out (-)
16	NC
17	NC
18	Left front in (+)
19	Right front in (+)
20	Ground
21	Ground
22	Right rear out (+)
23	Right rear out (-)

To Battery +

30A Fuse

To Right front speaker(34)
To Left front speaker(35)
To Left rear speaker(37)

To 27-17
To 27-1
To Right front speaker(34)
To Left front speaker(35)
To Left rear speaker(37)

Twisted
pair

To 27-16
To 27-18

To Gnd 2

To Right rear speaker(36)

185A
(XM/SIRIUS radio)

NC	1
	2
	3
	4
	5
XM Sdcar right	6
XM Sdcar left	7
XM Sdcar shield	8
Battery	9
Ground	10
Can (+)	11
Can (-)	12

184A
(CB radio)

1	Rt rear spkr (+)
2	Left rear spkr (+)
3	CB/GRMS audio (+)
4	HFM audio (+)
5	Left rear hdset spkr (+)
6	Left frt hdset spkr (+)
7	Left XM
8	NC
9	Frt mic (+)
10	Rear mic (+)
11	RR2 (RR Cntl Matrix)
12	RC4 (RR Cntl Matrix)

Optional
XM module
connector
(violet)

185C

185D
XM antenna

50B
CB antenna

XM
Antenna

XM

CB

Optional
GPS
connector

GPS
Antenna

193A

193B
GPS
antenna

27

28
(Ultra only)

51B

Radio, CB/Intercom/XM

2012 TOURING MODELS CLASSIC/ULTRA RADIO ANTENNAS, RADIO, CB, XM AND GPS
CONNECTOR DETAILS CIRCUIT DIAGRAM

2012 ALL TOURING MODELS

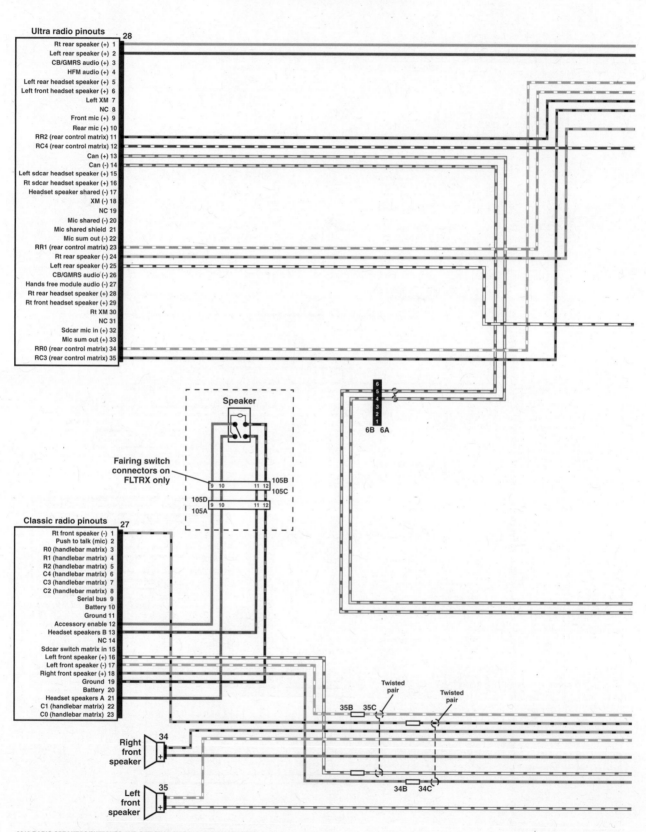

Ultra radio pinouts 28

Rt rear speaker (+)	1
Left rear speaker (+)	2
CB/GMRS audio (+)	3
HFM audio (+)	4
Left rear headset speaker (+)	5
Left front headset speaker (+)	6
Left XM	7
NC	8
Front mic (+)	9
Rear mic (+)	10
RR2 (rear control matrix)	11
RC4 (rear control matrix)	12
Can (+)	13
Can (-)	14
Left sdcar headset speaker (+)	15
Rt sdcar headset speaker (+)	16
Headset speaker shared (-)	17
XM (-)	18
NC	19
Mic shared (-)	20
Mic shared shield	21
Mic sum out (-)	22
RR1 (rear control matrix)	23
Rt rear speaker (-)	24
Left rear speaker (-)	25
CB/GMRS audio (-)	26
Hands free module audio (-)	27
Rt rear headset speaker (+)	28
Rt front headset speaker (+)	29
Rt XM	30
NC	31
Sdcar mic in (+)	32
Mic sum out (+)	33
RR0 (rear control matrix)	34
RC3 (rear control matrix)	35

Speaker

Fairing switch
connectors on
FLTRX only

105B
105C
105D
105A

9 10 11 12
9 10 11 12

6
5
4
3
2
1

6B 6A

Classic radio pinouts 27

Rt front speaker (-)	1
Push to talk (mic)	2
R0 (handlebar matrix)	3
R1 (handlebar matrix)	4
R2 (handlebar matrix)	5
C4 (handlebar matrix)	6
C3 (handlebar matrix)	7
C2 (handlebar matrix)	8
Serial bus	9
Battery	10
Ground	11
Accessory enable	12
Headset speakers B	13
NC	14
Sdcar switch matrix in	15
Left front speaker (+)	16
Left front speaker (-)	17
Right front speaker (+)	18
Ground	19
Battery	20
Headset speakers A	21
C1 (handlebar matrix)	22
C0 (handlebar matrix)	23

**Right
front
speaker** 34

**Left
front
speaker** 35

Twisted
pair

Twisted
pair

35B 35C

34B 34C

2012 RADIO SPEAKERS/SWITCHES AND OPTIONAL SIDECAR RADIO SPEAKERS
AND CONTROL CONNECTOR DETAILS CIRCUIT DIAGRAM

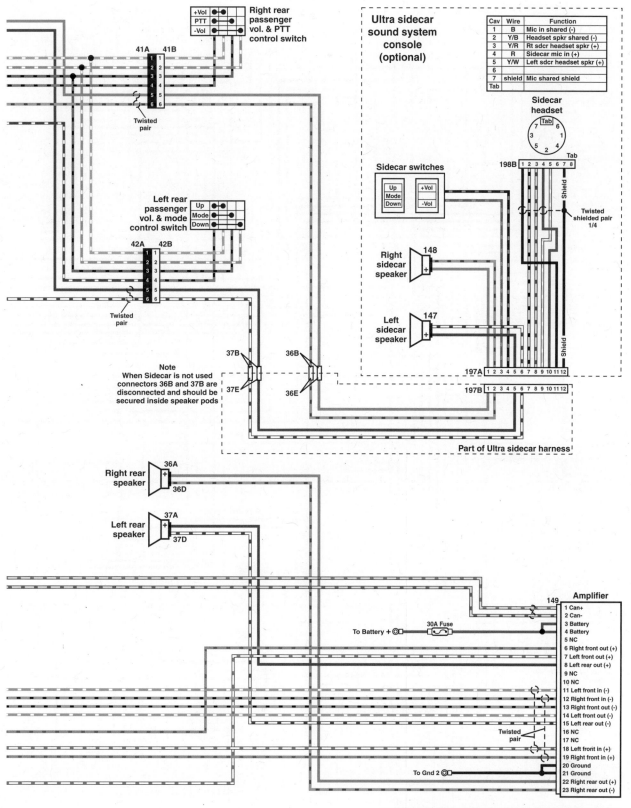

Cav	Wire	Function
1	B	Mic in shared (-)
2	Y/B	Headset spkr shared (-)
3	Y/R	Rt sdcr headset spkr (+)
4	R	Sidecar mic in (+)
5	Y/W	Left sdcr headset spkr (+)
6		
7	shield	Mic shared shield
Tab		

Right rear passenger vol. & PTT control switch

+Vol
PTT
-Vol

41A 41B

Twisted pair

Ultra sidecar sound system console (optional)

Sidecar headset

Sidecar switches

Up
Mode
Down

+Vol
-Vol

Left rear passenger vol. & mode control switch

Up
Mode
Down

42A 42B

Twisted pair

198B

Shield

Twisted shielded pair 1/4

Right sidecar speaker 148

Left sidecar speaker 147

Shield

37B 36B

37E 36E

197A

197B

Note
When Sidecar is not used connectors 36B and 37B are disconnected and should be secured inside speaker pods

Part of Ultra sidecar harness

Right rear speaker 36A
36D

Left rear speaker 37A
37D

Amplifier
1 Can+
2 Can-
3 Battery
4 Battery
5 NC
6 Right front out (+)
7 Left front out (+)
8 Left rear out (+)
9 NC
10 NC
11 Left front in (-)
12 Right front in (-)
13 Right front out (-)
14 Left front out (-)
15 Left rear out (-)
16 NC
17 NC
18 Left front in (+)
19 Right front in (+)
20 Ground
21 Ground
22 Right rear out (+)
23 Right rear out (-)

149

30A Fuse

To Battery +

Twisted pair

To Gnd 2

16

2012 RADIO SPEAKERS/SWITCHES AND OPTIONAL SIDECAR RADIO SPEAKERS
AND CONTROL CONNECTOR DETAILS CIRCUIT DIAGRAM

2013 ALL TOURING MODELS

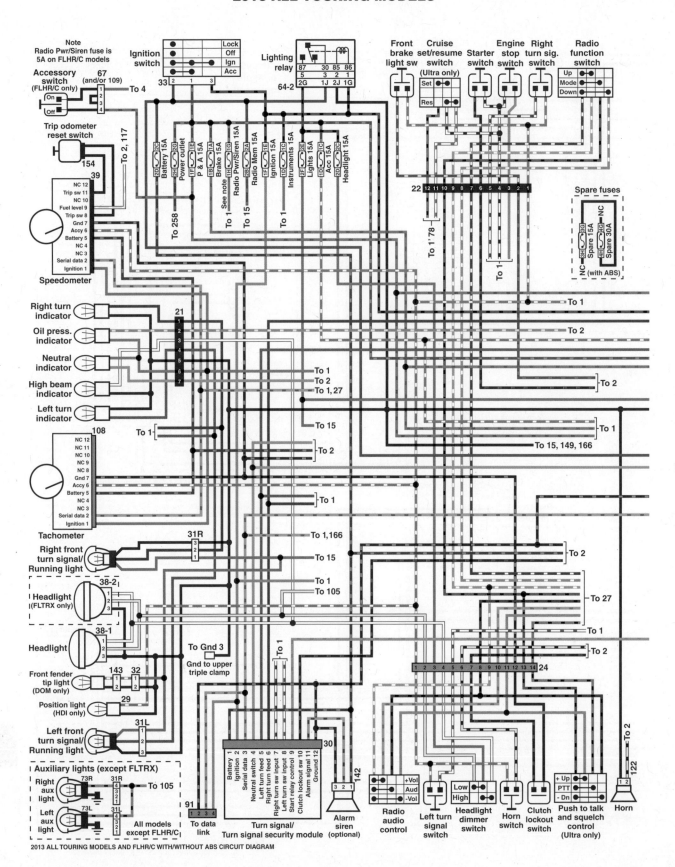

2013 ALL TOURING MODELS AND FLHR/C WITH/WITHOUT ABS CIRCUIT DIAGRAM

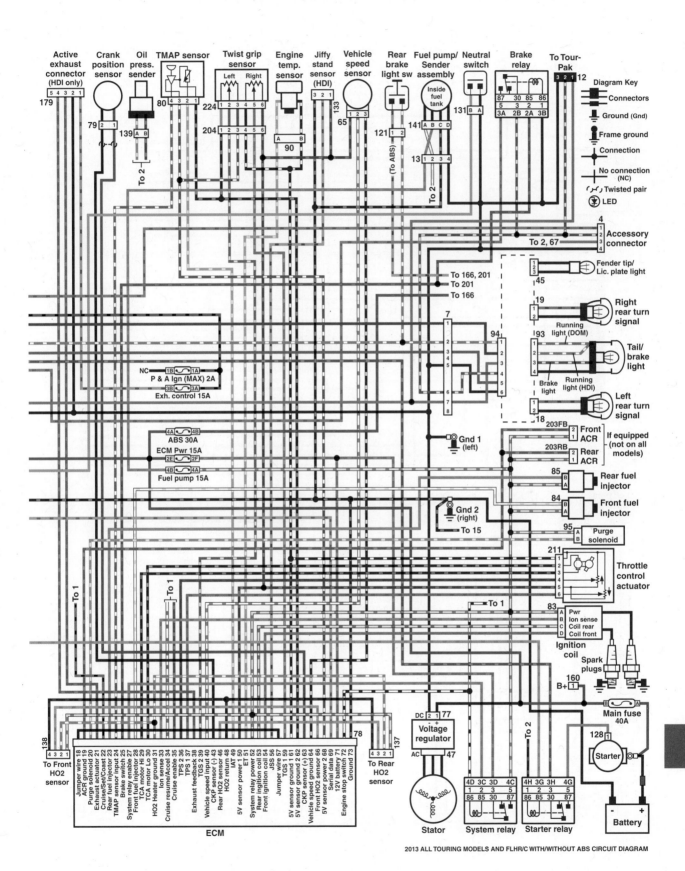

2013 ALL TOURING MODELS AND FLHR/C WITH/WITHOUT ABS CIRCUIT DIAGRAM

16

2013 FLHX, FLHT, FLHTC, FLHTCU, FLTRX AND FLHTK MODELS

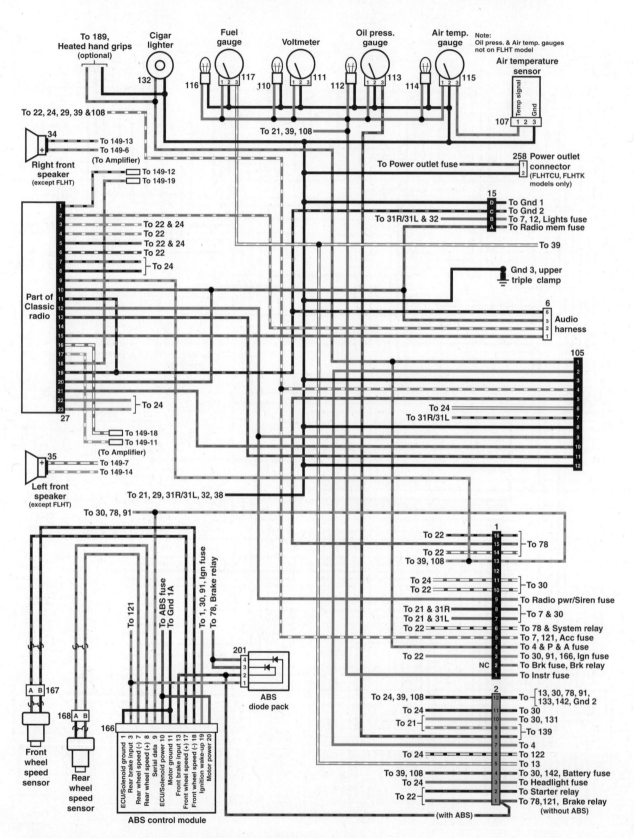

2013 FLHX, FLHT, FLHTC, FLHTCU, FLTRX AND FLHTK GAUGES, RADIO, FRONT SPEAKERS AND ABS CIRCUIT DIAGRAM

2013 ALL TOURING MODELS

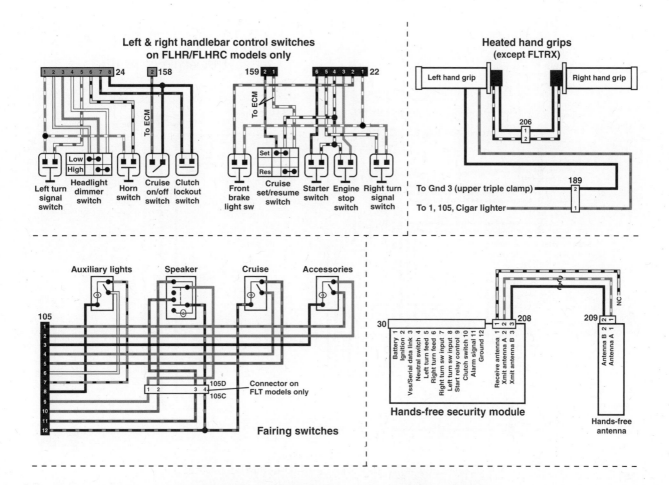

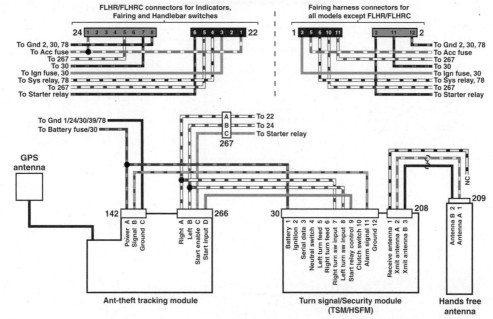

2013 TOURING MODELS LEFT/RIGHT HANDLE BAR SWITCHES, HEATED HAND GRIPS, FAIRING SWITCHES,
HANDS FREE SECURITY MODULE AND SECURITY CIRCUIT WITH ANTI-THEFT TRACKING MODULE CIRCUIT DIAGRAMS

16

2013 FLHR AND FLHRC MODELS

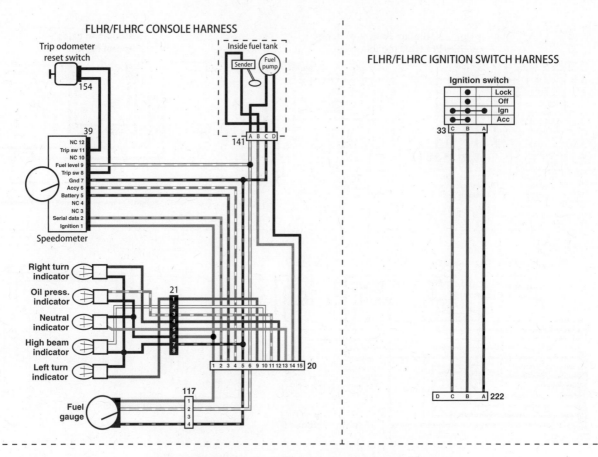

FLHR/FLHRC CONSOLE HARNESS

FLHR/FLHRC IGNITION SWITCH HARNESS

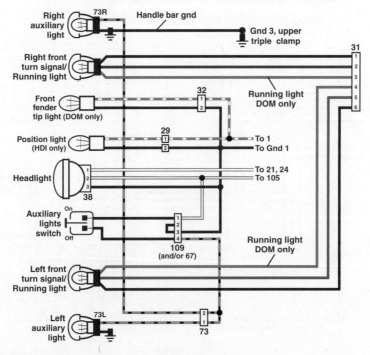

FLHR/FLHRC AUXILIARY LIGHT AND TURN SIGNAL HARNESS

2013 FLHR, FLHRC CONSOLE, IGNITION SWITCH AND AUXILIARY LIGHTS WITHOUT/WITH ABS CIRCUIT DIAGRAMS

2013 DOMESTIC, CANADA AND INTERNATIONAL MODELS

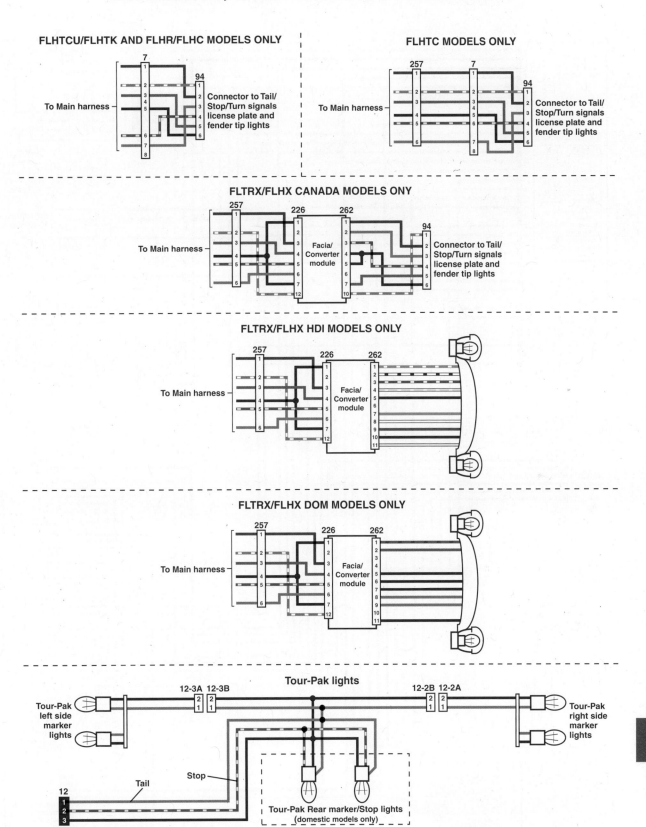

2013 DOMESTIC, CANADA AND INTERNATIONAL REAR LIGHTING HARNESSES
AND TOUR-PAK CIRCUIT DIAGRAMS

16

2013 ALL TOURING MODELS

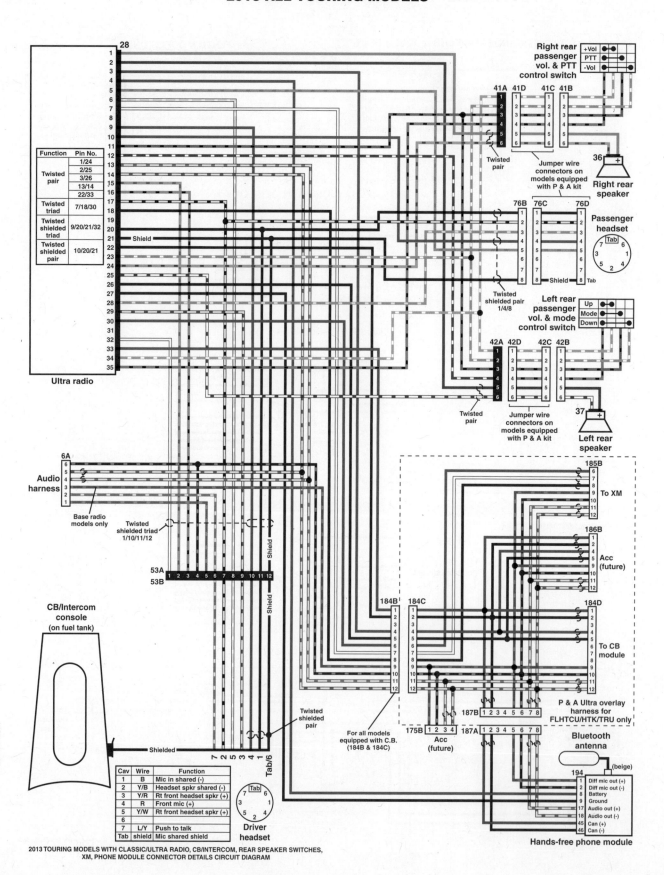

Function	**Pin No.**
Twisted pair	1/24
	2/25
	3/26
	13/14
	22/33
Twisted triad	7/18/30
Twisted shielded triad	9/20/21/32
Twisted shielded pair	10/20/21

Ultra radio

Right rear passenger vol. & PTT control switch

+Vol		
PTT		
-Vol		

Jumper wire connectors on models equipped with P & A kit

Right rear speaker

Passenger headset

Twisted shielded pair 1/4/8

Left rear passenger vol. & mode control switch

Up		
Mode		
Down		

Jumper wire connectors on models equipped with P & A kit

Left rear speaker

Audio harness

Base radio models only

Twisted shielded triad 1/10/11/12

To XM

Acc (future)

To CB module

P & A Ultra overlay harness for FLHTCU/HTK/TRU only

CB/Intercom console (on fuel tank)

Twisted shielded pair

For all models equipped with C.B. (184B & 184C)

Acc (future)

Bluetooth antenna

(beige)

Cav	Wire	Function
1	B	Mic in shared (-)
2	Y/B	Headset spkr shared (-)
3	Y/R	Rt front headset spkr (+)
4	R	Front mic (+)
5	Y/W	Rt front headset spkr (+)
6		
7	L/Y	Push to talk
Tab	shield	Mic shared shield

Driver headset

1	Diff mic out (+)
2	Diff mic out (-)
9	Battery
16	Ground
17	Audio out (+)
18	Audio out (-)
45	Can (+)
46	Can (-)

Hands-free phone module

2013 TOURING MODELS WITH CLASSIC/ULTRA RADIO, CB/INTERCOM, REAR SPEAKER SWITCHES, XM, PHONE MODULE CONNECTOR DETAILS CIRCUIT DIAGRAM

2013 ALL TOURING MODELS

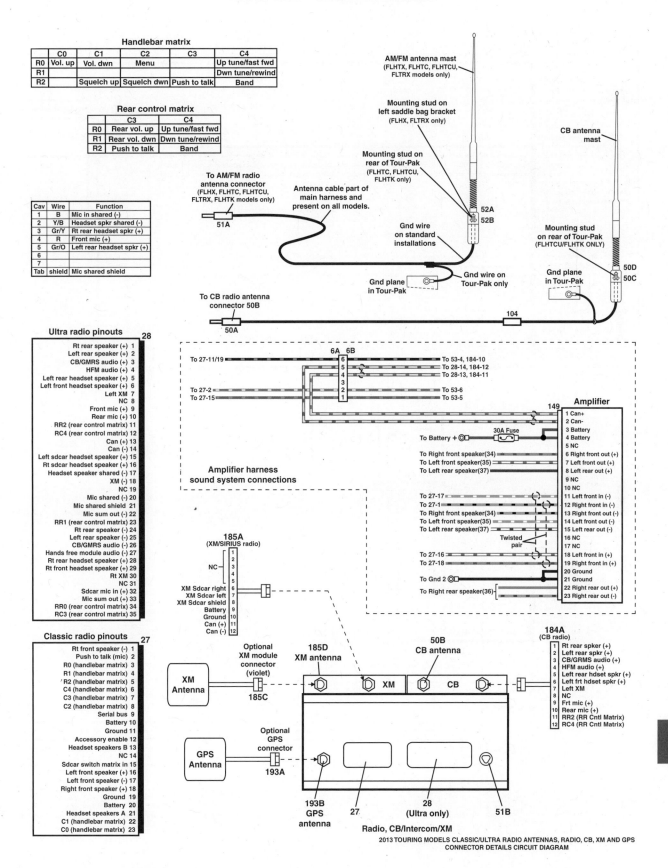

Handlebar matrix

	C0	C1	C2	C3	C4
R0	Vol. up	Vol. dwn	Menu		Up tune/fast fwd
R1					Dwn tune/rewind
R2		Squelch up	Squelch dwn	Push to talk	Band

Rear control matrix

	C3	C4
R0	Rear vol. up	Up tune/fast fwd
R1	Rear vol. dwn	Dwn tune/rewind
R2	Push to talk	Band

Cav	Wire	Function
1	B	Mic in shared (-)
2	Y/B	Headset spkr shared (-)
3	Gr/Y	Rt rear headset spkr (+)
4	R	Front mic (+)
5	Gr/O	Left rear headset spkr (+)
6		
7		
Tab	shield	Mic shared shield

Ultra radio pinouts 28

Rt rear speaker (+) 1
Left rear speaker (+) 2
CB/GMRS audio (+) 3
HFM audio (+) 4
Left rear headset speaker (+) 5
Left front headset speaker (+) 6
Left XM 7
NC 8
Front mic (+) 9
Rear mic (+) 10
RR2 (rear control matrix) 11
RC4 (rear control matrix) 12
Can (+) 13
Can (-) 14
Left sdcar headset speaker (+) 15
Rt sdcar headset speaker (+) 16
Headset speaker shared (-) 17
XM (-) 18
NC 19
Mic shared (-) 20
Mic shared shield 21
Mic sum out (-) 22
RR1 (rear control matrix) 23
Rt rear speaker (-) 24
Left rear speaker (-) 25
CB/GMRS audio (-) 26
Hands free module audio (-) 27
Rt rear headset speaker (+) 28
Rt front headset speaker (+) 29
Rt XM 30
NC 31
Sdcar mic in (+) 32
Mic sum out (+) 33
RR0 (rear control matrix) 34
RC3 (rear control matrix) 35

Classic radio pinouts 27

Rt front speaker (-) 1
Push to talk (mic) 2
R0 (handlebar matrix) 3
R1 (handlebar matrix) 4
R2 (handlebar matrix) 5
C4 (handlebar matrix) 6
C3 (handlebar matrix) 7
C2 (handlebar matrix) 8
Serial bus 9
Battery 10
Ground 11
Accessory enable 12
Headset speakers B 13
NC 14
Sdcar switch matrix in 15
Left front speaker (+) 16
Left front speaker (-) 17
Right front speaker (+) 18
Ground 19
Battery 20
Headset speakers A 21
C1 (handlebar matrix) 22
C0 (handlebar matrix) 23

AM/FM antenna mast
(FLHTX, FLHTC, FLHTCU, FLTRX models only)

Mounting stud on
left saddle bag bracket
(FLHX, FLTRX only)

Mounting stud on
rear of Tour-Pak
(FLHTC, FLHTCU,
FLHTK only)

CB antenna
mast

To AM/FM radio
antenna connector
(FLHX, FLHTC, FLHTCU,
FLTRX, FLHTK models only)

Antenna cable part of
main harness and
present on all models.

51A

52A
52B

Gnd wire
on standard
installations

Gnd wire on
Tour-Pak only

Gnd plane
in Tour-Pak

Mounting stud
on rear of Tour-Pak
(FLHTCU/FLHTK ONLY)

Gnd plane
in Tour-Pak

50D
50C

To CB radio antenna
connector 50B

50A

104

**Amplifier harness
sound system connections**

To 27-11/19
To 27-2
To 27-15

6A 6B
6
5
4
3
2
1

To 53-4, 184-10
To 28-14, 184-12
To 28-13, 184-11

To 53-6
To 53-5

149
Amplifier

1 Can+
2 Can-
3 Battery
4 Battery
5 NC
6 Right front out (+)
7 Left front out (+)
8 Left rear out (+)
9 NC
10 NC
11 Left front in (-)
12 Right front in (-)
13 Right front out (-)
14 Left front out (-)
15 Left rear out (-)
16 NC
17 NC
18 Left front in (+)
19 Right front in (+)
20 Ground
21 Ground
22 Right rear out (+)
23 Right rear out (-)

To Battery +
30A Fuse

To Right front speaker(34)
To Left front speaker(35)
To Left rear speaker(37)

To 27-17
To 27-1
To Right front speaker(34)
To Left front speaker(35)
To Left rear speaker(37)

Twisted
pair

To 27-16
To 27-18

To Gnd 2

To Right rear speaker(36)

185A
(XM/SIRIUS radio)

NC
1
2
3
4
5
6
XM Sdcar right 7
XM Sdcar left 8
XM Sdcar shield 9
Battery 10
Ground 11
Can (+) 12
Can (-)

Optional
XM module
connector
(violet)

185C

185D
XM antenna

50B
CB antenna

184A
(CB radio)

1 Rt rear spker (+)
2 Left rear spker (+)
3 CB/GMRS audio (+)
4 HFM audio (+)
5 Left rear hdset spkr (+)
6 Left frt hdset spkr (+)
7 Left XM
8 NC
9 Frt mic (+)
10 Rear mic (+)
11 RR2 (RR Cntl Matrix)
12 RC4 (RR Cntl Matrix)

XM
Antenna

XM

CB

GPS
Antenna

Optional
GPS
connector

193A

**193B
GPS
antenna**

27

**28
(Ultra only)**

51B

Radio, CB/Intercom/XM

2013 TOURING MODELS CLASSIC/ULTRA RADIO ANTENNAS, RADIO, CB, XM AND GPS
CONNECTOR DETAILS CIRCUIT DIAGRAM

16

2013 ALL TOURING MODELS

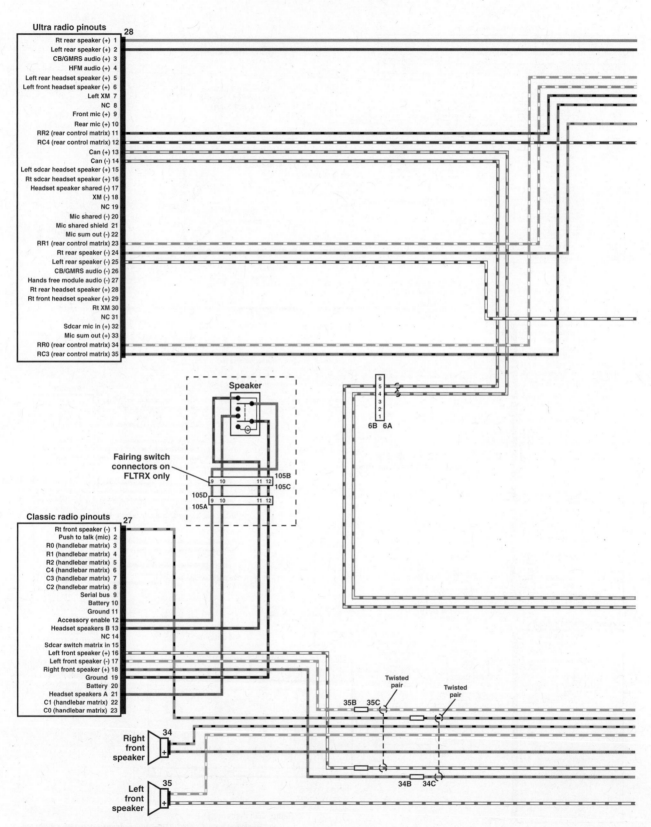

Ultra radio pinouts

Rt rear speaker (+)	1
Left rear speaker (+)	2
CB/GMRS audio (+)	3
HFM audio (+)	4
Left rear headset speaker (+)	5
Left front headset speaker (+)	6
Left XM	7
NC	8
Front mic (+)	9
Rear mic (+)	10
RR2 (rear control matrix)	11
RC4 (rear control matrix)	12
Can (+)	13
Can (-)	14
Left sdcar headset speaker (+)	15
Rt sdcar headset speaker (+)	16
Headset speaker shared (-)	17
XM (-)	18
NC	19
Mic shared (-)	20
Mic shared shield	21
Mic sum out (-)	22
RR1 (rear control matrix)	23
Rt rear speaker (-)	24
Left rear speaker (-)	25
CB/GMRS audio (-)	26
Hands free module audio (-)	27
Rt rear headset speaker (+)	28
Rt front headset speaker (+)	29
Rt XM	30
NC	31
Sdcar mic in (+)	32
Mic sum out	33
RR0 (rear control matrix)	34
RC3 (rear control matrix)	35

Speaker

Fairing switch connectors on FLTRX only

105B
105C
105D
105A

9 10 11 12
9 10 11 12

6B 6A

Classic radio pinouts

Rt front speaker (-)	1
Push to talk (mic)	2
R0 (handlebar matrix)	3
R1 (handlebar matrix)	4
R2 (handlebar matrix)	5
C4 (handlebar matrix)	6
C3 (handlebar matrix)	7
C2 (handlebar matrix)	8
Serial bus	9
Battery	10
Ground	11
Accessory enable	12
Headset speakers B	13
NC	14
Sdcar switch matrix in	15
Left front speaker (+)	16
Left front speaker (-)	17
Right front speaker (+)	18
Ground	19
Battery	20
Headset speakers A	21
C1 (handlebar matrix)	22
C0 (handlebar matrix)	23

Right front speaker 34

Left front speaker 35

Twisted pair

Twisted pair

35B 35C

34B 34C

2013 RADIO SPEAKERS/SWITCHES AND OPTIONAL SIDECAR RADIO SPEAKERS AND CONTROL CONNECTOR DETAILS CIRCUIT DIAGRAM

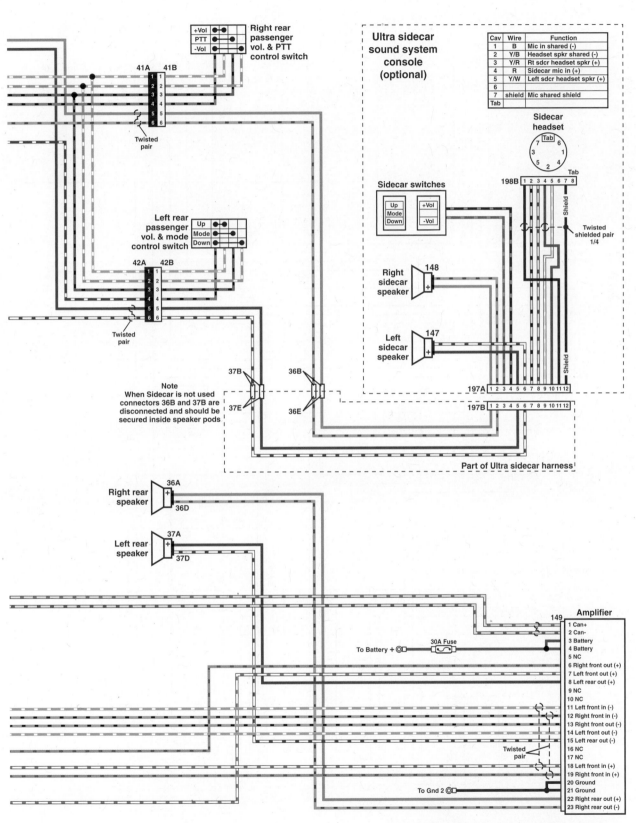

2013 RADIO SPEAKERS/SWITCHES AND OPTIONAL SIDECAR RADIO SPEAKERS AND CONTROL CONNECTOR DETAILS CIRCUIT DIAGRAM

2011-2013 FLHT CUSE6, FLHT CUSE7 AND FLHT CUSE8

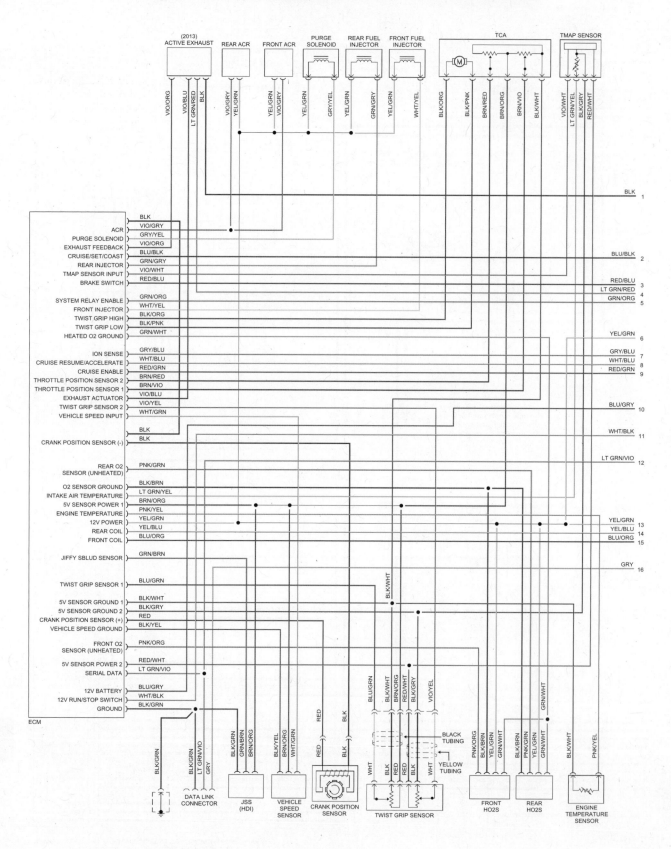

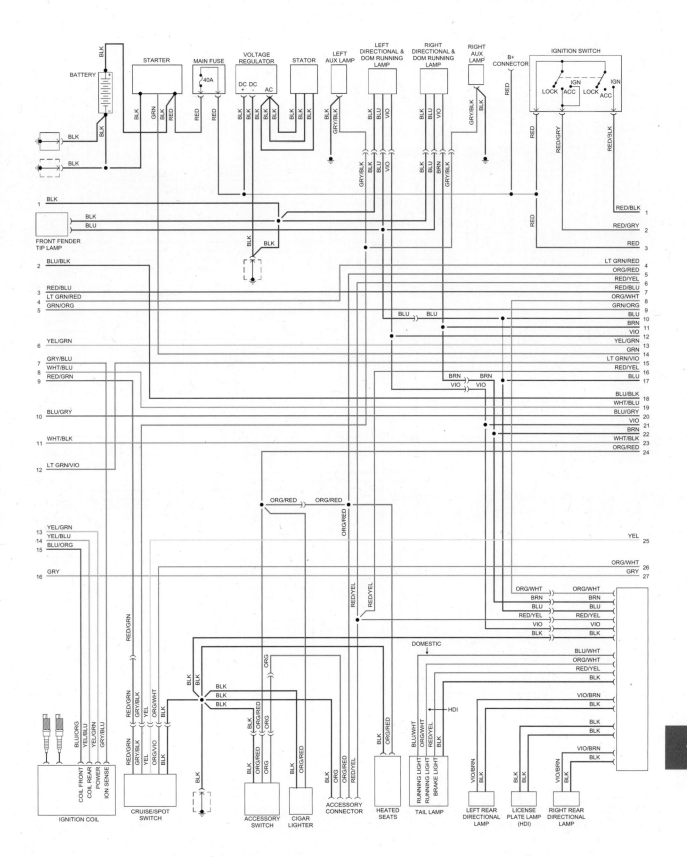

16

2011-2013 FLHT CUSE6, FLHT CUSE7 AND FLHT CUSE8 (CONTINUED)

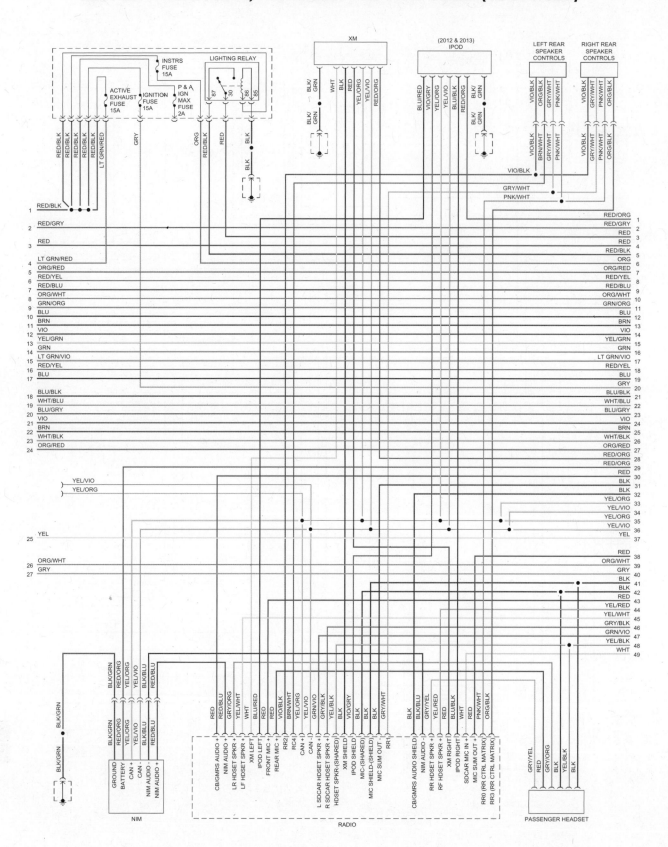

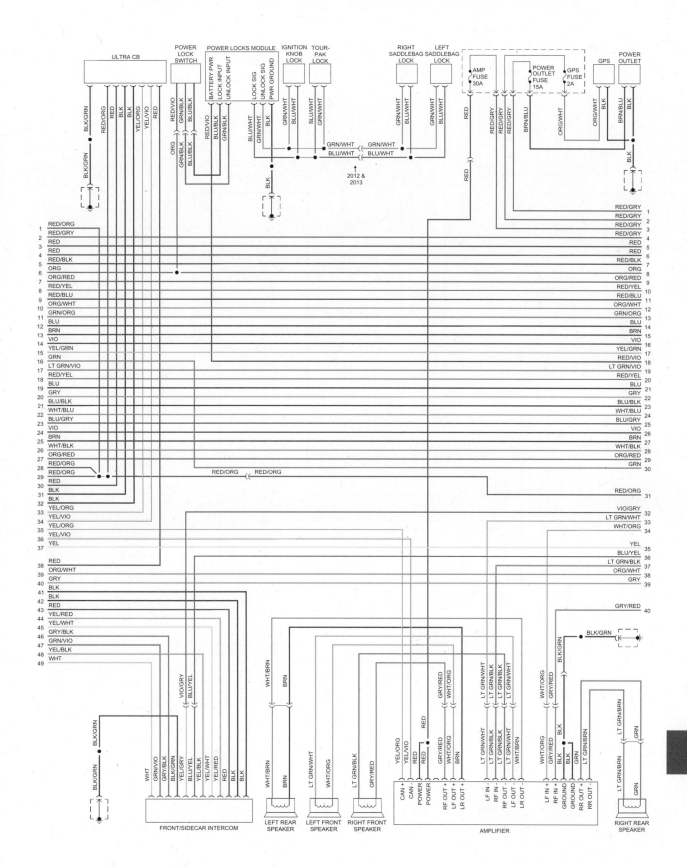

2011-2013 FLHT CUSE6, FLHT CUSE7 AND FLHT CUSE8 (CONTINUED)

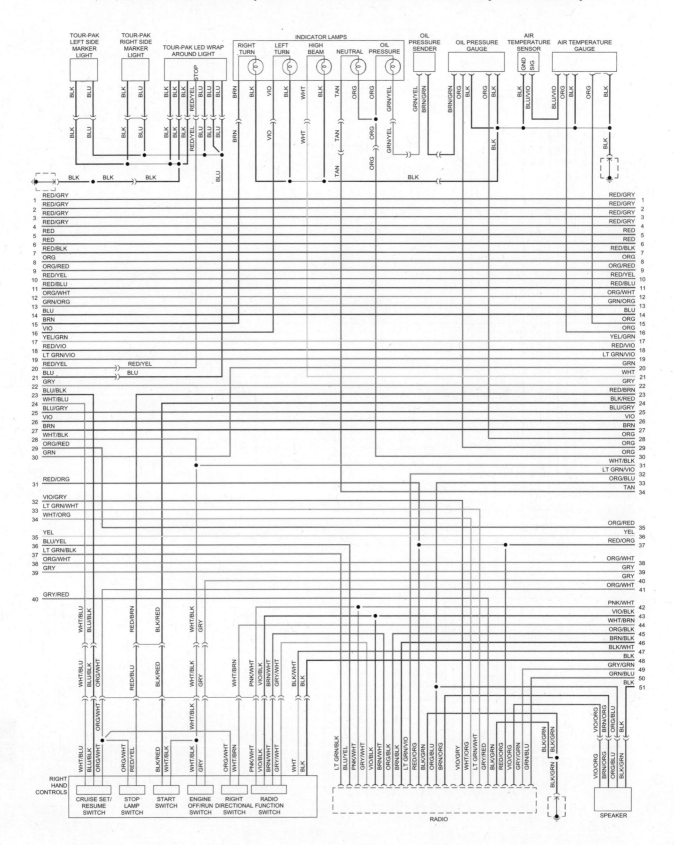

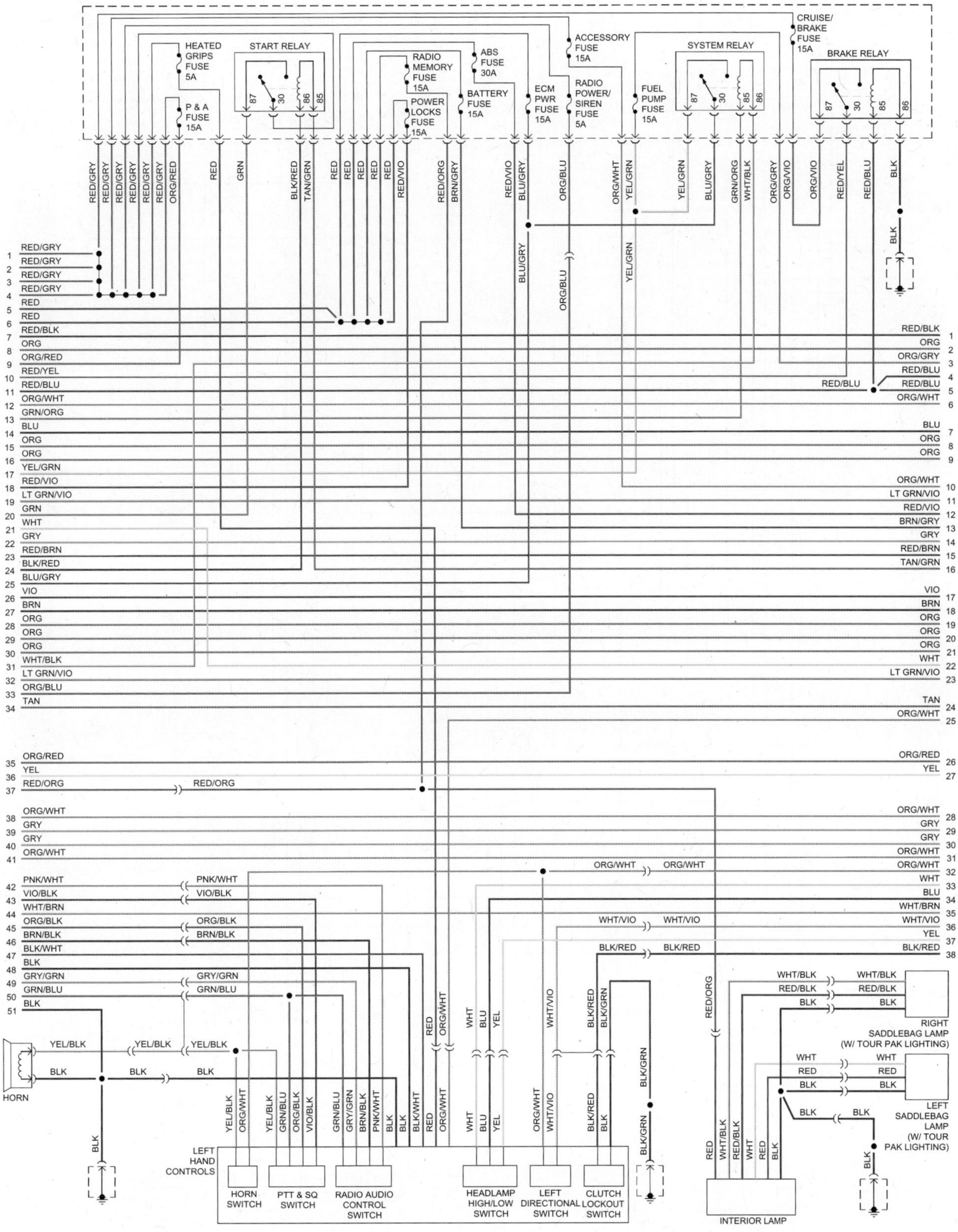

START RELAY

HEATED GRIPS FUSE 5A

P & A FUSE 15A

87 30 86 85

RADIO MEMORY FUSE 15A

POWER LOCKS FUSE 15A

ABS FUSE 30A

BATTERY FUSE 15A

ECM PWR FUSE 15A

ACCESSORY FUSE 15A

RADIO POWER/ SIREN FUSE 5A

SYSTEM RELAY

FUEL PUMP FUSE 15A

87 30 85 86

CRUISE/ BRAKE FUSE 15A

BRAKE RELAY

87 30 85 86

RED/GRY RED/GRY RED/GRY RED/GRY RED/GRY ORG/RED RED GRN BLK/RED TAN/GRN RED RED RED RED RED/VIO RED/ORG BRN/GRY RED/VIO BLU/GRY ORG/BLU ORG/WHT YEL/GRN YEL/GRN BLU/GRY GRN/ORG WHT/BLK ORG/GRY ORG/VIO RED/YEL RED/BLU BLK

BLK

BLU/GRY

ORG/BLU

YEL/GRN

1 RED/GRY
2 RED/GRY
3 RED/GRY
4 RED/GRY
5 RED
6 RED
7 RED/BLK
8 ORG
9 ORG/RED
10 RED/YEL
11 RED/BLU
12 ORG/WHT
13 GRN/ORG
14 BLU
15 ORG
16 ORG
17 YEL/GRN
18 RED/VIO
19 LT GRN/VIO
20 GRN
21 WHT
22 GRY
23 RED/BRN
24 BLK/RED
25 BLU/GRY
26 VIO
27 BRN
28 ORG
29 ORG
30 ORG
31 WHT/BLK
32 LT GRN/VIO
33 ORG/BLU
34 TAN

35 ORG/RED
36 YEL
37 RED/ORG

38 ORG/WHT
39 GRY
40 GRY
41 ORG/WHT

42 PNK/WHT
43 VIO/BLK
44 WHT/BRN
45 ORG/BLK
46 BRN/BLK
47 BLK/WHT
48 BLK
49 GRY/GRN
50 GRN/BLU
51 BLK

RED/ORG

PNK/WHT
VIO/BLK

ORG/BLK
BRN/BLK

GRY/GRN
GRN/BLU

ORG/WHT ORG/WHT

WHT/VIO WHT/VIO

BLK/RED BLK/RED

RED/BLK RED/BLK
1 ORG
2 ORG/GRY
3 RED/BLU
4 RED/BLU
5 ORG/WHT
6
7 BLU
8 ORG
9 ORG
10 ORG/WHT
11 LT GRN/VIO
12 RED/VIO
13 BRN/GRY
14 GRY
15 RED/BRN
16 TAN/GRN
17 VIO
18 BRN
19 ORG
20 ORG
21 WHT
22 LT GRN/VIO
23
24 TAN
25 ORG/WHT
26 ORG/RED
27 YEL
28 ORG/WHT
29 GRY
30 GRY
31 ORG/WHT
32 ORG/WHT
33 WHT
34 BLU
35 WHT/BRN
36 WHT/VIO
37 YEL
38 BLK/RED

RED/BLU RED/BLU

HORN

YEL/BLK YEL/BLK YEL/BLK

BLK BLK BLK

BLK

LEFT HAND CONTROLS

YEL/BLK ORG/WHT

YEL/BLK GRN/BLU ORG/BLK VIO/BLK

HORN SWITCH

GRN/BLU GRY/GRN BRN/BLK PNK/WHT BLK

PTT & SQ SWITCH

RADIO AUDIO CONTROL SWITCH

BLK BLK RED ORG/WHT

WHT BLU YEL

RED ORG/WHT

HEADLAMP HIGH/LOW SWITCH

ORG/WHT WHT/VIO

LEFT DIRECTIONAL SWITCH

BLK/RED BLK

CLUTCH LOCKOUT SWITCH

BLK/GRN

BLK/GRN

RED/ORG

ORG/WHT

WHT/BLK WHT/BLK
RED/BLK RED/BLK
BLK BLK

RIGHT SADDLEBAG LAMP (W/ TOUR PAK LIGHTING)

WHT WHT
RED RED
BLK BLK

LEFT SADDLEBAG LAMP (W/ TOUR PAK LIGHTING)

RED WHT/BLK RED/BLK WHT RED BLK

BLK BLK

BLK

INTERIOR LAMP

16

2011-2013 FLHT CUSE6, FLHT CUSE7 AND FLHT CUSE8 (CONTINUED)

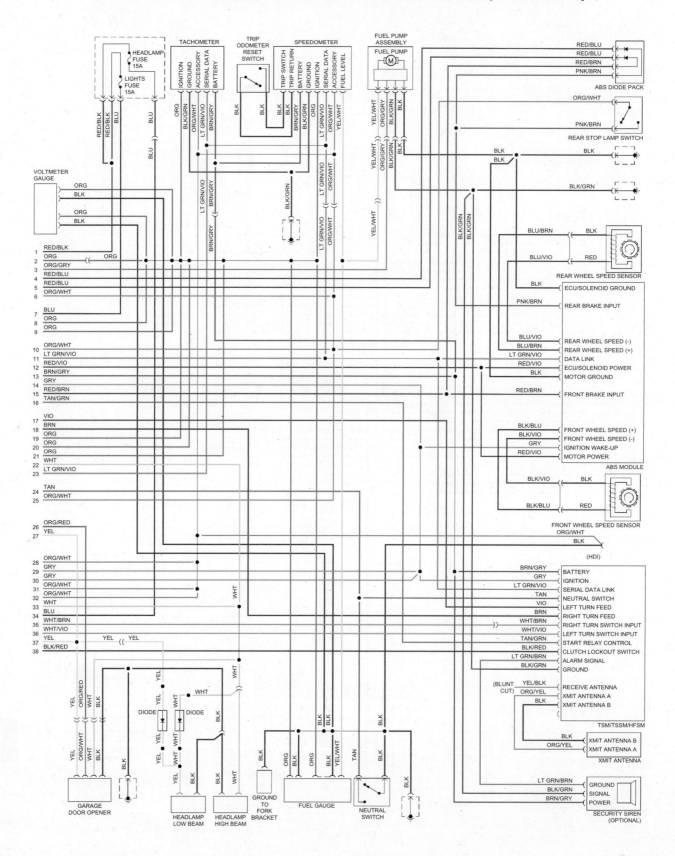

2010-2011 FLXHSE AND FLHXSE2

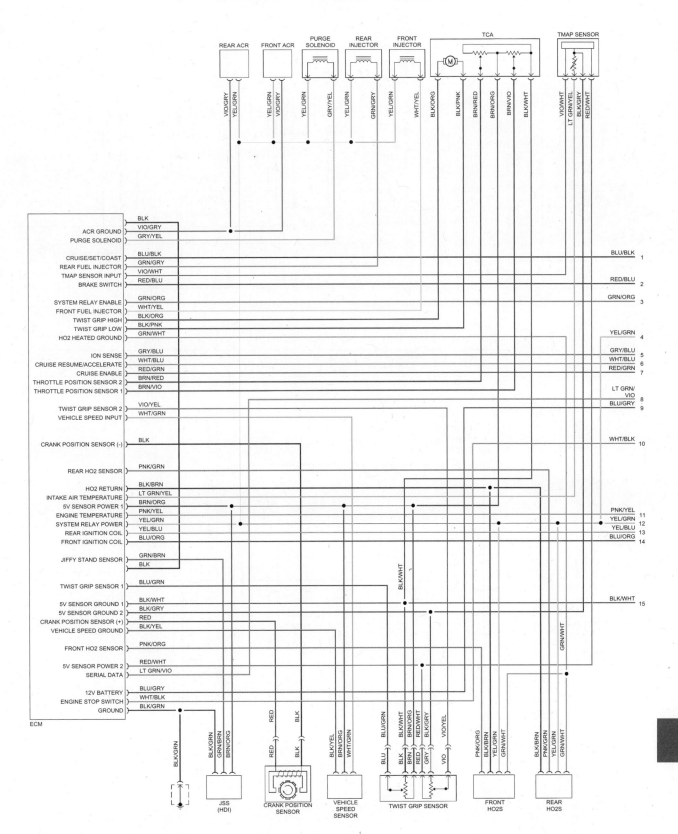

2010-2011 FLXHSE AND FLHXSE2 (CONTINUED)

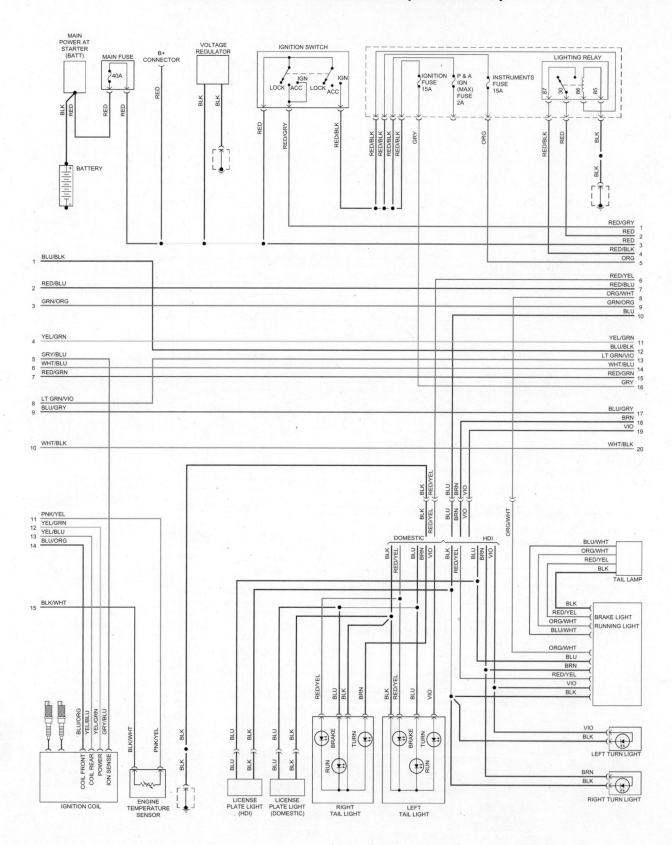

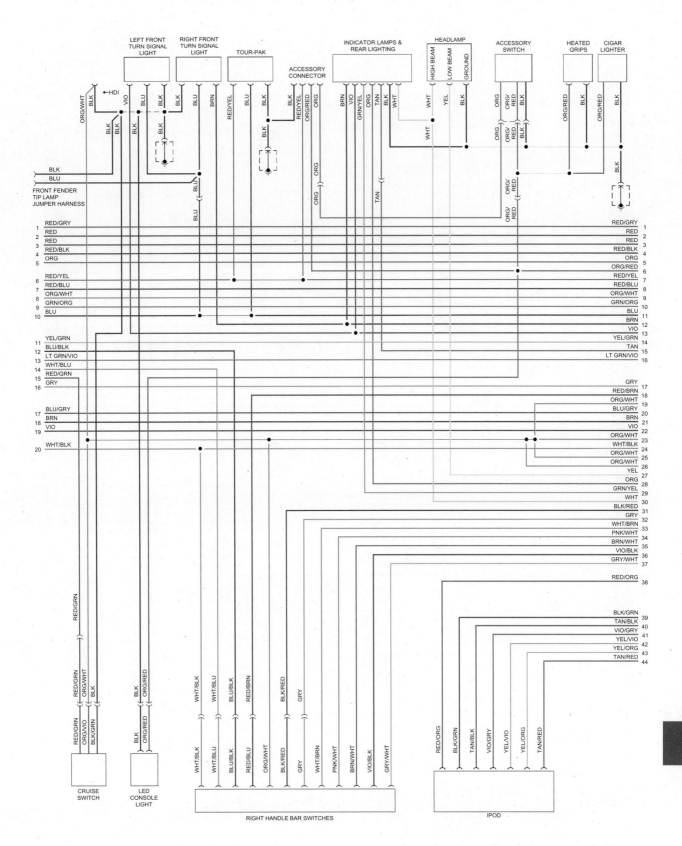

2010-2011 FLXHSE AND FLHXSE2 (CONTINUED)

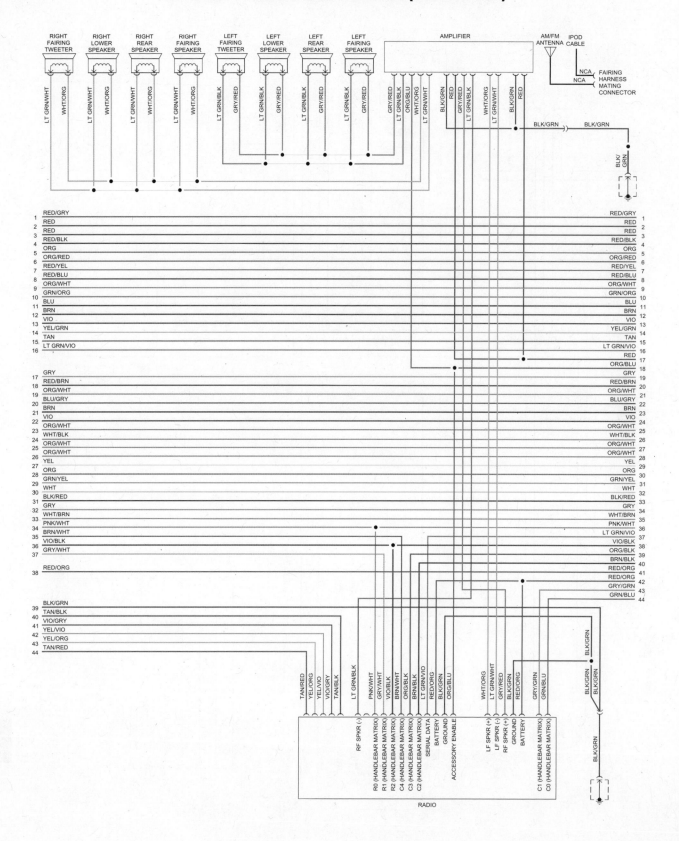

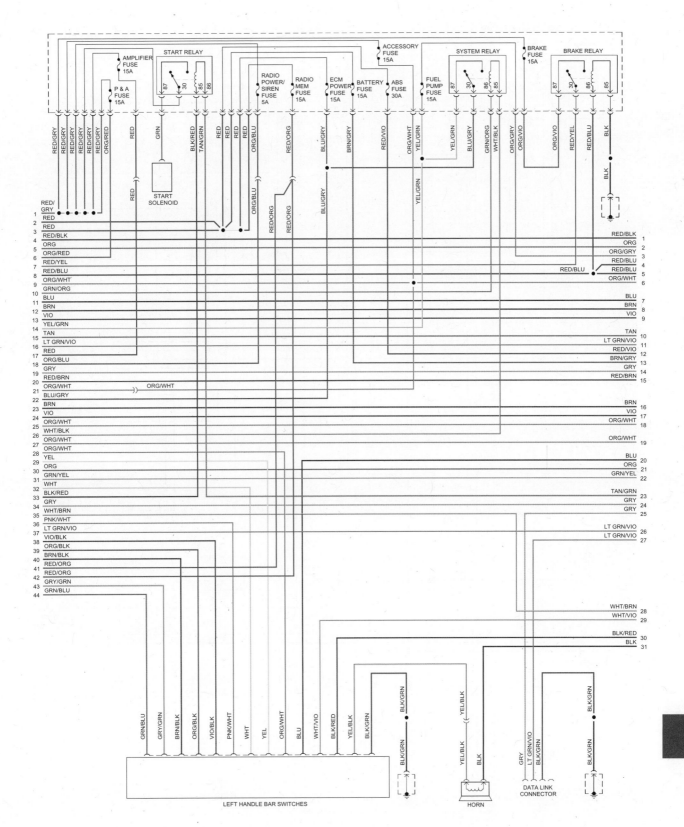

2010-2011 FLXHSE AND FLHXSE2 (CONTINUED)

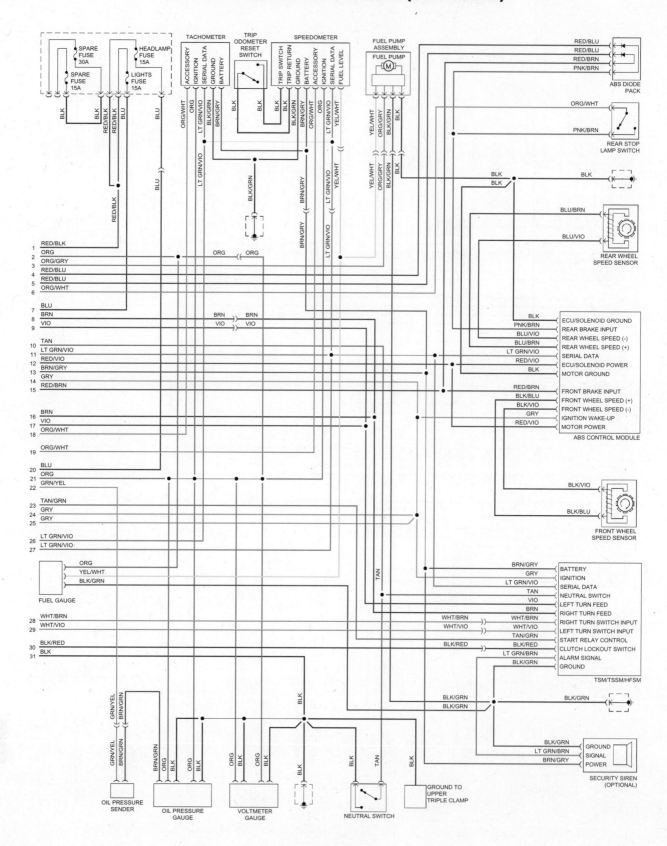

2013 FLHRCSE5

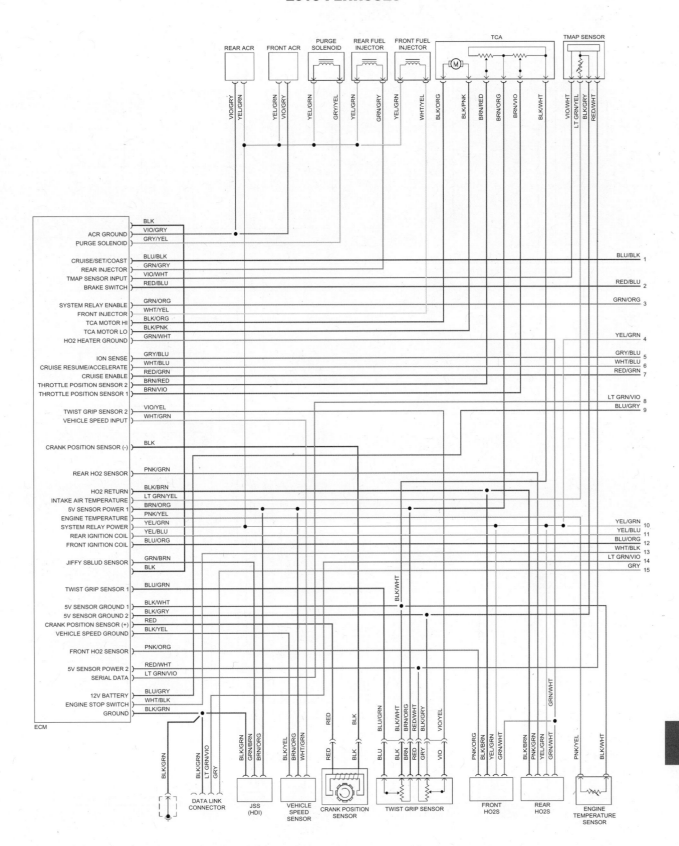

WIRING DIAGRAMS

2013 FLHRCSE5 (CONTINUED)

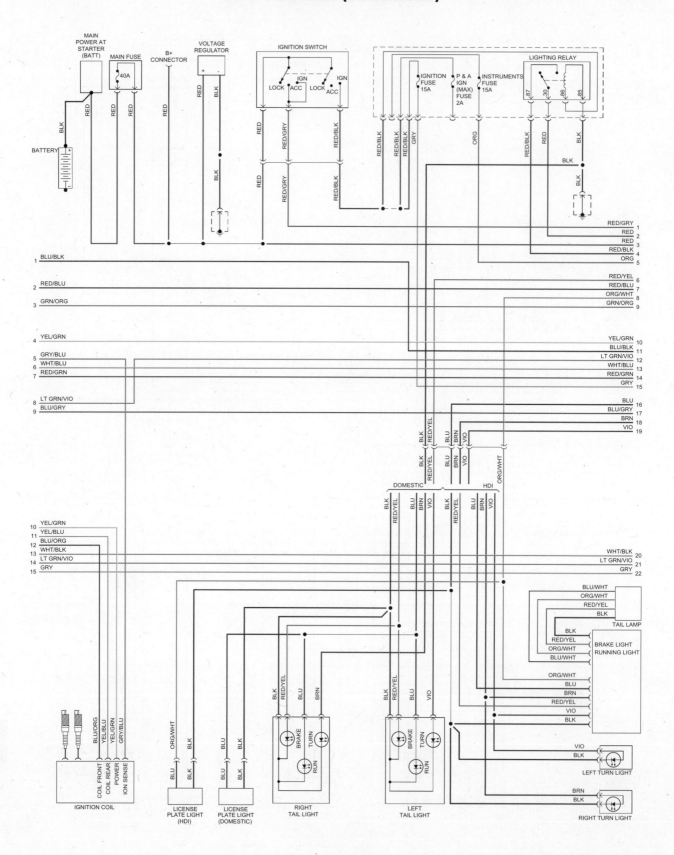

LEFT TURN &
DOM RUNNING LIGHT

RIGHT TURN &
DOM RUNNING LIGHT

INDICATOR LAMPS

| RIGHT TURN | LEFT TURN | HIGH BEAM | NEUTRAL | OIL PRESSURE |

OIL PRESSURE

VIO BLU BLK

BLK BLU BRN

VIO BLU BLK

BLK BLU BRN

BLK

BLK

BRN BLK VIO BLK BLK WHT TAN ORG ORG GRN/YEL

GRN/YEL

BRN

VIO

BLK

WHT TAN ORG

GRN/YEL

BRN

VIO

BLK/GRN

WHT TAN

1 RED/GRY
1 RED
2 RED
3 RED/BLK
4 ORG
5
6 RED/YEL
7 RED/BLU
8 ORG/WHT
9 GRN/ORG

10 YEL/GRN
11 BLU/BLK
12 LT GRN/VIO
13 WHT/BLU
14 RED/GRN
15 GRY
16 BLU
17 BLU/GRY
18 BRN
19 VIO

RED/GRY 1
RED 2
RED 3
RED/BLK 4
ORG 5
ORG/RED 6
RED/YEL 7
RED/BLU 8
ORG/WHT 9
GRN/ORG 10
BLU 11
BRN 12
VIO 13
YEL/GRN 14
TAN 15
LT GRN/VIO 16
BLK/GRN 17
RED/GRN 18
GRY 19
RED/BRN 20
BLK/RED 21
BLU/GRY 22
BRN 23
VIO 24
ORG 25
BRN 26
WHT 27

20 WHT/BLK
21 LT GRN/VIO
22 GRY

YEL 28
WHT/BLK 29
LT GRN/VIO 30
GRY 31
GRY 32
ORG/WHT 33
VIO 34
WHT/BRN 35
GRY/WHT 36
PNK/WHT 37
VIO/BLK 38

ORG/RED

ORG ORG ORG/RED

YEL BLK GRY/BLK

BLK BLK BLK BLK

BLK BLK BLK BLK

W/ ACCESSORY FRONT LIGHTING

W/ AUXILIARY FRONT LIGHTING

WHT/BLU BLU/BLK
RED/BRN
BLK/RED
WHT/BLK GRY
ORG/WHT WHT/BRN

GRY/WHT PNK/WHT VIO/BLK BRN/WHT

BRN/WHT

BLK BLK

BLK BLK

GRY/BLK GRY/BLK

BLK

ORG/RED
RED/YEL
ORG
BLK

BLK BLK

NORMAL CLOSED

NORMAL OPEN

WHT/BLU BLU/BLK WHT/BLK

ORG/WHT RED/YEL

BLK/RED WHT/BLK

WHT/BLK GRY

ORG/WHT WHT/BRN

GRY/WHT PNK/WHT VIO/BLK BRN/WHT

BLK/GRN

ACCESSORY CONNECTOR

ACCESSORY/ AUXILIARY LAMP SWITCH

AUXILIARY LAMPS

CRUISE SET/ RESUME SWITCH

FRONT STOP LAMP SWITCH

START SWITCH

ENGINE STOP SWITCH

RIGHT TURN SWITCH

MODE SWITCH

RIGHT HAND CONTROLS

16

2013 FLHRCSE5 (CONTINUED)

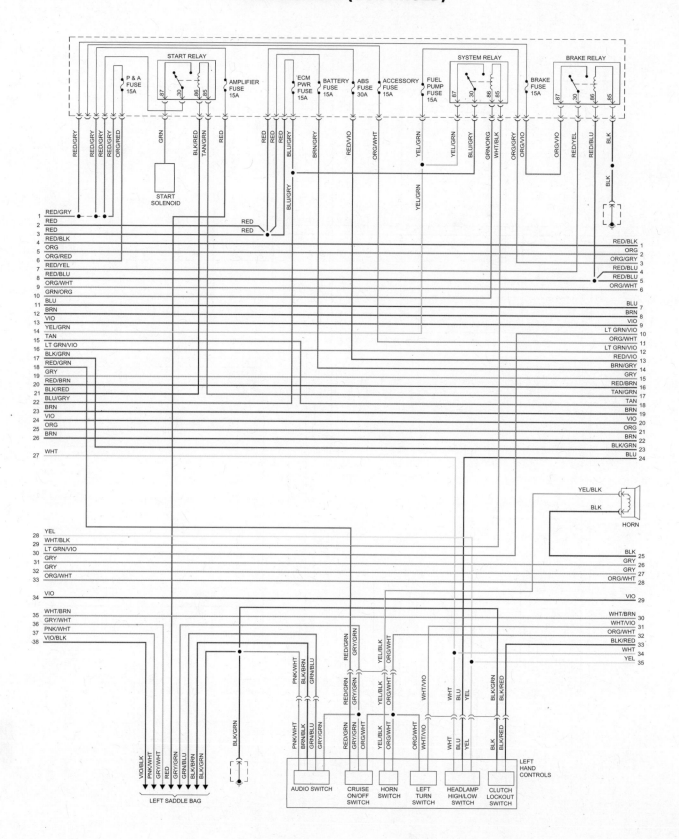

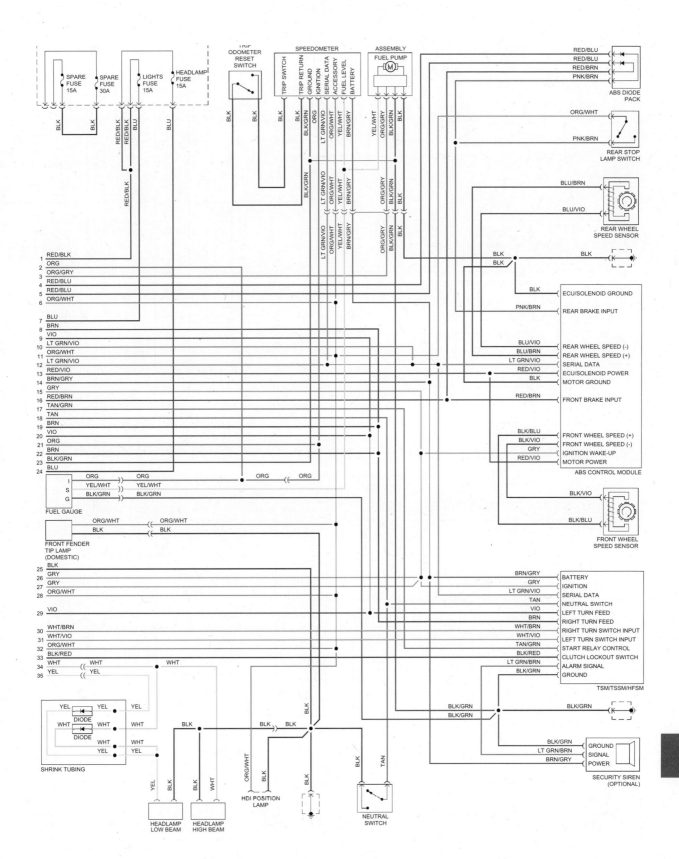

2011, 2013 FLTRUSE

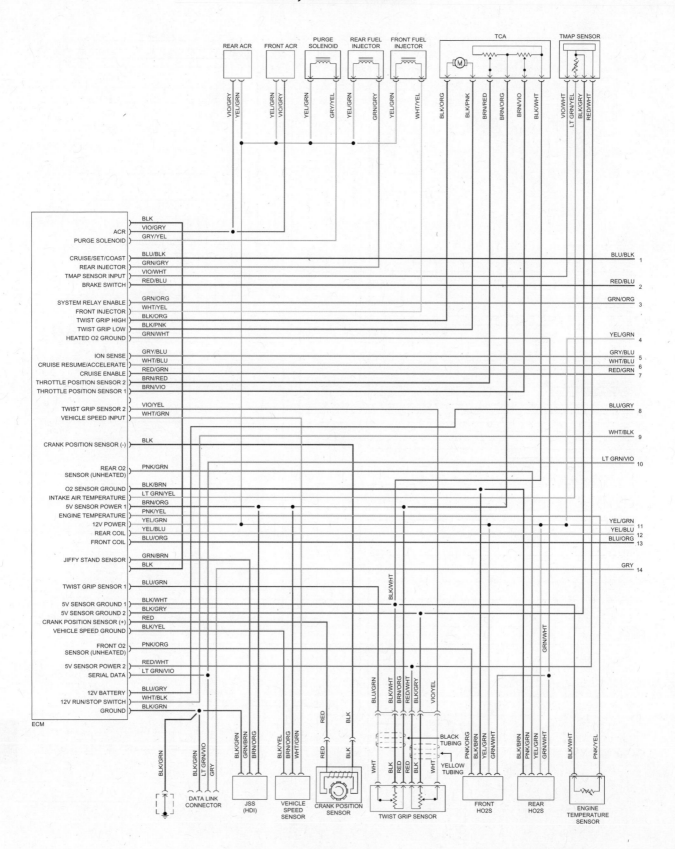

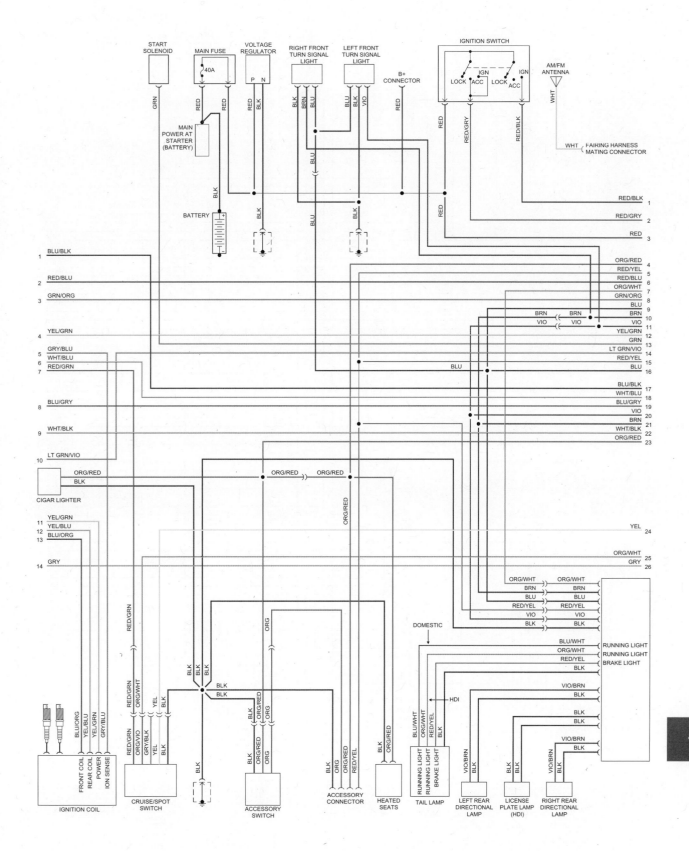

2011, 2013 FLTRUSE (CONTINUED)

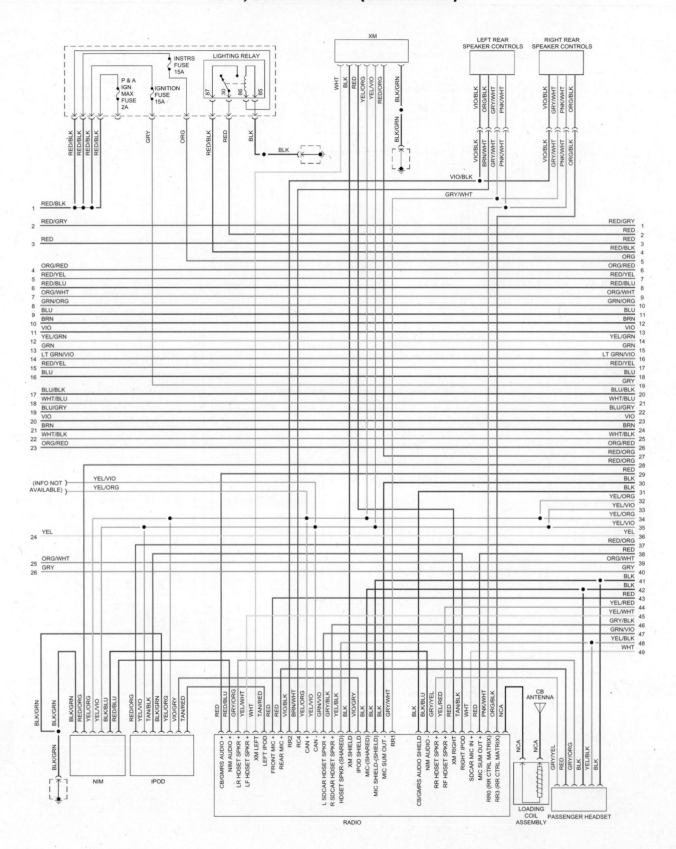

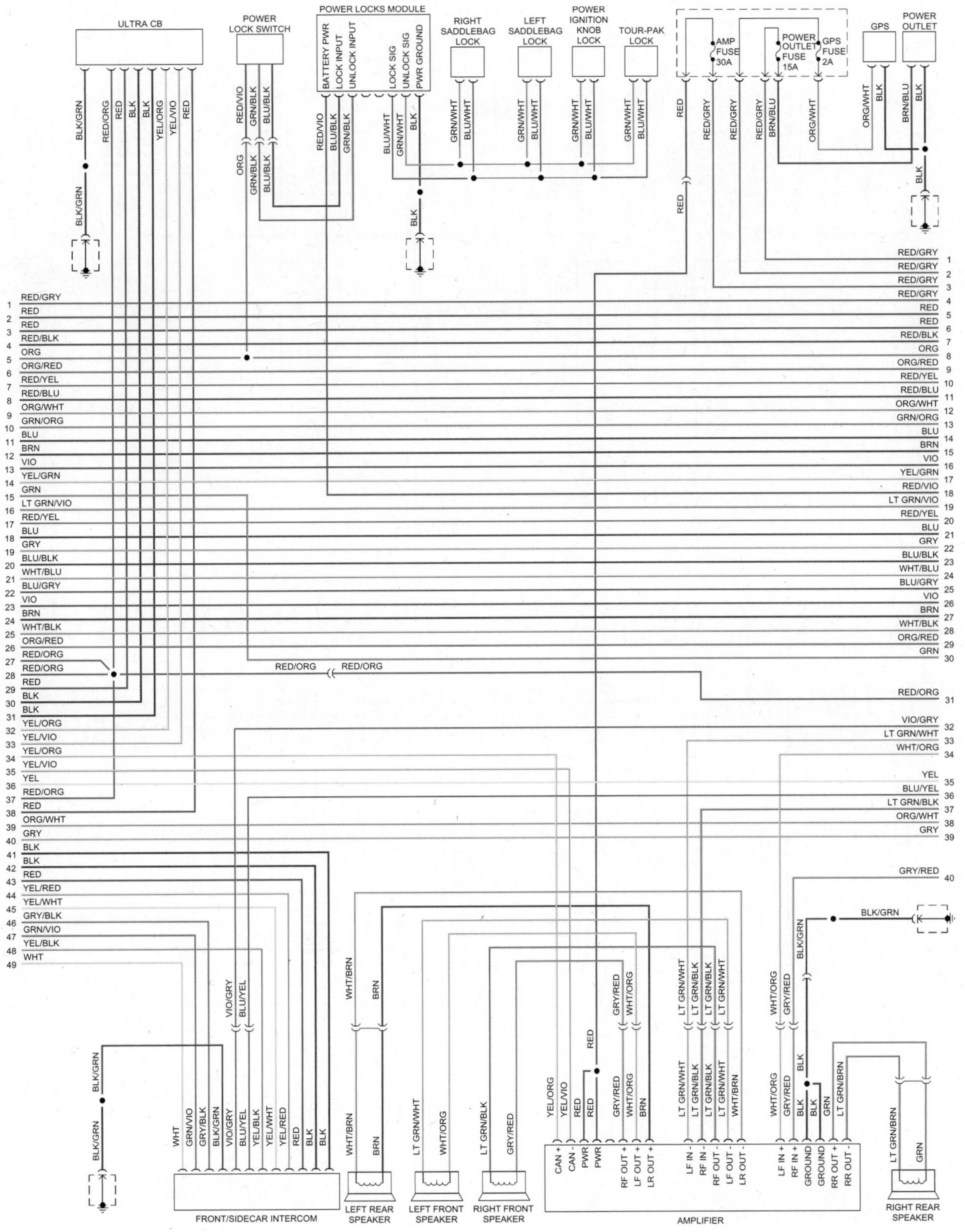
ULTRA CB
POWER LOCK SWITCH
POWER LOCKS MODULE
BATTERY PWR
LOCK INPUT
UNLOCK INPUT
LOCK SIG
UNLOCK SIG
PWR GROUND
RIGHT SADDLEBAG LOCK
LEFT SADDLEBAG LOCK
POWER IGNITION KNOB LOCK
TOUR-PAK LOCK
AMP FUSE 30A
POWER OUTLET FUSE 15A
GPS FUSE 2A
GPS
POWER OUTLET
FRONT/SIDECAR INTERCOM
LEFT REAR SPEAKER
LEFT FRONT SPEAKER
RIGHT FRONT SPEAKER
AMPLIFIER
RIGHT REAR SPEAKER
CAN +
CAN -
PWR
RF OUT +
LF OUT +
LR OUT +
LF IN -
RF IN -
RF OUT -
LF OUT -
LR OUT -
LF IN +
RF IN +
GROUND
RR OUT +
RR OUT -

2011, 2013 FLTRUSE (CONTINUED)

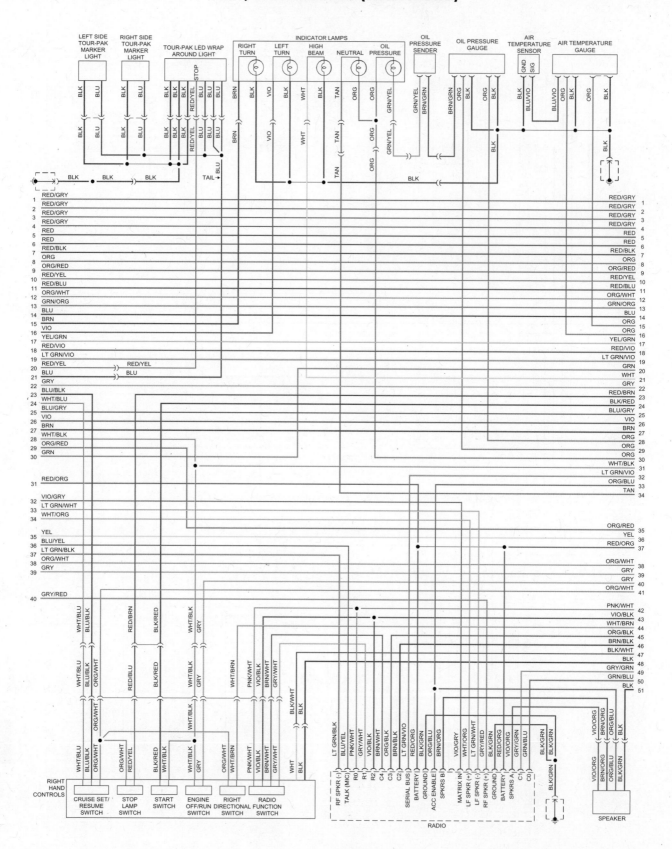

HEATED GRIPS FUSE 5A

START RELAY

RADIO MEMORY FUSE 15A

ABS FUSE 30A

ACCESSORY FUSE 15A

SYSTEM RELAY

CRUISE/ BRAKE FUSE 15A

BRAKE RELAY

P & A FUSE 15A

POWER LOCKS FUSE 15A

BATTERY FUSE 15A

ECM POWER FUSE 15A

RADIO POWER/ SIREN FUSE 15A

FUEL PUMP FUSE 15A

30 86 85 | 87 30 86 85 | 87 30 85 86 | 87 30 85 86

RED/GRY RED/GRY RED/GRY RED/GRY RED/GRY ORG/RED

RED GRN BLK/RED BLU/GRN RED RED RED RED RED/VIO RED/ORG BRN/GRY RED/VIO BLU/GRY ORG/BLU ORG/WHT YEL/GRN YEL/GRN BLU/GRY GRN/ORG WHT/BLK ORG/GRY ORG/VIO ORG/VIO RED/YEL RED/BLU BLK

BLU/GRY ORG/BLU YEL/GRN BLK

#	Left labels	#	Right labels
1	RED/GRY	1	RED/BLK
2	RED/GRY	2	ORG
3	RED/GRY	3	ORG/GRY
4	RED/GRY	4	RED/BLU
5	RED	5	
6	RED/BLK	6	ORG/WHT
7	ORG	7	BLU
8	ORG/RED	8	ORG
9	RED/YEL	9	ORG
10	RED/BLU	10	ORG/WHT
11	ORG/WHT	11	LT GRN/VIO
12	GRN/ORG	12	RED/VIO
13	BLU	13	BRN/GRY
14	ORG	14	GRY
15	ORG	15	RED/BRN
16	YEL/GRN	16	BLU/GRN
17	RED/VIO	17	VIO
18	LT GRN/VIO	18	BRN
19	GRN	19	ORG
20	WHT	20	ORG
21	GRY	21	WHT
22	RED/BRN	22	LT GRN/VIO
23	BLK/RED	23	
24	BLU/GRY	24	TAN
25	VIO	25	ORG/WHT
26	BRN	26	ORG/RED
27	ORG	27	YEL
28	ORG	28	ORG/WHT
29	ORG	29	GRY
30	WHT/BLK	30	GRY
31	LT GRN/VIO	31	ORG/WHT
32	ORG/BLU	32	ORG/WHT
33	TAN	33	WHT
34		34	BLU
35	ORG/RED	35	WHT/BRN
36	YEL	36	WHT/VIO
37	RED/ORG	37	YEL
38	ORG/WHT	38	BLK/RED
39	GRY		
40	GRY		
41	ORG/WHT		
42	PNK/WHT		
43	VIO/BLK		
44	WHT/BRN		
45	ORG/BLK		
46	BRN/BLK		
47	BLK/WHT		
48	BLK		
49	GRY/GRN		
50	GRN/BLU		
51	BLK		

RED/ORG

PNK/WHT VIO/BLK ORG/BLK BRN/BLK

ORG/WHT ORG/WHT

WHT/VIO WHT/VIO

BLK/RED BLK/RED

WHT/BLK WHT
RED/BLK RED
BLK BLK

RIGHT SADDLEBAG LAMP

WHT WHT
RED RED
BLK BLK

LEFT SADDLEBAG LAMP

HORN

YEL/BLK YEL/BLK YEL/BLK
BLK BLK BLK

BLK

LEFT HAND CONTROLS

YEL/BLK ORG/WHT YEL/BLK GRN/BLU ORG/BLK VIO/BLK GRN/BLU GRY/GRN BRN/BLK PNK/WHT BLK BLK/WHT RED ORG/WHT

HORN SWITCH

PTT & SQ

RADIO AUDIO CONTROL

WHT BLU YEL

HEADLAMP HIGH/LOW SWITCH

ORG/WHT WHT/VIO

LEFT DIRECTIONAL SWITCH

BLK/RED BLK

CLUTCH LOCKOUT SWITCH

BLK/GRN

RED WHT/BLK RED/BLK WHT RED BLK

INTERIOR LAMP

BLK BLK

16

2011, 2013 FLTRUSE (CONTINUED)

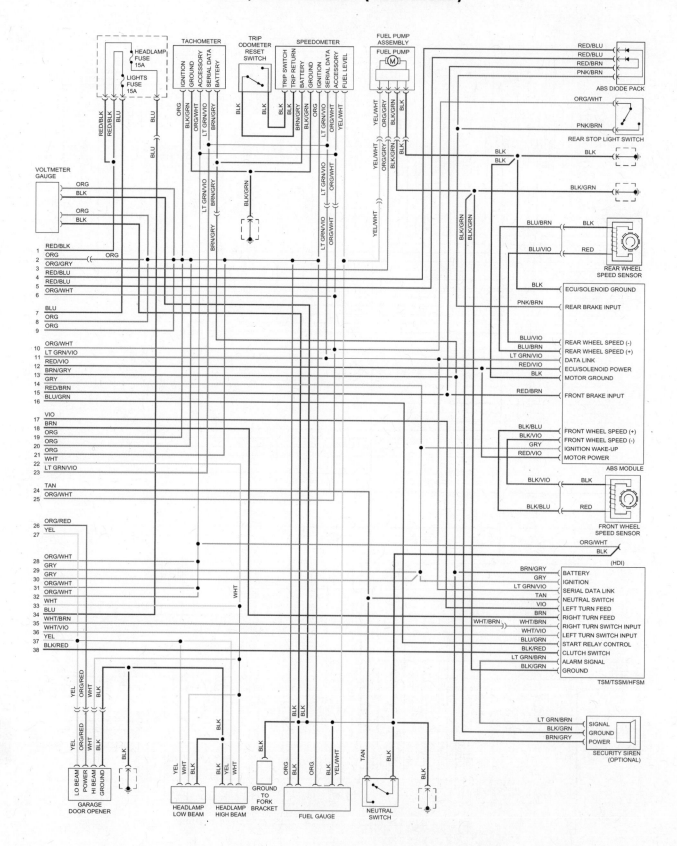

2012 FLTRXSE

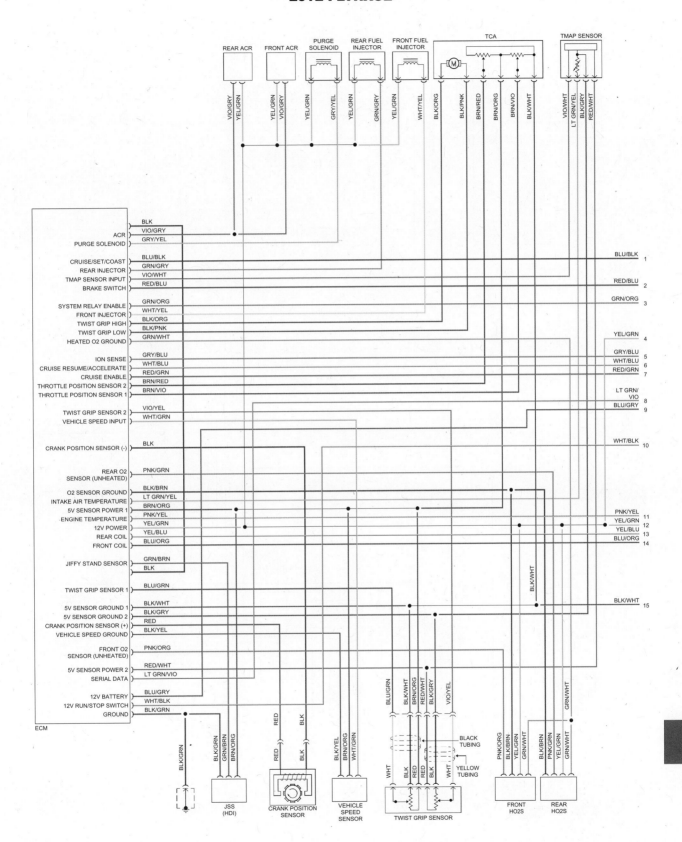

2012 FLTRXSE (CONTINUED)

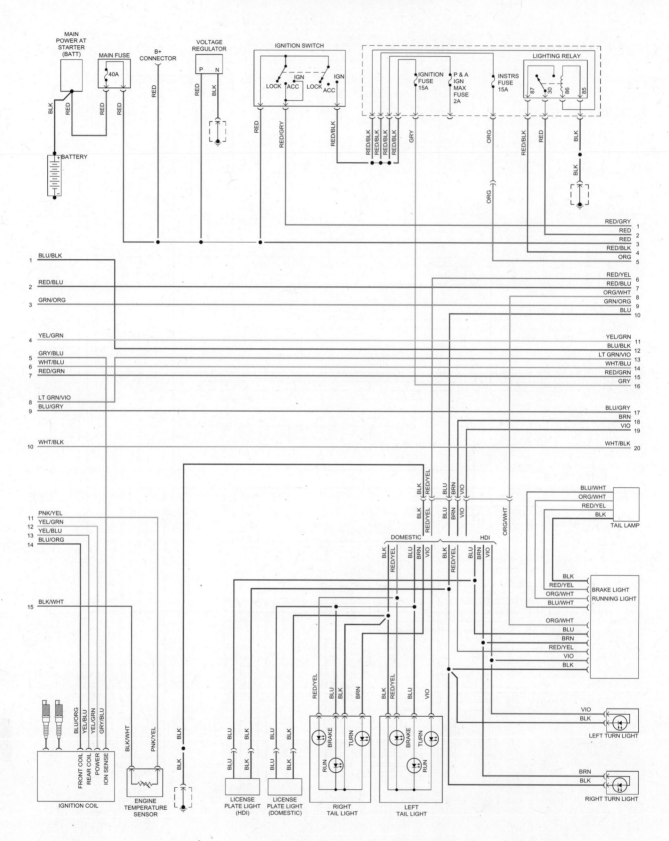

LEFT FRONT TURN SIGNAL LIGHT   RIGHT FRONT TURN SIGNAL LIGHT   TOUR-PAK   P & A ACCESSORY   INDICATOR LAMPS   HIGH BEAM HEADLAMP   LOW BEAM HEADLAMP   DASH PANEL SWITCHES   CIGAR LIGHTER

VIO BLU BLK   BLK BLU BRN   RED/YEL BLU BLK   BLK RED/YEL ORG/RED ORG   BRN VIO GRN/YEL ORG TAN BLK WHT   WHT YEL BLK   WHT YEL BLK   ORG/RED RED/GRN ORG ORG/WHT BLK BLK   ORG/RED BLK

BLK   BLK   BLU   ORG ORG   TAN   WHT YEL   ORG/RED RED/GRN   BLK

BLU   BLU

#	Left labels	Right labels	#
1	RED/GRY	RED/GRY	1
2	RED	RED	2
3	RED	RED	3
4	RED/BLK	RED/BLK	4
5	ORG	ORG	5
		ORG/RED	6
6	RED/YEL	RED/YEL	7
7	RED/BLU	RED/BLU	8
8	ORG/WHT	ORG/WHT	9
9	GRN/ORG	GRN/ORG	10
10	BLU	BLU	11
		BRN	12
		VIO	13
11	YEL/GRN	YEL/GRN	14
12	BLU/BLK	TAN	15
13	LT GRN/VIO	LT GRN/VIO	16
14	WHT/BLU		
15	RED/GRN		
16	GRY	GRY	17
		RED/BRN	18
		ORG/WHT	19
17	BLU/GRY	BLU/GRY	20
18	BRN	BRN	21
19	VIO	VIO	22
		ORG/WHT	23
20	WHT/BLK	WHT/BLK	24
		ORG/WHT	25
		ORG/WHT	26
		YEL	27
		ORG	28
		GRN/YEL	29
		WHT	30
		BLK/RED	31
		GRY	32
		WHT/BRN	33
		PNK/WHT	34
		BRN/WHT	35
		VIO/BLK	36
		GRY/WHT	37
		RED/ORG	38
		TAN/BLK	39
		VIO/GRY	40
		YEL/WHT (OR YEL/VIO)	41
		YEL/ORG	42
		TAN/RED	43

BLK   BLK   BLK   ORG/WHT   ←HDI

WHT/BLK WHT/BLU BLU/BLK RED/BRN ORG/WHT BLK/RED GRY WHT/BRN PNK/WHT BRN/WHT VIO/BLK GRY/WHT

WHT/BLK WHT/BLU BLU/BLK RED/BLU ORG/WHT BLK/RED GRY GRY WHT/BRN PNK/WHT BRN/WHT VIO/BLK GRY/WHT

RIGHT HAND CONTROLS

BLK/GRN   BLK/GRN

BLK/GRN RED/ORG TAN/BLK VIO/GRY YEL/WHT (OR YEL/VIO) YEL/ORG TAN/RED NCA

BLK/GRN RED/ORG TAN/BLK VIO/GRY YEL/VIO YEL/ORG TAN/RED NCA

GROUND BATTERY AUDIO (R) SHIELD (-) CAN (-) CAN (+) AUDIO (L)

IPOD MODULE

NCA   NCA

IPOD MEDIA PLAYER

16

2012 FLTRXSE (CONTINUED)

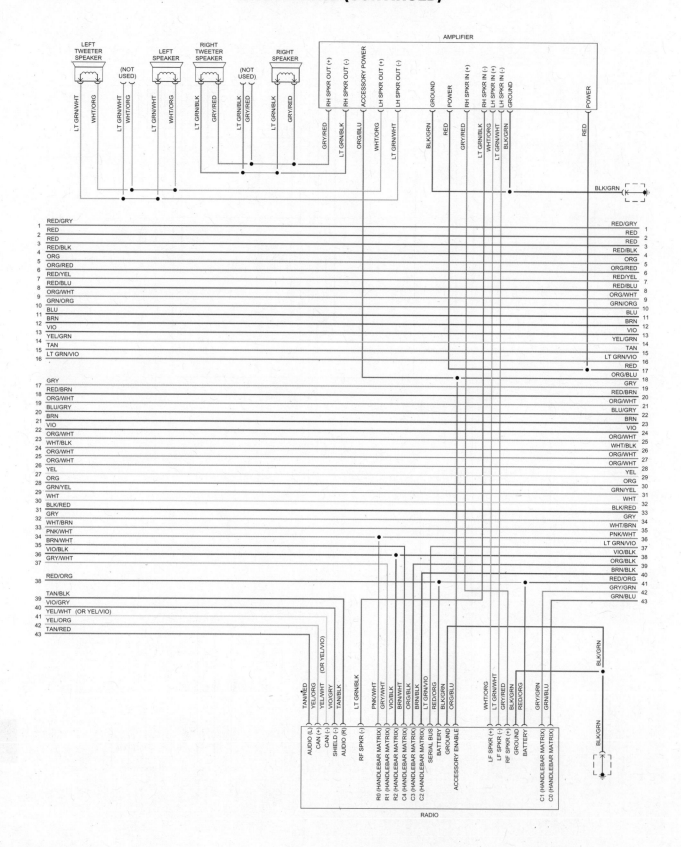

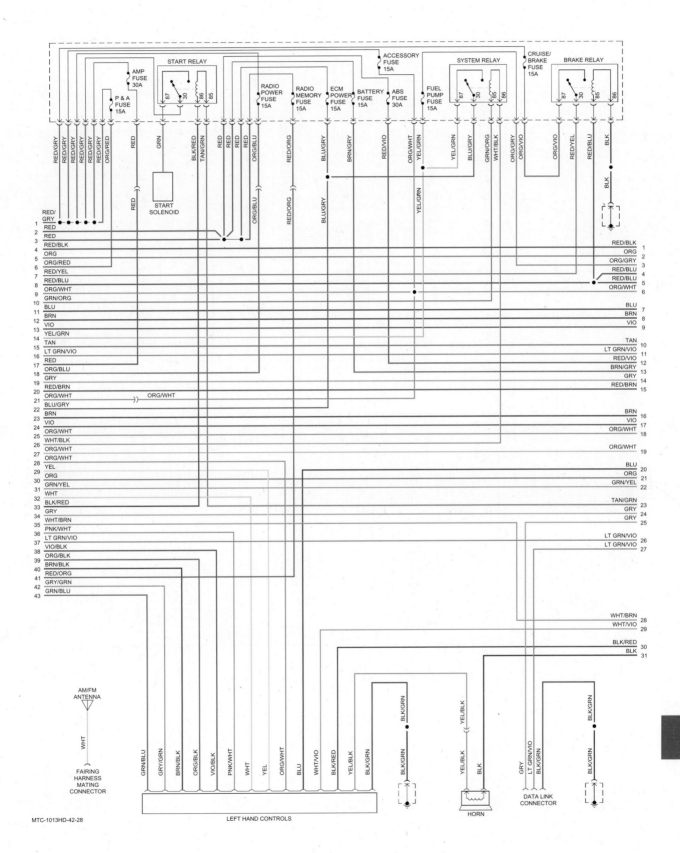

MTC-1013HD-42-28

16

2012 FLTRXSE (CONTINUED)

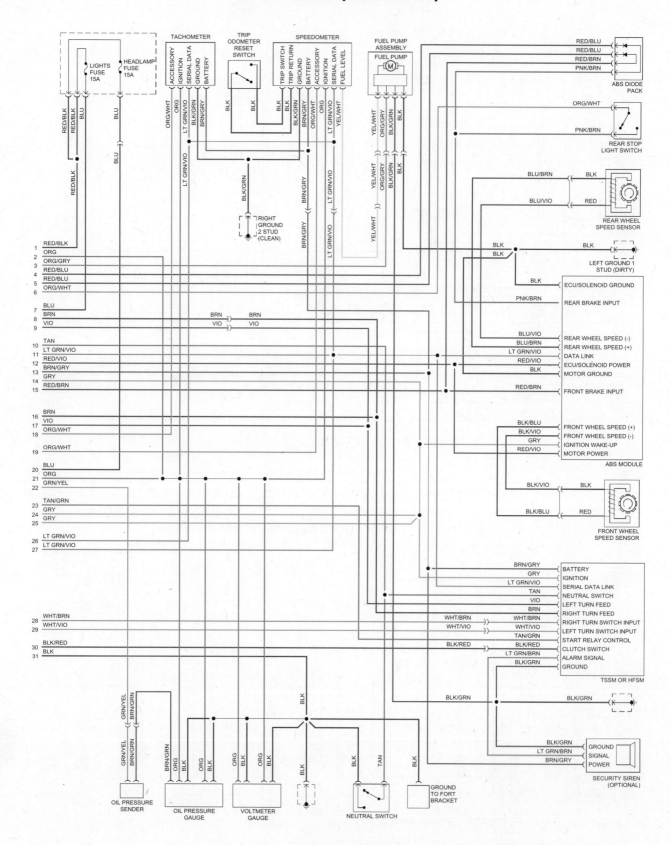

2013 FLTRXSE

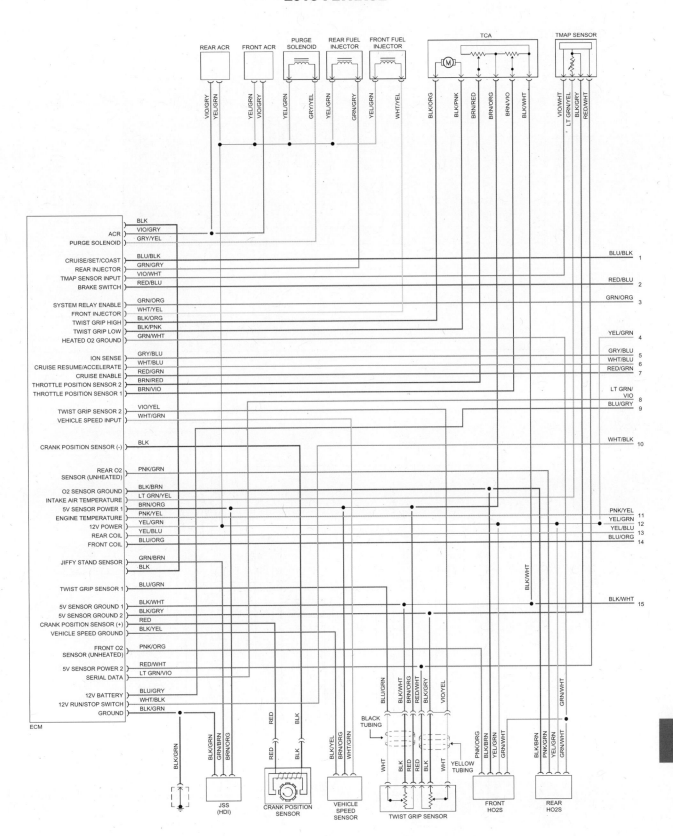

2013 FLTRXSE (CONTINUED)

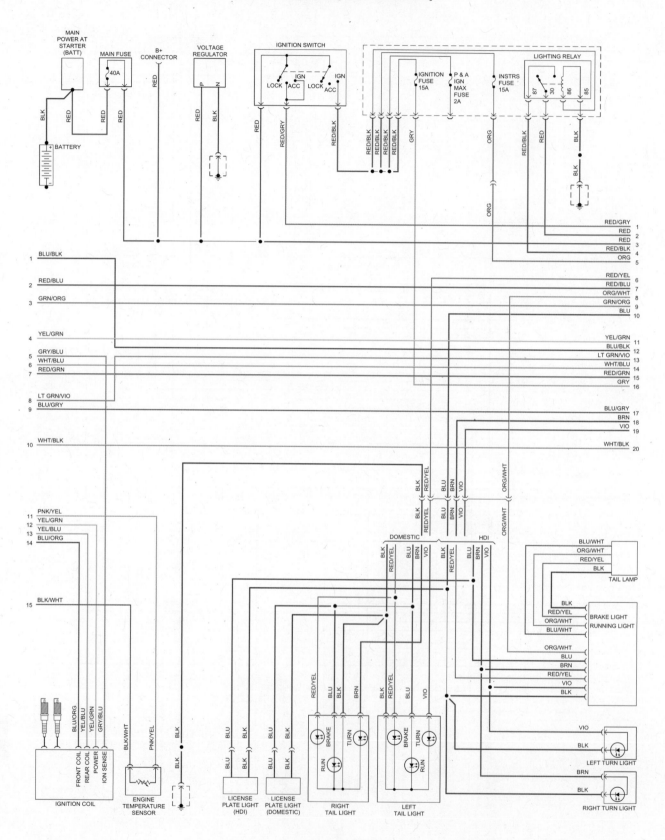

LEFT FRONT TURN SIGNAL LIGHT

RIGHT FRONT TURN SIGNAL LIGHT

TOUR-PAK

P & A ACCESSORY

INDICATOR LAMPS

HIGH BEAM HEADLAMP

LOW BEAM HEADLAMP

DASH PANEL SWITCHES

CIGAR LIGHTER

POWER ANTENNA

VIO · BLU · BLK · BLK · BLU · BRN · RED/YEL · BLU · BLK · BLK · RED/YEL · ORG/RED · ORG · ORG · BRN · VIO · GRN/YEL · ORG · TAN · BLK · WHT · WHT · YEL · BLK · ORG/WHT · ORG/WHT · WHT · YEL · BLK · ORG/RED · RED/GRN · ORG · ORG/WHT · BLK · BLK · ORG/RED · BLK · ORG/RED · BLK

BLK · BLK · BLK · WHT · YEL · ORG/RED · RED/GRN · ORG · ORG · TAN · BLU · BLU · BLU

#	Left	Right #
1	RED/GRY	RED/GRY 1
2	RED	RED 2
3	RED	RED/BLK 3
4	RED/BLK	ORG 4
5	ORG	ORG/RED 5
6	RED/YEL	RED/YEL 6
7	RED/BLU	RED/BLU 7
8	ORG/WHT	ORG/WHT 8
9	GRN/ORG	GRN/ORG 9
10	BLU	BLU 10
		BRN 11
		VIO 12
11	YEL/GRN	YEL/GRN 13
12	BLU/BLK	TAN 14
13	LT GRN/VIO	LT GRN/VIO 15
14	WHT/BLU	16
15	RED/GRN	
16	GRY	GRY 17
		RED/BRN 18
		ORG/WHT 19
17	BLU/GRY	BLU/GRY 20
18	BRN	BRN 21
19	VIO	VIO 22
		ORG/WHT 23
20	WHT/BLK	WHT/BLK 24
		ORG/WHT 25
		ORG/WHT 26
		YEL 27
		ORG 28
		GRN/YEL 29
		WHT 30
		BLK/RED 31
		GRY 32
		WHT/BRN 33
		PNK/WHT 34
		BRN/WHT 35
		VIO/BLK 36
		GRY/WHT 37
		RED/ORG 38
		WHT/BLK 39
		VIO/GRY 40
		YEL/VIO 41
		YEL/ORG 42
		TAN/RED 43

BLK · BLK · BLK · ORG/WHT · ←HDI

WHT/BLK · WHT/BLU · BLU/BLK · RED/BRN · ORG/WHT · BLK/RED · GRY · WHT/BRN · PNK/WHT · BRN/WHT · VIO/BLK · GRY/WHT

16 · 3

RIGHT HAND CONTROLS

BLK/GRN · RED/ORG · WHT/BLK · VIO/GRY · YEL/VIO · YEL/ORG · TAN/RED

BLK/GRN

GROUND · BATTERY · AUDIO (R) · SHIELD (-) · CAN (-) · CAN (+) · AUDIO (L) · NCA

IPOD MODULE

NCA · NCA

IPOD MEDIA PLAYER

2013 FLTRXSE (CONTINUED)

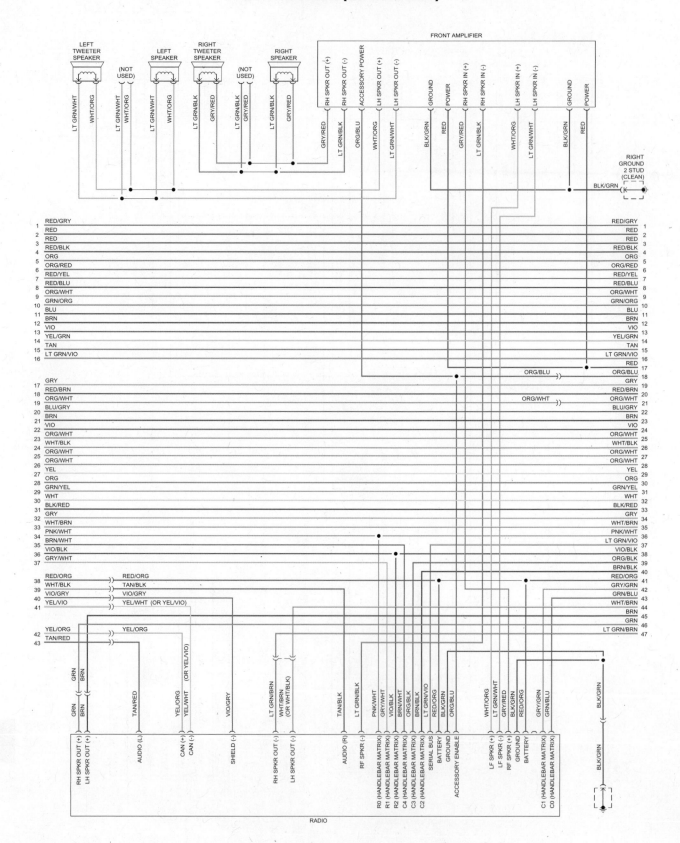

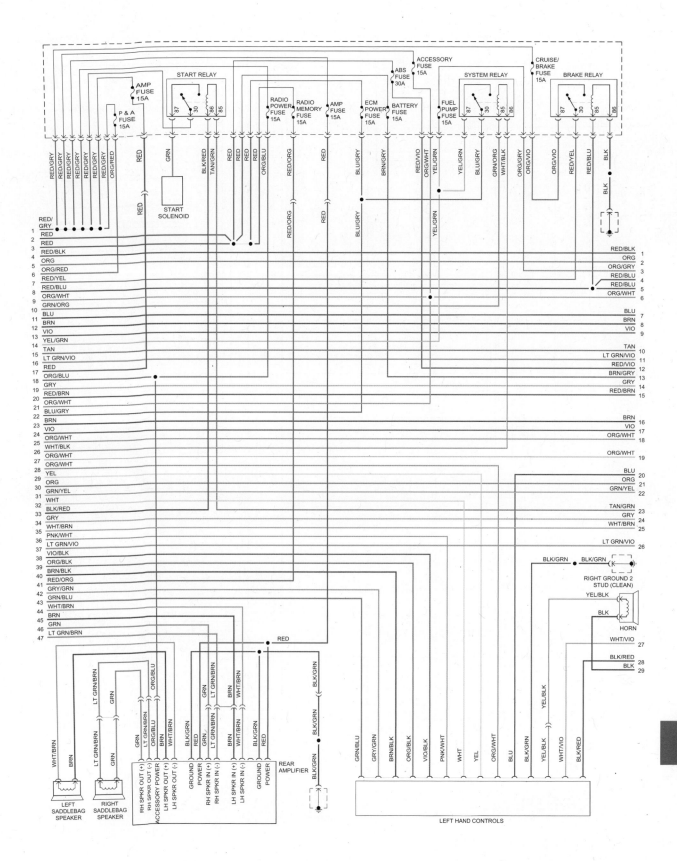

2013 FLTRXSE (CONTINUED)

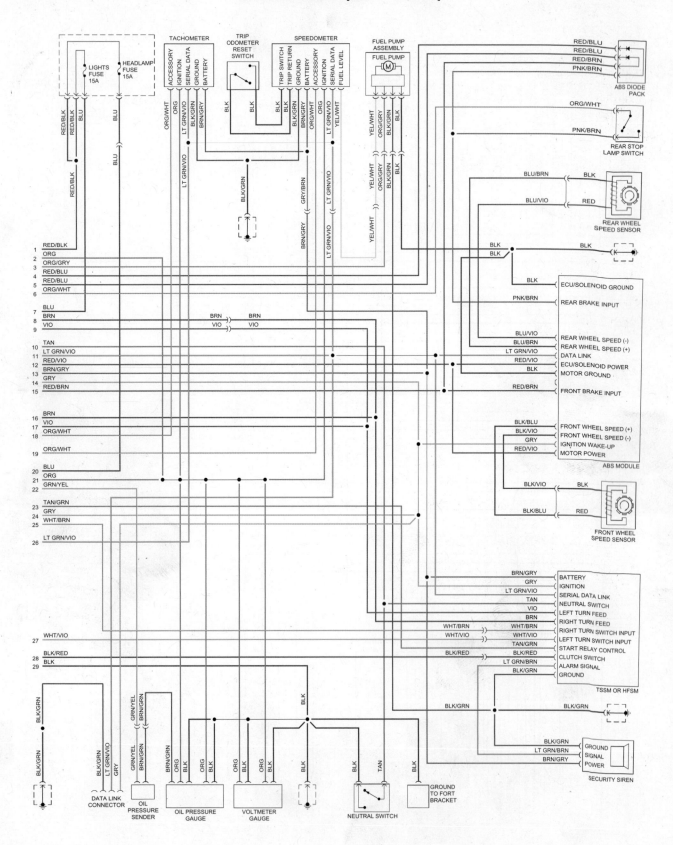